Psychology

Phoebe Beasley, an American artist and lithographer created the collages that appear on the cover and chapter-opening pages of this book. She has been named Woman of the Year by the Los Angeles *Sentinel* and Black Woman of Achievement by the NAACP Legal Defense and Education Fund. Ms. Beasley's luminous collages bring the viewer face to face with all kinds of people and their unique, yet universal, stories. Similarly, psychologists study a variety of experiences—love, hate, sexuality, growing up and growing old, dreaming —looking for general patterns underlying human individuality. The personal narratives portrayed in Ms. Beasley's work, like those in the chapter prologues, reflect common experiences and help us in our quest to understand humankind.

Psychology

Don H. Hockenbury

Tulsa Community College

Sandra E. Hockenbury

WORTH PUBLISHERS

Psychology

Copyright © 1997 by Worth Publishers

All rights reserved

Manufactured in the United States of America

Library of Congress Catalog Card Number: 96-60601

ISBN: 1-57259-140-4

Printing: 1 2 3 4 5   01 00 99 98

Executive Editor: Thomas O. Gay

Development Editor: Rochelle Diogenes

Design: Malcolm Grear Designers

Art Director: George Touloumes

Production Editor: Margaret Comaskey

Production Supervisor: Sarah Segal

Layout: Fernando Quiñones

Picture Editor: June Lundborg Whitworth

Line Art: Demetrios Zangos and Monotype Composition Company, Inc.

Illustrations: J/B Woolsey Associates

Cover and Chapter Opener Art: Phoebe Beasley

Composition and Prepress: Monotype Composition Company, Inc.

Printing and Binding: R. R. Donnelley and Sons

Worth Publishers

33 Irving Place

New York, NY 10003

To Laura

About the Authors

Don H. Hockenbury has been an Assistant Professor of Psychology at Tulsa Community College since 1978. He completed both his undergraduate and graduate training in psychology at the University of Tulsa. Don's clinical psychology research on social skills and loneliness has been published in the *Journal of Personality and Social Psychology*. In 1990, he chaired a roundtable session on "The Psychology Major in Community Colleges" at the annual Teaching of Psychology conference. Don is an associate member of the American Psychological Association and a member of the American Psychological Society.

Sandra E. Hockenbury is a science writer and former psychology editor. She received her undergraduate degree from Shimer College. She did her graduate work at the University of Chicago, where she was a Research Associate at the Institute of Social and Behavioral Pathology. Sandy has also been an adjunct instructor at Tulsa Community College. She is a member of the American Psychological Society.

Contents in Brief

Contents

CHAPTER 3

Sensation and Perception

CHAPTER 4

Consciousness and Its Variations

CHAPTER 5

Learning

CHAPTER 6

Memory

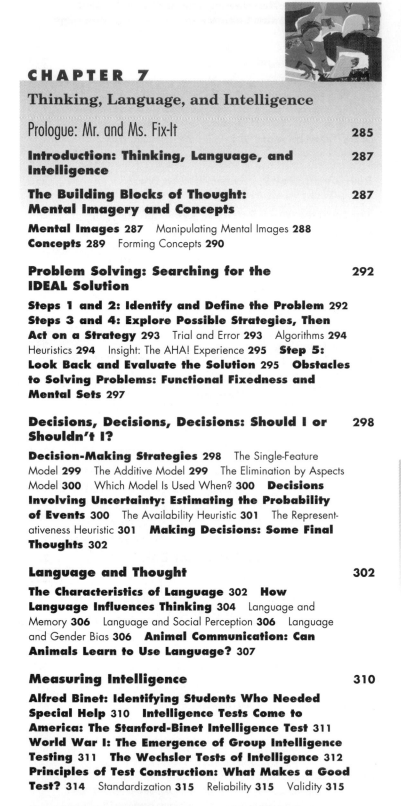

CHAPTER 9

Lifespan Development

CHAPTER 10

Gender and Sexuality

CHAPTER 11

Personality

CHAPTER 12

Social Psychology

Preface

Why did we write this text? Fate, love, and idealism. But in order for that answer to make sense, we should probably begin at the beginning.

Long before we wrote the first word of this text, we had both been actively involved in trying to improve the quality of psychology textbooks—Don as a reviewer and ancillary author for other psychology texts, and Sandy as the senior developmental editor for psychology at a college textbook publishing company. Between the two of us, those efforts added up to almost twenty years of involvement with psychology textbooks. We were both keenly aware of the problems that instructors encountered in their classrooms with introductory psychology texts. In fact, that's how we first met over the phone during the summer of 1988.

Don had just adopted a new edition of an introductory psychology text when he discovered that many of the test items had nothing to do with the text's content. He fired off a testy letter to the publisher, which eventually landed on Sandy's desk. After verifying that Don was right, Sandy enlisted Don's help in correcting the problem before adopters began using the text that fall. We had several long-distance phone conversations that summer. During those conversations, it became apparent that we shared a genuine concern with improving the quality of psychology textbooks.

The following January, we both attended the Teaching of Psychology Conference, which is held every year in St. Petersburg Beach, Florida. Neither of us was aware that the other was going to be at the conference until we got to Florida. But when Don spotted Sandy's name on the list of publishers' representatives, and Sandy spotted Don's name on the list of conference participants, we both wanted to meet the person who had been on the other end of those summer phone conversations. So at the noisy reception on the first evening of the conference, we both casually scanned the faces in the crowd. Standing on opposite sides of the room while we talked psychology with other conference participants, our eyes met and we both smiled. (Luckily, we were smiling at the right person!)

Within minutes of our first face-to-face conversation, we discovered that we both loved psychology, teaching, and writing. (We also fell in love, but that's another story.) Seven months later, we were married. Little did we know that our honeymoon in the Canadian Rockies would be the only vacation we would take for years to come.

Three months after we were married, we had dinner with Tom Gay from Worth Publishers. Tom had flown to Tulsa to try to persuade us to write an introductory psychology text. We sat in a restaurant and talked for over five hours about the Hockenburys' favorite topics—psychology, teaching, and textbooks. Throughout that conversation, we kept coming back to the same general theme: how to create a new introductory psychology text that would meet the needs of the diverse student audience that characterizes today's college classrooms.

As we walked out of the restaurant that evening, Tom challenged us to write an introductory psychology text that would achieve the goals we felt so many texts failed to accomplish. It was not a challenge we took lightly. We knew that if we accepted the challenge, it would dominate our lives for years.

And it did.

For the last seven years, we have immersed ourselves in researching and writing the text that you are holding. From its inception, we had a clear vision of the goals we wanted to achieve. We wanted to write an introductory psychology textbook that would:

- Actively engage diverse students, including adult learners
- Create a warm, personal learning atmosphere
- Communicate the scientific rigor *and* the personal relevance of psychology
- Clearly explain psychological concepts and how they are linked
- Show how classic psychological studies set the stage for today's research
- Encourage and model critical thinking
- Expand students' awareness of cultural and gender differences
- Provide an effective pedagogical system to help students test for retention *and* help them learn how to learn

To achieve those goals, we drew upon our classroom experiences in teaching multiple sections of general psychology every semester. We talked to other instructors and listened carefully to what they had to say. We surveyed the research literature on how students learn. We enlisted the help of more than sixty reviewers from all sectors of the academic spectrum, who gave us invaluable feedback at every step of the writing process. And we immersed ourselves in the research of every core topic in this text to develop a fresh appreciation for how that topic evolved into the role it plays in contemporary psychology.

Did we achieve our goals over the course of seven years? We could certainly tell you what our reviewers have said, but we think it's much more important that you decide for yourself.

We invite you to explore *every* element of this book. Look up the topics that your students find most difficult, and see how we met the challenge of explaining material clearly, thoroughly, and in an engaging fashion. Look at the contemporary design and the book's visual appeal. Take a look at the illustration program, carefully designed to help students understand complex material. Look at a chapter from front to back. Or, better yet, read one of our chapters and compare it to the corresponding chapter in the text you are using. We think you will discover, as our reviewers did, just why this textbook is special.

Features of This Text

Every feature and element in this text serves a specific purpose. From comprehensive surveys, reviewers, and our many discussions with faculty and students, we learned what features people wanted in a text and why they thought those features were important tools that enhanced the learning process. Armed with that information, we surveyed the research literature again, this time focusing on text comprehension, learning, and memory. We acquired many valuable insights from the work of cognitive and educational psychologists. Described below are the features that we decided to incorporate into our book.

A Narrative Approach

As you'll quickly discover, our book has a truly distinctive voice. From the very first page of this text, the reader comes to know us as people and teachers through our stories and anecdotes. Many of our friends and relatives also graciously allowed us to tell their stories. The stories are quite varied—some are funny, others are dramatic, and some are deeply personal. All of them are true.

The stories we tell reflect one of the most effective methods of teaching—the narrative approach. In addition to engaging the reader, each story serves as a pedagogical springboard to illustrate important concepts and ideas. Every story is used to connect new ideas, terms, and ways of looking at behavior to information with which the student is already familiar.

Prologues

As part of the narrative approach, every chapter begins with a **Prologue,** a true story about ordinary people with whom students can identify. The Prologue begins the teaching process. Each Prologue effectively introduces the chapter's themes and lays the groundwork for explaining why the topics treated by the chapter are important. The Prologue establishes a link between familiar experiences and the new information that is to come—a key ingredient in effective learning. Throughout the chapter, we return to the people and stories introduced in the Prologue, further reinforcing the link between the familiar and the unfamiliar. At the end of each chapter, we return once again to the Prologue, drawing closure on the chapter and its themes.

Logical Organization, Continuity, and Clarity

Every chapter tells the story of a particular topic in psychology in a logical way that flows continuously from beginning to end. Themes are clearly established in the first pages of the chapter. Throughout the chapter, we come back to those general themes as we weave in subtopics and specific research studies. Chapters are very thoughtfully organized so that students can easily see how themes evolve and ideas are connected. The writing is very carefully paced to maximize student interest and comprehension. And, rather than simply mentioning terms and findings, we explain concepts thoroughly. Analogies and everyday examples are used to help the student grasp abstract concepts and ideas.

Integrated Visual Program

One of the first things that you will notice about this textbook is its stunning visual program. Every visual element of this text was designed to enhance learning. The art, photographs, and design are content-driven. As you'll see again and again, text and visuals interact, each reinforcing the other.

The innovative illustrations are original to this text. Working closely with artist John D. Woolsey, we carefully developed the illustrations to

Associate the new with the old in some natural and telling way, so that the interest, being shed along from point to point, finally suffuses the entire system of objects. . . . Anecdotes and reminiscences [should] abound in [your] talk; and the shuttle of interest will shoot backward and forward, weaving the new and the old together in a lively and entertaining way.

William James *Talks to Teachers* (1899)

increase students' comprehension of difficult concepts and processes. The illustrations often clarify psychological processes through concrete (and sometimes humorous) examples—just as we do in our writing.

We use photographs as an additional vehicle to convey information and enhance comprehension. The captions are thoughtful, not merely descriptive, and provide another way to encourage active learning. The photographs were also carefully chosen to help students relate new concepts to other situations, and often provide vivid visual examples to help students remember new ideas.

Boxes

Boxes serve a very useful purpose in our chapters. Paradoxically, they allow us to maintain continuity from topic to topic, idea to idea, without losing the narrative thread of the chapter. Our boxes are substantive, and they provide an opportunity to explore a particular topic in depth.

The **Critical Thinking boxes** are designed to encourage students to think about the implications of psychological research—to stretch their minds a bit by pondering questions and issues that don't always have easy answers. Often, we leave the student with issues or questions to think about, questions that you can use in classroom discussions.

The **Science Versus Pseudoscience boxes** model and encourage another dimension of critical thinking: how to critically examine claims and weigh evidence. They focus on popular pseudosciences like astrology, subliminal motivation, and iridology—the kinds of topics that students frequently ask about in class.

The **In Focus boxes** do just that—they focus on an interesting topic in more depth than the chapter's organization would allow. Sometimes they highlight ingenious or interesting research. Others answer questions that students commonly ask. Some show students how psychological research can be applied in their lives.

Culture and Gender Issues

We weave cross-cultural research and gender issues throughout many chapter discussions. To increase student awareness of cross-cultural psychology, we also use **Culture and Human Behavior boxes** to highlight cultural and gender issues. Our Culture and Human Behavior boxes are unique in that they go beyond simply describing behavior that is different in other cultures. Rather, they show readers how culture plays a critical role in shaping behavior and attitudes, including the attitudes and behavior of students who are part of the cultural mainstream. As just one example to show you what we mean, take a look at the two Culture and Human Behavior boxes in Chapter 9 on Lifespan Development.

Chapter Applications

Among all the sciences, psychology is unique in the degree to which it speaks to our daily lives and applies to everyday problems and concerns. The **Application** at the end of each chapter provides an opportunity for us to present the findings from psychological research that address a wide variety of problems and concerns. In every Application, we present information in a form that students can actually use. Topics range from improving self-control to overcoming gender differences in handling interpersonal conflict.

The Pedagogical System

The pedagogical system in this textbook was carefully designed to help students identify important information, test for retention, and learn how to learn. It is easily adaptable to an SQ3R approach, for those instructors who have had success with that technique. Our pedagogical system has two key components—Advance Organizers and Concept Reviews—and several supporting features.

We designed the unique **Advance Organizers** several years ago. Every major section is introduced by an Advance Organizer that consists of a one-sentence summary or definition followed by three or four focus questions. The Advance Organizer mentally primes the student for the important information that is to follow, and does so in a way that encourages active learning. Students often struggle with trying to determine what's important to learn in a particular section or chapter. As a pedagogical technique, the Advance Organizer provides a guide that directs the reader toward the most important ideas, concepts, and information in the section. It helps students identify main ideas and distinguish them from supporting evidence and examples.

To further reinforce active learning, we often pose additional questions in the text discussion that encourage students to process information in a way that is personally meaningful, such as coming up with examples from their own lives. By actively processing information at a "deep" level rather than merely memorizing a string of definitions, students significantly enhance their comprehension of the material.

The **Concept Reviews** encourage students to review and check their learning. Every chapter contains a generous supply of Concept Reviews. As you look through the text, you'll see that the Concept Reviews vary in format. They include multiple choice, matching, short answer, and true/false questions. Many of the Concept Reviews are interactive exercises that help students transfer their learning to new situations or examples.

Supporting the Advance Organizers and Concept Reviews are several other pedagogical aids. Every chapter begins with a **Chapter Outline** that provides an overall view of topics and organization. Within the chapter, **Key Terms** are set in boldface type and defined in the margin. **Pronunciation guides** are included for difficult or unfamiliar words. Because students often have trouble identifying the most important theorists and researchers, names of **Key People** are set in boldface type within the chapter. We provide a brief biography of each key person at the end of each chapter, mentioning again why the person is important. A comprehensive **Chapter Summary** includes key points bulleted under each major section heading. We also provide a **page-referenced list of Key Terms** at the end of each chapter.

Taken together, the different elements of this text form a pedagogical system that is very student-friendly, straightforward, *and* effective. We've found that it appeals to diverse students with varying academic and study skills, enhancing the learning process without being gimmicky or condescending.

The Supplements Package

A comprehensive teaching package accompanies this textbook. The supplements have been designed to help you save time and teach more effectively. Many elements of the supplements package will be particularly helpful to the adjunct or part-time instructor. This superb teaching package includes the following elements:

Student Study Guide, prepared by Cornelius Rea, Douglas College, New Westminster, British Columbia, Canada. The

Study Guide has been carefully designed to help students understand text information and prepare for exams. It includes note-taking exercises for each chapter and progress tests.

- **Instructor's Resource Manual,** prepared by Wayne Hall and Granville Sydnor, San Jacinto College, Pasadena, Texas. The Instructor's Resource Manual includes an abundance of materials to aid instructors in planning their course, including detailed chapter outlines, lecture guides highlighting common student problems, classroom demonstrations, student exercises, advice on teaching the nontraditional student, and "Psychology in the News" topics.

- **Test Bank,** prepared by Marie Waung, University of Michigan–Dearborn, and Thomas Brice, University of Michigan–Flint and the Polk Company. The Test Bank contains over 1,800 multiple choice, fill-in-the-blank, true/false, and short-answer essay questions.

- A **Computerized Test Bank** is available for Macintosh, Windows, and DOS platforms. The software program allows instructors to edit, add, or scramble questions.

- **Second edition of *The Brain* videocassettes.** Along with new modules from the acclaimed PBS series, the second edition of *The Brain* package includes a guide for faculty that links the modules to specific topics in the textbook.

- *The Mind* **videocassettes** contain 38 short modules that dramatically enhance and illustrate important points in a lecture.

- **The Psychology Videodisc** contains brief, exciting video clips and a library of still images.

- **Full-color transparencies** with illustrations from the textbook include tables, photographs, and artwork.

- **CD-ROM** with art and illustrations from the text.

- **Psych-Sim Interactive Computer Simulations 4.0** contains nineteen programs in Macintosh or Windows format. These programs place the student in the role of the experimenter or the subject in simulated research, or provide dynamic demonstrations illustrating fundamental psychology principles.

- **The Critical Thinking Companion for Introductory Psychology,** by Jane Halonen, Alverno College, is a handbook for the student that includes critical thinking exercises that are keyed to main topics in introductory psychology.

These teaching aids are available to all qualified adopters of this text. For more information, or to examine any of these supplements, get in touch with your regional Worth sales representative or Worth Publishers.

Acknowledgments

Many talented people contributed to this project. First, we would like to thank **Marie Waung,** University of Michigan–Dearborn, for writing an exceptional appendix on industrial/organizational psychology. And thanks to

Marie D. Thomas at California State University, San Marcos, who provided a truly student-friendly statistics appendix.

We would also like to acknowledge the efforts of our supplements team, who have embraced our goals and incorporated them into the supplements package. Our thanks to: **Cornelius Rea,** of Douglas College in British Columbia, Canada, for writing a superb Student Study Guide; **Wayne Hall** and **Granville Sydnor** of San Jacinto College, Pasadena, Texas, for preparing a comprehensive Instructor's Resource Manual; and to **Marie Waung** of the University of Michigan–Dearborn and **Thomas Brice** of the University of Michigan–Flint and the Polk Company for preparing an excellent Test Bank. Con Rea also contributed to several of the Concept Reviews in the text. As colleagues who care as much as we do about teaching, they all have our gratitude for their hard work and commitment to excellence.

We are indebted to our many colleagues in the United States and Canada who acted as reviewers in the development of this text. Your suggestions and advice were invaluable in helping us create chapter discussions that were comprehensive, balanced, and accurate. Your enthusiastic response to our approach helped keep us going and intensified our commitment to the goals we had set for ourselves. To each and every reviewer, thank you for generously sharing your time and candid thoughts with us:

Lynn Haller Augsbach, Morehead State University

Susan J. Bartzak-Graham, Roxbury Community College

Brian R. Bate, Cuyahoga Community College, Western Campus

Michael G. Bergmire, Jefferson College

Connie Bosworth, El Paso Community College

Saundra K. Ciccarelli, Gulf Coast Community College

Marie G. Cisneros-Solis, Austin Community College

John M Clark, Macomb Community College

Lorry Cology, Owens Community College

Dana H. Davidson, University of Hawaii, Manoa

Kaye K. Diefenderfer, Seminole Community College

George J. Downing, Gloucester County College

Gilles O. Einstein, Furman University

Linda L. Faldetta, Fernald School

Michael K. Garza, Brookhaven College

Larry Goff, El Centro College

Peter Gram, Pensacola Junior College

Eddie M. Griggs, Abraham Baldwin Agricultural College

Phyllis Grilikhes-Maxwell, City College of San Francisco

Jim Hail, McLennan Community College

Gilmer Hall, University of Virgina, Charlottesville

Wayne W. Hall, San Jacinto College Central

Jane S. Halonen, Alverno College

William Hampes, Black Hawk College

Joseph J. Hanak, Corning Community College

William T. Hardy, Sierra College

Hope Hartman, City University of New York, City College

Matthew Hogben, State University of New York, Albany

Teri Hudson, Diablo Valley College

Richard A. Hughes, Laredo Community College

Doris Ivie, Pellissippi State Technical Community College

Andrew Kinney, Mohawk Valley Community College

Richard J. Klimck, Montgomery College

Gloria J. Lawrence, Wayne State College

Thomas W. Lombardo, The University of Mississippi

Joan Lovensheimer, Butler County Community College

Robert F. Massey, Saint Peter's College

Douglas G. Mook, University of Virginia, Charlottesville

Edward R. Mosley, Passaic County Community College

Melinda L. Myers-Johnson, College of the Redwoods, Humboldt State University

William C. Owen, Virginia Western Community College

Elizabeth Weiss Ozorak, Allegheny College

Gregory Pezzetti, Rancho Santiago College

Peter H. Platenius, Queens University

Christopher Potter, Harrisburg Area Community College

Sandra Prince-Madison, Delgado Community College

Cornelius P. Rea, Douglas College

Theresa J. Reis, Eastern Washington University

Valda Robinson, Hillsborough Community College

Paul Rosenfeld, Navy Personnel Research and Development Center

Marcia J. Rossi, Tuskegee University

Alan M. Schultz, Prince George's Community College

Richard Seefeldt, University of Wisconsin, River Falls

Betty Sunerton, Dawson College

Margaret Johnson Thornburg, Henry Ford Community College

Mary Trahan, Randolph-Macon College

M. Lisa Valentino, Seminole Community College

Wayne Van Zomeran, Northwest Missouri State University

John Vitkus, Case Western Reserve University

Scott D. Wright, University of Utah

Cecelia K. Yoder, Oklahoma City Community College

Matthew J. Zagumny, Tennessee Technological University

We are also thankful for the help we received on many other fronts. We are grateful for the support that Don has received from **Tulsa Community College. Dr. Dean P. VanTrease,** the President of Tulsa Community College, is strongly committed to academic excellence in serving the needs of our diverse student population. He also actively encourages and supports various forms of professional development for the faculty. In keeping with those commitments, Dr. VanTrease generously arranged for Don to have a reduced teaching load during three semesters.

At the Northeast Campus of Tulsa Community College, **John Kontogianes,** Provost, and **Kathy Purser,** Dean of Instruction, recognized the academic value of this undertaking and supported it in numerous ways. Special thanks go to our friend and Don's Division Chair, **Diane Potts,** who was enthusiastic in her encouragement. Our friends and psychology colleagues, especially **Camille Quinn, Cathy Furlong,** and **Brenda Vance,** continue to inspire us with their dedication to excellence in teaching.

At the **University of Tulsa,** we are indebted to our colleague and friend **Robert Hansson** in the Department of Psychology for numerous favors, big and small. The exceptional psychology collection at McFarlin Library was invaluable, and the helpful staff in the Interlibrary Loan Department tracked down elusive and obscure references from all corners of the globe. **Reed Davis,** Assistant Provost for Computer Resources, graciously arranged for us to have access to the University of Tulsa's Internet services, another invaluable resource.

The remarkable people who constitute **Worth Publishers** are dedicated to quality in the college textbooks they produce. From the earliest stages of the editorial process to the last stages of the production process, their attention to the details of this book was unwavering. Although they operate largely behind the scenes, they played critical roles in helping us to produce the best possible first-edition textbook that we could write.

No author could ask for a better sponsoring editor than **Tom Gay.** From the very beginning, Tom has believed in us and guided us with wisdom, wit, and integrity. In one way or another, every aspect of this project has benefited from Tom's involvement. On a more personal level, our lives have been enriched by Tom's friendship. It is impossible to convey the many ways that Tom has touched our lives, all for the good. To say that he is a special person would be an understatement. To say that he is our friend is a privilege. Thank you, Thomas, for being you.

Our developmental editor, **Rochelle Diogenes,** not only embraced our project but us, too. She wholeheartedly dedicated herself to our project and championed our ideas at every critical juncture. With editorial candor that can only be described as loving, she helped us keep our chapters to a manageable length, made certain we were listening to our reviewers, and kept us true to our goals. In more ways than we can describe here, she helped us turn our vision for this book into reality. And, like Tom, she knew how to make us laugh and stay motivated.

We spent countless hours on the phone with **June Lundborg Whitworth,** our photo researcher. June's gentle voice disguised her undaunted determination to track down just the right photos. Her tenacity is as admirable as her eye for visually stunning images. Director of photo research **Cindy Joyce** also made many contributions to the photo program of this text. It was Cindy who suggested artist **Phoebe Beasley's** wonderful collages for the cover and the opening pages of each chapter. We thank Phoebe Beasley for graciously allowing us to use her artwork.

The remarkable illustrations in this text reflect the talents of **John D. Woolsey** and his colleagues at **J/B Woolsey Associates.** John embraced our goals and approach with enthusiasm. His creative and innovative illustrations help teach psychological concepts better than any other drawings we have ever seen.

Every page of this book is a testament to the extraordinary abilities of art director **George Touloumes,** his assistants **Demetrios Zangos** and **Fernando Quiñones,** and designer **Pat Appleton** of **Malcolm Grear Designers.** George and Demetri worked and reworked every page of this demanding layout until they achieved the stunning results that you see in each chapter. They rose to the challenge of creating a book in which the content and visuals are perfectly integrated.

Many other people made important contributions to the successful completion of this book. The new president of Worth Publishers, **Susan Driscoll,** enthusiastically supported our project from her first day on the job. Like the eye in the center of a hurricane, managing editor **Suzanne Thibodeau** was a pillar of calm professionalism who kept everything from spinning out of control. She solved problems before we even knew they existed, always with grace and humor. **Cecilia Gardner** skillfully copyedited the entire manuscript with care and sensitivity to our unique writing style.

Working with production editor **Margaret Comaskey** was wonderful. Margaret calmly and cheerfully coordinated a bewildering array of manuscript pages, galleys, artwork, photos, and corrections. She helped us track down and tie up innumerable loose ends. Production supervisor **Sarah Segal** never wavered in her commitment to quality as she performed one miracle after another to bring the book to press. Supplements editor **Gerry Benedict** supervised the development of the supplements package, coordinating the diverse elements and maintaining a consistent level of excellence. We would also like to thank an unsung hero named **Tristan Ing.** Tristan managed a mountain of paperwork, reviews, and manuscript with remarkable efficiency, never losing his cool—or anything else, either.

Finally, a few personal acknowledgments are in order. Our friends and members of our extended family kindly allowed us to share their stories with you, the reader. Sandy's parents, **Erv** and **Fern,** deserve particular thanks for their helpfulness, good humor, and constant support. Fern and Erv, we hope that our respect, love, and appreciation for you comes through every time we tell a funny story about you! We thank **Janet, Janeen** and **Marty, Judy** and **Dean,** and the other members of our extended family for their support and encouragement—and for putting up with our absences from family gatherings over the past seven years. We thank our good friends **Asha** and **Paul, Marcia** and **Bill, David** and **Marie, Randy,** and **Warren** for allowing us to tell their stories in the pages of our book. Special thanks to our friends **Mike Needham, Henry Staat,** and **Jonelle Calon,** who provided invaluable advice and support at a critical stage in this book's development.

Last but not least, our daughter **Laura** has lived with this project since its inception and her own conception, as the two events very nearly coincided. Over the years, Laura became accustomed to postponing many simple pleasures of childhood "until the chapter was done." Now six years old and an exuberant first-grader, Laura has been a source of joy and happiness, laughter and love throughout the arduous process of putting this book together. Perhaps more so than anyone else, Laura's life has been affected by our writing this book, which is why it is dedicated to her.

An Invitation

We've devoted the last seven years of our lives to creating the introductory psychology text that you now hold in your hands. We hope that you will take the time to look at our book and discover its distinctive features for yourself. And, most important, we hope you adopt this book for use in your classroom and let us know how you and your students like it.

In a matter of months, we will begin the process of revising this book for the second edition. We welcome your thoughts, suggestions, and comments! You can write to us in care of Worth Publishers, 33 Irving Place, New York, NY 10003, or send your comments to our e-mail address:

psychology@aol.com

Above all, we hope that your semester is an enjoyable and successful one as you introduce your students to the most fascinating and personally relevant science that exists.

With best wishes,

To the Student: How to Use This Book

Welcome to psychology! Our names are Don and Sandy Hockenbury, and we're the authors of your textbook. Every semester we teach several sections of introductory psychology, and we wrote this text to help you succeed in the class you are taking. We carefully designed every aspect of this book to help you get the most out of your introductory psychology course. Before you begin your reading, you will find it well worth your time to take a few minutes to familiarize yourself with the special features and learning aids.

First, take a look at the **Chapter Outline** at the very beginning of each chapter. The Chapter Outline shows you the progression of topics and subtopics that will be covered in the chapter. You might also want to flip through the chapter and browse a bit so you have an idea of what's to come.

Next, read the chapter **Prologue,** which is a true story about real people. Some of the stories are humorous, some dramatic. We think you will enjoy this very special feature, but it will also help you to understand the material in the chapter, and why the topics are important. The Prologue will help you relate the new information in this book to experiences that are already familiar to you. Throughout each chapter, we return to the people and stories introduced in the Prologue to illustrate important concepts and ideas.

As you begin reading the chapter, you will notice several special elements. Every major section begins with an **Advance Organizer**—a short section preview that looks like this one:

> *Social support refers to the resources provided by other people. How does social support benefit health? How can social support sometimes increase stress? What gender differences have been found in social support?*

The first sentence of the Advance Organizer provides a definition or summary statement of the material in the section that follows. This summary statement is followed by focus questions. Read the questions and try to keep them in mind as you read the section. They will help you identify important points being discussed in each section. When you finish a section, look again at the Advance Organizer. Make sure that you can comfortably answer each question before you go on to the next section. Ideally, you should answer each question in an Advance Organizer in writing. You can also use the questions in the Advance Organizer to aid you in taking notes or outlining chapter sections.

You will also notice that some terms in the chapter are printed in **boldface,** or darker, type. Some of these **Key Terms** may already be familiar to you, but most will be new. The dark type signals that the term has a specialized meaning in psychology. Each Key Term is formally defined within a sentence or two of being introduced. The Key Terms are also defined in the margins, usually on the page upon which they appear. Some Key Terms include a **pronunciation guide** to help you say the word correctly. Occasionally, we also print words in *italic type* to signal either that they are boldfaced terms in another chapter or that they are specialized terms in psychology.

Certain names also appear in boldface type. These are the **Key People**—the researchers or theorists who are especially important within a given area of psychological study. Typically, Key People are the psychologists or other researchers whose names your instructor will expect you to know.

A **Concept Review** appears several times in every chapter. The Concept Reviews contain exercises that allow you to test yourself to make certain that you understand and remember important information. Write out your answers by filling in the blanks before you check your answers against the correct ones that are provided at the end of each chapter.

Each chapter has from three to five boxes that focus on specific topics. Take the time to read the boxes, because they are an integral part of each chapter. They also present important information that you may be expected to know. There are four types of boxes:

- **Critical Thinking boxes** ask you to stretch your mind a bit, by presenting issues that are provocative or controversial. They will help you actively question the implications of the material that you are learning.

- **Science Versus Pseudoscience boxes** examine the evidence for various popular pseudosciences—from astrology to subliminal motivation tapes. In addition to being interesting in themselves, these boxes will help teach you how to critically evaluate evidence.

- **Culture and Human Behavior boxes** are a special feature of this text. Many students are unaware of the importance of cross-cultural research in contemporary psychology. These boxes highlight cultural differences in thinking and behavior, and they will also sensitize you to the ways in which people's behavior, including your own, has been influenced by cultural factors.

- **In Focus boxes** present interesting information or research. Think of them as sidebar discussions. They deal with topics as diverse as sexual fantasies, whether animals dream, and how to help a stressed-out friend.

We think you'll find the **Application** section at the end of each chapter particularly helpful. Each Application provides concrete suggestions to help you deal with a real-life problem or issue. These suggestions are based upon actual psychological research, rather than opinions, anecdotes, or self-help philosophies. The Applications show you how psychology can be applied to a wide variety of everyday concerns. We hope that the Applications make a difference in your life. Because the Applications for Chapters 5 and 6 deal with study skills, motivation, and memory, you may want to skip ahead and read those right away.

Several elements are placed at the end of the chapter to help you review what you've learned. The **Chapter Summary** provides a concise overview of the main points of the chapter. All of the chapter's **Key Terms** are listed, along with the pages on which they appear and are defined. You can check your knowledge of these terms by going down the list and defining each term in your own words, then comparing it to information on the page where it is discussed. Brief biographical sketches of each chapter's **Key People** also appear at the end of the chapter; this will help you remember why they are important.

There are two special appendices at the back of this text. The **Statistics: Understanding Data** appendix discusses how psychologists use statistics to summarize and draw conclusions from the data they have gathered. The **Industrial/Organizational Psychology** appendix describes the branch of psychology that studies human behavior in the workplace. Your instructor may assign one or both of these appendices, or you may wish to read them on your own.

Also at the back of this text is an alphabetical **Glossary** containing the definitions for all Key Terms in the book. You can use the **Subject Index** to locate discussions of particular topics.

Finally, an excellent **Student Study Guide** accompanies this text. The Study Guide was written by our colleague, Cornelius Rea, at Douglas College in New Westminster, British Columbia, Canada. Your bookstore should have copies available or will be happy to order it.

That's it! We hope you enjoy reading and learning about psychology from our text. If you want to share your thoughts or suggestions for the next edition of this book, you can write to us at the following address:

Don & Sandy Hockenbury
c/o Worth Publishers
33 Irving Place
New York, NY 10003

If you have access to e-mail, our e-mail address is easy to remember:

psychology@aol.com

Chapter

Introducing Psychology

Prologue: April 19, 1995: Oklahoma City

It was a little after 10:30 a.m. when the phone rang in your author Sandy's office. It was Fern, Sandy's mother, calling from Chicago. Sandy immediately knew that something was wrong—Fern never made long-distance phone calls during the day. Fern's usually cheery voice was shaking. "Are you all right? Where's Laura? Is she OK? Where's Don?"

"I'm fine, Mom. Laura's at day care. She's *fine*. And Don's at the college. What's wrong, Mom?"

"Don't you know what happened?" Fern blurted out, her voice frantic. "Aren't you listening to the news? Turn on your TV! Somebody blew up a big office building in Oklahoma!" Fern started to cry. "They bombed a day-care center! They killed *children* and *babies*."

Like millions of other Americans, we later watched in horror as the aftermath of the Oklahoma City bombing unfolded on television. Oklahoma City was not much more than an hour's drive from our home in Tulsa. Psychologically, it felt much closer on that day. Too close. Was some deranged person targeting day-care centers in Oklahoma? Was our four-year-old daughter safe?

Sandy immediately called her school, and was relieved to hear that everything was fine. But like other schools and day-care centers in Oklahoma, our daughter's school had received telephoned bomb threats within hours of the blast. All the doors were locked and two armed guards were patrolling the grounds. When we picked Laura up that afternoon, every car was stopped at the entrance to the parking lot and checked by the guards.

1

Why Do People Risk Their Lives to Help Others? From all over the country, rescue workers volunteered to come to Oklahoma City to help in the search for survivors buried in the rubble. Working around the clock, these men and women risked their lives to help complete strangers. What motivated their behavior? And why is it that in other situations, people will ignore people who clearly need help? This is just one of the many issues about human behavior that we will explore in this text.

We knew several people who lived in the Oklahoma City area. Many of our neighbors had friends and relatives who worked in downtown Oklahoma City, and some knew people who worked in the Murrah Federal Building itself. Our friend Bob, who lives across the street, counted a childhood friend among the missing and, eventually, among the dead. His friend was a young woman who had just started as an engineer for the Army Corps of Engineers.

The immediate response to the tragedy was as dramatic as the bomb blast itself. Rescue teams, doctors, nurses, and trauma specialists, including psychologists, flew in from all over the country. In Tulsa, people stood in line for hours to donate blood to the Red Cross. Churches, schools, and businesses collected money, food, clothing, and medical supplies to help the victims.

Thunderstorms hit Oklahoma City that night, yet the rescue workers continued their efforts around the clock. Working under massive floodlights, they refused to sleep, risking their own lives in the unstable building in a desperate attempt to find and rescue survivors. And in their efforts to save others, some died. One man, Michael Loudenslager, survived the immediate blast. He helped free some of his co-workers from the rubble. Then, rather than leaving the unsafe building, he headed to the area where the day-care center had been. As he tried to make his way toward the trapped children, he was crushed by a heavy concrete block (Irving, 1995). A rescue worker, a nurse named Rebecca Anderson, was killed when she was hit by falling debris.

Rescue workers from out of town were offered free hotel rooms, boots, clothing, food, and even haircuts. Amid the outpouring of public support, rumors ran rampant. At first, many people believed that the bombing was the result of an international terrorist attack of some sort, like the World Trade Center bombing in New York City. Arab-Americans living in and near Oklahoma City, including college students, were afraid to leave their homes. Some had their windows shot out. Some Muslim organizations received bomb threats.

After the initial shock came the questions: What kind of a person would do such a thing? And why? Beyond the inevitable questions about the bomber's identity and motives came a host of others: How will the survivors cope with the tragedy? How can they be helped? More than 200 children had lost a parent. Thirty children had lost *both* parents. Will those children be psychologically scarred for life? How will their future relationships and emotional development be affected?

Broader questions were also being raised. Why would people travel across the country to risk their lives to help complete strangers? Why were Arab-Americans threatened even though they had been members of the community for years?

You probably have your own personal story to tell of the day that Oklahoma City was bombed—your emotions, thoughts, and attempts to explain what happened. Perhaps you remember exactly where you were when you first heard the news of the bombing. Some psychologists believe that we form "flashbulb" memories of dramatic, upsetting national events like the Oklahoma City bombing. Do you have a "flashbulb" memory of the morning of April 19, 1995? Where were you when you found out about the bombing? What were you doing?

The Aftereffects of Trauma What will be the long-term effects of the Oklahoma City bombing on the survivors, rescue workers, and those who lost family members, friends, and co-workers? How can they best be helped in dealing with the aftereffects of this tragedy? These are just some of the kinds of questions that psychologists study.

The kinds of questions and issues that the Oklahoma City bombing raises are often studied by psychologists. Throughout this text, we'll explore what psychologists have learned about human behavior, both in crisis situations such as the Oklahoma City bombing and in more commonplace circumstances.

In this chapter, we'll introduce you to the field of psychology. We'll consider how the definition of psychology has changed since it was founded as a science. And we'll look at how psychologists study behavior and mental processes. As we do so, you'll see that there are many different kinds of psychologists working in a variety of settings. Yet they all contribute to psychology as it exists today—a remarkably diverse discipline.

Introduction

What Is Psychology?

Psychology is now defined as the science of behavior and mental processes, but the definition has changed throughout psychology's short history. How did philosophy and physiology influence the evolution of psychology? What roles did Wilhelm Wundt and William James play in the founding of psychology?

Psychology is now formally defined as *the science of behavior and mental processes*. However, the definition of psychology has changed radically over the past century. Indeed, psychology has *not* evolved in a smooth fashion. The history of psychology is the history of a field struggling to define itself as a separate and unique scientific discipline (Hilgard, 1987).

Psychology has always focused on the scientific study of human experience. However, the definition of *which* areas of human experience should be studied, and *how* they should be studied, has changed and evolved. What is the proper subject matter of psychology? What methods should psychologists use? What should the nature of psychology be? As you'll see in the next few sections, the first psychologists struggled with these questions.

The Early History of Psychology

We begin this introductory chapter with a brief overview of psychology's history. Why is the history of psychology important? Students and others are often surprised at the wide range of topics studied by psychologists. As you'll see later in this chapter, psychology's subject area is extremely broad. It ranges from the behavior of a single brain cell to the behavior of people in groups. The topics that fall within psychology today, the emphasis that is given to particular areas, and the diverse methods that psychologists use to study these different areas are all the result of the shifting concerns of psychologists over the past century.

It was a famous German psychologist named Hermann Ebbinghaus (1908) who wrote, "Psychology has a long past, but only a short history." As a formal scientific discipline, psychology has existed for only about 120 years. Compared to other scientific disciplines, such as biology and chemistry, psychology is still a relative newcomer to the scientific community. But in a broader sense, psychology has existed for as long as people have tried to explain human behavior and thinking. That's what Ebbinghaus meant in writing that psychology has a long past. Indeed, the beginnings of psychology can be traced back for centuries to the writings of the great philosophers.

The Influence of Philosophy

Many great philosophers and scholars concerned themselves with issues that are still important in psychology. For example, three centuries before the birth of Christ, the Greek philosopher Aristotle (384–323 B.C.) wrote extensively about topics like sleep, dreaming, the senses, memory, and learning (Watson & Evans, 1991). Some 1,400 years later, the French philosopher René Descartes (1596–1650) promoted a doctrine called *dualism*—the idea that mind and body are separate entities. Today, psychologists continue to debate the relationship between mind and body or brain (Damasio, 1994; Sperry, 1995).

psychology
The scientific study of behavior and mental processes.

Nature or Nurture? Both mother and daughter are clearly enjoying the experience of painting together. Is the child's interest in painting an expression of her natural tendencies, or is it the result of her mother's encouragement and teaching? Parental influence is just one of many environmental factors that can nurture the developing child's talents, interests, and motives. Are such environmental factors more important than the child's inborn abilities? Originally posed by philosophers hundreds of years ago, such questions continue to interest psychologists today.

Aristotle, Descartes, and other philosophers and scholars laid the groundwork for many questions that have been central to psychology. For example, philosophers have debated for centuries which was more important: the inborn *nature* of the individual, or *nurture,* the environmental influences on the individual (Kimble, 1993). Psychologists continue to focus on this question, which is called the *nature/nurture issue* (see Plomin, 1993). We, too, will discuss the nature/nurture issue in relation to various topics throughout this text, including intelligence (Chapter 7), human development (Chapter 9), gender and sexuality (Chapter 10), and personality (Chapter 11).

Although such issues are still unresolved, there is a key difference between the philosophical debates of centuries ago and the scientific debates of today. The philosophical debates about such issues relied largely on observation, intuition, and logical reasoning. However, logic and intuition could only advance the understanding of human behavior to a certain point. In contrast, modern psychological debates are based on the systematic gathering of evidence to test and support ideas.

Two hundred years ago, many influential scientists doubted that human behavior and mental processes could be studied scientifically. Thus, the eventual emergence of psychology as a science hinged on advances in already established sciences, particularly physiology.

The Influence of Physiology

Of all the other sciences, the one that is most responsible for the emergence of psychology as a scientific discipline is physiology. *Physiology* is a branch of biology that studies the functions and parts of living organisms, including humans. Beginning in the 1600s, physiologists were becoming interested in the human brain and its relation to behavior. By the early 1700s, intriguing discoveries had already been made. For example, it was discovered that damage to one side of the brain produced a loss of function in the opposite side of the body (Fancher, 1990). By the early 1800s, the idea that different brain areas were related to different behavioral functions was being vigorously debated, as we'll discuss more fully in Chapter 2.

Physiologists were also beginning to understand the functioning of the senses, like vision and hearing. In the mid-1800s, for example, a German physiologist named Hermann von Helmholtz developed an explanation for color vision, which we'll discuss in Chapter 3. Collectively, the early scientific discoveries made by physiologists were establishing the foundation for an idea that was to prove critical to the development of psychology: that scientific methods could be applied to issues of human behavior and thinking.

Wilhelm Wundt:
The Founder of Psychology

By the late 1800s, the stage was set for the emergence of psychology as a separate scientific discipline. The leading proponent of this idea was a German physiologist named **Wilhelm Wundt,** who had been an assistant to Helmholtz. Like Helmholtz, Wundt applied experimental methods to the study of fundamental psychological processes, such as mental reaction times in response to visual or auditory stimuli. For example, Wundt tried to measure precisely how long it took to consciously detect the sight and sound of a bell being struck.

In 1874, Wundt published the first bona fide psychology textbook, *Principles of Physiological Psychology,* in which he outlined the connections between physiology and psychology. In his book he promoted his belief that psychology should be established as a separate scientific discipline, one that would use experimental methods to study mental processes (Fancher, 1990). Wundt also opened the first working research laboratory in the new field at the University of Leipzig in March 1879, which is regarded by many as the formal beginning of psychology as a science.

Wundt, Titchener, and Structuralism

Wilhelm Wundt's most devoted student, Edward B. Titchener (1867–1927), established structuralism, the first major approach, or "school," in psychology. **Structuralism** held that even our most complex conscious experiences can be broken down into elemental *structures*, or component parts, of sensations and feelings. To identify these structures of conscious thought, Wundt and Titchener trained subjects in a procedure called *introspection*. The subjects would view a simple stimulus, such as an apple, then try to reconstruct their sensations and feelings immediately after viewing it (Hilgard, 1987). They might first report on the colors they saw, then the smells, and so on, to create a total description of their experience.

Along with being the first school of thought in early psychology, structuralism also holds the dubious distinction of being the first school to disappear. The structuralists relied heavily on the method of introspection. However, introspection had many limitations. First, even a subject who was well trained in introspection varied in his responses to the same stimulus from trial to trial. And different subjects often provided very different introspective reports about the same stimulus. Thus, introspection did not seem to be a very reliable method of investigation.

Second, introspection could not be used to study children or animals. And third, complex topics such as learning, development, mental disorders, and personality did not lend themselves to be investigated using introspection. Structuralism was simply too limited to accommodate the rapidly growing field of psychology.

Wilhelm Wundt (1932–1920) German physiologist Wilhelm Wundt is generally credited as being the founder of the new science of psychology. In 1879, he established the first psychology research laboratory in Leipzig, Germany. Wundt's student, Edward Titchener, founded the first major school or approach in psychology, called structuralism.

Seize the very first possible opportunity to act on every resolution you make, and on every emotional prompting you may experience in the direction of the habits you aspire to gain.

William James Principles of Psychology, 1890

structuralism
Early school of psychology which emphasized studying the most basic components, or structures, of conscious experiences.

functionalism
Early school of psychology which emphasized studying the purpose, or function, of behavior and mental experiences.

William James and Functionalism:
Establishing Psychology in America

Psychology may have officially begun in Germany in 1879, but it was already well on its way to being established in the United States through the efforts of Harvard professor **William James.** James began teaching a physiology and anatomy class at Harvard University in the 1870s. He was an intense, enthusiastic teacher who actively engaged his students in the quest for new knowledge. James was also prone to changing the subject matter of his classes as his own interests changed (B. Ross, 1991).

Gradually, his lectures came to focus more on psychology than physiology. By the late 1870s, James was teaching classes devoted exclusively to the topic of psychology (Fancher, 1990). Around this time, James also began writing a comprehensive textbook of psychology, a task that would take him over a decade to complete. Finally published as two volumes in 1890, it was entitled *Principles of Psychology* and was over 1,400 pages long! Despite its length, James's *Principles of Psychology* quickly became the leading psychology textbook and had an enormous impact on the development of psychology in the United States (B. Ross, 1991).

James's ideas became the basis for functionalism, an approach to psychology that differed from structuralism. **Functionalism** stressed the importance of how behavior *functions* to allow people and animals to adapt to their environment. The functionalists did not limit their methods to introspection.

William James (1842–1910) Harvard professor William James was instrumental in establishing psychology in the United States. In 1890, James published a highly influential text, *Principles of Psychology*. James's ideas became the basis of another early school of psychology called functionalism, which stressed studying the adaptive and practical functions of human behavior.

They expanded the scope of psychology research to include direct observation of living creatures in natural settings. Functionalists also examined how psychology could be applied to areas such as education, child rearing, and the work environment.

Like the structuralists, the functionalists thought that psychology should focus on conscious experiences. But rather than trying to identify the fundamental "structures" of consciousness, William James saw consciousness as an ongoing "stream" of mental activity. As James wrote in *Talks to Teachers* in 1899:

> Now the immediate *fact which psychology, the science of mind, has to study is also the most general fact. It is the fact that in each of us, when awake (and often when asleep),* some kind of consciousness is always going on. *There is a stream, a succession of states, or waves, or fields (or whatever you please to call them), of knowledge, of feeling, of desire, of deliberation, etc., that constantly pass and repass, and that constitute our inner life. The existence of this is the primal fact, [and] the nature and origin of it form the essential problem, of our science.*

In Chapter 4, on consciousness, we'll encounter James's views on consciousness again. For now, simply understand that both the functionalists and the structuralists saw the study of consciousness as a fundamental goal of the new science of psychology. However, they had very different ideas about how and why consciousness should be studied.

Like structuralism, functionalism no longer exists as a school of thought in contemporary psychology. Nevertheless, functionalism's twin themes of (1) the importance of the adaptive role of behavior and (2) the emphasis upon applying psychology to enhancing human behavior continue to be evident in many areas of modern psychology (D. N. Robinson, 1993).

William James and His Students

James also profoundly influenced American psychology through his students, many of whom became prominent American psychologists. Two of James's most notable students were G. Stanley Hall and Mary Whiton Calkins.

In 1878 **G. Stanley Hall** received the first Ph.D. in psychology to be awarded in America. Hall founded the first psychology research laboratory in the United States. He also began publishing the *American Journal of Psychology*, the first U.S. journal devoted to psychology. Most important, in 1892, Hall founded the American Psychological Association (Street, 1994). Today, the American Psychological Association is one of the world's leading professional organizations of psychologists, with over 130,000 members (APA, 1995a).

In 1890 **Mary Whiton Calkins** was assigned the task of teaching experimental psychology at a new women's college—Wellesley College. Calkins studied with James at nearby Harvard University. She completed all the requirements for a Ph.D. in psychology. However, Harvard refused to officially grant her the Ph.D. degree

G. Stanley Hall (1844–1924) G. Stanley Hall helped organize psychology in the United States. Among his achievements, Hall established the first psychology research laboratory in the United States, started publishing the *American Journal of Psychology*, and founded the American Psychological Association.

Mary Whiton Calkins (1863–1930) Under the direction of William James, Mary Whiton Calkins completed all the requirements for a Ph.D. in psychology. Calkins had a distinguished professional career, establishing a psychology laboratory at Wellesley College and becoming the first woman president of the American Psychological Association.

because she was a woman. At the time, Harvard was not coeducational (Brennan, 1991).

Despite the fact that she was never awarded the degree she had earned, Calkins went on to make several notable contributions to psychology (Stevens & Gardner, 1982). She conducted research in many areas, including dreams, memory, and personality. In 1891 she established a psychological laboratory at Wellesley College, one of the first in the United States. At the turn of the century, she wrote a well-received textbook herself, titled *Introduction to Psychology*. In 1905 Mary Whiton Calkins was elected president of the American Psychological Association—the first woman, but not the last, to hold that position (Street, 1994).

Psychology in the Twentieth Century

> *Behaviorism dominated American psychology until the 1960s, but psychology was also influenced by psychoanalysis, Gestalt psychology, and humanistic psychology. What were the key ideas stressed by each approach? Who were the key proponents of each approach?*

Beginning in the early 1900s, new approaches emerged that challenged the principles of structuralism and functionalism. In this section, we will focus on four of these approaches: behaviorism, psychoanalysis, Gestalt psychology, and humanistic psychology.

Behaviorism

The course of psychology changed dramatically in the early 1900s, when another approach, called **behaviorism,** emerged as a dominating force. Behaviorism rejected the emphasis on consciousness promoted by the structuralists and the functionalists. Instead, behaviorism contended that psychology should focus its scientific investigations on observable behavior that could be objectively measured and verified.

Behaviorism grew out of the pioneering work of a Russian physiologist named **Ivan Pavlov.** Pavlov demonstrated that dogs could learn to associate a neutral stimulus, such as the sound of a bell, with an automatic behavior, such as salivating to food. Once the association was formed, the sound of the bell alone would make the dog salivate. Pavlov enthusiastically believed he had discovered the mechanism by which all behaviors were learned.

In the United States, Pavlov's enthusiasm was shared by a young, dynamic psychologist named **John Watson.** Watson championed behaviorism as a new school, or approach to psychology. Behaviorism rejected both introspection as a method and the idea that consciousness or mental processes should be studied by psychology. As Watson wrote in his classic 1924 book entitled *Behaviorism*:

> *Behaviorism, on the contrary, holds that the subject matter of human psychology is the behavior of the human being. Behaviorism claims that consciousness is neither a definite nor a usable concept. The behaviorist, who has been trained always as an experimentalist, holds, further, that belief in the existence of consciousness goes back to the ancient days of superstition and magic.*

behaviorism
School of psychology and theoretical viewpoint that emphasizes the study of observable behaviors, especially as they pertain to the process of learning.

Ivan Pavlov

John B. Watson

B.F. Skinner

Three Key Figures in the Development of Behaviorism Based on the pioneering research of Russian physiologist Ivan Pavlov (1849–1936), American psychologist John B. Watson (1878–1958) founded the school of behaviorism. Behaviorism advocated that psychology should study observable behaviors, not mental processes. Following Watson, B.F. Skinner (1904–1990) continued to champion the ideas of behaviorism, and became one of the most influential psychologists of the twentieth century. Like Watson, Skinner strongly advocated the study of observable behaviors rather than mental processes.

The influence of behaviorism on American psychology was enormous. Although Watson left academic psychology in the early 1920s, behaviorism was later championed by an equally forceful proponent—the famous American psychologist **B. F. Skinner.** Between Watson and Skinner, behaviorism largely dominated American psychology for almost half a century. During that time, the study of conscious experiences was virtually ignored as a topic in psychology (Hilgard, 1992; Leahey, 1992).

Instead of mental processes, the early behaviorists focused exclusively on overt behavior. Their goal was to discover the fundamental principles of *learning*—how behavior is acquired and modified in response to environmental influences. For the most part, the behaviorists studied animal behavior under carefully controlled laboratory conditions. In Chapter 5, on learning, we'll look at the lives and contributions of Pavlov, Watson, and Skinner in greater detail.

Psychoanalysis

While Watson and others studied directly observable behaviors, across the Atlantic Ocean an Austrian physician named **Sigmund Freud** focused on uncovering causes of behavior that were *unconscious*—that is, hidden from the person's conscious awareness. Freud's school of psychological thought was called **psychoanalysis,** and it emphasized the role of unconscious conflicts in determining behavior and personality.

Freud's theories about personality and behavior were based largely on his work with his patients and on insights derived from self-analysis. Freud believed that human behavior was motivated by unconscious conflicts that were almost always sexual or aggressive in nature. Past experiences, especially childhood experiences, were thought to be critical in the formation of adult personality and behavior. According to Freud (1904), glimpses of these unconscious impulses are revealed in everyday life in dreams, memory blocks, slips of the tongue, and spontaneous humor. Freud believed that when unconscious conflicts become extreme, psychological disorders can be the result.

Many of the basic ideas of psychoanalysis continue to influence psychologists and other professionals in the mental health field. Along with being a form of psychotherapy, Freud's psychoanalysis also provided a landmark theory of personality. In Chapter 11, on personality, and Chapter 15, on psychotherapy, we'll explore Freud's ideas in more detail.

Sigmund Freud (1856–1939) Sigmund Freud began his career as a neurologist and physician in Vienna, Austria. Freud's probing of the unconscious conflicts of his patients led him to the formulation of psychoanalysis, his influential theory of personality and psychotherapy.

Gestalt Psychology

Another early influence on American psychology was the school of Gestalt psychology. Founded by German psychologist **Max Wertheimer** in the early 1900s, **Gestalt psychology** emphasized the perception of whole figures rather than the individual elements of conscious experiences stressed by the structuralists (Leahey, 1992). After Wertheimer and other Gestalt psychologists immigrated to the United States during the rise of the Nazis in Germany in the 1930s, Gestalt psychology helped advance the study of perception and problem solving in American psychology. Unlike behaviorism,

psychoanalysis
Personality theory and form of psychotherapy that emphasizes the role of unconscious factors in personality and behavior.

Gestalt psychology
(Guess-TALT) School of psychology that emphasized the perception of whole figures rather than the individual elements of conscious experiences.

humanistic psychology
School of psychology and theoretical viewpoint that emphasizes each person's unique potential for psychological growth and self-direction.

Gestalt psychology assigned an important role to mental activities in organizing sensations into meaningful perceptions (Hilgard, 1987). In Chapter 3, on sensation and perception, we'll encounter some of the contributions of the Gestalt psychologists.

Humanistic Psychology

Behaviorism and psychoanalysis were the two perspectives that dominated the thinking of most American psychologists for several decades. In the 1950s a new school of thought emerged, called **humanistic psychology.** Because humanistic psychology was distinctly different from both psychoanalysis and behaviorism, it was sometimes referred to as the "third force" in American psychology (Maslow, 1970).

Humanistic psychology was largely founded by American psychologist **Carl Rogers.** Like Freud, Rogers was heavily influenced by his experiences with his psychotherapy clients. However, rather than emphasizing unconscious conflicts, Rogers emphasized the *conscious* experiences of his patients, including each person's unique potential for psychological growth and self-direction. In contrast to the behaviorists, who saw human behavior as being determined solely by environmental influences, Rogers emphasized *self-determination*, free will, and the importance of choice in human behavior (Leahey, 1992).

Abraham Maslow, another humanistic psychologist, developed a theory of motivation that emphasized psychological growth, which we discuss in Chapter 8. Like psychoanalysis, humanistic psychology included both influential theories of personality and a form of psychotherapy, which we'll discuss in later chapters.

The history of psychology has included considerable debate about the proper course that the new science should follow. Each of the schools that we've briefly described helped shape the focus of psychology in the first half of the twentieth century. And, as you'll see throughout this textbook, psychological research has been strongly influenced by the changing perspectives in psychology.

Carl Rogers (1902–1987)

Two Key Figures in the Development of Humanistic Psychology Carl Rogers and Abraham Maslow were key figures in establishing humanistic psychology. Humanistic psychology emphasized the importance of self-determination, free will, and human potential. The ideas of Carl Rogers have been particularly influential in modern psychotherapy. Abraham Maslow's theory of motivation emphasized the importance of psychological growth.

Abraham Maslow (1908–1970)

Major Schools in Psychology

Identify the school or approach *and* the founder associated with each of the following statements.

1. Psychology should study how behavior and mental processes allow organisms to adapt to their environments.
School/Approach _____
Founder _____

2. Psychology should emphasize each person's unique potential for psychological growth and self-directedness.
School/Approach _____
Founder _____

3. Psychology should focus on the elements of conscious experiences, using the method of introspection.
School/Approach _____
Founder _____

4. Human behavior is strongly influenced by unconscious sexual and aggressive conflicts.
School/Approach _____
Founder _____

5. Psychology should scientifically investigate observable behaviors that can be measured objectively, and should not study consciousness or mental processes.
School/Approach _____
Founder _____

6. Rather than studying the individual elements of conscious experience, psychology should emphasize the role of active mental processes in organizing sensations into meaningful perceptions.
School/Approach _____
Founder _____

Psychology Today

Psychology today is a very diverse field. What important influences have helped shape psychology in the last few decades? What are the six major perspectives in psychology, and what are some of psychology's most important specialty areas?

Since the 1960s, several approaches have emerged as important influences on contemporary psychology. In this section, we'll take a look at some of these recent developments in psychology's continuing evolution as a science.

Biological Psychology

Biological psychology emphasizes studying the physical bases of human and animal behavior. Psychologists have always been interested in biological influences on behavior, but several factors have contributed to the growth of biological psychology in the last few decades. For example, during the late 1950s and early 1960s, drugs were developed that helped control the symptoms of serious psychological disorders like schizophrenia and depression. The relative success of these new drugs led psychologists to focus on the important interaction between biological factors and human behavior. By the 1970s, researchers had begun to identify the behavioral effects of chemical messengers in the brain.

Equally important were technological advances that allowed psychologists and other researchers to explore the human brain as never before. For example, the development of a computerized X-ray procedure called the *CAT scan* allowed researchers to study the structures of the intact brain. Gradually, the complex functions of the brain were beginning to be unraveled, producing new understandings about the biological bases of memory, learning, emotions, mental disorders, and other behaviors.

Today, biological psychologists study the nervous system, genetics, the endocrine system, and the immune system. Throughout this textbook, we'll describe the biological factors that are involved in behavior and mental processes.

Cognitive Psychology

The 1960s also witnessed a return to the study of how mental processes influence behavior. Often called "the cognitive revolution" because it represented a break from traditional behaviorism, cognitive psychology focused once again on the important role of mental processes in how people process information, develop language, solve problems, and think (Anderson, 1995).

One important factor in the cognitive revolution was the development of the first computers in the 1950s (Ellis & Hunt, 1992). This gave psychologists a new model for conceptualizing human mental processes. Much like a computer, human thinking, memory, and perception could be understood in terms of an "information processing" model.

Cross-Cultural Psychology

More recently, psychologists began to take a closer look at how cultural factors influence patterns of behavior. By the late 1980s, cross-cultural psychology had emerged in full force as large numbers of psychologists began studying the diversity of human behavior in different cultural settings and countries (Triandis, 1994, 1996). In the process, some well-established psychological findings that were thought to be true for all humans around the world turned out not to be so.

For example, one well-established psychological finding was that people will exert more effort on a task when working alone than when working as part of a group, a phenomenon called *social loafing*. Social loafing was originally demonstrated in research conducted in North America during the 1970s, and it has been a common finding in many psychological studies conducted in North America and Europe. But can we safely assume that social loafing is a universal phenomenon?

Before you answer that question, keep in mind that about 70 percent of the world's population does *not* live in North America or Europe. When similar studies were conducted with Chinese participants in Taiwan during the 1980s, the exact *opposite* was found to be true (see Moghaddam & others, 1993). Chinese participants worked harder on a task when they were part of a group than when they were working alone.

As it turned out, such findings were just the tip of the iceberg. Today, psychologists have become very sensitive to the influence of cultural and ethnic factors on behavior. We have included "Culture and Human Behavior" boxes throughout this textbook to help sensitize you, as well, to the influence of culture on behavior—including your own. Because cross-cultural psychology is a relatively new specialty in psychology, we describe it in more detail in Culture and Human Behavior Box 1.1: "What Is Cross-Cultural Psychology?"

CULTURE AND HUMAN BEHAVIOR 1.1

What Is Cross-Cultural Psychology?

Culture is a broad term that refers to the attitudes, values, beliefs, and behaviors shared by a group of people and communicated from one generation to another (Matsumoto, 1994). A person's sense of *cultural identity* is influenced by such factors as ethnic background, nationality, race, religion, and language. When this broad definition is applied to people throughout the world, about 4,000 different cultures can be said to exist. Studying the differences between those cultures as well as the

more general issue of how culture influences behavior are the fundamental goals of *cross-cultural psychology* (Betancourt & López, 1993).

On the one hand, people around the globe share many attributes: we all eat, sleep, form families, seek happiness, and mourn losses. After all, we are all members of the same species. On the other hand, the way we learn to express our human qualities can vary considerably from one culture to the next. What we eat, where we sleep, and

All cultures are simultaneously very similar and very different.

Harry Triandis (1994)

how we form families, define happiness, and express sadness can take very different forms in different cultures. That's why cross-cultural psychologist Harry Triandis (1994) writes that "All cultures are simultaneously very similar and very different."

As we grow up within a given culture, we learn our culture's *norms,* or rules of behavior. Once those cultural norms are understood and internalized, people tend to act in accordance with their cultural norms without too much thought. For example, cultural norms in the United States prescribe that small children do not sleep in the same room or bed as their parents. However, in many cultures around the world, it's taken for granted that parents and

Cultural Differences in Subway Norms
Like thousands of commuters in major cities in the United States, commuters in Tokyo take the subway to work each day. In Japan, however, commuters line up politely behind white lines on the subway platform and patiently wait their turn to board the train. White-gloved conductors obligingly "assist" passengers in boarding by shoving them in from behind, cramming as many people into the subway car as possible. Clearly, the norms that govern "subway-riding behavior" are very different in American and Japanese cultures.

children will sleep in the same bed (Morelli & others, 1992). In these cultures, people are shocked at the North American practice of separating infants from family members during the night.

Most people share a natural tendency to accept their own cultural rules as defining what's "normal". The tendency to use your own culture as the standard for judging other cultures is called **ethnocentrism** (Triandis, 1994). Ethnocentrism can lead to the inability to separate ourselves from our own cultural backgrounds and biases so that we can understand the behaviors of others (Matsumoto, 1994). Thus, ethnocentrism may prevent you from being aware of how your behavior has been shaped by your own culture.

Some degree of ethnocentrism is probably inevitable, but extreme ethnocentrism can lead to intolerance for other cultures (Moghaddam & others, 1993). If you believe that your way of seeing things or behaving is the only proper one, other ways of behaving and thinking may seem not only foreign but ridiculous, wrong, or immoral.

With technological advances in communication, trade, and travel, the world is rapidly becoming a global village. Ethnocentric intolerance for other ways of thinking and behaving can undermine appreciation for and acceptance of diversity within the new global community. In the United States, as in many other countries, we can no longer afford to be ignorant or intolerant of other cultures.

Along with influencing how we behave, culture also affects the way we define our sense of personal identity (Markus & Kitayama, 1991; Matsumoto, 1994). For the most part, the dominant cultures of North America, Australia, New Zealand, and Europe can be described as individualistic cultures (Brislin, 1993). **Individualistic cultures** emphasize the needs and goals of the individual over the needs and goals of the group (Triandis, 1996). In such cultures, the self is seen as *independent,* autonomous, and distinctive. Much of a person's identity is defined by his or her individual achievements, abilities, and occupation.

In contrast, **collectivistic cultures** emphasize the needs and goals of the group over the needs and goals of the individual. The cultures of Asia, Africa, and Central and South America tend to be collectivistic (Brislin, 1993). In a collectivistic culture, the self is seen as being much more *interdependent* with others (Markus & Kitayama, 1991; Simon & others, 1995). Your relationships with others, and your identification with a larger group, such as the family or tribe, are key components of your personal identity (Triandis, 1996).

Like all psychologists, cross-cultural psychologists look for consistent patterns in human behavior. Although cross-cultural psychologists make generalizations about the behaviors and attitudes of people in different cultures, they recognize that there is a great deal of individual variation among the members of *every* culture.

Our own culture is no exception. For example, suppose we made the statement, "American college students like pizza." Is it true that *every* college student in the United States likes pizza? No, of course not. But as a general statement, it is reasonably accurate to say that *many* or *most* American college students like pizza.

The same is true when cross-cultural psychologists make generalizations about cultural attributes: general statements may be valid yet still allow for individual variation. It's important that you keep that qualification in mind when cross-cultural findings are discussed, as they will be throughout this text.

The Culture and Human Behavior boxes that we have included in this book will help you learn about human behavior in other cultures. They will also help you understand how culture affects *your* behavior, beliefs, attitudes, and values as well. We hope you find this feature to be both interesting and enlightening!

Perspectives and Specialty Areas in Psychology

In the last few decades, the scope of topics in psychology has become progressively more diverse. And, as psychology's knowledge base has increased, psychology itself has become more specialized (Bower, 1993). Rather than being dominated by a particular school of thought, today's psychologists tend to characterize themselves according to (1) the *perspective* they emphasize in investigating psychological topics and (2) the *specialty area* in which they practice.

Major Perspectives in Psychology

Any given topic in contemporary psychology can be approached from a variety of perspectives. Traditionally, five major perspectives have been identified in psychology: *biological, behavioral, psychoanalytic, humanistic,* and *cognitive.* Because of the increasing importance of cross-cultural research in

TABLE 1.1 Perspectives in Psychology

Perspective	Emphasis
Biological	Physical bases of behavior
Behaviorial	Environmental influences on behavior
Psychoanalytic	Unconscious influences on behavior and personality
Humanistic	Psychological growth and personal potential
Cognitive	Mental processes
Cross-cultural	Influence of culture on behavior

psychology, some psychologists have added a sixth: the *cross-cultural perspective*. As you can see in Table 1.1, each perspective reflects a particular emphasis in studying a given topic or issue.

Let's illustrate how the different perspectives might approach studying the developmental period that spans the first two years of life—infancy.

- From a *biological perspective*, a psychologist might investigate brain changes during infancy, sensory abilities, or the influence of genetics.

- Taking a *behavioral perspective*, a psychologist might focus on how the infant's behavior is influenced by facial expressions and other responses of the caregiver.

- From a *psychoanalytic perspective*, a psychologist might study the impact of the infant's emotional relationship with his mother or father on his developing personality.

- From a *humanistic perspective*, a psychologist might be interested in how different parenting practices promote or restrict a child's striving to reach her potential.

- From the *cognitive perspective*, a psychologist would study how the infant processes, stores, and remembers information. She might investigate when the infant understands that objects continue to exist even if he can't see them, or how the infant gradually acquires an understanding of words.

- From a *cross-cultural perspective*, a psychologist might study the influence of culturally specific child-rearing practices, such as being raised in a kibbutz, a collective community in Israel.

FIGURE 1.1 Specialty Areas and Employment Settings
You can see the approximate percentage of psychologists in each of the major specialty areas in the chart on the left. Although many psychologists work in more than one setting, the chart on the right shows their primary place of employment.
(Adapted from Thurgood & Clarke, 1995, and APA Research Office, 1995)

Specialty Areas

Listed below are some of the important specialty areas in contemporary psychology, which reflect the enormous diversity of psychology today. Figure 1.1 shows the approximate percentage of U.S. psychologists working in different specialty areas.

Specialty Areas of Psychologists

Employment Settings of Psychologists

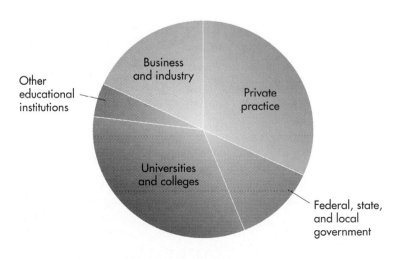

- **Biological psychology** focuses on the relationship between behavior and the body's physical systems, including the brain and the rest of the nervous system, the endocrine system, the immune system, and genetics.

- **Cognitive psychology** investigates mental processes, including reasoning and thinking, problem solving, memory, perception, mental imagery, and language.

- **Experimental psychology** is the term that has been traditionally used to describe research focused on such basic topics as sensory processes, principles of learning, emotion, and motivation. It's important to note, however, that experimental psychologists are *not* the only psychologists who perform experiments. Experiments are used by psychologists in every area of psychology.

- **Developmental psychology** studies the physical, social, and psychological changes that occur at different ages and stages over the lifespan, from conception to old age.

- **Social psychology** explores how people are affected by their social environments, including how people think about and influence others. Topics as varied as conformity, obedience, persuasion, interpersonal attraction, helping behavior, prejudice, aggression, and social beliefs are studied by social psychologists.

- **Personality psychology** examines individual differences and the characteristics that make each person unique, including how those characteristics originated and developed.

- **Health psychology** focuses on the role of psychological factors in the development, prevention, and treatment of illness. Health psychology includes areas like stress and coping, the relationship between psychological factors and health, patient/doctor relationships, and ways of promoting health-enhancing behaviors.

- **Educational psychology** studies how people of all ages learn. Educational psychologists help develop the instructional methods and materials used to train people in both educational and work settings. A related field, *school psychology,* focuses on designing programs that promote the intellectual, social, and emotional development of children, including those with special needs.

- **Industrial/organizational psychology** is concerned with the relationship between people and work. This specialty includes such topics as worker productivity and job satisfaction, personnel selection and training, consumer reactions to a company's products or services, and the interaction between people and equipment. Industrial/organizational psychology is discussed in Appendix B.

- **Clinical psychology** studies the causes, treatment, and prevention of different types of psychological disorders, such as debilitating anxiety or depression, eating disorders, and chronic substance abuse. A related specialty area is *counseling psychology,* which aims to improve everyday functioning by helping people solve problems in daily living and cope more effectively with challenging situations.

Like clinical psychologists, psychiatrists also study the causes, treatment, and prevention of psychological disorders. How are clinical psychologists and psychiatrists different? A *clinical psychologist* typically has a doctorate in psychology, which includes intensive training in treating people with psychological disorders. In contrast, a *psychiatrist* has a medical degree plus years of specialized training in the treatment of psychological disorders. While both clinical psychologists and psychiatrists can treat patients with psychological disorders, only psychiatrists can prescribe medications and order medical procedures, such as electroshock treatments. Finally, a *psychoanalyst* is a clinical psychologist, psychiatrist, or other mental health professional with extensive training in Freud's psychoanalytic method of psychotherapy. In Chapter 15 we'll describe other workers in the mental health field, such as clinical social workers and psychiatric nurses.

Clinical Psychologists Working in private practice, hospitals, or community mental health centers, clinical psychologists have extensive training in psychological disorders, psychotherapy techniques, and psychological testing. Along with conducting psychotherapy with individuals, clinical psychologists also work with married couples, families, and groups of unrelated people.

In Figure 1.1, you can see the settings in which psychologists work. Despite diverse work settings and interests, psychologists share the methods by which they investigate facets of human behavior and mental processes. In the next section, we'll look at how psychologists are guided by the scientific method in their efforts to understand behavior and mental processes.

CONCEPT REVIEW 1.2

Major Perspectives and Specialty Areas in Psychology

1. Dr. Chan conducts research on specialized cells in the brain and nervous system. Which perspective in psychology does Dr. Chan's research best represent?
  a. biological   **c.** cognitive
  b. behavioral   **d.** cross-cultural

2. A North American researcher found that when workers were part of a group, they were less productive than when working alone. However, researchers in Taiwan reported the opposite finding. These contradictory findings emphasize the importance of the _____ perspective in psychological research.
  a. cognitive   **c.** behavioral
  b. cross-cultural   **d.** humanistic

3. Dr. Wittlesea focuses her research on the use of mental images in problem solving and memory. Dr. Wittlesea is most likely a _____ psychologist.
  a. biological   **c.** humanistic
  b. behavioral   **d.** cognitive

4. Recently David has begun to feel so tense, anxious, and depressed that he sometimes spends the whole day in bed and can no longer study or work. It would be most beneficial for David to be examined by a(n) _____ psychologist.
  a. experimental   **c.** social
  b. developmental   **d.** clinical

5. Dr. Sharma and Dr. Wilcox both work in a mental health clinic. Dr. Sharma routinely prescribes medications to help alleviate the symptoms of mental disorders. Dr. Wilcox cannot prescribe drugs and relies primarily on psychotherapy to treat patients. It is most likely that Dr. Sharma is a _____ and Dr. Wilcox is a _____.
  a. cognitive psychologist; behavioral psychologist
  b. psychiatrist; clinical psychologist
  c. social psychologist; developmental psychologist
  d. social psychologist; health psychologist

The Scientific Method

The scientific method is a set of assumptions, attitudes, and procedures that guide scientists as they conduct research. What are the four goals of psychology? What assumptions and attitudes are held by psychologists? What characterizes each step of the scientific method?

The four basic goals of psychology are to (1) describe, (2) explain, (3) predict, and (4) control or influence behavior and mental processes. For example, a psychologist might try to *describe* people's reactions to the Oklahoma City bombing, *explain* why they reacted the way they did, *predict* how survivors will cope with their experience, and *influence* them by offering counseling. In fact, psychologists were actively engaged in all of these pursuits during the aftermath of the bombing.

In trying to achieve these four goals, psychologists rely on the scientific method. The **scientific method** refers to a set of assumptions, attitudes, and procedures that guide researchers in creating questions to investigate, generating evidence, and drawing conclusions (Heiman, 1995). Even though some psychologists do not conduct research, all psychologists have been extensively trained in the scientific method. In this section, we'll look at what that means.

Assumptions and Attitudes of Psychologists

Like all scientists, psychologists are guided by the basic scientific assumption that *events are lawful* (American Association for the Advancement of Science, 1989). When this scientific assumption is applied to psychology, it means that *psychologists assume that behavior and mental processes follow consistent patterns*.

Psychologists are also guided by the scientific assumption that *events are explainable*. Thus, *psychologists assume that behavior and mental processes have a cause or causes*. Although psychology may not currently be able to explain the causes of a particular phenomenon, psychologists move on the premise that an explanation does exist and will ultimately be discovered.

Along with these basic assumptions, psychologists share a particular group of attitudes in trying to achieve the goals of psychology. In striving to discover and understand consistent patterns of behavior, psychologists are *open-minded*. They are willing to consider new explanations of behavior and mental processes. However, their open-minded attitude is tempered by a healthy sense of *scientific skepticism*. That is, psychologists *critically evaluate the evidence* for new findings, especially those that seem contrary to established knowledge. And in promoting new ideas and findings, psychologists are *cautious* in the claims they make.

Ideally, you should assume the same set of attitudes as you approach the study of psychology. To learn how to be a better critical thinker, see Critical Thinking Box 1.2.

Finally, all psychologists are professionally obligated to follow a *code of ethical principles and conduct*. This code prescribes that psychologists respect the fundamental rights, dignity, and worth of all people (American Psychological Association, 1992a). When psychologists conduct research with animals, they follow another strict code of ethics that governs the humane treatment of animal subjects (American Psychological Association, 1992b). Later in the chapter, we'll discuss research ethics in more detail.

scientific method
A set of assumptions, attitudes, and procedures that guide researchers in creating questions to investigate, generating evidence, and drawing conclusions.

CRITICAL THINKING 1.2

What Is Critical Thinking?

As you'll see throughout this text, many issues in contemporary psychology are far from being settled; many questions have no clear-cut answer. And although research findings may have been arrived at in a very objective manner, the *interpretation* of what findings mean and how they should be applied can be a matter of considerable debate. In short, there is a subjective side to *any* science. This is especially true in psychology because it tackles questions and issues that concern people in all walks of life, everything from child rearing to the treatment of the mentally ill.

As you look at the evidence that psychology has to offer on many topics, we want to encourage you to engage in critical thinking. Just exactly what does *critical thinking* mean? There are many definitions of critical thinking (e.g., Halpern & Nummedal, 1995; Halonen, 1995). However, some common themes emerge.

In general, *critical thinking* refers to *actively questioning* statements rather than blindly accepting them. More precisely, we define **critical thinking** as the active process of:

- Trying to minimize the influence of preconceptions and biases while rationally evaluating evidence;
- Determining the conclusions that can be drawn from the evidence;
- Considering alternative explanations.

In the following list we summarize some of the key attitudes and mental skills that characterize critical thinking (R. A. Smith, 1995; Mayer & Goodchild, 1990; Halonen, 1986). You probably already use many of these skills in everyday life to make decisions and form opinions. Let's briefly consider five key critical thinking skills and the conditions under which it can be especially challenging to apply that particular skill.

1. The critical thinker can assume other perspectives. Critical thinkers are not imprisoned by their own point of view. Nor are they limited in their capacity to imagine life experiences and perspectives that are fundamentally different from their own. Rather, the critical thinker strives to understand and evaluate issues from many different angles. This can be particularly challenging when the issue is an emotionally charged one, especially if you have strong personal feelings about the topic.

2. The critical thinker is aware of biases and assumptions. In evaluating evidence and ideas, critical thinkers strive to identify the biases and assumptions that are inherent in any argument. Critical thinkers also try to identify and minimize the influence of their *own* biases. It's difficult to apply this critical thinking skill when you are attempting to rationally evaluate ideas that contradict your own biases.

3. The critical thinker is flexible, yet maintains an attitude of healthy skepticism. Critical thinkers are open to new information, ideas, and claims. They genuinely consider alternative explanations and possibilities. However, this open-mindedness is tempered by a healthy sense of skepticism as the critical thinker consistently asks, "What evidence supports that claim?" It's especially challenging to evaluate critically new claims that you *hope* are true, like "Learn while you sleep!" or "Shed pounds effortlessly!"

4. The critical thinker engages in reflective thinking. Critical thinkers avoid knee-jerk responses. Instead, critical thinkers are *reflective*. Most complex issues are unlikely to have a simple resolution. Therefore, critical thinkers resist the temptation to sidestep complexity by boiling an issue down to an either/or, yes/no kind of proposition. Instead, the critical thinker *expects* and *accepts* complexity. It's not always easy to think reflectively and accept complexity when what you really want is a simple or instant answer.

5. The critical thinker scrutinizes the evidence before drawing conclusions. Critical thinkers strive to weigh all the available evidence *before* arriving at conclusions, rather than moving on the presumption that they already know the answer. And in evaluating evidence, the critical thinker distinguishes between empirical evidence and opinions based on feelings or personal experience. It can be particularly difficult to scrutinize the evidence when the opinions and feelings that are used to bolster an argument happen to be the same as your own private opinions and feelings.

As you can see, critical thinking is not a single skill, but rather a *set* of attitudes and thinking skills that you can actively apply in logically evaluating the pros and cons of arguments. As is true with any set of skills, you can get better at critical thinking with practice. That's one of the reasons that we've included Critical Thinking boxes in every chapter of this text.

You'll discover that these Critical Thinking boxes are very diverse, rather than following a rigid formula. Some will challenge your preconceptions on certain topics. Others will invite you to take sides in the debates of some of the most important contributors to modern psychology. For example, in Chapter 5, you'll get the opportunity to debate the issue of "free will" with one of the most influential psychologists of the twentieth century, B. F. Skinner. Other Critical Thinking boxes will help you identify and critically evaluate the evidence for various phenomena, ranging from iridology to ESP and subliminal motivation tapes. In every case, our goal is to encourage you to actively engage in the attitudes and skills that characterize critical thinking.

We hope you enjoy this feature!

BIZARRO

The Steps in the Scientific Method:

Seeking Answers

Like any science, psychology is based on *empirical evidence,* or evidence that is the result of observation, measurement, and experimentation. As part of the overall process of producing empirical evidence, psychologists follow the steps of the scientific method. In a nutshell, these steps are: (1) creating testable questions, (2) designing a study to collect data, (3) analyzing the data to arrive at conclusions, and (4) reporting the results. While not foolproof, the basic guidelines of the scientific method help minimize the chance for error and faulty conclusions. Let's look at some of the key concepts associated with each step of the scientific method.

Step 1. Formulate a Hypothesis That Can Be Tested Empirically

Once a researcher has identified a question or an issue that he or she wishes to investigate, it must be posed in the form of a hypothesis that can be tested empirically. Formally, a **hypothesis** is a tentative statement that describes the relationship between two or more variables. A hypothesis is often posed in terms of a specific prediction that can be empirically tested, such as the hypothesis "mental distraction increases pain tolerance." (We discuss this particular hypothesis in Chapter 3.)

The **variables** contained in any given hypothesis are simply the factors that can vary, or change. These changes must be capable of being observed, measured, and verified. In describing the variables to be investigated, the psychologist must provide an operational definition of each variable. An **operational definition** defines the variable in terms of how the factor is to be measured or manipulated.

Operational definitions are critical because many of the concepts that psychologists investigate—like memory, happiness, or stress—can be measured in more than one way. In providing operational definitions of the variables in the study, the researcher spells out in very concrete and precise terms how the variables will be manipulated or measured. This allows other researchers to understand exactly how the variables were measured or manipulated in a particular study.

For example, consider the hypothesis that "negativity reduces marital stability" (see Karney & Bradbury, 1995). To test this hypothesis, you would need to operationally define each variable. How could you operationally define "negativity" and "marital stability"? What could you measure?

You could operationally define "negativity" any number of ways, such as the number of critical comments the couple made to each other during an hour-long interview. Or "negativity" could be operationally defined as the score on a 1-to-10 scale, where the couple rated each other from low negativity (1) to high negativity (10). Or you might operationally define "negativity" as the number of arguments the couple has per month. In a similar way, you would have to devise an operational definition for "marital stability," such as the number of times the couple discussed getting divorced or the number of times the couple separated.

Although operational definitions may sometimes sound completely arbitrary, they usually are not. As research develops on a particular topic in psychology, whether that topic is happiness, creativity, or loneliness, methods of measuring the variable in question become established. For example, a standard measurement of loneliness is the 20-item *UCLA Loneliness Scale* (see Gambrill, 1995a). The scale produces a loneliness score between 20 (very low loneliness) and 80 (very high loneliness). Thus, a widely accepted operational definition of loneliness is a person's score on the UCLA Loneliness Scale.

hypothesis
(high-POTH-eh-sis) A tentative statement about the relationship between two or more variables.

variable
A factor that can vary, or change, in ways that can be observed, measured, and verified.

operational definition
A precise description of how the variables in a study will be manipulated or measured.

Formulating a Hypothesis Hypotheses are often generated from casual observations. For example, do you think this accomplished young musician processes music differently from someone who is just beginning to learn to play a musical instrument? How could a psychologist investigate this question? What variables would need to be operationally defined?

Step 2. Design the Study and Collect the Data

This step involves deciding which research method will be used for collecting data. There are two basic categories of research methods—*experimental* and *descriptive*. Each research method answers different kinds of questions and provides different kinds of evidence.

The *experimental method* is used to show that one variable *causes* change in a second variable. In an experiment, the researcher deliberately and systematically varies one factor, then measures the changes produced in a second factor. For example, to study the effect of the number of bystanders on a person's willingness to help a stranger, the researcher would deliberately vary the number of bystanders (Latané & Darley, 1970). Then, he would measure how the willingness to help a stranger was affected by the change in the number of bystanders.

Ideally, all experimental conditions are kept as constant as possible except for the factor that is deliberately changed. Then, if changes occur in the second factor, those changes can be attributed to the variations in the first factor. In the next main section, we'll take a detailed look at how the experimental method provides evidence of a *cause-and-effect relationship* between two variables.

In contrast to the experimental method, *descriptive methods* are research strategies for *observing and describing behavior,* including identifying the factors that seem to be associated with a particular phenomenon. Descriptive methods answer the *who, what, where,* and *when* kinds of questions about behavior. Who engages in a particular behavior? What factors or events seem to be associated with the behavior? Where does the behavior occur? When does the behavior occur? How often? In a later section, we'll discuss commonly used descriptive methods, which include *naturalistic observation, surveys, case studies,* and *correlational studies.*

Step 3. Analyze the Data and Draw Conclusions

Once the observations and measurements have been collected, the "raw" data need to be summarized and analyzed in a way that allows overall conclusions to be drawn. To do so, researchers rely on **statistics,** which are mathematical methods that are used to summarize, analyze, and draw conclusions about data.

Researchers use statistics to determine if the results support the hypothesis. Statistics are also used to determine whether the findings are statistically significant. If the finding is **statistically significant,** it means the results are not very likely to have occurred by chance (Grimm, 1993). As a rule, statistically significant results confirm the hypothesis. If you're interested in the use of statistics in the scientific method, we provide an introduction to the basic principles of statistics in the Statistics Appendix at the back of the book.

Keep in mind, statistical significance and practical significance are not necessarily the same. If a study involves a large number of participants, even small differences among groups of subjects may result in a statistically significant finding. But the actual average differences may be so small that they have little practical significance or importance. So remember that a statistically significant result is simply one that is not very likely to have occurred by chance. Whether the finding is significant in the everyday sense is another matter altogether.

A statistical technique called **meta-analysis** is increasingly being used in psychology to analyze the results of many research studies on a specific topic (Rosenthal, 1994; Schmidt, 1992). Meta-analysis is also useful when a

statistics
Mathematical methods used to summarize data and draw conclusions based on the data.

statistical significance
A mathematical indication that research results are not very likely to have occurred by chance.

meta-analysis
A statistical technique that involves combining and analyzing the results of many research studies on a specific topic in order to identify overall trends.

replicate
To repeat or duplicate a scientific study in order to increase confidence in the validity of the original findings.

large number of studies have produced inconsistent or contradictory results. Basically, meta-analysis involves pooling the results of several studies into a single analysis. By creating one large pool of data to be analyzed, meta-analysis can sometimes reveal overall trends that are not evident in individual studies.

For example, a recent meta-analysis combined 286 different studies investigating gender differences in spatial abilities (Voyer & others, 1995). The meta-analysis revealed that males have an advantage over females on some tests of spatial ability, but not others. However, the meta-analysis also showed that gender differences in spatial skills have decreased in recent years, suggesting that educational practices and changing social attitudes are having an impact on cognitive abilities. In Chapter 10, we discuss such gender differences in more detail.

Step 4. Report the Findings

For advances to be made in any scientific discipline, researchers must publish or share their findings with other scientists. Psychologists report or publish their results along with a detailed explanation of the exact methods and procedures that were used. Describing the methods in detail makes it possible for other investigators to **replicate,** or repeat, the study. Replication is an important part of the scientific process. When a study is replicated and the same basic results occur again, it increases scientific *confidence* that the results are accurate. And, obviously, if the replication of a study fails to produce the same basic findings, it reduces confidence in the original findings.

One way that psychologists report their findings is by formally presenting their research at a professional conference. For example, hundreds of psychologists gather every year at the annual meetings of the *American Psychological Association (APA)* and the *American Psychological Society (APS)* to share and discuss new research findings.

Researchers can also report their findings by writing a paper summarizing the study and submitting it for publication in one of the many psychology journals. Most of these scientific journals have the research reviewed by other psychologists before accepting it for publication. Reviewers critically evaluate different aspects of a study, including how the results were analyzed. If the study conforms to the principles of sound scientific research and contributes to the existing knowledge base, it is accepted for publication.

Some of the leading psychology journals include the *Journal of Personality and Social Psychology, Developmental Psychology, Health Psychology,* and the *Journal of Abnormal Psychology.* These journals represent forums for presenting research in different specialty areas of psychology. Other important psychology journals, such as *Psychological Bulletin, Psychological Review, American Psychologist,* and *Psychological Science,* are broader in the scope of topics covered. If you flip to the References section at the back of this book, you'll see a lengthy list of scientific research publications.

Throughout this text, you'll see citations like the one at the end of this sentence (Leichtman & Ceci, 1995). These citations identify the sources of the research and ideas that we discuss. The citation tells you the author or authors of the published study (Leichtman & Ceci) and the year (1995) in which the study was published. Using this information, you can go to the alphabetized References section at back of this text and find the complete reference, which lists the authors' full names, the article title, and the journal or book in which it was published. In Figure 1.2, you can see how to interpret the different parts of a typical journal reference.

Year study published   Authors   Title of study

Leichtman, Michelle D., & Ceci, Stephen J.
(1995). The effects of stereotypes and suggestions on preschoolers' reports.
Developmental Psychology, *31* (4), 568–578.

Title of scientific journal   Volume number   Issue number   Page numbers

FIGURE 1.2 How to Read a Journal Reference
Using the references section at the back of this text, you can find the complete source for each citation that appears in a chapter. The figure above shows what the different components of a typical journal reference mean. In the chapter itself, the citation for this particular reference would read "(Leichtman & Ceci, 1995)."

theory
A tentative explanation that tries to integrate and account for the relationship among various findings and observations.

To underscore the contribution of women to psychological research, we include the first name of researchers in both the References and the Name Index at the back of this book. Although the traditional citation style calls for first initials only, too often students assume that the researchers are male when the first name is not given.

Hypotheses, Theories, and the Scientific Method:

Putting It All Together

As research findings accumulate from individual studies, eventually theories develop. A **theory,** or *model,* is a tentative explanation that tries to account for diverse findings on the same topic. Note that theories are *not* the same as hypotheses. As we said earlier, a hypothesis is a specific question or prediction to be tested. A theory, in contrast, integrates and summarizes a large number of findings and observations. Along with explaining existing results, a good theory generates *new* hypotheses to be tested by further research. In every chapter in this text, you'll encounter theories that try to account for the diverse evidence on particular topics, such as why we need to sleep (Chapter 4) and how people and animals learn new behaviors (Chapter 5).

As you encounter different theories, try to remember that theories are *tools* for explaining behavior and mental processes, not statements of absolute fact. A theory's usefulness is judged by how much it furthers understanding of behavior and stimulates new research. Often more than one theory is useful in understanding a particular area of behavior or mental processes.

Theories evolve and change as new findings are reported. When new research results challenge the established way of thinking about a phenomenon, theories are expanded, modified, and even replaced. Put simply, the knowledge base of psychology is constantly evolving.

At this point, you should have a good basic understanding of the assumptions, attitudes, and steps that are inherent in the scientific method. In the next couple of sections, we'll look at the scientific method in action as we describe the experimental method and descriptive methods in more detail.

CONCEPT REVIEW 1.3

The Scientific Method

Identify the step of the scientific method that each of the following items represents, writing the appropriate letter in each blank:
(A) analyze the data
(B) report the findings
(C) design the study and collect data
(D) formulate a hypothesis

_____ **1.** A psychologist is interested in testing the idea that spaced practice results in greater learning than massed practice. She operationally defines spaced practice as studying one hour a day for five days and massed practice as five hours of study on one day. The measure of learning would be the number of correct answers on a recall test of the material studied.

_____ **2.** The psychologist assigns the research participants to two different groups by picking their names out of a hat. She instructs one group of students to study material one hour a day for five days. On the sixth day they are tested on the material. The other group is instructed to study the material for five hours on one day, and they are tested the following day.

_____ **3.** After she collects all the data, the psychologist calculates the average number of correct responses for each group and then does some further analyses to determine if the difference between the two groups is statistically significant.

_____ **4.** Finally, the psychologist writes a report, presents her findings at a regional psychology conference, and submits her report to a psychology journal for publication.

The Experimental Method

The experimental method is used to demonstrate a cause-and-effect relationship between two variables. What are the hypothesis, independent variable, and dependent variable in the Sam Stone experiment? What are the roles of random assignment, the control group, the experimental groups, and inter-rater reliability in an experiment?

The **experimental method** is a research method that is used to demonstrate a cause-and-effect relationship between changes in one variable and the effects on another. Essentially, conducting an experiment involves *deliberately varying* one factor, which is called the **independent variable,** then *measuring* the effects on another factor, called the **dependent variable.** The dependent variable is so named because it "depends" on the changes in the independent variable. Assuming that all other conditions in the experiment have been held constant, any changes that occur in the dependent variable can be attributed to the changes in the independent variable. That's how an experiment can demonstrate a cause-and-effect relationship between the independent and dependent variables.

To help you understand important aspects of the experimental method, we will look at an ingenious experiment recently conducted by psychologists Michelle Leichtman and Stephen Ceci. They were interested in the reliability of young children's memories in court cases.

Leichtman and Ceci (1995) found that like adult witnesses, children are often repeatedly questioned over the course of several weeks by people involved in the case, such as police officers, social workers, psychotherapists, lawyers, and family members. Sometimes, interviewers use *suggestive questioning.* That is, they may word their questions in such a way that the questions suggest to the child what the interviewer thinks happened. Leichtman and Ceci were interested in whether suggestive questioning, especially when it takes place on several occasions, could influence a preschooler's later memory of an event.

In some court cases, children are repeatedly exposed to negative information about a person that can potentially distort a young child's interpretations of actual events (Ceci & Bruck, 1993). For example, in custody court battles, children often hear one parent openly criticizing the other parent. In turn, this negative pre-information can influence how the child perceives the subsequent actions of the parent who has been criticized. So, Leichtman and Ceci were also interested in whether negative pre-information could influence a young child's memory of a later event.

Leichtman and Ceci's experiment was designed to realistically create both these conditions—suggestive questioning and exposure to pre-information—and then measure their effect on the accuracy of young children's memories of a neutral event. They refer to their experiment as the "Sam Stone study" because the event in question involved the visit of a stranger called Sam Stone.

The Sam Stone Study

The 176 preschoolers who participated in the study were enrolled in private day-care centers. All the children experienced the visit of a stranger named Sam Stone to their day-care classroom. Here is how psychologists Michelle Leichtman and Stephen Ceci (1995) describe Sam Stone's visit:

> *First, he entered the classroom and said hello to a teacher or aide who sat amidst the assembled children during a story-telling session, and he was in-*

experimental method
A method of investigation used to demonstrate cause-and-effect relationships by purposely manipulating a factor thought to produce change in a second factor.

independent variable
The purposely manipulated factor thought to produce change in an experiment.

dependent variable
The factor that is observed and measured for change in an experiment; thought to be influenced by the independent variable.

random assignment
Assigning subjects to experimental conditions in such a way that all subjects have an equal chance of being assigned to any of the conditions or groups in the study.

control group
The group of subjects who are exposed to all experimental conditions, except the independent variable.

troduced by the teacher or aide to the children [as Sam Stone]. Next, he commented on the story that was being read to the children by the teacher or aide ("I know that story; it's one of my favorites!") and strolled around the perimeter of the classroom. Finally, he departed, waving goodbye to the children. In each case, the entire event was timed and lasted approximately 2 minutes.

FIGURE 1.3 **The Experimental Design of the "Sam Stone" Study**
The diagram shows the basic design of the "Sam Stone" study. Two independent variables were manipulated: (1) whether the children received information about Sam Stone before his visit; and (2) whether suggestive questioning of the children occurred after Sam Stone's visit. This created four experimental conditions, the control group and three experimental groups, as shown here.

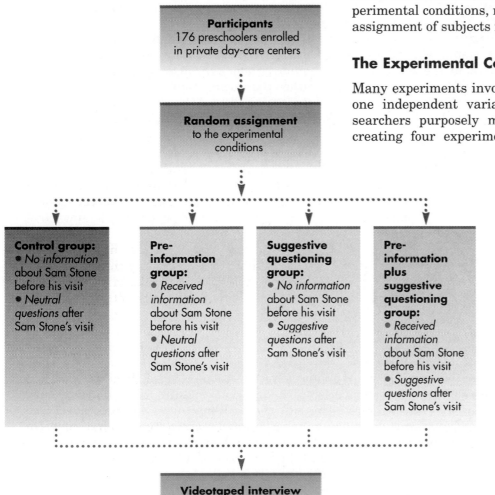

Random Assignment

Collectively, the preschoolers represented a wide range of social and ethnic groups. The researchers used a process called *random assignment* to assign each class of preschoolers to one of the four different experimental conditions. **Random assignment** means that all subjects have an equal chance of being assigned to any of the experimental conditions.

Random assignment is an important element of good experimental design. First, randomly assigning subjects ensures that differences among the subjects are spread out across all experimental conditions. And second, because the same criteria are used to assign all subjects to the experimental conditions, random assignment helps ensure that the assignment of subjects is done in an unbiased manner.

The Experimental Conditions

Many experiments involve deliberately manipulating more than one independent variable. In the Sam Stone study, the researchers purposely manipulated two independent variables, creating four experimental conditions. The first independent variable was whether the children received *information* about Sam Stone before his visit. The second independent variable was whether the children were exposed to *suggestive questioning* after Sam Stone's visit. Take a moment to look at Figure 1.3, which depicts the study's design and summarizes the four different experimental conditions.

Let's describe the four experimental conditions in more detail. The children randomly assigned to the **control group** did *not* experience either of the independent variables. In other words, the children in the control group received *no* information about Sam Stone before his visit. Following Sam Stone's visit, the control-group children were individually questioned once per week for four weeks with simple, neutral questions about what Sam Stone had done during his visit. During this neutral questioning, *no* suggestions were given to the control-group children about how Sam Stone behaved during his visit.

In any experiment, the control group serves several important functions. First, it serves as a *baseline* to which changes in the other experimental groups can be compared. Second, the control group can be used to check for changes that occur naturally or spontaneously over time. Because the control group is *not* exposed to the independent variable, whatever changes occur in the dependent variable in the control group cannot have been caused by the independent variable. So, in the Sam Stone study, the control group was used as a way to detect changes in the memories of preschoolers who were *not* exposed to information or suggestive questioning.

In addition to the control group, there were three **experimental groups** in the Sam Stone study. Each experimental group was exposed to one or both of the independent variables. The children assigned to the first experimental group represented the *pre-information group*. These children were repeatedly told stories about Sam Stone before his visit to their classroom. Each week during the month before Sam Stone's visit, a research assistant told the children a different, carefully scripted story. Each story depicted Sam Stone as a kind and well-meaning, but very clumsy and bumbling, person.

The children in the pre-information group were also individually interviewed every week during the month following Sam Stone's visit. Like the children in the control group, the children in the information group were asked neutral questions about what Sam Stone had done during his visit to their classroom. The interviewers made no suggestions about what Sam Stone had done.

The second experimental group represented the *suggestive questioning condition*. The preschoolers assigned to this condition did *not* receive any information about Sam Stone before his visit. After Sam Stone's visit, the children in the suggestive questioning group were also interviewed once per week for a month. However, rather than being neutral, the questions were *suggestive*. For example, the interviewer showed the child the torn page of a book and a stained teddy bear. Then the interviewer asked suggestive questions like these:

- When Sam Stone ripped the book, did he do it alone or with a helper?

- When Sam Stone got the bear dirty, was he wearing long or short pants?

The children in the third experimental group represented the *pre-information-plus-suggestive-questioning* condition. These children were exposed to both independent variables: (1) pre-information about Sam Stone before his visit *and* (2) suggestive questioning during the four weekly interviews after Sam Stone's visit.

The Dependent Variable

After the month of weekly interviews, there was a lapse of six weeks. Then each child was questioned by a new interviewer about what had happened during Sam Stone's visit. This fifth, critical interview was videotaped. The dependent variable was the number of factual errors the children made in the fifth interview. Specifically, the researchers measured how many of the children erroneously reported that Sam Stone had (1) torn the book page, (2) soiled the teddy bear, or (3) committed both of these acts.

Each videotaped interview was scored by an observer who rated whether the child claimed that Sam Stone had torn the page, soiled the teddy bear, or both. To help ensure the rater's objectivity, the rater was *blind,* or unaware of the experimental condition to which the child had been assigned. If the rater knew a participant's experimental condition, it could inadvertently influence the rating. Thus, having judges or raters "blind" to the participants' experimental condition makes it more likely that evaluations will be objective and unbiased.

experimental group
The group of subjects who are exposed to all experimental conditions, including the independent variable.

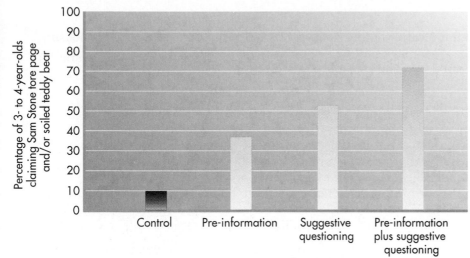

FIGURE 1.4 The Results of the Sam Stone Study

In the Sam Stone study, the results were analyzed separately for the youngest preschoolers in the 3-to-4 age range and for older preschoolers in the 5-to-6 age range. Above, you can see the results for the youngest preschoolers. Clearly, the greatest effect can be seen with those preschoolers who were exposed to both pre-information about Sam Stone and suggestive questioning. In general, the older preschoolers were about half as likely as the youngest preschoolers in each condition to claim that Sam Stone had committed the acts.

(Adapted from Leichtman & Ceci, 1995)

The Results of the Sam Stone Study

The results of the Sam Stone study are shown in Figure 1.4. As you can see, the young children were clearly influenced by both pre-information and suggestive questioning. In comparison to the control group, the most dramatic effect was for the children in the pre-information-plus-suggestive-questioning group: 72 percent of them claimed that Sam Stone had torn the book page or soiled the teddy bear (Leichtman & Ceci, 1995). Keep in mind that *neither* of these events occurred during Sam Stone's visit to their classroom.

Leichtman and Ceci (1995) note several implications of their findings. First, the study replicates, or repeats, the findings of earlier studies showing that young children's memories can be influenced by the suggestions of an adult. Second, the low rate of errors made by children in the control group demonstrates that even young children can accurately report an event if the situation remains free of added information and suggestive or leading questions.

Variations in Experimental Design

Experimental designs can vary, depending on the question to be investigated. What is a placebo control group, and when is it likely to be used? What is the expectancy effect? Why do researchers use the double-blind technique, and how can demand characteristics influence the outcome of an experiment? What are some limitations to the experimental method?

Depending on the research question, experimental designs can vary. For example, experiments designed to assess the effectiveness of a treatment, such as a particular drug, often involve the use of a **placebo control group.** The participants assigned to this experimental condition receive a *placebo,* which is a fake treatment or a substance with no known effects. However, the subjects don't know whether they are receiving the actual or fake treatment.

Why is a placebo control group important in experiments designed to assess the effectiveness of a treatment? A placebo control group helps check for **expectancy effects,** which refer to changes that may occur simply because subjects expect change to occur. Thus, researchers can compare the effects of the actual treatment versus the expectancy effects, if any, that are demonstrated by the placebo control group.

In such studies, researchers often use a double-blind technique. A *double-blind* study is one in which neither the participants nor the researcher who interacts with them is aware of which experimental condition each participant has been assigned to. For example, in a study with a placebo control group, the researcher who interacted with the subjects would not know which subjects got the placebo and which subjects received the actual treatment. The researchers who *do* know which participants have been assigned to each experimental condition do not interact with or evaluate the participants. In contrast, a *single-blind study* is one in which the researcher, but not the subjects, is aware of critical information.

The purpose of the double-blind technique is to guard against the possibility that the researcher will inadvertently display subtle cues or signals

placebo control group
(pluh-SEE-bo) An experimental control group in which subjects are exposed to a fake independent variable.

expectancy effect
Change in a subject's behavior produced by the subject's belief that change should happen.

that communicate what is expected of particular subjects. A behavior as subtle as the researcher smiling when dealing with certain participants, but not others, could bias the outcome of a study.

Limitations of Experiments

The strength of a well-designed experiment is that it can provide convincing evidence of a cause-and-effect relationship between the independent and dependent variables. However, experiments are not without their limitations. Because experiments are often conducted in highly controlled laboratory situations, they are frequently criticized for having little to do with actual behavior. That is, the artificial conditions of some experiments may produce results that do not *generalize* well, or apply to real situations or populations beyond the participants in the study.

In order to make experimental conditions less artificial, sometimes experiments are conducted in a natural setting rather than in a laboratory. This strategy was used in the Sam Stone study: all experimental manipulations and measurements were conducted at the childrens' preschools. The researchers also tried to create conditions that realistically reflected those faced by young children in the judicial process, such as being questioned on several occasions by different interviewers. However, experiments conducted in natural settings have their own disadvantages, such as a decrease in experimental control. For example, in the Sam Stone study, it was impossible to control for what the preschoolers might have said to one another between the interviews.

Another limitation of the experimental method is that it's not always feasible to study a particular issue experimentally. For example, if participants would be harmed by being exposed to a variable or experimental condition, the experiment could not ethically be performed. Later in the chapter we'll discuss ethics in psychological research in more detail.

Finally, it may be impossible to create experimentally the kinds of conditions that researchers want to study. For example, in the prologue to this chapter we described the Oklahoma City bombing. The effects of that disaster on the lives of those directly and indirectly affected will be the subject of psychological study for many years to come. Obviously, the conditions involved in the Oklahoma City bombing could not be experimentally manipulated. Thus, psychologists must also rely on other research methods to advance the understanding of human behavior. We'll look at these alternative research methods, called *descriptive methods,* in the next section.

CONCEPT REVIEW 1.4

The Experimental Method

Reread the example given in Concept Review 1.3 and then answer the following questions, choosing from these alternatives:

(A) dependent variable   (B) experimental group
(C) independent variable   (D) control group
(E) random assignment

1. The condition manipulated in the experiment, whether spaced practice or massed practice was used for studying, is the _____.

2. The participants in each group were determined by picking their names out of a hat.

This is an example of _____.

3. The score on the recall test constitutes the _____.

4. In a later variation, the psychologist compared a group of students who studied the material one hour a day for five days and a group of students who were simply tested on the same material with no special instructions as to how they should study the material. In this study, the first group was the _____, and the second group represented the _____.

descriptive methods
Scientific procedures that involve systematically observing behavior in order to describe the relationships among behaviors and events.

naturalistic observation
The systematic observation and recording of behaviors as they occur in their natural setting.

Descriptive Methods

Descriptive methods are research methods used to observe and describe behavior. How is naturalistic observation usually conducted? What are case studies, and when are case studies typically used?

The **descriptive methods** do *not* involve deliberately manipulating the variables to which subjects are exposed. Rather, they are research strategies for observing and describing behavior. Using descriptive methods, researchers can answer important questions, such as when certain behaviors take place, how often they occur, and whether they are related to other factors, such as a person's age, race, and educational level. As you'll see, descriptive methods can provide a wealth of information about behavior, especially behaviors that would be difficult or impossible to study experimentally.

Naturalistic Observation:
The Science of People- and Animal-Watching

When psychologists systematically observe and record behaviors as they occur in their natural settings, they are using the descriptive method called **naturalistic observation.** Usually, the researcher tries to avoid being detected by the subjects, whether they are people or animals. The basic goal of naturalistic observation is to detect the behavior patterns that exist naturally—patterns that might not be apparent in a laboratory or if the subjects knew they were being watched.

As you might expect, psychologists very carefully define the behaviors that they will observe and measure before they begin their research. Often, two or more observers are used to increase the accuracy of the observations. In some studies, the observations are videotaped or audiotaped, so that the researchers can record and carefully analyze the details of the behavior they are studying.

Naturalistic observation can be used to study many different kinds of behavior and subjects. For example, psychologist Jane Goodall and her colleagues have used naturalistic observation as their primary research method to study chimpanzee behavior in Tanzania. Shortly after beginning her naturalistic observation studies in the early 1960s, she discovered that chimpanzees, like humans, use objects as tools. For example, she observed chimps using saliva-coated sticks to fish termites out of their nests, then eating them off the sticks. Such tool-using behavior was long thought to be a characteristic that distinguished humans from animals (see Peterson & Goodall, 1993).

One advantage of naturalistic observation is that it can allow researchers to study human behaviors that could not be ethically manipulated in an experiment. For example, suppose a psychologist wanted to study bullying behavior in children. It would be completely unethical to deliberately create a prolonged situation in which one child is aggressively bullied by another child. However, psychologists *could* ethically study bullying by observing aggressive behavior in children on crowded school playgrounds.

Psychologists Debra Pepler and Wendy Craig (1995) did just that. From their vantage point on the second floor of the school, they used a camcorder with a telephoto lens and small, wireless microphones to observe the spontaneous interactions of school children. Using

Naturalistic Observation Since 1960, Jane Goodall has been observing the behavior of chimpanzees in the wild. Goodall, shown here in an early photograph with a young chimp she named Flint, made many discoveries about chimpanzee behavior in the wild through the use of naturalisitc observation. Most psychologists engaged in naturalistic observation, however, would never get this close to their subjects. Ideally, the observer tries to avoid disturbing or interfering with the natural behavior pattern that she is investigating.

this naturalistic observation strategy, they discovered that physical and verbal aggressive incidents are far from rare. Even among children whom teachers regarded as nonaggressive, instances of physical aggression occurred about once every 11 minutes, and verbal aggression about once every 5 minutes. And, contrary to what many people assume, Pepler and Craig found that girls bully other children at the same rate as boys.

As a research tool, naturalistic observation can be used virtually anywhere that patterns of behavior can be openly observed—from fast-food restaurants, college campuses, or singles bars to the jungles of Tanzania. And because the observations occur in the natural setting, the results of naturalistic observation studies can often be generalized more confidently to real-life situations than can artificially manipulated or staged situations (see Pepler & Craig, 1995).

Case Studies:
Details, Details, Details

A **case study** is an intensive, in-depth investigation of an individual. Case studies involve compiling a great deal of information, often from a variety of different sources, to construct a detailed picture of a single subject. For example, the subject may be intensively interviewed, and his or her friends, family, and co-workers may be interviewed as well. Psychological records, medical records, and even school records may be examined. Other sources of information can include extensive psychological testing and observations of the person's behavior.

Case studies are most often used to investigate rare, unusual, or extreme conditions. Sometimes, case studies can provide psychologists with information that can be used to help understand normal behavior. For example, as you'll see in Chapter 2, case studies of people with injury or damage to a specific part of the brain are often used to study how the brain and behavior are related.

By combining the information from several case studies focusing on the same type of behavior, it is possible to engage in *case study research*. Psychologists look for patterns or characteristics that are consistent across the individual cases. For example, case study research has played an important role in understanding the progression of mental disorders, including patterns of recovery. In future chapters, you'll see how the rich descriptions provided by case studies have contributed to the understanding of many topics, including memory, development, personality, and psychotherapy (Adler, 1993).

Surveys, Questionnaires, and Interviews:
(A) Always (B) Sometimes (C) You've Got to Be Kidding!

> *Surveys, questionnaires, and interviews are descriptive methods that involve directly asking people about their behavior. Why is random selection important in choosing a sample? What does it mean to say that a sample is representative of a larger population, and why is it important?*

A direct way to find out about the behavior, attitudes, and opinions of people is simply to ask them. **Surveys** and *questionnaires* typically involve a paper-and-pencil format in which the subjects respond to a structured set of questions about their experiences, beliefs, behavior, or attitudes. One key

case study
A highly detailed description of a single individual or event.

survey
A questionnaire or interview designed to investigate the opinions, behaviors, or characteristics of a particular group.

CALVIN AND HOBBES

advantage offered by survey research is that researchers are able to gather information from a much larger group of people than could be obtained through other research methods.

An *interview* is a survey that is conducted in person, with the interviewer recording the person's responses. As with surveys and questionnaires, the interviewer usually asks a structured set of questions in a predetermined order. Although they are more expensive and time-consuming than surveys and questionnaires, interviews have some unique advantages.

First, the interviewer can be certain the person understands the questions being asked. Second, the interviewer can note responses to questions that are different from the predetermined options. And third, the interviewer can directly observe the behaviors and reactions of the person responding. The person's spontaneous comments and behaviors, as well as the interviewer's subjective impressions, can all be recorded as part of the interview process.

Surveys, questionnaires, and interviews are seldom administered to everyone within the particular group or population under investigation. Instead, the researchers usually select a **sample**—a segment of the larger group or population. Selecting a sample that is representative of the larger group is the key to getting accurate survey results. A **representative sample** very closely parallels, or matches, the larger group on relevant characteristics, such as age, sex, race, marital status, and educational level.

How do researchers select the participants for the sample so that they end up with a sample that is representative of the larger group? The most common strategy is to randomly select the sample participants. *Random selection* means that every member of the larger group has an equal chance of being selected for inclusion in the sample.

To illustrate how random selection works, let's look at how the sample was created for the *National Health and Social Life Survey* (abbreviated *NHSLS*). Conducted by researcher Robert T. Michael and his colleagues (1994) at the University of Chicago, the NHSLS focused on the sexual practices of American adults between the ages of eighteen and fifty-nine. Here is Michael's description of how his team used random selection to choose the survey participants:

> *Essentially, we chose at random geographic areas of the country, using the statistical equivalent of a coin toss to select them. Within these geographic regions, we randomly selected cities, towns, and rural areas. Within those cities and towns we randomly select neighborhoods. Within those neighborhoods, we randomly select households.*
>
> *. . . If there were two people living in a household who were in our age range, we flipped a coin to select which one to interview. If there were three people in the household, we did the equivalent of flipping a three-sided coin to select one of them to interview.*

Notice that the participants who were interviewed in the NHSLS did *not* volunteer to participate in the survey. A specific individual was randomly selected through the process described above. If that person refused to participate, someone else in the household could *not* substitute for that person. Using this random selection process, over 3,000 people were interviewed for the National Health and Social Life Survey.

How closely did the NHSLS sample match important characteristics of the U.S. population? You can judge for yourself in Table 1.2. Clearly, the

sample
A selected segment of the population used to represent the group that is being studied.

representative sample
A selected segment that very closely parallels the larger population being studied on relevant characteristics.

TABLE 1.2 Comparing the Social Characteristics of the NHSLS Sample and the U.S. Population

	NHSLS	U.S. Population
Gender		
Men	44.6%	49.7%
Women	55.4	50.3
	100 %	100 %
Age		
18–24	15.9%	18.2%
25–29	14.5	14.3
30–39	31.3	29.5
40–49	22.9	22.7
50–59	15.3	15.3
	100 %	100 %
Education		
Less than high school	13.9%	15.8%
High school or equivalent	62.2	64.0
Any college	16.6	13.9
Advanced	7.3	6.3
	100 %	100 %
Marital Status		
Never married	28.2%	27.7%
Currently married	53.3	58.3
Divorced, separated	16.2	12.4
Widowed	2.3	1.6
	100 %	100 %
Race/Ethnicity		
White	76.5%	75.9%
Black	12.7	11.7
Hispanic	7.5	9.0
Other	3.3	3.3
	100 %	100 %

SOURCE: Michael & others, 1994.

Using random selection, approximately 3,000 people were chosen for the sample used in the National Health and Social Life Survey (NHSLS). In this table, you can see that the overall characteristics of those in the NHSLS sample were very representative of the U.S. population as a whole.

random selection process used in the NHSLS study resulted in a sample that was representative of the American population as a whole.

Contrast the procedures used in the NHSLS with surveys of sexual behavior conducted by popular magazines, such as *Redbook* and *Playboy*. In the *Playboy* survey, about 1 percent of 5 million readers returned the survey, which was included in an issue of the magazine. With the *Redbook* survey, the response was slightly higher—about 2 percent of *Redbook* readers returned the survey (Michael & others, 1994). What problems do you see with this approach?

One problem is that the survey participants were limited to the readership of the magazines. While *Redbook* and *Playboy* readers may reflect a certain segment of the larger population, they are certainly not representative of the U.S. population as a whole. For example, *Redbook* readers tend to be affluent white women who are married and in their late twenties and thirties (Michael & others, 1994). Second, the people who participated in these magazine surveys were *self-selected:* they voluntarily filled out the survey and mailed it in. There may be important differences between the 2 percent of people who volunteered to describe their sexual practices and the 98 percent of those readers who did not volunteer.

Thus, the *Redbook* and *Playboy* surveys can tell us something about the sexual practices of the people who responded to those surveys. But such surveys have no scientific basis for making generalizations about the American population as a whole, because the sample does not accurately represent the larger population. And, in fact, neither *Redbook* nor *Playboy* magazine presented its survey results as representative of the American population as a whole.

Another potential problem with surveys and questionnaires is that people do not always answer honestly. Subjects can misrepresent their personal characteristics or lie in their responses. This problem, too, can be addressed in a well-designed survey. The NHSLS incorporated several ways to check participants' responses (Michael & others, 1994). For example, the same basic question was asked at different points during the interview and was posed in slightly different ways. Thus, the researchers were able to compare the two responses to make sure that the participant was responding honestly and consistently.

At this point, you're probably wondering just what the National Health and Social Life Survey *did* reveal about the sexual practices of Americans. Well, let's just say that the NHSLS results did not support media images of sex-crazed adults occupying America's bedrooms. In Table 1.3, you can see how often men and women of different ages reported having had sex during the previous year. In Chapter 10, on gender and sexuality, we'll look at other NHSLS findings on sexual practices and preferences of American adults. Stay tuned!

TABLE 1.3 Frequency of Sex by Gender and Age

	Not at All	A Few Times per Year	A Few Times per Month	2 or 3 Times a Week	4 or More Times a Week
Gender					
Men	14%	16%	37%	26%	8%
Women	10	18	36	30	7
Age					
Men					
18–24	15	21	24	28	12
25–29	7	15	31	36	11
30–39	8	15	37	33	6
40–49	9	18	40	27	6
50–59	11	22	43	20	3
Women					
18–24	11	16	32	29	12
25–29	5	10	38	37	10
30–39	9	16	36	33	6
40–49	15	16	44	20	5
50–59	30	22	35	12	2

SOURCE: Michael & others, 1994.

Correlational Studies:
Looking at Relationships and Making Predictions

Correlational studies show how strongly two factors are related to one another. What is a correlation coefficient? What is the difference between a positive correlation and a negative correlation? Why can't correlational studies be used to demonstrate cause-and-effect relationships?

Along with answering who, what, where, and when, the data gathered by descriptive research techniques can be analyzed to show how various factors are related. A **correlational study** is one that examines how strongly two variables are related to, or associated with, each other. Probably the best way to develop an appreciation of correlational studies, including their limitations, is to look at a simple example.

Many people believe that there is a relationship between stress and susceptibility to colds—that the more stress you're under, the more likely you are to catch a cold. How could we investigate the relationship between stress and colds? First, we could survey people on the number of stressful events they've experienced in the last six months, such as financial troubles, relationship problems, job-related pressures, and so on. Second, we could ask them how many colds and respiratory infections they've had during the same time period.

With these data in hand, we could use a statistical procedure to calculate a figure called a correlation coefficient. A *correlation coefficient* is a numerical indicator of how strongly related two factors seem to be. A correlation coefficient always falls in a range from –1.00 to + 1.00. There are two parts to any correlation coefficient—the number and the sign. The number tells us about the *strength* of the relationship and the sign indicates the *direction* of the relationship between the two variables.

More specifically, the closer a correlation coefficient is to 1.00, whether it is positive or negative, the stronger the correlation or association between two factors. Hence, a correlation coefficient of +.80 or –.80 would represent a strong association, while a correlation of +.20 or –.20 would represent a weak correlation.

Notice that correlation coefficients do not function like the algebraic number line. A correlation of –.80 represents a stronger relationship than a correlation of +.20. That's because the plus or minus sign in a correlation coefficient simply tells you the direction of the relationship between the two variables. A **positive correlation,** like a +.60, is one in which the two factors vary in the same direction. That is, the two factors increase or decrease together. For example, there's a positive correlation between years of education and average annual earnings. As years of education increase, average yearly earnings also increase.

In contrast, a **negative correlation** is one in which the two variables move in *opposite* directions. For example, a negative correlation exists between marital satisfaction and rate of divorce. As the degree of reported marital satisfaction *increases,* the rate of divorce *decreases* (Karney & Bradbury, 1995). Thus, when two factors are negatively correlated, the two factors vary in opposite directions.

Given the basics of correlation coefficients, let's go back to our example. After crunching the data, let's assume that we found a very strong, positive correlation of +.90 between the number of stressful events that people have experienced and the number of colds people have. That is, people who

correlational study
A research strategy that allows the precise calculation of how strongly related two factors are to one another.

positive correlation
A finding that two factors vary systematically in the same direction, increasing or decreasing together.

negative correlation
A finding that two factors vary systematically in opposite directions, one increasing as the other decreases.

experienced a high number of stressful events also have a higher number of colds than people who experienced a lower number of stressful events. Now, here's the critical question: Can we conclude that stress *causes* susceptibility to colds?

Not necessarily. Even if stressful life events and colds are very strongly correlated, it's completely possible that some other factor is involved. For example, it may be that people who are under a great deal of stress have more contact with other people and thus are more frequently exposed to cold germs. Or it could be that people who are under a great deal of stress engage in more unhealthy behaviors, such as smoking, eating a poor diet, or getting inadequate sleep. Rather than stress, it may be that unhealthy behaviors increase vulnerability to colds.

The critical point here is that even if two factors are very strongly correlated, *correlation does not necessarily indicate causality*. All a correlation tells you is that two factors seem to be related or co-vary in a systematic way. Although two factors may be very strongly correlated, different evidence is required to demonstrate a true cause-and-effect relationship. As we discussed earlier in the chapter, experimental evidence is required to demonstrate a cause-and-effect relationship between two variables.

Even though you can't draw conclusions about causality with correlational research, correlational research is still very valuable for two reasons. First, correlational research can be used to rule out some factors and identify others that merit more intensive study. For example, correlational research has been used to identify which factors contribute the most to episodes of depression (Kendler & others, 1993a).

Second, the results of correlational research can allow you to make meaningful predictions. As you'll see in Chapter 13, on stress, health, and coping, there is compelling evidence demonstrating a strong positive correlation between stress and susceptibility to colds and infections (e.g., Cohen & others, 1993). Thus, how much stress you are under *is* a good predictor of susceptibility to colds and infections.

Even though all the descriptive methods are limited by the fact that they don't provide evidence of causality, they can provide important information about when behavior happens, how often it happens, and if other factors or events are related to the behavior being studied. Finally, if you want to know more about correlation coefficients, they are discussed in greater detail in the Statistical Appendix.

CONCEPT REVIEW 1.5

Descriptive Methods and Correlational Studies

Read the following statements and fill in each blank with one of these terms: naturalistic observation, the case study method, the survey method, correlational research, positive correlation, negative correlation.

1. A psychologist discovers that as negative life events increase, episodes of depression also increase. He concludes that there is a _____ between negative life events and episodes of depression.

2. A psychologist is interested in what hospital staff members say about their patients while riding in hospital elevators. His team of research assistants dress in ordinary street clothes and spend four hours each day riding elevators in various hospitals and unobtrusively recording the public conversations. This psychologist is using _____ to investigate public conversations about hospitalized patients.

3. The college admissions office is interested in finding out which students are going to do well in their first academic year at the college. They have a considerable amount of information about the new students, including their high school GPA. The admissions office would be well advised to use _____ to address this question.

4. Researchers have found that the more credit cards people have, the less money they tend

to have in their savings accounts. These researchers have discovered a _____ between the number of credit cards and the amount of savings.

5. Dr. Romano conducts in-depth interviews and gives extensive psychological tests to individuals who claim to have been abducted by aliens. He also collects information from their friends and family members. Dr. Romano is using the

_____ in his investigations of alien abductees.

6. To find out more about students' attitudes regarding their educational experience, researchers select a random, representative sample of students who are about to graduate. They send them each a three-page questionnaire and follow it up with a structured telephone interview. The researchers are using _____ to measure student attitudes.

Ethics in Psychological Research

All psychological research is subject to ethical guidelines developed by the American Psychological Association. What are five key provisions of the APA guidelines for research involving humans? Why do psychologists sometimes conduct research with animal subjects?

What might happen if you were to volunteer to participate in a psychology experiment or study? Are psychologists allowed to manipulate or control you without your knowledge or consent? Could a psychologist force you to reveal your innermost secrets? Could he or she administer electric shocks? Trick you into doing something weird against your will?

The answer to all these questions is "No." The American Psychological Association has developed a strict code of ethics for conducting research with both human and animal subjects. This code is contained in a document called *Ethical Principles of Psychologists and Code of Conduct* (APA, 1992a).

In general, psychologists must respect the dignity and welfare of their subjects. Psychologists cannot expose research participants to dangerous or harmful conditions that might cause either physical or emotional harm. And any psychological research using human or animal subjects must be approved by an ethics panel at the institution where the study is to be conducted.

Here are five of the key provisions in the most recent version of the APA ethical guidelines regulating research with human participants:

- **Informed consent and voluntary participation.** In reasonably understandable language, the psychologist must inform the participants of the nature of the research, including significant factors that might influence a person's willingness to participate in the study, such as physical risks, discomfort, or unpleasant emotional experiences. The psychologist must also explain to the participants that they are free to decline to participate or to withdraw from the research at any time.

- **Students as research participants.** When research participation is a course requirement or an opportunity for extra credit, the student must be given the choice of an alternative activity to fulfill the course requirement or earn extra credit.

- **The use of deception.** Psychologists can use deceptive techniques as part of the study only when two conditions have been met: (1) when it is not feasible to use alternatives that do not involve deception; (2) when the potential findings justify the use of deception because of their scientific, educational, or applied value.

- **Confidentiality of records.** Psychologists do not publicly disclose personally identifiable information about research participants.

- **Information about the study and debriefing.** All participants are provided with the opportunity to obtain information about the nature, results, and conclusions of the research. Psychologists are also obligated to *debrief* the participants—that is, to correct any misconceptions that participants may have had about the research.

Who makes sure that these ethical guidelines are followed? First, the institution or organization where psychological research is conducted has usually established an ethics committee that must review and approve research proposals. Second, the APA has established the Committee on Scientific and Professional Ethics, which investigates all complaints it receives. If a psychologist is found to be in violation of the ethics code, that person may be suspended or expelled from the APA.

Not surprisingly, the ethical guidelines for research with human and animal subjects are somewhat different. However, the use of animals in psychological research is also governed by specific ethical guidelines (APA, 1992b). These guidelines, as well as other issues, are discussed in Box 1.3.

IN FOCUS 1.3

Questions About the Use of Animals in Psychology Research

Is animal research condoned in psychology?

The American Psychological Association (1992b) does condone the use of animals in psychological research—but only under certain conditions. First, research using animal subjects must have an *acceptable scientific purpose.* Second, there must be a reasonable expectation that the research will (a) increase knowledge about behavior; (b) increase understanding of the species under study; or (c) produce results that benefit the health or welfare of humans or other animals.

Are there standards that psychologists must meet in using animal subjects?

The American Psychological Association publishes a document entitled *Guidelines for Ethical Conduct in the Care and Use of Animals,* which was revised in 1992. You can request a free copy of this document by writing to the American Psychological Association, 750 First Street N.E., Washington, D.C. 20002-4242. The APA Guidelines for animal care have been praised as being the most comprehensive set of guidelines of their kind (Fisher, 1986). In addition, federal and state laws govern the care and use of research animals.

How are these requirements enforced?

First, any psychologist who conducts research with animals is required to have the research approved in advance by a panel at the institution where the research is to be done. Second, any research using animals that is published in an APA journal must be in compliance with the ethical standards.

How many animal subjects are used in psychological research?

The vast majority of psychological research involves human subjects, not animals. Animals are used in only about 7 to 8 percent of psychological studies conducted in a given year. Most psychological research with animal subjects does *not* involve pain, suffering, or deprivation (APA, 1995b; Shapiro, 1991; Coile & Miller, 1984).

In the most recent survey conducted by the APA, the total number of animals used by psychology departments throughout the United States was about 200,000. Of these, about 170,000 were rats, mice, or other rodents. There were approximately 1,200 primates, 800 dogs, and about 600 cats.

The rest of the total was made up of a variety of creatures, from bats to sea snails (APA, 1986). In comparison, over *20 million* dogs and cats are destroyed in pounds every year.

Why are animals used in psychological research?

Here are a few of the key reasons that psychologists might use animal subjects rather than human subjects in research:

1. *Many psychologists are interested in the study of animal behavior for its own sake.* The branch of psychology that focuses on the study of the behavior of different species is called *comparative psychology.* Some psychologists also do research in the area called *animal cognition,* which is the study of animal learning, memory, thinking, and language.

Animal research is also pursued for its potential benefit to animals themselves (Azar, 1994b). For example, information gained from psychological research on animal behavior has been used to improve the quality of life and survival of animals in zoos and to increase the likelihood of survival of endangered species in the wild.

2. *Research on animal subjects is sometimes conducted that would not be feasible or possible to conduct on human subjects* (Heiman, 1995; Gallup & Suarez, 1985). Here are a few of the types of instances in which this might apply:

- There are many similarities between human and animal behavior. Human behavior, however, tends to be much more complex than animal behavior. So it's often easier to identify basic elements and principles of behavior by studying animals.

- Most species of animals commonly used in psychological research have a much shorter lifespan than humans. Psychologists can observe animals throughout their entire lifespan, from the prenatal stage through old age. Multiple generations can also be studied. To track such changes in human subjects might take decades of research (Miller, 1985).

- A psychologist can exercise much greater control over animal subjects. In a laboratory, the researcher can control all aspects of the animal subjects' environment, including lighting, diet, temperature, and so forth. If necessary, psychologists can also control for the genetic background of the animals.

3. *Research that would be ethically unacceptable to conduct on humans can be conducted using animal subjects. How-*

ever, research conducted on animal subjects is still subject to ethical constraints. The use of animal subjects in psychology (and other research) is based on the premise that human life is intrinsically more valuable than animal life. Not everyone agrees with this position (Finsen & Finsen, 1994; Singer, 1990; Rollin, 1992). However, as the APA's guidelines make clear, cruel or inhumane treatment of animal subjects cannot be justified under *any* circumstances.

In what areas of psychology has research using animals produced significant and valuable information?

Psychological research with animal subjects has made essential contributions to virtually every area of psychology (Domjan & Purdy, 1995). Along with con-

tributing to knowledge of the workings of the human brain, animal research has contributed to psychological knowledge in the areas of learning, memory, cognition, psychological disorders, therapies, and stress. Research with animals has produced significant gains in the treatment of many human conditions, from premature infants to people who suffer from chronic migraines, hypertension, or insomnia. Significant gains have also been made in helping animals, including the successful breeding and preservation of endangered species, improvements in the care of zoo animals, and the prevention of animal diseases (APA, 1995b; Miller, 1985).

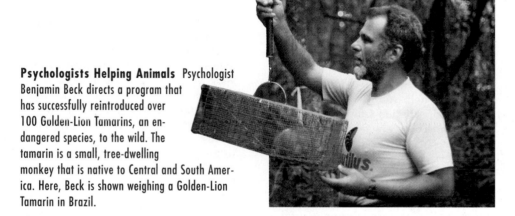

Psychologists Helping Animals Psychologist Benjamin Beck directs a program that has successfully reintroduced over 100 Golden-Lion Tamarins, an endangered species, to the wild. The tamarin is a small, tree-dwelling monkey that is native to Central and South America. Here, Beck is shown weighing a Golden-Lion Tamarin in Brazil.

Summing Up: Introducing Psychology

In this chapter we've laid the foundation for exploring a wide range of topics in the coming chapters. At this point, you should have a good understanding of how psychology came into existence and how it has become progressively more diverse as a scientific discipline. You should also have an appreciation for how psychologists rely on the scientific method in their efforts to gather evidence and answer questions.

In chapter after chapter of this book, you'll see how psychologists have applied these basic scientific tools, sometimes very ingeniously, to further the understanding of why we humans do what we do. Whether it is dealing with the common experiences of everyday life or with more extreme events like the Oklahoma City bombing, psychology can provide many insights into human behavior and mental processes. And, as you'll discover, psychology has much to teach you, not only about other people but about yourself as well. It's a fascinating journey and one that we look forward to sharing with you.

Welcome to psychology!

APPLICATION

Thinking Critically About Psychology and the Media

Discussions about psychological findings and issues are common in the popular media, but they aren't always presented accurately. How can you critically evaluate psychological research reported in the popular media?

Discussions about psychology abound in the popular media. Whether it's your local newspaper, the *New York Times, Newsweek,* or *USA Today,* articles appear proclaiming the latest psychological findings with headlines designed to grab your attention. The same can be said of talk shows, where "experts" try to enlighten the audience by discussing unusual aspects of human behavior.

Given all this attention to psychology and psychology-related topics in the popular press, how can you determine if the information being presented has any credibility? There are several ways to be a more informed consumer of psychology-related information in the mass media. The guidelines that follow will help you assess whether or not the information is worthy of your attention. These suggestions will also help you critically evaluate the claims and information you may encounter in the media.

1. Avoid being duped by "pseudosciences." A **pseudoscience** is a fake or a false science. Often, a pseudoscience displays all the trappings of the stereotype that many people have about a "real" science, such as sophisticated technical jargon, researchers with impressive-sounding credentials, striking statistical graphs, and elaborate theories (Hines, 1988). In reality, a pseudoscience has little or no scientific basis, and its proponents are often unwilling to submit their claims to scientific scrutiny (Jacobson & others, 1995).

For example, *graphology* is a pseudoscience that claims to be able to assess personality, health, and abilities through analysis of a person's distinctive handwriting, doodles, and drawing style (Beyerstein, 1996). This particular pseudoscience is extremely popular and has been widely publicized in business journals, magazines, and newspapers (e.g., Zweig & Clash, 1993). Graphology is used by an estimated

3,000 companies in the United States to hire new personnel, make promotions, assess aptitudes, and predict job success (Basil, 1991; Neter & Ben-Shakhar, 1989).

Graphology's popularity is particularly alarming because scientific studies have repeatedly shown that it fails to predict job success and personality characteristics (e.g., Edwards & Armitage, 1992). Other popular pseudosciences include astrology, numerology, palmistry, and biorhythms (Hines, 1988).

2. Be especially skeptical of sensationalistic findings or claims. As a matter of professional ethics, psychologists are obligated to avoid misrepresenting scientific findings through sensationalism, exaggeration, or superficiality. Headlines proclaiming "discoveries" or "breakthroughs" in psychological research are designed to grab your attention. Almost always, if you listen or read further, you'll encounter a much more conservative tone in the statements of the researchers themselves. As scientists, psychologists tend to be conservative in stating their research results, their purpose being not to mislead the public. Reporters, on the other hand, are sometimes more interested in attracting readers or viewers than they are in accurately portraying scientific results (Connor-Greene, 1993; McCall, 1988).

3. Consider the motivations of the researchers. Always consider the source of the information (Carlson, 1995). It's difficult to put much stock in research that was funded by a company or agency whose motive is to convince you to buy some product, service,

or device. Training courses, products, or devices are often marketed with convincing-looking research studies to back up their claims.

For example, an advertisement for cassette tapes proclaimed the following: "Neuroscientists have recently discovered that special music calibrated at a specific beat per second merge the right and left hemispheres of your brain into a cohesive unit. Studies have shown that this synchronization can speed up the learning process two to five times while dramatically increasing the receptivity of your subconscious mind" ("Supercharge your mind," 1995). By listening to tapes that use this "special music," you can supposedly have "super intelligence," acquire "laser concentration," *and* have a "flat stomach." Quite a deal, for only $12.95 per tape plus $3.00 postage and handling!

It's difficult to imagine that such research, if funded by the same company, was done objectively or that negative findings were also noted. For that matter, you have to wonder if the "studies" even exist when any details about them are conveniently left out.

4. Separate opinions from data. Testimonials, isolated cases, and conjecture are not the same as scientifically gathered data. The essence of any science is objective data gathering that supports or refutes the ideas being tested. It's difficult for individuals to be objective about events with which they are directly connected. Emotions, points of view, past history, and culture can all play a part in the misinterpretation of events.

Try to avoid committing the *inductive fallacy:* Do not assume that be-

GEECH®

cause an event was experienced one way by a particular individual it's experienced the same way by everyone. For example, even though you know someone who conquered a fear of flying by being hypnotized, don't assume the same strategy will work for everyone.

5. Look for the original source of professional publication. When the study has been conducted by a reputable researcher, whether it's reported in print or on television, the original source of professional publication is almost always noted. Usually, psychological research is first published in a professional psychology journal before it is shared with the general public.

Typically, a report in the popular media will include a sentence like, "In this month's issue of the *Journal of Personality and Social Psychology,* it was reported that . . . ," which identifies the original source. Knowing that the research has been scrutinized by other psychologists before publication can give you increased confidence in the findings. Keep in mind, however, that reporters may add their own interpretation to those of the researchers, thereby distorting or misrepresenting

the actual findings (Connor-Greene, 1993; McCall, 1988). If the original source is identified, you can locate the actual study and read it yourself.

6. Consider the methods and operational definitions used. At this point you should understand the importance of such elements as control groups in experiments, the use of multiple observers in descriptive research, random assignment of subjects, and the use of a sample that is representative of the population being studied. Look for these elements in the description of the study to increase your confidence in the research findings. Also, try to identify how the researchers operationally defined the variables in the study. For example, if the study is investigating whether being married affects a person's level of happiness, you'd be wise to try to identify how the researchers operationally defined and measured the emotion of happiness.

7. Remember the difference between correlation and causality. Many of the research results reported in the mass media are correlational studies. Yet the reports often imply that

a cause-and-effect relationship has been discovered (Connor-Greene, 1993). From our earlier discussion, you now understand that just because two factors are correlated, one does not necessarily cause the other. It is entirely possible that a third factor is responsible for the behavior in question. As a general rule, whenever the words *link, tie, connection, association,* and *relationship* are used in describing psychological findings, the research being described is correlational.

8. Skepticism is the rule, not the exception, in science. It seems as if it is basic to human nature to look for easy answers to life's dilemmas— whether it's increasing motivation and self-discipline, improving your memory, combating stress, or enhancing relationships. As you'll see in these Application sections at the end of each chapter, psychological research has much to say about these and other practical topics. But achieving these goals is rarely as simple as is portrayed in the popular press. Therefore, remember one final axiom: If it sounds too good to be true, it probably is!

Summary Introducing Psychology

What Is Psychology?

- Psychology is now defined as the science of behavior and mental processes. However, the definition of psychology has evolved over time.

The Early History of Psychology

- Early philosophers, such as Aristotle and Descartes, used observation, logic, and intuition to understand psychological topics. In later centuries, the discoveries of physiologists demonstrated that scientific methods could be applied to psychological topics.

- Wilhelm Wundt, a German physiologist, is credited with formally founding the science of psychology. Wundt's student, Edward B. Titchener, established structuralism, the first school of psychology. The structuralists focused on studying the "structure" of conscious experience; their primary research method was introspection.

- William James was the founder of psychology in the United States. James established functionalism, a school of psychology that emphasized the adaptive role of behavior. James's students, G. Stanley Hall and Mary Whiton Calkins, were two important early figures in American psychology.

Psychology in the Twentieth Century

■ Behaviorism emerged in the early 1900s, based on Ivan Pavlov's research. Behaviorism was first championed by John Watson and further developed by B. F. Skinner. Behaviorism rejected the study of mental processes and emphasized the study of observable behavior, especially the principles of learning.

■ Other influences on psychology during the first half of the twentieth century were Sigmund Freud and psychoanalysis; Max Wertheimer and Gestalt psychology; and Carl Rogers and Abraham Maslow and humanistic psychology.

Psychology Today

■ Advances in drug treatments and technology increased the influence of biological psychology, the study of the physical bases of behavior.

■ Breaking with the behaviorists, cognitive psychologists focus on the role of mental processes in behavior.

■ The insights of cross-cultural psychology have revealed that psychological findings cannot always be universally applied, and emphasize the importance of human diversity and cultural influences in psychology.

■ Psychology today is very diverse. Topics can be approached from different perspectives. These include the biological, behavioral, psychoanalytic, humanistic, cognitive, and cross-cultural perspectives.

■ Some of the important specialty areas of psychology include the following: biological psychology; cognitive psychology; experimental psychology; developmental psychology; social psychology; personality psychology; health psychology; educational psychology; industrial/organizational psychology; and clinical psychology. Although their training is different, both clinical psychologists and psychiatrists treat people with mental disorders.

The Scientific Method

■ The four goals of psychology are to describe, explain, predict, and influence human behavior and mental processes. Despite the diversity of contemporary psychology, all psychologists have been trained in the scientific method, which guides scientists in their research.

■ Psychology is based on empirical evidence. The four steps of the scientific method are as follows: generate a hypothesis that can be tested empirically; design the study and collect the data; analyze the data and draw conclusions; and report the findings. The variables must be operationally defined as to how they will be measured or manipulated.

■ Research methods include the experimental method and descriptive methods. Statistics are used to analyze the data and to determine whether findings are statistically significant. Meta-analysis can be used to combine and analyze multiple studies on a single topic. Reporting the results of a study in a professional publication allows other researchers to replicate the study.

■ As research findings accumulate from individual studies, theories or models develop to explain the different findings on a related topic. Theories are tools for understanding and explaining behavior and mental processes. Theories evolve and change as new evidence emerges.

The Experimental Method

■ The experimental method is a research method that demonstrates a cause-and-effect relationship between one variable and another. Experiments involve manipulating the independent variable and measuring the effects of the manipulation on the dependent variable. A model experiment is the Sam Stone study by Leichtman & Ceci (1995).

■ A well-designed experiment includes the following characteristics: random assignment of subjects to experimental conditions; experimental groups compared to a control group; systematic manipulation of the independent variable; and objective measurement of the dependent variable.

■ There are many variations in experimental design. A placebo control group is included to check for expectancy effects. The double-blind technique helps ensure objectivity. Although experiments can provide evidence of causality, they do have certain limitations. Not all questions can be studied experimentally.

Descriptive Methods

■ Descriptive methods are research strategies to observe and describe behavior. Descriptive methods include naturalistic observation, case studies, and surveys.

■ Surveys, questionnaires, and interviews are administered to a sample of the larger group to be investigated. For results to be generalizable to the larger population, the sample must be representative. Participants are usually chosen through random selection.

Correlational Studies:
Looking at Relationships and Making Predictions

■ Correlational studies investigate how strongly two factors are related to each other, and the relationship is expressed in terms of a correlation coefficient. A positive correlation indicates that two factors vary in the same direction, while a negative correlation indicates that two factors vary in opposite directions.

■ Even when two factors are strongly related, conclusions cannot be drawn about causality; a third factor may actually be responsible for the association. However, correlational evidence can be used to identify important relationships and to make meaningful predictions.

Ethics in Psychological Research

■ All psychological research is subject to regulations contained in an ethical code developed by the American Psychological Association. For research with human subjects, the ethical code requires that: informed consent and voluntary participation must be ensured; student subjects must be given alternatives to participating in research; deceptive techniques can be used only under specific conditions; records are kept confidential; participants are to be debriefed and given the opportunity to learn more about the study.

■ Research with animal subjects is also governed by an ethical code developed by the American Psychological Association.

Key Terms

psychology (p. 3)

structuralism (p. 5)

functionalism (p. 5)

behaviorism (p. 7)

psychoanalysis (p. 8)

Gestalt psychology (p. 8)

humanistic psychology (p. 9)

culture (p. 11)

ethnocentrism (p. 12)

individualistic cultures (p. 12)

collectivistic cultures (p. 12)

scientific method (p. 16)

critical thinking (p. 17)

hypothesis (p. 18)

variable (p. 18)

operational definition (p. 18)

statistics (p. 19)

statistical significance (p. 19)

meta-analysis (p. 19)

replicate (p. 20)

theory (p. 21)

experimental method (p. 22)

independent variable (p. 22)

dependent variable (p. 22)

random assignment (p. 23)

control group (p. 23)

experimental group (p. 24)

placebo control group (p. 25)

expectancy effect (p. 25)

descriptive methods (p. 27)

naturalistic observation (p. 27)

case study (p. 28)

survey (p. 28)

sample (p. 29)

representative sample (p. 29)

correlational study (p. 31)

positive correlation (p. 31)

negative correlation (p. 31)

pseudoscience (p. 36)

Key People

Mary Whiton Calkins (1863–1930) American psychologist who conducted research on memory, personality, and dreams; established one of the first U.S. psychology research laboratories; first woman president of the American Psychological Association.

Sigmund Freud (1856–1939) Austrian physician and founder of psychoanalysis.

G. Stanley Hall (1844–1924) American psychologist who established the first psychology research laboratory in the United States; founded the American Psychological Association.

William James (1842–1910) American philosopher and psychologist who founded psychology in the United States and established the psychological school called functionalism.

Abraham Maslow (1908–1970) American humanistic psychologist who developed a theory of motivation.

Ivan Pavlov (1849–1936) Russian physiologist whose pioneering research on learning contributed to the development of behaviorism; discovered the basic learning process that is now called classical conditioning.

Carl Rogers (1902–1987) American psychologist who founded the school of humanistic psychology.

B. F. Skinner (1904–1990) American psychologist and leading proponent of behaviorism; developed a model of learning called operant conditioning; emphasized studying the relationship between environmental factors and observable behavior.

John B. Watson (1878–1958) American psychologist who founded behaviorism, emphasizing the study of observable behavior and rejecting the study of mental processes.

Max Wertheimer (1880–1943) German psychologist who founded the school of Gestalt psychology.

Wilhelm Wundt (1832–1920) German physiologist who founded psychology as a formal science; opened first psychology research laboratory in 1879.

CONCEPT REVIEW 1.1 Page 9

1. functionalism; William James
2. humanistic psychology; Carl Rogers
3. structuralism; Edward Titchener
4. psychoanalysis; Sigmund Freud
5. behaviorism; John Watson
6. Gestalt psychology; Max Wertheimer

CONCEPT REVIEW 1.2 Page 15

1. a
2. b
3. d
4. d
5. b

CONCEPT REVIEW 1.3 Page 21

1. D. formulate a hypothesis
2. C. design the study and collect data
3. A. analyze the data
4. B. report the findings

CONCEPT REVIEW 1.4 Page 26

1. C. independent variable
2. E. random assignment
3. A. dependent variable
4. B. experimental group; D. control group

CONCEPT REVIEW 1.5 Page 32

1. positive correlation
2. naturalistic observation
3. correlational research
4. negative correlation
5. the case study method
6. the survey method

2 The Biological Foundations of Behavior

Prologue: Asha's Story

The headaches began without warning. A pounding, intense pain just over Asha's left temple. Asha just couldn't seem to shake it—the pain was unrelenting. She was uncharacteristically tired, too.

But our friend Asha, a healthy, active 32-year-old, chalked up her constant headache and fatigue to stress and exhaustion. After all, she *was* under considerable stress. The end of her demanding first semester of teaching and research at a major university was drawing near. Except for problems with allergies, Asha had always been extremely healthy and usually tolerated stress well. She didn't drink or smoke or take any kind of drugs, except for her allergy medications. And no matter how late she stayed up working on her lectures and research proposals, she still got up at 5:30 every morning to work out at the university gym.

There were other, more subtle signs that something was wrong. Asha's husband, Paul, noticed that she had been behaving rather oddly in recent weeks. For example, at Thanksgiving dinner, Asha had picked up a knife by the wrong end and tried to cut her turkey with the handle instead of the blade. A few hours later, Asha had made the same mistake in trying to use a scissors: she held the blades and tried to cut with the handle.

Asha laughed these incidents off, and for that matter, so did Paul. They both thought she was simply under too much stress. And when Asha occasionally got her words mixed up, neither Paul nor anyone else was terribly surprised. Asha was born in India, and her first language was Tulu. Although Asha was extremely fluent in English, she often got English phrases slightly wrong—like the time she said that Paul was a "straight dart" instead of a "straight arrow." Or when she said that it was "storming cats and birds" instead of "raining cats and dogs."

There were other odd lapses in language. "I would say something thinking it was correct," Asha recalled, "and people would say to me: 'What are you saying?' I wouldn't realize I was saying something wrong. I would open my mouth and just nonsense would come out. But it made perfect sense to me. At other times, the word was on the tip of my tongue—I knew I knew the word, but I couldn't find it. I would fumble for words but it would come out wrong. Sometimes I would slur words, like I'd try to say Saturday, only it would come out 'salad-day.'"

The day before Paul and Asha were due to leave for a Christmas visit to Paul's parents in another state, Asha went to her allergist, thinking that perhaps the headache was due to sinus problems. She told the allergist about her chronic headache and he took several X-rays, which showed that her sinuses were clear. Somewhat alarmed, Asha's allergist made an appointment for her to see a neurologist at the hospital emergency room that night. Uncharacteristically, Asha adamantly refused to keep the appointment, despite Paul's urging. Instead, she insisted on going shopping to buy new clothes for the Christmas trip.

As Asha recalled, "I remember that all my decisions were very impulsive. One minute I would say I was very tired, the next minute I'd say I wanted to go to the mall. My mind was racing so fast. At the mall, I was totally confused. The noise and the lights and all the people confused me. And I couldn't make up my mind, which is very unusual for me. The entire time at the mall, I kept telling Paul that my head was pounding."

Paul and Asha left the next morning on the long drive to Paul's parents' home. About midway, they stopped and picked up Paul's sister. Throughout the drive, Asha held her hand to her left temple, trying to ease the pain. As Asha recalls, "My sister-in-law kept telling me I was talking nonsense. The words were just coming out all wrong."

On Christmas morning, Paul and Asha were sitting with Paul's family, opening presents. Asha walked over to Paul's father to look at the pool cue he had received as a gift. As she bent down, she fell forward onto her father-in-law. At first, everyone thought Asha was just joking around. But then she fell to the floor, her body stiff. Seconds later, it was apparent that Asha had lost consciousness and was having a seizure.

Asha remembers nothing of the seizure or of being taken by ambulance to the hospital intensive care unit. She floated in and out of consciousness for the first day and night. Tests were run. A CAT scan showed some sort of blockage in her brain. An MRI scan showed a large white spot on the left side of Asha's brain. At only 32 years of age, Asha had suffered a stroke.

She remained in the hospital for twelve days. It was only after she was transferred out of intensive care that both Asha and Paul began to realize just how serious the repercussions of the stroke were. Asha couldn't read or write and had difficulty comprehending what was being said. Although she could speak, she couldn't name even simple objects, such as a tree or a clock. As Paul describes, "It was as if in her mind she knew what it was, but she just couldn't find the right word. The connection between memory and vocabulary was gone."

When Asha and Paul finally returned to their home, Asha went to her new neurologist—the same doctor that she had so adamantly refused to see two days before her stroke. At that point, Asha was convinced that her life was over. As she explains, "I had a doctorate and I was an assistant professor at the university. But I couldn't read, write, or talk! I had to have constant help." Asha's mother, Nalini, came from India to stay with Asha. There was no way Asha could go back to teaching that semester. Instead, she began the difficult, painstaking task of relearning how to speak, read, recognize, and name common objects.

In this chapter, you'll learn more about Asha's experience. You'll also learn why the brain damage she experienced impaired her ability to speak, read, and name objects. At the end of this chapter, we'll tell you what happened to Asha, and how she's doing now.

Introduction

The Scope of Biological Psychology

As Asha's story demonstrates, even simple behaviors and psychological processes are intimately connected to the workings of the brain. If we showed you a picture of a bicycle, you would not find it difficult to verbally identify it. If we handed you today's newspaper, you could read the headlines back to us and explain what they meant. You could easily follow the rapid exchange of dialogue between two riled-up guests on a TV talk show. But for months after her stroke, Asha found it impossible to perform any of these simple tasks.

In this chapter, you will discover why the brain damage that Asha experienced impaired her ability to perform simple behaviors like the ones above. You'll also gain a better understanding of the biological bases of your own behavior. Indeed, one important way to make sense out of your experiences is to understand the physical structures and processes that are responsible for them.

From the simple to the complex, the workings of the brain and the rest of the nervous system are apparent in every action, thought, or feeling you experience. Your ability to process new information and experiences, your memory of previous experiences, your sense of who you are and what you know, your actions and reactions—all of these are products of the brain and the rest of the nervous system working in harmony.

As we discussed in Chapter 1, **biological psychology** is the study of the internal physical events and processes that correspond with our experiences and behavior. It may surprise you to learn that psychology is so closely related to biology. But if you think about it, the "psychological you" is really inseparable from the "biological you." Psychological processes are closely linked to biological processes, and biological processes can profoundly influence human behavior. In this chapter, you will encounter some of the questions and issues that are most fundamental to biological psychology, questions like:

- How does communication occur in the nervous system and endocrine system? How is the nervous system organized?

- How do scientists study the brain and the rest of the nervous system?

- How are different brain areas specialized to perform different functions?

- How does environmental stimulation affect brain structure and function?

Biological psychology is not limited to the study of the brain and the rest of the nervous system. Throughout this text, you'll encounter issues that are addressed by biological psychology. Here are just a few of the issues you'll encounter in later chapters:

- How do we tell the difference between red and blue, cold and hot, loud and soft? (Chapter 3)

- How are body functions and processes altered during sleep? Why is it so difficult to change our "body clock" when we change time zones? What are dreams and what causes them

The Scope of Biological Psychology Maintaining your balance on a bicycle, smiling, talking with a friend, avoiding other vehicles—all of our behaviors involve the complex integration of many physical processes working in harmony. For that matter, so does your ability to perceive and recognize the image in this photograph. What kinds of questions might biological psychologists ask about the common behaviors shown here?

biological psychology
Specialized branch of psychology that studies the relationship between behavior and body processes and systems.

to occur? How does sleep differ from waking consciousness? (Chapter 4)

- What exactly is a "memory" and where is it stored in the brain? (Chapter 6)

- Why do we get hungry? How do emotions occur? (Chapter 8)

- Can our emotions affect our vulnerability to infection and disease? If so, how? (Chapter 13)

- How does heredity influence our development? Does genetics play a role in personality traits? Is heredity involved in mental disorders? (Chapters 9, 11, and 14)

- What role does abnormal brain chemistry play in psychological disorders? How do antianxiety, antidepressant, and antipsychotic medications work to alleviate the symptoms of serious psychological disorders? (Chapters 14 and 15)

As you'll see, most of these issues are far from being completely resolved. Nevertheless, biological psychology has contributed important insights about many different dimensions of human behavior. This area of research reflects the contributions of psychologists as well as other kinds of scientists, including biologists, chemists, neurologists, and psychiatrists.

In this chapter, we'll lay an important foundation for the rest of this book by helping you develop a broad appreciation of the *nervous system*—the body's most important communication network. We'll start by looking at the most important cells of the nervous system, called *neurons*. We'll also consider the organization of the nervous system and another important communication network—the *endocrine system*. We'll then move on to a guided tour of the brain. We'll look at how certain areas in the brain are specialized to handle different functions, like language and vision. In the chapter's Application, we discuss how the brain responds to environmental stimulation by literally altering its structure. And at several points, we'll return to Asha's story and tell you how she fared after her stroke.

The Neuron: The Basic Unit of Communication

Information in the nervous system is transmitted by the neuron, a type of cell that is specialized for communication. What are the three main types of neurons? What are the basic components of the neuron, and what are their functions? What are glial cells, and what is their role in the nervous system?

Communication throughout the nervous system takes place via **neurons**—cells which are highly specialized to receive and transmit information from one part of the body to another. The number of neurons in the nervous system is astronomical. The human brain is estimated to have 100 billion neurons (Fischbach, 1992). To help put this in perspective, if you could count neurons at the rate of one per second, it would take over 3,000 years to count the neurons in a human brain!

For the record, no one has actually counted all of the neurons in the nervous system because most neurons are extremely small, especially many of

neuron
Highly specialized cell that communicates information in electrical and chemical form; a nerve cell.

glial cells
(GLEE-ull) Support cells that assist neurons by providing structural support, nutrition, and removal of cell wastes; manufacture myelin.

sensory neuron
Type of neuron that conveys information to the brain from specialized receptor cells in sense organs and internal organs.

motor neuron
Type of neuron that signals muscles to relax or contract.

interneuron
Type of neuron that communicates information from one neuron to the next.

those in the compact area that the brain occupies. Special magnifying equipment, like the electron microscope, is often needed to study them.

Fortunately for neuroscientists, there are often striking similarities between the workings of the human nervous system and the nervous systems of many other creatures in the animal kingdom. Very simple creatures, such as sea snails and squids, tend to have larger neurons and simpler nervous systems than humans. Neuroscientists have been able to observe the actions and reactions of a single neuron by studying the nervous systems of such simple animals.

Along with neurons, the human nervous system is made up of another type of specialized cell, called **glial cells.** Glial cells outnumber neurons by about ten to one, but are much smaller than neurons (Kalat, 1995). Unlike neurons, glial cells do not send or receive information. Rather, they are cast in supporting roles to the major player, the neuron. *Glia* is Greek for "glue," and at one time it was believed that glial cells were the "glue" that held the neurons of the brain together. While they don't actually glue neurons together, glial cells do provide structural support for neurons. Glial cells also help neurons by providing nutrition, enhancing the speed of communication between neurons, and removing waste products, including neurons that have died or been damaged (Kandel, 1995a; Lees, 1993).

There are three basic types of neurons, each communicating different kinds of information. **Sensory neurons** convey information about the environment, such as light or sound, from specialized receptor cells in the sense organs to the brain. Sensory neurons also carry information from the skin and internal organs to the brain. **Motor neurons** communicate information to the muscles and glands of the body. Simply blinking your eyes activates thousands of motor neurons. Finally, **interneurons** communicate information *between* neurons. By far, most of the neurons in the human nervous system are interneurons, and many interneurons connect to other interneurons. As you can see in Figure 2.1, individual neurons vary greatly in size and shape—a variety that reflects their specialized functions.

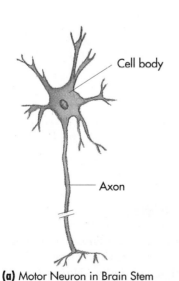

(a) Motor Neuron in Brain Stem

(b) Purkinje cell

(c) Pyramidal Cell

FIGURE 2.1 The Diversity of Neurons
Neurons come in a surprising variety of shapes and sizes. A neuron's structure reflects its specialized function. A simple motor neuron is shown in **(a).** An actual motor neuron is likely to have an axon that is much longer in proportion to the rest of its structures than is shown here. The neurons shown in **(b)** and **(c)** have widely branching dendrites. Thus they are capable of receiving and integrating a tremendous amount of information from many sources.

FIGURE 2.2 The Parts of a Neuron
The location and function of key parts of a neuron are depicted in the figure. With the aid of an electron microscope, it is possible to see actual cell bodies, dendrites, and axons in the cluster of brain neurons shown in the photograph. The green color is added to provide contrast in the photograph and make the neurons more visible.

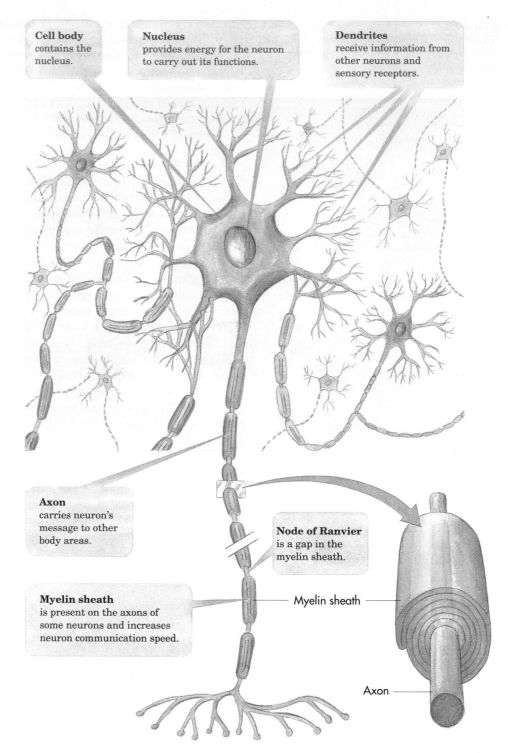

Cell body contains the nucleus.

Nucleus provides energy for the neuron to carry out its functions.

Dendrites receive information from other neurons and sensory receptors.

Axon carries neuron's message to other body areas.

Node of Ranvier is a gap in the myelin sheath.

Myelin sheath is present on the axons of some neurons and increases neuron communication speed.

Myelin sheath

Axon

Characteristics of the Neuron

Most neurons have three basic components: a *cell body, dendrites,* and an *axon* (see Figure 2.2). The **cell body** contains the nucleus, which provides energy for the neuron to carry out its functions. The cell body also contains genetic material and other structures that are found in virtually all the cells in the body.

Extending out from the cell body are many short, branching fibers, called **dendrites.** The term *dendrite* comes from a Greek word meaning "tree," and the intricate branching of the dendrites does often resemble the branches of

cell body
The part of a neuron that contains the nucleus.

dendrites
Multiple short fibers that extend from the neuron's cell body and receive information from other neurons or sensory receptor cells.

a tree or bush. Dendrites *receive* messages from other neurons or specialized cells (Johnston & others, 1996). Dendrites with many branches have a greater surface area, which increases the amount of information that the neuron can receive (Kalat, 1995). Some neurons have thousands of dendrites.

The **axon** is a single, elongated tube that extends from the cell body in most, though not all, neurons. (Some neurons do not have axons.) Axons carry information *from* the neuron *to* other cells in the body, including other neurons, glands, and muscles. In contrast to the potentially large number of dendrites, a neuron has no more than one axon exiting from the cell body. However, many axons have branches near their tips that allow the neuron to communicate information to more than one target (Kandel, 1995a).

Axons can vary enormously in length. Most axons are very small; some are no more than a few thousandths of an inch long. Other axons, however, are quite long. For example, the longest axon in your body is that of the motor neuron that controls your big toe. This neuron extends from the base of your spine into your foot. If you happen to be a seven-foot-tall basketball player, this axon could be four feet long! For most of us, of course, this axon is closer to three feet in length.

The axons of many, though not all, neurons are surrounded by the **myelin sheath.** The myelin sheath is a white, fatty covering manufactured by special glial cells. In much the same way that you can bundle together electrical wires if they are each insulated with plastic, myelin helps insulate one axon from the axons of other neurons. Rather than being a continuous coating of the axon, the myelin sheath occurs in segments that are separated by small gaps where the myelin is missing. The small gaps are called the *nodes of Ranvier* or simply *nodes* (see Figure 2.2). Neurons wrapped in myelin communicate their messages up to twenty times faster than unmyelinated neurons (Schwartz, 1995b).

The importance of myelin becomes readily apparent when it is damaged. For example, *multiple sclerosis* is a disease that involves the degeneration of patches of the myelin sheath. This degeneration causes the transmission of neural messages to be slowed or interrupted, resulting in disturbances in sensation and movement. Muscular weakness, loss of coordination, and speech and visual disturbances are some of the symptoms that can characterize multiple sclerosis.

Communication Within the Neuron:
The All-or-None Action Potential

Neurons communicate information in the form of brief electrical impulses called action potentials. How is the action potential produced, and how does it "travel" down the axon? What factors affect the speed at which the nerve impulse travels?

Essentially, the function of neurons is to transmit information throughout the nervous system. But exactly *how* do neurons transmit information? What form does this information take? In this section, we'll consider the nature of communication *within* a neuron, and in the following section we'll describe communication *between* neurons. As you'll see, communication in and between neurons is an electrochemical process.

In general, messages are gathered by the dendrites and cell body and then transmitted along the axon in the form of a brief electrical impulse called an **action potential** (Fischbach, 1992). The action potential is produced by the movement of electrically charged particles, called *ions,* across the membrane of the axon. Some ions are negatively charged, others positively charged.

axon
The long, fluid-filled tube that carries a neuron's messages to other body areas.

myelin sheath
(MY-eh-linn) A white, fatty covering wrapped around the axons of some neurons that increases their communication speed.

action potential
A brief electrical impulse by which information is transmitted along the axon of a neuron.

Think of the axon membrane as a gatekeeper that carefully controls the balance of positive and negative ions on the interior and exterior of the axon. As the gatekeeper, the axon membrane opens and closes *ion channels* that allow ions to flow in and out of the axon (Koester & Siegelbaum, 1995).

Each neuron requires a minimum level of stimulation from other neurons or sensory receptors to activate it. This minimum level of stimulation is called the neuron's **stimulus threshold.** While waiting for sufficient stimulation to activate it, the neuron is said to be *polarized.* This means that the axon's interior is more negatively charged than the exterior fluid surrounding the axon.

Just in case you're wondering, scientists have measured the negative electrical charge of the neuron's interior, using giant squid neurons to do so. And how much electricity are we discussing? About −70 millivolts (or thousandths of a volt). The −70 millivolts is referred to as the neuron's **resting potential** (Koester, 1995a).

This polarized, negative-inside/positive-outside condition is primarily due to the different concentrations of two particular ions: sodium and potassium. The fluid surrounding the axon contains a larger concentration of sodium ions than the fluid within the axon. The fluid within the axon contains a larger concentration of potassium ions than the fluid outside the axon.

When sufficiently stimulated by other neurons or sensory receptors, the neuron *depolarizes,* beginning the action potential. At each successive axon segment, sodium ion channels open for a mere 1/1000 of a second. The sodium ions rush to the axon interior from the surrounding fluid, and then the sodium ion channels close. Less than a thousandth of a second later, the potassium ion channels open, allowing potassium to rush out of the axon and into the fluid surrounding it. Then the potassium ion channels close (see Figure 2.3a). This sequence of depolarization and ion movement continues in a self-sustaining fashion down the entire length of the axon (Koester, 1995a, 1995b).

As sodium ions penetrate the axon membrane and potassium ions exit, the electrical charge on the inside of the axon momentarily changes to a positive electrical charge of about +30 millivolts. The result is a brief positive electrical impulse that progressively occurs at each segment down the axon—the action potential.

Keep a couple of things in mind. First, although it's tempting to think of the action potential as being conducted in much the same way that electricity is conducted through a wire, that's *not* what takes place in the neuron. The axon is actually a poor conductor of electricity. At each successive segment of the axon, the action potential is *regenerated* in the same way that it was generated in the previous segment—by depolarization and the movement of ions (Kalat, 1995).

Second, once the action potential is started, it is self-sustaining and continues to the end of the axon. In other words, there is no such thing as a partial action potential. Either the neuron is sufficiently stimulated and an action potential occurs, or the neuron is not sufficiently stimulated and an action potential does not occur. This principle is referred to as the **all-or-none law.**

Following the action potential, a *refractory period* occurs during which the neuron is unable to fire. This refractory period lasts for a mere 1/1000 of a second or less. During the refractory period, the neuron *repolarizes* and reestablishes the negative-inside/positive-outside condition. Like depolarization, repolarization occurs progressively at each segment down the axon. This process of "pumping" sodium ions out and drawing potassium ions back in reestablishes the resting potential conditions so that the neuron is capable of firing again (Carlson, 1994). Figure 2.3b depicts the complete sequence from resting potential to action potential and back to resting potential again.

stimulus threshold
The minimum level of stimulation required to activate a particular neuron.

resting potential
State in which a neuron is prepared to activate and communicate its message if it receives sufficient stimulation.

all-or-none law
The principle that either a neuron is sufficiently stimulated and an action potential occurs or a neuron is not sufficiently stimulated and an action potential does not occur.

(a)

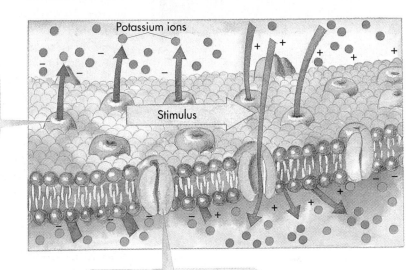

Sodium ions

Stimulus arrives

Sodium channels open and sodium ions rush in.

Sodium ions

Potassium ions

Stimulus

A mere 1/1000th second later, potassium channels open and potassium ions rush out of the axon.

The first sodium channels have closed, but those further down the axon open, carrying the movement of depolarization along.

FIGURE 2.3 Communication Within the Neuron

(a) The Action Potential When sufficiently stimulated, a neuron depolarizes and an action potential begins. At each progressive segment of the axon's membrane, sodium ion channels open and sodium ions rush in to the interior of the axon. A split-second later, the sodium ion channels close and potassium ion channels open, allowing potassium ions to rush out of the axon. As this sequence occurs, the electrical charge on the interior of the axon changes from negative to positive. Once started, an action potential is self-sustaining and continues to the end of the axon.

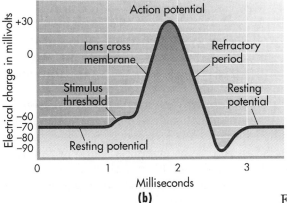

(b)

(b) Electrical Changes During an Action Potential This graph shows the changing electrical charge of the neuron during an action potential. When the neuron depolarizes and ions cross the axon membrane, it results in a positive electrical impulse of +30 millivolts—the action potential. During the refractory period, the neuron reestablishes the resting potential negative charge of −70 millivolts, and then is ready to activate again.

For clarity, we've simplified many of the details involved in the action potential (see, for example, Barinaga, 1995). However, that's basically how information is communicated *within* a neuron. Remember, action potentials are generated in mere thousandths of a second. Thus, a single neuron can generate hundreds of neural impulses per second. Given these incredibly small increments of time, just how fast do neural impulses zip around the body?

The fastest neurons in your body communicate at speeds of up to 270 miles per hour. In the slowest neurons, messages creep along at about 2 miles per hour. This variation in communication speed is due to two factors: the axon diameter and the myelin sheath. The greater the axon's diameter, the faster the axon conducts action potentials. And, as we said earlier, myelinated neurons communicate faster than unmyelinated neurons. In myelinated neurons, the sodium ion channels are concentrated at each of the nodes of Ranvier where the myelin is missing. So in myelinated neurons the action potential "jumps" from node to node rather than progressing down the entire length of the axon (Koester & Siegelbaum, 1995b).

Communication Between Neurons:
Bridging the Gap

Communication between neurons takes place at the synapse, the junction between two adjoining neurons. How is information communicated at the synapse? What is synaptic transmission, and how does it occur? What is a neurotransmitter, and what is its role in synaptic transmission?

The primary function of a neuron is to communicate information to other cells, most notably other neurons. The point of communication between two neurons is called the **synapse.** At this communication junction, the message-*sending* neuron is referred to as the *presynaptic neuron.* The message-*receiving* neuron is called the *postsynaptic neuron.* For cells that are specialized to communicate information, neurons have a surprising characteristic: they don't touch each other. The presynaptic and postsynaptic neurons are separated by a tiny fluid-filled space, called the **synaptic gap,** which is only about *five-millionths* of an inch wide.

The transmission of information between two neurons occurs in one of two possible ways: electrically or chemically. When communication is electrical, the synaptic gap is extremely narrow, and special ion channels serve as a bridge between the neurons. Electrical communication between the two neurons is virtually instantaneous (Kandel & Siegelbaum, 1995).

Although some neurons communicate electrically in the human nervous system, the most common form of communication between neurons is chemical. Chemical communication occurs when the presynaptic neuron creates a chemical substance that diffuses across the synaptic gap and is detected by the postsynaptic neuron. This one-way communication process has many important implications for human behavior.

More specifically, here's how chemical communication takes place between neurons: As we've seen, when the presynaptic neuron is activated, it generates an action potential that travels to the end of the axon. At the end of the axon are several small branches called **axon terminals.** Floating in the interior fluid of the axon terminals are tiny sacs called **synaptic vesicles** (see Figure 2.4). The synaptic vesicles hold special chemical messengers manufactured by the neuron, called **neurotransmitters.**

When the action potential reaches the axon terminals, some of the synaptic vesicles "dock" on the axon terminal membrane, then release their neurotransmitters into the synaptic gap (Kandel, 1995c). These chemical messengers cross the synaptic gap. Then they attach to receptor sites on the dendrites of the surrounding neurons. This neurotransmitter "journey" across the synaptic gap takes less than 10 millionths of a second. This entire process of transmitting information at the synapse is called **synaptic transmission.**

What happens to the neurotransmitter molecules after they've attached to the receptor sites of the postsynaptic neuron? Most commonly, they detach from the receptor and are reabsorbed by the presynaptic neuron so they can be recycled and used again. This process is called **reuptake.** Reuptake also occurs with many of the neurotransmitters that failed to attach to a receptor and are left floating in the synaptic gap. Neurotransmitter molecules that are not reabsorbed or that remain attached to the receptor site are broken down or destroyed by enzymes (Schwartz, 1995a). As you'll see in the next section, certain drugs can interfere with both of these processes, prolonging the presence of the neurotransmitter in the synaptic gap.

The number of neurotransmitters that a neuron can manufacture varies. Some neurons produce only one type of neurotransmitter, while others manufacture three or more (Kalat, 1995).

The Brain Capturing a Thought In the brain, as in the rest of the nervous system, information is transmitted by electrical impulses (red area) that speed from one neuron to the next.

synapse
(SIN-aps) The point of communication between two neurons.

synaptic gap
(sin-AP-tick) The tiny space between the axon terminal of one neuron and the dendrite of an adjoining neuron.

axon terminals
Branches at the end of the axon that contain tiny pouches or sacs called synaptic vesicles.

synaptic vesicles
(sin-AP-tick VESS-ick-ulls) Tiny pouches or sacs in the axon terminals that contain chemicals called neurotransmitters.

neurotransmitter
Chemical messenger manufactured by a neuron.

synaptic transmission
(sin-AP-tick) The process in which neurotransmitters are released by one neuron, cross the synaptic gap, and affect adjoining neurons.

reuptake
The process by which neurotransmitter molecules detach from a postsynaptic neuron and are reabsorbed by a presynaptic neuron so they can be recycled and used again.

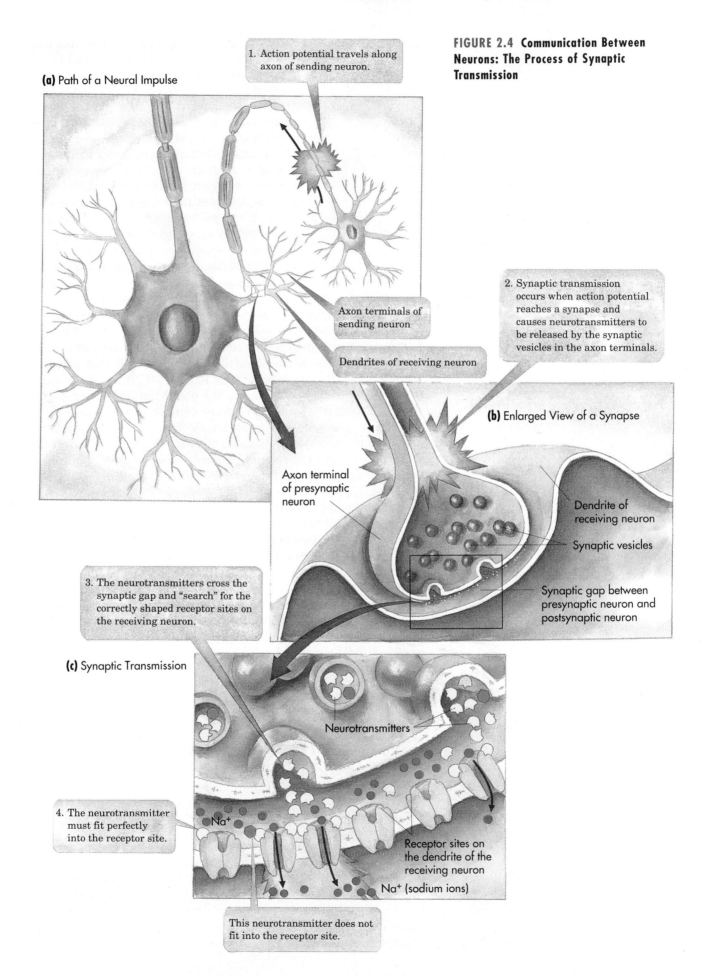

FIGURE 2.4 Communication Between Neurons: The Process of Synaptic Transmission

(a) Path of a Neural Impulse

1. Action potential travels along axon of sending neuron.

Axon terminals of sending neuron

Dendrites of receiving neuron

2. Synaptic transmission occurs when action potential reaches a synapse and causes neurotransmitters to be released by the synaptic vesicles in the axon terminals.

(b) Enlarged View of a Synapse

Axon terminal of presynaptic neuron

Dendrite of receiving neuron

Synaptic vesicles

Synaptic gap between presynaptic neuron and postsynaptic neuron

3. The neurotransmitters cross the synaptic gap and "search" for the correctly shaped receptor sites on the receiving neuron.

(c) Synaptic Transmission

Neurotransmitters

4. The neurotransmitter must fit perfectly into the receptor site.

Na^+

Receptor sites on the dendrite of the receiving neuron

Na^+ (sodium ions)

This neurotransmitter does not fit into the receptor site.

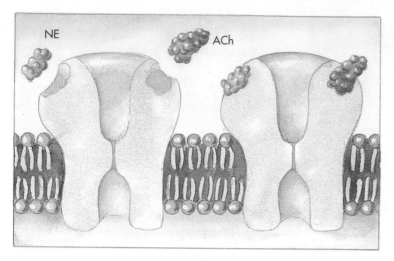

FIGURE 2.5 Neurotransmitter and Receptor Site Shapes
NE is the abbreviation for the neurotransmitter norepinephrine and ACh is the abbreviation for acetylcholine. Each neurotransmitter has a chemically distinct shape. Like a key in a lock, a neurotransmitter must fit the receptor site on the receiving neuron perfectly for its message to be communicated.

Each type of neurotransmitter has a chemically distinct, different shape. When released by the presynaptic neuron, neurotransmitters "search" for the correctly shaped receptor sites on the dendrites of the postsynaptic neurons. Like a key in a lock, a neurotransmitter's shape must precisely match that of receptor sites on the postsynaptic neuron's dendrites for the neurotransmitter to affect that neuron. Keep in mind that the postsynaptic neuron can have many differently shaped receptor sites on its dendrites, thereby accommodating several different neurotransmitters (see Figure 2.5).

A given neurotransmitter can communicate either an excitatory or an inhibitory message to a postsynaptic neuron. An *excitatory message* increases the likelihood that the postsynaptic neuron will activate and generate an action potential. Conversely, an *inhibitory message* decreases the likelihood that the postsynaptic neuron will activate. If a postsynaptic neuron simultaneously received an excitatory and inhibitory message, the two messages would cancel each other out (see Kandel, 1995b).

Thus, depending on the number and kind of neurotransmitter chemicals that are taken up by the dendrites of the adjoining neurons, the postsynaptic neurons are more or less likely to activate. If the net result is a sufficient number of excitatory messages, the postsynaptic neuron depolarizes, generates an action potential, and releases its own neurotransmitters.

When released by a presynaptic neuron, neurotransmitter chemicals cross hundreds, even thousands, of synaptic gaps and affect the intertwined dendrites of adjacent neurons. Because the receiving neuron can have thousands of dendrites that intertwine with the axon terminals of many presynaptic neurons, the number of potential synaptic interconnections between neurons is mind-boggling. In your brain alone, there are up to 100 *trillion* synaptic interconnections (Kandel & Siegelbaum, 1995; Koester, 1995b). To help put this in perspective, look up at the sky on a clear, dark night. There are nearly a thousand times more synaptic connections in your brain than there are stars in our entire galaxy.

Once again, we've simplified many details, but at this point you should have a basic understanding of how communication occurs within a neuron and between neurons. In the next section, we'll look at what roles are played by specific kinds of neurotransmitters and how drugs can affect the process of synaptic transmission.

CONCEPT REVIEW 2.1

The Neuron

Match the part of the neuron in the list with its function in neural communication.

a. action potential   **b.** myelin sheath
c. axon   **d.** neurotransmitters
e. synapse   **f.** dendrite

1. _____ A fluid-filled tube that carries information to other neurons, glands, and muscles

2. _____ Receives information from other neurons

3. _____ Brief electrical charge that communicates information within the neuron

4. _____ Fluid-filled space between sending and receiving neurons

5. _____ Chemical messengers manufactured by a neuron

6. _____ White, fatty covering surrounding an axon that increases speed of neural communication

Effects of Neurotransmitters

Neurotransmitters play a key role in the transmission of information throughout the nervous system. How do drugs affect neurotransmitters and synaptic transmission? What are five important neurotransmitters, and in what general functions are they involved?

FIGURE 2.6 How Drugs Can Affect Synaptic Transmission
Drugs can exert their effects on the brain by interfering in a number of ways with neurotransmitter functioning in the synapse. Drugs may also affect synaptic transmission by increasing or decreasing the amount of a particular neurotransmitter that is produced.

Dendrite of receiving neuron

Axon terminal of sending neuron

Synaptic gap

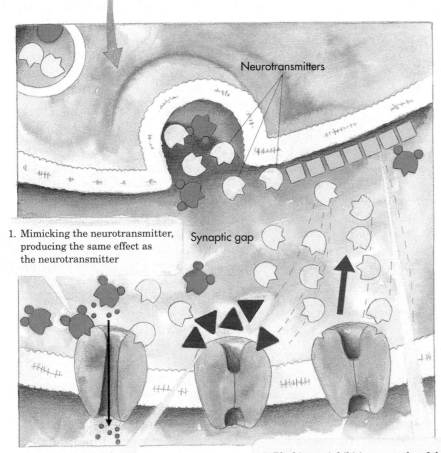

Neurotransmitters

Synaptic gap

1. Mimicking the neurotransmitter, producing the same effect as the neurotransmitter

2. Blocking the receptor site on the receiving neuron, preventing or inhibiting the effect of the neurotransmitter

3. Blocking or inhibiting reuptake of the neurotransmitter, increasing the amount of time the transmitter substance remains in the synaptic gap, thus increasing its effects

Neurotransmitters play a crucial role in communication between neurons. Because the activation of most neurons is determined by the messages delivered by neurotransmitters, neurotransmitters have profound effects on our physical and psychological functioning. Our ability to perceive, feel, think, move, act, and react depends on the delicate balance of neurotransmitters in the nervous system. Too much or too little of a given neurotransmitter can have devastating effects.

Yet neurotransmitters are present in only minuscule amounts in the human body. Imagine trying to detect a pinch of salt dissolved in an Olympic-sized swimming pool. That gives you some idea of the amounts of certain neurotransmitters that are present in brain tissue. Despite the challenge of isolating substances found in such low concentrations, scientists have identified about fifty neurotransmitters to date, and expect to find many more (Fischbach, 1992).

Although scientists have learned a great deal about neurotransmitters and their effects, much remains unknown. The action of neurotransmitters is extremely complex. A single neurotransmitter substance can have many different effects, depending on which area of the brain or nervous system is targeted. However, the effect of any particular neurotransmitter depends on the *receptor* to which it binds (Kandel & Siegelbaum, 1995). Thus, the same neurotransmitter can have an inhibitory effect on one neuron and an excitatory effect on another. So, while researchers have linked abnormal levels of specific neurotransmitters to various behavioral or physical problems, the connection between specific neurotransmitters and specific behaviors is rarely a simple one-to-one relationship.

Much of what we know about different neurotransmitters has come from observing the effects of drugs and other substances. Many drugs, especially those that affect moods or behavior, work by interfering with the normal functioning of neurotransmitters in the synapse (Julien, 1995). As Figure 2.6 illustrates, some drugs increase or decrease the amount of neurotransmitter produced by neurons. Drugs may also affect the length of time that the neurotransmitter remains in the synaptic gap, either increasing or decreasing the amount available to the postsynaptic receptor. Some drugs prevent the reuptake of the neurotransmitter by the sending neuron, thus prolonging and intensifying the effects of the neurotransmitter.

Drugs can also affect information transmission between neurons by *mimicking* specific neurotransmitters. When a drug is chemically similar to a specific neurotransmitter, it may produce the *same* effect as the neurotransmitter. Alternatively, the drug can *block* the effect of the neurotransmitter by fitting into receptor sites and preventing the neurotransmitter from acting (Julien, 1995).

We'll come back to neurotransmitters many times throughout this book. At this point, it's important that you understand how neurotransmitters can affect behavior. In this section, we'll look at the behavioral effects of some of the better-understood and more important neurotransmitters: acetylcholine, dopamine, serotonin, norepinephrine, and the endorphins.

Acetylcholine: From Eye Blinks to Black Widow Spider Bites

The first neurotransmitter discovered was **acetylcholine.** Acetylcholine is found in certain groups of neurons in the brain and in all motor neurons. It stimulates muscles to contract, including the stomach and heart muscles. Whether a movement is as simple as the flick of an eyelash or as complex as a back flip, it involves acetylcholine.

Because of acetylcholine's effects on muscle movement, drugs that block acetylcholine can cause paralysis. The drug *curare,* used by a South American Indian tribe to poison the tips of their hunting arrows, produces almost instant paralysis by blocking acetylcholine receptor sites on motor neurons. The brain sends signals to the motor neurons, but the muscles can't respond because the motor neuron receptor sites are blocked by the curare. The animal goes limp and quickly suffocates because its respiratory muscles are paralyzed.

Botulism, a disease caused by a toxin produced by bacteria in improperly canned foods, also causes paralysis because of its effect on acetylcholine. But rather than blocking acetylcholine receptors, the botulin toxin blocks the *release* of acetylcholine from the *sending* neuron (Thompson, 1993).

The opposite effect is produced by the bite of the black widow spider. The black widow's venom causes acetylcholine to be continuously released by the motor neurons, producing severe, uncontrollable muscle spasms. Nerve gases used in chemical weapons produce a similar result. Excessive acetylcholine builds up in the synaptic gap. This causes muscle spasms that can become so severe that the victim is unable to breathe and dies quickly from suffocation. *Atropine,* a drug that was carried by the U.S. troops in the Persian Gulf war, is an effective antidote for nerve gas. When injected, atropine counteracts the effects of nerve gas by blocking acetylcholine receptor sites *without* producing paralysis.

The nicotine found in cigarettes and other forms of tobacco is chemically similar to acetylcholine. Nicotine can occupy acetylcholine receptor sites in certain neurons in the brain and throughout the nervous system (Julien, 1995). By mimicking acetylcholine, nicotine causes the heart muscle to beat more quickly and artificially stimulates the skeletal muscles. That's why you'll sometimes notice a heavy smoker's hands trembling slightly.

Acetylcholine is also involved in *Alzheimer's disease,* which is characterized by the progressive loss of memory and general deterioration of intellectual functioning. The exact cause of Alzheimer's disease has yet to be identified. However, it's known that in Alzheimer's disease, brain neurons degenerate into tangled clumps. Neurons that produce acetylcholine are especially affected. The result is that acetylcholine levels in the brain are greatly reduced in Alzheimer's disease (see Thompson, 1993).

acetylcholine
(uh-*seet*-ull-KO-leen) Neurotransmitter that produces muscle contractions and is involved in memory functions.

Dopamine

Another neurotransmitter that is implicated in a wide range of behaviors and psychological processes is **dopamine.** Dopamine seems to be involved in a number of important functions, including movement, attention, and learning (Carlson, 1994). There's also evidence that abnormal dopamine levels are involved in some mental disorders.

The degeneration of the neurons that produce dopamine in one area of the brain causes a disorder called *Parkinson's disease.* Parkinson's disease is characterized by rigidity, muscle tremors, poor balance, and difficulty in initiating movements. These disruptions in movement are the result of the diminished dopamine production in that brain area. Symptoms can be alleviated by a drug called *L-dopa,* which stimulates the production of dopamine in the brain by the surviving neurons.

Interestingly, it seems that an *excess* of dopamine in another part of the brain is at least partly involved in the hallucinations and perceptual distortions that characterize the severe mental disorder called *schizophrenia.* Antipsychotic drugs that relieve certain schizophrenic symptoms seem to work by blocking dopamine receptors and reducing dopamine activity in the brain (Julien, 1995). In the chapters on psychological disorders (Chapter 14) and therapies (Chapter 15), we'll discuss schizophrenia, dopamine, and antipsychotic drugs in more detail.

Unfortunately, these antipsychotic drugs also have some potentially undesirable side-effects. Because the drugs reduce dopamine activity in several different areas of the brain, some patients develop symptoms that are very similar to those of Parkinson's disease. This is but one example of the complexity of the relationship between neurotransmitters and behavior, and of the delicate balance that must be maintained for normal functioning to occur.

Serotonin and Norepinephrine

Two other important neurotransmitters are *serotonin* and *norepinephrine.* Because these neurotransmitters are found in many different brain areas, they have been implicated in many different behaviors (see Groves & Rebec, 1992). For example, **serotonin** is involved in sleep, moods, and emotional states. Antidepressant drugs like *Prozac* increase the availability of serotonin in certain regions of the brain. These serotonin-increasing drugs can often help alleviate symptoms of depression and other mental disorders.

Norepinephrine seems to be involved in the activation of neurons throughout the brain. Norepinephrine is also involved when the body "gears up" in the face of danger or threat. For example, norepinephrine increases heartbeat (Thompson, 1993). Norepinephrine also seems to be a key player in the processes of learning and memory retrieval. Finally, like serotonin and dopamine, norepinephrine has been implicated in some mental disorders.

Endorphins: The Brain's Natural High

In 1973 researchers Candace Pert and Solomon Snyder of Johns Hopkins University made the startling discovery that there were receptor sites in the brain that were specific for pain-killing drugs called *opiates* (Pert & Snyder, 1973). The opiates include morphine, heroin, and codeine, all derived from the opium poppy. Along with alleviating pain, the opiates frequently produce states of euphoria. Why would the brain have neurotransmitter receptor sites for specific drugs like morphine? Pert, Snyder, and other researchers concluded that the brain must manufacture its own painkillers, morphine-like chemicals that act as neurotransmitters.

dopamine
(DOPE-uh-meen) Neurotransmitter that is involved in the regulation of bodily movements and thought processes.

serotonin
(ser-ah-TONE-in) Neurotransmitter that is involved in sleep and emotions.

norepinephrine
(nor-ep-in-EF-rin) Neurotransmitter involved in learning and memory; also a hormone manufactured by the adrenal glands.

TABLE 2.1 Summary of Important Neurotransmitters

Neurotransmitter	Primary Roles	Associated Disorders
Acetylcholine	Muscle contractions Memory	Alzheimer's disease
Dopamine	Movement Thought processes	Parkinson's disease Schizophrenia
Serotonin	Sleep Emotional states	Depression
Norepinephrine	Physical arousal Learning Memory	Depression
Endorphins	Pain perception Positive emotions	None

Within a few years, researchers identified a number of such chemicals manufactured by the brain (Snyder, 1984). Collectively, they are called **endorphins,** a term that is a combination of the words "endogenous morphines." (The word *endogenous* means "produced internally in the body.") Although chemically similar to morphine, endorphins are 100 times more potent than morphine. Today, endorphins are known to play a key role in the perception of pain (Barondes, 1993).

Following the discovery of endorphins in the mid-1970s, there was a flood of research investigating their effects. In trying to determine whether endorphins play a role in a particular process, researchers devised an ingenious strategy using a drug called *naloxone,* which blocks the effects of endorphins. If endorphins are involved in a particular phenomenon, then administering naloxone should diminish their effects.

For example, researchers found that endorphins are involved in the pain-reducing effects of *acupuncture,* an ancient Chinese medical technique that involves inserting needles at various points in the body. Giving naloxone blocks the pain-relieving effects of acupuncture (Watkins & Mayer, 1982). It has also been found that endorphins are involved in the "placebo effect," in which patients who are given a fake painkiller still experience significant reductions in pain. Such placebo effects are blocked when patients are first given the drug naloxone (Fields & Levine, 1984).

Along with pain perception, the endorphins are associated with positive mood. For example, the "runner's high" associated with aerobic exercise has also been attributed to endorphins (see Julien, 1995). In marathon runners, endorphin levels have been found to increase up to four times over their normal levels. When naloxone is given prior to such activities, researchers have found that the positive moods are blocked (Hopson, 1988).

The Nervous System and the Endocrine System: Communication Throughout the Body

Information is transmitted throughout the body by way of the nervous system and the endocrine system. The nervous system includes the central and peripheral nervous systems. What are the spinal cord's functions? What are the key components of the peripheral nervous system, and what are their functions?

endorphins
(en-DORF-ins) Neurotransmitters that regulate pain perception.

nervous system
The primary internal communication network of the body; divided into the central nervous system and the peripheral nervous system.

Specialized for communication, up to one *trillion* neurons are linked throughout your body in a complex, organized communication network called the **nervous system.** The human nervous system is divided into two main divisions: the *central nervous system* and the *peripheral nervous system.* In order for even simple behaviors to occur, such as curling your toes or scratching your nose, these two divisions must function as a single, integrated unit. Yet each of these divisions is highly specialized, performing different tasks (see Figure 2.7).

The neuron is the most important transmitter of messages in the central nervous system. In the peripheral nervous system, communication occurs along **nerves.** Nerves and neurons are not the same thing (see Figure 2.8). Nerves are made up of large bundles of neuron axons. Unlike neurons, many nerves are large enough to be seen easily with the unaided eye.

Central nervous system

Peripheral nervous system

FIGURE 2.7 The Nervous System
The nervous system is a complex organized communication network that is divided into two main divisions: the central nervous system (shown in yellow) and the peripheral nervous system (shown in blue).

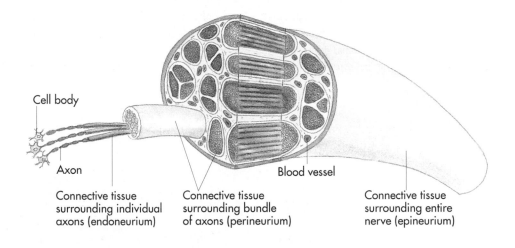

Cell body

Axon

Connective tissue surrounding individual axons (endoneurium)

Connective tissue surrounding bundle of axons (perineurium)

Blood vessel

Connective tissue surrounding entire nerve (epineurium)

FIGURE 2.8 Nerves and Neurons Are Not the Same
A cross section of a peripheral nerve is shown in both the figure and the electron micrograph. In both images, you can see that a nerve is actually composed of bundles of neuron axons that are held together by connective tissue.

nerve
Bundle of neuron axons that carries information in the peripheral nervous system.

central nervous system
Division of the nervous system that consists of the brain and spinal cord.

The Central Nervous System

The **central nervous system** includes the brain and the spinal cord. The central nervous system is so critical to your ability to function that it is entirely protected by bone—the brain by your skull, and the spinal cord by your spinal column. As an added measure of protection, the brain and spinal cord are suspended in *cerebrospinal fluid* to protect them from being jarred.

The central nervous system is aptly named. It is "central" to all your behaviors and mental processes. And it is the "central" processing center—every action, thought, feeling, and sensation you experience is processed through the central nervous system. The most important element of the central nervous system is, of course, the brain, which acts as the command center. We'll take a tour of the human brain in a later section.

Think of the spinal cord as a very busy telephone switchboard, handling both incoming and outgoing messages. Sensory receptors send messages along sensory nerves to the spinal cord, then up to the brain. To activate muscles, the brain sends signals down the spinal cord, which are relayed out along motor nerves to the muscles.

Most behaviors are controlled by your brain. However, the spinal cord can produce **spinal reflexes**—simple, automatic behaviors that occur without any brain involvement. One of the simplest spinal reflexes involves a three-neuron loop of rapid communication—a *sensory neuron* that communicates sensation to the spinal cord, an *interneuron* that relays information within the spinal cord, and a *motor neuron* leading from the spinal cord that signals muscles to react.

The spinal reflex shown in Figure 2.9 illustrates your author Don's recent attempt to rescue his English muffin, trapped in a life-or-death struggle with an obstinate toaster. Half-awake, he poked his coffee spoon into the toaster to pry out the smoking English muffin. The resulting electrical shock, de-

FIGURE 2.9 A Spinal Reflex Arc
A spinal reflex is a simple, involuntary behavior that is processed in the spinal cord without brain involvement. As you follow the sequence shown here, you can see that the withdrawal reflex occurs before the brain processes the conscious perception of pain.

A nasty shock

A quick motor response

A slower pain response

1. Skin receptors in the fingertips detect the electric shock, sending messages to sensory neurons.

2. Sensory neurons carry messages to the spinal cord.

3. Interneurons in the spinal cord relay messages to motor neurons.

4. Motor neurons send messages to hand muscles, causing a withdrawal reflex *before* the brain consciously registers the sensation of pain.

5. A moment *after* the spinal reflex has occurred, sensory neurons send messages up the spinal cord to the brain.

6. The brain structure called the thalamus identifies the sensory messages as pain and relays the information to the appropriate higher brain center.

7. In the brain structure called the somatosensory cortex, the messages are consciously interpreted as "PAIN IN HAND!"

tected by sensory receptors in his hand, sent a barrage of neural impulses along his sensory neurons to his spinal cord. Interneurons relayed the information within his spinal cord, and motor neurons leading from his spinal cord signaled his muscles to jerk back.

The result? Don reflexively pulled his hand away *before* becoming consciously aware of either the sensation or his own movement. This spinal reflex occurred in just a fraction of a second, without involving your author's brain (which was obviously not fully functioning anyway). A moment later, the stimulus was interpreted by his brain ("PAIN IN HAND!") as he danced around the kitchen, shaking his tingling hand ("YEOW! That #%!* toaster attacked me!").

Spinal reflexes are crucial to your survival. The additional few seconds that it would take you to consciously process sensations and decide how to react could result in serious injury. Spinal reflexes are also important as indicators that the nerves in your spinal cord are working correctly. That's why physicians test spinal reflexes during neurological examinations by tapping just below your kneecap for the knee-jerk spinal reflex, or scratching the sole of your foot for the toe-curl spinal reflex.

The Peripheral Nervous System

The **peripheral nervous system** is the other major division of your nervous system. The word *peripheral* means "lying at the outer edges." Thus, the peripheral nervous system comprises all the nerves outside the central nervous system that extend to the outermost borders of your body, including your skin. The communication functions of the peripheral nervous system are handled by its two subdivisions: the *somatic nervous system* and the *autonomic nervous system.*

The **somatic nervous system** takes its name from the Latin word *soma,* which means "body." It plays a key role in communication throughout the entire body. First, the somatic nervous system communicates sensory information received by sensory receptors along sensory nerves *to* the central nervous system. And second, it carries messages *from* the central nervous system along motor nerves to perform voluntary muscle movements. All the different sensations that you're experiencing right now are being communicated by your somatic nervous system to your spinal cord and on to your brain. When you perform a voluntary action, such as turning a page of this book, messages from the brain are communicated down the spinal cord, then out to the muscles via the somatic nervous system.

The other subdivision of the peripheral nervous system is the **autonomic nervous system.** The word *autonomic* means "self-governing." Thus, the autonomic nervous system regulates *involuntary* functions, such as heartbeat, blood pressure, breathing, and digestion. These processes occur with little or no conscious involvement. This is fortunate, because if you had to mentally command your heart to beat or your stomach to digest the pizza you had for lunch, it would be difficult to focus your attention on anything else.

However, the autonomic nervous system is not completely self-regulating. By engaging in physical activity or purposely tensing or relaxing your muscles, you can increase or decrease autonomic activity. You can also influence your autonomic nervous system with mental imagery. Vividly imagining a situation that makes you feel angry, frightened, or even sexually aroused can dramatically increase heartbeat and blood pressure. A peaceful mental image can lower many autonomic functions.

The involuntary functions regulated by the autonomic nervous system are controlled by two different branches: the *sympathetic* and *parasympathetic nervous systems.* These two systems control many of the same organs in your body, but cause them to respond in opposite ways (see Figure 2.10).

spinal reflexes
Simple, automatic behaviors that are processed in the spinal cord.

peripheral nervous system
(per-IF-er-ull) Division of the nervous system that includes all the nerves lying outside the central nervous system.

somatic nervous system
Subdivision of the peripheral nervous system that communicates sensory information to the central nervous system and carries messages from the central nervous system to the muscles.

autonomic nervous system
(aw-toe-NOM-ick) Subdivision of the peripheral nervous system that regulates involuntary functions.

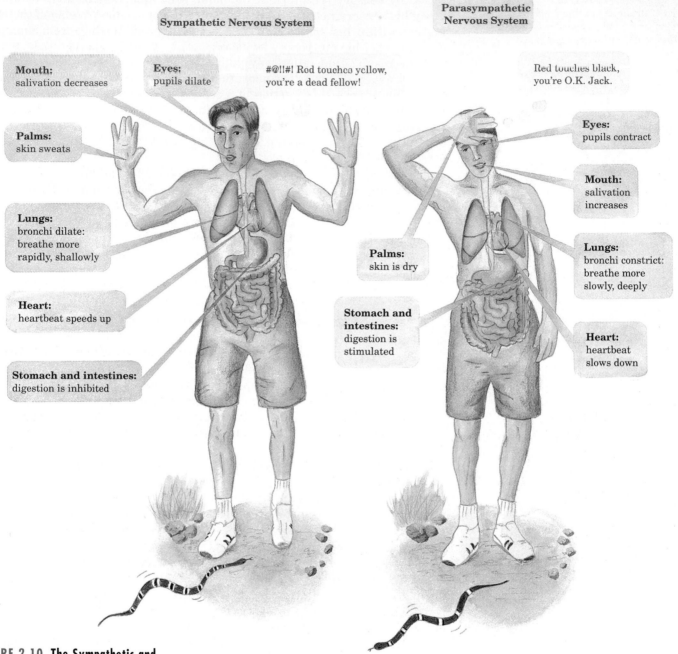

Sympathetic Nervous System

Parasympathetic Nervous System

Mouth; salivation decreases

Eyes: pupils dilate

#@!!#! Rod touches yellow, you're a dead fellow!

Red touches black, you're O.K. Jack.

Palms: skin sweats

Eyes: pupils contract

Mouth: salivation increases

Lungs: bronchi dilate: breathe more rapidly, shallowly

Palms: skin is dry

Lungs: bronchi constrict: breathe more slowly, deeply

Heart: heartbeat speeds up

Stomach and intestines: digestion is stimulated

Heart: heartbeat slows down

Stomach and intestines: digestion is inhibited

FIGURE 2.10 The Sympathetic and Parasympathetic Branches of the Autonomic Nervous System
Hikers in the southern United States memorize a simple rhyme to distinguish the poisonous coral snake (red stripes touch yellow stripes) from its harmless mimic, a scarlet king snake (red stripes touch black stripes). Arousal of the sympathetic nervous system (left) prepares the hiker to fight or flee the dangerous snake. When he realizes that the snake is harmless (right), the parasympathetic nervous system calms the body and restores functioning to normal.

In general, the sympathetic nervous system arouses the body to expend energy, while the parasympathetic nervous system helps the body conserve energy.

The **sympathetic nervous system** is the body's emergency system, rapidly activating body systems to meet threats or emergencies. When you are frightened, your breathing accelerates, your heart beats faster, digestion stops, and the bronchial tubes in your lungs expand. All these physiological responses increase the amount of oxygen available to your brain and muscles. Your pupils dilate to increase your field of vision, and your mouth becomes dry, because salivation stops. You begin to sweat in response to your body's expenditure of greater energy and heat. These bodily changes collectively represent the *fight-or-flight response*—they physically prepare you to fight or flee from a perceived danger (Cannon, 1932).

As a short-term response, the fight-or-flight response helps you cope with

sympathetic nervous system
Branch of the autonomic nervous system that produces rapid physical arousal in response to perceived emergencies or threats.

parasympathetic nervous system
Branch of the autonomic nervous system that maintains normal body functions and conserves the body's physical resources.

an emergency situation. However, if this heightened physiological arousal continues, such as during times of prolonged stress, you can suffer from mental and physical deterioration or exhaustion (see Stein & Miller, 1993). We'll discuss the fight-or-flight response in greater detail in later chapters on emotion (Chapter 8) and stress (Chapter 13).

Other types of emotional arousal also involve your sympathetic nervous system. The anxiety that you feel when you have to make an important presentation, the anger you experience during a heated argument with a loved one, and the acute discomfort you feel when your boss chews you out—all these unpleasant emotions involve physical arousal due to the activation of your sympathetic nervous system.

Heightened arousal of the sympathetic nervous system can sometimes work against you. For example, have you ever found yourself "choking" while taking an important exam? Your hands begin to sweat, your mouth becomes dry, your heart pounds, and, of course, your mind goes blank. These are all symptoms of your sympathetic nervous system going into high gear.

While the sympathetic nervous system mobilizes your body's physical resources, the **parasympathetic nervous system** conserves and maintains your physical resources. It calms you down after an emergency. Acting much more slowly than the sympathetic nervous system, the parasympathetic nervous system gradually returns body systems to normal. Heartbeat, breathing, and blood pressure level out. Pupils constrict back to their normal size. Saliva returns, and the digestive system begins operating again.

Although the sympathetic and parasympathetic nervous systems produce opposite effects, they act together, keeping the nervous system in balance. For example, consider the potentially lethal effects of cocaine. It has long been known that cocaine stimulates the sympathetic nervous system, producing mental and physiological arousal. But cocaine also *inhibits* the *parasympathetic* nervous system, preventing it from calming the system back down (Bouman & others, 1994). When cocaine speeds up heartbeat while inhibiting the mechanism that slows heartbeat down, "sudden death" can occur—unpredictable, sudden heart failure in an otherwise healthy individual.

To summarize, the human nervous system is a complex, finely balanced communication system, the basic unit of which is the neuron. The different divisions of the nervous system, as shown in Figure 2.11, are specialized to perform different tasks in the body. Although each division handles different functions, the whole nervous system works in unison so that both automatic and voluntary behaviors are carried out smoothly. In the next section, we'll look at the second major communication system in the body: the endocrine system.

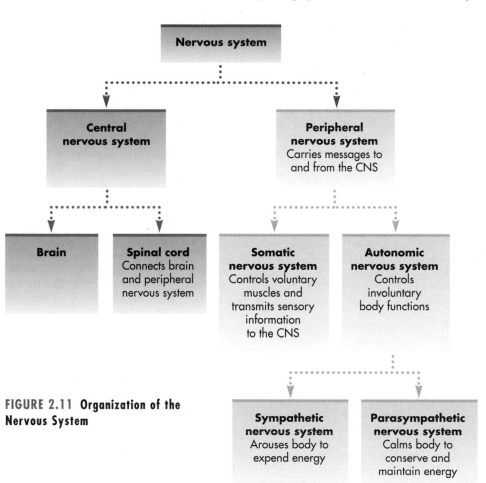

FIGURE 2.11 Organization of the Nervous System

The Endocrine System

The endocrine system is made up of glands that transmit information via chemical messengers called hormones. How does information transmission in the endocrine system differ from that in the nervous system? What roles are played by the pituitary gland, the hypothalamus, the gonads, and the adrenal glands?

FIGURE 2.12 The Endocrine System
The endocrine system and the nervous system are directly linked by the hypothalamus in the brain, which controls the pituitary gland. In turn, the pituitary releases hormones that affect the hormone production of several other endocrine glands. In the male and female figures shown here, you can see the location and main functions of several important endocrine glands.

The nervous system is not the only "information network" in the body. Another important communication system is the endocrine system. The **endocrine system** is made up of glands that are located throughout the body (see Figure 2.12). Like the nervous system, the endocrine system involves the use of chemical messengers to transmit information from one part of the body to the other. While the endocrine system is not part of the nervous system, it interacts with the nervous system in some important ways, as you'll see in this section.

Endocrine glands communicate information from one part of the body to another by secreting messenger chemicals called **hormones** into the bloodstream. The hormones circulate throughout the bloodstream until they reach specific hormone receptors on target organs or tissue. By interacting with the nervous system and affecting internal organs and body tissues, hormones regulate physical processes and influence behavior in a variety of ways. Metabolism, growth rate, digestion, blood pressure, and sexual development and reproduction are just some of the processes that are regulated by the endocrine hormones. Hormones are also involved in emotional response and the response to stress (Thompson, 1993).

Endocrine hormones are also closely linked to the workings of the nervous system. For example, the release of hormones may be stimulated or inhibited by certain parts of the nervous system. In turn, hormones can promote or inhibit the generation of nerve impulses. Finally, some hormones and neurotransmitters are chemically identical. That is, the same molecule can act as a hormone in some locations and act as a neurotransmitter in the nervous system (Kalat, 1995).

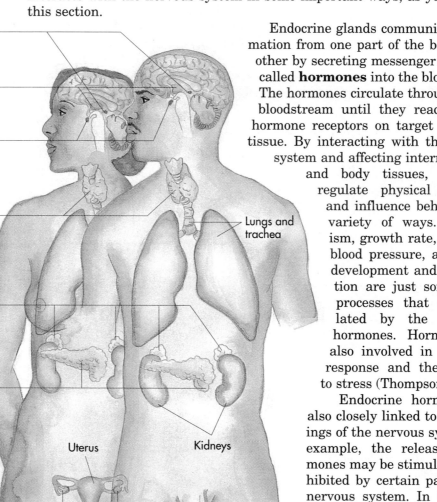

Pineal gland
regulates sleep/wake cycles

Hypothalamus
controls the pituitary gland; links endocrine system with nervous system

Pituitary gland
regulates physical growth and the activities of several other glands; stimulates milk production in nursing mothers

Thyroid gland
controls body metabolism rate

Lungs and trachea

Adrenal glands
(adrenal cortex and adrenal medulla) arouse body when physically threatened or emotionally excited; involved in physical response to stress

Pancreas
regulates blood sugar and insulin levels; involved in hunger

Uterus

Kidneys

Ovaries
regulate development of female reproductive organs; influence sexual behavior and secondary sex characteristics, such as breast development and body hair

Testes
regulate development of male reproductive organs; influence sexual behavior and secondary sex characteristics, such as facial hair, body hair, and deepening of voice

endocrine system
(EN-doe-krin) A communication system composed of glands located throughout the body that secrete hormones into the bloodstream.

hormones
Chemical messengers secreted into the bloodstream by endocrine glands.

pituitary gland
(pi-TOO-ih-tare-ee) Endocrine gland attached to the base of the brain that secretes hormones that affect the function of other glands as well as hormones that act directly on physical processes.

adrenal glands
Pair of endocrine glands that are involved in the human stress response.

adrenal cortex
The outer portion of the adrenal gland.

adrenal medulla
The inner portion of the adrenal gland; secretes epinephrine and norepinephrine.

In contrast to the rapid speed of information transmission in the nervous system, communication in the endocrine system takes place much more slowly. Because hormones rely upon the circulation of the blood to deliver their chemical message to target organs, it may take a few seconds or longer for the hormone to reach its target organ once it is secreted by the originating gland.

The signals that trigger the secretion of hormones are regulated by the brain, primarily by a brain structure called the *hypothalamus.* (You'll learn more about the hypothalamus later in the chapter.) The hypothalamus serves as the main link between the endocrine system and the nervous system. The hypothalamus directly regulates the release of hormones by the **pituitary gland,** a small, pea-sized gland just under the brain. The pituitary's hormones, in turn, regulate the production of other hormones by many of the glands in the endocrine system. Thus, under the direction of the hypothalamus, the pituitary gland directly controls hormone production in other endocrine glands.

The pituitary gland also produces some hormones that act directly. For example, the pituitary produces *growth hormone,* which stimulates growth. In nursing mothers, the pituitary produces both *prolactin,* the hormone that stimulates milk production, and *oxytocin,* the hormone that produces the "let-down reflex," in which stored milk is "let down" into the nipple.

Breast feeding is a good example of the complex interaction among the nervous system, the endocrine system, and behavior. When an infant nurses at its mother's breast, a message is sent by the hypothalamus to the pituitary to produce oxytocin, leading to the let-down of milk (see Figure 2.13). In a nursing mother, a baby's cry, the sight of her infant, or just the thought of her infant can stimulate this complex chain of internal events and lead to milk production even in the absence of physical stimulation of the nipple.

Hypothalamus

Posterior pituitary

Release of oxytocin

Nerve impulses to hypothalamus

FIGURE 2.13
Breast-Feeding
Here is an example of the complex interaction among the nervous system, the endocrine system, and behavior. Nerve impulses from sensory receptors in the mother's skin are sent to the brain. The hypothalamus signals the production of oxytocin by the pituitary gland, which causes the mother's milk to "let-down" and begin flowing.

Another set of glands called the **adrenal glands** are of particular interest to psychologists. The adrenal glands consist of the **adrenal cortex,** which is the outer portion, and the **adrenal medulla,** which is the inner portion of the gland. Both the adrenal cortex and the adrenal medulla produce hormones that are involved in the human stress response (Thompson, 1993). As you'll see in Chapter 13, on stress, hormones secreted by the adrenal cortex also interact with the *immune system,* the body's defense against invading viruses or bacteria.

The adrenal medulla plays a key role in the fight-or-flight response, described earlier. When aroused, the sympathetic nervous system stimulates the adrenal medulla. In turn, the adrenal medulla produces *epinephrine* and *norepinephrine.* (You may be more familiar with the word *adrenaline,* which is another name for epinephrine.)

As they circulate through the bloodstream to the heart and other target organs, epinephrine and norepinephrine complement and increase the effects of the sympathetic nervous system. These hormones also act as neurotransmitters, stimulating activity at the synapses in the sympathetic nervous system. The action of epinephrine and norepinephrine is a good illustration of the long-lasting effects of hormones. If you've noticed that it takes a while for you to calm down after a particularly upsetting or stressful experience, it's because of the lingering effects of epinephrine and norepinephrine in your body.

gonads
The endocrine glands that secrete hormones that regulate sexual characteristics and reproductive processes; ovaries in females and testes in males.

brain
The main organ of the nervous system, made up of billions of neurons organized into a complex, integrated hierarchy of structures.

Also important are the **gonads,** or sex organs—the *ovaries* in women and the *testes* in men. The pituitary gland secretes hormones called *gonadotrophins.* The gonadotrophins, in turn, regulate the secretions of sex hormones by the gonads. In males, the testes secrete the hormone *testosterone.* In females, the ovaries secrete the hormones *estrogen* and *progesterone.* These sex hormones have profound effects on sexual development, reproduction, and sexual behavior. For example, the sexual development of the fetus is determined by the prenatal activity of testosterone or estrogen. The development of secondary sexual characteristics at puberty is caused by increased levels of sex hormones. And the cyclical release of estrogen and progesterone, directed by the pituitary, produces the menstrual cycle in women.

Other important endocrine glands include the *thyroid,* which controls metabolism, and the *pancreas,* which regulates blood sugar levels and plays a key role in hunger and eating. Finally, the tiny *pineal gland,* located in the center of the brain, is involved in the regulation of sleep and wakefulness. (We'll discuss the pineal gland's role in body rhythms in Chapter 4.)

The endocrine system plays an important role in regulating many functions and behaviors. And, as we noted, some of the hormones secreted by endocrine glands can even function as neurotransmitters that influence the communication of the nervous system. Thus, the nervous system, the endocrine system, and behavior form a highly interdependent network.

Still, the most critical component of the body's communication systems remains the **brain.** As the main command center of the nervous system *and* the endocrine system, the brain is the source of consciousness, thoughts, creativity, emotions, and the variety of behaviors that make humans unique among all other creatures. As we turn our attention to the brain, you'll see that unraveling the complexities of the brain continues to be one of science's greatest challenges.

CONCEPT REVIEW 2.2

The Nervous System and the Endocrine System

Circle the letter of the item that correctly completes each statement.

1. While watching a suspenseful video late at night, you hear a sudden crash in another room. You leap out of your chair in fear, then realize that your dog has knocked over his water bowl again. Your fear reaction involved the activation of the _____ of the nervous system. Calming down involved the _____ of the nervous system.
   a. hypothalamus; endocrine branch
   b. somatic branch; sympathetic division
   c. sympathetic division; parasympathetic division
   d. parasympathetic division; sympathetic division

2. The part of the nervous system that controls voluntary movement is the:
   a. parasympathetic nervous system
   b. somatic nervous system
   c. autonomic nervous system
   d. fight-or-flight response

3. The glands of the endocrine system communicate via:
   a. electrically charged ion channels
   b. neural impulses along the axon
   c. spinal reflexes
   d. messenger chemicals called hormones

4. The main link between the nervous system and the endocrine system occurs at the:
   a. adrenal glands
   b. pineal gland
   c. somatic nervous system
   d. hypothalamus

5. In response to stress, epinephrine (or adrenaline) is pumped into the bloodstream by the:
   a. adrenal glands
   b. pineal gland
   c. thyroid gland
   d. pituitary gland

Studying the Brain: The Toughest Case to Crack

Because the brain is encased by bone, it is difficult to study. What methods have scientists used to study the brain, and how has each method contributed to knowledge of the brain?

Even as a child, your author Don was known for his curiosity about how things worked. Along with systematically dismantling a variety of discarded objects, such as an old manual typewriter and a broken lawn mower, he also took his mother's vacuum cleaner apart. (Don's mother wasn't too happy about that one.) Clocks and radios were also fair game.

Now imagine how difficult it would be for Don—or anyone else—to try to figure out how something works without being able to open it, take it apart, or watch it operate. Such has long been the challenge faced by scientists investigating the workings of the human brain. Because the brain is encased entirely by bone, it has been impossible to directly observe a normal, living brain in action. One early approach to "mapping" brain functions involved examining the bumps on a person's skull. As you can see in Critical Thinking Box 2.1, this approach was not very successful.

CRITICAL THINKING 2.1

Phrenology: The Bumpy Road to Scientific Progress

Are people with large foreheads smarter than people with small foreheads? Does the shape of your head provide clues to your abilities, character, and personality characteristics? Such notions were at the core of phrenology, an extremely popular pseudoscience founded by Franz Gall, a German physician and brain anatomist.

In the early 1800s, Gall made several important contributions to the understanding of brain anatomy. He correctly noted, for example, that the cortex of animals was smaller and less developed than the cortex of intellectually superior humans. Eventually, he became convinced that the size and shape of the cortex were reflected in the size and shape of the skull. Taking this notion a step further, he suspected that variations in the size and shape of the human skull might reflect individual differences in abilities, character, and personality.

To gather evidence for this notion, Gall went to hospitals, prisons, asylums, and schools to examine people with oddly shaped heads. Gall noted the association between a particular person's characteristics and any distinctive bulges and bumps on the per-

son's skull. Based on these observations, he identified 27 personality characteristics, or "faculties," that he believed could be diagnosed by examining specific areas of the head. Gall devised elaborate maps showing the skull location of various personality characteristics and abilities. For instance, Gall believed that a thick neck was as-

sociated with increased sexual motivation, and that a prominent forehead was associated with greater intellectual ability (McCoy, 1996).

Gall's methods of testing his theory were both careless and highly subjective. When confronted with evidence that seemed to contradict his theory, Gall merely dismissed it (Fancher, 1990). And when his theory of phrenology was ridiculed by other scientists for lack of adequate evidence, Gall took his ideas to the general public by presenting lectures and demonstrations. He lectured widely, and gave "readings" in which he provided a personality description based on measuring the bumps on a person's head.

In the early 1900s, phrenology continued to be popular with the general public. It was around that time that Henry Lavery of Wisconsin set out to invent a machine to improve the accuracy of phrenology readings. It took Lavery many years to perfect his invention, which he called the "Psycograph." Ultimately, forty of the machines were built, and became popular attractions in department stores and theater lobbies throughout the country. Today, you can still find one of Lavery's Psyco-

The Psycograph Intended to increase the accuracy of phrenology measurements, the helmetlike headpiece of the Psycograph contained over thirty probes that made contact with the skull. The machine then stamped out brief statements summarizing the different "faculties" measured, such as, "You are fairly secretive but can improve" (McCoy, 1996).

graph machines at the Museum of Questionable Medical Devices in Minneapolis (McCoy, 1996).

Is phrenology merely a historical curiosity? Actually, phrenology played a significant role in advancing the scientific study of the human brain (Zola-Morgan, 1995). When it first appeared in the early 1800s, phrenology triggered scientific interest in the possibility of cortical localization—the idea that different brain areas are specialized for specific functions (Hilgard, 1987). Gall's belief that personality characteristics were reflected in the bumps of the skull was discredited. However, scientists began to debate the more general notion of cortical localization. By the mid-1800s, scientific evidence for cortical localization began to emerge (Damasio & others, 1994). Later in the chapter, we'll look at some of that evidence.

Another obstacle is the complexity of the brain itself—complex not only in its enormous number of interconnected neurons, but also in the intricate structures, regions, and pathways formed by those neurons. But scientists are not an easily discouraged lot. When direct methods of studying the brain were unavailable, indirect methods were found. In this section, we will see how researchers have risen to the challenge of unlocking the brain's mysteries.

Case Studies:
Evidence from the Damaged Brain

Some of the oldest methods of studying the brain are still commonly used. Using the *case study,* researchers systematically observe and record the behavior of people whose brains have been damaged by illness or injury. These case studies of individuals with brain damage have provided valuable insights into behavior in such areas as memory, speech, emotion, motor function, and personality. As you'll see later, the knowledge gained from such observations allowed scientists to begin mapping the functions of the brain.

However, there are limits to the knowledge that can be gained using the case study method. By their very nature, case studies usually focus on unusual situations or behaviors—in this case, brain disease or injury. Because these behaviors or situations are out of the ordinary, they may not reflect typical behavior. Therefore, generalizing results from a case study must be done cautiously.

Another potential limitation to the case study method in brain research is that injuries to the brain are rarely limited to specific, localized areas or contained within well-defined anatomical boundaries. It's often difficult to be sure exactly which brain area is responsible for specific behavioral problems. In addition, many individual regions of the brain are linked to other areas of the brain. Damage in one area may also disrupt functioning in another, otherwise normal area. And finally, for reasons that are not completely understood, similar injuries often have very different effects on different people. So, while case studies are still widely used in brain research, they have distinct limitations.

electroencephalograph
An instrument that uses electrodes placed on the scalp to record the brain's electrical activity.

CAT scan (computerized axial tomography)
An instrument that produces two-dimensional pictures of brain structures using multiple X-rays that are reassembled by a computer.

magnetic resonance imaging scanner (MRI)
An instrument that provides three-dimensional, highly detailed views of the brain using electrical signals generated by the brain in response to magnetic fields.

PET scan (positron emission tomography)
An instrument that provides color-coded images of brain activity by measuring the amount of glucose or oxygen used in different brain regions.

A related method involves producing *lesions*—surgically altering or destroying specific portions of the brain, then observing the subsequent effects on behavior. In humans, lesions are sometimes produced for medical reasons, such as when part of the brain is surgically altered or removed to relieve uncontrollable seizures. To experimentally investigate the effects of brain lesions on different aspects of behavior, animals are used.

Researchers have also studied the behavioral effects of electrically stimulating specific brain areas with small electrified discs or wires called *electrodes* (e.g., Penfield & Perot, 1963; Delgado, 1969). Although each of these techniques has limitations, they have produced valuable insights into the brain's role in such diverse functions as memory, speech, emotion, personality, and sleep.

Imaging the Brain

As technology has become more advanced, so have the tools that can be used to study the brain. A variety of techniques have been developed to study the normal, living brain.

The **electroencephalograph** records the brain's electrical activity through the use of electrodes placed harmlessly on a person's scalp. The graphic record of the brain's electrical activity that this instrument produces is called an *electroencephalogram,* abbreviated *EEG.* Modern electroencephalographs provide sophisticated computerized analyses of the brain's electrical activity, recording the electrical activity of the brain from millisecond to millisecond (see Azar, 1994a).

The **CAT scan** (*CAT* stands for *C*omputerized *A*xial *T*omography) allows researchers to make images of the brain's structure. CAT scans work by taking multiple X-rays of the brain from different angles. These multiple images are reassembled by computer. Researchers can look at a picture of the brain from any angle, viewing a "slice" of the brain. CAT scans can detect brain abnormalities and are widely used in medicine and in research.

CAT Scan of the Normal Brain

Another advanced instrument for viewing the brain's structure is the **magnetic resonance imaging scanner,** or **MRI.** While a person lies motionless in a long, magnetic tube, his brain is bombarded with harmless magnetic fields. In response to these magnetic fields, the molecules of the brain generate electromagnetic signals that are analyzed by computer to create highly detailed images of the brain. Like the CAT scan, MRI is a harmless, noninvasive technique that can be used to study brain structures and to detect abnormalities (Weinberger & others, 1990).

MRI Scan of the Normal Brain

One of the most exciting techniques to investigate brain functioning is **positron emission tomography,** commonly called the **PET scan.** Unlike MRI and CAT scans, which provide pictures of the brain's structure, the PET scan generates images of the brain's *activity.* The PET scan tracks the brain's use of glucose, a type of sugar that is the brain's main source of energy. Brain regions use more glucose when they are actively functioning

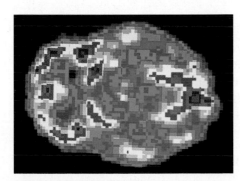

PET Scan of the Normal Brain

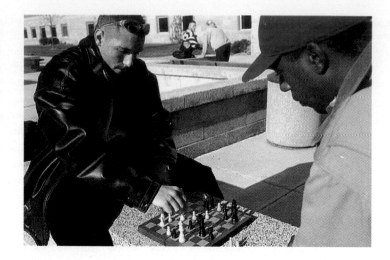

Where Chess Players Think PET scans allow psychologists and other scientists to identify the specific brain areas that are activated by different tasks. For example, researchers have used PET scans to identify the brain areas involved in the complex mental activities during a chess game (Nichelli and others, 1994). In **(a),** areas at the back of the brain, where visual information is processed, are most active when a player distinguishes between black and white chess pieces. In **(b),** the lower middle region of the brain is more active when a player is determining if a particular chess piece can capture another piece.

than when they are inactive. The PET scan measures the amount of radioactively tagged glucose or oxygen used in thousands of different brain areas while the subject reads, talks, or engages in other kinds of mental activity. This information is analyzed by computer to create dramatic color-coded images showing the brain areas that are active during different tasks, such as those of chess players in the photographs above.

The use of PET scans has had a tremendous impact on the field of neuroscience. Recently, a new technique has become available that holds even greater promise than the PET technology. *Functional MRI* refers to a new kind of MRI that can, like a PET scan, reveal the activity of the working brain (Naeye, 1994). One key difference is that in functional MRI, researchers take a rapid series of brain images. When put together by computer, these images create a sort of "movie" of brain activity. Because MRI scanners are less costly and more widely available than PET scanners, many researchers believe that functional MRI will be the dominant brain-mapping technique in years to come (see Azar, 1994a). Functional MRI also produces a much sharper picture than PET scans and can be used to image much smaller brain structures (see Naeye, 1994).

Sophisticated techniques for imaging the brain continue to be developed (Cohen & others, 1995). With the availability of ever more precise and sophisticated instruments to study the living brain, neuroscientists believe that a new era in brain research has begun. But even the most sophisticated technological device is simple in comparison to the phenomenal complexity of the brain itself.

CONCEPT REVIEW 2.3

Brain Imaging Techniques

Match each of the following terms with the correct description below: EEG, CAT, PET, MRI.

1. A technique that provides color-coded images of brain activity by measuring the amount of glucose used in different regions of the brain. _____

2. An technique that creates three-dimensional, detailed views of the brain using electrical signals generated by the brain in response to magnetic fields. _____

3. An instrument that uses electrodes placed on the scalp to record the brain's electrical activity. _____

4. A technique that uses a computer to create two-dimensional pictures of brain structures from multiple X-rays. _____

A Guided Tour of the Brain

Although particular areas of the brain correspond with particular functions, multiple brain areas are involved in most behaviors. What are neural pathways? What do we mean when we say that the brain is an integrated system? How does the brain develop?

Forget all the hype about the Internet. The *real* information superhighway is the human brain. In fact, the most complex mass of matter known to exist sits right between your two ears: your brain.

Neuroscientists have made enormous advances in the past decades in understanding the brain structures and neural pathways involved in behavior. New discoveries are made so frequently that even experts find it hard to keep up with the explosion of research on the brain. All the same, a great deal remains to be explained about how the brain processes information and translates neural impulses into complex behavior (Bullock, 1993).

In this section, we'll take you on a guided tour of the human brain. As your tour guides, our goal here is not to tell you everything that is known or suspected about the human brain. Such an endeavor would take multiple books rather than a single chapter in a college textbook. Instead, our first goal is to familiarize you with the basic organization and structures of the brain. In later chapters, we'll add to your knowledge of the brain as we discuss the brain's involvement in specific psychological processes in more detail. Our second goal is to give you a general sense for *how* the brain works.

Along the tour, we'll take a few side trips. We'll look at how the accidental injury of a railroad worker in the 1800s has contributed to our understanding of the brain structures involved in emotional control and social behavior. We'll also look at the discovery of "pleasure centers" in the brain.

At the beginning of this tour, it's important to note that the brain generally does not lend itself to simple explanations. As we describe the different areas of the brain, we'll identify important centers where particular functions seem to be localized. Nevertheless, bear in mind that specific functions seldom correspond neatly to a single, specific brain site (Farah, 1994). Many psychological processes, particularly complex ones, involve multiple brain structures and regions. Even simple tasks—such as watching TV, carrying on a conversation, or walking down the street—involve the smoothly coordinated synthesis of information among many different areas of your brain.

How is information communicated and shared among these multiple brain regions? Many brain functions involve the activation of *neural pathways* that link different brain structures. Neural pathways are formed by groups of neuron cell bodies in one area of the brain that project their axons to other brain areas. Like the transcontinental telephone system that links different parts of the world, these neural pathways form communication networks and circuits that link different brain areas. As a result, damage to one area of the brain may disrupt many neural pathways and affect many different functions.

Even though we'll talk about brain centers and structures that are involved in different aspects of behavior, the best way to think of the brain is as an *integrated system* (Farah, 1994; Bullock, 1993). Imagine a simple behavior, such as running your finger over the coarse side of a piece of sandpaper. Perceiving the sandpaper's rough texture, moving your finger, recognizing the scratchy substance, and knowing the uses of sandpaper involves the seamless interaction of numerous brain areas. At the end of this section, we'll come back to the sandpaper example and use it to illustrate how different regions of the brain interact.

Our guided tour will follow the same general sequence that the brain follows in its development before birth. The human brain begins as a fluid-filled

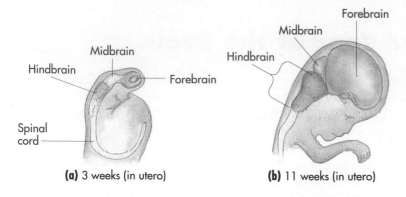

(a) 3 weeks (in utero)

(b) 11 weeks (in utero)

(c) At birth

FIGURE 2.14 The Sequence of Fetal Brain Development
The human brain begins its development as a fluid-filled tube at about two weeks after conception. The hindbrain structures are the first to develop, followed by midbrain structures. The forebrain structures develop last, eventually coming to envelop and surround the hindbrain and midbrain structures.

Human Embryo at Six Weeks Though the embryo is less than an inch long, the prominent structures of the hindbrain and the beginnings of the forebrain can clearly be seen at this early stage of prenatal development.

tube that forms about two weeks after conception. Gradually, the tube expands and develops into separate fluid-filled cavities called *ventricles,* which are at the core of the fully developed brain. *Cerebrospinal fluid* is manufactured in the ventricles. We noted previously that cerebrospinal fluid acts as a shock absorber for the central nervous system and cushions the brain (Kalat, 1995).

As the human fetus develops, brain cells multiply, differentiate, and migrate to their final locations (Jessell, 1995a). Between conception and birth, the number of neurons is increasing in the developing person by an average of 250,000 neurons per *minute* (Thompson, 1993). During this phase, there is an overabundance of neurons, which compete to form synaptic connections (Rakic, 1995). Neurons that fail to form connections are eliminated. Progressively, the three major divisions of the brain develop—the *hindbrain,* the *midbrain,* and the *forebrain.* As you can see in Figure 2.14, during the course of fetal brain development, the forebrain structures eventually surround and envelop the midbrain and hindbrain structures.

At birth, the infant's brain weighs less than a pound. Virtually all the neurons that a person will ever have are present at birth, but the newborn brain is only about one-fourth the size of an adult brain. The number of neurons does not increase after birth; rather, the neurons grow in size. The neurons continue to develop new dendrites (Johnston & others, 1996). Axons also grow longer, and the branching at the ends of axons becomes more dense (Shatz, 1992). By adulthood, the fully mature human brain weighs about three pounds.

In the next section, we'll begin our guided tour of the brain. Following the general sequence of the brain's development, we'll start with the structures at the base of the brain and work our way up to the "higher" brain regions that are responsible for complex mental activity.

The Brainstem:
Hindbrain and Midbrain Structures

> *The brainstem includes the hindbrain and midbrain, which are located at the base of the brain. Why does damage to one side of the brain affect the opposite side of the body? What are the key structures of the hindbrain and midbrain, and what functions are associated with each structure?*

The major regions of the brain are illustrated in Figure 2.15, which can serve as a map to keep you oriented during our tour. At the base of the brain lie the hindbrain and, directly above it, the midbrain. Combined, the structures of the hindbrain and midbrain make up the brain region that is also called the **brainstem.**

The Hindbrain

The **hindbrain** connects the spinal cord with the rest of the brain. It is through the hindbrain that sensory and motor pathways pass to and from regions that are situated higher up in the brain. Sensory information coming in from one side of the body crosses over at the hindbrain level, projecting to the opposite side of the brain. And outgoing motor messages from one side of

Forebrain
Uppermost and largest brain region composed of several structures, the most prominent being the cerebral cortex

Corpus callosum
Thick band of axons connecting the two hemispheres of the cerebral cortex

Cerebral cortex
Divided into two hemispheres and responsible for sophisticated mental functions

Hindbrain
Region at base of brain that connects the brain to the spinal cord

Pons
Helps coordinate movements on left and right sides of body

Cerebellum
Coordinates movement, balance, and posture

Midbrain
Middle region of brain; coordinates visual and auditory information

Reticular formation
Helps regulate attention, alertness, and incoming sensory information

Medulla
Controls breathing, heartbeat, and other vital life functions

FIGURE 2.15 Major Regions of the Brain
This cross section of the human brain shows the primary structures that make up the hindbrain region (yellow), the midbrain region (blue), and the forebrain region (pink). The hindbrain and midbrain regulate many of the most basic life functions, while the forebrain is involved in more sophisticated behaviors and higher mental processes.

brainstem
A region of the brain made up of the hindbrain and the midbrain.

hindbrain
A region at the base of the brain that contains several structures that regulate basic life functions.

medulla
(meh-DULL-uh) A hindbrain structure that controls vital life functions such as breathing, circulation, and muscle tone.

the brain also cross over at the hindbrain level, controlling movement and other motor functions on the opposite side of the body

That's why people who suffer strokes on one side of their brain experience muscle weakness or paralysis on the opposite side of their body. Our friend Asha, for example, suffered only minor damage to motor control areas in her brain. However, because the stroke occurred on the *left* side of her brain, what muscle weakness she did experience was localized on the *right* side of her body, primarily in her right hand.

Three structures make up the hindbrain—the medulla, pons, and cerebellum. The **medulla** lies directly above the spinal cord and contains centers involved in the control of such vital autonomic functions as breathing, heart rate, and digestion. Because the medulla is involved in such critical life functions, damage to the medulla can result in death. The medulla also controls a number of vital reflexes, such as swallowing, coughing, vomiting, and sneezing.

Above the medulla is a swelling of tissue called the **pons,** which represents the uppermost level of the hindbrain. Bulging out behind the pons is the large **cerebellum.** On each side of the pons, a large bundle of axons connects the pons to the cerebellum. The word *pons* means "bridge," and the pons is a bridge of sorts: Information from various other brain regions located higher up in the brain is relayed to the cerebellum via the pons.

The cerebellum functions in the control of balance, muscle tone, and coordinated muscle movements. It's also involved in the learning of habitual or automatic movements and motor skills, such as typing, writing, or gracefully backhanding a tennis ball.

Jerky, uncoordinated movements can result from damage to the cerebellum. Simple movements such as walking or standing upright may become difficult or impossible. The cerebellum is also one of the brain areas that is affected by alcohol consumption. That's why a person "under the influence" may stagger and find it impossible to walk a straight line or stand on one foot. (That's also why a police officer will ask a suspected drunk driver to execute these normally effortless movements.)

At the core of the medulla and the pons is a network of neurons called the **reticular formation,** or the *reticular activating system.* The reticular formation is composed of many groups of specialized neurons that project up to higher brain regions and down to the spinal cord. The reticular formation plays an important role in regulating attention and sleep.

In regulating attention, the reticular formation helps screen the flood of sensory information picked up by sensory receptors and directed to the midbrain and forebrain regions. Although the neural pathways involved are far from thoroughly understood, the reticular formation seems to help filter out unimportant sensory information (see Schneider & Tarshis, 1995; Carlson, 1994). However, when you deliberately, *consciously* focus your attention on specific aspects of your environment, other brain areas come into play, particularly forebrain regions (Hillyard & others, 1995; Stein & others, 1995).

Although other brain areas are also involved, the role of the reticular formation in regulating sleep and arousal has been known for some time. In a famous experiment, the reticular formation of a sleeping cat was electrically stimulated by an electrode that had been implanted in the cat's brain. The cat instantly woke up, fully alert (Moruzzi & Magoun, 1949). The researchers also found that damage to the reticular formation could cause a permanent state of sleep, from which a cat could not be awakened, no matter what the stimulation. In Chapter 4, we'll discuss the hindbrain's role in sleep, dreaming, and sleep disorders in more detail.

The Midbrain

The **midbrain** is an important relay station, where auditory and visual information is integrated. Auditory sensations from the left and right ears are coordinated in the midbrain, allowing you to detect the direction of a sound. The midbrain also coordinates visual information, including eye movements, helping you to locate objects and track their movement. Once coordinated at the midbrain level, auditory and visual information is relayed to sensory processing centers farther up in the forebrain region.

A midbrain area called the **substantia nigra** is involved in motor control and contains a large concentration of dopamine-producing neurons. *Substantia nigra* means "dark substance," and as the name suggests, this area is darkly pigmented. The substantia nigra is part of a larger neural pathway that is involved in preparing other brain regions to initiate organized movements or actions (Kalat, 1995). In the section on neurotransmitters, we noted that Parkinson's disease involves symptoms of abnormal movement. Many of those movement-related symptoms are associated with the degeneration of dopamine-producing neurons in the substantia nigra.

pons
A hindbrain structure that connects the medulla to the two sides of the cerebellum; helps coordinate and integrate movements on each side of the body.

cerebellum
(sare-uh-BELL-um) A large, two-sided hindbrain structure at the back of the brain responsible for muscle coordination, fine motor movements, and maintaining posture and equilibrium.

reticular formation
(reh-TICK-you-ler) A network of nerve fibers located in the center of the medulla that helps regulate attention, arousal, and sleep.

midbrain
The smallest brain region, which helps coordinate auditory and visual sensations.

substantia nigra
(sub-STANCE-ee-uh NEE-gruh) An area of the midbrain that is involved in motor control and contains a large concentration of dopamine-producing neurons.

forebrain
The largest and most complex brain region, which contains centers for complex behaviors and mental processes.

cerebral cortex
(suh-REE-brull or SARE-uh-brull) The wrinkled outer portion of the forebrain, which contains the most sophisticated brain centers.

cerebral hemisphere
The nearly symmetrical left and right halves of the cerebral cortex.

corpus callosum
A thick band of nerve fibers that connects the two cerebral hemispheres and acts as a communication link between them.

The Forebrain

> *The forebrain includes the cerebral cortex and the limbic system structures. What are the four lobes of the cerebral cortex, and what functions have been identified with each lobe? What functions are associated with the thalamus, hypothalamus, hippocampus, and amygdala? What is the limbic system?*

Situated above the midbrain is the largest region of the brain: the **forebrain.** In humans, the forebrain represents about 90 percent of the brain. Many important structures are found in the forebrain. We'll start by describing the forebrain's most prominent structure.

The Cerebral Cortex

The outer portion of the forebrain is called the **cerebral cortex,** which is divided into two **cerebral hemispheres.** The word *cortex* means "bark," and much like the bark of a tree, the cerebral cortex is the outer covering of the forebrain. A thick bundle of axons called the **corpus callosum** connects the two cerebral hemispheres, as shown in Figure 2.16. The corpus callosum serves as the primary communication link between the left and right cerebral hemispheres (Hoptman & Davidson, 1994).

The cerebral cortex is only about a quarter of an inch thick. It is mainly composed of glial cells and neuron cell bodies and axons, giving it a grayish appearance—which is why the cerebral cortex is sometimes described as being composed of *gray matter*. Extending inward from the cerebral cortex are white myelinated axons that are sometimes referred to as *white matter*. These myelinated axons connect the cerebral cortex to other brain regions.

Numerous folds, grooves, and bulges characterize the human cerebral cortex (see Figure 2.17). The purpose of these ridges and valleys is easy to illustrate. Imagine a flat, three-foot by three-foot piece of paper. You can compact the surface area of this piece of paper by scrunching it up into a wad. In much the same way, the grooves and bulges of the cerebral cortex allow about three square feet of surface area to be packed into the small space of the human skull.

FIGURE 2.16 The Cerebral Hemispheres and the Corpus Callosum
This transparent view of the brain shows the corpus callosum, the C-shaped bundle of axons that links the left and right hemispheres of the cerebral cortex.

FIGURE 2.17 Corticalization in Humans and Other Animals
Corticalization refers to the degree of wrinkling of the cerebral cortex. Note that the bass, pigeon, cat, chimpanzee, and human each have a medulla, a cerebellum, and a cerebral cortex. However, the cerebral cortex makes up a much greater proportion of the human brain, and it has many more wrinkles and folds. As the degree of corticalization increases in different species, so does intelligence and the capacity for sophisticated behaviors.

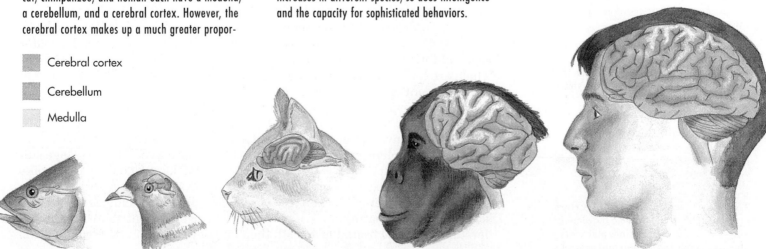

- Cerebral cortex
- Cerebellum
- Medulla

Bass   Pigeon   Cat   Chimpanzee   Human

Each cerebral hemisphere can be roughly divided into four regions, or *lobes*: the *temporal, occipital, parietal, and frontal* lobes (see Figure 2.18). Each lobe is associated with distinct functions. Located near your temples, the **temporal lobe** contains the *primary auditory cortex,* which receives auditory information. At the very back of the brain is the **occipital lobe.** The occipital lobe includes the *primary visual cortex,* where visual information is received.

FIGURE 2.18 Lobes of the Cerebral Cortex
Each hemisphere of the cerebral cortex can be divided into four regions or *lobes,* as shown. Each lobe is associated with distinct functions. The association areas, shaded in purple, make up most of the cerebral cortex.

Parietal lobe

Frontal lobe

Occipital lobe

Temporal lobe

Primary motor cortex (on frontal lobe) controls voluntary movement

Somatosensory cortex (on parietal lobe) receives information about body sensations

Association areas (on all four lobes) combine sensory and motor information; coordinate interaction among different brain areas

Primary visual cortex (on occipital lobe) processes visual information

Primary auditory cortex (on temporal lobe) processes auditory information

temporal lobe
An area on each hemisphere of the cerebral cortex near the temples which is the primary receiving area for auditory information.

occipital lobe
(ock-SIP-it-ull) An area at the back of each cerebral cortex hemisphere that is the primary receiving area for visual information.

parietal lobe
(puh-RYE-et-ull) An area on each hemisphere of the cerebral cortex located above the temporal lobe that processes somatic sensations.

frontal lobe
The largest lobe of the cerebral cortex; processes voluntary muscle movements and is involved in thinking, planning, and emotional expression and control.

The **parietal lobe** is involved in processing bodily or *somatosensory information,* including touch, temperature, pressure, and information from sense receptors in the muscles and joints. A band of tissue on the parietal lobe, called the *somatosensory cortex,* receives information from touch receptors in different parts of the body.

Each part of the body is represented on the somatosensory cortex, but this representation is not equally distributed. Instead, body parts are represented in proportion to their sensitivity to somatic sensations. For example, your hands and face, which are very responsive to touch, have much greater representation on the somatosensory cortex than the backs of your legs, which are far less sensitive to touch. If body areas were actually proportional to the amount of representation on the somatosensory cortex, humans would resemble the misshapen character on the right side of Figure 2.19.

The largest lobe of the cerebral cortex is called the **frontal lobe.** The frontal lobe is involved in planning, initiating, and executing voluntary movements. In the nineteenth century, a railroad worker named Phineas Gage suffered a devastating injury to part of his frontal lobe when an iron spike accidentally blasted through his brain. Gage survived, but a section of his frontal lobe was seriously damaged, producing dramatic changes in his personality. The fascinating story of how Phineas Gage has contributed to the understanding of the frontal lobe, both then and now, is told in In Focus Box 2.2.

Motor Cortex

Somatosensory Cortex

FIGURE 2.19 Body Representation on the Primary Motor Cortex and Somatosensory Cortex
Touch, temperature, pressure, and pain sensations for different body areas occur at distinct locations on the parietal lobe's somatosensory cortex. Similarly, the initiation of movement for different body parts occurs at distinct locations on the frontal lobe's primary motor cortex. If body parts were proportional to their representation on the somatosensory and primary cortex, they would look like the misshapen human figures on the outer edge in the drawing.

Like the somatosensory cortex on the parietal lobe, the movements of different body parts are represented in a band of tissue on the frontal lobe called the *primary motor cortex*. The degree of representation on the primary motor cortex for a particular body part reflects the diversity and precision of its potential movements, as shown on the left side of Figure 2.19. Thus, it's not surprising that almost one-third of the primary motor cortex is devoted to the hands and another third is devoted to facial muscles. The disproportionate representation of these two body areas on the primary motor cortex is reflected in the human capacity to produce an extremely wide range of hand movements and facial expressions.

The primary sensory and motor areas found on the different lobes represent just a small portion of the cerebral cortex. The remaining bulk of the cerebral cortex consists mostly of three large **association areas.** These areas are generally thought to be involved in processing and integrating sensory and motor information (see Jessell, 1995b; Carlson, 1994). For example, the *prefrontal association cortex,* situated in front of the primary motor cortex, is involved in the planning of voluntary movements. Another association area includes parts of the temporal, parietal, and occipital lobes, and is involved in the formation of perceptions and in the integration of perceptions and memories.

Beneath the cerebral cortex are several important forebrain structures, including the *thalamus,* the *hypothalamus,* the *hippocampus,* and the *amygdala.* Collectively, these structures make up what is called the *limbic system.* Before we describe the limbic system as a whole, we'll briefly consider each of these brain structures.

association areas
Areas of the cerebral cortex where information from different brain centers is combined and integrated.

IN FOCUS 2.2

Phineas Gage, Then and Now

A landmark event in understanding the brain's role in behavior occurred on September 13, 1848. A 25-year-old railroad worker named Phineas Gage was the foreman of a railroad crew that was blasting out rock near Cavendish, Vermont. Their method was to drill a hole in the rock, fill it with gunpowder, and cover the gunpowder with a layer of sand. Then, using a fine-pointed, three-and-a-half-foot-long iron rod, Gage would pack the sand and gunpowder down into the hole. The sand was used to keep sparks from igniting the gunpowder when Gage tamped it down with the iron rod.

On this particular day, Gage and a crew member were momentarily distracted while filling the hole. When Gage turned back from the distraction, he thought his assistant had already poured the sand into the hole. But such was not the case. Gage tamped the iron rod down the hole, and a spark from the rod scraping the rock ignited the gunpowder.

The iron rod blew out like a javelin, striking Gage just below his left eye. The rod went completely through Gage's skull and ripped out a hole in the top of his head, landing some fifty feet away. Gage himself was thrown back by the explosion and the massive iron rod catapulting through his skull. His crew stared in horror at him lying on the ground, knowing that surely Gage was dead.

But after a few minutes, Gage began to speak. His crew, astonished that he was still alive, rushed him to the town of Cavendish. The town doctors, John Harlow and Edward Williams, helped Gage walk up three flights of stairs to an attic room where they cleaned his wounds (Harlow, 1848).

Miraculously, Phineas Gage survived despite his massive brain injury. In fact, Gage's recovery was near complete. Movements, speech, memory, and the ability to learn new information were not impaired. He appeared to be as intelligent as he had been before the accident.

But the accident had seriously damaged Gage's frontal lobes, producing a profound change in Gage's personality. The previously friendly, competent, responsible foreman became stubborn, bad-tempered, profane, and unreasonable. Gage also became incapable of carrying out plans, and could no longer hold down a job. As Dr. Harlow (1868) later wrote, "His mind was radically changed, so decidedly that his friends and acquaintances said he was 'no longer Gage.'"

Gage survived for more than twelve years after the accident, dying in 1861. After Gage's death, Harlow persuaded Gage's family to have the body exhumed so that Gage's skull could be recovered and kept as a medical record. The tamping iron, which had been buried with Gage, was also recovered. Today, Gage's skull and the tamping iron are on exhibit at a medical museum at Harvard University.

In 1868, Harlow wrote a paper detailing the accident. He suggested that the changes in Gage's behavior and cognitive functioning were related to the specific location of brain damage. In effect, Harlow proposed that the frontal lobes were involved in social and emotional behavior, reasoning, the abilities to think and plan, and decision-making.

At the time, Harlow's ideas about the frontal lobes were dismissed. Why? One reason was that Harlow had not performed an autopsy. Without anatomical evidence, critics discounted Harlow's suggestions. However, phrenology also played a role in the rejection of Harlow's suggestion (see Box 2.1). Claims for brain specialization were viewed with great skepticism by scientists because of the rejection of the pseudoscientific claims of phrenology. Harlow's ideas were too close to Gall's notion of "faculties" that could be determined from the bumps on a skull (see Damasio & others, 1994; Fancher, 1990).

Harlow's suspicions were finally confirmed almost 125 years after Gage's death. In 1994, Drs. Hanna and Antonio Damasio, a husband-and-wife team at the University of Iowa Department of Neurology, reexamined Phineas Gage's skull. Using X-rays

and sophisticated computerized brain-modeling techniques, they created a three-dimensional model of the injury to Gage's brain, which is shown here. In effect, the Damasios simulated the autopsy that was never performed on Phineas Gage.

The Damasios found that the specific brain damage that Gage sustained and the subsequent behavioral changes fit the pattern found in other individuals with frontal lobe damage (Damasio & others, 1994, 1991). This damage is not associated with an impaired ability to perform logical operations or learn new information, or with disruptions in memory or speech abilities (see Shimamura, 1995). Instead, this damage is associated with an impaired ability to make rational decisions in personal and social matters, and it compromises the processing of emotions (see Robin & Holyoad, 1995).

Although Dr. Harlow's ideas about the role of the frontal lobe in behavior and emotions were initially rejected, over a hundred years later the Damasios have confirmed that Harlow's proposal was accurate. As Hanna Damasio and her colleagues (1994) write, "The mysteries of frontal lobe functioning are slowly being solved, and it is only fair to establish, on a more substantial footing, the roles that Gage and Harlow played in the solution."

A Model of Gage's Injury Computer-simulated reconstruction of Gage's skull by Damasio and her colleagues (1994) suggests that Gage's left and right frontal lobes were both damaged.

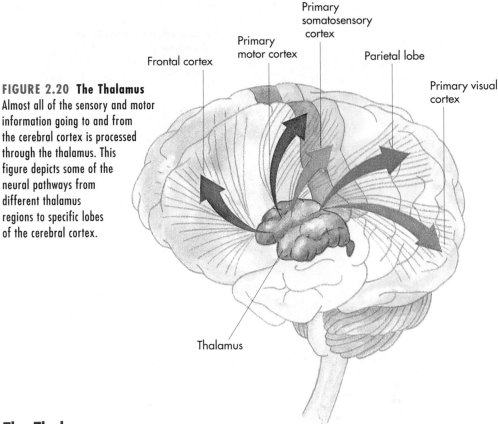

FIGURE 2.20 The Thalamus Almost all of the sensory and motor information going to and from the cerebral cortex is processed through the thalamus. This figure depicts some of the neural pathways from different thalamus regions to specific lobes of the cerebral cortex.

Karen Ann Quinlan After ingesting liquor, Darvon, and Valium, Karen Ann Quinlan lapsed into a permanent coma that lasted for many years. Thirteen years after her death in 1985, Quinlan's brain was examined. Although her cerebral cortex was relatively intact, her thalamus was badly damaged. This and other evidence suggests that the thalamus plays a key role in the regulation of human awareness (Fackelmann, 1994).

The Thalamus

The word *thalamus* comes from a Greek word meaning "inner chamber." And indeed, the **thalamus** is a rounded mass of cell bodies located within each cerebral hemisphere. The thalamus processes and distributes almost all of the sensory and motor information going to and from the cerebral cortex (Jessell, 1995). Figure 2.20 depicts some of the neural pathways going from the thalamus to the different lobes of the cerebral cortex. However, the thalamus is more than just a sensory relay station. The thalamus is also thought to be involved in regulating levels of awareness, attention, motivation, and emotional aspects of sensations (Jessell, 1995; Schneider & Tarshis, 1995). Some of the evidence for the role of the thalamus in awareness involves the famous case of Karen Ann Quinlan (see the photograph at the left).

The Hypothalamus

Hypo means "beneath" or "below." As its name implies, the **hypothalamus** is located below the thalamus (see Figure 2.21). Although it is only about the size of a peanut, the hypothalamus contains many neural connections. These neural pathways ascend to other forebrain areas and descend to the midbrain, hindbrain, and spinal cord.

The hypothalamus regulates both divisions of the autonomic nervous system, increasing and decreasing such functions as heartbeat and blood pressure. It is also involved in regulating a variety of behaviors related to survival, such as eating, drinking, frequency of sexual activity, fear, and aggression. In the motivation chapter (Chapter 8), we'll describe the role of the hypothalamus in more detail.

The hypothalamus exerts considerable control over the secretion of endocrine hormones throughout the body by directly influencing the *pituitary gland*. The *pituitary gland* is situated just below the hypothalamus and is attached to the hypothalamus by a short stalk. The hypothalamus produces both neurotransmitters and hormones that directly influence the pituitary gland. As we noted in the section on the endocrine system, the

thalamus
(THAL-uh-muss) A forebrain structure that processes sensory information for all senses, except smell, and relays it to the cerebral cortex.

hypothalamus
(hi-poe-THAL-uh-muss) A peanut-sized forebrain structure that is part of the limbic system and regulates behaviors related to survival, such as eating, drinking, and sexual activity.

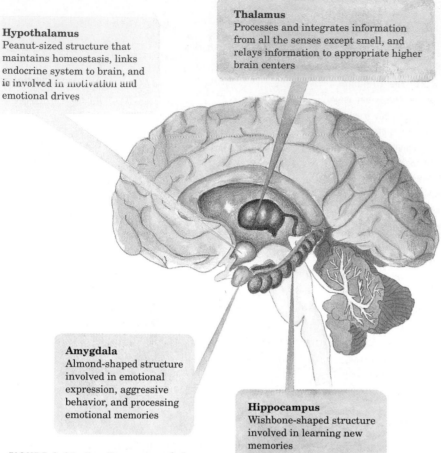

Hypothalamus
Peanut-sized structure that maintains homeostasis, links endocrine system to brain, and is involved in motivation and emotional drives

Thalamus
Processes and integrates information from all the senses except smell, and relays information to appropriate higher brain centers

Amygdala
Almond-shaped structure involved in emotional expression, aggressive behavior, and processing emotional memories

Hippocampus
Wishbone-shaped structure involved in learning new memories

FIGURE 2.21 Key Structures of the Forebrain and Limbic System
In the cross-sectional view shown here, you can see the locations and functions of four important subcortical brain structures. In combination, these structures make up the *limbic system,* which regulates emotional control, learning, and memory.

hippocampus
A curved forebrain structure that is part of the limbic system and is involved in learning and forming new memories.

amygdala
(uh-MIG-dull-uh) An almond-shaped forebrain structure that is part of the limbic system and involved in emotion and memory.

limbic system
A group of forebrain structures that form a border around the brainstem and that are involved in emotion, motivation, learning, and memory.

pituitary gland, in turn, releases hormones that influence the activity of other glands.

The Hippocampus

The **hippocampus** is located beneath the temporal lobe in each cerebral hemisphere (see Figure 2.21). The word *hippocampus* comes from a Latin word meaning "seahorse." If you have a vivid imagination, the hippocampus sort of looks like the curved tail of a seahorse. The hippocampus plays an important role in the ability to form new memories. In Chapter 6, we'll take a closer look at the role of the hippocampus and other brain structures in memory.

The Amygdala

The **amygdala** is an almond-shaped clump of neuron cell bodies at the base of the temporal lobe. The amygdala is involved in controlling a variety of emotional response patterns, including fear, anger, and disgust (LeDoux, 1994; Aggleton, 1992). Studies with animals have shown that electrical stimulation of the amygdala can produce these emotions. In contrast, destruction of the amygdala reduces or disrupts behaviors that are linked to fear and rage. For example, when the amygdala is destroyed in monkeys, they lose their fear of natural predators, like snakes. In humans, electrical stimulation of the amygdala produces feelings of fear and apprehension (see Kandel & Kupfermann, 1995). The amygdala is also involved in learning and in memory formation, especially memories with a strong emotional component (LeDoux, 1994a, 1994b).

The Limbic System

In combination, the hypothalamus, hippocampus, amygdala, and parts of the thalamus and frontal cortex represent some of the key structures of the **limbic system.** The word *limbic* means "border," and as you can see in Figure 2.21, the structures that make up the limbic system form a border of sorts around the brainstem.

In various combinations, the limbic system structures form complex neural circuits that play critical roles in learning, memory, and emotional control (Squire & Knowlton, 1995; Kupfermann & Kandel, 1995; Kalin, 1993). The limbic system is not just involved in negative emotions like fear and aggression. It's been known for some time that limbic system areas are also involved in pleasurable or rewarding sensations. In the 1950s, neuropsychologist James Olds discovered that rats could be trained to perform a task, such as pressing a bar, in order to receive electrical stimulation to certain regions in the limbic system (Olds, 1958, 1962).

In their early work, Olds and other researchers found that the rats preferred brain stimulation to food—even when the rats were extremely hungry (Olds & Fobes, 1981). This finding led the researchers to speculate that there might be some sort of "pleasure center" located in the limbic system. Since their initial discovery, the existence of such pleasure centers has also been demonstrated in other animals, including rabbits, cats, dogs, monkeys, and even goldfish. During the 1960s, the effects of rewarding brain stimulation were tried in humans, with mixed results (see Kalat, 1995).

Today, it's known that electrical stimulation of *many* different parts of the brain can produce similar effects (Olds & Fobes, 1981). Exactly how electrical stimulation produces rewarding sensations is still not completely understood, but neural pathways involving the neurotransmitter dopamine seem to play a prominent role (Wise, 1996).

The Brain as an Integrated System

At this point, you should be in a better position to follow the neurological circuit of the simple behavior we mentioned at the beginning of this section—detecting the roughness of sandpaper with your finger.

The general organization of the sensory system for touch is shown in Figure 2.22. Basically, three neurons link the skin with the somatosensory cortex in the parietal lobe (see Martin & Jessell, 1995). The first neuron carries the neural impulse from the sensory receptor in the fingertip to the hindbrain. The second neuron crosses over to the opposite side of the brain and projects upward through the brainstem to the thalamus. The third neuron extends from the thalamus to the somatosensory cortex. When the neural signal is received by the somatosensory cortex, you experience the sensation of touch. In Chapter 3, sensation and perception, we'll take a detailed look at how our different sensory systems process information.

FIGURE 2.22 The Sensory System for Touch An action as simple as detecting the roughness of sandpaper requires the processing and integration of information along pathways in both the peripheral and central nervous systems. Beginning at the fingertips of the right hand, the information is routed to the spinal cord, then to the brainstem, where it crosses to the opposite side of the body. The information is forwarded to the thalamus, which directs it to the somatosensory cortex on the left parietal lobe.

A safecracker sandpapers his fingertips to increase sensitivity.

Somatosensory cortex

Thalamus

Brain stem

Spinal cord

Sensory neuron

Stimulation of sensory receptor in skin

The Brain

Fill in the blanks in the following statements.

1. The three major regions of the brain are the
   _____, _____, and
   _____.

2. Coordinated muscle movements and balance
   are regulated by the _____.

3. The _____ connects the two cerebral hemispheres.

4. Auditory information is processed in the
   _____ lobe.

5. The signals for voluntary movements originate
   in the _____, which is located on
   the _____ lobe.

6. The _____ plays a critical role in
   the formation of new memories.

7. The hypothalamus, hippocampus, amygdala,
   and parts of the thalamus and frontal cortex
   make up the _____.

Specialization in the Cerebral Hemispheres

Over a hundred years ago, Broca and Wernicke provided the first evidence that the left and right hemispheres were specialized for different functions. What are Broca's and Wernicke's areas? How did clinical findings on aphasia contribute to our knowledge of the brain?

The most sophisticated cognitive and behavioral functions are processed in the cerebral cortex. As we mentioned in the last section, the cerebral cortex is divided into two distinct hemispheres that communicate with one another primarily through a thick bundle of axons called the corpus callosum (Hoptman & Davidson, 1994). We also noted that each hemisphere processes sensory and motor functions for the opposite side of the body.

Although the two cerebral hemispheres appear to be symmetrical, they are *not* symmetrical in their functioning. Each cerebral hemisphere is specialized for certain abilities. Here's a rough analogy: Imagine two computers that are linked through a network. One computer is optimized for handling word processing, the other for handling graphic design. Although specialized for different functions, the two computers actively share information and can "talk" to each other across the network. In this analogy, the computers correspond to the left and right hemispheres, and the network that links them is the corpus callosum.

The first discoveries about the dramatic differences between the two hemispheres of the brain were made more than a hundred years ago by two important pioneers in brain research, Pierre Broca and Karl Wernicke.

Language and the Left Hemisphere:
The Early Work of Broca and Wernicke

Earlier in the chapter we discussed phrenology, a pseudoscience that became popular in the early 1800s. The basic premise of phrenology was that personality characteristics and cognitive abilities were reflected in the bumps on

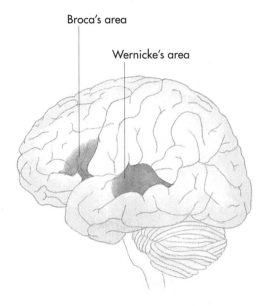

Broca's area

Wernicke's area

FIGURE 2.23 Broca's and Wernicke's Areas of the Cerebral Cortex
Broca's area, located in the lower frontal lobe, is involved in the production of speech. Wernicke's area, found in the temporal lobe, is important in the comprehension of written or spoken language. Damage to either of these areas will produce different types of speech disturbances or aphasia. In most people, both of these areas are found on the left hemisphere.

aphasia
(uh-FAZE-yuh) The partial or complete inability to articulate ideas or understand spoken or written language due to brain injury or damage.

a person's skull. Although that idea was eventually discredited, phrenology drew scientific attention to the notion of cortical localization (Hilgard, 1987). *Cortical localization* refers to the idea that specific areas of the cerebral cortex are associated with specific behaviors or psychological processes, such as language use or perception (Springer & Deutsch, 1993).

Even when phrenology was first becoming popular, the idea of cortical localization was not completely without precedent. It was already well established that injury to one side of the brain could produce muscle paralysis or loss of sensation on the opposite side of the body (Fancher, 1990). By the early 1800s, animal experiments had shown the loss of specific functions when particular brain areas were selectively destroyed. And in the mid-1800s, the Phineas Gage story told in Box 2.2 had become famous. The changes in Gage's personality following his injury gave support to the notion that the frontal lobes are associated with emotional control and the ability to plan future actions (see Damasio & others, 1994).

Although these events helped provide momentum for the idea of cortical localization, they lacked the scientific precision that clinical evidence can provide. That clinical evidence began to be gathered in the 1860s. At that time, a French surgeon and neuroanatomist named **Pierre Paul Broca** (1824–1880) treated a series of patients who had great difficulty speaking but could comprehend written or spoken language. Subsequent autopsies of these patients revealed a consistent finding—brain damage to an area on the lower *left frontal lobe.* Today, this area on the left hemisphere is referred to as *Broca's area,* and it is known to play a crucial role in speech production (see Figure 2.23).

About a decade after Broca's discovery, a young German neurologist named **Karl Wernicke** (1848–1905) discovered another left hemisphere area that, when damaged, produced a *different* type of language disturbance. Unlike Broca's patients, Wernicke's patients could not understand spoken or written communications. They could speak quickly and easily, but their speech sometimes made no sense. Their sentences seemed to be grammatical, but the patients would use meaningless words or even nonsense syllables (Fancher, 1990). If asked how he was feeling, the patient might respond by saying something like, "Don't glow glover. Yes, uh, ummm, bick, bo chipickers the dallydoe mick more work mittle." Autopsies of these patients' brains revealed consistent damage to an area on the *left temporal lobe* that today is called *Wernicke's area* (see Figure 2.23).

The discoveries of Broca and Wernicke provided the first compelling clinical evidence showing the specialized language abilities of the left hemisphere. If damage occurs in the exact same locations on the *right* hemisphere, language and speech functions are *not* affected. The general pattern of language abilities in the left hemisphere is typical for virtually all right-handed individuals and the majority of left-handed people (see Damasio & Damasio, 1992). What about the left-handed people who don't fit this pattern? For more insights on hand preference and brain organization, see Box 2.3, "The Puzzle of the Left-Hander."

The language disruptions that Broca and Wernicke's patients demonstrated represent different types of aphasia. **Aphasia** refers to the partial or complete inability to articulate ideas or understand spoken or written language due to brain injury or damage. There are many different types of aphasia. Victims of *Broca's aphasia* find it difficult or impossible to produce speech, but their comprehension of verbal or written words is unaffected. Victims of *Wernicke's aphasia* can speak, but they often have trouble finding the right words and have great difficulty comprehending written or spoken communication. In more severe cases of Wernicke's aphasia, speech can be characterized by nonsensical, meaningless, incoherent words, as in the example given above.

IN FOCUS 2.3

The Puzzle of the Left-Hander

Anatomically, our two hands are mirror images. Nevertheless, the vast majority of people use their right hand exclusively for tasks requiring dexterity.

Humans are unique in their strong tendency to be right-handed. Animals also show a preference for one paw over the other, but rats, cats, dogs, and other animals are just as likely to be left-pawed as right-pawed. In humans, only about 8% of the population is left-handed. Remarkably, this percentage has been consistent for over fifty centuries. Even Stone Age cave drawings and tools indicate that our prehistoric ancestors were predominantly right-handed (Coren, 1992).

Almost twice as many men as women are left-handed. Some researchers believe this occurs because males are exposed to higher levels of testosterone during prenatal development. Prenatal testosterone exposure could also possibly account for the fact that left-handers tend to display higher rates of learning disorders, allergic disorders, and immune system disorders than right-handers (Geschwind & Galaburda, 1987). On a more positive note, there are twice as many left-handed artists, musicians, mathematicians, and engineers as would be expected in the general population (Kilshaw & Annett, 1983).

Almost all right-handers display left hemisphere dominance for language functions. However, neurosurgeons have discovered a surprising pattern of differences in brain organization among left-handers. Before brain surgery, each hemisphere can be separately anesthetized, allowing the hemisphere that controls language functions to be identified.

Using this technique, it was found that about 70% of left-handers show the same pattern as right-handers, with the left hemisphere dominant for language. But about 15% of left-handed individuals show the opposite pattern, with language functions localized in their right hemisphere. The remaining 15% of left-handed individuals process language in both hemispheres (Springer & Deutsch, 1993; Damasio & Damasio, 1992).

This variability in brain organization may explain why left-handers are a more diverse group in their degree of hand preference. Right-handers consistently perform virtually all tasks requiring dexterity with their right hands. But many left-handers prefer their right hand for some tasks (Springer & Deutsch, 1993). Your author Don, for example, writes and holds a fork with his left hand. But he uses his right hand to move the computer mouse, throw a ball, and play tennis.

What causes hand preference? Some researchers contend that environmental influences cause handedness (e.g., Collins, 1970, 1975). However, evidence also points to a genetic influence. If both parents are right-handed, the odds of a having a left-handed child are only about 1 in 50. If one parent is left-handed and the other right-handed, the odds of having a left-handed child are about 1 in 6. And, if both parents are left-handed, the odds are approximately 1 in 2 (Springer & Deutsch, 1993).

Adding support to the idea of genetic involvement, hand preference has been demonstrated before birth. Psychologist Peter G. Hepper and his colleagues (1990) used ultrasound to observe over 200 developing fetuses. Approximately 95% preferred sucking their right thumb, while 5% preferred their left thumb. These figures correspond very closely to the number of left and right-handed people in the population.

HAGAR

At the beginning of this chapter, we described the symptoms experienced by our friend Asha in the weeks before and the months following her stroke. Asha, who is right-handed, experienced the stroke in her left hemisphere. About three days after her stroke, an MRI brain scan showed where the damage had occurred: the left temporal lobe.

Asha experienced many symptoms of Wernicke's aphasia. Talking was difficult, not because Asha couldn't speak, but because she had to stop frequently to search for the right words. Asha was unable to name even simple objects, like the cup on her dinner tray at the hospital or her doctor's necktie. She "recognized" the objects but was unable to say what they were. Asha also had a great deal of difficulty following a normal conversation or understanding speech, whether it was in English or her native language, Tulu. Telephone conversations were virtually impossible.

Asha also discovered that she had lost the ability to read. That is, she could see the words on the page, but they seemed to have no meaning. Paul brought some of their Christmas cards to the hospital. As Asha recalls, "When I realized I couldn't read the Christmas cards, I thought my life was over. I just lost it. I remember crying and telling the nurse, 'I have a doctorate and I can't read, write, or talk!'"

When we visited Asha in the hospital, we brought her a Christmas present: a portable cassette tape player with headphones and some tapes of relaxing instrumental music. Little did we realize how helpful the music would be for Asha. One tape was a recording of Native American flute music called *Sky of Dreams*. The music was very beautiful and rather unusual, with intricate melodies and unexpected, complex harmonies. Although it was very difficult for Asha to follow normal speech, listening to *Sky of Dreams* was an entirely different experience. As Asha explains:

> *I tried cranking up the music very high and it soothed me. I could sleep. At the time, the flute music seemed to be just perfectly timed with the way my brain was working. It was tuning out all the other noises so I could focus on just one thing and sleep. So I would play the music over and over again at a very high level. I did that for a long time because my mind was so active and jumbled that I couldn't think.*

Asha's language functions were severely disrupted. Yet she was able to listen to and appreciate instrumental music—even very complex music. Why? At the end of the next section, we'll offer some possible explanations for what seems to have been a disparity in Asha's cognitive abilities after her stroke.

Cutting the Corpus Callosum:
The Split Brain

> *In the split-brain operation, the corpus callosum is cut. How were split-brain patients tested to reveal differences in the abilities of the two hemispheres? How do the left and right hemispheres differ?*

Since the discoveries made by Broca and Wernicke, the most dramatic evidence illustrating the independent functions of the two cerebral hemispheres has come from a surgical procedure called the **split-brain operation.** This operation is used to stop or reduce recurring seizures in severe cases of epilepsy that can't be treated in any other fashion. The procedure involves surgically cutting the corpus callosum, the thick band of axons that connects the two hemispheres.

What was the logic behind cutting the corpus callosum? An epileptic seizure typically occurs when neurons begin firing in a disorganized fashion in one region of the brain. The disorganized neuronal firing quickly spreads from one hemisphere to the other via the corpus callosum. If the corpus callosum is cut, seizures should be contained in just one hemisphere, reducing their severity or eliminating them altogether. This is exactly what happened when the split-brain operation was first tried in this country in the 1940s (see Springer & Deutsch, 1993).

split-brain operation
A surgical procedure that involves cutting the corpus callosum.

Roger Sperry (1913–1994) For his pioneering research using split-brain patients to investigate the relationship between brain and behavior, Sperry received the 1981 Nobel Prize in Physiology or Medicine.

Surprisingly, cutting the corpus callosum initially seemed to produce no noticeable effect on the patients, other than to reduce their epileptic seizures. Their ability to engage in routine conversations and tasks seemed to be unaffected. On the basis of these early observations, some brain researchers speculated that the corpus callosum served no function whatsoever (see Gazzaniga, 1995). One famous psychologist, Karl Lashley, joked that its primary function seemed to be to keep the two hemispheres from sagging (Hoptman & Davidson, 1994).

In the 1960s, however, psychologist and neuroscientist **Roger Sperry** (1913–1994) and his colleagues began unraveling the puzzle of the left and right hemispheres. Using simple but ingenious research techniques, Sperry systematically tested the abilities of the split-brain patients. In one experiment, Sperry asked a split-brain patient to close her eyes and then placed a fork in her left hand. When asked to identify the object, she was unable to answer. Can you explain why?

Remember, sensations and movements on the *left* side of the body are processed by the *right* hemisphere. The sensation of the spoon in the split-brain subject's left hand was directed to her *right* hemisphere. But, as Broca and Wernicke had discovered, the *left* hemisphere is responsible for language functions. Because the split-brain subject's corpus callosum had been cut, her right hemisphere had no way of sharing the information with her verbal left hemisphere. Hence, the right hemisphere could not "say" what the left hand was holding, and the verbal left hemisphere could feel nothing. In this experimental situation, split-brain subjects would often deny that anything was in their left hands, or they would make random guesses (Gazzaniga, 1995).

In other experiments, Sperry and his colleagues used the apparatus shown in Figure 2.24. They would direct a split-brain subject to focus on a point in the middle of a screen, while briefly flashing a word or picture to the left or right of the midpoint. In this procedure, visual information to the right of the midpoint is projected to the person's *left* hemisphere, and visual information to the left of the midpoint is projected to the *right* hemisphere. Behind the screen were several objects that were hidden from the split-brain subjects. The split-brain subject could reach under a partition below the screen to pick up the concealed objects, but could not see them (Sperry, 1982).

In a typical experiment, Sperry projected the image of an object concealed behind the screen, such as a hammer, to the left of the midpoint. Thus, the image of the hammer was sent to the right, nonverbal hemisphere. If a split-brain subject was asked to *verbally* identify the image flashed on the screen, he could not do so, and often denied that anything had appeared on the screen. Once again, his verbal left hemisphere had no way of knowing the information that had been sent to his right hemisphere. However, if a split-brain subject was asked to use his left hand to reach under the partition for the object that had been displayed, he would correctly pick up the hammer. Why? Because his left hand was controlled by the same right hemisphere that saw the image of the hammer.

Sperry's experiments reconfirmed the specialized language abilities of the left hemisphere that Broca and Wernicke had discovered over a hundred years earlier. But notice, even though the split-brain subject's right hemisphere could not express itself verbally, it still processed information and expressed itself *nonverbally*—the subject was able to pick up the correct object.

Does our right hemisphere have any role in communication? Working with a female split-brain subject, Sperry flashed a picture of a female nude to the left of the screen's midpoint, sending the information to the subject's right, nonverbal hemisphere (see Springer & Deutsch, 1993). When asked what she had seen, the woman, as expected, said she saw nothing. But moments later she blushed, smiled, and giggled. When asked why she was laughing, she could only say, "Oh, doctor, you have some machine!"

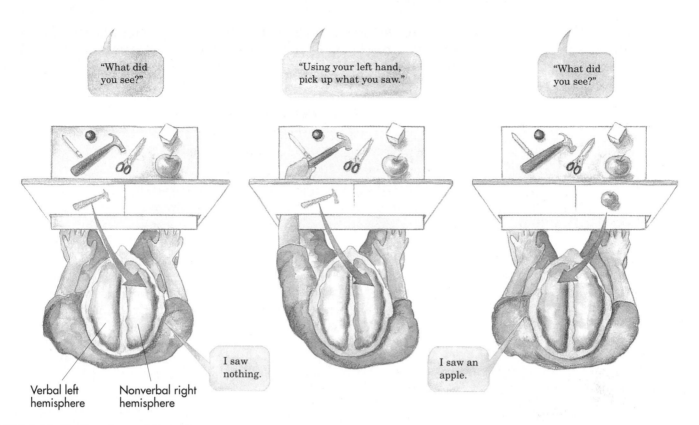

FIGURE 2.24 The Experimental Setup in Split-Brain Research

In a typical split-brain experiment, as shown here, the participant focuses his attention on the midpoint of the screen. Notice that he is unable to verbally identify the picture that is flashed to his nonverbal right hemisphere, but he is able to grasp the hammer with his left hand. In contrast, when the image of the apple is flashed to his verbal left hemisphere, he can easily name it.

The Specialized Abilities of the Left and Right Hemispheres The red arrow at the top of each PET scan is pointing to the front of the brain. The red and yellow colors show the areas of greatest brain activity. Listening to speech involves the language processing functions of the left hemisphere, while listening to music activates the nonverbal functions of the right hemisphere.

Her right hemisphere, which saw the picture of the nude, displayed the emotional reactions of amusement and embarrassment, which it expressed *nonverbally*. Such observations have led researchers to believe that the right hemisphere is involved in regulating the emotional and nonverbal aspects of communication, such as tone of voice and the use of gestures, or "body language." The right hemisphere is also thought to be involved in interpreting the nonverbal cues of others (Springer & Deutsch, 1993).

For his pioneering research on split-brain subjects and brain specialization, Roger Sperry received the 1981 Nobel Prize in physiology and medicine. His findings spurred other researchers to investigate whether the same patterns of brain specialization occurred in normal individuals as well as split-brain subjects. More than three decades of research have confirmed that similar patterns of specialization exist in individuals whose corpus callosum has *not* been cut (see Gazzaniga, 1995).

On the basis of this and other evidence, researchers have concluded that—in most people—the left hemisphere is superior at language abilities, speech, and writing. The right hemisphere is superior at nonverbal emotional expression and visual perception tasks that involve deciphering visual clues, such as completing a puzzle or manipulating blocks to match a particular design (Gazzaniga, 1995).

A dramatic demonstration of right hemisphere superiority in visual perception tasks was captured on film (Gazzaniga, 1977). A split-brain patient was given the task of arranging colored blocks to match the design shown on a card. At the beginning of the film, the patient is shown readily assembling the blocks with his left hand, which is controlled by his right hemisphere. But when told to use his right hand, which is controlled by his left hemisphere, he fumbles with the blocks and is plagued by indecision. When the left hand tries to help, the researcher gently but firmly removes it from the table, leaving the right hand to continue fumbling with the task.

The right hemisphere also excels at other visual perception tasks such as face recognition, reading maps, copying designs, and drawing. Finally, the right hemisphere shows a higher degree of specialization for musical and artistic appreciation or responsiveness—but not necessarily for musical or artistic ability, which often involves the use of the left hemisphere as well. The different "talents" of the two hemispheres are summarized in Table 2.2.

TABLE 2.2 The Specialized Abilities of the Two Hemispheres

Left Hemisphere Superiority	Right Hemisphere Superiority
Language abilities	Visual perception tasks
Speech	Nonverbal emotional expression
Writing	Artistic and musical appreciation

Given the basic findings of the split-brain research, can you speculate why Asha was unable to read or follow a simple conversation, but could easily concentrate on a complex piece of music? Why were her language abilities so disrupted, while her ability to appreciate music remained intact?

A plausible explanation has to do with the location of the stroke's damage on Asha's left temporal lobe. Because the left hemisphere is specialized for language, the stroke produced serious disruptions in Asha's language abilities. However, her *right* cerebral hemisphere sustained no detectable damage. Because one of the right hemisphere's abilities is the appreciation of musical sounds, Asha retained the ability to understand and appreciate music.

CONCEPT REVIEW 2.5

Specialization in the Cerebral Hemispheres

Match each of the following terms to the correct statement below: Broca's area, Wernicke's area, left hemisphere, right hemisphere, corpus callosum.

1. This area is superior at visual perception tasks and at musical and artistic appreciation.

2. Damage to this specific area disrupts the ability to understand spoken or written communication.

3. This area is surgically cut in the split-brain operation.

4. Damage to this specific area disrupts the ability to speak but not the ability to understand spoken or written communication.

5. This area is superior at language tasks.

Summing Up: The Biological Foundations of Behavior

Asha's stroke changed her life. She came to realize, she told us, "just how fragile life can be." We've seen throughout this chapter that our physical survival and our conscious experience are mediated by the delicate balance of chemicals and the complex, intricate connections in our nervous system.

Asha's story also illustrates the interdependence of mind and brain. On the one hand, there are the physical "wiring" and chemistry of the human nervous system. On the other hand, there are the mental events and abilities that we experience as the conscious mind. Between the two, there is an ongoing and complex interaction, one that is only beginning to be understood (see Gazzaniga, 1995; Horgan, 1994; Crick & Koch, 1992).

What happened to Asha? Fortunately, Asha's story has a happy ending. After being discharged from the hospital, she began several months of intensive speech therapy. She set a very high goal for herself: to return to teaching at the university by the fall semester. With the help of her husband, Paul, and her mother, who traveled from India to stay with her for four months, Asha made remarkable gains. Her speech therapist assigned a great deal of "homework" that consisted of repetitiously pairing pictures with words, objects with words, and words with objects. Especially at first, it was frustrating for Asha. But gradually, she made significant gains.

Asha reached the goal that she had set for herself. With remarkable determination, she returned to her teaching and research at the university the following fall semester. Today, more than two years after her stroke, you would be unable to detect any signs of impairment indicating that Asha had sustained significant brain damage.

What Asha's story illustrates is that the brain has an incredible ability to recover and regain functions after an injury. Even more astonishing, these same abilities are also at work in the *uninjured* brain. Not the least of the brain's marvels is its ability to change and grow throughout life. As researchers have only recently discovered, the brain literally changes its structure in response to the quality of environmental stimulation. In the chapter Application, we'll take a look at how researchers have documented the remarkable plasticity of which the brain is capable. And you'll learn how research findings on brain plasticity can be used to enhance *your* dendritic potential!

Asha Today

APPLICATION

Pumping Neurons: Keeping Your Brain in Shape

Some brain structures can change in response to experience. What are the effects of environmental enrichment on the brain?

It's established medical wisdom that if you don't use your muscles, they become weak. Can the same be said of the brain? Neuropsychologist Marilyn Albert (1994) comments, "People used to ask me that years ago and I would say that we don't have enough data to say one way or another. I don't say that anymore. I tell them what the data looks like—use it or lose it."

Neuroscientists have discovered how the brain changes in response to mental stimulation, and how important it is to "exercise" the brain. At the end of the Application, we'll provide you with a variety of ways to give your brain a good workout.

The Flexible Brain: Structural Plasticity

Researchers once believed that by early adulthood the brain's physical structure was "hard-wired" for life. It's now known that exposure to stimulating or unstimulating environmental conditions actually causes some *brain structures to physically change* throughout the lifespan. Called **structural plasticity,** this phenomenon was first demonstrated in the early 1960s in studies with rats (see Rosenzweig, 1996).

The basic experimental procedure was relatively simple. Rats were systematically exposed to either an "enriched" or an "impoverished" environment at different ages and for varying lengths of time. As the accompanying photograph shows, the "enriched" environment is spacious, houses several rats, and has assorted wheels, ladders, tunnels, and objects to explore, which are regularly changed to add further variety. In the "impoverished" environment, a solitary rat lives alone in a small laboratory cage with only a water bottle and food tray to keep it company.

Using this basic design, researchers found that enrichment increases the number and length of dendrites, enlarging the size of neurons and increasing the number of potential connections with other neurons (see Johnston & others, 1996). Enrichment also increases the number of glial cells, which manufacture the myelin sheath that increases communication speed between neurons. And because the enriched conditions promote physical activity, cerebral blood flow is also enhanced, which increases the vitality of brain structures and their functions (Diamond, 1988).

In simple terms, all these changes result in increased communication capacity in the brain. Enrichment produces *more synaptic connections* between brain neurons; impoverishment decreases synaptic connections. With more synapses, the brain has a greater capacity to integrate and process information, and to do so more quickly. The cerebral cortex, where sophisticated mental functions occur, is the area most strongly affected by enrichment or impoverishment. Structures below the cerebral cortex, such as those in the limbic system, apparently change very little in response to environmental enrichment or impoverishment.

Even the aged brain can change in response to environmental stimulation. Researchers investigated that issue by raising rats in impoverished environments until the rat's age was equivalent to that of seventy-five-year-old humans. (Ten days of rat life is roughly equivalent to one year of the human lifespan.) The rats were then placed in enriched environments until they reached the equivalent of ninety human years of age.

The result? Despite the normal decline expected in the aged brain, the senior-citizen rats showed *significant increases* in brain growth and synaptic interconnections. In fact, no matter what age was studied, environmental enrichment or impoverishment had a significant impact on brain structure (Diamond, 1993, 1988). As psychologist William Greenough (1993) summarizes, "What we know from animals suggests that the harder you use your brain, the more in shape it's going to be."

From Animal Studies to Humans

Can the conclusions drawn from studies on rats and other mammals be applied to human brains? Obviously, researchers cannot directly study the immediate effects of enriched or impoverished environments on human brain tissue as they can with rats. However, psychologists and other researchers have amassed an impressive array of correlational evidence showing that the human brain also seems to benefit from enriched, stimulating environments (Rosenzweig, 1996). As neuroscientist Michael Merzenich (1994) commented, "People don't think about the power that they have within themselves to change their brains."

For example, autopsy studies have compared the brains of university graduates versus high school dropouts. The brains of university graduates had up to 40 percent more synaptic connections than those of high school dropouts (see Jacobs & others, 1993). According to UCLA neuroscientist Bob Jacobs (1993), "This is the human equivalent of the animals exposed to enriched environments having smarter brains. As you go up the

educational ladder there is a dramatic increase in dendritic material."

However, the key is not just getting a higher education. University graduates who lead mentally unstimulating lives had fewer dendritic connections than did those who remained mentally active throughout their lives. According to Jacobs (1993), "The bottom line is that you have to use it or you lose it."

Another line of evidence comes from studies comparing symptoms of Alzheimer's disease in elderly individuals with different levels of education (see Katzman, 1993; Stern & others, 1994, 1992). Autopsies showed that the more educated individuals had just as much damage to their brain cells as the poorly educated individuals. However, the better-educated people had *not* suffered the devastating memory losses or other symptoms of Alzheimer's disease, while the poorly educated people had. In simple terms, because the better-educated had more synaptic connections, they did not suffer as much when brain cells began to degenerate due to Alzheimer's.

More broadly, other research has shown that environmental stimulation of the brain is critical for normal development, even from the first day of life (Stromswold, 1995; Shatz, 1992). Infants and children should be exposed to a wide variety of experiences to enhance brain connections and intellectual development (Greenough, Black, &

Wallace, 1987). The intellectual and social development of mentally retarded people, especially children, has been significantly improved by enrichment programs. A stimulating environment can have a beneficial effect on brain functions in someone who has sustained brain damage from injury or disease (Rosenzweig, 1996; Renner & Rosenzweig, 1987).

Over the lifespan, the degree to which a person remains mentally active can act as an insulator against intellectual decline (White & others, 1994; Inouye & others, 1993). Since 1956, psychologist K. Warner Schaie and his colleagues have followed some 5,000 people as they have aged to learn what happens to intellectual abilities (see Schaie, 1994). Contrary to what is commonly believed, Schaie found that intellectual decline is not an inevitable result of aging. Rather, intellectual decline depends to a large degree on whether a person is a mental athlete— or a cerebral couch potato. Among the factors that can help protect a person from intellectual decline is being involved in a complex and stimulating environment, including being married to a smart spouse (see Schaie, 1995a).

Rats in an Enriched Environment Compared to rats raised in solitary lab cages, rats raised in an enriched environment, like the one shown here, show significant increases in brain growth and synaptic interconnections.

Pumping Neurons: Exercising Your Brain

Whatever your age, there seems to be a simple, basic prescription for keeping your brain fit. According to neuroscientist Arnold Scheibel (1994), "The important thing is to be actively involved in areas unfamiliar to you. Anything that's intellectually challenging can probably serve as a kind of stimulus for dendritic growth, which means it adds to the computational reserves in your brain." In short, keep your brain active and flexible. On a regular basis, try the new and unfamiliar. Here are some possible suggestions:

- Learn to play a musical instrument.

- If you are a "number" or "word" person, sign up for an art class.

- If you are an "art" person, start a personal journal or take a creative writing class.

- Listen to different radio stations.

- Buy a newspaper or magazine you've never read before.

- Read books with new ideas that challenge your opinions or beliefs.

- Talk to people of a different ethnic or religious background about their upbringing or family holidays.

- Take up a new hobby.

- Try to fix something.

- Attend a play or a performance of the symphony.

- Try all kinds of puzzles—word, visual, matching, and maze puzzles.

- Go to the library and browse until you find at least three books that spark your interest, then check them out and read them.

- Sign up for a class on a topic that you want to know more about.

- Go to the library and check out cassettes or CDs with different kinds of ethnic or cultural music.

- Set aside a day in which you may communicate in any manner except speaking.

- Unplug your television set for a week.

This list represents just a few of the possible ways you can stimulate your own brain. The brain is never too old to learn and change in response to new and mentally stimulating experiences.

Never Too Old to Learn
At 102 years of age, Gemisto Villani returned to school to complete his education. Intellectual decline is not an inevitable consequence of aging, especially if your environment is mentally challenging.

Summary
The Biological Foundations of Behavior

The Scope of Biological Psychology

- Psychological and biological processes are closely linked. Biological psychologists investigate the physical processes that underlie psychological experience and behavior.

The Neuron: The Basic Unit of Communication

- Information in the nervous system is transmitted via cells specialized for communication, called neurons. Glial cells help neurons by providing nutrition, removing waste products, and producing the myelin sheath.

- Most neurons have three basic components. The neuron's cell body provides energy and directs the neuron's activity. Dendrites receive information from other neurons or sensory receptors. And the axon carries the information away from the neuron's cell body toward other locations. The

axons of some neurons are wrapped in a myelin sheath, which speeds the rate at which neural messages are sent.

- Within the neuron, information is communicated in the form of brief electrical messages called action potentials. When prepared to activate, the neuron carries a slight negative electrical charge, which is referred to as the resting potential. If sufficiently stimulated, the neuron activates and depolarizes. Electrically charged ions rush into and out of the axon, changing the electrical charge of the neuron from negative to positive. After a brief pause, the neuron reestablishes the resting potential so that it can activate again.

- The point of communication between two neurons is called the synapse. Neurons communicate information to other neurons either electrically or chemically. The most common process is chemical communication involving neurotransmitters, which cross the fluid-filled space and affect neighboring neurons. There are many different kinds of neurotransmitters, each capable of sending either an excitatory or inhibitory message to the receiving neuron. Certain drugs can influence behavior and mental processes by mimicking neurotransmitters, by occupying receptor sites, or by blocking the reuptake of neurotransmitters.

The Nervous System and the Endocrine System: Communication Throughout the Body

- The nervous system is divided into two main divisions, the central nervous system and the peripheral nervous system. The central nervous system is composed of the brain and the spinal cord. Some simple forms of behavior, such as spinal reflexes, occur in the spinal cord without brain involvement.

- The peripheral nervous system consists of all the nerves outside the central nervous system. The two main subdivisions of the peripheral nervous system are the somatic nervous system, which communicates sensory and motor information, and the autonomic nervous system, which regulates involuntary functions like heartbeat and respiration. The autonomic nervous system is divided into the sympathetic nervous system, which arouses the body to meet threats or emergencies, and the parasympathetic nervous system, which maintains normal functions and conserves physical energy.

- The endocrine system is composed of glands that secrete hormones into the bloodstream, regulating a diverse range of body functions including physical growth, stress responses, and sexual development. The endocrine system is regulated by the hypothalamus in the brain. The hypothalamus produces neurotransmitters and hormones that influence the pituitary gland. In turn, the pituitary gland releases hormones that influence the other endocrine glands.

Studying the Brain: The Toughest Case to Crack

- Because the brain is encased by bone, it has been especially challenging for scientists to study. Among the first techniques were case studies of people with brain damage or disease. In animal studies, researchers would produce lesions in a particular brain area, then observe the behavioral effects. Researchers have also used electrodes to electrically stimulate specific areas of the brain.

- Technological advances have produced a variety of techniques to image the brain's structures and activity. The electroencephalograph records the brain's electrical activity. CAT scans use X-rays to make images of the brain's structures. MRI scanners use magnetic signals to produce highly detailed images of the brain's structures. PET scans use radioactive oxygen or glucose to produce color-coded images of the brain's activity. Functional MRI scans take rapid, multiple MRI images that are computer-assembled to create a "movie" of brain activity.

A Guided Tour of the Brain

- Most psychological processes involve the integrated processing of information via neural pathways in multiple brain structures and regions. During the earliest stages of prenatal development, the human brain begins as a fluid-filled tube, which ultimately forms the three key brain regions: the hindbrain, midbrain, and forebrain.

- Combined, the hindbrain and midbrain structures constitute the brainstem. Sensory and motor pathways cross over in the hindbrain so that each side of the body is controlled by the opposite side of the brain. The key structures of the hindbrain are the medulla, which helps control autonomic functions such as breathing and digestion; the cerebellum, which is involved in muscle movements and balance; and the pons, which relays information from higher brain regions to the cerebellum. Located in the core of the medulla and the pons is the reticular formation, which is involved in attention and filtering incoming sensory information.

- The midbrain contains areas where auditory and visual information is integrated and coordinated. A darkly pigmented area called the substantia nigra contains a concentration of neurons that produce the neurotransmitter called dopamine.

- The outer portion of the forebrain is called the cerebral cortex, which is divided into two cerebral hemispheres. Each hemisphere is roughly divided into four lobes. The temporal lobe contains the primary auditory cortex, where auditory information is received. The occipital lobe contains the primary visual cortex, where visual information is received. The parietal lobe contains the somatosensory cortex, where body sensations are registered. And the frontal lobe contains the primary motor cortex, where voluntary muscle movements originate. The remainder of the cerebral cortex is composed of association areas, which are thought to be involved in processing and integrating sensory and motor information.

- Beneath the cerebral cortex are several important structures. The thalamus distributes sensory and motor information going to and from the cerebral cortex, and is involved in regulating attention, awareness, motivation, and emotional aspects of sensations. The hypothalamus regulates the autonomic nervous system and the endocrine system, and is involved in behaviors related to survival, including hunger, fear, and aggression. The hippocampus is involved in the ability to form new memories. The amygdala helps control emotional response patterns involving fear, anger, or disgust. Combined, these structures along with regions of the frontal cortex, form the limbic system. The limbic system structures form neural circuits that play critical roles in learning, memory, and emotional control.

Specialization in the Cerebral Hemispheres

- The first clinical evidence for the specialized abilities of the two cerebral hemispheres occurred in the mid-1800s, when it was discovered that damage to the left hemisphere produced different forms of aphasia, such as Broca's aphasia and Wernicke's aphasia.

- More evidence for the specialized abilities of the two hemispheres has resulted from the split-brain operation, in which the corpus callosum connecting the two hemispheres is cut to reduce epileptic seizures. Using special testing procedures that directed information to just one hemisphere, Roger Sperry and his colleagues demonstrated the different strengths of each hemisphere. The left hemisphere is specialized for language tasks, while the right hemisphere is superior at visual-spatial tasks.

Key Terms

biological psychology (p. 43)

neuron (p. 44)

glial cells (p. 45)

sensory neuron (p. 45)

motor neuron (p. 45)

interneuron (p. 45)

cell body (p. 46)

dendrites (p. 46)

axon (p. 47)

myelin sheath (p. 47)

action potential (p. 47)

stimulus threshold (p. 48)

resting potential (p. 48)

all-or-none law (p. 48)

synapse (p. 50)

synaptic gap (p. 50)

axon terminals (p. 50)

synaptic vesicles (p. 50)

neurotransmitter (p. 50)

synaptic transmission (p. 50)

reuptake (p. 50)

acetylcholine (p. 54)

dopamine (p. 55)

serotonin (p. 55)

norepinephrine (p. 55)

endorphins (p. 56)

nervous system (p. 56)

nerve (p. 57)

central nervous system (p. 57)

spinal reflexes (p. 58)

peripheral nervous system (p. 59)

somatic nervous system (p. 59)

autonomic nervous system (p. 59)

sympathetic nervous system (p. 60)

parasympathetic nervous system (p. 61)

endocrine system (p. 62)

hormones (p. 62)

pituitary gland (p. 63)

adrenal glands (p. 63)

adrenal cortex (p. 63)

adrenal medulla (p. 63)

gonads (p. 64)

brain (p. 64)

electroencephalograph (p. 67)

CAT scan (computerized axial tomography) (p. 67)

magnetic resonance imaging scanner (MRI) (p. 67)

PET scan (positron emission tomography) (p. 67)

brainstem (p. 70)

hindbrain (p. 70)

medulla (p. 71)

pons (p. 72)

cerebellum (p. 72)

reticular formation (p. 72)

midbrain (p. 72)

substantia nigra (p. 72)

forebrain (p. 73)

cerebral cortex (p. 73)

cerebral hemispheres (p. 73)

corpus callosum (p. 73)

temporal lobe (p. 74)

occipital lobe (p. 74)

parietal lobe (p. 74)

frontal lobe (p. 74)

association areas (p. 75)

thalamus (p. 77)

hypothalamus (p. 77)

hippocampus (p. 78)

amygdala (p. 78)

limbic system (p. 78)

aphasia (p. 81)

split-brain operation (p. 83)

structural plasticity (p. 87)

Key People

Pierre Paul Broca (1824–1880) French surgeon and neuroanatomist who in 1861 discovered an area on the lower left frontal lobe of the cerebral cortex that, when damaged, produces speech disturbances but no loss of comprehension.

Roger Sperry (1913–1994) American psychologist who received the Nobel Prize in 1981 for his pioneering research on brain specialization in split-brain patients.

Karl Wernicke (1848–1905) German neurologist who in 1874 discovered an area on the left temporal lobe of the cerebral cortex that, when damaged, produces meaningless or nonsensical speech and difficulties in verbal or written comprehension.

CONCEPT REVIEW 2.1 Page 52

1. c
2. f
3. a
4. e
5. d
6. b

CONCEPT REVIEW 2.2 Page 64

1. c
2. b
3. d
4. d
5. a

CONCEPT REVIEW 2.3 Page 68

1. PET
2. MRI
3. EEG
4. CAT

CONCEPT REVIEW 2.4 Page 80

1. hindbrain; midbrain; forebrain
2. cerebellum
3. corpus callosum
4. temporal
5. primary motor cortex; frontal
6. hippocampus
7. limbic system

CONCEPT REVIEW 2.5 Page 86

1. right hemisphere
2. Wernicke's area
3. corpus callosum
4. Broca's area
5. left hemisphere

Chapter

3 Sensation and Perception

Prologue: Don't Ask These Guys to Stop and Smell the Roses

We have two good friends, quite dissimilar in most ways, who share one common characteristic—they have no sense of smell. Paul is an electrical engineer in his late twenties; Warren is a well-known professor of psychology some twenty years older. Although you might guess this condition to be extremely rare, the inability to smell (called *anosmia*) is relatively common, occurring in about 1 in 500 people (Engen, 1991).

Paul was born without a sense of smell, a fact he was completely unaware of until he was about ten years old. Paul's mother asked him to smell an arrangement of freshly cut flowers, but the puzzled child could detect nothing. Paul wasn't particularly concerned by the realization, but he did learn to compensate for his lack of smell.

For example, one day in high school chemistry class, the instructor picked Paul to demonstrate the distinctiveness of certain chemical odors. The teacher placed a beaker on the table in front of Paul with the label facing away from him and asked him to identify the chemical by its smell. Paul reached for the beaker, turned it slightly so that he could sneak a quick glance at the label, and sniffed deeply. "Ammonia," he said.

Because Paul has never experienced smell, it's impossible for him even to imagine what a smell smells like. Friends have tried to describe the aroma of garlic, flowers, burning leaves, and so forth. But, like trying to describe the color red to someone who's been blind since birth, it's almost impossible to describe one smell without relating it to another. Try it and you'll see what we mean. How would you describe the smell of steaks barbecuing? a new car? a locker room? sour milk?

As you'll discover in this chapter, the senses of taste and smell are closely related, and the flavor of a food is strongly tied to its aroma. That's part of the reason that food often tastes bland or "cardboardy" when you have a bad head cold. What does food taste like for Paul? Just as it's hard for us to describe odors to Paul, it's hard for Paul to describe the way he experiences food.

Paul is married to Asha, whom you met in Chapter 2. Asha cooks some wonderfully spicy Indian meals. When she tries out different Indian dishes on Paul, Asha has discovered that Paul bases many of his food preferences on the *texture* of foods instead of on their flavor. For example, Paul dislikes noodles because their texture seems "slimy" to him. He also dislikes the sensation of certain textures combined, like nuts in ice cream or brownies. Other foods, like chocolate, have no taste at all.

Unlike Paul, Warren knows what he's missing. Warren was born with a normal sense of smell, but as a young man he underwent major surgery to repair an artery at the front of his brain. To get to the artery, the surgeon had to cut through the sensory nerves for smell, destroying Warren's sense of smell.

For several days following the surgery, Warren's eyes were swollen shut. Deprived of both visual and odor cues, he was unable to identify many of the foods he was fed. For example, he couldn't tell the difference among strawberry, chocolate, and vanilla pudding—they all tasted the same to him. And like Paul, Warren found that the texture of different foods became much more significant. For example, peanut butter now tasted like "oily sand" to Warren.

At first, the experience of taste was very different for Warren than it had been before the surgery. He experimented with familiar as well as new and unusual foods to see how they would taste. However, in the years following his surgery, Warren learned to compensate for the missing sense of smell, at least for its role in taste. Now, many years later, Warren has become accustomed to the way things taste, despite the lack of smell cues.

Another aspect of Warren's experience illustrates the critical role played by the brain in interpreting our sensations. Even today, years after the surgery, Warren is still able to reconstruct memories of a few very specific smells when the stimulus is presented. What stimulus produces the most powerful memory trigger for Warren? The sight of the litter box for the family cats.

In this chapter we'll explore how we sense the world around us and how the brain integrates and interprets those sensory signals to form meaningful perceptions. As we go along, we'll tell you more about our friends Paul and Warren.

Introduction
Sensation and Perception

Glance around you. Notice the incredible variety of colors, shades, shadows, and images. Listen carefully to the diversity of sounds, loud and soft, near and far. Focus on everything that's touching you—your clothes, your shoes, the chair you're sitting on. Now, inhale deeply through your nose and identify the aromas in the air.

With these simple observations you have exercised four of your senses: vision, hearing, touch, and smell. As we saw in Chapter 2, the primary function of the nervous system is communication—the transmission of information from one part of the body to the other. Where does that information come from? Put simply, your senses are the gateway through which your brain receives all its information about the environment. It's a process that is so nat-

sensation
The process of detecting a physical stimulus, such as light, sound, heat, or pressure.

perception
The process of integrating, organizing, and interpreting sensations.

sensory receptors
Specialized cells unique to each sense organ that respond to a particular form of sensory stimulation.

ural and automatic that we typically take it for granted until something happens, as it did to Paul and Warren. As Paul and Warren demonstrate, people with one nonfunctional sense are amazingly adaptive. Other senses may compensate for the missing environmental information.

In this chapter, we will explore the overlapping processes of *sensation* and *perception*. **Sensation** refers to the sensory processes—the virtually instantaneous and basic experiences generated by environmental stimuli, such as sounds, objects, and airborne molecules. **Perception** occurs when we integrate, organize, and interpret sensory information in a way that is meaningful (Matlin & Foley, 1992). Here's a simple example to contrast the two terms. Being able to detect splotches of color and edges reflects *sensation*. Integrating and organizing those sensations so that we interpret the splotches of color and edges as a painting, a flag, a calendar, or some other object reflects *perception*.

Where does the process of sensation leave off and the process of perception begin? There is no clear boundary line between the two processes as we actually experience them. In fact, many researchers in this area of psychology regard sensation and perception as a single process (Coren & others, 1994).

Although the two processes overlap, in this chapter we will present sensation and perception as separate discussions. In the first half we'll discuss the basics of *sensation*—how our sensory receptors respond to stimulation and transmit that information in usable form to the brain. In the second half of the chapter, we'll explore *perception*—how the brain actively organizes and interprets the signals sent from our sensory receptors.

Some Basic Principles of Sensation

Sensation is the result of stimulation of sensory receptors by some form of physical energy, which is converted into neural impulses and transmitted to the brain. What are the two types of sensory thresholds? How do Weber's Law and sensory adaptation demonstrate that the experience of sensation is relative?

Imagine biting into a crisp red apple. You experience a broad range of sensations: the sound of the apple crunching, the sweet-sour taste of the apple, its distinctive aroma, the smooth feel of the apple's skin against your hand, the mellow red of the apple's skin. We're accustomed to thinking of these sensory experiences as quite different. However, all of our senses involve some common processes.

All sensation is a result of the stimulation of specialized cells called **sensory receptors** by some form of *energy*. Your experience of hearing the apple crunching is a response to the physical energy of vibrations in the air, or *sound waves*. The sweet taste of the apple is a response to the physical energy of *dissolvable chemicals* in your mouth, just as the distinctive sharp aroma of the apple is a response to *airborne chemical molecules* that you inhale through your nose. The smooth feel of the apple's skin is a response to the *pressure* of the apple against your hand. And the red color is a response to the physical energy of *light waves* reflecting from the irregularly shaped object that you've just bitten into.

Sensory receptors convert the different forms of physical energy into electrical impulses that are then transmitted via neurons to the brain. The process by which a form of physical energy is converted into a coded neural

Experiencing the World Through Our Senses Imagine biting into a crisp, red apple. All of your senses are involved in your experience—vision, smell, taste, hearing, and touch. Although we're accustomed to thinking of our different senses as being quite distinct, all forms of sensation involve the stimulation of specialized cells called sensory receptors.

Sensation → Perception

We experience some type of stimulus, usually in the form of environmental information such as sounds, light, or odors.

The stimulus activates specialized receptor cells in the appropriate sense organ.

A coded neural message is sent along a specific sensory nerve to the brain.

The neural message is decoded and interpreted in the brain as a meaningful perception.

It's a rose!

FIGURE 3.1 How We Sense and Perceive the World
For all of our senses, moving from sensation to perception is a continuous process that involves four basic steps.

signal that can be processed by the nervous system is called **transduction.** These neural signals are sent to the brain, where the perceptual processes of organizing and interpreting the coded messages occur. In Figure 3.1, you can see the basic steps involved in sensation and perception.

We are constantly being bombarded by many different forms of energy. For instance, at this very moment radio and television waves are bouncing around the atmosphere and passing through your body. However, sensory receptors are so highly specialized that they are only sensitive to very specific types of energy (which is lucky, or you might be hearing Top 40 tunes or seeing *I Love Lucy* reruns in your brain right now). The important point here is that for any type of stimulation to be sensed, the stimulus energy must first be in a form that can be detected by our sensory receptor cells. Otherwise, transduction cannot occur.

TABLE 3.1 Absolute Thresholds

Sense	Absolute Threshold
Vision	A candle flame seen from thirty miles away on a clear, dark night
Hearing	The tick of a watch at twenty feet
Taste	One teaspoon of sugar in two gallons of water
Smell	One drop of perfume throughout a three-room apartment
Touch	A bee's wing falling on your cheek from a height of about half an inch

Psychologist Eugene Galanter (1962) has provided these examples of the absolute thresholds for our senses. In each case, people are able to sense these faint stimuli at least half the time.

Sensory Thresholds

Along with being specialized as to the types of energy that can be detected, our senses are specialized in other ways as well. We do not have an infinite capacity to detect all levels of energy. If we did, you would probably find it hard to concentrate on studying because you might hear not just your next-door neighbor's stereo but also the hum of her computer and the sound of her breathing. To be sensed, a stimulus must first be strong enough to be detected—loud enough to be heard, concentrated enough to be smelled, bright enough to be seen. The point at which a stimulus is strong enough to be detected by activating a sensory receptor cell is called a **sensory threshold.** There are two general kinds of sensory thresholds for each sense—the absolute threshold and the difference threshold.

The **absolute threshold** refers to the smallest possible strength of a stimulus that can be detected half the time. Why just half the time? Because the minimum level of stimulation that can be detected varies from person to person and from trial to trial. Because of such human variability, researchers have arbitrarily set the limit as the minimum level of stimulation that can be detected half the time. Under ideal conditions (which rarely occur in normal daily life), our sensory abilities are far more sensitive than you might think. Table 3.1 provides examples of the absolute thresholds for our senses.

While absolute thresholds describe the minimum levels of stimuli that we can detect, another important threshold involves detecting the *difference* be-

transduction
The process by which a form of physical energy is converted into a coded neural signal that can be processed by the nervous system.

sensory threshold
The level at which a stimulus is strong enough to be detected by activating sensory receptors.

absolute threshold
The smallest possible strength of a stimulus that can be detected half the time.

difference threshold
The smallest possible difference between two stimuli that can be detected half the time. Also called **just noticeable difference.**

just noticeable difference (jnd)
The smallest possible difference between two stimuli that can be detected half the time. Also called **difference threshold.**

Weber's Law
A principle of sensation that holds that the size of the just noticeable difference will vary depending on its relation to the strength of the original stimulus.

sensory adaptation
The decline in sensitivity to a constant stimulus.

tween two stimuli. The **difference threshold** is the smallest possible difference between two stimuli that can be detected half the time. Another term for difference threshold is **just noticeable difference,** which is abbreviated **jnd.**

The just noticeable difference will *vary* depending on its relation to the original stimulus. This principle of sensation is called **Weber's Law.** It holds that for each sense, the size of a just noticeable difference is a constant proportion of the size of the initial stimulus. So, whether or not we can detect a change in the strength of a stimulus depends on the intensity of the *original* stimulus. For example, if you are holding a pebble (the original stimulus), you will notice an increase in weight if a second pebble is placed in your hand. But if you start off holding a very heavy rock (the original stimulus), you probably won't detect an increase in weight when the same pebble is balanced on it.

What Weber's Law underscores is that our psychological experience of sensation is *relative*. There is no simple one-to-one correspondence between the objective characteristics of a physical stimulus, such as the weight of a pebble, and our psychological experience of it.

Sensory Adaptation

Suppose your best friend has invited you over for a spaghetti dinner. As you walk in the front door, you're almost overwhelmed by the odor of onions and garlic cooking on the stove. However, after just a few moments, you no longer notice the smell. This example demonstrates another characteristic of our senses. After being exposed to a steady stimulus for a time, we become less aware of it. Why? Because our sensory receptor cells become less responsive to a constant stimulus. This gradual decline in sensitivity to a constant stimulus is called **sensory adaptation.** Once again, this illustrates that our experience of sensation is relative—in this case, relative to the *duration of exposure*.

Because of sensory adaptation, we become accustomed to constant stimuli. This allows us to quickly notice new or changing stimuli. This makes sense: if we were continually aware of *all* incoming stimuli, we'd be so overwhelmed with sensory information that we wouldn't be able to focus our attention. Thus, once we manage to land our posterior on the sofa, we don't need to be constantly reminded that the sofa is beneath us.

CONCEPT REVIEW 3.1

Introduction and Vision

1. Sensation is to perception as _____ is to _____.
   a. detection; interpretation
   b. interpretation; organization
   c. integration; interpretation
   d. adaptation; transduction

2. When a researcher presented many sounds at very low levels of intensity, Natalie could detect them less than 50 percent of the time. These sounds were below Natalie's
   a. difference threshold
   b. just noticeable difference level
   c. sensory adaptation level
   d. absolute threshold

3. Which of the following is an example of sensory adaptation?
   a. not noticing how cold the water is after you have been in the pool for a while
   b. increased reliance on hearing when you are blindfolded
   c. exiting the building immediately when you hear the fire alarm
   d. covering your ears at an extremely loud rock concert

4. Sensory receptors convert different forms of physical energy into neural signals through the process of
   a. sensory adaptation   c. transduction
   b. accommodation   d. Weber's Law

Vision: From Light to Sight

*The sense organ for vision is the eye, which contains receptor cells
that are sensitive to the physical energy of light. What is the visible spectrum? What are the key structures of the eye, and how is
each structure involved in vision?*

A lone caterpillar on the screen door, the pile of dirty laundry in the corner of
the closet, a spectacular autumn sunset, the bowl of multicolored Sugar
Bombs in front of you at breakfast. You glance at the Sunday comics or examine the intricate play of color, light, and texture in a painting by Monet.
All these sensations involve vision; but what is vision and how does it occur?

The sense organ for vision is the eye, which contains receptor cells that
are sensitive to the physical energy of *light*. Before we can talk about how the
eye functions, we need to discuss briefly some characteristics of light as the
visual stimulus.

What We See:

The Nature of Light

Light is just one of many different kinds of electromagnetic energy that travel
in the form of waves. Other forms of electromagnetic energy include X-rays,
the microwaves you use to bake a potato, and the ultraviolet rays that give
you a sunburn. These different types of electromagnetic energy differ in terms
of their **wavelength,** which is the distance from one wave peak to another.
Figure 3.2 shows the spectrum of different forms of electromagnetic energy.

Humans are capable of visually detecting only a minuscule portion of the
electromagnetic energy range. In Figure 3.2, notice that the *visible* portion of
the electromagnetic energy spectrum can be further divided into different
wavelengths. As we'll discuss in more detail later, the different wavelengths
of visible light correspond to our psychological perception of different colors.

FIGURE 3.2 The Electromagnetic Spectrum
We are surrounded by different kinds of electromagnetic energy waves, yet we are able to see
only a tiny portion of the entire spectrum of electromagnetic energy. Electronic instruments, like
radio and television, are specialized receivers that
detect a specific wavelength range. In a similar
fashion, the human eye is sensitive to only a very
narrow range of wavelengths.

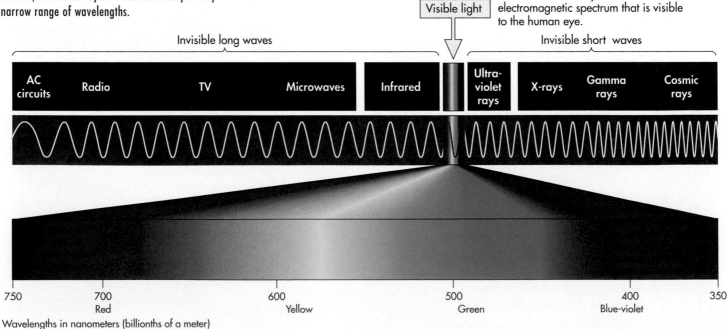

Notice the incredibly narrow band of the
electromagnetic spectrum that is visible
to the human eye.

Visible light

Invisible long waves

Invisible short waves

| AC circuits | Radio | TV | Microwaves | Infrared | | Ultra-violet rays | X-rays | Gamma rays | Cosmic rays |

750   700   600   500   400   350
Red   Yellow   Green   Blue-violet

Wavelengths in nanometers (billionths of a meter)

How a Pit Viper Sees a Mouse at Night
Does the world look different to other species? In many cases, yes. Each species has evolved a unique set of sensory capabilities. Pit vipers "see" infrared light, which we sense only as warmth. In the photo, the mouse has been photographed through an infrared viewer. The image shows how a pit viper uses its infrared "vision" to detect warm-blooded prey at night (Gould & Gould, 1994). Similarly, many insect and bird species can detect ultraviolet light, which is invisible to humans.

How We See:
The Human Visual System

Suppose you're watching your neighbor's yellow and white tabby cat sun himself on the front steps. How do you "see" the cat? Simply to see a yellow tabby cat involves a complex chain of events. We'll describe the process of vision from the object to the brain. You can trace the path of light waves through the eye in Figure 3.3.

First, lightwaves reflected from the cat enter the eye, passing through the *cornea, pupil,* and *lens.* The **cornea** is a clear membrane that covers the eye and that helps gather and direct incoming light. The **pupil** is the black opening in the middle of your eye. The pupil is surrounded by the **iris,** the colored structure that we refer to when we say that someone has brown or blue eyes. The iris is actually a ring of muscles that contracts or expands to precisely control the size of the pupil, and thus the amount of light entering the eye. In dim light, the iris widens the pupil to let light in; in bright light, the iris narrows the pupil.

FIGURE 3.3 Path of a Light Wave Through the Human Eye
Light waves pass through the cornea, pupil, and lens. The iris controls the amount of light entering the eye by controlling the size of the pupil. The lens changes shape to focus the incoming light onto the retina. As the light strikes the retina, the light energy activates the rods and cones. Information from the rods and cones is collected by the bipolar cells, which transmit the information to the ganglion cells. The ganglion cell axons are bundled together to form the optic nerve, which transmits the information to the brain. There is a "blind spot" in our field of vision where the optic nerve leaves the eye (see Figure 3.5).

CRITICAL THINKING 3.1

Iridology: Science Versus Pseudoscience

A *pseudoscience* is a fake science that makes extraordinary claims on the basis of little or no scientific evidence (see Chapter 1). To appear credible, pseudoscientists use lots of scientific terminology and often create elaborate charts or graphs. They frequently refer to commonly known scientific facts, which they intertwine with unproven or disproven pseudoscientific notions. When confronted with objective evidence that disputes their claims, pseudoscientists tend to ignore it, dismiss it, or create new unfounded claims (Hines, 1988).

The currently popular pseudoscience called **iridology** (pronounced EYE-ruh-*doll*-uh-jee) demonstrates all

An Iridologist's Map of the Eye According to proponents of iridology, specific areas of the iris correspond to areas of the body and psychological functions. Using elaborate maps of the iris like the one shown here, iridologists look for irregularities in the flecks of color in the iris to evaluate physical and mental health.

these qualities. Iridology is based on the unproven notion that physical and psychological functioning are reflected in the iris, the colored part of your eye (Barrett, 1996). Iridologists claim that simply examining the color and markings of your iris with a magnifying glass can supposedly reveal a wealth of information about you—including your level of mental stress and the presence of mental disorders; your personality characteristics, genetic tendencies, nutritional deficiencies, and drug history; and your past diseases and injuries (Jackson, 1993; Jensen & Bodeen, 1992). Iridologists use highly detailed charts, like the one shown, to "diagnose" such characteristics. They also recommend that you have your eyes "read" about once a year to detect any significant changes.

How have the notions of iridology stood up to scientific investigation? In one study, iridologists were asked to evaluate iris photographs of subjects taken before and after they had developed an acute disease (see Worrall, 1986). They were asked to state whether a change in the iris had occurred and which organ was affected. The iridologists found that one before-and-after set of photographs indicated clear-cut changes. Unfortunately for the iridologists, those two photographs of the same individual had been taken only two minutes apart and were part of the control conditions for the experiment.

In another study, three iridologists and three ophthalmologists (physicians with specialized training in diseases of the eye) were asked to judge iris photographs of 143 subjects. Of these subjects, 48 had kidney disease, which can supposedly be detected quite easily

using iridology. The ophthalmologists acted as an expert control group in the study. Ophthalmologists do not normally claim to be able to diagnose kidney disease from examining the eye, but in this case they were instructed to try to judge kidney function with "whatever methods they could best do so" (Simon & others, 1979).

The iridologists correctly predicted whether subjects had kidney disease 49 percent of the time. The ophthalmologists were equally unimpressive, correctly identifying the subjects with kidney disease 53 percent of the time. In other words, both groups were about as accurate as you would be if you simply flipped a coin.

Such controlled scientific studies have failed to confirm the extraordinary claims of iridology. How do iridologists respond to such scientific scrutiny? One leading iridology expert defensively countered: "Iridology is based on scientific observation. It is the kind of science that cannot be related through scientific tests" (Jensen, 1980). Evidently so. Since iridology was founded over a hundred years ago, advocates of iridology have failed to publish even one well-documented study to support their claims (Worrall, 1986).

At best, iridology is simply another popular, though ludicrous, fad. At worst, it is a potentially dangerous pseudoscience. Individuals with serious physical or psychological problems may delay consulting legitimate professionals, instead relying on the "expert" advice of an iridologist. Or people with no actual health problems may spend money on expensive medical tests solely on the basis of an iridologist's "diagnosis" of the iris. Perhaps the most disturbing aspect of popular pseudosciences like iridology and graphology (discussed in Chapter 1) is how easily many people will suspend their abilities to question evidence and think critically.

Slim Rods and Fat Cones The rods and cones in the retina are the sensory receptors for vision, converting light into electrical impulses that are transmitted, ultimately, to the brain. This photograph shows the rods and cones magnified about 45,000 times. The rods are long and thin; the cones are shorter, fatter, and tapered at one end. As you can see, the rods and cones are densely packed in the retina, with many rods surrounding a single cone or pair of cones.

lens
A transparent structure located behind the pupil that actively focuses, or bends, light as it enters the eye.

accommodation
The process by which the lens changes shape to focus incoming light so that it falls on the retina.

retina
(RET-in-uh) A thin, light-sensitive membrane located at the back of the eye that contains the sensory receptors for vision.

rods
The long, thin, blunt sensory receptors of the eye that are highly sensitive to light but not color and are primarily responsible for peripheral vision and night vision.

cones
The short, thick, pointed sensory receptors of the eye that detect color and are responsible for color vision and visual acuity.

Behind the pupil is the **lens,** another transparent structure. In a process called **accommodation,** the lens thins or thickens in order to bend or focus the incoming light so that the light falls on the retina. The **retina** is a thin, light-sensitive membrane that lies at the back of the eye, covering most of its inner surface (see Figure 3.3). The retina contains the two kinds of sensory receptors for light: the **rods** and **cones.** When exposed to light, the rods and cones undergo a chemical reaction that results in a neural signal. The rods and cones play an extremely important role in vision, so we'll describe them in some detail.

Rods and Cones

> *The sensory receptors for vision are the rods and cones in the retina. How are rods and cones different? What is their role in the adaptation to bright and dim light and in peripheral vision?*

Rods and cones differ in many ways. First, as their names imply, rods and cones are shaped differently. Rods are long and thin, with blunt ends; cones are shorter and fatter, with one end that tapers to a point. The eye contains far more rods than cones. It is estimated that each eye contains about 7 million cones and about *125 million* rods!

Rods and cones are specialized for different visual functions. Rods are hundreds of times more sensitive to light than cones are. We rely on the rods for our vision in dim light and at night. However, rods are *not* involved in color vision. Cones require much more light than rods to function effectively. We rely on our cones for vision in bright light, for seeing fine details, and for color vision.

Adaptation to Light and Dark

Rods and cones also react differently to changes in the amount of light. You may have noticed that it takes you a long time to become accustomed to the dimness of a dark movie theater. That's because it takes about thirty minutes for the rods to reach maximum sensitivity to light. Once the rods are fully adapted to the dark, they are about a thousand times better at detecting weak visual stimuli than cones are (Uttal, 1981).

You've probably also noticed that when the lights are turned on at the end of the film, you adapt quickly, blinking only for a few moments. That's because the cones adapt much more quickly than the rods do. It only takes about five minutes for the cones to reach their maximum sensitivity to the available light.

Peripheral Vision

Rods are most prevalent in the *periphery,* or outlying areas, of the retina. When you see something "out of the corner of your eye," you are using your peripheral vision and relying primarily on your rods. However, there are a few cones in the peripheral areas of the retina. That's why the world doesn't suddenly become black and white on the edges of your visual field.

Because rods are more sensitive to light than cones, at night or in a dimly lit room you will actually be able to see better if you use peripheral vision (relying on your rods) than if you look directly in front of you (using your cones). If there's a particular object that you want to view in dim light, look slightly above, below, or to the side of it. Try this when looking at a star at night—a trick that astronomers and sailors have known for hundreds of years.

Visual Processing in the Retina

Signals from the rods and cones undergo preliminary processing in the bipolar and ganglion cells of the retina before being transmitted to the brain. How are signals processed in the bipolar and ganglion cells? What is the fovea? How does information travel from the retina to the brain?

Visual information is mostly processed in the brain. However, before the visual information is sent to the brain, it undergoes some preliminary processing in the retina (see Figure 3.3). Information from the sensory receptors, the rods and cones, is collected by specialized neurons called *bipolar cells.* The bipolar cells, in turn, funnel the information to other specialized neurons called *ganglion cells.* The signals from the rods and the cones are combined and integrated in the bipolar and ganglion cells of the retina before they are sent to the brain. This preliminary processing of visual data in the cells of the retina is possible because the retina actually developed from a bit of brain tissue that "migrated" to the eye during fetal development (see Hubel, 1995).

When the number of rods and cones are combined, there are over 130 million receptor cells. However, there are only about one million ganglion cells. How do just one million ganglion cells transmit messages from 130 million visual receptor cells?

The answer has to do with an important difference in the way that signals from rods and cones are processed in the bipolar and ganglion cells. For the most part, a single ganglion cell receives information from only one or two cones. However, a single ganglion cell might well receive information from a *hundred* or more rods. Because the messages from many different rods are combined in the retina before being sent on to the brain, the visual information transmitted by the rods is far less specific. The cones can send messages of much greater visual detail to the brain.

As an analogy to how rod information is processed, imagine a hundred people trying to talk at once over the same telephone line. You would hear the sound of many people talking, but individual voices would be blurred. With cone vision, imagine the voice of a single individual being transmitted across the same telephone line. Every syllable and sound would be clear and distinct. In much the same way, cones use the ganglion cells to provide the brain with much more specific visual information than do rods.

Because of this difference in the way information is processed, the cones are especially important in *visual acuity,* which refers to the ability to see fine details. Most of the cones are concentrated in the **fovea,** which is a tiny region in the very center of the retina. There are *no* rods in the fovea. If you watch a friend read, you'll notice that his eyes make small movements as he follows the letters across the page. That's because he is moving the fovea of each eye into position over the words that he is reading. Visual acuity is strongest when images are focused on the fovea because of the high concentration of cones there.

Cones become less and less frequent as you move away from the fovea to the periphery of the retina. Focus your eyes on a single word on this page. You'll notice that words a bit to the left and right are somewhat blurry in contrast to the sharpness of the word you're focusing on. That's because the image of the "outlying" words is striking the peripheral areas of the retina, where cones are much less common.

Images that do not fall on the fovea tend be perceived as blurry or indistinct. Visual problems such as *nearsightedness* and *farsightedness* result when images are not properly focused on the retina. These common disorders are explained in Figure 3.4.

fovea
(FOH-vee-uh) A small area in the center of the retina that is composed entirely of cones where visual information is most sharply focused.

optic nerve
The thick nerve that exits from the back of the eye and carries visual information to the visual cortex in the brain.

blind spot
The point where the optic nerve leaves the eye, producing a small gap in the field of vision.

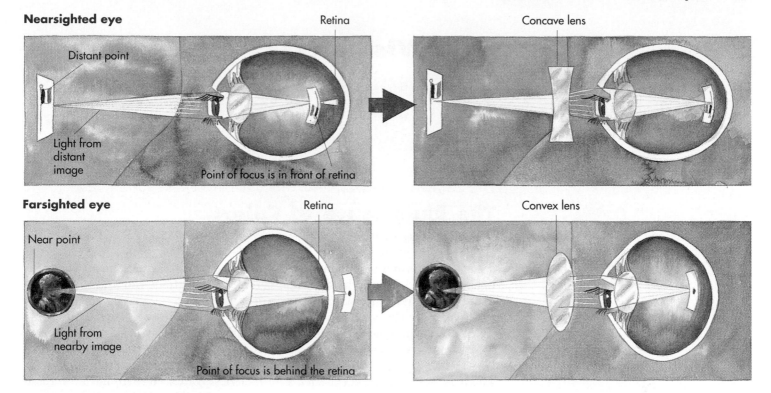

Nearsighted eye

Distant point

Retina

Light from distant image

Point of focus is in front of retina

Concave lens

Farsighted eye

Near point

Retina

Light from nearby image

Point of focus is behind the retina

Convex lens

FIGURE 3.4 Common Visual Disorders: Nearsightedness and Farsightedness
Nearsightedness and farsightedness, common visual disorders, are both caused by an abnormally shaped eyeball. In each case, the lens does not properly focus the incoming light onto the retina. Corrective lenses intercept and bend the light before it reaches the eye, so that the image falls properly on the retina. The thickness and curvature of the corrective lens determines where the image falls.

From Eye to Brain

How does information travel from the retina to the brain? The axons of the ganglion cells are bundled together to form the **optic nerve,** a thick nerve that exits from the back of the eye and extends to the brain. About the diameter of a pencil, the optic nerve transmits messages from the rods and cones to the thalamus in the brain. From the thalamus, the signals are sent to the visual cortex, where they are decoded and interpreted. Most of the receiving neurons in the visual cortex of the brain are highly specialized (Logothetis & Sheinberg, 1996). Each responds to a particular type of visual stimulation, such as angles, edges, lines, and other forms, and even to the movement and distance of objects (Hubel, 1995; Livingstone & Hubel, 1988).

Interestingly, there are no rods and cones in the area where the optic nerve leaves the eye. Consequently, there is a tiny hole or **blind spot** in your field of vision. Try the demonstration described in Figure 3.5 to locate your blind spot (and prove to yourself that it really exists!).

Why don't we notice this "hole" in our visual images? Some researchers have suggested that we simply don't notice that any information is missing because the blind spot is located in an area where there are few receptors. Another explanation is that the brain actually "fills in" the missing information (Ramachandran, 1992a, 1992b). In effect, the brain "paves over" the blind spot with the colors and patterns of the surrounding visual information.

FIGURE 3.5 Demonstration of the Blind Spot
To prove to yourself that you really do have a blind spot, try this simple demonstration. Hold the book a few feet in front of you. Close your right eye and stare at the insect spray can with your left eye. Slowly bring the book toward your face. At some point the spider will disappear, because you have focused it onto the part of your retina where the blind spot is. Notice, however, that you still perceive the spiderweb. That's because information has been "filled in" from the surrounding area.

Color Vision

Different wavelengths of light correspond to our perceptual experience of different colors. What three properties of light determine the color that is perceived? What is white light? What determines the color of an object?

The Experience of Color:

What Makes an Orange Orange?

We see images of an apple, a banana, and an orange because these objects reflect light waves. But why do we perceive the apple to be red and the banana to be yellow? What makes an orange orange?

To explain the nature of color, we must go back to the visual stimulus—light. Our experience of **color** involves three properties of the light wave. First, what we usually refer to as color is a property more accurately termed **hue.** Hue varies with the wavelength of light. *Different wavelengths correspond to our subjective experience of different colors.* Wavelengths of about 400 nanometers are perceived as violet; wavelengths of about 700 nanometers are perceived as red. In between are orange, yellow, green, and blue.

Second, the **saturation,** or *purity,* of the color corresponds to the purity of the light wave. Pure red, for example, produced by a single wavelength, would be more *saturated* than pink, which is produced by a combination of wavelengths (red plus white light). In everyday language, saturation refers to the richness of a color. A highly saturated color is vivid and rich, while a less saturated color is faded and washed out.

The third aspect of color is its **brightness** or its perceived intensity. Brightness corresponds to the amplitude of the light wave. These three properties of color—hue, saturation, and brightness—are responsible for the amazing range of colors we experience. If you have normal color vision, you can discriminate from 120 to 150 color differences based on differences in hue, or wavelength, alone. When saturation and brightness are also factored in, you can potentially perceive millions of different colors (Bornstein & Marks, 1982).

Many people mistakenly believe that white light contains no color. White light actually contains *all wavelengths,* and thus *all colors,* of the visible part of the electromagnetic spectrum. A glass prism placed in sunlight creates a rainbow because it separates sunlight into all the colors of the visible light spectrum.

So we're back to the question: Why is an orange orange? Common sense tells us that the color of an object is an inseparable property of the object (unless we paint it, dye it, or spill spaghetti sauce on it). But actually, *the color of any object is determined by the wavelength of light that the object reflects.* If your T-shirt is red, it's red because the cloth is *reflecting* only the wavelength of light that corresponds to the red portion of the spectrum. The T-shirt is *absorbing* the wavelengths that correspond to all other colors. An object appears white because it *reflects* all the wavelengths of visible light and absorbs none. An object appears black, on the other hand, when it *absorbs* all the wavelengths of visible light and reflects none. In reality, color corresponds to our perception of certain wavelengths of light.

When Red + Blue + Yellow = White
When light waves of different wavelengths are combined, the wavelengths are added together, producing the perception of a different color. Thus, when green light is combined with red light, yellow light is produced. When the wavelengths of red, green, and blue light are added together, we perceive the blended light as being white.

How We See Color:
The Process of Color Vision

Color vision has been explained by two competing theories: the trichromatic theory and the opponent-process theory. How does each theory explain color vision? Why are both theories said to be correct?

Color vision has interested scientists for hundreds of years. The first truly scientific theory of color vision was proposed by Hermann von Helmholz (1821–1894) in the mid-1800s and was called the *trichromatic theory*. A rival theory, the *opponent-process theory,* was proposed in the late 1800s. Each theory was capable of explaining some aspects of color vision, but neither theory could explain all aspects of color vision. Technological advances in the last few decades allowed researchers to gather direct physiological evidence to test both theories. That research evidence showed that *both* theories of color vision are accurate; each theory simply describes color vision at a different stage of processing.

The Trichromatic Theory: Color Sensation at the Receptor Level

As you'll recall, only the cones are involved in color vision. According to the **trichromatic theory of color vision,** cones come in three varieties. Each variety of cone is especially sensitive to red light (long wavelengths), green light (medium wavelengths), or blue light (short wavelengths). For the sake of simplicity we will refer to red-sensitive, green-sensitive, and blue-sensitive cones, but keep in mind that there is some overlap in the wavelengths that each cone is sensitive to (Abramov & Gordon, 1994). A given cone will be *very* sensitive to one of the three colors and only slightly responsive to the other two.

When a color other than one of these three strikes the retina, it stimulates a *combination* of cones. For example, if yellow light strikes the retina, both the red-sensitive and green-sensitive cones are stimulated; purple light evokes strong reactions from red-sensitive and blue-sensitive cones. The trichromatic theory of color vision received compelling research support in 1964, when George Wald was able to show that different cones were indeed activated by red, blue, and green light. Wald later received the Nobel Prize for his work.

The trichromatic theory provides a good explanation for the most common form of **color blindness,** which is red-green color blindness. People with this deficiency cannot discriminate between red and green. That's because they have normal blue-sensitive cones, but their other cones are *either* red-sensitive or green-sensitive. Thus, red and green look the same to them.

color
The perceptual experience of different wavelengths of light, involving hue, saturation (purity), and brightness (intensity).

hue
The property of wavelengths of light known as color, with different wavelengths corresponding to our subjective experience of different colors.

saturation
The property of color that corresponds to the purity of the light wave.

brightness
The perceived intensity of a color that corresponds to the amplitude of the light wave.

trichromatic theory of color vision
The theory that the sensation of color is due to cones in the retina that are especially sensitive to red light (long wavelengths), green light (medium wavelengths), or blue light (short wavelengths).

color blindness
One of several inherited forms of color deficiency or weakness in which an individual cannot distinguish between certain colors.

The Most Common Form of Color Blindness To someone with red-green color blindness, the most common type of color deficiency, these two photographs look almost exactly the same. People with this form of color blindness have normal blue-sensitive cones, but their other cones are sensitive to either red or green.

What we commonly refer to as color blindness is really misnamed. People who are completely color-blind and only see the world in shades of gray are extremely rare—roughly one in a million persons suffer from this disorder (Hurvich, 1981). Most instances of color blindness would more accurately be described as *color deficiency.*

Color blindness is a genetically transmitted disorder. Because of the way in which it is inherited, red-green color blindness is relatively common in males, but extremely rare in females. Less than half of one percent of women are color-blind. However, approximately 8 percent of white males, and a slightly lower percentage of Asian, black, and Native American males, have some form of color deficiency (Sekuler & Blake, 1994). Because red-green color blindness is so common, most stoplights are designed so that the red light is always on top. Color-blind individuals can thus interpret traffic signals by the location of the light rather than the color.

The Opponent-Process Theory: Color Sensation Beyond the Receptors

The trichromatic theory cannot explain all aspects of color vision. One important phenomenon that it cannot account for is the afterimage. An **afterimage** is a visual experience that occurs after the original source of stimulation is no longer present. To experience an afterimage firsthand, follow the instructions in Figure 3.6. What do you see?

FIGURE 3.6 Demonstration of Afterimage
Stare at the white dot in the center of this oddly colored flag for about 30 seconds, then look at a white wall or white sheet of paper. What do you see?

Afterimages can be explained by the opponent-process theory of color vision, which proposes a mechanism of color detection entirely different from the one set forth in the trichromatic theory. According to the **opponent-process theory of color vision,** there are four basic colors, which are divided into two pairs of color-sensitive neurons: red-green and blue-yellow. The members of each pair *oppose* each other. If red is stimulated, green is inhibited. If green is stimulated, red is inhibited. Green and red cannot both be stimulated simultaneously. The same is true for the blue-yellow pair. In addition, black and white act as an opposing pair. Color, then, is sensed and encoded in terms of its proportion of red OR green, and blue OR yellow.

For example, red light would evoke a response of RED–YES • GREEN–NO in the red-green opponent pair. Yellow light would evoke a response of BLUE–NO • YELLOW–YES. Colors other than red, green, blue, and yellow activate one member of each of these pairs to differing degrees. Purple stimulates the *red* of the red-green pair *plus* the *blue* of the blue-yellow pair. Orange activates *red* in the red-green pair and *yellow* in the blue-yellow pair.

afterimage
A visual experience that occurs after the original source of stimulation is no longer present.

opponent-process theory of color vision
The theory that color vision is the product of opposing pairs of color receptors, red/green, blue/yellow, and black/white; when one member of a color pair is stimulated, the other member is inhibited.

Afterimages can easily be explained when the opponent process theory is combined with the general principle of sensory adaptation (Jameson & Hurvich, 1989). If you stare continuously at one color, sensory adaptation occurs and your visual receptors become less sensitive to that color. What happens when you subsequently stare at a white surface?

If you remember that white light is made up of the wavelengths for *all* colors, you may be able to predict the result. The receptors for the original color have adapted to the constant stimulation and are temporarily "off duty." Thus, they do not respond to that color. Instead, only the receptors for the opposing color will be activated, and you perceive the wavelength of only the *opposing* color. For example, if you stare at a patch of green, your green receptors eventually become "tired." The wavelengths for both green and red light are reflected by the white surface, but since the green receptors are "off," only the red receptors are activated. This is exactly what occurred in Figure 3.6, when staring at a green, black, and yellow flag produced an afterimage of opposing colors—in the form of a red, white, and blue American flag.

The Theories Combined: An Integrated View of Color Processing

At the beginning of this section we said that current research has shown that *both* the trichromatic theory and the opponent-process theory of color vision are accurate. How can both theories be right? It turns out that each theory correctly describes color vision at a *different level* of visual processing.

As described by the *trichromatic* theory, the cones of the retina do indeed respond to and encode color in terms of red, green, and blue. But recall that signals from the cones and rods are partially processed in the ganglion cells before being transmitted along the optic nerve to the brain. Researchers now believe that an additional level of color processing takes place in the ganglion cells.

As described by the *opponent-process* theory, the ganglion cells respond to and encode color in terms of opposing pairs (De Valois & De Valois, 1975). In the brain, the thalamus and visual cortex also encode color in terms of opponent pairs (Boynton, 1988). Consequently, both theories contribute to our understanding of the process of color vision. Each theory simply describes color vision at a different stage of visual processing (Hubel, 1995).

CONCEPT REVIEW 3.2

Vision and Color Vision

Fill in the blanks using the correct term.

1. The sensory receptors for vision are contained in the _____.

2. When a red pen was displayed in Barry's peripheral vision, he correctly identified the object but was unable to name its color. The explanation for this is that there are very few _____ in the periphery of the retina.

3. Information travels from the retina to the brain via the _____.

4. All the wavelengths of the visible part of the electromagnetic spectrum are contained in _____ light.

5. According to the _____ theory of color vision, the person with red-green color blindness has normal blue-sensitive cones.

6. When people stare at a blue circle and then shift their eyes to a white surface, the afterimage of the circle appears _____. This phenomenon can best be explained by the _____ theory of color vision.

Hearing: From Vibration to Sound

Sound waves are the physical stimuli that produce the sensation of sound. What properties of a sound wave correspond to our perception of sound?

We have hiked in a desert area that was so quiet we could hear the whir of a single grasshopper's wings in the distance. And we have waited on a subway platform where the screech of metal against metal forced us to cover our ears. The sense of hearing, or **audition,** is capable of responding to a wide range of sounds, from very soft to very loud, simple to complex, harmonious to discordant. The ability to sense and perceive very subtle differences in sound is important to physical survival, social interactions, and language development. Most of the time, all of us are bathed in sound—so much so that moments of near-silence, like our experience in the desert, can seem almost eerie.

What We Hear:

The Nature of Sound

Whether it's the ear-splitting screech of metal on metal or the subtle whir of a grasshopper's wings, *sound waves* are the physical stimuli that produce our sensory experience of sound. Usually, sound waves are produced by the rhythmic vibration of air molecules, but sound waves can be transmitted through other media too, such as water. Our perception of sound is directly related to the physical properties of sound waves (see Figure 3.7).

One of the first things that we notice about a sound is how loud it is. **Loudness** is determined by the intensity, or **amplitude,** of a sound wave, and is measured in units called **decibels.** Zero decibels represents the loudness of the softest sound that humans can hear, or the absolute threshold for hearing. As decibels increase, perceived loudness increases (see Table 3.2). For example, while a routine conversation is about 60 decibels, the loudest human scream ever recorded was measured at 128 decibels (McFarlan, 1991).

Pitch refers to the relative "highness" or "lowness" of a sound. The rumble of thunder is an example of a low-pitched sound; a child's squeal of delight is a high-pitched sound. Pitch is determined by the frequency of a sound wave. **Frequency** refers to the rate of vibration, or number of waves per second, and is measured in units called *hertz*. Hertz simply refers to the number of wave peaks per second. The faster the vibration, the higher the frequency, the closer together the waves are—and the higher is the tone produced. You can demonstrate this for yourself by paying close attention as you pluck the high E and the low E strings on a guitar. The low E vibrates much more slowly—far fewer times per second—than the high E.

Most of the sounds we experience do not consist of a single frequency but are *complex,* consisting of several sound-wave frequencies. This combination of frequencies produces the distinctive quality, or **timbre,** of a sound. For example, you can easily distinguish among the same note played on a saxophone, piano, or electric guitar. Every

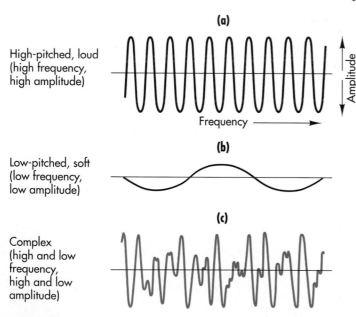

High-pitched, loud (high frequency, high amplitude)

Low-pitched, soft (low frequency, low amplitude)

Complex (high and low frequency, high and low amplitude)

FIGURE 3.7 Characteristics of Sound Waves
The length of a wave, its height, and its complexity determine the loudness, pitch, and timbre that we hear. In **(a)** the sound would be high-pitched and loud. In **(b)** the sound would be soft and low. The sound in **(c)** is complex, like the sounds we usually experience in the natural world.

TABLE 3.2 Decibel Level of Some Common Noises

Decibels	Examples	Exposure Danger
180	Rocket launching pad	Hearing loss inevitable
140	Shotgun blast, jet plane	Any exposure is dangerous
120	In front of speakers at rock concert, sandblasting, thunderclap	Immediate danger
100	Chain saw, boiler shop, pneumatic drill	2 hours
90	Truck traffic, noisy home appliances, shop tools, lawn mower	Less than 8 hours
80	Subway, heavy city traffic, alarm clock at 2 feet, factory noise	More than 8 hours
70	Busy traffic, office tabulator, noisy restaurant (constant exposure)	Critical level begins
60	Air conditioner at 20 feet, conversation, sewing machine	
50	Light traffic at a distance, refrigerator, gentle breeze	
40	Quiet office, living room, bedroom away from traffic	
30	Quiet library, soft whisper	
0	Lowest sound audible to human ear	

audition
The technical term for the sense of hearing.

loudness
The intensity (or amplitude) of a sound wave, measured in decibels.

amplitude
The intensity or amount of energy of a wave, reflected in the height of the wave; the amplitude of a sound wave determines a sound's loudness.

decibel
(DESS-uh-bell) The unit of measurement for loudness.

pitch
The relative highness or lowness of a sound, determined by the frequency of a sound wave.

frequency
The rate of vibration, or the number of sound waves per second.

timbre
(TAM-ber) The distinctive quality of a sound, determined by the complexity of the sound wave.

outer ear
The part of the ear that collects sound waves and consists of the pinna, the ear canal, and the eardrum.

eardrum
A tightly stretched membrane at the end of the ear canal that vibrates when sound waves hit it.

human voice has its own distinctive timbre, which is why you can immediately identify a friend's voice on the telephone from just a few words, even if you haven't talked to each other for years.

How We Hear:
The Path of Sound

Sound waves are collected in the outer ear, amplified in the middle ear, and converted to neural messages in the inner ear. What are key structures involved in hearing, and what is their function? How do place theory and frequency theory explain pitch? What are some common causes of hearing loss?

The human ear is made up of the outer ear, the middle ear, and the inner ear. In general, sound waves are *collected* in the outer ear, *amplified* in the middle ear, and *transduced* or *transformed into neural messages* in the inner ear. You can trace the path taken by sound waves through the ear in Figure 3.8.

The **outer ear** includes the *pinna*, the *ear canal*, and the *eardrum*. The *pinna* is that oddly shaped flap of skin and cartilage that's attached to each side of your head. The pinna helps us pinpoint the location of a sound (see Sekuler & Blake, 1994). But the pinna's primary role is to catch sound waves and funnel them into the *ear canal*. The sound wave travels down the ear canal, then bounces into the **eardrum,** a tightly stretched membrane. When sound waves hit the eardrum, it vibrates, matching the vibrations of the sound wave in both intensity and frequency.

FIGURE 3.8 (a) The Path of Sound Through the Human Ear A complex chain of events leads to the perception of sound. Sound waves are caught by the outer ear, funneled down the ear canal, and ultimately stimulate the hair cells, the sensory receptors in the cochlea (see inset). **(b) The Hair Cells** Magnified thousands of times, this photograph shows the hair cells, embedded in the basilar membrane in the cochlea. As the basilar membrane ripples, the hair cells bend, stimulating the auditory nerve, which transmits neural messages to the auditory cortex of the brain.

Sound waves are collected in the **outer ear.**

Sound waves are amplified in the **middle ear.**

Sound waves are transformed into coded neural messages in the **inner ear.**

Hammer

Anvil

Semicircular canals

Oval window

Auditory nerve

To brain

Cochlea

Ear drum

Stirrup

Ear canal

Sound waves

(a)

Outer ear   **Middle ear**   **Inner ear**

Stirrup

Hammer

Anvil

Cochlea, partially uncoiled

Sound waves

Auditory canal

Sound waves

Fluid

Ear drum

Hair cells

Basilar membrane

Vibrations in fluid cause the basilar membrane to wave up and down.

(b)

As you can see in Figure 3.8, the eardrum separates the outer ear from the middle ear. As the eardrum vibrates, the vibration is transferred to the **middle ear,** which contains three tiny bones —the *hammer,* the *anvil,* and the *stirrup,* named after the objects they resemble. Each bone sets the next bone in motion. The joint action of these three bones almost doubles the amplification of the sound. The innermost bone, the stirrup, transmits the amplified vibration to the *oval window.* Like the eardrum, the oval window is a membrane, but it is many times smaller than the eardrum.

The oval window separates the middle ear from the **inner ear.** As the oval window vibrates, the vibration is next relayed to an inner structure called the **cochlea,** a fluid-filled tube that's coiled in a spiral. The word "cochlea" comes from the Greek word for "snail," and the spiral shape of the cochlea does resemble a snail's shell. Although the cochlea is a very complex structure, it is quite tiny—no larger than a pea.

As the fluid in the cochlea ripples, the vibration in turn is transmitted to the **basilar membrane.** The basilar membrane runs the length of the coiled cochlea. Embedded in the basilar membrane are the sensory receptors for sound, called **hair cells,** which have tiny, projecting fibers that look like hairs. The hair cells bend as the basilar membrane ripples. It is here that transduction finally takes place: the physical vibration of the sound wave is converted into neural impulses. As the hair cells bend, they stimulate the cells of the auditory nerve, which carries the neural information to the brain.

Distinguishing Pitch:
Two Theories

How do we distinguish between the low-pitched throb of a bass guitar and the high-pitched tones of a flute? Remember, pitch is determined by the *frequency* of a sound wave. The basilar membrane is a key structure involved in our discrimination of pitch. Two complementary theories describe the role of the basilar membrane in the transmission of differently pitched sounds.

According to **frequency theory,** the basilar membrane vibrates at the *same* frequency as the sound wave. Thus, a sound wave of about 100 hertz would excite each hair cell along the basilar membrane to vibrate 100 times per second, and neural impulses would be sent to the brain at the same rate. However, there's a limit to how fast neurons can fire: individual neurons cannot fire faster than about 1,000 times per second. But we can sense sounds with frequencies that are many times higher than 1,000 hertz. A child, for example, can typically hear pitches ranging from about 20 to 20,000 hertz. Frequency theory explains how *low*-frequency sounds are transmitted to the brain, but cannot explain the transmission of higher-frequency sounds.

So how *do* we distinguish higher-pitched sounds? According to **place theory,** different frequencies cause larger vibrations at different *locations* along the basilar membrane. High-frequency sounds, for example, cause maximum vibration near the stirrup end of the basilar membrane. Lower-frequency sounds cause maximum vibration at the opposite end. Thus, different pitches excite different hair cells along the basilar membrane. Higher-pitched sounds are interpreted according to the *place* where the hair cells are most active.

Thus, *both* frequency theory and place theory are involved in explaining our discrimination of pitch. Frequency theory helps explain our discrimination of frequencies lower than 500 hertz. Place theory helps explain our discrimination of higher-pitched sounds. And for intermediate frequencies or mid-range pitches, both place and frequency are involved.

Hearing Disorders

Given the large number of moving parts that are involved in hearing, it's not surprising that many things can go wrong. Hearing loss, or **deafness,** can be either partial or total. Deafness can be caused by genetic defects, injury or illness, or brain damage. Sometimes only very specific frequency ranges, such as high-pitched tones, are involved.

Conduction deafness is hearing loss due to "mechanical" problems that prevent the parts of the ear from conducting vibrations to the hair-cell sensory receptors of the inner ear. Conduction deafness has many possible causes, such as eardrum damage, damage to the tiny bones of the middle ear, or even a buildup of ear wax! In old age, the hammer, anvil, and stirrup often

middle ear
The part of the ear that amplifies sound waves and consists of three small bones, the hammer, the anvil, and the stirrup.

inner ear
The part of the ear where sound is transduced into neural impulses; consists of the cochlea and semicircular canals.

cochlea
(COKE-lee-uh) The coiled, fluid-filled inner-ear structure that contains the sensory receptors for sound.

basilar membrane
(BASE-uh-ler) The membrane within the cochlea of the ear that contains the hair cells.

hair cells
The hairlike sensory receptors for sound, found in the basilar membrane of the cochlea.

frequency theory
The view that the basilar membrane vibrates at the same frequency as the sound wave.

place theory
The view that different frequencies cause larger vibrations at different locations along the basilar membrane.

deafness
The complete or partial loss of hearing.

become brittle, so that the ear's ability to conduct and magnify sounds is reduced (see Sekuler & Blake, 1994). Conduction deafness is often helped by a hearing aid, which artificially amplifies sounds.

Nerve deafness, in contrast, is due to damage to the hair cells or auditory nerve. Varying degrees of permanent nerve deafness can be caused by regular exposure to extremely loud noises, such as music played above 90 decibels or factory machinery. Hearing aids are of no use in this form of deafness because the neural messages cannot reach the brain.

CONCEPT REVIEW 3.3

Hearing

Complete the following sentences using the correct term from this list: conduction deafness, loudness, amplitude, basilar, frequency, pitch, nerve deafness, place, cochlea, middle ear.

1. Frequency is to _____ as amplitude is to _____.

2. The sensory receptors for hearing are embedded in the _____ membrane in the _____.

3. After playing with a heavy-metal rock band for many years, Sly is experiencing a severe hearing loss that cannot be helped by wearing a hearing aid. Most likely, Sly suffers from a hearing disorder called _____.

4. The _____ theory of hearing best explains how we hear the low-frequency sound of thunder rumbling.

5. Neurons cannot fire faster than about 1,000 times per second, yet humans can sense high-pitched sounds up to 20,000 hertz. The _____ theory of hearing explains how people hear high-pitched sounds.

6. Marcel's hearing loss has improved now that he has been fitted with a hearing aid that artificially amplifies sound. Marcel's hearing loss was probably due to a disorder called _____.

Smell and Taste: The Chemical Senses

Unlike hearing and vision, smell and taste receptors are specialized to respond to different types of chemical stimulation. How do airborne molecules result in the sensation of an odor? What are pheromones?

Remember Paul and Warren, who both lack a sense of smell? As Paul and Warren are well aware, the senses of smell and taste are closely linked. If you've ever temporarily lost your sense of smell because of a bad cold, you've probably noticed that your sense of taste was also disrupted. Even a deluxe hamburger tastes sort of like cardboard.

Smell and taste are linked in other ways, too. Unlike vision and hearing, which involve sensitivity to different forms of energy, the sensory receptors for taste and smell are specialized to respond to different types of *chemical* substances. That's why smell, or *olfaction,* and taste, or *gustation,* are sometimes referred to as "the chemical senses" (Bartoshuk & Beauchamp, 1994).

As the cases of Paul and Warren illustrate, people can get along quite well without a sense of smell. In fact, a surprisingly large number of people completely lack a sense of smell or are unable to smell specific odors (see Sekuler & Blake, 1994). Although humans gather most of their information about the world through hearing and vision, many animal species depend on chemical signals as their primary source of information (Agosta, 1992). Moles, for example, make up for their poor eyesight with an extremely acute sense of smell.

CALVIN AND HOBBES

However, even for humans, smell and taste can provide important information about the environment. Tastes help us determine whether a particular substance is to be savored or spit out. Smells alert us to potential dangers, such as the odor of a smoldering fire, leaking gas, or spoiled food. For example, shortly after Paul and Asha built a new house, Paul noticed water seeping up into the lawn and called the builder to complain about the leaking underground sprinkler system. But when the builder came out to check on it, he quickly informed Paul that it wasn't the sprinkler system that was leaking— it was the *septic* system. Paul, of course, could not smell the distinctive odor of sewage.

Our senses of smell and taste are very important to the quality of everyday life. The sweet taste of chocolate melting on your tongue, the soft scent of a baby's skin just after a bath, or the delightful smell and taste of fresh popcorn—these are just a few examples of the indescribable pleasures that we experience through our senses of smell and taste.

How We Smell (Don't Answer That!)

What do we smell when we smell a smell? The sensory stimuli that produce our sensation of an odor are *molecules in the air*. These airborne molecules are emitted by the substance we are smelling. We inhale them through the nose and through the opening in the palate at the back of the throat. In the nose, the molecules encounter millions of olfactory receptor cells located high in the nasal cavity.

Unlike the sensory receptors for hearing and vision, the olfactory neurons are constantly being replaced, each lasting for only about 30 to 60 days (Buck, 1996). In 1991, neuroscientists Linda Buck and Richard Axel identified the odor receptors that are present on the hairlike fibers of the olfactory neurons. Like synaptic receptors, each odor receptor seems to be specialized to respond to molecules of a different chemical structure. When these receptor cells are stimulated by the airborne molecules, the stimulation is converted into neural messages that travel down the axons that make up the *olfactory nerve* (Buck 1996).

So far, hundreds of different odor receptors have been identified. We probably don't have a separate receptor for each of the estimated 10,000 different odors that we can identify, however. Rather, it seems that a given smell activates a *group* of different receptors. Specific odors are identified by the brain as it interprets the pattern of receptors that are stimulated (Buck, 1996).

The olfactory nerve directly connects to the **olfactory bulb** in the brain, which is actually the enlarged ending of the *olfactory cortex* at the front of the

olfactory bulb
(ole-FACK-toe-ree) The enlarged ending of the olfactory cortex at the front of the brain where the sensation of smell is registered.

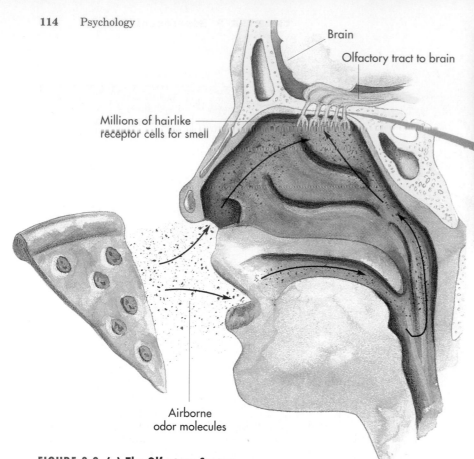

(a)

(b)

FIGURE 3.9 (a) The Olfactory System
Inhaled through the nose or the mouth, airborne molecules travel to the top of the nasal cavity, and stimulate the olfactory receptors. When stimulated, these receptor cells communicate neural messages to the olfactory bulb, which is part of the olfactory cortex of the brain, where the sense of smell is registered. **(b) The Olfactory Receptor Cells** More than five million olfactory neurons make up a moist, mucus-bathed tissue at the back of the nose. Projecting from the olfactory neurons are the fiber-like olfactory hairs, which can be clearly seen in this photograph. Olfactory neurons are replaced every month or two.

brain (see Figure 3.9). It's here that smells are perceived in the brain. Our friend Warren lost his sense of smell because the surgeon cut through the nerves leading to his olfactory bulb. Axons from the olfactory bulb also project to structures in the limbic system of the brain (see Angier, 1995).

The direct connection of receptor cells to the cortex and limbic system is unique to our sense of smell. As discussed in Chapter 2, all other body sensations are first processed in the thalamus before being relayed to the higher brain centers in the cortex. Olfactory neurons are unique in another way, too. They are the only neurons that *directly* link the brain and the outside world (Axel, 1995). The axons of the sensory neurons that are located in your nose extend directly into your brain!

Sensitivity to and Recognition of Smells

Human sensitivity to odors varies widely. Several studies have demonstrated that women tend to be more sensitive to smells than men (see Sekuler & Blake, 1994). Our sensitivity also varies for *different* odors. For example, *National Geographic* magazine included a selection of different odors in "scratch and sniff" panels for a survey on smell (Gibbons, 1986). One particular odor required less than an ounce of the substance to be perceptible in the *11 million* copies of the magazine! Yet even large quantities of certain other substances, such as carbon monoxide, are completely odorless to humans.

Although humans are highly sensitive to odors, many animals display even greater sensitivity (Agosta, 1992). Dogs, for example, have about 200 million receptor cells, compared to the approximately 10 million receptors that humans have.

Given the small number of smell receptors we have relative to other animals, humans have a remarkable ability to recognize familiar smells. And, in fact, every individual has a unique, genetically determined scent (Axel, 1995). In one study children were presented with two T-shirts, one worn by their sibling for the past three nights and the other worn by an unrelated child. When asked to identify which T-shirt had been worn by their sibling, the children answered correctly almost 80 percent of the time. When the children's mothers were asked which T-shirt had been worn by their child, the mothers answered correctly almost 95 percent of the time. In a related test, parents were also highly accurate in distinguishing between their children solely on the basis of smell (Porter & Moore, 1981).

As with the other senses, we experience sensory adaptation to odors when exposed to them for a period of time. Perhaps you've visited a friend in an industrial section of town and commented on the strong smell of air pollution, while your friend had no idea what you were talking about. In general, we reach maximum adaptation to an odor in less than a minute. We continue to smell the odor, but we have become about 70 percent less sensitive to it (Sekuler & Blake, 1994). Keep that reassuring thought in mind the next time you squeeze onto a crowded bus in the middle of a heat wave!

Pheromones

Many animals communicate by producing **pheromones,** chemical scents that linger in the air. Pheromones are used to mark territories and serve as warning signals to other members of the same species (Agosta, 1992). They are also extremely important in regulating mating and reproductive behavior in many animals. The male cabbage moth, for example, can detect pheromones released from a sexually receptive female cabbage moth that is several miles away (Lerner & others, 1990).

Do humans, like other animals, produce pheromones that serve as sexual signals? A popular notion among some teenage males is that the aroma of male sweat is sexually exciting to women, but this has never been substantiated scientifically. The human sexual response is much more complex than that of other animals, and it is unlikely that pheromones alone could be the powerful stimulus that they are elsewhere in the animal kingdom. So, until researchers do discover human sex pheromones, your best bet is to just go ahead and throw those sweaty socks in the washer.

This is *not* to say, however, that human pheromones do not exist, or that chemical signals do not affect human behavior. For example, while still a college student, neurobiologist Martha McClintock (1971) set out to scientifically investigate the folk notion that women who lived in the same dorm eventually developed synchronized menstrual periods. McClintock was able to show that the more time the women spent together, the more likely their cycles were to be in sync. She also discovered that women who spent more time with *males* had shorter and more regular menstrual cycles. It turned out that the women's sense of smell was related to both phenomena.

Research later showed that smelling an unknown chemical substance in underarm sweat from female donors was responsible for synchronizing menstrual cycles (Preti & others, 1986). And smelling an unknown chemical substance in underarm sweat from *male* donors was responsible for producing shorter and more regular menstrual cycles (Cutler & others, 1986). So, even though no one has been able to isolate human sex pheromones that will make you irresistible to members of the preferred sex, there is substantial evidence that chemical signals can affect human hormones and behavior (McClintock, 1992).

Taste

> *Taste results from the stimulation of specialized receptors in the the taste buds. What are the primary tastes? How do we perceive tastes?*

When people talk about how a food tastes, they often use the words "'taste" and "flavor" interchangeably. But to psychologists there is a difference between taste and flavor. Strictly speaking, our sense of taste, or *gustation,* results from the stimulation of special receptors in the mouth. The perception of *flavor* goes beyond the sensation of taste and involves several other sensations, including the smell, temperature, texture, and appearance of the food.

pheromones
(FARE-uh-mones) Chemical signals used by animals to communicate territorial boundaries and sexual receptiveness.

The importance of texture, temperature, and appearance in the perception of flavor should not be underestimated. For example, when your author, Don, had oral surgery that required him to be on a liquid diet for two weeks, your other author, Sandy, cheerfully surprised him with a blenderized pizza for dinner. Although all the ingredients (and, consequently, all the tastes) were present, his response was less than enthusiastic: the liquefied pizza somehow lacked the same appeal as a freshly baked one. In the symphony of food, taste represents the individual notes, while flavor is the entire performance.

How We Taste: This Bud's for You

The stimuli that produce the sensation of taste are chemical substances in whatever you eat or drink. These substances are dissolved by saliva, which allows the chemicals to activate the **taste buds,** which contain the specialized receptors for taste.

Stick out your tongue and look at it in the mirror. (Oh, go ahead and look. We did. If anyone notices, just tell them it's a psychology experiment.) You'll see that the surface of the tongue is covered with thousands of little bumps that have grooves between them (see Figure 3.10). These grooves are lined with the taste buds. Taste buds are also located on the insides of your cheeks, on the roof of your mouth, and in your throat (Oakley, 1986). When activated, special receptors cells in the taste buds send neural messages along nerves to the thalamus in the brain. In turn, the thalamus directs the information to several higher brain regions in the cortex.

There are four primary taste qualities: sweet, salty, sour, and bitter. All other tastes are actually a combination of the four primary taste qualities. Each taste bud shows maximum sensitivity to one particular taste quality and lesser degrees of sensitivity to the other three taste qualities (Arvidson & Friberg, 1980). More complex tastes are a result of the activation of different combinations of these four types of receptors (Martin & Jessell, 1995).

The specialized sensitivity of taste buds is easy to demonstrate. Brush your teeth, then taste some orange juice. Why does the orange juice taste so bitter right after you've brushed your teeth? The culprit is a chemical that is present in most brands of toothpaste. It intensifies bitter tastes, while disrupting the binding of sweet-tasting substances to the sweetness receptors (Schiffman, 1983). Because the sweetness receptors are temporarily blocked, you can taste only the bitter chemical substances that are present in the orange juice.

Bump on the surface of the tongue

Taste buds

(b)

FIGURE 3.10

Taste Buds (a) The photograph shows the surface of the tongue magnified hundreds of times. Taste buds are located in the grooves of the bumps on the surface of the tongue. **(b)** Embedded in the surface of the tongue are thousands of taste buds, the sensory receptor organs for taste. Each taste bud contains an average of fifty taste receptor cells. When activated, the taste receptor cells send messages to adjoining sensory neurons, which relay the information to the brain. Taste buds, like the olfactory neurons, are constantly being replaced. The life expectancy of a particular taste bud is only about 10 days.

taste buds
The specialized sensory receptors for taste that are located on the tongue and inside the mouth and throat.

Skin and Body Senses

The skin senses include touch, temperature, and pain; the body senses include movement, position, and balance. What are some sensory receptors for touch? How do we experience the sensations of cold, warm, and hot?

While vision, hearing, smell, and taste provide you with important information about your environment, another group of senses provide you with information that comes from a source much closer to home: your own body. Without looking, can you tell where your left knee is right now? Are you sitting up straight or lying down? Are you wearing shoes? These questions may sound silly, but think about how difficult life would be if you were unable to answer them. In this section, we'll first consider the *skin senses*, which provide essential information about your physical status and your physical interaction with objects in your environment. We'll next consider the *body senses,* which keep you informed as to your position and orientation in space.

Touch and Temperature

As you grope around the bottom of your lukewarm dirty dishwater for stray silverware, you cringe at the squishy sensation of cold spaghetti noodles, and then wince with pain as you cut yourself on a paring knife. This simple example illustrates the skin sensations—*touch, temperature,* and *pain.* We usually don't think of our skin as a sense organ. But in fact the skin is the largest and heaviest sense organ. The skin of an average adult covers about 20 square feet of surface area and weighs about 6 pounds.

There are many different kinds of sensory receptors in the skin. Some of these sensory receptors are specialized to respond to just one kind of stimulus, such as pressure or temperature. Other skin receptors respond to more than one type of stimulus (see Kalat, 1995).

IN FOCUS 3.2

The Power of Touch

Touch is an important source of information about the world. It can also be the source of great pleasure or great pain. Psychologist Tiffany Field and pediatrician Saul Schanberg discovered that touch can have a positive impact on the growth and development of premature babies.

Schanberg and Field (1987) studied 40 premature infants with very low birth weights. Their medical condition had stabilized, but the infants still had to be kept in incubators in a special hospital nursery. According to the prevailing medical wisdom at that time, infants who were that premature were rarely handled. Field and Schanberg wanted to see if sensory stimulation—specifically, touch—would affect the infants' growth and development (see Field, 1993).

For a period of 10 days, half of the preterm infants were gently massaged for 15 minutes three times a day. That is, the infants' head, neck, shoulders, arms, legs, and back were gently but firmly stroked. The results were impressive. Compared to the control infants, who did not receive the massage, the massaged infants averaged 47 percent more weight gain. This weight gain did not occur because the massaged babies ate more. Both the massaged and the control infants ate the same amount of food. The weight gain appeared to be due to the effect of touch on their metabolism (Schanberg & Field, 1987).

Additional benefits were equally impressive. The massaged infants were more active and spent longer periods awake than the control infants. They were more responsive to people and objects, such as a rattle, and had higher scores on tests that measured mental and motor development. Finally, they were hospitalized an average of six fewer days than the control infants (Field & others, 1986).

Remarkably, these benefits seemed to be long-term (Field, 1993). At eight months of age, the massaged infants continued to weigh more and to show better performance on tests that assessed mental and motor development than did the babies who had not been massaged.

Infant massage is common in many cultures, and need not be limited to premature babies. In India, for example, infant massage is a common practice. In her research, Field (1993) found that infants respond best to gentle, firm, and slow strokes, much like a Swedish massage. When touch is too light, it tends to be overstimulating and may even be irritating.

Not surprisingly, different areas of the infant's body respond differently to touch. Stroking the face, stomach, or feet tends to stimulate babies; stroking the back or legs tends to soothe and relax them. Touch may be especially important in early infancy because it is the most mature sensory system for the first few months of life (Goleman, 1991b).

The Power of Touch Psychologist Tiffany Field, shown here, massages a premature infant in an incubator.

One important receptor involved with the sense of touch is called the *Pacinian corpuscle,* which is located beneath the skin. When stimulated by pressure, the Pacinian corpuscle converts the stimulation into a neural message that is relayed to the brain. If a pressure is constant, sensory adaptation takes place. The Pacinian corpuscle either reduces the number of signals sent or quits responding altogether (which is fortunate, or you'd be unable to forget the fact that you're wearing underwear).

Sensory receptors are distributed unevenly among different areas of the body. That's why sensitivity to touch and temperature sensations varies from one area of the body to another. Your hands, face, and lips, for example, are much more sensitive to touch than your back, arms, and legs. That's because your hands, face, and lips are much more densely packed with sensory receptors.

Just as different areas of the body are especially sensitive to touch, different body areas are more responsive to either warmth or cold. For example, your back is much more responsive to cold than to warmth, which is why you react so strongly when someone drops an ice cube down the back of your shirt.

How do we sense temperature? A given section of skin is like a patchwork of small but specific spots which, when stimulated, produce *either* cold or warm sensations, but not both. "Cold spots" can actually be activated by either a *cold* (around 50°F.) or *hot* stimulus (around 125°). When a cold spot is stimulated with *either* a cold or hot stimulus, it produces the sensation of cold. But "warm spots" only seem to respond to warm stimuli, reaching peak sensitivity at around 105°.

How do we experience hot sensations? Surprisingly, there do *not* appear to be "hot spots" on our skin. Instead, the sensation of "hot" occurs when warm and cold spots are *simultaneously* stimulated (see Figure 3.11). That's because a cold spot will activate in response to either a cold or a hot stimulus, but a warm spot can be activated only by a stimulus that is warm. Thus, if both warm and cold receptors are simultaneously activated, the brain makes the most logical interpretation of the pattern of stimulation: the stimulus must be hot.

There is one exception to this pattern, however. An extremely cold or extremely hot stimulus does not produce the sensation of either hot or cold. Instead, it produces an entirely different skin sensation—pain.

FIGURE 3.11
The Sensation of "Hot"
The sensation of "hot" occurs when warm and cold spots on the skin are simultaneously stimulated. This can be demonstrated with two intertwined metal pipes, one containing cold water and the other containing warm water. A person who grasps both pipes will immediately react as though he's touched a very hot surface, quickly yanking his hand away.

Cold water   Warm water

Pain

Pain can be produced by a wide variety of stimuli. What is the gate-control theory of pain? How do psychological factors affect the pain experience? What is the role of substance P and the endorphins in pain?

A wide variety of stimuli can produce **pain**—the sensation of discomfort or suffering. Virtually any external stimulus that can produce tissue damage can cause pain, including certain chemicals, electric shock, and extreme heat, cold, pressure, or noise. Pain can also be caused by internal stimuli, such as disease, infection, or deterioration of body functions.

Without question, pain is important to our survival. It provides us with important information about our body, telling us to pay attention, to stop what we are doing, or to pull away from some object or stimulus that is injuring us.

How is pain processed in the body? To date, the most influential model for understanding how pain is processed is called the **gate-control theory,** developed by psychologist Ronald Melzack and anatomist Patrick Wall (1965,

pain
The unpleasant sensation of physical discomfort or suffering that can occur in varying degrees of intensity.

gate-control theory
The theory that pain is a product of both physiological and psychological factors that cause spinal "gates" to open and relay patterns of intense stimulation to the brain, which perceives them as pain.

substance P

A neurotransmitter that is involved in the transmission of pain messages to the brain.

1983). The gate-control theory suggests that the sensation of pain is controlled by a series of "gates" that open and close in the spinal cord. If the spinal "gates" are open, pain is experienced. If the spinal "gates" are closed, no pain is experienced.

The obvious next question is, What opens or closes the gates? According to gate-control theory, both physical and psychological factors are involved in the brain's interpretation of painful sensations, influencing whether the gates are open or closed. Thus, the experience of pain is not strictly a sensory phenomenon. Rather, it is a highly personal and variable experience that is influenced by diverse psychological factors (Turk, 1994).

To understand how psychological factors can mediate the sensation of pain, we first need to look at how the gate-control process is believed to work. Pain begins when an intense stimulus activates small-diameter sensory fibers, called *free nerve endings,* in the skin, muscles, or internal organs. The free nerve endings carry their messages to the spinal cord, releasing a neurotransmitter called **substance P.** In the spinal cord, substance P causes other neurons to become activated, sending their messages through open spinal gates to the *thalamus* in the brain (see Kalat, 1995; Julien, 1995; Turk & Nash, 1993).

Unless you've somehow managed to get through life so far without an injury, you already know that there seem to be two different kinds of pain: sudden, sharp pain and dull, steady pain. These two different types of pain are carried to the brain via different pathways in the spinal cord. *Phasic pain,* commonly called *acute pain,* is sudden and sharp, and is carried on one neural tract in the spinal cord. *Tonic pain,* commonly called *chronic pain,* is persistent and steady, and is carried on a different neural tract. Each neural pathway sends information to the thalamus, which processes and routes the information to different areas of the brain (Melzack, 1990).

When the sensory pain signals reach the brain, the sensory information is integrated with psychological information. Depending on a person's current psychological and emotional state, the perception of pain can be lessened or intensified. Psychological and emotional factors that can *intensify* the experience of pain include anxiety, fear, a sense of helplessness, and unpleasant memories of previous painful experiences. Psychological and emotional factors that can *reduce* the experience of pain include positive emotions; a sense of control; the belief that one has the personal resources to cope with pain; distraction; and laughter. The pain experience is also influenced by social and cultural learning experiences about the meaning of pain and how people should react to pain (see Turk, 1994; Turk & Rudy, 1992; Taylor, 1995).

How can psychological and emotional factors influence the experience of pain? First, depending on how the brain interprets the pain experience, it regulates pain by sending signals down the spinal cord that either "open" or "close" the gates. If, because of psychological factors, the brain signals the gates to open, pain is experienced or intensified.

TABLE 3.3 The Body's Most and Least Sensitive Areas to Pain

| **Body areas MOST SENSITIVE to pain:** |
| Back of the knee |
| Neck region |
| Bend of the elbow |
| **Body areas LEAST SENSITIVE to pain:** |
| Tip of the nose |
| Sole of the foot |
| Ball of the thumb |

SOURCE: Based on Geldard, 1972.

Second, psychological factors can influence the release of *endorphins,* the body's natural painkillers which are produced in many parts of the brain and the body (see Chapter 2). Endorphins are released as part of the brain's overall response to physical pain or stress (see Taylor, 1995). In the brain, endorphins can inhibit the transmission of pain signals. And in the spinal cord, endorphins inhibit the release of substance P (see Schneider & Tarshis, 1995).

Finally, a person's mental or emotional state can influence other bodily processes, such as muscle tension, blood flow, heart rate, and respiration. Physiological arousal and muscle tension play important roles in the production of pain (Turk & Nash, 1993).

Today, a variety of techniques and procedures can effectively eliminate or reduce pain (Melzack, 1993). These techniques are explored in the chapter Application, entitled "Controlling Pain."

kinesthetic sense
(*kin*-ess-THET-ick) The technical name for the sense of location and position of body parts in relation to one another.

vestibular sense
(vess-TIB-you-ler) The technical name for the sense of balance, or equilibrium.

Movement, Position, and Balance

The kinesthetic sense involves the location and position of body parts in relation to one another, while the vestibular sense involves balance and equilibrium. What are the kinesthetic receptors? What structures are involved in the vestibular sense?

The phone rings. Without looking up from your textbook, you reach for the receiver, pick it up, and guide it to the side of your head. You have just demonstrated your **kinesthetic sense**—the sense that involves the location and position of body parts in relation to one another. The word "kinesthetics" literally means "feelings of motion."

The kinesthetic sense involves specialized sensory neurons, called *proprioceptors,* that are located in your muscles and joints. The proprioceptors constantly communicate information to the brain about changes in your body position and muscle tension.

The kinesthetic sense helps you keep track of the position and movement of different parts of your body. Closely related is the **vestibular sense,** which provides a sense of balance or equilibrium by responding to changes in gravity, motion, and body position.

There are two sources of vestibular sensory information, which are both located in the ear: the *semicircular canals* and the *vestibular sacs* (see Figure 3.12). These structures are filled with fluid and lined with hairlike receptor cells that shift in response to motion, changes in body position, or changes in gravity. When you experience environmental motion, like the rocking of a boat in choppy water, the fluids in the vestibular canals and the vestibular sac are affected. Changes in your body position, such as falling backward in a heroic attempt to return a volleyball serve, also affect the fluids. Your vestibular sense supplies the critical information that allows you to compensate for such changes and quickly reestablish your sense of balance.

Maintaining our equilibrium also involves information from other senses, particularly vision. Under normal circumstances, this works to our advantage. However, when information from the eyes conflicts with information from the vestibular system, the result can be dizziness, disorientation, and nausea. These are the symptoms that are commonly experienced in motion sickness, the bane of many travelers, whether they are in cars, on planes, on boats, or even in space. One strategy to combat motion sickness is to minimize sensory conflicts by focusing on a distant point or an object that is fixed, such as the horizon.

Semicircular canals

Vestibular sacs

(a)

FIGURE 3.12 (a) The Vestibular Sense
The vestibular sense provides our sense of balance, or equilibrium. Shown here are the two sources of vestibular sensory information, both located in the ear: the semicircular canals and the vestibular sacs. Both structures are filled with fluids that shift in response to changes in body position or gravity, and motion. **(b) A Balancing Act** These talented circus acrobats at Montreal's famous *Cirque du Soleil* (Circus of the Sun) are performing a difficult four-person tower—a feat that pushes the sense of balance to its limits. Maintaining equilibrium involves the kinesthetic sense, the vestibular sense, and vision. Signals from the proprioceptors in the muscles and joints (the kinesthetic sense), the fluids in the semicircular canals and the vestibular sacs (the vestibular sense), and visual information must all be integrated to keep the human tower from toppling.

(b)

Smell, Taste and Touch

Fill in the blanks using the correct term from this list: gate-control, olfactory, cold, warm, hot, kinesthetic, taste, touch, olfactory nerve, pheromones, vestibular, substance P.

1. With your eyes closed you would probably have little problem touching your chin with your index finger. This ability is due to your _____ sense.

2. Most people can detect the presence of invisible substances such as gasoline vapors because of their _____ sense.

3. Even with her eyes closed Charmagne felt dizzy and disoriented during a roller coaster ride. Her loss of balance and equilibrium was a function of her _____ sense.

4. When warm and cold receptors on our skin are simultaneously stimulated, we feel the sensation of _____.

5. Olfactory receptors transmit information via the _____ to the brain structure called the olfactory bulb.

6. The neurotransmitter called _____ plays an important role in the processing of pain signals.

7. According to the _____ theory of pain, psychological factors can lessen or intensify the experience of pain.

From Sensation to Perception . . .

In the first part of this chapter, we've described how the body's senses respond to stimuli in the environment. Table 3.4 summarizes the different sensory systems that we have discussed. The information that is detected and collected by the specialized receptors in the sense organs is transduced into neural messages, and ultimately, transmitted to the brain. To make use of this raw sensory data, we must organize, interpret, and relate the data to existing knowledge. But how is this sensory information organized and interpreted? In the next part of this chapter, we'll look at the process of *perception*—how we make sense out of the information we receive about our environment.

TABLE 3.4 Summary Table of the Senses

Sense	Stimulus	Sense Organ	Sensory Receptor Cells
Hearing (audition)	Sound waves	Ear	Hair cells in cochlea
Vision	Light waves	Eye	Rods and cones in retina
Color vision	Different wavelengths of light	Eye	Cones in retina
Smell (olfaction)	Airborne odor molecules	Nose	Hairlike receptor cells at top of nasal cavity
Taste (gustation)	Chemicals dissolved in saliva	Mouth	Taste buds
Touch	Pressure	Skin	Pacinian corpuscle
Temperature	Warmth, cold	Skin	No specific receptor; warm and cold "spots" on skin
Pain	Tissue injury or damage; varied	Skin, organs, and other body sites	No single specific receptor; pattern of messages from many kinds of receptors
Movement (kinesthetic sense)	Movement of the body	None; muscle and joint tissue	Proprioceptors in muscle and joint tissue
Balance (vestibular sense)	Changes in position, gravity	Semicircular canals and vestibular sacs	Hairlike receptor cells in semicircular canals and vestibular sacs

Perception

Perception refers to the process of integrating, organizing, and interpreting sensory information in a way that is meaningful. As we move about the world, what three basic perceptual questions must we routinely answer? Who were the Gestalt psychologists?

As we've seen, our various senses are constantly registering a diverse range of stimuli from the environment and transmitting that information to the brain. But as we interact with our environment, we don't experience isolated bits and pieces of sensory data. Early in this chapter, we defined *perception* as the process of integrating, organizing, and interpreting sensory information in a way that is meaningful. Thus, we perceive a meaningful environment: objects, people, events. As a simple illustration, look at the photograph at the left, which sits on Don's desk. In the photo you can see our daughter, Laura, holding her cat, Nubbin.

Effortlessly, you reached a number of complex perceptual conclusions about the image. You perceived Laura as a whole object, despite the fact that Nubbin is actually blocking a good portion of the view of Laura. You perceived the Christmas tree as being behind Laura and Nubbin and farther away. And although the Christmas tree ornaments, lights, and packages are really just fuzzy images at best, you still deciphered and perceived those fuzzy images as ornaments, lights, and packages. How did you arrive at these perceptual conclusions?

Cognitive processes, such as learning and memory, are involved in determining the "meaning" of an object (Logothetis & Sheinberg, 1996). Our learning experiences create a knowledge base from which we can identify and interpret many objects, including kids, cats, and Christmas trees. But now take a look at the gizmo pictured at the bottom of this page. Even if you have no idea what the object is, the simple fact remains that you perceive it as an object, not as random bits and pieces of sensory information. How do we accomplish these perceptual feats?

A useful way to think about the process of perception is to consider the basic perceptual questions that we must answer in order to survive. We exist in an ever-changing environment that is filled with objects that may be standing still or moving, just like ourselves. Whether it's a brown bear or a bowling ball, we need to be able to identify objects, locate objects in space, and, if they are moving, track their motion. Thus, our perceptual processes must help us organize our sensations to answer three basic but important questions: (1) How far away is the object? (2) Where is it going? and (3) What is it?

In the next few sections, we will look at what psychologists have learned about how we perceptually answer those three questions. Much of our discussion reflects the work of the early **Gestalt psychologists,** a group of German psychologists who investigated the basic rules of perceptual organization in the early 1900s (see Chapter 1). Roughly translated, the German word *Gestalt* means a unified whole. The Gestalt psychologists emphasized that we perceive whole objects or figures (*gestalts*) rather than isolated bits and pieces of sensory information. As you'll see, their pioneering work established many of the basic principles of perception.

Organizing Sensations into Meaningful Perceptions With virtually no conscious effort, the psychological process of perception allows you to integrate, organize, and interpret the lines, colors, and contours in this image as meaningful objects—a smiling child holding a black cat in front of a Christmas tree. How did you reach those perceptual conclusions?

Gestalt psychology
(geh-SHTALT) A school of psychology founded in Germany in the early 1900s that maintained that our sensations are actively processed according to consistent perceptual rules that result in meaningful whole perceptions, or *gestalts*.

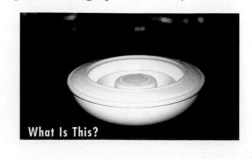

What Is This?

CRITICAL THINKING 3.3

ESP: Can Perception Occur Without Sensation?

Do you believe in ESP? If you do, you're not alone. A Gallup poll found that almost half of American adults "believed in ESP" and another quarter thought ESP might exist (Gallup & Newport, 1991). Another poll found that 67 percent of Americans said that they had "experienced ESP" in some form (Greeley, 1987).

ESP, or extrasensory perception, is based on the idea that sensory information can be detected by some means other than through the normal processes of sensation. Forms of ESP supposedly include:

- *Telepathy*—the direct communication between the minds of two individuals.

- *Clairvoyance*—the perception of a remote object or event, such as "sensing" that a friend has been injured in a car accident.

- *Psychokinesis*—the ability to influence a physical object, process, or event without touching it, such as the ability to bend keys or spoons or stop clocks without touching them.

- *Precognition*—the ability to predict future events.

The general term for such unusual abilities is *paranormal phenomena,* meaning that they are "outside the range of normal experience" and thus unexplainable using known laws of science and nature. **Parapsychology** refers to the investigation of claims of various paranormal phenomena. Only a small percentage of psychologists are parapsychologists.

Have you ever felt as if you had just experienced ESP? Consider the following two examples.

- Your sister was supposed to stop by around 7 p.m. It's now 7:15 and you "sense" that something has happened to her. Shortly after 8 o'clock she calls, informing you that she's been involved in a fender-bender about six blocks away. Did you experience clairvoyance?

- Your author Sandy had a vivid dream that Nubbin the Tailless Cat got lost. The next morning, Nubbin sneaked out the back door,

went for an unauthorized stroll in the woods, and was gone for three days. Did Sandy have a precognitive dream?

Such common experiences are often used as "proof" that ESP exists. However, there are two less extraordinary concepts that can explain both occurrences: coincidence and the fallacy of positive instances. *Coincidence* is the term that describes an event that occurs simply by chance. For example, you have over a thousand dreams per year, most of which are about familiar people and situations. By mere chance alone, *some* aspect of *some* dream will occasionally correspond with reality.

The same is true of "hunches." Every once in a while, a hunch is bound to appear right on target. In response to such experiences, we often engage in the *fallacy of positive instances.* This is our tendency to remember coincidental events that seem to *confirm* our belief about unusual phenomena, like clairvoyance or precognition.

Think of the number of times you've thought something happened to someone but nothing did, or the number of dreams that you've had that did not correspond to subsequent events. These situations are far more common, but we quickly forget about dreams or hunches when nothing happens.

Why do people attribute chance events to ESP? Research has shown that believers in ESP are less likely to accurately estimate the probability of an event occurring by chance alone. Nonbelievers tend to be more realistic about the probability of events occurring simply by chance (Blackmore, 1985).

When confronted with an event that strikes us as extremely unlikely to occur by chance alone, such as a dream predicting the future, we often hypothesize a "nonchance" explanation, such as clairvoyance or precognition (Hines, 1988). Such ESP explanations may strike us as more plausible (and intriguing) than the idea of mere coincidence.

Parapsychologists attempt to study ESP in the laboratory under controlled conditions. Many initially convincing demonstrations of ESP are later shown

to be the result of research design problems or the researchers' unintentional cueing of the subject. Occasionally, outright fraud is involved on the part of either the ESP subject or experimenter (Randi, 1982, 1980).

Another problem involves one of the basic principles of the scientific method, discussed in Chapter 1. To be considered valid, experimental results must be demonstrations that can be *replicated* or repeated by other scientists under identical laboratory conditions. ESP experiments have been particularly problematic in this regard. To date, replication has not been achieved for *any* parapsychology experiment that claims to show evidence of the existence of ESP (Hyman, 1994; Hansel, 1991; Hoppe, 1988).

You must keep in mind, though, that the history of science is filled with examples of phenomena that were initially scoffed at and later found to be real. For example, the pain-relieving effects of acupuncture were initially dismissed by Western scientists as mere "superstition" or the power of "suggestion" (Zusne & Jones, 1989).

Conversely, paranormal explanations are sometimes proposed for normal phenomena when no other explanation is available. For example, it was widely believed earlier in this century that bats navigate in the dark by some sort of "sixth sense" or ESP (Alcock, 1987). We now know that bats emit high-frequency sound waves and use the echoes to navigate and hunt prey.

So keep an open mind about ESP, but also maintain a healthy sense of scientific skepticism (Kurtz, 1994). It is entirely possible that someday convincing experimental evidence will demonstrate the existence of ESP abilities (see Bem & Honorton, 1994; Hyman, 1994; Bem, 1994). In the final analysis, all psychologists, including those who accept the possibility of ESP, recognize the need for evidence that meets the requirements of the scientific method (Bem & Honorton, 1994; Blackmore, 1987). Until such evidence appears, many psychologists will remain unconvinced of the existence of extrasensory perception (Hyman, 1994).

Texture Gradient, Overlap, and Aerial Perspective When you look at a photograph, you rely on monocular cues to gauge the distance of objects depicted. The details of the tall grass are crisp in the foreground, fuzzy in the background, an example of texture gradient. The bushes are perceived as closer than the house they overlap. Finally, the haze of the low hanging cloud blurs the foothills, contributing to the perception of even greater distance. Linear perspective is also evident in the parallel wheel tracks in the grass that seem to converge.

depth perception
The use of visual cues to perceive the distance or three-dimensional characteristics of objects.

monocular cues
(moe-NOCK-you-ler) Distance or depth cues that can be processed by either eye alone.

binocular cues
(by-NOCK-you-ler) Distance or depth cues that require the use of both eyes.

Depth Perception: "How Far Away Is It?"

Depth perception refers to the ability to perceive the distance of objects. What are monocular cues and binocular cues, and how do they differ? How is binocular disparity involved in our ability to see three-dimensional images in stereograms?

Look around you. Notice that you can easily perceive that some objects are close to you and some farther away. Being able to perceive the distance of an object has obvious survival value, especially regarding potential threats, such as snarling dogs, lurking snakes, or oncoming trains. But simply walking through your house or apartment also requires that you accurately judge the distance of furniture, walls, other people, and so forth. Otherwise you'd be constantly bumping into doors, walls, and tables. The ability to perceive the distance of an object as well as the three-dimensional characteristics of an object is called **depth perception.**

Monocular Cues

We use a variety of different cues to judge the distance of objects. The cues listed below require the use of only one eye; hence they are called **monocular cues** ("mono" means "one"). After you've become familiar with these cues, look again at the photograph of Laura and Nubbin. Try to identify the monocular cues you used to determine the distance of each object in that photograph.

1. *Relative size.* If two or more objects are assumed to be similar in size, the object that appears larger is perceived as being closer.

2. *Overlap.* When one object partially blocks or obscures the view of another object, the partially blocked object is perceived as being farther away.

3. *Aerial perspective.* Faraway objects often appear hazy or slightly blurred by the atmosphere.

4. *Texture gradient.* As a surface with a distinct texture, such as a gravel road or a carpet, extends into the distance, the details of the surface texture gradually become less clearly defined. The texture of the surface seems to undergo a gradient, or continuous pattern of change, from crisp and distinct when close to you to fuzzy and blended when farther away.

5. *Linear perspective.* Parallel lines seem to meet in the distance. For example, if you stand in the middle of a railroad track and look down the rails, you'll notice that the parallel rails seem to meet in the distance. The closer together the lines appear to be, the greater the perception of distance.

6. *Motion parallax.* When you are moving, you use the speed of passing objects to estimate the distance of the objects. Nearby objects seem to zip by faster than distant objects. While you are riding in a commuter train, for example, houses and parked cars along the tracks seem to whiz by, while the distant downtown skyline seems to move very slowly.

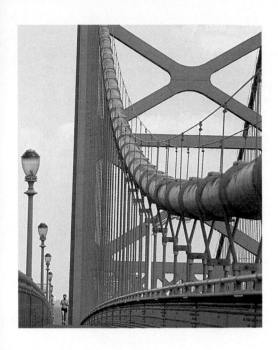

Relative Size and Linear Perspective Several monocular depth cues operate in this photograph, especially relative size. The very small image of the jogger and the decreasing size of the street lamps contribute to the perception of distance. Linear perspective is evident in the apparent convergence of the walkway railings. And, aerial perspective contributes to the perception of depth from the hazy background.

When any of these same cues are used by artists to create the perception of distance or depth in paintings, they are referred to as *pictorial cues*. If you look at the cover of this book, you can see how artist Phoebe Beasley used pictorial cues, like overlap and relative size, to create the perception of depth in her artwork.

Another monocular cue is called *accommodation*. Unlike the pictorial cues described above, accommodation utilizes information about changes in the shape of the lens of the eye to help us estimate distance. When you focus on a distant object, the lens is flat. But focusing on a nearby object causes the lens to thicken. Thus, to some degree we use information provided by the muscles controlling the shape of the lens to judge depth. In general, however, we rely more on pictorial cues than on accommodation for depth perception (see Matlin & Foley, 1992).

Motion Parallax This photograph of waiters passing a tray from one train car to the next captures the visual flavor of motion parallax. Objects that whiz by faster are perceptually judged as being closer, as in the case here of the blurred ground and bushes. Objects that pass by more slowly are judged as being further away, as conveyed by the clearer details of buildings and more distant objects.

Binocular Cues

In contrast to the monocular cues, **binocular cues** for distance or depth perception require information from both eyes. One binocular cue is *convergence*—the degree to which muscles rotate your eyes to focus on an object. The more the eyes converge, or rotate inward, to focus on an object, the greater the strength of the muscle signals, and the closer the object is perceived to be. For example, if you hold a dime about six inches in front of your nose, you'll notice the slight strain on your eye muscles as your eyes converge to focus on the coin. If you hold the dime at arm's length, less convergence is needed. Perceptually, the information provided by these signals from your eye muscles is used to judge the distance of an object.

Another binocular distance cue is *binocular disparity*. Because our eyes are set a couple of inches apart, a slightly different image of an object is cast on the retina of each eye. When the two retinal images are very different, we perceptually interpret the object as being close to us. When the two retinal images are more nearly identical, the object is perceived as being farther away.

Here's a simple example that illustrates how we use binocular disparity to perceive distance. Hold a pencil just in front of your nose. Close your left eye, then your right. These images are quite different—that is, there is a great deal of binocular disparity between them. Thus, we perceive the pencil as being very close. Now focus on another object across the room and look at it with first one eye closed, then the other. These images are much more similar. Because there is less binocular disparity between the two images, the object is perceived as being farther away. Finally, notice that with both eyes open, the two images are fused into one.

A ViewMaster works on the same principle. Thanks to binocular disparity, you can experience the perceptual illusion of three-dimensional depth from two two-dimensional scenes. As you look through a ViewMaster, each eye sees a slide that is photographed or drawn from a slightly different angle so as to mimic the slightly different views that each eye detects when you look at a scene in a natural setting. When the brain fuses the two different ViewMaster images, it creates the illusion of three-dimensional depth.

The object on page 122 is a liquid fabric softener dispenser for a washing machine.

A *stereogram* works in exactly the same way as a ViewMaster, except that all the disparate information is contained in a single two-dimensional picture rather than in two separate pictures. Look directly at the stereogram shown at the right, which was created by Hiroshi Kunoh and is entitled *Rustling Hares* (Kunoh & Takaoki, 1994). When you first look at the image, you perceive a two-dimensional picture of leaves. The pictorial cues are arranged so that each element in the picture appears to be the same distance from you.

However, a stereogram is actually composed of repeating columns of carefully arranged visual information. If you focus as though you were looking at some object that is farther away than the stereogram, the repeating columns of information will present a slightly different image to each eye. This disparate visual information then fuses into a single image, enabling you to perceive a three-dimensional image—three rabbits. To see the rabbits, follow the directions in the caption to the stereogram.

CONCEPT REVIEW 3.5

Depth Perception

Several monocular depth cues are evident in this photograph of the Ginza, a major shopping and entertainment district of Tokyo, Japan. After studying the photograph, identify examples of the following monocular depth cues:

1. Relative size
2. Overlap
3. Aerial perspective
4. Texture gradient
5. Linear perspective

The Perception of Motion:
"Where Is It Going?"

The perception of motion involves the integration of information from several sources. What are key sources of information in perceiving movement? What is induced motion? What is stroboscopic motion? How do we use auditory cues to perceive distance and location?

Along with perceiving the distance of stationary objects, we also need to be able to gauge the path of moving objects, whether it's a baseball whizzing through the air, a falling tree branch, or the egg about to roll off the kitchen counter. How do we perceive movement?

As we follow a moving object with our gaze, the image of the object moves across the retina. Our eye muscles make micro-fine movements to keep the object in focus. We also compare the moving object to the background, which is usually stationary. Complex neural pathways in the brain combine information about eye-muscle activity, the changing retinal image, and the contrast of the moving object with its stationary background (Livingstone & Hubel, 1988; Wallach, 1987). The end result? We perceive the object as moving.

Binocular Disparity and the Perception of Depth in Stereograms This stereogram, *Rustling Hares,* was created by artist Hiroshi Kunoh (1994). To see the three-dimensional rabbits, first hold the picture close to your face. Focus your eyes as though you are looking at an object that is beyond the book and farther away. Without changing your focus, slowly extend your arms and move the picture away from you. The image of the leaves will initially be blurry, then details will come into focus and you should see three rabbits. The three-dimensional images that can be perceived in stereograms occur because of binocular disparity—each eye is presented with slightly different visual information.

Beyond this basic explanation, researchers are still trying to understand exactly how the brain's visual system processes movement. It's known, for example, that some neurons are highly specialized to detect motion in one direction but not the opposite direction. Other neurons are specialized to detect motion at one particular speed, but not faster or slower. Research also shows that different neural pathways in the cerebral cortex process information about the depth of objects, movement, form, and color (see Coren & others, 1994; Livingstone & Hubel, 1988).

Psychologically, we tend to make certain assumptions when we perceive movement. For example, we typically assume that the *object* moves while the background or frame remains stationary (see Rock, 1995). Thus, as you visually follow a billiard ball ricocheting around a pool table, you perceive the ball as moving and not the table, which serves as the background.

Induced Motion

Because we have a strong tendency to assume that the background is stationary, we sometimes experience an illusion of motion called *induced motion*. Induced motion was first studied by Gestalt psychologist Karl Duncker in the 1920s. Duncker (1929) had subjects sit in a darkened room and look at a luminous dot that was surrounded by a larger luminous rectangular frame. When the *frame* slowly moved to the right, the subjects perceived the *dot* as moving to the left. The dot, of course, had not moved.

Why did subjects perceive the dot as moving? Perceptually, Duncker's subjects expected to see the smaller dot move within the larger rectangular frame, not the other way around. If you've ever looked up at a full moon on a windy night when the clouds were moving quickly across the face of the moon, you've probably experienced the induced motion effect. The combination of these environmental elements makes the moon appear to be racing across the sky. Or perhaps you've had an experience similar to the one we had recently: We were sitting in a plane that was parked at the gate. As we waited for the plane to leave the gate, a large delivery truck just outside our plane window began slowly backing up. Because of the phenomenon of induced motion, we perceived the *plane* to be moving, rather than the delivery truck.

Stroboscopic Motion

Another illusion of motion is called *stroboscopic motion*. First studied by Gestalt psychologist Max Wertheimer in the early 1900s, stroboscopic motion creates a compelling illusion of movement with two carefully timed flashing lights (Wertheimer, 1912). A light briefly flashes at one location, followed about a tenth of second later by another light briefly flashing at a second location. If the time interval and distance between the two flashing lights are just right, a very compelling illusion of movement is created.

What causes the perception of stroboscopic motion? Although different theories have been proposed, researchers aren't completely sure (see Coren & others, 1994). The perception of motion typically involves the movement of an image across the retina. However, during stroboscopic motion the image does *not* move across the surface of the retina. Rather, the two different

Stroboscopic Motion and Movies The perception of smooth movements in a motion picture is due to stroboscopic motion. Much like this series of still photographs of a gymnast performing a front flip, a motion picture is actually a series of static photographs that are projected on the screen at the rate of 24 frames per second, producing the illusion of smooth motion.

flashing lights are detected at two different points on the surface of the retina. Somehow the brain's visual system combines this rapid sequence of visual information to arrive at the perceptual conclusion of motion, even though no movement has actually occurred.

Electronic signboards with a "rolling" message are based on the principle of stroboscopic motion. The rapidly changing sequence of flashing lights produces the illusion of words moving from left to right across the signboard. The perception of smooth motion in a movie also is due to stroboscopic motion.

Auditory Cues

We also use *auditory* information to judge distance and direction. Much as we can use information from one or both eyes in perceiving the distance of an object, we can use information from one or both ears to detect the distance of a sound. If you use only one ear, the louder the sound, the closer it is perceived to be. Hence, the faint sound of a dog barking is judged to be far away, while a loud yelping is perceived to be close at hand.

Using both ears allows us to more accurately locate the direction as well as the distance of a sound (Konishi, 1993). For example, when a sound is directly to your left, the sound wave reaches your left ear a few thousandths of a second before it reaches your right ear. Because your left ear is closer to the source, the sound it detects is also slightly louder. Your brain calculates these differences in time lag and loudness, quickly perceiving that the source of the sound is to your left (Phillips & Brugge, 1985). Notice that when you are trying to determine the direction of a sound, such as an ambulance siren a few blocks away, you instinctively tilt your head to one side. Doing so adds to the contrast between the information received by your two ears and helps you to perceive the distance and direction of the sound.

The Perception of Shape: "What Is It?"

> *To identify an object, we rely primarily on its shape. What is the figure–ground relationship, and what is its significance? What perceptual principles do we follow in determining figure–ground relationships?*

figure–ground relationship
A Gestalt principle of perceptual organization that states that we automatically separate the elements of a perception into the feature that clearly stands out (the figure) and its less distinct background (the ground).

When you look around your world, you don't see random edges, curves, colors, or splotches of light and dark. Rather, you see countless distinct objects against a variety of backgrounds. Although to some degree we rely on size, color, and texture to determine what an object might be, we rely primarily on an object's *shape* to identify it. This tendency is evident at a very early age, and becomes even more pronounced as we get older (Landau & Jackendoff, 1993).

FIGURE 3.13 The "Dax" Experiment

(a) Original dax — 2.5 inches
(b) 24 inches — Objects also identified as a dax
(c) 2.5 inches
(d) 2.5 inches — Rejected

A clever series of experiments demonstrated the importance of shape in object identification (see Landau, 1994; Landau & Jackendoff, 1993). Three-year-olds were shown a blue, wooden object like the one depicted in Figure 3.13a. The experimenter told the children that the object was a "dax." Then the children were shown a variety of other objects, like the ones depicted in Figure 3.13b, c, and d. Some objects had the same shape as the dax, but were made of different materials or were a different color or size. Other objects were identical to the original dax in every way except that they were shaped a little differently. The experimenter asked the children which of these objects was a dax. It turned out that as long as the object had the same *shape* as the original dax, the children identified it as a dax.

FIGURE 3.14 **A Classic Example of Figure–Ground Reversal** Figure–ground reversals illustrate the psychological nature of our ability to perceptually sort a scene into the main element and the background. With a little psychological effort, it is possible to perceive either the face or the vase as the main element.

Figure–Ground Relationship

Whether we focus on a "dax," a duck, or some other object, how do we organize our perceptions so that we see the object as separate from other objects? The early Gestalt psychologists established an important perceptual principle called the **figure–ground relationship.** This term refers to the fact that when we view a scene, we automatically separate the elements of that scene into the *figure*, which is the main element of the scene, and the *ground,* which is its background.

You can illustrate the figure–ground relationship for yourself by looking at a coffee cup on a table. The coffee cup is the figure, and the table is the ground. Notice that usually the "figure" has a definite shape, such as the distinct contours of the coffee cup. As you focus on the cup, it tends to stand out clearly and is perceptually meaningful in some way. In contrast, the "ground" tends to be less clearly defined, even fuzzy, and it usually appears to be behind and farther away than the figure (Matlin & Foley, 1992).

The separation of a scene into figure and ground is not really a property of the actual elements of the scene we're looking at. Rather, our ability to separate a scene into figure and ground is a psychological accomplishment. To illustrate, look at the classic example shown in Figure 3.14. If you perceive the white area as the figure and the dark area as the ground, you'll perceive a vase. If you perceive the dark area as the figure and the white as the ground, you'll see the silhouettes of two faces. Regardless of which figure you saw first, with a little mental effort you can "force" yourself to perceive the other figure–ground relationship.

The perception of an image in two different ways like this is called a *figure–ground reversal.* Figure–ground reversals underscore that our perception of figure and ground is a psychological phenomenon. Artists like M. C. Escher have used the principle of figure–ground reversal to produce some intriguing effects (see the photograph at the left).

Figure–Ground Reversal in Art The Dutch artist M. C. Escher (1898–1972) is perhaps best known for creating complex visual puzzles. In Winged Lion, Escher uses figure–ground reversal to create a compelling image. Along with psychologists, mathematicians and biologists have been influenced by Escher's work (Schattschneider, 1990).

In nature, ambiguous figure–ground relationships are quite common. Many insects and animals have markings that act as natural camouflage and prevent them from being detected by predators. Because the animal blends in with the background, the predator cannot distinguish the animal (the *figure*) from the natural background (the *ground*). In much the same way, military personnel and equipment are often concealed from enemy forces by clothing or tarps that are designed to blend in with the terrain, whether jungle or desert.

Perceptual Grouping

When we perceive a form, we often group different elements of it together. What perceptual principles or laws do we follow when we group visual elements?

Many of the forms that we perceive are composed of a number of different elements that seem to "go together" (Prinzmetal, 1995). It would be more accurate to say that we actively organize the elements to try to produce the stable perception of well-defined, whole objects. This is what perceptual psychologist Stanley Coren (Coren & others, 1994) refers to as "the urge to organize." What sort of principles do we follow when we try to organize visual elements?

The Gestalt psychologists studied how the perception of visual elements becomes organized into patterns, shapes, and forms. They identified several "laws" or principles that we tend to follow in grouping elements together to arrive at the perception of forms, shapes, and figures. Examples of these perceptual laws are shown in Figure 3.15.

The Gestalt psychologists also formulated a general principle called the *law of Prägnanz,* or the *law of simplicity* (Matlin & Foley, 1992). This law states that when

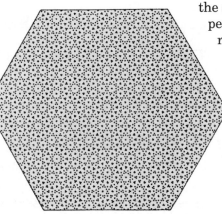

The Perceptual Urge to Organize As you scan this image, you'll experience firsthand the strong psychological tendency to organize visual elements to arrive at the perception of whole figures, forms, and shapes. Notice that as you shift your gaze across the pattern, you momentarily perceive circles, squares, and other geometric forms.

(a) The Law of Similarity

(b) The Law of Closure

(c) The Law of Good Continuation

(d) The Law of Proximity

FIGURE 3.15 The Gestalt Principles of Organization

The Gestalt psychologists formulated several basic principles of perceptual organization, which are illustrated above. We tend to follow these principles in grouping elements together to arrive at the perception of shapes, forms, and figures. **(a)** The Law of Similarity is the tendency to perceive objects of similar size, shape, or color as a unit or a figure. Thus, you perceive four horizontal rows of holiday cookies rather than six vertical columns of cookies. **(b)** The Law of Closure is the tendency to fill in the gaps or contours in an incomplete image. Thus, you perceive the two circles on the face of the clock as smooth, continuous circles, even though the curved lines are actually interrupted by the hands of the clock, the hands of the person, and the edge of the photograph. **(c)** The Law of Good Continuation is the tendency to group elements that appear to follow in the same direction as a single unit or figure. In this image, good continuation is reflected in the strong tendency to perceptually identify the straight sections of highway as continuous units, and the curved sections of highway as continuous units. **(d)** The Law of Proximity is the tendency to perceive objects that are close to one another as a unit or a figure. Thus, you perceive these six people as two groups of three.

FIGURE 3.16 What Do You See?
The law of simplicity is our tendency to efficiently organize the visual elements of a scene in a way that produces the simplest and most stable forms or objects. You probably perceived the image as that of three overlapping squares rather than as two six-sided objects and one four-side object.

several perceptual organizations of an assortment of visual elements are possible, the perceptual interpretation that will occur will be the one that produces the "best, simplest, and most stable shape" (Koffka, 1935). To illustrate, consider Figure 3.16. Do you perceive that image as two six-sided objects and one four-sided object? If you are following the law of Prägnanz, you don't. Instead, you perceptually organize the elements in the most cognitively efficient and simple way, perceiving them as three overlapping squares.

The law of Prägnanz encompasses all the other Gestalt principles, including the figure–ground relationship (see Matlin & Foley, 1992). The implication of the law of Prägnanz is that our perceptual system works in an economical way to promote the interpretation of stable and consistent forms. The ability to efficiently organize elements into stable objects helps us to perceive the world accurately. In effect, we actively and automatically construct a perception that reveals "the essence of something," which is roughly what the German word *Prägnanz* means (Coren & others, 1994).

Perceptual Constancies

> *Perceptual constancy refers to the tendency to perceive objects as unchanging despite changes in sensory input. What principles guide our perceptions of size constancy? What are shape constancy and brightness constancy?*

Consider this scenario. As you're driving on a flat stretch of highway, a red van zips past you and speeds far ahead. As the distance between you and the van grows, its image becomes progressively smaller until the van is no more than a dot on the horizon. Yet, even though the image of the van on our retinas has become progressively smaller, we don't perceive the van as shrinking. Instead, we perceive its shape, size, and brightness to be unchanged.

This tendency to perceive objects, especially familiar objects, as constant and unchanging despite changes in sensory input is called **perceptual constancy.** Without this perceptual ability, our perception of reality would be in a constant state of flux. If we simply responded to retinal images, our perceptions of objects would continually change as lighting, viewing angle, and distance from the object changed from moment to moment. Instead, the various forms of perceptual constancy promote a stable view of the world.

Size Constancy

Size constancy is the perception that an object remains the same size despite its changing image on the retina. When our distance from an object changes, the image of the object that is cast on the retinas of our eyes also changes, yet we still perceive it to be the same size. The red van example reflects the perception of size constancy. As the distance between you and the red van increased, you could eventually block out the retinal image of the van with your hand. However, you don't believe that your hand has suddenly become larger than the van. Instead, the perception of size constancy occurs: The brain automatically adjusts your perception of an object's size by combining information about retinal image size and distance.

perceptual constancy
The tendency to perceive objects, especially familiar objects, as constant and unchanging despite changes in sensory input.

size constancy
The perception of an object as maintaining the same size despite changing images on the retina.

Shape Constancy Each door in the photograph is positioned at a different angle and thus produces a differently shaped image on your retinas. Nevertheless, because of the perceptual principle of shape constancy, you easily identify all five objects as rectangular doors.

An important principle of size constancy is that if the retinal image of an object does *not* change but the perception of its distance *increases,* we will perceive an object as larger. That's not as complicated as it sounds. It's also easy to demonstrate. Stare at a 75-watt light bulb for about ten seconds. Then focus on a bright, distant wall. You should see an afterimage of the light bulb on the wall that will look several times larger than the original light bulb. Why? When you looked at the wall, the lingering afterimage of the light bulb on your retina remained constant but your perception of distance increased. When your brain combined and interpreted this information, your perception of the light bulb's size increased. Remember this demonstration; we'll mention it again when we explain how some perceptual illusions occur.

Shape Constancy

Shape constancy is the tendency to perceive familiar objects as having a fixed shape regardless of the image they cast on our retinas. You can easily demonstrate shape constancy by viewing any familiar object, such as a door, from different angles (see the photograph at the top of the page). Our perception of the door's rectangular shape remains constant despite changes in its retinal image. That's shape constancy.

Shape constancy has a greater influence on your perceptions than you probably realize. Look at Figure 3.17, count the right angles, and write the number in the margin. If you're like most people, you probably counted twelve right angles in the drawing of the slightly tilted cube. Now look at it again, this time more carefully. There are *no* right angles in the drawing. Because of shape constancy, you perceived an image of a cube with right angles despite the lack of sensory information to support that perception.

FIGURE 3.17 How Many Right Angles Do You See?

Brightness Constancy

Another kind of perceptual constancy is **brightness constancy,** in which the perceived brightness of an object seems to stay the same even though the lighting conditions change. The white sheet on a bed is perceived as equally bright whether seen in full sunlight or in the dim light of a night light. A black outdoor grill or crow is perceived as equally dark during the day or at night. The perception of brightness constancy occurs because objects always reflect the same *proportion* of available light, even if the lighting conditions change dramatically.

shape constancy
The perception of a familiar object as maintaining the same shape regardless of the image produced on the retina.

brightness constancy
The perception that the brightness of an object remains the same even though the lighting conditions change.

perceptual illusion
The misperception of the true characteristics of an object or an image.

Müller-Lyer illusion
A famous visual illusion involving the misperception of the identical length of two lines, one with arrows pointed inward, one with arrows pointed outward.

Perceptual Illusions

Perceptual illusions involve the misperception of a stimulus and are used to study perceptual principles. What is the Müller-Lyer illusion? How can it be explained?

Our perceptual processes are largely automatic and unconscious. On the one hand, this arrangement is very mentally efficient. With a minimum of cognitive effort, we decipher our surroundings, answering important perceptual questions and making sense of the environment. On the other hand, because perceptual processing is largely automatic, we can inadvertently arrive at the wrong perceptual conclusion. When we misperceive the true characteristics of an object or an image, we experience a **perceptual illusion.**

During the last century, well over 200 perceptual illusions have been discovered. The perceptual contradictions of illusions are not only fascinating, but can also shed light on how the normal processes of perception guide us to perceptual conclusions. Given the basics of perception that we've covered thus far, you're in a good position to understand how and why some famous illusions seem to occur. In this section, we'll consider two of the best-known perceptual illusions: the Müller-Lyer illusion and the moon illusion. Then we'll look at the perceptual puzzles posed by impossible figures. At the end of this section, we'll return to the issue of what perceptual illusions and impossible figures tell us about the process of perception.

FIGURE 3.18 The Müller-Lyer Illusion
Compare the two photographs. Which corner line is longer? Now compare the two line drawings. Which center line is longer? In reality, the center lines in the photographs and the line drawings are all exactly the same length, which you can prove to yourself with a ruler.

The Müller-Lyer Illusion

Look at the center line in each of the two photographs in Figure 3.18. Which line is longer? If you said the one in the bottom photo, then you just experienced the **Müller-Lyer illusion.** In fact, the two center lines are the same length, even though they *appear* very different in length. If you measure the corner line in each photograph, you'll confirm that they are the same length. The same illusion occurs when you look at a simple drawing of the Müller-Lyer illusion, which is also shown in Figure 3.18.

Part of what contributes to the Müller-Lyer illusion are visual depth cues that promote the perception that the bottom line is *farther* from us (Rock, 1995; Gregory, 1968). When you look at the bottom photograph, the center line is that of a wall jutting away from you. When you look at the bottom part of the drawing of the Müller-Lyer illusion, the outward-pointing arrows create much the same visual effect—a corner jutting away from you. In the top photograph and line drawing, visual depth cues promote the perception of *lesser* distance—a corner that is jutting toward you.

Size constancy also seems to play an important role in the Müller-Lyer illusion (see Coren & others, 1994). Because they are the same length, the two center lines in the photographs and the line drawings produce retinal images that are the same size. However, we noted in our earlier discussion of size constancy that if the retinal size of an object stays the same but the perception of its distance increases, we will perceive the object as larger. Previously, we demonstrated this with the afterimage of a light bulb that seemed much larger when viewed against a distant wall.

The same basic principle seems to occur with the Müller-Lyer illusion. Although the two corner lines produce retinal images that are the same size, the bottom corner line is embedded in visual depth cues that make us perceive it as farther away. Hence, we perceive the bottom corner line as longer, just as you perceived the afterimage of the light bulb as larger when viewed on a distant wall.

Keep in mind, it is the arrows pointing inward or outward that are responsible for creating the illusion in the Müller-Lyer illusion: take away those potent depth cues and the Müller-Lyer illusion evaporates. You perceive the two lines just as they are—the same length.

The Moon Illusion

The moon illusion is the misperception that a full moon is larger when viewed on the horizon than in the overhead sky. How can the moon illusion be explained? What do perceptual illusions and impossible figures reveal about normal perceptual processes?

Another famous illusion is one that you've probably experienced firsthand: the **moon illusion,** shown in Figure 3.19. When a full moon is rising on a clear dark night, it appears much larger when viewed on the horizon against buildings and trees than it does in the night sky overhead. But the moon, of course, doesn't shrink as it rises. The fact of the matter is that *the retinal size of the full moon is the same in all positions.* Still, if you've ever watched the moon rise from the horizon to the night sky, it does *appear* to shrink in size. What causes this illusion?

Part of the explanation has to do with how far away we perceive objects to be at different locations in the sky (see Rock, 1995; Kaufman & Rock, 1989). Put simply, researchers have found that people perceive objects on the horizon as farther away than objects that are directly overhead in the sky. The horizon contains many familiar distance cues, such as faraway buildings, trees, and the "smoothing" of the texture of the landscape as it fades into the distance. Of course, the moon on the horizon is perceived as being *behind* these depth cues. The depth-perception cue of overlap adds to the perception that the moon on the horizon is farther away.

The Moon Illusion When viewed on the horizon, the moon appears considerably larger than when it is viewed higher in the sky. Why does the moon illusion occur?

The moon illusion also involves the misapplication of size constancy, much like the explanation for our perception of the afterimage of a glowing light bulb as larger when it is viewed against a distant wall. Remember, the retinal image of the moon is the *same* in all locations, just like the afterimage of the light bulb. Thus, even though the retinal image of the moon remains constant, we perceive the moon as larger because it seems farther away on the horizon.

If you could somehow remove the additional distance cues that the horizon seems to contain, would the moon appear to be the same size in all locations? Here's one way to find out. Look at a full moon on the horizon through a cardboard tube or through your cupped hands. Either strategy will effectively remove the distance cues provided by trees, faraway buildings, and other objects on the horizon that the moon appears to be behind. When you do this, the size of the moon on the horizon will rapidly shrink—and look the same size as it does when directly overhead.

Impossible Figures

Artists have created a variety of "impossible figures." Though not illusions in the true sense, these figures baffle our natural tendency to perceptually organize a scene. The artist most famous for his elaborate impossible figures was Dutch artist M. C. Escher (1898–1970). You can see Escher's work entitled *Waterfall* at the left. When you look at the image, you try to perceptually sort and integrate the different visual elements to arrive at a stable, well-organized, whole image. However, that's not possible with impossible figures. As you study one area of the picture and try to integrate it with other parts of the picture, perceptual contradictions arise—such as the conclusion that water is running uphill.

In effect, impossible figures are visual riddles that capitalize on our urge to perceptually organize visual elements into a meaningful whole. Try making sense of the picture below, which is entitled *Doric Dilemma* and was created by psychologist Roger Shepard (1990). As you can see, what appears to be a column is not a column. Faced with that paradox, we immediately begin scanning another section of the image to try to find areas that do make perceptual sense. If nothing else, impossible figures remind us that we should carefully consider our "first glance" perceptual conclusions.

Perceptual illusions like the Müller-Lyer illusion underscore the fact that what we see is *not* merely a simple reflection of the world, but rather our subjective perceptual interpretation of it. And although seeing is said to be believing, in the case of illusions, believing can lead to seeing something that isn't really there. Nevertheless, impossible figures remind us that we actively construct perceptual conclusions about the information detected through our

Artist M. C. Escher's Lithograph *Waterfall* (1961) Misleading depth cues in this lithograph by Escher trick the viewer into perceiving the water as flowing uphill. ©1996 M. C. Escher/ Cordon Art—Baarn—Holland. All rights reserved.

moon illusion
A visual illusion involving the misperception that the moon is larger when it is on the horizon that when it is directly overhead.

Doric Dilemma At first glance, the image in this drawing by psychologist Roger Shepard (1991) seems to be simple enough. However, if you look at the columns carefully, you'll see that figure and ground are constantly shifting. Hence, it is impossible to arrive at a stable perception of the image.

senses. In arriving at those perceptual conclusions, we are guided by well-established perceptual principles, such as the cues that typically indicate distance, movement, and form.

The various illusions, impossible figures, and other perceptual demonstrations we've looked at in the second half of this chapter clearly illustrate the fundamental difference between sensation and perception. Through our senses we detect different forms of energy—light waves, sound waves, airborne chemicals, pressure, and so on. But it is the brain that integrates and interprets that information, giving it a meaning that is a reasonably accurate reflection of the physical world.

As we said at the beginning of this section, our perceptual processes are largely automatic and unconscious. In fact, it's often difficult to override or correct the automatic processes of perception. There is no better demonstration of this principle than the kinds of simple illusions we've described. Even when you consciously know that the two lines are the same length in the Müller-Lyer illusion, the largely automatic and unconscious processes of perception leave us with the compelling perceptual conclusion that one line *seems* longer.

Clearly, then, perception is a psychological process. And like any psychological process, perception can be influenced by many factors, such as our expectations (Bruner, 1992). In the final section of this chapter, we'll consider how our prior experiences and cultural factors can influence our perceptions of reality.

The Effects of Experience on Perceptual Interpretations

Perception can be influenced by a variety of learning experiences. How does culture affect perception? What role do perceptual sets play in perception?

In the broadest sense, our educational, cultural, and life experiences shape what we perceive. As a simple example, consider airplane cockpits. If your knowledge of the instruments contained in an airplane cockpit is limited, as is the case with your author Sandy, an airplane cockpit looks like a confusing, meaningless jumble of dials. But your author Don, who is a pilot, has a very different perception of an airplane cockpit. Rather than a blur of dials, he sees altimeters, VORs, air speed and RPM indicators, and other instruments, each with a specific function. Our different perceptions of an airplane cockpit are shaped by our prior learning experiences.

Learning experiences can vary not just from person to person but also from culture to culture. In Culture and Human Behavior Box 3.4, entitled "Culture and Visual Illusions," we discuss the important role that experiences unique to a particular culture can play in the perception of illusions.

Past experience often predisposes us to perceive a situation in a particular way, even though other perceptions are possible. Consider the recent experience of one of our students. As he was driving home late at night, he stopped at a convenience store to buy a pack of cigarettes. Standing at the counter and rummaging through his wallet for some cash, he requested "a pack of Nows." When he looked up, the young female clerk had put a copy of *Penthouse* on the counter. Obviously, the clerk perceived what she had expected to hear.

CULTURE AND HUMAN BEHAVIOR 3.4

Culture and Visual Illusions

Suppose you showed the Müller-Lyer illusion to a friend or relative. Do you think they would perceive the illusion in the same way as you do—that one line is significantly longer than the other? Do you think people from *any* culture would be equally susceptible to the Müller-Lyer illusion? These questions reflect a longstanding debate on whether perceptual principles are universal or vary from one culture to the next.

On one side of this debate were the Gestalt psychologists, who believed that the rules of perception reflected the way the human perceptual system was "hard-wired" in the brain (see Segall, 1994; Hilgard, 1987). This view is called the *nativist* position, because it argues that perceptual processes are inborn. According to the nativists, people everywhere, whatever their background, "see" the world in the same way because they share the same perceptual rules.

On the other side of the debate were psychologists and others who advocated the *empiricist* position. The empiricists believed that perception is strongly influenced by experience, including cultural experience. According to this perspective, people actively construct their perceptions, drawing on their prior learning experiences to arrive at perceptual conclusions. As cross-cultural psychologist Marshall Segall (1994) summarizes this view, "Every perception is the result of an interaction between a stimulus and a perceiver shaped by prior experience." Thus, people from very different backgrounds might well perceive the world differently.

Because visual illusions are ambiguous figures that can be interpreted in more than one way, psychologists believed that illusions could be useful in investigating whether perceptual principles are universal or culture-specific. According to the nativists, the response to illusions should be universal. According to the empiricists, cross-cultural differences might influence susceptibility to specific illusions.

Of all the illusions, the Müller-Lyer has been studied most extensively (see Figure 3.18). Since the early 1900s, it has been known that people in industrialized societies are far more susceptible to the Müller-Lyer illusion than people in some nonindustrialized societies (see Matsumoto, 1994). Segall and his colleagues (1963, 1966) proposed that this difference might be due to different perceptual experiences.

More specifically, Segall proposed *the carpentered-world hypothesis*: the idea that people living in urban, industrialized environments have a great deal of perceptual experience in judging lines, corners, edges, and other rectangular, manmade objects. Thus, people in "carpentered" cultures would be more susceptible to the Müller-Lyer illusion. (Remember, the Müller-Lyer illusion seems to occur because the arrows mimic a corner that is jutting toward or away from the perceiver.)

In contrast, people who live in very "*non*-carpentered" cultures more frequently encounter natural objects. In these cultures, perceptual experiences with straight lines and right angles are relatively rare. In these cultures, Segall predicted, people would be less susceptible to the Müller-Lyer illusion.

To test this idea, Segall and his colleagues (1963, 1966) compared the responses of people in "carpentered" societies, such as Evanston, Illinois, with those of people living in "non-carpentered" societies, such as African tribes living in remote areas. The results confirmed their hypothesis. The Müller-Lyer illusion was stronger for those living in carpentered than non-carpentered societies. The findings provided strong support for the idea that culture could influence perception.

However, the nativists were quick to suggest that Segall's results might be due to racial differences rather than cultural differences. After all, they pointed out, the non-Western subjects in Segall's research were mostly Africans, and racial differences in eye pigmentation had been shown to affect the ability to visually detect contours (see

Segall, 1994). Could the difference in illusion susceptibility be due to some sort of physiological difference rather than a cultural difference?

To address that issue, psychologist V. M. Stewart (1973) compared groups of African-American and white schoolchildren living in the "carpentered" society of Evanston, Illinois. Stewart found that, regardless of their race, the Evanston children were equally susceptible to the Müller-Lyer illusion. She then compared groups of black African children in five different areas of Zambia—ranging from the very "carpentered" capital city of Lusaka to very rural, "non-carpentered" areas of the country.

The results of this second comparison? The African children living in the "carpentered" society of Lusaka were just as susceptible to the illusion as the white and African-American children in Evanston. And the children living in the rural, non-carpentered countryside were far less susceptible. In other words, the children's race made *no* difference at all. What mattered was the children's experience, or lack of experience, with a carpentered environment.

The Müller-Lyer illusion has played a key role in the debate about whether perceptual processes are universal and inborn or are influenced by learning experiences. Clearly, the evidence supports the latter conclusion, emphasizing once again the important role of culture and learning.

Visitors from Another Planet? Perceptual set may lead the avid believer in UFOs to see this photograph of unusual cloud formations as evidence for the existence of flying saucers. Then again, take another look at the photo on page 122. Your perceptual set might also lead you to believe that these white shapes were really fabric softener dispensers flying through the air.

This example illustrates the notion of **perceptual set**—the expectancies and predispositions that the observer brings to a perceptual situation. We're often mentally primed to interpret a particular perception a particular way. Our perceptual sets are, of course, influenced by our prior learning experiences. To use an example discussed in an earlier section, an oddly shaped piece of a wood might be a "dax" to one child and simply an oddly shaped piece of wood to another child. One person's mystery dial is another person's altimeter.

Perceptual sets can exert a strong influence on the perceptual conclusions we reach. Our perceptual sets usually lead us to reasonably accurate conclusions. If they didn't, we would develop new perceptual sets that were more accurate. But sometimes a perceptual set can lead us astray. For example, when the partially decomposed body of a large, hairy creature was discovered in upper New York state, it generated much excitement because the remains were perceived by several people as proof of the existence of "Bigfoot" (Hines, 1988). Scientists operating with a different perceptual set examined the dead creature and duly proclaimed it for what it was—the remains of a brown bear.

Similar examples of erroneous perceptual set have occurred with supposed "sightings" of UFOs, the Loch Ness monster, mermaids, and ghosts. In each case, observers interpreted ambiguous stimuli in terms of the perceptual set they held in that situation and saw what their expectations led them to see.

CONCEPT REVIEW 3.6

Perceptual Principles

Fill in the blanks using the correct terms from this list: perceptual set; closure; similarity; figure; shape constancy; ground; size constancy; proximity; stroboscopic motion; brightness constancy; good continuation.

1. At the end of many airport runways is a line of strobe lights that flash in rapid succession. From the cockpit of an airplane approaching to land, the flashing strobe lights look like a white ball repeatedly zooming toward the end of the runway. This illusion of movement is caused by _____.

2. When Jenny was flying to the South Pacific she saw several lush green islands that stood out in a sea of bright blue. In this example the islands are the _____ and the sea is the _____.

3. As you watch four-year-year Jason cling to his horse on a turning Merry-Go-Round, you perceive Jason's form as being continuous and unchanging despite the different images that are cast on the retinas of your eyes. This perceptual tendency is called _____.

4. As the football is hurtling toward you, it creates a progressively larger image on your retina, and the angle of the ball is constantly changing. Despite these drastic changes in sensory input, the joint phenomena of _____ and _____ enable you to continue to perceive the object as a football.

5. •••• •••• •••• If you followed the law of _____, you perceived this arrangement as three groups of four dots.

6. ○○○○●●●○○○○●●●● If you followed the law of _____, you perceived this arrangement as two groups of four circles and two groups of four dots.

7. Hundreds of people flocked to an Indiana town when it was reported that the face of a religious figure appeared in a rust stain on the side of a water tower. This perception was probably an example of _____.

perceptual set
The influence of prior assumptions and expectations on perceptual interpretations.

Summing Up: Sensation and Perception

In this chapter, we've seen the interaction of biological, behavioral, and psychological factors. We come to know and experience the world by detecting various forms of energy through our sense organs. With each of our senses, the process of sensation ultimately results in the transmission of neural messages to the brain, where the psychological process of perception occurs. The process of perception follows consistent patterns of organization as we draw perceptual conclusions about objects, including their distance and direction of movement.

That the process of perception is a psychological phenomenon is underscored by the fact that we can sometimes arrive at more than one perceptual conclusion for a given stimulus. And, as perceptual illusions and impossible figures demonstrate, our perceptual conclusions sometimes represent inaccurate reflections of physical reality. Our perceptual conclusions can also be influenced by a variety of psychological factors, including our expectations, learning experiences, and experiences that are unique to our culture. In the final analysis, sensation and perception reflect, once again, the profound interdependence of body, brain, and mind.

APPLICATION

Controlling Pain

Occasional pain is an unavoidable fact of life, but many strategies can be used to control or minimize pain. What techniques can you use to reduce your subjective experience of pain? What techniques do experts use to manage and reduce pain?

Pain is the body's way of indicating that something is wrong. Whether it's being stung by a bee, having wisdom teeth pulled, getting a bad sunburn, or suffering a sprained ankle, we all experience episodes of acute pain now and again. And pain can be recurring, chronic, or progressive for some people, such as those who suffer from sporadic migraine headaches, unremitting back pain, or rheumatoid arthritis. There are many strategies for controlling pain, whether acute or chronic. First we'll look at several techniques that can be used by virtually anyone to help reduce pain, especially acute pain. Then we'll examine some of the pain-reducing techniques used by pain specialists.

Pain-Reducing Techiques You Can Use

Research has shown that each of the following simple self-administered techniques can be useful for dealing with the everyday pain of a headache, an injury, or a trip to the dentist. Of course the techniques described here are *not* a substitute for seeking appropriate medical attention, especially when pain is severe, recurring, or of unknown origins.

1. Distraction. By actively focusing your attention on some nonpainful stimulus, you can often reduce pain (Turk & Nash, 1993; Fernandez, 1986). For example, you can mentally count backward by 7s from 901; multiply pairs of two-digit numbers, such as 14×23; mentally draw different geometric figures, such as a circle with a triangle in it; count ceiling tiles; or sing "The Star Spangled Banner." You can also stare at the details of a picture or another object, or intently listen to music.

2. Imagery. One form of distraction is *imagery.* Creating a vivid mental image can help control pain or other unpleasant physical symptoms (Rossman, 1993). Usually people create a pleasant and progressive scenario, such as walking along the beach, hiking in the mountains, or enjoying a gathering of friends. Aggressive or arousing imagery can also be useful, such as imag-

ining a heated argument, fighting off an enemy, or driving a race car at high speeds (Lyles & others, 1982). Whatever imaginary scenario you use, try to visualize all the different sensations involved, including the sights, sounds, aromas, touches, and tastes. The goal is to become so absorbed in your fantasy that you distract yourself from the pain sensations.

3. Positive Self-Talk. This strategy involves making positive coping statements, either silently or out loud, during a painful episode or procedure (see Cioffi & Holloway, 1993; Fernandez, 1986). Examples of positive self-talk include statements such as "It hurts but I'm okay, I'm in control"; "I'm uncomfortable, but I can handle it"; "The pain is uncomfortable but not unbearable"; and "I can tolerate anything for five minutes."

Such self-talk can also include *redefining the pain.* By using realistic and constructive thoughts about the pain experience in place of threatening or harmful thoughts, you can minimize pain (McCaul & Malott, 1984). For example, an athlete in training might say, "The pain means my muscles are getting stronger." Someone wearing orthodontic braces might tell himself that the pain means that his teeth are moving into place; a woman during childbirth might redefine the painful contractions of labor as work or effort.

4. Counter-irritation. The technique of counter-irritation has been used for centuries. *Counter-irritation* involves decreasing pain by creating a strong, competing sensation that's mildly stimulating or irritating (Sarafino, 1994). People often do this naturally, as when they vigorously rub an injury or bite their lip during an injection. How does rubbing the area where an injury has occurred reduce pain? The intense sensations of pain and the normal sensations of touch are processed through different nerve fibers going to the spinal cord. Increasing normal sensations of touch interferes with the transmission of high-intensity pain signals (Coren & others, 1994).

Other possible counter-irritation strategies include scratching, massaging, or applying very cold water, ice packs, or heat. While undergoing a painful procedure, you can create and control a competing discomfort by pressing your thumbnail into your index finger. Focusing your attention on the competing discomfort may lessen your overall experience of pain.

5. Relaxation. Deep relaxation can be a very effective strategy for deterring pain sensations (Turk & Nash, 1993; Benson, 1993). Relaxation procedures can be used in a particular situation or repeatedly practiced during prolonged pain. One simple strategy to achieve relaxation is *deep breathing:* inhale deeply, then exhale very slowly and completely, releasing tension throughout your body, especially in your neck, shoulders, and chest. As you exhale, consciously note the feelings of relaxation and warmth you've produced in your body (Turk & others, 1983).

Techniques Used by Pain Specialists

There are many different kinds of pain specialists, including physicians, psychologists, nurses, and physical therapists. Medical techniques to control pain include painkilling drugs, some of which will be discussed in the next chapter. Here we look at nondrug pain relievers used by pain specialists.

1. *Biofeedback* is a process of learning voluntary control over largely automatic body functions such as heartbeat, blood pressure, and muscle tension (M.S. Schwartz & N.M. Schwartz, 1993). Using sensitive equipment that signals very subtle changes in a specific body function, biofeedback augments the body's natural internal feedback system. Through biofeedback, an individual can learn to become more aware of body signals and exercise conscious control over a particular body process. For example, an individual who experiences chronic tension headaches might use biofeedback to learn to relax shoulder, neck, and facial muscles. Biofeedback has proven to be effective in helping many people who experience tension headaches, migraine headaches, jaw pain, and back pain (Turk & Nash, 1993; M.S. Schwartz & N.M. Schwartz, 1993).

2. *Hypnosis* is an induced, trancelike state of relaxation during which an individual is highly focused on the suggestions of the hypnotist (Olness, 1993). Although people vary in their susceptibility to hypnotic suggestions, hypnosis has been used to reduce pain associated with a variety of conditions, including dental procedures, childbirth, headaches, and cancer (Spira & Spiegel, 1992; Hilgard & Hilgard, 1983). We'll discuss hypnosis in more detail in Chapter 4.

3. *Acupuncture* is a procedure that involves inserting long, thin needles at specific points in the body which are then twirled, heated, or stimulated with a mild electrical current (Taylor, 1995; Duffin, 1985). Acupuncture origi-

nated in China over 2,000 years ago. Acupuncture can significantly reduce pain and has been used as the sole analgesia (painkiller) in some cases of surgery (Sarafino, 1994). Acupuncture seems to produce pain reduction partly by increasing endorphin levels in the body (see Schneider & Tarshis, 1995).

4. *TENS* stands for *transcutaneous electrical nerve stimulation* and is an electrical form of counter-irritation (Hare & Milano, 1985). This procedure involves placing electrodes on the skin close to where a person feels pain. The electrodes stimulate the skin with a mild electric current, producing counter-irritation. Research has shown that TENS also reduces pain partly by increasing endorphin levels (see Cailliet, 1993).

Using Acupuncture for Pain Relief For thousands of years, acupuncture has been used in traditional Chinese medicine for pain relief and other medical treatments. Shown here is a modern acupuncture method in which the acupuncture needles are stimulated with a mild electrical current.

Summary

Sensation and Perception

Sensation and Perception

- *Sensation* refers to the response of sensory receptors in the sense organs to stimulation and the transmission of that information to the brain.

- *Perception* refers to the process through which the brain organizes and interprets sensory information.

- Sensation is the result of the stimulation of sensory receptors by some form of energy. Through the process of transduction, this energy is converted and coded into neural impulses, and then sent to the brain.

- Each sense is specialized in terms of the form of energy to which it will respond. The senses are also responsive only to particular levels of stimulation, called sensory thresholds. Two types of sensory thresholds are the absolute threshold and the difference threshold, or just noticeable difference (jnd). Weber's Law states that the just noticeable difference will vary depending on the strength of the original stimulus.

- Sensory adaptation takes place when the sensory receptor cells gradually decline in sensitivity to a constant stimulus.

Vision: From Light to Sight

- The sensory receptors for vision respond to light waves. Visible light is only a tiny part of the electromagnetic energy spectrum, which is described in terms of wavelength.

- Light waves enter the eye and pass through the cornea, pupil, and lens, which focuses the light on the retina. The retina contains the sensory receptors for vision, the rods and cones.

- Rods are specialized for vision in dim light; cones for color vision and for vision in bright light. We rely on the rods for peripheral vision and on the cones for seeing fine detail. Cones adapt quickly to bright light, while rods adapt slowly to dim light.

- The rods and cones send information to the bipolar and ganglion cells, where it undergoes preliminary processing before being sent to the brain via the optic nerve. There is a much smaller ratio of cones than rods to ganglion cells; thus, cones are important to visual acuity. Cones are concentrated in the fovea. The optic nerve transmits information to the thalamus. From the thalamus, information is sent to the visual cortex. There are no rods or cones in the blind spot, which is where the optic nerve exits the eye.

Color Vision

- Color is the psychological experience of different wavelengths of light, and involves hue, brightness, and saturation. White light contains all the wavelengths of the visible spectrum. The color of an object is determined by the light wave it reflects.

- In combination, the trichromatic theory and the opponent-process theory explain color vision. Trichromatic theory explains red-green color blindness and color processing in the retina; opponent-process theory explains afterimages and color processing in the ganglion cells and the brain.

Hearing: From Vibration to Sound

- Sound waves are the physical stimuli that produce the sensation of sound. The amplitude, frequency, and complexity of a sound wave determine the loudness, pitch, and timbre of the sound that we hear.

- Sound waves are collected in the outer ear, amplified in the middle ear, and transduced in the inner ear. The sensory receptors for hearing are the hair cells, which are located on the basilar membrane in the cochlea. In combination, frequency theory and place theory explain the sensation of pitch.

- Hearing loss, or deafness, may be either partial or total. Conduction deafness results when vibrations are not adequately conducted to the hair cells. Nerve deafness results from damage to the hair cells or the auditory nerve.

Smell and Taste: The Chemical Senses

- The sensory receptors for smell and taste are specialized to respond to chemical substances. The sensation of smell is caused by airborne molecules stimulating odor receptors that are located on the olfactory receptor cells in the lining of the nose; information is transmitted directly to the olfactory bulb in the brain via the olfactory nerve.

- Women are generally more sensitive to smells than men. Many animals communicate information about territory and reproduction through pheromones, which are chemical scents. Human sex pheromones have not been discovered, but chemical signals have been shown to affect the menstrual cycle in women.

- Taste results from the stimulation of sensory receptors in the taste buds, which are located on the tongue and the inside of the mouth. When activated by chemical substances dissolved in saliva, the taste buds send neural messages to the thalamus in the brain. There are four primary tastes: sweet, salty, sour, and bitter.

Skin and Body Senses

- The skin and body senses provide important information about the body and include the senses of touch, temperature, pain, movement, position, and balance.

- The skin includes several kinds of sensory receptors, which are unevenly distributed among the parts of the body. The Pacinian corpuscle is the skin receptor that is sensitive to pressure. Cold temperatures are sensed when cold spots are stimulated; warm temperatures when warm spots are stimulated; and hot temperatures when cold and warm spots are stimulated simultaneously.

■ Pain sensation is partly explained by the gate-control theory. Psychological factors are involved in the experience of pain. Pain sensations also result from the release of a neurotransmitter called substance P. The transmission of pain signals is inhibited by the release of endorphins, which can also be influenced by psychological factors.

■ The kinesthetic sense involves the location and position of body parts in relation to one another. The sensory receptors for the kinesthetic sense are the proprioceptors, which are located in the muscles and joints. The sense of balance, equilibrium, and orientation is due to the vestibular sense. The vestibular sensory receptors are located in the semicircular canals and the vestibular sacs in the inner ear.

Perception

■ Perception refers to the process of integrating, organizing, and interpreting sensory information in a meaningful way. Our perceptual processes help us answer important questions about objects in the environment. The Gestalt psychologists studied perception in the early twentieth century, emphasizing the perception of *gestalts,* or whole forms.

Depth Perception: "How Far Away Is It?"

■ Depth perception refers to the perception of the distance of an object or its three-dimensional characteristics. Monocular depth cues include relative size, overlap, aerial perspective, texture gradient, linear perspective, motion parallax, and accommodation. Binocular depth cues include convergence and binocular disparity.

The Perception of Motion: "Where Is It Going?"

■ The perception of movement involves integrating information from the eye muscles, the retina, and the environment. The illusion of induced motion is a result of our assumption that the background is stationary. The perception of stroboscopic motion results from images being rapidly registered on the retina. We also use auditory cues to judge the distance and direction of an object.

The Perception of Shape: "What Is It?"

■ We rely primarily on shape to identify an object. Figure–ground relationships are important in distinguishing an object from its background.

■ We actively organize visual information and group different visual elements together. The Gestalt principles of organization include proximity, similarity, closure, good continuation, and the law of Prägnanz.

Perceptual Constancies

■ Perceptual constancy refers to the tendency to perceive objects as unchanging despite changes in sensory input and retinal image. Size constancy, shape constancy, and brightness constancy are three important forms of perceptual constancy. Size constancy results from the combination of information about the size of the retinal image and about the distance of the object. When the retinal image does not change but the perception of distance increases, the object is perceived as larger.

Perceptual Illusions

■ Perceptual illusions can be used to study perceptual principles. The Müller-Lyer illusion involves the principles of depth cues and size constancy. The moon illusion results from the principles of overlap, depth cues, and the misperception of the shape of the sky. Impossible figures challenge our ability to organize a scene into a stable and meaningful perception.

The Effects of Experience on Perceptual Interpretations

■ Perception can be influenced by learning experiences, including experiences that are unique to one's culture. *Perceptual set* refers to the expectations that a person brings to a situation, which can affect his or her interpretation of the situation.

Key Terms

sensation (p. 95)

perception (p. 95)

sensory receptors (p. 95)

transduction (p. 96)

sensory threshold (p. 96)

absolute threshold (p. 96)

difference threshold (p. 97)

just noticeable difference (jnd) (p. 97)

Weber's Law (p. 97)

sensory adaptation (p. 97)

wavelength (p. 98)

cornea (p. 99)

pupil (p. 99)

iris (p. 99)

iridology (p. 100)

lens (p. 101)

accommodation (p. 101)

retina (p. 101)

rods (p. 101)

cones (p. 101)

fovea (p. 102)

optic nerve (p. 103)

blind spot (p. 103)

color (p. 104)

hue (p.104)

saturation (p. 104)

brightness (p. 104)

trichromatic theory of color vision (p. 105)

color blindness (p. 105)

afterimage (p. 106)

CONCEPT REVIEW 3.1 Page 97

1. a
2. d
3. a
4. c

CONCEPT REVIEW 3.2 Page 107

1. retina
2. cones
3. optic nerve
4. white
5. trichromatic
6. yellow; opponent-process

CONCEPT REVIEW 3.3 Page 112

1. pitch; loudness
2. basilar; cochlea
3. nerve deafness
4. frequency
5. place
6. conduction deafness

CONCEPT REVIEW 3.4 Page 121

1. kinesthetic
2. olfactory
3. vestibular
4. hot
5. olfactory nerve
6. substance P
7. gate-control

CONCEPT REVIEW 3.5 Page 126

1. *Relative size.* The cars, people, street posts, and banners at the bottom of the photo seem closer because they are larger than those toward the top of the photo.
2. *Overlap.* Many objects in the photograph are partially obscured by other objects—such as the signs, people, and vehicles. In each case, the object that is not obscured is perceived as being closer.
3. *Aerial perspective.* The buildings in the upper middle of the photograph are fuzzy and slightly blurred, and thus are perceived as farther away.
4. *Texture gradient.* Details of the sidewalk, street, and cars are crisp in the foreground, but become progressively more blurred as you move toward the top of the photograph.
5. *Linear perspective.* The parallel boundaries of the street, the lines of yellow and orange banners, and the lines of parked cars seem to converge at the top of the photo, creating a sense of greater distance.

CONCEPT REVIEW 3.6 Page 138

1. stroboscopic motion
2. figure; ground
3. shape constancy
4. size constancy; shape constancy
5. proximity
6. similarity
7. perceptual set

4

Consciousness and Its Variations

Prologue: Glimpses of the Mind at Night

Still half asleep, we could hear them upstairs, talking and giggling as they traded stories of dreams they remembered. Of course, our four-year-old daughter did not have so long a legacy of dream memories to draw from as did Grandma Fern, Sandy's mom. Downstairs, the brain fog was still pretty thick, but your author Don dragged himself out of the lumpy sleeper sofa, pulled on some clothes, and trudged upstairs in search of a potent antidote to morning brain fog—Fern's strong coffee.

Grandma Fern and Laura were, of course, disgustingly alert as Don joined them at the small kitchen table. Fern mentioned that she had heard Laura calling out in her sleep during the night. Laura had awakened during a bad dream. Right on cue, Laura excitedly retold the details of her dream:

> There was a big monster chasing me and Nubbin the Cat! And we jumped on a golden horse but the monster kept chasing us! Then Nubbin jumped off and started to eat the monster. And then my Mommy came and saved me! And then Daddy took a sword and killed the monster! And then me and Mommy and Nubbin rode the horse into the clouds.

As for most children, nightmares could be frighteningly real to Laura. But even though she was just barely four years old, Laura already had a good grasp of the difference between dreams and actual events—at least once she completely woke up. And, fortunately, the recognition of that difference provides considerable comfort to her when she has an occasional bad dream.

A short while later Sandy trudged upstairs, still in her bathrobe, also in search of Fern's coffee. As Grandma Fern and Laura continued to chatter about monsters and golden horses and other imaginary creatures, Sandy described the dream she had been having shortly before she woke up:

> I was back in high school. The building was huge and old and dark and gloomy. I went to my locker but I couldn't remember the locker combination and I couldn't find my books or my shoes. Then I couldn't find my classroom. The hallways were dark and had very high ceilings. I would turn a corner and keep getting lost. Once I finally got to class, I tried to sneak in the back because I was so late. Then I realized that I hadn't come to class for weeks! And everybody was supposed to turn in a term paper that day—but I didn't even know what the topic was! I slumped at my desk, trying to hide. Then the teacher, who was very stern and wore glasses and a crewcut, announced that we were having an essay exam. In my dream, I was trying to figure out how to get out of this mess and I think I just got up and bolted out the door. Then I woke up—intensely relieved to discover that I was no longer in high school!

The experience of dreams is, of course, a universal one. Although everybody dreams, some people are like Don, who seldom remembers his dreams. Perhaps you're like Sandy and Laura, who vividly recall several dreams a week.

In this chapter, we'll consider the naturally occurring variations in the everyday experience of consciousness, including sleep and dreaming. We'll tackle such issues as why we sleep, the nature of sleep, and the significance of dreams. We've made an effort to try to answer many of the questions that students often ask about sleep and dreaming, such as whether animals dream. And, yes, we will answer the famous question, "If I fall off a cliff in my dreams and I don't wake up before I hit the bottom, will I die?"

Beyond sleep and dreaming, we'll also look at variations in consciousness that are deliberately induced: hypnosis, meditation, and the effects of drugs. In the chapter Application, we'll provide some practical suggestions for dealing with "morning brain fog" and improving the quality of your sleep.

Introduction

Consciousness: Experiencing the "Private I"

> *Consciousness refers to your immediate awareness of internal and external stimuli. What did William James mean by the phrase "stream of consciousness"? Why was psychological research on consciousness abandoned for a time, and why did research on consciousness regain legitimacy?*

Your immediate awareness of thoughts, sensations, memories, and the world around you represents the experience of **consciousness.** That the experience of consciousness varies enormously from moment to moment is easy to illustrate. Imagine that we could videotape three one-minute segments of your conscious activities at different times while your psychology instructor lectures in class. What might those three one-minute segments of consciousness reveal? Here are just a few of the possibilities:

consciousness
Personal awareness of mental activities, internal sensations, and the external environment.

- Focused concentration on your instructor's words and gestures.
- Mental drifting from one fleeting thought, memory, or image to another.
- Awareness of physical sensations, such as the beginnings of a headache or the sharp pain of a paper cut.
- Active mental problem solving, as you try to think of a topic for your humanities term paper.
- Sexual fantasies.
- Mental rehearsal of what you'll say and how you'll act when you meet a friend for dinner later that night.
- Replaying of an emotionally charged conversation.
- Wishful, grandiose daydreams of a future that is fundamentally different from your current situation.
- Obsessive worry about a family member.

Most likely, the three video clips would reveal very different scenes, dialogues, and content as your consciousness changed from one minute to the next. If we could examine your conscious awareness an hour or two later, the focus of your awareness might be completely different. However, even though your conscious experience is constantly changing, you don't experience your personal consciousness as disjointed. Rather, the subjective experience of consciousness has a sense of continuity. One stream of conscious mental activity seems to effortlessly, and seamlessly, blend into another.

It was this characteristic of consciousness that led the influential American psychologist **William James** (1892) to describe consciousness as a "river" or "stream." Although always changing, consciousness is perceived as unified and unbroken, much like a stream. Despite the changing focus of our awareness, our experience of consciousness as unbroken helps provide us with a sense of personal identity that has continuity from one day to the next.

The nature of human consciousness was one of the first topics to be tackled by the fledgling science of psychology in the late 1800s (Schneider, 1993). In Chapter 1, we discussed how the first psychologists tried to determine the nature of the human mind through *introspection*—verbal self-reports that tried to capture the "structure" of conscious experiences (see page 5). But because such self-reports were not objectively verifiable, many of the leading psychologists at the turn of the century emphasized the scientific study of *behavior*, which could be directly observed, measured, and verified.

In the second half of this century, many psychologists once again turned their attention to the study of consciousness (Hilgard, 1992; Schacter, 1995a). This occurred for a couple of reasons. First, it was becoming abundantly clear that a complete understanding of behavior was *not* possible for psychologists unless they considered the role of conscious mental processes in behavior.

Second, although the experience of consciousness is personal and subjective, psychologists devised more objective ways to study conscious experiences. For example, psychologists often *infer* the conscious experience that seems to be occurring by carefully observing behavior. Technological advances in studying brain activity were also producing intriguing correlations between brain activity and different states of consciousness, some of which we'll consider in this chapter.

Today, the scientific study of consciousness is incredibly diverse. Working from a variety of perspectives, psychologists and other researchers are piecing together a picture of consciousness that takes into account the role of

The "Stream" of Consciousness The famous American psychologist William James compared consciousness to a flowing stream. Like a stream, the contents of consciousness are always changing, yet are experienced as unbroken and continuous.

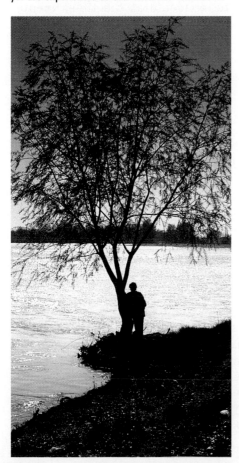

psychological, physiological, social, and cultural influences (Schacter, 1995a; Farber & Churchland, 1995; Horgan, 1994).

The Biological and Environmental "Clocks" Regulating Consciousness

Circadian rhythms are biological processes that systematically vary over a 24-hour period. What roles do the suprachiasmatic nucleus, sunlight, and melatonin play in regulating circadian rhythms? How do "free-running" conditions affect circadian rhythms?

Throughout the course of the day there is a natural ebb and flow to consciousness. The most obvious variation in consciousness that we experience is the daily sleep/wake cycle. But conscious states also change in more subtle ways.

For example, you've probably noticed that your mental alertness varies throughout the day in a relatively consistent way. Most people experience two distinct peaks of mental alertness: one in the morning, usually around 9:00 or 10:00 a.m., and one in the evening, around 8:00 or 9:00 p.m. In between these two peaks, you'll experience a slump in mental alertness at about three o'clock in the afternoon. And, should you manage to stay awake, your mental alertness will probably reach its *lowest* point at about three o'clock in the morning. One practical implication of this consistent daily pattern is the increase in the number of traffic accidents at the times mental alertness is at its lowest points (see Figure 4.1).

Mental alertness and the sleep/wake cycle are just two examples of the daily highs and lows you experience in a wide variety of bodily processes. These daily cycles are called **circadian rhythms.** The word *circadian* combines the Latin words for "about" and "day." So, the term *circadian rhythms* refers to biological processes that systematically vary over a period of about 24 hours (Thorpy & Yager, 1991).

You actually experience many different circadian rhythms that ebb and flow over the course of any given 24-hour period (see Table 4.1). In fact, researchers have discovered over 100 bodily processes that rhythmically peak and dip each day, including blood pressure, the secretion of different hormones, and pain sensitivity (see Schneider & Tarshis, 1995). Normally, your circadian rhythms are closely synchronized with one another. For example, the circadian rhythm for the release of growth hor-

FIGURE 4.1 Mental Alertness and Traffic Accidents
Time of day was analyzed in over 6,000 fatigue-related traffic accidents in Israel, Texas, and New York. The number of accidents peak when mental alertness is typically at its lowest levels. During the day, accidents are most frequent at about 3:00 p.m. At night, the peak rate of accidents occurs at about 3:00 a.m.
(Data reported in Mitler, 1994.)

TABLE 4.1 Examples of Human Circadian Rhythms

Function	Typical Circadian Rhythm
Peak mental alertness and memory functions	Two daily peaks: around 9:00 a.m. and 9:00 p.m.
Lowest body temperature	About 97° around 3:00 a.m. to 4:00 a.m.
Highest body temperature	About 99° around 5:00 p.m. to 6:00 p.m.
Peak physical strength	Two daily peaks: around 11:00 a.m. and 7:00 p.m.
Peak hearing, visual, taste, and smell sensitivity	Two daily peaks: around 3:00 a.m. and 6:00 p.m.
Lowest sensitivity to pain	Around 3:00 p.m. to 5:00 p.m.
Peak sensitivity to pain	Around 3:00 a.m. to 5:00 a.m.
Peak degree of sleepiness	Two daily peaks: around 3:00 a.m. and 3:00 p.m.
Peak melatonin hormone in blood	Between 1:00 a.m. and 3:00 a.m.
Peak allergic sensitivity to pollen and dust	Between 11:00 p.m. and 1:00 a.m.

SOURCES: Mitler, 1994; Dinges & Broughton, 1989; and Rose, 1988.

mone is synchronized with the sleep/wake circadian rhythm, so that growth hormone is released only during sleep.

The Suprachiasmatic Nucleus:
The Body's "Clock"

Your many circadian rhythms are controlled by a master "biological clock"— a tiny cluster of neurons in the hypothalamus in the brain. This cluster of neurons is called the **suprachiasmatic nucleus,** abbreviated **SCN.** Put simply, the SCN is the internal pacemaker that governs the timing of circadian rhythms, including the sleep/wake cycle and the mental alertness cycle (Klein & others, 1991).

Keeping the circadian rhythms synchronized to one another and on a 24-hour schedule also involves environmental time cues. The most important of these environmental cues is bright light, especially sunlight. In people, light detected by special photoreceptors in the eye is communicated via the visual system to the SCN in the hypothalamus (Foster, 1993; Card & Moore, 1991).

How does sunlight help regulate the sleep/wake cycle and other circadian rhythms? In somewhat simplified terms, the connection works like this: As the sun sets each day, the decrease in available light is detected by the SCN through its connections with the visual system. In turn, the SCN triggers an increase in the production of a hormone called **melatonin** by the *pineal gland,* an endocrine gland located in the brain (Zoltoski & Gillin, 1994; Illnerová, 1991).

Increased blood levels of melatonin make you sleepy and reduce activity levels. At night, blood levels of melatonin rise, peaking between 1:00 and 3:00 a.m. Shortly before sunrise, the pineal gland all but stops producing melatonin, and you soon wake up. As the sun rises, exposure to sunlight and other bright light suppresses melatonin levels, and they remain very low throughout the day (G. Brown, 1994; Boivin & others, 1994; Lewy & others, 1990). Thus, sunlight *entrains,* or sets, the SCN so that it keeps circadian cycles synchronized and operating on a 24-hour schedule.

circadian rhythm
(ser-KADE-ee-en) A cycle or rhythm that is roughly 24 hours long; refers to daily fluctuations in many biological and psychological processes.

suprachiasmatic nucleus (SCN)
(soup-rah-*kye*-az-MAT-ick) A cluster of neurons in the hypothalamus in the brain that governs the timing of circadian rhythms.

melatonin
(mel-uh-TONE-in) A hormone manufactured by the pineal gland that produces sleepiness.

Life Without a Sundial:
"Free-Running" Circadian Rhythms

Given that sunlight is responsible for "setting" the internal clock, what would happen to the timing of circadian rhythms if they were allowed to "run free" in the absence of environmental time cues like sunlight and clocks? To create *free-running conditions,* researchers have constructed rooms in underground caves. Volunteers live in these underground bunkers for weeks or months at a time, deprived of all environmental time cues (Webb, 1994).

Under free-running conditions, two distinct effects occur (Kronauer, 1994; Lewy & Sack, 1987). First, in the absence of normal light/darkness and other time cues, people tend to drift to the natural rhythm of the suprachiasmatic nucleus. What's intriguing is that the SCN naturally tends toward roughly a *25-hour* day, not a 24-hour day. Thus, people in a free-running condition go to sleep about an hour later each day. Exactly why the human sleep/wake cycle gravitates toward a 25-hour cycle rather than a 24-hour cycle remains a mystery (Thompson, 1993).

The second effect that consistently occurs when people are placed in a free-running condition is that their circadian rhythms lose their normal synchronization with one another (Aschoff, 1994, 1993). All of a person's circadian rhythms become longer, but they do not become longer in the same way (Schneider & Tarshis, 1995). For example, normally the sleep/wake cycle, body temperature, and the melatonin cycle are closely coordinated. At about 3 o'clock in the morning your body temperature dips to its lowest point just as melatonin is reaching its highest level and you are the sleepiest (Empson, 1993). But in the absence of environmental cues, the sleep/wake, body temperature, and melatonin circadian rhythms become "desynchronized," so that they are no longer properly coordinated with one another (Anch & others, 1988).

What happens when people leave the free-running condition and are once again exposed to normal daylight and darkness cues? Within days, sunlight "resets" the biological clock. Circadian rhythms become synchronized again, and they resume operating on a 24-hour cycle rather than a 25-hour cycle (Lewy & Sack, 1987).

Like the experimental subjects temporarily housed in the underground caves, many blind people have free-running circadian cycles because they are unable to detect the light that normally sets the SCN. Thus, they often suffer from recurring bouts of insomnia and other sleep problems (Sack & others, 1992a, 1992b). Like people deprived of environmental time cues, many blind people experience free-running melatonin, body temperature, and sleep/wake circadian cycles (Czeisler & others, 1995; Sack & Lewy, 1993).

Sunlight and the Body Clock Sunlight plays a key role in setting circadian rhythms. When volunteers are deprived of sunlight and other time cues for weeks or months, their circadian rhythms tend to drift to a 25-hour cycle.

Circadian Rhythms and Sunlight:
Some Practical Implications

> *When environmental time cues are out of sync with our internal biological clock, symptoms of jet lag can result. What four common situations can produce jet-lag symptoms? How is melatonin involved in jet-lag symptoms?*

Most of us are unlikely to spend much time in an underground bunker, isolated from sunlight and other time cues. Nevertheless, the close tie between our internal biological clock and environmental time cues has some very important practical applications.

Jet Lag

Consider what happens when your biological clock gets seriously out of whack with your environmental clock. Such disruptions often occur when people travel across multiple time zones. For example, imagine that you leave Denver at 2 o'clock in the afternoon on a 10-hour flight to London. When you arrive in London, it's 7:00 a.m. and the sun is shining. However, your body is still on Denver time. As far as your internal biological clock is concerned, it's midnight.

The result? Your circadian rhythms are drastically out of synchronization with daylight/darkness cues. The psychological and physiological effects of this disruption in circadian rhythms can be severe. Thinking, concentration, and memory get fuzzy. You experience physical and mental fatigue, depression or irritability, and disrupted sleep (Anch & others, 1988). Collectively, these symptoms are called *jet lag*.

Although numerous physiological variables are involved in jet lag, the circadian cycle of the hormone melatonin seems to play a key role. When it's 10:00 a.m. in London, it's 3:00 a.m. in Denver. Since your body is still operating on Denver time, your melatonin production is peaking. Rather than feeling awake, you feel very sleepy, sluggish, and groggy. For many people, it can take a week or longer to adjust to such an extreme time change (Moore-Ede, 1993).

Night Shifts

You don't need to travel across multiple time zones to experience symptoms of jet lag. Nurses, doctors, and other medical personnel often have to work night shifts or rotating shifts. So do people working in law enforcement and the military, broadcasting and weather services, and other businesses that operate around the clock. Night-shift workers in these and other occupations often suffer from jet-lag symptoms because their circadian rhythms are out of sync with daylight/darkness time cues (Scott, 1994; Sack, Blood, & Lewy, 1992).

For the night worker, the problem of being out of sync with the environmental clock is compounded every morning when she returns home in the bright morning light. Exposure to the bright morning light is a potent stimulus that can reset the person's body clock to a day schedule (Shanahan & Czeisler, 1991). And unless the person can completely darken the bedroom, even traces of sunlight through curtains can prevent her body clock from staying in sync with the night work schedule (Czeisler & others, 1989). Because sunlight time cues exert such a powerful influence on circadian rhythms, many night-shift workers never fully adjust to a nighttime work schedule (Harma, 1993; Empson, 1993).

However, research is turning up ways to minimize or eliminate the negative effects of rotating shifts. The Application at the end of the chapter provides some suggestions for minimizing jet-lag symptoms caused by night work.

Monday-Morning Brain Fog

Do Monday mornings make you miserable? Many people experience "Monday-morning brain fog"—grogginess, dulled reactions, and sometimes even mild depression. No, it's not just because you have to return to work or classes. Because of our inclination to drift toward longer days, it's easy to stay up late on the weekend socializing with friends or watching the late, late movie. But if you follow your natural inclination to stay up late when you have the opportunity on the weekend, you can inadvertently "reset" your biological clock and shift your melatonin cycle. Consequently, when your alarm clock goes off at 6:00 a.m. on Monday morning after a weekend of staying up until 2:00 a.m.

and sleeping in until 10:00, your melatonin levels may still be elevated. The result? Monday-morning brain fog. In the Application section, we offer some suggestions for minimizing the effects of morning brain fog.

There are several practical implications of the role played by circadian rhythms in the daily ebb and flow of our overall experience of consciousness. However, we should point out that circadian rhythms have *no* connection to *biorhythms,* a popular pseudoscience discussed in Box 4.1.

SCIENCE VERSUS PSEUDOSCIENCE 4.1

Biorhythms Versus Circadian Rhythms

Biorhythms is a pseudoscience based on the unproven notion that from birth onward, three rigidly fixed "natural biorhythms" reflect high, low, and critical periods of a person's physical, emotional, and intellectual functioning. The timing of these biorhythms is presumably determined by your date of birth. Physical functioning supposedly follows a 23-day cycle; emotional, a 28-day cycle; and intellectual, a 33-day cycle (Lester, 1990).

As in other pseudosciences, biorhythms practitioners use scientific-looking charts, like the one shown at the right, to plot an individual's three cycles. If a particular cycle is above the horizontal midline on a given day, it's a good day to engage in behaviors related to that particular cycle; below the midline is a bad indicator. "Critical days" supposedly occur when a cycle crosses the midpoint. If two cycles cross the midpoint simultaneously, it's a double critical day; when all three cross the midpoint, it's a triple critical day.

According to one biorhythms expert, "A person should be more careful during these critical days because his system seems to be in a state of flux and to have a considerable degree of instability" (Thommen, 1987). To underscore the seriousness of single, double, or triple critical days, biorhythms proponents cite examples of airplane crashes, athletic losses, deaths of famous people, space travel mishaps, industrial accidents, and so forth (Hines, 1996). Along with causing disasters, biorhythms cycles also purportedly influence your mental health, marital compatibility, the day on which a woman gives birth, and the sex of the offspring!

Although "biorhythms" and "biological rhythms" *sound* very similar,

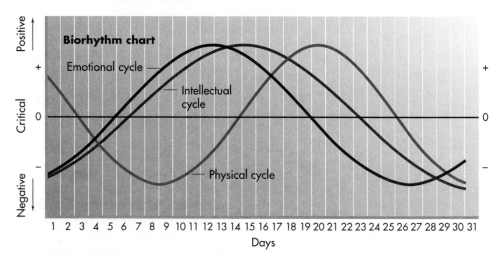

A Sample Biorhythm Chart
The green line represents the 23-day physical cycle, the purple line represents the 28-day emotional cycle, and the red line represents the 33-day intellectual cycle. Performance is presumably better than average on positive days, and worse than average on negative days. Performance is supposed to be particularly poor on "critical days," when the cycle crosses the midline. Biorhythm proponents predict that accidents and other mishaps are especially likely on critical days.

they have about as much in common as mold and gold. The legitimate scientific study of *biological rhythms* examines the consistent but potentially varying cycles of living organisms over time, including plants, animals, insects, and humans (Webb, 1994; Wheeler, 1990). Circadian rhythms, discussed in the chapter, are an example of scientifically verified biological rhythms that are highly consistent but certainly not rigidly fixed like the supposed 23-, 28-, and 33-day cycles of biorhythms.

In an effort to appear scientifically credible, biorhythms proponents often refer to biological rhythms, like the sleep/wake circadian rhythm or the menstrual cycle. To avoid confusion between the science and the pseudoscience, many psychologists, biologists, and other scientists now use the term *chronobiology* to refer to the scientific study of biological rhythms over time (Thorpy & Yager, 1991).

Scientific investigations of biorhythms are certainly not in short supply (Hines, 1996). Psychologist Terence Hines (1988) has summarized over thirty well-designed scientific investigations evaluating the effects of biorhythms. Researchers have studied the relationship between biorhythms and: automobile, aircraft, and industrial accidents; sports, academic, and intelligence test performance; the timing of births, deaths, and suicides; and the sex of newborn babies. Each of these scientific investigations found no relationship at all between biorhythms and any of these events. It seems that biorhythms are about as real as talking horses (sorry, Mr. Ed).

The Biological and Environmental "Clocks" Regulating Consciousness

Complete the sentences below using the following terms: melatonin, jet lag, suprachiasmatic nucleus, sunlight, circadian rhythm, 24, 25, growth hormone.

1. Mark notices that he consistently feels awake and alert in his 9:00 a.m. algebra class, mentally sluggish in his 2:00 p.m. philosophy class, and wide awake again when he studies later in the evening. This consistent daily pattern is an example of a _____.

2. Sheila works the night shift. Despite getting adequate sleep before going to work, Sheila feels very sleepy and physically tired at about 3:00 a.m. Her fatigue at 3:00 a.m. is most likely caused by increased blood levels of _____.

3. Wilhelm has just arrived in Berlin after a

10-hour flight from Seattle. His thinking, concentration, and memory are not very clear. He is physically tired and irritable. Taken together, Wilhem's symptoms are referred to as _____.

4. As a research volunteer, Keith has agreed to live in an underground bunker for two months. The underground environment contains everything he needs except any means to tell the time. Over the first few weeks, his _____ will naturally drift to a _____-hour cycle and his circadian rhythms may become desynchronized.

5. When the study concludes, Keith leaves the underground bunker. Within days, exposure to _____ resets his circadian rhythms so they become synchronized and operate on a _____-hour cycle.

Sleep

The invention of the electroencephalograph and the discovery of REM sleep marked the beginning of modern sleep research. What was the significance of these two discoveries? What are the two basic types of sleep? What are hypnagogic hallucinations?

Birds do it. Giraffes do it. Cats do it a lot, mostly during the day. Dolphins do it too, but only one brain hemisphere at a time. And, of course, you do it and we do it but not as much as we'd like to. Sleep, that is. In fact, if you live a long life, you'll spend approximately 22 years of your life sleeping.

As you'll see in this section, technological advances during this century have allowed scientists to unravel many of the mysteries of sleep. We'll start by looking at some of the major milestones in the modern study of sleep. Then we'll detail the systematic changes that occur during the course of a normal night's sleep. We'll also describe how the normal patterns of sleep can become disrupted by sleep disorders.

The Beginnings of Modern Sleep Research:
Measuring Sleep

From Aristotle to Shakespeare to Freud, history is filled with examples of scholars, writers, and scientists who have been fascinated by sleep and dreams (Thorpy, 1991). But prior to the twentieth century, there was no objective way to study the internal processes that might be occurring during sleep. So, traditionally, sleep was largely viewed as a period of restful inactivity in which dreams sometimes occurred.

Monitoring Sleep Using electrodes that are attached harmlessly to the face and scalp, the electroencephalograph records the brain's electrical activity throughout the night. Although this may look uncomfortable and cumbersome, people generally sleep just fine with all the wires attached.

electroencephalograph
(electro-en-SEFF-uh-low-graph) An instrument that uses electrodes placed on the scalp to measure and record the brain's electrical activity.

EEG
The graphic record of brain activity produced by an electroencephalograph.

REM sleep
Type of sleep during which rapid eye movements and dreaming occur.

NREM sleep
Nondreaming quiet sleep, which is divided into four stages.

beta brain waves
Brain wave pattern associated with alert wakefulness.

alpha brain waves
Brain wave pattern associated with relaxed wakefulness and drowsiness.

hypnagogic hallucinations
(hip-nah-GO-jick) Vivid sensory phenomena that can occur during the onset of sleep.

The Invention of the Electroencephalograph

The invention of the **electroencephalograph** by German psychiatrist Hans Berger in the 1920s gave sleep researchers an important tool for measuring the rhythmic electrical activity of the brain. These rhythmical patterns of electrical activity are referred to as *brain waves.* The electroencephalograph produces a graphic record called an **EEG,** or *electroencephalogram.* By studying EEGs, sleep researchers firmly established that brain-wave activity systematically changes throughout sleep (Empson, 1993).

Along with brain activity, today's sleep researchers monitor a variety of other physical functions during sleep (Cooper & Bradbury, 1994). Eye movements, muscle movements, breathing rate, air flow, pulse, blood pressure, amount of exhaled carbon dioxide, body temperature, and breathing sounds are just some of the body functions that are measured in contemporary sleep research.

The Discovery of REM Sleep

The next milestone in sleep research occurred in the early 1950s. Eugene Aserinsky, a graduate student at the University of Chicago, was working in the laboratory of renowned sleep researcher Nathaniel Kleitman (Hobson, 1988). Using his ten-year-old son as a subject, Aserinsky discovered that particular EEG patterns during sleep were often associated with rapid movements of the sleeper's eyes. Moreover, these periods of rapid eye movement were highly correlated with the subject's reports of dreaming. In 1953, Aserinsky and Kleitman published their findings, heralding the discovery of *rapid eye movement sleep,* usually abbreviated *REM sleep.*

Today, sleep researchers distinguish between two basic types of sleep. **REM sleep** is often called *active sleep* or *paradoxical sleep* because it is associated with heightened body and brain activity during which dreaming consistently occurs. **NREM sleep,** or *non-rapid-eye-movement sleep,* is often referred to as *quiet sleep* because the body's physiological functions and brain activity slow down during this period of slumber. NREM sleep is further divided into four stages, as we'll describe shortly.

As you'll see, normal sleep follows a consistent pattern. In the next section, we'll look at what happens when we fall asleep. Then we'll explore the cycle of brain activity during the first 90 minutes of sleep and the rest of the night.

The Onset of Sleep and Hypnagogic Hallucinations

Awake and reasonably alert as you prepare for bed, your brain generates small, fast brain waves, called **beta brain waves.** After your head hits the pillow and you close your eyes, your muscles relax. Your brain's electrical activity gradually gears down, generating slightly larger and slower **alpha brain waves.** As drowsiness sets in, your thoughts may wander and become less logical.

During this drowsy, presleep phase, you may experience odd but vividly realistic sensations. You may hear your name called or a loud crash, feel as if you're falling or floating, smell something burning, or see kaleidoscopic patterns or an unfolding landscape. These vivid sensory phenomena that occasionally occur during the transition from wakefulness to light sleep are called **hypnagogic hallucinations** (Mavromatis, 1987). Although most tend to be rather ordinary, hynagogic hallucinations can sometimes be so vivid or startling that they cause a sudden awakening (Thorpy & Yager, 1991).

GARFIELD

Probably the most common hypnagogic hallucination is the vivid sensation of falling. The sensation of falling is often accompanied by a *myoclonic jerk*—an involuntary muscle spasm of the whole body that jolts the person completely awake (Cooper, 1994; Empson, 1993). Although this experience can seem really weird (or embarrassing) when it occurs, you can rest assured that it's not abnormal. The vast majority of people occasionally experience the hypnagogic hallucination of falling combined with a myoclonic jerk (Mavromatis, 1987).

The First 90 Minutes of Sleep and Beyond

> *During the first 90 minutes of sleep, the sleeper progresses through the four stages of NREM and then enters REM sleep. What are the characteristics of NREM and REM sleep stages? How do sleep cycles vary throughout the remainder of the night? How do sleep patterns change over the lifespan?*

The course of a normal night's sleep follows a relatively consistent cyclical pattern. As the person drifts off to sleep, she initially enters NREM sleep and begins a progression through the four NREM sleep stages (see Figure 4.2). In general, the progression through each NREM sleep stage is characterized by corresponding decreases in brain and body activity. For example, during NREM sleep, the sleeper is virtually motionless. On the average, the progression through the first four stages of NREM sleep occupies the first 50 to 70 minutes of sleep (Cooper, 1994). We'll briefly describe the characteristics of each stage of NREM sleep.

Stage 1 NREM

As the alpha brain waves of drowsiness are replaced by even slower *theta brain waves,* you enter the first stage of sleep. Lasting only a few minutes, stage 1 is a transitional stage during which you gradually disengage from the sensations of the world around you. Familiar sounds, such as the hum of the refrigerator or the sound of traffic, gradually fade from conscious awareness.

During stage 1 NREM, you can easily regain conscious alertness if the phone rings or your three-year-old wanders into your bedroom to ask if Big Bird likes Fruit Loops. Although hypnagogic experiences can also occur in stage 1, less vivid mental imagery is common, such as imagining yourself engaged in some everyday activity. While dreamlike, these images lack the unfolding, sometimes bizarre, details of a true dream (Hobson, 1988).

Stage 2 NREM

Stage 2 represents the onset of true sleep. Stage 2 sleep is marked by the appearance of **sleep spindles,** which are bursts of brain activity that last a second or two (see Figure 4.2). Other than these occasional sleep spindles, brain activity continues to slow down considerably. Breathing becomes rhythmical. Slight muscle twitches may occur. Theta waves are predominant in stage 2, but large, slow brain waves called *delta brain waves* also begin to emerge. During the 15 to 20 minutes initially spent in stage 2, the amount of delta brain waves gradually increases.

sleep spindles
Short bursts of brain activity that characterize stage 2 NREM sleep.

Synchronized Sleepers As these time-lapse photographs show, couples who regularly sleep in the same bed tend to have synchronized sleep cycles. Since bed partners fall asleep at about the same time, they are likely to have similarly timed NREM/REM sleep cycles. The body movements of this couple are also synchronized: Both sleepers shift position just before and after episodes of REM sleep.

FIGURE 4.2 The First 90 Minutes of Sleep From wakefulness to the deepest sleep of stage 4 NREM, the brain's activity, measured by EEG recordings, progressively diminishes, as demonstrated by larger and slower brain waves. The four slow-wave, NREM stages occupy the first 50 to 70 minutes of sleep. Then, in a matter of minutes, the brain cycles back to smaller, faster brain waves and the sleeper experiences the night's first episode of dreaming REM sleep, which lasts 5 to 15 minutes. During the rest of the night, the sleeper continues to experience 90-minute cycles of alternating NREM and REM sleep.

(Based on Hobson, 1989.)

Stage 3 and Stage 4 NREM

Stages 3 and 4 of NREM are physiologically very similar. Both stages are defined by the amount of delta brain wave activity. Thus, in combination, stages 3 and 4 are sometimes referred to as *slow-wave sleep* (Thorpy & Yager, 1991). When delta brain waves represent more than 20 percent of total brain activity, the sleeper is said to be in stage 3 NREM. When delta brain waves exceed 50 percent of total brain activity, the sleeper is said to be in stage 4 NREM (Cooper, 1994).

During the 20 to 40 minutes spent in the night's first episode of stage 4 NREM, delta waves eventually come to represent 100 percent of brain activity. At that point, the sleeper's heart rate, blood pressure, and breathing rate drop to their lowest levels. Not surprisingly, the sleeper in stage 4 NREM is virtually oblivious to the world; noises as loud as 90 decibels often fail to wake the sleeper (Empson, 1993). However, the sleeper's muscles are still capable of movement. For example, sleepwalking occurs during stage 4 NREM sleep (see Box 4.2).

It can easily take 15 minutes or longer to regain full waking consciousness from stage 4. It's even possible to answer a ringing phone, carry on a conversation for several minutes, and hang up without ever leaving stage 4 sleep—and without remembering it the next day. When people are briefly awakened by sleep researchers during stage 4 NREM and asked to perform some simple task, they often don't remember it the next morning (see Goodenough, 1991; Dinges, 1990).

| 50 to 70 minutes | 5 to 15 minutes |

Awake and Alert: Beta brain waves

Awake but Drowsy: Alpha brain waves

Stage 1 NREM Sleep: Mixture of alpha and theta brain waves

Sleep spindle

Stage 2 NREM Sleep: Sleep spindles, theta brain waves, and beginnings of delta waves

Stage 3 NREM Sleep: Mixture of theta and delta brain waves

Stage 4 NREM Sleep: Delta brain waves

REM Sleep: Fast, active brain waves accompanied by rapid eye movements (REMs)

IN FOCUS 4.2

What You *Really* Want to Know About Sleep

Is it true that there are some people who never sleep?

No. There are people who *claim* to never sleep (usually on talk shows to promote the book they've written while supposedly awake all night). Such people seldom volunteer for study in sleep labs. When they do, of course, they eventually fall asleep.

However, there is a very rare and lethal disease called *fatal familial insomnia.* Fewer than ten families worldwide are known to have this disease, most of whom seem to be of Italian descent. The disease begins with severe insomnia and progresses to a dreamlike stupor. Other symptoms develop, such as tremors, episodes of fever, unexplained sweating, depression, and memory loss. The disorder progressively destroys brain cells, leading to coma. Ultimately, death occurs.

Is it true that some people are "morning larks" while others are "night owls"?

Morning people follow the "early to bed, early to rise" axiom. They have sleep/wake circadian cycles that are set ahead of most people's. Night or evening people tend to follow the maxim "the night is still young." They go to bed and arise later than most people. The circadian rhythms of night people are delayed in comparison to most people.

As a general rule, the older you get, the more you tend to follow a "morning lark" schedule. Whether this happens because of changing life demands as you get older, as a matter of preference, or for other reasons seems less clear.

Sometimes in the morning when I first wake up, I can't move. I'm literally paralyzed! Is this normal?

REM sleep is characterized by paralysis of the voluntary muscles, which keeps you from acting out your dreams.

In a relatively common phenomenon called *sleep paralysis,* the paralysis of REM sleep carries over to the waking state for up to 10 minutes. If preceded by an unpleasant dream or hypnagogic experience, this sensation can be frightening. Sleep paralysis can also occur as you're falling asleep. In either case, the sleep paralysis lasts only for a few minutes. So, if this happens to you, relax: voluntary-muscle control will soon return.

If I tape-record my chemistry class notes and play them while I sleep, can I learn the material without studying?

Not a chance. Although some perceptual processing can occur during sleep, the ability to learn and recall information requires wakefulness.

Is it true that you can "program" yourself to wake up at a certain time?

Most of us have some ability to judge the passage of time while we're asleep and can exert some control over when we wake up. Some people *do* have the ability to very accurately control when they wake up, without cheating by waking up throughout the night and peeking at a bedside clock.

Do deaf people who use sign language sometimes "sleep sign" during sleep?

Yes.

Do the things that people say when they're sleeptalking make any sense? Can you get them to answer questions?

In one experiment, sleep researchers recorded the utterances of sleeptalkers, then awakened them and asked them what they were thinking. The greatest agreement was found for sleeptalking during REM sleep, followed by sleeptalking that occurred during stage 2 NREM sleep. Sleeptalking during the slow-wave sleep of NREM stages 3 and 4 is best described as incoherent ramblings, with no apparent relationship to what the person reported when awakened.

There are many anecdotes of spouses who have supposedly engaged their sleeptalking mates in extended conversations, but sleep researchers have been unsuccessful in having extended dialogues with chronic sleeptalkers. As far as the truthfulness of the sleeptalker's utterances go, they're reasonably accurate insofar as they reflect whatever the sleeptalker is responding to while asleep. If you're looking for a confession as to what your mate was *really* doing when they got home late last Thursday night, you're better off asking them when they're awake.

By the way, not only do people sleeptalk, they can also sleep-*sing*! In one case we know of, a little boy sleep-sang "Frosty the Snowman."

Is it dangerous to wake a sleepwalker?

It's not dangerous to wake a sleepwalker; it's just difficult, because they are in deep sleep. Sleepwalkers will usually respond to verbal suggestions, so it's relatively easy to guide them back to bed.

Sleepwalking may be genetically determined. Identical twins are much more likely to share this characteristic than are nontwin siblings. One college student confided to sleep researcher Jacob Empson (1993) that her whole family sleepwalked. She reported that on one occasion her entire family woke up in the early-morning hours seated around the kitchen table, where they had all gathered in their sleep!

SOURCES: Ozbayrak & Berlin, 1995; Empson, 1993; Takeuchi & others, 1992; Ishihara & others, 1992; Arkin, 1991, 1981; Thorpy & Yager, 1991; Larson & others, 1991; Lugaresi & Montagna, 1990; Hobson, 1989.

Thus far in our description, the sleeper is approximately 70 minutes into a typical night's sleep and immersed in deeply relaxed stage 4 NREM sleep. At this point, the sequence reverses. In a matter of minutes the sleeper cycles back from stage 4 to stage 3 to stage 2, and enters a dramatic new phase: the night's first episode of REM sleep.

REM Sleep

During REM sleep, the brain becomes more active, generating smaller and faster brain waves. Visual and motor neurons in the sleeper's brain fire repeatedly, just as they do during wakefulness. Dreams usually occur during REM sleep. Although the brain is very active, voluntary muscle activity is suppressed, which prevents the dreaming sleeper from acting out her dreams (Cooper, 1994).

REM sleep is accompanied by considerable physiological arousal. The sleeper's eyes dart back and forth behind closed eyelids. Heart rate, blood pressure, and respirations can fluctuate up and down, sometimes extremely. Muscle twitches occur. In both sexes, sexual arousal may occur, which is not necessarily related to dream content (Hobson, 1989).

This first REM episode tends to be brief—about 5 to 15 minutes. From the beginning of stage 1 NREM sleep through the completion of the first episode of REM sleep, about 90 minutes elapse.

Beyond the First 90 Minutes

Throughout the rest of the night, the sleeper cycles between NREM and REM sleep. Each cycle lasts about 90 minutes on the average, but the duration of cycles may vary from 70 to 120 minutes (Morin, 1993). Usually, four more 90-minute cycles of NREM and REM sleep occur during the night. Just before and after REM periods, the sleeper shifts position (Hobson, 1989).

The progression of a typical night's sleep cycles is depicted in Figure 4.3. Stage 3 and 4 NREM, slow-wave sleep usually occurs only during the first two 90-minute cycles. As the night progresses, episodes of REM sleep become increasingly longer, and less time is spent in NREM. During the last two 90-minute sleep cycles before awakening, periods of REM sleep can last as long as 40 minutes, and NREM sleep is composed primarily of stage 2 sleep. In a later section, we'll look at dreaming and REM sleep in more detail.

FIGURE 4.3 The 90-Minute Cycles of Sleep
During a typical night, you experience five 90-minute cycles of alternating NREM and REM sleep. The deepest stages of NREM sleep, stages 3 and 4, occur during the first two 90-minute cycles. Dreaming REM sleep episodes become progressively longer as the night goes on. Sleep position shifts, indicated by the dots, usually occur immediately before and after REM episodes.

(Based on Hobson, 1989.)

Changes in Sleep Patterns over the Lifespan

Over the course of our lives the quantity and quality of sleep change considerably. REM sleep begins long before birth, as scientists have discovered by using ultrasound to document fetal eye movements and by studying the sleep of premature infants. Four months before birth, REM sleep seems to constitute virtually all of fetal life (see Figure 4.4). By one month before birth, the fetus demonstrates distinct wake/sleep cycles, spending around 12 hours each day in REM sleep (Williams & others, 1994).

At birth, a newborn sleeps about 16 hours a day, up to 80 percent of which is REM sleep. By the end of the first year of life, total sleep time drops to around 13 hours a day, a third of which is spent in REM sleep.

FIGURE 4.4 Changes in REM and NREM Sleep over the Lifespan
Both the quality and quantity of sleep change over the lifespan. Even before birth, the cycles of REM and NREM sleep are evident. A newborn infant sleeps about 16 to 17 hours per day, with up to 80 percent of sleep time devoted to REM. From birth onward, total sleep time, REM sleep, and NREM sleep slowly decrease. The amount of time spent in stages 3 and 4, the deepest stages of NREM, also decreases over the lifespan.

(Based on Hobson, 1989.)

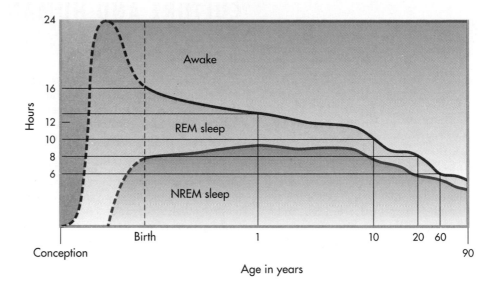

The Beginnings of REM Sleep By studying premature infants and using ultrasound to create images of the developing fetus in utero, researchers have documented the beginnings of REM sleep and rapid eye movements long before birth.

In general, from birth onward the average amount of time spent sleeping each day gradually decreases (see Figure 4.4). The amount of time devoted to REM sleep and slow-wave NREM sleep each night also gradually decreases over the lifespan. Young children can easily spend two hours or more each night in the deep sleep of stage 3 and 4 NREM. By early adulthood, about an hour is spent in deep sleep each night. But by late adulthood, only about 20 minutes of a night's sleep is spent in stage 3 and 4 NREM sleep (Williams & others, 1994).

As the amount of deep sleep and REM sleep decreases throughout adulthood, more time is spent in lighter, stage 2 NREM sleep. Consequently, sleep becomes more fitful as people get older. Beginning in their forties, people wake up more easily during the night and sleep tends to feel less satisfying (see Figure 4.5). People also tend to wake up feeling less rested and find it harder to regain alertness and get their brains in gear each morning (Williams & others, 1994). By the time people reach their sixties, total sleep time averages about 6 hours per night and the quality of sleep is much more shallow. Older people often spend part of the night simply resting with their eyes closed rather than sleeping (see Morin, 1993).

FIGURE 4.5 Never Wake a Sleeping Adult?
As we get older, the overall quality of our sleep diminishes. Beginning in our forties, the number of awakenings during the night increases steadily.

(Data reported in Williams & others, 1994.)

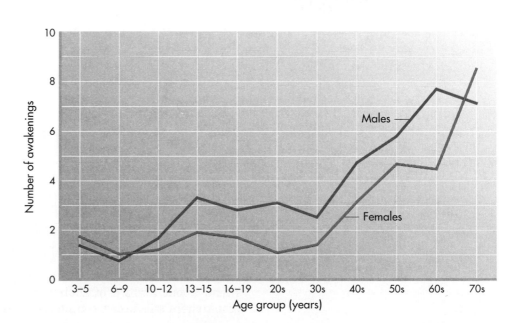

CULTURE AND HUMAN BEHAVIOR 4.3

Siestas and Naps

For the first year or two of life, babies take a morning and afternoon nap. Toddlers gradually outgrow their need for a morning nap, but most children continue to take an afternoon nap through the preschool years. Adults in the United States are not expected to take naps, unless they're sick, elderly, or college students who have stayed up all night studying for a final. Yet throughout our lives, most of us continue to get sleepy around the middle of the afternoon. In fact, many of us (your authors included) would take an afternoon nap if we could get away with it (Dinges, 1989; Webb, 1989).

Eating a big lunch and getting inadequate sleep the night before are

Nap Time We expect infants and preschoolers to take a daily afternoon nap, but most adults get sleepy in the afternoon, too. In siesta cultures, an afternoon nap is a well-established part of the daily routine. Many adults in nonsiesta cultures would take a daily nap if they could get away with it!

often blamed for the 3 o'clock slump in our mental alertness, but neither of these factors is the culprit. Instead, as we discussed earlier in the chapter, our circadian rhythm dictates reduced mental alertness around midafternoon each day (Moore-Ede, 1993). This midafternoon sleepiness seems to occur regardless of how much food we've consumed or how much sleep we've had the night before (Broughton, 1989; Lavie, 1989). In fact, the human brain seems to be "programmed" for an afternoon siesta (Carskadon, 1989).

In many Latin American, Mediterranean, and Spanish cultures, the society as a whole has adapted to this midafternoon slump in mental alertness. The same is true in some regions of Greece, Italy, and many Middle Eastern countries, including Israel. For about two hours in the afternoon, which is also the hottest part of the day in tropical climates, the traditional siesta occurs.

During the siesta period, shops, banks, government offices, and restaurants may close for a few hours. Evening events, such as the nightly meal, tend to occur later than in nonsiesta cultures. In cultures where a siesta is taken, it's common for people to eat their last meal of the day at about 10:00 p.m., go to bed very late, and get up early in the morning (Thorpy & Yager, 1991; Webb & Dinges, 1989). Businesses may be closed from 2 until 4 o'clock, but remain open during the evening hours. So, in some

cities, it's impossible to buy a postage stamp at 3 o'clock in the afternoon, but you can go to the bank at 11 o'clock at night!

However, even the siesta culture is not immune to change. In some developing countries, the incidence of afternoon naps has declined as the countries have become more urban and more industrialized (Webb & Dinges, 1989). In most industrialized cultures, including American culture, afternoon naps are discouraged. The emphasis on productivity in these countries has created a "24-hour society," where people are working around the clock (Moore-Ede, 1993). Even though a strategically timed nap might improve overall productivity, naps are simply not acceptable in the Westernized workplace.

This is too bad, because research has shown that many people fail to get adequate sleep at night, and an afternoon nap has many benefits. Naps reduce fatigue and sleepiness, and improve a person's mood and mental alertness. A regular afternoon nap can also reduce the amount of sleep that you need at night (Webb & Dinges, 1989). And, contrary to popular belief, taking an hour's nap does not make it more difficult to fall asleep at night (Dinges, 1989).

The tendency to take an afternoon nap is a normal, even beneficial, aspect of our daily sleep/wake circadian rhythm. Just don't do it while driving, interviewing for a job, or attending psychology class.

The Functions of Sleep

Sleep deprivation studies demonstrate that we have a biological need for sleep. What is REM and NREM rebound? What is the restorative theory of sleep? How does the evolutionary theory of sleep account for the varied patterns of sleep observed in different animals?

Why do we sleep? What's sleep good for, anyway? Given that most people spend about a third of their lives asleep, it may surprise you that sleep researchers still aren't completely sure why we need to sleep. That we have a biological need for sleep is clearly demonstrated by *sleep deprivation studies*. After as little as one day's sleep deprivation, research subjects will develop *microsleeps*, which are episodes of sleep lasting only a few seconds that occur during wakefulness. People who go without sleep for a day or more also experience disruptions in mood, mental abilities, reaction time, perceptual skills, and complex motor skills (Gökcebay & others, 1994).

Sleep researchers have also selectively deprived people of different *components* of normal sleep. For example, to study the effects of REM deprivation, researchers wake the subject whenever the monitoring instruments indicate that he is entering REM sleep. After several nights of being selectively deprived of REM sleep, the subject is allowed to sleep uninterrupted. What happens? The first time the subject is allowed to sleep without interruption, he experiences **REM rebound**—the amount of time spent in REM sleep increases by as much as 50 percent (Ellman & others, 1991).

The same effect occurs when people are selectively deprived of NREM stages 3 and 4. When given the opportunity for uninterrupted sleep, the amount of time spent in deep, slow-wave sleep shows a sharp increase in comparison to the normal durations of time spent in NREM stages 3 and 4 (Empson, 1993). The phenomena of REM and NREM rebound seem to indicate that the brain needs to "make up" for the missing sleep components.

Clearly, we need to both sleep and experience the full range of sleep stages. But what particular functions does sleep serve? Although the exact physiological functions of sleep have yet to be firmly established, two general theories have been proposed: the *restorative theory of sleep* and the *evolutionary theory of sleep*.

The Restorative Theory of Sleep

The **restorative theory of sleep** suggests that sleep promotes physiological processes that restore and rejuvenate the body and the mind (Gökcebay & others, 1994). The restorative theory of sleep has considerable intuitive appeal. After all, billions of people go to bed every night feeling tired and wake the next morning feeling refreshed.

According to the restorative theory of sleep, NREM and REM sleep serve different purposes. NREM sleep is thought to be important for restoring the body, while REM sleep is thought to restore mental and brain functions.

Evidence supporting the role of NREM sleep in body restoration comes from studies demonstrating increased deep sleep following sleep deprivation, starvation, and strenuous athletic activity. The secretion of growth hormone, testosterone, prolactin, and other hormones increases during NREM sleep (Anch & others, 1988).

The importance of REM sleep in mental and brain functions is suggested by the fact that REM sleep is abundant in the developing fetus, infants, and young children, then decreases throughout adulthood (see Figure 4.4). Tentatively, this suggests that REM sleep plays some role in the peak rates of brain development that occur in the early stages of the lifespan. The abundant REM sleep that the developing fetus, infants, and young children experience may provide needed stimulation for brain development (Empson, 1993; Hobson, 1989).

The Evolutionary Theory of Sleep

As its name implies, the **evolutionary theory of sleep** suggests that the sleep patterns exhibited by different animals, including humans, are the result of evolution (Webb, 1975). The basic idea is that different sleep patterns evolved as way of preventing a particular species from interacting with the environment when doing so is most hazardous. Animals with few natural predators, such as gorillas and lions, sleep as much as 15 hours a day. In

REM rebound
A phenomenon in which a person who is deprived of REM sleep greatly increases the amount of time spent in REM sleep at the first opportunity to sleep uninterrupted.

restorative theory of sleep
The view that sleep and dreaming are essential to normal physical and mental functioning.

evolutionary theory of sleep
The view that the unique sleep patterns of different animals evolved over time to help promote survival and environmental adaptation.

Nap, Anyone? From anteaters to zebras, virtually all animals share the need for rest and periodic sleep. Sleep patterns vary greatly from one species to another. According to the evolutionary theory of sleep, animals with few predators have the luxury of sleeping unprotected in broad daylight, like this lion and polar bear. Animals who are vulnerable to predators, like giraffes and shrews, sleep only fitfully, or in well-protected nests.

contrast, grazing animals, such as cattle and horses, tend to sleep in short bursts that total only about four hours per day. Hibernation patterns of animals like bears and gophers also coincide with periods during which environmental conditions pose the greatest threat to survival.

There is evidence to support both the restorative and the evolutionary theories of sleep. Sleep does seem to restore the body, but exactly how it does so remains uncertain. And the variations in sleep patterns exhibited by different animals seem to reflect an adaptive process that promotes survival. Researchers still aren't sure exactly what physiological functions are served by sleep. Sleep may well fulfill multiple purposes (Gökcebay & others, 1994).

CONCEPT REVIEW 4.2

The Stages of Sleep

Fill in the blanks using the proper terms from this list: REM, myoclonic jerk, stage 2 NREM, stage 4 NREM, dreaming, hypnagogic hallucination.

1. You have been asleep for about 10 minutes and are experiencing bursts of brain activity, called sleep spindles, which last a few seconds. It is likely that you are in _____ sleep.

2. Joe is just drifting off to sleep when he experiences a sudden sensation of falling and an involuntary muscle spasm that jolts him awake. Joe has experienced the _____ of falling combined with a _____.

3. Marsha has been asleep for well over an hour. Her eyes start to dart back and forth beneath her closed eyelids. Her heart rate and blood pressure fluctuate up and down, yet her voluntary muscle activity is suppressed. Most likely, Marsha is experiencing _____ sleep, and _____ is occurring.

4. You have volunteered to be a subject in a sleep research lab. At some point during your first night's sleep, you answer the phone and have a brief conversation with the research assistant but remember nothing about this incident the next morning. It is most likely that the phone conversation occurred during _____ sleep.

Troubled Sleep: Sleep Disorders

Sleep disorders are serious disturbances in normal sleep patterns that interfere with daytime functioning and cause subjective distress. How is insomnia defined, and what are its causes and effects? What characterizes sleepwalking, night terrors, REM sleep behavior disorder, sleep apnea, and narcolepsy?

While a good night's sleep can be wonderfully refreshing, a night of fitful or otherwise poor sleep has a variety of negative effects. Although this will probably not come as a great shock to you, people who sleep poorly are not happy campers the next day. They complain of feeling unhappy, listless, socially withdrawn, inattentive, and mentally sluggish (Zammit, 1988; Kales & others, 1984).

"There is no part of society where sleep disorders and sleep deprivation are not serious problems, and there is no component of society where there is adequate awareness of sleep disorders and sleep deprivation."

William C. Dement, M.D., Ph.D. (1993b)

In this section, we'll go beyond the occasional night of lousy sleep to look at the most common sleep disorders. **Sleep disorders** are serious disturbances in the normal sleep pattern that interfere with daytime functioning and cause subjective distress (American Psychiatric Association, 1994). Virtually everyone is seriously troubled by the quality or quantity of their sleep at some point. For example, a 1991 survey sponsored by the National Sleep Foundation found that 36 percent of Americans suffer from some type of sleep problem (Gallup Organization, 1991). Similar surveys have found that better than 25 percent of children, including preschoolers, suffer from sleep disruptions (see Chambers, 1995; Morin, 1993).

Insomnia

By far the most common sleep complaint among adults is insomnia. Insomnia is not defined solely on the basis of amount of time spent sleeping. Put simply, people vary in how much sleep they need to feel refreshed. Rather, people are said to suffer from **insomnia** when they repeatedly complain about the quality or duration of their sleep, have difficulty going to sleep or staying asleep, or wake before it is time to get up (Morin, 1993).

Over the course of any given year, about a third of the adult population is troubled by a bout of insomnia (Mellinger & others, 1985). Not surprisingly, such sleeping difficulties can often be traced to stressful life events, such as job or school difficulties, troubled relationships, the death of a loved one, or financial problems. As we noted earlier, insomnia can also occur as one of the symptoms of jet lag due to travel or night-shift work (Buysse & Reynolds, 1990). When sleep disturbance is related to stressful life events, it is termed *situational* or *transient insomnia* (Morin, 1993). As a general rule, when the stressful events are resolved, the quality of sleep improves.

Concerns about sleeping can add to whatever waking anxieties the person may already be experiencing. This can create a vicious cycle—worrying about the inability to sleep makes troubled sleep even more likely, further intensifying anxiety (Roemer & Borkovec, 1993; Spielman & Glovinsky, 1991).

When a person experiences sleep difficulties three or more nights per week and the sleep disturbances continue for six months or more, the condition is classified as *chronic insomnia* (American Psychiatric Association, 1994). Approximately 10 percent of the adult population is affected by chronic insomnia (Bearpark, 1994).

Sleep disorder specialists use a variety of behavioral and psychological techniques to treat insomnia and help people develop better sleep habits. Educating people on sleep "hygiene" is often part of the successful treatment of insomnia. For example, many people troubled by insomnia use alcohol or over-the-counter sleep medications to induce sleep. Although such remedies may help people sleep in the short run, they can disrupt normal sleep cycles, including REM sleep. Even the sleep-inducing medications sometimes prescribed by physicians must be carefully managed to avoid drug dependence (Morin, 1993; Dement, 1992a; Buysse & Reynolds, 1990).

Sleepwalking and Night Terrors

Unlike insomnia, *sleepwalking* and *night terrors* are sleep disturbances that are much more common in children than adults (Lask, 1995; Mindell, 1993). These sleep disturbances occur during the deepest stages of NREM sleep, stages 3 and 4. As noted previously, young children spend considerably more time each night in deep sleep than adolescents or adults (Whyte & Schaefer, 1995). Not surprisingly, most instances of bedwetting, or *nocturnal enuresis,* also tend to occur when the child is in deep sleep (Barclay & Houts, 1995a; Empson, 1993).

sleep disorders
Serious disturbances in the normal sleep pattern that interfere with daytime functioning and cause subjective distress.

insomnia
A condition in which a person regularly experiences the inability to fall asleep, stay asleep, or feel adequately rested by sleep.

About 25 percent of all children have at least one episode of **sleepwalking,** also known as *somnambulism.* Sleepwalking typically occurs during the first three hours after the child has gone to sleep. After sitting up and getting out of bed, the child moves about in a slow, poorly coordinated, automatic manner, usually with a blank, staring look on his face. Surprisingly, the sleepwalking child is able to navigate around objects without much difficulty. However, the sleepwalker's general lack of awareness of his surroundings is evident: he may try to dress, eat, or go to the bathroom in the wrong location (Ozbayrak & Berlin, 1995).

Night terrors, or *sleep terrors,* also typically occur during stage 3 or 4 NREM sleep in the first few hours of sleep. Physiologically, a night terror is much more intense than a run-of-the-mill nightmare. The first sign of a night terror is sharply increased physiological arousal—restlessness, sweating, and a racing heart. Typically, the child abruptly sits up in bed and lets out a panic-stricken scream or cry for help as she thrashes about in bed or even sleepwalks. Terrified and disoriented, the child may struggle with a parent who tries to calm her down (Lask, 1995).

Night terrors tend to be brief, usually lasting only a matter of seconds (Ferber, 1994). Amazingly, the child almost immediately goes back to quiet sleep, and wakes in the morning with no recollection of the incident (Lask, 1995). Unlike the unfolding dream story of a nightmare, night terrors are usually accompanied by a single but terrifying sensation, such as being crushed or falling. Often, the child imagines that she is choking or that a frightening figure is present, such as a threatening animal or "monster" (Kahn & others, 1991). Though dramatic, night terrors are not regarded as a true sleep disorder or psychological problem unless they occur regularly (Wiedemann, 1987). For the vast majority of children who experience regular night terrors, the problem resolves itself by early adolescence (Lask, 1995).

Terror in the Night French artist Jean Ignace Gérard created this print, entitled "The Nightmare." However, the image of a monster lowering a weight on the sleeper's chest suggests instead the frightening experience of a night terror. Night terrors occur during NREM sleep, and are almost always accompanied by sensations of being crushed or smothered.

REM Sleep Behavior Disorder

A more serious sleep disorder that has only recently been recognized by sleep researchers is called **REM sleep behavior disorder** (Mahowald & Schenck, 1990). This sleep disturbance typically affects males over the age of 60 and is characterized by the brain's failure to suppress muscle movements during REM sleep. The dreamer acts out his dreams, sometimes leaping out of bed, running across the bedroom, lashing out at imagined intruders, or tackling a chest of drawers. Such behavior might seem quite comical if the potential for serious injury to the sleeper or the sleeper's bed partner weren't so great. Evidence suggests that the cause of REM sleep behavior disorder is deterioration or damage in lower brain centers that control physical and mental arousal during sleep (Zoltoski & Gillin, 1994; Chase & Morales, 1990).

Sleep Apnea

In **sleep apnea,** the sleeper repeatedly stops breathing during the night (Krieger, 1990). Carbon dioxide builds up in the blood, causing a momentary awakening during which the sleeper snorts or gulps in air (Empson, 1993). Breathing may stop for as little as 10 seconds or for so long that the sleeper's skin turns blue before he wakes up. During a single night, over 300 sleep

sleepwalking
A sleep disturbance characterized by an episode of walking or performing other actions during stage 3 or stage 4 NREM sleep; also called *somnambulism.*

night terrors
A sleep disturbance characterized by an episode of increased physiological arousal, intense fear and panic, frightening hallucinations, and no recall of the episode the next morning; typically occurs during stage 3 or stage 4 NREM sleep; also called *sleep terror.*

REM sleep behavior disorder
A sleep disorder in which the sleeper acts out his dreams.

sleep apnea
(APP-nee-uh) A sleep disorder in which the person repeatedly stops breathing during sleep.

narcolepsy
A sleep disorder characterized by excessive daytime sleepiness and brief lapses into sleep throughout the day.

apnea attacks can occur. Often the person has no recollection of the repeated awakenings, but feels sleepy throughout the following day.

Like REM sleep behavior disorder, sleep apnea is more common in older men, especially those with a weight problem. Special mouthpieces, weight loss, and surgical intervention have been effectively used to treat sleep apnea. For people who suffer sleep apnea only when they sleep on their backs, treatment is sometimes as simple as sewing a tennis ball to the back of their pajama tops, which forces them to sleep on their sides (Thorpy & Ledereich, 1990).

Narcolepsy

Unlike the sleep disorders discussed so far, the symptoms of **narcolepsy** are experienced during the day. The most common symptom of narcolepsy is excessive daytime sleepiness and brief lapses into sleep throughout the day, usually lasting an hour or less. However, some narcoleptics experience dramatic, sudden daytime "sleep attacks" that last up to several minutes. Laughter, anger, surprise, and other forms of emotional arousal, including sexual arousal, can trigger the sleep attacks. During sleep attacks, narcoleptics instantly enter REM sleep and experience *sleep paralysis*—their muscles go limp and they collapse. Vivid and sometimes terrifying hypnagogic hallucinations are common during sleep attacks.

The onset of narcolepsy typically occurs during adolescence and is considered a chronic, lifelong condition. Genetics seem to play an important role, as the disorder tends to run in families. Although narcolepsy cannot be cured, scheduled daytime naps increase alertness for narcoleptics. Stimulants and other psychoactive drugs can also help minimize narcoleptic symptoms (Gibbons & Kotagal, 1995; Broughton, 1990).

CONCEPT REVIEW 4.3

Sleep Disorders

Imagine that you are a sleep disorders specialist and you have to diagnose these clients as suffering from one of the following: situational insomnia, sleep apnea, narcolepsy, chronic insomnia, night terror, REM sleep behavior disorder.

1. Jerry is sixty-four years old. According to his wife, Jerry sometimes jumps out of bed during the night and appears to act out his dreams. He waves his arms, shoves the bedroom furniture, speaks to people who aren't present, and so forth. It is very likely that Jerry suffers from _____.

2. Nicholas is in the tenth grade. While giving his first presentation in speech class, he suddenly went limp and collapsed on the floor, unable to move. After a few minutes, Nicholas seemed to recover completely. Similar incidents have happened when Nicholas was laughing with his friends. Nicholas probably has _____.

3. Mrs. Jones complains that her somewhat overweight husband snores and snorts throughout the night as though he is gasping for air, especially when he sleeps on his back. Mr. Jones has a disorder called _____.

4. After being asleep for almost an hour, young Indira suddenly sits up in bed and lets out a bloodcurdling scream. Surprisingly, she quickly returns to a quiet state of sleep and in the morning has no recollection of the event. Indira has experienced a _____.

5. Patricia experienced a great deal of stress during her first semester at college. On many nights, she was so anxious about her heavy course load that she had trouble falling asleep and woke frequently during the night. When the semester was over, she spent the vacation with her family and had no sleep problems. It appears that Patricia was suffering from _____.

Dreams and Mental Activity During Sleep

A dream is an unfolding episode of mental images that occurs during REM sleep. What are the characteristics of dreams? What do people dream about and what factors influence whether a dream is remembered? What is a lucid dream?

Dreams have fascinated people since the beginning of time. On the average, about 25 percent of a night's sleep is spent dreaming, or almost two hours every night. So, assuming you live to a ripe old age, you'll devote more than 50,000 hours, or about six years of your life, just to dreaming.

Although dreams may be the most spectacular brain productions during sleep, they are not the most common mental activity during sleep. More prevalent is **sleep thinking,** which occurs during NREM sleep and consists of vague, uncreative, bland, and thoughtlike ruminations about real-life events (Hobson & Stickgold, 1995; Schatzman & Fenwick, 1994; Hobson, 1988). For example, just before an important exam, students may review terms and concepts during NREM sleep.

In contrast to sleep thinking, a **dream** is an unfolding episode of mental images that is storylike, involving characters and events. According to sleep researcher Allan Hobson (1988), dreams have five basic characteristics:

- Emotions can be intense.
- Content and organization are usually illogical.
- Sensations are sometimes bizarre.
- Even bizarre details are uncritically accepted.
- The dream images are difficult to remember.

Usually, dreams occur during REM sleep, but dreams can also occasionally occur during NREM sleep (Schatzman & Fenwick, 1994). When people are awakened during REM sleep, up to 90 percent of the time they will report a dream—even people who claim that they never dream. In fact, you usually have four or five episodes of dreaming each night, even if you don't remember the dreams. Early-morning dreams, which can last as long as 40 minutes, are the dreams that you're most likely to remember. Contrary to popular belief, dreams happen in real time, not split seconds. In fact, dreamers tend to be quite accurate in estimating how long they've been dreaming (Empson, 1993).

What Do We Dream About?

Although nearly everyone can remember an unusually bizarre dream, most dreams are a reflection of everyday life, including people we know and familiar settings (Weinstein & others, 1991). Remember Sandy's "high school" dream, described in the prologue to this chapter? Before she went to sleep that night, Sandy had been talking with her parents about some old friends from high school. The dark hallways, high ceilings, and gloomy classrooms, while somewhat exaggerated in her dream, were a fairly accurate depiction of the public high school she attended in Chicago years ago.

Dream researcher Calvin Hall collected and analyzed over 10,000 dreams from hundreds of people. He found that a dream's themes often reflect the

sleep thinking
Repetitive, bland, and uncreative ruminations about real-life events during sleep.

dream
A story-like episode of unfolding mental imagery during sleep.

TABLE 4.2 Common Dream Themes Across Cultures

Although thousands of miles apart and immersed in two very different cultures, American and Japanese college students share many dream themes, as shown in these survey results.

	Percentage Saying Yes	
Have you ever dreamed of . . . ?	American	Japanese
1. being attacked or pursued	77	91
2. falling	83	74
3. trying again and again to do something	71	87
4. school, teachers, studying	71	86
5. being frozen with fright	58	87
6. sexual experiences	66	68
7. arriving too late, e.g., missing train	64	49
8. dead people as though alive	46	57
9. loved person being dead	57	42
10. being on verge of falling	47	45
11. failing an examination	39	41
12. flying or soaring through air	34	46
13. being smothered, unable to breathe	44	33
14. seeing self as dead	33	35
15. being nude	43	17

SOURCE: Adapted from data reported in Empson, 1993.

daily concerns of the dreamer (Hall & Van de Castle, 1966). Worries about exams, money, health, or troubled relationships are all likely to be reflected in our dreams. And as you can see in Table 4.2, certain themes, such as falling or being chased or attacked, are surprisingly common across cultures.

Sleep researchers can successfully influence dream content *during* dreaming. In sleep labs, researchers have played recordings of a rooster crowing, a bugle playing reveille, and a dog barking, and have even sprayed water on sleeping research subjects. Depending on the stimulus, up to half of the dreamers incorporated the external stimulation into their dream content (Dement, 1992b, 1978; Arkin & Antrobus, 1991).

Why Don't We Remember Our Dreams?

Even in the best dream recallers, the vast majority of dreams are forgotten—at least 95 percent, by one estimate (Hobson, 1989). Why are dreams so much more difficult to remember than waking experiences? Several theories have been proposed, each with at least some evidence to support them, but the bottom line is that no clear answer has yet emerged from sleep research.

Even so, several generalizations are possible (Goodenough, 1991). First, you're much more likely to recall a dream if you wake up during it. When subjects are intentionally awakened during REM sleep, they usually recall the dream content. There are also individual differences in dream recall. Some people, like your author Sandy, frequently remember their dreams in vivid detail. Other people, like your author Don, hardly ever remember their dreams.

Second, the more vivid, bizarre, or emotionally intense a dream is, the more likely it is to be recalled the following morning. Vivid dreams are also more likely to be remembered days or weeks after the dream has occurred. In many respects, this is very similar to waking experiences: whether we're awake or asleep, mundane and routine experiences are most likely to be forgotten.

Third, distractions upon awakening interfere with our ability to recall dreams. This fact was noted by psychologist Mary Calkins (1893) over a century ago:

> To recall a dream requires usually extreme and immediate attention to the content of the dream. Sometimes the slight movement of reaching for paper and pencil or of lighting one's candle seems to dissipate the dream-memory, and one is left with the tantalizing consciousness of having lived through an interesting dream-experience of which one has not the faintest memory.

Finally, it's difficult to remember *any* experience during sleep, not just dreams. Sleep researchers have also found that subjects who are briefly awakened during the night to give reports or perform simple tasks frequently do not remember the incident the next morning (Goodenough, 1991).

It seems clear, then, that the brain is largely "programmed" to forget not only the vast majority of dream experiences but other experiences during sleep as well. As we'll discuss in more detail in the memory chapter (Chapter 6), memory requires that information be processed and stored in such a way that it can be retrieved at a later time. Possibly, the fundamental changes in brain chemistry and functioning that occur during sleep fail to support such information processing and storage, except when dreams are especially vivid. One theory is that the neurotransmitters needed to create new memories are not available during sleep (Hobson & Stickgold, 1995; Hobson, 1990).

IN FOCUS 4.4

What You *Really* Want to Know About Dreams

If I fall off a cliff in my dreams and don't wake up before I hit the bottom, will I die?

The first obvious problem with this bit of folklore is that if you did die before you woke up, how would anyone know what you'd been dreaming about? Beyond that basic contradiction, studies have shown that about a third of dreamers can recall a dream in which they died or were killed. And such dream sensations as falling, soaring through the air, and being paralyzed seem to be universal.

When my dog yips, twitches his nose, and moves his paws as if he's running while he's asleep, is he dreaming?

Virtually all mammals experience sleep cycles in which REM sleep alternates with slow-wave NREM sleep. Animals clearly demonstrate perception and memory. They also communicate using vocalizations, facial expressions, posture, and gestures to show territoriality and sexual receptiveness. Thus, it's quite reasonable to conclude that the brain and other physiological changes that occur during animal REM sleep are coupled with mental images. One bit of anecdotal evidence supporting this idea involved a gorilla that had been taught basic sign language to communicate. The gorilla signed "sleep pictures," presumably referring to REM dream activity while it slept. Finally, when sleep researchers have altered the brain area in cats that normally suppresses movements during REM sleep, the cats acted out instinctual behaviors during REM periods, including swiping at mice that were not there!

What do people who have been blind all their lives "see" when they dream?

People who become totally blind before the age of five typically do not have visual dreams as adults. Even so, their dreams are just as complex and vivid as sighted people's; they just involve other sensations, especially sound and touch.

If I'm really hungry when I go bed, will I dream about food?

Not necessarily. When sleep researchers have deprived subjects of food or water, food- or water-related dreams don't substantially increase. But historically, examples of widespread food-related dreaming have been reported during periods of food shortages and among people who are severely malnourished, such as those in concentration camps or prisons. While participants in sleep research know that they're eventually going to be fed or handed a glass of water, the same can't be said of people who are living in extremely impoverished conditions or who are actually in danger of starving. Thus, the *meaning* of the hunger or thirst seems to be what's most important. Similarly, a cigarette smoker may rarely dream of smoking—until he tries to quit!

Can you predict the future with your dreams?

History is filled with stories of dream prophecies. Over the course of your life, you will have over 100,000 dreams. Simply by chance, it's not surprising that every now and then a dream contains elements that coincide with future events.

Are dreams in color or black and white?

Up to 80 percent of our dreams contain color. When dreamers are awakened and asked to match dream colors to standard color charts, soft pastel colors are frequently chosen.

SOURCES: Halliday, 1995; Schatzman & Fenwick, 1994; Empson, 1993; Weinstein & others, 1991; Hobson, 1989, 1988; Anch & others, 1988.

Nightmares

An unpleasant anxiety dream that occurs during REM sleep is called a **nightmare.** Nightmares often produce spontaneous awakenings, during which the vivid and frightening dream content is immediately recalled (Thorpy & Yager, 1991). Nightmares are especially common in young children (Halliday, 1995). The general theme of nightmares is of being helpless or powerless in the face of great danger or destruction. Like Laura's dream, described in the prologue, children often have nightmares in which they are attacked by an animal or "monster."

In dealing with a child who has experienced a nightmare, simple reassurance is a good first step, followed by an attempt to help the child understand the difference between an imaginary dream and a real waking experience (Halliday, 1995; Josephs, 1987). In adults, an occasional nightmare is a natural and relatively common experience (Wood & Bootzin, 1990). Nightmares are not considered to be indicative of a psychological or sleep disorder unless they frequently cause personal distress.

nightmare
A frightening or unpleasant anxiety dream that occurs during REM sleep.

Lucid Dreams

In contrast to the unpleasantness of nightmares, lucid dreams can be fun. A **lucid dream** is one in which a person becomes aware that he is dreaming. What makes lucid dreams fun is that the dreamer can often guide the course of the dream (Green & McCreery, 1994; Schatzman & Fenwick, 1994).

While it's only relatively recently that sleep and dream researchers have "discovered" the phenomenon of lucid dreaming, lucid dreaming has been part of some cultures for centuries. For example, Tibetan Buddhist monks in the eighth century described techniques for passing directly from waking into lucidly dreaming sleep without losing conscious awareness (Gillespie, 1988).

About half of all people can recall at least one lucid dream, and some people frequently have lucid dreams. Sleep researchers have worked with lucid dreamers to study dream length, physical correlates of dream actions, and the degree of muscle-activity suppression during REM (Green & McCreery, 1994; LaBerge, 1992).

Would you like to try to have a lucid dream? Lucid-dream researchers Celia Green and Charles McCreery (1994) offer these simple suggestions to increase the possibility of lucid dreaming:

1. Observe your own mind as you fall asleep. Try to retain self-awareness while watching dream associations and images as they arise.

2. Become more aware of consciousness while you are awake. Throughout the day, repeatedly ask yourself if you are dreaming. Then imagine that you are dreaming at the present moment and pretend that everything you are perceiving is illusionary.

3. Resolve to carry out some specific task in a dream as a test of whether you are in a dream state or not. For example, resolve to imagine that you are picking up something that is really too heavy for you to lift. When the same event occurs in a dream, it can signal you to ask yourself, "Is this a dream?"

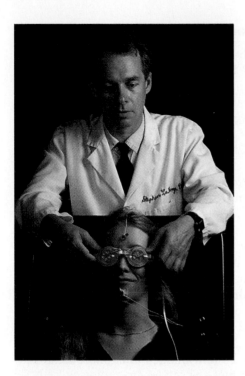

Leap Skyscrapers in a Single Bound? Lucid dream researcher Stephen LaBerge, shown here, has developed computerized goggles that help dreamers hone their lucid dreaming skills. The goggles signal the sleeper by flashing lights during episodes of REM sleep, increasing the likelihood of lucid dreams. Experienced lucid dreamers can exert conscious control over dream contents. Many lucid dreamers try to soar through the air in their dreams.

The Significance of Dreams

Dreams have been thought to be meaningful for centuries. What was Sigmund Freud's explanation for dreams? How does the activation-synthesis model explain dreaming? What conclusions can we draw about the meaning of dreams?

Just as sleep researchers aren't exactly sure why we sleep, they also do not know why we dream every night. However, the idea that dreams are meaningful has a long history. In the Bible, for example, there are numerous references to information being communicated through dreams, either directly or symbolically.

For thousands of years and throughout many cultures, dreams have been thought to contain highly significant, cryptic messages. Do dreams mean anything? Do they contain symbolic messages? In this final section on dreaming, we will look at two theories that try to account for the purpose of dreaming, starting with the most famous one.

lucid dream
A dream in which the sleeper is aware that he is dreaming.

Sigmund Freud: Dreams as Fulfilled Wishes

In the chapters on personality and psychotherapy (Chapters 11 and 15), we'll look in detail at the ideas of **Sigmund Freud** (1856–1939), the founder of psychoanalysis. As we discussed in Chapter 1, Freud believed that sexual and aggressive instincts are the motivating forces that dictate human behavior. But because these instinctual urges are so consciously unacceptable, sexual and aggressive thoughts, feelings, and wishes are pushed into the unconscious, or *repressed*. However, Freud believed that these repressed urges and wishes could surface in dreams.

In his landmark work, *The Interpretation of Dreams* (1900), Freud wrote that dreams are the "disguised fulfillments of repressed wishes" and provide "the royal road to a knowledge of the unconscious mind." Thus, Freud believed that dreams function as a sort of psychological "safety valve" for the release of unconscious and unacceptable urges.

Freud (1904) believed that dreams have two components: the *manifest content,* or the dream images themselves, and the *latent content,* which is the disguised psychological meaning of the dream. Like a detective searching for clues, Freud carefully analyzed the dreams of his patients, looking for symbolic expressions of repressed urges and wishes. For example, Freud (1911) believed that dream images of sticks, swords, and other elongated objects are phallic symbols, representing the penis. Dream images of cupboards, boxes, and ovens supposedly symbolize the vagina.

Freud's notions are certainly intriguing and consistent with the ancient belief that dream symbols must be interpreted to reveal the dream's meaning. In many types of psychotherapy today, especially those that follow Freud's ideas, dreams are still seen as an important source of information about psychological conflicts. That said, let's consider a very different view of the meaning of dreams.

Hobson & McCarley: The Activation-Synthesis Model of Dreaming

Armed with an array of evidence that dreaming involves the activation of different brain areas during REM sleep, researchers **J. Allan Hobson** and Robert McCarley (1977) proposed a new model of dreaming, called the **activation-synthesis model of dreaming.** Put simply, this model maintains that dreaming is our subjective awareness of the brain's internally generated signals during sleep (see Hobson & Stickgold, 1995; Hobson, 1990).

More specifically, the activation-synthesis model maintains that the experience of dreaming sleep is due to the automatic activation of brainstem circuits at the base of the brain (see Figure 4.6). These brainstem circuits arouse more sophisticated brain areas, such as visual centers, that normally register stimuli from the external world. But rather than responding to stimulation from the external environment, the dreaming brain is actually responding to its own internally generated signals.

Different elements of dreams correspond to the activation of particular brain areas. For example, the activation of emotion centers in the brain is reflected in emotionally intense dreams; visual dream elements are due to activation of the brain's visual centers; and so forth.

In the absence of external sensory input, the activated brain combines, or "synthesizes," these internally generated sensory signals and imposes meaning on them. The dream story itself is derived from a hodgepodge of memories and sensations that are triggered by the brain's activation and chemical changes during sleep. According to this model, then, dreaming is nothing more than the brain synthesizing and integrating memory fragments and sensations that are internally triggered (Hobson & Stickgold, 1995).

activation-synthesis model of dreaming
The theory that brain activity during sleep produces dream images (*activation*), which are combined by the brain into a dream story (*synthesis*).

Stimulation from the external environment is blocked

Primary auditory center

Primary visual center

A dream story is created from the brain's own internally generated signal during sleep

Body movement is suppressed

However, the activation-synthesis theory does *not* state that dreams are completely meaningless (Hobson & Stickgold, 1995). As Hobson (1989) observes, "For all their nonsense, dreams have a clear import and a deeply personal one." But, if there is a meaning to dreams, that meaning lies in the deeply personal way in which the images are organized or "synthesized." In other words, the meaning is to be found not by "decoding" the dream symbols, but by analyzing the way the dreamer makes sense out of the chaos of dream images.

Some Observations About the Meaning of Dreams

So we're back to our original question: Do dreams mean anything? First, the meaning of some dreams seems self-evident. You dream that you're being hassled by the same person with whom relationship difficulties already exist. You're worried about your job, and you dream that your boss is chewing you out. Subjectively, it seems obvious that at least some of our dreams mirror our real-life concerns, frustrations, anxieties, and desires. Less subjectively, this is consistent with sleep research on the content of dreams (Weinstein & others, 1991).

But that's not the same as suggesting that dreams are highly symbolic. Are they? As dream researchers Morton Schatzman and Peter Fenwick (1994) point out:

> It is impossible to test the idea that a particular dream chosen at random has a meaning because it cannot be proven that it does not. . . . Offered a dream, a resourceful interpreter can almost always find a message. But was the message really there or did the interpreter invent a message in the course of looking for one?

If nothing else, remember that the interpretation of dreams occurs when you're awake. It seems reasonable, then, to suggest that conscious speculations about the meaning of these elusive nightly productions might reveal more about the psychological characteristics of the interpreter than about the dream itself (Cartwright & Kaszniak, 1991).

Dreams

1. Lisa is asleep and is having a very frightening dream in which she is being chased by a large dog with big fangs. Lisa is most likely in _____ sleep and experiencing a _____.
   a. stage 4 NREM; night terror
   b. stage 1 NREM; hypnogogic hallucination
   c. REM; nightmare
   d. REM; night terror

2. Jeff enjoys his dreams very much and claims he can often guide the course of his dreams even while he is asleep and experiencing the dream. Jeff is _____.
   a. suffering from narcolepsy
   b. a lucid dreamer
   c. probably using hallucinogenic drugs
   d. lying

3. Mark's psychotherapist suggests that the images in Mark's dreams are actually symbolic of significant people and events in his life. As part of Mark's therapy, his therapist tries to uncover the hidden meaning, or _____ content, of the dream images.
   a. lucid
   b. latent
   c. manifest
   d. restorative

4. Although Monica is a straight-A student, she had a vivid dream in which she failed an important statistics exam and her statistics instructor was yelling at her in front of the other students in the class. According to Freud's theory, the specific images that Monica remembers from her dream are called the _____ content.
   a. lucid
   b. latent
   c. manifest
   d. restorative

5. The night before an important job interview, Marjorie doesn't sleep well and repeatedly awakens for brief periods throughout the night. Each time she briefly awakens, the vague, thoughtlike imagery filling her mind is that of rehearsing details she wants to remember to say during the interview. These ruminations during sleep about the next day's events represent _____.
   a. dreams
   b. nightmares
   c. lucid dreams
   d. sleep thinking

Hypnosis

Hypnosis refers to an unusual state of awareness in which a person responds to suggestions with changes in perception, memory, and behavior. Who can be hypnotized? What are the primary effects of hypnosis? How has hypnosis been explained?

Hypnosis is an unusual and controversial state of awareness that has been the focus of a great deal of scientific research. **Hypnosis** can be defined as a cooperative social interaction in which one person, the subject, responds to suggestions by another person, the hypnotist, which produce changes in perception, memory, and behavior (Kihlstrom, 1987). Hypnosis can also be self-induced.

Hypnosis is characterized by highly focused attention, increased responsiveness to suggestions, vivid images and fantasies, and a willingness to accept distortions of logic or reality. During hypnosis, the subject temporarily suspends his or her sense of initiative, voluntarily accepting and following the hypnotist's instructions (Hilgard, 1986a).

The history of hypnosis has been checkered with skepticism and claims of fraud, partly because of its unconventional origins. The origins of hypnosis can be traced to the eighteenth-century practices of an Austrian physician named *Anton Mesmer,* who was living in Paris (Riskin & Frankel, 1994; Fancher, 1990). Mesmer would fill a tub with magnetized iron filings and iron rods. His patients would hold on to the iron rods. Then Mesmer would induce

hypnosis
(hip-NO-sis) A cooperative social interaction in which a person responds to suggestions with changes in perception, memory, and behavior.

"The Banquet of Mesmer" Anton Mesmer (1734–1815) believed that he could cure people through the application of magnetism. In groups, patients would sit around a wooden tub filled with water and iron filings and rods. Mesmer would point his finger or an iron rod at his patient's bodies, inducing what he called a "crisis" state. The room was soon filled with convulsing, trembling patients. After the treatment, some patients claimed to be cured of their ailments (Fancher, 1990).

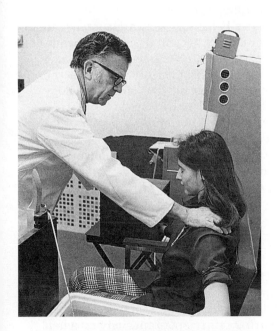

Hypnotic Suppression of Pain After inducing hypnosis in this young woman, Ernest Hilgard instructs her that she will feel no pain in her arm. The subject's arm is then immersed in circulating ice water for several minutes, and she reports that she does not experience any pain. In contrast, a non-hypnotized subject perceives the same experience as being extremely painful, and can keep his arm in the ice water for no more than a few seconds.

what he called a "crisis" state, during which patients experienced trembling, twitching, and even convulsions. In many instances, the procedure seemed to cure the patients' various symptoms.

Mesmer concluded that these results occurred because he was a highly magnetized person, a characteristic he called "animal magnetism." This claim gave rise to the common misconception that the hypnotist has unusual abilities or powers and can "mesmerize" people (Fancher, 1990).

When skepticism was expressed, Mesmer invited a scientific examination of his claims. In 1784, a blue-ribbon scientific commission, which included Benjamin Franklin, concluded that the cures were the result of the patients' imaginations. Not easily discouraged, Mesmer founded a school where his students learned and practiced "animal magnetism" (Fancher, 1990; Hilgard, 1987).

Although hypnosis today is accepted as a legitimate area of scientific study, many psychologists remain skeptical about hypnotic phenomena (see Spanos, 1994; Baker, 1996, 1990). As you'll see later in this section, hypnosis continues to be a controversial subject.

Who Can Be Hypnotized?

People vary in their susceptibility to hypnosis. Psychologists have found that about 15 percent of adults are highly susceptible to hypnosis, 10 percent are difficult or impossible to hypnotize, and most adults are somewhere in between (Hilgard, 1982). Children tend to be more responsive to hypnosis than adults, and children as young as five years old can be hypnotized (L. Cooper, 1979). Some evidence suggests that the degree of hypnotic susceptibility tends to run in families (Wallace & Persanyi, 1989).

The best candidates for hypnosis are individuals who approach the hypnotic experience with positive, receptive attitudes (Spanos & others, 1987). The subject's expectations of being responsive to hypnosis also plays an important role (Spanos & others, 1993; Silva & Kirsch, 1992). Most important, highly susceptible people have the ability to become deeply absorbed in fantasy and imaginary experience. They easily become absorbed in reading fiction, watching movies, and listening to music (Nadon & others, 1991; Roche & McConkey, 1990).

Effects of Hypnosis

Deeply hypnotized subjects sometimes experience profound changes in their subjective experience of consciousness. They may report feelings of detachment from their bodies, profound relaxation, or sensations of timelessness (Tart, 1979). More often, hypnotized people converse normally and remain fully aware of their surroundings.

Sensory and Perceptual Changes

Some of the most dramatic effects that can be produced with hypnosis are alterations in sensation and perception. Sensory changes that can be induced through hypnosis include temporary blindness, deafness, or a complete loss of sensation in some part of the body (Hilgard, 1986a). When the suggestion is made to a highly responsive subject that her arm is numb and cannot feel pain, for example, she will not consciously experience the pain of a pinprick or the pain of having her arm immersed in ice water. This property of hypnosis has led to its use as a technique in pain control. Painful dental and medical procedures, including surgery, have been successfully performed with hypnosis as the only anesthesia (Hilgard & Hilgard, 1983).

People can also experience hallucinations under hypnosis (Kihlstrom, 1985). A highly responsive hypnotic subject can be told that his closest friend is sitting in a chair on the other side of the room. Not only will the hypnotic subject report seeing his friend in vivid detail, he will walk over and "touch" the other person. Under hypnosis, people can also *not* perceive something that *is* there. For example, if the suggestion is made that a jar of rotten eggs has no smell, a highly suggestible subject will not consciously perceive any odor.

Posthypnotic Suggestions

Hypnosis can also influence behavior *outside* of the hypnotic state. When a **posthypnotic suggestion** is made during hypnosis, the subject will carry out that specific suggestion after the hypnotic session is over. For example, under hypnosis, a subject was given the posthypnotic suggestion that the number 5 no longer existed. He was brought out of hypnosis and then asked to count his fingers. The subject counted 11 fingers! Counting again, the baffled subject was at a loss to explain his results.

Most posthypnotic suggestions last only a few hours or days before they wear off, although some posthypnotic suggestions have been reported to last over a year (Kihlstrom, 1984). So, even if the hypnotist does not include some posthypnotic signal to trigger rediscovery of the number 5, the subject will eventually recall that the number 5 exists.

Although the effects of hypnosis can be dramatic, there are limits to the behaviors that can be influenced by hypnosis. First, contrary to popular belief, a person cannot be hypnotized against his or her will. Second, hypnosis cannot make you stronger than your physical capabilities or induce talents that are not already present (Bowers, 1976). However, hypnosis *can* enhance physical skills or athletic ability by increasing motivation and concentration, or by reducing anxiety (LeUnes & Nation, 1989; Stanton, 1989a).

Third, hypnosis cannot make you perform behaviors that are contrary to your morals and values. Thus, you're very unlikely to commit criminal or immoral acts under the influence of hypnosis—unless, of course, you find such actions acceptable. Hypnosis researcher Ernest Hilgard (1986b) tells the story of a colleague who hypnotized a female student in front of a psychology class and then told her to take off her clothes. Normally, this is a foolproof demonstration of a hypnotic subject's unwillingness to commit an action that conflicts with the subject's values. Instead of spontaneously coming out of hypnosis, however, the female student began unbuttoning her blouse! The professor, of course, immediately stopped her. As it turned out, the student had a part-time job as a nightclub stripper.

Hypnosis and Memory

Memory can be significantly affected by hypnosis. In **posthypnotic amnesia,** a subject is unable to recall specific information or events that occurred before or during hypnosis (Kihlstrom, 1984). Posthypnotic amnesia is produced by a hypnotic suggestion that suppresses the memory of specific information, such as the subject's street address. The effects of posthypnotic amnesia are usually temporary, disappearing either spontaneously or when a posthypnotic signal is suggested by the hypnotist (Kihlstrom, 1983). When the signal is given, the information floods back into the subject's mind.

The opposite hypnotic effect is called **hypermnesia,** which is enhancement of memory for past events (Kihlstrom, 1985). Police investigators sometimes use hypnosis in an attempt to enhance the memories of crime victims and witnesses. Despite the common belief that you can "zoom in" on briefly seen crime details under hypnosis, such claims are extremely exaggerated (M. Smith, 1983). When compared to regular police interview methods, hypnosis does not significantly enhance memory or improve the accuracy of memories (see Kihlstrom & Barnhardt, 1993; Sloane, 1981).

Hypnosis and Memory Many people believe that hypnosis can be used to enhance recall, particularly of upsetting or traumatic events. However, research has shown that hypnosis is no more effective than other types of memory-enhancing methods. Simply looking at a family photograph album can provide potent cues to help retrieve once-forgotten memories.

posthypnotic suggestion
A suggestion made during hypnosis that the person carry out a specific instruction following the hypnotic session.

posthypnotic amnesia
A hypnotic suggestion that suppresses the ability to recall specific information.

hypermnesia
(high-perm-NEES-zha) A hypnotic suggestion to enhance a person's memory for past events.

TABLE 4.3 Help Through Hypnosis

Trained professionals have successfully used hypnosis to:

- Reduce the pain and discomfort of cancer treatments in children
- Remove warts
- Reduce stress in secretaries
- Reduce use of narcotics to relieve postoperative pain
- Improve the concentration and motivation of athletes
- Diminish anxiety and fear in the terminally ill
- Lessen maternal depression after childbirth
- Modify behavior in eating disorders
- Eliminate recurring nightmares
- Help insomniacs fall asleep faster
- Lessen the severity and frequency of asthma attacks
- Decrease the intensity and frequency of headaches
- Eliminate or reduce stuttering
- Suppress the gag reflex during dental procedures

dissociation
The splitting of consciousness into two or more simultaneous streams of mental activity.

hidden observer
Hilgard's term for the hidden, or dissociated, stream of mental activity during hypnosis.

Many studies have shown that efforts to enhance memories hypnotically can lead to distortions and inaccuracies. In fact, hypnosis can greatly increase confidence in memories that are actually incorrect (Kihlstrom, 1985; Kihlstrom & Barnhardt, 1993). False memories, also called *pseudomemories,* can be inadvertently created when hypnosis is used to aid recall (see Yapko, 1994a; Lynn & Nash, 1994).

For example, in one study it was suggested to hypnotized subjects that they had been awakened one night during the previous week by loud noises (Laurence & Perry, 1983). Following hypnosis, almost half of the subjects claimed that loud noises had disturbed their sleep during the previous week. Even *after* the subjects were told the loud noises had been hypnotically suggested, several subjects persisted in the belief that the disturbance had actually taken place.

The problem of inaccurate, distorted, or contrived memories also frequently occurs in *age regression*—the use of hypnosis to recall or re-experience an earlier developmental period (Nash, 1987). When hypnotized people are age-regressed, they confidently "relive" experiences from early childhood and display childlike behaviors and abilities. However, when attempts are made to objectively verify specific details from the experience, they are generally inaccurate, as are the adult subject's depictions of how a small child thinks or behaves (Spanos, 1987–1988). Just as deafness or blindness is not actually produced by hypnotic suggestion, neither is an actual return to childhood. Instead, the subject combines fragments of actual memories with fantasies and information about how he or she thinks children at a particular age will behave.

We can summarize the effects of hypnosis on memory in this way: As a general rule, hypnosis is much more effective in enhancing *confidence* in memories than in enhancing the *accuracy* of memories (see Kihlstrom & Barnhardt, 1993). Thus, the use of hypnosis by therapists to recover "repressed" memories from early childhood can be extremely problematic. We deal with the issue of repressed memories in greater depth in Chapter 6, on memory.

Explaining Hypnosis:
Consciousness Divided?

According to psychologist **Ernest Hilgard** (1992, 1991, 1986a), the hypnotized person experiences **dissociation**—the splitting of consciousness into two or more simultaneous streams of mental activity. While hypnotized, a person consciously experiences one stream of mental activity that is responding to the hypnotist's suggestions. But a second, dissociated stream of mental activity is also operating, processing information that is unavailable to the consciousness of the hypnotized subject. Hilgard (1992, 1986a) refers to this second, dissociated stream of mental activity as the **hidden observer.** (The phrase "hidden observer" does *not* mean that the hypnotized person has multiple personalities.)

Hilgard accidentally discovered the "hidden observer" while conducting a classroom demonstration (see Hilgard, 1992, 1986a). Hilgard hypnotized the student and induced hypnotic deafness. Seated before the class, the student was completely unresponsive to very loud, sudden sounds, such as the sound of a starter pistol firing or of wooden blocks being banged together.

Another student, observing the demonstration, asked Hilgard if "some part" of the hypnotized subject was actually aware of the sounds. Hilgard instructed the hypnotized student to raise his right index finger if some part of him could still hear. To Hilgard's surprise, the hypnotized student's right index finger rose! When brought out of hypnosis, the student had no recall of any sounds during hypnotically induced deafness, *including* Hilgard's suggestion to raise his index finger. Hypnosis, it seemed, had produced a split in consciousness. A conscious segment complied with the hypnotic suggestion of deafness, but a separate, dissociated segment unavailable to consciousness continued to process information. This was the "hidden observer."

Not all psychologists agree that hypnotic phenomena are due to dissociation, divided consciousness, or a "hidden observer" (see Kirsch & others, 1995; Spanos, 1994; Fellows, 1990). Rather, some researchers believe that hypnotic phenomena can be understood in terms of social factors. In Critical Thinking Box 4.5, we examine this controversy more fully.

Regardless of how hypnotic phenomena are ultimately explained, the fact remains that hypnosis works. As research has more clearly defined the effects and limits of hypnotic suggestions, the use of hypnosis in medicine, dentistry, and psychotherapy has become more common. Hypnosis has also been used in sports and business to improve performance and enhance motivation. Table 4.3 lists just a few of the situations in which hypnosis has been successfully used to help people.

CRITICAL THINKING 4.5

Hypnosis: A Special State of Consciousness?

As we discussed in the chapter, the research of Ernest Hilgard and others suggests that hypnotic effects are the result of mental activity occurring on multiple levels of consciousness. This viewpoint has not gone unchallenged (see Baker, 1996, 1990). Some psychologists, such as Nicholas Spanos (1994, 1989, 1986), have contended that hypnotically produced changes can be explained using well-established concepts in *social psychology*, a branch of psychology that investigates how people influence, think about, and relate to one another.

Because hypnosis involves a voluntary social interaction between two people, Spanos (1994) argued that hypnotic subjects are simply responding to *social demands*. They are motivated to be "good" subjects and to cooperate with the hypnotic suggestions. Thus, they act the way that they think good hypnotic subjects are supposed to act, conforming to the expectations of the hypnotist, their own expectations, and situational cues.

As you'll see in the chapter on social psychology (Chapter 12), there is ample evidence that people will obey an authority figure to a surprising extent, sometimes performing very uncharacteristic and extreme behaviors. Under enough social pressure, people will alter, distort, or lie about their perceptions of objective events to conform to the majority view. When these findings are extrapolated and applied to hypnotic phenomena, social-psychological influences seem to provide a simpler and more logical explanation of hypnotic phenomena than notions like a "dissociation in consciousness" and the "hidden observer."

To back up their social-psychological interpretation of hypnotic phenomena, Spanos (1994, 1989) and his colleagues have amassed an impressive array of evidence showing that highly motivated people often perform just as well as hypnotized subjects in demonstrating pain reduction, amnesia, age regression, and hallucinations. Studies of people pretending to be hypnotized have shown similar results.

Are hypnotic effects the result of social-psychological influences that motivate people to conform, role-play, or act in ways that fulfill the expectations inherent in the situation? Or is hypnosis a special state of consciousness that involves a dissociative "split" in awareness?

Both positions have a long history in psychology, and both are supported by experimental evidence. Advocating the "dissociation" explanation of hypnosis, Hilgard (1992, 1986b) makes the common-sense point that it is unlikely that people would undergo surgery without anesthesia simply to please a hypnotist.

There is a possible middle ground. Psychologist and hypnosis researcher John Kihlstrom (1986) has argued that a comprehensive understanding of hypnotic phenomena requires a combination of *both* explanations. The importance of social influences is recognized by many hypnosis researchers. However, as Kihlstrom points out, social influences alone seem inadequate to account for the extraordinary phenomena sometimes demonstrated under hypnosis.

What do you think? Research has shown that highly motivated subjects can mimic the effects of hypnosis, but does that invalidate the notion that hypnotic effects are the result of a dissociation in consciousness? What kinds of evidence would prove or disprove the notion that hypnotic effects involve a special dissociative state of consciousness?

meditation
Any one of a number of sustained concentration techniques that focus attention and heighten awareness.

Meditation

Meditation refers to techniques used to control or retrain attention so as to induce an altered state of focused attention and awareness. What are two general types of meditation? What are the effects of meditation?

Meditation is not easy to define. In general, **meditation** refers to a group of techniques that induce an altered state of focused attention and heightened awareness. Meditation takes many forms, and has been used for thousands of years as part of religious practices throughout the world. Virtually every major form of religion has a rich tradition of meditative practices—whether Hindu, Taoist, Buddhist, Jewish, Christian, or Muslim. However, many people practice meditation independent of any religious tradition or spiritual context. Some forms of psychotherapy also include meditative practice as a component of the overall therapy (Epstein, 1995).

Common to all forms of meditation is the goal of controlling or retraining attention (West, 1987). During waking consciousness, we're engaged in a continual stream of mental activities and self-talk, such as problem solving and daydreaming. The goal of meditation is to quiet the mental chatter—to experience a "pure awareness" that is free of our usual mental activity (Schuman, 1980).

Although meditation techniques vary a great deal, they can be divided into two general categories (West, 1987). *Concentration techniques* involve focusing awareness on a visual image, your breathing, a word, or a phrase. When a sound is used, it is typically a short word or a religious phrase, called a *mantra,* that is mentally repeated. *Opening-up techniques* involve a present-centered awareness of the passing moment without mental judgment (see Tart, 1994). Rather than concentrating on an object, sound, or activity, the meditator engages in quiet awareness of the "here and now" without distracting thoughts (West, 1987).

Meditation in Different Cultures Meditation is an important part of many cultures. On the left, a holy man in Katmandu, Nepal, sits motionless, practicing solitary meditation in a Buddhist temple garden. On the right, a group of women are practicing tai chi in a public park in Hong Kong. Tai chi is a form of meditation that involves a structured series of slow, smooth movements. Throughout China, many people begin their day with tai chi, often meeting in parks and other public places.

Effects of Meditation

During the 1970s, Western researchers began studying the physiological effects of meditation (Wallace & Densen, 1972). One meditation technique that has been widely used in research is called *transcendental meditation,* or *TM.* TM is a form of concentrative meditation that can be quickly mastered, follows a simple format, and does not require any changes in lifestyle or beliefs (Wallace, 1987). Meditators sit quietly with eyes closed, mentally repeat the mantra they have been given, and are taught to allow distracting thoughts to simply "fall away." If you'd like to try a simple meditative technique, follow the instructions in Table 4.4.

TABLE 4.4 How to Meditate

Here is a simple but effective meditation technique that was developed by British psychologist and meditation researcher Michael A. West. Practice the technique for 15 to 20 minutes twice a day, and continue to do so for at least two weeks.

1. Sit quietly in an upright position in a room where you are not likely to be disturbed.

2. Close your eyes and relax your body. Sit quietly for about half a minute.

3. Begin to easily repeat the word "one" silently to yourself. Or choose some other simple word, like "peace" or "calm."

4. Don't concentrate too hard on the sound. The word need only be a faint idea at times—you don't have to keep repeating it clearly.

5. Think the word easily. It may change by getting louder or softer, longer or shorter, or it may not change at all. In every case, just take it as it comes.

6. Remember, the word has no special meaning or special significance. It is a simple device which helps in meditation.

7. Continue the meditation in this way for about 15 minutes. Don't worry about achieving a deep level of meditation or about whether you are concentrating on the sound.

8. Don't try to control thoughts. If thoughts come during meditation, don't worry about it. When you become aware that you have slipped into a train of thought, just go very easily back to the sound. Don't make great efforts to exclude thoughts—just favor the sound.

9. If you become aware of outside noises or other distracting sounds, go easily back to the word; don't fight to exclude those distractions. Do the same as you would with thoughts. Accept them but favor the sound.

10. Above all, you are meant to enjoy the meditation, so don't try too hard, just take it easily as it comes.

SOURCE: West, 1987.

Numerous studies have shown that even beginning meditators practicing TM experience a state of lowered physiological arousal, including decreased blood pressure, heart rate, and changes in brain waves (Dillbeck & Orme-Johnson, 1987). Advocates of TM have claimed that such physical changes produce a unique state of consciousness with a wide variety of benefits, including stress reduction. However, in terms of simply reducing physiological arousal, TM appears to be no more effective than merely resting with your eyes closed (Holmes, 1987, 1984). Does this mean that simple rest or relaxation is the *same* as transcendental meditation? Not necessarily.

Like other forms of meditation, TM has diverse effects. Meditators show EEG patterns that are dominated by alpha brain-wave activity, which is similar to the state of drowsiness that precedes stage 1 sleep (Fenwick, 1987). However, experienced meditators tend to describe meditation in very different subjective terms than drowsiness (Pekala, 1987). Often, the meditative experience is described as simultaneously producing relaxation *and* a state of wakeful alertness. In contrast, people who practice mental relaxation with their eyes closed often describe the experience as relaxing but boring (Alexander & others, 1989).

Does meditation produce beneficial effects? One long-range study involved elderly nursing home residents with an average age of eighty-one (Alexander & others, 1989). The residents were randomly assigned to one of four groups. One group was taught TM. A second group, called the mindfulness group, was taught to engage in mental exercises, like word games. A third group was taught a simple relaxation procedure. The fourth group

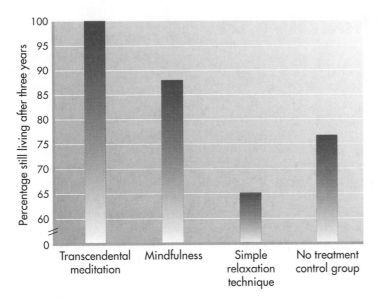

FIGURE 4.7 Beneficial Effects of Meditation in an Elderly Population Elderly nursing home residents were randomly assigned to one of four groups: transcendental meditation, mindfulness, simple relaxation, or a no-treatment control group. Subjects in the three experimental groups practiced their technique for 20 minutes, twice a day, for 12 weeks. Depicted here are the percentages of elderly nursing home residents who were alive three years later. Of the elderly subjects who practiced TM, all were still alive three years later, compared to 77 percent of the no-treatment control group and 65 percent of the subjects who were taught the simple relaxation technique.

(Alexander & others, 1989.)

acted as the no-treatment control group. For a period of 12 weeks, members of the experimental groups practiced their assigned techniques for 20 minutes twice a day.

The results? The elderly subjects in the TM group and the mindfulness group showed significant improvements in blood pressure, cognitive functioning, and mental health ratings. But the most dramatic finding was the survival rate three years later, as shown in Figure 4.7. Of the elderly subjects who practiced TM, *all* were still alive three years later, compared to 65 percent of the simple relaxation group (Alexander & others, 1989). These findings are consistent with other studies that have shown that TM enhances physical and psychological functioning (Jedrczak, 1986; Orme-Johnson, 1987).

Meditation and hypnosis are similar in that both involve the deliberate use of mental techniques to change the experience of consciousness. In the final section of this chapter, we'll consider one of the oldest and most widely used strategies for deliberately altering conscious awareness—psychoactive drugs.

Hypnosis and Meditation

1. The common misconception that a hypnotist can hypnotize people because he possesses special powers or abilities can be traced back to the activities of _____.
   a. Sigmund Freud
   b. Anton Mesmer
   c. Ernest Hilgard
   d. Svengali

2. Jill is very responsive to hypnotic suggestions. Jill probably _____.
   a. has a very vivid imagination and a rich fantasy life
   b. has a very negative attitude toward hypnosis
   c. is easily distracted
   d. can be easily hypnotized against her will

3. While Glenda is under hypnosis, the hypnotist tells her that she remembers being lost in a shopping mall as a young child. After being brought out of hypnosis, Glenda is completely convinced that the event occurred. She describes being found by a mall security guard and other details of the event. The hypnotist has successfully created _____.

   a. an age regression   **c.** hypermnesia
   b. posthypnotic amnesia   **d.** a pseudomemory

4. Dr. Kildare used hypnosis instead of an anesthetic when setting a patient's broken toe. The patient insisted that she felt no pain, but when instructed to raise her right index finger if some part of her felt any pain, she raised her finger. This example best illustrates the notion of _____.
   a. age regression
   b. posthypnotic suggestion
   c. the hidden observer
   d. transcendental meditation

5. To help deal with the stress of his busy schedule, Dean meditates for about 15 minutes on the commuter train as he is going to and from work. His meditation consists of focusing his awareness on mentally repeating the word "peace." Dean is using a(n) _____ technique of meditation.
   a. concentration   **c.** opening-up
   b. mindfulness   **d.** Zen

Psychoactive Drugs

Psychoactive drugs alter consciousness by changing arousal, mood, thinking, sensation, and perception. What are the common properties of psychoactive drugs? What factors influence the effects, use, and abuse of drugs?

Do you start your day with a cup of coffee? We do. (Actually, to be honest, we tend to start our mornings with a *pot* of coffee.) Most people sip (or gulp) coffee to help them wake up in the morning and stay alert throughout the day. In the evening, many people drink a beer or a glass of wine to help them relax. Caffeine and alcohol are two of the most widely used psychoactive drugs. **Psychoactive drugs** are chemical substances that can alter arousal, mood, thinking, sensation, and perception. In this section, we'll look at a variety of consciousness-altering psychoactive drugs, both legal and illegal.

Common Properties of Psychoactive Drugs

Addiction is a broad term that refers to a condition in which a person feels psychologically and physically compelled to take a specific drug. When an individual experiences **physical dependence,** his body and brain chemistry has physically adapted to the drug (Berridge & Robinson, 1995). Many physically addictive drugs gradually produce **tolerance,** which means that increasing amounts of the drug are needed to gain the original, desired effect.

When a person is physically dependent on a drug, abstaining from the drug produces withdrawal symptoms. **Withdrawal symptoms** are unpleasant physical reactions to the lack of the drug plus an intense craving for it. Withdrawal symptoms are alleviated by taking the drug again. Often, the withdrawal symptoms are opposite to the drug's action, a phenomenon called the **drug rebound effect.** For example, withdrawing from stimulating drugs, like the caffeine in coffee, may produce depression and fatigue. Withdrawal from depressant drugs, like alcohol, may produce excitability.

Biological Effects of Drugs

Each psychoactive drug has a distinct biological effect. Psychoactive drugs may influence many different body systems, but their consciousness-altering effects are primarily due to their effect on the brain. Typically, these drugs influence brain activity by altering synaptic transmission among neurons (see Julien, 1995). As we discussed in Chapter 2, drugs can affect synaptic transmission by blocking, mimicking, increasing, or decreasing neurotransmitters (see Figure 2.6 on page 53).

The biological effects of a given drug can also vary somewhat from one person to another. The drugtaker's size, gender, and age may influence the intensity of the drug's effects. So can individual metabolism, and whether the person is taking the drug on a full or empty stomach or in combination with other drugs.

Psychological and Environmental Influences

Along with biological factors, psychological and environmental factors influence the effects of a drug. The response to a drug can be significantly affected by the drugtaker's personality characteristics, mood, expectations, experience with the drug, and the setting in which the drug is taken (see Marlatt

psychoactive drug
A drug that alters normal consciousness, perception, mood, and behavior.

physical dependence
A condition in which a person has physically adapted to a drug so that he must take the drug regularly in order to avoid withdrawal symptoms.

tolerance
A condition in which increasing amounts of a physically addictive drug are needed to produce the original, desired effect.

withdrawal symptoms
Unpleasant physical reactions, combined with intense drug cravings, that occur when a person abstains from a drug on which she is physically dependent.

drug rebound effect
Withdrawal symptoms that are the opposite of a physically addictive drug's action.

& others, 1988; Stacy & others, 1990). For example, what kind of effect do you think three drinks would have on each of the following individuals?

- A college student at an end-of-semester bash the night final exams are over.

- A depressed woman, recently separated, drinking alone at a bar until closing time.

- A father toasting his youngest daughter at her bat mitzvah.

- A man having an escalating argument with his wife on a hot summer night.

Even though the physiological effect of alcohol is essentially the same for each individual, the behavioral and psychological response would clearly be different. One drinker feels joyously uninhibited; another is contemplating suicide; the third is feeling sentimental and proud; and the fourth may be close to committing homicide. Although alcohol may provide the most familiar example, individual responses to other psychoactive drugs are also subject to psychological and environmental influences.

Why Do People Abuse Drugs?

There is no easy answer to that question. First of all, it's difficult to draw a hard-and-fast line between drug *use* and drug *abuse*, especially when the drug in question is a legal one, like alcohol. Most people would not consider having a cold beer at a summer picnic an instance of drug abuse. Chug-a-lugging three six-packs, however, falls into a different category altogether. So a distinction must first be made between moderate drug *use* and drug *abuse*. This distinction is not always clear-cut. Generally, however, **drug abuse** refers to recurrent drug use that results in disruptions in academic, social, or occupational functioning, or in legal or psychological problems (American Psychiatric Association, 1994).

Second, many factors are involved in drug abuse. Listed below are some of the most important factors that have been found to be involved in drug abuse (Petraitis & others, 1995; Hawkins & others, 1992):

- Social and cultural norms that are favorable toward drug taking.

- Availability and cost of the drug.

- Drug-taking behavior of role models and family members.

- Occupational, social, and academic problems.

- Association with drug-using peers.

- Rebelliousness or alienation from society as a whole.

Finally, both culture and ethnicity can affect drug use. Many traditional societies use psychoactive substances in structured religious rituals or social ceremonies. Because the use of psychoactive drugs under these circumstances is tightly controlled, abuse is rare or nonexistent. However, when traditional restrictions imposed by a particular society begin to break down, ritual use may degenerate into drug abuse.

For example, *kava* is an intoxicating but nonalcoholic drink that has been used for hundreds of years in ritual ceremonies in the South Pacific islands. In the past, abuse of kava was rare and, when it occurred, was not tolerated by the community. In recent years, kava abuse has become a major social problem as younger people have begun to use kava to "get high" rather than using it within the context of religious ceremonies (Trimble, 1994).

Dangerous Drugs, Tragic Deaths Drug abuse can result in lethal consequences, such as the tragic 1993 death of the talented young actor, River Phoenix. Phoenix ingested a lethal mixture of Valium (a barbiturate), cocaine (a stimulant), and heroin (an opiate) (Robb, 1994).

drug abuse
Recurrent drug use that results in disruptions in academic, social, or occupational functioning, or in legal or psychological problems.

The norms of many cultural and ethnic groups also have a strong influence on drug use and abuse. The media typically present stereotypes of drug abuse as occurring largely among members of minorities. However, national surveys have consistently shown that a much higher percentage of white teenagers use illegal drugs than African-American teenagers (Substance Abuse and Mental Health Services Administration, 1994).

Clearly, a wide range of factors are involved in drug use. Equally clear is that drug abuse poses a serious threat to many societies, including our own. In the remainder of this section, we will look at the characteristics of four broad categories of psychoactive drugs:

1. *Depressants*—drugs that *depress,* or inhibit, brain activity.

2. *Opiates*—drugs that are chemically similar to morphine and that relieve pain and produce euphoria.

3. *Stimulants*—drugs that *stimulate,* or excite, brain activity.

4. *Psychedelic drugs*—drugs that distort sensory perceptions.

The Depressants:
Alcohol, Barbiturates, and Inhalants

Depressants inhibit central nervous system activity. What characterizes alcohol use and abuse? How does alcohol affect the body and psychological functioning? What are the effects of barbiturates, tranquilizers, and inhalants?

The **depressants** are a class of drugs that depress or inhibit central nervous system activity. In general, depressants produce drowsiness, sedation, or sleep. Depressants also relieve anxiety and lower inhibitions. All the depressant drugs are potentially physically addictive. Finally, the effects of depressant drugs are *additive.* That is, the sedative effects are increased when depressants are combined.

Alcohol

Alcohol provides a good example of the potential for a psychoactive drug to be misused. Used in small amounts, alcohol reduces tension and anxiety. Evidence even exists that light drinking reduces the risk of heart disease, probably because of its beneficial effects on cholesterol levels (Rimm, 1991; Gordon & Doyle, 1987). Weddings, parties, and other social gatherings often include alcohol, a tribute to its relaxing and "social lubricating" properties. Yet consider these points:

- Drug experts believe that alcohol abuse has the highest social cost of all drug addictions (Marlatt & others, 1988).

- Every year, alcohol is implicated in over 25,000 fatal automobile accidents and 12,000 murders in the United States.

- Approximately two-thirds of all cases of spouse abuse and violent child abuse involve alcohol use (Steele & Josephs, 1990).

- Drinking by pregnant women is the third leading cause of birth defects producing mental retardation—and the only preventable one (Julien, 1995).

depressants
A category of psychoactive drugs that depress or inhibit brain activity.

Thus, even though alcohol is a legal and readily available drug for adults, it's also a dangerous drug with a high potential for abuse.

Who Drinks and Why? More than two-thirds of the Americans who are old enough to drink do so at least occasionally. Of those, an estimated 14 million Americans have serious alcohol problems. They may drink excessively on a regular basis and suffer social, occupational, and health problems as a result of drinking (Rosenberg, 1993). About half of these, or 7 million people, are considered to be *alcoholic*—they are physically addicted to alcohol (Julien, 1995).

Is alcoholism hereditary? There's no clear answer to that question (Holden, 1994). Twin and adoption studies have convinced some researchers that there is a genetic tendency to abuse alcohol (Crabbe & others, 1994). Other researchers disagree (Plomin & others, 1994). Of course, even if there is a genetic predisposition to abuse alcohol, genetics would be only one of the factors contributing to the development of alcoholism. As noted earlier, the abuse of any substance, including alcohol, involves many different psychological and social factors.

How Does Alcohol Affect the Body? Generally, it takes about one hour to metabolize the alcohol in one drink, which is defined as the amount of alcohol in one ounce of 80-proof whiskey, four ounces of wine, or 12 ounces of beer. All three drinks contain the same amount of alcohol; it's simply more diluted in beer than in hard liquor.

Factors such as body weight, gender, food consumption, and the rate of alcohol consumption also affect blood alcohol levels. A slender person who quickly consumes three drinks on an empty stomach will become more than twice as intoxicated as a heavier person who consumes three drinks with food. Women metabolize alcohol more slowly than men. If a man and a woman of equal weight consume the same number of drinks, the woman will become more intoxicated.

Alcohol depresses the activity of neurons throughout the brain. Alcohol impairs cognitive abilities such as concentration, memory, and speech, and physical abilities such as muscle coordination and balance (Julien, 1995). As blood levels of alcohol rise, more brain activity is impaired, until the person loses consciousness. If blood alcohol levels continue to rise, death can occur because the brain's respiratory center can no longer function. This is why drinking "contests" are potentially lethal.

Because alcohol is physically addictive, the alcoholic who stops drinking may suffer from physical withdrawal symptoms. The severity of the withdrawal symptoms depends on the level of physical dependence. With a low level of dependence, withdrawal may involve disrupted sleep, anxiety, and mild tremors ("the shakes"). At higher levels of physical dependence on alcohol, withdrawal may involve confusion, hallucinations, and severe tremors or

The Social and Personal Costs of Alcohol Abuse The bereaved family attending the funeral of a son killed by a drunk driver (left) and the family and friends of victims of another accident (right) can testify to the high costs associated with alcohol abuse. An intoxicated driver has impaired perceptual ability and psychomotor functions, delayed reaction time, and poor coordination. He or she also is likely to display impaired judgment, poor impulse control, and an inflated self-image. This deadly combination results in more than 25,000 traffic deaths each year.

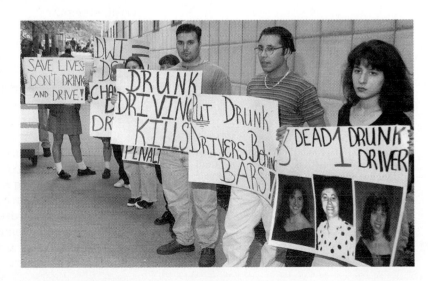

seizures. Collectively, these severe symptoms are sometimes called the *delirium tremens,* or *DTs.* Alcohol withdrawal causes rebound hyperexcitability in the brain. In cases of extreme physical dependence, withdrawal can cause seizures, convulsions, and even death in the absence of medical supervision (Julien, 1995).

What Are Alcohol's Psychological Effects?

People are often surprised that alcohol is classified as a depressant. Initially, alcohol produces mild euphoria, talkativeness, and feelings of good humor and friendliness, leading many people to think of alcohol as a stimulant. But these subjective experiences occur because alcohol *lessens inhibitions* by depressing the brain centers responsible for judgment and self-control. Reduced inhibitions and self-control are involved in the aggressive and violent behavior sometimes associated with alcohol abuse (Steele, 1986; Steele & Josephs, 1990). But the individual effects of the loss of inhibitions are unpredictable and depend on the person's environment and his expectations regarding alcohol's effect (Bushman, 1993; Marlatt & Rohsenow; 1980).

Barbiturates and Tranquilizers

Barbiturates are powerful depressant drugs that reduce anxiety and promote sleep, which is why they are sometimes called "downers." Barbiturates depress activity in the brain centers that control arousal, wakefulness, and alertness (Julien, 1995; Barondes, 1993). Barbiturates also depress the brain's respiratory centers.

Like alcohol, barbiturates at low doses cause relaxation, mild euphoria, and reduced inhibitions. Larger doses produce a loss of coordination, impaired mental functioning, and depression. High doses can produce unconsciousness, coma, and death. Barbiturates also produce a very deep but abnormal sleep; REM sleep is greatly reduced. Because of the additive effect of depressants, barbiturates combined with alcohol are particularly dangerous.

Common barbiturates include the prescription sedatives *Seconal* and *Nembutal.* The illegal drug *methaqualone* (street name *Quaalude*) is almost identical chemically to barbiturates and has similar effects.

Barbiturates produce both physical and psychological dependence. Withdrawal from low doses of barbiturates produces irritability and REM rebound nightmares. Withdrawal from high doses of barbiturates can produce hallucinations, disorientation, restlessness, and life-threatening convulsions.

Tranquilizers are depressants that are prescribed to relieve anxiety. Common tranquilizers include Xanax, Valium, Librium, and Ativan. We will discuss these drugs in more detail in Chapter 15, on therapies. Chemically different from barbiturates, tranquilizers produce similar, although less powerful, effects.

Inhalants

Inhalants refer to a number of chemical substances that are inhaled to produce an alteration in consciousness (Carroll, 1993). Paint solvents, model airplane glue, gasoline, nitrous oxide, and certain aerosol sprays are just a few of the substances that are abused in this way.

Although the inhalants do not have a common chemical structure, they generally act as central nervous system depressants (Julien, 1995). At low doses, they may cause relaxation, giddiness, and reduced inhibition. At higher doses, inhalants can lead to hallucinations and a loss of consciousness.

The inhalants are also quite dangerous. Suffocation is one hazard. Many inhaled substances are toxic to the liver and other body organs. Inhalants are inexpensive and readily available, and inhalant abuse is most prevalent among male teenagers (Julien, 1995).

barbiturates
(barb-ITCH-yer-ets) A category of depressant drugs that reduce anxiety and produce sleepiness.

tranquilizers
Depressant drugs that relieve anxiety.

inhalants
Chemical substances that are inhaled to produce an alteration in consciousness.

opiates
(OH-pee-ets) A category of psychoactive drugs that are chemically similar to morphine and have strong pain-relieving properties.

The Opiates:

From Poppies to Demerol

The opiates are a group of addictive drugs that relieve pain and produce euphoria. How do opiates affect the brain and relieve pain?

Often called *narcotics,* the **opiates** refer to a group of addictive drugs that relieve pain and produce feelings of euphoria. Natural opiates include: *opium,* which is derived from the opium poppy; *morphine,* the active ingredient in opium; and *codeine,* which can be derived from either opium or morphine. Synthetic and semisynthetic opiates include *heroin, methadone,* and the prescription painkillers *Percodan* and *Demerol.*

Opiates produce their powerful effects by mimicking the brain's own natural painkillers, called *endorphins.* Opiates occupy endorphin receptor sites in the brain (Snyder, 1986). As you may recall from Chapter 2, the word *endorphins* literally means "the morphine within."

When used medically, opiates alter an individual's reaction to pain not by acting at the pain site, but by reducing the brain's perception of pain.

Many people recovering from surgery experience a wave of pain relief after receiving narcotics such as morphine, Demerol, or Percodan. People who take opiates in such circumstances rarely develop drug tolerance or dependence (Jacox & others, 1994).

The most frequently abused opiate is heroin. When injected into a vein, heroin reaches the brain in seconds, creating an intense "rush" of euphoria that is followed by feelings of contentment, peacefulness, and warmth. Withdrawing from heroin is not life-threatening, but it does produce unpleasant drug rebound symptoms. Withdrawal symptoms include an intense craving for heroin, fever, chills, muscle cramps, and gastrointestinal problems.

Heroin Cough Syrup Opium and its derivatives, including heroin, morphine, and codeine, were legal in the United States until 1914. In the late nineteenth and early twentieth century, opiates were commonly used in over-the-counter medications for a variety of ailments, from sleeplessness to "female problems" (Musto, 1991). This ad for "Glyco-Heroin" cough syrup appeared in 1904. Codeine is still used in some prescription cough syrups

Cocaine Toothache Drops? Prior to 1914, cocaine was legal in the United States and, like the opiates, was widely used as an ingredient in over-the-counter medicines. From this 1885 advertisement for Cocaine Toothache Drops, it's clear that cocaine was used in treating children as well as adults. Cocaine derivatives are still used medically as anesthetics, such as Novocain and Lidocaine. Cocaine was also part of Coca-Cola's original formula in 1888. It was replaced in 1903 with another stimulant, caffeine. Coca leaves, with the cocaine extracted for medical purposes, are still used for flavoring cola drinks.

stimulants
A category of psychoactive drugs that increase brain activity, arouse behavior, and increase mental alertness.

The Stimulants:
Caffeine, Nicotine, Amphetamines, and Cocaine

Stimulant drugs increase brain activity. What are the effects of caffeine and nicotine? How does nicotine affect the brain? What are the effects of amphetamines and cocaine?

Stimulants vary in the strength of their effects, legal status, and the way they are taken. All stimulant drugs, however, are at least mildly addicting, and all tend to increase brain activity. We'll first look at the most widely used and legal stimulants, caffeine and nicotine. Then we'll examine much more potent stimulants, cocaine and the amphetamines.

Caffeine and Nicotine

Caffeine is found in coffee, tea, cola drinks, chocolate, and many over-the-counter medications. Most Americans consume caffeine in some form every day (DeAngelis, 1994a). In fact, caffeine is the most widely used psychoactive drug in the world.

Caffeine stimulates the cerebral cortex in the brain, resulting in an increase in mental alertness and wakefulness (Julien, 1995). Even a single cup of coffee has a noticeable effect on the cerebral cortex.

Yes, coffee drinkers, caffeine *is* physically addictive. Regular coffee, tea, or cola drinkers will experience withdrawal symptoms if they abruptly stop their caffeine intake: headaches, irritability, drowsiness, and fatigue may last up to a week (Goldstein, 1994; Griffiths, 1994). At high doses, caffeine can produce anxiety, restlessness, insomnia, and increased heart rate—symptoms that are collectively called "coffee nerves."

Nicotine is another widely used, legal, and extremely addictive stimulant. Nicotine is found in all tobacco products, including pipe tobacco, cigars, cigarettes, and smokeless tobacco. Like coffee, nicotine increases mental alertness and reduces fatigue or drowsiness. About 25 percent of American adults use tobacco regularly. The proportion of smokers is much higher in Japan, many European countries, and developing countries (Bartecchi & others, 1995).

When cigarette smoke is inhaled, nicotine reaches the brain in seconds. But within 30 minutes or so, nicotine has left the brain (Ashton & Stepney, 1983). Thus, the addicted "pack-a-day" smoker will light a cigarette every thirty to forty minutes to maintain a relatively constant nicotine level in the brain.

TABLE 4.5 Common Sources of Caffeine

Item	Caffeine Content (Average, in mg)
Coffee (5-ounce cup)	100
Tea (5-ounce cup)	50
Cocoa (5-ounce cup)	5
Chocolate (semisweet, baking) (1 ounce)	25
Chocolate milk (1 ounce)	5
Cola drink (12 ounces)	40
Over-the-counter stimulants (No Doz, Vivarin)	100+
Over-the-counter analgesics (Excedrin, Anacin, Midol, Vanquish)	65 / 33
Over-the-counter cold remedies (Coryban-D, Triaminicin)	30
Over-the-counter diuretics (Aqua-ban)	100

SOURCE: Julien, 1995.

Caffeine and Conversation Caffeine is the most widely used psychoactive drug in the world and is commonly consumed in social settings. These French college students are enjoying a cup of espresso at an outdoor cafe. Thousands of miles away, the gentlemen in Egypt shown on page 187 are relaxing in a corner cafe over a glass of mint tea.

Over the course of a year, that averages out to 70,000 "hits" of nicotine (Carroll, 1993).

Although nicotine is classified as a stimulant, many smokers claim that smoking is relaxing. They're right. In *small* doses, nicotine acts as a stimulant, but in *large* doses, nicotine acts as a depressant (Hamilton & Timmons, 1990; Bartecchi & others, 1995).

Nicotine is extremely addictive, both physically and psychologically. People who start smoking for nicotine's stimulating or relaxing properties often continue smoking to avoid the withdrawal symptoms—jumpiness, irritability, tremors, craving for cigarettes, headaches, drowsiness, brain fog, and light-headedness (Shiffman & others, 1995).

(a)

Amphetamines and Cocaine

Like caffeine and nicotine, amphetamines and cocaine stimulate brain activity, increasing mental alertness and reducing fatigue. However, amphetamines and cocaine also elevate mood and produce a sense of euphoria (Snyder, 1986). When abused, they can produce severe psychological and physical problems.

Common amphetamines are the prescription drugs *Benzedrine* and *Dexedrine*. Sometimes called "speed" or "uppers," **amphetamines** suppress appetite and were once widely prescribed as diet pills. Tolerance to the appetite-suppressant effects occurs quickly, so progressive increases in amphetamine dosage are required to maintain the effect. Consequently, amphetamines are rarely prescribed today for weight control.

Cocaine is an illegal stimulant that is derived from the leaves of the coca tree, found in South America. (The coca plant is not the source of cocoa or chocolate, which is made from the beans of the *cacao* plant.) When "snorted" in purified, powdered form, cocaine reaches the brain within a few minutes. Inhaling cocaine provides intense euphoria, mental alertness, and self-confidence, which lasts for several minutes.

Tobacco Use Around the World
(a) To compensate for decreased cigarette consumption in the United States, American tobacco companies have increased their exports of cigarettes to other countries. This Marlboro man appears on the side of a building in Luxor, Egypt. **(b)** Egyptian cafe patrons enjoying a glass of tea with their tobacco.

(b)

caffeine
(kaff-EEN) A stimulant drug found in coffee, tea, cola drinks, chocolate, and many over-the-counter medications.

nicotine
A stimulant drug found in tobacco products.

amphetamines
(am-FET-uh-mins) A class of stimulant drugs that arouse the central nervous system and suppress appetite.

cocaine
A stimulant drug derived from the coca tree.

stimulant-induced psychosis
Schizophrenia-like symptoms that can occur as the result of prolonged amphetamine or cocaine use.

A more concentrated form of cocaine called *crack* is smoked rather than inhaled. Crack reaches the brain in seconds, producing a short, intense, electrifying feeling of euphoria. This high is quickly followed by a severe "crash" characterized by deep depression, irritability, and a strong craving for another hit. Some experts believe crack cocaine is more addictive than heroin, barbiturates, or alcohol (Carroll, 1993).

Prolonged use of either amphetamines or cocaine can result in **stimulant-induced psychosis,** also called *amphetamine psychosis* or *cocaine psychosis* (Snyder, 1986). Schizophrenia-like symptoms develop, including auditory hallucinations of "voices" and bizarrely paranoid ideas. "Cocaine bugs" refers to an unusual tactile hallucination that occurs in stimulant-induced psychosis but not in schizophrenia: people itch and tingle, claiming that insects or small animals are crawling on or under their skin.

Psychedelic Drugs:
Mescaline, LSD, and Marijuana

The psychedelic drugs create perceptual distortions, alter mood, and affect thinking. What are the effects of mescaline, LSD, and marijuana?

The term **psychedelic** was coined in the 1950s to describe a group of drugs that create profound perceptual distortions, alter mood, and affect thinking. *Psychedelic* literally means "mind-manifesting" (Tart, 1990).

Peyote-Inspired Visions The Huichol Indians of Mexico have used peyote in religious ceremonies for hundreds of years. Huichol yarn paintings, like the one shown here, are flat pieces of wood inlaid with designs made with colored yarn. The yarn paintings often depict imagery and scenes inspired by traditional peyote visions, which resemble the geometric shapes and radiating patterns of hallucinations induced by psychedelic drugs.

Mescaline and LSD

Naturally occurring psychedelic drugs have been used for thousands of years. **Mescaline,** which is derived from the peyote cactus, has been used for centuries in the religious ceremonies of Mexican Indians. Another psychedelic drug called *psilocybin* is derived from the psilocybe mushroom. Sometimes called "magic mushrooms," psilocybin has been used since 500 B.C. in religious rites in Mexico and Central America (Snyder, 1986).

In contrast to these naturally occurring psychedelics, **LSD** (or *lysergic acid diethylamide*) is a powerful psychedelic drug that was first synthesized in the late 1930s. LSD is far more potent than mescaline or psilocybin. Just 25 micrograms, or one-millionth of an ounce, of LSD can produce profound psychological effects with relatively few physiological changes (Julien, 1995).

LSD and psilocybin are very similar chemically to the neurotransmitter *serotonin,* which is involved in regulating moods and sensations (see Chapter 2). LSD and psilocybin mimic serotonin in the brain, stimulating serotonin receptor sites (Aghajanian, 1994; Jacobs, 1987).

The effects of a psychedelic experience vary greatly, depending on an individual's personality, current emotional state, surroundings, and the other people present (see Smith & Seymour, 1994). When a "bad trip" occurs, it can produce extreme anxiety, panic, and even psychotic episodes.

Tolerance to psychedelic drugs may occur after heavy use. However, even heavy users of LSD do not develop physical dependence, nor do they experience withdrawal symptoms if the drug is not taken.

Adverse reactions to LSD include "flashbacks" (recurrences of the drug's effects), depression, long-term psychological instability, and prolonged psychotic reactions (Smith & Seymour, 1994). In a psychologically unstable or susceptible person, even a single dose of LSD can precipitate a severe psychotic reaction.

Marijuana

The common hemp plant, *Cannabis sativa,* is used to make rope and cloth. But when its leaves, stems, flowers, and seeds are dried and crushed, the mixture is called **marijuana,** one of the most widely used illegal drugs. Marijuana's active ingredient is the chemical *THC*. When marijuana is smoked, THC reaches the brain in less than 30 seconds. One potent form of marijuana, *hashish,* is made from the resin of the hemp plant. Hashish is sometimes eaten.

psychedelic drugs
A category of psychoactive drugs that create sensory and perceptual distortions, alter mood, and affect judgment.

mescaline
A psychedelic drug derived from the peyote cactus.

To lump marijuana with the highly psychedelic drugs mescaline and LSD is somewhat misleading. At high doses, marijuana can sometimes produce sensory distortions that resemble a mild psychedelic experience. Low to moderate doses of THC produce a sense of well-being, mild euphoria, and a dreamy state of relaxation. Senses become more attuned and vivid. Taste, touch, and smell may be enhanced; time perception may be altered.

Most marijuana users do not develop tolerance or physical dependence. Chronic users of extremely high doses *can* develop some tolerance to THC and may experience withdrawal symptoms when its use is discontinued. Such symptoms include irritability, restlessness, insomnia, tremors, and decreased appetite.

Marijuana and its active ingredient, THC, have been shown to be helpful in the treatment of pain, epilepsy, hypertension, nausea, glaucoma, and asthma (Snyder, 1990). In cancer patients, it can prevent the nausea and vomiting caused by chemotherapy. However, at the present time, the medical use of marijuana is extremely limited and politically controversial.

On the negative side, marijuana interferes with muscle coordination and perception and may impair driving ability. When combined with alcohol, marijuana's effects are intensified—a dangerous combination for drivers. Marijuana has also been shown to interfere with learning, memory, cognitive functioning, and reproductive processes (see Julien, 1995; Goldstein, 1994).

CONCEPT REVIEW 4.6

Psychoactive Drugs

For each of the following descriptions, name the drug class and give two (or more) examples.

		Drug Class	Examples
1.	Drugs that create perceptual distortions, alter mood, and affect thinking.	_____	_____
2.	Drugs that inhibit central nervous system activity; produce drowsiness, sedation, or sleep; and may reduce anxiety and lower inhibitions.	_____	_____
3.	Addictive drugs that mimic endorphins and can relieve pain and produce euphoria.	_____	_____
4.	Drugs that increase brain activity, are at least mildly addictive, increase mental alertness, and reduce fatigue.	_____	_____

Summing Up: Consciousness and Its Variations

In this chapter, we've surveyed consciousness in its many different forms. We've looked at how the experience of consciousness can be deliberately influenced by chemical substances like psychoactive drugs, or by practices like hypnosis and meditation. We've explored the variations in consciousness that naturally occur throughout the cycles of everyday life. We've seen that a full understanding of consciousness must also consider the important roles played by social, psychological, and cultural factors.

LSD
A synthetic psychedelic drug.

marijuana
A psychoactive drug derived from the hemp plant.

In the prologue to this chapter, we described a fairly typical morning—family members struggling to wake up, drinking coffee together, talking about their dreams. We hope that you now have a much fuller appreciation of the variety of complex psychological processes involved in just such a "normal" morning. Perhaps you, like your authors, have trouble waking up in the morning. In the Application, we'll give you some simple suggestions for improving the quality of *your* consciousness.

APPLICATION

Improving Sleep and Mental Alertness

Many environmental cues affect circadian rhythms. How can you enhance mental alertness, improve the quality of your sleep, and minimize the negative effects of shift work?

In this Application we'll give you some research-based, practical suggestions to help wake up in the morning, improve the quality of your sleep, and minimize the mental and physical disruptions that can occur when your body clock is out of sync with environmental time cues.

Dealing with Morning Brain Fog

There is surprisingly little research on how to deal with **sleep inertia**—sleepiness upon awakening that interferes with your ability to perform mental or physical tasks (Hobson & Stickgold, 1995). For some people, "morning brain fog" can last half an hour or more before they feel fully alert (Little, 1993; Dinges, 1989).

The simplest antidote for sleep inertia seems to be the passage of time. People who have trouble getting up in the morning tend to stay in bed until the last possible moment. This strategy, of course, only intensifies their disorientation because they are forced to hustle out the door before they are fully awake.

So, if you suffer from sleep inertia, try setting your alarm clock (and possibly a second one in the next room) to wake you 15 minutes *earlier* than usual. Resolve to hit the floor when the alarm goes off. The extra 15 minutes will help give your mind time to clear.

During that 15 minutes, sip a cup of coffee or tea. It will take you approximately half an hour to feel the full effects of the caffeine (Julien, 1995). If

the sun is up, sit near a window; if it's not, turn on the lights. Bright light, especially sunlight, helps brain fog dissipate by reducing blood levels of the hormone melatonin (Brown, 1994). To help engage your brain, glance at the newspaper or start a list of what you want to accomplish for the day. Though simple, these suggestions really do help, as your night-owl authors, neither of whom exactly greets the morning with enthusiasm, have discovered.

Improving the Quality of Your Sleep

Sleep researchers have identified a variety to ways to improve the quality of your sleep.

- Timing is more important than you probably realize. In the early evening hours, usually between 8:00 and 10:00 p.m., we normally experience a daily period of *increased* wakefulness that occurs prior to sleepiness. Sleep researchers call this presleep burst of wakefulness the "forbidden zone for sleep" (Lavie, 1989). So to avoid suddenly feeling wide awake in bed, you should go to bed *after* the forbidden zone, when your brain has begun to gear down to sleepiness.

- Going to bed very hungry or very full will disrupt sleep, but a light snack will help reduce nighttime restlessness and increase total sleep time (Empson, 1993).

- Moderate exercise during the day seems to promote deep sleep, but exercise in the evening or shortly before going to bed may rev you up and keep you awake.

- Soaking in a very warm bath shortly before retiring promotes

deep sleep by raising your core body temperature (Empson, 1993).

- A consistent bedtime routine and familiar surroundings enhance the quality of sleep. Try to go to bed at about the same time each night and get up at approximately the same time every morning so that you stay in sync with your own pattern of circadian rhythms.

- Depressant drugs, such as alcohol and barbiturates, may produce drowsiness but they also reduce REM sleep, disrupting the quality of your sleep. Hence, they should be avoided.

- Recent research indicates that taking supplemental melatonin, which can be purchased at health food stores, may promote a better night's sleep (Zhdanova & others, 1995; Brown, 1994). However, the Food and Drug Administration has warned people who take supplemental melatonin that they do so "without any assurance that it is safe or that it will have any beneficial effect" (Cowley, 1995).

Finally, you may be pleased to discover that sex promotes sleep. For example, rabbits tend to sleep very little—with the exception of quickly nodding off into REM sleep after some amorous activity in the old rabbit hutch. The same phenomenon also seems to occur in humans, which may be why sleep so often follows sexual interaction. As sleep researcher J. Allan Hobson (1989) put it, sex "not only leads to muscle relaxation, but also clears the cerebral circuits of tedious humdrum."

Working the Night Shift and Rotating Shifts

People vary in the ease with which they develop tolerance for working the night shift or rotating shifts (Harma, 1993). Here are four suggestions for minimizing the negative effects that night work can produce:

- If you have a choice in your work schedule, the longer you can stay with one shift, the better. Frequent shift changes, such as every other week, increase jet-lag symptoms (Wilkinson, 1992).

- If you work rotating shifts, try to make your schedule changes more compatible with circadian rhythms (Czeisler & others, 1982). Because of our natural tendency to drift toward longer days, it is easier to lengthen our days than to shorten them artificially. Therefore, try to arrange it so that your shift changes progress from the morning to evening to night shifts, rather than the other way around (Gallo & Eastman, 1993).

- If you work the midnight to 8:00 a.m. shift, bright lights in the workplace, especially during the early part of the shift, will help you and your co-workers' circadian cycles adjust to the night schedule (Dawson & Campbell, 1991; Czeisler & others, 1990).

- To promote sleep during the daytime, ask your doctor about the pros and cons of taking supplemental melatonin. Some researchers have found that melatonin supplements can help induce daytime sleep, improving mental alertness during night shifts (Dawson, 1995; Folkard & others, 1993).

Summary
Consciousness and Its Variations

Consciousness: Experiencing the "Private I"

- Consciousness refers to the immediate awareness of internal and external stimuli. Early psychologists studied consciousness, but the behaviorists believed that consciousness was not an appropriate topic for psychology. Today, consciousness is regarded as an important subject for psychological research.

The Biological and Environmental "Clocks" Regulating Consciousness

- We experience a variety of circadian rhythms, which are regulated by the suprachiasmatic nucleus (SCN), the "master clock" located in the hypothalamus of the brain. In response to light detected by visual receptors, the SCN reduces the production of melatonin by the pineal gland. Increased melatonin makes you sleepy.

- Under free-running conditions, human circadian rhythms seem to drift toward a 25-hour day. Circadian rhythms become disrupted when environmental time cues are out of sync with the body clock. Symptoms of jet lag can be produced by travel across time zones, night-shift or rotating-shift work, and disruption of normal sleep patterns caused by staying up late on the weekends.

Sleep

- The traditional view of sleep as a period of inactivity was changed by the invention of the electroencephalograph and the discovery of rapid eye movements (REM). The two basic types of sleep are REM sleep and NREM sleep.

- As people fall asleep, brain activity slows down. The first 90 minutes of sleep include four different stages of NREM sleep followed by a brief episode of REM sleep. As the night progresses, episodes of REM sleep become longer and NREM episodes become shorter.

- As people age, periods of REM sleep and deep sleep generally become shorter and more time is spent in stage 2 NREM.

- Sleep deprivation studies have demonstrated that people have a biological need to sleep. The restorative theory of sleep proposes that sleep promotes physiological processes that restore the body and mind. NREM seems particularly important in physical restoration, and REM seems important in brain development. The evolutionary theory of sleep suggests that the varying sleep patterns of different animals evolved as a means of promoting survival and adapting to environmental conditions.

Troubled Sleep: Sleep Disorders

- Sleep disorders are serious disturbances in the normal sleep pattern that interfere with daytime functioning and cause subjective distress.

- The most common sleep disorder is insomnia. Children are most likely to experience sleepwalking and night terrors. Other sleep disorders include REM sleep behavior disorder, sleep apnea, and narcolepsy.

Dreams and Mental Activity During Sleep

- Sleep thinking occurs during NREM sleep. A dream is a storylike unfolding episode of mental images. Dreams are characterized by intense emotions, illogical content and organization, bizarre sensations, and outlandish details that are uncritically accepted. Dreams are also difficult to remember.

- Most dreams reflect everyday concerns and include familiar people and settings. There are individual differences in dream recall. Several factors contribute to our general lack of ability to recall dreams, including changes in brain chemistry and functioning that occur during sleep.

- Nightmares are unpleasant anxiety dreams. During lucid dreams, people are consciously aware that they are dreaming.

- Sigmund Freud believed that dream symbols represent, in disguised form, the expression of repressed, unconscious wishes. The activation-synthesis model of dreaming proposes that dreams reflect our subjective awareness of brain activation during sleep. The activated brain combines internally generated sensory signals and imposes meaning on them.

Hypnosis

- Hypnosis is an unusual state of awareness, defined as a cooperative social interaction in which one person responds to suggestions made by another person (the hypnotist). Changes in perception, memory, and behavior may be produced. People vary in their susceptibility to hypnosis.

- Under hypnosis, profound sensory and perceptual changes may be experienced, including hallucinations. Hypnosis has been used in pain control. Posthypnotic suggestions influence behavior outside of the hypnotic state. Hypnosis cannot be used to make people perform behaviors that are contrary to their morals or values.

- Memory effects include posthypnotic amnesia. However, hypermnesia has not been substantiated as an effect of hypnosis. Hypnosis does not increase the accuracy of memories, but it does increase confidence in memories, even when they are demonstrated to be false.

- Ernest Hilgard explained hypnosis as involving dissociation and the "hidden observer." Not all psychologists agree that hypnosis is a special state of consciousness or awareness.

Meditation

- Meditation refers to techniques used to control attention so as to induce an altered state of focused attention and awareness.

- Research on the effects of transcendental meditation suggests that regular meditation enhances physical and psychological functioning. Some researchers believe that meditation is no more effective than simple rest.

Psychoactive Drugs

- Psychoactive drugs can alter arousal, mood, thinking, sensation, and perception. Many psychoactive drugs are addictive, producing physical dependence and tolerance. The physically dependent person who stops taking a drug experiences withdrawal symptoms, which often include the drug rebound effect.

- Biologically, psychoactive drugs disrupt brain activity by interfering with synaptic transmission. Drug effects can be influenced by the person's size, gender, metabolism, and whether the drug is taken alone or in combination with other drugs. Personality characteristics, mood, expectations, experience with the drug, and the setting in which the drug is taken can also affect the drug response.

- Drug abuse refers to recurrent drug use that leads to disruptions in academic, social, or occupational functioning and to legal or psychological problems. Drug abuse results from a wide variety of factors, including social and cultural influences.

- The depressants inhibit central nervous system activity. Depressants include alcohol, barbiturates, tranquilizers, and inhalants.

- The physical effects of alcohol depend on the level of alcohol in the blood. Psychologically, alcohol lessens inhibitions. Psychological effects depend on the person's environment and expectations.

- Barbiturates and inhalants produce relaxation and reduce inhibitions. Barbiturates are physically addictive.

- The opiates refer to a group of addictive drugs that relieve pain and produce feelings of euphoria. The opiates include opium, morphine, codeine, heroin, methadone, and the prescription painkillers Demerol and Percodan. Opiates relieve pain by mimicking the effect of endorphins in the brain.

- The stimulants include caffeine, nicotine, amphetamines, and cocaine. The stimulants increase brain activity, and all stimulants are addictive to some degree.

- The psychedelic drugs include mescaline, LSD, and marijuana. The psychedelics create perceptual distortions, alter mood, and affect thinking. While the psychedelic drugs are not physically addictive, they can cause a variety of harmful effects.

Key Terms

consciousness (p. 146)

circadian rhythm (p.148)

suprachiasmatic nucleus (SCN) (p. 149)

melatonin (p. 149)

electroencephalograph (p. 154)

EEG (p. 154)

REM sleep (p.154)

NREM sleep (p. 154)

beta brain waves (p. 154)

alpha brain waves (p. 154)

hypnagogic hallucinations (p. 154)

sleep spindles (p. 155)

REM rebound (p. 161)

restorative theory of sleep (p. 161)

evolutionary theory of sleep (p. 161)

sleep disorders (p. 163)

insomnia (p. 163)

sleepwalking (p. 164)

night terrors (p. 164)

REM sleep behavior disorder (p. 164)

sleep apnea (p. 164)

narcolepsy (p. 165)

sleep thinking (p. 166)

dream (p. 166)

nightmare (p. 168)

lucid dream (p. 169)

activation-synthesis model of dreaming (p. 170)

hypnosis (p. 172)

posthypnotic suggestion (p. 174)

posthypnotic amnesia (p. 174)

hypermnesia (p. 174)

dissociation (p. 175)

hidden observer (p. 175)

meditation (p. 177)

psychoactive drug (p. 180)

physical dependence (p. 180)

tolerance (p. 180)

withdrawal symptoms (p. 180)

drug rebound effect (p. 180)

drug abuse (p. 181)

depressants (p. 182)

barbiturates (p. 184)

tranquilizers (p. 184)

inhalants (p. 184)

opiates (p. 185)

stimulants (p. 186)

caffeine (p. 186)

nicotine (p. 186)

amphetamines (p. 187)

cocaine (p. 187)

stimulant-induced psychosis (p. 187)

psychedelic drugs (p. 188)

mescaline (p. 188)

LSD (p. 188)

marijuana (p. 188)

sleep inertia (p. 190)

Key People

Sigmund Freud (1856–1939) Founder of psychoanalysis, who proposed that dream images are disguised and symbolic expressions of unconscious wishes and urges (see Chapter 11).

Ernest R. Hilgard (b. 1904) Contemporary American psychologist who extensively studied hypnosis and advanced the dissociation theory of hypnosis.

J. Allan Hobson (b. 1933) Contemporary American psychiatrist and neurobiologist who extensively researched sleep and dreaming; proposed the *activation-synthesis model* of dreaming with co-researcher Robert W. McCarley.

William James (1842–1910) American psychologist and philosopher who proposed that the subjective experience of consciousness is an ongoing "stream" of mental activity (see Chapter 1).

CONCEPT REVIEW 4.1 Page 153

1. circadian rhythm
2. melatonin
3. jet lag
4. suprachiasmatic nucleus; 25
5. sunlight; 24

CONCEPT REVIEW 4.2 Page 162

1. stage 2 NREM
2. hypnagogic hallucination; myoclonic jerk
3. REM; dreaming
4. stage 4 NREM

CONCEPT REVIEW 4.3 Page 165

1. REM sleep behavior disorder
2. narcolepsy
3. sleep apnea
4. night terror
5. situational insomnia

CONCEPT REVIEW 4.4 Page 172

1. c
2. b
3. b
4. c
5. d

CONCEPT REVIEW 4.5 Page 179

1. b
2. a
3. d
4. c
5. a

CONCEPT REVIEW 4.6 Page 189

1. Psychedelic drugs: LSD, mescaline, marijuana
2. Depressants: alcohol, barbiturates, tranquilizers, inhalants
3. Opiates: opium, morphine, heroin, methadone, Demerol, Percodan
4. Stimulants: caffeine, nicotine, amphetamines, cocaine

Chapter

5 Learning

Prologue: The Killer Attic

Sandy's parents, Erv and Fern, have been married for almost fifty years. Sometimes it seems truly amazing that they've managed to survive so long together, as you'll see from this true story.

It was a warm summer morning in Chicago. Erv and Fern drank their coffee and made plans for the day. The lawn needed mowing, the garage needed cleaning, and someone had to go to the post office to buy stamps. Fern, who doesn't like driving, said that she would mow the lawn if Erv would go to the post office. Erv, who doesn't like yard work, readily agreed to the deal.

As Erv left for the post office, Fern started cutting the grass in the back yard. When Erv returned, he parked the car around the corner under some large shade trees so that the car would stay cool while he puttered around in the garage. He walked through the front door to drop off the stamps, and noticed that the attic fan was squeaking loudly. Switching it off, Erv decided to oil the fan before he tackled the garage. Fetching the stepladder and oil from the basement, he propped the ladder under the attic trap door, climbed up, and gingerly crawled through the trap door, leaving it open.

Meanwhile, Fern was getting thirsty. As she walked past the garage on the way into the house, she noticed that the car was still gone. "Why isn't he back yet? Erv must have stopped somewhere on the way back from the post office," she thought. As she got a glass of water, she noticed the stepladder and the open attic door. Muttering that Erv never put anything back, Fern latched the attic trap door shut and dragged the ladder back down to the basement.

Erv, who had crawled to the other side of the attic to oil the fan, never heard the attic trap door shut. It was very hot in the well-insulated, airless attic, so he tried to work fast. After oiling the fan, he crawled back to the attic door—only to discover that it was latched shut from the outside! "Fern," he hollered, "open the door!" But Fern was already back outside, mowing away, and couldn't hear Erv over the noise of the lawn mower. Erv, dripping with sweat, kept yelling and pounding on the trap door.

Outside, Fern was getting hot too. She stopped to talk to a neighbor, leaving the lawn mower idling. He offered Fern a cold beer, and the two of them leaned over the fence, laughing and talking. From a small, sealed attic window, Erv watched the whole scene. Jealousy was now added to his list of discomforts. He was also seriously beginning to think that he might sweat to death in the attic heat. He could already see the tabloid headlines in the supermarket checkout line: LAUGHING WIFE DRINKS BEER WHILE HUSBAND COOKS IN ATTIC!

Finally, Fern went back to mowing, wondering what in the world had happened to Erv. Meanwhile, up in the attic, Erv promised God he'd never complain about Chicago winters again. At last, Fern finished the lawn and walked back to the house. Hearing the back door open, Erv began to yell and pound on the trap door again.

"Hey, Fern! Fern!"

Fern froze in her tracks.

"Fern, let me out!"

"Erv! Is that you? Where are you?" she called, looking around.

"I'm in the attic! Let me out!"

"What are you doing in the attic? I thought you were at the store!"

"What do you *think* I'm doing? Let me out of here!"

Once Fern was reassured that Erv had suffered no ill effects from his experience, she burst out laughing. Later that day, still grumbling about Fern's harebrained sense of humor, Erv removed the latch from the attic door. Ever since, whenever Erv goes up in the attic, he posts a sign on the ladder that reads MAN IN THE ATTIC! And, even today, Erv breaks into a sweat whenever he has to go up in the attic.

For her part, Fern is careful to check on Erv's whereabouts before she closes the attic door. But she still laughs when she tells the story of the "killer attic"—which she does frequently, as it never fails to crack up her listeners. Luckily, Erv is a good sport and is used to Fern's sense of humor.

Erv and Fern have both learned from their experience, as is reflected in the changes in their behavior. As you'll see, learning can take place in many ways, but it almost always helps us to adapt to changing circumstances.

Introduction
What Is Learning?

Learning refers to a relatively permanent change in behavior as a result of experience. What is conditioning? What are the different psychological perspectives in learning research?

Psychologists define **learning** as a relatively permanent change in behavior that is due to past experience. Erv has learned to feel anxious and uncomfortable whenever he has to work in the attic. He's also learned to take simple precautions, like posting his MAN IN THE ATTIC sign, to avoid getting locked in the attic again. As Erv's behavior demonstrates, the learning of new

learning
A relatively permanent change in behavior as a result of past experience.

behavioral perspective
In learning theory, a general explanation of learning that emphasizes the relationship between outwardly observable behaviors and environmental events, rather than mental processes.

behavior often reflects some kind of *adaptation to the environment*. On the basis of experience, we acquire new behaviors or modify old behaviors so as to better cope with our surroundings.

When students first encounter the topic of "learning" in psychology, they sometimes mistakenly think that it focuses on formal classroom methods of acquiring new knowledge or skills, such as taking lecture notes or learning how to play the piano. Indeed, these activities reflect learning in the everyday sense of the word. In this chapter, however, we'll focus on a more basic form of learning, referred to as *conditioning*. Conditioning is the process of learning associations between environmental events and behavioral responses.

This description may sound as if it has only limited application to your life. But conditioning is reflected in most of your everyday behavior, from your simplest habits, such as answering the telephone, to complex skills, such as using a computer word-processing program. Even emotional reactions, such as feeling anxious when your instructor uses the word *test,* often involve conditioning.

Earlier in this century, psychologists distinguished between two forms of conditioning: classical conditioning and operant conditioning (Skinner, 1935, 1938; Hilgard & Marquis, 1940). As you'll see in the next section, *classical conditioning* can help explain why climbing into the attic makes Erv anxious. And, as you'll see in a later section, *operant conditioning* will help us understand why Erv now puts up a sign whenever he feels the urge to rummage around in the attic.

We'll structure our discussion of classical and operant conditioning around three key perspectives in the scientific study of learning: the behavioral, the cognitive, and the ecological perspectives. Each of these perspectives emphasizes different aspects of learning, and each has added to our understanding of the factors involved in classical and operant conditioning.

The *behavioral perspective* emphasizes studying the relationship between environmental events and outward behaviors that can be objectively observed and measured. In contrast, the *cognitive perspective* stresses the role played by mental processes in conditioning. Finally, the *ecological perspective* emphasizes the study of an animal's natural behavior patterns and environment as influences in the learning process. As you'll see later in the chapter, different animal species are biologically prepared to learn certain types of associations more easily than others.

John Broadus Watson (1878–1958)
Watson founded behaviorism in the early 1900s, emphasizing the scientific study of observable behaviors rather than subjective mental processes. His influence spread far beyond the academic world. He wrote many books and articles for the general public on child-rearing and other topics, popularizing the findings of the "new" science of psychology.

The Behavioral Perspective

The behavioral perspective defines learning in terms of an observable change in behavior. Who founded behaviorism? What are the basic assumptions and beliefs of the behavioral perspective?

As we discussed in Chapter 1, the **behavioral perspective** is a broad approach to the study of learning that emphasizes changes in outwardly observable behaviors. The roots of this perspective can be traced to one of the earliest schools of psychology, called *behaviorism*.

Behaviorism was founded in the early 1900s by the American psychologist **John B. Watson** (1878–1958). Watson (1913) strongly opposed the views of the earliest psychologists, who believed that psychology should study conscious experiences, such as perception and thought processes. Watson—and the behaviorists who followed him—believed that internal mental processes were far too subjective to be included in a scientific study of behavior.

He maintained that thoughts, feelings, and other conscious experiences were not appropriate subject matter for the young science of psychology. Instead, Watson (1924/1970) wrote, "Let us limit ourselves to things that can be observed, and formulate laws concerning only those things. Now what can we observe? We can observe *behavior—what the organism does or says.*"

Watson, along with other behaviorists, believed that virtually *all* human behavior is a result of learning—that is, due to past experience and environmental influences. He claimed that neither talent, personality, nor intelligence was inherited. In a characteristically bold statement, Watson (1930) proclaimed:

> I should like to go one step further now and say, "Give me a dozen healthy infants, well-formed, and my own specified world to bring them up in and I'll guarantee to take any one at random and train him to become any type of specialist I might select—doctor, lawyer, artist, merchant-chief and yes, even beggar-man and thief, regardless of his talents, penchants, tendencies, abilities, vocations, and race of his ancestors." I am going beyond my facts and I admit it, but so have the advocates of the contrary and they have been doing it for many thousands of years.

Needless to say, Watson never actually carried out such an experiment. And his boast was clearly exaggerated to make his point. Nevertheless, Watson's influence on psychology cannot be overemphasized: Behaviorism dominated American psychology for more than fifty years. Watson's ideas, however, were based on the earlier work of another scientist. The origins of behaviorism can be traced to a physiologist studying the digestive system of dogs in turn-of-the-century Russia—which is where our story now turns.

Ivan Pavlov (1849–1936) In his laboratory, Pavlov was known for his meticulous organization, keen memory, and attention to details (Windholz, 1990). But outside his lab, Pavlov was absent-minded, forgetful, and impractical, especially regarding money. He often forgot to pick up his paycheck, and when he did, he sometimes loaned money to people with hard luck stories who couldn't possibly pay him back (Fancher, 1990). On a trip to New York City, Pavlov carried his money so carelessly that he had his pocket picked in the subway and his American hosts had to take up a collection to pay for his expenses.

Classical Conditioning:
Associating Stimuli

> *Classical conditioning describes a process of learning associations between stimuli. Who discovered classical conditioning, and how did he investigate it? How does classical conditioning occur? How can classically conditioned responses be weakened or eliminated?*

One of the major contributors to modern psychology was not a psychologist, but a Russian physiologist who was awarded a Nobel Prize for his work on digestion. **Ivan Pavlov** (1849–1936) was a brilliant scientist who directed several research laboratories in St. Petersburg, Russia, at the turn of the century. Pavlov's involvement with psychology began as a result of an observation he made while investigating the role of saliva in digestion, using dogs as his experimental subjects.

In order to get a dog to produce saliva, Pavlov (1904/1965) would put food on the dog's tongue. After he had worked with the same dog for several days in a row, Pavlov noticed something curious. The dog would begin salivating *before* Pavlov put the food on his tongue. In fact, the dogs would begin salivating when Pavlov entered the room, or even at the sound of his approaching footsteps. But salivating is a *reflex*—a largely involuntary, automatic response to an external stimulus. The dogs should salivate only *after* the food was presented, not before. Why would the reflex occur before the stimulus was presented? What was causing this unexpected behavior?

If you own a dog, you've observed the same basic phenomenon that Pavlov did. Your dog gets excited and begins to slobber when you shake the bag of dog food and pour it into a bowl. In everyday language, the animal has learned to anticipate food in association with some signal—namely, the sound you make when you pour food into the dog's bowl.

Pavlov's extraordinary gifts as a researcher enabled him to recognize the important implications of what had at first seemed a problem—a reflex (salivation) occurring *before* the appropriate stimulus (food) was presented. He also had the discipline to systematically study how such associations are formed. In fact, Pavlov (1928) abandoned his research on digestion and spent the remaining thirty years of his life investigating this phenomenon. Let's look at what he discovered in more detail.

Principles of Classical Conditioning

The process of conditioning that Pavlov discovered was the first model of learning to be extensively studied in psychology. Thus, it's called **classical conditioning** (Hilgard & Marquis, 1940). Classical conditioning deals with behaviors that are elicited automatically by some stimulus. *Elicit* means draw out or bring forth. That is, the stimulus doesn't produce a "new" behavior, but rather *causes an existing behavior to occur.*

Classical conditioning often involves reflexive behaviors. Remember, a reflex is a relatively simple unlearned behavior, governed by the nervous system, that occurs *automatically* when the appropriate stimulus is presented. In Pavlov's (1904) original studies of digestion, the dogs salivated reflexively when food was placed on their tongues. But when the dogs began salivating in response to the sight of Pavlov or to the sound of an experimenter's footsteps, a new, *learned* stimulus elicited the salivary response. Thus, in classical conditioning, a *new* stimulus–response sequence is learned.

How does this kind of learning take place? Essentially, classical conditioning is a process of learning an *association between two stimuli.* Classical conditioning involves pairing a *neutral* stimulus (the sight of Pavlov) with an *unlearned, natural* stimulus (food in the mouth) that automatically elicits a reflexive response (the dog salivates). If the two stimuli (Pavlov + food) are repeatedly paired, eventually the neutral stimulus (Pavlov) elicits the same reflexive response as the natural stimulus (food)—even in the absence of the natural stimulus. So, when the dog in the laboratory started salivating at the sight of Pavlov *before* the food was placed on its tongue, it was because the dog had formed a new, *learned association* between the sight of Pavlov and the food.

The classical conditioning model of learning uses special terms to describe each element of the conditioning process. The natural stimulus that reflexively produces a response without the necessity of prior learning is called the **unconditioned stimulus** (abbreviated **UCS**). In this example, the unconditioned stimulus is the food in the dog's mouth. The unlearned, reflexive response is called the **unconditioned response** (or **UCR**). The unconditioned response is the dog's salivation.

To learn more about his discovery, Pavlov (1927/1960) controlled the stimuli that preceded the appearance of food. For example, in one set of experiments, he used a bell as a neutral stimulus—neutral because dogs don't normally salivate to the sound of a bell ringing. Pavlov would first ring the bell and then give the dog food. After this procedure was repeated several times, the dog would begin to salivate when the bell was rung, before the food was put in its mouth. At that point, the dog was *classically conditioned* to salivate to the sound of a bell alone. That is, the dog had learned a new association between the sound of the bell and the presentation of food.

classical conditioning
The basic learning process that involves repeatedly pairing a neutral stimulus with a response-producing stimulus until the neutral stimulus elicits the same response.

unconditioned stimulus (UCS)
The natural stimulus that reflexively elicits a response without the necessity of prior learning.

unconditioned response (UCR)
The unlearned, reflexive response that is elicited by an unconditioned stimulus.

conditioned stimulus (CS)
A formerly neutral stimulus that acquires the capacity to elicit a reflexive response.

conditioned response (CR)
The learned, reflexive response to a conditioned stimulus.

Pavlov called the sound of the bell the **conditioned stimulus** (or **CS**). The conditioned stimulus is the stimulus that is originally neutral but comes to elicit a reflexive response. He called the dog's salivation to the sound of the bell the **conditioned response** (or **CR**), which is the *learned* reflexive response to a previously neutral stimulus. The steps of Pavlov's conditioning process are outlined in Figure 5.1.

Classical conditioning terminology can be confusing. You may find it helpful to think of the word "conditioned" as meaning the same as "learned." Thus, the "conditioned stimulus" would be the "learned stimulus," the "unconditioned response" would be the "unlearned response," and so forth.

It's also important to note that the unconditioned response and the conditioned response describe virtually the same behavior—the dog salivating. Which label is applied depends on which stimulus elicits the response. If the dog is salivating in response to a *natural* stimulus that it had not acquired through learning, it is an *unconditioned* response. If, however, the dog has learned to salivate to a *neutral* stimulus that doesn't normally produce the automatic response, it is a *conditioned* response.

FIGURE 5.1 The Process of Classical Conditioning
The diagram shows Pavlov's classical conditioning procedure. As you can see, classical conditioning involves the learning of an association between a neutral stimulus (the ringing bell) and a natural stimulus (food).

Before Conditioning
Prior to conditioning, the dog notices the bell ringing, but does not salivate. Here, the bell is a neutral stimulus. Food placed in the dog's mouth (the UCS) naturally produces the salivation reflex (the UCR).

Neutral stimulus (ringing bell) → No salivation

Natural reflex — UCS (food in mouth) → UCR (salivation)

During Conditioning
In the conditioning phase, the neutral stimulus (the ringing bell) is repeatedly sounded immediately before food is placed in the dog's mouth (the UCS), which produces the natural reflex of salivation (the UCR).

Neutral stimulus (ringing bell) + UCS (food in mouth) — Natural reflex → UCR (salivation)

After Conditioning
The ringing bell is no longer neutral. It is now called a CS because, when the bell is rung, the dog reacts with a conditioned reflex: It salivates even though no food is present. The salivation response is now called a CR.

CS (ringing bell) — Conditioned reflex → CR (salivation)

CONCEPT REVIEW 5.1

Identifying Elements of Classical Conditioning

Identify the UCS, the UCR, the CS, and the CR in each of the following examples.

1. Before each of his chemotherapy sessions, Allen, a young cancer patient, is given a bowl of ice cream. The chemotherapy makes Allen nauseous. Now just seeing the bowl of ice cream makes him feel queasy.

UCS: _____   UCR: _____.
CS: _____   CR: _____.

2. Frank loved to swim in the lake near his house. After swimming in the lake one afternoon, he discovered two big, slimy, blood-sucking leeches firmly attached to his leg. He was revolted by the experience of touching the slimy bodies and pulling them off his leg. Now every time he drives by the lake, he shudders in disgust.

UCS: _____   UCR: _____.
CS: _____   CR: _____.

3. Every time two-year-old Jodie heard the doorbell ring she raced to open the front door. On Halloween night, Jodie answered the doorbell and encountered a scary monster with ten flashing eyes. Jodie screamed in fear and ran away. For the next year Jodie screamed and hid in the corner of her bedroom whenever the doorbell rang.

UCS: _____   UCR: _____.
CS: _____   CR: _____.

Factors That Affect Conditioning

Over the three decades that Pavlov (1928) spent studying classical conditioning, he discovered many factors that could affect the strength of the conditioned response. For example, he discovered that the more frequently the conditioned stimulus and the unconditioned stimulus are paired, the stronger the association between the two.

Pavlov also discovered that the *timing* of stimulus presentations affected the strength of the conditioned response. He found that conditioning is most effective when the conditioned stimulus is presented immediately *before* the unconditioned stimulus. In his early studies, Pavlov found that a half-second was the optimal time interval between the onset of the conditioned stimulus and the beginning of the unconditioned stimulus. Later, Pavlov and other researchers found that the optimal time interval could vary in different conditioning situations, but was never more than a few seconds.

Pavlov (1927/1960) also noticed that once a dog was conditioned to salivate to a particular stimulus, new stimuli that were similar to the original conditioned stimulus could also elicit the conditioned salivary response. For example, Pavlov conditioned a dog to salivate to a low-pitched tone. When he sounded a slightly higher-pitched tone, the conditioned salivary response would also be elicited. Pavlov called this phenomenon **stimulus generalization.** Stimulus generalization occurs when stimuli that are similar to the original conditioned stimulus also elicit the conditioned response, even though they have never been paired with the unconditioned stimulus.

Just as a dog can learn to respond to similar stimuli, so it can learn the opposite—to *distinguish* between similar stimuli. For example, Pavlov repeatedly gave a dog some food following a high-pitched tone, but did not give the dog any food after a low-pitched tone. The dog learned to distinguish between the two tones, salivating to the high-pitched tone but not to the low-pitched tone. This phenomenon, **stimulus discrimination,** occurs when a particular conditioned response is made to one stimulus but not to other, similar stimuli.

stimulus generalization
The occurrence of a learned response not only to the original stimulus but to other, similar stimuli as well.

stimulus discrimination
The occurrence of a learned response to a specific stimulus but not to other, similar stimuli.

Here's an example of stimulus generalization versus stimulus discrimination: Suppose your dog begins to drool whenever you shake his box of doggie treats. If he also drools one morning when you shake a box of Wheaties and pour some into *your* bowl, that would be an example of *stimulus generalization*. Eventually Fido learns that the sound of Wheaties rattling in a box is not followed by food, but the slightly different sound of doggie treats rattling in a box is. Fido no longer drools when you pour out your cereal, but still slobbers when you shake the box of doggie treats. That would be an example of *stimulus discrimination*. He's learned to discriminate between two similar stimuli—the sound of a box of Wheaties being shaken versus the sound of a box of doggie treats being shaken.

Once learned, can conditioned responses be eliminated? Pavlov (1928) found that conditioned responses could be gradually weakened. If the conditioned stimulus, like the ringing bell, was repeatedly presented *without* being paired with the unconditioned stimulus (the food), the conditioned response seemed to gradually disappear. Pavlov called this process of decline and eventual disappearance of the conditioned response **extinction.**

But Pavlov also found that a dog does not simply return to its unconditioned state following extinction. If an animal is allowed a period of rest (such as a few hours) after a response has been extinguished, the conditioned response will reappear when the conditioned stimulus is again presented. This reappearance of a previously extinguished conditioned response after a period of time without exposure to the conditioned stimulus is called **spontaneous recovery.**

Applications of Classical Conditioning

Classical conditioning can explain many aspects of human behavior. How do classically conditioned emotional reactions form? How can classical conditioning affect physiological reactions?

Classical conditioning always involves the learning of some type of relatively automatic stimulus–response sequence. This may sound like a fairly limited type of learning. But classical conditioning has wide application beyond training dogs to drool on command. In this section, we'll explore some of the ways that classical conditioning has been used to both explain and influence human behavior.

Conditioned Emotional Reactions

One of the most famous experiments in the history of psychology was conducted in 1920 by behaviorist John B. Watson and his graduate student, Rosalie Rayner. Watson and Rayner (1920) demonstrated that classical conditioning could be used to deliberately establish a conditioned emotional response in a human subject. Their subject was a baby whom they called "Albert B.," but who is now more popularly known as "Little Albert."

Watson and Rayner first assessed Little Albert when he was only nine months old. Little Albert was a healthy, unusually calm baby who showed no fear when presented with a tame white rat, a rabbit, a dog, and a monkey. He was also unafraid of cotton, masks, and even burning newspapers! However, Watson and Rayner did discover one stimulus that made Little Albert fearful: loudly clanging a steel bar behind his head. Here, the clanging noise is the unconditioned stimulus, and the unconditioned response is fear.

extinction
The gradual weakening and disappearance of conditioned behavior. In classical conditioning, extinction occurs when the conditioned stimulus is repeatedly presented without the unconditioned stimulus.

spontaneous recovery
The reappearance of a previously extinguished conditioned response after a period of time without exposure to the conditioned stimulus.

(a)

Two months after their initial assessment, Watson and Rayner attempted to condition Little Albert to fear the white rat (the conditioned stimulus). Watson stood behind Little Albert. Whenever Little Albert reached toward the rat, Watson clanged the steel bar with a hammer. Just as before, of course, the loud CLANG! (the unconditioned stimulus) scared the daylights out of Little Albert (the unconditioned response).

During this first conditioning session, Little Albert experienced two pairings of the white rat with the loud clanging sound. A week later, he experienced five more pairings of the two stimuli. After only these seven pairings of the loud noise and the white rat, the white rat alone made Little Albert display extreme fear (the conditioned response). Little Albert had developed a classically conditioned fear response to the white rat (see Figure 5.2).

Watson and Rayner found, too, that stimulus generalization had taken place: Little Albert was also afraid of other furry animals, a dog and a rabbit. He had even developed a classically conditioned fear response to a variety of fuzzy objects—a sealskin coat, cotton, Watson's hair, and a white-bearded Santa Claus mask!

Although the Little Albert study has achieved legendary status in psychology, there were a number of problems with it (Paul & Blumenthal, 1989; Harris, 1979). One criticism is that the experiment was not carefully designed or conducted. For example, Albert's "fear and distress" were not objectively measured, but were subjectively evaluated by Watson and Rayner.

The experiment is also open to criticism on ethical grounds. Watson and Rayner did not extinguish Little Albert's fear of furry animals and objects, even though they believed that such conditioned emotional responses would "persist and modify personality throughout life" (Watson & Rayner, 1920). Whether they had intended to do so is not completely clear (see Paul & Blumenthal, 1989). Little Albert left the hospital shortly after the completion of the experiment. Watson (1930) later wrote that he and Rayner could not try to eliminate Albert's fear response because the infant had been adopted by a family in another city shortly after their experiment had concluded. Today, such an experiment could not be ethically conducted under *any* circumstances.

Perhaps you can think of objects, people, situations, or even locations in your own experience that evoke a classically conditioned fear. For example, one of our students told us that whenever he drove past a certain intersection where he had experienced a serious auto accident, his heart would begin to race and his hands would tremble. In this chapter's Prologue, "The Killer Attic," Erv was classically conditioned to feel anxious whenever he entered the attic.

Sexual responses are also commonly subject to classical conditioning. Suppose a particular neutral stimulus, like a particular aroma or song, is frequently paired with a person with whom you are romantically involved. That stimulus may become a conditioned stimulus that evokes feelings of romantic excitement or sexual arousal even in that person's absence. For example, you may have found yourself feeling attracted to another person simply because he or she wore the same cologne as someone with whom you were involved in the past. See if you can come up with additional examples of conditioned emotional reactions.

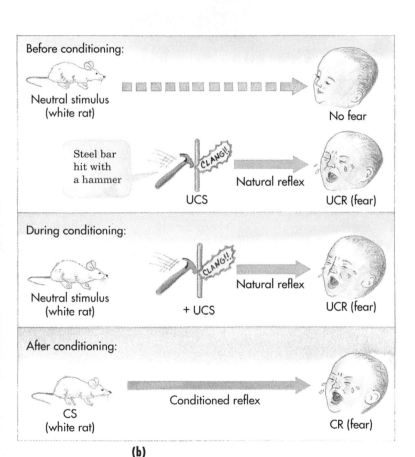

(b)

FIGURE 5.2 A Classically Conditioned Fear Response

(a) In the photograph, Rosalie Rayner holds Little Albert as John Watson looks on. Little Albert is petting the white rat, clearly not afraid of it. **(b)** By repeatedly pairing the white rat with the UCS (a loud noise), the white rat becomes a CS. After conditioning, Little Albert is terrified of the rat and other furry white objects, like rabbits, cotton, Rayner's white fur coat, and Watson in a Santa Claus beard.

IN FOCUS 5.1

Watson, Classical Conditioning, and Advertising

From cars to colas, advertising campaigns often use sexy models to promote their products. Today, we take this phenomenon for granted. But it's actually yet another example of Watson's influence.

Shortly after the Little Albert experiment, Watson's wife discovered that he was having an affair with his graduate student Rosalie Rayner. Following a scandalous and highly publicized divorce, Watson was fired from his academic position. Despite his international fame as a scientist, no other university would hire him. Banned from academia, Watson married Rayner and joined the J. Walter Thompson advertising agency (Buckley, 1989).

Watson was a pioneer in the application of classical conditioning principles to advertising. "To make your consumer react," Watson told his colleagues at the ad agency, "tell him something that will tie up with fear, something that will stir up a mild rage, that will call out an affectionate or love response, or strike at a deep psychological or habit need" (quoted in Buckley, 1982).

Watson applied this technique in ad campaigns he worked on in the 1920s for Johnson & Johnson Baby Powder and Pebeco toothpaste. For the baby powder ad, Watson intentionally tried to stimulate an anxiety response in young mothers by creating doubts about their ability to care for their infants.

The Pebeco toothpaste ad campaign targeted the newly independent young woman who smoked. The ad raised the fear that attractiveness might be diminished by the effects of smoking—and Pebeco toothpaste was promoted as a way of increasing one's sexual attractiveness. One ad read, "Girls! Don't worry any more about smoke-stained teeth or tobacco-tainted breath. You can smoke and still be lovely if you'll just use Pebeco twice a day."

While Watson may have pioneered the strategy of associating products with "sex appeal," modern advertising has taken this technique to an extreme.

Similarly, some ad campaigns pair products with images of adorable babies, happy families, or other "natural" stimuli that elicit warm, emotional responses. If classical conditioning occurs, the product by itself will also elicit a warm emotional response. It's not clear whether such strategies are actually effective in producing a classically conditioned response to particular brands of burgers or bulldozers, but they are certainly in wide use.

Conditioned Physiological Responses

Classical conditioning can also influence physiological responses that we're not even aware of. If you're as caffeine-dependent as your authors, perhaps you've noticed that after just a few groggy sips of your first cup of coffee in the morning, you begin to feel more alert. In reality, it takes about 30 to 45 minutes after drinking a cup of coffee for the caffeine to reach significant levels in your bloodstream (Julien, 1995). Your sense of increased alertness may be due to a classically conditioned response to the sight, smell, and taste of your morning cup of coffee. Sandy's conditioned response to coffee is so strong that she can't drink even *decaffeinated* coffee in the evening, because she'll have trouble falling asleep later.

The potential for physiological responses to become classically conditioned is finding new applications in medicine. For example, patients who were taking medication to treat their high blood pressure were switched, without their knowledge, to a placebo—a fake pill. These patients maintained healthy blood pressures longer than other patients who were taken off their medication but not given placebos. The patients' decrease in blood pressure had apparently become a classically conditioned response to the cues associated with taking their medicine (Ader, 1993a; Suchman & Ader, 1989).

Researchers have been able to classically condition a drop in immune response in rats and mice (see Ader & Cohen, 1993). Human subjects can also display classically conditioned decreases in immune response. For example, one study involved a group of cancer patients who had undergone a series of chemotherapy treatments (Bovbjerg & others, 1990). Each chemotherapy treatment temporarily lowered the cancer patients' immune response. After a few chemotherapy treatments, researchers found that the patients' immune response dropped when measured in the hospital *before* the chemotherapy treatment was administered.

How can this be explained in terms of classical conditioning? Initially, only the chemotherapy treatments (the unconditioned stimulus) produced a drop in the patients' immune response (the unconditioned response). But with repeated treatments, cues related to the hospital environment (the conditioned stimulus) became associated with the chemotherapy treatments. Now, the conditioned stimulus alone—the hospital environment—produced a conditioned response of reduced immune functioning. Similarly, many chemotherapy patients experience nausea and vomiting—common side-effects of the treatments—simply at the sight of the hospital clinic, the sound of the nurse's voice, or other hospital-related cues (see Ader & Cohen, 1993).

Operant Conditioning: Associating Behaviors and Consequences

Operant conditioning deals with the learning of active, non-reflexive behaviors. Who was the first psychologist to experimentally study how voluntary behaviors are influenced by their consequences, and what conclusions did he reach? What were B. F. Skinner's key assumptions?

Classical conditioning plays a role in a wide range of emotional and physiological responses. However, it cannot account for all learned behaviors, especially the nonreflexive, or voluntary, actions often exhibited by humans and animals. In this section we'll look at another form of learning that describes how we acquire and maintain active, voluntary behaviors.

Thorndike and the Law of Effect

Edward L. Thorndike (1874–1949) was the first psychologist to systematically investigate how voluntary behaviors are influenced by their consequences. Thorndike was interested in determining whether animals, like humans, use reasoning to solve problems. In an important series of experiments, Thorndike (1898) put hungry cats in specially constructed cages that he called "puzzle boxes." A cat could escape the cage by some simple act, such as pulling a loop or pressing a lever that would unlatch the cage door. A plate of food was placed just outside the cage, where the cat could see and smell it.

Law of Effect
Learning principle proposed by Thorndike that responses followed by a satisfying effect become strengthened and are more likely to recur in a particular situation, while responses followed by a dissatisfying effect are weakened and less likely to recur in a particular situation.

operant
Skinner's term for an actively emitted (or voluntary) behavior that operates on the environment to produce consequences.

B. F. Skinner (1904–1990) As a young adult, Skinner had hoped to become a writer. When he graduated from college, he set up a study in the attic of his parents' home and waited for inspiration to strike. After a year of "frittering" away his time, he decided that there were other ways to learn about human nature. As Skinner (1967) later wrote, "A writer might portray human behavior accurately, but he did not understand it. I was to remain interested in human behavior, but the literary method had failed me; I would turn to the scientific. . . . The relevant science appeared to be psychology, though I had only the vaguest idea of what that meant."

Thorndike found that when the cat was first put into the puzzle box, it would engage in many different, seemingly random behaviors. For example, the cat would scratch at the cage door, claw at the ceiling, and try to squeeze through the bars (not to mention complain at the top of its lungs). Eventually, however, the cat would accidentally pull on the loop or step on the lever, opening the door latch and escaping the box. After several trials in the same puzzle box, a cat gradually took less and less time to get the cage door open.

Thorndike (1898) concluded that the cats did not display any humanlike insight or reasoning unlatching the puzzle box door. Instead, Thorndike explained the cats' learning as a process of *trial and error*. The cat gradually learned to associate certain responses with successfully escaping the box and gaining the food reward. According to Thorndike, these successful behaviors became "stamped in" so that the cat was more likely to repeat these behaviors when placed in the puzzle box again. Unsuccessful behaviors, in contrast, were gradually eliminated.

On the basis of his observations, Thorndike (1898, 1911) formulated the **Law of Effect:** Responses followed by a "satisfying state of affairs" are "strengthened" and more likely to occur again in the same situation. Conversely, responses followed by an unpleasant or "annoying state of affairs" are "weakened" and less likely to occur again.

Thorndike's Law of Effect was the first step in the development of a model to describe how active, voluntary behaviors are influenced by their consequences. Thorndike (1903) later applied his findings to education and published many books on educational psychology. The task of developing a formal model of learning to explain the acquisition of voluntary behaviors was taken up by another American psychologist, B. F. Skinner.

B. F. Skinner and the Search for "Order in Behavior"

From the time he was a graduate student in psychology until his death, the famous American psychologist **B. F. Skinner** (1904–1990) searched for the "lawful processes" that would explain "order in behavior" (Skinner, 1956, 1967). Skinner was a staunch behaviorist. Like Watson, Skinner believed that psychology should restrict itself to studying only phenomena that could be objectively measured and verified—outwardly observable behavior. Skinner acknowledged the existence of "internal factors" such as thoughts, expectations, and perceptions (Skinner, 1974; Delprato & Midgley, 1992). But "private events" like thoughts and feelings defy direct scientific observation. Thus, Skinner believed that such subjective factors should not be included in an objective, scientific explanation of behavior (Baum & Heath, 1992).

Skinner acknowledged that classical conditioning could explain the learned association of stimuli in certain reflexive responses (Iversen, 1992). But classical conditioning was limited to existing behaviors that are reflexively elicited. Skinner was interested in a different category of behavior. To Skinner, the most important form of learning was demonstrated by *new* behaviors that were actively *emitted* by the organism, like the active behaviors produced by Thorndike's cats in trying to escape the puzzle boxes.

Skinner coined the term **operant** to describe active behaviors that "operate upon the environment to generate consequences." In everyday language, Skinner's operant conditioning model of learning explains how we acquire the wide range of *voluntary* behaviors we perform in daily life. As a staunch behaviorist, Skinner avoided the term "voluntary," because it would imply that behavior was due to a conscious choice or intention.

As Skinner developed his operant conditioning model, he defined concepts in very objective terms. He emphasized outward behavior that could be

The practice of looking inside the organism for an explanation of behavior has tended to obscure the variables which are immediately available for a scientific analysis. These variables lie outside the organism, in its immediate environment and in its environmental history.

B. F. Skinner Science and Human Behavior, 1953

observed and measured, and he avoided references to subjective mental states. In our explanation of operant conditioning, we'll try to stay close to Skinner's original terminology and definitions.

Reinforcement:
Increasing Future Behavior

The basic premise of operant conditioning is that behavior is shaped and maintained by its consequences. What is reinforcement, and what effect does it produce? How are positive and negative reinforcement similar, and how are they different? Why are conditioned reinforcers important?

In a nutshell, Skinner's **operant conditioning** model explains learning as a process in which behavior is shaped and maintained by its consequences. One possible consequence of a behavior is reinforcement. **Reinforcement** is a stimulus or an event that follows an operant and increases the likelihood of the operant being repeated. Notice that reinforcement is defined by the effect that it produces—increasing or strengthening the occurrence of a behavior in the future.

Let's look at reinforcement in action. Suppose you put your money into a soft-drink vending machine and push the button. Nothing happens. You push the button again. Nothing. You try the coin-return lever. Still nothing. Frustrated, you slam the machine with your hand. Bingo! Your can of pop rolls down the chute. In the future, if another vending machine swallows your money without giving you what you want, what are you likely to do? Hit the machine, right?

In this example, slamming the vending machine with your hand is the operant—the active response you emitted. The can of pop is the reinforcing stimulus—the stimulus or event that is sought in a particular situation. In everyday language, a reinforcing stimulus is typically something desirable, satisfying, or pleasant. Skinner, of course, wouldn't use those terms, because they reflect subjective emotional states.

Positive and Negative Reinforcement

Reinforcement can take two forms: positive reinforcement and negative reinforcement. Both forms of reinforcement increase future behavior, but they do so in different ways. **Positive reinforcement** involves following an operant with the *addition of a reinforcing stimulus*. For example, suppose you study with a friend for your psychology midterm (the operant), which is followed by your receiving an A on the exam (the reinforcing stimulus). If the addition of this consequence makes you more likely to study with a friend in the future, then positive reinforcement has occurred. The vending machine example also illustrates positive reinforcement. The operant (hitting the machine) was followed by the addition of a reinforcing stimulus (the can of pop), making you more likely to behave the same way in similar situations in the future.

It's important to note that the reinforcing stimulus is not necessarily something that we usually consider to be "positive" or "desirable." For example, most teachers would not think of a scolding as being a reinforcing stimulus to a child. But to a child, adult attention can be a powerful reinforcing stimulus. If a child receives attention from the teacher only when he misbehaves, then the teacher may unwittingly be reinforcing misbehavior. The child may actually increase his disruptive behavior in order to get the sought-after reinforcing stimulus—adult attention, even if it's in the form of being scolded. To reduce the child's disruptive behavior, the teacher would do

operant conditioning
The basic learning process that involves changing the probability of a response being repeated by manipulating the consequences of that response.

reinforcement
The occurrence of a stimulus or event following a response that increases the likelihood of the response being repeated.

positive reinforcement
A situation in which a response is followed by the addition of a reinforcing stimulus, increasing the likelihood of the response being repeated in similar situations.

Process	Operant	Consequence	Effect on Behavior
Positive reinforcement	Studying to make dean's list	Make dean's list	Increase studying in the future
Negative reinforcement	Studying to avoid losing academic scholarship	Avoid loss of academic scholarship	Increase studying in the future

FIGURE 5.3 Comparing Positive and Negative Reinforcement
Both positive and negative reinforcement increase the likelihood of a behavior being repeated. Positive reinforcement involves a behavior that leads to a reinforcing or rewarding event. In contrast, negative reinforcement involves behavior that leads to the avoidance or escape of an aversive or punishing event. Ultimately, both positive and negative reinforcement involve outcomes that strengthen future behavior.

better to reinforce the child by paying attention to him when he's behaving appropriately, such as working quietly or helping another child.

Negative reinforcement involves the *removal of an unpleasant or aversive stimulus* from a situation, thereby strengthening future occurrences of the behavior that brings about this removal. Like positive reinforcement, negative reinforcement *increases* the likelihood of a behavior being repeated (see Figure 5.3). For example, you take two aspirin (the operant) to remove a headache (the aversive stimulus). Are you more likely to take aspirin to deal with pain in the future? If you are, then negative reinforcement has occurred.

Aversive stimuli typically involve physical or psychological discomfort that an organism seeks to avoid or escape. Consequently, behaviors are said to be negatively reinforced when they let you either (1) *escape* aversive stimuli that are already present or (2) *avoid* aversive stimuli before they occur. That is, we're more likely to repeat the same avoidance or escape behaviors in similar situations in the future. The headache example illustrates the negative reinforcement of *escape behavior*. By taking two aspirin, you "escaped" the headache. Returning your library books on time to avoid an overdue fine illustrates the negative reinforcement of *avoidance behavior*.

Like positive reinforcement, negative reinforcement can be used to *increase* socially desirable behaviors. For example, Keith Allen and his colleagues (1992) used negative reinforcement to increase cooperative behavior in young dental patients who had a history of crying and squirming when the dentist tried to work on their teeth. When the child cooperated with the dentist, the dentist would say, "You are sitting so nice and still and quiet that we're going to take a little rest break!" If the child was disruptive, the dentist would continue working, but remind her that he would stop for a rest break when she calmed down. In this way, cooperative behavior was negatively reinforced: the child was allowed a few minutes of escape from the discomfort of dental treatment. The result? Each child showed an immediate, marked increase in cooperative behavior (see Figure 5.4).

Positive or Negative Reinforcement?
Is this student studying late at night in the college library to avoid losing his academic scholarship, or because studying will be rewarded with high grades and academic success?

FIGURE 5.4 Using Negative Reinforcement to Increase Cooperative Behavior
This graph shows the progressive increase in cooperative behavior over four treatment sessions with a four-year-old dental patient named Jenny. Beginning with the second session, the dentist used a negative reinforcement procedure in which Jenny was allowed to briefly "escape" the dental treatment if she behaved cooperatively by sitting still, not crying, and not complaining. As you can see, cooperative behavior increased dramatically.

(Adapted from Allen & others, 1992.)

Primary and Conditioned Reinforcers

Skinner also distinguished between reinforcing stimuli that were primary and conditioned. A **primary reinforcer** is one that is *naturally* reinforcing for a given species. Even if the species had no prior experience with the stimulus, the stimulus or event would still have reinforcing properties. For example, food, water, adequate warmth, and sexual contact are primary reinforcers for most animals, including humans.

Primary and Conditioned Reinforcers
Primary reinforcers, like hugs, are naturally reinforcing; they don't need to be learned. In contrast, you must learn the value of conditioned reinforcers, like these trophies and ribbons awarded to the teen-ager swimmers shown on the right. Conditioned reinforcers acquire their reinforcing value through being associated with primary reinforcers.

A **conditioned reinforcer,** also called a *secondary reinforcer,* is one that has acquired reinforcing value by being associated with a primary reinforcer. The classic example of a conditioned reinforcer is money. Money is reinforcing not because those flimsy bits of paper and little pieces of metal have value in and of themselves, but because we've learned that we can use them to acquire primary reinforcers and other conditioned reinforcers. Awards, frequent flyer points, and college degrees are just a few other examples of conditioned reinforcers.

Sometimes there are many links in the association between a conditioned reinforcer and a primary reinforcer. You can't plunk your college degree down on the counter to purchase a loaf of bread at the grocery store, but your college degree can lead to a job that provides you with money to exchange for the primary reinforcer of food.

Conditioned reinforcers need not be as tangible as money or college degrees. The respect of your peers and the approval of your instructors or managers are powerful conditioned reinforcers. Conditioned reinforcers can be as subtle as a smile, a touch, or a nod of recognition. Fern, for example, is reinforced by the laughter of her friends and relatives each time she tells the "killer attic" story—so she keeps telling the story!

Every day, your behavior is influenced by countless conditioned reinforcers. To help you see how this concept applies to daily life, try making a list of conditioned reinforcers that have influenced your behavior over the last few days.

negative reinforcement
A situation in which a response results in the removal, avoidance, or escape of a punishing stimulus, increasing the likelihood of the response being repeated in similar situations.

primary reinforcer
A stimulus or event that is naturally or inherently reinforcing for a given species, such as food, water, or other biological necessities.

conditioned reinforcer
A stimulus or event that has acquired reinforcing value by being associated with a primary reinforcer; also called a *secondary reinforcer.*

punishment
The presentation of a stimulus or event following a behavior that acts to decrease the likelihood of the behavior being repeated.

Punishment:
Using Aversive Consequences to Decrease Behavior

> *Punishment is a process that decreases the occurrence of a behavior. What factors influence the effectiveness of punishment? What negative effects are associated with the use of punishment, and why is punishment not the best method for changing behavior?*

Positive and negative reinforcement are processes that *strengthen* future behavior. The opposite effect is produced by punishment. **Punishment** refers to the presentation of an event or stimulus following a behavior that acts to *decrease* the likelihood of the behavior being repeated. Many people tend to confuse punishment and negative reinforcement, but these two processes produce entirely different effects on behavior (see Figure 5.5). Negative reinforcement *always increases* the likelihood that an operant will be repeated in the future. Punishment *always decreases* the future performance of an operant.

Process	Operant	Consequence	Effect on Behavior
Punishment	Using radar detector	Receive ticket and fine for illegal use of radar detector	Decrease use of radar detector in the future
Negative reinforcement	Using radar detector	Avoid speeding ticket and fine	Increase use of radar detector in the future

FIGURE 5.5 Comparing Punishment and Negative Reinforcement
Punishment and negative reinforcement are two different processes that produce *opposite* effects on a given behavior. Punishment *decreases* the future performance of the behavior, while negative reinforcement *increases* it.

Skinner (1974) identified two types of aversive events that can act as punishment. *Punishment by application* involves the presentation of a punishing stimulus following a response. If an employee is reprimanded for tardiness, causing tardiness to decrease, the reprimand is a punishing stimulus. Punishing stimuli also occur as natural consequences for some behaviors, such as being burned when you touch a hot pan.

The second type of punishment is *punishment by removal,* which involves the loss or withdrawal of a reinforcing stimulus following a response. In other words, the consequence of the operant is the loss of privileges, possessions, or some other desirable outcome. The child who forfeits her dessert for slinging mashed potatoes at her sister is being punished by the *removal* of a reinforcing stimulus. So is the guy whose driver's license is suspended as a consequence of reckless driving.

Like reinforcement, punishment is defined by the effect it produces. In everyday usage, people often refer to a particular consequence as a punishment when, strictly speaking, it's not—because the consequence has *not* reduced future occurrences of the behavior. For example, drivers often continue to speed despite receiving fines, tardy employees may continue to show up late to work despite being reprimanded, and ex-cons may continue to break the law after being released from prison.

Why is it that aversive consequences don't always function as effective punishments? Several factors influence the effectiveness of punishment (see Axelrod & Apsche, 1983; Goodall, 1984; Azrin & Holz, 1966). For example, punishments are more effective if they immediately follow a response than if they are delayed. Punishment is also more effective if it consistently, rather than occasionally, follows a response. Given these factors, can you see why consequences such as speeding tickets and prison sentences are often ineffective? Though commonly referred to as punishments, these aversive consequences are inconsistently applied and often administered only after a long delay. Thus, they don't always effectively decrease specific behaviors.

Even when punishment works, its use has several drawbacks. First, punishment may decrease a specific response, but it doesn't teach or promote a more appropriate response to take its place. Second, punishment that is intense may produce undesirable results, such as complete passivity, fear, anxiety, or hostility (Skinner, 1974). Finally, the effects of punishment are likely to be temporary (Skinner, 1938; Estes & Skinner, 1941). A child who is sent to her room for teasing her little brother may well repeat the behavior when her mother's back is turned. As Skinner (1971) wrote, "Punished behavior is likely to reappear after the punitive consequences are withdrawn."

Throughout his life, Skinner remained strongly opposed to the use of punishment. Instead, he advocated the greater use of positive reinforcement to strengthen desirable behaviors (Skinner, 1971; Dinsmoor, 1992). For some suggestions on changing behavior without applying punishing stimuli, see In Focus Box 5.2, "Changing the Behavior of Others: Alternatives to Punishment."

IN FOCUS 5.2

Changing the Behavior of Others: Alternatives to Punishment

Whether it's a friend, classmate, co-worker, or child whose behavior annoys us, we'd often like to change the behavior of others. Sometimes we respond to an undesirable behavior with a punishing stimulus, such as anger or criticism. However, punishment has several drawbacks, not the least of which is that it can make the person who has been punished feel fearful, anxious, or angry. And even though punishment may temporarily decrease the occurrence of the problem behavior, it doesn't promote more desirable or appropriate behaviors in its place.

In this box, we'll briefly describe four alternative strategies that can be used to reduce undesirable behaviors. We'll also give you some tips to enhance the effectiveness of positive reinforcers to increase the occurrence of desirable behaviors.

Strategy #1: Stop Reinforcing the Problem Behavior

Technically, this strategy is called *extinction.* The first step in effectively applying extinction is to observe the behavior as carefully and objectively as you can, and try to identify exactly what reinforcer is maintaining the behavior. If the reinforcer is one that can be easily controlled, eliminate it.

For example, suppose a co-worker is wasting your time with gossip. You want to extinguish his behavior of interrupting your work with needless chitchat. In the past, trying to be polite, you've responded to his behavior by acting interested (a reinforcer). You could eliminate the reinforcer by responding to his interruptions as noncommittally as possible and continuing to work while he talked.

It's important to note that when the extinction process is initiated, the problem behavior often *temporarily* increases. This is especially true if the problem behavior has been only occasionally reinforced in the past. Thus, once begun, it's critical that nonreinforcement of the problem behavior be consistent (see Lawton & others, 1991).

For example, if parents decide to extinguish their young child's emotional outbursts at bedtime, they should initially expect the child to wail longer and louder to get their attention. But if the parents remain consistent in *not* reinforcing the child's outbursts with parental attention, the problem behavior will eventually decrease.

Strategy #2: Remove the Opportunity to Obtain Positive Reinforcement

It's not always possible to identify and eliminate all the reinforcers that maintain a behavior. For example, a child's obnoxious behavior might be reinforced by the laughter and social attention he gets from siblings or classmates.

In a procedure called *time-out from positive reinforcement,* the child is removed from the reinforcing situation for a short time, so that the access to reinforcers is eliminated. When the undesirable behavior occurs, the child is immediately sent to a time-out area, such as a chair in a remote corner. The time-out area should be free of distractions, activities, and social contact. The time-out period begins when the child's behavior is under control—for example, once he is sitting quietly. For children, a good rule of thumb is one minute of time-out per year of age.

Strategy #3: Reinforce the Nonoccurrence of the Problem Behavior

This strategy involves setting a specific time period after which the individual is reinforced if the unwanted behavior has *not* occurred. For example, if you're trying to reduce bickering between your children, set an appropriate time limit, and then provide positive reinforcement if they have *not* squabbled during that interval.

At first, reinforce the nonoccurrence of the behavior after a relatively short time, and use a highly valued reinforcer. With success, you can gradually increase the time span required for reinforcement, and scale back the reinforcer. This strategy requires closely monitoring the individual to ensure that a positive reinforcer is delivered only after the behavior has not occurred.

Strategy #4: Reinforce an Incompatible Behavior

The best method to reduce a problem behavior is to reinforce an *alternative* behavior that is both constructive and incompatible with the problem behavior (Reese, 1986). For example, if you're trying to decrease a child's whining, respond to her requests (the reinforcer) only when she talks in a normal tone of voice. If the goal is to increase cooperative play, reinforce sharing and taking turns rather than quarreling and bullying. As with the other strategies, this procedure works best when it is used very consistently and potent positive reinforcers are initially used.

Enhancing the Effectiveness of Positive Reinforcement

Often, these four strategies are used in combination (see Burgio & Sinnott, 1990; Babbitt & Parrish, 1991). However, remember the most important behavioral principle: *Positively reinforce the behaviors that you want to increase.* There are several ways you can enhance the effectiveness of positive reinforcement.

First, make sure that the reinforcer is strongly reinforcing to the individual whose behavior you're trying to modify. Second, the positive reinforcer should ideally be delivered *immediately* after the preferred behavior occurs. Third, the positive reinforcer should initially be given *every* time the preferred behavior occurs. When the desired behavior becomes well established, *gradually reduce the frequency of reinforcement.*

Fourth, try to use a *variety* of positive reinforcers, such as tangible items, praise, special privileges, recognition, and so on. Keep in mind that you can use a more preferred activity (watercoloring) to reinforce a less preferred activity (picking up one's toys). Finally, encourage the individual to engage in *self-reinforcement* in the form of pride, a sense of accomplishment, and feelings of self-control.

discriminative stimulus
A specific stimulus in the presence of which a particular response is more likely to be reinforced, and in the absence of which a particular response is not reinforced.

Discriminative Stimuli:
Setting the Occasion for Responding

Discriminative stimuli refer to environmental cues in the presence of which a particular response is likely to be reinforced. What important role do discriminative stimuli play in operant conditioning?

The third component of the operant conditioning model of learning is what Skinner called the **discriminative stimulus**—the specific stimulus in the presence of which a particular operant is more likely to be reinforced. For example. When do you pick up the telephone and say hello? When it rings, of course. The ringing phone is a discriminative stimulus that sets the occasion for a particular response: picking up the telephone and speaking.

This example illustrates how we've learned from experience to associate certain environmental cues or signals with particular operant responses. We've learned that we're more likely to be reinforced for performing an operant response when we do so in the presence of the discriminative stimulus. Thus, you've learned that you're more likely to be reinforced for screaming at the top of your lungs at a football game (one discriminative stimulus) than in the middle of class (a different discriminative stimulus).

In this way, according to Skinner (1974), behavior is determined and controlled by the stimuli that are present in a given situation. In Skinner's view, an individual's behavior is not determined by a personal "choice" or a conscious "decision." Instead, individual behavior is determined by environmental stimuli and the person's reinforcement history in that environment. Skinner's views on this point have some very controversial implications (see Critical Thinking Box 5.3: "Is Human Freedom Just an Illusion?").

We now have all the fundamental components of the operant conditioning model (see Figure 5.6). Basically, it works like this: In the presence of a specific environmental stimulus (the discriminative stimulus), we emit a particular behavior (the operant), which is followed by a consequence (reinforcement or punishment). If the consequence is either positive or negative reinforcement, we are *more* likely to repeat the operant when we encounter the same or similar discriminative stimuli in the future. If the consequence is some form of punishment, we are *less* likely to repeat the operant when we encounter the same or similar discriminative stimuli in the future.

Next, we'll build on the basic operant conditioning model by considering how Skinner explained the acquisition of complex behaviors.

FIGURE 5.6 The Operant Conditioning Model of Learning
The examples given here illustrate the three key components involved in the operant conditioning model of learning. The basic operant conditioning process works like this: In the presence of a specific discriminative stimulus, an operant response is emitted, which is followed by a consequence. Depending on the consequence, we are more or less likely to repeat the operant when we encounter the same or similar discriminative stimuli in the future.

	Discriminative Stimulus	Operant Response	Consequence	Effect on Future Behavior
Definition	The environmental stimulus that precedes an operant response	The actively emitted or voluntary behavior	The environmental stimulus or event that follows the operant response	Reinforcement increases the likelihood of operant being repeated; punishment or lack of reinforcement decreases the likelihood of operant being repeated.
Examples	Neighbor in yard	Talk to neighbor	Pleasant conversation	Positive reinforcement: More likely to talk to neighbor in the future when he is out in the yard.
	Red oil light	Shut off car engine	Avoid engine damage	Negative reinforcement: More likely to shut off car in the future when red oil light is present.
	Poison ivy plant	Touch plant	Painful, itchy rash on hand	Punishment: Less likely to touch poison ivy plant in the future.

CRITICAL THINKING 5.3

Is Human Freedom Just an Illusion?

Had B. F. Skinner been content to confine his observations to pigeon or rat behavior, his career might have been relatively uncontroversial. But Skinner was intensely interested in human behavior and social problems. He believed that operant conditioning principles could, and *should,* be applied on a broad scale to help solve society's problems.

Skinner's most radical—and controversial—stance involved his belief that ideas like free will, self-determination, and individual choice are just an illusion. Skinner (1971) argued that behavior is not simply influenced by the environment, but is *determined* by it. Control the environment, he said, and you will control human behavior. As he bluntly asserted in his controversial best seller, *Beyond Freedom and Dignity* (1971), "A person does not act upon the world, the world acts upon him."

Skinner's ideas clashed with traditional American ideals of personal responsibility, individual freedom, and self-determination. Such ideals are based on the assumption that behavior arises from causes that are *within* the individual. All individuals are held responsible for their conduct and given credit for their achievements. Skinner labeled such notions the "traditional prescientific view" of human behavior.

Skinner advocated an entirely different philosophy, one based on scientific evidence. As he put it, "A scientific analysis [of behavior] shifts both the responsibility and the achievement to the environment." Applying his ideas to social problems such as alcoholism and crime, Skinner (1971) wrote, "It is the environment which is 'responsible' for objectionable behavior, and it is the environment, not some attribute of the individual, which must be changed."

To understand Skinner's point of view, it helps if you can think of society as being a massive, sophisticated Skinner box. From the moment of birth, the environment shapes and determines your behavior through reinforcing or punishing consequences. Taking this view, you are no more personally responsible for your behavior than a rat in a Skinner box. Just like a rat, your behavior is simply a response to the unique patterns of environmental consequences to which you have been exposed.

Skinner (1971) proposed that "a technology of behavior" be developed, one based on a scientific analysis of behavior. He believed that society could be redesigned using operant conditioning principles to produce more socially desirable behaviors—and happier citizens. He described such an ideal, utopian society in *Walden Two,* a novel he published in 1948. Critics of Skinner charged him with advocating a totalitarian state. They asked who would determine which behaviors were shaped and maintained (see Todd & Morris, 1992).

As Skinner pointed out, however, human behavior is *already* controlled by various authorities: parents, teachers, politicians, religious leaders, employers, and so forth. Such authorities regularly use reinforcing and punishing consequences to shape and control the behavior of others. Skinner insisted that it is better to control behavior in a rational, humane fashion than to leave the control of behavior to the whims and often selfish aims of those in power. Skinner himself was adamantly opposed to the use of punishment and other aversive stimuli to control behavior. Instead, he repeatedly advocated the greater use of positive reinforcement (Dinsmoor, 1992).

On the one hand, it may seem convenient to "blame" your history of environmental consequences for your failures and misdeeds. On the other hand, that means you can't take any credit for your accomplishments and good deeds either! Given this summary of Skinner's ideas, what do you think? Is your behavior determined by the environment? Are human freedom and personal responsibility just illusions? Or is human behavior fundamentally different from a rat's behavior in a Skinner box? Think about it carefully. After all, exactly *why* are you reading this box?

NON SEQUITER

Recognizing Components of Operant Conditioning: Reinforcement and Punishment

1. Josh studies to avoid the aversive or unpleasant consequence of bad grades. His studying behavior is maintained by:
   a. positive reinforcement
   b. negative reinforcement
   c. punishment
   d. primary reinforcement

2. Katie's room is a mess. Her parents agree to increase her allowance by $5 each week if she cleans her room every Tuesday.
   a. positive reinforcement
   b. negative reinforcement
   c. punishment by application
   d. punishment by removal

3. Judy's dog, Murphy, will roll over, beg, and do other tricks for a food reward. However, when offered a $10 bill, he won't do any of these tricks. It appears that Murphy is more responsive to _____ than to _____.
   a. positive reinforcers; negative reinforcers
   b. bribery; corruption

   c. primary reinforcers; conditioned reinforcers
   d. punishment; positive reinforcement

4. Zachary works on a cattle ranch. When the chuck wagon comes around, the cook rings a big metal bell to signal that the food is ready. Whenever Zak and the other cowhands hear the sound of the bell, they head straight for the chuck wagon. In this example, the sound of the bell is a(n):
   a. primary reinforcer
   b. negative reinforcer
   c. unconditioned stimulus
   d. discriminative stimulus

5. Seeing a stranded motorist, Dean stopped to see if he could help. The stranded motorist robbed Dean and stole his car. Dean no longer stops to help strangers. This is an example of:
   a. positive reinforcement
   b. primary reinforcement
   c. punishment
   d. negative reinforcement

Shaping Behavior:
Getting Closer All the Time

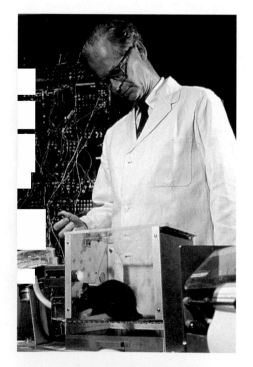

The Skinner Box Popularly called a Skinner box after its inventor, an operant chamber is used to experimentally study operant conditioning in laboratory animals.

> *New behaviors can be acquired through the process of shaping. How does shaping work? What is a Skinner box, and how is it used to study learning?*

To scientifically study the relationship between behavior and its consequences in the laboratory, Skinner invented the *operant chamber,* more popularly known as a **Skinner box.** A Skinner box is a small glass cage with a food dispenser. Attached to the cage is a device that automatically records the number of operants made by an experimental animal, usually a rat or pigeon. For a rat, the typical operant is to press a bar; a pigeon usually pecks at a small disk. Food pellets are used for positive reinforcement. Often, a light in the cage functions as a discriminative stimulus: When the light is on, pressing the bar or pecking the disk will be reinforced with a food pellet; when the light is off, responses will not result in reinforcement.

When a rat is first placed in a Skinner box, it typically will explore its new environment, occasionally nudging or pressing the bar in the process. The researcher can hasten the rat's bar-pressing behavior by using a process called shaping. **Shaping** involves reinforcing successively closer approximations of a behavior until the correct behavior is displayed. For example, a researcher might first reinforce the rat with a food pellet whenever it moved to the half of the Skinner box in which the bar was located; other responses would be ignored. Once that response had been learned, reinforcement would be withheld until the rat moved even closer to the bar. Then the rat might be

Shaping Operant Behavior Shaping is often used to train animals to perform impressive tricks, like this dolphin jumping through a hoop high above the water. To shape this behavior, the dolphin was first reinforced for swimming through the hoop underwater. Progressively, the hoop is raised until it is above the water. As the shaping process continues, reinforcement is delivered only for behaviors that become closer to the ultimate goal behavior.

reinforced only when it touched the bar. Step by step, the rat is reinforced for behaviors that correspond ever more closely to the final goal behavior: pressing the bar.

Skinner believed that shaping could explain how people acquire a wide variety of abilities and skills—everything from tying your shoes to operating sophisticated computer programs. To illustrate, consider how parents can use shaping to teach a toddler to dress herself. At first they might praise her for simply picking up a shirt, and then for managing to pull it over her head. Once that had been mastered, she would be reinforced only when she poked her head and arms through the appropriate shirt holes. Eventually, praise would be forthcoming only when, as a preschooler, she picked out clothes that matched, or when, as an older child, she chose an outfit that didn't mortify her parents.

Athletic coaches, teachers, parents, and child-care workers all use shaping techniques. Psychologist Judith Mathews and her colleagues (1992) used shaping to teach visually impaired children as young as two years of age to wear contact lenses. Toys, bubbles, and stars were used as reinforcers. First, the children were positively reinforced for allowing their faces to be touched. Then the children were reinforced for pulling open an eyelid, having an adult's finger approach their eyes, touching the contact lens, and so forth. By the end of the study, the children were wearing their contact lenses every day, and it took an average of only two minutes for an adult to insert or remove the children's contact lenses.

Maintaining Behavior:
The Schedules of Reinforcement

> *Once acquired, behaviors are maintained through different schedules or patterns of reinforcement. What is the partial reinforcement effect? What are the four basic schedules of reinforcement, and what pattern of responses does each schedule produce? How did Skinner explain superstitious behavior?*

Once a rat had acquired a bar-pressing behavior, Skinner found that the most efficient way to strengthen the response was to immediately reinforce *every* occurrence of bar pressing. This pattern of reinforcement is called **continuous reinforcement.** In everyday life, of course, it's common for responses to be reinforced only sometimes—a pattern called **partial reinforcement.** For example, practicing your basketball skills isn't followed by putting the ball through the hoop on every free throw. Sometimes you're reinforced by making a basket, and sometimes you're not.

Now suppose that despite all your hard work, your basketball skills were dismal. If practicing free throws was *never* reinforced by making a basket, what would you do? You'd probably eventually quit playing basketball. This is an example of **extinction:** In operant conditioning, when a learned response no longer results in reinforcement, the likelihood of the behavior being repeated gradually declines.

Skinner box
The popular name for an *operant chamber,* the experimental apparatus invented by B. F. Skinner to study the relationship between environmental events and active behaviors.

shaping
The operant conditioning procedure of selectively reinforcing successively closer approximations of a goal behavior until the goal behavior is displayed.

continuous reinforcement
A schedule of reinforcement in which every occurrence of a particular response is reinforced.

partial reinforcement
A situation in which the occurrence of a particular response is only sometimes followed by a reinforcer.

extinction
The gradual weakening and disappearance of conditioned behavior. In operant conditioning, extinction occurs when an emitted behavior is no longer followed by a reinforcer.

The Partial Reinforcement Effect:

Building Resistance to Extinction

Skinner (1956) first noticed the effects of partial reinforcement when he began running low on food pellets one day. Rather than reinforcing every bar press, Skinner tried to stretch out his food pellet supply by rewarding responses only periodically. He found that the rats not only continued to respond, but actually increased their rate of bar pressing.

One important consequence of partially reinforcing behavior is that such behaviors tend to be more resistant to extinction than behaviors conditioned using continuous reinforcement. This phenomenon is called the **partial reinforcement effect.** For example, when Skinner shut off the food-dispensing mechanism, a pigeon conditioned using *continuous reinforcement* would continue pecking at the disk 100 times or so before the behavior decreased significantly, indicating extinction. In contrast, a pigeon conditioned with *partial reinforcement* continued to peck at the disk thousands of times! If you think about it, this is not surprising. When pigeons, rats, or humans have experienced partial reinforcement, they've learned that reinforcement may yet occur, despite delays and nonreinforced responses, if persistent responses are made.

In everyday life, the partial reinforcement effect is reflected in behaviors that persist despite the lack of reinforcement. For example, parents who *occasionally* give in to their child's whining are inadvertently strengthening the behavior by putting it on a partial reinforcement schedule. If the parents then try to extinguish the behavior by consistently refusing to reinforce it, the whining will persist for a longer period of time than if they had previously reinforced *every* instance of whining. Similarly, gamblers may persist despite a string of losses, writers will persevere in the face of repeated rejection slips, and the family dog will continue begging for the scraps of food that it has occasionally received at the dinner table in the past.

Skinner (1956) found that specific preset arrangements of partial reinforcement produce different patterns and rates of responding. Collectively, these different reinforcement arrangements are called **schedules of reinforcement.** As we describe the four basic schedules of reinforcement, you'll find it helpful to refer to Figures 5.7 and 5.8, which show the typical pattern of responses produced by each schedule.

Fixed-Ratio Schedule

With a **fixed-ratio (FR) schedule,** reinforcement occurs after a fixed number of responses. For example, a rat might be on a 25-to-1 fixed-ratio (abbreviated FR-25), meaning it has to press the bar 25 times in order to receive one food pellet. Not surprisingly, it usually requires shaping to get a rat to the point where it will press the bar 25 times in order to get one food pellet. Initially the rat may have been on continuous reinforcement, followed by an FR-2 schedule, then an FR-4 schedule, and so on. Eventually, the rat's behavior is shaped to produce responding on an FR-25 schedule of reinforcement. Once the behavior is shaped, the ratio of reinforcements to responses is fixed and predictable.

Fixed-ratio schedules typically produce a high rate of responding that follows a burst-pause-burst pattern. The rat displays a burst of bar pressing, receives a pellet of food, pauses briefly, then displays another burst of responding (see Figure 5.7). In everyday life, the fixed-ratio schedule is reflected in any activity that requires a precise number of responses in order to obtain reinforcement. Piecework—being paid for producing a specific number of items, such as being paid $1 for every 100 envelopes you stuff—is an ex-

partial reinforcement effect
The phenomenon by which behaviors that are conditioned using partial reinforcement are more resistant to extinction than behaviors that are conditioned using continuous reinforcement.

schedule of reinforcement
The delivery of a reinforcer according to a preset pattern based on the number of responses or the time interval between responses.

fixed-ratio (FR) schedule
A reinforcement schedule in which a reinforcer is delivered after a fixed number of responses has occurred.

variable-ratio (VR) schedule
A reinforcement schedule in which a reinforcer is delivered after an average number of responses that varies unpredictably from trial to trial.

fixed-interval (FI) schedule
A reinforcement schedule in which a reinforcer is delivered for the first response that occurs after a fixed time interval has elapsed.

ample of an FR-100 schedule. On this sort of schedule, you might work steadily until you'd stuffed 100 envelopes, and then take a short break before you began working again (Mazur, 1994).

Variable-Ratio Schedule

With a **variable-ratio (VR) schedule,** reinforcement occurs after an average number of responses that *varies* from trial to trial. For example, a rat on a variable-ratio-20 schedule (abbreviated VR-20) would be reinforced after an average of 20 responses. But the rat might have to press the bar 25 times on the first trial before being reinforced and only 15 times on the second trial before reinforcement. While the number of responses required on any specific trial is *unpredictable,* over repeated trials the ratio of responses to reinforcers works out to the predetermined average.

As you can see in Figure 5.7, variable-ratio schedules of reinforcement produce high, steady rates of responding with hardly any pausing between trials or after reinforcement. Why do variable-ratio schedules produce such persistent responses? One explanation is that it's impossible to predict *which* response will result in reinforcement, but the more responses that are made, the greater the likelihood of reinforcement. The combination of these two factors can make some behaviors, such as gambling, "addictive" for some people (Mazur, 1994). Gambling is the classic example of a variable-ratio schedule in real life. Each spin of the roulette wheel, toss of the dice, or purchase of a lottery ticket could be the big one, and the more you gamble, the greater your chances to win. (And lose, as casino owners are well aware.)

FIGURE 5.7 Fixed-Ratio and Variable-Ratio Schedules of Reinforcement
The predictable nature of fixed-ratio schedules produces a high rate of responding with a pause after the reinforcer is delivered. In contrast, the unpredictable nature of variable-ratio schedules produces high, steady rates of responding with hardly any pausing between reinforcers.
(Based on Skinner, 1961.)

Fixed-Interval Schedule

With a **fixed-interval (FI) schedule,** a reinforcer is delivered for the first response emitted *after* the preset time interval has elapsed. A rat on a two-minute fixed-interval schedule (abbreviated FI-2 minutes) would receive no food pellets for any bar presses made during the first two minutes, whether it pressed the bar twice or 100 times. But the first bar press *after* the two-minute interval had elapsed would be reinforced.

Fixed-interval schedules typically produce a pattern of responding in which the number of responses tends to increase as the time for the next reinforcer draws near. As you can see in Figure 5.8, this produces a scallop-shaped pattern of responses. Long pauses in responding after reinforcement are especially common when the fixed interval is large. For example, a rat conditioned to an FI-10 minutes schedule may go for several minutes without pressing the bar. But as the end of the 10-minute interval draws near, bar pressing steadily increases until reinforcement occurs.

FIGURE 5.8 Fixed-Interval and Variable-Interval Schedules of Reinforcement
The predictable nature of fixed-interval schedules produces a scallop-shaped pattern of responding. As the end of the interval draws near, the rate of responding steadily increases until a reinforcer is delivered; then comes a sharp decrease in responding until the end of the interval draws near again. In contrast, the unpredictable nature of variable-interval schedules produces a moderate but steady rate of responding.
(Based on Skinner, 1961.)

Daily life contains examples of reinforcement that follow a very similar pattern to the laboratory example of fixed-interval reinforcement. For instance, if your instructor gives you a test every four weeks, studying behavior would probably follow the same scallop-shaped pattern of responding as the rat's bar-pressing behavior. As the end of the four-week interval draws near, studying behavior increases. After the test, studying behavior drops off until the end of the next four-week interval draws near. The same effect can occur with an employee's annual performance review. As the time for the performance review gets closer, the employee's productive behaviors (the operant) tend to increase.

Variable-Interval Schedule

On a **variable-interval (VI) schedule,** reinforcement occurs for the first response emitted after an *average* amount of time has elapsed, but the interval varies from trial to trial. In other words, the length of time that must pass before a particular reinforcement is delivered is unpredictable—but over a *series* of trials, it works out to a predetermined average. A rat on a VI-30 seconds schedule might be reinforced on trial 1 for the first bar press after only 10 seconds have elapsed, for the first bar press after 50 seconds have elapsed on trial 2, and for the first bar press after 30 seconds have elapsed on trial 3. This works out to an average of one reinforcer every 30 seconds.

Generally, the unpredictable nature of variable-interval schedules tends to produce moderate but steady rates of responding, especially when the average interval is relatively short (see Figure 5.8). In daily life, variable-interval schedules are reflected in situations where we must wait for events that follow an approximate, not a precise, schedule. Trying to call a friend whose phone is busy is one example: You periodically try dialing your friend's number, because you know that at some point you'll get through. However, it's impossible to predict exactly when your dialing (the operant response) will be reinforced (your friend answering the phone).

On a variable-interval schedule, reinforcement depends on the passage of time, rather than on the number of responses. Dramatically increasing the number of responses probably won't result in increased reinforcement. But reinforcement is unpredictable, and *might* occur at any time. Thus, a moderately steady rate of responses will pay off in the long run.

CONCEPT REVIEW 5.3

Recognizing Schedules of Reinforcement in Operant Conditioning

Indicate which schedule of reinforcement is being used in the following examples:

Variable interval (VI)
Fixed interval (FI)
Variable ratio (VR)
Fixed ratio (FR)

1. _____ A keypunch clerk is paid $1 for every 100 correct accounting entries made on the computer.

2. _____ At the beginning of the new term, your instructor announces that there will be five surprise quizzes over the course of the semester.

3. _____ At the beginning of the semester, your instructor announces that there will be a test every two weeks.

4. _____ On the average, the campus shuttle bus passes the library about every hour.

5. _____ Michael loves to play the slot machines, and, occasionally, he wins.

6. _____ Miguel gets paid every Friday afternoon.

Superstitious Behavior Professional athletes sometimes develop quirky superstitious rituals, such as these New York Mets baseball players balancing baseballs on their caps. How can this behavior be explained by accidental reinforcement?

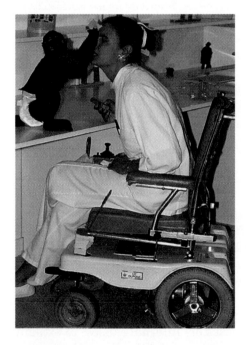

Using Operant Conditioning An organization called "Helping Hands," founded by behavioral psychologist Mary Joan Willard, trains capuchin monkeys to help people who are paralyzed or otherwise disabled. During the training phase, operant conditioning is used to teach the monkey a wide range of helping skills, such as feeding a person, turning lights on and off, and so forth. The training process may take up to four years before a monkey is placed with a disabled person.

behavior modification
The application of learning principles to help people develop more effective or adaptive behaviors.

Accidental Reinforcement and Superstitious Pigeons

Your friend wears his red T-shirt and pitches a no-hitter. You play your "lucky number" in the lottery and win $100. Will your friend wear his red T-shirt again the next time he pitches in an important game? Will you play your "lucky number" again in the next lottery? Quite possibly. Sometimes it only *appears* as if a particular response has resulted in reinforcement. In reality, the consequence is just a coincidence—the result of *accidental reinforcement.*

One of Skinner's (1948/1992) most clever demonstrations was to show how accidental reinforcement could lead to superstitious behaviors. Placing a food-deprived pigeon in a Skinner box, he set a timer so that every 15 seconds a food reinforcer was automatically dispensed. The pigeon's behavior and the delivery of the food reinforcer were completely independent of each other. Can you predict what happened?

Just as the basic principles of operant conditioning would predict, whatever behavior happened to be occurring when the food pellet was dispensed became strengthened and more likely to be repeated. Over time, six of the eight pigeons in this conditioning situation developed what Skinner called "a sort of superstition." One bird hopped sideways from one foot to the other. Another turned in counterclockwise circles. As Skinner (1948/1992) explained, "The bird behaves as if there is a causal relation between its behavior and the presentation of food, although such a relation is lacking."

The resemblance to the development of human superstitions should be obvious. As Skinner pointed out, the bowler who gestures at the bowling ball rolling down the alley after he's released it has no effect on the ball's motion. But a few "accidental connections" between such a ritual and favorable consequences may be enough to maintain the behavior, even though the behavior is often *not* reinforced. So the good luck that seems to follow when you drop a penny in a wishing well or eat black-eyed peas on New Year's Day, although simply a coincidence, may "reinforce" the behavior, leading you to repeat it.

Accidental reinforcement is yet another example of partial reinforcement. Thus, superstitious behaviors can be extremely resistant to extinction—as Skinner's superstitious pigeons demonstrated. After Skinner turned off the food dispenser, one pigeon continued to perform its side-to-side hop over 10,000 times! The partial reinforcement effect may help explain the persistence of various superstitious beliefs and ritualistic practices in many cultures, including our own. So the next time you're staring at a final exam paper face-down on your desk, knock on wood, cross your fingers, and remember Skinner's dancing pigeons.

Applications of Operant Conditioning

Applications of operant conditioning principles include behavior modification and animal training. What is behavior modification, and how has it been used to change human behavior?

In previous sections we described how operant conditioning principles have been applied in attempts to increase cooperative behavior in young dental patients and to help visually impaired children to wear contact lenses. Both of these examples illustrate **behavior modification,** the application of learning principles to help people develop more effective or adaptive behaviors. Most often, behavior modification involves applying the principles of operant conditioning to bring about changes in behavior.

Behavior modification has been used in such diverse situations as increasing social skills in school children, promoting sleep at night, and increasing automobile seatbelt use (Martens & others, 1992; Kamps & others, 1992; Lilie & Rosenberg, 1990). Behavior modification has even been used to reduce "goofing off" by competitive athletes during practice sessions (Hume & Crossman, 1992). When swimmers were reinforced with music for focusing on practicing their skills, productive behavior increased dramatically. In each of these situations, the systematic use of reinforcement and shaping has resulted in the increased occurrence of desirable behaviors.

The principles of operant conditioning have also been used in the specialized training of animals to help people who are physically challenged in some way. Seeing-eye dogs for the blind and dogs who assist people who are deaf are just a few examples.

Before you go on to the next section, take a few minutes to review Table 5.1, and make sure you understand the differences between classical and operant conditioning.

TABLE 5.1 Comparing Classical and Operant Conditioning

	Classical Conditioning	Operant Conditioning
Type of behavior	Reflexive, involuntary behaviors	Nonreflexive, voluntary behaviors
Source of behavior	Elicited by stimulus	Emitted by organism
Basis of learning	Associating two stimuli	Associating a response and the consequence that follows it
Responses conditioned	Physiological and emotional responses	Active behaviors that lead to reinforcers
Extinction process	Conditioned response decreases when conditioned stimulus is repeatedly presented alone	Responding decreases with elimination of reinforcing consequences

The Cognitive Perspective

According to the cognitive perspective, learning involves mental processes. What kinds of cognitive processes seem to be involved in classical conditioning, and how have they been demonstrated experimentally? What is meant by the phrase, "The animal behaves like a scientist" in classical conditioning?

In our discussion of the behavioral perspective, we noted that the behaviorists saw no need to resort to mental processes or "internal causes" to explain behavior (Skinner, 1987; Blumberg & Wasserman, 1995). From the behavioral perspective, classical conditioning results from a simple association of the conditioned stimulus and the unconditioned stimulus. In operant conditioning, learning results from the association of an operant and its consequence. Hence, the behavioral perspective maintains that learning is accomplished in both classical and operant conditioning without the involvement of mental or cognitive processes.

However, not all psychologists were convinced that mental processes were uninvolved in learning. Some wondered whether conditioning procedures do more than simply change how an organism responds. Could conditioning procedures change what the organism *knows* as well as what it *does*? According to the **cognitive perspective,** mental processes as well as external events are an important component of learning. In this section, we'll look first at the role cognitive processes seem to play in classical and operant conditioning. Then we'll consider how cognitive processes are involved in learning through the observation and imitation of the behaviors of others.

cognitive perspective
In learning theory, a general approach to the study of learning that stresses the role of expectations, mental representation, and other mental processes in learning.

Cognitive Aspects of Classical Conditioning:
Reliable Predictors

According to Pavlov, classical conditioning occurs simply because two stimuli are associated closely in time: the conditioned stimulus (the bell) precedes the unconditioned stimulus (the food) by no more than a few seconds. But is it possible that Pavlov's dogs were learning more than the mere association of two stimuli that occurred very close together in time?

To answer that question, let's begin with an analogy. Suppose that on your way to class you had to go through a railroad crossing. Every time a train approaches the crossing, warning lights flash. Being rather intelligent for your species, after a few weeks you conclude that the flashing lights will be quickly followed by a freight train barreling down the railroad tracks. You've learned an association between the flashing lights and an oncoming train, because the lights are a *reliable predictor* of the train.

Now imagine that a friend of yours also has to cross train tracks, but at a different location. The railroad has had nothing but problems with the warning lights at that crossing. Sometimes the warning lights flash before a train roars through, but sometimes they don't. And sometimes they flash when no train is coming. Does your friend learn an association between the flashing lights and oncoming trains? No, because here the flashing lights are an *unreliable predictor;* they seem to have no relationship to a train's arrival.

Psychologist **Robert A. Rescorla** (b. 1940) demonstrated that classically conditioned rats also assess the reliability of predictors, much like you and your friend at the different railroad crossings. In Rescorla's 1968 experiment, one group of rats heard a tone (the conditioned stimulus) that was paired twenty times with a brief shock (the unconditioned stimulus). A second group of rats experienced the *same* number of tone–shock pairings, but they also experienced an *additional* twenty shocks with *no* tone (see Figure 5.9).

FIGURE 5.9 Reliable and Unreliable Predictors
In Rescorla's experiment, both groups of rats experienced the same number of shock–tone pairings. However, the rats in group 1 received a shock only when the tone was sounded, while the rats in group 2 experienced additional shocks that were not paired with the tone. Subsequently, the rats in group 1 displayed a conditioned fear response to the tone, while the rats in group 2 did not. Why did only the rats in group 1 become conditioned to display fear when they heard the tone?

Then Rescorla tested for the conditioned fear response by presenting the tone alone to each group of rats. According to the traditional classical conditioning model, both groups of rats should have displayed the same levels of conditioned fear. After all, each group had received twenty tone–shock pairings. However, this is not what Rescorla found. The rats in the first group displayed a much stronger fear response to the tone than did the rats in the second group. Why?

According to Rescorla (1988), classical conditioning depends on the *information* the conditioned stimulus provides about the unconditioned stimulus.

For learning to occur, the conditioned stimulus must be a *reliable predictor* of the unconditioned stimulus. For the first group of rats, that was certainly the situation: every time the tone sounded, a shock followed. But for the second group, the tone was an unreliable predictor: sometimes the tone preceded the shock, and sometimes the shock occurred without warning.

Rescorla concluded that the rats in both groups were *actively processing information* about the reliability of the signals they encountered. Rather than merely associating two closely paired stimuli, as Pavlov suggested, the animal assesses the *predictive value* of stimuli. Applying this interpretation to classical conditioning, we can conclude that Pavlov's dogs learned that the bell *reliably predicted* food would follow.

According to this view, animals use cognitive processes to draw inferences about the signals they encounter in their environment. To Rescorla (1988), classical conditioning "is not a stupid process by which the organism willy-nilly forms associations between any two stimuli that happen to co-occur." Rather, his research suggests that "the animal behaves like a scientist, detecting causal relations among events and using a range of information about those events to make the relevant inferences" (Rescorla, 1980).

Because of studies by Rescorla and other researchers, today's understanding of how learning occurs in classical conditioning is very different from the explanations offered by Pavlov and Watson. Simply pairing events in time may not be enough for classical conditioning to occur. Instead, a conditioned stimulus must *reliably signal* that the unconditioned stimulus will follow. Put simply, classical conditioning seems to involve *learning the relations between events* (see Rescorla, 1988; Klein & Mowrer, 1989).

Cognitive Aspects of Operant Conditioning:
Rats! I Thought *You* Had the Map!

> *According to the cognitive perspective, operant conditioning involves forming a mental representation of the relationship between a behavior and its consequence. What is a cognitive map? What is latent learning, and how was it demonstrated?*

If cognitive processes are involved in classically conditioned behaviors, what about operant behaviors? Many early behaviorists believed that complex, active behaviors were no more than a chain of stimulus–response connections that had been "stamped in" by their effects. But one early learning researcher, **Edward C. Tolman** (1898–1956), had a different view of learning. Tolman believed that, even in the lowly rat, cognitive processes were involved in the learning of complex behaviors. According to Tolman, although such cognitive processes could not be observed directly, they could still be experimentally verified and inferred by careful observation of outward behavior (Tolman, 1932).

Much of Tolman's research involved rats in mazes. When Tolman began his research in the 1920s, many studies of rats in mazes had been done. In a typical experiment, a rat would be placed in the "start" box, and a food reward would be put in the "goal" box at the end of the maze. The rat would initially make many mistakes in running the maze. After several trials, it would eventually learn to run the maze quickly and with very few errors.

But what had the rats learned? According to traditional behaviorists, the rats had learned a *sequence of responses,* such as "first corner—turn left; second corner—turn left; third corner—turn right," and so on. Each response was associated with the "stimulus" of the rat's position in the maze. And the entire sequence of responses was "stamped in" by the food reward at the end of the maze.

Edward Chace Tolman (1898–1956)
Although he looks rather solemn, Tolman was known for his openness to new ideas, energetic teaching style, and playful sense of humor. During an important speech, he showed a film of a rat in a maze with a short clip from a Mickey Mouse cartoon spliced in at the end (Gleitman, 1991). Tolman's research demonstrated that cognitive processes are an important part of learning, even in the rat.

cognitive map
Tolman's term to describe the mental representation of the layout of a familiar environment.

latent learning
Tolman's term to describe learning that occurs in the absence of reinforcement but is not behaviorally demonstrated until a reinforcer becomes available.

Tolman (1948) disagreed with that view. He noted that several investigators had reported as incidental findings that their maze-running rats had occasionally taken their own shortcuts to the food box. In one case, an enterprising rat had knocked the cover off the maze, climbed over the maze wall and out of the maze, and scampered directly to the food box (Lashley, 1929; Tolman & others, 1946/1992). To Tolman, such reports indicated that the rats had learned more than simply the sequence of responses required to get to the food. Instead, Tolman believed that the rat eventually builds up, through experience, a **cognitive map** of the maze—a mental representation of its layout.

As an analogy, think of the route that you typically take to get to your psychology classroom. If a hallway along the way were blocked off for repairs, you would use your "cognitive map" of the building to come up with an alternative route to class. Tolman showed experimentally that rats, like people, seem to form cognitive maps (Tolman, 1948). And, like us, rats can use their cognitive maps to come up with an alternate route to a goal when the customary route is blocked (Tolman & Honzik, 1930a).

Tolman challenged the prevailing behaviorist model on another important point. According to Thorndike, for example, learning would not occur unless the behavior was "strengthened" or "stamped in" by a rewarding consequence. But Tolman showed that this is not necessarily the case. In a classic experiment, three groups of rats were put in the same maze once a day for several days (Tolman & Honzik, 1930b). For group 1, a food reward awaited the rats at the end of the maze. Their performance in the maze steadily improved; the number of errors and the time it took the rats to reach the goal box showed a steady decline with each trial. The rats in group 2 were placed in the maze each day with *no* food reward. They consistently made many errors, and their performance showed only slight improvement. The performance of the rats in groups 1 and 2 is exactly what the traditional behaviorist model would have predicted.

Now consider the behavior of the rats in group 3. These rats were placed in the maze with no food reward for the first ten days of the experiment. Like the rats in group 2, they made many errors as they wandered about the maze. But, *beginning on day 11*, they received a food reward at the end of the maze. As you can see in Figure 5.10, there was a dramatic improvement in group 3's performance between day 11 and day 12. Once the rats had discovered that food awaited them at the end of the maze, they made a beeline for the goal. On day 12, the rats in group 3 ran the maze with very few errors, improving their performance to the level of the rats in group 1 that had been rewarded on every trial!

Tolman concluded that *reward*—or reinforcement—is *not necessary* for learning to take place (Tolman & Honzik, 1930b). The rats in group 3 had learned the layout of the maze, and formed a cognitive map of the maze, simply by exploring it for ten days. However, they had not been motivated to *demonstrate* that learning until a reward was introduced. Rewards, then, seem to affect *performance* of what has been learned rather than *learning* itself. To describe learning that is not immediately demonstrated in overt behavior, Tolman used the term **latent learning.**

FIGURE 5.10 Latent Learning
Beginning with day 1, the rats in group 1 received a food reward at the end of the maze, and the number of errors they made steadily decreased each day. The rats in group 2 never received a food reward; they made many errors as they wandered about in the maze. Beginning on day 11, the rats in group 3 received a food reward at the end of the maze. Notice the sharp decrease in errors on day 12 and thereafter. According to Tolman, the rats in group 3 had formed a cognitive map of the maze during the first 11 days of the experiment. Learning had taken place, but this learning was not demonstrated until reinforcement was present—a phenomenon that Tolman called latent learning.
(Tolman & Honzik, 1930b.)

Group 2
Never received food reward.

Group 1
Received food reward every day.

Group 3
No food reward until the 11th day.

Food reward introduced for Group 3.

Average errors in maze

Days of training in maze

IN FOCUS 5.4

The Discovery of Learned Helplessness

In the 1960s, University of Pennsylvania psychologist Richard L. Solomon was studying the transfer of learning in dogs from a classical conditioning situation to an operant conditioning situation. Dogs were first classically conditioned to display an emotional reaction of fear to a tone. This was accomplished by repeatedly exposing the dogs to a tone followed by a mild electric shock, which produced fear—the dogs whimpered. This conditioning process continued for several days.

Once the fear response was classically conditioned, Solomon transferred the dogs to a shuttlebox, which is an operant chamber with a low barrier in the middle. The dogs now had to learn a simple escape behavior—to jump over the barrier when the floor on one side became electrified. Normally, dogs quickly learn this simple operant response. Once the dogs had learned this operant behavior, Solomon wanted to see if the tone would produce the same classically conditioned fear reaction in the shuttlebox situation.

However, a problem arose. When the classically conditioned dogs were placed in the shuttlebox and one side became electrified, the dogs just lay down and whimpered. They didn't try to jump to the other side. To Martin Seligman, a young psychology graduate student, the explanation of the dogs' passive behavior was obvious. As Seligman (1990) recalls:

Accidentally, during the early part of the experiment, the dogs must have been taught to be helpless. That's why they had given up. The tones had nothing to do with it. During Pavlovian conditioning they felt the shocks go on and off regardless of whether they struggled or jumped or barked or did nothing at all. They had concluded, or "learned," that nothing they did mattered. So why try?

In effect, Seligman was suggesting that the dogs' expectations in the situation were guiding their behavior. This notion, however, flew in the face of traditional behaviorism. To behaviorists, all behavior, including passive behavior, is determined by its environmental consequences, not by conscious thoughts, feelings, and expectations. If passive behavior increases, behaviorists maintained, it is because passive behavior has been reinforced.

Undaunted, Seligman and fellow graduate student Steven Maier designed a relatively simple experiment to test the idea that expectations were involved in the learning of helpless behavior. Dogs were arranged in groups of three. The first dog received shocks that it could escape by pushing a panel with its nose. The second dog was "yoked" to the first dog and received the same number of shocks as the first dog. However, nothing the second dog did would stop the shock. The shock stopped only when the first dog pushed the panel. The third dog in the group got no shocks at all.

After this initial training, the dogs were transferred to the shuttlebox. As Seligman and Maier predicted, the first and third dogs quickly learned to jump over the barrier when the floor became electrified. But the second dog, the one that had learned that nothing it did would stop the shock, made no effort to jump over the barrier. Because the dog had developed the expectation that its behavior had no effect on the environment, it had become passive. As Seligman (1990) recalls:

Pathetically, it soon gave up and lay down, though it was regularly shocked by the box. It never found out that the shock could be escaped merely by jumping to the other side. Clearly, animals can learn their actions are futile, and when they do, they no longer initiate action; they become passive. We had taken the central premise of learning theory—that learning occurs only when a response produces reward or punishment—and proved it wrong.

Seligman and Maier published their results in 1967 in the *Journal of Experimental Psychology*. They dubbed the dogs' reaction **learned helplessness**—a phenomenon in which exposure to inescapable and uncontrollable aversive events produces passive behavior (Maier & others, 1969). Their demonstration of the role of cognitive expectations in the acquisition of learned helplessness created an uproar among behaviorists.

But much to the chagrin of the leading behaviorists in the 1960s, the two young graduate students *had* successfully demonstrated that mental processes do play an important role in learning. Since the initial discovery of the phenomenon, there have been thousands of studies of learned helplessness (Peterson & others, 1993). Today, learned helplessness is seen as yet another example of the important role played by cognitive factors in classical and operant conditioning (Maier, 1989).

From these and other experiments, Tolman concluded that learning involves the acquisition of knowledge rather than simply changes in outward behavior. According to Tolman (1932), an organism essentially learns "what leads to what." It learns to "expect" that a certain behavior will lead to a particular outcome in a specific situation.

Tolman is now recognized as an important forerunner of modern cognitive theories of learning (Olton, 1992; Gleitman, 1991). Many contemporary cognitive learning theorists follow Tolman in their belief that operant conditioning involves the *cognitive representation* of the relationship between a behavior and its consequence. Other psychologists have also identified conditions under which cognitive expectations influence learning (see In Focus Box 5.4, "The Discovery of Learned Helplessness"). Today, operant conditioning is seen as involving the cognitive *expectancy* that a given consequence will follow a given behavior (Dickinson, 1989; Bolles, 1972).

Observational Learning:
Imitating the Actions of Others

> *In observational learning, we learn by watching others. What does Bandura's theory have in common with Tolman's ideas? What four mental processes are involved in observational learning? How has observational learning been applied?*

When your author Don was eleven years old, he had a paper route. Through rain, sleet, blizzards, and summer heat, the *Sioux City Journal* would get delivered every day after school. On Sundays, however, Don had to get up at 4:00 a.m. to deliver the papers by 6:00 a.m. The only incentive for doing so (outside of keeping his paper route) was that on his way home he could stop by the kitchen of a local bakery and snarf down a half dozen freshly baked, warm, glazed doughnuts—a potent positive reinforcer.

One particularly cold, wintry Sunday morning Don was trudging home after delivering the Sunday papers, slightly delirious from sugar shock. As he approached his house, he paused in front of the garage where his father's Oldsmobile Delta 98 was parked. He looked around. The house was completely dark. Everyone was still sound asleep. It was 5:45 a.m., and the streets were deserted because of a fresh snowfall during the night. After a microsecond of careful consideration, he decided to take the Delta 98 out for a little spin. After all, who'd ever find out?

Don carefully lifted the garage door, started the car, backed it out, and quietly glided down Ingleside Avenue. Exhilarated, he cruised through town. Driving to a deserted grocery store parking lot, he gunned the old Delta 98 around in the fresh snow, making perfect snow doughnuts! Eventually, he headed back home. The house was still dark. Ever so quietly, he eased the Oldsmobile safely back into the garage, shut off the engine, closed the garage door, and smiled. The perfect adventure!

Well, *almost* the perfect adventure. As he walked toward the house, two Sioux City police cars pulled up simultaneously from different directions. The front door of the house opened to reveal his father standing in his bathrobe and slippers. Don froze in his tracks, and saw his brief life pass before his eyes. Suffice it to say, Don's driving days were over until he got his driver's permit a few years later.

How did your author learn to drive his father's Delta 98 when he was only eleven years old? He had never been reinforced for getting behind the steering wheel of a car, much less for doing doughnuts in a grocery store parking lot. Nor had he learned through trial and error. Don's ability to take the family car out for an unauthorized spin illustrates many aspects of **observational learning.** In this model, learning takes place through observing the actions of others.

Classical conditioning and operant conditioning emphasize the role of direct experiences in learning, such as directly experiencing a reward following

observational learning
Learning that occurs through observing the actions of others.

Albert Bandura (b. 1925) Bandura contends that most human behavior is acquired through observational learning rather than trial and error or directly experiencing the consequences of our actions. Watching and processing information about the actions of others, including the consequences that occur, influences the likelihood that behavior will be imitated.

a particular behavior. But much human learning occurs *indirectly* by watching what others do, then imitating it. It's a capacity that humans develop at a very early age. Studies of twenty-one-day-old infants have shown that they will imitate a variety of actions, including opening their mouths, sticking out their tongues, and making other facial expressions (Meltzoff & Moore, 1977, 1983; Field & others, 1982).

Albert Bandura (b. 1925) is the psychologist most strongly identified with observational learning. Bandura (1974) believes that observational learning is the result of cognitive processes that are "actively judgmental and constructive," not merely "mechanical copying." To illustrate his theory, let's consider a famous Bandura (1965) experiment involving the imitation of aggressive behaviors. In the experiment, four-year-old children separately watched a short film showing an adult playing aggressively with a Bobo doll. A Bobo doll is a large, inflated balloon doll that stands upright because it has sand in the bottom. In the film, each child observed the adult hit, kick, and punch the Bobo doll.

However, different versions of the film had different endings. Some of the children saw the adult *reinforced* with soft drinks, candy, and snacks after performing the aggressive actions. Other children saw a version in which the aggressive adult was *punished* for the actions with a scolding and a spanking by another adult. Finally, some children watched a version of the film in which *no consequences* occurred to the aggressive adult.

After seeing the film, each child was allowed to play alone in a room with several toys, including a Bobo doll. The playroom was equipped with a one-way window so that the child's behavior could be observed. Can you predict how the children behaved?

As you've probably already anticipated, the consequences the children observed in the film made a difference. Children who watched the film in which the adult was punished were much less likely to imitate the aggressive behaviors than children who watched either of the other two film endings. So far, these results aren't especially surprising.

But then Bandura added an interesting twist to the experiment. Each child was asked to show the experimenter what the adult did in the film. For every behavior they could imitate, the child was rewarded with snacks and stickers. Now, virtually *all* of the children imitated the adult's behaviors that they had observed in the film, including the aggressive behaviors. Which version of the film the child had seen made no difference.

Bandura (1965) explained these results in much the same way that Tolman explained latent learning: Reinforcement is *not* essential for learning to occur. Rather, the *expectation of reinforcement* affects the *performance* of what has been learned.

Bandura (1986) suggests that four cognitive processes interact to determine whether imitation will occur. First, you must pay *attention* to the other person's behavior. Second, you must *remember* the other person's behavior so that you can perform it at a later time. That is, you must form and store a mental representation of the behavior to be imitated. Third, you must be able to transform this mental representation into *actions you are capable of reproducing*. These three factors—attention, memory, and motor skills—are necessary for learning to take place through observation.

Fourth, there must be some *motivation* to imitate the behavior. This factor is crucial to the actual performance of the learned behavior. An individual is more likely to imitate a behavior if there is some expectation that doing so will produce reinforcement or reward. Thus, all the children were capable of imitating the adult's aggressive behavior. But the children who saw the aggressive adult being rewarded were much more likely to imitate his behavior than the children who saw him punished. Table 5.2 summarizes other factors that increase the likelihood of imitation.

The Classic Bobo Doll Experiment Bandura demonstrated the powerful influence of observational learning in a series of experiments conducted in the early 1960s. Children watched a film showing an adult playing aggressively with an inflated Bobo doll. If they saw the adult experience no consequences or rewarded with candy for the aggressive behavior, the children were much more likely to imitate the behavior than if they saw the adult punished for the aggressive behavior (Bandura & others, 1963; Bandura, 1965).

Like classical and operant conditioning, observational learning has been applied in a variety of settings. For example, observational learning has been used to help people develop more effective interpersonal skills through assertiveness training. Such training typically involves observing a therapist behave in an assertive way in a specific situation, such as refusing an unreasonable request. The individual then role-plays (or imitates) the therapist's actions. The therapist provides feedback on the individual's performance. Assertiveness training can produce long-term changes in a person's interpersonal skills (see Gambrill, 1995b).

TABLE 5.2 Factors That Increase the Likelihood of Imitation

You're more likely to imitate . . .
- People who are rewarded for their behavior.
- Warm, nurturant people.
- People who have control over you or have the power to influence your life.
- People who are similar to you in terms of age, sex, and interests.
- People you perceive as having higher social status.
- When the task to be imitated is not extremely easy or difficult.
- If you lack confidence in your own abilities in a particular situation.
- If the situation is unfamiliar or ambiguous.
- If you've been rewarded for imitating the same behavior in the past.

SOURCE: Based on research summarized in Mazur, 1994; Bandura, 1986, 1977.

Social skills, manual skills, and academic skills are often acquired by observing and imitating the successful actions of another person. You can even learn from watching public television, whether you're observing the cooking techniques of *The Frugal Gourmet* or the remodeling techniques used on *This Old House*.

When you begin a new job, your first few weeks often involve observing an experienced employee. Training for nurses, electricians, pilots, and police officers routinely involves watching an experienced professional correctly perform a particular task, then imitating it. Clearly, this is advantageous. After all, would you want to be operated on by a surgeon who was learning strictly by trial and error?

CONCEPT REVIEW 5.4

Identifying Factors in Observational Learning

Reread the story of Don's adventure in his father's car. Bandura described four processes that are involved in observational learning: attention, memory, transforming the mental representation into actions you are capable of performing, and motivation. Which of the following statements best represents each process?

1. Don thought that driving would be fun and that he was unlikely to get caught. _____

2. Don had frequently watched how his father started and drove the car. _____

3. At the age of eleven, Don had the motor skills required to drive the car. _____

4. Don could vividly picture in his mind how his father drove the car. _____

The Ecological Perspective:
Biological Predispositions to Learn

According to the ecological perspective, an animal's natural behavior patterns and other unique characteristics influence what it is able to learn. How do taste aversions challenge the principles of classical conditioning? How does biological preparedness explain taste aversions?

The traditional behaviorist view maintains that the general principles of learning apply to virtually all species and all learning situations. By studying drooling dogs, pecking pigeons, or bar-pressing rats, the behaviorists believed that they could discover these general principles of learning. Once discovered, these principles could supposedly be applied with equal validity to pigs, hummingbirds, whales, and other species, including humans. As B. F. Skinner (1956) wrote:

> *Pigeon, rat, monkey, which is which? It doesn't matter. Of course, these species have behavioral repertoires which are as different as their anatomies. But once you have allowed for differences in the ways in which they make contact with the environment, and in the ways in which they act upon the environment, what remains of their behavior shows astonishingly similar properties.*

Skinner's contention that the particular species studied "doesn't matter" began to be challenged in the 1960s when researchers first reported "exceptions" to the well-established learning principles. As more exceptions were reported, some psychologists began to question just how general the general principles of learning really were (Lockard, 1971; Seligman, 1970).

ecological perspective
In learning theory, a general approach that emphasizes that the study of learning must consider the unique behavior patterns of different species that have evolved in relation to the species' natural environment.

In this section, we'll consider some findings that challenge the generality of learning principles involving classical and operant conditioning. These findings helped give rise to the ecological perspective. The **ecological perspective** stresses that the study of learning must consider the unique behavior patterns and capabilities of different species. As the result of evolution, animals have developed unique forms of behavior to adapt to their natural environment, or *ecology*. Thus, according to the ecological perspective, an animal's natural behavior patterns and unique characteristics can influence what it is capable of learning (Bolles, 1985).

Ecological Aspects of Classical Conditioning:
Spaghetti? No, Thank You!

A few months ago, Sandy made a pot of super spaghetti, with lots of mushrooms, herbs, spices, and some extra-spicy sausage. Being very fond of Sandy's spaghetti, Don ate a few platefuls. Several hours later, in the middle of the night, Don came down with a nasty case of stomach flu. Predictably, Sandy's super spaghetti came up—a colorful spectacle, to say the least. As a result, Don has developed a *taste aversion*—he now avoids eating spaghetti and feels "queasy" whenever Sandy suggests spaghetti for dinner. He cannot abide the taste, the smell, or even the thought of spaghetti.

Such learned taste aversions are relatively common. Our students have told us about episodes of motion sickness, morning sickness, or illness that resulted in taste aversions to foods as varied as cotton candy, strawberries, and chicken soup. At first glance, it seems as if taste aversions can be explained by classical conditioning. In Don's case, a neutral stimulus (spaghetti sauce) was paired with an unconditioned stimulus (a stomach virus) which produced an unconditioned response (nausea). Now a conditioned stimulus, the spaghetti sauce by itself elicits the conditioned response of nausea.

But notice that this explanation seems to violate two basic principles of classical conditioning. First, conditioning did not require repeated pairings. Conditioning occurred in *a single pairing* of the conditioned stimulus and the unconditioned stimulus. Second, the time span between these two stimuli was *several hours*—not a matter of seconds. Is this possible? The anecdotal reports of people who develop specific taste aversions seem to suggest that it is. But such reports lack the objectivity and systematic control that a scientific explanation of behavior requires.

Enter psychologist **John Garcia** (b. 1917), who demonstrated that taste aversions could be produced in laboratory rats under controlled conditions (Garcia & others, 1966). Garcia's procedure was straightforward: Rats first drank saccharine-flavored water (the neutral stimulus) and then, hours later, were injected with a drug (the unconditioned stimulus) that produced gastrointestinal distress (the unconditioned response). When the rats recovered from their illness, they refused to drink the flavored water. The rats had developed a taste aversion to the flavored water—which had become a conditioned stimulus.

At first, many psychologists were very skeptical of Garcia's findings because they seemed to violate the basic principles of classical conditioning. Several leading psychological journals refused to publish Garcia's research, saying the results were impossible (Garcia, 1981). But Garcia's results have been replicated many times. In fact, later research showed that taste aversions could develop even when a full twenty-four hours separated the presentation of the flavored water and the drug that produced illness (Etscorn & Stephens, 1973). Clearly, the phenomenon of taste aversions challenges some basic tenets of classical conditioning.

John Garcia (b. 1917) Garcia was one of the first researchers to experimentally demonstrate the existence of taste aversions and other "exceptions" to the general laws of classical conditioning.

Conditioning Taste Aversions in Coyotes
To control coyote predation without killing the coyotes, sheep carcasses are injected with a drug that produces extreme nausea and left where coyotes can find and eat them. In one study, captive coyotes were fed such poisoned rabbit and sheep carcasses. When placed in a pen with live rabbits and sheep, the coyotes avoided them rather than attack them. In fact, some of the coyotes threw up at the sight of a live rabbit (Gustavson & others, 1976).

Conditioned taste aversions also challenge the traditional behaviorist notion that associations can be learned between virtually any stimulus and any response. As Pavlov (1928) wrote, "Any natural phenomenon chosen at will may be converted into a conditioned stimulus . . . any visual stimulus, any desired sound, any odor, and the stimulation of any part of the skin." After all, Pavlov had demonstrated that dogs could be classically conditioned to salivate to a ringing bell, a ticking metronome, and even the sight of geometric figures.

But if this is the case, then why didn't Don develop an aversion to other stimuli he encountered between the time he ate the spaghetti and when he got sick? Why was it that only the spaghetti sauce became a conditioned stimulus that triggered nausea, rather than the dinner table, the silverware—or even Sandy, for that matter?

Contrary to what Pavlov suggested, Garcia and his colleagues demonstrated that the conditioned stimulus that is used *does* make a difference in classical conditioning (Garcia & Koelling, 1966). In another series of experiments, Garcia found that rats did *not* learn to associate a taste with a painful event, like a shock. Nor did they learn to associate a flashing light and noise with illness. Instead, rats were much more likely to associate a *painful stimulus* like a shock with *external stimuli*—flashing lights and noise. And to associate a *taste* stimulus with *internal stimuli*—the physical discomfort of illness. Garcia and Koelling (1966) humorously suggested that a sick rat, like a sick person, speculates, "It must have been something I ate."

Why is it that certain stimuli are more easy to associate than others? One explanation is **biological preparedness**—the idea that an organism is innately predisposed to form associations between certain stimuli and responses. If the particular stimulus and response combination is not one that an animal is biologically prepared to associate, then the association may not occur or may occur only with great difficulty.

When this concept is applied to taste aversions, rats (and people) seem to be biologically prepared to associate an illness with a taste rather than with a location or an object. Hence, Don developed an aversion to the spaghetti sauce and not to the fork he used to eat it. And, because humans and rats are biologically prepared to learn taste aversions, it's not surprising that taste aversions can be classically conditioned more readily than more arbitrary associations, such as that between a ringing bell and a plate of food.

Associations that are easily learned may reflect the evolutionary history and survival mechanisms of the particular animal species. For example, rats in the wild eat a wide variety of foods. If a rat eats a new food and gets sick several hours later, it's likely to survive longer if it learns from this experience to avoid that food in the future (Kalat, 1985; Seligman, 1970).

biological preparedness
In learning theory, the idea that an organism is innately predisposed to form associations between certain stimuli and responses.

IN FOCUS 5.5

Biological Preparedness and Conditioned Fears: What Gives You the Creeps?

Do these photographs make you somewhat uncomfortable?

A *phobia* is an extreme, irrational fear of a specific object, animal, or situation. It was once believed that all phobias were acquired through classical conditioning, like Little Albert's fear of white rats. But many people develop phobias without having experienced a traumatic event in association with the object of their fear (Merckelbach & others, 1992). Obviously, other forms of learning, such as observational learning, are involved in the development of some fears.

When people do develop conditioned fears as a result of traumatic events, they are more likely to associate fear with certain stimuli rather than others. Erv, not surprisingly, has acquired a conditioned fear response to the "killer attic." But why doesn't Erv shudder every time he hears a lawn mower or sees a ladder, the clothes he was wearing when he got trapped, or his can of oil?

Psychologist Martin Seligman (1971) noticed that phobias seem to be quite selective. Extreme, irrational fears of snakes, spiders, heights, and small enclosed places (like Erv and Fern's attic) are relatively common. But very few people are phobic of stairs, ladders, electrical outlets or appliances, or sharp objects, even though these things are far more likely to be associated with traumatic experiences or accidents.

Seligman has proposed that humans are biologically prepared to develop fears of objects or situations—like snakes, spiders, and heights—that may have once posed a threat to humans' evolutionary ancestors. As Seligman (1971) puts it, "The great majority of phobias are about objects of natural importance to the survival of the species." According to Seligman, people don't commonly develop phobias of knives, stoves, or cars because they're not biologically prepared to do so.

Support for this view is provided by early studies that tried to replicate Watson's Little Albert research. Elsie Bregman (1934) was unable to produce a conditioned fear response to wooden blocks and curtains, although she followed Watson's procedure carefully. And Horace English (1929) was unable to produce a conditioned fear of a wooden duck. Perhaps we're more biologically prepared to learn a fear of furry animals than wooden ducks, blocks, or curtains!

More recently, Swedish psychologists Arne Ohman and Joaquim Soares (1994) have accumulated experimental evidence that seems to support the biological preparedness hypothesis of phobias. For example, people more readily acquire conditioned fear responses to pictures of snakes and spiders paired with an electric shock than they do to pictures of mushrooms and flowers. Furthermore, the conditioned fears of spiders and snakes are much more resistant to extinction (Soares & Ohman, 1993). Ohman and Soares suggest that unconscious perceptual mechanisms in the brain may be "prewired" to react quickly and intensely to threatening environmental stimuli, such as poisonous reptiles and insects.

Not surprisingly, animals also seem to be biologically prepared to fear certain types of stimuli that represent natural threats to survival. For example, researchers have found that monkeys readily learn a conditioned fear response to images of snakes and crocodiles. But under the same conditions, monkeys do *not* acquire a conditioned fear response to images of flowers or toy rabbits (Mineka & Cook, 1993; Cook & Mineka, 1990).

Do Either of These Photos Give You the Creeps?

That different species form some associations more easily than others also probably reflects the unique sensory capabilities and feeding habits that have evolved as a matter of environmental adaptation. Bobwhite quail, for instance, rely primarily on vision for identifying potential meals. In contrast, rats have relatively poor eyesight and rely primarily on taste and odor cues to identify food. Given these species differences, it shouldn't surprise you that quail, but not rats, could easily be conditioned to develop a taste aversion to blue-colored water—a *visual* stimulus. On the other hand, rats learn more readily than quail to associate illness with sour water—a *taste* stimulus (Wilcoxon & others, 1971). In effect, quail are more biologically prepared than rats to associate visual cues with illness. And rats are more biologically prepared than quail to associate taste cues with illness.

Ecological Aspects of Operant Conditioning:
Misbehaving Chickens

> *Operant conditioning can be influenced by an animal's natural behavior patterns. What is instinctive drift, and how does it challenge the behavioral view of operant conditioning? What general conclusions can we draw about the validity of the principles of classical and operant conditioning?*

Psychologists studying operant conditioning also found that an animal's natural behavior patterns can interfere with the learning of new behaviors. Consider the experiences of Keller and Marian Breland, two of B. F. Skinner's students. The Brelands established a successful business training animals for television commercials, trade shows, fairs, and even displays in department stores (Breland & Breland, 1961; Bailey & Bailey, 1993). The Brelands used operant conditioning to train thousands of animals of many different species to perform all sorts of complex tricks.

But the Brelands weren't always successful in training particular animals. For example, they tried to train a chicken to play baseball. The chicken learned to pull a loop that activated a swinging bat. After hitting the ball, the chicken was supposed to run to first base. The chicken had little trouble learning to pull the loop, but instead of running to first base, the chicken would chase the ball.

The Brelands also tried to train a raccoon to pick up two coins and deposit them in a metal box. The raccoon easily learned to pick up the coins, but seemed to resist putting them into the box. Like a furry little miser, it would rub the coins together. And rather than dropping the coins in the box, it would dip the coins in the box and take them out again. As time went on, this behavior became more persistent, despite the fact that the raccoon was not being reinforced for it. In fact, the raccoon's "misbehavior" was actually *preventing* it from getting reinforced for correct behavior.

The Brelands noted that such nonreinforced behaviors seemed to reflect innate, instinctive responses. The chicken chasing the ball was behaving like a chicken instinctively chasing a bug. Raccoons in the wild instinctively clean and moisten their food by dipping it in streams or rubbing it between their forepaws. These natural behaviors interfered with the operant behaviors the Brelands were attempting to condition—a phenomenon called **instinctive drift.**

The biological predisposition to perform such natural behaviors was strong enough to overcome the lack of reinforcement. These instinctual behaviors also prevented the animals from engaging in the learned behaviors that would result in reinforcement. Clearly, reinforcement is not the sole determinant of behavior. And inborn or instinctive behavior patterns can interfere with the operant conditioning of arbitrary responses.

instinctive drift
The tendency of an animal to revert to instinctive behaviors which can interfere with the performance of an operantly conditioned response.

Exploring the Cognitive and Ecological Perspectives

For each of the situations described below, name the process involved (latent learning, taste aversions, or instinctive drift) and the psychologist(s) associated with it.

1. Lisa transfers to a new college and spends her first few days on campus getting oriented. At the beginning of her second week, she decides to have lunch at the cafeteria. Although she has never eaten there before, she has no problem finding the cafeteria.

2. One of Jordan's first jobs as an animal trainer was to train a pig to pick up a coin and deposit it in a "piggy bank." Through shaping and reinforcement with food, Jordan had some initial

success, but soon the pig was more interested in pushing the coin along the ground with its snout than in putting it in the bank.

3. Roger wanted to impress his girl friend by taking her to an expensive Indian restaurant, even though he was experiencing some symptoms of the flu. After the meal Roger got quite sick. Now even the smell of curry makes him feel nauseous.

Process	Psychologist(s)
1.	
2.	
3.	

Summing Up: Learning

Researchers who take the ecological perspective focus on natural behavior patterns of various species, especially as those behaviors occur in their natural environment, or ecology. Equipped by their distinct biological heritage, different species have evolved unique abilities to find food, attract mates, avoid predators, and survive in their natural habitat. To fully understand the process of learning, the ecological perspective maintains that you must consider the innate behavior patterns that have evolved in relation to a species' natural environment (Johnston, 1985). When learning is viewed in this context, miserly raccoons and bobwhite quail who develop taste aversions to blue-colored water begin to make sense.

Do the exceptions and conditioning "failures" that gave rise to the ecological perspective invalidate the principles of classical and operant conditioning? Not at all. Thousands of laboratory experiments have shown that behavior can be reliably and predictably influenced by classical and operant conditioning procedures. By and large, the general principles of classical and operant conditioning hold up quite well. However, a particular species may have evolved specialized behavior patterns and other characteristics that make it biologically prepared to learn certain types of associations or responses more easily than others. So the general principles of learning are just that—general, not absolute.

The fact that the basic principles of classical and operant conditioning hold up quite well is not necessarily a contradiction of the ecological perspective. After all, the general principles of learning are adaptive in almost any conceivable environment. Clearly, there are survival advantages in being able to learn that a neutral stimulus can signal an important upcoming event, as in classical conditioning. An organism also enhances its odds of survival by being responsive to the positive and negative consequences of its actions, as in operant conditioning. Thus, it is probably because these abilities are so useful in so many environments that the basic principles of learning are demonstrated with such consistency across so many species (Staddon, 1988; Beecher, 1988).

In the final analysis, the most important consequence of learning may be that it promotes the adaptation of many different species, including humans, to their unique environments. Were it not for the adaptive nature of learning, Erv would probably get trapped in the attic again!

APPLICATION

Using Learning Principles to Improve Self-Control

Self-control often involves choosing long-term reinforcers over appealing short-term reinforcers. How can learning principles be used to help you achieve long-term goals?

Do any of these examples have a familiar ring?

■ You sign up for an 8:00 a.m. class that meets on Tuesdays and Thursdays. Each Monday night you set your alarm clock for 6:00 a.m. But on Tuesday morning, when the alarm goes off, the bed feels so warm and cozy that you shut off the alarm, go back to sleep, and miss the class . . . again.

■ You work out a strict budget that will allow you to save enough money for next semester's tuition. Feeling virtuous, you stop at the mall on the way home from class and shop the sale racks.

■ You're determined to lose some weight. But your mother invites you over for dinner and makes your favorite dessert. How can you resist an extra slice of double chocolate cream pie?

Self-control often involves choosing between a *short-term reinforcer* that provides immediate gratification and a *long-term reinforcer* that will provide gratification at some point in the future. Objectively, the benefits of the long-term reinforcer far outweigh the benefits associated with the short-term, immediate reinforcer. Yet despite our commitment to the long-term goal, sometimes we choose a short-term reinforcer that conflicts with it. Why?

The Shifting Value of Reinforcers

The key is that *the relative value of reinforcers can shift over time* (Rachlin, 1974; Ainslie, 1975). Let's illustrate

how this can happen using the 8:00 a.m. Tuesday-morning class example. On Monday night, the short-term reinforcer (getting extra sleep on Tuesday morning) and the long-term reinforcer (getting a good course grade at the end of the semester) were both potential future reinforcers. Neither reinforcer was immediately available. So, when you compared these two future reinforcers, the value of making a good grade easily outweighed the value of getting extra sleep on Tuesday morning. That's why you duly set the alarm clock for 6:00 a.m. so you would get to class on time.

However, as the availability of a reinforcer gets closer, the subjective value of the reinforcer increases. Consequently, when your alarm goes off on Tuesday morning, the situation is fundamentally different. The short-term reinforcer is now immediately available: staying in that warm, comfy bed and going back to sleep. Compared to Monday night when you set the alarm, the subjective value of extra sleep has increased significantly. While making a good grade in the course is still important to you, its subjective value has not increased on Tuesday morning. After all, that long-term reinforcer is still in the distant future.

At the moment you make your decision, you will choose whichever reinforcer has the greatest subjective value to you. At that moment, if the subjective value of the short-term reinforcer outweighs that of the long-term reinforcer, you're very likely to choose the short-term reinforcer (Ainslie, 1975; Rachlin, 1974). In other words, you'll probably stay in bed.

When you understand how the subjective values of reinforcers shift over time, the tendency to cave in to available short-term reinforcers starts to make more sense. The availability of an

immediate, short-term reinforcer can temporarily outweigh the subjective value of a long-term reinforcer in the distant future. How can you counteract these momentary surges in the subjective value of short-term reinforcers? Fortunately, there are several strategies that can help you overcome the temptation of short-term reinforcers and improve self-control.

1. Precommitment

Precommitment involves making an advance commitment to your long-term goal, one that will be difficult to change when a conflicting reinforcer becomes available. In the case of getting to class on time, a precommitment could involve setting multiple alarms and putting them far enough away that you will be forced to get out of bed to shut each of them off. Or you could ask an early-rising friend to call you on the phone and make sure you're awake. If you want to lose weight by changing your eating habits, make a precommitment by buying only healthy food when you go to the grocery store, skipping the snack aisle altogether.

2. Self-Reinforcement

Sometimes long-term goals seem so far away that your sense of potential future reinforcement seems weak compared to immediate reinforcers. One strategy to increase the subjective value of the long-term reinforcer is to use self-reinforcement for current behaviors related to your long-term goal. For example, promise yourself that if you spend two hours studying in the library, you'll reward yourself by watching a favorite television show or spending time with friends.

It's important, however, to reward yourself only *after* you perform the desired behavior. If you say to yourself,

"Rather than study tonight, I'll go to this party and make up for it by studying tomorrow," you've blown it. You've just reinforced yourself for *not* studying! This would be akin to trying to increase bar-pressing behavior in a rat by giving the rat a pellet of food *before* it pressed the bar. Obviously, this contradicts the basic principle of positive reinforcement in which behavior is *followed by* the reinforcing stimulus.

3. Stimulus Control

Remember, environmental stimuli can act as discriminative stimuli that "set the occasion" for a particular response. In effect, the environmental cues that precede a behavior can acquire some control over future occurrences of that behavior. So be aware of the environmental cues that are likely to trigger unwanted behaviors. Then replace those cues with others that will help you achieve your long-term goals.

For example, studying in an easy chair might "set the occasion" for watching a little television or taking a nap. Before you know it, you've blown off a couple of hours that you had planned to spend studying. Instead, always study in a specific location, whether it's the library, an empty class-room, or at a table or desk in a certain corner of your apartment. Over time, these environmental cues will become associated with the behavior of studying. Similarly, you can apply stimulus control to impulsive spending by not going window shopping at the mall or browsing through the ads in the Sunday newspaper.

4. Focus on the Delayed Reinforcer

The cognitive aspects of learning also play a role in choosing behaviors associated with long-term reinforcers (Mischel, 1983, 1981). When faced with a choice between an immediate and a delayed reinforcer, selectively focus on the delayed reinforcer. You'll be less likely to impulsively choose the short-term reinforcer (Ainslie, 1975; Watson & Tharp, 1985).

Practically speaking, this means that if your goal is to save money for school, don't fantasize about new clothes or expensive running shoes. Focus instead on the delayed reinforcement of achieving your long-term goal (see Mischel & others, 1989). Imagine yourself proudly walking across the stage and receiving your diploma. Visualize yourself fulfilling your long-term career goals. The idea in selectively focusing on the delayed reinforcer is to mentally bridge the gap between the present and the ultimate attainment of your future goal. One of our students, a biology major, put a picture of a famous woman biologist next to her desk to help inspire her to study.

5. Observe Good Role Models

Observational learning is another strategy you can use to improve self-control. Psychologist Walter Mischel (1966) found that children who observed others choose a delayed reinforcer over an immediate reinforcer were more likely to choose the delayed reinforcer themselves. So look for good role models. If your goal is to study more, try to get to know other students who are serious about their studies and academic goals, rather than hanging out with people who never crack a book. Establish a study group so that you're frequently in contact with serious students. If a regular exercise program is your goal, join an exercise class or running club. Observing others who are currently behaving in ways that will ultimately help them realize their long-term goals can make it easier for you to do the same.

Summary
Learning

What Is Learning?

▪ *Learning* is defined as a relatively permanent change in behavior that is due to past experience. Learning often reflects adaptation to the environment. Three perspectives on learning are the behavioral perspective, the cognitive perspective, and the ecological perspective.

The Behavioral Perspective

▪ The behavioral perspective emphasizes changes in observable behaviors, and was founded by John B. Watson. According to the behavioral perspective, all human behavior is a result of learning.

Classical Conditioning: Associating Stimuli

▪ Ivan Pavlov, a Russian physiologist, discovered the principles of classical conditioning while studying the digestive system in dogs.

▪ Classical conditioning deals with reflexive behaviors that are elicited by a stimulus, and results from learning an association between two stimuli. A neutral stimulus is repeatedly paired with an unlearned, natural stimulus (the unconditioned stimulus), producing a reflexive response (the unconditioned response). Eventually, the neutral stimulus (or conditioned stimulus) elicits the same reflexive response (the conditioned response) as the natural stimulus.

■ Factors that affect the strength of the conditioned response include the frequency with which the unconditioned and conditioned stimuli are paired, and the timing of the stimulus presentations.

■ When a new stimulus that is similar to the conditioned stimulus produces the conditioned response, stimulus generalization has occurred. In stimulus discrimination, one stimulus elicits the conditioned response but another, similar stimulus does not.

■ In classical conditioning, extinction occurs when the conditioned stimulus no longer elicits the conditioned response. However, spontaneous recovery of the conditioned response may occur.

■ Applications of classical conditioning include conditioned emotional reactions and advertising. Physiological responses can also be classically conditioned.

Operant Conditioning: Associating Behaviors and Consequences

■ Edward Thorndike investigated the learning of active behaviors and formulated the Law of Effect. B. F. Skinner developed the operant conditioning model of learning to explain how voluntary, active behaviors are acquired.

■ Operant conditioning is a model of learning that explains learning as a process in which behavior is shaped and modified by its consequences. Reinforcement increases the likelihood of an operant being repeated. Two forms of reinforcement are positive reinforcement and negative reinforcement. Reinforcers may be either primary or conditioned reinforcers.

■ Punishment decreases the likelihood of an operant being repeated. Two forms of punishment are punishment by removal and punishment by application.

■ Aversive consequences do not always function as effective punishments. As a method of controlling behavior, punishment has many limitations.

■ The discriminative stimulus is the stimulus in the presence of which a particular operant is likely to be reinforced; it sets the occasion for a particular response.

■ New behaviors can be acquired through the process of shaping. A Skinner box is often used to study the acquisition of new behaviors by laboratory animals. Shaping is frequently used in everyday life to teach new behaviors.

■ Once acquired, behaviors are maintained through different schedules of reinforcement. Behaviors on a partial reinforcement schedule are more resistant to extinction than are behaviors on a continuous reinforcement schedule, as demonstrated by the partial reinforcement effect. Schedules of reinforcement include the fixed-ratio, variable-ratio, fixed-interval, and variable-interval schedules. When behavior is accidentally reinforced, superstitious behavior may result.

■ In behavior modification, the principles of operant conditioning are applied to help people develop more adaptive behaviors.

The Cognitive Perspective

■ According to the cognitive perspective, mental processes are involved in learning.

■ Robert Rescorla has demonstrated that classical conditioning involves learning the reliability of predictors rather than simply associating two stimuli.

■ Edward Tolman demonstrated that the learning of active behaviors also involves cognitive processes, such as forming cognitive maps and latent learning.

■ Albert Bandura demonstrated that new behaviors can be learned through observational learning. Observational learning involves the cognitive processes of attention, memory, motor skills, and motivation.

The Ecological Perspective: Biological Predispositions to Learn

■ According to the ecological perspective, natural behavior patterns influence conditioning and the learning of new behaviors.

■ Taste aversions violate key principles of classical conditioning. As John Garcia demonstrated, classical conditioning is affected by biological preparedness: some stimuli are more readily associated with conditioned responses than others.

■ Operant conditioning can also be affected by natural behavior patterns, as shown by the phenomenon of instinctive drift.

Key Terms

learning (p. 196)

behavioral perspective (p. 197)

classical conditioning (p. 199)

unconditioned stimulus (UCS) (p. 199)

unconditioned response (UCR) (p. 199)

conditioned stimulus (CS) (p. 200)

conditioned response (CR) (p. 200)

stimulus generalization (p. 201)

stimulus discrimination (p. 201)

extinction (in classical conditioning) (p. 202)

spontaneous recovery (p. 202)

Law of Effect (p. 206)

operant (p. 206)

operant conditioning (p. 207)

reinforcement (p. 207)

positive reinforcement (p. 207)

negative reinforcement (p. 208)

primary reinforcer (p. 208)

conditioned reinforcer (p. 209)

punishment (p. 209)

discriminative stimulus (p. 212)

Skinner box (p. 214)

shaping (p. 214)

continuous reinforcement (p. 215)

partial reinforcement (p. 215)

extinction (in operant conditioning) (p. 215)

partial reinforcement effect (p. 216)

schedule of reinforcement (p. 216)

fixed-ratio (FR) schedule (p. 216)

variable-ratio (VR) schedule (p. 217)

fixed-interval (FI) schedule (p. 217)

variable-interval (VI) schedule (p. 218)

Key People

Albert Bandura (b. 1925) American psychologist who experimentally investigated observational learning, emphasizing the role of cognitive factors.

John Garcia (b. 1917) American psychologist who experimentally demonstrated the learning of taste aversions in animals, a finding that challenged several of the basic assumptions of classical conditioning.

Ivan Pavlov (1849–1936) Russian physiologist who first described the basic learning process of associating stimuli that is now called *classical conditioning.*

Robert A. Rescorla (b. 1940) American psychologist who experimentally demonstrated the involvement of cognitive processes in classical conditioning.

B. F. Skinner (1904–1990) American psychologist who developed the operant conditioning model of learning and emphasized studying the relationship between environmental factors and observable actions, not mental processes, in trying to achieve a scientific explanation of behavior.

Edward L. Thorndike (1874–1949) The first American psychologist to experimentally study animal behavior and document how active behaviors are influenced by their consequences; postulated the Law of Effect.

Edward C. Tolman (1898-1956) American psychologist who used the terms *cognitive map* and *latent learning* to describe experimental findings that strongly suggested that cognitive factors play a role in animal learning.

John B. Watson (1878-1958) American psychologist who founded behaviorism in the early 1900s, an approach which emphasized the scientific study of outwardly observable behavior rather than subjective mental states.

CONCEPT REVIEW 5.1 Page 201

1. chemotherapy; nausea; ice cream; nausea
2. slimy leeches; disgust; the lake; disgust
3. scary monster; fear; doorbell; fear

CONCEPT REVIEW 5.2 Page 214

1. b
2. a
3. c
4. d
5. c

CONCEPT REVIEW 5.3 Page 218

1. Fixed ratio
2. Variable interval
3. Fixed interval
4. Variable interval
5. Variable ratio
6. Fixed interval

CONCEPT REVIEW 5.4 Page 228

1. motivation
2. attention
3. transforming mental representations into actions you are capable of performing
4. memory

CONCEPT REVIEW 5.5 Page 233

1. latent learning; Tolman
2. instinctive drift; Brelands
3. taste aversion; Garcia

Chapter

6 Memory

Prologue: The Drowning

Elizabeth was only fourteen years old when her mother drowned. Although Elizabeth remembers many things about visiting her Uncle Joe's home in Pennsylvania that summer, her memory of the details surrounding her mother's death had always been hazy. As she explains:

> In my mind I've returned to that scene many times, and each time the memory gains weight and substance. I can see the cool pine trees, smell their fresh tarry breath, feel the lake's algae-green water on my skin, taste Uncle Joe's iced tea with fresh-squeezed lemon. But the death itself was always vague and unfocused. I never saw my mother's body, and I could not imagine her dead. The last memory I have of my mother was her tiptoed visit the evening before her death, the quick hug, the whispered, "I love you."

It was some thirty years later that Elizabeth began to remember the details surrounding her mother's death. While at her Uncle Joe's ninetieth birthday party, Elizabeth learned from a relative that she had been the one to discover her mother's body in Uncle Joe's swimming pool. With this realization, memories that had eluded Elizabeth for decades began to come back.

> The memories began to drift back, slow and unpredictable, like the crisp piney smoke from the evening campfires. I could see myself, a thin, dark-haired girl, looking into the flickering blue-and-white pool. My mother, dressed in her nightgown, is floating face down. "Mom? Mom?" I ask the question several times, my voice rising in terror. I start screaming. I remember the police cars, their lights flashing, and the stretcher with the clean, white blanket tucked in around the edges of the body. The memory had been there all along, but I just couldn't reach it.

As the memory crystallized, it suddenly made sense to Elizabeth why she had always felt haunted by her vague memories of the circumstances surrounding her mother's death. And it also seemed to partly explain why she had always been so fascinated by the topic of memory.

However, several days later, Elizabeth learned that the relative had been wrong—it was *not* Elizabeth who discovered her mother's body, but her Aunt Pearl. Other relatives confirmed that Aunt Pearl had been the one who found Elizabeth's mother in the swimming pool. Yet Elizabeth's memory had seemed so real.

The Elizabeth in this true story is none other than Elizabeth Loftus, a psychologist who is nationally recognized as the leading expert on the distortions that can occur in the memories of eyewitnesses. Loftus shares this personal story in her book *The Myth of Repressed Memory: False Memories and Allegations of Sexual Abuse,* which she co-wrote with science writer Katherine Ketcham in 1994.

Even though Loftus is an expert on memory distortions and false memories, she wasn't immune to the phenomenon herself. Loftus experienced firsthand just how convincing a false memory can be. In retrospect, Loftus can see how she actively created information in her own mind that corresponded to the inaccurate information that she had been the one to discover her mother's body. As Loftus writes, "That elaborate but completely fabricated memory confronted me with its detail and precision, its utter lack of ambiguity" (Loftus & Ketcham, 1994).

In this chapter, we'll consider the psychological and biological processes that underlie how memories are formed and forgotten. As you'll see, memory distortions like the one that Elizabeth Loftus experienced are not uncommon. By the end of this chapter, you'll have a much better understanding of the memory process, including the reason Elizabeth's "memory" of finding her mother's body could seem so real.

Introduction

The Everyday Nature of Memory

As Elizabeth's story in our prologue demonstrates, memory is a fascinating and unpredictable phenomenon. Your very sense of identity relies on the memory of your personal history. Without memory, who would you be?

Memories can be vivid, almost three-dimensional, and evoke intense emotions. Yet memories can also be vague, elusive, fleeting, and frustratingly unreliable. Everyday life is filled with examples of embarrassing memory lapses. Have you ever put a cup of coffee on top of a car, then watched it roll down your back windshield as you drove off? Or shown up on the wrong day for a final exam? Or driven three miles back to your home because you couldn't remember whether you'd locked the back door or turned off the coffeepot?

On the one hand, it's incredible how much information is stored in memory, and how much we rely on those memories. With next to no conscious effort, you can remember how to operate a VCR, what you did last Saturday night, and the names of hundreds of relatives, friends, and acquaintances. On the other hand, some memories seem to evaporate quickly, such as the all-too-familiar experience of realizing that you can't remember the name of the person you were just introduced to and have been talking to for the last five minutes.

Memories Can Involve All Your Senses Think back to a particularly memorable experience from your high school years. Can you conjure up vivid memories of smells, tastes, sounds, or emotions associated with that experience? In the years to come, these teenagers may remember many sensory details associated with this impromptu football game on a crisp autumn afternoon.

THE FAR SIDE

© Chronicle Features, 1983 *Larson*

First pants, THEN your shoes

Along with information, we also form vivid memories of personal experiences that involve all our senses, like Loftus's memories of her uncle's home in Pennsylvania. You, too, can conjure up vivid memories, possibly from many years ago, that include smells, sounds, and even tactile sensations. The feeling of rain-soaked clothes against your skin or how cold your feet felt the day you went ice skating as a child are examples.

In this chapter we will explore what psychologists and other researchers have discovered about how human memory works. We encourage you to take a few minutes to try each of the memory demonstrations included in this chapter. These demonstrations will help you gain firsthand insights into fundamental memory processes as well as memory quirks, such as how memories can get distorted and the familiar feeling of having a memory on the tip of your tongue.

We'll also consider some unusual and controversial memory experiences, such as "memories" of previous lives and the recovery of "repressed" memories. Toward the end of the chapter, we'll discuss the brain's role in memory. And in the chapter's Application, we'll provide several suggestions for improving your memory.

Memory Processes and Stages:
An Overview

> *Memory is a group of related mental processes that enable us to acquire, retain, and retrieve information. What are encoding, storage, and retrieval? What is the three-stage model of memory? How do the stages differ, and how do they interact?*

memory
The mental processes that enable us to retain and use information over time.

encoding
The process of transforming information into a form that can be entered into and retained by the memory system.

storage
The process of retaining information in memory so that it can be used at a later time.

retrieval
The process of recovering information stored in memory so that we are consciously aware of it.

Memory refers to the mental processes that enable us to acquire, retain, and retrieve information. Rather than being a single process, memory involves three fundamental processes: *encoding, storage,* and *retrieval.*

Encoding refers to the process of transforming information into a form that can be entered and retained by the memory system. For example, if you were trying to memorize the definition of a key term that appears on a text page, you would visually *encode* the patterns of lines and dots on the page as meaningful words that can be retained by your memory. **Storage** is the process of retaining information in memory so that it can be used at a later time. **Retrieval** involves recovering the stored information so that we are consciously aware of it (Butters & Delis, 1995).

The Stage Model of Memory

Researchers have yet to settle on any one model that seems to capture exactly how human memory works (Anderson, 1995). However, one very influential model, called the **stage model of memory,** continues to be useful in explaining the basic workings of memory. In this model, memory involves three distinct stages: *sensory memory, short-term memory,* and *long-term memory* (Atkinson & Shiffrin, 1968). As shown in Figure 6.1, the stage model is based on the idea that information is *transferred* from one memory stage to another. Each memory stage is thought to differ in terms of the following:

- *Capacity:* how much information can be stored
- *Duration:* how long the information can be stored
- *Function:* what is done with the stored information

The first stage of memory is called *sensory memory*. **Sensory memory** registers a great deal of information from the environment and holds it for a very brief period of time. After a few seconds or less, the information fades. Think of your sensory memory as an internal camera that continuously takes "snapshots" of your surroundings. With each snapshot, you momentarily focus your attention on specific details. Almost instantly, the snapshot fades, only to be replaced by another.

Sensory Memory
- Environmental information is registered.
- Large capacity for information
- Duration: 1/4 second to 3 seconds

Attention →

Short-Term (Working) Memory
- New information is transferred from sensory memory.
- Old information is retrieved from long-term memory.
- Limited capacity for information
- Duration: approx. 30 seconds

Encoding and Storage →
← Retrieval

Long-Term Memory
- Information that has been encoded in short-term memory is stored.
- Unlimited capacity for information
- Duration: potentially permanent

FIGURE 6.1 Overview of the Stage Model of Memory

During the very brief time that the information is held in sensory memory, you "select," or pay *attention* to, just a few aspects of all the environmental information that's being registered. While studying, for example, you focus your attention on one page of your textbook, ignoring other environmental stimuli. The information that you select from sensory memory to pay attention to is important, because it is this information that is transferred to the second stage of memory, *short-term memory.*

Short-term memory refers to the active, working memory system (Cowan & others, 1994). Your short-term memory temporarily holds all the information that you are currently thinking about or consciously aware of. Information is stored briefly in short-term memory—for up to about 30 seconds (Cowan, 1994). Because you use your short-term memory to actively process conscious information in a variety of ways, today short-term memory is often referred to as **working memory** (Baddeley, 1995, 1990). Imagining, remembering, and problem solving all take place in short-term memory.

Over the course of any given day, vast amounts of information are temporarily held in your short-term memory. Most of this information quickly fades and is forgotten in a matter of seconds. However, some of the information that is actively processed in short-term memory may be encoded for storage in long-term memory.

stage model of memory
A model describing memory as consisting of three distinct stages: sensory memory, short-term memory, and long-term memory.

sensory memory
The stage of memory that registers information from the environment and holds it for a very brief period of time.

short-term memory (working memory)
The active stage of memory in which information is stored for about 30 seconds.

The Interaction of Memory Stages in Everyday Life Imagine driving on a busy street in a pouring rain. How might each of your memory stages be involved in successfully navigating the wet streets? What kinds of information would be transferred from sensory memory and retrieved from long-term memory?

Long-term memory is the third memory stage, and it represents what most people typically think of as memory—the long-term storage of information, potentially for a lifetime. It's important to note that the transfer of information between short-term and long-term memory is a two-way street. Not only does information flow from short-term memory to long-term memory, but much information also flows in the other direction—from long-term memory to short-term memory (Shiffrin & Nosofsky, 1994).

If you think about it, this makes a great deal of sense. Consider a routine cognitive task like carrying on a conversation. Such tasks involve processing current sensory data and the retrieval of stored information relevant to the task at hand, such as the meaning of individual words (Goldman-Rakic, 1992).

Let's use the Gary Larson cartoon that appeared at the beginning of this chapter to illustrate how the three memory stages work together. First, the visual image of the cartoon was momentarily stored in *sensory memory*. If you paid *attention* to it, the information was *transferred* to *short-term memory*. To interpret the cartoon, considerable information was also *retrieved* from *long-term memory* and transferred into short-term memory. That is, you retrieved information from long-term memory to understand what the words on the sign meant, to infer that the man was just waking up, and even to recognize that the lines on the page were a cartoon that was supposed to be humorous. Actively thinking about what the cartoon meant and interpreting it as funny all took place in short-term memory.

In the next few sections, we'll describe each of the stages of memory in more detail.

Sensory Memory: Fleeting Impressions of Reality

> *The first stage of memory, called sensory memory, holds sensory information from the environment for a few seconds or less. How did Sperling's experiment establish the duration of visual sensory memory? What are the functions of sensory memory?*

Has something like this ever happened to you? You're engrossed in a suspenseful movie on television. From another room, a family member calls out, "Where'd you put the phone book?" You respond with, "What?" Then, a split second later, the question registers in your mind. Before the other person can repeat the question, you respond, "Oh, the phone book. It's on the kitchen counter."

You were able to answer the question because your *sensory memory* registered and preserved the other person's words for a few fleeting seconds—just long enough for you to recall what had been said to you while your attention was focused on the movie. Sensory memory stores a detailed record of a sensory experience after it happens, but only for a few seconds at the most (Crowder, 1992).

long-term memory
The stage of memory that represents the long-term storage of information.

The Duration of Sensory Memory:

It Was There Just a Split Second Ago!

It was largely through the research of psychologist **George Sperling** (b. 1934) in 1960 that the characteristics of visual sensory memory were first identified. Sperling would flash the image of twelve letters on a screen for one-twentieth of a second (see Figure 6.2). The letters were arranged in four rows of three letters each. Subjects would focus their attention on the screen and, immediately after the screen went blank, report as many letters as they could remember.

On the average, the subjects could report only four or five of the twelve letters. However, several subjects claimed that they had actually seen *all* the letters. But the complete image faded from their memory as they spoke, disappearing before they could verbally report more than four or five letters.

With this clue, Sperling tried a simple variation on the original experiment. He arranged the twelve letters in three rows of four letters each. Then, immediately *after* the screen went blank, he sounded a high-pitched, medium-pitched, or low-pitched tone. If the subjects heard the high-pitched tone, they were to report the letters in the top row. The medium-pitched tone signaled the middle row, and the low-pitched tone signaled the bottom row. If the subjects actually did see all the letters, Sperling reasoned, then they should be able to report the letters in a given row by focusing their attention on the indicated row *before* their visual sensory memory faded.

This is exactly what Sperling found. If the tone followed the letter display within less than one-third of a second, subjects could accurately report about three of the four letters in whichever row was indicated by the tone. Sperling found that if the interval between the screen going blank and the sound of the tone was more than one-third of a second, the accuracy of the subjects decreased dramatically. By one second, the afterimage in their visual sensory memory had already faded beyond recall.

Sperling's classic experiment demonstrated that our *visual sensory memory* holds a great deal of information very briefly—for about half a second. This information is available just long enough for us to select and pay attention to specific elements that are significant to us at that moment. It is this meaningful information that is transferred from the very brief storage of sensory memory to the somewhat longer storage of short-term memory.

FIGURE 6.2 Sperling's Experiment Demonstrating the Duration of Sensory Memory

In George Sperling's (1960) classic experiment, subjects stared at a screen on which rows of letters were projected for just one-twentieth of a second (1). The screen then went blank (2). After intervals varying up to one second, a tone was sounded that indicated the row of letters the subject should report (3). If the tone was sounded within about one-third of a second, subjects were able to report the letters in the indicated row (4), because the image of *all* the letters was still in sensory memory.

1. Letters are displayed on a screen for 1/20 of a second

Q C F T
S K G O
W R J B

2. Screen is blank

Length of time varies up to one second

3. Tone is sounded, indicating row

HIGH
MEDIUM
LOW

4. Subject reports letters in row indicated by tone

S, K, G, . . .

Perceiving Sensory Memory Traces A bolt of lightning is actually three or more separate bolts of electricity. Why do we see a continuous lightning bolt streaking across the sky instead of a series of separated flashes? Because our visual sensory memory holds information for a fraction of a second, the separate flashes overlap and we perceive a single bolt of lightning.

Types of Sensory Memory:
Pick a Sense, Any Sense!

Memory researchers believe there is a separate sensory memory for each sense—vision, hearing, touch, smell, and so on (Crowder, 1992). Of the different senses, however, visual and auditory sensory memories have been the most thoroughly studied. *Visual sensory memory* is sometimes referred to as *iconic memory*, because it is the brief memory of an image, or *icon. Auditory sensory memory* is sometimes referred to as *echoic memory*, meaning a brief memory that is like an *echo*.

Researchers have found slight differences in the duration of sensory memory for visual and auditory information. Your visual sensory memory typically holds an afterimage of your environment for about one-quarter to one-half second before it is replaced by yet another overlapping "snapshot." This is easy to demonstrate. Quickly wave a pencil back and forth in front of your face. Do you see the fading image of the pencil trailing behind it? That's your visual sensory memory at work. It momentarily holds the "snapshot" of the environmental image you see before it is almost instantly replaced by another overlapping image.

Your auditory sensory memory holds sound information a little longer—up to a few seconds (Crowder, 1992). This brief auditory sensory trace for sound allows us to hear speech as continuous words, or a series of musical notes as a melody, rather than as disjointed sounds. That's also why you are able to "remember" something that you momentarily don't "hear," as in our example of the family member asking you where the phone book was.

An important function of sensory memory is to very briefly store our sensory impressions so that they overlap slightly with one another. Thus, we perceive the world around us as continuous, rather than as a series of disconnected visual images or disjointed sounds (Ashcraft, 1994).

Short-Term, Working Memory:
The Workshop of Consciousness

> *Short-term, or working, memory provides temporary storage for information transferred from sensory and long-term memory. What is the duration and capacity of short-term memory? How do we overcome the limitations of short-term memory?*

You can think of *short-term memory*, or *working memory*, as the "workshop" of consciousness. It is the stage of memory in which information transferred from sensory memory *and* information retrieved from long-term memory becomes conscious. When you consider solutions to a problem, recall a past event, or mentally add two numbers, the information is temporarily held and processed in your short-term memory. Your short-term memory also allows you to make sense out of this sentence by holding the beginning of the sentence in active memory while you read the rest of the sentence. So an important function of working memory is that it provides temporary storage for information that is currently being used in some conscious cognitive activity (Baddeley, 1995, 1992).

Short-term memory almost continually interacts with long-term memory, retrieving information that is used temporarily (Ericsson & Kintsch, 1995).

For example, to successfully multiply two numbers, you need to retrieve multiplication tables from long-term memory. To read and understand this sentence, you retrieve the meaning of the letters, words, and punctuation from long-term memory. By combining previously stored information with the new information, you often create new memories.

The Duration of Short-Term Memory:
Going, Going, Gone!

Information in short-term memory lasts longer than information in sensory memory, but its duration is still very short. At best, you can hold most types of information in short-term memory up to about 30 seconds before it's forgotten (Cowan, 1994). However, information can be maintained in short-term memory longer than 30 seconds if it is *rehearsed,* or repeated, over and over again. Because consciously rehearsing information will maintain it in short-term memory, this process is called **maintenance rehearsal.**

You use maintenance rehearsal all the time to increase the length of time you can hold information in short-term memory. For example, when you look up an office number on a building directory, you use maintenance rehearsal to maintain it in short-term memory until you reach the office. Another example is repeating an unfamiliar phone number until you dial it.

As you're well aware, information that is not actively rehearsed quickly fades, or *decays,* from short-term memory (Cowan, 1994). That's why you sometimes forget an important point that came to mind while you waited for a talkative friend to pause. Your idea quickly faded from short-term memory because listening to your friend's comments prevented you from rehearsing—and remembering—the point you wanted to make.

The Capacity of Short-Term Memory:
So That's Why There Were Seven Dwarfs!

Along with having a relatively short duration, short-term memory also has a relatively limited capacity. This is easy to demonstrate. Take a look at the numbers in Figure 6.3. If you've got a friend handy who's willing to serve as your research subject, simply read the numbers out loud to her, one row at a time, and ask her to repeat them back to you in the same order. Try to read the numbers at a steady rate—about one per second. Note each row that she correctly remembers. You can also be your own research subject: Simply read the numbers in each row once, then look away from your book and try to record them in the correct order on a piece of paper.

How many numbers could your friend repeat accurately? Most likely, she could correctly repeat between five and nine numbers. That's what psychologist George Miller (1956/1994) described as the limits of short-term memory in a classic paper entitled "The Magical Number Seven, Plus or Minus Two." Miller found that the capacity of short-term memory is limited to about seven items, or bits of information, at one time. So it's no accident that local telephone numbers are seven digits long. And had Snow White met more than seven dwarfs, it would be even more difficult to remember all their names.

This seven-item limit to short-term memory also seems to be universal. For example, it's been demonstrated in non-Western cultures in studies using Chinese characters instead of English-language materials (Yu & others, 1985).

So what happens when your short-term memory store is filled to capacity? New information will *displace,* or bump out, currently held information.

Row 1 — 8 7 4 6
Row 2 — 3 4 9 6 2
Row 3 — 4 2 7 7 1 6
Row 4 — 5 1 4 0 8 1 3
Row 5 — 1 8 3 9 5 5 2 1
Row 6 — 2 1 4 9 7 5 2 4 8
Row 7 — 9 3 7 1 0 4 2 8 9 7
Row 8 — 7 1 9 0 4 2 6 0 4 1 8

FIGURE 6.3 Demonstration of Short-Term Memory Capacity

maintenance rehearsal
The mental or verbal repetition of information in order to maintain it beyond the usual 30-second duration of short-term memory.

Maintenance rehearsal is one way to avoid the loss of information from short-term memory. By consciously repeating the information you want to remember, you keep it active in short-term memory and prevent it from being displaced by new information (Cowan & others, 1994).

S-t-r-e-t-c-hing the Capacity of Short-Term Memory:

Chunking

Although the capacity of your short-term memory is limited, there are ways to increase the amount of information that you can hold in short-term memory at any given moment. To illustrate this point, let's try another short-term memory demonstration. Read the following sequence of letters, then close your eyes and try to repeat the letters out loud in the same order:

U V A F C I C R B S A I

How many letters were you able to remember? Unless you have an exceptional short-term memory (or watch *Wheel of Fortune* too much), you probably could not repeat the whole sequence correctly. Now try this sequence:

V C R F B I U S A C I A

You probably managed the second sequence with no trouble at all, even though it is made up of exactly the same letters as the first sequence. The ease with which you handled the second sequence demonstrates **chunking**—the grouping of related items together into a single unit. The first letter sequence was perceived as twelve separate items and probably exceeded your short-term memory's capacity. But the second letter sequence was perceived as only four "chunks" of information, which you easily remembered: VCR, FBI, USA, and CIA. Thus, chunking can increase the amount of information held in short-term memory. But to do so, chunking also often involves the retrieval of meaningful information from *long-term memory,* such as the meaning of the initials FBI (Ericsson & Kintsch, 1995).

The basic principle of chunking is incorporated into many important numbers that we need to remember. Long strings of identification numbers, such as social security numbers or bank account numbers, are usually broken up by hyphens so that you can chunk them easily. Notice, however, that short-term memory is still limited to seven chunks. It's as if short-term memory has about seven mental slots for information. Each slot can hold a simple message or a complex message, but only about seven slots are available.

Long-Term Memory

> *When information is encoded, it is stored in long-term memory over time. What factors increase the efficiency of encoding? How does the levels-of-processing framework explain the relationship between coding and storage?*

Long-term memory refers to the storage of information over extended periods of time. Technically, any information stored longer than the roughly 30-second duration of short-term memory is considered to be stored in long-term memory. So a long-term memory can be recalling what you were doing five minutes ago or ten years ago. In terms of maximum duration, some long-term memories can last a lifetime.

chunking
Increasing the amount of information that can be held in short-term memory by grouping related items together into a single unit, or "chunk."

Compared to the limited bits of information that can be stored in sensory memory and short-term memory, the amount of information that can be held in long-term memory is limitless. Granted, it doesn't always feel limitless, but consider this: Every day, you effortlessly remember the directions to your college, the names of your instructors, and the faces of your fellow students. You remember how to tie your shoes, zip up your coat, and lock your front door. And simply to read this chapter, you will have retrieved the meaning of thousands of words from your long-term memory. These examples illustrate not only the range and quantity of information stored in long-term memory, but also the fact that retrieving information from long-term memory happens quickly and with little effort—most of the time.

Encoding and Long-Term Memory Storage

How does information get "into" long-term memory? One very important function that takes place in short-term memory is *encoding,* or transforming the new information into a form that can be retrieved later. As a student, you may have tried to memorize dates, facts, or definitions by simply repeating them to yourself over and over again. This strategy reflects an attempt to use maintenance rehearsal to encode material into long-term memory. However, maintenance rehearsal is *not* a very effective strategy for encoding information into long-term memory (see Anderson, 1995).

Elaborative Rehearsal: Encoding for Meaning

A much more effective encoding strategy is **elaborative rehearsal,** which involves focusing on the *meaning* of information to help encode and transfer it to long-term memory (Ashcraft, 1994). Elaborative rehearsal involves relating the information to other information that you already know (Ellis & Hunt, 1993a). Rather than simply repeating the information over and over to yourself, you *elaborate* on the new information in some meaningful way.

Elaborative rehearsal significantly improves memory for new material (Solso, 1991). This point is especially important for students, because elaborative rehearsal is a helpful study strategy. Here's an example of how you might use elaborative rehearsal to improve your memory for new information: In Chapter 2 we discussed three brain structures that are part of the limbic system: the *hypothalamus,* the *hippocampus,* and the *amygdala.* If you tried to memorize the definitions of these structures by reciting them over and over to yourself, you engaged in the not-so-effective memory strategy of maintenance rehearsal.

But if you elaborated on the information in some meaningful way, you would be more likely to recall it. For example, you could think about the limbic system's involvement in emotions, memory, and motivation by constructing a simple story: "I knew it was lunchtime because my hypothalamus told me I was *hu*ngry, *thi*rsty, and cold. My hippocampus helped me remember a new restaurant that opened on *campus,* but when I got there I had to wait in line and my amygdala reacted with *anger.*" The story may be a bit silly, but many studies have shown that elaborative rehearsal leads to better retention (Lockhart & Craik, 1990).

Creating this simple story to help you remember the limbic system illustrates two additional factors that enhance encoding (Lockhart, 1992). First, applying information to yourself, called the *self-reference effect,* improves your memory for information (Rogers & others, 1977). And second, the use of *visual imagery,* especially vivid images, also enhances encoding (Paivio, 1986; Marschark, 1992).

elaborative rehearsal
Rehearsal that involves focusing on the meaning of information to help encode and transfer it to long-term memory.

levels of processing framework
The view that information that is processed at a "deeper" (more meaningful) level is more likely to be remembered than information that is processed at a "shallow" level.

Levels of Processing

Why should elaborative rehearsal be a more effective way of encoding new information than maintenance rehearsal? Psychologists Fergus Craik and Robert Lockhart (1972) proposed that the *level* at which new information is processed determines how well the new information will be encoded and remembered. Craik and Lockhart's approach to understanding the relationship between coding processes and memory is called the **levels of processing framework** (Lockhart, 1992).

According to the levels of processing framework, information that is processed at a "deeper" level is more likely to be remembered than information that is processed at a "shallow" level (Craik & Tulving, 1975). Deep processing involves processing the *meaning* of the new information, rather than its more superficial characteristics. According to this framework, simple repetition, or maintenance rehearsal, would represent shallow processing of the information. In contrast, elaborative rehearsal would represent deep processing of material.

The fact that deep processing results in more effective encoding and better memory of new information has many practical applications for students. How can you process new information at a "deep" rather than a "shallow" level? You can:

- Actively question new information.
- Think about its implications.
- Figure out how new information relates to information you already know.
- Try to generate your own examples of the concept, especially examples from your own experiences.
- Make sure you understand and question the evidence.

Such mental activities promote "deeper" processing and enhance your memory for new information. In the Application, we'll give you more suggestions for strategies you can use to improve your memory.

FIGURE 6.4 The Role of Sensory and Short-Term Memory in the Memory System Model

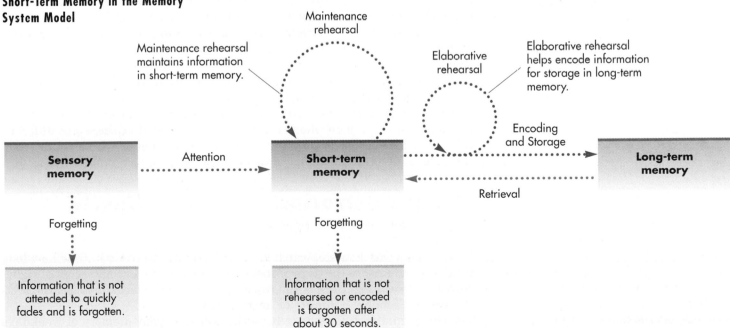

Types of Information in Long-Term Memory

> *Three basic categories of information are stored in long-term memory: procedural, episodic, and semantic. How do these categories differ? How is information organized in long-term memory? What is a semantic network?*

There are three major categories of information stored in long-term memory (Tulving, 1995, 1985). **Procedural information** refers to the long-term memory of how to perform different skills, operations, and actions. Typing, riding a bike, running, and making scrambled eggs are all examples of procedural information stored in long-term memory. We begin forming procedural memories early in life when we learn to walk, talk, feed ourselves, and so on.

Often, we can't recall exactly when or how we learned a skill or action. And usually, it's difficult to describe procedural memories in words. For example, try to describe *precisely* and *exactly* what you do when you blow-dry your hair, play the guitar, or ride a bicycle. You'll find that it's not as easy as you might think. A particular skill may be easy to demonstrate, but very difficult to describe.

Partly, this is because well-rehearsed skills become *automatic*. We're so accustomed to riding a bike or drying our hair that we no longer have to think consciously about how to perform the action. For example, both your authors type at about seventy words per minute. For each of us, typing involves automatic procedural memories that are executed without consciously thinking about the location of the keyboard letters. In fact, neither of us can consciously recite the location of all the keyboard letters and symbols from memory. And if we do consciously think about how and where we are moving our fingers, it interferes with our automatic ability to type accurately.

In contrast to procedural information, **episodic information** refers to your long-term memory of events or episodes in your life, such as when you registered to take this class or when you attended a friend's wedding (Squire & others, 1993). Also called *autobiographical memory,* such information is usually stored along with knowledge about when and where the event occurred (K. Nelson, 1993; Robinson, 1986).

The third kind of information stored in long-term memory is **semantic information**—general knowledge that includes facts, names, definitions, concepts, and ideas. Semantic information represents your personal encyclopedia of accumulated data and trivia that is stored in your long-term memory. Typically, you store semantic information in long-term memory *without* remembering when or where you originally stored the information. For example, can you remember when or where you learned that there are different time zones across the United States? How about when or where you learned the difference in the meanings of *there, their,* and *they're*? Probably not.

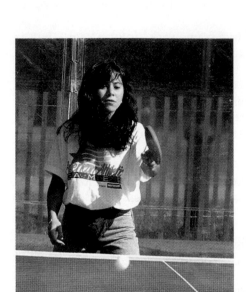

Types of Information Stored in Long-Term Memory Playing ping-pong involves all three types of information stored in long-term memory. Examples of *procedural information* might be how to hold the paddles and hit the ball. Remembering the rules of the game would be an example of *semantic information*. And, your vivid recollection of the time you beat your brother-in-law in a close game right before Thanksgiving dinner would be an example of *episodic information*.

The Organization of Information in Long-Term Memory

You'll need a watch or stopwatch for this demonstration. First, time how long it takes you to recite the days of the week. About three or four seconds, right? Now time how long it takes you to verbally recite the weekdays in alphabetical order. Probably a minute or longer, right?

The dramatic difference reflects the fact that your memory of weekdays is organized sequentially rather than alphabetically. Trying to arrange the

procedural information
Long-term memory of how to perform different skills, operations, and actions.

episodic information
Long-term memory of personally experienced events; also called *autobiographical memory.*

semantic information
General knowledge of facts, names, and concepts stored in long-term memory.

week days alphabetically requires considerable mental juggling. This simple demonstration illustrates that information in long-term memory is *organized*—not just a random jumble of information. Exactly *how* information is organized is not completely understood by memory researchers (see Ashcraft, 1994). Nevertheless, memory researchers have several clues to the organization of long-term memory.

Clue #1: Clustering

Before reading any further, try the demonstration in Figure 6.5. Now, look at the list of words that you were able to recall. Is there a pattern to your answers? If you're like most people, you probably listed several animals together, several cities, a group of colors, and different sports. This pattern of answers demonstrates **clustering,** which refers to organizing items into related groups or clusters during recall (Romney & others, 1993). Even though the words were presented in random order, you organized and clustered them in your long-term memory. Of course, the words in Figure 6.5, although random, do fall into fairly obvious categories.

What would happen if you presented people with a list of random words that had *no* obvious similarities or relationships? People still tend to organize information to help themselves remember it. When they recall unrelated items, people create their own subjective, organizational clusters that make sense to them. For example, they might create a sentence, story, or visual image that linked some of the words together. This tendency to organize even unrelated items in memory is called *subjective organization* (Tulving, 1962). The key point here is that we have a strong tendency to actively organize information in long-term memory, even when the components of the information are fundamentally unrelated.

Clue #2: Associations

Four words are listed in Figure 6.6. Your task is to read each word, then write down the first word that comes into your mind. Do this before reading any further.

Can you explain why you responded with the words you did? Most likely, each of your responses was based on some kind of logical *association* between the two words. This simple word-association task demonstrates that different bits of information in long-term memory are linked, or associated. Perhaps you even responded with one of the associations that our students commonly pick, as shown in Figure 6.7. But even if you didn't, each of your responses was based on some kind of logical association that you could explain if asked. For example, some of the not-so-common but logical associations that our students give to the word *red* are *hair, coat, hot, flag, tag, wine, alert, embarrassment,* and *ink.*

On the basis of finding that items stored in long-term memory are both organized and associated, memory researchers have developed several models to show how long-term memory is organized (see Ashcraft, 1994; Ratclif & McKoon, 1994). One of the best-known models is called the **semantic network model** (Collins & Loftus, 1975).

A semantic network works like this: There are many kinds of associations we can make between concepts. A *concept* is simply a cluster of related bits of information. For example, we can associate an object with its characteristics (ball → round), a location with an activity (library → study), or an activity

chair	apple
boat	car
footstool	airplane
orange	lamp
pear	banana
peach	dresser
bed	sofa
bus	bookcase
train	truck
plum	table
grapes	strawberry
motorcycle	bicycle

FIGURE 6.5 Clustering Demonstration
Study the words on this list for one minute. Then, beginning with the letter *Z*, write the alphabet in correct backwards order on a piece of paper. When you've completed that task, turn the paper over and write down as many of the words from the list as you can remember.

truck _____
red _____
apple _____
flower _____

FIGURE 6.6 Word Associations

FIGURE 6.7 Common Word Association Responses
Listed here are the five most common word associations given by 224 college students surveyed in your authors' classes. Word associations demonstrate how information stored in long-term memory is logically linked together.

truck	red	apple	flower
car	blue	orange	rose
Ford	apple	red	pretty
pickup	color	tree	smell
Chevy	green	fruit	daisy
semi	rose	round	pot

clustering
Organizing items into related groups during recall from long-term memory.

semantic network model
A model that describes units of information in long-term memory as being organized in a complex network of associations.

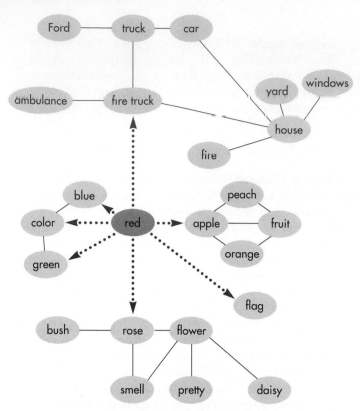

FIGURE 6.8 A Semantic Network Model
The semantic network is one model that has been proposed to show how information in long-term memory is organized through associations and clustering. Activating one concept can trigger a variety of other concepts, which, in turn, can spread throughout the network.
(Based on Collins & Loftus, 1975.)

with an emotion (gambling → excitement). All these associations can in turn be linked with additional associations in a massive network in long-term memory. However, some concepts in the network are more strongly linked than others.

When one concept is activated in the semantic network, it can *spread* in any number of directions, *activating* other associations in the semantic network. For example, the word *red* might activate *blue* (another color), *apple* or *fire truck* (objects that are red), or *alert* (as in the phrase, "red alert").

Figure 6.8 illustrates the potential associations in a greatly simplified semantic network. Each oval represents a piece of information stored in long-term memory. The lines connecting the ovals represent a network of possible associations. The length of the lines between the ovals indicates the strength of the association between two concepts. The shorter the line, the stronger the association, and the less time it takes to make that association. Thus, in the semantic network shown in Figure 6.8, if the concept *red* is activated in long-term memory, it's more likely to activate an association with the concepts *apple* or *blue* than with the concepts *fire truck* or *flag*.

The fact that information is organized in long-term memory has some very important implications for the retrieval process, as you'll see in the next section.

FIGURE 6.9 The Role of Long-Term Memory in the Memory System Model

Comparing the Three Stages of Memory

Identify each of the following descriptions as characteristic of sensory memory (SM), short-term memory (STM), or long-term memory (LTM).

Function

1. Encoded information is stored for possible retrieval later _____

2. Brief storage of overlapping sensory impressions _____

3. Temporary storage of incoming information and interaction with permanently stored information _____

Duration

4. Potentially permanent _____

5. Approximately 20 to 30 seconds _____

6. Approximately ½ to 3 seconds _____

Capacity

7. Limited capacity of about 7 items _____

8. Large but fleeting capacity _____

9. Unlimited capacity _____

retrieval
The process of accessing stored information.

retrieval cue
A clue, prompt, or hint that helps trigger recall of a given piece of information stored in long-term memory.

retrieval cue failure
The inability to recall long-term memories because of inadequate or missing retrieval cues.

Retrieval: Getting Information from Long-Term Memory

> *Retrieval refers to the process of retrieving or accessing stored information from long-term memory. What is a retrieval cue? What does the TOT experience tell us about the nature of memory? How is retrieval tested, and what is the serial position effect?*

So far, we've discussed some of the important factors that affect encoding and storing information in memory. In this section, we will look at the other side of the coin and consider factors that influence the retrieval process. **Retrieval** refers to the process of accessing, or *retrieving,* stored information.

Before you read any further, try the demonstration in Figure 6.10(a) and (b). Part (a) of the demonstration is on this page. After completing it, go on to part (b) on the next page. We'll refer to this demonstration throughout this section, so please take a shot at it. After you've completed both parts of the demonstration, continue reading.

FIGURE 6.10a Demonstration of Retrieval Cues

This demonstration illustrates the importance of retrieval cues. You'll need a blank sheet of paper and a pencil. Please follow the instructions exactly.

Instructions: Spend 3 to 5 seconds reading each of the sentences below, and read through the list only once. As soon as you are finished, cover the list and write down as many of the sentences as you can remember (you need not write "can be used" each time). Please begin now.

A brick can be used as a doorstop.
A ladder can be used as a bookshelf.
A wine bottle can be used as a candleholder.
A pan can be used as a drum.
A record can be used to serve potato chips.
A guitar can be used as a canoe paddle.
A leaf can be used as a bookmark.
An orange can be used to play catch.
A newspaper can be used to swat flies.
A TV antenna can be used as a clothes rack.
A sheet can be used as a sail.
A boat can be used as a shelter.
A bathtub can be used as a punch bowl.
A flashlight can be used to hold water.
A rock can be used as a paperweight.
A knife can be used to stir paint.
A pen can be used as an arrow.
A barrel can be used as a chair.
A rug can be used as a bedspread.
A telephone can be used as an alarm clock.
A scissors can be used to cut grass.
A board can be used as a ruler.
A balloon can be used as a pillow.
A shoe can be used to pound nails.
A dime can be used as a screwdriver.
A lampshade can be used as as a hat.

Now that you've recalled as many sentences as you can, turn to Figure 6.10b on page 254.

(From Bransford & Stein, 1984.)

The Importance of Retrieval Cues

There's a vast difference between what is stored in our long-term memory and what we can actually access. In many instances, our ability to retrieve stored memories hinges on having an appropriate retrieval cue. A **retrieval cue** is a clue, prompt, or hint that can help trigger recall of a stored memory. If your performance on the demonstration experiment in Figure 6.10 was like ours, the importance of retrieval cues should have been vividly illustrated.

Let's compare results. How did you do on the first part of the demonstration in Figure 6.10(a)? Don remembered 12 pairs of items. Sandy blew Don out of the water on the first part—she remembered 19 pairs of items. (No bets were riding on the outcome, as Don has learned not to bet Sandy on memory tasks.) Like us, you undoubtedly reached a point at which you were unable to remember any more pairs. At that point, you experienced **retrieval cue failure,** which refers to the inability to recall long-term memories because of inadequate or missing retrieval cues.

Your authors both did much better on the demonstration in Figure 6.10(b), and you probably did, too. (Sandy got 24 out of 26 words, and Don got 26 out of 26 words, except that he remembered *clothes rack* as *clothes line.*) Why the improvement? Because you were presented with retrieval cues that helped you access your stored memories.

The point of this exercise is to demonstrate the difference between information that is *stored* in long-term memory and information that you can *access.* Notice, many of the items on the list that you could not recall in Figure 6.10(a) were not forgotten. They were simply inaccessible—until you had a retrieval cue to work with. This illustrates that many memories only *appear* to be forgotten. As Figure 6.10(b) demonstrated, with the right retrieval cue, you can often access stored information that seemed to be completely unavailable.

FIGURE 6.10b Demonstration of Retrieval Cues (Continued)

Instructions: *Do not* look back at the list of sentences in Figure 6.10a. Use the following list as retrieval cues, and now write as many sentences as you can. Be sure to keep track of how many you can write down.

flashlight	lampshade
sheet	shoe
rock	guitar
telephone	scissors
boat	leaf
dime	brick
wine bottle	knife
board	newspaper
pen	pan
balloon	barrell
ladder	rug
record	orange
TV antenna	bathtub

(From Bransford & Stein, 1984.)

tip-of-the-tongue (TOT) experience
A memory phenomenon that involves the sensation of knowing that specific information is stored in long-term memory but being temporarily unable to retrieve it.

recall
A test of long-term memory that involves retrieving information without the aid of retrieval cues.

cued recall
A test of long-term memory that involves remembering an item of information in response to a retrieval cue.

recognition
A test of long-term memory that involves identifying correct information out of several possible choices.

Retrieval Glitches in Daily Life: The Tip-of-the-Tongue Experience

One of the most common, and most frustrating, experiences of retrieval failure is called the **tip-of-the-tongue (TOT) experience.** The TOT experience refers to the inability to get at a bit of information that you're absolutely certain is stored in your memory. Subjectively, it feels as though the information is very close, but just out of reach—or on the tip of your tongue (Koriat, 1993).

When experiencing this sort of retrieval failure, people can almost always dredge up partial responses or related bits of information from their memory. About half the time, people can accurately identify the first letter of the target word and the number of syllables in it. They can also often produce words with similar meanings or sounds (A. S. Brown, 1991). While momentarily frustrating, most TOT experiences are quickly resolved, sometimes within a few minutes. In one study, more than half of the blocked words spontaneously came to participants' minds within two days (D. M. Burke & others, 1991).

Tip-of-the-tongue experiences illustrate several aspects of the retrieval process. First, retrieving information is not an all-or-nothing process. Often, we remember bits and pieces of what we want to remember. Second, in many instances, information is stored in memory but not accessible without the right retrieval cues. Third, TOT experiences emphasize a point that we made earlier: Information stored in memory is *organized* and connected in relatively logical ways. As you mentally struggle to retrieve the blocked information, logically connected bits of information are frequently triggered. In many instances, these related tidbits of information act as additional retrieval cues, helping you access the desired memory.

Testing Retrieval: Recall, Cued Recall, and Recognition

The first part of the demonstration in Figure 6.10 illustrated the use of recall as a strategy to measure memory. **Recall** (also called *free recall*) involves producing information using no retrieval cues. This is the memory measure that's used on essay tests. Other than the questions themselves, an essay test provides no retrieval cues to help jog your memory. Recall tests demonstrate, once again, that retrieving information from long-term memory is not an all-or-nothing process. Often, you remember related bits of information on essay tests but not the desired information. (Thus the common student strategy of trying to dazzle your professor with what you *can* recall in hopes of a few sympathy points.)

The second part of the demonstration used a different memory measurement called **cued recall.** Cued recall involves remembering an item of information in response to a retrieval cue. Fill-in-the-blank and matching questions are examples of cued-recall tests.

A third memory measurement is **recognition,** which involves identifying the correct information out of several possible choices. Multiple-choice tests involve recognition as a measure of long-term memory. The multiple-choice question provides you with one correct answer and several wrong answers. If the information is committed to long-term memory, you should be able to recognize the correct answer.

From a student's perspective, cued-recall and recognition tests are clearly to your advantage. Because these kinds of tests provide retrieval cues, the likelihood that you will be able to access stored information is increased.

The Serial Position

Notice that the first part of the demonstration in Figure 6.10 did not ask you to recall the sentence in any particular order. Instead, the demonstration tested *free recall*—you could recall the items in any order. Take another look at your answers to Figure 6.10(a). Do you notice any sort of pattern to the items that you did recall?

Both of your authors were least likely to recall items from the middle of the list. This pattern of responses is called the **serial position effect,** which refers to the tendency to retrieve information more easily from the beginning and the end of a list rather than the middle. The serial position effect is especially prominent when you have to engage in *serial recall*—that is, when you need to remember a list of items in their original order. Remembering speeches, ordered lists, and directions are a few examples of serial recall.

A Demonstration of the Serial Position Effect Without singing them, try to recite the words of The Star-Spangled Banner. If you're like most of our students, you'll correctly remember the words at the beginning and the end of The Star-Spangled Banner but have difficulty recalling the words and phrases in the middle—the essence of the serial position effect.

There are two parts to the serial position effect. The tendency to recall the first items in a list is called the *primacy effect,* while the tendency to recall the final items in a list is called the *recency effect.* The recency effect was evident in Don's pattern of answers: Nine of the 12 pairs of items he recalled were from the second half of the list.

The Encoding Specificity Principle

According to the encoding specificity principle, recreating the original learning conditions improves retrieval effectiveness. What are the context effect, state-dependent retrieval, mood-dependent retrieval, and mood congruence? What role does distinctiveness play in retrieval, and how accurate are flashbulb memories?

serial position effect
The tendency to remember items at the beginning and end of a list better than items in the middle.

encoding specificity principle
The principle that when the conditions of information retrieval are similar to the conditions of information encoding, retrieval is more likely to be successful.

One of the best ways to increase access to information in memory is to recreate the original learning conditions. That simple idea is formally called the **encoding specificity principle** (Tulving, 1983). As a general rule, the more closely retrieval cues match the original learning conditions, the more likely it is that retrieval will occur. The encoding specificity principle can take several forms. Examples include the context effect, state-dependent retrieval, mood-dependent retrieval, and mood congruence.

The Context Effect

The encoding specificity principle can help explain some common experiences, such as the one where you can't remember some bit of information during a test but immediately recall it as you walk into the library where you normally study.

The explanation? When you intentionally try to remember some bit of information, such as the definition of a particular key term, you often encode into memory much more than just that isolated bit of information. As you study in the library, for example, at some level you're aware of all kinds of environmental cues. These cues might include the sights, sounds, and aromas within that particular situation. *The environmental cues in a particular context can become encoded as part of the unique memories you form while in that context.* These same environmental cues can act as retrieval cues to help you access the memories that were formed in that context. This particular form of encoding specificity is called the context effect. The **context effect** is the tendency to remember information more easily when the retrieval occurs in the same setting in which you originally learned the information (see Figure 6.11)

The context effect explains why you were able to recall the information in the library but not during the test in the classroom. The environmental cues in the library where you normally study act as additional retrieval cues that helped jog your memory. Of course, it's too late to help your test score, but the memory *was* there. Just for the record, studies have confirmed that when students are tested in the same room where they learned the material, they perform better (e.g., Saufley & others, 1985). In the Application, we discuss how you can use the context effect to your advantage even when the context is different from the one in which you learned the information.

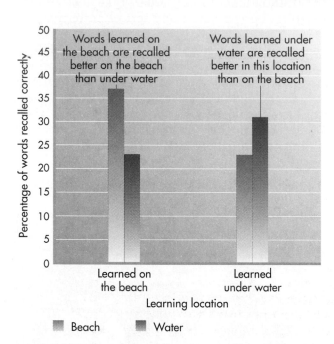

FIGURE 6.11 The Context Effect

The influence of the context effect was seen in a clever study in which subjects learned lists of words either while on the beach or while submerged under 15 feet of water. In this graph, you see that when the conditions of learning and retrieval matched, subjects were able to remember more words.

(From Godden & Baddeley, 1975.)

*Graph labels:*
Percentage of words recalled correctly

Words learned on the beach are recalled better on the beach than under water

Words learned under water are recalled better in this location than on the beach

Learned on the beach   Learned under water

Learning location

Beach   Water

State-Dependent Retrieval

Whereas context effects are due to *external* environmental cues, state-dependent retrieval is a form of encoding specificity in which the critical factor is the influence of drugs on a person's *internal* state. Taking a drug can produce an internal state with unique psychological and physiological characteristics, aspects of which can become encoded with new memories. At a later point, the same intoxicated state can provide additional retrieval cues. Thus, **state-dependent retrieval** involves better recall of information when the pharmacological states of learning and retrieval match (Roediger, 1992).

Studies have shown that when subjects learn information while under the influence of alcohol or marijuana, they recall the information better when they are under the influence of the drugs than when they are sober (Roediger, 1992; Baddeley, 1990). Similar effects have been shown with caffeine, nicotine, and other drugs (Horton & Mills, 1984; Peters & McGee, 1982; Eich, 1980).

Does this mean that drugs such as alcohol or marijuana improve memory? Absolutely not. As we noted in Chapter 4, on consciousness, these drugs tend to *impair* memory. It's also important to note that state-dependent effects are very weak and limited to free-recall tasks. On cued-recall or recognition memory tasks, performance is superior when a person is in a *sober* state, even if the information was encoded in an *intoxicated* state (Roediger, 1992). That's because the strong retrieval cues of recognition or cued-recall tasks easily outweigh the very weak state-dependent retrieval effect (Eich, 1989).

context effect
The tendency to recover information more easily when the retrieval occurs in the same setting as the original learning of the information.

state-dependent retrieval
An encoding specificity phenomenon in which information that is learned in a particular drug state is more likely to be recalled while the person is in the same drug state.

Mood and Memory Your emotional state tends to evoke memories that are consistent with the mood you are experiencing. When you're in a good mood, happy memories more easily come to mind. When you're feeling despondent, you're more likely to recall sad memories.

Mood-Dependent Retrieval

Mood-dependent retrieval is very similar to state-dependent retrieval. Here, the critical internal factor is the person's *mood* at the time of memory encoding and retrieval. Thus, **mood-dependent retrieval** occurs when information encoded in a certain emotional state is most retrievable when in the same emotional state (Eich & others, 1994). If you're very happy when you encode a particular memory, retrieval of that memory is more likely when you're in a very happy mood.

Overall, findings on mood-dependent retrieval have been mixed. Still, several experiments have successfully demonstrated mood-dependent memory. When moods match at the time of encoding and retrieval, recall is somewhat better than when they don't match (see Eich, 1995; Blaney, 1986). However, like state-dependent retrieval, the effect is most pronounced on free-recall tasks rather than recognition or cued-recall tasks. Also like state-dependent retrieval, the effects of mood-dependent retrieval are not that strong. Recall is *modestly* better when encoding/retrieval moods match than when encoding/retrieval moods are mismatched.

Mood Congruence

Mood congruence refers to the idea that a given mood tends to evoke memories that are consistent with that mood. In contrast to the mixed research results on mood-dependent effects, research has consistently shown that your current mood does influence the kinds of memories you recall (Eich & others, 1994; Johnson & Magaro, 1987; Blaney, 1986). A particular emotional state can act as a retrieval cue that evokes memories of events involving the same emotion. So when you're in a positive mood, you're more likely to recall positive memories. When you're feeling blue, you're more likely to recall negative or unpleasant memories.

In seriously depressed individuals, the mood-congruent effect can actually prolong depression (Baddeley, 1989). The depressed mood enhances memory retrieval of sad experiences, like memories of personal failures or losses. In turn, dwelling on negative memories can intensify or prolong the depression.

Distinctiveness and Flashbulb Memories:
Vivid Events, Vivid Memories

If you simply rummage around your own memories, you'll quickly discover that highly unusual, surprising, or even bizarre experiences are easier to retrieve from memory than routine events (Ellis & Hunt, 1993a). Such memories are said to be characterized by a high degree of *distinctiveness*. That is, the encoded information represents a unique, different, or unusual memory. In the retrieval cue demonstration in Figure 6.10, if you were more likely to remember the unusual combinations than the ordinary combinations, distinctiveness probably played a role.

Here's another example of the importance of distinctiveness: Imagine that several months ago you had to call the social security office to replace a lost social security card. As you were talking with the clerk, the line suddenly disconnected. You tried calling back, but the line was busy. Not that unusual, right? Feeling frustrated, you simply decided to try again some other time.

Usually, if something like this happened to you, you wouldn't remember much about the particular incident. But let's assume that you discovered a few hours later why the phone disconnected—somebody blew up the building. In fact, this is exactly what happened to an Oklahoma City caller on the morning of April 19, 1995, when the Murrah Federal Building was bombed.

mood-dependent retrieval
An encoding specificity phenomenon in which information encoded in a certain emotional state is most retrievable when the person is in the same emotional state.

mood congruence
An encoding specificity phenomenon in which a given mood tends to evoke memories that are consistent with that mood.

flashbulb memory
The recall of very specific images or details surrounding a vivid, rare, or significant personal event.

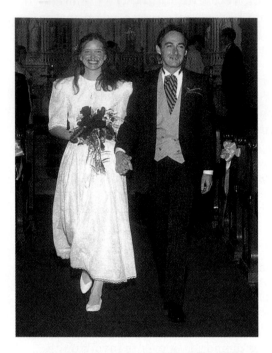

Flashbulb Memories Significant events, such as your wedding day, your high school graduation, or a national tragedy can trigger vivid flashbulb memories.

If that event had happened to you, you would probably easily be able to retrieve vivid memories of calling the federal building that day. Why? Because the retrieval cues themselves would be so distinctive (Ross, 1992). Such vivid memories are sometimes referred to as *flashbulb memories* (Brown & Kulik, 1982). Just as a camera flash captures the specific details of a scene on film, a **flashbulb memory** is thought to involve the recall of very specific images or details surrounding a significant, rare, or vivid event.

Do flashbulb memories literally capture specific details, like the details on a photograph, that are unaffected by the passage of time? National tragedies have provided psychologists with a unique opportunity to study the accuracy of flashbulb memories. When the space shuttle *Challenger* exploded in January 1986, psychologists Ulric Neisser and Nicole Harsch asked college students to write down how they had heard the news (Neisser & Harsch, 1992). Three years later, the same students were asked to recall the episode.

The results? Most of the students were very confident of their recollections, but fully one-third of them were wrong in what they remembered. Over a span of three years, some of the details of their memories had changed. When the students were shown their own handwritten accounts from the day after the explosion, many were so confident that their inaccurate memories were correct that they claimed that their own *original* accounts were wrong (Neisser & Harsch, 1992). Clearly, confidence in a memory is no guarantee of accuracy.

Other studies have also confirmed that flashbulb memories are less than picture-perfect. Although flashbulb memories can seem incredibly vivid, they appear to function just like normal, everyday memories: we remember some details, forget some details, and *think* we remember some details. What does seem to distinguish flashbulb memories from ordinary memories is the high degree of confidence that the person has in the accuracy of these memories (Weaver, 1993).

CONCEPT REVIEW 6.2

Recognizing Factors That Affect Retrieval

1. While looking at some old vacation pictures, Jim was flooded with very clear memories of the people he had met, the excitement of surfing, the fun beach parties, and the warm tropical weather. The pictures acted as
   a. retrieval cues
   b. tip-of-the-tongue cues
   c. serial position cues
   d. chunking cues

2. Janice rushed to the supermarket but forgot her shopping list. When she got home, she discovered that she had remembered most of the items at the beginning and the end of the list but had forgotten most of the items in the middle. Her pattern of remembering is
   a. due to state-dependent retrieval
   b. the result of mood-dependent retrieval
   c. referred to as the serial position effect
   d. called tip-of-the-tongue recall

3. Juan did all his studying for the final exam in the library and was surprised when he had difficulty remembering some information during the exam, which was held in the gym. His problem in retrieval is most likely due to
   a. context effects
   b. state-dependent retrieval
   c. mood-dependent retrieval
   e. mood congruence

4. The more depressed Jody feels, the easier it is for her to remember sad and unhappy events in her life. This best illustrates
   a. context effects
   b. state-dependent retrieval
   c. mood congruence
   d. tip-of-the-tongue retrieval

5. An eyewitness to a bank robbery is asked to identify the suspects in a police lineup. Which type of memory test is being used?
   a. free recall
   b. serial position test
   c. cued recall
   d. recognition

Reconstructing Memories:
Sources of Potential Errors

Because retrieval involves the active reconstruction of memories, details of memories can change. What are schemas, and how can they contribute to memory distortions? What is source confusion, and how can it produce false memories? What factors can reduce the accuracy of eyewitness testimony?

For the most part, you remember the general gist of what you see or hear. But the specific details that you remember can change over time. Unintentionally and without your awareness, details can get added, subtracted, exaggerated, or downplayed in your memories (Loftus & Ketcham, 1994).

How do errors and distortions creep into your memories? First, you need to understand that every new memory you form is not simply recorded, but *actively constructed.* To form a new memory, you actively organize and encode information. When you later attempt to retrieve those details from memory, you *actively reconstruct,* or rebuild, the memory (Barclay, 1986). In the process of constructing and reconstructing a memory, two general factors can contribute to errors and distortions: (1) the information you have stored *before* the memory occurs and (2) the information you acquire *after* the memory occurs (Ashcraft, 1994). Let's look at how each of these factors can contribute to memory errors and distortions.

The Psychology Professor's Office in the Brewer and Treyens (1981) Study Take a few moments to "look around" the office, then continue reading.

Schemas and Memory Distortions

Since very early in life, you have been actively forming **schemas**—organized clusters of knowledge and information about particular topics (Ashcraft, 1994). The topic can be almost anything, such as a particular event, an object, a situation, or a concept. For example, consider the schema you have for a typical kitchen. It probably includes food, a refrigerator, stove, sink, cabinets, pots, pans, silverware, and so forth. You started forming your kitchen schema early in life by gradually identifying the common elements first in your own kitchen, then in other people's. Over time, these common elements became associated and organized into a cluster of knowledge, producing the working schema you have for a kitchen.

On the one hand, schemas are useful in forming new memories. Using the schemas you already have stored in long-term memory allows you to quickly integrate new experiences into your knowledge base (Ellis & Hunt, 1993a). So if you read about some handy new cooking gadget like a breadmaking machine, you can quickly incorporate that new bit of information into your kitchen schema.

Although useful, schemas can also contribute to memory distortions. To illustrate this point, let's try to recreate some of the conditions in an ingenious study by William Brewer and James Treyens (1981). Imagine that you've signed up to participate in a psychology experiment. When you show up at the psychology professor's office for the study, the professor asks you to wait briefly in his office. Take a few moments to "glance around" the office, which is depicted in the accompanying photograph.

The professor comes back and escorts you to a different room. After you sit down, you are told the real purpose of the study: to test your memory of

schema
(SKEE-muh) An organized cluster of information about a particular topic.

the details of the professor's office. Without looking at the photograph again, take out a piece of paper and write down as many details as you can remember about the office, then continue reading.

Did you remember that the office contained books, a filing cabinet, a telephone, a lamp, pens, pencils, and a coffee cup? That's what many of the participants in this study remembered. But *none* of these items were in the professor's office. Compare what you remembered with what is actually shown in the photograph. How accurate was *your* memory?

Why did the participants in this study erroneously "remember" items that weren't there? When the participants reconstructed their memories of the office, they remembered objects that were not in the room but that *did* fit their schema of a professor's office. Thus, the incorrect details that they thought they remembered were all items that would be consistent with a typical professor's office.

Schemas can also contribute to memory distortions when we learn new information that is inconsistent with previously learned information. When we try to account for or incorporate the new information, memories can become distorted to resolve the inconsistencies.

In one clever study, subjects read a brief story about "Bob" and "Margie," a happy, compatible couple who were engaged to be married (Spiro, 1980). Just before the subjects left the experiment, however, the experimenter "casually" mentioned that Bob and Margie broke up and never did get married. When the subjects were later tested for their recall of the written story, they introduced new, inaccurate details to make the story more consistent with the experimenter's remark. For example, one subject recalled that there were problems with Bob's or Margie's parents, and that these troubles led to the breakup. Unknowingly, the subjects fabricated or distorted details of the story to make it consistent with the experimenter's remark and with their own schemas about relationships and marriage.

In combination, the office study and the Bob and Margie study underscore several important points. First, they show how the schemas we already hold can influence what we remember. Second, they demonstrate that once a memory is formed, it has the potential to be changed by new information. And third, they demonstrate how easily memories can become distorted. Notice that neither of these studies involved elaborate efforts to get subjects to distort the memories being formed or remembered.

Source Confusion and False Memories

Memory distortions can also occur because of **source confusion,** which arises when the true source of the memory is forgotten (Johnson & others, 1993; Leichtman & Ceci, 1995). That's because one of the most easily forgotten parts of a memory is its source—how, when, or where you acquired it (Goleman, 1994). Elizabeth's story in the prologue demonstrated how confusion about the source of a memory can give rise to an extremely vivid, but inaccurate, recollection. Vivid and accurate memories of her uncle's home, like the smell of the pine trees and the feel of the lake water, became blended with her fantasy of finding her mother's body. The result was a *false memory*—a distorted or inaccurate memory that feels completely real and is often accompanied by all the emotional impact of a real memory.

Confusion about the source of a memory is a common cause of false memories. Such false memories can arise when you confuse something that you've only heard about, read about, or seen in a film with something that really happened to you (Johnson & others, 1993). In Critical Thinking Box 6.1, "Science Versus Pseudoscience: Remembering Past Lives," we discuss some unusual examples of false memories that seem to involve source confusion.

source confusion
A memory distortion that occurs when the true source of the memory is forgotten.

CRITICAL THINKING 6.1

Science Versus Pseudoscience: Remembering Past Lives

While under hypnosis, people sometimes recover memories of past lives (Baker, 1992; Spanos, 1987–1988). When such memories surface, individuals may report very specific details about the time period of their previously remembered life. Current events, buildings, local customs, people's names, and even previously spoken languages are sometimes recalled. Consider the following representative cases:

Case #1. Under hypnosis, a Colorado housewife named Virginia Tighe recalled her previous life in Ireland in the 1800s (Rogo, 1985). Speaking with an Irish accent, Tighe remembered many details of her past life as Bridey Murphy, including her marriage to a Brian Joseph McCarthy.

Case #2. Jane Evans, a Welsh housewife, recalled several previous lives (Hines, 1988). In one past life, Evans was a fifteenth-century maid to the wealthy Frenchman Jacques Coeur. Evans recalled very specific details of Coeur's magnificent home, such as carvings over the fireplace. She also remembered that the Frenchman was unmarried and had no children.

Case #3. An American woman recalled a past life during which she lived in Bulgaria. While recounting the previous life, the woman supposedly spoke Bulgarian. Three other individuals had memories of past lives that they described in a foreign language, sup-

posedly speaking Swedish, Apache, and German (Thomason, 1986–1987; 1984).

Past-life memories like these are frequently offered as evidence of reincarnation. Whether or not you believe in reincarnation, consider the most basic evidence that any reasonably objective person would need to regard such memories as credible.

First, the reincarnation memory must contain information that could not be obtained through relatively ordinary means, such as books, conversations, movies, and newspaper articles. Second, it should not be possible to attribute the demonstration of a complex skill, such as recalling a foreign language, to learning acquired in the person's current life.

Third, the individual reporting the reincarnation memory should be able to provide ordinary information that virtually anyone living at that time would know. So if a person reports that he was a Japanese fighter pilot during World War II, he could reasonably be expected to know who the emperor of Japan was at the time.

Fourth, most of the information in a previous-life memory should mesh with valid historical records. If an individual reports a previous life as the composer Wolfgang Amadeus Mozart living in England in the 1400s, there are some credibility problems, because Mozart was born in 1756 and lived most of his life in Vienna, Austria.

Given these basic criteria, let's look at each of our reincarnation cases again.

Case #1 Reconsidered. In the Virginia Tighe case, historical searches failed to uncover evidence for many details of her past-life memories, including any records of either Bridey Murphy or her husband (Rogo, 1985). But investigators learned that while Virginia Tighe was growing up, she lived across the street from an Irish woman who told her stories about Ireland. The neighbor's name? Bridie Murphy. It also turns out that in high school, Virginia Tighe had been involved in theater and had performed several Irish monologues, complete with Irish accent (Alcock, 1978–1979).

Case #2 Reconsidered. Jane Evans's reincarnation memories seem pretty convincing, especially to those of us who have never heard of the fifteenth-century Frenchman Jacques Coeur. But as it turns out, Coeur's home still exists today and is one of France's most photographed homes. The other problem with Evans's recollections of her life as Coeur's maid is that they are incorrect: for instance, Coeur was married and had five children. Jane Evans's memories do, however, mesh very nicely with a detailed novel about Coeur's life entitled *The Moneyman* by Thomas B. Costain—which makes no mention of Coeur's wife or five children (Hines, 1988).

Case #3 Reconsidered. Linguist Sarah Thomason (1984) carefully analyzed the "Bulgarian" that one woman spoke during the recounting of a previous-life memory. Unfortunately, the woman's speech didn't contain common Bulgarian sounds, and she couldn't provide the correct Bulgarian translation for even common words. Another individual recalled a previous life as a nineteenth-century Apache-speaking "squaw." However, she could not produce any true Apache but instead preferred the Hollywood version of a Native American's broken English: "He ride ponies for white man. I no care. He scout for white man. I go to happy hunting ground." The perfor-

CHANNELLING ON THE CHEAP

MY NAME IS EUNICE. I HAVE LIVED MANY PAST LIVES, MOST OF THEM IN TRENTON, NEW JERSEY,....

Drawing by M. Stevens; © 1987 The New Yorker Magazine, Inc.

mance of the German or Swedish that other subjects supposedly spoke in a previous life was equally dismal (Thomason, 1986–1987).

So how are we to explain these memories of past lives? Although reincarnation "evidence" initially sounds impressive, there is good reason to believe that many reincarnation memories are examples of cryptomnesia, which literally means "hidden memories" (Baker, 1992). **Cryptomnesia** is a memory distortion in which a seemingly "new" or "original" memory is actually based on an unrecalled previous memory. In each of the cases we've described, existing information seems to form the basis for what the person believes is a genuine reincarnation memory.

Notice that this explanation doesn't necessarily rule out the possibility of reincarnation, which is a religious belief held by many people. It just means that pseudoscientific claims of "proof" for reincarnation are often made with little or no objective consideration of the evidence. In many cases, common psychological processes, such as cryptomnesia, seem to provide simpler and more likely explanations of the phenomenon. So beware. The past life that you remember just might be your own.

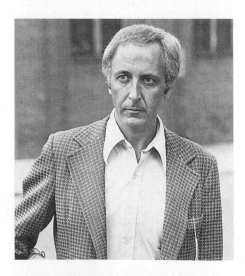

Do These Men Look Alike? Seven eyewitnesses identified Father Pagano (top photo) as the armed robber that the press dubbed the "Gentleman Bandit." But Robert Clouser (lower photo) confessed to the crimes during Pagano's trial. How could seven eyewitnesses confuse these two men?

Distortions in Eyewitness Testimony

Given the fallibility of human memory, it's understandable that precautions are often taken when specific details may be critically important. For example, a voice and flight recorder in the cockpit of every commercial airplane documents the details of a flight. If you dial 911, your emergency report and the dispatcher's response are recorded. In these situations and others, steps have been taken to guard against memory distortions *before* a crucial event or dialogue occurs.

One important area where it's often impossible to take such precautions is eyewitness testimony. The guilt or innocence of people in criminal and civil cases often hinges on the accuracy of people's memories. Researchers are well aware of how easily memories can be distorted in the laboratory. If such distortions also occur in real life, they could have serious implications.

As a case in point, consider the differences in appearance between the two men in the accompanying photographs. The older, bald man in the top picture is Father Bernard Pagano, a Roman Catholic priest who was arrested and charged with six armed robberies (Beck & Borger, 1979). It was dubbed the trial of the "Gentleman Bandit" because the robber was very polite and courteous to his victims. At Father Pagano's trial, not one but *seven* eyewitnesses positively identified the priest as the robber.

Now look at the lower picture. That man is Ronald Clouser, the man who actually committed the robberies. Had Ronald Clouser not confessed to the robberies during Father Pagano's trial, Father Pagano would probably have been convicted of the crimes. But Clouser reported specific details of the robberies that were known only by the police, so there was no doubt that he was the real crook.

How could seven eyewitnesses positively identify Father Pagano as the robber? Before we answer that question, we need to consider some of the research investigating how the memory of eyewitnesses can become distorted. Psychologist **Elizabeth Loftus** (b. 1944), whose story we told in the prologue, is one of the most widely recognized authorities on eyewitness testimony. Loftus not only has conducted extensive research in this area, but has also testified as an expert witness in many high-profile cases (Loftus & Ketcham, 1991).

To illustrate how eyewitness testimony can become distorted, let's consider a Loftus study that has become a classic piece of research (Loftus & Palmer, 1974). Loftus had subjects watch a film of an automobile accident, write a description of what they saw, and then answer a series of questions. There was one critical question in the series: "About how fast were the cars going when they contacted each other?" Different subjects got different versions of that question. For some subjects, the word *contacted* was replaced with *hit,* while other subjects were given *bumped, collided,* or *smashed.*

Depending on the specific word used in the question, subjects gave very different estimates of the speed at which the cars in the film were traveling. As shown in Figure 6.12, the subjects who gave the highest speed estimates got *smashed* (so to speak). Clearly, how a question is asked can influence what is remembered.

A week after seeing the film, the subjects were asked another series of questions. This time, the critical question was, "Did you see any broken glass?" Although no broken glass was shown in the film, the majority of the subjects whose question had used the word *smashed* a week earlier said yes. Once again, this demonstrates that following the initial memory (the film of the automobile accident), new information (the word *smashed*) can distort the reconstruction of the memory (remembering broken glass that wasn't really there).

More recently, Loftus and her colleagues have demonstrated that subjects can intentionally be led to make inaccurate reports after being exposed to misleading information (Loftus, 1992; Loftus & others, 1989). This **misinformation effect** is relatively easy to produce. In one study, subjects watched a series of slides about a burglary in which a screwdriver was a key element. The subjects then read a written account of the event. However, the written account contained misleading information: it referred to a hammer instead of a screwdriver. The subjects were then tested for their memory of the event.

The results? After exposure to the misleading information, about 60 percent of the subjects quickly and confidently said that a hammer, rather than a screwdriver, had been used in the burglary. In fact, subjects were as confident about their fabricated memories as they were about their genuine memories of other details of the original event. Many other studies have confirmed that misleading questions, misinformation, and other factors can distort eyewitness memories (see Pendergrast, 1995; Loftus & Ketcham, 1991; Wells, 1993; Baker, 1992).

Now we can begin to make sense of Father Pagano's experience. Remember, seven eyewitnesses *confidently,* but *mistakenly,* identified him as the armed robber. As you consider the following additional bits of information that led to his arrest, notice the roles played by schemas and misinformation:

- After the victims experienced the robberies (the original memories), the local media showed a composite sketch of the robber (potentially inaccurate information) based on details remembered by the victims.

- A former member of Father Pagano's parish "recognized" the priest from the sketch and notified the police (Beck & Borger, 1979).

- The behavior of the "Gentleman Bandit" fit the schema of a priest: the robber was very courteous and even apologetic when robbing people, saying he needed the money (schema distortion).

FIGURE 6.12 Estimated Speeds
(After Loftus & Palmer, 1974.)

Word Used in Question	Average Speed Estimate
smashed	41 m.p.h.
collided	39 m.p.h.
bumped	38 m.p.h.
hit	34 m.p.h.
contacted	32 m.p.h.

Misleading information can turn a lie into memory's truth. It can cause people to believe that they saw things that never really existed, or that they saw things differently from the way things actually were. It can make people confident about these false memories and also, apparently, impair earlier recollections. Once adopted, the newly created memories can be believed as strongly as genuine memories.

Elizabeth Loftus, 1992

Memory Researcher Elizabeth Loftus
Research by Loftus has shown how easily memories can become distorted. In the chapter prologue, we told you the story of her own experience with a false, but utterly convincing, memory.

misinformation effect
A memory-distortion phenomenon in
which people's existing memories can be
altered by exposing them to misleading
information

- When police investigators interviewed the witnesses, the officers mentioned that the robber *might* be a priest (misleading information; source confusion).

- *After* witnesses saw news photos of the priest being arrested (more misleading information), they were shown photographs of possible suspects. Only *one* photograph showed a suspect wearing a clerical collar—the picture of Father Pagano.

In combination, these factors contributed to the memory distortions of the seven eyewitnesses. Is the case of Father Pagano an isolated example of eyewitnesses mistakenly identifying the wrong person? Not at all. Psychologist Gary Wells (1993) notes that in more than 1,000 convictions of people who turned out to be innocent, the single largest factor leading to those false convictions was eyewitness error.

How Reliable *Is* Memory?

Given the different ways in which memories can become distorted, several points need to be emphasized as we summarize this section. First, we don't want to leave you with the impression that it's astonishing that anybody ever remembers *anything* accurately. In reality, people's memories tend to be quite accurate for overall details. If asked, you could correctly recall many details related to the way you spent last Thanksgiving or your last birthday. In general, the more meaningful or important the details were to you, the more likely it is that you'll be able to recall them (Baddeley, 1990).

Second, under normal circumstances, there are limits to the degree to which ordinary memories can become distorted. Memory distortions usually involve limited bits of information. In all the examples we've discussed, the general memories were accurate, even though specific details were wrong. Granted, those specific details can sometimes be crucial, but they are a far cry from being outrageous memory distortions. For example, none of the subjects in the office study reported seeing a couch or B. F. Skinner sitting in the office, even though both are consistent with the schema of a psychologist's office.

Third, the astonishing ease with which bits of memory can become distorted is unnerving. Yet the distorted memories ring true in our minds; they feel just as "real" as accurate memories. In the prologue, you saw how easily Elizabeth Loftus, herself a noted researcher on memory distortions, created a false memory. You also saw how quickly she became convinced of the false memory's authenticity and the strong emotional impact it had on her. Fortunately, however, memory researchers have also discovered a number of ways we can guard against inadvertently producing memory distortions (Wells, 1993). For example, being careful to ask neutral rather than leading questions can protect against the misinformation effect (Leichtman & Ceci, 1995).

Finally, it's important to point out that not all memory distortions are undesirable. Sometimes, memories of past events can become distorted in psychologically beneficial ways. One study looked at the memories of well-adjusted adults who, as children, had been treated for significant problems (Robins & others, 1985). Many of these adults did *not* remember spending time in a juvenile detention center, living with foster parents, or growing up in an unstable household. Instead, they tended to remember their parents as performing their roles adequately and providing sufficient supervision. Their childhood memories had become distorted so that they were more consistent with their current, well-adjusted adult lives.

The Accuracy of Memory Will these people accurately remember the details of this day? Despite the potential for errors in the recall of specific details, our memories are usually accurate for overall themes and general information.

Forgetting: You *Forgot* the Plane Tickets?!

> *Forgetting is common, and can also be adaptive. Many factors contribute to forgetting. What was Ebbinghaus's contribution to the study of forgetting? What roles do encoding failure, interference theory, motivated forgetting, and decay play in forgetting?*

In the everyday sense, forgetting is simply not being able to remember some piece of information. Often, this involves information we intended to remember, such as removing the brownies from the oven before they're burned to a crisp (again). More formally, **forgetting** is the inability to recall information that was previously available (Solso, 1991).

Forgetting is so common that our lives are filled with automatic reminders to safeguard against forgetting important information. Cars are equipped with buzzers so you don't forget to put on your seatbelt or turn off your lights. News announcements remind you to reset your clocks as Daylight Savings Time begins or ends. Dentists thoughtfully send brightly colored postcards so that your root canal appointment doesn't slip your mind.

Sometimes, of course, we *want* to forget. From the standpoint of a person's psychological well-being, it's probably just as well that we tend to forget the details of unpleasant memories, such as past failures, social embarrassments, and unhappy relationships. Even more generally, it's easy to argue that our minds would be cluttered with mountains of useless information if we remembered every television program, magazine article, billboard, or conversation we've ever experienced. So forgetting *does* have some adaptive value.

CALVIN AND HOBBS

Herman Ebbinghaus:
The Forgetting Curve

German psychologist **Herman Ebbinghaus** (1850–1909) began the scientific study of forgetting over a century ago. Because there was a seven-year gap between his completion of college and his first university teaching position, Ebbinghaus couldn't use university students for experimental subjects (Fancher, 1990). So to study forgetting, Ebbinghaus had to rely on the only available research subject: himself.

Ebbinghaus's goal was to determine how much information was forgotten after different lengths of time. But he wanted to make sure that he was studying the memory and forgetting of completely new material, rather than information that had pre-existing associations in his memory. To solve this problem, Ebbinghaus (1885/1987) created new material to memorize: thousands of nonsense syllables. A *nonsense syllable* is a three-letter combination, made up of two consonants and a vowel, like WIB or MEP. It almost sounds like a word, but is meaningless.

Ebbinghaus carefully noted how many times he had to repeat a list of thirteen nonsense syllables before he could recall the list perfectly. To give you a feeling for this task, here's a typical list:

ROH, LEZ, SUW, QOV, XAR, KUF, WEP, BIW, CUL, TIX, QAP, WEJ, ZOD

forgetting
The inability to recall information that was previously available.

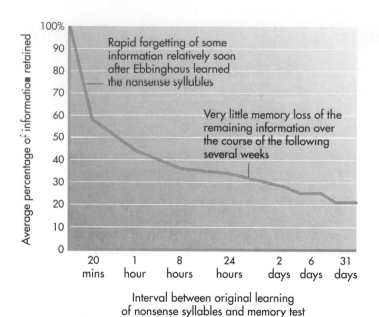

Rapid forgetting of some information relatively soon after Ebbinghaus learned the nonsense syllables

Very little memory loss of the remaining information over the course of the following several weeks

Average percentage of information retained

Interval between original learning
of nonsense syllables and memory test

(a)

Rapid forgetting of some information during the first several months after the psychology class

Very little memory loss over a period of 10 years for the remaining concepts and names learned in the psychology class

Names

Concepts

Average percentage of information recalled

Interval in months between completion of psychology class
and memory test for concepts and names

(b)

FIGURE 6.13 (a) The Famous Ebbinghaus Forgetting Curve

Ebbinghaus's research demonstrated the basic pattern of forgetting: relatively rapid loss of some information, followed by stable memories of the remaining information.

(Adapted from Ebbinghaus, 1885/1987.)

(b) Forgetting Information Learned in a Psychology Class

Most of the information that the students forgot was lost during the first several months immediately following the class, followed by a ten-year period during which the memories for the remaining information showed little loss. Notice that the curve closely parallels the shape of the Ebbinghaus forgetting curve.

(Adapted from Conway & others, 1991.)

Once the nonsense syllables were learned, Ebbinghaus tested his recall of them after varying amounts of time, ranging from 20 minutes to 31 days. He plotted his results in the now-famous Ebbinghaus *forgetting curve,* shown in the left graph in Figure 6.13.

The Ebbinghaus forgetting curve reveals two distinct patterns in the relationship between forgetting and the passage of time. First, much of what we forget is lost relatively soon after we originally learn it. How quickly we forget material depends on several factors, such as how well the material was encoded in the first place, how deeply it was processed, and how often it was rehearsed.

In general, if you learn something in a matter of minutes on just one occasion, most forgetting will occur very soon after the original learning—also in a matter of minutes. However, if you spend many sessions over weeks or months encoding new information into memory, the period of most rapid forgetting will be the first several months after such learning.

The basic pattern of Ebbinghaus's forgetting curve has been demonstrated using a wide variety of learning materials. For example, a similar pattern emerged when researchers measured the retention of psychology concepts from three months to over ten years after students took a psychology course (Conway & others, 1991). Memory for names and concepts learned in the course declined very rapidly over the first several months, as shown in the right graph in Figure 6.13.

Second, the Ebbinghaus forgetting curve shows that the amount of forgetting eventually levels off. As you can see in Figure 6.13, there's very little difference between how much Ebbinghaus forgot eight hours later and a month later. The information that is *not* quickly forgotten seems to be remarkably stable in memory over long periods of time. This same pattern is also evident in the study of former psychology students. The amount of forgotten psychology information leveled off after about three years, then remained essentially the same for the next seven years (Conway & others, 1991).

Ebbinghaus was a pioneer in the study of memory. His major contribution was to identify the basic pattern of forgetting: rapid forgetting of some information relatively soon after the original learning, followed by stability of the memories that remain.

Factors That Influence Forgetting

Why do we forget? Research on forgetting, both in the laboratory and in everyday life, has identified four potential causes of forgetting: encoding failure, interference, motivated forgetting, and decay. Let's consider how each of these causes can help explain instances of forgetting.

Encoding Failure: It Never Got to Long-Term Memory

You know what a penny looks like, right? Without rummaging through your loose change, look at each drawing in Figure 6.14, then circle the one that accurately depicts the details of a penny. How confident are you in your answer? Now, check your answer against a real penny. Was your answer correct?

When this task was presented to subjects in one study, less than half of them picked the correct drawing (Nickerson & Adams, 1982). The explanation: Unless you're a coin collector, you've probably never really looked carefully at a penny. Even though you've handled thousands of pennies, you've only encoded the most general and important details about a penny—like its color, size, and texture—into your long-term memory.

As this simple demonstration illustrates, one of the most common reasons for forgetting is that we never *encoded* the information into long-term memory in the first place. This phenomenon is called **encoding failure.** Encoding failure explains why you forget where you put your car keys or a person's name five minutes

FIGURE 6.14 Test for Memory of Details of a Common Object
Which of these drawings is an accurate picture of a real penny?

after meeting him. The information momentarily entered your short-term memory, but it was never encoded into long-term memory. As we discussed earlier, information that is not transferred from short-term memory to long-term memory lasts up to about 30 seconds, then evaporates. (You *do* remember that, don't you?) Although we may notice important details, the memory of those details will be fleeting if we don't quickly make a conscious effort to store it.

Interference Theory: Memories Interfering with Memories

A second reason for forgetting is that memories can interfere with one another. According to the **interference theory** of forgetting, forgetting is caused by one memory competing with or replacing another memory. Probably the most critical influence on whether one memory will create interference with another memory is the similarity of the information. Memory researchers have repeatedly demonstrated that the more similar the information is in two memories, the more likely it is that interference will be produced (Ashcraft, 1994).

There are two basic types of interference. **Retroactive interference** occurs when a *new* memory (your new phone number) interferes with remembering an *old* memory (your old phone number). Retroactive interference can also help explain how misinformation can contribute to the distortions that sometimes occur in eyewitness memories. After the original memory (being robbed), the witness is given inaccurate information that forms a new memory (the robber might be a priest). The new memory then interferes with the old memory, causing the forgetting of details or distortions of the old memory (Riccio & others, 1994). Thus, the misinformation effect that we discussed earlier can be a form of retroactive interference (Ashcraft, 1994).

encoding failure
The inability to recall specific information because of insufficient encoding for storage in long-term memory.

interference theory
The theory that forgetting is caused by one memory competing with or replacing another.

retroactive interference
Forgetting in which a new memory interferes with remembering an old memory.

proactive interference
Forgetting in which an old memory interferes with remembering a new memory.

motivated forgetting
The theory that forgetting occurs because an undesired memory is held back from awareness.

suppression
Motivated forgetting that occurs consciously.

repression
Motivated forgetting that occurs unconsciously.

Proactive interference is the opposite of retroactive interference. It occurs when an *old* memory interferes with a *new* memory. This is a relatively common experience. For example, proactive interference can occur when you get a new car or borrow someone else's car. You want to switch on the headlights, but you keep turning on the windshield wipers. The old memory (the switch's location in your car) interferes with the more recent memory (the switch's location in the new car). A rather embarrassing example of proactive interference occurs when you refer to your current partner by a previous partner's name. Such momentary memory glitches seem to occur spontaneously, often in the thralls of passion or anger.

Motivated Forgetting

Motivated forgetting refers to the idea that we forget because we are motivated to forget, usually because a memory is unpleasant or disturbing. In one form of motivated forgetting, called **suppression,** a person makes a deliberate, conscious effort to forget information. Although the person remains aware that a particular event did occur, he or she consciously chooses not to think about it (Loftus & Ketcham, 1994). In effect, the goal is to "put it out of your mind." However, research is mixed on whether it's really possible to deliberately forget information (H. Johnson, 1994; Wegner, 1989).

Another form of motivated forgetting is much more controversial. **Repression** is motivated forgetting that occurs *unconsciously*. When repression occurs, all awareness of an event or experience is blocked from conscious awareness. Thus, repression is fundamentally different from suppression, in which people know that a particular event happened but intentionally avoid thinking about it (Ceci & Loftus, 1994). As we'll discuss in greater detail in Chapters 11 and 15, the idea of repression is the cornerstone of Sigmund Freud's famous psychotherapy called *psychoanalysis.*

Freud (1904/1965) believed that psychologically threatening feelings and traumatic events, especially ones that occurred during childhood, become repressed. Even though such memories are blocked and unavailable to consciousness, the repressed memories continue to unconsciously influence the person's behavior and personality, often in maladaptive or unhealthy ways.

Among clinical psychologists who work with seriously disturbed people, the notion that a person's behavior can be influenced by repressed memories is widely, but certainly not universally, accepted (Yapko, 1994a, 1994b). Among the general public, many people believe that we are capable of repressing memories of unpleasant events (Loftus & others, 1994). However, trying to scientifically study the influence of memories that a person does *not* remember is tricky, if not impossible (Loftus, 1993b).

Today, much remains unknown about repression, and the topic is very controversial (Yapko, 1994b; Erdelyi, 1993). At one extreme are many psychologists who do not believe that true repression ever occurs (Holmes, 1990). At the other extreme are psychologists who are convinced that repressed memories are at the root of many psychological problems, particularly repressed memories of childhood sexual abuse (Briere & Conte, 1993). In the middle are memory researchers who agree that extreme emotion can disrupt memory, yet believe that the evidence for repression is far from conclusive (see Baddeley, 1990; Loftus, 1993b; Yapko, 1994b).

In the past several years, a type of psychotherapy that focuses on the recovery of repressed memories of sexual abuse has become widespread (Pendergrast, 1995). This therapy has led to a heated controversy: Are the "recovered" memories true memories, or have they been inadvertently created by the therapist's suggestions? In Critical Thinking Box 6.2, "Recovering 'Repressed' Memories of Childhood Sexual Abuse," we explore this controversy.

DOONESBURY

CRITICAL THINKING 6.2

Recovering "Repressed" Memories of Childhood Sexual Abuse

Sexual abuse of children is a serious problem in our society. It is estimated that approximately 25 percent of all girls and about 10 percent of all boys have been sexually abused (Zgourides, 1996). Sexually abusive acts range from inappropriate touching to vaginal, oral, or anal penetration. Every year, approximately 45,000 cases of childhood sexual abuse are reported to the authorities (Nevid & others, 1995). However, that number may only be the tip of the iceberg. Of adults who remember being sexually abused as a child, only about one out of eight reported the incident to authorities (Janus & Janus, 1993). Without question, the physical and sexual abuse of children can contribute to psychological problems in adulthood (Wenar, 1994; Brewin & others, 1993).

In recent years, many psychotherapists, counselors, social workers, and other mental health workers have embraced a new form of treatment, called *recovery therapy, trauma therapy,* or *repressed memory therapy.* Recovery therapy assumes that most adult "survivors" of childhood sexual abuse have completely repressed all memories of the sexual abuse, although it may have gone on for years and involved multiple family members. Because they are "in denial," these adults consciously remember their childhood as being relatively uneventful—until they enter therapy.

Although all memories of the abuse are blocked, recovery therapists claim that the repressed memories cause a wide range of psychological problems. Symptoms of repressed childhood sexual abuse range from eating disorders, substance abuse, and sexual problems to headaches, anxiety, lack of motivation, relationship problems, and career problems (see Pendergrast, 1995).

The goal of repressed memory therapy is to help adults "recover" their memories of childhood sexual abuse that have presumably been repressed from conscious awareness. As they do so, they can begin "the healing process" of working through the anger and other intense emotions that are related to these repressed memories (Bass & Davis, 1994).

The Controversy: Methods Used to "Recover" Repressed Memories

Repressed memory therapy is at the center of what has become a highly publicized and emotionally charged controversy. At the heart of this controversy are the methods that are used to help people "unblock" or "recover" repressed memories. Repressed memory therapists routinely use hypnosis, automatic writing, guided imagery visualization, and other highly suggestive techniques (Pendergrast, 1995; Yapko, 1994b). For example, recovery therapist Wendy Maltz (1991) advises patients who are unable to remember being sexually abused during childhood to do the following:

> . . . *Spend time imagining that you were sexually abused, without worrying about accuracy, proving anything, or having your ideas make sense. As you give rein to your imagination, let your intuition guide your thoughts.*

Through the use of hypnosis and other highly suggestive techniques, vivid memories of childhood sexual abuse can supposedly be recovered and brought to conscious awareness. In extreme cases, patients have even recovered repressed memories of years of ritual satanic abuse involving secret cults practicing infanticide (the murder of babies), torture, and ritual murder (Sakheim & Devine, 1994).

Repressed memory therapists insist that the recovered memories, however farfetched, are authentic (see Pendergrast, 1995; Loftus & Ketcham, 1994). As evidence of the credibility of the memories, they cite the intense emotional pain experienced by patients, the vividness of the recall, and the fact that thousands of survivors describe similar stories of hidden, repeated abuse going on for years while their families outwardly led normal lives (Bass & Davis, 1994). No one, the repressed memory therapists claim, could invent such vivid, emotional stories.

When patients become convinced of the validity of their memories, they often confront their parents and other family members with detailed accusa-

tions of the abuse. When the accusations are vehemently denied, extreme ruptures in family relationships often result. Families are shattered, and sometimes legal action is taken against the accused family members (Pendergrast, 1995). To date, hundreds of civil and criminal cases have been filed based on the retrieved memories of child abuse. And some of the accused have been sentenced to prison solely on the basis of the evidence of recovered memories (Ofshe & Watters, 1994).

The Critical Issue: Recovered Memories or False Memories?

Many psychologists, including many psychotherapists, are very skeptical of the techniques used in repressed memory therapy. These critics contend that many of the supposedly "recovered" memories are actually *false memories* produced by the suggestions of well-intentioned but misguided therapists (Ofshe & Watters, 1994).

Critics note that in documented cases of trauma, most survivors are troubled by the *opposite* problem—they cannot forget their traumatic memories (Pendergrast, 1995; Yapko, 1994b). Rather than being unable to remember the traumatic experiences, the person suffers from recurring flashbacks, intrusive thoughts and memories of the trauma, and nightmares (Loftus & Ketcham, 1994; Loftus, 1993b).

The issue of repression in general is also controversial. Although psychologists generally accept the notion that repression can occur, there are important qualifications to that statement (Schacter, 1995b). For example, it is relatively common for a person to be unable to remember *some* of the specific details of a traumatic event (Ofshe & Watters, 1994; Loftus, 1993b). The person who is injured in an automobile accident may be unable to remember the actual collision. The woman who is brutally raped may remember the events leading up to and following the attack, but not specific details of the rape itself.

Thus, people might experience amnesia for a single traumatic incident or the events surrounding the incident (Schacter, 1995b). However, memory researchers as a whole are extremely

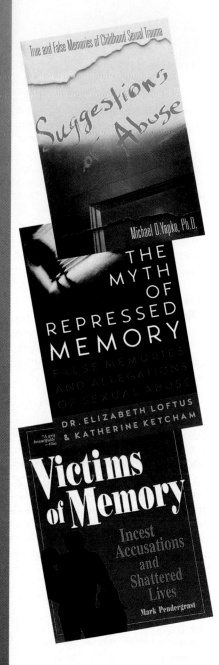

As we've seen in this chapter, compelling evidence exists to support the power of suggestion and misinformation in the creation of vivid but false memories. A fascinating experiment by memory researchers Maryanne Garry and Elizabeth Loftus (1994) demonstrated how easily false memories of a mildly traumatic childhood event could be created in some adults.

Each volunteer suggested to another family member that he or she had been lost in a shopping mall at the age of five. The critical issue was whether the other family member would create false memories to support this inaccurate information. The results? Vivid false memories of being lost in a shopping mall were confidently "remembered" by 24 men and women, ages eighteen to sixty-three (Garry & Loftus, 1994).

Advocates of repressed memory therapy have been quick to respond to the results of the shopping mall study. In particular, they stress that there is little parallel between being lost in a shopping mall and the extreme trauma that can accompany childhood sexual abuse (see Bass & Davis, 1994; Loftus & Ketcham, 1994).

What Conclusions Can Be Drawn?

There is no question that physical and sexual abuse of children occurs, and that it can contribute to psychological problems in adulthood (Wenar, 1994). And many psychologists believe it is possible for childhood memories of abuse to become repressed, only to surface many years later in adulthood (see Yapko, 1994a). Nevertheless, it's clear that repressed memories that have been recovered in psychotherapy need to be regarded with caution. Here are some key points to remember in weighing such claims:

First, having confidence in a memory is no guarantee that a memory is accurate. False or fabricated memories can seem just as detailed, vivid, and real as accurate ones. As you've seen in this chapter, the ease with which the details of memories can be distorted is disturbing. Consequently, the use of highly suggestive techniques to "recover" abuse memories raises serious concerns about the accuracy of such memories.

Second, keep in mind that every act of remembering involves reconstructing a memory. The human memory system does not function like a video camera, perfectly preserving the details of an experience. Remembering an experience is not like popping a videotape into your VCR. As we saw when we looked at flashbulb memories, memories can change over time. Without our awareness, memories grow and evolve, sometimes in unexpected ways.

In the last few years, three major books have been published that describe the problems inherent in repressed memory therapy (see the accompanying photographs). Many articles criticizing repressed memory therapy have also appeared in both professional journals and the popular media. These critical attacks have helped sensitize many therapists to the possibility of inadvertently creating false memories. Psychotherapists are also developing guidelines to help mental health professionals avoid inadvertently creating false memories (Byrd, 1994; Gold & others, 1994; Morokoff, 1994). Finally, some leaders of the incest-survivor recovery movement have significantly toned down their more extreme claims.

Clinical psychologist Michael Yapko (1994b) has eloquently summarized the concerns of many mental health professionals about this issue:

> I am deeply concerned that therapy clients will be led to believe destructive things that are untrue, to recall memories of terrible things that never actually happened, to jump to conclusions that are not warranted, and to destroy the lives of innocent people—including their own—in the process.
>
> I am all too aware that the abuse of children is a huge problem growing to ever more sickening proportions. I am also aware that people can be led to believe things that are not true. Abuse happens, but so do false accusations.
>
> The important task of mental health professionals is to sort out which is which with a considerably greater degree of responsibility than we have demonstrated thus far. I hope we are up to the challenge, because the integrity of families and individuals rests on the outcome.

skeptical that anyone could repress all memories of *repeated* incidents of abuse, especially when they stretch over a period of several years (see Pendergrast, 1995; Loftus & Ketcham, 1994).

Memory experts also have many objections to the use of hypnosis and other highly suggestive techniques to "recover" repressed memories. As discussed in Chapter 4, hypnosis has not been shown to increase the accuracy of memories, including memories of being "regressed" back to early childhood (Kihlstrom & Barnhardt, 1993; Nash, 1987; Spanos, 1987–1988). However, hypnosis does increase a person's *confidence* in the memories that are recalled.

Decay Theory

Earlier in the chapter we noted that information in sensory memory and short-term memory quickly fades, or *decays,* if it is not transferred to long-term memory. Can the same thing happen with information that *is* stored in long-term memory?

According to **decay theory,** we forget memories because we don't use them and they fade away over time as a matter of normal brain processes. The idea is that when a new memory is formed, it creates a *memory trace*—a distinct change in brain structure or chemistry. Through disuse over time, the normal metabolic processes of the brain are thought to erode the memory trace. The gradual fading of memories, then, would be similar to the fading of letters on billboards or newsprint exposed to environmental elements, like sunlight.

Like motivated forgetting, decay theory makes a good deal of sense intuitively. However, most memory researchers today do not think that long-term memories simply fade or "decay" from disuse (Ellis & Hunt, 1993a; Solso, 1991). Why? Because too much evidence contradicts the basic assumptions of decay theory.

For example, many studies have shown that information can be remembered for decades after it was originally learned, even though it has not been rehearsed or recalled since the original memory was formed (Bahrick & Hall, 1991; Bahrick & Phelps, 1987). As we discussed earlier, the ability to access memories is strongly influenced by the kinds of retrieval cues that are provided when memory is tested (Slamecka, 1992). If the memory trace simply decayed over time, the presentation of potent retrieval cues should have no effect on the retrieval of information or events experienced long ago—but, in fact, they do.

Although researchers have not been able to muster compelling evidence for decay theory, there has been enormous interest in trying to explain the physiological basis of memory and forgetting. In the final section of this chapter, we'll look at how memories seem to be created and stored in the brain.

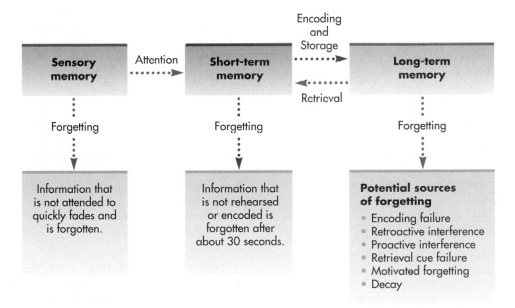

decay theory
The view that forgetting is due to normal metabolic processes that occur in the brain over time.

FIGURE 6.15 Forgetting in the Memory System Model

Identifying Influences on Forgetting

Pick one of the following explanations for each of the examples of forgetting given below: A = encoding failure, B = suppression, C = repression, D = retroactive interference, E = proactive interference.

1. After studying chemistry all afternoon, Brittany is having trouble remembering details of the biology lecture she heard that morning. _____

2. At Drew's ten-year high school reunion, some of his old high school buddies were laughing about an embarrassing incident that happened to Drew at the senior prom. Drew could not remember the incident. _____

3. When asked, you are not able to say which letter of the alphabet is missing from your telephone keyboard. _____

4. Professor Ivanovich has many vivid memories of her students from last semester and can recall most of their names. As a result, she is having problems remembering her new students' names this semester. _____

5. Alayna did very poorly on her statistics midterm exam; now, while she is studying for the final, she makes a deliberate effort not to even think about her low midterm score. _____

The Search for the Biological Basis of Memory

Early researchers believed that memory is associated with physical changes in the brain, but these changes have only recently begun to be discovered. How are memories both "localized" and "distributed"? How do neurons change when a memory is formed?

Does the name *Ivan Pavlov* ring a bell? We hope so. As you should recall from Chapter 5, Pavlov was the Russian physiologist who classically conditioned dogs to salivate to the sound of a bell and other neutral stimuli. Without question, learning and memory are intimately connected. Learning an adaptive response depends on our ability to form new memories in which we associate environmental stimuli, behaviors, and consequences.

Pavlov (1927/1960) believed that the memory involved in learning a classically conditioned response would ultimately be explained as a matter of changes in the brain. However, Pavlov only speculated about the kinds of brain changes that would produce the memories needed for classical conditioning to occur. Other researchers would take up the search for the physical changes that were associated with learning and memory. In this section, we look at some of the key discoveries that have been made in trying to understand the biological basis of memory.

The Search for the Elusive Memory Trace

It was an American physiological psychologist named **Karl Lashley** (1890–1958) who set out to find evidence for Pavlov's speculations (Thompson, 1994). Beginning in the 1920s, Lashley began the search for the **memory trace,** or *engram*—the brain changes associated with the formation of a long-term memory. Guiding Lashley's research was his belief that memory is *localized,* meaning that a particular memory is stored in a specific brain area.

memory trace
The brain changes associated with a particular stored memory.

Lashley searched for the specific location of the memory that a rat forms for running a maze. Lashley (1929) suspected that the specific memory was localized at a specific site in the *cerebral cortex,* the outermost covering of the brain that contains the most sophisticated brain areas. Once a rat had learned to run the maze, Lashley surgically removed tiny portions of the rat's cortex. After the rat recovered, Lashley tested the rat in the maze again. Obviously, if the rat could still run the maze, then the portion of the brain removed did not contain the memory.

Over the course of thirty years, Lashley systematically removed different sections of the cortex in trained rats. The result of Lashley's painstaking research? No matter which part of the cortex he removed, the rats were still able to run the maze (Lashley, 1929, 1950). At the end of his professional career, Karl Lashley concluded that memories are not localized in specific locations, but instead are *distributed,* or stored throughout the brain.

Lashley was wrong, but not completely wrong. Some memories *do* seem to be localized at specific spots in the brain. Some twenty years after Lashley's death, psychologist **Richard F. Thompson** (b. 1930) and his colleagues resumed the search for the location of the memory trace that would confirm Pavlov's speculations. Thompson classically conditioned rabbits to perform a very simple behavior—an eyeblink. By pairing a tone with a puff of air to the rabbit's eye, he classically conditioned the rabbit to blink reflexively in response to the tone alone (Thompson, 1994, 1993).

Thompson discovered that after a rabbit learned this simple behavior, there was a change in the brain activity in a small area of the rabbit's *cerebellum,* a lower brain structure involved in physical movements. When this tiny area of the cerebellum was removed, the rabbit's memory of the learned response disappeared. It no longer blinked at the sound of the tone. However, the puff of air still caused the rabbit to blink reflexively, so the reflex itself had not been destroyed.

Thompson and his colleagues had confirmed Pavlov's speculations: The long-term memory trace of the classically conditioned eyeblink was formed and stored in a very localized region of the cerebellum. So why had Karl Lashley failed? Unlike Thompson, Lashley was working with a relatively complex behavior. Running a maze involves the use of several senses, including vision, smell, and touch. In comparison, Thompson's rabbits learned a very simple reflexive behavior—a classically conditioned eyeblink.

Thus, part of the reason Lashley failed to find a specific location for a rat's memory of a maze was that the memory was not a single memory. Instead, the rat had developed a complex set of *interrelated memories* involving information from multiple senses. These interrelated memories were processed and stored in different brain areas. The result was that the rat's memories were *distributed* and stored across multiple brain locations. Hence, no matter which small brain area Lashley removed, the rat could still run the maze. So Lashley seems to have been right in suggesting that some memories are distributed throughout the brain.

When you combine the findings of Lashley and Thompson, they suggest that memories have the potential to be *both localized and distributed* (Squire, 1987). Very simple memories may be localized in a specific area, while more complex memories seem to be distributed throughout the brain. A complex memory involves clusters of information, and each part of the memory may be stored in the brain area that originally processed the information (Squire & Butters, 1992).

More recently, researchers have used PET scans to confirm that many kinds of memories are distributed in the human brain. As you can see in the accompanying photograph, when we are performing a relatively complex memory task, multiple brain regions are activated—evidence of the distribution of memories involved in complex tasks (Squire & others, 1992).

Brain Activity During a Memory Task This PET scan shows a left-to-right cross section of the brain. During a memory task, multiple brain areas are activated. The greatest activity occurs in the hippocampus, the white area that is ringed in red, yellow, green, and blue.

The Role of Neurons in Long-Term Memory

What exactly is it that is localized or distributed? Memories don't just float around in your brain. The notion of a memory trace suggests that some change must occur in the workings of the brain when a new long-term memory is stored. Logically, two possible changes could occur. First, the *functioning* of the neurons in the brain could somehow change. Second, the *structure* of the neurons could somehow change.

Given those two possibilities, the challenge for memory researchers has been to identify the specific neurons involved in a given memory, a task that is virtually impossible with the human brain because of its enormous complexity. What would be required is a creature with a limited number of neurons that is also capable of learning new memories.

Enter *Aplysia,* a gentle, seaweed-munching sea snail that resides off the California coast. The study of *Aplysia* in the last thirty years has given memory researchers important clues to the brain changes involved in memory (Kandel & Hawkins, 1993; Bailey, 1992). *Aplysia* has only about 20,000 good-sized neurons. Thus, memory researchers like Eric Kandel (1995d) at Columbia University have been able to study the neuronal changes that occur when *Aplysia* forms a new memory for a simple classically conditioned response.

If you give *Aplysia* a gentle squirt with a WaterPik, followed by a mild electric shock to its tail, the snail reflexively withdraws its gill flap. When the process is repeated several times, *Aplysia* wises up and acquires a new memory of a classically conditioned response—it withdraws its gill when squirted with the WaterPik alone. This learned gill-withdrawal reflex seems to involve a circuit of just three neurons: one that detects the water squirt, one that detects the tail shock, and one that signals the gill-withdrawal reflex (see Figure 6.16).

When *Aplysia* acquires this new memory through repeated training trials, significant changes occur in the three-neuron circuit (Kandel, 1995d).

Aplysia, the Super-Snail of Memory Research Eric Kandel holds *Aplysia,* the sea snail that is used to study how neurons change when simple behaviors are learned and remembered.

First, the *function* of the neurons is altered; there is an increase in the amount of the neurotransmitters produced by the neurons. Second, the *structure* of the snail's neurons changes. The number of interconnecting branches between the neurons increases, along with the number of synapses or communication points on each branch. These changes allow the neurons involved in the particular memory circuit to communicate more easily.

The same kinds of brain changes have been observed in more sophisticated mammals. Chicks, rats, and rabbits also show structural and functional neuron changes associated with new learning experiences and memories (Rosenzweig, 1996; Greenough, 1992; Alkon, 1989). And, as you may recall from the Chapter 2 Application, "Pumping Neurons: Keeping Your Brain in Shape," there is indirect evidence that the same kinds of changes also occur in humans (Jacobs & others, 1993; Stern & others, 1994, 1992).

In terms of our understanding of the memory trace, what do these findings suggest? Although there are vast differences between a simple creature such as *Aplysia* and the enormous complexity of the human brain, some tentative generalizations are possible. Forming a memory seems to produce distinct functional and structural changes in specific neurons. These changes create a memory circuit. Each time the memory is recalled, the neurons in this circuit are activated. As the structural and functional changes in the neurons strengthen the communication links in this circuit, the memory becomes established as a long-term memory (Rose, 1993; Lynch, 1986).

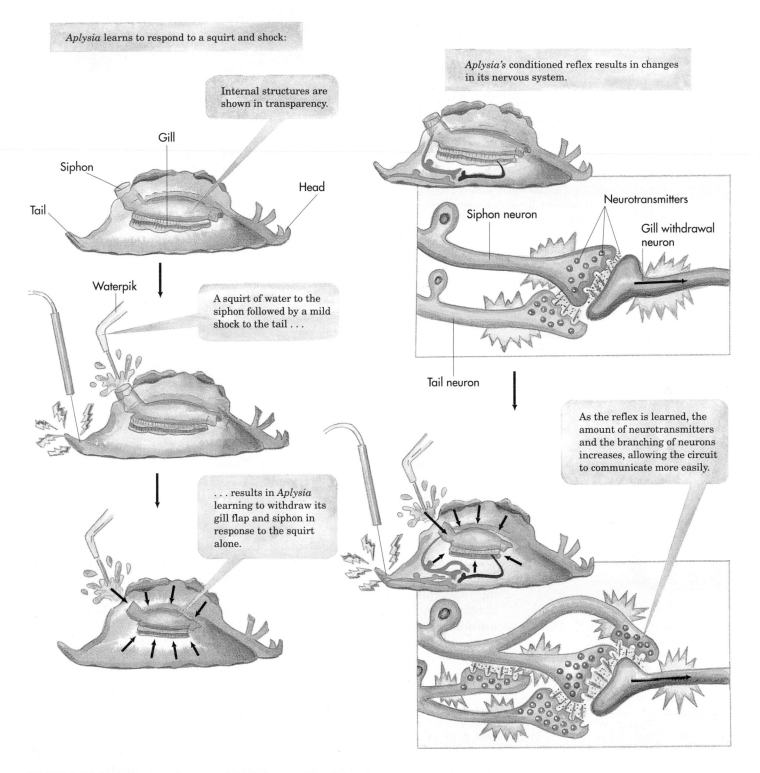

Aplysia learns to respond to a squirt and shock:

Internal structures are shown in transparency.

Gill

Siphon

Tail

Head

Waterpik

A squirt of water to the siphon followed by a mild shock to the tail . . .

. . . results in *Aplysia* learning to withdraw its gill flap and siphon in response to the squirt alone.

Aplysia's conditioned reflex results in changes in its nervous system.

Siphon neuron

Neurotransmitters

Gill withdrawal neuron

Tail neuron

As the reflex is learned, the amount of neurotransmitters and the branching of neurons increases, allowing the circuit to communicate more easily.

FIGURE 6.16 How Neurons Change as Aplysia Forms a New Memory
When *Aplysia* is repeatedly squirted with water, and each squirt is followed by a mild shock to its tail, the snail learns to withdraw its gill flap if squirted with the water alone. Three neurons are involved in acquiring this conditioned reflex: a sensory neuron in the tail that detects the shock; a sensory neuron that detects the squirt of water; and a motor neuron that signals the gill-withdrawal reflex. Conditioning leads to structural and functional changes in the three neurons involved in the memory circuit.

Remembering Famous Names

Match each of the following names with one of the descriptions below: Herman Ebbinghaus, Richard F. Thompson, George Sperling, Elizabeth Loftus, Karl Lashley.

1. The psychologist who identified the duration of visual sensory memory _____

2. One of the most widely recognized experts on memory distortions, eyewitness testimony, and false memories _____

3. The psychologist who was one of the first people to scientifically study memory and forgetting _____

4. The physiological psychologist who tried but failed to find the specific location of individual memories in the brain _____

5. The physiological psychologist who succeeded in identifying the specific brain location of a simple classically conditioned response _____

Processing Memories in the Brain:
Clues from Amnesia

Case studies of people with amnesia have provided important insights into the brain structures involved in memory. What has been learned from cases of retrograde and anterograde amnesia? What is meant by memory consolidation? What roles do the hippocampus and amygdala seem to play in normal memory?

The complexity and inaccessibility of the human brain has made it virtually impossible to study the role of individual neurons in human memory. However, memory researchers have been able to study the role of specific brain structures in processing memories. Much of this research has involved studying individuals who have sustained brain injury or had part of their brain surgically removed for medical reasons. Often, such individuals experience **amnesia,** or severe memory loss (Butters & Delis, 1995). By relating the type and extent of amnesia to the specific brain areas that have been damaged, researchers have uncovered clues as to how the human brain processes memories.

Retrograde Amnesia: The Consolidation of Memories

One type of amnesia is **retrograde amnesia.** People who suffer from retrograde amnesia are unable to remember some or all of their past, especially episodic memories for recent events. Retrograde amnesia often results from a blow to the head. Boxers sometimes suffer such memory losses after years of fighting. Head injuries from automobile and motorcycle accidents are another common cause of retrograde amnesia (Levin & others, 1984).

The most important clue that retrograde amnesia has provided about the brain processes of memory has to do with which memories are most often lost. Typically, memories of the events that immediately preceded the injury are completely lost, as in the case of accident victims who cannot remember details about what led up to the accident.

Apparently, establishing a long-term memory is like creating a cement wall—it needs time to "set" before it becomes permanent. This process of "set-

amnesia
(am-NEE-zha) Severe memory loss.

retrograde amnesia
Loss of memory, especially for episodic information.

Disrupting the Consolidation of Memories
A football player suffers a concussion during a game and is carried off the field. Football players who were questioned immediately after their injury could remember how they were injured and the name of the play just performed. But if questioned thirty minutes later for the same information, they could not. Because the head injury had disrupted the memory consolidation process, the memories were permanently lost (Yarnell & Lynch, 1970).

memory consolidation
The gradual, physical process of converting new long-term memories to stable, enduring long-term memory codes.

anterograde amnesia
Loss of memory caused by the inability to store new memories.

ting" a new memory permanently in the brain is called memory consolidation. More specifically, **memory consolidation** is the gradual, physical process of converting new long-term memories to stable, enduring memory codes. If memory consolidation is disrupted before the process is complete, a long-term memory is vulnerable and may be lost. In humans, memory consolidation can be disrupted by brain trauma, such as a sudden blow, concussion, electric shock, or encephalitis (Squire & Butters, 1992; Squire, 1987).

Anterograde Amnesia: The Case of H.M.

Another form of amnesia is **anterograde amnesia**—the inability to form new memories. The most famous case of anterograde amnesia involves a man who is known only by the initials H.M. to protect his identity. In 1953, H.M. was twenty-seven years old and had a history of untreatable epileptic seizures. H.M.'s doctors located the brain area where the seizures seemed to originate. In desperation, they surgically removed portions of the temporal lobe on each side of H.M.'s brain, including the brain structure called the *hippocampus* (Ogden & Corkin, 1991).

After the surgery the frequency and severity of H.M.'s seizures were greatly reduced. However, it was quickly discovered that the surgery had produced another effect: the destruction of H.M.'s ability to form new memories of events and information. Although intended to treat H.M.'s seizures, the surgery dramatically revealed the role of the hippocampus in forming new memories.

Canadian psychologist Brena Milner (1965, 1970) has studied H.M. extensively over the last forty years. If you were to meet H.M. today, you could carry on a conversation with him and he would appear normal enough. H.M. has a good vocabulary, normal language skills, and above-average intelligence. But he lives in the eternal present. If you left his room and returned five minutes later, he wouldn't remember having seen you before. In fact, he must be reintroduced to his doctors each time he sees them, even though some of them have been treating him for years (Ogden & Corkin, 1991).

For the most part, H.M.'s short-term memory seems to work just fine. If he actively repeats or rehearses information in short-term memory, he can hold information in short-term memory for an hour or more. However, he forgets the information if he switches his attention to something else and stops rehearsing it (Ogden & Corkin, 1991). H.M.'s long-term memory is also relatively intact. He can retrieve long-term memories from before the time he was sixteen years old, when the severe epileptic seizures began.

H.M.'s case suggests that the hippocampus is not involved in most short-term memory tasks or in the storage and retrieval of long-term memories. The critical role played by the hippocampus seems to be the *encoding* of new memories for events and information and the *transfer* of them from short-term to long-term memory (Squire & Knowlton, 1995). When the same brain sections are surgically removed in monkeys, they show the same kinds of massive anterograde amnesia that H.M. displays (Zola-Morgan & Squire, 1993).

However, H.M. can form new long-term *procedural* memories, such as the procedural memories involved in learning a new skill. For example, when H.M. was given the same logical puzzle to solve several days in a row, he was able to solve it in less time each day, showing that he remembered the procedures involved to some degree. But, of course, he could not remember having learned how to do it, or having solved the puzzle before (Cohen, 1984). What this shows is that the hippocampus is critical in forming new episodic memories, but not new procedural memories (Zola-Morgan & Squire, 1992). For more on the role of the hippocampus in episodic memories, see In Focus Box 6.3, "Infantile Amnesia and the Hippocampus."

IN FOCUS 6.3

Infantile Amnesia and the Hippocampus

What's your very first memory? Usually, our earliest memories are for events that took place between the ages of three and five (Bruhn, 1990; Sheingold & Tenney, 1982). Some researchers have found evidence for first memories as early as age two to three, especially for distinct events such as the birth of a sibling or a hospitalization (Usher & Neisser, 1993). And occasionally, adults report early memories from ages as young as one year. However, such recollections usually turn out to be a matter of memory reconstruction. In other words, the person has so often heard a story about an incident involving her as an infant or a toddler, she *thinks* she can remember it (Loftus, 1993a).

As a general rule, when we try to remember events from our first few years of life, we draw a complete blank. This loss of memory for our experiences during infancy is called *infantile amnesia*. There are several different explanations for infantile amnesia, two of which we'll consider here (see Howe & Courage, 1993).

First, there is Sigmund Freud's (1904/1965) explanation of the "strange riddle" of infantile amnesia. Freud saw infantile amnesia as an important example of motivated forgetting. In Freud's (1940/1949) view, the experiences of infancy are repressed, banished from conscious memory, because the infant's sexual impulses and fantasies are too psychologically threatening to be consciously remembered.

One problem with Freud's explanation is that we don't just have amnesia for threatening or disturbing memories. Rather, we have amnesia for *all* memories, including pleasant experiences and commonplace events. And as you saw earlier in the chapter, the evidence for repressed memories is mixed at best. So although Freud's ideas are intriguing, memory researchers are not inclined to put much stock in Freud's explanation of infantile amnesia (Neisser, 1992).

A second, much more plausible explanation for infantile amnesia involves brain development (C. A. Nelson, 1995). In the developing infant, the hippocampus does not mature until about two years of age (Kalat, 1995; Nadel & Zola-Morgan, 1984). This suggests that the infant's hippocampus is simply not able to encode and store events and experiences in long-term memory. Other late-maturing brain structures, such as the cortex, may also play a role in memory development (C. A. Nelson, 1995; Goldman-Rakic, 1992).

Supporting the hippocampus explanation is the striking parallel between infant amnesia and the memory capabilities of adult anterograde amnesia victims with hippocampus damage, such as H.M. Both infants and adults with hippocampus damage lack the ability to encode and store new *episodic* memories—conscious recollections of events and information (Moscovitch, 1985; Schacter & Moscovitch, 1984).

However, victims of anterograde amnesia have not lost their ability to form new *procedural* memories. Even though they may not consciously recall the experiences involved in learning the new skill, they do show improvement in the skill with repeated practice. This suggests that new procedural memories are being formed even though new episodic memories of the learning experience itself are not encoded and stored.

In many respects, infant memory seems to correspond to the procedural memory system that remains intact in adults with hippocampus damage. The first few years of life involve learning many new skills, such as walking, talking, and feeding yourself. These skills are represented in the procedural memory system rather than the episodic memory system. Thus, it's very unlikely that you can recall your first steps or your first attempts to feed yourself with a spoon. However, you did get better at these skills as procedural memories were formed.

Infantile amnesia, then, may not reflect the *forgetting* of events from the first few years of life. Rather, the inability to remember explicit information may be due to the fact that the events were never effectively encoded and stored in the first place. As the critical brain structures necessary for episodic memory become more fully functional around the age of two to three, the very beginnings of episodic memory traces become solidified as long-term memories.

Another brain structure involved in processing memories is the *amygdala,* which is situated very close to the hippocampus (see Figure 6.17). The amygdala seems to be responsible for associating memories that involve different senses (see Aggleton, 1992). For example, when the amygdala is removed, monkeys seem to lose their ability to link different sensory memories associated with a familiar object. When they see a banana, they behave as if they can't recall how it smells or tastes.

Amygdala
Associates memories formed involving different senses; encodes emotional aspects of memories

Hippocampus
Encodes and transfers new memories to long-term memory

Cerebellum
Memories involving movement

FIGURE 6.17 Brain Structures Involved in Human Memory
In this midline cross-sectional view of the brain, you can see some of the key brain structures involved in encoding and storing memories.

The amygdala also seems to encode the emotional qualities associated with particular memories, such as fear or anger (LeDoux, 1994b; Davis, 1992). Normally, monkeys are afraid of snakes. But if the amygdala is damaged, a monkey loses its fear of snakes and other natural predators.

Although we've simplified many details, this brief section on the biological basis of memory gives you some idea of the promising leads that biopsychologists and other neuroscientists are pursuing. Neuroscientists are far from a comprehensive understanding of the brain mechanisms involved in memory. Nevertheless, enormous strides have been made in the last thirty years. Clearly, certain brain structures, most notably the hippocampus, are involved in the initial processing of episodic memories (Squire & Knowlton, 1995). Distinct structural and functional changes in circuits of neurons seem to be associated with enduring memories (Bailey, 1992; Greenough, 1992). Researchers are also making gains in understanding which neurotransmitters seem to be most involved in the memory process (Baudry & Davis, 1992).

The overall goal of such research is far from being purely academic. For example, progressive memory loss is the hallmark of *Alzheimer's disease*. *Dementia* is another condition that is characterized by numerous cognitive deficits, of which amnesia is the primary symptom. The prevalence of each of these conditions increases with advancing age (Butters & Delis, 1995). Through the efforts of memory researchers, combined with advances in technology, it may one day be possible to treat these conditions or at least minimize the devastating loss of human memory that accompanies them.

Summing Up: Memory

Human memory is at once both perfectly ordinary and quite extraordinary. With next to no mental effort, you form and recall countless memories as you go through daily life. As you've seen in this chapter, psychologists have made enormous progress in explaining how those memories are encoded, stored, retrieved, and forgotten.

Yet perhaps the most fascinating aspect of human memory is its fallibility. Memory is surprisingly susceptible to errors and distortions. Under some conditions, completely false memories can be experienced, like Elizabeth Loftus's memory of discovering her mother's body in the swimming pool. Such false memories can be so subjectively compelling that they feel like authentic memories.

Many mysteries of human memory remain, including exactly how memories are stored in and retrieved from the brain. Nevertheless, reliable ways to improve memory in everyday life have been discovered. In the chapter Application, "How to Make Those Memories Last," we provide several suggestions to enhance your memory for new information.

APPLICATION

How to Make Those Memories Last

Several strategies can be used to improve memory for important information. How can the principles discussed in this chapter be used to study more effectively?

None of us are immune to the pitfalls of forgetting. Fortunately, there are several very effective strategies to boost your memory for important information, whether it's textbook material or the location of that extra set of house keys. Based on the memory research, we've compiled ten effective techniques to enhance your memory.

1. Focus Your Attention

Problems in absorbing new information arise when distracting thoughts, background noise, and other interruptions sidetrack your attention. Television is one common culprit. When the television is on in the background, reading comprehension and other cognitive skills involved in the memory process drop significantly (Armstrong & Greenberg, 1990).

Rather than studying in front of the tube, locate a quiet study space that's free from distractions so you can focus your attention. If distracting thoughts are competing for your attention, start your study session by reading aloud part of what you need to study. Doing so can help you focus on the task rather than on your distracting thoughts (Hertel & Rude, 1991).

2. Commit the Necessary Time to Remember Information

There is a direct relationship between the amount of time you spend learning material and the length of time you remember it (Baddeley, 1990). In other words, the more time you spend learning material, the better you will understand it, and the longer you will remember it. So don't rely on skimming material the night before a test. Budget enough time to carefully read the assigned material. If you read material faster than you can comprehend it, you not only won't understand the material, you also won't remember it.

3. Space Your Study Sessions

Distributed practice means that you learn information over several sessions, which gives you time to mentally process and incorporate the information. Students who take the distributed-practice approach to learning retain significantly more information than students who use cramming, or *massed practice* (Baddeley, 1990). It's also been shown experimentally that sleep, particularly REM or dreaming sleep, helps consolidate new memories (Gokcebay & others, 1994; Smith & Lapp, 1994). All-night cram sessions just before an exam are one of the least effective ways to learn or memorize new material.

4. Organize the Information

We have a strong natural tendency to organize information in long-term memory into categories. Think about it this way: You organize your belongings so that you can find your socks when you need them, right? You very naturally do the same thing with your memories—you mentally organize information so that it can be retrieved more easily.

You can capitalize on this tendency by actively organizing information you want to remember. One way to accomplish this is by outlining chapters or your lecture notes (Reed, 1996). Use the chapter headings and subheadings as categories or, better yet, create your own categories. Under each category, list and describe the relevant terms, concepts, and ideas. Create additional subcategories if needed. This strategy can double the amount of information you can recall.

5. Elaborate the Material

Maintenance rehearsal, or simple repetition, is fine if all you want to do is maintain information in short-term memory. But once you stop repeating it, the information is usually gone in about 30 seconds. So, unless you're going to be tested in the next 30 seconds, forget maintenance rehearsal.

Instead, use elaborative rehearsal by looking for meaning in what you're studying. You've probably noticed that virtually every term or concept in this text is formally defined in just a sentence or two. But we also spend a paragraph or more explaining what the concept means. In order to remember the information you read, you have to do the same thing—engage in elaborative rehearsal and actively process the information for meaning.

How can you actively process information for meaning? Form memory associations by relating the material to what you already know. Try to come up with examples that relate to your own life. React to what you read by writing your comments or questions in the margin of the textbook. Create sentences that accurately use the concept or term.

6. Use Visual Imagery

Two memory codes are better than one (Paivio, 1986). Rather than just encoding the information verbally, use mental imagery. Much of the information in this text as well as other college texts easily lends itself to visual imagery. At the very least, use the text photographs and other illustrations to help you form visual memories of the information.

7. Explain It to a Friend

Memory research clearly supports the benefits of explaining new material out loud (Muth & others, 1988). After you read a section of material, stop. Summarize what you have read in your mind. Then, when you think you understand it, try to verbally explain the information to a friend or a family member. This strategy improves memory in three ways. First, it acts as a reality check to see if you understand what you think you've committed to memory. If you can't explain the information to someone else, you probably don't really understand it. Second, putting concepts and information in your own words is an effective form of elaborative rehearsal. And third, it's another way to rehearse the information.

8. Reduce Interference Within a Topic

Students sometimes complain that information or concepts in a textbook chapter are hard to remember because they are simply too similar. If you occasionally confuse related terms and concepts, it may be because you're experiencing *interference* in your memories for similar information.

To minimize memory interference for related information, first break the chapter into manageable sections, then learn the key information one section at a time. As you encounter new concepts, contrast them with previously learned concepts, looking for differences and similarities. By building distinct memories for important information as you progress through a topic, you're more likely to distinguish between concepts so they don't get confused in your memory. A simple way to make text information visually distinct is by using different-colored highlighters for different concepts.

9. Counteract the Serial Position Effect

The serial position effect is our tendency to remember information at the beginning and end of a sequence. To counteract it, spend extra time with the information that falls in the middle. Once you've initially mastered a sequence of material, start at a different point each time you review the information.

10. Use Contextual Cues to Jog Memories During a Test

Ideally, study in the setting where you're going to be tested. As we noted in the chapter, details of your physical surroundings can act as additional retrieval cues when you try to recall memories. If that's not possible, when you're taking a test and a specific memory gets blocked, imagine that your books and notes are in front of you and that you're sitting where you normally study. Simply imagining the surroundings where you learned the material can help jog those memories (S. M. Smith & others, 1978).

Summary Memory

Memory Processes and Stages: An Overview

- Memory refers to the mental processes that enable us to acquire, retain, and retrieve information. Key memory processes are encoding, storage, and retrieval.

- The stage model of memory describes human memory as the process of transferring information from one memory stage to another. The three stages of memory are sensory memory, short-term memory, and long-term memory. Short-term memory is also referred to as working memory.

Sensory Memory: Fleeting Impressions of Reality

- Sensory memory stores information about the environment for a very brief period. Information that we pay attention to is transferred from sensory memory to short-term memory; other information fades quickly.

- George Sperling discovered that visual sensory memory holds information for about half a second before the information fades.

- Although there is a separate sensory memory for each sense, visual and auditory sensory memory are the most thoroughly studied. Auditory sensory memory lasts slightly longer than visual sensory memory—up to a few seconds.

Short-Term, Working Memory: The Workshop of Consciousness

- Short-term memory provides temporary storage for information transferred from sensory memory and long-term memory that we are currently using in some conscious cognitive activity. Most information fades from short-term memory within about 30 seconds. Maintenance rehearsal can be used to keep information active in short-term memory.

- The capacity of short-term memory is limited to about seven items, plus or minus two. When the capacity of short-term memory is reached, new information will displace existing information. Chunking can be used to increase the amount of information held in short-term memory.

Long-Term Memory

- Long-term memory stores a limitless amount of information for extended periods of time.

- Encoding transforms information into a form that can be stored and retrieved later. The most effective encoding strategies involve elaborative rehearsal. The levels of processing framework suggests that information that is processed "deeply" will be encoded more effectively.

■ Long-term memory includes procedural, episodic, and semantic information. Information in long-term memory is both clustered and associated; thus, long-term memory is organized. The semantic network model is one description of how information is organized in long-term memory.

Retrieval: Getting Information from Long-Term Memory

■ Retrieval refers to the process of accessing information stored in long-term memory.

■ Retrieval cues are hints that help us retrieve stored memories. Sometimes, stored memories cannot be retrieved because of retrieval cue failure. Tip-of-the-tongue experiences are everyday examples of retrieval failure.

■ Retrieval can be tested using recall, cued recall, and recognition measures. The serial position effect is our tendency to remember best the first and last items in a series.

■ According to the encoding specificity principle, recreating aspects of the original learning conditions is one way to increase retrieval effectiveness. There are several different forms of the encoding specificity principle, including the context effect, state-dependent retrieval, mood-dependent retrieval, and mood congruence.

■ Memories that are highly unusual tend to be easier to retrieve from long-term memory. Although flashbulb memories can be extremely vivid, they seem to function like normal memories and are not always accurate.

Reconstructing Memories: Sources of Potential Errors

■ Because retrieval involves the reconstruction of memories, memory details can change. Memories can be distorted by schemas and other preexisting information that we have stored before acquiring a new memory. Schemas can also contribute to memory distortions when we learn new information that is inconsistent with previously learned information. Source confusion occurs when we either don't remember or misidentify the source of a memory.

■ There are many potential causes of inaccuracies in eyewitness testimony, including the misinformation effect, schema distortion, and source confusion.

■ Despite the potential for memories to become distorted, memory tends to be fairly accurate for the general gist of experiences. Meaningful or important details are least likely to be forgotten. Distorted or false memories can be just as vivid as accurate memories. Memories sometimes become distorted in psychologically beneficial ways.

Forgetting: You *Forgot* the Plane Tickets?!

■ Forgetting refers to the inability to recall information that was previously available. The general pattern of forgetting is reflected in the forgetting curve, which is based on the research of Herman Ebbinghaus.

■ Several factors can contribute to forgetting. Encoding failure is one important cause. According to interference theory, forgetting results from retroactive and proactive interference with other information. Motivated forgetting is the result of suppression and repression. Research support for repression is mixed. Decay theory is another explanation for forgetting, but it is contradicted by some of the findings of memory research.

The Search for the Biological Basis of Memory

■ Pavlov believed that learning and memory are associated with physical changes in the brain. Karl Lashley conducted extensive research searching for the memory trace, but finally concluded that memories are distributed rather than localized. Richard Thompson showed the physical changes that are associated with a simple conditioned reflex in rabbits. Today it is believed that memories are both localized and distributed. Complex memories involve interrelated changes among many different brain areas.

■ Eric Kandel showed that functional and structural changes in neurons are associated with acquiring a conditioned reflex in the sea snail *Aplysia*. These changes in the neurons create a memory circuit. Many researchers believe that similar changes occur in the human brain when memories are formed.

■ Case studies of people with amnesia have provided important insights into the brain structures involved in normal human memory. Amnesia affects episodic memories rather than procedural memories. Retrograde amnesia results when the consolidation of memories is disrupted. When the hippocampus is damaged or removed, anterograde amnesia results, as in the case of H.M. The hippocampus is involved in the processing of new episodic memories, and the amygdala seems to be involved in encoding the emotional qualities of memories.

Key Terms

memory (p. 241)

encoding (p. 241)

storage (p. 241)

retrieval (p. 241)

stage model of memory (p. 242)

sensory memory (p. 242)

short-term memory (working memory) (p. 242)

long-term memory (p. 243)

maintenance rehearsal (p. 246)

chunking (p. 247)

elaborative rehearsal (p. 248)

levels of processing framework (p. 249)

procedural information (p. 250)

episodic information (p. 250)

semantic information (p. 250)

clustering (p. 251)

semantic network model (p. 251)

retrieval (p. 253)

retrieval cue (p. 253)

retrieval cue failure (p. 253)

tip-of-the-tongue (TOT) experience (p. 254)

recall (p. 254)

cued recall (p. 254)

recognition (p. 254)

serial position effect (p. 255)

encoding specificity principle (p. 255)

context effect (p. 256)

state-dependent retrieval (p. 256)

mood-dependent retrieval (p. 257)

mood congruence (p. 257)

flashbulb memory (p. 258)

schema (p. 259)

source confusion (p. 260)

cryptomnesia (p. 262)

misinformation effect (p. 263)

forgetting (p. 265)

encoding failure (p. 267)

interference theory (p. 267)

retroactive interference (p. 267)

proactive interference (p. 268)

motivated forgetting (p. 268)

suppression (p. 268)

repression (p. 268)

decay theory (p. 271)

memory trace (p. 272)

amnesia (p. 276)

retrograde amnesia (p. 276)

memory consolidation (p. 277)

anterograde amnesia (p. 277)

Key People

Herman Ebbinghaus (1850–1909) German psychologist who originated the scientific study of forgetting; plotted the first "forgetting curve," which describes the basic pattern of forgetting learned information over time.

Karl Lashley (1890–1958) American physiological psychologist who attempted to find the specific brain location of particular memories.

Elizabeth F. Loftus (b. 1944) American psychologist who has conducted extensive research on the memory distortions that can occur in eyewitness testimony.

George Sperling (b. 1934) American psychologist who identified the duration of visual sensory memory in a series of classic experiments in 1960.

Richard F. Thompson (b. 1930) American psychologist and neuroscientist who has conducted extensive research on the neurobiological foundations of learning and memory.

CONCEPT REVIEW 6.1 Page 252

1. LTM
2. SM
3. STM
4. LTM
5. STM
6. SM
7. STM
8. SM
9. LTM

CONCEPT REVIEW 6.2 Page 258

1. a
2. c
3. a
4. c
5. d

CONCEPT REVIEW 6.3 Page 272

1. D
2. C
3. A
4. E
5. B

CONCEPT REVIEW 6.4 Page 276

1. George Sperling
2. Elizabeth Loftus
3. Herman Ebbinghaus
4. Karl Lashley
5. Richard F. Thompson

Chapter

Thinking, Language, and Intelligence

Prologue: Mr. and Ms. Fix-It

"I found it! The rubber gasket between the sink and faucet is leaking!" Don yelled from under the kitchen sink.

"The *basket* is leaking!" our three-year old daughter, Laura, who was holding the flashlight, enthusiastically relayed to Sandy.

"The *basket* is leaking?" Sandy asked. "What basket?"

"No, it's called a *gasket,* not a basket, honey," Don explained to Laura, who looked very puzzled about this new concept.

"Can you fix it?" Sandy asked.

"Piece of cake," Don replied as he crawled out from under the sink. "Laura and I will run down to the hardware store and buy a new gasket."

Of course, the solution turned out *not* to be that simple. "They don't sell *just* the gasket," the man at the hardware store explained. "You gotta buy a whole new faucet."

"What's that going to run me?"

"Kitchen faucets start at $39.95 plus tax," the hardware guy smiled. "Then you'll need some replacement tubing for when you weld the new faucet in place. You got a welding torch, don't you? If you don't, a plumber probably wouldn't charge more than $150 or so to install it, not including the cost of the parts."

"Let me think about it," Don replied, frowning.

"Why didn't we buy a new basket?" Laura asked as she and Don walked out of the hardware store.

"It's called a *gasket,* sweetie," Don explained. "It's just a piece of rubber that fits between two pieces of metal. It keeps the water that splashes around the faucet from dripping under the sink. Does that make sense?"

"I think so," Laura said thoughtfully. "Why didn't we buy one?"

"Because they want too much money for it," Don answered as he buckled Laura into her car seat.

As Laura chattered away on the drive home, Don mulled over calling a plumber. *A couple hundred bucks to replace a lousy piece of rubber. That's ridiculous.*

"We'll make one!" Don suddenly exclaimed.

"Make what, Daddy?" Laura responded, slightly startled.

"A new gasket! And best of all, Laura, it won't cost a cent!"

Less than five minutes later, Don and Laura were at a General Tire store. "Help yourself," the manager replied when he asked if he could have a discarded inner tube. About an hour later, the new "gasket" was in place—a piece of black rubber inner tube that Don had cut to the same shape as the original gasket. It worked like a charm. No drips.

"You missed your calling in life," Sandy quipped as Don stood basking in the glory of the moment.

"Hey, you just have to think creatively," Don smiled back.

Unfortunately, creative thinking is not always the answer. A few weeks later, when the upstairs toilet wouldn't flush properly, Mr. Fix-It spent almost two hours dismantling and lifting the entire toilet off the floor drain in search of the cause.

"You're sure you didn't flush one of your toys down the toilet?" Don asked Laura again.

"No, Daddy," Laura said solemnly, shaking her head, as she peered down the ominous-looking drain in the floor with her Barney flashlight.

"Well, I don't know what the hell is wrong with it," Don announced in frustration, wiping the sweat from his brow.

Sitting in the corner of the bathroom, Sandy flipped through the pages of a book called *The Complete Home Fix-It-Yourself Manual*. "Did you look at this book? There's a troubleshooting guide for toilets on this page."

"No, I did *not* look at it," Don huffed cynically. "I *know* how to unblock a toilet. First, you try a plunger. If that doesn't work, then you take the toilet off to find whatever is blocking the drain."

"That's what it lists to try *third* in this book," Sandy pointed out calmly. "What was the water level inside the tank?"

"It was a couple inches down from the fill line," Don answered.

"Well, it says here that if the water level is too low, the toilet bowl will drain sluggishly," Sandy explained matter-of-factly, then glanced up. "Did you try raising the water level to the fill line *before* you took the toilet apart?"

Silence loomed in the bathroom.

It was well over an hour later that Laura excitedly called downstairs to Sandy: "Momma! Momma! Come see! Daddy fixed the toilet!"

"What was wrong with it?" Sandy innocently asked as she watched the toilet flush perfectly.

"The water level was just too low," Don replied, then cleared his throat.

"You're kidding!" Sandy feigned disbelief. "That must have been why it was listed as the *first* thing to check in that troubleshooting guide."

"I think you missed your calling in life," Don muttered.

"Well, you know what I always say: 'When in doubt, look it up!'" Sandy smiled.

All of us rely on a variety of cognitive processes to imagine, think, make decisions, and solve problems in daily life. In this chapter, we'll look at the broad issue of how we think, including how we solve problems, make decisions, and occasionally arrive at creative solutions. In the process, we'll come back to this story of Mr. and Ms. Fix-It to illustrate several important concepts and ideas.

Introduction

Thinking, Language, and Intelligence

cognition
The mental activities involved in acquiring, retaining, and using knowledge.

thinking
The manipulation of mental representations of information in order to draw inferences and conclusions.

mental image
A mental representation of objects or events that are not physically present.

Cognition is a general term that refers to the mental activities involved in acquiring, retaining, and using knowledge (Matlin, 1989). In previous chapters, we've looked at such fundamental cognitive processes as perception, learning, and memory. Without question, these processes are critical in order for us to acquire and retain new knowledge.

In this chapter we will focus on how we *use* that knowledge to think, solve problems, make decisions, and use language. As you'll see, such cognitive abilities are widely regarded as key dimensions of *intelligence*—a concept that has proven difficult to define. Later in this chapter, we will explore the different ways in which psychologists have tried to define and measure intelligence. Finally, in the chapter Application, we'll present a workshop on enhancing your capacity to think more creatively.

The Building Blocks of Thought:
Mental Imagery and Concepts

> *Thinking typically involves the manipulation of mental images and concepts. What are some of the basic characteristics of mental images? How do we manipulate mental images?*

"Let me think about it." "I think so." "You just have to think creatively." "I think you missed your calling in life." Intuitively, we all seem to have an understanding of what the word *think* means. But what do psychologists mean by the term?

In the most general sense, thinking is involved in all conscious mental activity, whether we are acquiring new knowledge, remembering, planning ahead, or daydreaming (Holyoak & Spellman, 1993). More narrowly, we can say that **thinking** involves manipulating mental representations of information in order to draw inferences and conclusions (Kosslyn, 1995). Thinking, then, involves active mental processes, and is often directed toward some goal, purpose, or conclusion.

What exactly is it that we think *with*? Thinking often involves the manipulation of two forms of mental representations: *mental images* and *concepts*. We'll look first at mental images.

Mental Images

When you read the chapter's prologue, did you see a mental picture of a little girl peering down a cavernous floor drain with her Barney the dinosaur flashlight? Or Sandy sitting in the corner of the bathroom, looking at the home repair manual? The stories we tell in our prologues typically lend themselves to the creation of a mental image. Formally, a **mental image** is a mental representation of objects or events that are not physically present.

A Flower for Your Thoughts? What types of cognitive activities might be involved in growing an elaborate flower garden? Planning, forming mental images, making decisions, and problem solving are some of the mental activities involved.

You can easily form images of objects, events, or experiences that you have actually experienced. When someone asks you to give them directions to where you live, the request usually triggers a series of familiar mental images as you describe the route to the other person. But you also have an enormous capacity to form vivid mental images of objects, events, and locations you've never directly experienced, such as the sequence of mental images you probably created in reading the prologue.

Often, we rely on mental images to accomplish some cognitive task (Farah, 1995). For example, try reciting the letters of the alphabet that only include curved lines. To accomplish this task, you have to mentally visualize and then inspect an image of each letter of the alphabet.

Note that mental imagery is not strictly limited to visual "pictures." Most people are able to form images that involve senses other than vision (McKellar, 1972). For example, you can probably easily create a mental representation for the taste and texture of a chocolate milkshake, or the feel of wet clothing sticking to your skin. All the same, most research on mental images has involved how we manipulate visual images (Ochsner & Kosslyn, 1994). Thus, we'll focus on visual images in our discussion.

Manipulating Mental Images

Do you manipulate mental images in the same way that you manipulate your visual images of actual objects? One line of evidence comes from studies that compare the scanning of mental images to the scanning of actual pictures or visual images, such as maps. *Scanning* simply means shifting your visual attention or focus across an image or picture.

To illustrate, suppose we gave you a map of the United States and asked you to visually locate San Francisco. Then suppose we asked you to fix your gaze on another city. If the other city was far away from San Francisco (like New York), it would take you longer to visually locate it than if it was located close by (like Los Angeles). Given that, here's the question: If you were scanning a *mental* image rather than a visual image of an actual map, would it also take you longer to scan across a greater distance?

A classic study by Stephen Kosslyn and his colleagues (1978) was designed to answer this question. Participants in this study first memorized a map of a fictitious island with distinct locations—a sandy beach, a lake, a hut, a tree, a well, a rock, and grass (see Figure 7.1). After the map was removed, subjects were asked to imagine a specific location on the island, such as the sandy beach. Then a second location, such as the rock, was named. The participants mentally scanned across their mental image of the map and pushed a button when they reached the rock.

The results? The researchers found that the amount of time it took to mentally scan to the new location was directly related to the distance between the two points. The greater the distance between the two points, the longer it took to scan the mental image of the map (Kosslyn & others, 1978).

It seems, then, that we tend to scan a mental image in much the same way that we visually scan an actual image (Ochsner & Kosslyn, 1994). However, we don't just look at mental images in our minds. Sometimes thinking involves the *manipulation* of mental images before we can arrive at an answer. For example, take a look at Figure 7.2. Two of the *3*'s are backward. Which ones?

FIGURE 7.1 Mentally Scanning Images
This is a reduced version of the map used by Stephen Kosslyn and his colleagues (1978) to study the scanning of mental images. After subjects memorized the map, the map was removed. Subjects then mentally scanned from one location to another. As you can see in the average scanning times, it took subjects longer to scan greater distances on their mental images of the map, just as it takes longer to visually scan greater distances on an actual map.

FIGURE 7.2 Manipulating Mental Images
Two of these threes are backward. Which ones?

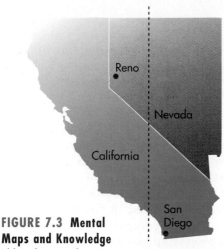

FIGURE 7.3 Mental Maps and Knowledge
Although most subjects thought that San Diego is west of Reno and Montreal is north of Seattle, neither statement is true. As these maps show, Reno is west of San Diego and Montreal is south of Seattle.
(Adapted from Stevens & Coupe, 1978.)

Did you find that it took you longer to determine that the *3* in the middle was backward than to determine that the *3* on the far left was backward? If you did, here's why: In order to determine which of the *3*'s were backward, you probably had to mentally *rotate* each one to an upright position. And, just as it takes time to rotate a physical object, it takes time to mentally rotate an image. Furthermore, the greater the degree of rotation required, the longer it takes you to rotate the image mentally (see Kosslyn & Sussman, 1995; Stillings & others, 1987). Thus, it probably took you longer to mentally rotate the *3* in the middle, which you had to rotate 180 degrees, than it did to mentally rotate the *3* on the far left, which you only had to rotate 60 degrees.

Collectively, experiments on our cognitive ability to manipulate mental images by scanning or rotating them seem to indicate that we treat mental images pretty much like the actual objects they represent (Farah, 1995; Kosslyn & Sussman, 1995). Of course, this doesn't mean that our mental images are always perfect duplicates of our actual sensory experiences. To illustrate this point, imagine a map of the United States and Canada. Now answer two questions. Which city is farther west, San Diego or Reno? And which city is farther north, Montreal or Seattle?

Most of the participants in a study that posed these questions answered that San Diego was west of Reno and that Montreal was north of Seattle (Stevens & Coupe, 1978). But as you can see by looking at the maps in Figure 7.3, both of those answers are wrong.

What this illustrates is that our memories of visual images, like our memories in general, are less than picture perfect. The mental images that we use in thinking share some features in common with actual visual images, but they are not like photographs. They are not exact duplicates of real images (Chambers & Reisberg, 1985). Instead, like memories, mental images are actively constructed (Reisberg & Chambers, 1991).

Concepts

> *A concept is a mental category that groups objects, events, or situations that share similar characteristics. What are natural concepts, and how do they differ from formal concepts? What role do prototypes play in concept formation?*

Along with mental images, thinking also involves the use of concepts. A **concept** is a mental category we have formed to group objects, events, or situations that share similar features or characteristics. Concepts provide a kind of mental shorthand, economizing the cognitive effort required for thinking and communication.

For example, the concept *food* might include anything from a loaf of bread to a fresh rutabaga. Although these items are far from identical, we can still group them together because they share the central feature of being edible. When someone introduces us to a new delicacy and tells us it is *food,* we immediately know that it is something to eat—even if it is something we've never seen before. Thus, using concepts makes it easier to communicate with others, remember information, and learn new information.

Adding to the efficiency of our thinking is our tendency to organize the concepts we hold into orderly hierarchies composed of main categories and subcategories. Thus a very general concept, like *furniture,* can be mentally divided into a variety of subcategories: *tables, chairs, lamps,* and so forth. As we learn the key properties that define general concepts, we also learn how members of the concept are related to one another (Reed, 1996).

concepts
The mental categories of objects or ideas based on properties that they share.

formal concept
A mental category that is formed by learning the rules or features that define it.

natural concept
A mental category that is formed as a result of everyday experience.

prototype
The most typical instance of a particular concept.

Forming Concepts

When you form a concept by learning the *rules* or *features* that define the particular concept, it is called a **formal concept.** As children, we were taught the specific rules or features that defined many simple formal concepts, such as shapes, numbers, and days of the week.

The rules or features that define a formal concept can be very simple, such as the rules that define a triangle. Or the rules can be complex, such as the features that define the visible portion of the electromagnetic spectrum, which we discussed in Chapter 3. In either case, the rules are logical but rigid. If the defining features or *attributes* are present, then the object is included as a member or example of that concept. If the defining features or attributes are missing, then the object is not included in the concept. For some formal concepts this rigid all-or-nothing categorization procedure works well. For example, a substance can be categorized as a *solid, liquid,* or *gas.* The rules defining these formal concepts are very clear-cut.

However, psychologist Eleanor Rosch (1973) pointed out that the features that define categories of natural objects and events in everyday life are seldom as clear-cut as the features that define formal concepts. A **natural concept** is one that is formed as a result of everyday experience rather than by logically determining whether an object or event fits a specific set of rules. Rosch suggested that, unlike logical concepts, natural concepts have "fuzzy boundaries." That is, the rules or attributes that define the natural concept are not always sharply defined.

Because natural concepts have fuzzy boundaries, it's often easier to classify some members of natural concepts than others (Rosch & Mervis, 1975). To illustrate this point, think about the defining features or rules that you usually associate with the natural concept of *vehicle.* With virtually no hesitation, you can say that *car, truck,* and *bus* are all examples of this natural concept. How about *sled? wheelbarrow? raft? elevator?* It probably took you a few seconds to determine whether these objects are also *vehicles.* Why are some members of natural concepts easier to classify than others?

According to Rosch (1978), some members are better representatives of a natural concept than others. The "best," or most typical, instance of a particular concept is called a **prototype** (Mervis & Rosch, 1981; Rosch, 1978). We tend to determine whether an object is an instance of a natural concept by comparing it to the prototype we have developed, rather than by logically evaluating the object in terms of whether the defining features or attributes are present or absent.

The more closely an item matches the prototype, the more quickly we can identify it as being an example of that concept. In Table 7.1, the first few items listed under each concept tend to be the ones that most people list as the prototypes for that concept. The items farther

TABLE 7.1 From Prototypes to Atypical Examples

| Sequence of Items | Concept | | |
	Furniture	Vehicles	Fruit
1	chair	car	orange
2	sofa	truck	apple
3	table	bus	banana
4	dresser	motorcycle	peach
5	desk	train	pear
6	bed	trolley car	apricot
7	bookcase	bicycle	plum
8	footstool	airplane	grape
9	lamp	boat	strawberry
10	piano	tractor	grapefruit
11	cushion	cart	pineapple
12	mirror	wheelchair	blueberry
13	rug	tank	lemon
14	radio	raft	watermelon
15	stove	sled	honeydew
16	clock	horse	pomegranate
17	picture	blimp	date
18	closet	skates	coconut
19	vase	wheelbarrow	tomato
20	telephone	elevator	olive

SOURCE: Rosch & Mervis, 1975.

The first items listed under each general concept are the ones that most people tend to think of as the prototype examples of that concept. As you move farther down the list, the items become progressively more dissimilar from the prototype examples.

down each list tend to deviate more from the items we think of as prototypes (Rosch & Mervis, 1975). Consequently, it usually takes us longer to identify an *olive* or a *coconut* as being a *fruit* because they are so dissimilar from the prototypes we typically think of as fruit, like apples and oranges (Rosch, 1975).

As two of the basic building blocks of thinking, mental images and concepts help us impose order on the phenomena we encounter and think about. We often rely on this knowledge when we engage in complex cognitive tasks, such as solving problems and making decisions, which we'll consider next.

Are These Mammals? The more closely an item matches the prototype of a concept, the more quickly we can identify the item as being an example of that concept. In the case of the concept *mammal,* a dog is much closer to the prototype that most people have of a mammal than is a bat or a dolphin.

Identifying the Building Blocks of Thought

For each of the following, decide which term best applies. Choose from: formal concept, natural concept, prototype, or mental image.

1. You are asked how many windows you have in your home. To answer this question, you probably rely on a _____.

2. In question 1, the word *home* is used to describe the place where you usually sleep, eat, and keep your belongings. *Home* is an example of a _____.

3. When Mary is asked what object comes to mind in response to the word *furniture,* she immediately says, "Chair." For Mary, *chair* is a _____.

4. In his geometry class, Karl has learned the rules and features that define a parallelogram. Karl has learned a _____.

Problem Solving: Searching for the IDEAL Solution

Problem solving refers to thinking and behavior directed toward attaining a goal that is not readily available. What are the basic steps in problem solving? What are advantages and disadvantages of each problem-solving strategy? How can functional fixedness and mental set interfere with problem solving?

Problem solving refers to thinking and behavior directed toward attaining a goal that is not readily available. From fixing flat tires to figuring out how to pay for college classes, we engage in the cognitive task of problem solving so routinely that we often don't even notice the processes we follow.

One useful way to conceptualize (and remember) the steps involved in problem solving was devised by psychologists John Bransford and Barry Stein (1984). In their formulation, called the *IDEAL problem solver,* each letter of the word *IDEAL* represents a step in the problem-solving process:

Step 1. **I**dentify the problem.

Step 2. **D**efine and represent the problem.

Step 3. **E**xplore possible strategies or solutions.

Step 4. **A**ct on a selected strategy or solution.

Step 5. **L**ook back and evaluate the solution.

In this section, we'll refer to the chapter prologue to illustrate some important aspects of problem solving. We'll also present you with some of the kinds of problems and tasks that researchers use to study how people solve problems.

Steps 1 and 2:
Identify and Define the Problem

Before you can begin to solve any problem, you have to (1) recognize that a problem exists, then (2) develop an accurate understanding of the problem (Ellis & Hunt, 1993b). In the prologue, the problems were obvious and easy to recognize: we discovered a sizable puddle under the kitchen sink, and the water drained sluggishly in the upstairs toilet. As was the case in these examples, identifying that a problem exists is often the easiest part of problem solving.

The second step is more critical. Once a problem has been identified, you have to accurately *define* it, which involves creating a mental representation of it. You must sort out the important and unimportant information, and determine which aspects of the problem are relevant to its solution (Sternberg, 1988a).

If you evaluate the information too quickly, you can hamper your ability to properly define a problem. If you don't pay careful attention to all the information provided, your interpretation of the information can lead to a faulty mental representation of the problem.

This is exactly what occurred when Mr. Fix-It attempted to fix the upstairs toilet. Because the water drained sluggishly, your author Don immediately assumed that something was blocking the drain. Armed with an erroneous representation of the problem, Don launched a strategy to fix a problem that did not even exist.

problem solving
Thinking and behavior directed toward attaining a goal that is not readily available.

trial and error
A problem-solving strategy that involves attempting different solutions and eliminating those that do not work.

With practice, people can get better at sorting out the important and irrelevant information in a problem. Simply listing all the relevant information can help you focus your attention on critical details, which can improve your accuracy in interpreting a problem (Sternberg, 1988a). Try this suggestion if you have difficulty solving the problems 1 and 2 in Figure 7.4. When problems are complicated or involve weighing many different factors, creating a graph or table can be useful for identifying the relationships between the important elements of the problem. Try this suggestion if you have difficulty mentally visualizing problem 3 in Figure 7.4.

FIGURE 7.4 Strategies for Defining and Representing Problems
If you have difficulty solving problems 1 and 2, try listing the important information. Problem 3 is easier to solve if you draw a table or a diagram to help you keep track of the information. Try to solve the problems without looking at the solutions on page 294.

(Adapted from Halpern, 1989, pp. 392, 400.)

Problem 1 If you follow Interstate 25, the distance between Albuquerque and Denver is 437 miles. At 9:00 a.m., Mary leaves Albuquerque for Denver driving a U-haul truck at 50 miles per hour. At 11:00 a.m., Frank leaves Albuquerque for Denver driving a minivan at 65 miles per hour. At noon, Mary stops for 30 minutes for lunch. Who is closer to Denver when the two vehicles pass each other?

Problem 2 Imagine you are the pilot of a corporate jet. When you leave Tampa, you have 5 male passengers and 3 female passengers. At Memphis, 2 men get off, and 2 women get on. At Houston, 4 male passengers get on, and 1 female passenger gets off. Upon landing at Phoenix, 3 male passengers board, 1 male passenger gets off, and 2 female passengers board. At Salt Lake City, no male passengers get on or off, but 1 woman boards the jet. At Sacramento, 2 men and 2 women get off the jet. How old is the pilot?

Problem 3 Four dogs are sitting in front of their doghouses. From left to right, the dogs are named Pizza, Tiger, Lady, and Sancho. On the basis of the following information, figure out which dog eats Crunchy Blend dog food and which dog lives in the green house.
• Pizza lives in a blue doghouse.
• Sancho eats Butcher Boy dog food.
• The dog in the white house is next to the dog that eats Butcher Boy.
• The dog that eats medium-rare steak is farthest away from the dog that eats Butcher Boy.
• The dog that lives in a red house eats Yummies.
• Lady lives next to the dog with the green house.
• Tiger lives next to the dog that eats Crunchy Blend.

Steps 3 and 4:
Explore Possible Strategies, Then Act on a Strategy

As a general rule, people tend to attack a problem in an organized or systematic way. Usually, the strategy we select is influenced by the nature of the problem and the amount of time we're willing to invest in solving it. In this section, we'll look at some of the common strategies used in problem solving.

Trial and Error

The strategy of **trial and error** involves actually trying a variety of solutions and eliminating those that don't work. When there is a limited range of possible solutions, trial and error can be a useful problem-solving strategy. If you were trying to develop a new spaghetti recipe, for example, you might use trial and error to fine-tune the seasonings.

DRABBLE

DRABBLE reprinted by permission of United Feature Syndicate, Inc.

© 1995 United Feature Syndicate, Inc.

http://www.unitedmedia.com

Problem 1   When the two vehicles pass each other, they'll be the *same* distance from Denver.

Problem 2   You're the pilot of the jet, so the answer is your age.

Problem 3   Solving this problem is much easier if you create a simple table to help you keep track of the information. Start by listing the names of the four dogs from left to right. On the next row, list the color of the doghouses as they become known. On the third row, list the name of the dog food as it becomes known. As you progressively fill in each blank, the answer will become apparent: Lady eats Crunchy Blend, and Sancho lives in the green doghouse.

	Pizza	Tiger	Lady	Sancho
Doghouse Color	Blue	Red	White	Green
Dog Food	Steak	Yummies	Crunchy Blend	Butcher Boy

Solutions to the Problems in Figure 7.4

When the range of possible answers or solutions is large, however, trial and error can be very time-consuming. For example, our friend Thomas typically learns new computer programs by trial and error. Rather than read the manual, he'll spend hours trying different menu commands to see if he can make the software do what it's supposed to do.

Algorithms

Unlike trial and error, an **algorithm** is a procedure or method that, when followed step by step, always produces the correct solution. Programming a VCR so that it displays the correct time is a simple example of using an algorithm to solve a problem. By following the steps described in the VCR manual, you can solve the problem. Mathematical formulas are another example of algorithms, like the formula used to convert temperatures from Celsius to Fahrenheit (multiply C by nine-fifths, then add 32).

Even though an algorithm may be guaranteed to eventually produce a solution, using an algorithm is not always practical. For example, imagine that while rummaging in a closet you find a combination lock with no combination attached. Using an algorithm will eventually produce the correct combination. You can start with 0–0–0, then try 0–0–1, followed by 0–0–2, and so forth, and systematically work your way through combinations to 36–36–36. But this solution would take a while, because there are 46,656 potential combinations to try. So while using an algorithm to generate the correct combination for the combination lock is guaranteed to work eventually, it's not a very practical approach to solving this particular problem.

Heuristics

In contrast to algorithms, a **heuristic** is a general rule-of-thumb strategy that may or may not work. Although heuristic strategies are not guaranteed to solve a given problem, they tend to simplify problem solving because they let you reduce the number of possible solutions. With a more limited range of solutions, you can use trial and error to arrive eventually at the correct one.

Here's an example: Creating footnotes is described somewhere in the manual for a word-processing computer program. If you use the algorithm of reading every page of the manual, you're guaranteed to solve the problem eventually. But you can greatly simplify your task by using a heuristic, such as looking in the index for the page number for footnoting. This strategy does not guarantee success, because the procedure may not be listed in the index.

The prologue contained a couple of examples of heuristics. In the case of the leaking faucet, Don resorted to the familiar homeowner's heuristic of going to the hardware store to buy a replacement. Notice, however, that this heuristic did not result in an acceptable solution. And in trying to solve the problem of the malfunctioning toilet, Sandy relied on her favorite heuristic: she looked for potential solutions in a book on the subject. Of course, this particular heuristic will work only when there's a book available that describes how to solve a specific problem.

One common heuristic is to break a problem into a series of *subgoals* (Reed, 1996). This strategy is often used in writing a term paper. Choosing a

algorithm
A problem-solving strategy that involves following a specific rule, procedure, or method, which inevitably produces the correct solution.

heuristic
A problem-solving strategy that involves following a general rule of thumb to reduce the number of possible solutions.

GARFIELD®

topic, locating information about the topic, organizing the information, and so on becomes a series of subproblems. As you solve each subproblem, you move closer to solving the larger problem.

Another useful heuristic involves *working backward* from the goal. Starting with the end point, you determine the steps necessary to reach your final goal. For example, when making a budget, people often start off with the goal of spending no more than a certain total each month, then work backward to determine how much of the target amount they will allot for each category of expenses.

Insight: The AHA! Experience

Finally, the solution to some problems seems to arrive in a sudden realization, or flash of **insight,** that happens after you mull a problem over (Kaplan & Simon, 1990). Sometimes an insight will occur when you recognize how the problem is similar to a previously solved problem. Or an insight can involve the sudden realization that an object can be used in a novel way, such as using a can of hair spray as a rolling pin to squeeze the toothpaste to the top of tube. Don's realization that he could make an inexpensive replacement gasket for the kitchen sink from a discarded inner tube is an example of problem solving through insight. Try your hand at the three problems in Figure 7.5. The solution to each of those problems is often achieved by insight.

Insights rarely occur through the conscious manipulation of concepts or information (Schooler & others, 1993). Rather, we're usually not aware of the thought processes that led to an insight (Ellis & Hunt, 1993b). Increasingly, cognitive psychologists are investigating nonconscious mental processes, including unconscious problem solving and insight (see Underwood, 1996).

FIGURE 7.5 A Demonstration of Insightful Solutions
The solution to the following problems is often characterized by sudden flashes of insight. See if you have the "That's it!" experience in solving the following problems without looking at the solutions on page 296.
(Adapted from Ashcraft, 1994. Problem 3 adapted from Sternberg, 1986.)

Problem 1	A police car involved in a high-speed chase of two armed bank robbers crashed into the car of a father who was driving his eight-year-old son to soccer practice. As they pulled the child from the mangled wreckage, it was quickly apparent that the boy was gravely injured and bleeding internally. Transported by air ambulance to a major hospital, the unconscious boy was rushed into surgery. As the surgical nurses were preparing the boy, the surgeon scrubbed for surgery in an adjacent room, yelling orders for specific instruments and drugs. Gloved and gowned, the surgeon hurried into the operating room, then froze with shock. "I can't operate on this child. This child is my son," the surgeon declared. How can this be?
Problem 2	Six drinking glasses are lined up in a row. The first three are full of water, the last three are empty. By handling and moving only one glass, change the arrangement so that no full glass is next to another full one, and no empty glass is next to another empty one.
Problem 3	A man who lived in a small town married twenty different women in that same town. All of them are still living, and he never divorced any of them. Yet he broke no laws. How could he do this?

Step 5:

Look Back and Evaluate the Solution

The final step in problem solving is to look back and evaluate the solution. If the problem is clearly defined, like fixing a leaky faucet, it's relatively easy to determine whether a solution is effective—either water continues to drip or it doesn't. In everyday life, many problems are not so simple. Often, a range of potential solutions exist, each with advantages and disadvantages. Picking among the solutions can itself become a problem, especially if the goal is vague or poorly defined (Ellis & Hunt, 1993b). Later in the chapter, we'll discuss strategies that can help you choose from a range of potential solutions.

insight
The sudden realization of how a problem can be solved.

IN FOCUS 7.1

Intuition: Knowing Without Knowing How You Know

"Hunches" often play a role in our decisions and judgments. For example, you may have a hunch that someone is lying to you, even though you have no proof. Or a hunch that someone else is attracted to you, even though they outwardly act the same around you as others. A scientist's hunch may determine the direction of his research. The common element in these examples is that you can't immediately explain *why* the hunch occurred to you, but it did. Is there a scientific explanation for the cognitive processes that lead to hunches?

Such hunches are examples of **intuition**—coming to a conclusion or making a judgment without conscious awareness of the thought processes involved. Canadian psychologist Kenneth Bowers and his colleagues (1990) have proposed a two-stage model of intuition. In the first stage, called the *guiding stage,* you perceive a pattern in the information you're contemplating, but not consciously. Your perception of such patterns is based on your expertise in a given area and your memories of related information.

For example, when a doctor makes a medical diagnosis, she does so by recognizing a pattern in the patient's symptoms. She integrates a wide range of clues, both obvious and subtle, into a meaningful pattern that gives her a hunch about what the illness may be. An experienced physician will accurately recognize the pattern more quickly than an intern still in training, who has to consciously and methodically compare each symptom to a checklist of possible illnesses.

In the second stage, the *integrative stage,* a representation of the pattern becomes conscious, usually in the form of a hunch or hypothesis. At this point, conscious, analytic thought processes take over: you systematically attempt to prove or disprove the hypothesis. Thus, the doctor orders lab tests to confirm or disconfirm her hunch.

To test the hypothesis that patterns can be recognized unconsciously, Bowers and his colleagues (1990) devised an ingenious experiment. Using introductory psychology students as their subjects, they showed students pairs of three-word trigrams, like the ones shown in the next column. For one of the trigrams, there was a solution: a word that could be associated with all three members. For example, the solution to the trigram *goat/pass/climber* is the word *mountain.* But for the other trigram, no solution existed.

The subjects saw each pair of trigrams for 8 seconds, then had another 12 seconds to come up with a solution. Whether they could solve the trigram or not, they had to indicate which of the two trigrams they thought was solvable. On the average, the subjects were able to solve less than one-third of the trigrams. But they were surprisingly accurate at judging which trigram was solvable. In other words, they could not consciously describe the pattern, but they unconsciously recognized that a pattern existed.

According to Bowers, the fact that the initial, guiding stage of intuition is unconscious doesn't mean it's irrational. Intuition is an orderly phenomenon. The intuitive process that generates a hunch is based on an organized network of information in long-term memory. As you try to solve a problem, "clues," or available evidence, activate relevant information networks in memory.

An intuitive hunch, then, is a new idea that integrates new information with existing knowledge stored in long-term memory. Such hunches are likely to be accurate only in contexts in which you already have a broad base of knowledge and experience (Benderly, 1989). Thus, an expert stockbroker's hunch that a certain stock is likely to skyrocket in value is very different from a hunch that a certain number will prove to be a lottery winner!

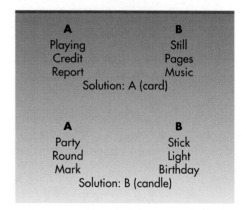

A	B
Playing	Still
Credit	Pages
Report	Music
Solution: A (card)	

A	B
Party	Stick
Round	Light
Mark	Birthday
Solution: B (candle)	

Sample Trigrams Used in Experiment on Unconscious Pattern Recognition

(From Bowers & others, 1990.)

Problem 1	The surgeon was the boy's mother.
Problem 2	Pour the water in glass number 2 into glass number 5.
Problem 3	The man is a minister.

Solutions to the Problems in Figure 7.5

Obstacles to Solving Problems:

Functional Fixedness and Mental Sets

A common obstacle to problem solving is illustrated in a humorous story told by psychologist Mark Ashcraft (1994). A candidate for a faculty position was making a presentation of his research to the psychology faculty and students. But when the candidate switched on the slide projector, the slide image was projected too low on the screen. According to Ashcraft:

> *A flurry of activity around the projector ensued, one professor asking out loud, "Does anyone have a book or something?" Someone volunteered a book, the professor tried it, but it was too thick—the slide image was now too high. "No, this one's too big. Anyone got a thinner one?" he continued.*
>
> *After several more seconds of hurried searching for something thinner to put under the projector, another professor finally exclaimed, "Well, for Pete's sake, I don't believe this!" Marching over to the projector, he grabbed the book, opened it halfway, and then put it under the projector. He looked around the lecture hall and shook his head, saying, "A room full of Ph.D.s, and no one knows how to open a book!"*

When we view objects as functioning only in the usual or customary way, we're engaging in a tendency called **functional fixedness.** Functional fixedness often prevents us from seeing the full range of ways in which an object can be used. To get a feel for how functional fixedness can potentially interfere with our ability to find a solution, try solving the problem described in Figure 7.6.

Here's another example of functional fixedness. When pilots fly through clouds, they watch an instrument called an "artificial horizon," which shows an outline of an airplane against a horizontal line that represents the horizon. By watching the movement of the outline, they can tell if the aircraft is tilting up or down, or banking to the left or right.

When Don was first learning to fly, he was publicly chastised by a salty old flight instructor for failing to wear a St. Christopher's medal around his neck when flying. Since St. Christopher is the patron saint of travelers, Don assumed that the flight instructor was a bit superstitious. Don's functional fixedness kept him from thinking of any other reason for a pilot to wear a St. Christopher's medal. Finally, Don asked the instructor.

It turned out that a St. Christopher's medal or any other object on a chain can be used to create a makeshift artificial horizon if the flight instrument should fail. You simply drape the chain over the throttle stick. If the aircraft starts pointing down, the medal swings forward; if the aircraft starts pointing upward, the medal swings back. When the aircraft banks, the medal swings to one side or the other. This novel use of an object could literally save the lives of the people in the plane.

Another common obstacle to problem solving is **mental set**—the tendency to persist in solving problems with solutions that have worked in the past. Obviously, if a solution has worked in the past, there's good reason to consider using it again. However, if we approach a problem with a mental set already in mind, it can work against our ability to see other possible solutions. For example, Don's initial attempt to fix the toilet reflected his mental set that when the water in a toilet doesn't drain properly, the drain is probably clogged. Since using a plunger had solved such problems in the past, it made sense to try that solution again.

Mental sets can sometimes suggest a useful heuristic. But they can also prevent us from coming up with new, and possibly simpler or more effective, solutions. If we try to be flexible in our thinking and overcome the tendency toward mental sets, we can often identify simpler solutions to many common

FIGURE 7.6 Overcoming Functional Fixedness
Here's a problem for you to solve: You are given two candles, some thumbtacks, and a box of matches. Using just these objects, try to figure out how to mount the candles on a wall. (Solution is on p. 299.)
(Adapted from Duncker, 1945.)

functional fixedness
The tendency to view objects as functioning only in their usual or customary way.

mental set
The tendency to persist in solving problems with solutions that have worked in the past.

problems. Because Sandy did not have any particular mental sets about malfunctioning toilets, she was able to search for and identify an alternative solution that not only worked but was also much simpler than Don's attempt to solve the problem.

Comparing Problem-Solving Strategies

Identify what is demonstrated in each of the following examples and fill in the blank with the appropriate letter: (A) trial and error, (B) algorithm, (C) heuristic, (D) insight, (E) functional fixedness, or (F) mental set.

_____ **1.** As you try to spell the word *deceive,* you recite the phrase "*i* before *e* except after *c*."

_____ **2.** You are asked to complete the following sequence: O, T, T, F, F, ____ , ____ , ____ , ____ , ____ . After puzzling over the answer, you suddenly realize, without knowing why, that you are looking at the number series depicted by their first letters and the answer is obvious: S,S,E,N,T.

_____ **3.** One by one, Professor Goldstein tries each key on the keychain until she finds the one that opens her new filing cabinet.

_____ **4.** A scientist tests thousands of different chemical combinations, trying to find the one that will work best as a nonpolluting fuel.

_____ **5.** At the laundromat, Tom fails to realize that he can straighten a wire coat hanger and use it to retrieve the sock that has fallen behind the washing machine.

_____ **6.** When asked if the phrase "Time flies. I can't, they're too fast" makes sense, Roberta says "No." Roberta does not realize that the word *flies* in this case refers to small flying insects whose speed is difficult to measure, rather than to the passage of time.

Decisions, Decisions, Decisions:
Should I or Shouldn't I?

We use a variety of cognitive strategies to make decisions. What are the single-feature model, the additive model, and the elimination by aspects model of decision making? Under what conditions is each strategy most appropriate?

Who hasn't felt like flipping a coin when faced with an important or complicated decision? Fortunately, most of the decisions we make in everyday life are pretty minor, such as deciding what to wear, where to eat lunch, or which brand of toothpaste to buy.

But every now and then we have to make a decision where much more is at stake. Choosing a major, deciding whether to get married, and determining which job to accept are just a few examples of decisions that can have a large impact on our lives. Not surprisingly, when a decision is both important and complex, we're more likely to invest time, effort, and other resources in considering different options. Doing so can increase our chances of making a correct decision. But how do we make decisions?

Decision-Making Strategies

The decision-making process is often complicated by the fact that each option has several features or aspects that can be considered. It's rare that one alternative is superior in every category. What do you do when each alternative has pros and cons?

The Single-Feature Model

One decision-making strategy is called the *single-feature model*. In order to simplify the choice among many alternatives, you base your decision on a single feature (Reed, 1996). When the decision is a minor one, the single-feature model can be a good decision-making strategy. For example, you could simplify your decision among an entire aisle of laundry detergents by deciding to buy the cheapest brand. When a decision is important or complex, however, making decisions on the basis of a single feature can increase the riskiness of the decision.

The Additive Model

A better strategy for complex decisions is to systematically evaluate the important features of each alternative. One such decision-making model is called the *additive model* (Reed, 1996).

In this model, you first generate a list of the factors that are most important to you. Then, you rate each alternative on each factor using an arbitrary scale, such as –5 to +5. If a particular factor has strong advantages or appeal, you give it the maximum rating (+5). If a particular factor has strong drawbacks or disadvantages, you give it the minimum rating (–5). Finally, you add up the ratings for each alternative. This strategy can often reveal the best overall choice.

Suppose you were trying to decide which college to attend. You've been accepted by two colleges, each having advantages and disadvantages. To help you make your decision, you could apply the additive model as follows:

Important Factors	College A	College B
Cost of tuition	+5	–5
Availability of financial aid	+1	+4
Academic ranking	–2	+4
Availability of desired program	+1	+5
Cost/availability of housing	+4	–3
Sum of ratings	+9	+5

On the basis of the factors listed, college A would clearly be the better choice.

Notice that this example assumes that all the features are equally important to you. Often, however, decisions involve situations in which some factors are more important than others. You can emphasize the more important factors by multiplying the rating. For instance, if the academic ranking of the college is twice as important as any other factor, you can multiply the rating by 2 to emphasize it. If you do this with the above example, the sum of the ratings would now be +7 for college A and +9 for college B, changing your decision. It is also possible that factors can interact. Although the tuition of college B is very unattractive, the greater availability of financial aid might offset this disadvantage.

Taking the time to apply the additive model to important decisions can greatly improve your decision making. By allowing you to evaluate the features of one alternative at a time, then comparing the alternatives, the additive model provides a logical strategy for identifying the most acceptable choice among a range of possible decisions. Although we seldom formally calculate the subjective value of individual features for different options, we often informally use the additive model by comparing two choices feature by feature (Reed, 1996). The alternative with the "best" collection of features is then selected.

Solution to Figure 7.6

The Elimination by Aspects Model

Psychologist Amos Tversky (1972) proposed another decision-making model called the *elimination by aspects model*. Using this model, we evaluate all the alternatives on one characteristic at a time, typically starting with the feature we consider most important. If a particular alternative fails to meet that criterion, we scratch it off our list of possible choices even if it possesses other desirable attributes. As the range of possible choices is narrowed down, we continue to compare the remaining alternatives, one feature at a time, until just one alternative is left.

For example, suppose you wanted to buy a new television set. You might initially eliminate all the TV sets that won't fit on the table in your living room. You then eliminate all the models with less than a 19-inch screen. Next you exclude all models that cost more than $300. Models without a full year's warranty are then scratched off the list. Continuing in this fashion, you progressively narrow down the range of possible choices to the one choice that satisfies all your criteria.

Which Model Is Used When?

Do people tend to use the additive model or the elimination by aspects model when making a decision among several choices? The answer seems to depend on the complexity of the decision (Payne, 1985, 1976). Good decision makers adapt their strategy to the demands of the specific situation (Payne & others, 1993).

If there are just a few choices and features to compare, we tend to use the additive method, at least informally. However, when the decision is complex, involving the comparison of many choices that have multiple features, people often use *both* strategies (Reed, 1996). That is, we usually begin by focusing on the critical features, using the elimination by aspects strategy to quickly narrow down the range of acceptable choices. Once we have narrowed the list of choices down to a more manageable "short list," we tend to use the additive model to make a final decision.

Decisions Involving Uncertainty:
Estimating the Probability of Events

> *Some decisions must be made under conditions of uncertainty, in which we must estimate the probability of a particular event's occurring. How do we use the availability and representativeness heuristics to help us estimate the likelihood of an event?*

Some decisions involve a high degree of uncertainty. In these cases, you need to make a decision, but you are unable to predict with certainty that a given event will occur. Instead, you have to estimate the probability of an event's occurring. But how do you actually make that estimation?

For example, imagine that you're running late for a very important appointment. You may be faced with this decision: Should I risk a speeding ticket to get to the appointment on time? In this case, you would have to estimate the probability of a particular event's occurring—getting pulled over for speeding.

In such instances, we often estimate the likelihood that certain events will occur, then gamble. In deciding what the odds are that a particular gamble will go our way, we tend to rely on two rule-of-thumb heuristics to help us estimate the likelihood of events (Tversky & Kahneman, 1982). These two heuristics are the *availability heuristic* and the *representativeness heuristic*.

The Availability Heuristic

When we use the **availability heuristic,** we estimate the likelihood of an event on the basis of how easily other instances of the event are available in our memory. When instances of an event are easily recalled, we tend to consider the event as being more likely to occur. So we're less likely to exceed the speed limit if we can easily remember recent occurrences of other drivers getting speeding tickets, such as having heard that a friend got a speeding ticket or having seen a car pulled over by a state trooper.

However, the availability heuristic can produce inaccurate estimates. When a rare event makes a vivid impression on us, we may overestimate its likelihood (Tversky & Kahneman, 1982). This is why companies like Publisher's Clearinghouse and American Publishers run so many TV commercials showing that lucky person who won the $10 million sweepstakes prize. A vivid memory is created, which leads viewers to an inaccurate estimate of the likelihood that the event will happen to them.

The key point here is that the less accurately our memory of an event reflects the actual frequency of the event, the less accurate our estimate of the event's likelihood will be. That's why the sweepstakes commercials don't show the other 50 million or so people staring dejectedly at their mailboxes because they did *not* win the $10 million.

The Representativeness Heuristic

The other heuristic we often use to make estimates is called the **representativeness heuristic** (Kahneman & Tversky, 1982). Here, we estimate an event's likelihood by comparing how similar its essential features are to our prototype of the event. (Remember, a *prototype* is the most typical example of an object or an event.)

To go back to our example of deciding whether to speed, we are more likely to risk speeding if we think that we're somehow significantly different from the prototype of the driver who is caught for speeding. If our prototype is a teenager driving a flashy, high-performance car, and we're an adult driving a minivan with a baby seat, then we will probably estimate the likelihood of our getting a speeding ticket as low.

Like the availability heuristic, the representativeness heuristic can lead to inaccurate judgments. Consider the following description:

> *Maria is a perceptive, sensitive, introspective woman. She is very articulate, but measures her words carefully. Once she's certain she knows what she wants to say, she expresses herself easily and confidently. She has a strong preference to work alone.*

Given the above description, which is more likely: that Maria is a successful fiction writer, or that Maria is a nurse? If you responded like most of our students, you probably guessed that she is a successful fiction writer. Why? Because the description seems to mesh with what many people think of as the typical characteristics of a writer.

However, when you compare the number of nurses (which is very large) to the number of successful female fiction writers (which is very small), it's actually much more likely that Maria is a nurse. So it's important to keep in mind that the representativeness heuristic can produce faulty estimates if (1) we fail to consider possible variations from the prototype or (2) we fail to consider the approximate number of prototypes that actually exist.

Vivid Images and the Availability Heuristic More than a hundred people died when this jet broke up while landing in Sioux City, Iowa. After media coverage of a plane crash, we may exaggerate the dangers of air travel, overestimating the likelihood that the plane we're traveling in might crash. How does the availability heuristic explain this phenomenon?

availability heuristic
A strategy in which the likelihood of an event is estimated on the basis of how easily other instances of the event are available in memory.

representativeness heuristic
A strategy in which the likelihood of an event is estimated by comparing how similar it is to the typical prototype of the event.

Making Decisions:

Some Final Thoughts

First, although there are many pitfalls to making risky decisions, a range of acceptable results often exists. Although one outcome may be the most desirable, less desirable outcomes might still be acceptable. For example, in deciding which car to buy, you try to pick the model that offers you the most for your money. But in choosing among five different models, it may well be that any one of the cars would be likely to meet your needs.

Second, in everyday life we often make decisions based on inadequate evidence or by using heuristics that lead us to inaccurate conclusions. Moreover, several psychological factors can influence the way that we evaluate evidence. Box 7.2, "The Persistence of Unwarranted Beliefs," discusses some of the less-than-logical processes that can affect judgment and decisions.

Third, rational calculation is not always the best way of making a risky decision. If people relied only on objective criteria in making decisions, few people would attempt such risky ventures as becoming a creative writer or actor, marketing a new invention, or starting a business (Goleman & others, 1992).

Finally, despite pitfalls in decision making, most of us make reasonable and workable decisions that produce successful outcomes to life's dilemmas.

Language and Thought

> Language is a system for combining arbitrary symbols to produce an infinite number of meaningful statements. What are five characteristics of language? How does language affect thinking? Can animals use language?

The human capacity for language is surely one of the most remarkable of all our cognitive abilities. With little effort, you produce hundreds of new sentences every day. And you're able to understand the vast majority of the thousands of words contained in this chapter without consulting a dictionary.

The primary function of language is, of course, to communicate. Human language has many special qualities—qualities that make it flexible, versatile, and complex. **Language** can be formally defined as a system for combining arbitrary symbols to produce an infinite number of meaningful statements. We'll begin our discussion of language and thought by describing these special characteristics of language. In Chapter 9, we'll discuss language development.

The Characteristics of Language

The purpose of language is to communicate—to express meaningful information in a way that can be understood by others. To do so, language requires the use of *symbols*. These symbols may be sounds, written words, or, as in American Sign Language, formalized gestures.

A few symbols may be similar in form to the meaning that they signify, such as the English words *boom* or *pop*. However, for the vast majority of words, the connection between the symbol and the meaning is completely *arbitrary* (Pinker, 1995). For example, *ton* is a small word that stands for a

language
A system for combining arbitrary symbols to produce an infinite number of meaningful statements.

CRITICAL THINKING 7.2

The Persistence of Unwarranted Beliefs

Throughout this text, we've shown how many pseudoscientific claims have been scientifically investigated and disproven. However, once a belief in a pseudoscience or paranormal phenomenon is established, the presentation of contradictory evidence often has little impact. Ironically, contradictory evidence can actually *strengthen* a person's established beliefs (Lord & others, 1979). How do psychologists account for this?

Several psychological studies have explored how people deal with evidence—specifically, evidence that contradicts their beliefs (see Zusne & Jones, 1989; Ross & Anderson, 1982). The four obstacles to logical thinking described below can account for much of the persistence of unwarranted beliefs in pseudosciences.

Obstacle 1: The Belief-Bias Effect

The *belief-bias effect* occurs when people accept only the evidence that conforms to their belief, rejecting or ignoring any evidence that doesn't (Matlin, 1989). For example, in a study conducted by Warren Jones and Dan Russell (1980), ESP-believers and ESP-disbelievers watched two attempts at telepathic communication. In each attempt, a "receiver" tried to indicate what card the "sender" was holding.

In reality, both attempts were rigged. One attempt was designed to appear to be a successful demonstration of telepathy, with a significant number of accurate responses. The other attempt was designed to convincingly demonstrate failure. In this case, the number of accurate guesses was no more than chance and could be produced by simple random guessing.

Following the demonstration, the subjects were asked what they believed

had taken place. Both believers and disbelievers indicated that ESP had occurred in the successful attempt. But only the believers said that ESP had *also* taken place in the clearly *unsuccessful* attempt. In other words, the ESP-believers ignored the evidence in the failed attempt. This is the essence of the belief-bias effect.

Obstacle 2: Confirmation Bias

Confirmation bias is the strong tendency to search for information or evidence that confirms a belief, while making little or no effort to search for information that might disprove the belief (Myers, 1996). For example, we tend to read the newpaper and magazine columns of editorial writers who interpret events from our perspective and to avoid the columns of writers who don't see things our way.

Obstacle 3: The Fallacy of Positive Instances

The *fallacy of positive instances* is the tendency to remember uncommon events that seem to confirm our beliefs, while forgetting events that disconfirm our beliefs. Often, the occurrence is really nothing more than coincidence. For example, you find yourself thinking of an old friend. A few moments later, the phone rings and it's him. You remember this seemingly telepathic event, but forget all the times that you've thought of your old friend and he did *not* call. In other words, you remember the positive instance but fail to notice the negative instances when the anticipated event did not occur.

Obstacle 4: The Overestimation Effect

The tendency to overestimate the rarity of events is referred to as the *overestimation effect*. Suppose a "psychic" comes to your class, which consists of

23 students. Using his psychic abilities, he "senses" that two people in the class were born on the same day. A quick survey finds that, indeed, two people share the same month and day of birth. This is pretty impressive evidence of clairvoyance, right? After all, what are the odds that two people in a class of 23 would have the same birthday?

When we perform this "psychic" demonstration in class, our students usually estimate that it is very unlikely that 2 people in a class of 23 will share a birthday. In reality, the odds are *1 out of 2,* or 50-50 (Cole, 1995; Alcock, 1981). Our students' overestimation of the rarity of this event is an example of the *overestimation effect*.

Thinking Critically About the Evidence

On the one hand, it is important to keep an open mind. Simply dismissing an idea as "impossible" shuts out the consideration of evidence for new and potentially intriguing ideas or phenomena. At one time, for example, scientists thought it impossible that rocks could fall from the sky (Hines, 1988).

On the other hand, the four obstacles described here underscore the importance of choosing ways to gather and think about evidence that will help us avoid unwarranted beliefs and self-deception.

The critical thinking skills we described in Chapter 1 are useful in evaluating all claims, including pseudoscientific or paranormal claims. In particular, it's important to stress again that good critical thinkers strive to evaluate *all* the available evidence before reaching a conclusion, not just the evidence that supports what they want to believe.

vast quantity, while *millimicron* is a large word that stands for a very small quantity. Because the relationship between the symbol and its meaning is arbitrary, language is tremendously flexible (Ashcraft, 1994). New words can be invented, and the meanings of words can change and evolve (Pinker, 1994).

Speakers of the same language agree on the connection between the sound and what it symbolizes. If people who speak the same language are in agreement that *max* means "Wednesday," then Wednesday it is. This leads us to a second important characteristic of language: the meaning of these symbols is *shared* by others who speak the same language. A foreign language sounds like a stream of meaningless sounds because we do not share the memory of the connection between the arbitrary sounds and the concrete meanings they symbolize.

Third, language is a system. Language is highly structured and follows specific rules. That is, every language has its own unique *syntax,* which consists of rules for combining words (Ashcraft, 1994). Although you're usually unaware of these rules as you're speaking or writing, you immediately notice when a rule has been violated. For example, you instantly recognize that the sentence "The child is to the zoo gone" violates the rules of word order in English.

The rules of language help determine the meaning that is being communicated. Word-order rules are very important in determining the meaning of an English phrase. For example, "The boy ate the giant pumpkin" has an entirely different meaning than "The giant pumpkin ate the boy." Other languages are less dependent on word order than English (Hunt & Agnoli, 1991). Instead, meaning may be conveyed by other rule-based distinctions, such as the particular pronouns, the class or category of word, or the word endings that are used (Pinker, 1994).

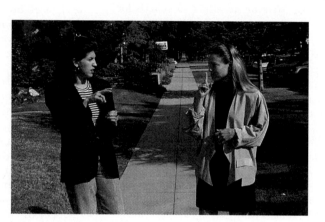

American Sign Language American Sign Language, used by the hearing impaired, meets all the formal requirements for language, including syntax, displacement, and generativity.

A fourth important characteristic of language is that it is creative, or *generative.* That is, you can generate an infinite number of new and different phrases and sentences (Anderson, 1995). Except for a few pat phrases like "Have a nice day" or "How's it going?" virtually every sentence you utter is new and unique, as are most of the sentences that you read in this textbook.

A final important characteristic of human language is called *displacement:* you can communicate meaningfully about ideas, objects, and activities that are not physically present. Rather than being limited to the here and now, you can refer to activities that will take place in the future or that took place in the past. You can even communicate meaningfully about activities that will never take place, or that will take place only if certain conditions are met ("If you get that promotion, maybe we can afford a new car"). You can also carry on a vivid conversation about abstract ideas ("What is justice?") or strictly imaginary topics ("If you were going to spend a year in a space station orbiting Mars, what would you bring along?").

How Language Influences Thinking

All your cognitive abilities are involved in understanding and producing language. You interpret the words you hear or read (or see, in the case of American Sign Language) through the use of perception. Using learning and memory, you acquire and remember the meaning of words. You use language to help you reason, represent and solve problems, and make decisions (Polk & Newell, 1995).

Language can influence thinking in several ways (Matlin, 1985). In this section, we'll consider just a few of the ways in which language affects cognitive processes, including memory and our perception of other people.

CULTURE AND HUMAN BEHAVIOR 7.3

The Effect of Language on Perception

Professionally, Benjamin Whorf was an insurance company inspector. But his passion was the study of languages, particularly Native American languages. In the 1950s, Whorf proposed an intriguing theory that became known as the *Whorfian hypothesis.*

Whorf (1956) believed that a person's language determines the very structure of his or her thought and perception. Your language, he claimed, determines how you perceive and "carve up" the phenomena of your world. He argued that people who speak very different languages have completely different world views. More formally, the Whorfian hypothesis is called the **linguistic relativity hypothesis**—the notion that differences among languages cause differences in the thoughts of their speakers (Pinker, 1994).

To illustrate his hypothesis, Whorf contended that the Eskimos had many different words for "snow." Each of these words supposedly described a specific type of snow—falling snow, drifting snow, snow you can use to make an igloo, and so forth. But English, he pointed out, has only the word *snow.* According to Whorf (1956):

> We have the same word for falling snow, snow on the ground, snow packed hard like ice, slushy snow, wind-driven flying snow—whatever the situation may be. To an Eskimo, this all-inclusive word would be almost unthinkable; he would say that falling snow, slushy snow, and so on, are sensuously and operationally different, different things to contend with; he uses different words for them and for other kinds of snow.

Whorf's example would be compelling except for one problem: the Eskimos do *not* have dozens of different words for snow. Rather, they have just a few words for snow (Martin, 1986; Pullum, 1991). Beyond that minor sticking point, think carefully about Whorf's example. Is it really true that English-speaking people have only a limited capacity to describe snow? Or that English-speaking people do not discriminate between different types of snow? The English language includes *snowflake, snowfall, slush, sleet, flurry, blizzard,* and *avalanche.* Avid skiers have many additional words to describe snow, from *powder* to *mogul* to *hardpack.*

More generally, people with expertise in a particular area tend to perceive and make finer distinctions than nonexperts do. This is true regardless of the language spoken. Experts are also more likely to have names for those different distinctions (Pinker, 1994). To the knowledgeable birdwatcher, for example, there are distinct differences between a cedar waxwing and a bohemian waxwing. To the nonexpert, they're just two brownish birds with yellow tail feathers.

Despite expert/nonexpert differences in noticing and naming details, we don't claim that the expert "sees" a different reality than a nonexpert. In other words, our perceptions and thought processes influence the language we use to describe those perceptions (Rosch, 1987). Notice that this conclusion is the exact *opposite* of the linguistic relativity hypothesis.

Whorf also pointed out that many languages have different color naming systems. English has names for eleven basic colors: *black, white, red, green, yellow, blue, brown, purple, pink, orange,* and *gray.* However, some languages have only a few color terms. Navajo, for example, has only one word to describe both blue and green, but two different words for black (Fishman, 1960/1974). Would people who had just a few words for colors "carve up" and perceive the electromagnetic spectrum differently?

Eleanor Rosch set out to answer this question ([Rosch] Heider & Olivier, 1972). The people of New Guinea who speak a language called Dani have words for only two colors. *Mili* is used for the dark, cool colors of black, green, and blue. *Mola* is used for light, warm colors, such as white, red, and yellow. According to the Whorfian hypothesis, the people of New Guinea, with names for only two classes of colors, should perceive color differently than English-speaking people, with names for eleven basic colors.

Rosch's procedure was simple: she tested the Dani speakers' ability to recognize and remember colors. She showed Dani speakers a brightly colored chip and then, 30 seconds later, asked them to pick out the color they had seen from an array of other colors. Her results? The Dani-speaking people perceived colors in much the same way as English-speaking people. For example, even though both red and yellow were called *mola,* the Dani could distinguish between them. Despite their lack of a specific word for the color they were shown, the Dani could remember and identify the color from a range of other colors as readily as English-speaking Americans given the same test.

Whorf's strong contention that language *determines* perception and the structure of thought has not been supported. Rather than *determining* perception and thought, language can *influence* our perception and thought (see Hunt & Agnoli, 1991). And, it seems more accurate to say that, rather than determining cultural differences, language *reflects* cultural differences (Pinker, 1994; Rosch, 1987).

1. :-D   **6.** :-)

2. :-(O)   **7.** :-P

3. :-(**8.** :-&

4. ;-)   **9.** =:-o

5. [ ]   **10.** :-x

Language and Memory

Language can affect our thoughts by influencing what we remember. As a demonstration, spend a few moments looking at the ten patterns of typing symbols in the margin. Then, without looking back, reproduce as many of the patterns as you can on a separate sheet of paper.

How many could you remember? If you had difficulty reproducing them exactly, it's not surprising. However, you may find these patterns easier to remember if we tell you that these symbols are used to represent facial expressions and emotions when people communicate via computer networks or send electronic mail. Called "smilies" or "emoticons," these symbols function as emotional signposts in on-line conversations (A. Nelson, 1995).

Turn your book sideways and look at the symbols again. According to computer expert Guy Kawasaki (1991) and others, the patterns mean the following:

1. :-D = laughing   **6.** :-) = smile

2. :-(O) = yelling   **7.** :-P = sticking out tongue

3. :-(= frown   **8.** :-& = tongue-tied

4. ;-) = wink   **9.** =:-o = EEK!

5. [ ] = hug   **10.** :-x = My lips are sealed.

Giving these patterns distinctive names makes it much easier to remember—and reproduce—them. The same is true of other patterns (Ellis & Hunt, 1993b).

As we noted in Chapter 6, language can also contribute to memory *distortions*. A classic experiment demonstrated this point. Participants in the study were shown a series of line drawings, each of which had one of two labels. For example, the simple line drawing "O—O" was labeled *either* "dumbbells" or "eyeglasses." Participants who had been shown the drawing with the "dumbbells" label were later likely to reconstruct it as "O———O". But participants who had been shown the drawing with the label "eyeglasses" were more likely to draw it as "O‿O" (Carmichael & others, 1932).

Language and Social Perception

Another important way in which language can influence thought has to do with our social perceptions of others. Consider the different images produced in your mind by these pairs of terms:

ambulance chaser	vs.	personal injury lawyer
statuesque brunette	vs.	tall, dark-haired woman
vivacious blonde	vs.	articulate light-haired woman
grease monkey	vs.	automotive technician

The nuances of the words we use can influence our social perceptions of others, reinforcing or minimizing negative stereotypes. Language that promotes stereotypical thinking can encourage discrimination against women, the elderly, and minorities or members of ethnic groups. In Chapter 12, we'll discuss the effects of stereotypes in more detail.

Language and Gender Bias

When you hear about a course titled, "Man and His Environment," what image comes to mind? Do you visualize a group of men tromping through the forest, or do you imagine a mixed group of males and females?

Technically, the word *man* or the pronoun *he* can refer to either a male or a female in English. That's because there is no gender-neutral pronoun in English. So, according to the rules of the English language, the course title "Man and His Environment" refers to both men and women, just as the sentence, "As man evolved, he developed language" does not apply to men alone, but rather to the entire human race.

However, what do people actually understand by this style of language? Most people are not equally likely to visualize a woman or group of women when they hear the course title "Man and His Environment." And, if using the masculine pronoun were truly gender-neutral, we would not be startled by sentences like these: "A secretary can increase his efficiency by using a computer," or "A receptionist should look his best when important clients are visiting the office."

Several studies have shown that using the masculine pronoun tends to produce images of males and exclude females (Gastil, 1990). In a study by Nancy Henley (1989), participants were given identical sentence fragments to complete. Examples included "If a writer expects to get a book published . . ." and "If an employee wants a raise . . ." But participants in the first group were given the masculine generic *he* to use in finishing the sentences. Participants in the second group were given either *they* or *he or she* to use in completing the sentences.

After completing the sentences, the subjects were asked to describe their mental imagery for each sentence and to provide a first name for the person they visualized. When the word *he* was used, subjects were much more likely to produce a male image and first name than a female image and name. When *he or she* was used, subjects were only slightly more likely to use a male rather than a female image or name.

Using the masculine generic pronoun influences people to visualize a male, even when they "know" that *he* supposedly includes both men and women (Hamilton, 1991, 1988). Thus, using *he* to refer to both men and women in speech and writing tends to increase male bias.

You may have noticed that we alternate the use of the pronouns *he* and *she* in this book, and sometimes put in a *he or she*. Now you know why! In teaching our classes, we've also found that students often erroneously assume that a researcher is male if only the first and middle initials are given. In the References at the back of the book, we list the first names of researchers, so that the many women who have made important contributions to psychology can be more easily recognized.

Animal Communication:
Can Animals Learn to Use Language?

Without question, animals communicate. Chimpanzees "chutter" to warn of snakes, "rraup" to warn of an eagle, and "chirp" to let the others know that a leopard is nearby (Marler, 1967). Each of the warning calls of the vervet monkey of East Africa triggers specific behaviors for a particular danger, such as scurrying for cover in the bushes when the warning for an airborne predator is sounded (Cheney & Seyfarth, 1990).

Animals also communicate with other species. The squirrels in our back yard will sit in the tree branches and scold our cat, Nubbin, with a brisk *chuk, chuk, chuk* if she gets too near the squirrel feeder. And to let us know that her food bowl is empty, Nubbin meows and rubs against our legs until we get the message.

Vervet Monkeys Vervet monkeys sound different alarm calls for different kinds of predators. The "leopard" call sends the troop into the trees to avoid leopards and other ground predators. In response to the "eagle" call, the monkeys look up and take cover in bushes to hide from aerial predators.

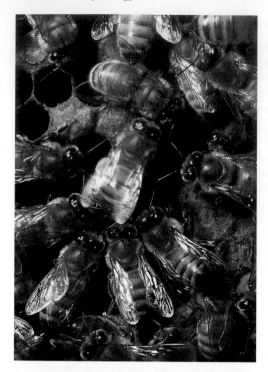

A Honeybee "Conversation?" Honeybees have a complex system of communication. The honeybee in the center is performing a "dance" that reports the location and distance of a pollen source to its nest mates. Information about the quality of the pollen sources is also communicated by the honeybee's dance (Gould & Gould, 1994).

Clearly, then, animals communicate, but can they learn to use language? In an attempt to answer this question, psychologists have taught chimpanzees and other primates to communicate simple messages by using American Sign Language, computer symbols, or plastic geometric shapes (Fouts & Rigby, 1977; Rumbaugh, 1977; Premack & Premack, 1983). In early studies conducted in the 1970s and 1980s, primates were found to be able to follow directions, respond to questions, request food and objects from their trainers, and even generate new combinations of words (see Candland, 1995). These early results seemed to show that primates were able to demonstrate the fundamental characteristics of using a language they had been taught.

But a considerable amount of controversy surrounded these early accomplishments. After training a chimpanzee named Nim to use sign language, Herbert Terrace concluded that Nim and the other primates were not truly producing language. Instead, Terrace concluded that they were merely imitating their trainers or producing learned behaviors in response to nonverbal cues (Terrace, 1985, 1981). Terrace pointed out that the sequences of "words" produced by the primates bore no resemblance to the rule-governed sentences of true language. Nor did the primate sequences seem to demonstrate even a rudimentary grasp of syntax.

Since these issues were raised, research in the area of animal language has proceeded more cautiously and under more carefully controlled conditions that guard against the inadvertent cueing of responses by experimenters. Some of the most promising results have come from the research of Sue Savage-Rumbaugh, Duane Rumbaugh, and their co-workers. These researchers are working with a rare chimpanzee species called the *bonobo*. In the mid-1980s, they taught a female bonobo named Matata to press symbols on a computer keyboard. While Matata did not learn many symbols, her infant son, Kanzi, appeared to learn how to use the keyboard simply from watching his mother and her caretakers (Savage-Rumbaugh & Lewin, 1994).

Although Kanzi never received formal training, he quickly learned many symbols. Altogether, Kanzi understands more than 150 spoken English words. Kanzi can respond to new, complex spoken commands like "Go to the refrigerator and get out a tomato" (Savage-Rumbaugh, 1993). These spoken commands are made by an assistant out of Kanzi's view, so he cannot be responding to nonverbal cues.

Kanzi also seems to demonstrate an elementary understanding of syntax. He is able to respond correctly to commands whose meaning is determined by word order. For example, using a toy dog and toy snake, he responds appropriately to commands like "Make the dog bite the snake" and "Make the snake bite the dog" (Savage-Rumbaugh, 1993). Kanzi seems to demonstrate a level of language comprehension that is roughly equivalent to that of a two-and-a-half-year-old human child.

Sue Savage-Rumbaugh with Kanzi
Kanzi, a bonobo, communicates by pressing symbols on a computer keyboard.

Research using other species has produced evidence that nonprimates can also acquire certain limited aspects of language. Louis Herman and his co-workers (1993) have trained bottle-nosed dolphins to respond to sounds and gestures, each of which stands for a word. The artificial languages taught to the dolphins incorporate rules governing syntax, or word order.

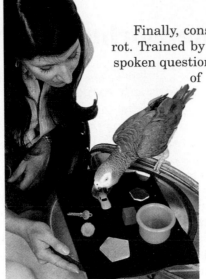

Irene Pepperberg with Alex In response to Pepperberg's request, Alex correctly selects the object that is "blue."

Finally, consider the case of Alex, an African gray parrot. Trained by Irene Pepperberg (1993), Alex can answer spoken questions with spoken words. After about ten years of training, Alex has about a seventy-word vocabulary, which includes the words for objects, names, shapes, and numbers and some simple phrases, like "come here," "how many," and "want to go."

Alex can answer questions about the color and number of objects, and even seems to comprehend certain simple concepts (Gould & Gould, 1994). When shown two objects, Alex can indicate how the objects are the same. For example, when shown a blue key and a blue cork and asked "What's the same?" Alex will respond "Color." Furthermore, Alex does just as well with novel objects that he's never seen before as he does with familiar objects. This implies that he understands the concepts of color and size, rather than memorizing stock phrases or responding to particular conditioning cues.

So we're back to our original question: Can animals learn to use language? Since the mid-1980s, the results of several ongoing studies have produced some compelling demonstrations of animal language learning. Just as important, this recent research seems to address many of the objections that were raised in response to the initial animal language studies. However, while recent results are promising, keep in mind that no animal has come close to developing or learning sophisticated language skills. Even the performance of primate superstars like Kanzi pales in comparison with the language learning demonstrated by a three-year-old child (Pinker, 1994).

Collectively, the animal language research reflects an active area of psychological research that is referred to as *animal cognition* or *comparative cognition*. While the results of these studies are fascinating, a great deal remains to be discovered about the limitations and potential of different species of animals to communicate, produce language, and solve problems (Wasserman, 1993; Povinelli, 1993). Many psychologists caution against jumping to the conclusion that animals can "think" or that they possess self-awareness, because such conclusions are far from proven (Blumberg & Wasserman, 1995).

CONCEPT REVIEW 7.3

Language

Match the following characteristics of language with each example.
(A) Syntax
(B) Meaning is shared among users of the same language.
(C) Generative
(D) Displacement

_____ **1.** This sentence has never been written before: Never stuff an artichoke into your floppy disk drive.

_____ **2.** Cele and Rochelle argue about what would have happened if Richard Nixon had not resigned as U.S. president.

_____ **3.** "John crushed the boulder" and "The boulder crushed John" have entirely different meanings.

_____ **4.** In response to a favor, people in Norway say, *"Tak!"* while people in France say, *"Merci beaucoup!"*

Measuring Intelligence

Intelligence can be defined as the global capacity to think rationally, act purposefully, and deal effectively with the environment. What roles did Binet, Terman, and Wechsler play in the development of intelligence tests? How did Binet, Terman, and Wechsler differ in their beliefs about intelligence and its measurement?

Up to this point, we have talked about a broad range of cognitive abilities—the use of mental images and concepts, problem solving and decision making, and the use of language. All these mental abilities are aspects of what we commonly call *intelligence*.

What exactly is intelligence? We will rely on a formal definition developed by psychologist David Wechsler. Wechsler (1977, 1944) defined **intelligence** as the global capacity to think rationally, act purposefully, and deal effectively with the environment. Although many people commonly equate intelligence with "book smarts," notice that Wechsler's definition is much broader. To Wechsler, intelligence is reflected in effective, rational, and goal-directed behavior.

Can such abilities be measured? If so, how? Intelligence tests attempt to measure general mental abilities, rather than accumulated knowledge or aptitude for a specific subject or area. In the next several sections, we will describe the evolution of intelligence tests, including the qualities that make any psychological test scientifically acceptable. Despite the existence of well-established intelligence tests, you'll see later that psychologists still disagree on the basic definition of intelligence and how intelligence should best be measured.

Just as important, the use of intelligence testing has sparked some highly charged debates over differences in the average intelligence of different racial groups. Are these differences primarily due to hereditary factors, environmental factors, or both? Is it even possible to determine how much of intelligence is due to hereditary factors? And just how much impact do environmental factors, such as discrimination against certain groups, play in the results of intelligence testing? Between now and the end of the chapter, we will tackle all of these issues. But first, we need to set the stage by looking at the evolution of the modern intelligence test.

Alfred Binet:

Identifying Students Who Needed Special Help

To judge well, to comprehend well, to reason well, these are the essential activities of intelligence.
Alfred Binet and Théodore Simon (1905)

One of the first attempts to scientifically measure intelligence arose from the need to solve a practical problem. In the early 1900s, the French government passed a law requiring all children to attend school. Faced with the need to educate children from a wide variety of backgrounds, the French government commissioned psychologist **Alfred Binet** (1857–1911) to develop procedures to identify students who might require special help.

Along with French psychiatrist Théodore Simon, Binet devised a series of tests to measure different kinds of mental abilities. Binet deliberately did not test abilities like reading or mathematics that the students might have already been taught. Instead, he focused on elementary mental abilities like memory, attention, and the ability to understand similarities and differences.

Binet arranged the questions on his test in order of difficulty, with the simplest tasks first. Simple problems included such tasks as visually following the movement of a lit match or pointing to different parts of the body. The tasks became progressively more difficult, such as stating the differences be-

intelligence
The global capacity to think rationally, act purposefully, and deal effectively with the environment.

Alfred Binet French psychologist Alfred Binet is shown here with an unidentified child. Although Binet developed the first systematic intelligence tests, he did not believe that he was measuring innate ability. Instead, he believed that his tests could identify schoolchildren who could benefit from special help.

tween a fly and a butterfly, copying a drawing from memory, or repeating a series of numbers (Aiken, 1994; Fancher, 1985).

Binet found that as children grew older, they were able to answer increasingly difficult questions. More important, Binet noticed that brighter children performed like older children, while less capable children performed like younger children. A bright seven-year-old might be able to answer the same number of questions as a typical nine-year-old, while a less capable seven-year-old might only do as well as an average five-year-old.

It was this observation that led Binet to the idea of a mental level or **mental age** that was different from a child's chronological age. An "advanced" seven-year-old might have a mental age of nine, while a "slow" seven-year-old might demonstrate a mental age of five.

It is somewhat ironic that Binet's early tests became the basis for the modern intelligence tests. First, Binet did *not* believe that he was measuring an inborn or permanent level of "intelligence" (Kamin, 1995). He believed that his tests could help identify "slow" children who could benefit from special help. In fact, he developed a program of special classes that would help such children "learn how to learn" (Fancher, 1985).

Second, Binet believed that intelligence was too complex a quality to describe with a single number (Siegler, 1992). He steadfastly refused to rank "normal" children on the basis of their scores, believing that such rankings would be unfair. He recognized that many individual factors, such as a child's level of motivation, might affect the child's score. Finally, Binet noted that an individual's score could vary from time to time (Gould, 1993; Fancher, 1985).

Intelligence Tests Come to America:
The Stanford-Binet Intelligence Test

There was enormous interest in Binet's test in the United States. Binet's test was translated and adapted by Stanford University psychologist **Lewis Terman** (1877–1956). Terman's revision was called the *Stanford-Binet Intelligence Scale.* First published in 1916, the Stanford-Binet was for many years the standard for intelligence tests in the United States.

Terman adopted the suggestion of a German psychologist that scores on the Stanford-Binet test be expressed in terms of a single number, called the **intelligence quotient,** or **IQ.** This number was derived by dividing the individual's mental age by the chronological age and multiplying the result by 100. Thus, a child of average intelligence, whose mental age and chronological age were the same, would have an IQ score of 100. A bright ten-year-old child with a mental age of thirteen would have an IQ of 130 (13/10 × 100). A slow child with a chronological age of ten and a mental age of seven would have an IQ of 70 (7/10 × 100). It was Terman's use of the intelligence quotient that resulted in the popularization of the phrase "IQ test."

World War I:
The Emergence of Group Intelligence Testing

When the United States entered World War I in 1917, the U.S. military was faced with the need to screen 2 million army recruits (Anastasi, 1988). Using a group intelligence test devised by one of Terman's students, army psychologists developed two group intelligence tests. The *Army Alpha* test was administered in writing, and the *Army Beta* test was administered orally to recruits and draftees who could not read.

mental age
A measurement of intelligence in which an individual's mental level is expressed in terms of the average abilities of a given age group.

intelligence quotient (IQ)
A global measure of intelligence derived by comparing an individual's score to that of others in the same age group.

Testing Immigrants at Ellis Island This photograph, taken in 1917, shows an examiner administering a mental test to a newly arrived immigrant at Ellis Island. According to one intelligence "expert" of the time, 80% of the Hungarians, 79% of the Italians, and 87% of the Russians were "feeble-minded" (see Kamin, 1995). The new science of "mental testing" was used to argue that immigration be restricted.

After World War I ended, the Army Alpha and Army Beta group intelligence tests were adapted for civilian use. The result was a tremendous surge in the intelligence testing movement. Group intelligence tests were designed to test virtually all ages and types of people, including preschool children, prisoners, and newly arriving immigrants (Kamin, 1995; Anastasi, 1988). However, the indiscriminate use of the tests also resulted in skepticism and hostility.

For example, newly arriving immigrants were screened as they arrived at Ellis Island. The result was sweeping generalizations about the intelligence of different nationalities and races. During the 1920s, a few intelligence testing experts even urged the U.S. Congress to severely limit the immigration of certain nationalities to keep the country from being "overrun with a horde of the unfit" (see Kamin, 1995).

Despite concerns about the misuse of the so-called IQ tests, the tests quickly became very popular. Lost was Binet's belief that intelligence tests were useful only to identify those who might benefit from special educational help. And, contrary to Binet's contention, it soon came to be believed that the IQ score was a fixed, inborn characteristic resistant to change (Gould, 1993).

Terman and other American psychologists also extended the meaning of the IQ score to apply to many realms outside of school. Believing that a high IQ was necessary for success in life, Terman went so far as to identify the minimum IQ that was required to succeed in different professions. He even proposed that businesses employ psychologists to screen applicants so that positions would be filled only by people of the appropriate IQ level (Gould, 1993).

To investigate the relationship between IQ and success in life, Terman (1926) identified 1,500 California schoolchildren with "genius" IQ scores. He set up a longitudinal research study to follow their careers throughout their lives—a study that is still in progress today. Some results of Terman's landmark study are described in Box 7.4, "Does a High IQ Predict Success in Life?"

The Wechsler Tests of Intelligence

The next major advance in intelligence testing came as a result of a young psychologist's dissatisfaction with the Stanford-Binet and other intelligence tests in widespread use. **David Wechsler** (1896–1981) was in charge of testing adults of widely varying cultural and socioeconomic backgrounds and ages at a large hospital in New York City. He designed a new intelligence test called the *Wechsler Adult Intelligence Scale (WAIS),* which was first published in 1955.

The WAIS had two advantages over the Stanford-Binet. First, the WAIS was specifically designed for adults rather than children. Second, Wechsler's test provided scores on eleven subtests measuring different abilities. The subtest scores were grouped to provide an overall "verbal score" and "performance score." The *verbal score* represented scores on subtests of vocabulary, comprehension, knowledge of general information, and other verbal tasks. The *performance score* reflected scores on largely nonverbal subtests, such as identifying the missing part in incomplete pictures, arranging pictures to tell a story, or arranging blocks to match a given pattern.

The design of the WAIS reflected Wechsler's belief that intelligence involves a variety of mental abilities. Because the WAIS provided an individualized profile of the subject's strengths and weaknesses on specific tasks, it marked a return to the attitudes and goals of Alfred Binet (Sternberg, 1990; Fancher, 1985).

David Wechsler Born in Romania in 1896, David Wechsler emigrated with his family to New York when he was 6 years old. Like Binet, Wechsler believed that intelligence involved a variety of mental abilities. He also strongly believed that IQ scores could be influenced by personality, motivation, and cultural factors (Matarazzo, 1981).

IN FOCUS BOX 7.4

Does a High IQ Score Predict Success in Life?

Starting in 1921, Lewis M. Terman set out to investigate the common notion that genius-level intelligence is related to social and personal maladjustment, physical weakness, and mental instability. Terman identified 1,500 California children between the ages of eight and twelve who had IQs above 140, the minimum IQ score for genius-level intelligence. The average IQ of the children was 150, and eighty children had scores above 170. Terman's goal was to track these children by conducting periodic surveys and interviews to see how genius-level intelligence would affect the course of their lives.

Within a few years, Terman (1926) showed that the highly intelligent children were far from being socially and physically inept. In fact, his findings indicated just the opposite. The children tended to be socially well-adjusted. They were also taller, stronger, and healthier than average children, with fewer illnesses and accidents. And as a group, not surprisingly, these children performed exceptionally well in school.

With the exception of moral character, there is nothing as significant for a child's future as his grade of intelligence.

Lewis M. Terman (1916)

Since Terman's death in 1956, the study has been continued by other psychologists, most notably Melita Oden, Robert Sears, and Pauline Sears. These collaborators in Terman's study kept track of the subjects, who were now well into adulthood. Today, more than seventy years after the study began, psychologists continue to assess the professional and personal accomplishments of the surviving original subjects (Holahan & Sears, 1995).

How did Terman's "gifted" children fare in the real world as adults? As a group, they showed an astonishing range of accomplishments (Terman & Oden, 1959, 1947). In 1955, when the average income was $5,000 a year, the average income for the group was $33,000. Two-thirds had graduated from college, and a sizable proportion had gone on to earn advanced academic or professional degrees. There were no "creative geniuses"—no Picassos, Einsteins, or Mozarts—but there were many doctors, lawyers, scientists, university professors, business executives, and other professionals in the group. Collectively, the gifted group had produced 2,200 scientific articles, 92 books, 235 patents, and 38 novels (Goleman, 1980). One individual had become a famous science fiction writer, and another was an Oscar-winning movie director.

However, not all of Terman's subjects were so successful. To find out why, Terman's colleague Melita Oden compared the 100 most successful men (the "A" group) and the 100 least successful men (the "C" group) in Terman's sample. Despite their high IQ scores, only a handful of the C group were professionals, and none was doing exceptionally well. Whereas the C's were

earning slightly above the national average income, the A's were earning almost five times the national income and better than three times the average C-group income. In terms of their personal lives, the C's were less healthy, had higher rates of alcoholism, and were three times as likely to be divorced as the A's (Terman & Oden, 1959).

Given that the IQ scores of the A and C group were essentially the same, what accounted for the difference in their level of accomplishment? As children, the A's were much more likely to display "prudence and forethought, will power, perseverance, and the desire to excel" (Terman & Oden, 1959). As adults, the A's were rated differently from the C's on only three traits: they were more goal-oriented, had greater perseverance, and had greater self-confidence. Overall, the A's seemed to have greater ambition and a greater drive to achieve. In other words, *personality factors* seemed to account for the differences in level of accomplishment between the A group and the C group (Terman & Oden, 1959).

As the general success of Terman's gifted children demonstrates, high intelligence can certainly contribute to success in life. But intelligence alone is not enough. Although IQ scores do reliably predict academic success, success in school is no guarantee of success beyond school. Many different personality factors are involved in achieving success, such as motivation, emotional maturity, commitment to goals, creativity, and—perhaps most important—a willingness to work hard (Goleman, 1995; Sternberg, 1985, 1982; Renzulli, 1986). None of these attributes are measured by traditional IQ tests.

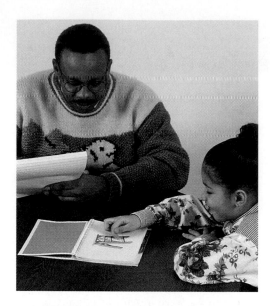

The Wechsler Intelligence Scale for Children (WISC) Revised and updated in 1991, the WISC-III is designed to assess the intelligence of children in the six to sixteen age range. This psychologist is administering the WISC-III picture completion subtest to a 6-year-old girl. Other WISC-III subtests include vocabulary, arithmetic, arranging blocks to match a design, and arranging pictures so that they correctly tell a story.

achievement test
A test designed to measure a person's level of knowledge, skill, or accomplishment in a particular area.

aptitude test
A test designed to assess a person's capacity to benefit from education or training.

standardization
The administration of a test to a large, representative sample of people under uniform conditions for the purpose of establishing norms.

normal curve (normal distribution)
A bell-shaped distribution of individual differences in a normal population in which most scores cluster around the average score.

reliability
The ability of a test to produce consistent results when administered on repeated occasions under similar conditions.

validity
The ability of a test to measure what it is intended to measure.

The subtest scores on the WAIS also proved to have practical and clinical value. Sharp differences among the scores could be revealing. For example, a pattern of low scores on some subtests combined with high scores on other subtests might indicate a specific learning disability (Kaufman, 1990). Or, someone who did well on the performance subtests but poorly on the verbal subtests might be unfamiliar with the culture rather than deficient in these skills (Aiken, 1994). That's because many items included on the verbal subtests draw on cultural knowledge.

Wechsler's test also provided a global IQ score, but he changed the way that the IQ score was calculated. On the Stanford-Binet and other early tests, the IQ represented the mental age divided by the chronological age. But this approach makes little sense when applied to adult subjects. Although a twelve-year-old is typically able to answer more questions than an eight-year-old because of developmental differences, such year-by-year age differences lose their meaning in adulthood.

Instead, Wechsler calculated the IQ by comparing an individual's score to the scores of others in the same general age group, such as young adults. The average score for a particular age group was statistically fixed at 100. The range of scores is statistically defined so that two-thirds of all scores fall between 85 and 115—the range that is considered to indicate "normal" or "average" intelligence. This procedure proved so successful that it was adopted by the administrators of other tests, including the current version of the Stanford-Binet. Today, IQ scores continue to be calculated by this method.

The WAIS was revised in 1981, so that today it is known as the WAIS-R. Since the 1960s, the WAIS has remained the most commonly administered intelligence test. Wechsler also developed two tests for children: the *Wechsler Intelligence Scale for Children* (WISC) and the *Wechsler Preschool and Primary Scale of Intelligence* (WPPSI).

Principles of Test Construction:
What Makes a Good Test?

Psychological tests must meet the requirements of standardization, reliability, and validity. What is the role of norms in standardization, and what is the normal curve? How are reliability and validity defined, and how are they determined?

There are many kinds of psychological tests that measure various aspects of intelligence or mental ability. **Achievement tests** are designed to measure a person's level of knowledge, skill, or accomplishment in a particular area, such as mathematics or a foreign language. You may remember periodically taking a battery of achievement tests during your elementary or high school years. There's a good chance that you took the Stanford Achievement Test, the Iowa Tests of Basic Skills, or the California Achievement Tests, three of the most commonly used achievement tests used by school systems (Aiken, 1994).

In contrast, **aptitude tests** are designed to assess a person's capacity to benefit from education or training. The overall goal of an aptitude test is to predict your ability to learn certain types of information or perform certain skills.

Regardless of whether it is an achievement, aptitude, or intelligence test, any psychological test must fulfill certain requirements to be considered scientifically acceptable. The three basic requirements of good test design are standardization, reliability, and validity. Let's briefly look at what each of those requirements entails.

"Normal" IQ scores range from 85 to 115—the average score of 100, plus or minus 15 points.

Number of scores →

68%

95%

| 0.1% | 2% | 14% | 34% | 34% | 14% | 2% | 0.1% |

0.1% 55   70   85   100   115   130   145 0.1%

IQ score

FIGURE 7.7 The Normal Curve of Distribution of IQ Scores
The distribution of IQ scores in the general population tends to follow a bell-shaped normal curve, with the average score defined as 100. Notice that 68 percent of the scores fall within the "normal" IQ range of 85 to 115. Ninety-five percent of the general population scores between 70 and 130, while only one-tenth of one percent score lower than 55 or higher than 145.

Demonstrating Validity A good test measures what it claims to measure. Shown here are sample items from an aptitude test, the Bennett Mechanical Comprehension Test. Because scores on this test are correlated with job performance in occupations requiring mechanical ability, the test is considered to be valid.

Look at Sample X on this page. It shows two men carrying a weighted object on a plank, and it asks, "Which man carries more weight?" Because the object is closer to man "B" than to man "A," man "B" is shouldering more weight; so blacken the circle under "B" on your answer sheet. Now look at Sample Y and answer it yourself. Fill in the circle under the correct answer on your answer sheet.

A   B

A   B   C
Municipal Bus Line

X

Which man carries more weight?
(If equal, mark C.)

EXAMPLES

A B C
X ○ ● ○
A B C
Y ○ ○ ○

Y

Which letter shows the seat where a passenger will get the smoothest ride?

Standardization

If you answer 75 out of 100 questions correctly, what does that score mean? Is it high, low, or average? In order to interpret an individual's test score, it has to be compared against some sort of standard of performance.

Standardization means that the test is given to a large number of subjects who are representative of the group of people for whom the test is designed. All the subjects take the same version of the test under uniform conditions. The scores of this group establish the *norms,* or the standards against which an individual score is compared and interpreted.

For IQ tests, such norms closely follow a pattern of individual differences called the **normal curve,** or **normal distribution.** In this bell-shaped pattern, most scores cluster around the average score. As scores become more extreme, fewer instances of the scores occur. In Figure 7.7, you can see the normal distribution of IQ scores on the WAIS-R. About 68 percent of subjects taking the WAIS-R will score between 85 and 115, the IQ range for "normal" intelligence. Less than 1 percent of the population have extreme scores that are above 145 or below 55.

Reliability

A good test must also have **reliability.** This means that the test must consistently produce similar scores on different occasions. How do psychologists determine if a psychological test is reliable? One way is to give two similar but not identical versions of the test at different times. Another procedure is to compare the scores on one half of the test to the scores on the other half of the test. A test is considered to be reliable if the test and retest scores are highly similar when such strategies are used.

Validity

Finally, a good test must demonstrate **validity,** which means that the test measures what it is supposed to measure. One way to establish the validity of a test is by demonstrating its predictive value. For example, if a test is designed to measure mechanical aptitude, the validity of the test could be demonstrated by comparing test scores with the degree of success that people ultimately have in jobs requiring mechanical skills. If people with high scores on the mechanical aptitude test ultimately become much more successful at mechanical jobs than people with low scores, the test would be considered valid.

In summary, if any psychological test is to be considered scientifically acceptable, the test must satisfy all three requirements of standardization, reliability, and validity. Keep that in mind the next time you encounter an "IQ test" or a "personality test" in a popular magazine or book. Although such tests may be entertaining, they usually lack any scientific basis because the essential requirements—standardization, reliability, and validity—have not been met.

Four Views on the Nature of Intelligence

Debate over the nature of intelligence centers on two key issues: (1) whether intelligence is a single factor and (2) how narrowly intelligence should be defined. How do Spearman, Thurstone, Gardner, and Sternberg differ in their views of intelligence?

The Wechsler Adult Intelligence Scale and the Stanford-Binet Intelligence Scale are standardized, reliable, and valid. But do they adequately measure intelligence? Psychologists do not agree on the answer to this question. Put simply, there is considerable disagreement about the nature of intelligence, including how intelligence should best be defined (Neisser & others, 1996).

Much of the controversy over the definition and nature of intelligence centers on two key issues:

1. Is intelligence a *single, general* ability? Or is intelligence a *cluster* of different abilities?

2. How *narrowly* should intelligence be defined? Does intelligence consist simply of mental abilities, like abstract reasoning, that are measured by IQ tests? Or does intelligence also involve practical skills that promote adaptation to a person's environment?

Although these issues have been debated for decades, they are far from being resolved (see Sternberg, 1995). In this section, we'll describe the views of four influential psychologists on both issues.

Charles Spearman:

Intelligence Is a General Ability

Some psychologists believe that a common factor, or general mental capacity, is at the core of different mental abilities. This approach originated with British psychologist **Charles Spearman** (1863–1945). While Spearman agreed that an individual's scores could vary on tests of different mental abilities, he found that the scores on different tests tended to be similar. That is, people who did well or poorly on a test of one mental ability, such as verbal ability, tended also to do well or poorly on the other tests.

Spearman recognized that particular individuals might excel in specific areas. However, Spearman (1904) believed that a factor he called **general intelligence,** or the **g factor,** was responsible for their overall performance on mental ability tests. Psychologists who follow this approach today think that intelligence can be described as a single measure of general cognitive ability, or g factor. Thus, general mental ability could accurately be expressed by a single number, such as the IQ score. Lewis Terman's approach to measuring and defining intelligence as a single, overall IQ score was in the tradition of Charles Spearman.

g factor (general intelligence)
The notion of a general intelligence factor that is responsible for a person's overall performance on tests of mental ability.

Examples of Gardner's Theory of Multiple Intelligences Gardner points out that many forms of mental ability are not adequately measured by traditional intelligence tests. Examples are the exceptional designs of this Navajo weaver (spatial intelligence), gifted jazz musician Wynton Marsalis (musical intelligence), and the poetic and storytelling genius of Maya Angelou (linguistic intelligence).

FIGURE 7.8 Gardner's "Multiple Intelligences"

Louis L. Thurstone:

Intelligence Is a Cluster of Abilities

Psychologist **Louis L. Thurstone** (1887–1955) flatly disagreed with Spearman's notion that intelligence is a single general mental capacity. Instead, Thurstone believed that there were seven different "primary mental abilities," each a relatively independent element of intelligence. Abilities such as verbal comprehension, numerical ability, reasoning, and perceptual speed are examples that Thurstone gave of independent "primary mental abilities."

To Thurstone, the so-called *g* factor was simply an overall average score of such independent abilities, and consequently was less important than an individual's specific *pattern* of mental abilities (Thurstone, 1937). David Wechsler's approach to measuring and defining intelligence as a pattern of different abilities was very similar to Thurstone's approach.

Howard Gardner:

"Multiple Intelligences"

More recently, **Howard Gardner** (b. 1943) has expanded Thurstone's basic notion of intelligence as different mental abilities that operate independently. However, Gardner has stretched the definition of intelligence. Rather than analyzing intelligence test results, Gardner (1985, 1993a) looked at the kinds of skills and products that are valued in different cultures. He also studied brain-damaged individuals, noting that some mental abilities are spared when others are lost. To Gardner, this phenomenon implies that different mental abilities are biologically distinct and controlled by different parts of the brain.

Like Thurstone, Gardner has suggested that such mental abilities are independent of each other, and cannot be accurately reflected in a single measure of intelligence. Rather than one intelligence, Gardner (1993a) believes there are "multiple intelligences." To Gardner, "an intelligence" is the ability to solve problems, or to create products, that are valued within one or more cultural settings. Thus, he believes that intelligence must be defined within the context of a particular culture. Gardner has proposed distinct, independent intelligences, which are summarized in Figure 7.8.

Some of the abilities emphasized by Gardner might be tapped by a standard intelligence test, such as logical-mathematical intelligence. However, other abilities, like bodily kinesthetic intelligence or musical intelligence, do not seem to be reflected on standard intelligence tests. Yet, as Gardner points out, such abilities are recognized and highly valued in many different cultures, including our own.

Linguistic intelligence	Adept at use of language: poet, writer, public speaker, native storyteller
Logical-mathematical intelligence	Logical, mathematical, and scientific intelligence: scientist, mathematician, navigator, surveyor
Musical intelligence	Musician, composer, singer
Spatial intelligence	Excels in ability to mentally visualize the relationships of objects or movements: sculptor, painter, expert chess player, architect
Bodily-kinesthetic intelligence	Control of bodily motions and capacity to handle objects skillfully: athlete, dancer, craftsperson
Personal intelligences	Understanding oneself and other people: politician, clinical psychologist, salesperson

triarchic theory of intelligence
Sternberg's theory that there are three forms of intelligence: componential, contextual, and experiential.

Robert Sternberg:
Three Forms of Intelligence

Robert Sternberg (b. 1949) agrees with Gardner that intelligence is a much broader quality than the narrow range of mental abilities tested by a conventional IQ test. However, Sternberg (1995, 1988a) disagrees with Gardner's notion of multiple, independent "intelligences." He believes that some of Gardner's "intelligences" are more accurately described as specialized "talents," while intelligence is a more general quality. Sternberg (1988a) points out that you would be able to manage just fine if you were tone-deaf and lacked "musical intelligence" in most societies. However, if you don't have the ability to reason and plan ahead, you would be unable to function in any culture.

Sternberg's **triarchic theory of intelligence** emphasizes both the universal aspects of intelligent behavior and the importance of adapting to a particular social and cultural environment. More specifically, Sternberg (1988a, 1985) contends that there are three forms of intelligence: componential, experiential, and contextual.

Componential intelligence refers to the mental processes used in learning how to solve problems, picking a problem-solving strategy, and solving problems. While conventional intelligence tests do measure mental abilities, they do not evaluate the strategies that are used to solve problems, which Sternberg considers important in determining componential intelligence.

Experiential intelligence is the ability to deal with novel situations by drawing on existing skills and knowledge. The intelligent person effectively draws on past experiences to cope with new situations, which often involves finding an unusual way to relate old information to new.

Contextual intelligence, also called *practical intelligence,* involves the ability to adapt to the environment. "Street smarts" is one way of describing contextual intelligence. Sternberg notes that what is required to adapt successfully in one particular situation or culture may be very different in another situation or culture. He stresses that the behaviors that reflect contextual intelligence can vary depending on the particular situation, environment, or culture. A person who is high in contextual intelligence functions effectively within a given cultural context.

Over 1,000 experts in intelligence testing were surveyed on their opinions about the most important elements of intelligence. As you can see, many experts agreed that some important elements of intelligence are *not* measured on intelligence tests.

TABLE 7.2 Important Elements of Intelligence and Intelligence Tests

Element of Intelligence	Percentage of Respondents Who Checked Item as an Important Element of Intelligence	Percentage Who Thought Item Was Important but Was Not Adequately Measured by IQ Tests
Abstract thinking or reasoning	99.3	19.9
Problem-solving ability	97.7	27.3
Capacity to acquire knowledge	96	42.2
Memory	80.5	12.7
Adaptation to one's environment	77.2	75.3
Mental speed	71.7	12.8
Linguistic competence	71	14
Mathematial competence	67.9	12.1
General knowledge	62.4	10.7
Creativity	59.6	88.3
Goal-directedness	24	64.1
Achievement motivation	18.9	71.7

SOURCE: Adapted from Snyderman & Rothman, 1987, Table 2, p. 140.

Looking Back:
The Nature of Intelligence

Despite disagreements on the specific nature and definition of intelligence, there is evidence that psychologists *do* generally agree on the characteristics of intelligent behavior. When several hundred psychologists who were experts in intelligence testing were surveyed, several points of agreement surfaced (Snyderman & Rothman, 1987, 1988). As shown in Table 7.2, the psychologists were virtually unanimous that factors such as abstract thinking, problem solving, and the capacity to acquire knowledge are important elements of intelligence. These aspects of intelligence are typically assessed in intelligence tests like the WAIS and Stanford-Binet.

However, many experts also agreed that other important aspects of intelligence exist but are *not* measured in conventional intelligence tests. These aspects include creativity, achievement motivation, and goal-directed behavior. While there was overall agreement that adaptation to one's environment was a significant factor in intelligence, three-fourths of those who agreed with this statement thought that existing tests do not adequately measure this quality. Thus, the respondents generally agreed that conventional intelligence tests have some important limitations.

The exact nature of intelligence will no doubt be debated for some time. However, the intensity of this debate pales in comparison to the next issue we consider: the origins of intelligence.

CONCEPT REVIEW 7.4

Identifying Major Contributors to the Intelligence Debate

Which person (Binet, Terman, Wechsler, Spearman, Thurstone, Gardner, Sternberg) is associated with each of the following descriptions?

_____ **1.** The contemporary American psychologist who believes that intelligence has three forms: componential, contextual, and experiential.

_____ **2.** The French psychologist who is credited with developing the first practical intelligence test.

_____ **3.** The American psychologist whose widely used intelligence test provides both a global IQ score and scores on verbal and performance tests.

_____ **4.** The British psychologist who advanced the theory that overall intellectual ability is a function of a general intelligence factor, called the *g factor*.

_____ **5.** The contemporary American psychologist who proposed that there are multiple independent intelligences, and that an intelligence is an ability that is valued within a particular cultural setting.

_____ **6.** The American psychologist who believed that there are seven different primary mental abilities rather than one *g factor*.

_____ **7.** The American psychologist who translated and adapted Binet's intelligence test for use in the United States.

What Determines Intelligence?

Most psychologists agree that both heredity and environment contribute to IQ. What factors contribute to the complexity of the relationship between genetics and environment, particularly with regard to intelligence? How are twin studies used in studying this relationship? What is heritability?

Given that psychologists do not agree on the definition or nature of intelligence, it probably won't surprise you that psychologists also do not agree on the *origin* of intelligence. On the surface, the debate comes down to this: Do we essentially *inherit* our intellectual potential from our parents, grandparents, and great-grandparents? Or is our intellectual potential primarily determined by our *environment* and upbringing?

The simple answer to both these questions is yes. In a nutshell, virtually all psychologists agree that *both* heredity and environment are important in determining intelligence level. Where psychologists disagree is in identifying how much of intelligence is determined by heredity, how much by environment. The implications of this debate have provoked some of the most heated arguments in the history of psychology. In this section, we'll try to clarify some of the critical issues involved in this ongoing controversy.

The Roles of Heredity and Environment

We will discuss the biological underpinnings of genetics and heredity in more detail in Chapter 9. To make sense out of the IQ controversy, however, a brief discussion of the interaction of environment and genes is required here.

Let's start with some simple examples illustrating the role of heredity and environment. Your eye color is completely genetically determined. If you were born with blue eyes, no level of environmental intervention will change your eyes to brown (colored contact lenses don't count).

Your height is also genetically determined, but to a different degree: you inherit a potential *range* for height, rather than an absolute number of inches. Thus, unlike eye color, your height can be affected by your environmental circumstances. If you are healthy and well-nourished, you may reach the maximum of your genetic height potential. But if you are poorly nourished and unhealthy, you probably won't.

To illustrate the interplay between heredity and environment, consider the fact that in the last fifty years, the average height of Americans has increased by several inches. The explanation for this increase is that nutritional and health standards have steadily improved, not that the genetic heritage of Americans has fundamentally changed. However, heredity does play a role in establishing some limits on height. If you're born with "short" genes (like your authors), you're unlikely to reach six foot four, no matter how good your nutrition.

The roles of heredity and environment in determining intelligence and personality factors are much more complex than the simple examples of height or eye color (Plomin & others, 1994). If you have brothers and sisters, you've probably been struck by the many physical and personality differences between you and your siblings. (We discuss this issue in greater detail in Chapter 11.) Assuming that you share the same set of biological parents, you and your siblings derived your genetic makeup from the same source: your mother and your father. However, the number of possible combinations of those genes is astronomical. Thus, the genetic makeup of you and your siblings is different, although it is more similar than that of unrelated people.

Furthermore, despite being raised in the same home, you and your siblings have each also experienced different environmental influences. First-born children typically get more attention from their parents; middle children have their siblings to contend with; sickly or "difficult" children may be treated differently from their healthier or less rambunctious siblings; and so forth.

In addition, your environment is not a single, stable factor, but is constantly changing. If your parents get divorced, for example, you might be affected in a very different way from your older or younger siblings. Even within the same family, the complexities of environmental influences are difficult to measure. Thus, both your genes *and* the influence of the environment are different from those of your siblings (Plomin & others, 1994; Plomin & Rende, 1991; Plomin & Daniels, 1987).

So what about the role of genetic factors in intelligence? However narrowly intelligence is defined, the genetic range of intellectual potential is influenced by *many* genes, not by just one single gene (Rose, 1995). No one knows how many genes might be involved. Like the influence of environment, the genetic aspect of intelligence is extremely complex. Given the complexities and interactions involved, how can scientists go about estimating how much of intelligence is due to genetics, how much to environment?

Genetics or Environment? These identical twins have a lot in common—including a beautiful smile. How do researchers determine the relative contributions of heredity and environment to personality and other characteristics?

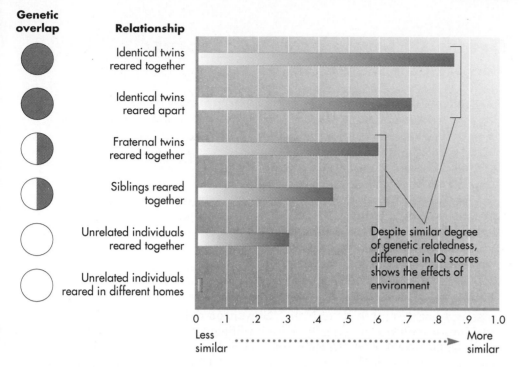

Genetic overlap | **Relationship**

Identical twins reared together
Identical twins reared apart
Fraternal twins reared together
Siblings reared together
Unrelated individuals reared together
Unrelated individuals reared in different homes

Despite similar degree of genetic relatedness, difference in IQ scores shows the effects of environment

0 .1 .2 .3 .4 .5 .6 .7 .8 .9 1.0
Less similar ← → More similar

FIGURE 7.9 Genetics, Environment, and IQ Scores

Comparing the IQ scores of individuals who are genetically related to differing degrees shows the effects of both heredity and environment. The more closely two individuals are related genetically, the more similar are their IQ scores. However, the environment also has an effect.

(Adapted from Bouchard & McGue, 1981.)

Twin Studies:

Sorting Out the Influence of Genetics Versus Environment

One way this issue has been explored is by comparing the IQ scores of individuals who are genetically related, but to different degrees. *Identical twins* share exactly the same genes, because they developed from a single fertilized egg that split into two. Hence, any dissimilarities between them must be due to environmental factors rather than hereditary differences. *Fraternal twins* are like any other pair of siblings, because they develop from two different fertilized eggs. As you can see from Figure 7.9, comparing IQ scores in this way shows the effects of both heredity and environment. Identical twins raised together have very similar IQ scores, while fraternal twins raised together have IQs that are less similar than those of identical twins.

However, notice that identical twins raised in separate homes have IQs that are slightly less similar, indicating the effect of different environments. And, although fraternal twins raised together are *less* similar in IQ scores than identical twins, they show *more* similarity in IQs than nontwin siblings. Recall that the degree of genetic relatedness between fraternal twins and nontwin siblings is essentially the same. However, because fraternal twins are the same age, their environmental experiences are likely to be more similar than that of siblings who are of different ages.

Thus, *both* genetic and environmental influences are important (Plomin & others, 1994). Genetic influence is shown by the fact that the closer the genetic relationship, the more similar the IQ scores. Environmental influences are demonstrated by two findings: Two people who are genetically identical but who are raised in different homes have different IQ scores. And two people who are genetically unrelated but who are raised in the same home have IQs that are much more similar than those of unrelated people from randomly selected homes.

Using studies based on degree of genetic relatedness, researchers have scientifically estimated **heritability**—the percentage of variation within a given population that is due to heredity. Using sophisticated statistical techniques to analyze such data, the currently accepted estimate is about 50 percent for the general population (Plomin and others, 1994).

In other words, approximately 50 percent of the difference among IQ scores *within* a given population is due to genetic factors. But there is disagreement even over this figure, depending on the statistical techniques and data sources used. Some researchers estimate the heritability of IQ as high as 65 percent (Bouchard & others, 1990a).

It is important to stress that the 50 percent figure does *not* apply to a single individual's IQ score. If Mike's IQ is 120, it does not mean that 60 IQ points are due to Mike's environment and 60 points are genetically inherited. Instead, the 50 percent heritability figure means that approximately 50 percent of the difference among IQ scores *within a specific group of people* is due to differences in their genetic makeup. More on this key point shortly.

heritabililiy
The percentage of variation within a given population that is due to heredity.

Group Differences in IQ Scores:
The Basic Controversy

While differences exist between the average IQ scores of different racial groups, it cannot be concluded that such group differences are genetic in origin. What do cross-cultural studies tell us about the effect of social discrimination on IQ? How might culture affect intelligence test results?

If the contributions of heredity and environment are roughly equal, why all the fuss? Much of the controversy over the role of heredity in intelligence is due to attempts to explain the differences in average IQ scores for different racial groups.

In comparing the *average IQ* for various racial groups, several studies have shown differences. For example, Japanese and Chinese schoolchildren tend to score above white American children on intelligence and achievement tests, especially in math (Lynn, 1987; Stevenson & Lee, 1990). Are Japanese and Chinese children genetically more intelligent than American children?

Consider this finding: In early childhood, there are *no* significant differences in IQ among American, Japanese, and Chinese schoolchildren. The three groups are essentially the same (Stevenson & Sigler, 1992). The gap begins to appear only after the children start school, and it increases with every year of school attended. By middle school, Asian students tend to score much higher than American students on both math and reading tests.

Why the increasing gap when Asian and American start school? Japanese and Chinese students spend more time in school, more time doing homework, and experience more pressure and support from their parents to achieve academically. Moreover, the Japanese and Chinese cultures place a high value on academic achievement (Gardner, 1995). Clearly, then, the difference between American and Asian students is due not to genetics, but to the educational system.

In this country, the most controversy has been caused by the differences in average IQ scores between black and white Americans. *As a group,* black Americans once scored about 15 points lower than white Americans *as a group* (MacKenzie, 1984). However, this gap has narrowed over the past few decades to 10 points or less (Neisser & others, 1996; Nisbett, 1995b).

Culture and Educational Achievement
These children attend kindergarten in Kawasaki, Japan. Children in Japan attend school six days a week. Along with spending more time in school each year than American children, Japanese children grow up in a culture that places a strong emphasis on academic success as the key to occupational success.

It's important to note that such group differences do not predict *individual* differences in IQ scores. Many individual black Americans receive higher IQ scores than many individual white Americans. Also, the range and degree of IQ variation *within* each group—the variation of IQs among individual blacks or among individual whites—is much greater than the 10-point average difference *between* the two groups.

How might these group differences in average IQ be explained? In the 1970s, educational psychologist Arthur Jensen (1969) created a public furor by claiming that these differences are primarily due to genetic factors. Jensen used evidence based on studies of similarity of IQ scores and degree of genetic relatedness among whites to conclude that intelligence is largely determined by heredity.

The same controversy erupted again in the mid-1990s with the publication of a book entitled *The Bell Curve: Intelligence and Class Structure in American Life,* written by psychologist Richard Herrnstein and political scientist Charles Murray. Much like Jensen, Herrnstein and Murray (1994) argue that the gap in black and white IQ scores is largely due to genetics and is unlikely to change. Based on this conclusion, Herrnstein and Murray advocate a variety of changes in social and public policy.

The Bell Curve has been heavily criticized by leading psychologists and researchers in genetics and intelligence testing (see Fraser, 1995; Jacoby & Glauberman, 1995). Psychologist Richard Nisbett (1995a) has expressed the sentiments of many experts in writing, "The book is full of . . . distortions and eccentric interpretations of evidence that are not shared by most experts, while evidence that undermines the conclusions of the authors is missing or dismissed on technical grounds."

Although there are many problems with the so-called evidence contained in *The Bell Curve* (Sternberg, 1995), the most fundamental problem is the inappropriate comparison of group differences in IQ scores. It is an important issue that you need to understand.

Differences *Within* Groups Versus Differences *Between* Groups

Although it is possible to estimate the degree of difference *within* a specific group that is due to genetics, it makes no sense to apply this estimate to the differences *between* groups. Why? An analogy provided by geneticist Richard Lewontin (1970) may help you understand this point.

Suppose that you have a 50-pound bag of corn seeds and two pots. A handful of the seeds is scooped out and planted in pot A, which has rich, well-fertilized soil. A second handful is scooped out and planted in pot B, which has poor soil with few nutrients (see Figure 7.10).

Because the seeds are not genetically identical, the plants *within group A* will vary in height. So will the plants *within group B*. Given that the environment (the soil) is the same for all the plants in each pot, this variation within each group of seeds is *completely* due to heredity—because nothing differs but the plants' genes.

However, when we compare the average height of the corn plants in the two pots, pot A's plants have a higher average height than pot B's. Can the difference in these average heights be explained in terms of overall genetic differences between the seeds in each pot? No. The overall differences can be attributed to the two different environments, the good soil and the poor soil. In fact, because the environments are so different, it is *impossible to estimate* what the overall genetic differences are between the two groups of seeds.

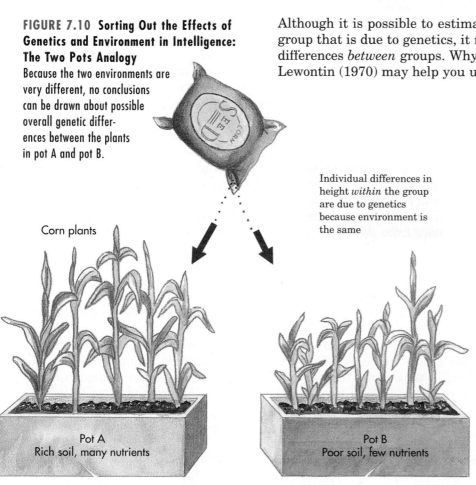

FIGURE 7.10 Sorting Out the Effects of Genetics and Environment in Intelligence: The Two Pots Analogy
Because the two environments are very different, no conclusions can be drawn about possible overall genetic differences between the plants in pot A and pot B.

Corn plants

Individual differences in height *within* the group are due to genetics because environment is the same

Pot A
Rich soil, many nutrients

Pot B
Poor soil, few nutrients

Difference in average height *between* groups is due to environment

Note also that even though, on the average, the plants in pot A are taller than the plants in pot B, some of the plants in pot B are taller than most of the plants in pot A. In other words, the average differences *within a group* of plants tell us nothing about whether an *individual* member of that group is likely to be tall or short.

The same point can be extended to the issue of average IQ differences between racial groups. Unless the environmental conditions of two racial groups are virtually identical, it is impossible to estimate the overall genetic differences between the two groups. Even if intelligence were *primarily* determined by heredity, which does not appear to be the case, IQ differences between groups could still be due entirely to the environment.

In the United States, black children, like members of many other minority groups, are more likely than white children to be raised in poverty and to have fewer educational opportunities. Environmental factors associated with poverty, such as poor nutrition and lack of prenatal care, can have a negative impact on intelligence. And, even when their socioeconomic status is roughly equal to that of white Americans, black Americans experience many forms of overt and subtle social discrimination (Steele & Aronson, 1995).

An important study by psychologists Sandra Scarr and Richard Weinberg (1976) explored the relationship between racial IQ differences and the environment in which children are raised. Scarr and Weinberg looked at the IQ scores of black children who had been adopted by white families that were highly educated and above average in occupational status and income. When tested, the black children's IQ scores were several points higher than the average scores of both blacks and whites.

Scarr and Weinberg also found that the younger the children were when they were adopted, the higher their IQ scores. They concluded that IQ differences are due not to race, but rather to the socioeconomic conditions and cultural values to which children are exposed. According to Weinberg (1989), the adopted black children performed well above average because they were provided with home environments in which the children were taught the vocabulary and cognitive skills that IQ and achievement tests reward. More important, a followup study of these same children a decade later indicated the "persisting beneficial effects [on IQ scores] of being reared in the culture of the school and tests" (Weinberg & others, 1992; Waldman & others, 1994).

Other evidence for the importance of the environment in determining IQ scores comes from the improvement in average IQ scores that has occurred in other cultures and countries during the last few generations (see Neisser & others, 1996). For example, average Japanese IQ scores have risen dramatically since World War II (Flynn, 1987).

In a survey of intelligence test scores around the world, 14 nations were found to have shown significant gains in average IQ scores in just one generation (Flynn, 1987). The average IQ in the United States has also steadily increased over the past century (see Kaufman, 1990). Such changes in a population can be accounted for only by environmental changes, because the amount of time is far too short for genetically influenced changes to have occurred.

Cross-Cultural Studies of Group Discrimination and IQ Differences

The effect of social discrimination on intelligence test scores has been shown in numerous cross-cultural studies (see Ogbu, 1986). In many different societies, average IQ is lower for members of a discriminated-against minority group, even when that group is not racially different from the dominant group.

For example, take the case of the Buraku people of Japan (De Vos & Wagatsuma, 1967). Americans typically think of Japan as being a relatively homogeneous culture, and indeed the Burakumin are not racially different from other Japanese. They look the same and speak the same language. However, the Burakumin are the descendants of an outcast group that for generations worked as tanners and butchers. Because they handled dead bodies and killed animals, the Burakumin were long considered to be unclean and unfit for social contact. Such work was viewed as dirty and violating Buddhist religious rules against killing animals and touching dead bodies. For centuries, the Burakumin were forced to live in isolated enclaves, apart from the rest of Japanese society.

Today, there are about 3 million Burakumin in Japan. Although the Buraku were legally emancipated from their outcast status many years ago, substantial social discrimination against them persists (Payton, 1992). Because there is no way to tell if a Japanese citizen is of Buraku descent, there are dozens of private detective agencies in Tokyo and other Japanese cities that openly specialize in tracking Burakumin who are trying to "pass" and hide their background. Corporations in Japan routinely consult computer databanks to identify Burakumin who apply for jobs, as do individuals who wish to investigate the ancestral background of prospective marriage partners.

The Buraku are the poorest people in Japan. They are only half as likely to graduate from high school or attend college as other Japanese. Although there are no racial differences between the Burakumin and other Japanese, the average IQ scores of the Burakumin in Japan are well below those of other Japanese, as shown in Table 7.3. However, when Buraku families immigrate to the United States, they are treated like any other Japanese. The children do just as well in school—and on IQ tests—as any other Japanese-Americans (Ogbu, 1986).

Of course, Japan is not the only society that discriminates against a particular social group, whether racially similar or dissimilar. Many societies discriminate against specific minority groups, such as the Harijans in India (formerly called the Untouchables), West Indians in Great Britain, the Maoris in New Zealand, and Oriental Jews in Israel.

The children of each of these minority groups score 10 to 15 points lower on intelligence tests than the dominant group's children in their society. Children of the minority groups are often one or two years behind dominant-group children in basic reading skills and mathematical skills. Minority-group children are overrepresented in remedial programs and in the number of school dropouts. They are also underrepresented among students in higher education. The impact of discrimination on group differences in IQ remains even when the minority-group and dominant-group members are of similar socioeconomic backgrounds (Ogbu, 1986). In many ways, the educational experiences of these minority groups seem to parallel those of black Americans, providing a cross-cultural perspective on the consistent effects of discrimination in many different societies.

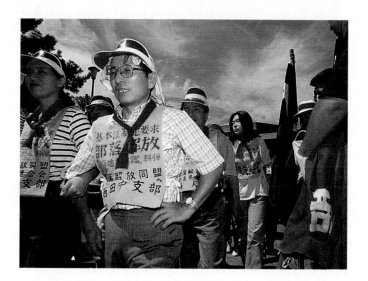

The Buraku Protest Centuries of Discrimination Members of the Burakumin Emancipation Alliance protest discrimination in a peaceful demonstration in Tokyo. Their vests proclaim their demand for basic human rights for the Buraku. Today, the Burakumin are the poorest group in Japan. Compared to the general population of Japan, only about half as many Burakumin graduate from high school or attend college.

TABLE 7.3 The Effects of Discimination on IQ Scores in Japan

Range of IQ Scores	Percentage of Children Scoring in a Given Range	
	Non-Buraku	Buraku
Above 125	23.3	2.6
124–109	31.8	19.5
108–93	23.3	22.1
92–77	11.7	18.2
Below 76	9.9	37.6

SOURCE: Adapted from De Vos & Wagatsuma, 1967, Table 2, p. 261.

The Buraku people of Japan are not racially different from other Japanese, but they have suffered from generations of discrimination. Their average IQ scores are about 10 to 15 points below those of mainstream Japanese (Ogbu, 1986). In many other cultures, a similar gap in IQ scores exists between the discriminated-against minority and the dominant group.

Are IQ Tests Culturally Biased?

Another approach to explaining group differences in IQ scores has been to look at cultural bias in the tests themselves. If standardized intelligence tests reflect white, middle class cultural knowledge and values, minority group members might do poorly on the tests not because of lower intelligence, but because of unfamiliarity with the white, middle-class culture.

Early intelligence tests were clearly culturally biased. Urban subjects did better than rural subjects, and middle-class subjects did better than lower-class subjects. For example, one question asked, "What would you do if you found a three-year-old child lost in the street?" The correct answer is "Call the police." But this might not be the most "intelligent" response if you lived in a rural area where a few police officers covered a large area, or if members of your ethnic group tended to perceive the police as unhelpful or even hostile (Scarr, 1984).

Researchers have also attempted to create tests that were "culture-fair" or "culture-free." However, it is now generally recognized that it is virtually impossible to design a test that is completely culture-free, because intelligence itself is not free of cultural influences (Sternberg, 1991). Quite simply, a test will tend to favor the people from the culture in which it was developed (Anastasi, 1988).

Cultural differences may also be involved in *test-taking behavior* (Sternberg, 1995). People from different cultural backgrounds may use strategies in solving problems or organizing information that are different from those required on standard intelligence tests (Miller-Jones, 1989). In addition, factors like motivation, attitudes toward test taking, and previous experiences with tests are all cultural factors that can affect performance and test scores (Anastasi, 1988).

And, as psychologist Claude Steele (1995) has discovered, simply being aware that you are not expected to do well on a particular test has the effect of lowering your score—whether you are black or white, male or female. Students' anxiety and apprehension over being evaluated when they feel that they are expected to perform poorly can lower both the speed and the accuracy of responses to standardized test questions (Steele & Aronson, 1995).

Psychologist Claude Steele Stanford University professor Claude Steele (1995) has found that being aware that you're expected to do poorly on a particular test can lower a person's score. His findings are providing new insights that help explain group differences in intelligence and achievement tests.

Some Concluding Thoughts on Group Differences in IQ

On the basis of our discussion about the influences of heredity and environment in intelligence, we can draw three broad conclusions about the debate surrounding intelligence and race.

First, it's clear that the IQ of any given individual, regardless of what racial group he or she may belong to, is the result of the complex interaction of hereditary and environmental factors. Second, as far as the IQ differences between racial groups are concerned, environmental factors are much more likely to account for such differences than genetics (Neisser & others, 1996). Third, within a given racial group, the differences among people are due at least as much to environmental influences as they are to genetic influences (Plomin & others, 1994).

CONCEPT REVIEW 7.5

Recognizing Important Determinants of Intelligence

1. Most intelligence experts agree that observed differences in average IQ scores between racial groups are probably due to
   a. genetic factors
   b. environmental factors
   c. the deliberate construction of biased tests
   d. the use of culture-free tests

2. A researcher tests a group of identical twins raised together and a different group of identical twins who were separated at birth and raised in different environments. She finds that the IQ scores of each pair of twins in the first group are more similar than the IQ scores of each pair of twins in the second group. These differences are the result of
   a. genetic influences
   b. environmental influences
   c. neither environmental nor genetic influences
   d. an equal degree of environmental and genetic influences

3. One scoop of seeds is planted in a plot of farmland with rich soil and adequate rainfall. Another scoop of seeds from the same batch is planted in a back yard with poor soil that is never watered or fertilized. On the average, the seeds in the rich soil grow taller than the seeds in the poor soil. The difference between the average height of the plants in the rich soil and that of the plants in the poor soil is best accounted for by:
   a. genetic factors
   b. environmental factors
   c. 30 percent genetics and 70 percent environment
   d. 70 percent genetics and 30 percent environment

4. In question 3, the plants in the rich farmland vary in height: some are taller than others. The same is true of the plants in the back yard. The difference among the heights of the plants in the same plot of soil is best accounted for by:
   a. genetics
   b. environment
   c. 30 percent genetics and 70 percent environment
   d. 70 percent genetics and 30 percent environment

Summing Up: Thinking, Language, and Intelligence

As we've seen, IQ scores measure only the selected aspects of intelligence they are designed to measure. In reality, each of us represents a unique constellation of genetic heritage and experience that influences our abilities, our choices, and our behaviors. We draw upon many different types of mental abilities to solve problems, adapt to our environment, and communicate with others. As the story of Mr. and Ms. Fix-It in the prologue to this chapter illustrated, solving even the most mundane problems of life often involves creative and flexible thinking. In the Application section, we provide a variety of suggestions that you can use to enhance your creativity.

APPLICATION

A Workshop on Creativity

Creativity refers to a group of cognitive processes used to generate useful and original ideas. What are six suggestions for increasing your potential to be creative?

As is the case with intelligence, there is no universally accepted definition of creativity (see Baer, 1993; Piirto, 1992). However, the following definition captures several of the important aspects that have been stressed by cognitive psychologists: **Creativity** is a group of cognitive processes used to generate useful, original, and novel ideas or solutions (Amabile & Tighe, 1993; Ochse, 1990).

Notice that usefulness, along with originality, is involved in judging creativity. An idea can be highly original, but if it lacks usefulness it is not regarded as creative.

Can you learn to be more creative? In general, creativity experts agree that you can (Cropley, 1992, 1991; Schank, 1988). Although there is no simple formula that guarantees creative success, a few basic ingredients are central to the process of creative thinking.

1. Choose the Goal of Creativity

Although we typically think of creativity in terms of artistic expression, the act of creativity is almost always linked to the process of solving some problem. In that sense, creativity can occur in virtually any area of life.

Psychologists have found that virtually everyone possesses the intelligence and cognitive processes needed to be creative to some degree (Weisberg, 1993, 1988). Often, what separates the individuals who achieve creative accomplishments from those who don't is that the creative individual values creativity as a personal goal (Hennessey & Amabile, 1988). Without the personal goal of creativity, the likelihood of doing something creative is slim.

2. Reinforce Intrinsic Motivation

People will be most creative when they are motivated by their own interest, the enjoyment of a challenge, and a personal sense of satisfaction and fulfillment. This is called *intrinsic motivation.* In contrast, when people are motivated by external rewards, such as money or grades, they are displaying *extrinsic motivation* (Amabile, 1989, 1983; Hennessey & Amabile, 1988).

If the goal of creative expression is not primarily the creative act itself, but the satisfaction of money, awards, or fame, then you're motivated by the factors that are *least* likely to produce creativity. The question you need to ask yourself is very simple: Are you more excited by the idea of doing something creative or by the thought of what the achievement will bring you?

3. Engage in Problem Finding

In many cases the real creative leap involves recognizing that a problem exists. This is referred to as *problem finding* (Brown, 1989; Getzels & Csikszentmihalyi, 1976). We often overlook creative opportunities by dismissing trivial annoyances rather than recognizing them as potential problems to be solved (Hayes, 1989).

For example, consider the minor annoyance experienced by a man named Art Fry (Kaplan, 1990). Fry, a researcher for 3M Corporation, regularly sang in his church choir. In order to locate the hymns quickly during the Sunday service, Fry would use little scraps of paper to mark their places. But the scraps of paper would sometimes fall out when Fry stood up to sing, and he'd have to fumble to find the right page.

While sitting in church, Fry recognized the "problem" and came up with a relatively simple solution. If you put a substance that is sticky, but not *too* sticky, on the scraps of paper, they'll stay on the page and you can take them off when they are not needed anymore.

If you haven't already guessed, Art Fry invented Post-It Notes. The formula for the adhesive had been discovered years earlier at 3M, but nobody could imagine a use for a glue that did not bond permanently. The mental set of the 3M researchers was to find *stronger* glues, not weaker ones. Fry's story demonstrates the creative value of recognizing problems instead of simply dismissing them.

A technique called *bug listing* is one useful strategy to identify potential problems (Adams, 1979). Bug listing involves creating a list of things that annoy, irritate, or bug you. Such everyday annoyances are problems in need of creative solutions.

4. Acquire Relevant Knowledge

It was the famous French chemist Louis Pasteur who said, "Chance favors the prepared mind." If you know little or nothing about a particular topic, it's tough to be creative in that area. Acquiring a solid knowledge base increases your potential for recognizing how to creatively extend your knowledge or apply it in a new way. In essence, creativity almost always requires a good deal of preparation (Weisberg, 1993).

5. Try Different Approaches

Creative people are flexible in their thinking. They step back from problems, turn them over, and mentally play with possibilities. By being flexible and imaginative, people seeking creative solutions generate many different responses. This is called *divergent thinking,* because it involves moving away (or diverging) from the problem and considering it from a variety of perspectives (Baer, 1993).

CALVIN AND HOBBES

IF YOU ASK *ME*, THESE ASSIGNMENTS DON'T TEACH YOU HOW TO WRITE. THEY TEACH YOU HOW TO *HATE* TO WRITE.

DEADLINES, RULES HOW TO DO IT, GRADES... HOW CAN YOU BE CREATIVE WHEN SOMEONE'S BREATHING DOWN YOUR NECK?

I GUESS YOU SHOULD TRY NOT TO THINK ABOUT THE END RESULT TOO MUCH AND JUST HAVE FUN WITH THE PROCESS OF CREATING.

EVERY TIME I DO THAT, I END UP IN THE SCHOOL PYSCHOLOGIST'S OFFICE.

WELL, MAYBE NOT *THAT* MUCH FUN.

Looking for analogies is one technique to encourage divergent thinking. In the context of problem solving, an *analogy* is the recognition of some similarity or parallel between two objects or events that are not usually compared. Similarities can be drawn in terms of the two objects' operation, function, purpose, materials, or other characteristics.

For example, Gay Balfour of Colorado recognized that a problem existed—the need to remove prairie dogs from an area without killing them (New Prairie Dog Vacuum, 1992). When trying to come up with a way to get the prairie dogs out of their holes, Balfour was struck by the analogy between a vacuum cleaner and the suction devices used to clean out septic tanks. Balfour devised a machine that sucks the critters out of the ground without harming them so they can be relocated. On one occasion, he vacuumed up 53 prairie dogs in a little over an hour. His company, called Dog-Gone, is doing quite well.

6. Expect Effort and Setbacks

We're often tempted to believe that the creative leap simply "happens" to peo-ple in a split second of inspiration. While flashes of insight can play a role in creativity, the creative process itself never occurs in just an instant. The flash of inspiration usually occurs after a great deal of thought and effort. Whether you're trying to build a better mousetrap, write a term paper that is uniquely different, or invent the next hula hoop or Trivial Pursuit, the simple fact is that creativity requires effort and persistence.

Finally, the creative process is typically filled with obstacles and setbacks. The best-selling novelist Stephen King endured years of rejection of his manuscripts and considered quitting writing before his first book was published. Thomas Edison tried thousands of filaments before he created the first working lightbulb. As Robert Sternberg (1988b) notes, "The question is not whether or not an individual will encounter these obstacles but rather how one will handle them. A creative individual perseveres."

To summarize our workshop on creativity, we'll use the letters of the word *create* as an acronym. Thus, the basic ingredients of creativity are:

- **C**hoose the goal of creativity.
- **R**einforce intrinsic motivation.
- **E**ngage in problem finding.
- **A**cquire relevant knowledge.
- **T**ry different approaches.
- **E**xpect effort and setbacks.

The Prairie Dog Vacuum Balfour's invention harmlessly sucks prairie dogs out of their burrows and deposits them into a holding tank in his truck so that they can be relocated. According to Balfour, "It's quite a ride but the prairie dogs are not too disturbed about it."

Summary

Thinking, Language, and Intelligence

The Building Blocks of Thought:
Mental Imagery and Concepts

- Thinking involves manipulating internal, mental representations of information in order to draw inferences and conclusions. Thinking often involves the manipulation of two kinds of mental representations: mental images and concepts.

- Most research has been done on visual mental images. We seem to treat mental images much as we do actual visual images or physical objects.

- Thinking also involves the use of concepts. Formal concepts are defined by logical rules. Natural concepts are likely to have fuzzy rather than rigid boundaries. We determine membership in natural concepts by comparing an object to our prototype for the natural concept. The more similar an item is to the prototype, the more quickly and easily we can determine whether it is an instance of the concept.

Problem Solving: Searching for the IDEAL Solution

- Problem solving refers to thinking and behavior directed toward attaining a goal that is not readily available. The IDEAL problem solver is a model describing the five steps followed in problem solving.

■ Strategies that are commonly used in problem solving include trial and error, algorithms, and heuristics. Heuristics include breaking a problem into a series of subgoals and working backward from the goal. Sometimes problems are resolved through insight. Evaluating a solution is easier when the problem is clearly defined.

■ Functional fixedness and mental set are two common obstacles to problem solving.

Decisions, Decisions, Decisions: Should I or Shouldn't I?

■ Decision-making models include the single-feature model, the additive model, and the elimination by aspects model. Different strategies may be most helpful in different situations.

■ When making risky decisions, we often use the availability heuristic and the representativeness heuristic to help us estimate the likelihood of events.

Language and Thought

■ Language is a system for combining arbitrary symbols to produce an infinite number of meaningful statements.

■ Language has the following characteristics: meaning is conveyed by arbitrary symbols; meaning is shared by speakers of the same language; language is a rule-based system; language is generative; and language involves displacement.

■ Language influences thinking by affecting what we remember and our perceptions of others.

■ Animals communicate with members of their own species and with members of other species, including humans. Whether animals can be taught to use language is controversial. Recent studies have been more carefully controlled than early studies. Bonobos and dolphins seem to have demonstrated an elementary grasp of the rules of syntax.

Measuring Intelligence

■ Intelligence can be defined as the global capacity to think rationally, act purposefully, and deal effectively with the environment. Intelligence tests are designed to measure general mental abilities.

■ Alfred Binet developed the first widely accepted intelligence test, which incorporated the idea of a mental age that was different from chronological age. Binet did not believe that intelligence was inborn or fixed, or that it could be described in a single number.

■ Lewis Terman adapted Binet's test for use in the United States and developed the concept of the intelligence quotient, or IQ score. Terman believed that success in life was primarily determined by IQ.

■ Group intelligence tests were developed for screening military recruits during World War I.

■ David Wechsler developed the Wechsler Adult Intelligence Scale (WAIS), which included scores on subtests that measured different mental abilities. Wechsler also changed the way that overall IQ scores were calculated.

■ Achievement tests and aptitude tests are two types of psychological tests. Psychological tests must meet the requirements of standardization, reliability, and validity. The norms, or standards, for intelligence tests follow the normal curve, or normal distribution of scores.

Four Views on the Nature of Intelligence

■ Debate over the nature of intelligence centers on two key issues: (1) whether intelligence is a single factor or a cluster of different abilities; and (2) how narrowly intelligence should be defined.

■ Charles Spearman believed that intelligence could be described as a single factor called general intelligence, or the g factor.

■ Louis L. Thurstone believed that there were seven primary mental abilities.

■ Howard Gardner believes that there are "multiple intelligences." He defines intelligence as the ability to solve problems or create products that are valued within a cultural setting.

■ Robert Sternberg's triarchic theory of intelligence emphasizes both the universal aspects of intelligence and the importance of adapting to a particular cultural environment. He identifies three forms of intelligence: componential, experiential, and contextual intelligence.

■ Despite continuing controversy, intelligence researchers generally agree that abstract thinking, problem solving, and capacity to acquire knowledge are important aspects of intelligence and are measurable by intelligence tests. However, they also agree that other important aspects of intelligence, like creativity, are not measured by intelligence tests.

What Determines Intelligence?

■ The IQ of any individual is the result of a complex interaction between heredity and environment. Intelligence is not determined by a single gene but by the interaction of multiple genes.

■ Twin studies are used to determine the degree to which genetics contribute to complex characteristics like intelligence. Heritability refers to the percentage of variation within a given population that is due to heredity. Within a given racial group, the effects of environment and genetics are roughly equal.

■ There are differences in the average IQ scores for different racial groups. However, there is more variation within a particular group than there is between groups.

■ While it is possible to calculate the differences within a given group that are due to heredity, it is not possible to calculate the differences between groups that are due to heredity. Unless the environments are identical, no comparisons can be drawn. Rather than genetic factors, environmental factors are more likely to be the cause of average IQ differences among groups.

■ Cross-cultural studies have demonstrated that the average IQ scores of groups who suffer social discrimination are frequently lower than the average IQ scores of the dominant social group, even when the groups are not racially different.

- Intelligence tests can be culturally biased. All intelligence tests reflect the culture in which they are developed. Cultural factors may also influence test-taking behavior and individual performance. IQ scores reflect only selected aspects of intelligence.

Key Terms

cognition (p. 287)

thinking (p. 287)

mental image (p. 287)

concepts (p. 289)

formal concept (p. 290)

natural concept (p. 290)

prototype (p. 290)

problem solving (p. 292)

trial and error (p. 293)

algorithm (p. 294)

heuristic (p. 294)

insight (p. 295)

intuition (p. 296)

functional fixedness (p. 297)

mental set (p. 297)

availability heuristic (p. 301)

representativeness heuristic (p. 301)

language (p. 302)

linguistic relativity hypothesis (p. 305)

intelligence (p. 310)

mental age (p. 311)

intelligence quotient (IQ) (p. 311)

achievement test (p. 314)

aptitude test (p. 314)

standardization (p. 315)

normal curve (normal distribution) (p. 315)

reliability (p. 315)

validity (p. 315)

g factor (general intelligence) (p. 316)

triarchic theory of intelligence (p. 318)

heritabilility (p. 321)

creativity (p. 328)

Key People

Alfred Binet (1857–1911) A French psychologist who, along with French psychiatrist Théodore Simon, developed the first widely used intelligence test.

Howard Gardner (b. 1943) A contemporary American psychologist whose theory of intelligence states that there is not one intelligence but multiple intelligences, the importance of each being determined by cultural values.

Charles Spearman (1863–1945) A British psychologist who advanced the theory that a general intelligence factor, called the *g factor,* is responsible for overall intellectual functioning.

Robert Sternberg (b. 1949) A contemporary American psychologist whose *triarchic theory of intelligence* includes three forms of intelligence (componential, contextual, and experiential).

Lewis Terman (1877–1956) An American psychologist who translated and adapted the Binet-Simon intelligence test for use in the United States; he also began a major longitudinal study of the lives of gifted children in 1921.

Louis L. Thurstone (1887–1955) An American psychologist who advanced the theory that intelligence is composed of several primary mental abilities, and cannot be accurately described by an overall general or *g* factor measure.

David Wechsler (1869–1981) An American psychologist who developed the Wechsler Adult Intelligence Scale, the most widely used intelligence test.

CONCEPT REVIEW 7.1 Page 291

1. mental image
2. natural concept
3. prototype
4. formal concept

CONCEPT REVIEW 7.2 Page 298

1. (C) heuristic
2. (D) insight (O = One, T = Two, etc.)
3. (B) algorithm
4. (A) trial and error
5. (E) functional fixedness
6. (F) mental set

CONCEPT REVIEW 7.3 Page 309

1. (C) Generative
2. (D) Displacement
3. (A) Syntax
4. (B) Meaning is shared among users of the same language.

CONCEPT REVIEW 7.4. Page 319

1. Sternberg
2. Binet
3. Wechsler
4. Spearman
5. Gardner
6. Thurstone
7. Terman

CONCEPT REVIEW 7.5. Page 327

1. b
2. b
3. b
4. a

8

Motivation and Emotion

Prologue: One Step at a Time

"Nonsmoking section, please," Randy said to the hostess.

The request caught Don off guard. "Quit smoking again?" Don asked, trying not to sound too unconvinced. This was not exactly the first time that Randy had "quit" smoking.

"Yep," Randy said flatly as we walked toward the table. "I'm going to clean up my act. I quit coffee about three weeks ago, cigarettes about two weeks ago, and I joined a health club one week ago."

"And what motivated you to make all these changes?"

"I'm going to run this year's Tulsa Run," Randy explained matter-of-factly.

Don looked at Randy with a deadpan expression. "The Tulsa Run? Let me get this straight. You quit smoking and joined a health club so you can run nine miles in a race with 10,000 other runners. Why?!"

Randy smiled his trademark funny little smile, the one that usually means he's thinking about four steps ahead of you. "To see if I can do it," he explained.

It was early May when we had that conversation. The Tulsa Run takes place every year on the last Saturday in October. That meant that Randy had about five months to train for the race. His training began very slowly at first, largely because he had no choice but to start slowly. The most he could jog was about half a block before he was gasping for breath. After regaining his breath, he'd jog another half a block. Nonetheless, Randy would jog/walk about three miles a day.

By late June, Randy had made significant progress. He also passed his first major mile stone. He was able to run a mile before he had to stop and catch his breath. Don assumed that Randy would abandon his Tulsa Run goal by midsummer, when the

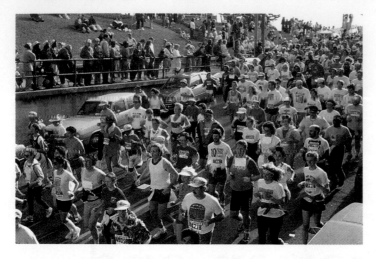

Motivation: What Makes Them Run?
Motivation researchers study the "why" of human behavior—the forces that motivate an individual to act.

sweltering Tulsa heat makes running at any time of the day uncomfortable. But Randy persevered. He started getting up at five o'clock every morning so that he could be on the running track by 5:30. By mid-July, Randy could jog two miles nonstop.

In early September, Randy ran in his first official race—a three-mile run. Although he had to stop once during the race, he finished with an average time of about nine minutes per mile. And in all fairness, it was pretty impressive for a guy who couldn't even run a block three months earlier.

In early October, Randy twisted an ankle while running, and Don was certain Randy's Tulsa Run goal would finally evaporate. It didn't. Instead, Randy worked out at the health club, "running" in the swimming pool as his ankle healed.

The last Saturday in October finally arrived. As the starting gun of the Tulsa Run sounded that morning, some 10,000 runners surged forward to cover 9.3 miles. Randy was somewhere in that throng of people. The professional runners, of course, always win the race with extraordinary times. So what are all of the other runners trying to accomplish? Many of them are trying to achieve a personal "best" time.

By his own admission, Randy had never run more than six miles at a time in all of his training. But he was certain he could finish the Tulsa Run. The critical issue in Randy's mind was whether he could complete the race in eight-minute miles or better—the goal he had set for himself back in May.

Randy sprinted the last four blocks of the Tulsa Run and crossed the finish line at 1 hour, 14 minutes, and 10 seconds. His average time? *Exactly* eight minutes per mile.

It is impossible to capture in words just how exhilarated Randy was on that Saturday. In fact, Randy was on an emotional high for the rest of the weekend. His sense of achievement was complete: he had set a very challenging goal for himself, worked toward it literally one step at a time, and attained it.

In this chapter, we will explore the two topics of motivation and emotion. These two topics are closely related, and each has a rich historical background in psychology. We'll come back to Randy's story now and then to illustrate some important concepts. In the chapter Application, we'll provide suggestions for increasing the emotional experience of happiness.

Introduction

Defining Motivation

> *Motivation refers to the forces acting on or within an organism to initiate and direct behavior. What are three characteristics associated with motivation?*

Without question, "something" triggered Randy to strap on his running shoes almost every day. If you think about it, "something" also triggered your behavior to get out of bed this morning, such as getting to work or class on time. That "something" is what the topic of **motivation** is about—the forces that act on or within an organism to initiate and direct behavior (Petri, 1996).

In everyday conversations, people often use the word *motivation* when they try to understand or explain the behavior of others. "And what motivated you to make all these changes?" "I can't believe how motivated he is to stick with it and succeed." "She seems highly motivated to finish school."

motivation
The forces that act on or within an organism to initiate and direct behavior.

instinct theories
The view that some motives are innate and due to genetic programming.

Such statements reflect three of the basic characteristics commonly associated with motivation: activation, persistence, and intensity (Geen, 1995).

Activation is demonstrated by the initiation or production of behavior, such as the motivated student who initiates going to the library to finish a term paper. *Persistence* is demonstrated by continued efforts or the determination to achieve a particular goal, often in the face of obstacles. Finally, *intensity* is seen in the greater vigor of responding that usually accompanies motivated behavior, such as the highly motivated student who studies harder than her classmates.

In the first chapter, we said that the four basic goals of psychology are to *describe, explain, predict,* and *influence* behavior. As you'll see in the next several sections, the topic of motivation reflects the essence of psychology's second goal: to explain the "why," or the motive behind behavior.

The Study of Motivation:
From Then to Now

> *Theories of motivation have included instinct, drive, incentive, and humanistic theories. How does each theory explain motivation, and what are the limitations of each theory? What is a drive, and how is it related to homeostasis? What is the hierarchy of needs? What characterizes the study of motivation today?*

In the early days of psychology, motivation theorists tried to create a single unified model that explained the motivation of *all* behaviors. Over the last century, several models of motivation have been proposed. Each model eventually proved to be inadequate, unable to explain certain aspects of motivation. However, key ideas from each model remained essential to a complete understanding of motivation, and were incorporated into the new models. As you'll see in this section, the study of motivation has progressively become more diverse and multifaceted.

Instinct Theories:
Is There a Jogging Instinct?

In the late 1800s, the newly founded science of psychology initially embraced instinct theories to explain motivation. According to **instinct theories,** people are motivated to engage in certain behaviors because of genetic programming. Just as animals display instinctive behavior patterns, like migration or mating behaviors, human behavior was also thought to be motivated by inborn instincts.

Drawing inspiration from the work of Charles Darwin and his scientifically based theory of evolution, psychologists devised lengthy lists of instincts to account for every conceivable human behavior (see Table 8.1). The behavior of a neat and tidy person, for example, was thought to be motivated by the "cleanliness instinct." Our friend Randy's behavior probably would have been explained as an expression of a "jogging" instinct.

By the early 1900s, thousands of instincts had been proposed in one expert's list or another. (The early instinct theorists were, no doubt, motivated by a "listing" instinct.) But what does it tell you to say that an assertive person has a "self-assertion instinct"? The obvious problem with the early

TABLE 8.1 Some Examples of Instincts Proposed by Instinct Theorists

rivalry	combativeness
sympathy	hunting
fear	acquisitiveness
constructiveness	play
curiosity	sociability
shyness	secretiveness
cleanliness	modesty
jealousy	parental love
self-assertion	submission
food-seeking	repulsion
escape	mating

SOURCE: Based on Petri, 1996, pp. 30–31.

CALVIN AND HOBBES

instinct theories was that such theories merely described and labeled behaviors, rather than actually explaining them (Petri, 1996).

By the 1920s and 1930s, instinct theories fell out of favor, primarily because of their lack of explanatory power. But the more general idea that some human behaviors are innate and genetically programmed remained an important element in the overall understanding of motivation.

Drive Theories:
Biological Needs as Motivators

Instinct theories were replaced during the 1940s and 1950s by drive theories. In general, **drive theories** assert that behavior is motivated by the desire to reduce internal tension caused by unmet biological needs, such as hunger or thirst. The basic idea is that these unmet biological needs "drive" or "push" us to behave in certain ways, leading to a reduction in the drive. When a particular behavior successfully reduces a drive, the behavior becomes more likely to be repeated when the same need state arises again.

Leading drive theorists, like psychologists Clark Hull (1943, 1952) and Robert Woodworth (1958), believed that drives are triggered by the internal mechanisms of homeostasis. The principle of **homeostasis** states that the body monitors and maintains relatively constant levels of internal states, such as body temperature, fluid levels, and energy supplies. If any of these internal conditions deviates very far from the optimal level, the body initiates processes to bring the condition back to the normal or optimal range. Thus, the body automatically tries to maintain a "steady state," which is what the word *homeostasis* means.

According to drive theorists, when an internal imbalance is detected by homeostatic mechanisms, a **drive** to restore balance is produced. The drive activates behavior to reduce the need and to reestablish the balance of internal conditions. For example, after you have not eaten anything for several hours, the internal pangs of hunger signal an imbalance in your body's energy level. According to the drive theorists, this unmet biological need creates a drive state—hunger—that motivates or energizes your behavior. And how might the drive of hunger energize you to behave? You might gravitate to the kitchen and forage in the refrigerator for some leftover guacamole dip or chocolate cake.

Today, the drive concept remains useful in the explanation of some motivated behaviors that have biological components, like hunger, thirst, and sexuality. However, the drive theories also have some limitations. Let's consider hunger again. Is the motivation of eating behavior strictly a matter of physiological need? Obviously not. People often eat when they're not hungry, and don't eat when they are hungry.

Beyond that observation, drive theories proved inadequate for other reasons. Rather than a reduction of tension, many behaviors seem to be directed toward *increasing* tension and physiological arousal. For example, how could drive theories account for such behaviors as buying a lottery ticket, running a marathon, or playing competitive tennis? It seems apparent that the motivation of such behaviors has to be explained in some other way.

drive theories
The view that behavior is motivated by the desire to reduce internal tension caused by unmet biological needs.

homeostasis
(home-ee-oh-STAY-sis) The notion that the body monitors and maintains internal states, such as body temperature and energy supplies, at relatively constant levels.

drive
An impulse that activates behavior to reduce a need and restore homeostasis.

incentive theories
The view that behavior is motivated by the "pull" of external goals, such as rewards.

hierarchy of needs
Maslow's hierarchical division of motivation into levels that progress from basic physical needs to psychological needs to self-fulfillment needs.

Incentive Motivation:

Goal Objects as Motivators

Building on the base established by drive theories, incentive theories emerged in the 1950s. **Incentive theories** proposed that behavior is motivated by the "pull" of external goals, such as rewards. Winning a million dollars in the state lottery, taking first place in a marathon or a tennis tournament, and being listed in the *Guinness Book of World Records* are potentially rewarding "pulls" that can motivate behavior. Indeed, it's easy to think of many situations in which a particular goal, such as good grades or a promotion at work, can serve as an external incentive that helps activate particular behaviors.

Incentive theories of motivation drew heavily from well-established learning principles, such as reinforcement, and the work of influential learning theorists, such as Pavlov, Watson, Skinner, and Tolman (see Chapter 5). Of particular note, Edward Tolman (1932) stressed the importance of cognitive factors in learning and motivation, especially the *expectation* that a particular behavior will lead to a particular goal.

When combined, drive and incentive theories seemed to account for a broad range of the "pushes" and "pulls" motivating many behaviors. Even in combination with drive theories, however, incentive explanations of motivation still had limitations. The most obvious shortcoming was the inability to explain behaviors that are not primarily motivated by any kind of external incentive—such as playing, mastering a new task, helping others for no apparent gain, or simply trying to satisfy curiosity. If you think about it, our friend Randy's decision to take up running was not motivated by either an internal, biological drive or an external incentive.

Psychological Motives:

Striving to Reach Our Potential

In the late 1950s, humanistic theories of motivation emerged. While not discounting the role of biological and external motivators, humanistic theories stressed the idea that we are innately motivated to strive for a positive self-concept and the realization of our personal potential (see Franken, 1994).

Humanistic motivational theories emphasized the importance of psychological and cognitive components in human motivation. Motivation was thought to be affected by how we perceive the world, how we think about ourselves and others, and our beliefs about our abilities and skills (Rogers, 1977, 1961). Although the motivation to strive for a positive self-concept and personal potential was thought to be inborn, humanistic theories also recognized the importance of the environment (Maslow, 1970). Without a supportive and encouraging environment—personal, social, and cultural—the motivation to strive toward one's highest potential could be jeopardized.

The most famous humanistic model of motivation is the **hierarchy of needs,** developed by **Abraham Maslow** (1908–1970) and summarized in Figure 8.1. In a nutshell, Maslow (1970, 1968)

FIGURE 8.1 Maslow's Hierarchy of Needs
Abraham Maslow believed that people are innately motivated to satisfy a progression of needs, beginning with the most basic physiological needs. Once the needs at a particular level are satisfied, the individual is motivated to satisfy the needs at the next level, steadily progressing upward. The ultimate goal is self-actualization, the realization of personal potential.
(Based on Maslow, 1970.)

Self-actualization: achieving one's full potential, including creative activities

Esteem needs: prestige and feeling of accomplishment

Belongingness and love needs: intimate relationships, friends

Safety needs: security, safety

Physiological needs: food, water, warmth, rest

Self-fulfillment needs

Psychological needs

Basic needs

TABLE 8.2 Maslow's Characteristics of Self-Actualized People

Realism and acceptance	Self-actualized people have accurate perceptions of themselves, others, and external reality. They easily accept themselves and others as they are.
Spontaneity	Self-actualized people are spontaneous, natural, and open in their behavior and thoughts. However, they can easily conform to conventional rules and expectations when situations demand such behavior.
Problem centering	Self-actualized people focus on problems outside themselves. They often dedicate themselves to a larger purpose in life, which is based on ethics or a sense of personal responsibility.
Autonomy	Although they accept and enjoy other people, self-actualized individuals have a strong need for privacy and independence. They focus on their own potential and development rather than the opinions of others.
Continued freshness of appreciation	Self-actualized people continue to appreciate the simple pleasures of life with awe and wonder.
Peak experiences	Self-actualized people commonly have *peak experiences,* or moments of intense ecstasy, wonder, and awe during which their sense of self is lost or transcended. The self-actualized person may feel transformed and strengthened by these peak experiences.

SOURCE: Based on Maslow, 1970.

believed that people are motivated to satisfy the needs at each level of the hierarchy before moving up to the next level. People progressively move up the hierarchy, striving to eventually reach *self-actualization.* Notice that the lowest levels of Maslow's hierarchy emphasize fundamental biological, safety, and social needs. At the highest levels, the needs become more individualized and growth-oriented.

What exactly is self-actualization? Maslow (1970) himself had trouble defining the term, saying that self-actualization is "a difficult syndrome to describe accurately." Nonetheless, Maslow defined **self-actualization** in the following way:

> *It may be loosely described as the full use and exploitation of talents, capacities, potentialities, etc. Such people seem to be fulfilling themselves and to be doing the best that they are capable of doing. . . . They are people who have developed or are developing to the full stature of which they are capable.*

Beyond that general description, Maslow's research identified several characteristics that self-actualized people seem to possess. Some of these qualities are summarized in Table 8.2.

Not surprisingly, humanistic models of motivation also have limitations (see Petri, 1996; Mook, 1996). For example, concepts like self-actualization are extremely vague and almost impossible to define in a way that would allow them to be tested scientifically. And Maslow's initial studies on self-actualization were based on limited samples with questionable reliability. For example, Maslow (1970) often relied on the life stories of acquaintances whose identities were never revealed. He also studied the biographies and autobiographies of famous historical figures who he believed had achieved self-actualization, such as Eleanor Roosevelt, Abraham Lincoln, and Albert Einstein.

A more important criticism is that the majority of people do not experience or achieve self-actualization, despite the claim that this is an inborn goal toward which all people supposedly strive. Maslow (1970) himself wrote that self-actualization "can seem like a miracle, so improbable an event as to be awe-inspiring." Maslow explained this basic contradiction in a number of different ways. For instance, he suggested that few people experience the supportive environment that is required for self-actualization.

Although Maslow's theory continues to generate research (e.g., Sumerlin & Norman, 1992; Neher, 1991), the humanistic model of motivation is not as influential as it once was. Nonetheless, Maslow's theory helped establish the important role played by psychological and cognitive factors in human motivation. Later in the chapter, we'll look at how psychological and cognitive factors influence other forms of human motivation, such as curiosity and the need for achievement.

The Study of Motivation Today:
A Diverse Enterprise

Rather than a single "grand" theory, motivation researchers today assume that *the motivation of any behavior is determined by multiple factors.* Such factors can include biological, behavioral, cognitive, and social components.

self-actualization
Defined by Maslow as "the full use and exploitation of talents, capacities, and potentialities."

Exactly how these different factors interact to energize and motivate behavior is still the subject of much research.

Rather than continuing to search for a grand theory of motivation, today's researchers focus on the study of specific types of motivated behavior (Petri, 1996). In the next several sections, we will examine several very different behaviors investigated by researchers in motivation. We'll survey such motivated behaviors as eating, curiosity, and competence and achievement motivation. In Chapter 10, we'll take an in-depth look at the motivation of sexual behavior.

CONCEPT REVIEW 8.1

Components of Motivation

1. Dr. Moretti studies the various forces acting on or within organisms that initiate and direct behavior. Her area of research is:
  a. emotion   **c.** motivation
  b. cognition   **d.** perception

2. It is an innate characteristic of robins to build nests. This is an example of:
  a. an instinct   **c.** incentive motivation
  b. a drive   **d.** homeostasis

3. After finishing a six-mile race, Bobby feels very thirsty. His desire to drink water is a function of:
  a. instinct   **c.** incentive motivation
  b. homeostasis   **d.** self-actualization

4. For the past several weeks, Lois has been working overtime on an important project, hoping to get a raise. Her behavior illustrates:
  a. instinct   **c.** incentive motivation
  b. drive   **d.** self-actualization

5. Dr. Kurtz argues that the need for physical safety and adequate food and shelter must be met before citizens will be motivated to start a community orchestra. His proposal is based on the notion of:
  a. instinct   **c.** incentive motivation
  b. drive   **d.** hierarchy of needs

The Motivation to Eat

The motivation to eat is influenced by psychological, biological, social, and cultural factors. How do oral signals, stomach signals, CCK, insulin, and the hypothalamus seem to influence hunger and eating behavior?

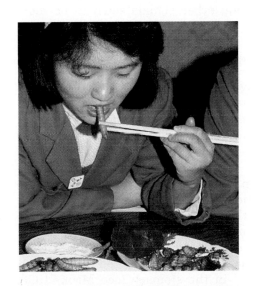

Delicious or Disgusting? The need to eat is a universal human motive. However, culture heavily influences *what* we eat, *when* we eat, and *how* we eat. This Chinese woman is clearly enjoying her meal of fried caterpillars and scorpions—a delicacy in her province.

On the surface, it seems simple: you eat because you're hungry. But it's not that simple. What, when, and how much you eat are influenced by diverse psychological, biological, social, and cultural factors.

For example, think about what you ate yesterday. Now contrast your choices with food preferences in other cultures. A typical diet for the Dusan of northern Borneo in Southeast Asia includes anteater, gibbon (a small ape), snake, mouse, and rat meat. After these meats have spoiled to point of being liquified, the Dusan consume them with rice. South American Indians consume head lice, bees, iguanas, and monkeys. The Guiana of South America eat pebbles as a regular part of their diet, while the Vedda of Sri Lanka like rotted wood (see Fieldhouse, 1986).

Psychologically, eating can be related to emotional states, such as depression, anxiety, or stress (Greeno & Wing, 1994). Interpersonally, eating is often used to foster relationships, as when you have friends over for dinner or take a potential customer to lunch. In describing others, we often rely on food-related adjectives, such as saying someone has a "sweet" or "sour" personality. Without question, the themes of food and eating permeate many different dimensions of our lives.

For psychologists, the study of eating behavior has focused on several critical issues. The most fundamental issue has been trying to understand what motivates us to eat on a day-to-day basis. What causes hunger? And how do we sense that we've eaten enough?

What Causes Us to Start and Stop Eating?

For most of this century, researchers have been searching for the source of the signals that trigger hunger and satiation. (*Satiation* is the feeling of fullness and diminished desire to eat.) Though the picture is far from complete, it's clear that multiple internal and external signals are involved in hunger and satiation. Let's briefly examine what these signals are and how they influence our motivation to eat.

Oral Signals: How About Some Liquid Pizza for Lunch?

The oral sensations involved in tasting and chewing food contribute greatly to the subjective pleasure and satisfaction of eating. They also contribute to the regulation of eating behavior. For example, subjects can be deprived of taste and chewing cues by having liquid food pumped directly into the stomach. Though subjects receive adequate nourishment to maintain their weight, they find the "meal" unsatisfying and express a strong desire to taste or chew something (Jordon, 1969).

More drastically, the relaying of oral sensations to the brain can be stopped altogether by cutting a particular nerve called the *vagus nerve*. When this nerve is cut in rats, their motivation to eat decreases. Though they continue to eat, the rats eat less and lose weight (Zeigler & others, 1985).

These and other studies suggest that oral sensations provide important sensory signals in eating behavior. However, oral sensations do *not* seem to be what causes us to start or stop eating. Instead, oral signals seem to help maintain or slow down eating behavior once it has begun (Bray, 1991). In terms of starting and stopping eating, other signals seem to be more influential.

Stomach Signals: Stretching It to the Limit

One common-sense explanation of hunger is that we start eating when our stomach "feels empty" and stop eating when we "feel full." In fact, the stomach has sensory neurons that detect the stretching of the stomach muscles. As the stomach stretches to accommodate food, signals from these neurons are relayed to the brain, helping to trigger feelings of satiation (Geliebter & others, 1987).

A hormone called **cholecystokinin,** thankfully abbreviated **CCK,** also seems to play a role in signaling satiation. As food moves from the stomach to the intestines, CCK is secreted into the bloodstream and conveyed to the brain, where CCK acts as a neurotransmitter (Kalat, 1995; Zhang & others, 1986). CCK seems to magnify the satiety-producing effects of food in the stomach by slowing the rate at which the stomach empties and by heightening the sensitivity of "stretch receptors" in the stomach (see Mook, 1996; Bray, 1991; McHugh & Moran, 1985).

Still, even if stretch signals from the stomach provide an important signal to stop eating, other signals must be involved. Why? Because it's long been known that people continue to experience hunger and satiation even after their stomachs have been removed for medical reasons (Wangensteen & Carlson, 1931).

cholecystokinin (CCK)

(*kole*-eh-*sist*-oh-KINE-in) A hormone that seems to play a role in signaling satiation, or fullness.

The Role of Insulin: Does the *Thought* of a Candy Bar Make You Hungry?

Try this: Imagine your favorite candy bar is sitting on the kitchen counter, unopened. Imagine picking it up and smelling the chocolate through the wrapper. Slowly, carefully, you peel the thin, crinkly wrapping paper back. You take a bite, savoring its sweet taste, appetizing texture, and mouth-watering aroma. As you slowly chew it, the taste of milk chocolate and caramel floods your senses. Are you starting to get hungry? If you are, it's probably because your levels of insulin just increased.

Insulin is a hormone secreted by the pancreas that helps regulate the metabolism of carbohydrates, fats, and starches in the body. Psychologist Judith Rodin (1985) has assembled an impressive array of evidence demonstrating that higher insulin levels lead us to experience more hunger and eat more food. Normally, insulin levels begin to rise shortly *after* we start eating. But Rodin has shown that we can become classically conditioned to produce increased insulin levels *before* consuming food.

Just as Pavlov's dogs became classically conditioned to salivate to the sound of a bell that had been repeatedly paired with food (see Chapter 5), people can become classically conditioned to associate environmental stimuli with eating. Stimuli such as the sight or smell of appealing food, other people eating, or even just the thought of food can trigger a surge of insulin in our bodies. Once such learned reflexes become firmly entrenched, we can experience increased insulin production and enhanced feelings of hunger before we've taken a single bite (Lucas & others, 1987).

In her studies, Rodin (1981, 1985) has found that people vary in their responsiveness to environmental stimuli associated with food. She refers to people who are highly responsive to food-related stimuli as *externals,* while people who are less responsive to food cues are called *nonexternals.* When externals are exposed to an environmental stimulus that they've learned to associate with food, they produce significantly more insulin in anticipation of eating than nonexternals do.

Rodin (1978) reported the different responses of externals and nonexternals in a clever study. External and nonexternal subjects were deprived of food for 18 hours. While blood samples were being drawn from the subjects, a steak was brought in, grilling and crackling in a frying pan. The externals responded to the sight, smell, and sound of the grilling steak with higher levels of insulin and greater feelings of hunger than the nonexternals did.

The Brain and Eating Behavior: No Simple Answers

The *hypothalamus,* a small structure buried deep within the brain, was first implicated in the regulation of eating behavior in the 1940s. Researchers found that when a particular area called the *ventromedial hypothalamus* (VMH) was damaged, an experimental animal would eat until it became obese (see Miller, 1995; Hetherington & Ranson, 1940). The photograph on page 342 shows a rat with VMH damage.

A decade later, it was discovered that damage to another area, called the *lateral hypothalamus* (LH), caused an animal to stop eating (Anand & Brobeck, 1951). With the LH damaged, a rat will starve to death if left to its own devices. If it is force-fed, the rat will eventually resume eating, but its body weight will drop to a much lower level.

On the basis of these initial findings, it became widely believed that the hypothalamus contained the "start eating" and "stop eating" centers. Though the simplicity of this model is appealing, later research cast serious doubts on its accuracy.

For example, it stands to reason that if the VMH alone provided the signal to stop eating, then rats with a destroyed VMH should eat everything in

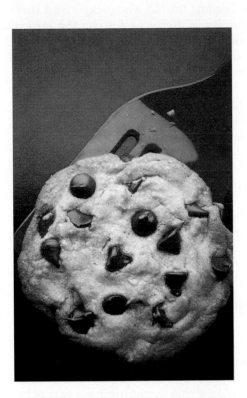

Is Your Mouth Watering? Researcher Judith Rodin has shown that the sight or thought of appetizing food can trigger a surge of insulin. That's why just looking at this photograph (assuming you like chocolate chip cookies) might make you feel hungry.

Rat with a Damaged VMH When a particular section of the hypothalamus called the ventromedial hypothalamus is destroyed, rats will eat until they become obese—but only if the food is appetizing. This particular rat tipped the scales at 1080 grams or almost two-and-a-half pounds!

sight because there would be no "stop eating" signal. In reality, such rats do not eat until they explode. Instead, they become finicky and picky about their food (Ferguson & Keesey, 1975). The quality of diet seems to be the critical factor. If the food is appealing, the rats make pigs of themselves (so to speak), blimp up, and eventually stabilize as very obese rats. But if the food is blah, at least as far as a rat is concerned, they maintain their normal weight or even lose weight. Thus, whether or not damage to the VMH produces obesity is strongly related to the appeal of the food (Keesey & Powley, 1986).

Other research cast doubt on the role of the lateral hypothalamus as the "start eating" center. As it turns out, damage to the LH not only reduces the drive to eat, it also reduces general arousal and other behaviors (Marshall & Teitelbaum, 1974). In other words, damage to the LH seems to reduce a wide variety of behaviors and drives, eating behavior among them.

While it seems reasonable to conclude that the hypothalamus and its surrounding regions play an important role in regulating eating behavior, the exact nature of that role remains unclear. It does seem clear, though, that the earlier notion that the hypothalamus contains specific "start eating" and "stop eating" centers is largely inaccurate.

The Daily Regulation of Eating Reconsidered

So what conclusions can we draw about the factors that regulate eating behavior? First, the physiological mechanisms underlying our motivation to eat are complex and not completely understood. Second, multiple signals appear to be involved, each providing some form of feedback to the brain. Oral signals, such as taste and chewing, seem to play a role in maintaining eating behavior. Stretch receptors and other sensory receptors in the stomach seem to play some role in signaling satiation (see Pennisi, 1994). Chemical signals involving the hormones CCK and insulin also seem to play pivotal roles (Bray, 1991).

Third, the role played by different brain regions remains unclear and is still being investigated. Tentatively, it appears that the hypothalamus and its surrounding regions detect these varied signals and, in turn, initiate or suppress eating behavior. And fourth, our psychological response to external signals—such as the smell of freshly popped popcorn—may trigger physiological changes in responsive individuals, such as increased insulin production, that lead to increased feelings of hunger.

While there's no question that physiological mechanisms are involved in regulating eating behavior, a simple fact remains. The decision to start or stop eating is ultimately made consciously, in the brain's most sophisticated centers, despite hunger or satiation signals from the stomach or hypothalamus. Our body may be signaling, "Full! Full! Enough, already!!" but we can still reach for another piece of pumpkin pie after a scrumptious Thanksgiving feast.

Likewise, even when you're very hungry, you may deliberately postpone or restrict eating, at least for a short period of time. (Ever sat through a noon class gnawing on your knuckles and hoping that no one could hear your stomach growl?) Dieters consciously restrain their appetites according to self-imposed limits, often establishing mental "boundaries" that define hunger and satiety (Herman & Polivy, 1984). As you'll see later, in the case of eating-related disorders, these self-imposed "boundaries" can become pathological for some people.

The bottom line: What motivates us to eat at a particular moment is governed by a complex system involving the *interaction* of physiological, behavioral, cognitive, and environmental factors. In the next section, we'll go beyond the short-term regulation of eating behavior and consider why our body weight seems to stay remarkably (and sometimes frustratingly) stable over time.

basal metabolic rate (BMR)
The rate at which the body uses energy for vital body functions when at rest.

The Regulation of Body Weight

The regulation of body weight has been explained in terms of the energy balance model. What role does basal metabolic rate play in weight regulation? What factors influence BMR? How does set-point theory account for the regulation of body weight?

How much do you weigh? Has your weight changed much over the past six months? Probably not, unless there's been a significant change in your health, activity level, or eating habits. (That's why body weight is listed as an identifying characteristic on driver's licenses—and on "Wanted" posters in the post office.) Over the course of a year, we typically gain a few pounds during the winter and shed a few pounds during the summer. But for the most part, our weight stays pretty much the same. Traditionally, this has been explained in terms of the *energy balance model:* If the food (energy) we consume equals the energy we expend, our weight remains constant (Salens, 1984).

Because it's so central to the discussion that follows, let's briefly consider each side of the energy balance equation. On the "energy supply" side, the food you eat is partially broken down into nutrients in your stomach. These nutrients are gradually absorbed in your intestines and converted into "fuel" that can be used by your body, such as amino acids and simple sugars. Of these fuels, the simple sugar called *glucose* is the main source of energy for humans and animals. If there is more glucose than your body needs for its energy requirements, the excess is converted into *fat*—stored energy for future use. On the average, people have about a month's supply of energy stored in their fat cells.

On the "energy expenditure" side, about one-third of your body's energy is used for routine physical activities, such as sitting, walking, standing in line at the grocery store, and running to class when you're late. The remaining two-thirds is used for continuous body functions that are essential to life, such as respiration, heartbeat, brain activity, and the production of body heat (Rodin, 1985; Corbett & Keesey, 1982). The rate at which your body uses energy for vital body functions when at rest is referred to as your **basal metabolic rate,** abbreviated **BMR.**

Factors Influencing Metabolism

People vary greatly in their basal metabolic rate. In a classic study, investigators tracked the food intake of pairs of same-sex subjects who were carefully matched for weight, age, height, and daily levels of activity (Rose & Williams, 1961). Over the course of several weeks, all subjects maintained their normal weight. Yet, in many cases, one member of the matched pairs was eating *twice as much* as the other member! This finding demonstrates that a constant body weight depends on the critical balance between food intake and BMR.

A variety of factors influence a person's basal metabolic rate. On the average, women have a lower metabolic rate than men. How much a person weighs also influences metabolism. Contrary to popular belief, heavy people typically have a *higher* metabolic rate than slender people (Franken, 1994). Basically, this is because a heavy person's body has to work harder to maintain vital body functions.

Metabolism also decreases with age. Between infancy and your early twenties, body metabolism declines steeply (see Figure 8.2). Consequently, it's not surprising that many people, upon reaching adulthood, suddenly must begin to watch how much they eat. As your BMR decreases with age, less food is

FIGURE 8.2 Age and Sex Differences in Metabolism From birth through adolescence, there is a steep decline in the rate at which your body uses energy for vital functions, such as heartbeat, breathing, and body heat. From early adulthood until old age, your basal metabolic rate continues to decrease, only more slowly. Regardless of age, females generally have a lower metabolic rate than males.

(Stuart & Davis, 1972, p. 166.)

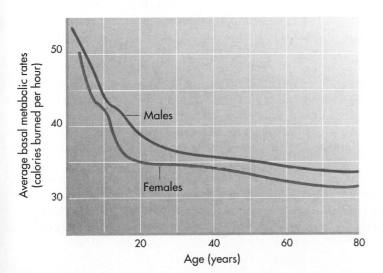

set-point weight
The particular weight that is set and maintained by increases or decreases in basal metabolic rate.

required to meet your energy needs. If, out of habit, you continue to eat as much as you did during your adolescence, it's almost a sure bet that you'll gain weight during early adulthood unless you increase your activity level. After your early twenties, your BMR continues to decline, but more gradually.

Genetics also seems to play a role in determining a person's BMR. For example, the adult weight of adopted individuals is strongly correlated with the adult weights of their biological parents, not their adoptive parents (Stunkard & others, 1986). Usually, a child's approximate adult weight can be reliably predicted from the adult weights of his or her biological parents.

Obviously, there are exceptions to such correlations: our neighbor, Bob, is very lean, but everyone in his immediate family is overweight, including his parents.

The influence of genetics in metabolism was also evident in a study of twelve pairs of male identical twins who ate an extra 1,000 calories a day for three months (Bouchard & others, 1990b). Though each twin pair gained virtually the same amount of weight, there was considerable variation *among* the twin pairs. Some twin pairs gained as little as 9 pounds, while other twin pairs gained as much as 29 pounds. Again, this result strongly suggests that we may be genetically predisposed to utilize food energy at a particular rate.

It's clear that basal metabolic rate plays an important role in the energy-balance model. But we still haven't addressed the critical question: How do we manage to maintain a steady body weight? Unless we're on a diet, most of us don't give a great deal of conscious consideration to how many calories we consume each day. Sometimes we eat more, sometimes we eat less. Despite these fluctuations in food consumption, body weight tends to remain remarkably stable. Why?

TABLE 8.3 Factors That Influence Basal Metabolic Rate (BMR)

Age	BMR slows down with increased age, especially during the first two decades of life.
Sex	Males generally have higher metabolic rates than females.
Body size	Heavier people have higher metabolic rates than slender people.
Genetics	Evidence strongly suggests that BMR is influenced by heredity.
Diet	Restricted food intake lowers BMR; excess food intake increases BMR.

Set-Point Theory: Are We "Set" to Maintain a Particular Weight?

Anyone who has ever tried to lose weight by dieting *or* to gain weight by eating more has experienced the body's "resistance" to establishing a new "standard" weight, whether it's lower or higher. According to Richard Keesey and Terry Powley (1986), this happens because each of us has a **set-point weight**—a particular weight that the body is naturally set to maintain by increasing or decreasing BMR (see Figure 8.3).

For example, assume that you've consistently weighed about 140 pounds for the past several years. This would be your set-point weight. Assume further that you've committed yourself to a New Year's resolution to go on a diet and lose 10 pounds by spring. After you have significantly reduced your normal food intake for a few weeks, your body weight begins to drop below your natural set-point weight.

At this point, your body initiates actions to "defend" and reestablish its set-point weight. Specifically, your body's regulatory mechanisms compensate by reducing your BMR and triggering feelings of hunger. With your body's energy requirements reduced, it becomes easier to return to your set-point weight *even though you're still eating less food than usual*. It's as though your body is programmed to monitor your weight and keep it within a predetermined range.

The opposite effect occurs if you try to gain weight. When you *increase* food consumption and your weight begins to rise above your set-point weight, your body *increases* its expenditure of energy (BMR), and feelings of hunger are reduced. Both actions function to reestablish your set-point weight. Once

FIGURE 8.3 Set-Point Theory

your set-point weight is reestablished, your BMR returns to its normal level if your food consumption returns to normal.

Set-point theory is based on the well-established principle of homeostasis, discussed earier. In support of set-point theory, many studies with both animals and humans have demonstrated that increases or decreases in body weight are followed by corresponding changes in the body's basal metabolic rate (Keesey & Powley, 1986).

What exactly does your body monitor to maintain your particular set-point weight? Several lines of research suggest that it's the number and size of fat cells (see Faust & others, 1976, 1977a). Both human and animal studies have demonstrated that the number and size of fat cells are established very early in life—by about the age of two (Knittle, 1975; Faust & others, 1977b). These studies suggest that both the number and size of fat cells are at least partly determined by genetic factors.

However, environmental factors, such as what and how much you eat, also play an important role in the amount of fat stored. At any age, if you consistently consume more food than is required to meet your body's energy needs, the excess becomes stored as fat. At first, overeating produces an increase in the *size* of fat cells. However, if overeating continues, fat cells start increasing in *number* (Macedonio, 1984).

Unfortunately, acquiring new fat cells is a one-way street. Once acquired, fat cells are with you for life (Salens, 1984). If you acquire more fat cells, your body essentially becomes programmed to maintain a higher set-point weight (Keesey & Powley, 1986). If you reduce your weight, even dramatically, the *number* of fat cells you have does not decrease—they simply decrease in *size*.

Although set-point theory has proved quite useful in helping us understand many aspects of body weight regulation, it is not without limitations. One criticism is that set-point theory merely describes what occurs rather than explaining the underlying mechanisms (see Graham, 1990).

When the Regulation of Body Weight Fails:
Obesity

Misconceptions about the causes of obesity are common. How do obese individuals differ from nonobese individuals in their response to food? Why is it difficult to maintain weight loss? What are the characteristics of anorexia and bulimia?

There is a great deal of societal pressure, often contradictory, on the estimated 30 million Americans who are obese (Brownell & Rodin, 1994). On the one hand, thinness represents the American ideal of beauty, health, and sex appeal. On the other hand, society provides a wide diversity of mouth-watering, easily attainable foods. Restaurant and food commercials are carefully designed to maximize the sensory appeal of food, increasing the temptation to overeat. And many activities provide the opportunity to overindulge ourselves in food, such as spectator sports, food courts in shopping malls, and even lunch with co-workers at all-you-can-eat restaurants.

Ironically, as the American ideal has gotten thinner, Americans themselves have gotten heavier (Brownell & Rodin, 1994; Rodin & others, 1985). Many Americans are obsessed with achieving, or at least getting closer to, the socially desirable goal of thinness. One survey, for example, revealed that 50 million Americans are trying to lose weight—approximately one-third of all American women and one-fifth of all American males (Levy & Heaton, 1992).

CATHY

This translates into over $30 *billion* dollars a year spent on diet aids and commercial weight-loss programs, such as Weight Watchers and Jenny Craig. If consistently followed, such programs can be very effective in reducing weight. Unfortunately, people are generally not very successful at keeping the excess weight off. Most people who lose weight eventually regain it (Nuckolls, 1992; Brownell, 1982).

Understanding Obesity: Some Common Misconceptions

Although definitions vary, people are said to be **obese** when their weight is 20 percent or more above their "ideal" weight (Metropolitan, 1983). For about 5 percent of obese individuals, some specific cause is responsible for the excessive weight, such as a brain tumor or a hereditary disease (Salens, 1984; Rodin, 1982). But for the vast majority of the obese, a specific cause cannot be identified.

There are many misconceptions about the causes of obesity. It is commonly believed, for example, that obese people lack will power and consistently eat much more than they should (Friedman & Brownell, 1995). There are two problems with this explanation. First, what constitutes overeating is not the same for everyone. Whether a given amount of food is excessive or not must be judged on an individual basis and depends on several factors, including the person's basal metabolic rate (Rodin, 1985). As we've already seen, the amount of food needed to maintain a stable body weight can vary enormously from one person to another.

Second, people often exaggerate the amount that obese people overeat (Rodin, 1982). Many obese people do not overeat *that* much (see Mook, 1996; Spitzer & Rodin, 1981). It's a mistake to assume that all obese people are obese because they consistently eat much more than they should. Other factors can be involved in maintaining obesity once it occurs, such as the type of foods consumed or a sedentary lifestyle (Epstein & others, 1995; Rodin, 1982).

We mentioned previously that genetics plays a role in influencing a person's basal metabolic rate. The role of genetics in obesity is still not fully understood, but obesity does tend to run in families (Rodin, 1982; Salens, 1984). Thus, it's possible that some people are genetically predisposed to obesity, which may be related to the genetic influence on metabolic rate. However, a family tendency toward obesity could also be explained in terms of environmental, social, or cultural factors (Brownell & Rodin, 1994). For example, family eating habits or the degree of importance placed on food could be involved.

The Regulation of Hunger, Body Weight, and Obesity

To get a better understanding of obesity, let's first consider how obese individuals differ from the nonobese in the daily regulation of hunger, then in the long-term regulation of body weight. Concerning the daily regulation of eating behavior, there are three pieces of evidence to consider.

First, several studies have demonstrated that many obese individuals tend to be *highly responsive to external cues* associated with food. Such cues include the time of day, how appetizing the food is, and the ease with which food can be obtained (Schachter, 1971a, 1971b; Rodin, 1981). Second, individ-

obese
Weighing 20 percent or more above one's "ideal" body weight.

uals who are highly responsive to food-related stimuli tend to *react physiologically with greater insulin production.* And third, obese individuals generally operate with *higher body levels of insulin* (Rodin, 1985; Rabinowitz, 1970).

Collectively, these three points suggest that obese individuals tend to respond with greater intensity to food-related cues and food itself, especially foods that are highly appetizing. Unfortunately, the more insulin that circulates throughout a person's body, the faster fat deposits build from glucose not used for energy. The more fat deposits a person acquires, the more weight is gained, and the easier it becomes to gain additional weight. As Rodin (1982) put it, "Our metabolic machinery is devised in such a way that the fatter we are, the fatter we are primed to become."

So what happens when an obese person restricts food intake, sometimes severely, to lose weight? As predicted by set-point theory, the body vigorously defends against the loss by sharply reducing the rate of metabolism. Within as little as two weeks after beginning a diet, an obese person's metabolic rate may drop by 20 percent or more (see Macedonio, 1984). Far fewer calories are now needed to maintain the obese weight because the body's expenditure of energy is sharply reduced. And fat requires less energy to maintain than lean body tissue does (Rodin, 1981).

Also critical is the finding that the metabolic rate *remains* decreased for as long as the person's body weight remains below the obese set-point weight. In one study of obese individuals who maintained their weight loss, their metabolic rate was still reduced *six years* later (Liebel & Hirsch, 1984).

The implications of all these findings are less than encouraging to obese individuals. Regardless of how an individual initially becomes obese, once obesity occurs it seems to be maintained by a complex system of environmental, psychological, and biological factors (Rodin, 1985). The obese person's body becomes primed to maintain and increase fat stores. When obese people diet to lose weight, they are often fighting their own uncooperative bodies. If they are successful in reducing their fat stores and body weight, they've only won the battle, not the war. To maintain their lower weight, people must permanently modify their eating patterns and follow a regular exercise program.

Because losing weight in the face of the multiple factors that maintain obesity represents a constant battle, many obese individuals have simply learned to accept their weight the way it is. This is no small psychological accomplishment. Obese people are on the opposite end of the media-manufactured "ideal" of physical attractiveness. When in public, obese people have virtually no opportunity to hide their condition. Developing a healthy sense of self-acceptance in the face of such societal pressure is not easy.

Finally, a thought for you. If you happen to be someone who is of normal weight or even slender, carefully consider the information we've shared with you in this section. More than once, we've encountered students who were very critical of obese individuals. Such criticisms reflect a lack of awareness of the information we've presented in this section. Ask yourself how you would want to be treated if you happened to be obese. Obese people live in a culture that condemns their physical appearance—and *blames* them for the way they look. In American culture, obese people are often the target of discrimination and criticism (Friedman & Brownell, 1995).

One of the most important themes that the science of psychology promotes is tolerance for individual differences. In the case of obese individuals, it may well be that psychologists and other researchers will eventually be able to provide a simple and safe way to control excess weight. Until that time, however, many obese people struggle to stay motivated to keep excess weight off or to accept themselves the way they are. Either way, insensitive and uninformed remarks do little to enhance the psychological well-being of the obese individual.

When the Regulation of Eating Behavior Fails:

Anorexia and Bulimia

Barbie, the American Ideal? If a normal-sized woman (left) was proportioned like a Barbie doll, she would look like the photograph on the right. Yale psychologist Kelly Brownell calculated that if a woman's hips stayed the same size, she would have to gain nearly a foot in height, add four inches to her chest, and lose five inches from her waist to meet the impossible standard set by Barbie. Many psychologists believe that such unrealistic standards contribute to the incidence of eating disorders in Western cultures.

anorexia nervosa
An eating disorder in which the individual refuses to maintain a minimally normal body weight, is extremely afraid of gaining weight or becoming fat, and has a distorted perception about the size of his or her body.

bulimia nervosa
An eating disorder in which a person engages in binge eating and then purges the excessive food consumption by self-induced vomiting or, less often, by taking laxatives or enemas.

Another disruption of normal weight lies at the opposite end of the spectrum from obesity. **Anorexia nervosa** is a life-threatening disorder that involves near self-starvation. This disorder has three key symptoms: the individual refuses to maintain a minimally normal body weight, is extremely afraid of gaining weight or becoming fat, and has a distorted perception about the size of his or her body. Approximately 90 percent of cases of anorexia nervosa occur in adolescent or young adult females (American Psychiatric Association, 1994). The characteristics of anorexia nervosa are very similar for males and females, but anorexia is much less common among males (Olivardia & others, 1995).

It's rare that a person with anorexia completely loses her appetite. Rather, she places herself on a very restricted diet that may be limited to just a few foods. Weight loss is also often accomplished by excessive exercise, fasting, self-induced vomiting, or the misuse of laxatives. By reducing total food intake, individuals with anorexia drop 15 percent or more below their ideal body weight. Depression, social withdrawal, insomnia, and, in women, failure to menstruate, frequently accompany the disorder (D. Sue & others, 1994).

A hallmark of anorexia is distorted self-perception. Despite her emaciated appearance, the person with anorexia looks in the mirror and sees herself as being overweight. Or she expresses displeasure with certain parts of her body, such as an abdomen or thighs that are "too fat." Weight loss is viewed with pride and regarded as an act of extraordinary self-discipline.

Individuals with anorexia also commonly become obsessed with food. The person may collect recipes and cookbooks, hoard food, or prepare elaborate meals for others. Despite this obsession with food, many individuals with anorexia do not admit to being hungry (Davison & Neale, 1994). Although estimates vary, approximately 10 percent of people with anorexia nervosa die from starvation, suicide, or physical complications accompanying extreme weight loss (American Psychiatric Association, 1994).

In contrast, people suffering from **bulimia nervosa** are within their normal weight range and may even be slightly overweight. Bulimic people engage in binge eating and then purge themselves of the excessive food consumption by self-induced vomiting. Less often, they may use laxatives or enemas to purge themselves of the food.

People suffering from bulimia usually conceal their eating problems from others. Episodes of binge eating typically occur in secrecy. When a binge occurs, it usually includes the consumption of high-caloric, sweet foods that can be swallowed quickly, such as ice cream, cake, and candy. Once they begin eating, they often feel as if they cannot control their food intake. Sometimes consuming as much as 50,000 calories at one time, they eat until they are uncomfortably, even painfully, full (American Psychiatric Association, 1994; Johnson & others, 1982).

What causes anorexia nervosa and bulimia nervosa? Diverse cultural, psychological, social, and genetic factors seem to be involved in both of these eating disorders (Steinhausen, 1994; North & others, 1995). For example, there is strong cultural pressure, especially for young women, to achieve the thinness ideal. Psychologically, there is often faulty thinking about food intake, distorted body perceptions, and a tendency toward perfectionism (Steinhausen & Vollrath, 1993; Steinhausen & Seidel, 1993).

Genetic factors also seem to play a role in eating disorders. Among female identical twins, when one develops anorexia, better than 50 percent of the time the other twin also develops anorexia. With nonidentical twins, the rate of co-occurrence of anorexia is only 5 percent (Holland & others, 1988).

The Motivation of Eating Behavior

Indicate whether each of the following statements is true or false.

___**1.** Higher insulin levels may lead you to eat more.

___**2.** All your fat cells are acquired by the age of two.

___**3.** Your basal metabolic rate decreases with age.

___**4.** Obese people typically have a lower basal metabolic rate than thin people.

___**5.** Physiological mechanisms control when you eat and how much you eat.

___**6.** The ventromedial hypothalamus is the brain area that provides the "start eating" signal.

___**7.** A couple of times each week, Jill stuffs herself with ice cream and cookies, then induces vomiting to purge herself of the food. Jill suffers from anorexia nervosa.

Arousal Motives: Curiosity and Sensation Seeking

According to arousal theory, people are motivated to maintain an optimal level of arousal. What factors influence curiosity and exploratory behavior? How does arousal theory help explain the pacing of curious behavior? What is sensation seeking?

Motivation researchers have long noted that people can be highly motivated to seek out experiences that *increase* tension, rather than reduce tension. Playing a video game, going to a suspenseful movie, hang gliding—none of these activities can be explained in terms of tension reduction or the satisfaction of some biological need. Incentive theories also fall short in explaining such behavior. Often, we solve puzzles, pursue hobbies, or try new things without being motivated by any kind of external reward.

Like people, animals also seem to seek out environmental stimulation. Rats, cats, dogs, and other animals will explore a novel environment. A monkey kept in a boring cage will "work" for the opportunity to open a window to peek into another monkey's cage or to watch an electric train run (Butler & Harlow, 1954). A monkey will also spend hours trying to open a complicated lock, even when there is *no* incentive or reward for doing so (Harlow, 1953).

Clearly then, behaviors like curiosity, exploration, and seeking stimulation cannot be adequately explained by drive theories of motivation (Loewenstein, 1994). In this section, we'll consider another approach to understanding motivation, one that is based on the premise that people are sometimes motivated to increase arousal by seeking out stimulation.

Curiosity: An Innate Motive Like humans, animals are also motivated to seek out stimulation and explore novel environments. In his research with monkeys, Harry Harlow (1953) found that simple curiosity was a powerful motive. These young monkeys are trying to open a complicated lock, despite the lack of an incentive or reward for their behavior.

Arousal Theory:

Seeking the "Optimal" Level

Arousal theory is based on the observation that people find both very high levels of arousal and very low levels of arousal quite unpleasant. When arousal is too low, we experience boredom and try to *increase* arousal by seeking out stimulating experiences. But when arousal is too high, we seek to *reduce* arousal in a less stimulating environment. Thus, according to this theory, people are motivated to maintain an *optimal* level of arousal, one that is neither too high nor too low (Hebb, 1955; see Petri, 1996). The optimal, or "just right," level of arousal can vary from person to person, from time to time, and from one situation to another.

According to psychologist Daniel Berlyne (1960, 1971), when arousal is unpleasantly low, one way that people and other animals increase arousal is by seeking out novel stimuli. Thus, arousal theory can help explain the next motive that we consider—curiosity (Spielberger & Starr, 1994).

Curiosity and Exploratory Behavior

Curiosity doesn't always seem to have a rational motive (Loewenstein, 1994). Why is it so hard to put down a suspenseful novel until we have read the very last page? Why do we strain to overhear that intriguing conversation of two strangers at the next table in a restaurant? Whether rational or not, there's no question that the motivational drive of curiosity can be very compelling. When something arouses our curiosity, the urge to "peek" can be irresistible. What compels this curiosity? What purpose is served by such behavior?

Curiosity is a motive that has a strong influence on human behavior at all stages of the life cycle (Loewenstein, 1994). Almost immediately after birth, human infants begin visually exploring the environment, their attention captured by the new, the different. Though only a few hours old, an infant will have its curiosity aroused by the sight of objects with relatively complex shapes, patterns, and contours (Fantz, 1963, 1965; Milewski, 1976).

Whoa! What's in Here? The joy of curiosity and discovery is evident in eleven-month-old Laura's face as she explores the fascinating contents of the kitchen pantry. Throughout the lifespan, curiosity is a compelling motive that helps us understand our environment.

We don't explore the world haphazardly. One purpose of curiosity and exploratory behavior is to become familiar with and understand our world (Loewenstein, 1994). In pursuit of this goal, we "pace" the rate at which we expose ourselves to increasing complexity and novelty (Dember & Earl, 1957). As we become familiar with a stimulus, we *gradually* move toward stimuli that are slightly more complex (Arkes & Boykin, 1971; May, 1963). This pacing produces the optimal level of physical and cognitive arousal that helps motivate curiosity (Berlyne, 1960, 1971).

If the pace of exposure to a complex stimulus is too fast, uncomfortable levels of physical or cognitive arousal can occur. When that happens, the curiosity drive becomes inhibited, and we withdraw from the stimulus. Intense anxiety and fear can even be triggered (Spielberger & Starr, 1994).

An example of this pattern often occurs during the holiday season, when a well-intentioned parent tries to prod his young child to sit in Santa's lap so the photographer can snap a picture. At a safe distance, the young child's pace of

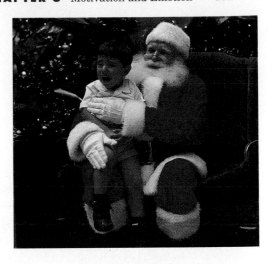

At My Own Pace, Please! At any age, people "pace" their exposure to new stimuli. For many young children, the prospect of a face-to-face encounter with Santa may be more novelty than they can handle comfortably.

curiosity remains comfortable. After all, the odd-looking, bearded guy in the red and white outfit with the black boots *is* a fascinating, novel stimulus to the young child.

To the parent, however, the situation is neither complex nor novel. So, in the interest of speeding things up, the parent lovingly carries Munchkin up to be deposited in the bearded guy's lap. Because the situation is moving faster than the child's exploratory pace, the child's physical and cognitive arousal accelerates exponentially. Curiosity rapidly gives way to extreme fear and the instinctual "flight" response. As the child's screams echo throughout the mall, the photographer captures this magical moment of childhood terror on film forever.

Individual Differences in Curiosity

Beyond illustrating the importance of pacing in curiosity, the Santa example underscores a few other important points. First, regardless of a person's age, what's considered "novel" or "complex" is relative to each individual's life experiences. As an individual becomes more familiar with his environment through exploratory behavior, the experience of new stimuli is combined with knowledge already established in memory. Curiosity also reflects the cognitive motivation to close the discrepancy, or information gap, between what people know and what they would like to know (Loewenstein, 1994). As the person's knowledge base increases, the complexity or novelty of the objects or situations that inspire her curiosity also progressively increases (Spielberger & Starr, 1994).

Second, the Santa example illustrates that the tendency to approach or withdraw from new situations varies from one person to another. Not all young children, of course, respond with terror to being placed in Santa's lap. As you'll see in Chapter 9, children differ in their response to novel stimuli. In a nutshell, some children respond positively to novel stimuli and easily adjust to changes in their environment, while other children do not. These temperamental differences seem to be based on genetic predispositions, and are often remarkably consistent throughout a person's life (Thomas & Chess, 1977, 1980).

Sensation Seeking

An arousal level that is too high can produce strong emotional and physical discomfort. When the level of arousal is too low, we experience boredom. Somewhere between these two extremes is a level of arousal that each of us experiences as comfortable or pleasurable—our "optimal" level of arousal.

sensation seeking
The degree to which an individual is motivated to experience high levels of arousal associated with varied and novel activities.

But even the casual observer of human behavior can see that some people seem motivated to take curiosity and exploratory behavior to a level of arousal that seems contradictory. For example, do you know people like your author Don, who has tried skydiving, aerobatic flying, white-water rafting, and scuba diving? (He also once ate a handful of biodegradable packing peanuts, much to the horror of a college secretary.)

Psychologist Marvin Zuckerman (1979) has extensively studied people who are highly motivated to try risky or exciting activities, whom he refers to as *sensation seekers*. People who are high in **sensation seeking** are motivated to experience the high levels of arousal that are associated with varied and novel activities that often involve some degree of physical or social risk. According to Zuckerman (1983), the tendency toward sensation seeking is an inborn personality trait.

On the surface, it would seem that sensation seekers are drawn to danger. But sensation seekers do not seem to be attracted to danger per se. Instead, they like novel experiences for their own sake and are not about to let a little danger stand in their way (see Franken, 1994).

Are you a sensation seeker? You can get a rough approximation of your tendency toward sensation seeking by completing the abbreviated version of Zuckerman's Sensation Seeking Scale in Table 8.4.

Sensation seekers tend to view themselves as independent, openminded, and unconventional. They like feeling uninhibited, especially in relaxed social situations. They tend to be flexible in their style of thinking, are tolerant of uncertainty, and enjoy the discovery of new knowledge. When they make decisions, they often give more consideration to their own sentiments than to the feelings of others. This characteristic, coupled with their tendency toward unconventional behavior, can sometimes put them in conflict with authority figures (see Franken, 1994). However, sensation seekers are not more likely than other people to commit antisocial acts or crimes (Levenson & others, 1995).

TABLE 8.4 An Abbreviated Version of the Sensation Seeking Scale

For each of the following items, decide which of the two choices best describes your likes and feelings. If neither choice applies, choose the one that *most* describes you. Answer all items.

1. a. I like the tumult of sounds in a busy city.
   b. I prefer the peace and quiet of the country.

2. a. I dislike the sensations one gets when flying.
   b. I enjoy many of the rides in amusement parks.

3. a. I would like a job that would require a lot of traveling.
   b. I would prefer a job in one location.

4. a. I often wish I could be a mountain climber.
   b. I can't understand people who risk their necks climbing mountains.

5. a. I get bored seeing the same old faces.
   b. I like the comfortable familiarity of everyday friends.

6. a. I like to explore a strange city or section of town by myself, even if it means getting lost.
   b. I prefer a guide when I am in a place I don't know well.

7. a. I find people who disagree with my beliefs more stimulating than people who agree with me.
   b. I don't like to argue with people whose beliefs are sharply divergent from mine, since such arguments are never resolved.

8. a. I prefer more subdued colors in decoration.
   b. I like to decorate with bright colors.

9. a. When I have nothing to do or look at for any length of time, I get very restless.
   b. I often enjoy just relaxing and doing nothing.

10. a. Most people spend entirely too much money on life insurance.
    b. Life insurance is something that no one can afford to be without.

11. a. I don't like to drink coffee because it overstimulates me and keeps me awake.
    b. I like to drink coffee because of the lift it gives me.

12. a. The worst social sin is to be rude.
    b. The worst social sin is to be a bore.

13. a. The most important goal of life is to live it to the fullest and experience as much of it as you can.
    b. The most important goal of life is to find peace and happiness.

14. a. If I were a salesperson, I would prefer working on commission if I had a chance to make more money than I could on a salary.
    b. If I were a salesperson, I would prefer a straight salary rather than the risk of making little or nothing on a commission basis.

15. a. I like sharp or spicy foods.
    b. I prefer foods with a minimum of seasoning.

Count one point for sensation seeking for each of the following: 1a, 2b, 3a, 4a, 5a, 6a, 7a, 8b, 9a, 10a, 11b, 12b, 13a, 14a, 15a. If you answered 11 or more items this way, you probably have a strong motive for sensation seeking. If you answered 5 items or less this way, you probably have a weak motive for sensation seeking. If you responded this way 6 to 10 times, you probably are in the average range of sensation seekers.

SOURCE: Zuckerman, 1979.

competence motivation
Motivated behavior directed toward demonstrating competence and exercising control in a situation.

Competence and Achievement Motivation

> Competence motivation is striving to be capable, while achievement motivation is striving to excel or outperform others. How is achievement motivation measured? How does culture affect achievement motivation? What is self-efficacy?

When you strive to use your cognitive, social, and behavioral skills to be capable and exercise control in a situation, you are displaying **competence motivation** (Bandura, 1990; de Charms, 1968; R. White, 1959). It is competence motivation that provides much of the "push" to prove to yourself that you can successfully tackle new challenges. Enrolling in this course, mastering algebra, or becoming proficient at a new computer program all reflect competence motivation.

SCIENCE VERSUS PSEUDOSCIENCE 8.1

Subliminal Self-Help Tapes

A typical subliminal self-help tape contains the sounds of ocean waves or relaxing music. "Subliminal messages," or messages that are below one's level of subjective awareness, are supposedly embedded in the sounds (Merikle, 1988).

The notion that simply listening to a subliminal self-help tape will quickly and easily produce changes in our motivation, behavior, and attitudes is very appealing. Who doesn't want to have "effortless weight control," "peak performance in work, studies, the arts, or sports," and the ability to "conquer habits like smoking, alcohol, and drugs without struggle," to quote a few claims we read in a recent advertisement.

As is the case with many pseudoscientific claims, the illusion of scientific credibility in selling subliminal self-help tapes is often promoted by the use of phrases that certainly *sound* scientific, like "technological breakthrough," "scientific research," and the testimony of "leading authorities." And, in fact, people spend millions of dollars each year on subliminal self-help tapes on the basis of the unsubstantiated claims contained in such ads (Dillingham, 1987). In the last few years, college and university bookstores have also begun selling subliminal motivation tapes. Our students often ask us

about the effectiveness of such tapes and whether or not they should spend their money on them.

How do subliminal self-help tapes stand up to scientific scrutiny? Consider a carefully controlled study involving 79 college students who were enrolled in a career development class (Russell & others, 1991). The students were randomly assigned to one of three groups. The experimental group listened to two subliminal self-help tapes, one on improving study habits and the other on passing exams. The placebo control group listened to what they *thought* were subliminal self-help tapes. In reality, the placebo tapes contained no subliminal messages, just the sound of ocean waves. The real and fake subliminal tapes were provided by the largest manufacturer of subliminal tapes in the United States. The third group was a no-treatment control group that didn't listen to any tapes.

According to the subliminal-tape manufacturer, an individual should listen to the tapes for 20 to 25 hours before expecting significant results. Over ten weeks of the semester, the students listened to the tapes for an average of *120* hours. Some students listened to the tapes for more than 250 hours. At the end of the semester, the final-examination scores of the students in the

three experimental groups were compared. The researchers also compared the three groups in terms of their semester grade point average.

The result? There were *no* significant differences among the three groups in terms of their final examination scores or their semester grade point average. In other words, the tapes produced none of the effects that the manufacturer claimed they produced. This finding is consistent with the conclusions of other researchers, who have also found no evidence to support the claim that subliminal self-help tapes can influence motivation or complex behaviors (see Moore, 1988; McConnell, 1989).

The moral? Don't be fooled by the advertising claims for subliminal self-help tapes. Their not-so-subliminal claims are designed to get you to spend your money by promising easy answers to life's difficulties. If you want to increase your motivation, implement the research-based suggestions that we present in Box 8.2. If you absolutely feel compelled to spend your money on something that will help you do better in your classes, buy a fluorescent highlighting pen to use when reading your textbooks. Plus, if you hold the pen's cap up to your ear, you can hear ocean waves. Honest!

Extraordinary Achievement Motivation
Gymnast Kerri Strug thrilled onlookers with her vault during the 1996 summer Olympics. Despite a badly sprained ankle, she flawlessly performed a difficult vault, believing that it was necessary for the U. S. team to win a gold medal. Strug's ankle was so badly injured that she had to be carried to the platform by her coach to receive her gold medal.

A step beyond competence motivation is **achievement motivation**—the drive to excel, succeed, or outperform others at some task. Finishing at the top of your class in college, creaming your rival in a competitive game, or trying to outdo your own previous level of performance, like our running friend Randy in the chapter prologue, are all examples of achievement motivation.

Henry Murray (1938) first defined the "need to achieve" as the tendency to "overcome obstacles, to exercise power, to strive to do something difficult as well and as quickly as possible." Since the 1950s, David McClelland (1985, 1984; McClelland & others, 1953) has been the leading researcher on the topic of achievement motivation.

Achievement motivation has been most commonly measured by a test called the *Thematic Apperception Test,* abbreviated *TAT.* Originally developed by Christiana Morgan and Henry Murray (1935), the TAT consists of a series of ambiguous pictures. The person being tested is asked to make up a story about each picture, and the story is then coded in terms of its achievement themes and imagery. (In Chapter 12, we discuss the TAT and similar tests in more detail.)

Several studies have shown that TAT measures of achievement do generally correlate well with various measures of success, such as school grades, job success, and performance in laboratory tests (see Spangler, 1992). For example, even simple arithmetic tasks are performed more rapidly by people with a high need to achieve than people with a low need to achieve (McClelland, 1985).

Achievement Motivation and Culture

When it is broadly defined as the "desire for excellence," achievement motivation is found in many, if not all, cultures. In individualistic cultures, like those that characterize North American and European countries, the need to achieve emphasizes personal, individual success rather than the success of the group. In these cultures, achievement motivation is also closely linked with succeeding on competitive tasks (Matsumoto & others, 1994; Markus & Kitayama, 1991).

In collectivistic cultures, like those of many Asian countries, achievement motivation tends to have a different focus. Instead of being individually oriented, achievement orientation is more *socially* oriented (Hawkins, 1994; Bond, 1986). The person strives to achieve not in order to promote himself

achievement motivation
Motivated behavior directed toward excelling, succeeding, or outperforming others at some task.

self-efficacy
The degree to which a person is subjectively convinced of his or her ability to effectively meet the demands of a situation.

or herself, but to promote the status or well-being of other members of the relevant social group, such as family members (Matsumoto & others, 1994). Individuals may persevere or aspire to do well in order to fulfill the expectations of family members and to fit into the larger group.

For example, the Japanese student who strives to do well academically is typically not motivated by the desire for personal recognition. Rather, the student's behavior is more likely to be motivated by the desire to enhance the social standing of his or her family by gaining admission to a top university (Hawkins, 1994).

Self-Efficacy

Competence and achievement motivation are closely linked to self-efficacy. Albert Bandura (1991a), whom you first encountered in Chapter 5, defines **self-efficacy** as the degree to which you are subjectively convinced of your ability to effectively meet the demands of a particular situation. If you have strong self-efficacy, you will exert greater motivational effort in trying to master a situation and will persist longer in the face of obstacles (Bandura, 1988). For example, if you believe strongly in your memory capabilities, you will invest more effort in trying to complete memory-related tasks, increasing the likelihood of success (Bandura, 1989b).

Not surprisingly, people who see themselves as competent and capable tend to strive for higher personal goals (Bandura & Wood, 1989; Mento & others, 1987). In choosing a career, for example, a person with strong self-efficacy will consider a wider range of options and prepare herself better educationally (Lent & Hackett, 1987; Wood & Bandura, 1991).

At virtually any age, we tend to avoid challenging situations or tasks that we *believe* exceed our capabilities (Bandura, 1989). The motivational effort of an individual with self-doubts quickly dwindles. Rather than persisting in trying to master a situation, the self-doubter will often settle for a half-baked solution that doesn't fully reflect his capabilities, or may abandon his efforts altogether. Even though he possesses the necessary skills, he may fail to perform up to his ability (Bandura, 1991a).

Increasing motivation, particularly achievement motivation, often involves convincing yourself that you *can* rise to a challenge. What can you do to increase your sense of self-efficacy? In Focus Box 8.2 presents some suggestions to counter that feeling of "I can't handle this!" that sometimes arises when you face a new challenge.

CONCEPT REVIEW 8.3

Identifying Arousal Motives

Identify what is demonstrated in each of the following situations. Choose from: curiosity, optimal arousal, sensation seeking, achievement motivation, or self-efficacy.

_____ **1.** Amani was bored, so she called a friend and went to a movie.

_____ **2.** Because Matthew had experience as a paramedic, he felt confident when he entered medical school.

_____ **3.** Ross can't dance, but he went to the prom just to see what it was like.

_____ **4.** Once Alexa perfected her cartwheel, she decided she would learn to do a back handspring within two weeks.

_____ **5.** Although they are mild-mannered accounting majors during the week, Tom, Suzanne, and Rochelle spend every weekend skydiving with other members of the Newark Skydiving Club.

IN FOCUS 8.2

Increasing Self-Efficacy

Have you ever failed to display competent behavior in a situation that you should have been able to handle? Feelings of self-efficacy help determine how well you will meet certain challenges and whether you will persist in your efforts to achieve important goals.

In many situations, the motivational drive to succeed is present, but the specific knowledge of what to do is not. After trying one tactic that fails, then another, motivation begins to erode and you may quit trying altogether.

Under such circumstances, it can be helpful to observe and imitate the behavior of someone who is already competent at the task you want to master (Bandura, 1986, 1990). For example, if you're not certain how to prepare effectively for a test or a class presentation, talk with fellow students who *are* successful. Ask how they study and what they do when they have difficulty understanding material. Knowing what works is often the critical element in ensuring success.

Our motivation and self-efficacy are also strongly influenced by the mental images that we create in anticipation of a situation (Ozer & Bandura, 1990). For example, students often un-

dermine their own performance by vividly imagining their worst fears, such as becoming overwhelmed by anxiety during a class presentation or going completely blank during a test.

Fortunately, the opposite is also true. Mentally visualizing yourself coping *effectively* with a situation can enhance your performance (Bandura, 1986; Feltz & Landers, 1983). Athletes, in particular, are aware of this and mentally rehearse their performance prior to competition. So strive to control your thoughts in a positive way by mentally focusing on your capabilities, not your limitations and worst fears. When you anticipate a challenging situation, mentally rehearse effectively using your skills.

Strive to be optimistic about your abilities, but not too optimistic. Developing strong self-efficacy is not the same as being completely free of self-doubt. As Bandura (1990) notes, "Students who greatly underestimate the difficulty of academic course demands and remain blissfully free of self-doubt are more likely to party than to hit the books to master the subject matter." In other words, don't be so optimistic that you delude yourself.

You can build confidence in your abilities by experiencing success at tasks that you perceive as moderately challenging (Bandura, 1991a, 1989a). When you approach a moderately challenging task, strive for progressive improvement, rather than perfection on the first attempt. You should understand that setbacks serve a useful purpose in teaching that success usually requires sustained effort. But in order for success to beget success, you must first genuinely *try* to succeed.

Finally, you can increase your sense of optimism and motivational perseverance by drawing inspiration from positive self-talk (Braiker, 1989). Like positive mental imagery, positive verbalizations can yield significant benefits. In everyday life, many people energize and sustain their motivational effort by using positive self-talk. Saying to yourself, "I can do this" or "It's hard by the yard, but a cinch by the inch" may seem simple. However, positive self-talk can provide the mental encouragement to help keep you motivated when trying to meet a challenge.

Go for it!

Emotion

Emotions serve many functions in human behavior and relationships. What are the three components of emotion? What are basic emotions? How do culture and individual differences influence emotional experience?

Emotions are closely tied to motivational processes. Put simply, we are motivated to seek out experiences that produce pleasurable emotions, such as happiness and pride. And we are motivated to avoid experiences that produce unpleasant emotions, such as anger or fear (Ekman & Davidson, 1994).

More generally, emotions give meaning to our daily experience (Izard, 1989). In fact, emotions are so important to human experience that it's hard to imagine a life without them. Even the thoroughly rational Vulcan, Mr.

The Many Functions of Emotion Emotions play an important role in relationships and social communication. If a friend tells you that she is thrilled, happy, or proud, you immediately understand her internal emotional state.

Spock, occasionally lost his cool on *Star Trek* (no doubt a result of his half-human parentage). Unlike Vulcans, humans seem to be born with a tendency to experience certain emotions, although the conditions that give rise to those emotions vary greatly from person to person.

How are emotions different from moods? Although *emotions* and *moods* are clearly related, psychologists draw a distinction between the two states. Generally, emotions are intense but rather short-lived. Emotions are also more likely to have a specific cause, to be directed toward some particular object, and to motivate a person to take some sort of action (Frijda, 1994). In contrast, a *mood* involves a milder emotional state that is more general and pervasive, such as gloominess or contentment, that lasts for a few hours or days (Watson & Clark, 1994).

Defining Emotion

Emotion can be formally defined as a psychological state involving three distinct components: subjective experience, physical arousal, and a behavioral or expressive response. To understand how these three components interact to produce a familiar emotional state, let's use a simple example. Imagine that you've just found out that your younger brother borrowed your car without asking you and wrapped it around a telephone pole, sideswiping a highway patrol car in the process. He walked away without even a bruise—but your car looks like it took last place in a demolition derby. How would you describe your reaction?

First, you would probably experience a sense of relief that your brother wasn't injured. But then, unless you're a close relative of Mr. Spock, you would probably respond with the emotion of *anger*. Your heart would pound and your blood pressure would rise. As you felt your face turn red, you would probably scowl, utter some unprintable words, and maybe even throw something across the room. And you'd probably say to yourself, "That #!&# idiot! This really makes me mad!"

This emotional response displays all three of the distinct components of emotion. First, you experienced a *subjective, conscious state* that you mentally labeled as "anger." Second, you experienced distinct *physical changes,* in this case physiological arousal. And third, you *expressed* the emotion in some sort of *behavior*—your words, actions, or facial expressions. We'll consider each of these components of emotion in turn. Then, in the last major section of the chapter, we'll look at four influential theories that attempt to explain emotion.

The Three Components of Emotion It's easy to detect this man's emotional state—he's furious! How are the three components of emotion being illustrated here?

emotion
A distinct psychological state that involves subjective experience, physical arousal, and a behavioral expression or response.

The Subjective Experience of Emotion:
Classifying Emotions

Given the central role that emotions play in our psychological experience, it may surprise you that considerable disagreement exists among psychologists regarding the definition and classification of emotions (LeDoux, 1995; Ekman & Davidson, 1994). Some psychologists assert that there are a limited number of universal, basic emotions. According to this view, the *basic emotions* are universal; they are biologically determined products of evolution (Ekman, 1992). Anger, happiness, sadness, and fear are most commonly cited as the basic emotions. To this list, other researchers add disgust, surprise, anxiety, shame, and interest (see Turner & Ortony, 1992; Ortony & Turner, 1990).

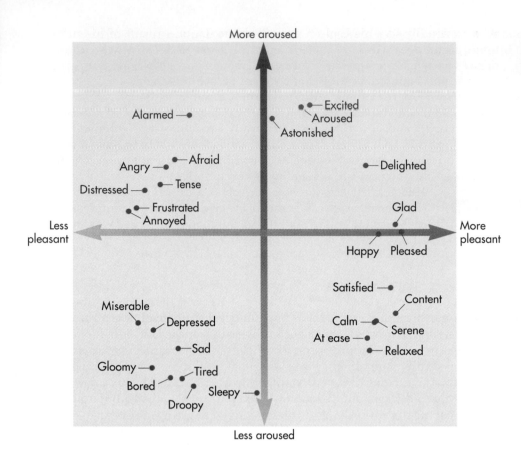

FIGURE 8.4 Comparing Emotions: The Dimensions of Emotion When emotions are compared, they can be arranged along two dimensions: how pleasant or unpleasant they are, and how much or how little arousal they involve.

(Adapted from Russell, 1980, p. 1168.)

According to some emotion theorists, more complex emotions are produced by various combinations of basic emotions. For example, combining anger and disgust yields contempt; sadness plus surprise equal disappointment; and love is the result of combining joy and acceptance (Plutchik, 1984). Other theorists, however, reject the idea of basic emotions. Instead, they believe that a large number of qualitatively different emotions exist (Turner & Ortony, 1992; Ortony & Turner, 1990).

People often experience a *blend* of emotions, rather than a "pure" form of any single given emotion. Thus, you might simultaneously feel unhappy, worried, and gloomy about a test that you have to take tomorrow. Or you might be feeling pleasantly excited about a lunch date along with feeling slightly anxious about the impression you're going to make. In more complex situations, we may experience *mixed emotions,* in which very different emotions are experienced simultaneously or in rapid succession. For example, ending a relationship might involve a bittersweet combination of anger, jealousy, sadness, nostalgia, and relief.

Emotions can be classified in an orderly way. When emotions are compared, they tend to be arranged along two dimensions: how pleasant or unpleasant the emotion is, and how much arousal is present (Russell, 1980). For example, how would you distinguish between the positive emotions of *contentment* and *joy*? Or the negative emotions of *rage* and *resentment*? Although each pair of emotions is alike in terms of being pleasant or unpleasant, they differ in terms of the intensity of the arousal experienced. Joy and rage involve high levels of arousal or intensity, while contentment and resentment involve relatively low levels of arousal. Other emotions can be arranged along the same dimensions (see Figure 8.4).

Culture and Emotional Experience

Are such emotional dimensions universal? Psychologist James Russell compared the emotion rankings of people from several different cultures. He found that they arranged emotions in much the same way as their American counterparts (Russell & others, 1989). Other researchers have found general agreement among cultures regarding the subjective experience of different basic emotions, such as joy, anger, fear, disgust, and sadness (Scherer & Wallbott, 1994).

Researchers have also found some key differences in cultural descriptions of emotion. For example, Hazel Rose Markus and Shinobu Kitayama (1991) found that Japanese subjects added a third dimension to Americans' two basic dimensions of pleasantness and arousal. The third dimension was *interpersonal engagement*—the degree to which each emotion involved relationships with others. For example, the Japanese rated anger and shame as being about the same in terms of unpleasantness and arousal, but they rated shame as being much higher than anger in terms of interpersonal engagement.

Why would the Japanese perceive this additional emotional dimension? As Markus and Kitayama (1991) point out, social relationships are extremely important in Japan. Because Japan is a collectivistic culture, one's identity is seen as *interdependent* with those of other people, rather than *independent,* as is characteristic of the more individualistic cultures of North America and Western Europe (see Chapter 1). Thus, interpersonal engagement is an important aspect of emotional experience in Japan and other collectivistic cultures.

Individual Differences in Emotional Experience

Do you know people who are very low-key and rarely seem to get very excited about anything? Or, at the other extreme, people who seem to be either on top of the world or in the depths of despair? Although people of a given culture may classify emotions in a similar way, individuals differ in how they experience emotion.

People vary greatly in the *intensity* of the emotions they experience. That is, some people really are "more emotional" than others (Larsen & Diener, 1987; Larsen & others, 1986). Along this line, many people believe that women are "naturally" more emotional than men. Are they? We explore this notion in Culture and Human Behavior Box 8.3, "Who's More Emotional, Men or Women?"

CULTURE AND HUMAN BEHAVIOR 8.3

Who's More Emotional—Men or Women?

"You *never* talk about your feelings!" *she* said. And *he* replied, "You're *so* emotional! It's impossible to discuss anything rationally with you!"

Sound familiar? One of the most pervasive gender stereotypes is that women are "more emotional" than men. That is, women supposedly experience more intense emotions, experience intense emotions more frequently, and are less able to control their emotions than men (Grossman & Wood, 1993). In contrast, men supposedly display greater emotional control—they are emotionally cool, calm, and collected. Women are easily swayed by their emotions and by appeals to emotion; men are more rational. Women cry easily; men don't cry at all.

What evidence is there to support these stereotypes? To begin with, when men and women rate their emotions, women subjectively rate themselves as being more emotionally intense than men (Grossman & Wood, 1993; Wood & others, 1989). Women are also more likely to report that they value emotional expressiveness in themselves and others (Shields, 1987). So, in terms

of self-perception, women *do* tend to see themselves as more emotional.

In terms of actual behavior, several studies have found that women more freely express emotions such as fear, sadness, happiness, and anxiety. Even as children, girls generally are more emotionally expressive than boys, and this difference seems to carry through to adulthood (Buck, 1988). In relationships, women often seem to play the role of the "emotion specialist." They tend to be more sensitive and more responsive to the emotional exchanges in a relationship (Gottsman, 1994). So, in general, it seems to be true that women are more emotionally expressive and responsive than men.

There is, however, one exception to this pattern. In contrast to other emotions, *anger* is more typically associated with men than women (Shields, 1987). That is, men are thought to experience anger more frequently, and more intensely, than women (Grossman & Wood, 1993).

Yet several studies have failed to find sex differences in the emotional experience of anger (see Cupach & Canary, 1995). In a study where men and women kept a diary of their angry episodes, no difference was found in the amount of anger *experienced* by men and women. But differences were found in how men and women *expressed* their anger. When they are the target of

MARVIN

another person's anger, women were more likely to feel hurt, while men were more likely to react with defiance. Women were also much more likely than men to cry when angry, often out of frustration (Averill, 1982).

Men and women also differ in where they felt comfortable displaying their anger. In *private* situations, such as the home, women express their anger in much the same way as men (Cupach & Canary, 1995). In *public* situations, men are much more likely than women to display their anger or to express anger toward a stranger (Frodi & others, 1977).

The expression of emotion is strongly influenced by cultural norms, or "rules" that tell us what is appropriate. In the United States, it's considered "unfeminine" for a woman to express anger publicly. And it's consid-

ered "unmasculine" for a man be too open in expressing emotions other than anger (Grossman & Wood, 1993). Thus, there are strong gender-role expectations concerning emotional sensitivity and emotional expressiveness. These cultural norms affect what parents teach their children about emotional expression and control, and what children see modeled by other adults.

Parents treat sons and daughters differently with regard to their emotions, even when the children are just toddlers. Mothers are more likely to pay attention to their male toddlers' angry displays and to give in to their angry demands. In contrast, mothers are more likely to either ignore their female toddlers' anger or tell them to stop. Thus, unlike little girls, little boys grow up feeling freer to express their anger and to expect that expressing

anger will be rewarded (Stenberg & Campos, 1990).

With regard to other emotions, parents often insist that boys control their emotions, but tend to emphasize emotional closeness to their daughters (see Goleman, 1991a). As a result, even preschoolers learn to associate anger with males and other common emotions—such as happiness, sadness, and fear—with females (Birnbaum & others, 1980).

What can we conclude about sex differences in emotionality? At least in American culture, women do tend to be more emotionally expressive than men. However, it's impossible to say whether women are naturally "more emotional" than men or if they have simply *learned* to express their emotions more freely—with the notable exception of anger.

People who experience very intense positive emotions also tend to experience very intense negative emotions (Diener & others, 1985; Diener & Emmons, 1984). When things go well, they're capable of experiencing great joy. But when things go poorly, they'll be equally miserable.

People also differ in their *expression* of emotions. Put simply, some people are more emotionally expressive than others. Emotionally expressive people tend to be better liked than people who are more inhibited in their expressions of emotions (DePaulo, 1992).

The Physiological Component of Emotion:
Hot Heads and Cold Feet

Intense emotions are accompanied by physiological changes. What physical changes are associated with different emotions? What evidence supports the idea that facial expressions of basic emotions are innate? How are facial expressions affected by cultural display rules?

The physiological, or physical, component of emotions is especially evident when you experience an intense emotion, such as anger or extreme fear. At those moments, you may become keenly aware of physical changes: your face may flush; your heart may pound; your muscles may tighten; you may get "goose bumps." In other words, you are experiencing physiological arousal.

As you read in Chapter 2, physiological arousal involves the activation of the sympathetic division of the *autonomic nervous system*. Arousal of the *sympathetic nervous system* triggers the "fight-or-flight" response and gears you up for action. Heartbeat and blood pressure increase; breathing quickens. You perspire, your mouth becomes dry, and the hairs on your skin stand up, causing goose bumps. Blood sugar levels increase, and blood is diverted from the stomach and intestines to the brain and skeletal muscles. Activation of the sympathetic nervous system makes sense for emotions such as anger and fear, because it prepares your body to take action: to fight (an "anger" response) or to take flight (a "fear" response).

Activation of the sympathetic nervous system is also involved in other emotions, such as excitement, passionate love, or extreme joy. Watching a suspenseful movie, being reunited with a lover, taking a roller-coaster ride all involve arousal of the sympathetic nervous system. Not all emotions involve extreme physical reactions, of course. And some emotions, such as contentment, are characterized by a *lowering* of body arousal, in which certain body processes slow down (Levenson, 1992).

The fact that changes in body functions accompany many emotions is the basis for the use of the *polygraph,* commonly called a *lie detector.* Can polygraphs accurately reveal whether a person is lying? We discuss this issue in Box 8.4.

Several studies have found that there are distinct differences in the patterns of physiological responses for different emotions (see Levenson, 1992; Scherer & Wallbott, 1994). In one group of studies, participants were asked to simulate the distinctive facial expression for six emotions—surprise, disgust, sadness, anger, fear, and happiness. While they held the expression for 10 seconds, their heart rate, skin temperature, and other measures of autonomic arousal were measured.

The results? Different physiological patterns were found for different emotions (see Figure 8.5). Anger, fear, and sadness all involved a significantly increased heart rate. Anger produced a dramatic increase in skin temperature, while fear involved a marked decrease in skin temperature (Levenson & others, 1990). No wonder angry people sometimes say they feel "hot under the collar," and those experiencing fear speak of feeling "a chill of fear," "clammy," or getting "cold feet."

Similar patterns of physiological arousal for different emotions were found in members of a remote culture in western Sumatra, an island in Indonesia (Levenson & others, 1992). Broader surveys of many different cultures have also suggested that distinct patterns of physiological changes may well be universal, at least for basic emotions like joy, fear, anger, sadness, and disgust (Scherer & Wallbott, 1994). However, whether there are unique patterns of physiological response for *every* emotion has not been demonstrated.

Do different emotions activate different parts of the brain? Using the EEG, psychologist Richard Davidson and others (1990) have measured brain activity while research participants are experiencing different emotions. R. J. Davidson (1993, 1994a) has found that activity increases in the *left* cerebral hemisphere when people experience joy, interest, and anger—emotions that represent the tendency to "approach" the emotion-producing stimulus. Activity increases in the *right* cerebral hemisphere when people experience distress, disgust, and fear—negative emotions that reflect the tendency to "withdraw" from the stimulus.

Heart rate

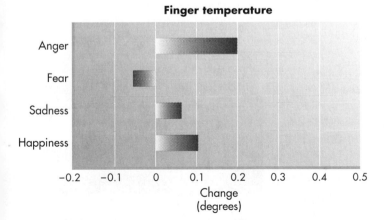

Finger temperature

FIGURE 8.5 Patterns of Physiological Arousal for Different Emotions Levenson and his colleagues (1990) found that different patterns of physical arousal accompanied different emotions. Anger, fear, sadness, and happiness all involved increases in heart rate. However, the three negative emotions elevated the heart rate much more than happiness did. Anger involved a strong increase in finger temperature, while fear produced a decrease in skin temperature.

(Levenson & others, 1990, p. 369.)

IN FOCUS 8.4

How Lie Detectors Work: Emotion Detectors in Action

The use of the polygraph, or lie detector, is based on the fact that changes in body functions accompany many emotions. Lie detectors might more accurately be called "emotion detectors." They do not actually detect lies, but rather measure arousal. A lie detector measures a few specific indicators of physiological arousal, usually changes in heart rate, blood pressure, respiration, and *galvanic skin response,* or *GSR*. Galvanic skin response refers to a change in the electrical conductivity of the skin that results from the increased perspiration associated with emotional arousal.

A lie detector is based on the idea that people will react emotionally, and with increased arousal, when lying in response to incriminating questions (Bashore & Rapp, 1993). The illustration shows a sample recording from a polygraph machine.

A little thought will reveal some of the problems with lie detectors that have, in fact, been shown to exist. One problem is that there is no specific pattern of physiological arousal that indicates that someone is lying (Bashore & Rapp, 1993). Rather, if a person responds with the physiological arousal that is associated with anxiety, lying is inferred (Rosenfeld, 1995). Whether this inference is justified or not is open to question.

Until recently, many companies used polygraphs to screen job applicants for a history of drug abuse or theft. But an innocent person who desperately needed a job, and knew that the lie detector test was important, might well respond anxiously when asked, "Have you ever stolen anything from an employer?" Or, if you know that you are suspected of committing a crime, you may well react emotionally to incriminating questions even though you're innocent.

To complicate matters, some people *are* able to lie without experiencing anxiety or arousal, whether they are guilty of a particular offense or not. An additional problem is that anxiety, irritation, and guilt are associated with similar patterns of physiological arousal—the polygraph cannot tell the difference (Lykken, 1983). Despite these problems, some people believe that polygraph tests can reliably detect lies. How accurate *are* polygraphs?

In one study, polygraph experts were asked to interpret the polygraph results of 50 people suspected of theft who later confessed and 50 people suspected of theft who were later shown to be innocent (Kleinmuntz & Szucko, 1984). Could the experts correctly identify the innocent or guilty suspects on the basis of polygraph results? Not very well. Although the experts correctly identified many of the suspects, they inaccurately judged one-third of the *innocent* people to be guilty and about one-fourth of the *guilty* people to be innocent!

In short, lie detectors are far from foolproof. Furthermore, innocent people are more likely to be falsely incriminated than guilty people are likely to be falsely let off. Many studies have shown that the use of lie detectors can result in a high rate of "false positives," in which an innocent person is judged to be guilty (see Bashore & Rapp, 1993).

Because of the high error rate, many states do not allow polygraph results to be used as evidence in court. The U.S. Congress passed a law in 1988 making it illegal for nongovernmental agencies and companies to use the lie detector to screen prospective employees for drug use or theft. However, the United States government itself continues its routine use of polygraph testing for a variety of purposes.

Respiration

Galvanic skin response

Heart beat

Increased arousal may indicate a lie

"How long have you lived at your current address?"   "Six years."   "Have you ever taken anything worth more than $20 from an employer?"   "No."

Caught in a Lie? The changes in physiological functioning detected by a polygraph are used as the basis for detecting deception or lies. Initially, the examiner asks a series of neutral questions to establish the person's baseline of physiological arousal. Then, the examiner asks the critical question. If a strong physiological reaction occurs, the person may be judged as lying.

Given these findings, Davidson (1994b, 1992) has proposed that the left hemisphere is specialized for emotions that are related to the tendency to *approach* a pleasant stimulus. The right hemisphere seems to be specialized for emotions that are related to the tendency to *withdraw* from an unpleasant stimulus.

The Expression of Emotion

In addition to their subjective and physiological components, emotions usually involve an *expressive,* or *behavioral,* component. When we experience an emotion, we often express it in some fashion. We talk about what we are feeling, hug another person, or slam a door. We also express our emotions by our nonverbal behavior, such as our gestures, changes in posture, and, most important, our facial expressions. Paul Ekman, a leading researcher in this area, has estimated that the human face is capable of creating over *7,000* different expressions (Ekman, 1980). This enormous flexibility allows us considerable versatility in expressing the subtleties of emotions.

A facial expression can display a single intense emotion, such as joy, anger, or disgust, but it can also communicate the subtleties involved in mixed or complex emotions. For example, the photographs below show smiles that are communicating very different emotions. Can you distinguish between the "true" smile of joy and the smile that is masking negative feelings?

Which Is the "True" Smile? The human face is capable of an amazing variety of facial expressions, and people are very adept at reading them. It's relatively easy to distinguish the "true" smile (left) from the fake smile that masks negative emotions (right), because of subtle differences in the facial muscles, especially around the eyes and lips.

Facial expressions are used to communicate with others, but people also express their emotions facially in nonsocial situations (Wagner, 1990). Suppose you were able to watch the faces of the audience during a suspenseful movie. Even though facial expressions were not being used to communicate with other people, you would still be able to watch the play of emotions in the faces in the audience as they watched a frightening or sentimental sequence.

How are facial expressions studied? Ekman and his colleagues have coded different facial expressions by carefully analyzing which facial muscles are involved in producing each expression (Ekman & Friesen, 1978). They've been able to precisely classify the facial expressions that characterize happiness, disgust, surprise, sadness, anger, and fear. When shown photographs of these expressions, a high percentage of subjects correctly identified the emotions depicted (Ekman, 1982).

Facial expressions for basic emotions seem to be innate or inborn rather than learned. Psychologist Carroll Izard (1989) found that the facial expressions of pain, interest, and disgust were present at birth. The social smile emerges by three or four weeks of age. By two months, sadness and anger are evident. And by six or seven months of age, infants display the facial expression indicating fear.

Facial Expressions Are Innate Born deaf and blind, this seven-year-old girl has never observed the facial expressions of those around her. Yet her smile and laughter are unmistakable and identical to that of other children. Facial expressions, especially for basic emotions, seem to be innate rather than learned.

Apparently, infants are not simply imitating the expressions of those around them or learning facial expressions from others. One line of evidence supporting this view comes from children who are born both blind and deaf (Goodenough, 1932; Eibl-Eibesfeldt, 1973). Despite being unable to observe facial expressions in others, these children express emotions such as joy, anger, and pleasure using the same facial expressions as other children.

Culture and Facial Expression

Are facial expressions universal across cultures? Ekman (1982) and his colleagues have found that people from many different cultures accurately recognize the emotions expressed in photographs of facial expressions. This held true even in remote, isolated villages of New Guinea where the inhabitants had not been exposed to Western culture.

In other research, people from Estonia, Germany, Greece, Hong Kong, Italy, Japan, Scotland, Sumatra, Turkey, and the United States were shown photographs of facial expressions that displayed *blends* of emotion. These expressions included combinations of disgust and contempt, fear and surprise, anger and disgust, and anger and surprise. The participants from all cultures generally agreed as to the identity of the two blended emotions, and also as to the relative intensity of the two emotions shown (Ekman & others, 1987).

Facial expressions for basic emotions may well be universal and, to some extent, biologically programmed. Nevertheless, people often exert control over their facial expressions. We adjust our expressions of emotion to make them appropriate to the situation. Even if deeply angered by the comments of your boss, for example, you might well smile and nod your head. Thus, social context can influence the expression of emotion.

Basic Emotions and Universal Facial Expressions Paul Ekman and his colleagues have precisely calibrated the muscles used in facial expressions for basic emotions. When photographs like these are shown to people in a wide variety of cultures, they recognize the basic emotions that are being expressed: happiness, surprise, sadness (top row); and anger, disgust, and fear (bottom row).

The expression of emotion is also strongly affected by culture. Cultural differences in the management of facial expressions are called **display rules** (Ekman & others, 1987). Recall our discussion of gender and emotional expression in Box 8.3. American men who cry in public and American women who express anger in public are examples of people violating cultural display rules.

Display rules can vary greatly from one culture to another. In one experiment, Japanese and Americans watched stress-inducing films alone, unaware of a hidden camera.

When alone, the Japanese and American subjects displayed virtually the same facial expressions. But when a scientist was present while the subjects watched the films, the Japanese subjects were far more likely than the American subjects to mask negative facial expressions (of disgust or fear, for example) with smiles. Why? Because for the Japanese, an important display rule is that you should not reveal negative emotions in the presence of an authority figure (see Ekman & others, 1987; Friesen, 1972).

Thus, although facial expressions of emotion seem to be innate and, to a certain degree, universal among human cultures, we are still able to exert control over our facial expressions. And when we do so, culturally determined display rules may come into play.

Explaining Emotions: Four Key Theories

Theories about emotion tend to differ in terms of which component of emotion they emphasize. What are the James-Lange and Cannon-Bard theories of emotion? How did Cannon refute the James-Lange theory? What is the facial feedback hypothesis?

Theories to explain the cause and nature of emotions have been debated throughout this century. In this section, we'll look at four of the most influential of these theories. As you'll see, the theories tend to differ in terms of which component of emotion receives the most emphasis—physical responses, expressive behavior, or subjective experience (Ellsworth, 1994).

The James-Lange Theory of Emotion: Do You Run Because You're Afraid? Or Are You Afraid Because You Run?

Imagine that you're walking to your car alone after a night class, later than usual because you stayed after the class to ask your professor a few questions. The now-deserted parking lot was crowded when you arrived at school, so you had to park in a distant corner of the lot that is not very well lit. You're feeling just a little apprehensive because in the last few weeks there has been a rash of muggings around your campus. As you get closer to your car, a shadowy figure suddenly appears from behind a parked car. As he starts to move toward you, you walk more quickly. "Hey, what's your hurry?" he calls out. He picks up his own pace, and it's clear that he's following you.

Your heart starts pounding as you break into a run. Reaching your car, you jump in and lock the door. Your hands are trembling so badly you can hardly get the key into the ignition. Within a few moments, you zoom out of the parking lot and onto a main street. You catch a look at yourself in the rear-view mirror and notice that you look wide-eyed and pale. Still feeling shaky, you turn on the radio and try to calm down. After several minutes, you breathe a sigh of relief.

In this example, all three of the components of emotion are present. You experienced a subjective feeling that you labeled as "fear." You experienced physical arousal—pounding heart, trembling, faster breathing, and dilated pupils. And you expressed the fear, both in your facial expression and in the

display rules
Social and cultural rules that regulate the expression of emotions, particularly facial expressions.

behavior of running. What caused the emotion of fear? What accounted for the three facets of the emotional reaction?

The common-sense view of emotion would suggest that you (1) recognized a threatening situation and (2) reacted by feeling fearful. The subjective feeling of fear triggered (3) arousal of the sympathetic nervous system and (4) fearful behavior.

In one of the first psychological theories of emotion, **William James** (1884) disagreed with this common-sense view, proposing a very different explanation of emotion. Danish psychologist Carl Lange proposed a very similar theory at about the same time (see James, 1894; Lange & James, 1922). Thus, this theory is known as the **James-Lange theory of emotion.**

Consider our example again. According to the James-Lange theory, your heart didn't pound and you didn't run because you were afraid. Rather, the James-Lange theory holds that you felt afraid *because* your heart pounded and you ran. Feedback from your physiological arousal and from the muscles involved in your behavior caused your subjective feeling of fearfulness. Thus, James believed that emotion follows this sequence: (1) we perceive a stimulus; (2) physiological and behavioral changes occur; and (3) we interpret our physiological and behavioral reaction as a particular emotion (see Figure 8.6).

FIGURE 8.6 The James-Lange Theory of Emotion According to William James, we don't tremble and run because we are afraid, we are afraid because we tremble and run. James believed that body signals triggered emotional experience. These signals included physiological arousal and feedback from the muscles involved in behavior. The James-Lange theory inspired a great deal of research, but only limited aspects of the James-Lange theory have been supported by research evidence.

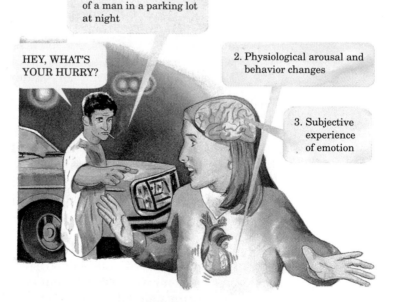

1. Stimulus: Shadowy figure of a man in a parking lot at night

HEY, WHAT'S YOUR HURRY?

2. Physiological arousal and behavior changes

3. Subjective experience of emotion

1. I see a man by that parked car.
2. I am trembling and running away.
3. I am afraid!

James-Lange theory of emotion
The theory that emotions arise from the perception and interpretation of bodily changes.

The James-Lange theory stimulated a great deal of research, much of it consisting of attempts to disprove the theory. In 1927 **Walter Cannon** (1871–1945) challenged the James-Lange theory, criticizing it on several grounds. First, Cannon pointed out that body reactions are similar for many emotions, yet our subjective experience of various emotions is very different. For example, both fear and rage are accompanied by increased heart rate, but we have no difficulty distinguishing between the two emotions.

Second, Cannon (1927) pointed out that our emotional reaction to a stimulus is often faster than our physiological reaction. Here's an example to illustrate this point: Not long ago, Sandy's car started to slide out of control on a wet road. She felt fear as the car began to skid, but it was only *after* the car was under control, a few moments later, that her heart began to pound and her hands started to tremble. Cannon correctly noted that it takes several seconds for the physiological changes caused by activation of the sympathetic nervous system to take effect, but the subjective experience of emotion is often virtually instantaneous.

Third, when physiological changes are artificially induced, the person does not necessarily report feeling a related emotion. Spanish psychologist Gregorio Marañon (1924) injected several subjects with epinephrine, the hormone that triggers activation of the sympathetic nervous system. When asked how they felt, the subjects did not report feeling any particular emotion. Instead, they simply reported the physical changes produced by the drug, saying, "My heart is beating very fast." Some reported feeling "as if" they should be feeling an emotion, but they said they did not feel the emotion itself: "I feel *as if* I were afraid."

James (1894) had proposed that if a person were cut off from feeling body changes, he would not experience true emotions. If he felt anything, he would experience only intellectualized, or "cold," emotions. To test this hypothesis, Cannon and his colleagues disabled the sympathetic nervous system of cats. But the cats still reacted with catlike rage when barking dogs were present: they hissed, growled, and lifted one paw to defend themselves (Cannon & others, 1927).

What about humans? The sympathetic nervous system operates via the spinal cord. Thus it made sense to James (1894) that people with spinal cord injuries would experience a decrease in emotional intensity, because they could not detect physical arousal.

Research with people who had spinal cord injuries at first seemed to support the James-Lange theory rather than Cannon's. In one widely cited study, George Hohmann (1966) interviewed paralyzed patients who had suffered spinal cord injuries which kept them from feeling body sensations. Hohmann asked them if their emotions—including fear, anger, and grief—were less intense than they had been before their injury. The greater the loss of sensation, the more likely the patients were to say that their subjective experience of emotion had significantly decreased. Some of the patients reported that they acted angry without really feeling angry, or that their anger had changed from a "hot" anger to a "cold," more mental kind of anger.

But Hohmann's research was criticized on many grounds, and many researchers do not accept his conclusions (see Lang, 1994; Chwalisz & others, 1988; Bermond & others, 1991). More recent studies have come up with very different results, finding *no* loss in subjective intensity of emotion in subjects with spinal cord injuries. For example, Dutch psychologist Bob Bermond and his colleagues (1991) found that individuals with spinal cord injuries reported that their experience of fear, anger, grief, sentimentality, and joyfulness had either increased in intensity or was unchanged since their injury.

Similarly, Kathleen Chwalisz and her colleagues (1988) compared spinal-cord-injured subjects with a control group of people who needed to use wheelchairs but who had not suffered spinal cord injuries or loss of sensation. There was little difference between the two groups in the intensity of emotions experienced, including love, joy, sentimentality, anger, sadness, and fear. The majority of the spinal-cord-injured patients reported feeling many emotions, especially fear, *more* intensely after their injury than before. In fact, one subject with very limited physical sensation reported feeling so angry at an instructor that he wanted to "run over him a few times" with his wheelchair.

Common-sense says we lose our fortune, are sorry and weep; we meet a bear, are frightened and run; we are insulted by a rival, are angry and strike. The hypothesis here to be defended says that this order of sequence is incorrect, that the one mental state is not immediately induced by the other, that the bodily manifestations must first be interposed between, and that the more rational statement is that we feel sorry because we cry, angry because we strike, afraid because we tremble.

William James, 1894

These two studies, then, point to the same conclusion: Although physiological arousal can amplify emotional feelings, the perception of physical arousal does not seem to be *essential* to the experience of emotion. In short, these findings seemed to undermine the James-Lange theory of emotion.

The Cannon-Bard Theory of Emotion

Along with challenging the James-Lange theory of emotion, Walter Cannon (1927) proposed his own theory. Because American physiologist Philip Bard later joined with him in endorsing this theory, it became known as the **Cannon-Bard theory of emotion.**

According to the Cannon-Bard theory of emotion, when an emotion-arousing stimulus is perceived, information is relayed *simultaneously* to the cortex in the brain and to the sympathetic nervous system (see Figure 8.7). The activation of the cortex causes the subjective experience of emotion, and the activation of the sympathetic nervous system causes the physical response, which takes a few seconds. Thus, according to Cannon and Bard, subjective experience and physiological arousal are triggered *at the same time:* neither causes the other.

1. Stimulus: Shadowy figure of a man in a parking lot at night

2. Simultaneous experience of:

Conscious emotion and

Physiological arousal

1. I see a man by that parked car.
2. I am afraid *and* trembling!

FIGURE 8.7 The Cannon-Bard Theory of Emotion According to Walter Cannon, emotion is a two-pronged response, including both conscious experience and physiological arousal. Cannon believed that the sympathetic nervous system and the cortex in the brain were simultaneously activated. The subjective, conscious experience of emotion and physiological arousal are triggered at the same time: neither causes the other.

The Facial Feedback Hypothesis:
Okay, Now Say "Cheese"

Although Cannon's critique of the James-Lange theory of emotion seemed at first to have effectively demolished it, new evidence seems to support some *limited* aspects of the James-Lange theory. First, as we have already seen, research indicates that different emotions *do* involve subtle differences in physiological response. However, these physiological differences are often too subtle for most people to consciously detect. Furthermore, people do not reliably associate specific emotions with a specific pattern of physiological arousal (Lang, 1994; Lang & others, 1993).

A second area of research supporting a modified James-Lange theory involves the effect of *behaviorally* expressing an emotion on subjective experience. When people *act* happy, they *feel* happier. And acting angry or fearful may lead you to feel angrier or more fearful (Duclos & others, 1989).

Why would acting happy make people feel happy? According to the **facial feedback hypothesis,** *expressing* a specific emotion, especially facially, causes us to *subjectively experience* that emotion. In testing this notion, researchers have asked people to manipulate their facial muscles to form a facial expression characteristic of a given emotion, such as a smile or a frown. But the researcher does not tell the subject what emotional expression the facial manipulations are supposed to represent. It's kind of like a professional photographer asking you to say "cheese" to get you to simulate a smile.

For example, to express anger, the participants were told, "Draw your eyebrows together and down. Contract the muscles at the corner of your jaw by clenching your teeth." Or try this one: "Lower your eyebrows, especially the outer corners. With your mouth closed, push up lightly with your lower lip."

Cannon-Bard theory of emotion
The theory that emotions arise from the simultaneous activation of the nervous system, which causes physical arousal, and the cortex, which causes the subjective experience of emotion.

facial feedback hypothesis
The view that expressing a specific emotion, especially facially, causes the subjective experience of that emotion.

Okay, Say "Cheese!" Misha obligingly demonstrates a simple test of the facial feedback hypothesis. In a study by Fritz Strack and others (1988), participants who held a pencil between their teeth (top) thought that cartoons were funnier than participants who held a pencil between their lips. How does this finding support the facial feedback hypothesis?

Did you feel your emotional state shift to sadness? Asking subjects to mimic the facial expression characteristic of a given emotion tends to influence subjects to report *feeling* that emotion (Izard, 1990b).

Now try this: Hold a pencil between your lips for 15 seconds. How do you feel? Now hold the pencil between your teeth for 15 seconds. Feel any different? Researchers Fritz Strack and his colleagues (1988) found that when subjects held the pencil between their teeth, which simulated a smile, they rated Gary Larson *Far Side* cartoons as funnier than did subjects who held the pencil between their lips, simulating a frown.

How can the facial feedback hypothesis be explained? One explanation is that feedback from the facial muscles is sent as signals to the brain, and this information affects our experience of the emotion (Izard, 1990b). Psychologists Paul Ekman and Richard Davidson (1993) have demonstrated that deliberately creating a "happy" smile tends to produce the same changes in some measures of brain activity as spontaneously producing a happy smile in response to a real event.

Collectively, such evidence lends limited support to one aspect of the James-Lange theory: Our body responses, including feedback from our muscles, *can* affect our subjective experience (Izard, 1990a). Keep in mind, the facial feedback hypothesis does not claim that facial expressions necessarily *cause* all emotional experiences. Rather, expressive behavior helps to activate and regulate emotional experience, intensifying or lessening emotion (Izard, 1990b).

The Two-Factor Theory of Emotion:
Is It Love? Or Too Much Coffee?

> *According to the two-factor theory of emotion, emotion results when a cognitive label is applied to physiological arousal. What aspects of the two-factor theory have been supported by research? What is the cognitive-mediational theory of emotion?*

A third important theory of emotion was proposed by psychologists Stanley Schachter and Jerome Singer. Schachter and Singer (1962) agreed with James that physiological arousal is a central element in emotion. But they also agreed with Cannon that physiological arousal is very similar for many different emotions. Thus, Schachter and Singer argued that arousal alone is not sufficient to produce a given emotion.

Instead, Schachter and Singer added a new element to the equation of emotion. They proposed that you label physiological arousal as a given emotion on the basis of your *cognitive interpretation* of your situation. The cognition determines what emotion will be experienced. For example, you might attribute your stirred-up state to joy, anger, or fear, depending on how you interpret your situational cues and your own thoughts. If you're watching a scary movie on television, you'll attribute your arousal to fear. If you're standing in a long checkout line at the grocery store and someone cuts in front of you, you'll attribute it to anger. And if you're spending an evening with an attractive person, you'll attribute your arousal to sexual excitement or attraction.

According to Schachter and Singer's (1962) **two-factor theory of emotion** (also called the *cognitive arousal theory of emotion*), emotion is a result of the *interaction* of physiological arousal and the cognitive label we attach to explain the stirred-up state. If one of these factors is absent, emotion will not be experienced (see Figure 8.8). Recall that in Marañon's (1924) experiment, arousal without a cognitive label did not produce a true emotional state, but only awareness of the arousal. Marañon's subjects felt *as if* they should be afraid. Likewise, a cognitive label without physiological arousal would not produce a true emotional experience (as in, "This should make me mad, but it doesn't").

Under normal circumstances, the two factors, cognitive labeling and physiological arousal, are interrelated. The cognition (man leaping out from behind car in deserted parking lot) triggers a state of physiological arousal. The arousal is interpreted in terms of the situation or condition that triggered it (knowledge about muggings on campus and the dangers of strange men in deserted parking lots). At that point, according to Schachter and Singer, the state of arousal is labeled as an emotion—fear.

Schachter and Singer (1962) tested their theory in an ingenious experiment. Male student volunteers were injected with epinephrine, a substance that produces trembling, pounding heart, and rapid breathing—the classic symptoms of physiological arousal. Only one group of subjects was accurately told that their symptoms were the result of the injection. The other subjects were told either that the injection would produce no effects or that the injection would produce entirely different effects, such as itching and numbness of the feet.

Then each subject was exposed to one of two conditions. In the "happy" condition, a confederate of the experimenters acted euphoric and, in fact, rather goofy: shooting paper airplanes, playing with hula hoops, and so forth. In the "angry" condition, a confederate complained about the experiment, objected to items on a questionnaire, and finally ripped up the questionnaire and stomped out of the room. Afterward, the mood of the subjects was assessed.

What were the results? In the "happy" condition, the uninformed subjects did report feeling happier than the informed subjects. In the "angry" condition, the uninformed subjects reported feeling angrier than the informed subjects. This part of the experimental results confirmed the hypothesis. However, other aspects of the experimental results were more problematic, and did not provide support for the Schachter-Singer theory (see Beck, 1990).

The Schachter-Singer two-factor theory inspired a great deal of research on the cognitive aspects of emotion. However, after reviewing two decades of related research, German psychologist Rainer Reisenzein (1983) concluded that there was little evidence to support the Schachter-Singer two-factor theory of emotion. More specifically, Reisenzein concluded there was little evidence for (1) the claim that arousal is a necessary condition for an emotional state or (2) the idea that emotional states can result from labeling unexplained arousal.

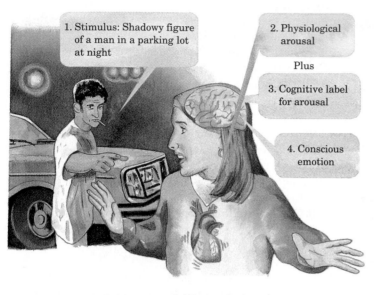

1. I see a man by that parked car.
2. I am trembling.
3. My trembling is CAUSED by fear.
4. I am afraid!

FIGURE 8.8 The Two-Factor Theory of Emotion According to Stanley Schachter and Jerome Singer, emotional experience requires the interaction of two separate factors: (1) physiological arousal and (2) a cognitive *label* for that arousal. *Both* factors are necessary for the subjective experience of emotion.

two-factor theory of emotion
Schachter and Singer's theory that emotion is a result of the interaction of physiological arousal and the cognitive label that we apply to explain the arousal.

cognitive-mediational theory of emotion
Lazarus's theory that emotions result from the cognitive appraisal of a situation's effect on personal well-being.

But as with the James-Lange theory, some limited aspects of the Schachter-Singer two-factor theory of emotion have received empirical support. Arousal from one source can spill over and increase your emotional response to a different situation (Sinclair & others, 1994; Reisenzein, 1983). For example, the arousal from strenuous physical exercise can spill over and intensify a negative emotional experience (Zillmann, 1983). Your response to an insult is likely to be much stronger if you had just finished a hard-fought tennis match than if you had been lying on the couch counting the cobwebs on the ceiling.

In much the same way, arousal from physical exercise can intensify positive feelings, such as sexual attraction (Zillmann, 1983). This is what regularly happens to a friend of ours who attends an aerobics class with an instructor he describes as only average-looking. "But by the end of each workout," he smiles, "I'm in love! She seems irresistible!" The physical arousal from exercise influenced his perception of her physical attractiveness. This casual observation has been confirmed by research showing that physical exercise can make males rate females as being more attractive (White & others, 1981). Thus, mislabeling the source of physiological arousal can affect an emotional response.

The Cognitive-Mediational Theory of Emotion:

Is That a Mugger? Or a Friend?

Although the two-factor theory of emotion received little support from subsequent research, it did stimulate a new line of research on the importance of cognition in emotion. Let's go back to the shadowy figure lurking in your college parking lot. Suppose that as the man called out to you, "Hey, what's your hurry?" you recognized his voice as that of a good friend. Would your emotional reaction be different? Of course. This simple observation is the basis for the fourth major theory of emotion that we'll consider.

Developed by psychologist **Richard Lazarus** (b. 1922), the **cognitive-mediational theory of emotion** emphasizes that the most important aspect of an emotional experience is our cognitive interpretation, or appraisal, of the emotion-causing stimulus. While related, Lazarus's theory is fundamentally different from the Schachter-Singer two-factor theory.

Both theories emphasize the importance of cognition. The two-factor theory says that emotion is the result of physiological arousal *plus* a cognitive label. Lazarus's theory states that cognitive appraisal is the *essential* trigger for an emotional response. All other components of emotion, including physiological arousal, follow from the initial cognitive appraisal (Lazarus, 1995).

For example, imagine two friends watching a very close basketball game, each passionately rooting for a different side. As the center scores the winning basket, their emotional response to the game's final score will be completely different—even though the emotion-producing stimulus is the same (Ortony & others, 1988). The person's thoughts about the situation determine the particular emotion that is experienced.

For Lazarus, *all* emotions are the result of cognitive appraisals of the personal meaning of events and experiences. If we think that we have something to gain or lose, we experience emotion. Thus, such appraisals are closely tied to motivation. The more personally important the outcome, the more intense the emotion (Lazarus, 1991a).

Appraisal and Emotion: Basket! Lazarus believes that how the individual cognitively appraises the personal significance of any event will determine the emotion experienced. Whether the sports fan experiences elation or dismay is likely to depend upon what the event means to him personally.

In the case of the shadowy figure in the parking lot, your relief that you were not on the verge of being attacked by a mugger could turn to another emotion very quickly, depending on the personal meaning of the encounter. If it's a good friend that you hadn't seen for a while, your relief might turn to pleasure, excitement, or even joy. If it's someone you'd prefer to avoid, your relief might turn to annoyance.

Some critics of the cognitive-mediational approach object that emotional reactions to a stimulus or event are virtually instantaneous—too rapid to allow for the process of cognitive appraisal. Instead, they suggest that we *feel first and think later* (Zajonc, 1984). While it's clear that cognitive appraisals can make a great deal of difference in emotional responses and experience, emotion researchers differ in how much they emphasize the role of cognition.

Some Final Thoughts:
An Interactive Approach to Emotion

No single theory of emotion has met with general acceptance in psychology. In some ways, this is not surprising. Emotion is a complex, multifaceted phenomenon, involving three very different processes: physiological, behavioral, and cognitive. These processes vary a great deal among individuals (Cacioppo & others, 1992). Furthermore, each element of the emotion equation serves different functions and can be studied separately (Izard, 1989). What continues to be debated is which process is *most* important in causing emotional experience.

Perhaps emotion can be best conceptualized as a dynamic system in which every component is important and can influence the others (Lazarus, 1991b; Carlson & Hatfield, 1992). An *interactive approach to emotion* might acknowledge that cognitive appraisals, physiological arousal, and behavioral expression all contribute to subjective emotional experience (Petri, 1996; Averill, 1994). Viewing emotion as the result of the dynamic interaction of different processes does have some practical applications, which we discuss in Box 8.5, "Managing Your Emotions."

CONCEPT REVIEW 8.4

Identifying Key Theories of Emotion

Read the following descriptions and decide which theory of emotion is being represented: (A) Lazarus's cognitive-mediational, (B) James-Lange, (C) Cannon-Bard, (D) facial feedback, or (E) Schachter-Singer two-factor theory.

_____ **1.** Tim and Kim both get a B+ grade in their statistics class. Tim is overjoyed at the news, but Kim, who plans to go to graduate school, is disappointed. Their different emotional reactions to exactly the same grade were obviously a result of their different interpretations.

_____ **2.** When Jim's car skidded on the icy road, he immediately felt fear and his heart began to pound and his hands started to sweat.

_____ **3.** Harry often hums the song "Put on a Happy Face," and when he does what the song suggests, he feels much happier.

_____ **4.** Jahoudi is halfway across the swaying suspension bridge 900 feet above the canyon when he realizes that his heart is racing, his legs are shaking, and his palms are sweating. Suddenly he feels afraid.

_____ **5.** Whenever she meets Rick in class or in the hallway, Sarah's heart beats faster and she gets a trembling feeling inside. Sarah now thinks she must be in love with Rick.

IN FOCUS 8.5

Managing Your Emotions

When we discuss the topic of emotion in our classes, we are commonly asked, "How can I learn to control my emotions?" What students often mean by this question is that their emotions sometimes cloud their judgment in some way, leading them to behave inappropriately.

The simple fact is that you cannot always *control* your emotions. Feelings of grief, anger, or fear can be overwhelming. But there are ways to *manage* your emotions more effectively.

When you find yourself feeling overwhelmed by your emotional response, remember that each component of emotional experience can intensify and influence the other. So you would do well to pay attention to *each* aspect of your emotion experience. Beyond that, here are a few concrete suggestions that may help you "get a grip" on yourself and help you avoid saying or doing something that you know you'll regret later.

1. Managing the Behavioral Expression of Emotion

When people say they'd like to be better able to control their emotions, often they're referring to having better control of the way they *express* their emotions. Remember that expressing an emotion can intensify it. And, even though you may not be able to control your emotional experience, you *can* control your behavior. If you're very angry, think twice before you slam that door or throw that coffee cup across the room. Doing so will just make you angrier (Tavris, 1989).

2. Managing Physiological Arousal

Feelings of physical arousal intensify emotion, especially anger. An old adage says that when you're angry, you should count to ten before you speak—and if you're *very* angry, count to fifty. But recall that physiological changes accompany other emotions besides anger, such as fear and sadness. Whatever the emotion, waiting until the physiological arousal has begun to ebb will give you better control over the way you express your emotion. You're also more likely to understand your emotions when you're physically calmer, so you'll be able to cope better with upsetting emotions.

Remember, too, that other mechanisms of physiological arousal can lead you to experience an emotion more intensely. If you are hyped up from exercise, too much caffeine, a wildly exciting basketball game, or a scary movie, your emotional experience may be more intense than it would have been otherwise.

Psychoactive drugs can also affect your subjective emotional experience—while simultaneously clouding your judgment (Bushman, 1993). In particular, alcohol may produce a triple whammy. Alcohol can (1) alter your mood, (2) reduce inhibitions, and (3) impair your thinking and judgment, including your willingness to take risks (see Chapter 3). In combination, these three effects can make you more likely to act on some of those disturbing emotions—and do or say something that you would not normally consider.

3. Managing Cognitive Appraisals

When an event or statement throws you into an emotional tizzy, pay attention to the way you evaluate what's happening. When you overreact emotionally to a situation or stimulus, it may be that you're evaluating it as more threatening, pervasive, or damaging than it really is. Is the breakup of a relationship *really* the end of the world? Does a bad grade on a single exam *really* mean that you're a complete failure who will never manage to graduate from college? Stop, take a breath, and pay attention to your thoughts, especially any tendency to view an event as more catastrophic than it really is (Seligman, 1990).

If you truly feel unable to control your emotions, or if your emotions are having an adverse impact on other areas of your life, it might be helpful to talk to a counselor or clinical psychologist. For help or a referral, check with the counseling center at your college or university.

Beyond the suggestions in this box, many techniques are available to help deal with emotional responses, ranging from relaxation exercises to learning how to change your cognitive appraisals of emotion-causing situations. We deal with some of these topics directly in Chapter 4, on states of consciousness, and Chapter 13, on stress, health, and coping.

Summing Up: Motivation and Emotion

Motivation and emotion are closely intertwined in every person's life. Like emotions, motives reflect the complex interaction of a variety of factors, including cognitive, biological, behavioral, and cultural factors. Think back to the story of Randy, whom we introduced in the prologue to this chapter. Randy's completion of the Tulsa Run is just one example of how motivational and emotional factors interact to cause behavior. As you've read this chapter, we hope you've also thought about the multiple factors that influence your own motivation and emotional experience.

In the chapter Application, we discuss another important topic that reflects the close ties between the topics of motivation and emotion: happiness. On the one hand, happiness is an emotional state. On the other hand, the desire for happiness is a motive that underlies a great deal of human behavior. In the Application, we'll tell you what researchers have discovered about happiness. We'll also provide you with some simple suggestions for increasing your own sense of personal happiness.

APPLICATION

Don't Worry, Be Happy!

Happiness is a subjective state that is not necessarily determined by objective conditions. How do life satisfaction and the experience of positive emotions contribute to happiness? How can emotional happiness be increased?

What would make you happy? Winning the lottery? Losing thirty pounds? A new car? These are common responses. You may be surprised to learn that psychologists have found that such positive events are not very likely to produce the long-term contentment that we commonly label "happiness."

Lottery winners, for example, illustrate the truth in the old adage that "money can't buy happiness." As one study found, lottery winners are no happier than subjects with average financial resources. In fact, the newly rich lottery winners reported *less* enjoyment of such everyday pleasures as talking with a friend and buying new clothes than did the ordinary people who served as control subjects (Brickman & others, 1978).

In contrast, doesn't it seem reasonable to think that becoming paralyzed would make a person miserable? Not

necessarily. The same researchers who studied lottery winners found that paraplegics and quadriplegics were only slightly less happy than noninjured control subjects (Brickman & others, 1978). Other researchers have found that disabled subjects were just as happy as nondisabled subjects (Chwalisz & others, 1988).

The common thread in these findings is that happiness is a subjective "state of mind," one that is not necessarily determined by objective conditions, whether favorable or unfavorable (Diener, 1984). Even physical attractiveness is not linked to happiness (Diener & others, 1995). Some people are relatively cheerful despite poverty, hardship, or poor health, while others are miserable no matter how privileged or fortunate their circumstances. So, as Hagar and people throughout history have pondered, What *is* the key to happiness?

The Basic Elements of Happiness: Life Satisfaction and Positive Emotions

There are two components underlying happiness: life satisfaction and the experience of positive emotions (Lewin-

sohn & others, 1991a). *Life satisfaction* has to do with how contented or pleased you are with your life as a whole (Argyle & Martin, 1991). Thus, your degree of life satisfaction reflects your *cognitive appraisal,* or evaluation, of your circumstances.

The other basic component of happiness is the *emotion* of happiness, measured by the amount of positive emotions, such as cheerfulness, that you experience on a daily basis. Obviously, there is a close connection between life satisfaction and the daily experience of positive emotions. If you're fundamentally dissatisfied with most aspects of your life, it's tough to be a happy camper.

The quality of your personal relationships makes the most important contribution to life satisfaction (Lewinsohn & others, 1991a). Many studies have found that being fundamentally satisfied with your close relationships is the strongest predictor of life satisfaction and happiness (see Myers & Diener, 1995; Diener, 1984). Not surprisingly, being in love is another strong predictor of happiness (Emmons & others, 1983). The social support provided by your family and network of friends also contributes to life satisfaction (Argyle & Martin, 1991).

Income affects life satisfaction, but not as strongly as is commonly believed. If you're very poor, your life satisfaction is likely to be low (Diener & Diener, 1995). But the effect of income on life satisfaction levels off once a reasonable standard of living is achieved (Diener & Diener, 1995; Myers &

HAGAR THE HORRIBLE

Diener, 1995). Determining what's "reasonable" is largely a matter of comparing yourself to others. If you're about as well off financially as your friends and neighbors, you're likely to be satisfied with your financial status. People who live in communities where the income levels are relatively uniform are more satisfied than people who live in areas where there is a large disparity in incomes (Morawetz, 1977).

Another factor contributing to life satisfaction is the degree to which you are pleased with your health and your work. Enjoyment of leisure activities also enhances overall life satisfaction (Diener, 1984; Lewinsohn & others, 1991a), as does having an active religious or spiritual faith (Myers & Diener, 1995; Poloma & Pendleton, 1988). While the quality of these diverse areas of your life is related to life satisfaction, they don't guarantee that you'll experience emotional happiness.

A common misconception is that "happiness" consists of intensely joyful experiences. However, brief but intensely positive emotional experiences are not necessarily associated with global, long-term happiness. In fact, such experiences can actually work against longlasting happiness (Diener & others, 1991). Extremely positive experiences that produce an emotional "high" tend to be quite rare. And when they do occur, the small pleasures of daily life may seem pale in comparison. For example, think of the letdown you may have experienced after a long-anticipated pleasant event, such as your high school graduation, your wedding, or a very special vacation trip.

Equally important is the finding that people who are prone to experience intense positive emotions are also prone to experience intense negative emotions (Diener & others, 1985). For these people, the intensely positive emotional experiences may be "canceled out" by equally frequent negative emotional experiences (Diener & others, 1991).

According to happiness researcher Ed Diener and his colleagues (1991), emotional happiness is primarily determined by *how often* a person has positive emotions. People who frequently experience positive emotions tend to score the highest on measures of happiness.

Increasing Happiness: Some Concrete Suggestions

Many of the findings we've discussed can be systematically applied to increase your degree of happiness. One program that has been shown to be effective has been developed by psychologist and happiness researcher Michael Fordyce (Fordyce, 1983, 1977; Diener, 1984).

Fordyce's program focuses on increasing emotional happiness through changes in attitudes and daily behavior. We'll present some of Fordyce's (1981) suggestions along with others from the happiness research. Following these simple suggestions will not guarantee you a life of bliss, of course. Rather, these suggestions should help you increase the frequency of positive emotions in daily life.

1. Strengthen Your Closest Relationships

Remember that your personal relationships have the greatest impact on your level of personal happiness. Thus, nurture your relationships with your family and friends. Spend quality time with the people who matter the most to you. Consciously strive to accept others for what they are, rather than becoming critical or angry with them for what they aren't.

2. Be More Social and Outgoing

People who are outgoing and sociable are happier than people who are not (Pavot & others, 1990). One way to become more outgoing is simply to *act* more outgoing: Smile and say hello to your classmates and neighbors, or join a group that shares your interests. If you're shy or find it difficult to join a group on your own, try volunteer work. Another pair of hands at a shelter for the homeless, food bank, or community center is always welcome.

4. Keep Busy Doing Things That You Enjoy

Happy people are often too busy to be bored. Rather than bemoaning the boredom of life, generate a list of activities that you enjoy, then incorporate at least one of them into each day. Taking a short walk, phoning an old friend, listening to music, and other simple activities can boost your spirits.

5. Engage in Activities That You Find Personally Meaningful

Choosing a career or a line of work that you think is important and meaningful will enhance your chances of long-term happiness. If you're fundamentally unhappy in your present career, try to train yourself for a new one. If that's not practical, look for ways outside your job to engage in meaningful pursuits, such as volunteer work, hobbies, or community involvement.

6. Stop Worrying and Develop Positive, Optimistic Thinking Patterns

As simple as it sounds, you're more likely to experience happiness if you engage in optimistic and pleasant thoughts. Make a list of the positive things in your life and, at least once a day, review that list. A few moments of reflection on the positive elements that already exist in your life can improve your perspective on life.

Worrying about the future and dwelling on negative past events are significant causes of unhappiness. But rather than simply worrying about your problems, focus your thoughts on concrete actions that will help you deal more effectively with the problem.

How effective are these simple suggestions? In Fordyce's happiness-training program, participants were instructed to change their everyday behavior by applying just one suggestion per day. Using that simple strategy, the majority of the participants significantly increased their happiness (Fordyce, 1983).

Summary
Motivation and Emotion

Defining Motivation

▨ *Motivation* refers to the forces that act on or within an organism to initiate and direct behavior. Three characteristics associated with motivation are activation, persistence, and intensity.

The Study of Motivation: From Then to Now

▨ Over the past century, psychologists tried to develop a single unified theory of motivation. Motivation theories included instinct theories, drive theories, incentive theories, and humanistic theories. Drive theories are based on the biological principle of homeostasis. Humanistic theories emphasize psychological motives, and include Maslow's hierarchy of needs.

▨ Today, motivation researchers assume that the motivation of any behavior is determined by the interaction of multiple factors, including biological, behavioral, cognitive, and social components.

The Motivation to Eat

▨ Psychologists have identified several internal and external signals involved in hunger and satiation. Oral sensations seem to help maintain or slow down eating behavior. Signals from sensory neurons in the stomach help to trigger feelings of satiation, as does a hormone called CCK. Increased insulin levels seem to lead to feelings of hunger. "Externals" and "nonexternals" vary in their insulin response to environmental stimuli associated with food.

▨ When the ventromedial hypothalamus or the lateral hypothalamus is damaged in rats, eating behavior is affected. However, the exact role played by the hypothalamus and surrounding brain regions in eating behavior remains unclear.

▨ The regulation of body weight can be explained by the energy balance model. The rate at which the body uses energy is called the basal metabolic rate (BMR). People vary greatly in their basal metabolic rate. Age, sex, genetics, and activity level all affect BMR.

▨ According to set-point theory, each person's body naturally tends to have a specific set-point weight. When food intake is reduced, BMR is also reduced. Set-point theory is based on the principle of homeostasis.

▨ Despite the value placed on being thin in American society, many people are obese. Obesity is not necessarily due to overeating. Obese people tend to respond differently to food cues than nonobese people and may have great difficulty maintaining weight loss.

▨ Eating disorders include anorexia nervosa and bulimia nervosa. In anorexia, people do not maintain a minimal body weight, are afraid of gaining weight, and have distorted perceptions about the size of their bodies. In bulimia, people engage in uncontrolled binge eating and then purge themselves of the excessive food by self-induced vomiting, laxatives, or enemas. The causes of anorexia and bulimia are still being investigated.

Arousal Motives: Curiosity and Sensation Seeking

▨ Human behaviors like curiosity, exploration, and stimulation seeking are characterized by an increase in tension, and cannot be adequately explained by either drive theories or incentive theories.

▨ According to arousal theory, people seek to maintain an optimal level of arousal, which sometimes involves seeking out stimulation.

▨ Along with increasing arousal, curiosity may be motivated by the urge to understand the environment. People differ in their tendency to approach or withdraw from novel stimuli.

▨ People who prefer a high level of arousal are high in sensation seeking. Sensation seekers are drawn to new and stimulating experiences.

Competence and Achievement Motivation

▨ Competence motivation refers to the drive to be capable, while achievement motivation refers to the desire to excel or outperform others. Achievement motivation can be measured by the Thematic Apperception Test (TAT). Achievement motivation is expressed differently in individualistic and collectivistic cultures.

▨ Competence motivation and achievement motivation are linked to one's belief of self-efficacy. People with a high degree of self-efficacy are more likely to strive for achievement than are people who doubt their abilities.

Emotion

▨ Emotions serve many different functions in human behavior and relationships, and have three basic components: subjective experience, physiological arousal, and a behavioral or expressive response.

▨ Some emotion theorists believe that there is a limited number of basic emotions that are universal across cultures. Emotions can be classified in terms of two dimensions: degree of pleasantness and level of arousal. Collectivistic cultures may add a third dimension of interpersonal engagement.

▨ People differ in the intensity of their emotional experience as well as in the ease with which they express their emotions.

■ Some emotions, like fear and anger, involve physiological arousal of the sympathetic nervous system. Psychologists have found specific physiological patterns that are associated with different basic emotions, including changes in brain activity.

■ Facial expressions for some basic emotions seem to be universal and innate, but expression is also influenced by cultural display rules.

Explaining Emotions: Four Key Theories

■ Emotion theories differ in terms of which component of emotion is emphasized. According to the James-Lange theory of emotion, emotion results from our perceptions of physical arousal. James predicted that people who have suffered spinal cord injury would experience dampened emotions, but research does not support this prediction. The Cannon-Bard theory of emotion holds that subjective experience and physiological arousal take place simultaneously.

■ The facial feedback hypothesis holds that expressing an emotion causes us to subjectively experience that emotion. Body responses affect the subjective experience of emotion, but do not necessarily cause emotions.

■ The two-factor theory of emotion, proposed by Stanley Schachter and Jerome Singer, holds that emotion results from applying a cognitive label to physiological arousal.

■ The cognitive-mediational theory of emotion, proposed by Richard Lazarus, holds that emotion results from the cognitive appraisal of emotion-causing stimuli.

■ An interactive approach to emotion emphasizes that cognitive appraisals, physiological arousal, and behavioral expression all contribute to subjective emotional experience.

Key Terms

motivation (p. 334)

instinct theories (p. 335)

drive theories (p. 336)

homeostasis (p. 336)

drive (p. 336)

incentive theories (p. 337)

hierarchy of needs (p. 337)

self-actualization (p. 338)

cholecystokinin (CCK) (p. 340)

basal metabolic rate (BMR) (p. 343)

set-point weight (p. 344)

obese (p. 346)

anorexia nervosa (p. 348)

bulimia nervosa (p. 348)

arousal theory (p. 350)

sensation seeking (p. 352)

competence motivation (p. 353)

achievement motivation (p. 354)

self-efficacy (p. 355)

emotion (p. 357)

display rules (p. 364)

James-Lange theory of emotion (p. 366)

Cannon-Bard theory of emotion (p. 368)

facial feedback hypothesis (p. 368)

two-factor theory of emotion (p. 370)

cognitive-mediational theory of emotion (p. 371)

Key People

Walter B. Cannon (1871–1945) American physiologist who developed an influential theory of emotion called the Cannon-Bard theory of emotion.

William James (1842–1910) American psychologist (see also Chapters 1 and 4) who developed an influential theory of emotion called the James-Lange theory of emotion.

Richard Lazarus (b. 1922) American psychologist who promoted the cognitive perspective in the study of emotion; proposed the cognitive-mediational theory of emotion.

Abraham Maslow (1908–1970) American psychologist and a founder of humanistic psychology who developed a hierarchical model of human motivation in which basic needs must first be satisfied before people can strive for self-actualization.

CONCEPT REVIEW 8.1   Page 339

1. c
2. a
3. b
4. c
5. d

CONCEPT REVIEW 8.2   Page 349

1. True
2. False
3. True
4. False
5. False
6. False
7. False

CONCEPT REVIEW 8.3   Page 355

1. optimal arousal
2. self-efficacy
3. curiosity
4. achievement motivation
5. sensation seeking

CONCEPT REVIEW 8.4.   Page 372

1. (A) Lazarus's cognitive-mediational theory
2. (C) Cannon-Bard theory
3. (D) Facial feedback hypothesis
4. (B) James-Lange theory
5. (E) Schachter-Singer two-factor theory

Lifespan Development

Prologue: Themes and Variations

"Daddy, will you play checkers with me?" Laura asked as she hung at the edge of my desk.

"In a while, Sweetie. I'm working on this prologue that Mom roughed out," Don replied as he paused to sip his coffee.

Laura got that inquisitive look on her face. "What's a prologue?" she asked.

Good question, Don thought. "A prologue is a story we tell at the beginning of a chapter that helps introduce some of the things we talk about in the chapter," Don explained.

"Is it a story about Aunt Janeenie's new baby?"

"That's a good idea," Don replied. "But no, Mom wrote a prologue about us."

"Is Nubbin in it?"

"Nope."

"Nubbin has to be in it if it's about us," Laura insisted.

"You want Nubbin Cat in the prologue? Let me see what I can do," Don replied.

"Then will you play checkers with me? Ple-e-e-ase?"

"Well, you've got be quiet and let me work on this for a while, and then I'll play checkers with you."

"Can I look at my Waldo book while you work?"

"If you're quiet," Don smiled.

"I'll be quiet, Daddy, I promise."

Laura kept her promise for almost 20 minutes, sitting on the couch, engrossed in looking for Waldo as Don typed. "Is the story done yet?" she finally asked.

"Well, I've got to let Mom read it, but it's done enough for right now," Don replied. "Do you want me to read it to you?"

"No! I want to play checkers!"

"But it's about you and me and Mama *and* Nubbin Cat, just like you wanted! Here, just listen for a minute."

It was on August 30, 1990, that our copies of the final contract to write this book arrived. It was a landmark event in our lives, and one that we knew required an enormous, long-term commitment. But there was to be more excitement that week. The very next day, our daughter was born, a few weeks ahead of schedule. Laura's early arrival caused a flurry of activity as Don raced around buying diapers and baby clothes.

Now, as we put the final touches on this manuscript, Laura is six years old. Her growth and development have been inextricably intertwined with the development of the book that you are holding in your hands. When Laura was a newborn, Sandy became very adept at typing with one hand so she could hold Laura in her lap with the other. As an infant, Laura would nap in her baby swing next to Don's desk as he worked. As a preschooler, Laura would sometimes "help" us work by practicing her alphabet on scratch paper at the corner of Sandy or Don's desk. And now, as a kindergartner, Laura helps us put journals and books back on the bookshelves.

As we've experienced Laura's development from infancy to early childhood, we've also experienced some transitions ourselves. Your authors met and married when we were in our mid-thirties. Laura was born a month after our first wedding anniversary. Thus, we were beginning our family at a relatively late age. In fact, we were the second-oldest couple in our childbirth class.

In one sense, the last seven years of our lives have been exciting and eventful. We've learned that you never know what lies around the corner (like Nubbin Cat, ready to pounce as you walk past). In another sense, the last seven years of our lives have been incredibly "normal." Just as Laura learned to walk, talk, and ride a tricycle in a predictable sequence, we've grown and developed as parents and marital partners in a relatively predictable fashion.

Without question, virtually every life follows well-established, sometimes universal, patterns of physical, social, and mental changes. Yet at the same time, every life is distinct and different—a unique combination of the predictable and the unexpected. So, although certain themes are common in the life stories of virtually every person, how those themes are played out remains highly individual. As you read this chapter, we hope you'll come to better understand some of the universal themes—and individual variations—in your life as well.

"Do you like it?"

"Can we play checkers *now*? *Ple-e-e-ease*?"

"Sure, Short Stuff, let's go play checkers."

Your Life Story

> *Developmental psychology is the study of how people change over the lifespan. What are the key themes in developmental psychology?*

One way to look at the "big picture" of your life is to think of your life as a story (Howard, 1991). You, of course, are the main character. Your life story so far has had a distinct plot, occasional subplots, and a cast of supporting characters, including family, friends, and lovers.

Like every other person, your life story has been influenced by factors beyond your control. One such factor is the unique combination of genes you inherited from your biological mother and father. Another is the historical era during which you grew up. Your individual development has also been shaped by the cultural, social, and family contexts within which you were raised (Bronfenbrenner, 1995, 1979).

At what point are you in your life story now? You may be at the brink of young adulthood, still trying to define who you are and what direction your story will take. Or you may have already accumulated life experiences in the realms of marriage, family, and career. Regardless, your unique story will continue to unfold with its own distinctive twists and turns.

The Scope of Developmental Psychology

The patterns of your life story, and the life stories of countless other people, are the focus of **developmental psychology**—the study of how people change physically, mentally, and socially throughout the lifespan. At every age and stage of life, developmental psychologists investigate the influence of multiple factors on development, including biological, environmental, social, cultural, and behavioral factors (Bronfenbrenner, 1995, 1979).

However, the impact of these factors on individual development is greatly influenced by attitudes, perceptions, and personality characteristics. For example, the adjustment to middle school is a breeze for one child, but a nightmare for another child. So while we are influenced by the events we experience, we also shape the meaning and consequences of life events.

Along with studying common patterns of growth and change, developmental psychologists look at the ways that people *differ* in their development and life stories. As our prologue illustrated, there is considerable individual variation during adulthood in the timing of social, occupational, and interpersonal accomplishments. As we'll note several times in this chapter, the typical or "normal" pattern of development can also vary among cultures.

Important Themes in Developmental Psychology

Developmental psychologists often conceptualize the lifespan in terms of basic *stages* of development. Traditionally, the stages of the lifespan are defined by age, which implies that we experience relatively sudden, age-related changes as we move from one stage to the next. Indeed, some of life's transitions *are* rather abrupt, such as entering the work force, becoming a parent, or retiring. And some aspects of development, such as prenatal development

---

The Eight Stages of the Lifespan

Stage	Age Range
Prenatal	Conception to birth
Infancy	0–2 years
Early childhood	2–6 years
Middle childhood	6–12 years
Adolescence	12–18 years
Young adulthood	18–40 years
Middle adulthood	40–65 years
Late adulthood	65+ years

One useful way to conceptualize the human lifespan is in terms of eight major developmental stages. Each stage is characterized by different kinds of physical, cognitive, and social changes, which we will explore in this chapter.

developmental psychology
The branch of psychology that studies how people change over the lifespan.

Continuity and Change over the Lifespan
The twin themes of continuity and change throughout the lifespan are evident in the changing nature of relationships. Childhood friendships center on sharing activities, while peer relationships in adolescence emphasize sharing thoughts and feelings. Early adulthood brings the challenge of forming intimate relationships and beginning a family. And close relationships with friends and family continue to contribute to psychological well-being in late adulthood.

chromosome
A long, threadlike structure composed of twisted parallel strands of DNA; found in the nucleus of the cell.

deoxyribonucleic acid (DNA)
The chemical basis of heredity; carries the genetic instructions in the cell.

gene
The basic unit of heredity that directs the development of a particular characteristic; the individual unit of DNA instructions on a chromosome.

and language development, are closely tied to *critical periods,* which are periods during which the child is maximally sensitive to environmental influences.

Still, most of our physical, mental, and social changes occur gradually. As we trace the typical course of human development in this chapter, the theme of *gradually unfolding changes* throughout the ages and stages of life will become more evident.

Another important theme in developmental psychology is the *interaction between heredity and environment.* Traditionally, this is called the *nature/nurture issue* (see Chapter 1). Although we are born with a specific genetic potential that we inherit from our biological parents, our environment influences and shapes how that potential is expressed. In turn, our genetic inheritance influences the ways in which we experience and interact with the environment (Scarr, 1992; Plomin & Neiderhiser, 1992).

For example, suppose you inherited a genetic predisposition to be very outgoing and sociable. The degree to which you express your outgoing nature has been affected by environmental factors, such as how much it has been encouraged and reinforced by your parents, teachers, and peers. But your genetic predisposition to be very sociable has also influenced the kinds of environments you seek out. In comparison to a very shy person, you have probably always been much more likely to seek out socially stimulating situations and people. Your sociable nature may even ultimately influence your career choice. As we've stressed in previous chapters, the relationship between genetics and environment is an interactive one (Bronfenbrenner & Ceci, 1994). In the next section, we'll look at the topic of genetics in more detail.

Genetic Contributions to Your Life Story

Your unique genetic makeup results from the pairing of one set of chromosomes from each biological parent at conception. What role does the environment play in the relationship between genotype and phenotype? How do dominant and recessive genes differ, and why are males more likely to display sex-linked recessive traits?

At the moment of your conception, you were a single cell no larger than the period at the end of this sentence. Packed in that tiny cell was the unique genetic blueprint that you inherited from your biological parents. Today, that

Human Chromosomes A person's unique genetic blueprint is contained in the 23 pairs of chromosomes found in every body cell. Chromosomes are numbered according to descending size. Hence, the first pair of chromosomes is the largest. The 23rd pair, which is labeled X in the above micrograph, determines a person's sex. An XX combination, which is shown, indicates a female. An XY combination indicates a male.

same genetic blueprint is found in the **chromosomes** in every cell of your body. Each chromosome is a long, threadlike structure composed of twisted parallel strands of **deoxyribonucleic acid,** abbreviated **DNA.** Put simply, DNA is the chemical basis of all heredity. It contains the chemical genetic code that has directed the growth and development of many of your unique characteristics.

The DNA code carried on each chromosome is arranged in thousands of segments called genes (see Figure 9.1). Each **gene** is a unit of DNA instructions pertaining to some characteristic, such as eye or hair color, height, or handedness.

At conception, the genes carried on the 23 chromosomes contributed by your biological mother's ovum were paired with the genes carried on the 23 chromosomes contributed by your biological father's sperm. The resulting 23 pairs of chromosomes contained an estimated 100,000 pairs of genes—your unique genetic blueprint.

Multiple gene pairs are involved in directing many complex features of development, such as brain organization, body build, and even some personality characteristics (Plomin & others, 1994). Height, for example, seems to be determined by four different pairs of genes (Hole, 1993). But some relatively simple traits are determined by the interaction of a single gene pair, such as light or dark eye color, freckles, and dimples. In the next section, we'll illustrate some basic genetic mechanisms by looking at a trait that is determined by a single gene pair: whether or not you have freckles.

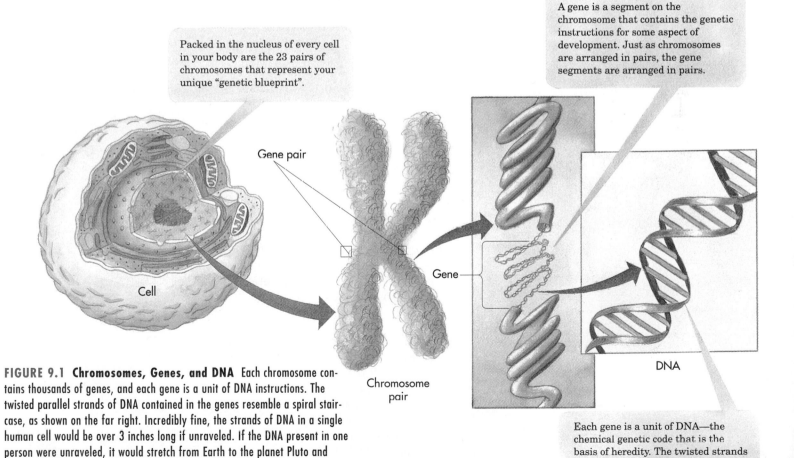

Packed in the nucleus of every cell in your body are the 23 pairs of chromosomes that represent your unique "genetic blueprint".

A gene is a segment on the chromosome that contains the genetic instructions for some aspect of development. Just as chromosomes are arranged in pairs, the gene segments are arranged in pairs.

Gene pair

Cell

Gene

Chromosome pair

DNA

Each gene is a unit of DNA—the chemical genetic code that is the basis of heredity. The twisted strands that make up the DNA molecule resemble a spiral staircase.

FIGURE 9.1 Chromosomes, Genes, and DNA Each chromosome contains thousands of genes, and each gene is a unit of DNA instructions. The twisted parallel strands of DNA contained in the genes resemble a spiral staircase, as shown on the far right. Incredibly fine, the strands of DNA in a single human cell would be over 3 inches long if unraveled. If the DNA present in one person were unraveled, it would stretch from Earth to the planet Pluto and back—*twice!*

Dominant and Recessive Characteristics

The term **genotype** refers to the underlying genetic makeup of a particular individual, while the term **phenotype** refers to the traits that are actually displayed. For the sake of our discussion, let's suppose that your genotype includes one gene from your mother with the genetic code for FRECKLES. This gene is paired with the gene you inherited from your father, which contains the genetic code for NO FRECKLES.

When a genotype combines such conflicting genetic information, the **dominant gene** will influence the trait you actually display. In this case, the dominant gene is the one for FRECKLES, and you'll inherit the tendency to develop freckles. Traits like freckles, dark eyes, dark hair, and dimples are referred to as *dominant characteristics* because they require *only one member of a gene pair to be dominant in order for the trait to be displayed.* If both members of the gene pair happen to be dominant, the genes will simply act in harmony. In either case, your phenotype will express the dominant characteristic.

So how do you get a phenotype displaying nondominant characteristics, like light hair, light eyes, and skin without freckles or dimples? *Each* gene in the gene pair must be a **recessive gene**—a gene whose instructions are not expressed if combined with a dominant gene. In other words, recessive genes are expressed only if paired with an identical recessive gene. In order to be freckle-free, you'd have to inherit a NO FRECKLES/NO FRECKLES gene combination as your genotype. Traits whose expression requires two identical recessive genes, like light hair and being dimple-free, are called *recessive characteristics.* Some examples of other dominant and recessive characteristics are listed in Table 9.1.

But let's not forget the interplay between heredity and environment. What we really inherit from our biological parents is a *genetic potential that can be influenced by environmental conditions.* For example, suppose you inherited a FRECKLES/FRECKLES genotype. Because both genes are dominant, you would be genetically "programmed" to develop freckles.

Would you be destined to have freckles? Not necessarily. The phenotype *expression* of that genetic programming could still be influenced by your environment. In the case of freckles, exposure to sunlight increases the phenotype expression of freckles. So, if you minimized your exposure to the sun, you might never develop freckles, despite being genetically programmed to do so (see Figure 9.2).

TABLE 9.1 Dominant and Recessive Characteristics

Dominant Characteristics	Recessive Characteristics
Full lips	Thin lips
Curly hair	Straight hair
Dark hair	Light hair
Free earlobes	Attached earlobes
Normal hearing	Congenital deafness
Freckles	No freckles
Ability to make U-shape with tongue	Lack of this ability
Dimples	No dimples
Feet with normal arches	Flat feet

SOURCE: Hole, 1993.

No sunlight

Exposed to sunlight

FIGURE 9.2 The Interaction of Heredity and Environment If you picked a pair of freckled parents, how many freckled kids would the freckled parents produce? The answer reflects the interactive role of genetics and environment. Even if you carried the genotype for freckles, freckles would develop only if environmental conditions supported the expression of the FRECKLES gene —in this case, exposure to sunlight.

The Sex Chromosomes and Sex-Linked Recessive Characteristics

Human Sex Chromosomes The human sex chromosomes are contained in the 23rd pair of chromosomes. On the left is the large X chromosome, which carries many more genes than the smaller Y chromosome, shown on the right.

Some recessive characteristics, such as color blindness and hemophilia (inability of the blood to clot properly), are much more common in men than women. Why? The answer has to do with the **sex chromosomes,** the 23rd pair of chromosomes—the ones that determine biological sex.

There are two types of sex chromosomes, the large *X chromosome* and the smaller *Y chromosome.* The large X chromosome carries more genes than the smaller Y chromosome, including genes for traits unrelated to sex. In females, the 23rd pair of chromosomes is made up of two large X chromosomes. In males, a large X chromosome and a smaller Y chromosome make up the 23rd pair.

As we've already seen, recessive characteristics normally require the presence of *two* identical recessive genes for the trait to be displayed, one on each chromosome in a particular pair. This pattern continues to hold for females for recessive characteristics communicated on the 23rd chromosome pair. Females require the presence of *two* recessive genes, one on each X chromosome.

For males, however, the smaller Y chromosome often does *not* contain a corresponding gene segment to match the one on their X chromosome. This means that a male can display certain recessive characteristics as the result of only *one recessive gene carried on the X chromosome of his XY pair.*

Traits determined by recessive genes on the X chromosomes are referred to as **sex-linked recessive characteristics.** Red-green color blindness, congenital night blindness, hemophilia, and brown tooth enamel are examples of sex-linked recessive characteristics. Because males require only one recessive gene on their X chromosome to display the recessive trait, they are more likely than females to display these sex-linked recessive characteristics. Thus, males and females show different patterns of inheritance for recessive characteristics that are communicted on the sex chromosomes.

Beyond the special case of sex-linked recessive characteristics, other patterns of genetic influence exist. Some traits, for example, are expressed as the *average* of the genetic instructions inherited from the mother and the father. For example, skin color is usually an intermediate value between the skin color of each parent. In addition, the genetic code can *mutate,* or spontaneously change, between one generation and the next.

The Human Genome Project:
Cracking the Genetic Code

The role of genetics in development and behavior is the focus of intensive ongoing research. One reflection of the intense interest in genetics is an international scientific effort called the *Human Genome Project.* The overall goal of the Human Genome Project is to identify all of the estimated 100,000 genes on the human chromosomes. In effect, researchers are trying to map out the complete genetic code for humans. Thus far, researchers have identified over 2,000 genes, about a fourth of which are disease-related (Marshall, 1996; NIH/CEPH, 1992).

Although it will be many years before the Human Genome Project is completed, the research has already produced numerous insights about the genetic underpinnings of many diseases. For example, chromosome 21 contains the genes for some forms of the memory-devastating Alzheimer's disease. Chromosome 21 also contains the genes for Lou Gehrig's disease, a rare but fatal disease involving a progressive degeneration of the spinal cord (see Ezzell,

genotype
(JEEN-oh-type) The underlying genetic makeup of a particular organism, including the genetic instructions for traits that are not actually displayed.

phenotype
(FEEN-oh-type) The observable traits or characteristics of an organism as determined by the interaction of genetics and environmental factors.

dominant gene
In a pair of genes, the gene containing genetic instructions that will be expressed whether paired with another dominant gene or with a recessive gene.

recessive gene
In a pair of genes, the gene containing genetic instructions that will not be expressed unless paired with another recessive gene.

sex chromosomes
Chromosomes designated as X or Y which determine biological sex; the 23rd pair of chromosomes in humans.

sex-linked recessive characteristics
Traits determined by recessive genes located on the X chromosome; in males, these characteristics require only one recessive gene to be expressed.

FIGURE 9.3 Amniocentesis In the course of development, the fetus sheds cells into the surrounding amniotic fluid. Amniocentesis involves removing some of the amniotic fluid. The fetal cells contained in the fluid are grown in a laboratory for about two to four weeks, after which the cells can be examined for evidence of chromosomal and genetic abnormalities.

Cells cultured for 2–4 weeks

Withdrawal of amniotic fluid

Fetal cell

Chromosome analysis

1992). And it has long been known that an extra copy of chromosome 21 produces a form of mental retardation called *Down syndrome.* As with many genetically related disorders, Down syndrome can be detected prenatally through genetic screening procedures, like *amniocentesis,* shown in Figure 9.3.

Being able to detect the genetic underpinnings of normal and abnormal development is an important advance. However, knowing what to do with that information is another matter altogether (Seachrist, 1995; Cotton, 1995). Knowing that a person is genetically predisposed to a particular condition, whether it's freckles or Alzheimer's disease, does not guarantee that he will display that trait. Ultimately, the expression of any trait is the result of the *interaction* between genetic inheritance and environmental conditions. As you'll see in the next section, environmental factors can influence the expression of our genetic potential even before we are born.

CONCEPT REVIEW 9.1

Genetic Contributions to Development

Answer *true* or *false* for each of the following statements. If a statement is false, write in the correct statement.

_____ **1.** The Human Genome Project is an intensive scientific effort to clone humans using the DNA of brilliant or gifted people.

_____ **2.** Mary's genotype (Dd) includes one dominant gene (D) for DIMPLES and a recessive gene (d) for NO DIMPLES. Mary's phenotype will be to have dimples.

_____ **3.** In order to display a sex-linked recessive characteristic, a male needs only one recessive gene to be present on his 23rd pair of chromosomes.

_____ **4.** In order for you to display a phenotype of flat feet, your genotype must be an (ff)—a flat feet/flat feet genetic combination. Hence, having flat feet must be a recessive characteristic.

_____ **5.** Sarah has an XY combination in her 23rd pair of chromosomes.

_____ **6.** Each chromosome has exactly 23 genes.

_____ **7.** The Y chromosome has twice as many genes as the X chromosome.

Prenatal Development

> *During the prenatal stage, the single-cell zygote develops into a full-term fetus. What are the three stages of prenatal development? What are teratogens, and what general principles seem to govern their impact on the fetus?*

At conception, chromosomes from the biological mother and father combine to form a single cell—the fertilized egg, or *zygote.* Over the relatively brief span of nine months, that single cell develops to the estimated trillion cells that make up a newborn baby. This **prenatal stage** has three distinct phases: the germinal period, the embryonic period, and the fetal period. In this section, we'll briefly describe the main characteristics of each period, noting some of the factors that can affect prenatal development.

The **germinal period,** also called the *zygotic period,* represents the first two weeks of prenatal development, or pregnancy. During this time, the zygote undergoes rapid cell division before becoming implanted on the mother's uterine wall. Some of the zygote's cells will eventually form the structures that house and protect the developing fetus and provide nourishment from the mother. By the end of the two-week germinal period, the single-celled zygote has developed into a cluster of cells called the *embryo.*

The **embryonic period** begins with week 3 and extends through week 8. During this time of rapid growth and intensive cell differentiation, the organs and major systems of the body form. Genes on the sex chromosomes and hormonal influences also trigger the initial development of the sex organs.

Protectively housed in the fluid-filled *amniotic sac,* the embryo's lifeline is the umbilical cord. Via the *umbilical cord,* the embryo receives nutrients, oxygen, and water, and gets rid of carbon monoxide and other wastes. The umbilical cord attaches the embryo to the *placenta,* a disk-shaped tissue on the mother's uterine wall. The placenta prevents the mother's blood from mingling with that of the developing embryo, acting as a filter to prevent harmful substances that might be present in the mother's blood from reaching the embryo.

The placenta cannot, however, filter out all harmful agents from the mother's blood. Harmful agents or substances that can cause abnormal development or birth defects are called **teratogens.** Generally, the greatest vulnerability to teratogens occurs during the embryonic stage, when major body systems are forming. Known teratogens include:

- exposure to radiation
- toxic industrial chemicals, such as mercury and PCBs
- diseases, such as rubella, syphilis, genital herpes, and AIDS
- drugs taken by the mother, such as alcohol, cocaine, and heroin

It's not always possible to predict the exact effects of a given teratogen, but a few general principles can be stated (see Moore, 1993). First, *the timing of exposure* during prenatal development is important. The period of greatest vulnerability seems to occur during the initial growth spurt of a particular body system. For example, the central nervous system is most vulnerable during the third to the sixth weeks of prenatal development; the teeth and palate are most vulnerable during the sixth to the tenth weeks.

Second, *a given teratogen tends to produce specific effects.* For example, regularly drinking alcohol during pregnancy can produce *fetal alcohol syndrome,* the most common cause of mental retardation. Individuals with fetal

prenatal stage
The state of development before birth; divided into the germinal, embryonic, and fetal periods.

germinal period
The first two weeks of prenatal development.

embryonic period
The second period of prenatal development, extending from the third week through the eighth week.

teratogens
Harmful agents or substances that can cause malformations or defects in an embryo or fetus.

fetal period
The third and longest period of prenatal development, extending from the eighth week until birth.

alcohol syndrome typically display a small head and facial deformities, retarded physical growth, central nervous system damage, and behavioral problems. Heavy drinking is most likely to damage the developing baby. However, even light drinking, especially during early pregnancy, may have long-term negative effects on behavioral and psychological functioning (Stratton & others, 1996; Nevitt, 1995).

Third, *the degree of susceptibility to teratogens is related to maternal factors,* such as the mother's age, physical health, and level of nutrition (Moore, 1993). For example, the greatest risk of giving birth to a child with birth defects occurs at the extremes of a woman's child-bearing years—during the teens and over age forty.

By the end of the embryonic period, the embryo has grown from a cluster of a few hundred cells no bigger than the head of a pin to over an inch in length. Now weighing about an ounce, the embryo looks distinctly human even though its head accounts for about half its body size.

The third month heralds the beginning of the **fetal period**—the final and longest stage of prenatal development. The main task during the next seven months is for body systems to grow and reach maturity in preparation for life outside the mother's body. By the end of the third month, the *fetus* can move its arms, legs, mouth, and head. It becomes capable of reflexive responses, such as fanning its toes if the sole of the foot is stroked and squinting if its eyelids are touched. During the fourth month, the mother experiences *quickening*—she can feel the fetus moving.

By the fifth month, essentially all the brain cells the person will ever have are present, though they will continue to develop long after birth (Shatz, 1992). The fetus has distinct sleep/wake cycles and periods of activity. During the sixth month, the fetus's brain activity becomes similar to that of a newborn baby.

Because of technological advances in the care of preterm infants, the seventh month is now considered to be a transitional month. That is, most fetuses born during the seventh month can survive outside the uterus with the help of intensive medical care and a protective environment. Although the fetus's respiratory system has not fully matured, with each passing week the odds of survival improve as its lungs become better equipped to breathe air (Mendelson & Boggaram, 1991).

During the final two months, the fetus will double its weight, gaining an additional three to four pounds of body fat. This additional body fat will help the newborn adjust to changing temperatures outside the womb. It also contributes to the newborn's chubby appearance. As birth approaches, growth slows and the fetus's body systems become more active.

Prenatal Development Although it is less than an inch long, the beginnings of arms, legs, and fingers can already be distinguished in the 7-week-old embryo (left). The amniotic sac and the placenta can be clearly seen in this photograph. The fetus at four months (right) now measures 6 to 10 inches long, and the mother may be able to feel the fetus's movements. Notice the well-formed umbilical cord. Near full-term (bottom photo), the 8-month-old fetus gains body fat to help it survive outside its mother's uterus.

Development During Infancy and Childhood

During **infancy**—the first two years of life—and early childhood, the dramatic pattern of rapid development continues on several fronts. In the next several sections, we'll explore physical, social, and cognitive development during infancy and childhood.

The Competent Newborn

While physically helpless, newborn infants are equipped with reflexes and sensory capabilities that enhance their chances for survival. How do the sensory capabilities of the newborn promote the development of relationships with caregivers? How does the brain develop after birth?

The newly born infant enters the world with an impressive array of physical and sensory capabilities. Initially, his behavior is mostly limited to reflexes that enhance his chances for survival. Touching the newborn's cheek triggers the *rooting reflex*—he turns toward the source of the touch and opens his mouth. Touching the newborn's lips evokes the *sucking reflex.* If you put a finger on each of the newborn's palms, he will display the *grasping reflex,* gripping your fingers so tightly that he can be lifted upright. As motor areas of the infant's brain develop over the first year of life, the rooting, sucking, and grasping reflexes are replaced by voluntary behaviors.

The newborn's senses—vision, hearing, smell, and touch—are keenly attuned to people, helping her quickly learn to differentiate between her mother and other humans. In a classic study, Robert Fantz (1961) demonstrated that the image of a human face holds the newborn's gaze longer than other images. Other researchers have also confirmed the newborn's visual preference for the human face. Newborns only 10 *minutes* old will turn their heads to continue gazing at the image of a human face as it passes in front of them, but they will not visually follow other images (Johnson & others, 1991).

Vision is the least developed sense at birth (Gottlieb & Krasnegor, 1985). The newborn is extremely nearsighted, meaning he can see near objects more clearly than distant objects. The optimal viewing distance for the newborn is about 6 to 12 inches, the perfect distance for a nursing baby to easily focus on his mother's face and make eye contact. Nevertheless, the infant's view of the world is pretty fuzzy for the first several months, even for objects that are within close range.

Interestingly, the interaction between adults and infants seems to naturally compensate for the newborn's poor vision. When adults interact with very young infants, they almost always position themselves so that their face is about 8 to 12 inches away from the baby's face. Adults also have a strong natural tendency to exaggerate head movements and facial expressions, such as smiles and frowns, again making it easier for the baby to see them.

The newborn also responds with increased alertness to the sound of human voices. Even at birth, he can distinguish between his mother's voice and that of another woman (DeCasper & Fifer, 1980). Especially if breast-fed, the newborn quickly becomes sensitized to the scent of his mother's body

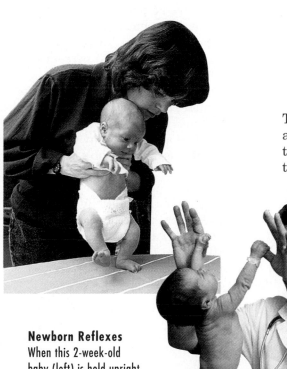

Newborn Reflexes
When this 2-week-old baby (left) is held upright with her feet touching a flat surface, she displays the *stepping reflex,* moving her legs as if she were trying to walk. Another reflex that is present at birth is the *grasping reflex* (right). The infant's grip is so strong that he can support his own weight. Thought to enhance the newborn's chances for survival, these involuntary reflexes disappear after the first few months of life.

infancy
The first two years of life.

That's Using Your Head! Although the sequence of motor development is universal, there is a great deal of individual variation in *when* and *how* these developmental milestones are reached. At eight months of age, Laura crawled like an inchworm, relying on her head and toes to get around instead of her hands and knees. Some children scoot or roll to get where they want to go.

(Makin, 1989). For her part, the mother becomes keenly attuned to her infant's characteristic appearance, smell, and skin texture (Kaitz & others, 1992).

Physical Development During Infancy and Childhood

By the time she begins crawling, at around seven to eight months of age, the infant's view of the world, including distant objects, will be as clear as that of her parents. The increasing maturation of the infant's visual system is a reflection of her developing brain. At birth, her brain is an impressive 25 percent of its adult weight. In contrast, her birth weight is only about 5 percent of her eventual adult weight. During infancy, her brain will grow to about 75 percent of its adult weight, while her body weight will reach only about 20 percent of her adult weight.

The newborn enters the world with essentially all the neurons his brain will ever have—an estimated 100 billion. After birth, however, the brain continues to develop rapidly. The number of *dendrites* increases dramatically during the first two years of life (Siegler, 1989). The axons of many neurons acquire *myelin*—the white, fatty covering that increases a neuron's communication speed (see Chapter 2).

Figure 9.4 illustrates the sequence and average ages of motor skill development during infancy. The basic *sequence* is universal, but the *average ages* can be a little deceptive. Infants vary a great deal in the ages at which they master each skill. While virtually all infants are walking well by fifteen months of age, some infants will walk as early as ten months. Each infant has her own genetically programmed timetable of physical maturation and developmental readiness to master different motor skills.

FIGURE 9.4 Milestones in Infant Motor Development Each bar in the graph below shows the typical range of ages for acquiring particular motor skills during infancy. Given the wide range of individual variation, can you see how simple statistical averages can be misleading?

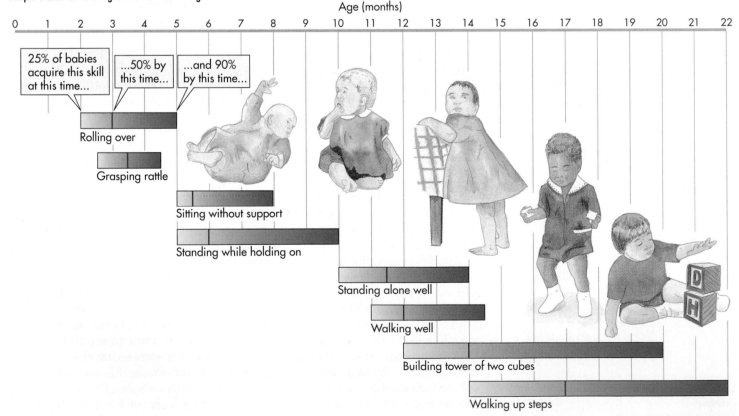

Age (months)

| 0 | 1 | 2 | 3 | 4 | 5 | 6 | 7 | 8 | 9 | 10 | 11 | 12 | 13 | 14 | 15 | 16 | 17 | 18 | 19 | 20 | 21 | 22 |

25% of babies acquire this skill at this time...

...50% by this time...

...and 90% by this time...

Rolling over

Grasping rattle

Sitting without support

Standing while holding on

Standing alone well

Walking well

Building tower of two cubes

Walking up steps

Early Development

1. Which of the following represents the correct sequence of periods in prenatal development?
   a. germinal, fetal, embryonic
   b. fetal, embryonic, germinal
   c. germinal, embryonic, fetal
   d. embryonic, germinal, fetal

2. Research on babies born with fetal alcohol syndrome suggests that alcohol is a
   a. teratogen　　　　c. dominant gene
   b. chromosome　　　d. recessive gene

3. Valerie touches her newborn baby's cheek, and he turns his head to the side that was touched and opens his mouth. Valerie has triggered the
   a. grasping reflex　　c. rooting reflex
   b. sucking reflex　　　d. startle reaction

4. Claudia is a healthy, normal newborn infant. She has
   a. less than 5 percent of her total brain cells
   b. approximately 25 percent of her total brain cells
   c. about 50 percent of her total brain cells
   d. essentially all the brain cells she will ever have

5. Which of the senses is least well developed in the newborn?
   a. vision　　　　c. taste
   b. touch　　　　d. hearing

6. All of the newborn's senses are keenly attuned to:
   a. bright objects　　c. food
   b. humans　　　　　d. the Disney channel

Aspects of Social and Personality Development in Infancy and Childhood

Temperament refers to inborn predispositions to behave and react in a particular way, while attachment refers to the emotional bond an infant forms with her primary caregivers. What temperamental patterns have been identified? What is the basic premise of attachment theory, and how is attachment measured?

From birth, forming close social and emotional relationships with caregivers is essential to the infant's physical and psychological well-being. Although physically helpless, the young infant does not play a passive role in forming these relationships. As you'll see in this section, the infant's individual traits play an important role in the development of the relationship between infant and caregiver.

Temperamental Qualities: Babies Are Different!

Infants come into the world with very distinct and consistent behavioral styles. Some babies are consistently calm and easy to soothe. Other babies are fussy, irritable, and hard to comfort. Some babies are active and outgoing; others seem shy and wary of new experiences. Psychologists refer to these inborn predispositions to consistently behave and react in a certain way as an infant's **temperament** (Bates, 1989, 1994).

Interest in infant temperament was triggered by a classic longitudinal study launched in the 1950s by psychiatrists Alexander Thomas and Stella Chess. The focus of the study was on how temperamental qualities influence adjustment throughout life. Chess and Thomas rated young infants on a variety of characteristics, such as activity level, mood, regularity, and attention span. They found that about two-thirds of the babies could be classified into one of three broad temperamental patterns: *easy, difficult,* and *slow-to-warm-up*. About a third of the infants were characterized as *average* babies

temperament
Inborn predispositions to consistently behave and react in a certain way.

The Importance of Attachment Secure attachment in infancy forms the basis for emotional bonds in later childhood. At one time, attachment researchers focused on the relationship between mothers and infants. Today, the importance of the attachment relationship between fathers and children is also recognized.

because they did not fit neatly into one of these three categories (Thomas & Chess, 1977).

Easy babies readily adapt to new experiences, generally display positive moods and emotions, and have regular sleeping and eating patterns. *Difficult* babies tend to be intensely emotional, are irritable and fussy, and cry a lot. They also tend to have irregular sleeping and eating patterns. *Slow-to-warm-up* babies have a low activity level, withdraw from new situations and people, and adapt to new experiences very gradually. After studying the same children from infancy through childhood, Thomas and Chess (1986) found that these broad patterns of temperamental qualities were remarkably stable.

Since the pioneering research of Thomas and Chess, other ways of categorizing temperamental patterns have been devised (see Wachs & King, 1994). For example, psychologist Jerome Kagan and his colleagues (1992) have classified infants as temperamentally *inhibited* or *uninhibited.*

Inhibited children tend to avoid unfamiliar stimuli and experiences; *uninhibited* children tend to approach them. Kagan and his colleagues have found several physiological differences between extremely inhibited and extremely uninhibited children and infants, suggesting that these differences are biological in nature (Kagan & Fox, 1995). For example, compared to uninhibited children, inhibited children respond to new stimuli with more intense physiological reactions, such as greater increases in heartbeat.

Virtually all temperament researchers agree that individual differences in temperament have a genetic and biological basis (see Rothbart & others, 1994; Calkins & Fox, 1994). However, researchers also agree that environmental experiences can modify a child's basic temperament (Gunnar, 1994; Goldsmith & others, 1987). For example, a child with a temperamental predisposition to be shy can be encouraged to be more sociable by his parents, and may well overcome much of his tendency toward shyness in a supportive environment (Kagan & Fox, 1995). Thus, the display of temperamental qualities is yet another example of the complex interaction between heredity and environmental factors.

Attachment: Forming Emotional Bonds

During the first year of life, the emotional bond that forms between the infant and his caregivers, especially his mother, is called **attachment.** According to *attachment theory,* an infant's ability to thrive physically and psychologically depends in part on the quality of attachment (Ainsworth & others, 1978).

In all cultures, the emotional bond between infants and caregivers is an important relationship (Grossmann & Grossmann, 1990). But not surprisingly, there are cultural differences in how the attachment relationship is conceptualized and encouraged. In Culture and Human Behavior Box 9.1, "Where Does the Baby Sleep?" we describe one example of how cultural differences in child-rearing practices reflect different ideas about the appropriate relationship between infants and parents.

In studying attachment, psychologists have typically focused on the infant's bond with the mother, since the mother is often the infant's primary caregiver. Still, it's important to note that many fathers today are also directly involved with the basic care of their infants and children (Blair & Lichter, 1991). In homes where both parents are present, infants who are attached to one parent are also attached to the other (Fox & others, 1991). Infants tend to form attachments to both parents at about the same time (Bornstein & Lamb, 1992). An infant is also capable of forming attachments to other consistent caregivers in his life, such as relatives or workers at a day-care center (Howes & Hamilton, 1992). Thus, an infant can form *multiple* attachments (Field, 1996).

attachment
The emotional bond that forms between an infant and her caretaker(s), especially her parents.

CULTURE AND HUMAN BEHAVIOR 9.1

Where Does the Baby Sleep?

In their best-selling guide to child care, Drs. Benjamin Spock and Michael Rothenberg (1985) offer this advice to parents:

> *Children can sleep in a room by themselves from the time they are born, if convenient, as long as the parents are near enough to hear them cry. . . . Otherwise there is a chance that they may become dependent upon [sleeping in the same room as their parents] and be afraid and unwilling to sleep anywhere else. The older they are, the harder it may be to move them. . . . I think it is a sensible rule not to take a child into the parents' bed for any reason.*

Most parents in the United States seem to be in full agreement with Dr. Spock's opinion. In most U.S. families, infants sleep in their own bed, usually in a separate room from their parents (Morelli & others, 1992).

It may surprise you to discover that the United States is very unusual in this respect. In one survey of 100 societies, the United States was the *only* one in which babies slept in separate rooms. Another survey of 136 societies found that in two-thirds of the societies, infants slept in the same beds as their mothers; in the remainder, infants generally slept in the same room as their mothers (Morelli & others, 1992).

Gilda Morelli and her colleagues (1992) compared the sleeping arrangements of several middle-class U.S. families with those of Mayan families in a small town in Guatemala. They found that infants in the Mayan families slept with their mothers until they were two or three, usually until another baby was about to be born. At that point, toddlers moved to the bed of another family member, usually the father or an older sibling. Children continued to sleep with other family members throughout childhood.

Mayan mothers were shocked when the American researchers told them that infants in the United States slept alone and often in a different room from their parents. The Mayan mothers reacted with disapproval and pity for the infant. They believed that the practice was cruel and unnatural, and would have negative effects on the infant's development.

In the United States, bedtime marks the separation of the infant or small child from the family. To ease the child's transition to sleeping—and to spending long hours alone—"putting the baby to bed" often involves lengthy bedtime rituals, like stories and lullabies. Small children often take comforting items, like a favorite blanket or teddy bear, to bed with them to ease the stressful transition to falling asleep alone. The child may also use the "security blanket" or "cuddly" to comfort himself when he wakes up in the night, as most small children do.

In contrast, the Mayan babies do not take cuddly items to bed, and no special routines marked the transition between wakefulness and sleep. Mayan parents were puzzled by the very idea. Instead, the Mayan babies simply go to bed when their parents do or fall asleep in the middle of the family's social activities.

Morelli and her colleagues (1992) found that the different sleeping customs of the U.S. and the Mayan families reflect different cultural values. Some of the U.S. babies slept in the same room as their parents when they were first born, which the parents felt helped foster feelings of closeness and emotional security in the newborns. Nonetheless, most of the U.S. parents moved their babies to a separate room when they felt that the babies were ready to sleep alone, usually by the time they were three to six months of age. These parents explained their decision by saying that it was time for the baby to learn to be "independent" and "self-reliant." Dr. Spock's advice well reflects these American values and beliefs.

In contrast, the Mayan parents felt that it was important to develop and encourage the infant's feelings of *interdependence* with other members of the family. Thus, in both Mayan and U.S. families, sleeping arrangements reflect goals for child rearing and cultural values for relations among family members (Morelli & others, 1992).

In general, when parents are consistently warm, responsive, and sensitive to their infant's needs, the infant develops a *secure attachment* to her parents (Goldsmith & Harman, 1994). The infant's expectations that her needs will be met are essential to forming a secure attachment to her parents (Thompson, 1986).

In contrast, *insecure attachment* may develop when an infant's parents are neglectful, inconsistent, or insensitive to his moods or behaviors. Insecure attachment seems to reflect an ambivalent or detached emotional relationship between an infant and his parents (Isabella & others, 1989; Ainsworth, 1979).

How do researchers measure attachment? The most commonly used procedure is called the *Strange Situation*, which was devised by **Mary Ainsworth** (b. 1913). The Strange Situation is typically used with infants who are between one and two years old (Ainsworth & others, 1978). In this technique, a baby and his mother are brought into an unfamiliar room with a variety of toys. A few minutes later, a stranger enters the room. The mother stays with the child for a few moments, then departs, leaving the child alone with the stranger. After a few more minutes, the mother returns, spends a few minutes in the room, leaves, and returns again. Through a one-way mirror, observers record the infant's behavior throughout this sequence of separations and reunions with his mother.

Psychologists assess attachment by observing the infant's behavior toward his mother during the Strange Situation procedure. When his mother is present, the *securely attached* infant will use her as a "secure base" from which to explore the new environment, periodically returning to her side. He will show distress when his mother leaves the room and will greet her warmly when she returns. A securely attached baby is easily soothed by his mother (Lamb & others, 1985; Ainsworth & others, 1979).

In contrast, an *insecurely attached* infant is less likely to explore the environment, even when her mother is present. In the Strange Situation, insecurely attached infants may appear either very anxious or completely indifferent. Such infants tend to ignore or avoid their mothers when they are present. Some insecurely attached infants become extremely distressed when their mothers leave the room. When insecurely attached infants are reunited with their mothers, they are hard to soothe, and may resist the mother's attempts to comfort them.

The quality of attachment during infancy is associated with a variety of long-term effects (Goldsmith & Harman, 1994). Preschoolers with a history of being securely attached tend to be more prosocial, empathic, and socially competent than preschoolers with a history of insecure attachment (Suess & others, 1992; Collins & Gunnar, 1990). Adolescents who were securely attached in infancy have fewer problems, do better in school, and have more successful relationships with their peers than do adolescents who were insecurely attached in infancy (Sroufe, 1995).

Because attachment in infancy seems to be so important, psychologists have extensively investigated the impact of day care on attachment. In Critical Thinking Box 9.2, "The Effects of Child Care on Attachment and Development," we take a close look at this issue.

CONCEPT REVIEW 9.3

Temperament and Attachment

Select the correct term—*easy, difficult, slow-to-warm-up, securely attached, insecurely attached*—for each of the following.

1. Instead of happily exploring the attractive toys in the doctor's waiting room, Ainslie clings to her mother's hand. It is likely that Ainslie is a(n) _____ child.

2. Joyce is generally a happy, cheerful child who is comfortable with new experiences and has regular sleeping and eating patterns. Joyce would probably be classified as having a(n) _____ temperament.

3. Manuel is hard to comfort, cries a lot, and is very emotional, irritable, and fussy. His eating and sleeping habits are irregular. Manuel would probably be classified as having a(n) _____ temperament.

4. When confronted with new situations, four-year-old Sam initially tends to withdraw but then gradually adapts to the situation. Sam is likely to be classified as having a(n) _____ temperament.

CRITICAL THINKING 9.2

The Effects of Child Care on Attachment and Development

The majority of infants and toddlers in the United States routinely experience care by someone other than their mother or father (Phillips, 1991). Given the importance of the emotional bond between infant and parent, should we be concerned that many young children experience daily separation from their parents?

Developmental psychologist Jay Belsky created considerable controversy when he published studies showing that infants under a year old were more likely to demonstrate insecure attachment if they experienced over 30 hours of day care per week (Belsky & Rovine, 1988; Belsky, 1986). Belsky also reviewed evidence showing that grade school children with extensive infant day-care experience were more aggressive and less compliant than children who had not been in day care. Belsky (1992) has concluded that children who entered full-time day care before their first birthday are "at risk" to be insecurely attached and to suffer later behavioral and emotional problems.

Needless to say, Belsky's conclusion sparked a heated debate over the effects of day care on infants. Does extensive experience with day care during the first year of life create insecurely attached infants and toddlers? Does it produce negative effects in later childhood? Let's look at the evidence.

High-Quality Day Care A high-quality day-care center offers a variety of age-appropriate activities and toys, and sometimes even a furry friend or two, as in this classroom. For toddlers and infants, consistency in caregivers is also extremely important.

Belsky did not claim that *all* infants in day care were likely to experience insecure attachment. Reviewing the data in Belsky's studies and others, psychologist Alison Clarke-Stewart (1989, 1992) pointed out that the actual difference in attachment was quite small when infants experiencing day care were compared to infants cared for by a parent. The proportion of insecurely attached infants in day care is only slightly higher than the proportion typically found in the general population (Lamb & others, 1992). In other words, *most* of the children who had started day care in infancy were securely attached, just like most of the children who had not experienced extensive infant day care.

So what about the long-term effects of day care? One study found that third graders with extensive infant day-care experience were more likely to demonstrate a variety of social and academic problems (Vandell & Corasaniti, 1990). However, these children were not enrolled in high-quality day care, as defined in the accompanying table. Rather, they experienced average day-care conditions in a state with relatively low standards for day-care centers. But even in this case, it's difficult to assign the cause of these problems to day care itself. Why? Because developmental problems in the third graders studied were also associated with being raised exclusively by their mothers at home.

Most psychologists today agree that the *quality* of child care is a key factor in promoting secure attachment in early childhood and preventing problems in later childhood (Scarr & Eisenberg, 1993). Many studies have found that children who experience high-quality care tend to be more sociable, better adjusted, and more academically competent than children who experience poor-quality care (Howes, 1991; Phillips & Howes, 1987). In fact, when psychologist Tiffany Field studied grade school children who had been enrolled in high-quality day care from infancy, she found *no* negative effects of their day-care experience. (Field, 1991; Field & others, 1988).

Swedish psychologist Bengt-Erik Andersson (1989, 1992) has arrived at

The Characteristics of High-Quality Day Care

- Whether care is in someone's home or in a day-care center, caregivers should be warm and responsive.
- Developmentally appropriate activities and a variety of play materials should be available.
- Caregivers should have some training and education in child development.
- Low staff turnover is essential, as consistency is especially important for infants and toddlers.
- The ratio of caregivers to children should be low. Two adults should care for no more than 8 infants, no more than 14 toddlers, or no more than 20 four- and five-year olds.

What constitutes high-quality day care? The National Association for the Education of Young Children (1990, 1989) has identified several key characteristics, which are supported by child development research.

the same conclusion. Andersson studied children who had experienced day care before one year of age in Sweden, where high-quality day care is widely available. When these children were assessed at the ages of eight and thirteen, they performed better in school and teachers rated them more highly on their social and emotional competence than children who had started day care later in childhood or who had stayed home with a parent until they entered grade school.

Clearly, then, day care in itself does not necessarily lead to undesirable outcomes. The quality of the care is the critical factor. High-quality day care can potentially benefit children, even when it begins in early infancy. In contrast, low-quality care can potentially contribute to social and academic problems in later childhood. Unfortunately, high-quality day care is not often readily available in the United States. High-quality day-care centers, where they exist, tend to be expensive and may have long waiting lists.

Language Development

> *Infants seem to be born with a biological predisposition to learn language. How is language development encouraged by caregivers? What are the stages of language development?*

Probably no other accomplishment in early life is as astounding as language development. By the time a child is three years old, he will have learned approximately 3,000 words and the complex rules of his language.

Biologically Programmed to Learn *Any* Language

How is it that language development seems to occur so effortlessly during the first few years of life? According to linguist **Noam Chomsky** (b. 1928), every child is born with a biological predisposition to learn language—*any* language (Chomsky, 1965). In effect, each child possesses a "universal grammar"—a basic understanding of the common principles of language organization. The infant is innately equipped not only to understand language but also to easily extract grammatical rules from what she hears.

At birth, infants can distinguish among the speech sounds of all the world's languages, no matter what language is spoken in their homes (Werker & Desjardins, 1995). For example, adult native speakers of English cannot distinguish between two different /t/ sounds in Hindi. And adult native speakers of Japanese cannot distinguish between /l/ and /r/ sounds: *rake* and *lake* sound the same. But infants just a few months old can distinguish among these different sounds.

Infants lose this ability by ten months of age (Werker & Desjardins, 1995; Kuhl & others, 1992). Instead, they can distinguish only among the speech sounds that are present in the language to which they have been exposed. Thus, during the first year of life, infants begin to master the sound structure of their native language.

Encouraging Language Development: Motherese

Just as infants seem to be biologically programmed to learn language, parents seem to be biologically programmed to encourage language development by the way they speak to infants and toddlers. People in every culture, especially parents, use a style of speech called *motherese,* or *infant-directed speech,* with babies (Bornstein & Lamb, 1992).

Motherese is characterized by very distinct pronunciation, a simplified vocabulary, short sentences, a high pitch, and exaggerated intonation and expression. Content is restricted to topics that are familiar to the child, and "baby talk" is often used—simplified words like "go bye-bye" and "night-night." Questions are often asked, encouraging a response from the infant. Research by psychologist Ann Fernald (1985) has shown that infants prefer infant-directed speech to language spoken in an adult conversational style.

The adult use of infant-directed speech seems to be instinctive. Deaf mothers who use sign language modify their hand gestures when they communicate with infants and toddlers in a way that is very similar to the infant-directed speech of hearing mothers (Bornstein & Lamb, 1992). Furthermore, as infants mature, the speech patterns of parents change to fit the child's developing language abilities (Papoušek & others, 1985).

The Cooing and Babbling Stage of Language Development

As with many other aspects of development, the stages of language development appear to be universal. In virtually every culture, infants follow the

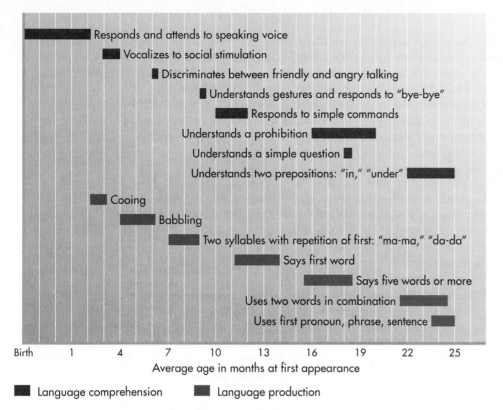

Responds and attends to speaking voice

Vocalizes to social stimulation

Discriminates between friendly and angry talking

Understands gestures and responds to "bye-bye"

Responds to simple commands

Understands a prohibition

Understands a simple question

Understands two prepositions: "in," "under"

Cooing

Babbling

Two syllables with repetition of first: "ma-ma," "da-da"

Says first word

Says five words or more

Uses two words in combination

Uses first pronoun, phrase, sentence

Birth   1   4   7   10   13   16   19   22   25

Average age in months at first appearance

■ Language comprehension   ■ Language production

FIGURE 9.5 Milestones in Language Comprehension and Production
Approximate average ages for the first appearance of different stages of language development. Notice that language comprehension occurs much earlier than language production.
(Based on Bornstein & Lamb, 1992, Fig. 9.1, p. 308.)

Deaf Babies Babble with Their Hands Deaf babies whose parents use American Sign Language (ASL) babble with their hands, rather than their voices. Just as hearing babies repeat the same syllables over and over, deaf babies repeat the same simple hand gestures. The hand shapes represent basic components of ASL gestures, much like the syllables that make up the words of spoken language. Here, a baby repeats the sign for "A."

comprehension vocabulary
The words that are understood by an infant or child.

production vocabulary
The words that an infant or child understands and can speak.

same sequence of language development, and at roughly similar ages (see Figure 9.5).

At about three months of age, the infant begins to "coo," repeating vowel sounds such as *ahhhhh* or *ooooo,* varying the pitch up or down. At about five months of age, the infant begins to *babble.* She adds consonants to the vowels and strings the sounds together in sometimes longwinded productions of babbling, such as *ba-ba-ba-ba, de-de-de-de,* or *ma-ma-ma-ma.*

When infants babble, they are not simply imitating adult speech. Infants all over the world use the *same* sounds when they babble, including sounds that do not occur in the language of their parents and other caregivers. At around nine months of age, babies begin to babble more in the sounds specific to their language (Cole & Cole, 1993). Babbling, then, seems to be a biologically programmed stage of language development.

Babbling also seems to be more than just the infant experimenting with her vocal cords and practicing sounds. Researcher Laura Ann Petitto and her colleagues (1991) discovered that deaf babies with hearing-impaired parents who communicated with American Sign Language *babbled with their hands.* Deaf babies repeatedly formed simple hand shapes that were components of sign-language words. These simple hand shapes are analogous to the repetitious syllables that hearing infants produce vocally.

And, just as a hearing infant develops a particular fondness for a certain syllable, often using it to produce early words (such as *da-da-da* and *daddy*), Petitto found that deaf infants preferred certain hand shapes, often incorporating the shape into their first meaningful words. So, even in the absence of the ability to hear human speech, the infant's developing brain seems predisposed to discover and express basic language patterns.

The One-Word Stage of Language Development

Long before a baby becomes an accomplished talker, she understands much of what is said to her (Woodward & others, 1994). Before they are a year old, most infants can understand simple commands, such as "Bring Daddy the block," even though they cannot *say* the words *bring, Daddy,* or *block.* This reflects the fact that an infant's **comprehension vocabulary** (the words she understands) is much larger than her **production vocabulary** (the words she can say). Generally, infants acquire comprehension of words more than twice as fast as they learn to speak new words (Bornstein & Lamb, 1992).

Somewhere around their first birthday, infants produce their first real words. First words usually refer to concrete objects or people that are important to the child, such as *mama, daddy,* or *ba-ba* (bottle). First words are also often made up of the syllables that were used in babbling.

During the *one-word stage*, babies use a single word and vocal intonation to stand for an entire sentence. With the proper intonation and context, *ba-ba* can mean "I want my bottle!" "There's my bottle!" or "Where's my bottle?"

The Two-Word Stage of Language Development

Somewhere around their second birthday, infants begin putting words together. During the *two-word stage*, infants combine two words to construct a simple "sentence," such as "Mama go," "Where kitty?" and "No potty!" During this stage, the words used are primarily content words—nouns, verbs, and sometimes adjectives or adverbs. Articles (*a, an, the*) and prepositions (*in, under, on*) are omitted.

Two-word sentences reflect the first understandings of grammar. Although these utterances include only the most essential words, they basically follow a grammatically correct sequence. In English, that means that subjects are placed before verbs, and verbs before objects. Thus, the infant says "Erika walk" rather than "walk Erika," and "throw ball" rather than "ball throw." Adjectives are typically placed before nouns, as in "big truck" rather than "truck big." Children born into non-English-speaking homes follow the syntactical patterns of their own language (Maratsos, 1983). Other than that difference, children around the world follow similar patterns in their use of two-word sentences.

At around two and a half years of age, children move beyond the two-word stage. They rapidly increase the length and grammatical complexity of their sentences. There is a dramatic increase in the number of words that they can comprehend and produce. By the age of three years, the typical child has a production vocabulary of over 3,000 words. Acquiring about a dozen new words per day, a child may have a production vocabulary of over 10,000 words by school age (Bjorklund, 1995).

Cognitive Development in Infancy and Childhood:
Piaget's Theory

> *According to Piaget, children progress through four distinct cognitive stages. Each stage marks a shift in how they think and understand the world. What characterizes each stage? What are three criticisms of Piaget's theory?*

When Laura was almost three, Sandy and Laura were investigating the tadpoles in the creek behind our home. "Do you know what tadpoles become when they grow up? They become frogs," Sandy explained. Laura looked very serious. After considering this new bit of information for a few moments, she asked, "Laura grow up to be a frog, too?"

Along with advancing in physical and language skills, the child develops increasing sophistication in *cognitive processes*—the mental functions used in thinking, remembering, and processing information. The most influential theory of cognitive development is that of the Swiss psychologist **Jean Piaget** (1896–1980). Originally trained as a biologist, Piaget combined a boundless curiosity about the nature of the human mind with a gift for scientific observation (Brainerd, 1996).

Piaget (1952, 1972) believed that children *actively* try to make sense out of their environment rather than passively soaking up information about the world. To Piaget, many of the "cute" things children say actually reflect their sincere attempts to make sense out of their world. In fact, Piaget carefully observed his own three children in developing his theory (Fischer & Hencke, 1996).

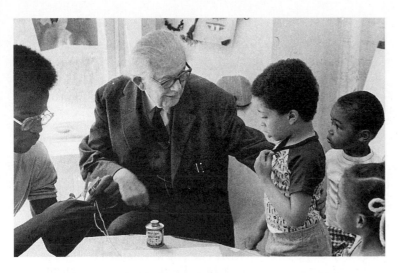

Jean Piaget Swiss psychologist Jean Piaget (1896–1980) viewed the child as a little scientist, actively exploring his or her world. Much of Piaget's theory was based upon his careful observation of individual children, especially his own children.

This Feels Different! During the sensorimotor stage, infants and toddlers rely on sensory and motor skills to explore and make sense out of the world around them.

sensorimotor stage
In Piaget's theory, the first stage of cognitive development, from birth to about age two; the period during which the infant explores the environment and acquires knowledge through sensing and manipulating objects.

object permanence
The understanding that an object continues to exist even when it can no longer be seen.

According to Piaget, children progress through four distinct cognitive stages: the sensorimotor stage from birth to age two; the preoperational stage from age two to age seven; the concrete operational stage from seven to eleven; and the formal operational stage, which begins during adolescence and continues into adulthood. As a child advances to a new stage, his thinking is *qualitatively different* from that of the previous stage. In other words, each new stage represents a fundamental shift in *how* the child thinks and understands the world.

Piaget saw this progression of cognitive development as a continuous, gradual process. As a child develops and matures, she does not simply acquire more information. Rather, she develops new understandings of the world in each progressive stage, building on the understandings acquired in the previous stage (Flavell, 1996; Siegler & Ellis, 1996). As the child assimilates new information and experiences, he eventually changes his way of thinking to accommodate new knowledge (P. H. Miller, 1993).

Piaget believed that these stages are biologically programmed to unfold at their respective ages (Flavell, 1996). He also believed that children in every culture progress through the same sequence of stages at roughly similar ages. However, Piaget also recognized that hereditary and environmental differences can influence the rate at which a given child progresses through the stages (Fischer & Hencke, 1996; Wadsworth, 1996).

For example, a "bright" child may progress through the stages faster than a child who is less intellectually capable. A child whose environment provides ample and varied opportunities to explore is likely to progress faster than the child who has limited environmental opportunities. Thus, even though the sequence of stages is universal, there can be individual variation in the rate of cognitive development.

The Sensorimotor Stage: From Birth to Age Two

The **sensorimotor stage** extends from birth until about two years of age. During this stage, the infant acquires knowledge about the world through actions that allow him to directly experience and manipulate objects. The infant discovers a wealth of very practical sensory knowledge, such as what objects look like and how they taste, feel, smell, and sound.

He also expands his practical knowledge about motor actions, like reaching, grasping, pushing, pulling, and pouring. In the process, the infant gains a basic understanding of the effects that his own actions can produce, such as pushing a button to turn on the television or knocking over a pile of blocks to make them crash and tumble.

At the beginning of the sensorimotor stage, the infant's motto seems to be, "Out of sight, out of mind." An object exists only if she can directly sense it. For example, if a four-month-old infant knocks a ball underneath the couch and it rolls out of sight, she will not look for it. Piaget interpreted this response to mean that, to the infant, the ball no longer exists.

However, by the end of the sensorimotor stage, the child acquires a new cognitive understanding, called object permanence. **Object permanence** is the understanding that an object continues to exist even if it can't be seen. Now, the infant will actively search for a ball that she has watched roll out of sight. Infants gradually acquire an understanding of object permanence as they gain experience with objects, as their memory abilities improve, and as they develop mental representations of the world, which Piaget called *schemas*.

FOR BETTER OR FOR WORSE

The Preoperational Stage: From Age Two to Age Seven

The **preoperational stage** lasts from roughly age two to age seven. In Piaget's theory, the word *operations* refers to logical, mental activities. Thus, the "preoperational" stage is a prelogical stage.

The hallmark of preoperational thought is the child's capacity to engage in symbolic thought. **Symbolic thought** refers to the ability to use words, images, and symbols to represent the world (DeLoache, 1995). One indication of the expanding capacity for symbolic thought is the child's impressive gains in language during this stage.

The child's increasing capacity for symbolic thought is also apparent in her use of fantasy and imagination while playing (Golomb & Galasso, 1995). A discarded box becomes a spaceship, a house, or a fort, as children imaginatively take on the roles of different characters. In doing so, a child imitates (or tries to imitate) actions she has mentally symbolized from situations she observed days, or even weeks, earlier.

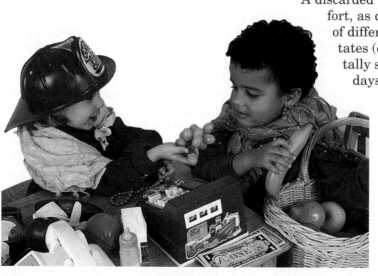

Still, the child's understanding of symbols remains immature. When a two-year-old is shown a picture of a flower, for example, he may try to smell it. A young child may be puzzled by the notion that a map symbolizes an actual location—as in the cartoon above. In short, the preoperational child is still actively figuring out the relationship between symbols and the actual objects they represent (see DeLoache, 1995).

preoperational stage
In Piaget's theory, the second stage of cognitive development, which lasts from about age two to age seven; characterized by increasing use of symbols and prelogical thought processes.

symbolic thought
The ability to use words, images, and symbols to represent the world.

egocentrism
In Piaget's theory, the inability to take another person's perspective or point of view.

irreversibility
In Piaget's theory, the inability to mentally reverse a sequence of events or logical operations.

centration
In Piaget's theory, the tendency to focus, or *center,* on only one aspect of a situation and ignore other important aspects of the situation.

The preoperational child's thought also often displays **egocentrism.** By *egocentrism,* Piaget did not mean selfishness or conceit. Rather, the egocentric child lacks the ability to consider events from another person's point of view. Thus, the young child genuinely thinks that Grandma would like a new Power Ranger video for her upcoming birthday because that's what *he* wants. Egocentric thought is also operating when the child silently nods his head in answer to Grandpa's question on the telephone.

The preoperational child's thought is also characterized by irreversibility and centration. **Irreversibility** means that the child cannot mentally reverse a sequence of events or logical operations back to the starting point. For example, they don't understand that adding "3 plus 1" and adding "1 plus 3" refer to the same logical operation. **Centration** refers to the tendency to focus, or center, on only one aspect of a situation, usually a perceptual aspect. In doing so, the child ignores other relevant aspects of the situation.

The classic demonstration of both irreversibility and centration involves a task devised by Piaget. When Laura was five, we tried this task with her. First, we showed her two identical glasses, each containing exactly the same amount of liquid. Laura easily recognized the two amounts of liquid as being the same.

Then, while Laura watched intently, we poured the liquid from one of the glasses into a third container that was much taller and narrower. Which container, we asked, holds more liquid? Like any other preoperational child, Laura answered confidently, "The taller one!" Even when we repeated the procedure, reversing the steps over and over again, Laura remained convinced that the taller container held more liquid than the shorter container.

This classic demonstration illustrates the preoperational child's inability to understand conservation. The principle of **conservation** holds that two equal physical quantities remain equal even if the appearance of one is changed, as long as nothing is added or subtracted (Piaget & Inhelder, 1974). Because of *centration,* the child cannot simultaneously consider the height and the width of the liquid in the container. Instead, the child focuses on only one aspect of the situation, the height of the liquid. And because of *irreversibility,* the child cannot cognitively reverse the series of events, mentally returning the poured liquid back to its original container. Thus, she fails to understand that the two amounts of liquid are still the same.

The Concrete Operational Stage: From Age Seven to Age Eleven

With the beginning of the **concrete operational stage,** at around age seven, the child becomes capable of true logical thought. The child is much less egocentric in his thinking, can reverse mental operations, and can focus simultaneously on two aspects of a problem. In short, he understands the principle of conservation. When presented with two rows of pennies, each row being equally spaced, the concrete operational child now understands that the number of pennies in each row remains the same even when the spacing between the pennies in one row is increased (Wadsworth, 1996).

As the name of this stage implies, the child's thinking and use of logic tend to be limited to concrete reality—to tangible objects and events. The child in the concrete operational stage cannot think logically about hypothetical situations or abstract ideas. For example, an eight-year-old will explain the concept of *friendship* in very tangible terms, such as saying "Friendship is when someone plays with me." In effect, the concrete operational child's ability to deal with abstract ideas and hypothetical situations is limited to his or her personal experiences and actual events.

The Formal Operational Stage: From Adolescence Through Adulthood

At the beginning of adolescence, the child enters the **formal operational stage.** In terms of problem solving, the formal operational adolescent is much more systematic and logical than the concrete operational child.

Formal operational thought reflects the ability to think logically even when dealing with abstract concepts or hypothetical situations (Piaget, 1972; Piaget & Inhelder, 1958). In contrast to the concrete operational child, the formal operational adolescent explains *friendship* by emphasizing more global and abstract characteristics, such as mutual trust, empathy, loyalty, consistency, and shared beliefs (Beal, 1994; Harter, 1990, 1983).

But like the development of cognitive abilities during infancy and childhood, formal operational thought emerges only gradually (Wood, 1988). Formal operational thought continues to increase in sophistication throughout adolescence and adulthood. While an adolescent may deal effectively with abstract ideas in one domain of knowledge, her thinking may not reflect the

With three-and-a-half-year-old Laura's help, Sandy opened the envelope and took out the wedding invitation. "Laura, your teacher is going to marry her boyfriend, and we're invited to her wedding! Do you know what it means to get married?" "Sure! It means that they can go to Wal-Mart," Laura replied.

conservation
In Piaget's theory, the understanding that two equal quantities remain equal even though the form or appearance is rearranged, as long as nothing is added or subtracted.

concrete operational stage
In Piaget's theory, the third stage of cognitive development, which lasts from about age seven to adolescence; characterized by the ability to think logically about concrete objects and situations.

formal operational stage
In Piaget's theory, the forth stage of cognitive development, which lasts from adolescence through adulthood; characterized by the ability to think logically about abstract principles and hypothetical situations.

same degree of sophistication in other areas (Keating, 1990; Case, 1985). Piaget (1973) acknowledged that even among many adults, formal operational thinking is often limited to areas in which they have developed expertise or a special interest.

TABLE 9.2 Piaget's Stages of Cognitive Development

Stage	Characteristics of the State	Major Change of the Stage
Sensorimotor (0–2 years)	Acquires understanding of object permanence. First understandings of cause-and-effect relationships.	Development proceeds from reflexes to actively using sensory and motor skills to explore environment.
Preoperational (2–7 years)	Symbolic thought emerges. Language development occurs (2–4 years). Thought and language both tend to be egocentric. Cannot solve conservation problems.	Development proceeds from understanding simple cause-and-effect relationships to prelogical thought processes involving the use of imagination and symbols to represent objects, actions, and situations.
Concrete operations (7–11 years)	Reversibility attained. Can solve conservation problems. Logical thought develops and is applied to concrete problems. Cannot solve complex verbal problems and hypothetical problems.	Development proceeds from prelogical thought to logical solutions to concrete problems.
Formal operations (from adolescence through adulthood)	Logically solves all types of problems. Thinks scientifically. Solves complex verbal and hypothetical problems. Is able to think in abstract terms.	Development proceeds from logical solving of concrete problems to logical solving of all classes of problems, including abstract problems.

SOURCE: Adapted from Wadsworth, 1996.

CONCEPT REVIEW 9.4

Piaget's Stages of Cognitive Development

Indicate by letter which stage of cognitive development is illustrated by each of the following examples: (A) sensorimotor; (B) preoperational; (C) concrete operational; (D) formal operations.

_____ **1.** When confronted with a lawn mower that would not start, Jason approached the problem very systematically, checking and eliminating possible causes one at a time.

_____ **2.** Lynn rolls identical amounts of playdough into two balls and is quite sure they are exactly the same. However, when her Dad flattens one ball into a pancake shape, Lynn is confident that the pancake has more playdough than the ball.

_____ **3.** When Carla's mother hides her favorite toy under a cushion, Carla starts playing with another toy and acts as though her favorite toy no longer exists.

_____ **4.** Andrew is told that Michael is taller than Bridget and Bridget is taller than Patrick. When asked who is the smallest child, Andrew thinks carefully, then answers, "Patrick."

Criticisms of Piaget's Theory

Since Piaget's theory first came to the attention of American psychologists in the 1950s, it has inspired hundreds of research studies (Kessen, 1996). Generally, scientific research has supported Piaget's most fundamental idea: that infants, young children, and older children use distinctly different cognitive abilities to construct their understanding of the world. However, other aspects of Piaget's theory have been criticized. We'll summarize three of the most important criticisms here.

Renée Baillargeon (b. 1954) Canadian-born psychologist Renée Baillargeon's ingenious studies of cognitive development during infancy, using visual rather than manual tasks, challenged Piaget's beliefs about the age at which object permanence first appears.

Criticism #1: Piaget Often Underestimated the Cognitive Abilities of Infants and Children. To test for object permanence during infancy, Piaget would show an infant an object, cover it with a cloth, and then observe whether the infant tried to reach under the cloth for the object. Obviously, this procedure requires the infant to have a certain level of motor skill development. Using this procedure, Piaget found that it wasn't until around nine months of age that an infant first behaved in a way that suggested she understood that the hidden object continued to exist. But even at nine months of age, Piaget maintained, the infant's understanding of object permanence was immature and wouldn't be fully developed for another year or so.

Today, many researchers believe that Piaget confused *motor incompetence* with *cognitive incompetence* in assessing object permanence during infancy (Mandler, 1990). In other words, perhaps the infant "knew" that the object was under the cloth, but simply lacked the physical coordination to reach for it.

To test this hypothesis, psychologist **Renée Baillargeon** (b. 1954) has used *visual* tasks, rather than *manual* tasks, in several studies to assess an infant's understanding of object permanence (1994, 1987). Baillargeon's research is based on the premise that infants, like adults, will look longer at "surprising" events that appear to contradict their understanding of the world.

Let's briefly examine a simple but ingenious study Baillargeon conducted with co-researcher Julie DeVos (1991), using three-and-a-half-month-old infants. During the pretest phase, the infants watched a short carrot as it moved behind a panel, briefly disappeared, and then reappeared on the other side of the panel, as depicted in the upper portion of Figure 9.6. After the babies became accustomed to the short carrot event, the same procedure was repeated using a tall carrot.

In the test phase, the event was changed slightly: a window was added to the panel. The window was too high for the short carrot to be seen as it passed behind the panel, but not the tall carrot. Now, as the infants watched, the tall carrot started to pass behind the screen. Although the tall carrot should have been visible in the window, it *failed* to appear in the window before reappearing on the opposite side (see the lower portion of Figure 9.6).

Baillargeon and DeVos (1991) reasoned that if three-and-a-half-month-old infants display object permanence, they would remember the size of the carrots. Because the short carrot was too short to be seen in the window, the infants should not have been surprised when the short carrot passed behind the panel without appearing in the window. However, they should have expected the tall carrot to appear in the window as it moved behind the panel—and should have been surprised when it didn't appear in the window before reappearing on the opposite side.

FIGURE 9.6 Testing Object Permanence In Very Young Infants

Pre-test Events

Short Carrot Event

Tall Carrot Event

Test Events

Possible Event

Impossible Event

This is exactly what Baillargeon and DeVos (1991) found. When infants *failed* to see the anticipated event—the tall carrot visibly passing the window—they looked much longer at the scene than when the short carrot passed behind the screen without being seen. This suggests that three-and-a-half-month-old infants mentally represented the existence, height, and path of each carrot as it moved behind the panel. Piaget believed that such cognitive understandings are not possible until infants are at least nine months old.

Other research has also demonstrated that infants have more sophisticated cognitive abilities than Piaget believed (see Siegal, 1991; Meltzoff, 1988; Gelman & Baillargeon, 1983). For example, children in the preoperational stage are less egocentric than Piaget believed (Newcombe & Huttenlocher, 1992). In one study, children as young as two years of age were asked to show a picture to an adult (Lemperers & others, 1977). Contrary to what Piaget would have predicted, the young children turned the picture so that it was oriented to the adult's perspective.

Criticism #2: Piaget's Stages Are Not as Universal as He Believed.

Piaget's contention that his stages are universal has also been called into question (Fischer & Hencke, 1996; Elkind, 1996). Researchers have found that many adults only display abstract-hypothetical thought in limited areas of knowledge, and some adults *never* display formal operational thought processes (Neimark, 1975, 1979). College students, for example, are much less likely to display formal operational thinking when given problems outside their major, as when an English major is presented with a physics problem (DeLisi & Staudt, 1980).

Such findings challenge Piaget's notion that his stages of cognitive development are universal and biologically programmed to unfold at certain ages. Late in his life, Piaget (1972, 1973) addressed this issue by suggesting that formal operational thinking may not be a universal phenomenon, but rather the product of an individual's expertise in a specific area. Research findings seem to support Piaget's later contention (Rogoff & Morelli, 1989; Fischer & others, 1984).

More important, many developmental psychologists reject the Piagetian notion of distinct stages, emphasizing instead the **information-processing model of cognitive development** (Siegler, 1991, 1983; Kail, 1991). The information-processing model of cognitive development focuses on investigating the development of fundamental mental processes like attention, memory, and problem solving (Rose & Feldman, 1995; Klahr, 1992). In this approach, cognitive development is viewed as a process of *continuous* change over the lifespan. Through life experiences, we continue to acquire new knowledge, including more sophisticated cognitive skills and strategies. In turn, this improves our ability to process, learn, and remember information (Siegler, 1991).

Criticism #3: Piaget Underestimated the Impact of the Social and Cultural Environment on Cognitive Development.

Piaget viewed the child as an independent little scientist who spontaneously discovers and constructs an understanding of the world. Accordingly, Piaget gave minimal attention to the role that social and cultural influences play in contributing to a child's understandings (Gopnik, 1996).

Other theorists have offered very different viewpoints, including the highly regarded Russian psychologist **Lev Vygotsky** (1896–1934). Vygotsky, who was born the same year as Piaget, developed his theory of cognitive development at about the same time as Piaget. Vygotsky's influence has increased dramatically in the last few decades (Wertsch & Tulviste, 1994).

Vygotsky agreed with Piaget that children may be able to reach a particular cognitive level through their own, independent efforts. However, unlike Piaget, Vygotsky (1978, 1987) believed that cognitive development is strongly influenced by social and culural factors such as the support and guidance

information-processing model of cognitive development
The model that views cognitive development as a continuous process over the lifespan and that studies the development of basic mental processes like attention, memory, and problem solving.

Lev Vygotsky Russian psychologist Lev Vygotsky was born in 1896, the same year as Piaget. He died in 1934 of tuberculosis, still a relatively young man. Recent decades have seen a resurgence of interest in Vygotsky's theoretical writings. Vygotsky emphasized the impact of social and cultural factors on cognitive development. To Vygotsky, cognitive development always takes place within a social and cultural context.

that children receive from parents, other adults, and older children. Such guidance can help "stretch" the child's cognitive abilities to new levels. Indeed, researchers have confirmed that such social interactions play a significant role in a child's cognitive development (Wertsch & Tulviste, 1992; Gopnik, 1996).

How these supportive social interactions are displayed varies from culture to culture (Rogoff & Chavajay, 1995). In middle-class American families, for example, adults often interact with children by posing questions to which the adult already knows the answer, such as asking, "How much is 2 times 2?" It's also considered culturally acceptable for children to show off their knowledge. In other cultures, however, these behaviors are not necessarily considered appropriate or acceptable (Rogoff & Morelli, 1989).

Cross-cultural studies have also shown that cognitive development is strongly influenced by the skills that are valued and encouraged in a particular environment. For example, Aboriginal children in Australia develop concrete operational reasoning on visual/spatial tasks earlier than Swiss children. In contrast, Swiss children develop numerical reasoning earlier than Aboriginal children (Dasen, 1994).

This cultural difference begins to make sense when you understand that Aborigines in traditional settings travel a great deal in an extremely harsh environment. Their survival depends on locating water, food, and each other over a fairly large territory. For Aboriginal children, remembering exactly *where* water is located is much more important than calculating its exact quantity. In contrast, the understanding of quantity and other numerical concepts is emphasized in the upbringing of Swiss children (Dasen, 1994).

So, while Piaget stressed the importance of actively exploring one's physical environment in promoting cognitive development, he largely overlooked the important roles that social interactions and cultural influences play in the process of cognitive development (see Rogoff & Chavajay, 1995). Despite this and other criticisms, Piaget's documentation of the many cognitive changes that occur during infancy and childhood ranks as one of the most outstanding contributions to developmental psychology (Beilin, 1994). With the exceptions that have been noted, Piaget's observations of the changes in children's cognitive abilities are fundamentally accurate.

Adolescence

> *Adolescence is the stage that marks the transition from childhood to adulthood. What characterizes relationships with parents and peers in adolescence? How do adolescents begin the process of identity formation? What is Erikson's psychosocial theory of lifespan development?*

Adolescence is the transitional stage between late childhood and the beginning of adulthood. Adolescence begins around age twelve and lasts until the individual assumes adult roles and responsibilities. Outwardly, the most noticeable changes that occur during adolescence are the physical changes that accompany the development of sexual maturity, a topic we'll discuss in detail in Chapter 10.

We'll start this section by looking at aspects of social development during adolescence, including the question of how the adolescent begins to build a unique sense of identity. Following that discussion, we'll consider some of the cognitive changes that occur during adolescence, especially the development of moral reasoning.

adolescence
The transitional stage between late childhood and the beginning of adulthood, during which sexual maturity is reached.

Aspects of Social Development in Adolescence

Think back to your own adolescence. Was it a time of emotional turmoil and psychological warfare with your parents? Or did you experience a relatively smooth transition to early adulthood? The still-popular notion that adolescence is a time of "storm and stress" originated with **G. Stanley Hall** (1844–1924). Hall began the study of developmental psychology in the United States (S. White, 1994).

Hall's landmark text, *Adolescence,* published in 1904, was instrumental in defining adolescence as a unique stage of development. Hall contended that the dramatic physical changes of adolescence produced psychological turmoil, emotional instability, and conflict with parents. Although his belief was not based on systematic research (Petersen, 1988), the "storm and stress" view of adolescence became very influential.

As you'll see in this section, there is little research support for Hall's "storm and stress" notion (Larson & Ham, 1993). Instead, contemporary psychologists see adolescence as a time of opportunities for growth and positive development (Compas & others, 1995).

Relationships with Parents and Peers

Are conflicts with parents inevitable during adolescence? Contrary to what many people think, parent–adolescent relationships are usually positive. In fact, most teenagers report that they admire their parents and turn to them for advice (Steinberg, 1990). As a general rule, when parent–child relationships have been good before adolescence, they continue to be relatively smooth during adolescence (Buchanan & others, 1992).

A small percentage of adolescents do display adjustment problems or antisocial behavior. In most of these cases, the problems are a continuation of psychological and behavior problems that first surfaced during childhood. Less than 10 percent of families report that parent–child relations dramatically deteriorate during adolescence (Steinberg, 1990).

Although parent–child relations are generally positive throughout the adolescent years, periodic bickering is virtually guaranteed, especially in early adolescence (Laursen & Collins, 1994; Buchanan & others, 1992). When skirmishes occur, they usually focus on whether the parent or the adolescent has final authority on a particular issue. One common area of conflict is the adolescent's choice of friends (Smetana & Asquith, 1994).

While parents remain influential throughout adolescence, relationships with friends and peers become increasingly important. Adolescents usually encounter greater diversity among their peers as they make the transitions to middle school and high school. To a much greater degree than during childhood, the adolescent's social network, social context, and community influence his or her values, norms, and expectations (Steinberg & others, 1995).

Parents often worry that peer influences will lead to undesirable behavior. Researchers have found, however, that peer relationships tend to *reinforce* the traits and goals that parents fostered during childhood (Steinberg & others, 1995). This finding is not as surprising as it might seem. Adolescents tend to form friendships with peers who are similar in age, social class, race, and beliefs about drinking, dating, church attendance, and educational goals (Savin-Williams & Berndt, 1990).

Friends often exert pressure on one another to study, make good grades, attend college, and engage in prosocial behaviors. So, while peer influence can lead to undesirable behaviors in some instances, peers can also influence one another in positive ways (Mounts & Steinberg, 1995; Berndt, 1992).

Peer Relationships in Adolescence Peer relationships become increasingly important in adolescence. Although parents often worry about the negative effects of peer influence, peers can also have a positive influence on one another. These teenage volunteers are helping plant trees in a public park in Austin, Texas.

identity
A person's definition or description of himself or herself, including the values, beliefs, and ideals that guide the individual's behavior.

Identity Formation: Erikson's Theory of Psychosocial Development

When psychologists talk about a person's **identity,** they are referring to the values, beliefs, and ideals that guide an individual's behavior (Marcia, 1991; Erikson, 1964a). Our sense of personal identity gives us an integrated and continuing sense of self over time. Identity formation is a process that continues throughout the lifespan. As we embrace new and different roles over the course of our lives, we define ourselves in new ways (Grotevant, 1992; Erikson & others, 1986).

For the first time in the lifespan, the adolescent possesses the cognitive skills necessary to deal with identity issues in a meaningful way (Dusek, 1996). Beginning in early adolescence, self-definition shifts. Preadolescent children tend to describe themselves in very concrete social and behavioral terms. An eight-year-old might describe himself by saying, "I play with Mark and I like to ride my bike." In contrast, the adolescent uses more abstract self-descriptions that reflect personal attributes, values, beliefs, and goals (Balk, 1995; Harter, 1990). Thus, a fourteen-year-old might say, "I have strong religious beliefs, love animals, and hope to become a veterinarian."

Some aspects of personal identity involve characteristics over which the adolescent has no control, such as gender, race, ethnic background, and socioeconomic level. In effect, these identity characteristics are fixed and already internalized by the time an individual reaches the adolescent years.

Beyond such fixed characteristics, the adolescent begins to evaluate herself on several different dimensions. Social acceptance by peers, academic and athletic abilities, work abilities, personal appearance, and romantic appeal are some important aspects of self-definition. Another challenge facing the adolescent is to develop an identity that is independent of her parents while retaining a sense of connection to her family. Thus, the adolescent has not one but several self-concepts that she must integrate into a coherent and unified whole to answer the question, "Who am I?"

The adolescent's task of achieving an integrated identity is one important aspect of psychoanalyst **Erik Erikson's** (1902–1994) influential theory of psychosocial development. Briefly, Erikson (1968) proposed that each of eight stages of life is associated with a particular psychosocial conflict that can be resolved in either a positive or negative direction (see Table 9.3). Relationships with others play an important role in determining the outcome of each conflict. According to Erikson, the key psychosocial conflict facing the adolescent is *identity versus identity diffusion.*

To successfully form an identity, an adolescent not only must integrate various dimensions of his personality into a coherent whole but must also define the roles that he will adopt within the larger society upon becoming an adult (Harter, 1990). To accomplish this, adolescents grapple with a wide variety of issues, such as selecting a potential career and formulating religious, moral, and political beliefs. They must also adopt social roles involving interpersonal relationships, sexuality, and long-term commitments like marriage and parenthood.

Psychoanalyst Erik Erikson (1902–1994)
Erikson is shown here with his wife Joan in 1988. Erikson's landmark theory of psychosocial development stressed the importance of social and cultural influences on personality throughout the stages of life.

TABLE 9.3 Erik Erikson's Psychosocial Stages of Development

Life Stage	Psychosocial Conflict	Positive Resolution	Negative Resolution
Infancy (birth to eighteen months)	Trust vs. mistrust	Reliance on consistent and warm caregivers produces a sense of predictability and trust in the environment.	Physical and psychological neglect by caregivers leads to fear, anxiety, and mistrust of the environment.
Toddlerhood (eighteen months to three years)	Autonomy vs. doubt	Caregivers encourage independence and self-sufficiency, promoting positive self-esteem.	Overly restrictive caregiving leads to self-doubt in abilities and low self-esteem.
Early childhood (three to six years)	Initiative vs. guilt	The child learns to initiate activities and develops a sense of social responsibility concerning the rights of others. Promotes self-confidence.	Parental overcontrol stifles the child's spontaneity, sense of purpose, and social learning. Promotes guilt and fear of punishment.
Middle and late childhood (six to twelve years)	Industry vs. inferiority	Through experiences with parents and "keeping up" with peers, the child develops a sense of pride and competence in schoolwork and home and social activities.	Negative experiences with parents or failure to "keep up" with peers leads to pervasive feelings of inferiority and inadequacy.
Adolescence	Identity vs. identity diffusion	Through experimentation with different roles, the adolescent develops an integrated and stable self-definition. Forms commitments to future adult roles.	An apathetic adolescent or one who experiences pressures and demands from others may feel confusion about his or her identity and role in society.
Young adulthood	Intimacy vs. isolation	By establishing lasting and meaningful relationships, the young adult develops a sense of connectedness and intimacy with others.	Because of fear of rejection or excessive self-preoccupation, the young adult is unable to form close, meaningful relationships and becomes psychologically isolated.
Middle adulthood	Generativity vs. stagnation	Through child rearing, caring for others, productive work, and community involvement, the adult expresses unselfish concern for the welfare of the next generation.	Self-indulgence, self-absorption, and a preoccupation with one's own needs lead to a sense of stagnation, boredom, and a lack of meaningful accomplishments.
Late adulthood	Ego integrity vs. despair	In reviewing his or her life, the older adult experiences a strong sense of self-acceptance and meaningfulness in his or her accomplishments.	In looking back on his or her life, the older adult experiences regret, dissatisfaction, and disappointment about his or her life and accomplishments.

SOURCE: Adapted from Erikson, 1964a.

In Erikson's (1968) theory, the adolescent's path to successful identity achievement begins with *identity diffusion,* which is characterized by little sense of commitment on any of these issues. This is followed by a *moratorium period,* during which the adolescent experiments with different roles, values, and beliefs. Gradually, by choosing among the alternatives and making commitments, the adolescent arrives at an *integrated identity.*

Psychological research has generally supported Erikson's description of the process of identity formation (Marcia, 1991, 1980; Grotevant, 1987). However, it's important to keep in mind that identity continually changes over the entire lifespan, not just during the adolescent years (Grotevant, 1992). Adolescents and young adults seem to achieve a stable sense of identity in some areas sooner than others, such as vocational choice. Far fewer adolescents and young adults have attained a stable sense of identity in the realm of religious and political beliefs (Waterman, 1985).

So, while Erikson believed that identity formation was a critical goal for the adolescent, it appears that the process of identity formation only begins to take on serious meaning during adolescence. For most people, a stable and fully integrated identity doesn't occur until well into the adult years.

moral reasoning
The aspect of cognitive development that has to do with the way an individual reasons about moral decisions.

Aspects of Cognitive Development in Adolescence:
The Development of Moral Reasoning

> *Kohlberg's theory of moral development describes the stages of development in moral reasoning. What are the stages and levels of moral development? How is moral reasoning influenced by gender and culture?*

An important aspect of cognitive development during adolescence is a change in **moral reasoning**—how an individual thinks about moral decisions. The adolescent's increased capacities to think abstractly, imagine hypothetical situations, and compare ideals to the real world all influence his thinking about moral issues (Darley & Shultz, 1990; Colby & others, 1983).

Kohlberg's Theory of Moral Development

The most influential theory of moral development was proposed by psychologist **Lawrence Kohlberg** (1927–1987). Kohlberg used stories like the one below to investigate moral reasoning. Read the story and then, before reading further, answer the questions at the end.

> *A woman was near death from a rare form of cancer. There was one drug that the doctors thought might save her, recently discovered by a druggist in the same town. The drug was expensive to make—about $400 for a small dose. But the druggist was charging ten times what the drug cost him to make— $4,000 for a small dose.*
>
> *The sick woman's husband, Heinz, went to everyone he knew to borrow the money, but he could only get together about $2,000, half of what the druggist was charging. He told the druggist that his wife was dying and asked him to sell it cheaper or let him pay the rest later. But the druggist refused, saying, "No, I discovered the drug and I'm going to make money from it." So Heinz gets desperate and considers breaking into the man's store to steal the drug for his wife.*
>
> *Should Heinz steal the drug? Why or why not? (Adapted from Colby & others, 1983.)*

In Kohlberg's (1984, 1976) theory, whether you think Heinz should or should not steal the drug is not the critical issue. Instead, it is the *reasoning* you use to justify your answer. Kohlberg analyzed the responses of children, adolescents, and adults to moral dilemmas like the Heinz story. He concluded that there were distinct *stages* of moral development. These stages unfold in an age-related, step-by-step fashion, much like Piaget's stages of cognitive development (Kohlberg, 1981).

Kohlberg proposed three distinct *levels* of moral reasoning: preconventional, conventional, and postconventional. Each level is based on the degree to which a person conforms to conventional standards of society. Furthermore, each level has two *stages* that represent different degrees of sophistication in moral reasoning. Table 9.4 describes the characteristics of the moral reasoning associated with each of Kohlberg's levels and stages.

HAGAR

TABLE 9.4 Kohlberg's Levels and Stages of Moral Development

I. Preconventional Level

Moral reasoning is guided by external consequences. No internalization of values or rules.

Stage 1: Punishment and Obedience

"Right" is obeying the rules simply to avoid punishment because others have power over you and can punish you.

Example:
Heinz shouldn't steal the drug because he'd go to jail if he got caught.

Stage 2: Mutual Benefit

"Right" is an even or fair exchange, so that both parties benefit. Moral reasoning guided by a sense of "fair play."

Example:
Heinz should steal the drug because the druggist is being greedy by charging so much.

II. Conventional Level

Moral reasoning is guided by conformity to social roles, rules, and expectations that the person has learned and internalized.

Stage 3: Interpersonal Expectations

"Right" is being a "good" person by conforming to social expectations, such as showing concern for others, and following rules set by others so as to win their approval. For example, behaving like a "good" child, student, citizen, spouse, friend, or employee.

Example:
Heinz should try to steal the drug because that's what a devoted husband would do.

Stage 4: Law and Order

"Right" is to help maintain social order by doing one's duty, obeying laws simply because they are laws, and showing respect for authorities simply because they are authorities.

Example:
Heinz should not steal the drug because it would be against the law and he has a duty to uphold the law.

III. Postconventional Level

Moral reasoning is guided by internalized legal and moral principles that protect the rights of all members of society.

Stage 5: Legal Principles

"Right" is to help protect the basic rights of all members of society by upholding legalistic principles that promote the values of fairness, justice, equality, and democracy.

Example:
Heinz should steal the drug because his obligation to save his wife's life must take precedence over his obligation to respect the druggist's property rights.

Stage 6: Universal Moral Principles

"Right" is determined by self-chosen ethical principles that underscore the person's profound respect for ideals such as the sanctity of human life, nonviolence, equality, and human dignity. If these moral principles conflict with democratically determined laws, the person's self-chosen moral principles would take precedence, such as the conscientious objector who refuses to be drafted because of his moral principles against war.

Example:
Even if it were a stranger and not his wife, Heinz should steal the drug because he must follow his own conscience and not let another person's desire for monetary gain outweight the value of a human life.

SOURCES: Based on Kohlberg, 1981; Colby & others, 1983.

Kohlberg and his colleagues found that the responses of children under the age of ten reflect *preconventional* moral reasoning based on self-interest —avoiding punishment and maximizing personal gain. Beginning in late childhood and continuing through adolescence and adulthood, responses typically reflect *conventional* moral reasoning, which emphasizes social roles, rules, and obligations. Thus, the progression from preconventional to conventional moral reasoning is closely associated with age-related cognitive abilities (Walker, 1989; Kohlberg, 1984; Colby & others, 1983).

Do people inevitably advance from conventional to *postconventional* moral reasoning, as Kohlberg once thought? In a twenty-year longitudinal study, Kohlberg followed a group of boys from late childhood through early adulthood. Out of the 58 subjects in the study, only 8 subjects occasionally displayed stage 5 reasoning, which emphasizes respect for legal principles that protect all members of society. And *none* of the subjects showed stage 6 reasoning, which reflects self-chosen ethical principles that are universally applied (Colby & others, 1983). Kohlberg and his colleagues eventually dropped stage 6 from the theory, partly because clear-cut expressions of "universal moral principles" were so rare (Rest, 1983).

Thus, Kohlberg's original belief that the development of abstract thinking in adolescence naturally and invariably leads people to the formation of idealistic moral principles has not been supported. Only a few exceptional people display the philosophical ideals in Kohlberg's highest level of moral reasoning. The normal course of changes in moral reasoning for most people seems to be captured by Kohlberg's first four stages (Colby & Kohlberg,

TABLE 9.5 Applying Kohlberg's Theory to Political Debates

Stage	Arguments Against U.S. Involvement	Arguments for U.S. Involvement
	"We shouldn't consider war . . .	"We should consider war . . .
1	"because it would hurt our economy."	"because our oil is threatened."
2	"because we'll have more money for domestic issues."	"because we can gain security of the oil supply."
3	"because we don't want to appear too militaristic."	"because we don't want the world to see us as weak."
4	"because war is killing and killing is against the law."	"because the U.N. has laid down written resolutions which should be upheld."
5	"even though the situation is bad, war is damaging to people and property and society agrees *that* is bad."	"the situation is extreme enough that society's rights are threatened and need to be defended."
6	"although atrocities have been committed, it would be an even greater atrocity to wage war."	"evil is on the march, and it would be morally wrong to allow it to continue."

SOURCE: Adapted from Shapiro, 1995.

Unlike the hypothetical dilemmas posed by Lawrence Kohlberg, political debates often focus on real-life moral decisions that affect many lives. When you apply Kohlberg's theory to just about any controversial political issue, such as abortion rights or gun control, it can help you identify different levels of moral reasoning used to support or oppose a particular decision. Psychology professor Johnna Shapiro (1995) did just that, asking her students to analyze U.S. congressional debates over the resolution to attack Iraq because of its invasion of Kuwait in 1990. Listed above are quotations that Shapiro's students compiled from those congressional debates, along with the stage of Kohlberg's theory that each quote reflects.

1984). By adulthood, the predominant form of moral reasoning is conventional moral reasoning, reflecting the importance of social roles and rules.

Gender and Moral Reasoning

Kohlberg's theory of moral development is not without its critics (see Modgil & Modgil, 1986). For example, psychologist Carol Gilligan (1982) points out that Kohlberg's early research was conducted entirely with male subjects, yet it became the basis for a theory applied to both males *and* females. Gilligan also notes that most of Kohlberg's stories involve a male as the main actor facing the moral dilemma to be resolved. When females are present in the stories, they often play a subordinate role, such as the female patient in the Heinz story. Thus, Gilligan believes that Kohlberg's model reflects a male perspective that may not accurately depict the development of moral reasoning in women.

To Gilligan, Kohlberg's model is based on an *ethic of individual rights and justice,* which is a more common perspective for males. In contrast, Gilligan has developed a model of women's moral development that is based on an *ethic of care and responsibility* (Gilligan, 1982). In her studies of women's moral reasoning, Gilligan found that women tended to stress the importance of maintaining interpersonal relationships and responding to the needs of others, rather than focusing primarily on individual rights (Gilligan & Attanucci, 1988).

Gilligan's model has sparked considerable research and debate. Several studies have reviewed gender differences in moral reasoning (see Walker & others, 1987; Ford & Lowery, 1986; Walker, 1984). In general, these researchers found that men and women may approach moral matters from slightly different perspectives. However, there do not seem to be systematic gender differences in moral reasoning when subjects are carefully matched on critical factors, such as level of education. Nevertheless, Gilligan and other researchers continue to study gender influences on the development of moral reasoning (e.g., Boldizar & others, 1989; Gilligan & others, 1988).

Culture and Moral Reasoning

Culture also seems to have an effect on moral reasoning (Eckensberger, 1994; Haidt & others, 1993). Some cross-cultural psychologists argue that Kohlberg's stories and scoring system reflect a Western emphasis on individual rights, harm, and justice that is not shared in many cultures (Triandis, 1994; Shweder & others, 1990a).

For example, Kohlberg's moral stages do not reflect the sense of interdependence and the concern for the overall welfare of the group that is more common in collectivistic cultures. Cross-cultural psychologist Harry Triandis (1994) reports an example of a response that does not fit into Kohlberg's moral scheme. In response to the scenario, "Heinz steals the drug to save his wife's life," a man in New Guinea said, "If nobody helped him, I would say that *we* had caused the crime." Thus, there are aspects of moral reasoning in other cultures that do not seem to be reflected in Kohlberg's theory (Matsumoto, 1994; Shweder & Haidt, 1993).

Stages of Moral Reasoning

The examples below represent moral reasoning typically associated with different levels in Kohlberg's stages of moral development. Identify each one as preconventional, conventional, or postconventional.

1. Because he believed that all war is immoral, Adrian burned his draft card and refused to be inducted into the military, even though he was risking imprisonment. _____

2. While his brother was in the washroom, Jerry resisted sneaking a bit of his dessert because he was afraid his brother would punch him if he did. _____

3. When her daughter chided her about driving so slowly, Barbara replied, "I can't drive faster than the posted speed limit because responsible drivers obey the traffic laws."
_____

Adult Development

Development continues throughout adulthood. What physical changes take place in adulthood? What are some general patterns of social development in adulthood? How does the transition to parenthood affect adults?

You can think of the developmental changes you experienced during infancy, childhood, and adolescence as early chapters in your life story. For the most part, your development during infancy, childhood, and adolescence occurred in a predictable sequence. Even so, your life story is still unique. You've experienced individual variation in the development of physical and cognitive changes. And, just as important, you have accumulated a unique combination of social and psychological experiences.

Those early life chapters helped set the tone and some of the themes for the primary focus of your life story—adulthood. During the half century or more that constitutes adulthood, predictable changes continue to occur. Self-definition evolves as people achieve independence and take on new roles and responsibilities. As you'll see in this section, the story of adulthood also reflects the increasing importance of individual variation. Although general patterns of aging exist, our life stories become more distinct and individualized with each passing decade of life (Schaie & Willis, 1996).

Physical Changes During Adulthood

Your unique genetic blueprint greatly influences the unfolding of certain physical changes during adulthood, such as when your hair begins to thin, lose its color, and turn gray. Such genetically influenced changes can vary significantly from one person to another. For example, **menopause,** the cessation of menstruation that signals the end of reproductive capacity in women, may occur anywhere from the late thirties to the early fifties.

But your destiny is not completely ruled by genetics. Your lifestyle is one key environmental factor that can influence the aging process. Staying men-

menopause
The natural cessation of menstruation and the end of reproductive capacity in women.

tally and physically active and eating a proper diet can both slow and minimize the degree of physical decline associated with aging.

Another potent environmental force is simply the passage of time. Decades of use and environmental exposure take a toll on the body. Wrinkles begin to appear as we approach the age of forty, largely due to a loss of skin elasticity combined with years of making the same facial expressions. With each decade after age twenty, the efficiency of various body organs declines. For example, lung capacity decreases, as does the amount of blood pumped by the heart.

Physical strength typically peaks in *early adulthood*, the twenties and thirties. By *middle adulthood*, roughly from the forties to mid-sixties, physical strength and endurance gradually decline. Physical and mental reaction times also begin to slow during middle adulthood. During *late adulthood*, from the mid-sixties on, physical stamina and reaction time tend to decline further and faster.

Some sensory capabilities decline with increasing age, especially during late adulthood. For example, our senses of smell and taste become less acute as we get older. Age-related declines in visual abilities also occur, which can have practical ramifications. Thus, older adults may have difficulty reading distant traffic signs (Owsley & others, 1991; Sivak & others, 1981). Some aspects of our sensory abilities, however, are remarkably resistant to change. For example, there is virtually no change in color vision over the course of adulthood (Fozard, 1990).

Social Development in Adulthood:
The Themes of Love and Work

In his theory of psychosocial development, Erik Erikson (1982) described the two fundamental themes that dominate adulthood: love and work. According to Erikson (1968, 1964b), the primary psychosocial task of early adulthood is to form a committed, mutually enhancing, intimate relationship with another person. During middle adulthood, the primary psychosocial task becomes one of *generativity*—to contribute to future generations through your children, your career, and other meaningful activities. In this section, we'll consider the themes of love and work by examining adult friendships, marriage, family life, and careers.

Friends and Lovers in Adulthood

Largely because of competing demands on their time, adults typically have fewer friends than adolescents do. Nonetheless, adults benefit from the social and emotional support of at least one close friend or confidant throughout adulthood (Arling, 1987; Holahan & Holahan, 1987).

The focus of friendships is somewhat different for each gender. Female friends tend to confide in one another about their feelings, problems, and interpersonal relationships. In contrast, male friends typically minimize discussions about relationships or personal feelings or problems. Instead, male friends tend to do things together that they find mutually interesting, such as activities related to sports or hobbies (Norris & Tindale, 1994; Winstead, 1986).

Beyond friendship, establishing a committed, intimate relationship takes on a new urgency in adulthood. Looking for Mr. or Ms. Right, getting married, and starting a family are the traditional tasks of early adulthood. However, in contrast to their parents, today's young adults are marrying at a later average age. As Table 9.6 shows, in 1960 the median age for a first marriage was 23 for males and 20 years for females. By 1993 those averages had

TABLE 9.6 Median Age at First Marriage: 1960 to 1993

Year	Men	Women
1993	26.5	24.5
1990	26.1	23.9
1985	25.5	23.3
1980	24.7	22.0
1975	23.5	21.1
1970	23.2	20.8
1965	22.8	20.6
1960	22.8	20.3

SOURCE: Saluter, 1994, p. vii.

increased to 27 for males and 25 for females (Saluter, 1994). Many young adults postpone marriage until their late twenties or early thirties so they can finish their education and become established in a career.

Whom are we most likely to marry? As a general rule, the old adage "Birds of a feather flock together" seems to hold. We tend to be attracted to and marry people who are similar to us on a variety of dimensions, including physical attractiveness, social and educational status, ethnic background, attitudes, values, and beliefs (Brehm, 1992).

And does the fairy tale ending "They got married and lived happily ever after" also hold true? Well, not exactly. Over the first year of marriage, newly-weds typically reduce the number of behaviors intended to please their partner, such as making them laugh, saying "I love you," or initiating sexual relations. The romantic excitement of the relationship also diminishes somewhat with the realization that the heretofore "perfect" mate has annoying little habits. More time is spent on the mundane tasks of daily life, like grocery shopping, cooking, and cleaning, than on doing enjoyable things together, like going to movies or parties. In short, the blissful "honeymoon" phase of marriage passes rather quickly as the couple faces the realities of daily life (Huston & others, 1986).

We don't want to leave you with the impression that most couples are miserable or disillusioned after the first year of marriage, because they are not. Most couples remain fundamentally positive about their relationship. They're just less positive than they were during courtship and the first months of marriage (Huston & others, 1986).

The Transition to Parenthood: Kids 'R' Us?

Although it is commonly believed that children strengthen the marital bond, marital satisfaction tends to decline after the birth of the first child (Levy-Shiff, 1994; Hackel & Ruble, 1992). For all the joy that can be derived from watching a child grow and experience the world, the first child's arrival creates a whole new set of responsibilities, pushes, and pulls on the marital relationship (Umberson & Gove, 1989).

Without question, parenthood fundamentally alters your identity as an adult. With the birth or adoption of your first child, you take on a commitment to nurture the physical, emotional, social, and intellectual well-being of the next generation. This change in your identity can be a struggle, especially if the transition to parenthood was more of a surprise than a planned event (Sandelowski & others, 1992; Mebert, 1991).

Parenthood is further complicated by the fact that children are not born speaking fluently so that you can immediately enlighten them about the constraints of adult schedules, deadlines, finances, and physical energy. Instead, you must continually strive to adapt lovingly and patiently to your child's needs while managing all the other priorities in your life.

Practically speaking, this means that you've got to learn to flow with the events of any given day. Some days, of course, the game plan flows better than others. In fact, as Don writes these words it is 4:52 a.m. Laura is sleeping much better since he gave her some cough syrup about 30 minutes ago. Unfortunately, Don couldn't get back to sleep.

Not all couples experience a decline in marital satisfaction after the birth of a child. The hassles and headaches of child rearing can be minimized if the marital relationship is warm and positive, and if both husband and wife share household and child-care responsibilities (Cowan & Cowan, 1992, 1988). It also helps if you're blessed with a child who is born with a good disposition and an easy temperament. When infants are irritable, cry a lot, or are otherwise "difficult," parents find it harder to adjust to their new role (van den Boom & Hoeksma, 1994; Wilkie & Ames, 1986).

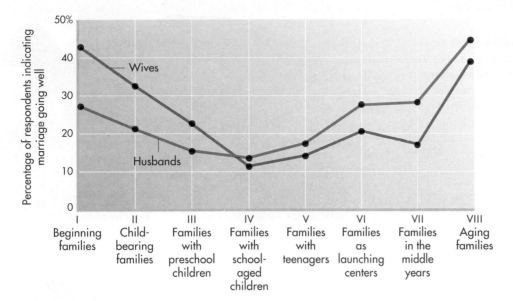

That many couples are marrying at a later age and waiting until their thirties to start a family also seems to be advantageous. Becoming a parent at an older age and waiting longer after marriage to start a family helps ease the adjustment to parenthood. Why? Largely because the couple is more mature and the marital relationship is typically more stable (Cowan & Cowan, 1992; Olds, 1989).

FIGURE 9.7 Marital Satisfaction at Different Stages in the Family Life Cycle
Researchers Boyd Rollins and Harold Feldman (1970) surveyed marital satisfaction at different stages in the family life cycle. The graph depicts the percentage of husbands and wives who reported that their marriage was going well "all the time" at these different stages. As you can see, over the course of the family life cycle, marital satisfaction tends to be highest before children are born and after children are "launched" into the world. Similar results were found in a more recent study by Anderson & others (1983).

Although marital satisfaction often declines when people first become parents, it rises again after children leave home (Norris & Tindale, 1994). As you can see in Figure 9.7, marital satisfaction seems to follow a U-shaped pattern across the life cycle of the family (Anderson & others, 1983). Successfully launching your children into the adult world represents the attainment of the ultimate parental goal. It also means there is more time to spend in leisure activities with your spouse. Not surprisingly, then, marital satisfaction tends to increase steadily once children are out of the nest and flying on their own.

Variations in the Paths of Adult Social Development

Up to this point, we've described the "traditional" track of adult social development: finding a mate, getting married, starting and raising a family. However, there is enormous diversity in how the goal of intimacy is realized during adulthood (Edwards, 1995b). The nature of intimate relationships and family structures varies widely in the United States (see Figure 9.8).

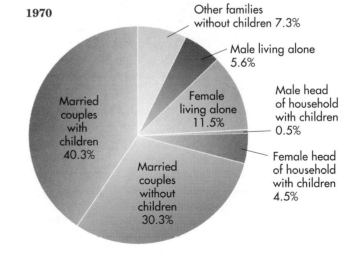

FIGURE 9.8 The Changing Structure of American Families and Households
Between 1970 and 1994, the number of American households increased from 63 million to 97 million. During that same period, however, the average size of the American household decreased from 3.14 to 2.67 persons. In the two pie charts above, you can see how the structure of American households has undergone major shifts during the last 25 years. Notice how the percentage of single-parent households has almost doubled, while the number of "traditional" families of a married couple with children has decreased dramatically.
(Rawlings & Saluter, 1995)

Single-Parent Families Today, more than thirty percent of all children are being raised by a single parent. Many single parents provide their children with a warm, stable, and loving environment. In terms of school achievement and emotional stability, children in stable single-parent households do just as well as the children with two parents living in the same home (see Berger, 1994).

For example, the number of unmarried couples living together has increased dramatically in the last twenty years—to well over 3 million couples in the 1990s. Currently, better than 30 percent of all children are being raised by a single parent (Rawlings & Saluter, 1995). As divorce has become more common, the number of single parents and stepfamilies has also risen. And among married couples, an increasing number are opting for a "child-free" life together (Macklin, 1987). There are also gay and lesbian couples who, like many married couples, are committed to a long-term, monogamous relationship with their partner (Kurdek, 1995).

Given that more than half of all first marriages end in divorce, the phenomenon of remarrying and having a "second family" later in life is not unusual (Karney & Bradbury, 1995). That's the case with our close friend, Joan. Joan has two children (by her second marriage) who are *younger* than her grandchildren (by her daughter from her first marriage). At forty-five, Joan was simultaneously the mother of a newborn and a grandmother.

Such diversity in adult relationships reflects the fact that adult social development does not always follow a predictable pattern. As you travel through adulthood, your life story may include many unanticipated twists in the plot and changes in the cast of characters. Just as the "traditional" family structure has its joys and heartaches, so do other configurations of intimate and family relationships. In the final analysis, *any* relationship that promotes the overall sense of happiness and well-being of the people involved is a successful one.

A "Blended" Family Another nontraditional family structure that has become more common is the so-called blended family. Sometimes, as with the family in this photograph, the children of the first marriage are much older than the children of the second marriage.

Careers in Adulthood

People follow a variety of routes in developing careers. Most people explore different career options, narrow down their options, and tentatively commit to a particular job in a particular field in young adulthood (Super, 1990). However, researchers have found that close to a third of people in their late twenties and early thirties do not just change jobs in a particular field, but completely switch occupational fields (Phillips & Blustein, 1994; Phillips, 1982). For example, our friend Bill got a degree in elementary education, pursued graduate training in clinical psychology, and then worked as a toy designer for many years. Today, in his forties, Bill is back in college, well on his way to beginning a new career as a registered nurse.

Establishing a Career Like this young man, a preschool teacher, many people commit to a particular career in young adulthood. However, it's common for people to change careers and even occupational fields in their late twenties and thirties.

Dual-career families have become increasingly common (Gilbert, 1993). However, the career tracks of men and women often differ if they have children. Although today's fathers are more actively involved in child rearing than fathers in previous generations, women still tend to have primary responsibility for child care. Thus, married women with children are much more likely than single women or childless women to interrupt their careers, leave their jobs, or switch to part-time work because of child-rearing responsibilities (Larwood & Gutek, 1987).

Do adults, particularly women, experience greater stress because of the conflicting demands of career, marriage, and family? Not necessarily. Generally, multiple roles seem to provide both men and women with a greater potential for increased feelings of self-esteem, happiness, and competence (Gilbert, 1994). The critical factor is not so much the number of roles that people take on, but the *quality* of their experiences on the job, in marriage, and as a parent (Barnett & others, 1992). When experiences in these different roles are positive and satisfying, psychological well-being is enhanced. However, when work is dissatisfying, finding high-quality child care is difficult, and making ends meet is a never-ending struggle, stress can escalate and psychological well-being can plummet—for either sex (Clay, 1995).

Especially for women, multiple roles have an added benefit. When career or work experiences are dissatisfying, the roles of marital partner and parent can act as a psychological buffer. In comparison, single or childless women tend to experience greater distress when the quality of job experiences declines (Barnett & others, 1992). Whether as a partner, a parent, or both, family roles seem to provide alternative sources of rewarding personal experiences when the negative aspects of jobs outweigh the positive aspects.

Late Adulthood and Aging

Late adulthood does not necessarily involve a steep decline in physical or cognitive capabilities. What cognitive changes take place in late adulthood? What factors can influence social development in late adulthood?

Stereotypes of Aging What are your thoughts about the personalities and abilities of these two gentlemen? When American college students were shown pictures of the same man at ages 25, 52, and 74, they rated the 74-year-old as least active, intelligent, healthy, and competent (Levin, 1988). After reading this section, can you explain why these stereotypes are inaccurate?

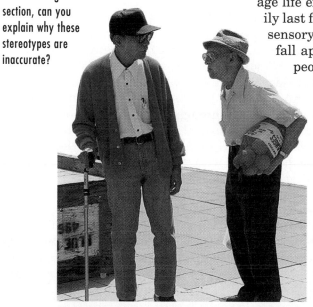

The average life expectancy for men is about 72 years. For women, the average life expectancy is about 79 years. So the stage of late adulthood can easily last for twenty years or more. Although we experience many physical and sensory changes throughout adulthood, that's not to say that we completely fall apart when we reach our sixties, seventies, or even eighties. In fact, people in their nineties or older are sometimes healthier and more active than people twenty years younger (Perls, 1995).

In American culture, but certainly not all cultures, "old age" is often associated with images of poor health, inactivity, social isolation, and mental and physical incompetence. Are those images accurate? Far from it. The majority of older adults live healthy, active, and self-sufficient lives (Schaie & Willis, 1996).

In fact, the stereotypical image that most of the elderly live in nursing homes is a myth. Only about 5 percent of people over age sixty-five live in nursing homes. This percentage increases with advancing age, but not as much as you might think. Even among those aged eighty-five and older, less than 25 percent live in nursing homes. Some older adults live with relatives, but most live in their own homes (U.S. Bureau of the Census, 1992).

Although they have more chronic medical conditions, the elderly tend to see themselves as relatively healthy, partly because they have fewer acute illnesses, such as colds and the flu, than younger people (U.S. National Center for Health Statistics, 1990). Even during the final year of life, the majority of older adults enjoy relatively good health, mental alertness, and self-sufficiency (Brock & others, 1994).

The number of older adults in the United States has been gradually increasing over the past several decades. At the turn of the century, only about one American in twenty was sixty-five or older; today, one out of every eight Americans is. By the year 2030, one out of five Americans will be an older adult (Human Capital Initiative, 1993).

Culture and Images of Aging   Some cultures hold the very old in great respect. Japan has a national holiday, "Respect for the Aged Day," celebrated each September. Shown here are Kin Narita and Gin Kanie, Japan's oldest twins, who celebrated their 104th birthday on August 1, 1996. Kin (which means "gold") and Gin (which means "silver") make regular appearances in Japanese television commercials and variety shows, and have even cut a CD.

Cognitive Changes in Late Adulthood

During which decade of life do you think people reach their intellectual peak? If you answered the twenties or thirties, you may be surprised by the results of longitudinal studies done by psychologist **K. Warner Schaie** (b. 1928). Since the 1950s, Schaie and his colleagues have followed some 5,000 people as they have aged to learn what happens to intellectual abilities.

Schaie (1995b) found that general intellectual abilities gradually increase until one's early forties, then become relatively stable until about age sixty. After age sixty, a small but steadily increasing percentage of older adults experienced slight declines on tests of general intellectual abilities, such as logical reasoning, math skills, word recall, and the ability to mentally manipulate images. But even after age sixty, most older adults maintain these abilities.

When declines in mental abilities occur during old age, Schaie found, the explanation is often simply a lack of practice or experience with the kinds of tasks on mental ability tests. Even just a few hours of training on mental skills can improve test scores for most older adults (Schaie & Willis, 1986).

Is it possible to minimize declines in mental abilities in old age? In a word, yes. Schaie (1994) found that those who were better educated and engaged in physical and mental activities throughout older adulthood showed the smallest declines in mental abilities. In contrast, the greatest intellectual declines tended to occur in older adults with unstimulating lifestyles, such as people who lived alone, were dissatisfied with their lives, and engaged in few activities.

So the bottom line here is that intellectual decline is *not* an inevitable result of aging. As we discussed in Chapter 2, keeping your mind active and stimulated throughout the entire lifespan is part of the prescription for keeping your brain fit (White & others, 1994). As you'll read in Culture and Human Behavior Box 9.3, cultural beliefs also seem to influence mental abilities in old age.

CULTURE AND HUMAN BEHAVIOR 9.3

Do Cultural Beliefs Affect Memory in Old Age?

Many researchers believe that declines in memory ability are part of the natural, biological aging process (Craik, 1994; Salthouse, 1993). However, psychologists Becca Levy and Ellen Langer have offered a very different explanation. Levy and Langer (1994) believe that cultural expectations about aging can affect memory abilities in the elderly.

While most Americans believe that memory loss inevitably accompanies old age (Ryan, 1992), Levy and Langer point out that this belief is far from universal. In many cultures, the elderly are accorded high status and revered for their wisdom and accumulated knowledge.

To test the notion that cultural stereotypes of the elderly can influence memory ability, Levy and Langer (1994) first identified two cultural groups that hold a very positive view of aging. One cultural group was people living in mainland China. The other cultural group consisted of hearing-impaired Americans who used American Sign Language and strongly identified with the Deaf culture.

Next, Levy and Langer recruited three groups of subjects: (1) residents of Beijing, China; (2) American members of the Deaf culture who communicated with American Sign Language; and (3) Americans who were part of the mainstream hearing culture. Half of each group consisted of younger people, aged fifteen to thirty; the other half consisted of older adults, aged fifty-nine to ninety-one. Participants in all groups were tested on four different memory tasks. In addition, their attitudes toward old age were measured.

On the memory tasks, Levy and Langer (1994) found no significant difference among all three groups of younger adults. But while the younger adults in the three cultural groups performed very similarly, the older adults did not. The older American hearing participants had the *lowest* memory test scores. The elderly Deaf participants had the next-highest memory test scores. And the elderly Chinese subjects had the *highest* scores of all the older adults. In fact, the elderly Chinese subjects performed so well on the memory tests that their scores did not differ from the scores of the young Chinese subjects.

Levy and Langer (1994) note that the pattern of memory test scores was directly correlated with each group's view of aging. The more positive each group's view of aging, the better was their performance on actual memory tasks. The Chinese reported the most positive view of aging, and the older Chinese participants scored the highest on the memory tasks. The hearing

Americans reported the *least* positive view of aging, and the elderly members of this group scored the lowest on the memory tasks of the three cultures studied. The Deaf participants' views about aging fell between the Chinese and the American hearing group; and their scores on the memory tests were also in the middle of the other two groups.

How can we interpret these findings? Levy and Langer point out that the Chinese and Deaf cultures have little in common other than their esteem for old age. If biological processes were responsible for memory loss in old age, the Chinese and Deaf participants should not have outperformed the older American hearing participants on all four memory tasks.

Levy and Langer (1994) conclude that cultural beliefs about aging may well play an important role in determining the degree of memory loss that people experience in old age. They suggest that the negative stereotypes about aging that are common in mainstream American culture may function as a self-fulfilling prophecy for many older Americans. Thus, if aging were viewed in a more positive light, cognitive functioning among the elderly might well be enhanced.

Social Development in Late Adulthood

At one time it was believed that older adults gradually "disengage," or withdraw from vocational, social, and relationship roles, as they face the prospect of their lives ending (Cumming & Henry, 1961). But consider Sandy's father, Erv, who, as we write these sentences, is about to turn seventy-seven. Erv and about a dozen other retired men in their seventies belong to what they call "the Golden Agers' Club." They regularly get together to play cards, go out to lunch, forage used bookstores and flea markets, and, about once a year, go on a fishing trip.

What Erv and his buddies epitomize is the activity theory of aging. According to the **activity theory of aging,** life satisfaction in late adulthood is highest when you maintain your previous level of activity, either by continuing old activities or finding new ones (Havighurst & others, 1968).

Just like younger adults, older adults differ in the level of activity they find personally optimal. Some older adults pursue a busy lifestyle of social activities, travel, college classes, and volunteer work. Other older adults are happier with a quieter lifestyle, pursuing hobbies, reading, or simply puttering around their homes. Such individual preferences reflect lifelong temperamental and personality qualities that continue to be evident as the person ages (Costa & McCrae, 1989).

For many older adults, caregiving responsibilities can persist well into late adulthood. Sandy's parents, Fern and Erv, for example, spend a great deal of time helping out with their young grandchildren and caring for some of their older relatives. They're not unusual in that respect. Many older adults who are healthy and active find themselves taking care of other older adults who are sick or have physical limitations (Norris & Tindale, 1994).

A Lifetime of Experience to Share Like many other senior adults, Ettore Buonomo of New York City derives great personal satisfaction as a volunteer helping grade-school students. Contributing to society, taking care of others, and helping people both younger and older than themselves often takes on renewed importance to senior adults.

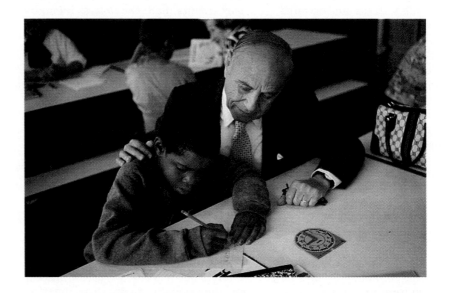

Even if an older adult is not very socially active, it's still important to have at least one confidant. Sometimes the confidant is simply a very close friend. For older men, the confidant is often the spouse. The social support provided by the confidant yields important psychological benefits for the older adult, such as higher morale, better mental health, and greater psychological well-being (Rawlins, 1992). A confidant can also provide an important buffer for the older adult in coping with stressful events, such as health problems or the deaths of friends or family members.

Along with satisfying social relationships, the prescription for psychological well-being in old age includes achieving what Erik Erikson called *ego integrity*—the feeling that one's life has been meaningful (Erikson & others, 1986). Older adults experience ego integrity when they look back on their lives and feel satisfied with their accomplishments, accepting whatever mistakes or missteps they may have made.

In contrast, those who are filled with regrets or bitterness about past mistakes, missed opportunities, or bad decisions experience *despair*—a sense of disappointment in life. Often the themes of ego integrity or despair emerge as older adults engage in a *life review,* thinking about or retelling their life story to others (Haight, 1992; Taft & Nehrke, 1990).

activity theory of aging
The psychosocial theory that life satisfaction in late adulthood is highest when people maintain the level of activity they displayed earlier in life.

Adulthood and Late Adulthood

Answer *true* or *false* for each of the following statements. If a statement is false, write in the correct statement.

___ **1.** The adage "Use it or lose it" seems to apply to your brain's abilities as you grow older.

___ **2.** In general, people tend to marry others like themselves.

___ **3.** Women tend to experience much greater stress than men when faced with the demands of career, marriage, and family roles.

___ **4.** Younger parents adjust more easily to parenthood than older parents do.

___ **5.** The percentage of married couples with children has remained very consistent since 1960.

___ **6.** After the last child leaves home, parents suffer from the "empty-nest syndrome," and marital satisfaction declines significantly.

The Final Chapter: Dying and Death

Attitudes toward death and dying are as diverse in late adulthood as they are throughout the lifespan. How did Kübler-Ross describe the stages of dying? Does her description accurately characterize the process of dying?

It is tempting to view death as the special province of the very old. Of course, death can occur at any point during the lifespan. It's also tempting to assume that older adults have come to a special understanding about death—that they view the prospect of dying with wisdom and serenity. In reality, attitudes toward death in old age show the same diversity that is reflected in other aspects of adult development. Not all older adults are resigned to death, even when poor health has severely restricted their activities (Kastenbaum, 1992, 1986).

As psychologist Robert Kastenbaum (1992) wrote, "Everyone lives in relationship to death at every point in the life span." In other words, long before encountering old age, each individual has a personal history of thinking about death. Some people are obsessed with issues of life and death from adolescence or early adulthood, while others, even in advanced old age, take more of a "one day at a time" approach to living.

In general, anxiety about death tends to peak in middle adulthood, then tends to *decrease* in late adulthood (Lonetto & Templer, 1986). At any age, people respond with a wide variety of emotions when faced with the prospect of imminent death, such as when they are diagnosed with a terminal illness.

Elisabeth Kübler-Ross (1969) interviewed over 200 terminally ill patients and proposed that the dying go through five stages. First, they *deny* that death is imminent, perhaps insisting that their doctors are wrong or denying the seriousness of their illness. Second, they feel and express *anger* that they are dying. Third, they *bargain*—they try to "make a deal" with doctors, relatives, or God, promising to behave in a certain way if only they may be allowed to live. Fourth, they become *depressed*. Finally, they *accept* their fate.

Although Kübler-Ross's research did much to sensitize the public and the medical community to the emotional experience of dying, it now seems clear that the dying individual in fact does not progress through a predictable sequence of stages (Kastenbaum, 1992). Dying is as individual a process as living. People cope with the prospect of dying much as they have coped with the stresses involved in living (Schulz & Schlarb, 1987–1988).

Faced with impending death, some older adults react with passive resignation, others with bitterness and anger. Some people plunge into activity and focus their attention on external matters, such as making funeral arrangements, disposing of their property, or arranging for the care of other family members. And others turn inward, searching for the meaning of their life's story as the close of the final chapter draws near (Kastenbaum, 1992).

But even in dying, our life story doesn't just end. Each of us leaves behind a legacy of memories in the minds of those who survive us. As we live each day, we are building this legacy, through our words, our actions, and the choices we make.

Each of us began life being completely dependent upon others for our survival. Over the course of our lifespan, others come to depend upon us. It is those people whose lives we have touched in some way, whether for good or for bad, who will remember us. In this sense, the final chapter of our lives will be written not by us, but by those whose life stories have intersected with our own.

Summing Up: Lifespan Development

Traditionally, development in childhood has received the most attention from developmental psychologists. Yet, as we have emphasized throughout this chapter, development is a lifelong process. Despite being firmly entrenched in middle adulthood, your authors, for example, have grown and changed at the same time that our daughter has developed from being a newborn to an exuberant kindergartner. And, as Sandy's parents, Erv and Fern, clearly demonstrate, development continues well beyond retirement. For many older adults, the responsibility for others does not end with retirement. Rather, it takes on new dimensions.

Throughout this chapter, you've seen that every life is a unique combination of universal and individualized patterns of development. While some aspects of development unfold in a predictable fashion, every life story, including yours, is influenced by unexpected events and plot twists. In our case, when we signed the contract to write this book, we never envisioned how dramatically it would affect our lives—and our daughter's life. So despite predictable changes, the wonderful thing about the developmental process is that you never *really* know what the next chapter of your life story may hold.

> "Daddy, can I ask you a question?"
> "Sure, Laura, just let me fix the typo in this sentence. Okay, shoot!"
> "Can we go visit Grandma and Grandpa?"
> "Well, you're in luck! Mom and Dad have to go to New York in about three weeks to talk to the book designers. And you, you lucky child, get to fly to Chicago and stay with Grandma Fern and Grandpa Erv for a few days!"
> "Can I bring Nubbin?"
> "Nope."
> "Darn. Is there snow in Chicago?"
> "There's mountains *of it!*"
> "Goodie! I can help Grandpa shovel the snow!"
> "I'm sure Grandpa Erv will appreciate that."
> "I'm going to go get my shovel right now!"
> "Hey! Wait a second! We're not leaving for a couple of weeks! Laura? Laura?"

Raising Psychologically Healthy Children

Parents differ in terms of their level of control of children's behavior and their responsiveness to children's needs. What are the basic parenting styles, and what effects do they have? What parenting strategies can you adopt to foster healthy psychological development in your child?

Unfortunately, kids don't come with owner's manuals. Maybe that's why if you walk into any bookstore and head for the "Parenting" section, you'll see shelves of books offering advice on topics ranging from "how to toilet-train your toddler" to "how to talk to your teenager." We're not going to attempt to cover that range in this brief chapter Application. However, we will present some basic principles of parenting that have been shown to foster the development of children who are psychologically well-adjusted, competent, and in control of their own behavior.

Basic Parenting Styles and Their Effects on Children

Psychologist Diana Baumrind (1971, 1967) has described three basic parenting styles: authoritarian, permissive, and authoritative. These parenting styles differ in terms of (1) *parental control* and (2) *parental responsiveness* to the child's needs and wishes.

Authoritarian parents are demanding but unresponsive to their children's needs or wishes. Authoritarian parents believe that they should shape and control the child's behavior so that it corresponds to an absolute set of standards. Put simply, they expect children to obey the rules, no questions asked. Rules are made without input from the child, and they are enforced by punishment, often physical.

At the opposite extreme are two types of **permissive parents** (Maccoby & Martin, 1983). *Permissive-indulgent parents* are responsive, warm, and accepting of their children, but impose few rules and rarely punish the child. *Permissive-indifferent parents* are both unresponsive and uncontrolling. Establishing firm rules and consistently enforcing them is simply too much trouble for permissive-indifferent parents. When

Situation: Nine-year-old Jeff wants to stay up late to watch a special program on television.

	Low responsiveness	High responsiveness
Low control	**Permissive-Indifferent** Doesn't notice that Jeff is up late; Jeff has no regular bedtime.	**Permissive-Indulgent** Says, "Fine, if it's that important to you."
High control	**Authoritarian** Says, "You know the rules. Bedtime is nine o'clock. No exceptions!"	**Authoritative** Asks why program is so important. Offers to tape program so Jeff can watch it at a later time, or agrees that Jeff can stay up late tonight if he promises to go to bed early tomorrow.

Four Parenting Styles
Researchers have identified four basic parenting styles, based on the dimensions of parental control and parental responsiveness.

the lack of involvement of permissive-indifferent parenting is taken to an extreme, it can amount to child neglect.

The third parenting style is authoritative. **Authoritative parents** are warm, responsive, and involved with their children. They set clear standards for mature, age-appropriate behavior and expect their children to be responsive to parental demands. However, authoritative parents also feel a *reciprocal* responsibility to consider their children's reasonable demands and points of view. Thus, there is considerable give and take between parent and child. Rules are firm and consistently enforced, but the reasons for the rules are discussed with the child (Maccoby & Martin, 1983).

How do these different parenting styles affect young children? Baumrind (1971) found that the children of authoritarian parents are likely to be moody, unhappy, fearful, withdrawn, unspontaneous, and irritable. The children of permissive parents tend to be more cheerful than the children of authoritarian parents, but they are more immature, impulsive, and aggressive. In contrast, the children of authoritative parents are likely to be cheer-

ful, socially competent, energetic, and friendly. They show high levels of self-esteem, self-reliance, and self-control (Buri & others, 1988).

These different parenting styles also affect school performance. In a nutshell, authoritative parenting is associated with higher grades than authoritarian or permissive parenting. In one study of several hundred adolescents, this finding was consistent for virtually all adolescents, regardless of ethnic or socioeconomic background (Dornbusch & others, 1987).

Adding to the evidence, psychologist Laurence Steinberg and his colleagues (1995) conducted a three-year longitudinal study involving over 20,000 U.S. high school students. Steinberg found that authoritative parenting is associated with a broad range of beneficial effects for the adolescent, regardless of socioeconomic or ethnic background. As Steinberg summarizes, "Adolescents raised in authoritative homes are better adjusted and more competent, they are confident about their abilities, competent in areas of achievement, and less likely than their peers to get into trouble" (Steinberg & others, 1995).

Why does an authoritative parenting style provide such clear advantages over other parenting styles? First, when children perceive their parents' requests as fair and reasonable, they are more likely to comply with the requests. Second, the children are more likely to *internalize* (or accept as their own) the reasons for behaving in a certain way and thus to achieve greater self-control (Hoffman, 1994, 1977).

In contrast, authoritarian parenting promotes resentment and rebellion (Hoffman, 1988, 1977). Because compliance is based on external control and punishment, the child often learns to avoid the parent rather than independently control his or her own behavior. Finally, the child with permissive parents may never learn self-control. And, because permissive parents have low expectations, the child may well live up to those expectations by failing to strive to fulfill his or her potential (Baumrind, 1971).

How to Be an Authoritative Parent: Some Practical Suggestions

Authoritative parents are high in both responsiveness and control. How can you successfully achieve that balance? Here are several suggestions based on psychological research.

1. *Let your children know that you love them.* Attention, hugs, and other demonstrations of physical affection, coupled with a positive attitude toward your child, are some of the most important aspects of parenting, aspects that have enduring effects. Over the long haul, children who experience warm, positive relationships with their parents are more likely to become

happy adults with stable marriages and good relationships with friends (Franz & others, 1991). So the question is simple: Have you hugged your kids today?

2. *Listen to your children.* Let your children express their opinions, and respect their preferences when it's reasonable to do so. In making rules and decisions, ask for their input and give it genuine consideration. Strive to be fair and flexible, especially on issues that are less than earthshaking, like which clothes they wear to school.

3. *Use induction to teach as you discipline.* The most effective form of discipline is called **induction,** because it *induces* understanding in the child. Induction combines controlling a child's behavior with *teaching* (Hoffman, 1994, 1977). Put simply, induction involves consistently explaining (a) the *reason* for prohibiting or performing certain behaviors; (b) the *consequences* of the action for the child; and (c) the *effect* of the child's behavior on others. With older children, induction can also involve describing how they can make *amends* for their misbehavior.

4. *Work with your child's temperamental qualities.* Think back to our earlier discussion of temperamental qualities. Be aware of your child's natural temperament and work with it, not against it. If your child is very active, for example, it is unrealistic to expect him to sit quietly during a four-hour plane or bus trip. Knowing that, you can increase the likelihood of positive experiences by planning ahead. Bring coloring books, picture books, or small toys to occupy the young child in

a restaurant or at a family gathering. Take frequent "exercise stops" on a long car trip. If your child is unusually sensitive, shy, or "slow-to-warm-up," give her plenty of time to make the transition to new situations, and provide lots of preparation so that she knows what to expect (Kurcinka, 1991).

5. *Understand your child's age-related cognitive abilities and limitations.* Some parents make the mistake of assuming that the child thinks in the same way as an adult. They may see a toddler or even an infant as purposely "misbehaving," "being naughty," or "rebelling" when the little one is simply doing what one-year-olds or three-year-olds do. Instead, your expectations for appropriate behavior should be geared to the child's age and developmental stage (see Barclay & Houts, 1995b). Having a thorough understanding of the information in this chapter is a good start. You might also consider taking a developmental psychology or child development class. Or go to your school library and check out some of the developmental psychology texts. By understanding your child's cognitive abilities and limitations at each stage of development, you're less likely to misinterpret his behavior or to place inappropriate demands on him.

6. *Don't expect perfection, and learn to go with the flow.* Accidents happen. Mistakes occur. Children get cranky or grumpy, especially when they're tired or hungry. Don't get too bent out of shape when your child's behavior is less than perfect. Be patient. Moments of conflict with children are a natural, inevitable, and healthy part of growing up. Look at them as part of the process by which a child achieves autonomy and a sense of self.

Finally, effective parenting is an ongoing process in which you, as the parent, should be regularly assessing your impact on your child. It's not always easy to combine responsiveness with control, or flexibility with an appropriate level of firmness. When you make a mistake, admit it not just to yourself but also to your child. In doing so, you'll teach your child how he should behave when he makes a mistake. As you'll discover, children are remarkably forgiving—and also resilient.

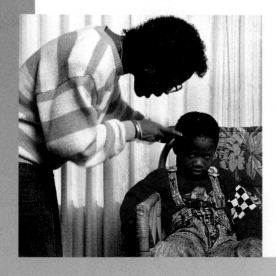

Using Induction to Teach as You Discipline
Through a combination of parental control and explanation why a certain behavior is not permitted and how it affects others, the child begins to understand that a parent's actions are not completely arbitrary or unfair. The child is also more likely to internalize the reasoning and apply it in new situations (Schulman & Mekler, 1985).

Summary

Lifespan Development

The Scope of Developmental Psychology

■ Developmental psychologists study the many ways in which people change over the lifespan. Key themes in developmental psychology include understanding the stages of lifespan development, the nature of change, and the interaction between heredity and environment.

Genetic Contributions to Your Life Story

■ The genetic blueprint is determined at conception by the pairing of chromosomes from the biological parents. The chromosomes are made of DNA, which is arranged in thousands of segments called genes.

■ The genotype refers to the underlying genetic makeup; the phenotype refers to the traits that are displayed. When paired with a recessive gene, a dominant gene determines the trait that will be displayed. Recessive traits are displayed only if there are two recessive genes. Environmental conditions can influence the phenotype.

■ The 23rd pair of chromosomes determines whether male or female sexual characteristics will develop. Females have two X chromosomes, while males have an X and a Y chromosome. Females require two recessive genes for sex-linked recessive characteristics to be displayed. However, males require only one recessive gene for the same sex-linked recessive characteristic.

■ The Human Genome Project is a group scientific effort to map all the genes on human chromosomes.

Prenatal Development

■ During the nine months that make up the prenatal stage, the zygote develops into a full-term fetus. The prenatal stage includes the germinal period, the embryonic period, and the fetal period. The effect of teratogens is influenced by the timing of exposure, the type of teratogen, and maternal factors.

Development During Infancy and Childhood

■ Although physically helpless, the newborn is equipped with various reflexes and sensory capabilities that seem to enhance his chances for survival. Vision, hearing, and smell are attuned to interaction with caregivers. The brain develops rapidly after birth. The sequence of motor skill development is generally universal, although there is individual variation in the rate of development.

Aspects of Social and Personality Development in Infancy and Childhood

■ Thomas and Chess demonstrated that infants seem to be born with different temperaments. They identified three basic temperamental patterns: easy, difficult, and slow-to-warm-up. Other researchers have identified two basic temperamental patterns, inhibited and uninhibited. Temperamental qualities seem to have a biological basis and persist through life, although they can be modified by environmental influences.

■ According to attachment theory, the infant's ability to thrive is dependent on the quality of her attachment to caregivers. Secure attachment develops when parents are sensitive and responsive to the infant's needs; insecure attachment may develop when parents are insensitive to the infant's needs. Attachment is measured using the Strange Situation.

■ Infants seem to be biologically predisposed to learn language. At birth, infants can distinguish between the sounds that are present in any language, but soon become sensitized to the sounds of the language that is spoken in their home. Adults encourage language development in infants by using motherese.

■ The stages of language development include cooing and babbling. Deaf infants exposed to American Sign Language babble with their hands, demonstrating that infants are not just imitating the sounds that they hear. Other stages of language development are the one-word stage and the two-word stage. At every stage, the infant's comprehension vocabulary is larger than her production vocabulary.

■ According to Jean Piaget's theory of cognitive development, children progress through distinct cognitive stages, each of which represents a shift in how they think and understand the world. These stages are the sensorimotor stage (from birth to age two); the preoperational stage (from two to seven); the concrete operational stage (from seven to eleven); and the formal operational stage (from adolescence through adulthood).

■ Object permanence is acquired during the sensorimotor stage. Symbolic thought is acquired during the preoperational stage. Preoperational thought is egocentric, and characterized by irreversibility and centration. Thus, the preoperational child is unable to grasp the principles of conservation. Children become capable of logical thought during the concrete operational stage, but thinking is limited to tangible objects and events. During the formal operational stage, the adolescent can engage in logical mental operations involving abstract concepts and hypothetical situations.

- Piaget's theory has been criticized because: Piaget underestimated the cognitive abilities of infants and children; Piaget's stages are not as universal as he believed; and Piaget underestimated the influence of social and cultural factors on cognitive development.

- Cross-cultural research has demonstrated that the skills that are valued in a particular culture may develop earlier than skills that are not emphasized.

- The information-processing model is an alternative description of cognitive development that emphasizes fundamental mental processes and stresses that cognitive development is a process of continuous change.

Adolescence

- Adolescence marks the transition from childhood to adulthood. Contemporary psychologists no longer view adolescence as inevitably a time of "storm and stress."

- Adolescent–parent relationships are generally positive, although minor conflicts are common, especially in early adolescence. Relationships with peers become increasingly important. Peer influence is just as likely to be positive as negative.

- Erik Erikson's theory of psychosocial development stresses that every stage of life is marked by a particular psychosocial conflict. Identity versus identity diffusion is the conflict associated with adolescence; however, the process of identity formation does not end in adolescence.

- Lawrence Kohlberg described the type of reasoning used in making moral decisions. His theory of moral development includes the preconventional, conventional, and postconventional levels, with each level having two stages. Some researchers believe that moral reasoning is affected by both gender and culture.

Adult Development

- Although there are general patterns in adult development, individual variation becomes increasingly significant in adulthood. The three phases of adulthood are early adulthood, middle adulthood, and late adulthood.

- Genetics, environment, and an individual's lifestyle all influence physical changes during adulthood and aging. Vision, hearing, and the sense of smell become less acute with age.

- Love and work are two key themes that dominate adult development. Although friends continue to be important in adulthood, forming a committed, intimate relationship is one important task traditionally associated with early adulthood. Marital satisfaction tends to decline after the first child is born and to increase after children leave home. Family structures and relationships have become increasingly diverse in the United States. Although the combination of work, marital, and family roles can be demanding, especially for women, multiple roles can lead to increased personal satisfaction when the quality of experience in each role is high.

Late Adulthood and Aging

- Late adulthood does not necessarily involve a steep decline in physical and cognitive functioning. Mental abilities only begin to decline slightly at around age sixty, and these declines can be minimized or eliminated with an active and mentally stimulating lifestyle.

- Many older adults do not disengage from life, but remain socially active. According to the activity theory of aging, life satisfaction in late adulthood is highest when people maintain their previous levels of activity. Older adults differ in their optimal level of activity. Erikson identified the task of ego integrity as the key psychosocial task of old age.

The Final Chapter: Dying and Death

- Although commonly associated with old age, death can occur at any point in the lifespan. Anxiety about death tends to peak in middle adulthood and decrease in late adulthood. Elisabeth Kübler-Ross proposed a five-stage model of dying: denial, anger, bargaining, depression, and acceptance. However, individuals respond in diverse ways to impending death.

Key Terms

developmental psychology (p. 381)

chromosome (p. 383)

deoxyribonucleic acid (DNA) (p. 383)

gene (p. 383)

genotype (p. 384)

phenotype (p. 384)

dominant gene (p. 384)

recessive gene (p. 384)

sex chromosomes (p. 385)

sex-linked recessive characteristics (p. 385)

prenatal stage (p. 387)

germinal period (p. 387)

embryonic period (p. 387)

teratogens (p. 387)

fetal period (p. 388)

infancy (p. 389)

temperament (p. 391)

attachment (p. 392)

comprehension vocabulary (p. 397)

production vocabulary (p. 397)

sensorimotor stage (p. 399)

object permanence (p. 399)

preoperational stage (p. 400)

symbolic thought (p. 400)

egocentrism (p. 400)

irreversibility (p. 400)

centration (p. 400)

conservation (p. 401)

concrete operational stage (p. 401)

formal operational stage (p. 401)

information-processing model of cognitive development (p. 404)

adolescence (p. 405)

identity (p. 407)

moral reasoning (p. 409)

menopause (p. 412)

activity theory of aging (p. 420)

authoritarian parenting style (p. 423)

permissive parenting style (p. 423)

authoritative parents (p. 423)

induction (p. 424)

Key People

Mary D. Salter Ainsworth (b. 1913) Psychologist who devised the Strange Situation procedure to measure attachment; contributed to attachment theory.

Renée Baillargeon (b. 1954) Canadian-born American psychologist whose highly original studies of cognitive development in infancy, using visual rather than manual tasks, challenged Piaget's beliefs about the age at which object permanence first appears.

Noam Chomsky (b. 1928) American linguist who proposed that people have an innate understanding of the basic principles of language, which he called a "universal grammar."

Erik Erikson (1902–1994) German-born American psychoanalyst who proposed an influential theory of psychosocial development throughout the lifespan.

G. Stanley Hall (1844–1924) American psychologist who founded developmental psychology in the United States and who was instrumental in defining adolescence as a distinct developmental stage. (Also see Chapter 1.)

Lawrence Kohlberg (1927–1987) American psychologist who proposed an influential theory of moral development.

Jean Piaget (1896–1980) Swiss child psychologist whose influential theory proposed that children progress through distinct stages of cognitive development.

K. Warner Schaie (b. 1928) American psychologist who has conducted longitudinal research on lifespan development, particulary intellectual development in adulthood and late adulthood.

Lev Vygotsky (1896–1934) Russian psychologist who stressed the importance of social and cultural influences in cognitive development.

CONCEPT REVIEW 9.1   Page 386

1. False. The goal of the Human Genome Project is to map the genes on all the human chromosomes.
2. True
3. True
4. True
5. False. Females have an XX combination in the 23rd pair of chromosomes.
6. False. With the exception of the Y chromosome, each human chromosome contains thousands of genes.
7. False. The larger X chromosome contains many more genes than the small Y chromosome.

CONCEPT REVIEW 9.2   Page 391

1. c
2. a
3. c
4. d
5. a
6. b

CONCEPT REVIEW 9.3   Page 394

1. insecurely attached
2. easy
3. difficult
4. slow-to-warm-up

CONCEPT REVIEW 9.4   Page 402

1. D
2. B
3. A
4. C

CONCEPT REVIEW 9.5   Page 412

1. postconventional
2. preconventional
3. conventional

CONCEPT REVIEW 9.6   Page 421

1. True
2. True
3. False. Rather than gender, the critical factor for both men and women is the quality of experiences in different roles.
4. False. Older parents tend to adjust more easily to parenthood than younger parents.
5. False. The percentage has decreased significantly.
6. False. Marital satisfaction typically increases after the last child leaves home.

Chapter

10

Gender and Sexuality

Prologue: Soaring with Angels

Richard and I had been best friends since our paths first crossed in high school. Even then, Richard was extraordinary. He was good-looking and liked by everyone. He maintained almost a straight-A average in his classes. In our senior year, he was student body president. (To be perfectly honest, he beat me in the race for student body president.) And his talent as a diver had attracted the attention of college swimming coaches. Coming from a family of very modest means, Richard hoped for an athletic scholarship to attend college. He got one: The University of Arkansas awarded him a four-year athletic scholarship.

Richard met Becky when they were both freshman at the University of Arkansas. They seemed like a good match. Becky was smart, pretty, athletic, and had a wonderful sense of humor. They were also both Catholic, which greatly pleased Becky's parents. So, it came as no surprise when Richard and Becky announced their plans to marry after graduating. But I can't help thinking in retrospect that Richard's timing was deliberate when he asked me, in front of Becky, to be the best man.

"You're *sure* you want to marry this guy?" I half-jokingly asked Becky.

"Only if he takes nationals on the three-meter board," Becky quipped. As it turned out, Richard did place third on the three-meter board the following spring at the national collegiate swimming competition.

Three months before their wedding, Richard and I had the only argument we've ever had. At the time we had the argument, the word *gay* meant lighthearted and cheerful, so the word never came up in our heated exchange.

"What do mean, you haven't told her!?"

"I don't need to tell her about the past," Richard insisted.

"That's bull, Richard," I shouted. "This woman loves you and if you don't tell her about your homosexual urges, then you are marrying her under false pretenses."

"I do *not* have those feelings anymore!" Richard yelled back.

"If that's true, then tell her!" I demanded.

But it wasn't true, of course. Although Richard would not admit it to himself, he had only become adept at suppressing his sexual attraction to other men. At the time we had that argument, I was still the only person who knew that Richard harbored what he called "homosexual urges." Richard had first told me when we were juniors in high school. I was stunned. But Richard was also adamant that he did not want to feel the way he did. In fact, he felt ashamed and guilty. Back then, being homosexual carried much greater social stigma than it does today.

So when Richard and I were still in high school, we scraped up enough money to secretly send him to a psychologist for a few sessions. Despite our naive hopes for a quick "cure," Richard's troubling feelings remained. When he got to the University of Arkansas, Richard saw a counselor on a regular basis. After months of counseling, Richard believed he was capable of leading a heterosexual life.

Richard and Becky's wedding was magnificent. And, yes, I was the best man. After the wedding, they decided to stay in Fayetteville so Richard could start graduate school. The inevitable happened less than a year later. Becky called me.

"I'm driving to Tulsa tonight. Don, you've *got* to tell me what's going on," she said, her voice strained, shaking. And I did, as gently as I could.

Richard and Becky's marriage was annulled. In time, Becky recovered psychologically, remarried, and had two children. Her bitterness toward Richard softened over the years. The last time I talked with her, she seemed genuinely forgiving of Richard.

For his part, Richard gave up trying to be something he was not. Instead, he came to grips with his sexual orientation, moved to San Francisco, and became a co-owner of two health clubs. True to form, Richard quickly became a respected and well-liked member of San Francisco's large gay community. He eventually met John, an accountant, with whom he formed a long-term relationship. But after Richard's move to San Francisco, our friendship faded.

It was our twenty-year high school reunion that triggered Richard's unexpected call. When I told Richard I simply did not have the time to go to Sioux City, he suggested stopping in Tulsa on his way to the reunion to see me again and to meet Sandy and our daughter, Laura.

So on a warm May evening, Richard, Sandy, and I drank some margaritas, ate Chinese carry-out, and talked until midnight. Just as I expected, Sandy was quite taken with Richard. Indeed, Richard *was* a wonderful man—smart, funny, thoughtful, and sensitive. And, just as I expected, Laura, who was not quite two years old, was also enchanted by Richard. My only regret about that evening is that I did not take a picture of Richard sitting on the deck as Laura brought him first one toy, then another, then another. As it turned out, it would be the last time I saw Richard.

About a year after he visited us in Tulsa, Richard was killed in a hang-gliding accident. As he was soaring over the rocky California coast, Richard swerved to miss an inexperienced flyer who crossed his path in the air. Richard lost control of his hang-glider and was killed on impact when he plummeted into the rocky coastline.

A week later, more than 300 people crowded into St. Mary's Catholic Church in Sioux City, where Richard had been an altar boy in his youth. The outpouring of love and respect for Richard at the memorial service was a testament to the remarkable man he was.

What Richard's story illustrates is that who we are in this life—our identity—is not determined by any single characteristic or quality. Richard was gay, but that's not all Richard was, just as your sexual orientation is not the only characteristic that defines you. Nonetheless, Richard's story illustrates that a person's sexual orientation and gender identity are potent forces that shape and direct each of our lives, including the relationships we form. In this chapter, we'll explore these topics in detail. In the process, we'll come back to Richard's story.

Introduction

Gender and Sexuality

> Sex *refers to the biological characteristics that define male and female, while* gender *refers to the cultural and social meanings that are associated with femininity and masculinity. How do the terms* gender roles, gender identity, *and* sexual orientation *differ in meaning?*

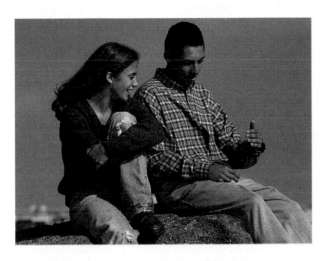

Life Themes: Gender and Sexuality From childhood to old age, gender identity and sexuality play an important role in our lives. How has your gender identity influenced the course of your life? The choices you've made? The relationships you've formed?

sex
(1) The biological category of male or female as defined by physical differences in genetic composition and in reproductive anatomy and function. (2) The behavioral manifestation of the sexual urge; sexual intercourse.

gender
The cultural, social, and psychological meanings that are associated with masculinity or femininity.

gender roles
The behaviors, attitudes, and personality traits that are designated as either masculine or feminine in a given culture.

gender identity
A person's psychological sense of being either male or female.

sexual orientation
The direction of a person's emotional and erotic attraction toward members of the opposite sex, the same sex, or both sexes.

As our description of Richard's life demonstrates, gender and sexuality are important components of everyone's personal destiny. As you read this chapter, we encourage you to think about how *your* life has been shaped by your sexual orientation and gender. Some of the information that we present in this chapter may challenge your preconceptions about sexual attitudes and behavior. Indeed, certain topics related to gender and sexuality are controversial for some people. Our primary goal in this chapter is to present research findings in an unbiased and evenhanded fashion.

Before we begin, we need to clarify terminology. The English language is less than precise in the arena of gender and sexuality. For example, the word *sex* can be used to describe an activity, as in the phrase "having sex." But the word *sex* is also used to indicate whether one is biologically male or female. In this sense, the term **sex** refers to biologically determined physical characteristics, such as differences in genetic composition and reproductive anatomy and function (Unger & Crawford, 1993).

In contrast, **gender** refers to the cultural and social meanings that are associated with maleness and femaleness (Eagly, 1995a). Think of "male" and "female" as designating the biological categories of *sex*, while "masculine" and "feminine" designate the social, cultural, and psychological categories of *gender*. As psychologists Rhoda Unger and Mary Crawford (1996) put it, "Gender is what culture makes out of the 'raw material' of biological sex."

Gender roles consist of the behaviors, attitudes, and personality traits that a given culture designates as either masculine or feminine (Bailey & Zucker, 1995). **Gender identity** refers to a person's psychological sense of being either male or female (Unger & Crawford, 1996). Finally, **sexual orientation** refers to whether a person's emotional and erotic attraction is directed toward members of the opposite sex, the same sex, or both sexes.

By the time most people reach adulthood, both gender identity and sexual orientation are well established. Often without our awareness, our behavior, attitudes, and aspirations have been strongly influenced by the gender-role expectations of our particular culture. But it's important to note that gender identity and sexual orientation can be independent of one another. For example, Richard's gender identity was very definitely male. He did not think of himself as anything but masculine. Nevertheless, his sexual orientation was toward other men, not women.

In this chapter, we'll take a close look at the development and consequences of male and female gender roles. We'll also examine how sexuality develops in our lives, and what's going in American bedrooms. Later in the chapter, we'll consider some of the ways in which the expression of sexuality can become disrupted and psychologically troubling. In the chapter Application, we'll look at how gender differences can short-circuit attempts to resolve conflicts in intimate relationships, and we'll show you how these communication problems can be overcome.

Gender Stereotypes and Gender Roles

Gender-role stereotypes are the beliefs and expectations that people hold about the characteristics and behaviors of each sex. How do men and women differ in terms of personality characteristics, cognitive abilities, and sexual attitudes and behaviors?

The beliefs that people have about the typical characteristics and behaviors of each sex are referred to as **gender-role stereotypes.** In our culture, gender-role stereotypes for men and women are very different. Women are thought (and expected) to be more emotional, nurturing, and patient than men. Men are thought (and expected) to be more aggressive, decisive, and mechanically minded than women. People often assume that gender stereotypes are derogatory toward women. In the United States, however, both men and women view the female gender-role stereotype more positively than the male gender-role stereotype (Swim, 1994; Unger & Crawford, 1996).

What about gender-role stereotypes in other cultures? In a survey of more than thirty cultures, psychologists John Williams and Deborah Best (1994, 1990) discovered a high degree of agreement on the characteristics associated with each sex (see Table 10.1). In general, the characteristics associated with males tended to be stronger and more active than the characteristics associated with females. In countries such as Japan, South Africa, and Nigeria, characteristics associated with the male stereotype were viewed more favorably than characteristics associated with the female stereotype. However, the reverse was true in other countries, such as Italy, Peru, and Australia.

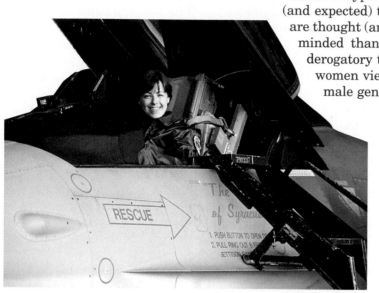

Gender Roles, Gender Stereotypes Lieutenant Susan Hart, a jet fighter pilot, is shown here in her F-16 jet. Many women have challenged traditional gender-role stereotypes in their choice of professions. How does Hart's occupation violate gender-role stereotypes?

Gender-Related Differences:
The *Opposite* Sex?

The notion that men and women are radically different is one that is routinely touted in the media. Consider John Gray's (1992) best-selling self-help book, entitled *Men Are from Mars, Women Are from Venus.* According to Gray:

> . . . *men and women differ in all areas of their lives. Not only do men and women communicate differently but they think, feel, perceive, react, respond, love, need, and appreciate differently. They almost seem to be from different planets, speaking different languages and needing different nourishment.*

When psychologists scientifically investigate the issue of gender differences, what do they find? *Are* men and women fundamentally different in *all* areas of their lives, as is often claimed in the popular media? Not at all. In fact, the exact opposite conclusion is much closer to the truth. In many aspects of behavior, including social, personality, and cognitive factors, men and women are very similar (see Hyde & Plant, 1995). And despite the claims of popular self-help books, men and women do not tend to *perceive* themselves as being diametrically opposite (Swim, 1994).

This doesn't mean that men and women are similar in every respect. Some significant differences between the sexes do exist (Eagly, 1995a). However, many psychologists (including those who write textbooks) are often reluctant to point out the gender differences that have been substantiated.

gender-role stereotypes
The beliefs and expectations that people hold about the typical characteristics, preferences, and behavior of men and women.

TABLE 10.1 Cross-Cultural Stereotypes of Men and Women

Characteristics Associated with Males		Characteristics Associated with Females	
active	loud	affected	modest
adventurous	obnoxious	affectionate	nervous
aggressive	opinionated	appreciative	patient
arrogant	opportunistic	cautious	pleasant
autocratic	pleasure-seeking	changeable	prudish
bossy	precise	charming	self-pitying
capable	progressive	complaining	sensitive
coarse	quick	complicated	sentimental
conceited	rational	confused	sexy
confident	realistic	curious	shy
courageous	reckless	dependent	softhearted
cruel	resourceful	dreamy	sophisticated
cynical	rigid	emotional	submissive
determined	robust	excitable	suggestible
disorderly	serious	fault-finding	superstitious
enterprising	sharp-witted	fearful	talkative
greedy	show-off	fickle	timid
hardheaded	steady	foolish	touchy
humorous	stern	forgiving	unambitious
indifferent	stingy	frivolous	understanding
individualistic	stolid	fussy	unintelligent
initiative	tough	gentle	unstable
interests wide	unfriendly	imaginative	warm
inventive	unscrupulous	kind	weak
lazy	witty	mild	worrying

SOURCE: Williams & Best, 1994, Table 1, p. 193.

Psychologists John Williams and Deborah Best (1994, 1990) surveyed gender stereotypes in thirty countries. They found a high level of agreement among these cultures. This table shows the items that were generally associated with the male and female gender roles. Williams and Best describe the characteristics associated with males as generally stronger and more active than those associated with women.

Why? Basically because some people are quick to equate a gender *difference* with a gender *deficiency*. For example, women's differences from men have historically been used to suggest that women are inferior to men (see Eagly, 1995b; Spence & Buckner, 1995). And, not surprisingly, the gender-difference-equals-inferiority argument has also been used to suggest that men are inferior to women.

Regardless of such inappropriate (and sexist) conclusions, we think it's important to present the findings on gender differences that have been supported by research. We've already noted some gender differences in previous chapters, such as our discussions of male/female differences in emotional expression (Chapter 8) and in friendship patterns (Chapter 9). But before we note other differences that seem to vary according to gender, two important qualifications need to be stressed.

First, the differences between men and women are *average* differences, not absolute differences. As with other generalizations in psychology, no single finding will apply to *all* men and women. For example, consider the general finding that men tend to think about sex more often than women (Michael & others, 1994). When you look at the actual data from one national survey in Figure 10.1, you quickly see that *some* women (19 percent) think about sex more often than almost half the male population. The point here is that on any given gender difference, there is a wide range of individual variation within each group. There is also quite a bit of overlap between men and women as groups.

Second, finding that a gender difference exists is one matter. It's another matter altogether to explain what *caused* that difference. For instance, consider the observation that women are more likely to wear earrings than

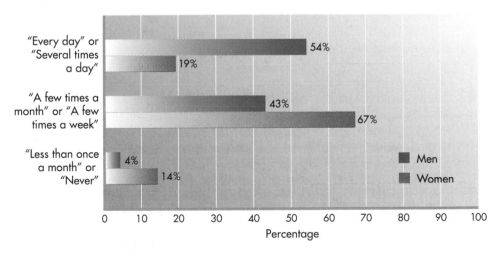

FIGURE 10.1 "How Often Do You Think About Sex?"
The percentages shown here were derived from a national survey based on a random sample of American adults between the ages of 18 and 59. As you can see, although *most* men seem to think about sex more than *most* women, there is overlap between the sexes in this respect.
(Michael & others, 1994.)

men. This finding, in itself, says nothing about the *cause* of that difference. Acknowledging that a gender difference exists does not automatically mean that such differences are "natural," "inevitable," or "unchangeable." Nor does it necessarily mean that the differences are biologically based.

Bearing these qualifications in mind, let's look at three areas of gender differences: personality, cognitive abilities, and sexual attitudes and behaviors. Although some differences do exist in these areas, men and women are more similar than they are different (Hyde & Plant, 1995; Tavris, 1992).

Personality Differences

On *most* personality characteristics, there are *no* significant average personality differences between men and women. For example, women and men are, on the average, very similar on such characteristics as impulsiveness and orderliness. However, there are two personality dimensions on which men and women consistently differ. The first is that women tend to be more *nurturant* than men. The second is that men tend to be more *assertive* than women (Feingold, 1994; Helgeson, 1994). As psychologist Alice Eagly (1995a) summarizes, "In general, women tend to manifest behaviors that can be described as socially sensitive, friendly, and concerned with others' welfare, whereas men tend to manifest behaviors that can be described as dominant, controlling, and independent."

Cognitive Differences

Is one sex smarter, more logical, or more creative than the other? In a word, no. On *most* cognitive abilities, there are *no* significant differences between males and females (Hyde, 1996; Hyde & Plant, 1995; Buss, 1995). However, once again, some limited differences do exist in this area. Here are some of the best-substantiated gender-related cognitive differences:

- **Verbal, reading, and writing skills.** Females consistently score much higher than males on tests of verbal fluency, reading comprehension, spelling, and, especially, basic writing skills (Eagly, 1995a; Hedges & Nowell, 1995). Although you rarely read about the "gender gap" in writing skills, researchers Larry Hedges and Amy Nowell (1995) point out, "The data imply that males are, on average, at a rather profound disadvantage in the performance of this basic skill."

- **Spatial skills.** Males outscore females on some, but not all, tests of spatial skills (Voyer & others, 1995). For example, males consistently outperform females on tests measuring the ability to mentally rotate three-dimensional figures (see Figure 10.2). On the other hand, women are significantly better than men at remembering the location of objects (Silverman & Eals, 1996).

- **Math skills.** On the average, males do slightly better than females on tests of mathematical ability (Hedges & Newell, 1995; Hyde, 1996).

The math difference deserves more comment. After all, hasn't everyone heard that "boys are much better than girls at math"? That assertion is simply not true. Over the last several decades, the so-called gender gap in mathematics has been steadily narrowing (see Murray, 1995; Hyde & Plant, 1995). Today, the average difference between males and females on national math tests is very small. However, it is true that twice as many males as females score in the very highest range—the top 3 percent—in math ability tests (Hedges & Nowell, 1995; Casey & others, 1995).

Women generally do better on tests of:

(a) Perceptual Speed

Which house on the right is exactly the same as the house on the far left?

(b) Verbal Fluency

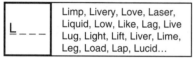

List as many words as you can think of that begin with the letter shown at left.

Men generally do better on tests of:

(c) Mental Rotation

Which item on the right is the rotated image of the item on the far left?

(d) Manipulating Mental Images

A hole has been punched through the folded sheet of paper on the far left. Which item on the right accurately shows where the holes will fall when the paper is unfolded?

FIGURE 10.2 Sample Test Items Favoring Females or Males
Women tend to outscore males on tests of verbal fluency, spelling, perceptual speed, and writing skills. Men, in contrast, tend to outscore women on some tests involving spatial skills, particularly mental rotation tasks.

(Kimura, 1992.)

Some researchers believe that cognitive differences between the sexes, such as the female advantage on verbal skills and the male advantage on spatial skills, are due to sex differences in brain function or organization (e.g., Kimura, 1993). For more on this controversial topic, see Critical Thinking Box 10.1, "'His' and 'Her' Brains?"

CRITICAL THINKING 10.1

"His" and "Her" Brains?

Sex Differences and the Brain Subtle gender differences in brain function and structure make headlines. This headline implies that new discoveries about the brain will explain "why men and women think differently." How valid is this conclusion?

On the average, men and women are very similar. But as we discussed in this chapter, researchers have consistently found differences in a few specific cognitive abilities. Some researchers, such as Canadian psychologist Doreen Kimura (1992), believe that these consistent differences are due to male–female differences in brain organization.

"Taken together," Kimura (1992) writes, "the evidence suggests that men's and women's brains are organized along very different lines from very early in life." How early? Kimura believes that the divergence begins prenatally, when male and female fetuses are exposed to different levels of sex hormones. Other researchers share her view (see Collaer & Hines, 1995).

The mass media have seized on the notion of sex differences in the human brain. The *Newsweek* cover reproduced here is just one example of the attention this issue has received in the popular press. Are there significant differences between male and female brain structure? And if so, do they demonstrate that "men and women think differently," as the headlines proclaim? Before we address those questions, let's consider just a few examples of what researchers have actually discovered:

- Men and women were found to use different parts of their brain when they read nonsense words and determined whether or not they rhymed (Shaywitz & others, 1995).

- The functions of the left and right cerebral hemispheres appear to be more integrated and symmetrical in women. Females tend to process information in both cerebral hemispheres. In men, the left and right hemispheres are more asymmetrical and more highly specialized for different tasks (Collaer & Hines, 1995; Springer & Deutsch, 1993).

- Some researchers have reported sex differences in the shape or number of neuronal fibers making up the *corpus callosum*, the structure that connects the left and right cerebral hemispheres (see Breedlove, 1994; Springer & Deutsch, 1993).

- Following comparable injuries to specific brain areas, men and women differ in the incidence of *aphasia*—speech and language disorders (Breedlove, 1994; Kimura, 1992). After a left-hemisphere stroke, men have a higher incidence of aphasia than women do, which suggests to some researchers that women's language functions are less dependent on the left hemisphere.

Do findings like these "explain" differences in cognitive abilities between the sexes? Do differences in brain structures demonstrate that men and women "think differently"? Before you swallow the headlines hook, line, and sinker, a more critical examination of the evidence is in order. Consider some additional points.

1. Studies showing anatomical and functional differences are typically based on very small samples. For example, the finding that men and women used different parts of their brain in a rhyming task involved just 19 men and 19 women (Shaywitz & others, 1995).

Perhaps the small sample sizes contribute to the inconsistent and contradictory findings in studies comparing male and female brains (Breedlove, 1994). For example, the difference in the corpus callosum is the most frequently reported sex difference. However, as psychologist Marc Breedlove (1994) notes, "The literature concerning the corpus callosum and possible sex differences in the corpus callosum in humans is filled with contradictory findings."

2. There are far more similarities than differences between male and female brains. Even when sex differences are found, there is often a great deal of overlap between men and women. For example, in the rhyming task cited above, 8 out of the 19 women displayed the *male* pattern of brain function rather than the female pattern (Shaywitz & others, 1995).

3. There is considerable individual variation in brain structure and function. The average range of difference *within* each sex is larger than the average difference *between* the sexes. That is, some individual females are found to be more similar to the average male pattern than to the average female pattern, and vice versa.

4. Other than a slight sex difference in weight, none of the sex differences in brain structure have been detected at birth or in the fetal brain (Breedlove, 1994). As we have repeatedly noted in this text, the brain's structure changes in response to experience (see Chapter 2). Therefore, it is entirely possible that brain differences in men and women could be due to different environmental and learning experiences.

5. Sex differences grab headlines. Similarities in male and female brains are much less likely to receive attention, even in scientific journals (Unger & Crawford, 1996).

Finally, just for the sake of argument, let's assume that a reliable sex difference in brain structure is found. For example, suppose the corpus callosum is consistently larger in one sex than in the other. What exactly does this mean? No one knows what the functional significance of such subtle differences in the corpus callosum—or any other brain structure—might be. As we stressed in Chapter 2, researchers are only beginning to unravel the incredibly complex and interrelated organization of the human brain. Even in animals whose brains have been studied for many years, researchers are still uncertain about the exact function of many brain areas (Gorski, 1995).

Undoubtedly, researchers will continue to uncover differences between male and female brains. As you encounter headlines proclaiming the significance of sex differences in the brain, the thoughtful reader should remember these key points: First, even the best-substantiated differences are small and inconsistent. Second, their meaning and practical significance are unclear. And third, the results are open to many different interpretations.

However, one thing *is* known with certainty: Male and female brains are *much* more alike than they are dissimilar. Given that, how well-justified do you consider the conclusion that subtle brain differences prove that "men and women think differently"?

Sexual Attitudes and Behaviors

Do men and women differ in their sexual attitudes, preferences, and behaviors? Psychologists Mary Beth Oliver and Janet Hyde (1993) conducted a meta-analysis to investigate that question. They combined and reanalyzed the results of over 170 previous studies that collectively involved more than 100,000 participants. Comparing males and females on a wide range of sexual attitudes and behaviors, Oliver and Hyde found that men and women were very similar on many dimensions. For example, there were no significant differences between men and women on measures of sexual satisfaction or incidence of oral sex.

In several areas, the data showed that certain male–female differences had become much less pronounced over the past few decades. In the 1960s, for example, men and women differed significantly on attitudes toward premarital sex. During the 1980s, this difference narrowed as both men and women became more accepting of premarital sex.

What differences did emerge? Oliver and Hyde's (1993) analysis found that men had more permissive sexual attitudes than women, including much greater acceptance of casual sex. Men also tended to have more sexual partners than women and experienced their first intercourse at an earlier average age. The most dramatic difference was the incidence of masturbation, with males reporting a higher incidence than women. Later in the chapter, we'll look at other patterns in the sexual behaviors and attitudes of men and women.

So there you have it: Men and women are *not* dramatically different. Women tend to be more nurturant, are much better at verbal, reading, and writing skills, and tend to be less sexually permissive. Men tend to be more assertive, are better at certain spatial skills, hold a slight (but shrinking) advantage on math skills, are more accepting of casual sex, and masturbate more often. In the chapter Application, we'll look at gender differences in communication style.

Even though men and women are more similar than dissimilar, there is a vast difference between growing up female and growing up male in most societies, including American society (see Unger & Crawford, 1996). In the next section, we'll look at how each of us learns to identify ourselves as either male or female.

Gender-Role Development:
Blue Bears and Pink Bunnies

Gender plays an important role in our culture. From birth, boys and girls are treated differently. What gender differences develop during childhood? How do social learning theory and gender schema theory explain the development of gender roles?

Being male or female *does* make a vast difference in our society. Put simply, males and females *are* treated differently. Within moments after birth, the newborn baby is "color coded" by gender. When our daughter was born, she was immediately wrapped in a pink blanket with bunnies, just like the other female infants in the nursery. The male infants were also color coded by gender—they had blue blankets with little bears. That, of course, is just the beginning.

When brand-new parents call family and friends to announce the birth of a new baby, what's the first question they are asked? In the overwhelming number of cases, the first question is, "Is it a boy or a girl?" (Intons-Peterson & Reddel, 1984). Given the importance that gender plays in most cultures, that's not a surprising finding. Infant boys and girls are virtually indistinguishable—except for their clothes, toys, and the furnishings in their room. If it weren't for the ruffled bonnet and pink booties, you wouldn't be able to tell that the infant in the grocery cart ahead of you was a girl from its size, appearance, or behavior.

Perhaps that's why the color coding that starts at birth continues throughout infancy and toddlerhood. In mainstream U.S. culture, girls are dressed in pink and other pastel colors, boys in blue and red (Shakin & others, 1985). Even disposable diapers come in blue for infant boys and pink for infant girls. Our friends Bill and Marcia described their efforts to raise their young daughter and infant son in a "gender-neutral, nonsexist environment." But, Marcia confessed, "I don't think I'm brave enough to dress Andrew in pink!"

Logically, of course, there is no reason why parents can't dress their newborn boys in pink overalls. The fact that they don't illustrates the pervasiveness and force of cultural and social expectations for appropriate male and female attire, attributes, and behavior.

When one-year-old infants are dressed identically, adults usually cannot tell male and female infants apart. However, in a series of studies, researcher T. G. R. Bower (1989) found that *other one-year-olds could* detect the difference. When one-year-old toddlers played with unfamiliar peers dressed in unisex clothes, the toddlers played more with toddlers of the same sex. And when watching videotapes of other toddlers, one-year-old girls stared more intently at films of other girls, and one-year-old boys looked more intently at films of other boys, no matter how the babies in the tapes were dressed.

Pink Bikes, Red Bikes Little boys and little girls clearly have a lot in common. All of these children are wearing blue jeans, and they all enjoy bicycling with their friends. Nevertheless, the girl's bike is pink with white tires, and the boy's bike is red with black tires. Why?

One-year-olds, of course, are unlikely to understand the concepts of "male" and "female." However, as research shows, one-year-olds are already sensitive to subtle gender differences in behavior and mannerisms (Poulin-Dubois & others, 1994). Clearly, then, gender awareness emerges at a very early age (Beal, 1994).

Gender Differences in Childhood Behavior:

Batman Versus Barbie

Roughly between the ages of two and three, children can identify themselves and other children as boys or girls, although the details are still a bit fuzzy to them (Fagot & others, 1992). Preschoolers don't yet understand that sex is determined by physical characteristics. This is not surprising, considering that the biologically defining sex characteristics—the sex organs—are hidden from view most of the time. Instead, young children identify the sexes in terms of external attributes, such as hairstyle, clothing, and activities.

A humorous story told by gender researcher Sandra Bem illustrates this point. Bem (1989) describes going along with her preschool son Jeremy's desire to wear barrettes to nursery school. Another little boy at the school repeatedly insisted that Jeremy "must be a girl, because only girls wear barrettes." So, Jeremy attempted to prove that he really was a boy by dropping his pants. The other little boy was not impressed. "Everybody has a penis, only girls wear barrettes," he countered.

From about the age of eighteen months to two years, sex differences in behavior begin to emerge. These differences become more pronounced throughout early childhood. Toddler girls play more with soft toys and dolls, and ask for help from adults more than toddler boys do. Toddler boys play more with blocks and transportation toys, such as trucks and wagons. They also play more actively than girls do (see Stern & Karraker, 1989).

Roughly between the ages of two and three, preschoolers start acquiring gender-role stereotypes for toys, clothing, household objects, games, and work (Poulin-Dubois & others, 1994; Huston, 1983). From the age of about three on, there are consistent gender differences in preferred toys and play activities. Boys play more with balls, blocks, and toy vehicles. Girls play more with dolls, domestic toys, dressing up, and art activities (Turner & Gervai, 1995). By the age of three, children have developed a clear preference for toys that are associated with their own sex. This tendency continues throughout childhood (see Figure 10.3).

Children also develop a strong preference for playing with members of their own sex—girls with girls and boys with boys (Thorne & Luria, 1986). It's not uncommon to hear boys refer to girls as "icky" and girls refer to boys as "mean" or "rough." And, in fact, preschool boys *do* play more roughly than girls, cover more territory, and play in larger groups (Block, 1983; Thorne,

FIGURE 10.3 Children's Letters to Santa Claus
Researchers John Richardson and Carl Simpson (1982) analyzed 750 letters to Santa Claus from boys and girls aged 5 to 9 years. They found sharp gender differences in the types of toys requested. However, more girls than boys asked for "opposite-sex" toys, reflecting girls' greater willingness to play with toys associated with the other sex. About 15 percent of girls asked for sports equipment or "spatial-temporal" toys like construction sets. In contrast, less than 1 percent of boys asked for a doll.
(Based on Richardson & Simpson, 1982.)

Separate Worlds? In childhood, boys tend to play in groups and prefer competitive games. In contrast, girls tend to establish close relationships with one or two other girls, and cement their friendship by sharing thoughts and feelings. How might such gender differences affect intimate relationships in adolescence and adulthood?

1986). Throughout the remainder of childhood, boys and girls play primarily with members of their own sex (Powlishta, 1995a, 1995b).

According to psychologist Carole Beal (1994), boys and girls almost seem to create separate "social worlds," each with its own style of interaction. They also learn particular ways of interacting that work well with other peers of the same sex. For example, boys learn to assert themselves within a group of male friends. Girls tend to establish very close bonds with one or two friends. Girls learn to maintain those close friendships through compromise, conciliation, and verbal conflict resolution. As we'll discuss in the chapter's Application, these gender differences in styles of social interaction persist into adulthood.

Children are far more rigid than adults in their beliefs in gender-role stereotypes. Children's strong adherence to gender stereotypes may be a necessary step in developing a gender identity (Powlishta, 1995a; Stangor & Ruble, 1987). Boys are far more rigid than girls in their preferences for toys associated with their own sex. Their attitudes about the sexes are also more rigid than those held by girls (Feinman, 1981). As girls grow older, they become even more flexible in their views of sex-appropriate activities and attributes, but boys become even less flexible (Katz & Ksansnak, 1994).

Girls' greater flexibility toward gender roles may reflect society's greater tolerance of girls who cross gender lines in attire and behavior. A girl who plays with boys, or who plays with boys' toys, may develop the grudging respect of both sexes. But a boy who plays with girls or with girls' toys may be ostracized by *both* boys and girls (Thorne, 1986). Girls are often proud to be labeled a "tomboy," but for boys, being called a "sissy" is the ultimate insult (Doyle & Paludi, 1995). One explanation may be that children of both sexes tend to value the male role more highly than the female role (Unger & Crawford, 1996).

As we've seen, there are very few significant differences between the sexes in either personality traits or intellectual abilities. Yet children's behavior mirrors, in many ways, the gender-role stereotypes that are predominant in our culture.

Explaining Gender Roles:
Two Contemporary Theories

Many theories have been proposed to explain the differing patterns of male and female behavior in our culture and others (see Unger & Crawford, 1996; Doyle & Paludi, 1995). Gender theories have included findings and opinions from anthropology, sociology, neuroscience, medicine, philosophy, political science, economics, and religion. (Let's face it, you probably have a few opinions on the issue yourself.) We won't even attempt to cover the full range of ideas. Instead, we'll describe two of the most influential psychological theories: social learning theory and gender schema theory. (In Chapter 11, on personality, we will discuss Freud's ideas on the development of gender roles.)

Social Learning Theory: Learning Gender Roles

social learning theory of gender-role development
The theory that gender roles are acquired through the basic processes of learning, including reinforcement, punishment, and modeling.

Based on the principles of learning, **social learning theory** contends that gender roles are learned through *reinforcement, punishment,* and *modeling.*

"Just One of the Guys" Today, girls receive more encouragement to compete in sports, including such previously male-dominated sports as soccer, basketball, and softball, than they did just a decade ago. A girl who successfully competes in a traditionally male game may earn the respect of both sexes.

From a very young age, children are reinforced or rewarded when they display gender-appropriate behavior and punished when they do not. For example, psychologists Beverly Fagot and Richard Hagan (1991) observed mothers and fathers interacting with their children in their homes. They found that eighteen-month-old boys received more positive reactions from their parents for playing with male-typed toys and for exhibiting aggressive or assertive behavior. In contrast, eighteen-month-old girls received more positive responses for attempts to communicate with their parents, while boys received more negative reactions for such attempts.

To what degree do such parental behaviors influence the development of gender differences? The effect is not as great as you might think. Psychologists David Lytton and David M. Romney (1992) conducted a meta-analysis of nearly 200 studies of parents' different treatment of boys and girls. They found that the actual effects of parental socialization in many areas of gender differences are relatively small. Yes, parents *do* tend to reinforce and encourage gender-appropriate play. But for the most part, parents treat their male and female children rather similarly.

If parents have only a minimal effect, how do children acquire their understanding of gender differences? Children are exposed to many other sources of information about gender roles, including television, children's books, and observation of same-sex adult role models. Hence, children also learn gender differences through *modeling,* in which they observe and then imitate the sex-typed behavior of significant adults and older children (Beal, 1994). By observing and imitating such models—whether it's Mom cooking, Dad fixing things around the house, or a male superhero rescuing a helpless female on television—children come to understand that certain activities and attributes are considered more appropriate for one sex than the other.

Gender Schema Theory: Constructing Gender Categories

Gender schema theory, developed by **Sandra Bem** (b. 1944), incorporates some aspects of social learning theory. However, Bem (1981) approaches gender-role development from a more strongly cognitive perspective. In contrast to the relatively passive role played by children in social learning theory, **gender schema theory** contends that children *actively* develop mental categories (or *schemas*) for masculinity and femininity (Martin & Halverson, 1981). That is, children actively organize information about other people and appropriate behavior, activities, and attributes into gender categories. Saying that "trucks are for boys and dolls are for girls" is an example of a gender schema.

According to gender schema theory, children, like many adults, look at the world through "gender lenses" (Bem, 1987). Gender schemas influence how people pay attention to, perceive, interpret, and remember gender-relevant behavior. Gender schemas also seem to lead children to perceive members of their own sex more favorably than members of the opposite sex (Powlishta, 1995a).

You've Come a Long Way, Baby? Children's books continue to reinforce gender stereotypes, sometimes in subtle ways. In this picture book for preschoolers, published in 1990, a little girl follows her big brother's lead. The boy is shown actively digging in the mud, happily getting dirty with his dog, bat, and ball nearby. In contrast, the little girl, dressed in pink, stays clean as she nurtures her kitten.

Who wants to sleep, anyway?
Not us! We want to be
busy, busy, busy!

Like schemas in general (see Chapter 6), children's gender schemas do seem to influence what they notice and remember. For example, five-year-olds were shown pictures of children engaged in activities that violated common gender stereotypes, such as girls playing with trucks and boys playing with dolls (Martin & Halverson, 1983, 1981). A few days later, the five-year-olds "remembered" that the boys had been playing with trucks and the girls with dolls!

Children also readily assimilate new information into their existing gender schemas. In one study, four- to nine-year-olds were given boxes of gender-neutral gadgets, such as hole punches (Bradbard & others, 1986). But some gadgets were labeled as "girl toys" and some as "boy toys." The boys played more with the "boy gadgets," and the girls played more with the "girl gadgets." A week later, the children easily remembered which gadgets went with each sex, and remembered more information about the gadgets that were associated with their own sex. Simply labeling the objects as belonging to boys or to girls had powerful consequences for the children's behavior and memory—evidence of the importance of gender schemas in learning and remembering new information.

Gender schemas also include a broad range of qualities and attributes that are less concrete, such as associating "gentleness" with females and "toughness" with males. Consider a study by Beverly Fagot and her colleagues (1992). Preschoolers were first shown a picture of a woman with a small girl and a picture of a man with a small boy, then asked to match drawings of various items to either picture: "Does this belong to the mommy and the little girl or to the daddy and the little boy?"

Some of the drawings were of objects like hammers and brooms that are conventionally associated with one sex rather than the other. These represented realistic associations that the children might have learned through observation. But other images were only *metaphorically* associated with one sex rather than the other, such as butterflies (female) or bears (male).

Fagot and her colleagues (1992) found that the children made both the concrete *and* the metaphoric associations to the appropriate sex. Children consistently matched the fierce-looking bear with males and the fluffy cat with females. Yet, as the researchers point out, "Few men keep bears, and cats do not belong only to women." Thus, beyond the concrete associations the children might have learned through reinforcement or observation, even preschoolers seemed to be aware of the *underlying meanings* of gender stereotypes.

Given the gender-schematized world we grow up in, it's not surprising that gender stereotypes remain so pervasive and influential. Are gender stereotypes as rigid as they once were? When our daughter Laura was about twenty months old, a substitute teacher at Laura's preschool commented to Sandy, "Laura is so feminine. It's really surprising how much she likes to play outside. And she's so fearless for a little girl. She'll climb higher than any of the boys!"

Startled by the comment, Sandy asked, "*Feminine*? She isn't even two years old yet! What do you mean by that?"

"Oh, she's so pretty and delicate-looking. And so gentle and affectionate with the other children. You know, *feminine*," the teacher replied.

The teacher's schema for a "feminine" girl—pretty, delicate, gentle, affectionate—did *not* include fearlessness and liking the outdoors, qualities that belonged to the teacher's schema for "masculinity." When children are routinely exposed to such comments and expectations, it's hard to avoid the effects of gender labeling.

gender schema theory
The theory that gender-role development is influenced by the formation of schemas, or mental representations, of masculinity and femininity.

Aspects of Gender and Sexuality

Decide which of the following terms applies to each of the examples below: gender schema theory, sex, gender-role stereotypes, social learning theory.

1. When John was born, the doctor saw his penis and said, "Mrs. McGillicuddy, it's a boy." _____

2. Michael thinks that women are more nurturing, patient, and emotional than men, and that men have greater mechanical aptitude and are more aggressive, logical, and rational than women. His expectations reflect _____.

3. Whenever Boris picked up a doll, he was scolded. Whenever he tried to throw a football to his father, his father beamed and praised him. As Boris grew up, he ignored dolls and took every opportunity to get involved in sports. _____

4. When Sarah first met Greg and Martha, Greg was carrying a doll and Martha was wearing a toy tool belt. The second time Sarah saw Greg, she asked, "Where's your tool belt?" _____

Human Sexuality

Multiple factors are involved in understanding human sexuality. What are the four stages of human sexual response? How does sexual motivation differ for lower and higher animals? What biological factors are involved in sexual motivation?

On the one hand, sexual feelings and relationships are very private and deeply personal. On the other hand, sexual behavior is very much in the public spotlight. Advertising and entertainment emphasize sexual themes. Sex-related issues and topics are regularly reported in the news media. And daytime talk shows compete for guests who engage in extreme and unusual sexual practices. Like it or not, virtually every aspect of human sexuality is a public topic in American society today.

Whether the media-manufactured images of sex in the United States are accurate, however, is a very different matter. From the standpoint of psychology, an accurate understanding of sexuality is essential to developing a comprehensive picture of behavior. After all, sexual feelings and relationships are an important part of being human.

As you'll see throughout the remainder of this chapter, the scientific study of sexuality is multidimensional. Biological, psychological, social, and cultural factors must all be taken into account to understand human sexuality. By the end of the chapter, you'll discover just how well the media images of sex in the United States stack up against the actual data.

Media Images of Sex and Sexuality Sexual themes and images are often used to sell products and movies and to boost TV ratings. How accurate are media images of human sexuality?

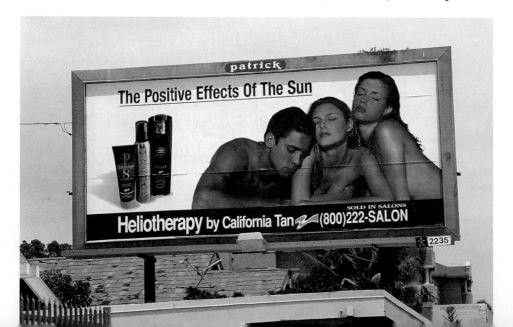

First Things First:

The Stages of Human Sexual Response

The human sexual response cycle was first mapped by sex research pioneers **William Masters** (b. 1915) and **Virginia Johnson** (b. 1925) during the 1950s and 1960s. Up until the 1950s, information about sexual response had been gathered by observing the behavior of different animal species. However, Masters and Johnson felt that a more direct approach was needed to further the understanding of human sexual anatomy and physiology. Thus, in the name of science, Masters and Johnson observed hundreds of people engage in more than 10,000 episodes of sexual activity in their laboratory. Their findings, published in 1966, indicated that the human sexual response can be described as a cycle with four stages.

As you read the descriptions of these stages, keep in mind that the transitions between stages are not as precise or abrupt as the descriptions might lead you to believe. Moreover, the duration of time spent in any particular stage can vary on different occasions of sexual interaction.

Stage 1: Excitement

The *excitement phase* marks the beginning of sexual arousal. Sexual arousal can occur in response to sexual fantasies or other sexually arousing stimuli, physical contact with another person, or masturbation. In both sexes, the excitement stage is accompanied by a variety of bodily changes in anticipation of sexual interaction. There is a rapid rise in pulse rate and blood pressure. The rate of breathing increases. Blood shifts to the genitals, producing an erect penis in the male and swelling of the clitoris in the female. The female's vaginal lips expand and open up, and her vagina becomes lubricated in preparation for intercourse. Her nipples and breasts may also become enlarged, and the nipples become erect and more sensitive.

Stage 2: Plateau

In the second, *plateau phase,* physical arousal builds as pulse and breathing rates continue to increase. The penis becomes fully erect and sometimes secretes a few drops of fluid (which may contain active sperm). The testes increase in size. The clitoris withdraws under the clitoral hood, but remains very sensitive to stimulation. The vaginal entrance tightens, putting pressure on the penis during intercourse. Vaginal lubrication continues. During the excitement and plateau stages, the degree of arousal may fluctuate up and down (Masters & others, 1995). During the plateau stage, the firmness of the male's erection may increase and decrease, and so may the female's degree of vaginal lubrication.

Stage 3: Orgasm

Orgasm is the third and shortest phase of the sexual response cycle. During orgasm, blood pressure and heart rate reach their peak. The muscles in the vaginal walls and the uterus contract rhythmically, as do the muscles in and around the penis as the male ejaculates. Other muscles may contract as well, such as those in the face, arms, and legs. Both men and women describe the subjective experience of orgasm in similar—and very positive—terms (see Masters & others, 1995).

The vast majority of men experience one intense orgasm. But many women are capable of experiencing multiple orgasms. If sexual stimulation continues following orgasm, women may experience additional orgasms within a short period of time.

Pioneers of Sex Research: William Masters and Virginia Johnson Masters and Johnson broke new ground with their scientific study of sexual behavior in the 1960s. Along with documenting and describing the human sexual response, they also developed many innovative techniques that are still used in sex therapy.

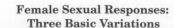

**Female Sexual Responses:
Three Basic Variations**

Typical Male Sexual Response

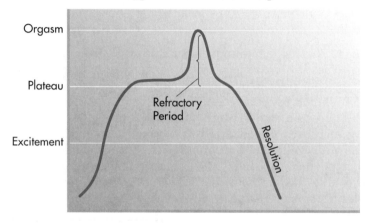

FIGURE 10.4 The Male and Female Sexual Response Cycle

The top figure depicts the three basic variations of the female sexual response. Pattern 1 shows multiple orgasms. Pattern 2 shows sexual arousal that reaches the plateau stage but not orgasm, followed by a slow resolution. Pattern 3 depicts brief reductions in arousal during the excitement stage, followed by rapid orgasm and resolution. The bottom figure depicts the most typical male sexual response, in which orgasm is followed by a refractory period.

(Masters & Johnson, 1966.)

Stage 4: Resolution

Following orgasm, both sexes tend to experience a warm physical "glow" and a sense of well-being. Arousal slowly subsides and returns to normal levels in the *resolution phase*. The male experiences a *refractory period,* during which he is incapable of having another erection or orgasm. The length of the refractory period varies; for one man it may last a matter of minutes, for another several hours. As men become older, the length of the refractory period tends to increase.

So, there you have it—the clinical, scientific description of the physiological changes that occur before, during, and after orgasm. Although it is simplified somewhat, Figure 10.4 depicts the basic pattern of sexual response for men and women. Somehow it lacks the lusty appeal of an erotic passage from a Danielle Steele best seller or D. H. Lawrence's (1928) classic novel, *Lady Chatterley's Lover.* Nonetheless, the early work of Masters and Johnson remains a landmark in the study of human sexuality.

What Motivates Sexual Behavior?

Psychologists consider the drive to have sex a basic human motive (Mook, 1996). But what exactly motivates that drive? Obviously, there are differences between sex and other basic motives, such as hunger. Engaging in sexual intercourse is essential to the survival of the human species, but it is not essential to the survival of any specific person. In other words, you'll die if you don't eat, but you won't die if you don't have sex (you may just *think* that you will).

In most animals, sexual behavior is biologically determined and triggered by hormonal changes in the female. During the cyclical period known as *estrus,* a female animal is fertile and receptive to male sexual advances. Roughly translated, the Greek word *estrus* means "frantic desire." Indeed, the female animal will often actively signal her willingness to engage in sexual activity—as the owner of any unneutered female cat or dog that's "in heat" can testify. In many, but not all, species, sexual activity only takes place when the female is in estrus (Rissman, 1995).

As you go up the evolutionary scale, moving from relatively simple to more sophisticated animals, sexual behavior becomes less biologically determined and more subject to learning and environmental influences (Mook, 1996). Sexual behavior also becomes less limited to the goal of reproduction. For example, in some primate species, such as monkeys and apes, sexual activity can occur at any time, not just when the female is fertile. In these species, sexual interaction serves important social functions, defining and cementing relationships among the members of the primate group (Feder, 1984).

One rare species of chimplike apes, the bonobos of the African country of Zaire, exhibits a surprising variety of sexual behaviors (de Waal, 1995). While most animals copulate, or have sex, with the male mounting the female from behind, bonobos often copulate face-to-face. Bonobos also engage in oral sex and intense tongue kissing. And bonobos seem to like variety.

Along with having frequent heterosexual activity, whether the female is fertile or not, bonobos also engage in homosexual and group sex.

Emory University psychology professor Frans de Waal (1995), who has extensively studied bonobos, observes that their frequent and varied sexual behavior seems to serve important social functions. Sexual behavior is not limited to fulfilling the purpose of reproduction. Among the bonobo, sexual interaction is used to increase group cohesion, avoid conflict, and decrease tension that might be caused by competition for food. According to de Waal (1995), the bonobos' motto seems to be "Make love, not war."

In humans, of course, sexual behavior is not limited to a female's fertile period. Nor is the motivational goal of sex limited to reproduction. While a woman's fertility is regulated by monthly hormonal cycles, these hormonal changes seem to have little or no effect on a female's sexual motivation (Davidson & Myers, 1988). Even when a woman's ovaries, which produce the female sex hormone *estrogen,* are surgically removed or stop functioning during menopause, there is little or no drop in sexual interest. In many nonhuman female mammals, however, removal of the ovaries results in a complete loss of interest in sexual activity. If injections of estrogen and other female sex hormones are given, the female animal's sexual interest returns (see Mook, 1996; Feder, 1984).

In male animals, removal of the testes (castration) typically causes a steep drop in sexual activity and interest, although the decline is more gradual in sexually experienced animals. Castration causes a significant decrease in levels of *testosterone,* the hormone responsible for male sexual development. When human males experience lowered levels of testosterone due to illness or castration, a similar drop in sexual interest tends to occur, although the effects vary among individuals. Some men continue to lead a normal sex life for years, while others quickly lose all interest in sexual activity (Feder, 1984). In castrated men who experience a loss of sexual interest, injections of testosterone restore the sexual drive.

Testosterone is also involved in female sexual motivation. Most of the testosterone in a woman's body is produced by her adrenal glands. If these glands are removed or malfunction, causing testosterone levels to become abnormally low, sexual interest often wanes (Mook, 1996; Gray & Gorzalka, 1980). When supplemental testosterone is administered, the woman's sex drive returns (Feder, 1984). Thus, in *both* men and women, sexual motivation is biologically influenced by body levels of the hormone testosterone.

Sexual behavior is also influenced by cultural factors. For more on the role of culture in sexual behavior see Culture and Human Behavior Box 10.2, "'Normal' Sexual Behavior: A Tale of Two Cultures."

The Bonobo of Zaire Bonobos demonstrate a wide variety of sexual interactions, including face-to-face copulation, kissing, and sexual interaction among same-sex pairs. Sexual behavior is not limited to reproduction, but seems to play an important role in maintaining peaceful relations among members of the bonobo group. As Frans de Waal (1995) writes, "For these animals, sexual behavior is indistinguishable from social behavior."

CULTURE AND HUMAN BEHAVIOR 10.2

"Normal" Sexual Behavior: A Tale of Two Cultures

What's considered "normal" sexual behavior is greatly influenced by culture and society (Davis & Whitten, 1987). For example, anthropologist John Messenger (1972) studied the sexual practices of the people living on a small island off the coast of Ireland. Among these people, deep kissing, breast fondling, and oral-genital contact were unknown. Because nudity was considered shameful, bathing was avoided. Even married couples were extremely modest in front of each other. Married couples changed clothes only in private, sometimes while under the blankets of their bed.

So much secrecy surrounded sexual activity on this small island that Messenger (1972) was unable to determine how frequently sexual interaction occurred. When sexual activity did occur, it took place in the dark with both the man and women wearing underwear or clothes. Sexual foreplay was limited, and intercourse lasted only a few minutes, with the male always on

top. Both males and females expressed amazement at the idea that women might enjoy sex, much less experience orgasm.

Now consider the very different cultural norms of the people living on the South Pacific island of Mangaia (Marshall, 1972). At puberty, both sexes receive detailed instructions about sexual techniques from older adults. Adolescent girls and boys are encouraged to have sex with several partners to ensure that they will find a compatible marriage partner. By being able to please his partner, a male gains social prestige. By age eighteen, it's not unusual for the typical Mangaian to have sex two or three times a night, several nights a week.

The wide variation among societies in what constitutes acceptable sexual behavior should not obscure the fact that *every* society controls sexuality to some extent. In all cultures, sexual behavior is regulated by social norms and customs. Many societies, including our

own, have formal laws governing sexual behavior. For example, virtually every society forbids *incest*—sexual relations between people who are closely related by blood or adoption. However, cultures vary in defining the degree of relatedness that constitutes an incestuous relationship.

Cultural norms of acceptable sexual behavior can also change over time. For example, during the 1940s and 1950s, only about 20 percent of American women and about 50 percent of American men under the age of nineteen had engaged in premarital sex (Kinsey & others, 1948, 1953). Those percentages have changed dramatically in the last four decades. Today, approximately 70 percent of women and 80 percent of men are sexually experienced by the age of nineteen (Michael & others, 1994). Clearly, what constitutes "normal" sexual behavior can vary from one culture to another, and from one time period to another within a given culture.

Sexual Orientation:

The Elusive Search for an Explanation

Sexual orientation refers to whether a person is attracted to members of the opposite sex, the same sex, or both sexes. Why is sexual orientation sometimes difficult to define? What factors have been associated with sexual orientation?

Given that biological factors seem to play an important role in motivating sexual desire, it only seems reasonable to ask if biological factors also play a role in *sexual orientation*—whether a person is sexually aroused by members of the same sex, the opposite sex, or both sexes (Bailey & Zucker, 1995). A *heterosexual* is sexually attracted toward individuals of the other sex, a *homosexual* toward individuals of the same sex, and a *bisexual* toward individuals of both sexes. Technically, the term *homosexual* can be applied to either males or females. However, female homosexuals are usually called *lesbians*. Male homosexuals typically use the term *gay* to describe their sexual orientation.

Sexual orientation is not nearly as cut and dried as many people believe. Some people *are* exclusively heterosexual or homosexual, but others are less

U.S. Congressman Barney Frank and His Companion Herb Moses Frank and Moses have shared a home since 1987. Frank realized he was gay in early adolescence. Was heterosexuality ever an option for him? As Frank (1996) explains, "I wished it was. But it wasn't. I can't imagine that anybody believes that a 13-year-old in 1953 thinks, 'Boy, it would really be great to be part of this minority that everybody hates and to have a really restricted life.' You can't make yourself a different person. I am who I am. I have no idea why."

easy to categorize. Many people who consider themselves to be heterosexual have had a homosexual experience at some point in their lives (Seidman & Rieder, 1994). The opposite is also true. Many people, like our friend Richard in the chapter's prologue, consider themselves to be homosexual but have had heterosexual relationships. The key point here is that there is not always a perfect correspondence between a particular person's sexual identity, sexual desires, and sexual behaviors (Laumann & others, 1994).

Determining the number of people who are homosexual or heterosexual is problematic for several reasons (Rogers & Turner, 1991). First, survey results vary depending on how the researchers define the terms *homosexual, heterosexual,* and *bisexual.* Second, gays and lesbians are not distributed evenly throughout the population. In rural areas and small towns, gays, lesbians, and bisexuals make up about 1 percent of the population. But in the largest U.S. cities, approximately one out of eight people (or 12 percent) consider themselves to be gay, lesbian, or bisexual (Michael & others, 1994). Thus, estimates of the size of the gay and lesbian population may vary, depending on:

- How researchers structure survey questions
- How they define the criteria for inclusion in gay, lesbian, or bisexual categories
- Where the survey is conducted
- How survey participants are selected

More important than the exact number of gays and lesbians is the recognition that gays and lesbians constitute a significant segment of the adult American population. According to the most reasonable estimates, it's safe to say that between 7 million and 15 million American men and women are gay or lesbian (Patterson, 1995a).

What Determines Sexual Orientation?

Despite considerable research on this question, psychologists and other researchers cannot say with certainty why people become homosexual or bisexual. For that matter, psychologists don't know exactly why people become *heterosexual* either. Still, research on sexual orientation has pointed toward several general conclusions, especially with regard to homosexuality.

Evidence from twin studies suggests that genetics plays a role in determining a homosexual orientation (Gladue, 1994; LeVay & Hamer, 1994). For example, psychologists Michael Bailey and Richard Pillard (1991) compared the incidence of male homosexuality among pairs of identical twins (who have identical genes), fraternal twins (who are genetically as similar as any two nontwin siblings), and adoptive brothers (who have no common genetic heritage but shared the same upbringing). The researchers found that the closer the degree of genetic relationship, the more likely it was that both brothers would be homosexual. Specifically, both brothers were homosexual in 52 percent of the identical twins, 22 percent of the fraternal twins, and 11 percent of the adoptive brothers.

Bailey and his colleagues (1993) discovered very similar results in twin studies of lesbians. In 48 percent of identical twins and 16 percent of fraternal twins, both sisters were lesbian, as compared to only 6 percent of adoptive sisters. While intriguing, such genetic studies are subject to criticisms about methodology and other issues (see Byne, 1994; Byne & Parsons, 1993). Furthermore, since only half of the identical twins were both homosexual, it's clear that genetic predisposition alone cannot explain sexual orientation. Nevertheless, these studies and others support the notion that sexual orientation is at least partly influenced by genetics (Gladue, 1994).

Another biological factor that has been investigated is differences in brain structure between heterosexuals and homosexuals (LeVay & Hamer, 1994). Neurobiologist Simon LeVay (1991) discovered a small but significant difference between male heterosexuals and homosexuals in a tiny cluster of neurons in the *hypothalamus,* which is known to be involved in sexual behavior. In male homosexuals and heterosexual women, the cluster was only half the size as in heterosexual men.

LeVay speculates that this tiny structure may be involved in determining sexual orientation (LeVay & Hamer, 1994). However, LeVay also carefully points out that there is no way of knowing if this difference in brain structure *causes* homosexual behavior in men. Conceivably, it might be the other way around—homosexual behavior might cause the difference in brain structure.

In general, the only conclusion we can draw from these studies is that some biological factors are *correlated* with a homosexual orientation (Byne, 1994). As we've stressed, correlation does not necessarily indicate causality, only that two factors *seem* to occur together. So stronger conclusions about the role of genetic and biological factors in determining sexual orientation await more definitive research findings (Baumrind, 1995; Gladue, 1994).

What about early life experiences? Is homosexuality due to abnormal parenting or early homosexual experiences? Alan Bell and his colleagues (1981) conducted a comprehensive study investigating these and other popular beliefs regarding the causes of homosexual orientation. On the basis of in-depth interviews of almost 1,000 homosexual men and women, and a comparison group of about 500 heterosexual men and women, they came to the following conclusions:

- Homosexuality is *not* due to an unpleasant early heterosexual experience, such as being sexually abused during childhood by a member of the opposite sex.

- Homosexuals are *not* more likely than heterosexuals to report a first sexual encounter with a member of the same sex, such as being seduced by an older member of the same sex.

- Homosexuality is *not* the result of an abnormal relationship between the parents and the child, such as having a father who is an inadequate male role model or having an overly dominant mother.

In short, Bell and his colleagues found *no* consistent differences between homosexual and heterosexual adults in their patterns of early experiences. It seems very unlikely, therefore, that homosexuality is caused by certain parenting styles, an unpleasant early heterosexual experience, or a pleasant early homosexual experience.

Bell and his colleagues (1981) also found that sexual orientation was determined before adolescence and long before the beginning of sexual activity. Gay men and lesbians typically became aware of homosexual feelings about three years before they engaged in any such sexual activity. In this regard, the pattern was very similar to that of heterosexual children, in whom heterosexual feelings are aroused long before the child expresses them in some form of sexual behavior.

Some researchers now believe that sexual orientation is established as early as age six (Strickland, 1995; Melton, 1989). Once sexual orientation is established, whether heterosexual or homosexual, it is highly resistant to change (American Psychiatric Association, 1994). The vast majority of homosexuals would be unable to change their orientation even if they wished to do so, just as the majority of heterosexuals would be unable to change their orientation even if *they* wished to do so. Thus, it's a mistake to assume that homosexuals have deliberately "chosen" their sexual orientation, any more than heterosexuals have. Indeed, when Richard was in high school, he would gladly have "chosen" to be heterosexual if the matter had been that simple.

It seems clear that no single factor determines whether people identify themselves as homosexual, heterosexual, or bisexual (Golombok & Tasker, 1996). Psychological, biological, social, and cultural factors are undoubtedly involved in determining sexual orientation. However, researchers are still unable to pinpoint exactly what those factors are and how they interact. As psychologist Bonnie Strickland (1995) points out, "Sexual identity and orientation appears to be shaped by a complexity of biological, psychological, and social events. Gender identity and sexual orientation, at least for most people, especially gay men, occur early, are relatively fixed, and are difficult to change." As Richard learned, changing his sexual orientation was simply not possible.

Lesbian Parents Are the children of gay or lesbian parents likely to become homosexual themselves? Apparently the children of homosexual parents are no more likely to be gay or lesbian in adulthood than children raised by heterosexual parents (Bailey & others, 1995; Golombok & Tasker, 1996). In fact, research studies to date show few differences among the children of gay, lesbian, or heterosexual parents (Strickland, 1995).

Homosexuality in itself is no longer considered a sexual disorder by clinical psychologists or psychiatrists (American Psychiatric Association, 1994). Many research studies have also found that homosexuals who are comfortable with their sexual orientation are just as well adjusted as heterosexuals (see Strickland, 1995).

Like heterosexuals, gays and lesbians can be found in every occupation and at every socioeconomic level in our society. And, like heterosexuals, many gays and lesbians are involved in long-term, committed, and caring relationships (Kurdek, 1995; Patterson, 1995b). Children who are raised by gay or lesbian parents are as well adjusted as children who are raised by heterosexual parents (Flaks & others, 1995; Patterson, 1995c, 1992). Furthermore, children who are raised by gay or lesbian parents are no more likely to be gay or lesbian in adulthood than are children who are raised by heterosexual parents (Golombok & Tasker, 1996; Bailey & others, 1995).

CONCEPT REVIEW 10.2

Elements of Human Sexuality and Sexual Orientation

1. Malcolm is a twenty-four-year-old heterosexual. His twenty-year-old brother, Morris, is homosexual. The brothers differ in their
   a. gender roles   **c.** sexual orientation
   b. gender identity   **d.** gender schemas

2. Jill and Joan are identical twins. Jill is a lesbian. What is the likelihood that Joan will also be homosexual?
   a. About a 50 percent chance.
   b. Almost a 100 percent chance.
   c. Less than a 10 percent chance.
   d. There is no correlation between genetic factors and sexual behavior.

3. Because of testicular cancer, twenty-five-year-old Arnie had to have his testicles removed. Research suggests that
   a he will very likely become homosexual.
   b. he may experience a decreased interest in sexual activity.
   c. he is very unlikely to experience any change in his sexual interest.
   d. injections of testosterone will have absolutely no effect on his sex drive.

4. What conclusions can be drawn concerning biological factors and homosexuality?
   a. Biological differences in the hypothalamus cause homosexuality.
   b. Sexual orientation is completely determined by genetics.
   c. Homosexuality is caused by insufficient amounts of testosterone.
   d. Some biological factors are correlated with homosexual orientation.

5. Maxwell is a homosexual. It is likely that
   a. he experienced some early childhood sexual abuse by a female.
   b. his first sexual experience occurred in childhood with a male.
   c. his mother was overly domineering and his father was ineffectual and provided him with a poor masculine role model.
   d. his sexual orientation was determined before adolescence and before any sexual activity occurred.

Sexual Behavior over the Lifespan

The development of sexuality begins in infancy. What elementary forms of sexuality appear during infancy and childhood?

Perhaps because sexual behavior tends to be a private matter, it's understandable that people (psychologists included) are curious about what other people do—and don't do—sexually. The mass media tend to offer overheated images of what people are supposedly doing. If you believe the not-so-subtle media messages, everyone (except you) has such an active, steamy, and varied sex life that you can't help wondering how anyone (except you) ever finds the time to get their laundry done.

So to prevent unnecessary despondency, let's deal with the "everybody's-sex-life-is-better-than-mine" issue at the beginning of this section. *Are* the media images accurate? Here's what sexual behavior expert Robert T. Michael and his colleagues (1994) have to say about the matter:

> *The public image of sex in America bears virtually* no *relationship to the truth. The public image consists of myths, and they are not harmless, for they elicit unrealistic and at worst dangerous misconceptions about what people do sexually. These resulting false expectations can badly affect self-esteem, marriages, relationships, even physical health.*

Possibly you recall Michael's name from Chapter 1. Michael, along with co-researcher Edward O. Laumann and their colleagues at the University of Chicago, conducted the *National Health and Social Life Survey (NHSLS)*—a state-of-the-art, scientifically constructed national survey of adult sexual behavior in America (Laumann & others, 1994; Michael & others, 1994). In Chapter 1, we described how participants were selected and how the research was conducted. Throughout this section, we'll rely on this landmark survey for help in accurately answering the "Who's doing what, when, how often, and with whom" questions about human sexuality.

As with other kinds of behavior, patterns of sexual behavior vary over the lifespan. So before we focus on the specifics of adolescent and adult sexuality, we'll start by looking at the emergence of sexuality during infancy and childhood.

Sexuality During Infancy and Childhood:
Discovering the Basics

Sexuality does not just magically appear with the onset of puberty during adolescence. Rather, the capacity of the human body to show reflexive sexual responses is present at birth. For example, female newborns can reflexively experience vaginal lubrication, and newborn males can reflexively experience firm erections. In fact, ultrasound studies have shown that male infants can experience erections while still in the womb (see Masters & others, 1995).

Infants commonly show reflexive signs of sexual activation while nursing or being bathed or diapered. Infants as young as three or four months of age will smile or coo as they engage in *genital play,* fondling their own genitals in a very elementary form of masturbation (Nevid & others, 1995). By the first birthday, genital play is a common occurrence, especially when the little one is being bathed.

Signs of sexual activation or genital play should not cause alarm in the parent, because such behaviors reflect completely *normal* developmental patterns. It's equally important to stress that the infant or young child is *not* experiencing sexual arousal or expressing a desire for erotic contact. Rather, the child has simply discovered, quite naturally, that such stimulation feels good (Masters & others, 1995).

During early childhood, roughly ages two to six, the child often becomes increasingly curious about his or her own body and its functions. Small children commonly explore their body parts while in the bathtub or on the toilet. Young children also become keenly attuned to parental attitudes, especially negative attitudes, concerning nudity, genital touching, and genital exploration (Hyde & Delamater, 1997). Gradually, the young child begins to notice the anatomical differences between males and females.

Although some parents are psychologically uncomfortable with their children's emerging interest in their own little bodies, human sexuality experts encourage parents to relax about such matters (see Masters & others, 1995). For example, there's really no reason to become frantic because your four-year-old walks in while you're just stepping out of the shower. One study found that childhood exposure to occasional instances of parental nudity, such as when the parents were getting dressed, was not associated with later sexual problems (Lewis & Janda, 1988).

Awareness of sexual matters expands during middle and late childhood. With each advancing year from about the age of five onward, children tend to show increased interest in exploring sexual topics (Goldman & Goldman, 1982). By about age eight, most children are aware that certain behaviors produce erotic feelings. Sexual curiosity is on the rise during the late childhood years, setting the stage for the attainment of sexual maturity during adolescence (Masters & others, 1995).

Sexuality During Adolescence

Sexual maturation begins during puberty in early adolescence. What are primary and secondary sex characteristics? What factors influence the onset of menarche? What are the effects of the timing of puberty? What characterizes the sexual relationships that develop in adolescence?

Nature seems to have a warped sense of humor when it comes to **puberty,** the physical process of attaining sexual maturation and reproductive capacity that begins during the early adolescent years. First, as you may well remember, physical development during adolescence sometimes proceeds unevenly (see Berger, 1995; Katchadourian, 1977). Feet and hands get bigger before legs and arms do. The torso typically develops last, so shirts and blouses sometimes don't fit quite right. And the left and right sides of the body can grow at different rates. The resulting lopsided effect can be quite distressing: one ear, foot, testicle, or breast may be noticeably larger than the other. Thankfully, such asymmetries tend to even out by the end of adolescence.

Second, nature's timetable seems to be quite whimsical. While one adolescent boy has a baritone voice, is shaving, and looks like he's ready to enlist in the Marines, another still sings soprano with the church choir and has less facial hair than the average cantaloupe. And because her best friend has been wearing a bra for almost a year, a female adolescent shuns her undershirts and hounds her mother for a "training" bra. Finally, nature literally gives girls a head start on puberty, which seems grossly unfair if you happen to be a sixth-grade boy who dwells much closer to ground level than his taller female classmates.

Just Friends? Interest in and affection for the opposite sex often begins in the early stages of adolescence. Because girls mature earlier than boys, they may be taller and heavier than boys of the same age.

puberty
The stage of adolescence in which an individual reaches sexual maturity and becomes physiologically capable of sexual reproduction.

Girls Get a Head Start These two eighth-graders are the same age! In terms of the progress of sexual and physical maturation, girls are usually about two years ahead of boys.

TABLE 10.2 The Typical Sequence of Puberty

Girls	Average Age
Ovaries increase production of estrogen and progesterone	9
Internal sex organs begin to grow larger	9½
Breast development begins	10
Peak height spurt	12
Peak muscle and organ growth, including widening of hips	12½
Menarche (first menstrual period)	12½
First ovulation (release of fertile egg)	13½
Boys	**Average Age**
Testes increase production of testosterone	10
External sex organs begin to grow larger	11
Production of sperm and first ejaculation	13
Peak height spurt	14
Peak muscle and organ growth, including broadening of shoulders	14½
Voice lowers	15
Facial hair appears	16

SOURCE: Based on data in Berger, 1995, and Brooks-Gunn & Reiter, 1990.

Physical and Sexual Development

Although nature's game plan for physical change during adolescence may seem haphazard, puberty actually tends to follow a predictable sequence for each sex. These changes are summarized in Table 10.2. Basically, the physical changes of puberty fall into two categories.

Internally, puberty involves the development of the **primary sex characteristics,** which are the sex organs that are directly involved in reproduction. For example, the female's uterus and the male's testes enlarge in puberty. Externally, development of the **secondary sex characteristics,** which are not directly involved in reproduction, signal increasing sexual maturity. Secondary sex characteristics include changes in height, weight, and body shape, appearance of body hair, voice changes, and, in girls, breast development.

As you can see in Table 10.2, females are typically about two years ahead of males in terms of physical and sexual maturation. For example, the period of marked acceleration in weight and height gains, called the **adolescent growth spurt,** occurs about two years earlier in females than in males. Much to the chagrin of many sixth- and seventh-grade males, it's not uncommon for their female classmates to be both heavier and taller than them.

The statistical averages in Table 10.2 are informative, but—because they are only averages—they cannot convey the normal range of individual variation in the timing of pubertal events (see Brooks-Gunn & Reiter, 1990). For example, a female's first menstrual period, which is termed **menarche,** typically occurs around age twelve or thirteen, but menarche may take place as early as age nine or ten or as late as age sixteen or seventeen. For boys, the testicles typically begin enlarging around age eleven or twelve, but the process can begin before age nine or after age fourteen. Thus, it's entirely possible for some adolescents to have already completed physical and sexual maturation before their classmates have even begun puberty. Yet they would all be considered well within the normal age range for puberty.

What determines when puberty will begin? Both genetics and environmental factors play a role in the timing of puberty. Girls often experience menarche at about the same age as their mothers did (Brooks-Gunn & Reiter, 1990). And, not surprisingly, the timing of pubertal changes tends to be closer for identical twins than for nontwin siblings.

Environmental factors, such as nutrition and health, also influence the onset of puberty (Hamburg & Takanishi, 1989). Generally, well-nourished and healthy children begin puberty earlier than do children who have experienced serious health problems or inadequate nutrition. In fact, as living standards and health care have improved, the average age for puberty has steadily decreased in the United States over the last century. For example, 150 years ago the average age of menarche in the United States was sixteen. Today it is about twelve and a half (Hamburg & Takanishi, 1989; Beal, 1994). In recent years, however, the trend toward earlier puberty seems to have slowed.

Body size and degree of physical activity are also related to the timing of puberty. In general, heavy children begin puberty earlier than lean children do. Girls who are involved in physically demanding athletic activities, such as gymnastics, figure skating, dancing, and competitive running, can experience delays in menarche of up to two years beyond the average age (Brooks-Gunn, 1988).

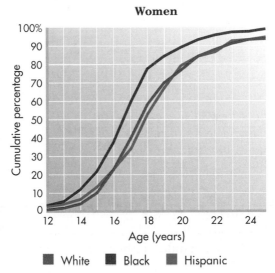

■ White   ■ Black   ■ Hispanic

FIGURE 10.5 Cumulative Percentages of People Who Have Had Sexual Intercourse, by Gender, Race, and Age

This figure is based on the responses of NHSLS participants who had reached their twenty-fifth birthday at the time of the interview. Although there is some variation by race and gender, about 90 percent of each group has had intercourse by age 22.

(Michael & others, 1994, Fig. 7, p. 91.)

primary sex characteristics
Sexual organs that are directly involved in reproduction, such as the uterus, ovaries, penis, and testicles.

secondary sex characteristics
Sexual characteristics that develop during puberty and are not directly involved in reproduction but differentiate between the sexes, such as male facial hair and female breast development.

adolescent growth spurt
The period of accelerated growth during puberty, involving rapid increases in height and weight.

menarche
A female's first menstrual period, which occurs during puberty.

The Timing of Changes: Early Versus Late Maturation

Adolescents tend to be keenly aware of the physical changes they are experiencing as well as the *timing* of those changes as compared to their peer group. Most adolescents are "on time," meaning that the maturational changes are occurring at roughly the same time for them as for others in their peer group. But some adolescents are "off time," experiencing maturation earlier or later than the majority of their peers.

Being off time has different consequences for boys and girls. For boys, early maturation is generally a plus. As compared to late-maturing boys, early-maturing boys tend to have the advantage in terms of popularity, social maturity, academic achievement, and athletics. However, early-maturing girls tend to be more likely than late-maturing girls to have negative feelings about their body image and pubertal changes, such as menarche. Compared to late-maturing girls, early-maturing girls are less likely to have received factual information concerning development. They may also feel embarrassed by unwanted attention from older males (Brooks-Gunn & Reiter, 1990). The positive or negative effects associated with early or late maturation are largely temporary. Eventually, of course, the late-maturers catch up with the early-maturers. By late adolescence, the individual physical differences in maturation that seemed so noticeable in the sixth or seventh grade have mostly evened out.

The Emergence of Sexual Relationships

Romantic and sexual relationships become increasingly important throughout the adolescent years. During early and middle adolescence, the physical changes of puberty prime the adolescent's interest in sexuality. But social and cultural factors also influence when, why, and how an adolescent initiates sexual behaviors (Brooks-Gunn & Furstenberg, 1989; Katchadourian, 1990). The beginning of dating, for example, coincides more strongly with social expectations and norms, such as when friends begin to date, than with an adolescent's degree of physical maturation (Garguilo & others, 1987).

Generally, age is a good predictor of when teenagers typically begin various sexual behaviors. With increasing age, there is a corresponding increase in the number of adolescents who have engaged in such sexual activities as kissing or petting (Katchadourian, 1990; Buhrmester & Furman, 1987). As you can see in Figure 10.5, the number of adolescents who have experienced sexual intercourse also corresponds closely to age (Michael & others, 1994). Between the ages of fifteen and eighteen, there is a sharp increase in the cumulative percentages of those who have had intercourse. Although it varies somewhat by race and gender, by age nineteen approximately 70 percent of females and 80 percent of males have lost their virginity.

It's often assumed that parents play a key role in the sexual socialization of their adolescent children, but there is usually little direct communication between parents and children regarding sexual matters (Hyde & Delamater, 1997; Katchadourian, 1990). Fathers, in particular, are not very likely to be involved in the sexual education of their children. When parents do respond to their children's questions about sexuality and reproduction, it is usually on a single occasion rather than as part of a continuing discussion about sexuality (Roberts, 1980).

It's not very surprising, then, that an adolescent's peer group gradually replaces his or her family as a source of sexual information (and misinformation), attitudes, and values (Katchadourian, 1990). For example, one study found that adolescents were just as likely to consult parents as peers about contraceptives. But on questions about sexual behavior, such as masturbation or homosexuality, peers were identified as the preferred source of information twice as often as parents (Coles & Stokes, 1985).

Sexuality During Adolescence

Apply the correct term to each of the examples below: (A) late maturation, (B) menarche, (C) puberty, (D) adolescent growth spurt, (E) early maturation.

_____ **1.** Jeanette, a typical twelve-year-old female, has noticed that her breasts have started to develop.

_____ **2.** Brian is only eleven years old, but is already taller than most thirteen-year-old boys.

_____ **3.** Noreen is almost thirteen and has just had her first menstrual period.

_____ **4.** During his fourteenth year, Adam grew almost five inches in height.

Sexuality in Early and Middle Adulthood

Intimate, committed relationships are typically established during early adulthood. What characterizes the sexual behavior patterns of adults? What are some important aspects of sexual relationships in late adulthood?

For most Americans, the onset of adulthood marks a commitment to the task of establishing long-term, intimate relationships. During their twenties, most men and women develop an intimate relationship with another adult. By the age of thirty, most Americans are part of a couple—either married or living with someone (Michael & others, 1994).

The NHSLS generated a mountain of data on the sexual practices of American adults between the ages of eighteen and fifty-nine. Our discussion is necessarily brief. We'll confine ourselves to the NHSLS findings on several key questions about the sexual practices of American adults. In doing so, we hope to dispel some of the media-manufactured myths about adult sexual behavior.

How Many Sex Partners Do People Have?

The notion that people today, especially younger people, have more sex partners than people did twenty or thirty years ago is fundamentally accurate. Among people aged thirty to fifty, about half have had five or more sexual partners. In contrast, only about a third of those over age fifty have had five or more sexual partners (Laumann & others, 1994).

Why the difference between age groups in the number of sexual partners? The vast majority of adults in the fifty to fifty-nine age range had their first sexual experience in the context of marriage. In contrast, only about a third of today's young adults had their first sexual experience in the context of marriage (Michael & others, 1994). Young adults today tend to become sexually active at an earlier age and are marrying at a later average age. Hence, younger people today tend to have more sexual partners than members of older generations.

Now consider a slightly different issue: the number of sexual partners in the past year. The vast majority of people—about 80 percent—had either _one_ sexual partner or _none_ in the previous year (see Figure 10.6). Why so few sexual partners in the last year? In a word, marriage. Marriage continues to be a cornerstone of American society as well as a major developmental milestone

	Number of Sex Partners in Past Twelve Months			
	0	1	2 to 4	5+
Total	12%	71%	14%	3%
By Gender				
Men	10	67	18	5
Women	14	75	10	2
By Age				
18–24	11	57	24	9
25–29	6	72	17	6
30–34	9	73	16	2
35–39	10	77	11	2
40–44	11	75	13	1
45–49	15	75	9	1
50–54	15	79	5	0
55–59	32	65	4	0

FIGURE 10.6 Number of Sex Partners During the Previous Year
In this chart, you can see that regardless of age or gender, about 80 percent of the people reported having had one or no sexual partners during the previous year.

(Adapted from data in Michael & others, 1994, Table 6, pp. 102–103.)

In real life, the unheralded, seldom discussed world of married sex is actually the one that satisfies people the most. It may not be an exciting picture of sex in Ameica, but if we look at the social forces that push us toward married life, it is an understandable, if not predicted, picture.

Robert T. Michael, 1994

for most people on the trek through adulthood. As people become adults, they experience considerable social pressure to find a partner and marry. Doing so confers numerous benefits, not the least of which is the social, legal, and moral acceptance of the sexual partnership.

By the age of thirty, about 90 percent of Americans have married. Regardless of age or number of previous partners, once most couples marry or start cohabiting, they feel strongly committed to being faithful to each other. As Michael and his colleagues (1994) explain:

> *Marriage regulates sexual behavior with remarkable precision. No matter what they did before they wed, no matter how many partners they had, the sexual lives of married people are similar. Despite the popular myth that there is a great deal of adultery in marriage, our data and other reliable studies do not find it. Instead, the vast majority are faithful while the marriage is intact.*

How Often Do People Have Sex?

Perhaps the widest disparity between the media images and the NHSLS results involves the issue of how often people have sex. Put simply, the media images that frequent, frolicking sex is "normal" do not reflect what is going on in America's bedrooms.

Here's what the NHSLS found: One-third of American adults have sex with a partner two or more times per week; one-third have sex a few times per month; and one-third have sex a few times a year or not at all (Michael & others, 1994). When the data are combined for all adults between eighteen and fifty-nine, men have sex an average of about seven times per month, while women have sex an average of about six times per month (Laumann & others, 1994). So any way you look at it, the most frequent activity in America's bedrooms is sleep, not sex.

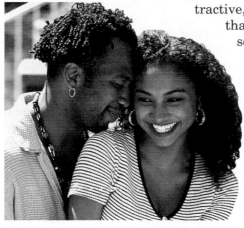

Intimacy, Love, and Sexuality in Adulthood Forming a long-term, committed relationship with another person is a key task of early adulthood. For many couples, the bonds of love and intimacy established in early adulthood last a lifetime.

Which Americans have the most active sex lives? Those young, attractive, footloose, swinging singles, right? Wrong. The fact is that married or cohabiting couples have the most active sex lives (Michael & others, 1994). If you think about it, this finding makes sense. Sexual activity is strongly regulated by the availability of a sex partner. Being a member of a stable couple is the social arrangement most likely to produce a readily accessible sexual partner.

Are people happy with their sex lives? The vast majority of the NHSLS respondents—about 85 percent—reported that they were physically and emotionally satisfied with their sexual relationships (Laumann & others, 1994). Part of the explanation for this high percentage is that in today's society there is considerably less social pressure to endure an unhappy marriage "until death do you part." Hence, those who are sexually dissatisfied with their relationship are likely to separate or get divorced—and try again with someone else. The net result is that most Americans are happily married or cohabiting.

What Do People *Actually* Do When They Have Sex?

Vaginal intercourse is nearly universal as the most practiced sexual activity among heterosexual couples. What about other practices? More than two-thirds of Americans have either given or received *oral sex* at some point in their lives. Fewer men (26 percent) and women (20 percent) have ever engaged in *anal sex* (that is, a penis inserted in the partner's anus) (Laumann & others, 1994).

What Would People *Like* To Do Sexually?

Given that most Americans seem to be having pretty traditional sex, you may be wondering whether they'd like to be a little more adventurous. After all, researchers have found that people do have sexual fantasies about a wide range of activities (see In Focus Box 10.3). So what do most people find appealing, and is that any different from what they actually do?

Although the list of potential sexual practices is varied, people prefer to stick with the tried and true. The most preferred sexual activities, in descending order for both sexes, are as follows: (1) having vaginal intercourse; (2) watching the partner undress; (3) receiving oral sex; and (4) giving oral sex.

In some ways, the flip side of the coin is more revealing. What do people find *un*appealing? Regardless of age, at least 90 percent of women found no appeal in the following sexual practices: (1) being forced to do something sexual; (2) forcing someone to do something sexual, (3) receiving anal intercourse; (4) having a same-gender sex partner; and (5) having sex with a stranger. With the exception of sex with a stranger, at least 90 percent of men also found these sexual practices unappealing. Other sexual practices that the majority of people do not find appealing include having group sex, using a vibrator or dildo (an object used as a substitute for an erect penis), and watching other people engage in sexual activity (Michael & others, 1994).

Sexual Relationships in Late Adulthood

The notion that sexual interest and potency disappear the day you become eligible for Medicare is a far cry from reality. One survey found that among adults age seventy and over, more than half reported engaging in sexual activity at least once a week (Brecher, 1984).

Even though there does not appear to be an upper age limit to sexuality, aging does have some effects on sexual behavior (see Masters & others, 1995). Older men and women take longer to become sexually aroused and achieve orgasm. For women, vaginal lubrication typically occurs more slowly, sometimes necessitating the use of lubricants during intercourse. For men, erections tend to be less firm, and longer refractory periods follow orgasm. Despite these physical changes, the majority of sexually active senior adults report a high level of sexual enjoyment (Brecher, 1984).

For older women, probably the biggest obstacle to enjoying sexual relations throughout old age is the lack of a sexual partner (see Figure 10.7). At age sixty, there are 89 men for every 100 women. By age seventy-five, the ratio is down to 68 men per 100 women (U.S. Bureau of the Census, 1995). Thus, the number of people with no sexual partner steadily climbs as people get older (Michael & others, 1994).

FIGURE 10.7 Where'd All the Guys Go?
Starting during the third decade of life, women outnumber men. By the eighth decade of life, women outnumber men by a margin of almost two to one. Not surprisingly, the number of older women without a sexual partner increases dramatically past retirement age.
(Michael & others, 1994.)

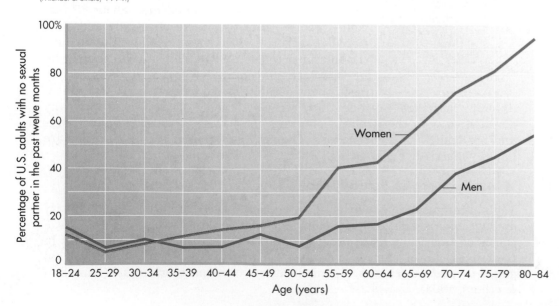

IN FOCUS 10.3

Everything You Wanted to Know About Sexual Fantasies

The brain is the most erotic organ in the human body. After all, the brain plays a pivotal role in the expression of human sexuality. What people think about and imagine influences how they behave sexually. And, in turn, people's sexual behavior can influence the content of their *sexual fantasies*—erotic or sexually arousing mental images (Leitenberg & Henning, 1995). In the realm of human sexuality, the mind–body connection is definitely a two-way street.

We experience sexual fantasies in the private theater of our own minds, but psychologists have discovered that sexual fantasies are a nearly universal human phenomenon. Using checklists and questionnaires, researchers have been able to answer various questions about people's sexual fantasies. In this box, with the help of an excellent research summary by University of Vermont psychologists Harold Leitenberg and Kris Henning (1995), we tackle some of the most intriguing questions about this private human experience.

When and How Often Do People Have Sexual Fantasies?

Sexual fantasies tend to begin during the adolescent years, and almost all adult men and women (95 percent) report having had sexual daydreams. It is very common for both men and women occasionally to engage in sexual fantasies during intercourse. But compared to women, men report a higher incidence of sexual fantasies during masturbation and nonsexual activities. In short, men tend to think about sex more often than women.

What Do People Have Sexual Fantasies About?

If you accept the notion that any fantasy, sexual or not, is based to some degree on life experiences, the three most common types of sexual fantasies that men and women have won't surprise you. They are: (1) reliving an exciting sexual experience; (2) imagining that you are having sex with your current partner; and (3) imagining that you are having sex with a different partner.

Do Male and Female Sexual Fantasies Differ?

There are some well-substantiated differences. First, men tend to fantasize themselves in active roles—that is, doing something sexual to their partner. In contrast, women tend to imagine themselves in sexually passive roles—that is, having something sexual done to them.

Second, men tend to have sexual fantasies with more explicit imagery, often involving specific sexual positions or anatomical details. Women are more likely to imagine romantic themes, including warm, loving feelings about their partner and details about the romantic ambiance of the scene.

Third, guys are more likely to imagine having sex with multiple partners. As Leitenberg and Henning (1995) put it, "Fantasizing about having sex with multiple partners at the same time appears to be more consonant with the male stereotype of being a 'superstud' than with the female stereotype of wanting a close, loving, monogamous relationship."

Are Sexual Fantasies Psychologically Unhealthy? Are They a Sign of Sexual Frustration or Dissatisfaction?

In a word, no. Neither of these notions has been supported by the research. In fact, the research has led to just the opposite conclusion: The people who engage in sexual fantasies the most often are those who exhibit the *least* number of sexual problems and the *least* sexual dissatisfaction.

Nonetheless, some people are troubled by their sexual fantasies. About 25 percent of people experience some degree of guilt over having sexual fantasies. The essence of this guilt is often the belief that sexual fantasies are immoral, will harm the relationship with their partner, or indicate that something is wrong with the person.

What About "Dominance" and "Submission" Sexual Fantasies?

Men are more likely to fantasize dominance themes (forcing someone to do something sexual) while women are more likely to report submission themes (being forced to do something sexual). However, it's important to stress that the fact that a woman might find submission fantasies sexually arousing does *not* indicate a desire to *actually* be forced into sexual submis-

sion, much less assaulted or raped (see Bond & Mosher, 1986; Kanin, 1982). As we note in the chapter, almost no women or men find appealing the idea of actually being forced to do something sexual or actually forcing someone to do something sexual (Michael & others, 1994).

Isn't This a Contradiction?

Not really. First, any kind of fantasy, whether it's sexual or not, allows us to imagine possibilities that may have little probability of occurring. Fantasy provides you with your own internal, private improvisational theater. As the lead character, director, and set designer, you control the plot, action, and dialogue without taking any *real* risks.

Given that, let's go back to the issue of female submission fantasies. The typical female submission fantasy is *not* one of being brutally forced to do something against the woman's will. Instead, as researchers Susan Bond and Donald Mosher (1986) point out, the typical female submission fantasy is one of an attractive man being overwhelmed by the woman's irresistible charms as she puts up a minimal effort to resist his sexual advances, finally allowing the handsome cad to have his way with her. Does this fantasy sound the least bit familiar? It should. It is a standard sexual fantasy that has been played out in many romantic novels and movies. Such fantasies have *nothing* in common with mental or actual scenes of brutal rape.

Sexuality in Late Adulthood Sexual interest and activity are important dimensions of the lives of many senior adults. Perhaps not surprisingly, sexual activity in old age is strongly correlated with the degree of sexual activity earlier in life (Bretschneider & McCoy, 1988).

Many people who have lost their spouse through death or divorce continue to date as they grow older. Older men date more often than older women, mostly because they have a larger pool of potential dating partners. Dating serves a different function in late adulthood than in early adulthood. For young adults, dating is part of the process of selecting a mate. For older adults, dating serves to fill the need for companionship and sexual intimacy. Many older adults have a serious relationship with a single, special dating partner, but have no intention of remarrying (Bulcroft & Bulcroft, 1991). In late adulthood, dating helps prevent loneliness and can meet the need for physical and emotional intimacy, a need which continues throughout the lifespan.

Sexual Behavior over the Lifespan:

Concluding Thoughts

The picture that emerges of sexuality over the lifespan does not seem to match the typical media images. For the most part, the development of sexual behavior follows a predictable sequence of events from infancy through adolescence. Upon reaching adulthood, the vast majority of Americans follow very traditional patterns of sexual behavior. Most people spend almost all their adult years involved in a stable sexual relationship with a single partner. Compared to single people, married or cohabiting couples have more active sex lives.

Most Americans are fundamentally happy with the relationship they have with their sexual partner. And, as this section has made clear, most American adults are not inclined toward kinky or unusual sexual practices. In fact, Americans tend to be conservative and traditional in their sexual practices and preferences.

To say that most American adults are happy with their sexual relationships is not to say that everyone is blissfully happy. Some people experience disruptions and difficulties in responding sexually to their partner. In the final section of this chapter, we'll look at sexual dysfunctions and other problems related to sexuality and gender.

CONCEPT REVIEW 10.4

Sexuality in Adulthood

On the basis of the research findings described in the text, indicate whether each of the following statements is true or false.

_____ **1.** Single people aged twenty to twenty-five have the most active and satisfying sex lives.

_____ **2.** Although vaginal intercourse was reported as the most common sexual activity, most people secretly preferred other forms of sexual expression.

_____ **3.** Most adults over the age of seventy are physically unable to have sexual intercourse.

_____ **4.** Almost half of all married people in the United States are dissatisfied with their sex lives.

_____ **5.** By the age of fifteen, about 90 percent of U.S. teenagers have had sexual intercourse at least once.

Sexual Disorders and Problems

> *Sexual dysfunctions are consistent disturbances in sexual desire, arousal, or orgasm that cause psychological distress. What are the sexual dysfunctions? What are the paraphilias, and how do they differ from dysfunctions? What is a gender identity disorder?*

Almost everyone experiences an occasional glitch in responding sexually, such as failing to feel sexually aroused on a particular occasion. What can cause this to happen? There are a number of rather ordinary reasons. You might be feeling tired or grumpy with your sexual partner. Anxiety, including anxiety over your sexual performance, can also interfere with sexual functioning. Drinking too much alcohol can disrupt the ability to achieve sexual arousal or orgasm. And, of course, it's possible that your well-intentioned partner is doing something that you don't find sexually stimulating, as in "Let's just skip the whipped cream next time, okay?"

For most people, such disruptions in sexual response are temporary. In contrast, some people experience persistent sexual problems, or sexual dysfunctions. **Sexual dysfunctions** are consistent disturbances in sexual desire, arousal, or orgasm that cause psychological distress and interpersonal difficulties (American Psychiatric Association, 1994). Researchers do not have reliable data on the prevalence of many sexual dysfunctions (see Hyde & Delamater, 1997). Nonetheless, in this section we'll describe some of the sexual dysfunctions that can occur.

Sexual Dysfunctions:
Consistent and Distressing Sexual Difficulties

Either men or women can experience psychological distress or interpersonal difficulties caused by having little or no sexual desire, a condition that is referred to as **hypoactive sexual desire disorder.** Keep in mind that the frequency with which people want to have sex varies over the lifespan and according to personal preference. In some instances, what seems like "low desire" in one partner may actually reflect "high desire" in the other partner. More extreme is **sexual aversion disorder,** in which a person actively avoids genital contact with a sexual partner because of extreme anxiety, fear, or disgust over sexual contact. Either men or women can chronically experience genital pain before, during, or after intercourse, a condition called **dyspareunia.**

Some sexual dysfunctions can be experienced only by either males or females. When a male experiences a recurrent inability to achieve or maintain an erection, it's called **male erectile disorder.** At the opposite extreme, an erect male may experience recurring delays or a complete absence of the ability to achieve orgasm through intercourse, a condition called **male orgasmic disorder.** Although the male may not be able to achieve orgasm during intercourse, he may be able to do so through other means, such as by being manually or orally stimulated by his partner. A man may experience considerable distress over recurrent episodes of **premature ejaculation,** in which he reaches sexual climax too soon, often immediately before or shortly after *penetration* (insertion of the penis into the partner's vagina).

When a female experiences distress over consistent delays in achieving orgasm, or the complete inability to achieve orgasm, it's called **female orgasmic disorder.** Women can also experience a condition called **vaginismus**—the persistent, involuntary contraction of the vaginal muscles, resulting in uncomfortable or painful intercourse. In severe cases, the vaginal muscle spasms may be so severe as to prevent penetration (American Psychiatric Association, 1994).

sexual dysfunction
A consistent disturbance in sexual desire, arousal, or orgasm that causes psychological distress and interpersonal difficulties.

hypoactive sexual desire disorder
A sexual dysfunction characterized by little or no sexual desire.

sexual aversion disorder
A sexual dysfunction characterized by active avoidance of genital sexual contact because of extreme anxiety, fear, or disgust.

dyspareunia
A sexual dysfunction characterized by genital pain before, during, or after intercourse.

male erectile disorder
In males, sexual dysfunction characterized by a recurring inability to achieve or maintain an erect penis.

male orgasmic disorder
In males, sexual dysfunction characterized by delayed orgasm during intercourse or the inability to achieve orgasm during intercourse.

premature ejaculation
In males, sexual dysfunction characterized by orgasm occurring before it is desired, often immediately or shortly after sexual stimulation or penetration.

female orgasmic disorder
In females, sexual dysfunction characterized by consistent delays in achieving orgasm or the inability to achieve orgasm.

vaginismus
Sexual dysfunction characterized by persistent, involuntary contractions or spasms of the vaginal muscles, which result in uncomfortable or painful intercourse.

What causes such sexual dysfunctions? Some sexual dysfunctions, such as male erectile disorder, may be the result of a physical or medical condition. In the case of male erectile disorder, two of the most prominent causes are diabetes and alcoholism. Other sexual dysfunctions, such as premature ejaculation and vaginismus, are more often the result of psychological factors than organic factors. Such psychological factors might include anxiety about sex or the association of pain with early sexual experiences. Fortunately, many sexual dysfunctions can be successfully treated by psychologists and physicians who have received specialized training in sex therapy (Masters & others, 1995; Nevid & others, 1995).

The Paraphilias:
Unusual Sexual Fantasies, Urges, or Behaviors

When a person's sexual gratification is highly or completely dependent on fantasies, urges, or behaviors that fall outside the socially accepted range of sexual behavior, the person is said to have a **paraphilia.** Such fantasies, urges, and behaviors may involve suffering or humiliation, children, another nonconsenting adult, or nonhuman objects (American Psychiatric Association, 1994). In general, the paraphilias are much more common among men than women.

Exactly what kinds of fantasies, urges, or behaviors are we talking about? Here are brief descriptions of the most common paraphilias:

- *Exhibitionism*: sexual arousal achieved by exposing one's genitals to shocked strangers.
- *Frotteurism*: sexual arousal from touching and rubbing against a nonconsenting person, usually in a crowded public situation, such as a crowded bus or subway car.
- *Fetishism*: sexual arousal in response to inanimate objects (e.g., female undergarments, shoes, leather) or body parts that are not typically associated with sexual arousal (e.g., feet, hair, legs).
- *Transvestic fetishism*: in heterosexual males, sexual arousal from cross-dressing in women's clothes.
- *Pedophilia*: sexual fantasies, urges, or behavior involving sexual activity with a prepubescent child (generally age thirteen or younger).
- *Voyeurism*: sexual arousal from observing an unsuspecting person who is disrobing, naked, or engaged in sexual activity.
- *Sexual sadism*: sexual arousal achieved through intentionally inflicting psychological or physical suffering on another person.
- *Sexual masochism*: sexual arousal in response to actually being humiliated, beaten, bound, or otherwise made to suffer.

Unlike the person with a sexual dysfunction, the person who has a paraphilia is often not psychologically distressed by it. Rather, these individuals typically come to the attention of mental health professionals only when their behavior has created a conflict with their sexual partner, has been discovered by a family member or co-worker, or has resulted in arrest (American Psychiatric Association, 1994; Masters & others, 1995). Some paraphilias, like pedophilia and voyeurism, are illegal.

paraphilia
(pair-uh-FILL-ee-uh) Any of several forms of nontraditional sexual behavior in which a person's sexual gratification depends on an unusual sexual experience, object, or fantasy.

What causes a particular paraphilia to develop? Theories involving biological and psychological causes exist, but there are no solid answers. At best, the exact causes of paraphilias remain obscure (Hyde & Delamater, 1997).

Gender Identity Disorder:

Feeling Trapped in the Wrong Body

As we noted at the beginning of the chapter, our sense of being male or female is referred to as our *gender identity*. When a person expresses persistent discomfort about his or her assigned gender, and repeatedly expresses a desire to be a member of the opposite sex, the person is said to have **gender identity disorder** (formerly called *transsexualism*).

When it occurs in children, gender identity disorder is marked by an intense preoccupation with the play activities, games, and toys traditionally associated with the opposite sex. Rather than play with same-sex playmates, the child expresses a strong desire to play with and dress like opposite-sex playmates. A boy may repeatedly voice the desire to be a girl, even insisting that he will grow up to be a woman. During the teenage years, he may exhibit other kinds of cross-gender behaviors, such as shaving his legs.

Adults with gender identity disorder are extremely uncomfortable about being regarded as a member of their assigned gender. In private, they may cross-dress and display mannerisms typical of the opposite sex. Some may do so publicly as well (American Psychiatric Association, 1994). Often, they resort to hormone treatments or surgical interventions, such as the surgical reduction of the Adam's apple in males, to appear more like the opposite gender. In some cases, they undergo *sex-reassignment surgery,* in which the existing genitalia are removed and the genitals of the opposite sex are surgically constructed. Although male-to-female surgery can result in a functional and authentic-looking vagina, the female-to-male surgery results in an artificial penis that cannot spontaneously become erect. Nonetheless, with an inflatable penile implant, artificial erections are often possible. Even so, ejaculation cannot occur (see Masters & others, 1995).

Sexually Transmitted Diseases

> *Sexually transmitted diseases can be bacterial, viral, or parasitic infections. Why do the STDs pose serious health problems? What effects does the HIV virus have on the body? Who is most at risk for AIDS?*

No discussion of human sexuality in the 1990s would be complete without noting the dangers of **sexually transmitted diseases,** abbreviated **STDs.** Transmitted primarily through sexual contact, STDs include bacterial, viral, and parasitic infections (see Table 10.3). Bacterial STDs include *gonorrhea, syphilis,* and *chlamydia. Pubic lice* is an example of a parasitic STD. Both bacterial and parasitic STDs can be cured with the appropriate treatment, such as antibiotic medications or anti-parasitic shampoos. In contrast, viral sexually transmitted diseases, such as *herpes* and *AIDS,* cannot be cured. However, their symptoms can often be reduced with treatment.

Left untreated, many STDs can eventually create significant health problems. This is especially troubling because it is completely possible for a person to be unaware that he or she is infected with an STD. For example, *chlamydia* often does not produce symptoms but can still damage reproductive organs if left untreated. Equally troubling is the fact that an infected person can unknowingly pass on an STD to sexual partners.

Self-Portrait by Photographer Loren Cameron Not all transsexuals feel that the desire to change sex is an illness, and some protest labeling transsexualism as a psychological disorder (Stryker, 1996). Loren Cameron, shown here, documented his own transformation from female to male. One of his goals was to communicate his sense of pride and satisfaction about his transformation: "It takes a lot of guts to acknowledge how uncomfortable you are before the transition, and to willfully accept the challenge of re-creating yourself."

gender identity disorder
A persistent discomfort about one's assigned gender along with the desire to be a member of the opposite sex.

sexually transmitted diseases (STDs)
Any of several infectious diseases that are primarily transmitted through sexual intercourse or other intimate sexual contact.

TABLE 10.3 Summary of Major Sexually Transmitted Diseases

STD	Symptoms	Treatment
Bacterial		
Gonorrhea	*Males:* yellowish penile discharge; burning or painful urination	Antibiotics
	Females: often no early symptoms; vaginal discharge; burning or painful urination	
Syphilis	Painless chancre, or sore; swollen lymph nodes	Antibiotics
Chlamydia	*Women:* most are symptom-free; painful urination and vaginal discharge	Antibiotics
	Men: many are symptom-free; burning or painful urination	
Parasitic		
Pubic lice	Intense itching in pubic area	Kwell shampoo, lotion, or cream; Lindane shampoo
Viral		
Genital herpes	Painful blisters on or inside the genitals; sometimes accompanied by fever, swollen lymph nodes, bodily aches and pains	Not curable, but antiviral drug Acyclovir shortens duration of initial symptom outbreak and reduces severity of recurrences
AIDS (acquired immune deficiency syndrome)	Initial HIV infection may be accompanied by mild flulike symptoms; HIV virus can be dormant for years; AIDS is characterized by severe weight loss and increased susceptibility to other diseases and infections.	Not curable, but antiviral drug AZT, in combination with other antivirals such as ddC, ddI, and 3TC, is effective in slowing the progress of the infection. Several promising new drugs, known as protease inhibitors, were approved by the Food and Drug Administration in early 1996. They appear to dramatically slow the progress of HIV; however, the long-term prognosis is not yet known.

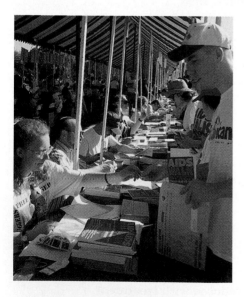

Increasing AIDS Awareness Benefits, concerts, and fund-raising events, such as the annual AIDS walk in New York City, have increased public awareness of the AIDS epidemic.

The AIDS Epidemic

AIDS, or **acquired immune deficiency syndrome,** is a disease caused when the *human immunodeficiency virus* (HIV) enters the bloodstream through the exchange of infected body fluids, primarily semen, blood, and blood products. Once a person is infected, the HIV virus can exist in his or her body for a decade or longer without causing any apparent symptoms. In other words, the infected person can look and feel perfectly healthy. Nonetheless, the person is an HIV carrier and can infect others.

When the virus becomes active, it selectively attacks a key component of the body's immune system: the *helper T cells.* As you'll see in Chapter 13, on stress, health, and coping, helper T cells mobilize other immune system cells to fight off diseases and infections. As the HIV virus weakens the immune system, the person becomes greatly susceptible to other diseases, including cancer, pneumonia, and encephalitis (inflammation of the brain and spinal cord). Eventually, the immune system becomes so weakened that the person succumbs to some opportunistic infection that overwhelms the body (Kalichman, 1995).

Gay men, intravenous drug users who share contaminated needles, and people with multiple sex partners are the groups most at risk of becoming infected by HIV (Centers for Disease Control and Prevention, 1993b). However, no one is immune to HIV. Among the various methods of HIV infection, heterosexual transmission is the fastest-growing category. According to the Centers for Disease Control and Prevention (1994), heterosexual contact now accounts for approximately 10 percent of the AIDS cases in this country. And cases of AIDS among U.S. women have been steadily rising. AIDS is now the fourth leading cause of death among women aged fifteen to forty-four (Centers for Disease Control and Prevention, 1993a).

Although there is no cure for AIDS yet, there is considerable reason for hope. The drug *AZT* is often effective in slowing the progression of the disease. Researchers believe they have developed, for the first time, an animal model to study AIDS (McClure & Novembre, 1996). New drugs and combinations of drugs hold the promise of improving both the quality and duration of life for those infected with HIV.

There are steps that any person can and should take to reduce the likelihood of getting a sexually transmitted disease, such as using condoms and spermicides and not engaging in high-risk sexual activity, such as anal sex, with new sexual partners. Unfortunately, despite widespread public awareness of the danger, engaging in risky, unprotected sexual behavior remains common (Fisher & others, 1995).

CONCEPT REVIEW 10.5

Identifying Sexual Disorders and Problems

Match the following terms with the descriptions below: female orgasmic disorder, premature ejaculation, gender identity disorder, sexual aversion disorder, paraphilia.

1. Lawrence is uncomfortable with his own assigned gender, dreams about being a female, and is considering sex-reassignment surgery. _____

2. Laverne is married, but she and her husband rarely have intercourse because the thought of any genital contact with her husband makes her very anxious and fearful. _____

3. Jack has been arrested twice for exposing his genitals to commuters on a subway platform, but he is unable to stop doing this. _____

4. George is very distressed because he frequently reaches sexual climax within seconds after beginning intercourse with his wife. _____

5. Although Eva has a warm, loving relationship with her husband, she has never experienced an orgasm during their sexual interactions. _____

Summing Up: Gender and Sexuality

From birth, each of us is profoundly influenced by the biological, social, cultural, and psychological forces that shape our gender identity and expression of sexuality. As you've seen in this chapter, a person's gender role identity is firmly entrenched by late childhood and adolescence.

Throughout adulthood, the expression of sexuality centers on stable interpersonal relationships that are based not just on physical intimacy but also on emotional and psychological intimacy. Even in old age, the need for physical, emotional, and psychological intimacy remains strong.

Over the course of life, much of who we are is defined by our gender and sexual identity. Often without our awareness, that identity shapes the activities we are drawn to, the relationships we form, and how we react in many situations. Most people develop a conventional sense of gender identity and sexual orientation, and form sexual relationships that follow the predominant patterns endorsed by society. But other people, like our friend Richard, are faced with the challenge of accepting themselves in a society that is often not very tolerant of sexual difference.

AIDS (acquired immune deficiency syndrome)
A disease caused by the exchange of body fluids (semen, blood, or blood products) containing the human immunodeficiency virus (HIV), which attacks and weakens the immune system.

We hope that, in reading this chapter, you've developed not only a greater appreciation of your own gender and sexual identity but also a better understanding of people whose gender identity or sexual orientation is different from your own. In the chapter Application, we'll provide suggestions for overcoming gender differences that can interfere with the resolution of conflicts in intimate relationships.

APPLICATION

Men, Women, and Conflict: Bridging the Gender Gap

Resolving conflict is a key ingredient in successful intimate relationships. How do the responses of men and women to interpersonal conflict differ? How can couples overcome these differences to resolve conflicts more constructively?

> *"What's bothering you?"*
>
> *"Me? Nothing. Why do you ask?"*
>
> *"You've got that look on your face."*
>
> *"What look?!"*
>
> *"You know—that I'm mad-as-hell-and-don't-talk-to-me look."*
>
> *"Just leave me alone, okay? What do you want to start a fight for?"*
>
> *"Who's starting a fight? I'm not trying to start a fight. I just want to know what's wrong."*
>
> *"Did I say there was anything wrong? There's nothing wrong. Can't I just sit here and read the paper without being hassled to death?"*
>
> *"I'm not trying to hassle you! I'm just trying to figure out what you're . . ."*
>
> *"Did you hear what I said? Leave me alone!"*
>
> *"Yeah, but if you're mad about something, then maybe we should talk about . . . "*
>
> *"Damn it! You just keep badgering me! Just leave me alone!" (Throws paper aside, gets up and storms out, slamming door.)*

Can you identify the male and female speaker in this exchange? That's probably not exactly a tough question. As we noted earlier in the chapter, women tend to be more comfortable about expressing their emotions than men are. Beyond this basic difference, re-

searchers have found that men and women communicate very differently, especially when they are trying to deal with problems, emotional issues, and interpersonal conflicts (Kalbfleisch & Cody, 1995; Brehm, 1992; Tannen, 1990). In this Application, we will look at some of those communication differences and consider how couples can learn to overcome them.

Conflict in Intimate Relationships

Being able to handle interpersonal conflict is important in any relationship, but especially in marriage. The demands and hassles of sharing and maintaining a household make occasional conflict in marriage virtually inevitable (Stafford & Dainton, 1994). Despite what many people think, the happiest marriages are not conflict-free. Instead, as psychologist John Gottman (1994) has discovered, conflict plays a key role in marital happiness and stability.

Gottman has intensively studied hundreds of married couples over the last twenty years (Gottman & Levenson, 1992; Levenson & others, 1994). He's found that a couple's relationship grows only if the couple successfully reconciles the inevitable differences that occur. As Gottman (1994) explains, "A certain amount of conflict is needed to help couples weed out actions and ways of dealing with each other that can harm the marriage in the long run."

Gottman and his colleagues have also found that men and women react differently to conflict, particularly conflicts that involve strong emotions (Levenson & others, 1994). Men have typically learned to suppress and con-

tain their emotions. In contrast, women tend to be more comfortable expressing their emotions. In general, women are more comfortable than men when it comes to dealing with emotional issues in intimate relationships.

According to Gottman (1994), women often become the "emotion managers" and "care-takers of intimacy" in close relationships. They tend to be more sensitive to problems that are developing in the relationship and more willing to talk about them. But when problems need to be resolved, Gottman has found, male and female patterns of reacting to and handling conflict often sabotage a couple's best efforts to resolve their differences.

What goes wrong when a couple tries to resolve their differences? First, consider the two types of responses that Gottman has found occur during emotional conflicts: flooding and stonewalling. *Flooding* means feeling overwhelmed (or "flooded") by your own emotions—feeling upset and out of control. When flooded, people experience high levels of physiological arousal. Heartbeat and blood pressure skyrocket.

People do vary in their thresholds for emotional overload. Some people can calmly listen to a long diatribe by a spouse, while others become flooded at the most minor criticism. And, not surprisingly, people become flooded more readily when they are already under pressure or stress.

As an argument or conflict heats up, both men and women can become flooded by their emotions. That said, which sex do you think is *more* likely to become flooded? Men are. In his lab, Gottman has found that during marital conflict a husband's heart rate and blood pressure increase faster, elevate higher, and stay elevated longer than his wife's (Gottman & Levenson, 1992). Not only is this high level of physiological arousal extremely unpleasant, it also makes it very difficult for a man to listen to his partner's words. Hence, because men physiologically react so strongly to conflict, they tend to be less willing to engage in it.

When flooded, what do men typically do? They go into the *stonewalling* mode—they withdraw to contain their uncomfortable emotions (Levenson & others, 1994). Women also stonewall, of course, but men are much more likely to resort to this strategy (Christensen & Heavey, 1993).

Now a vicious circle begins. Although stonewalling protects *him* from overwhelming stress and emotion, it creates enormous stress in *her*. She's accustomed to working through emotional problems. And she tends to experience his stonewalling as disapproval and rejection—and sometimes as the ultimate power play (Tannen, 1990). So how does she react to his stonewalling? Frustrated and angry, she now reacts by *flooding*.

If both the man and the woman reacted to flooding by stonewalling, the immediate tension would be diffused. But typically, they don't. Instead, when a woman experiences flooding, rather than withdraw she intensifies the expression of her emotions. This raises the temperature of the argument to a higher level and creates even more stress in the male, further increasing his urge to withdraw from the situation. In short, this is a very volatile scene. Each partner is exaggerating the frustration and emotional discomfort of the other. Especially in unhappily married couples, Gottman has found that even minor disagreements can quickly escalate in this way, ending up as a no-holds-barred, extremely unpleasant fight.

Breaking the Vicious Circle of Flooding-Stonewalling-Flooding

In his book *Why Marriages Succeed or Fail . . . and How You Can Make Yours Last,* Gottman (1994) offers many thoughtful and concrete suggestions for handling conflicts in a healthier manner. We'll summarize four of these suggestions, which are based on extensive research by Gottman and other psychologists.

The first step in breaking the vicious circle of flooding-stonewalling-flooding is to be *aware* of the gender differences in handling emotion. To men, stonewalling is a protective strategy. It represents an attempt to contain disturbing emotions before they become overwhelming and out of control. When women look at men's stonewalling in these terms, they're less likely to interpret it as rejection and as a refusal to try to resolve differences.

On their part, guys need to remember that women experience stonewalling as rejection, disapproval, and abandonment. Rather than abruptly stonewalling and withdrawing, men need to explain their withdrawal. The explanation can be as simple as saying, "Look, I need to be alone for a while so I can calm down and think about what you're saying. When I come back, we will keep talking." On their part, women need to accept men's need to temporarily withdraw from the situation.

Gottman (1994) advises that whenever either partner begins to feel overwhelmed or in danger of flooding, he or she should call a *time out*—a 20- to 30-minute intermission with an agreement to continue the discussion after the break. Remember, it takes at least 20 minutes for physiological arousal to subside completely. Because men are more likely to become emotionally flooded, calming down is especially important for them.

When a man agrees to continue the discussion later and explains why he needs the time out, his partner is less likely to feel angered and threatened by his withdrawal. As simple as the time-out strategy is, it can promote more constructive and rational discussions, increasing the likelihood that a mutually acceptable solution to the problem will be found.

Second, it is critical that you listen to what you're saying to yourself *during* the time out. Rather than rehearsing hateful or vengeful comments, use the time out to focus on calming thoughts about the immediate situation and on positive thoughts about your mate. For example, rather than saying to yourself, "He (she) is such a (fill in with an insult)," try saying to yourself, "Calm down and get a grip on things. This *is* basically a good marriage and I *do* love her (him)." The important point here is to spend the time out thinking about ways to *resolve* the conflict, not about ways to mount a more effective counterattack when the battle resumes.

Third, men need to make a conscious effort to embrace, rather than avoid, the problem at hand. As Gottman (1994) writes, "The most important advice I can give to men who want their marriages to work is to try *not* to avoid conflict. Sidestepping a problem won't make it go away." In other words, guys, you need to remember that your partner *really* cares about your relationship. That's why she keeps confronting you—so the two of you can resolve the problem *together*.

With practice, which may be difficult at first, men can get better at listening to their mate's concerns without feeling threatened or becoming defensive. Again, it helps if you mentally say constructive things to yourself, such as "I need to listen because it's important to her" and "She's confronting me because she wants the relationship to work."

Fourth, although women should not avoid raising issues that are in need of resolution, they should try to do it calmly, avoiding personal attacks. Gottman advises that issues be framed in the context of maintaining a loving relationship. As Gottman (1994) puts it, "It will be much easier for him to stay engaged if you let him know that talking together about what's bothering you is a way to keep the love between you alive."

Gottman's helpful book presents many other suggestions for improving communication and conflict resolution in marriage and other relationships. We highly recommend his book, which is founded on his many years of scientific research. However, simply being aware of the gender differences we've discussed in this Application may help you stay calm and cope better with the conflicts that are inevitable in any close relationship.

Summary
Gender and Sexuality

Gender and Sexuality

- Gender and sexuality are important components of everyone's life. The term *sex* refers to the biologically determined physical characteristics that define a person as male or female. *Gender* refers to the cultural and social meanings that are associated with masculinity and femininity.

Gender Stereotypes and Gender Roles

- According to gender-role stereotypes, men and women are very different. In reality, men and women are quite similar.

- Men and women are very similar in their cognitive abilities. On average, females outscore males on tests of verbal fluency, spelling, reading comprehension, and writing; males outscore females on mental rotation tasks. Average math scores of men and women are very similar, but more males score in the very highest range.

- Men and women are largely similar in their sexual attitudes and behaviors. Males have a higher incidence of masturbation and are more accepting of casual sex than females.

Gender-Role Development:
Blue Bears and Pink Bunnies

- Gender plays an important role in our culture. From birth, boys and girls are treated differently. During childhood, boys and girls develop different toy preferences and play with members of their own sex. Girls tend to be less rigid than boys in adhering to gender stereotypes.

- Two contemporary theories that explain gender-role development are social learning theory and gender schema theory. Social learning theory is based on the principles of learning. Through reinforcement, punishment, and modeling, children learn the appropriate behaviors for each gender.

- Gender schema theory is based on the idea that children actively develop mental categories for each gender. Children's gender schemas influence what they learn and remember. At a young age, children develop an awareness of the underlying meaning of gender categories.

Human Sexuality

- The four stages of human sexual response are excitement, plateau, orgasm, and resolution. Women are capable of multiple orgasms. Men experience a refractory period following orgasm.

- In animals, sexual behavior is biologically determined and typically triggered by hormonal changes in the female. In higher animals, sexual behavior is more strongly influenced by learning and environmental factors and less influenced by biological factors.

- Sexual orientation is not as cut and dried as many people think. More people have had some same-sex sexual experience than identify themselves as exclusively homosexual. Although psychologists do not know exactly what determines sexual orientation, genetics and differences in brain structure may be involved. Sexual orientation develops at a fairly early age and is difficult to change. In itself, homosexuality is not considered a psychological disorder.

Sexual Behavior over the Lifespan

- Sexual behavior varies over the lifespan. Infants experience reflexive sexual responses. During early and middle childhood, children become increasingly aware of their own bodies and curious about sexual matters.

- During puberty, adolescents reach sexual maturation. Puberty involves the development of primary and secondary sex characteristics, the adolescent growth spurt, and, in females, menarche. While the sequence of pubertal changes is relatively predictable, the timing of puberty varies. The consequences of early and late maturation tend to be different for boys and girls.

- Sexual and romantic relationships become increasingly important in adolescence. By the end of adolescence, most males and females have had sexual intercourse.

- Most adults are involved in an intimate relationship by the age of thirty. Young adults today tend to have more sexual partners than previous generations. Married people tend to have the most active sex lives and are the most satisfied with their sex lives. Vaginal intercourse is the most preferred sexual activity.

- In late adulthood, people experience physical changes that affect sexual response, but satisfying sexual relationships can continue throughout the lifespan.

Sexual Disorders and Problems

- A sexual dysfunction is a consistent disturbance in sexual response that causes the person psychological distress. Either sex can experience hypoactive sexual desire disorder, sexual aversion disorder, or dyspareunia. Men can experience male erectile disorder, male orgasmic disorder, or premature ejaculation. Women can experience female orgasmic disorder or vaginismus. Sexual dysfunctions may be caused by physical or psychological factors.

■ The paraphilias are unusual sexual fantasies, urges, or behaviors. They may involve nonhuman objects, suffering or humiliation, children, or another nonconsenting adult. Some paraphilias, such as pedophilia and voyeurism, are illegal.

■ In gender identity disorder, people are uncomfortable with their assigned gender and wish to be a member of the opposite sex. In some instances, the person undergoes sex-reassignment surgery.

■ Sexually transmitted diseases may be bacterial, viral, or parasitic. Some STDs have vague or nonexistent symptoms and can be unknowingly transmitted to a sex partner. Left untreated, some STDs can cause severe health problems.

■ AIDS is caused by the HIV virus, which is transmitted through the exchange of infected body fluids, such as semen and blood. After being infected, a person may not develop AIDS for several years, but can still infect others. When the virus becomes active, it attacks the immune system. No one is immune to HIV, but gay men, intravenous drug users who share contaminated needles, and people with multiple sex partners are most at risk to contract HIV. Choosing sex partners carefully and avoiding high-risk sexual behavior are two ways people can help protect themselves against AIDS and other STDs.

Key Terms

sex (p. 431)

gender (p. 431)

gender roles (p. 431)

gender identity (p. 431)

sexual orientation (p. 431)

gender-role stereotypes (p. 432)

social learning theory of gender-role development (p. 439)

gender schema theory (p. 440)

puberty (p. 451)

primary sex characteristics (p. 452)

secondary sex characteristics (p. 452)

adolescent growth spurt (p. 452)

menarche (p. 452)

sexual dysfunction (p. 459)

hypoactive sexual desire disorder (p. 459)

sexual aversion disorder (p. 459)

dyspareunia (p. 459)

male erectile disorder (p. 459)

male orgasmic disorder (p. 459)

premature ejaculation (p. 459)

female orgasmic disorder (p. 459)

vaginismus (p. 459)

paraphilia (p. 460)

gender identity disorder (p. 461)

sexually transmitted diseases (STDs) (p.461)

AIDS (acquired immune deficiency syndrome) (p. 462)

Key People

Sandra Lipsitz Bem (b. 1944) American psychologist who has conducted extensive research on sex roles and gender identity; proposed gender schema theory to explain gender role development.

Virginia E. Johnson (b. 1925) American behavioral scientist who, along with William H. Masters, conducted pioneering research in the field of human sexuality and sex therapy.

William H. Masters (b. 1915) American physician who, along with Virginia E. Johnson, conducted pioneering research in the field of human sexuality and sex therapy.

CONCEPT REVIEW 10.1 Page 442

1. sex
2. gender-role stereotypes
3. social learning theory
4. gender schema theory

CONCEPT REVIEW 10.2 Page 449

1. c
2. a
3. b
4. d
5. d

CONCEPT REVIEW 10.3 Page 454

1. C
2. E
3. B
4. D

CONCEPT REVIEW 10.4 Page 458

1. False
2. False
3. False
4. False
5. False

CONCEPT REVIEW 10.5 Page 463

1. gender identity disorder
2. sexual aversion disorder
3. paraphilia
4. premature ejaculation
5. female orgasmic disorder

468

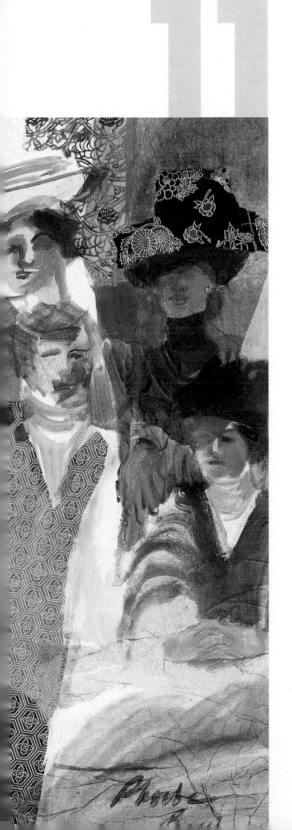

11

Personality

Prologue: The Secret Twin

The twins, Kenneth and Julian, were born a few years after the turn of the century. At first their parents, Gertrude and Henry, thought they were identical, because the twins looked exactly alike. Both had dark hair and deep brown eyes. Kenneth's son, your author Don, would later inherit these qualities.

But Gertrude and Henry quickly learned to tell the twins apart. Kenneth was slightly larger than Julian, and even as infants, their personalities were distinctly different. In the photographs of Kenneth and Julian as children, it's easy to see those personality differences. Julian is always smiling broadly, almost merrily, his head cocked slightly. Kenneth always looked straight at the camera, his expression thoughtful, serious, more intense.

We don't know much about Julian's childhood. Kenneth kept Julian's very existence a closely guarded secret for more than fifty years. In fact, it was only a few years before his own death that Kenneth even revealed that he had once had a twin brother named Julian.

Still, it's possible to get glimpses of Julian's early life from the letters they wrote home from summer camp in 1919 and 1920. Kenneth's letters to his mother are affectionate and respectful, telling her about their daily activities and reassuring her that he will look after his twin brother. "I reminded Julian about the boats and I will watch him <u>good</u>," Kenneth wrote in one letter. Julian's letters were equally affectionate, but shorter and filled with misspelled words. Julian's letters also reveal glimpses of his impulsive nature. He repeatedly promised his mother, "I will not go out in the boats alone again."

Julian's impulsive nature was to have a significant impact on his life. When he was twelve years old, Julian darted in front of a car and was seriously injured with a concussion. In retrospect, Kenneth believed that that was when Julian's problems began. Perhaps it was, because soon after the accident Julian first got into serious trouble: He was caught stealing money from the "poor box" at church.

469

Although Kenneth claimed that Julian had always been the smarter twin, Julian fell behind in high school and graduated a year later than Kenneth. After high school, Kenneth left the quiet farming community of Grinnell, Iowa, and moved to Minneapolis. He quickly became self-sufficient, taking a job managing newspaper carriers. In the meantime, Julian stayed in Grinnell and became apprenticed to learn typesetting. Given Julian's propensity for adventure, it's not surprising that he found typesetting monotonous. In the spring of 1928, Julian left Iowa, heading east to look for more interesting possibilities.

He found them in Tennessee. A few months after Julian left Iowa, Henry received word that Julian had been arrested for armed robbery and sentenced to fifteen years in a Tennessee state prison. Though Kenneth was only twenty-two years old, Henry gave him a large sum of money and the family car and sent him to try to get Julian released.

Kenneth's conversation with the judge in Knoxville was the first of many times in his life that he would deal with the judicial system on someone else's behalf. After much negotiation, Kenneth secured an agreement: If Julian promised to leave Tennessee and never return, and Kenneth paid the necessary cash "fines," then Julian would be released from prison.

When Julian walked through the prison gates the next morning, Kenneth stood waiting with a fresh suit of clothes. "Mother and Father want you to come back to Grinnell," he told Julian. But Julian would not hear of it, saying that instead he wanted to go to California to make his fortune.

"I can't let you do that, Julian," Kenneth said, looking hard at his twin brother.

"You can't stop me, brother," Julian responded, with a cocky smile.

Reluctantly, Kenneth kept just enough money to buy himself a train ticket back to Iowa. He gave Julian the rest of the money and the family car.

Julian got as far as Phoenix, Arizona, before he met his destiny. Julian robbed a drugstore at gunpoint in broad daylight. As he backed out of the store, he was spotted by a passing policeman. A brief gun battle followed, and Julian was shot twice. Somehow he managed to escape and holed up in a hotel room. Alone and untended, Julian died two days later from the bullet wounds. Once again, Kenneth was sent to retrieve his twin brother.

On a bitterly cold November morning in 1928, Julian's immediate family laid him to rest in the family plot in Grinnell. On the one hand, Kenneth felt largely responsible for Julian's misguided life. "I should have tried harder to help Julian," Kenneth later reflected. On the other hand, Julian had disgraced the family. Indeed, from the day that Julian was buried, the family never spoke of him again, not even in private.

Kenneth took it upon himself to atone for the failings of his twin brother. In the fall of 1929, Kenneth entered law school in Tennessee—the same state from which he had secured Julian's release from prison. Three years later, at the height of the Great Depression, Kenneth established himself as a lawyer in Sioux City, Iowa, where he would practice law for more than fifty years.

As an attorney, Kenneth Hockenbury was known for his integrity, his intensity in the courtroom, and his willingness to take cases regardless of the client's ability to pay. "Someone must defend the poor," he said repeatedly. In lieu of money, he often accepted labor from a working man or produce from farmers.

Almost sixty years after Julian's death, Kenneth died. But unlike the sparse gathering on that bitterly cold day that Julian was buried, scores of people came to pay their last respects to Kenneth Hockenbury. "Your father helped me so much," stranger after stranger said to Don at Kenneth's funeral. Without question, Kenneth had devoted his life to helping others.

Why did Kenneth and Julian turn out so differently? Two boys, born on the same day into the same middle-class family. Kenneth the conscientious, serious one; Julian the laughing boy with mischief in his eyes. How can we explain the fundamental differences in their personalities?

The Twins Julian (left) and Kenneth (right), with their father Henry, when they were about 10 years old. As boys, Kenneth and Julian were inseparable.

No doubt your family, too, is made up of people with very different personalities. By the end of this chapter, you'll have a much greater appreciation for how those personality differences might be explained. As the chapter proceeds, we'll come back to the story of Kenneth and Julian.

Introduction

What Is Personality?

Personality is defined as an individual's unique and relatively consistent patterns of thinking, feeling, and behaving. What are the four major theoretical perspectives in personality?

That you already have an intuitive understanding of the word *personality* is easy to demonstrate. Just from reading this chapter's prologue, you could easily describe different aspects of Kenneth's and Julian's personalities. Indeed, we frequently toss around the word *personality* in everyday conversations. "He's very competent, but he has an abrasive personality." "My boss and I have a major personality conflict." "She's got such a delightful personality, you can't help liking her."

Your intuitive understanding of personality is probably very similar to the way that psychologists define the concept. **Personality** is defined as an individual's unique and relatively consistent patterns of thinking, feeling, and behaving (Pervin, 1997). One way that psychologists study personality is by looking at specific personality *characteristics,* such as loneliness, shyness, or sensation seeking. In this chapter, however, we won't focus on specific personality characteristics. Rather, we'll take a close look at the most influential personality *theories.*

A **personality theory** is an attempt to describe and explain how people are similar, how they are different, and why every individual is unique. In short, a personality theory ambitiously tries to explain the *whole person* (Pervin, 1990). In many respects, personality theories are the grand theories of psychology, often tackling questions that have preoccupied philosophers for centuries: Is human nature inherently good or bad? What are the most fundamental motives of human behavior? Do hereditary or environmental factors have the greatest influence on personality?

Personality theories often reflect the work of a single individual or of a few closely associated individuals. Thus, it's not surprising that many personality theories bear the distinct personal stamp of their creators to a much greater degree than other kinds of psychological theories (Engler, 1995). Consequently, we've tried to let the theorists speak for themselves. Throughout this chapter, you'll encounter carefully chosen quotations from the theorists' own writings. These quotes will give you brief glimpses into the minds of some of the most influential thinkers in psychology. They'll offer some provocative insights about love, hate, lust, incest, anxiety, dreams, aggression, guilt, and creativity.

At the outset, it's important to stress that no single theory can adequately explain *all* aspects of human personality. Like the people who created them, every personality theory has its unique strengths and weaknesses. You may find some ideas to be very compelling, while others seem feeble or unconvincing. You may also find yourself strongly opposed to some ideas, which is another reason we've chosen to let the theorists speak for themselves. As your authors, we've tried to present accurately the core concepts of each

personality
An individual's unique and relatively consistent patterns of thinking, feeling, and behaving.

personality theory
A theory that attempts to describe and explain individual similarities and differences.

personality theory and to remain evenhanded in evaluating their strengths and weaknesses.

There are many personality theories, but they can be roughly grouped under four basic perspectives: the psychoanalytic, humanistic, social cognitive, and trait perspectives. In a nutshell, here's what each perspective emphasizes:

- The *psychoanalytic perspective* emphasizes the importance of unconscious processes and the influence of early childhood experience.

- The *humanistic perspective* represents an optimistic look at human nature, emphasizing the self and the fulfillment of a person's unique potential.

- The *social cognitive perspective* emphasizes learning and conscious cognitive processes, including the importance of beliefs about the self, goal setting, and self-regulation.

- The *trait perspective* emphasizes the description and measurement of specific personality differences among individuals.

After looking at some of the major personality theories that reflect each perspective, we'll consider a closely related topic: how personality is measured and evaluated. And yes, we'll talk about the famous inkblots there. But for the inkblots to make sense, we need to trace the evolution of modern personality theories. We'll begin with the tale of a bearded, cigar-smoking gentleman from Vienna of whom you just may have heard—Sigmund Freud.

The Psychoanalytic Perspective on Personality

> *Sigmund Freud was the founder of psychoanalysis, which stresses the influence of the unconscious, the importance of sexual and aggressive instincts, and early childhood experience. What were some key influences on Freud's thinking?*

Sigmund Freud (1856–1939) was one of the most influential figures of the twentieth century. Freud was the founder of *psychoanalysis*. **Psychoanalysis** is the theory of personality that stresses the influence of unconscious mental processes, the importance of sexual and aggressive instincts, and the enduring effects of early childhood experience on personality. Because so many of Freud's ideas have become part of our common culture, it is difficult to imagine just how radical a figure he appeared to his contemporaries. The following biographical sketch highlights some of the important influences that shaped Freud's own ideas and theory.

The Life of Sigmund Freud

Sigmund Freud was born in 1856 in what is today Pribôr, Czechoslovakia. When he was four years old, his family moved to Vienna, where he lived until he was forced to leave in the last year of his life. Freud was the firstborn child of Jakob and Amalia Freud. By the time Sigmund was ten years old, there were six more siblings in the household. Of the seven children, Sigmund was

psychoanalysis
Sigmund Freud's theory of personality, which emphasizes unconscious determinants of behavior, sexual and aggressive instinctual drives, and the enduring effects of early childhood experiences on later personality development.

his mother's favorite. As Freud later wrote, "A man who has been the indisputable favorite of his mother keeps for life the feeling of being a conqueror, that confidence of success that often induces real success" (Jones, 1953).

Freud the Outsider

Freud was extremely bright and intensely ambitious. He studied medicine, became a physician, and then proved himself to be an outstanding physiological researcher. Early in his career, Freud was among the first investigators of a new drug that had anesthetic and mood-altering properties (Fancher, 1973). That drug was cocaine, which is still used today as a topical anesthetic in eye surgery. One of Freud's colleagues, however, received credit for the discovery of the anesthetic properties of cocaine—a matter that left Freud bitter. On top of that, Freud's initial enthusiasm for the medical potential of cocaine quickly faded when he finally recognized that the drug was addictive.

Prospects for an academic career in scientific research were very poor, especially for a Jew in Vienna, which was intensely anti-Semitic at that time. So when he married Martha Bernays in 1886, Freud reluctantly gave up physiological research for a private practice in neurology. The income from private practice would be needed: Sigmund and Martha had six children, three sons and three daughters (Fancher, 1973). One of Freud's daughters, Anna Freud, was later to become an important psychoanalytic theorist in her own right.

Sigmund Freud always considered himself to be an outsider. First, he was Jewish and living at a time when anti-Semitism was strong in Europe. Even though he was a lifelong atheist, Freud remained proud of his Jewish heritage. Second, Freud's ideas, especially about the influence of unconscious sexual impulses, even in children, were unconventional and shocking. It was the Victorian era, and there was a strong taboo against discussing sexual matters. To some degree, however, Freud enjoyed his role as the isolated scientist—it served him well in trying to set himself, and his ideas on personality, apart from other researchers.

Influences in the Development of Freud's Ideas

Freud's theory evolved gradually during his first twenty years of private practice. He based his theory on observations of his patients as well as self-analysis. An early influence on Freud was Joseph Breuer, a highly respected physician in Vienna who had taken the struggling younger doctor under his wing, providing advice and even financial assistance (Fancher, 1973). Breuer described to Freud the striking case of a young woman with an array of puzzling psychological and physical symptoms. Breuer found that if he first hypnotized this patient, then asked her to talk freely about a given symptom, forgotten memories of traumatic events would emerge—memories that she could recall only under hypnosis. After she freely expressed the pent-up emotions associated with the event, her symptom would disappear. Breuer called this phenomenon *catharsis* (Freud, 1925).

At first, Freud embraced Breuer's technique but found that not all of his patients could be hypnotized. Eventually, Freud dropped the use of hypnosis and developed his own technique of **free association** to help his patients uncover forgotten memories. Freud's patients would spontaneously report their uncensored thoughts, mental images, and feelings as they came to mind. From these "free associations," the thread that led to the crucial long-forgotten memories could be unraveled. Breuer and Freud described several of their case studies in their landmark book *Studies on Hysteria*. Its publication in 1895 marked the beginning of psychoanalysis.

Freud the Outsider At the turn of the century, Freud was developing some of his most controversial ideas, including his belief that expressions of sexuality are reflected in the behavior of infants and young children. He is shown here with his wife Martha, and youngest child, Anna, in the garden of their Vienna home in 1898.

free association
A psychoanalytic technique in which the patient spontaneously reports all thoughts, feelings, and mental images as they come to mind.

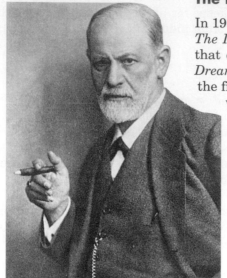

Freud the Leader In 1909, Freud visited the United States to lecture on his ideas at Clark University in Massachusetts. A year later, Freud and his many followers founded the International Psychoanalytic Association.

The Psychoanalytic Movement

In 1900 Freud published what many consider to be his most important work, *The Interpretation of Dreams*. As we discussed in Chapter 4, Freud argued that dreams symbolically reflect unconscious wishes. *The Interpretation of Dreams* was far from an instant best seller—it only sold 600 copies during the first eight years after publication. But ever so gradually, psychoanalysis was becoming more than a cluster of scientific ideas; it was becoming a movement (Gay, 1989). By the early 1900s, Freud had developed the basic tenets of his psychoanalytic theory and was no longer the isolated scientist. He was gaining international recognition and developing a following.

In 1904 Freud published what was to become one of his most popular books, *The Psychopathology of Everyday Life*. He described how unconscious thoughts, feelings, and wishes are often reflected in acts of forgetting, inadvertent slips of the tongue, accidents, and errors. By 1909 Freud's influence was also felt in the United States, when he and other psychoanalysts were invited to lecture at Clark University in Massachusetts.

Human Nature Versus Civilization

For the next thirty years Freud continued to refine his theory, publishing many books, articles, and lectures. Although he had achieved enormous international recognition, the last two decades of Freud's life were filled with many personal tragedies. The terrible devastation of World War I weighed heavily on his mind, especially because two of his sons were in the army. In 1920 one of Freud's daughters died from the flu at the age of twenty-six. In the early 1920s Freud developed cancer of the jaw, a condition for which he would ultimately undergo over thirty operations.

With all these matters weighing on his mind, Freud turned his attention to the problem of human destructiveness. For years he had asserted that sexuality was the fundamental human motive, but now he added aggression as a second powerful human instinct.

Given the climate of the times, it's not surprising that Freud came to focus on humanity's destructive tendencies. In the late 1920s, the Nazis were steadily gaining power in Germany. During this period, Freud wrote *Civilization and Its Discontents* (1930), in which he applied his psychoanalytic perspective to civilization as a whole. The central theme of the book is that human nature and civilization are in basic conflict—a conflict that is impossible to remedy.

Freud's extreme pessimism was undoubtedly a reflection of the destruction he saw all around him. By 1933 Adolf Hitler had seized power in Germany. In May of that year, there was a mass burning of Freud's books in Berlin. Five years later, the Nazis marched into Austria, seizing control of Freud's homeland.

Although Freud's life was clearly threatened, it was only after his youngest daughter, Anna, had been detained and questioned by the Gestapo that Freud reluctantly agreed to leave Vienna. In fact, four of Freud's sisters later died in Nazi extermination camps. Under great duress, Freud moved his family to the safety of England. Less than a year later, Freud's cancer returned. On September 23, 1939, he died at the age of eighty-three in London (Gay, 1988).

This brief sketch cannot do justice to the richness of Freud's life and the influence of his culture and society on his ideas. Even today, Freud's ideas remain provocative, and his legacy continues to influence psychology, literature, philosophy, and art. In the next section, we'll take a more detailed look at Freud's psychoanalytic theory.

Freud the Exile In the spring of 1938, Freud fled Nazi persecution for the safety of London on the eve of World War II. He is shown arriving in England, his eldest daughter, Mathilde, at his side. Freud died in London on September 23, 1939.

unconscious
In Freud's theory, a term used to describe thoughts, feelings, wishes, and drives that are operating below the level of conscious awareness.

Freud's Dynamic Theory of Personality

Psychoanalysis stresses the influence of unconscious mental processes. How do we get glimpses of unconscious mental processes? What are the three basic structures of personality, and what are their functions? What role is played by the defense mechanisms?

Freud (1940) saw personality and behavior as the result of a constant interplay between conflicting psychological forces. These psychological forces operate at three different levels of awareness: the conscious, the preconscious, and the unconscious. All the thoughts, feelings, and sensations that you're aware of at this particular moment represent the *conscious* level. The *preconscious* contains information of which you're not currently aware but which is easily capable of entering your consciousness, such as childhood memories or your social security number.

However, the conscious and preconscious are merely the visible tip of the iceberg of the mind. The bulk of this psychological iceberg is made up of the **unconscious,** which lies submerged below the waterline of the preconscious and conscious (see Figure 11.1). You're not directly aware of these submerged thoughts, feelings, wishes, and drives, but the unconscious exerts an enormous influence on your conscious thoughts and behavior.

Although it is not directly accessible, Freud (1904) believed that unconscious material often seeps through to the conscious level in distorted, disguised, or symbolic forms. Like a detective searching for clues, Freud carefully analyzed his patients' reports of dreams and free associations for evidence of unconscious wishes, fantasies, and conflicts. Dream analysis was particularly important to Freud. "The interpretation of dreams is the royal road to a knowledge of the unconscious activities of the mind," he wrote in *The Interpretation of Dreams*. Beneath the surface images, or *manifest content,* of a dream lay its *latent content*—the true, hidden, unconscious meaning of the dream symbols (see Chapter 4).

Ego: Rational, planful, mediating dimension of personality

Superego: Moralistic, judgmental, perfectionist dimension of personality

Id: Irrational, illogical, impulsive dimension of personality

Conscious: Information in your immediate awareness

Preconscious: Information which can easily be made conscious

Unconscious: Thoughts, feelings, urges, and other information that is difficult to bring to conscious awareness

FIGURE 11.1 Levels of Awareness and the Structure of Personality
Freud believed that personality is composed of three psychological processes—the Id, Ego, and Superego—that operate at different levels of awareness. If you think of personality as being like an iceberg, the bulk of this psychological iceberg is represented by the irrational, impulsive Id, which lies beneath the waterline of consciousness. Unlike the entirely unconscious Id, the rational Ego and moralistic Superego are at least partially conscious.

Freud (1904, 1933) believed that the unconscious could also be revealed in unintentional actions, such as accidents, mistakes, instances of forgetting, and inadvertent slips of the tongue, which are often referred to as "Freudian slips." For example, suppose you forget to set your alarm clock, oversleep, and miss an important exam. Forgetting to set your alarm reflects your possibly not-so-unconscious desire to avoid taking the exam. But it might also symbolize a deep unconscious conflict about academic success or your career choice. To Freud, seemingly accidental or unintentional actions were not accidental at all, but were determined by unconscious motives.

The Structure of Personality

According to Freud (1933), each person possesses a certain amount of psychological energy. This psychological energy evolves to form the three basic structures of personality—the Id, the Ego, and the Superego (see Figure 11.1). Understand that these are not separate identities or brain structures. Rather, they are distinct psychological processes.

The **Id,** the most primitive part of the personality, is entirely unconscious and present at birth. The Id is completely immune to logic, values, morality, danger, and the demands of the external world. It is the original source of psychological energy, parts of which will later evolve into the Ego and Superego (Freud, 1933, 1940).

The Id's reservoir of psychological energy is derived from two conflicting instinctual drives: the life instinct and the death instinct. The *life instinct,* which Freud called **Eros,** consists of biological urges that perpetuate the existence of the individual and the species—hunger, thirst, physical comfort, and, most important, sexuality. Freud (1915c) used the word **libido** to refer specifically to sexual energy or motivation. The *death instinct,* which Freud (1940) called **Thanatos,** is destructive energy that is reflected in aggressive, reckless, and life-threatening behaviors, including self-destructive actions.

Together, the life and death instincts represent the sheer, raw, conflicting psychological forces that fill the Id with a reservoir of dammed-up energy, energy that must be released. But because the Id resides completely in the unconscious, we're largely unaware of these psychological forces. The Id is rather difficult to describe in words. "We come nearer to the Id with images," Freud (1933) wrote, "and call it a chaos, a cauldron of seething excitement."

The Id is ruled by the **pleasure principle**—the relentless drive toward immediate satisfaction of the instinctual urges, especially sexual urges (Freud, 1920). Thus, the Id strives to increase pleasure, reduce tension, and avoid pain. Even though it operates unconsciously, Freud saw the pleasure principle as the most fundamental human motive.

Equipped only with the Id, the newborn infant is completely driven by the pleasure principle. When cold, wet, hungry, or uncomfortable, the newborn wants his needs addressed immediately. As the infant gains experience with the external world, however, he learns that his caretakers can't or won't always immediately satisfy those needs.

Thus, a new dimension of personality develops from part of the Id's psychological energy: the **Ego.** Partly conscious, the Ego represents the organized, rational, and planning dimensions of personality (Freud, 1933). As the mediator between the Id's instinctual demands and the restrictions of the outer world, the Ego operates on the reality principle. The **reality principle** is the capacity to postpone gratification until the appropriate time or circumstances exist in the external world (Freud, 1940).

As the young child gains experience, she gradually learns acceptable ways to satisfy her desires and instincts, such as finishing her dinner to get a cookie, saying "please," and waiting her turn rather than pushing another child off a playground swing. Hence, the Ego is the pragmatic part of the personality that learns various compromises to reduce the tension of the Id's instinctual urges. If the Ego can't identify an acceptable compromise to satisfy an instinctual urge, such as a sexual urge, it can *repress* the impulse, or remove it from conscious awareness (Freud, 1915a).

Appealing to the Id How would Freud explain the appeal of a billboard like this one? In Freud's theory, the Id is ruled by the pleasure principle—the instinctual drive to increase pleasure, reduce tension, and avoid pain. Advertisements like this one, which encourage us to be hedonistic, appeal to the pleasure principle.

LOVE THE SUN. WORSHIP YOUR SKIN.™

GREATER PIZ BUIN®
MOISTURIZING SUNCARE

Sav-on

patrick

Id
Latin for *the it;* in Freud's theory, the completely unconscious, irrational component of personality that seeks immediate satisfaction of instinctual urges and drives; ruled by the pleasure principle.

Eros
In Freud's theory, the self-preservation or life instinct, reflected in the expression of basic biological urges that perpetuate the existence of the individual and the species.

libido
In Freud's theory, the psychological and emotional energy associated with expressions of sexuality; the sex drive.

Thanatos
In Freud's theory, the death instinct, reflected in aggressive, destructive, and self-destructive actions.

pleasure principle
In Freud's theory, the motive to obtain pleasure and avoid tension or discomfort; the most fundamental human motive and the guiding principle of the Id.

CATHY

Establishing the Superego "Don't take something without asking" is just one of the many rules and values we learn as children from parents and other authorities. The internalization of such values is what Freud (1926) called the Superego —the inner voice that is our conscience. When we fail to live up to its moral ideals, the Superego imposes feelings of guilt, shame, and inferiority.

Ego
Latin for *I;* in Freud's theory, the partly conscious rational component of personality that regulates thoughts and behavior and is most in touch with the demands of the external world.

reality principle
In Freud's theory, the awareness of environmental demands and the capacity to accommodate them by postponing gratification until the appropriate time or circumstances exist.

Superego
In Freud's theory, the partly conscious self-evaluative, moralistic component of personality that is formed through the internalization of parental and societal rules.

In early childhood, the Ego must deal with external parental demands and limitations. Implicit in those demands are the parents' values and morals, their ideas of the right and wrong ways to think, act, and feel. Eventually, the child encounters other advocates of society's values, such as teachers and religious and legal authorities (Freud, 1926). Gradually, these social values move from being externally imposed demands to being *internalized* rules and values.

By about age five or six, the young child has developed an internal, parental voice that is partly conscious; this is the **Superego.** As the internal representation of parental and societal values, the Superego evaluates the acceptability of behavior and thoughts, then praises or admonishes. Put simply, your Superego represents your conscience, issuing demands "like a strict father with a child" (Freud, 1926). It judges your own behavior as right or wrong, good or bad, acceptable or unacceptable. And, should you fail to live up to these moral ideals, the Superego can be harshly punitive, imposing feeling of inferiority, guilt, shame, self-doubt, and anxiety. If we apply Freud's terminology to the twins described in the chapter prologue, Kenneth's Superego was clearly stronger than Julian's.

The Ego Defense Mechanisms: Unconscious Self-Deceptions

The Ego has a difficult task. It must be strong, flexible, and resourceful to successfully mediate conflicts between the instinctual demands of the Id, the moral authority of the Superego, and external restrictions. According to Freud (1923), everyone experiences an ongoing daily battle among these three warring personality processes.

Let's try to illustrate what Freud meant. Imagine lying in bed on a dark, cold morning. You promised to meet a friend on the running path in 20 minutes. On the one hand, your Id starts to whine, "I really want to go back to sleep. I'm tired, and it's dark and cold outside!" Your Superego, on the other hand, is scolding away: "Hey, you lazy slob! Get out of bed. Believe me, the cold air will be nothing compared to the guilt trip I'm going to lay on you if you don't keep your promise!" Your Ego must deal with these two warring factions, either by giving in to one side or the other or by finding a compromise that satisfies both Id and Superego (Freud, 1926).

When Id or Superego demands threaten to overwhelm the Ego, *anxiety* results (Freud, 1915a). If instinctual Id impulses overpower the Ego, a person may act impulsively and perhaps destructively. Using Freud's terminology, for example, you could say that Julian's Id was out of control when he stole from the church or tried to rob the drugstore. In contrast, when Superego demands overwhelm the Ego, an individual may suffer from guilt, self-reproach, or even suicidal impulses for failing to live up to the Superego's moral standards (Freud, 1933, 1936). Using Freudian terminology again, it is probably safe to say that Kenneth's feelings of guilt over Julian were Superego-inspired.

Ego defense mechanisms
In psychoanalytic theory, largely unconscious distortions of thought or perception that act to reduce anxiety.

repression
In psychoanalytic theory, the unconscious exclusion of anxiety-provoking thoughts, feelings, and memories from conscious awareness; the most fundamental Ego defense mechanism.

displacement
In psychoanalytic theory, the Ego defense mechanism that involves unconsciously shifting the target of an emotional urge to a substitute target that is less threatening or dangerous.

sublimation
In psychoanalytic theory, an Ego defense mechanism that involves redirecting sexual urges toward productive, socially acceptable, nonsexual activities; a form of displacement.

If a realistic solution or compromise is not possible, the Ego may temporarily reduce anxiety by *distorting* thoughts or perceptions of reality through processes that Freud called **Ego defense mechanisms** (Freud, 1915b; A. Freud, 1946). By resorting to these largely unconscious self-deceptions, the Ego can maintain an integrated sense of self while searching for a more acceptable and realistic solution to a conflict between Id and Superego.

The most fundamental Ego defense mechanism is **repression** (Freud, 1915a, 1936). To some degree, repression occurs in every Ego defense mechanism. In simple terms, repression is unconscious forgetting. Unbeknownst to the person, anxiety-producing thoughts, feelings, or impulses are pushed out of conscious awareness into the unconscious.

What kinds of information are likely to be repressed? Common examples include traumatic events, past failures, embarrassments, disappointments, the names of disliked people, episodes of physical pain or illness, and unacceptable urges. So if you "forget" a meeting, a deadline, or a dental appointment that you'd prefer to avoid, you may be experiencing a minor instance of repression.

Repression, however, is not an all-or-nothing psychological process. As Freud (1939) explained, "The repressed material retains its impetus to penetrate into consciousness." In other words, if you encounter a situation that is very similar to one you've repressed, bits and pieces of memories of the previous situation may begin to resurface. In such instances, the Ego may employ other defense mechanisms that allow the urge or information to remain partially conscious.

This is what occurs with the Ego defense mechanism of displacement. **Displacement** occurs when emotional impulses are redirected to a substitute object or person, usually one that is less threatening or dangerous than the original source of conflict (A. Freud, 1946). For example, the employee angered by his supervisor's unfair treatment may displace his hostility onto other drivers while driving home. He consciously experiences anger, but it is directed toward someone other than its true target, which remains unconscious.

Sublimation In Freud's view, creative or productive behaviors represented the re-channeling of sexual energy or *libido*—an Ego defense mechanism he termed sublimation. Later personality theorists, including the neo-Freudians and the humanistic theorists, criticized Freud's refusal to consider creativity a drive in its own right.

Freud (1930) believed that a special form of displacement, called *sublimation,* is largely responsible for the productive and creative contributions of people and even whole societies. **Sublimation** involves displacing sexual urges toward "an aim other than, and remote from, that of sexual gratification" (Freud, 1914). In effect, sublimation channels sexual urges into productive, socially acceptable, nonsexual activities.

A humorous example of sublimation was provided by a married couple in one of our classes. After the young woman had surgery, she was told to abstain from sexual intercourse for six weeks. As she explained in class, "It's amazing what got done around the house. Mark put flower boxes outside the windows, waxed the cars, trimmed the hedges, painted the house inside and out, and he even replaced the kitchen floor!" No doubt Freud would see this flurry of activity as the sublimation of sexual energy, or libido.

TABLE 11.1 The Major Ego Defense Mechanisms

Defense	Description	Examples
Repression	The complete exclusion from consciousness of anxiety-producing thoughts, feelings, or impulses. Most basic defense mechanism.	Three years after being hospitalized for back surgery, the person can remember only vague details about the event.
Displacement	Emotional impulses are redirected toward a substitute person or object, usually one that is less threatening or dangerous than the original source of conflict.	Angered by a neighbor's hateful comment, a mother spanks her daughter for accidentally spilling her milk.
Sublimation	A form of displacement in which sexual urges are rechanneled into productive, nonsexual activities.	A grad student works on her thesis 14 hours a day while her husband is on an extended business trip.
Rationalization	Justifying one's actions or feelings with socially acceptable explanations rather than consciously acknowledging one's true motives or desires.	After being rejected by a large, prestigious college, a student explains that he was glad it turned out that way because he'd be happier at a smaller, less competitive college.
Projection	The attribution of one's own unacceptable urges or qualities to others.	A married women who is sexually attracted to a co-worker accuses him of flirting with her.
Reaction formation	Thinking or behaving in a way that is the extreme opposite of unacceptable urges or impulses.	Threatened by their awakening sexual attraction to girls, adolescent boys often go out of their way to tease and torment adolescent girls.
Denial	The failure to recognize or acknowledge the existence of anxiety-provoking information.	An alcoholic fails to acknowledge that he is addicted to a drug.
Undoing	A form of unconscious repentance that involves neutralizing or atoning for an unacceptable action or thought with a second action or thought.	A woman who gets a tax refund by cheating on her taxes makes a larger than usual donation to the church collection on the following Sunday.

The major defense mechanisms are summarized in Table 11.1. In Freud's view, the drawback to using any defense mechanism is that maintaining these self-deceptions requires psychological energy. Regarding the most basic defense mechanism, repression, Freud (1936) pointed out that repression does not take place "on a single occasion," but rather demands "a continuous expenditure of effort." Such effort depletes psychological energy that is needed to cope effectively with the demands of daily life.

The use of defense mechanisms is very common. Many psychologically healthy people temporarily use Ego defense mechanisms to deal with stressful events. When Ego defense mechanisms are used in limited areas and on a short-term basis, psychological energy is not seriously depleted. Ideally, we strive to maintain realistic perceptions of the world and our motives, and search for workable solutions to conflicts and problems. Using Ego defense mechanisms is often a way of buying time while we consciously or unconsciously wrestle with more realistic solutions for whatever is troubling us. But when defense mechanisms delay or interfere with our use of more constructive coping strategies, they can be counterproductive.

Personality Development:
The Psychosexual Stages

The psychosexual stages include the oral, anal, phallic, latency, and genital stages. What are the core conflicts of the oral, anal, and phallic stages? What is the consequence of fixation? What role does the Oedipus complex play in personality development?

According to Freud (1905), people progress through five psychosexual stages of development. The foundations of adult personality are established during the first five years of life, as the child progresses through the *oral, anal,* and *phallic* psychosexual stages. The *latency stage* occurs during late childhood, while the fifth and final stage, the *genital stage,* begins in adolescence.

Each psychosexual stage represents a different focus of the Id's sexual energies. Freud (1940) contended that "sexual life does not begin only at puberty, but starts with clear manifestations after birth." This statement is often misinterpreted. Freud was *not* saying that an infant experiences sexual

psychosexual stages
In Freud's theory, age-related developmental periods in which the child's sexual urges are expressed through different body areas and the activities associated with those body areas.

Oedipus complex
In Freud's theory, a child's unconscious sexual desire for the opposite-sex parent, usually accompanied by hostile feelings toward the same-sex parent.

identification
In psychoanalytic theory, an Ego defense mechanism that involves reducing anxiety by modeling the behavior and characteristics of another person.

urges in the same way as an adult. Instead, Freud believed that the infant or young child expresses primitive sexual urges by seeking sensual pleasure from different body areas. Thus, the **psychosexual stages** are age-related developmental periods in which sexual impulses are focused on different body zones and are expressed through activities associated with these body areas.

Over the first five years of life, the expression of primitive sexual urges progresses from one bodily zone to another in a distinct order: the mouth, the anus, and the genitals. The first year of life is characterized as the *oral stage.* During this time the infant derives pleasure through the oral activities of sucking, chewing, and biting. During the next two years, pleasure is derived through elimination and acquiring control over elimination—the *anal stage.* In the *phallic stage,* pleasure seeking is focused on the genitals.

Fixation: Unresolved Developmental Conflicts

At each psychosexual stage, Freud (1905) believed that the infant or young child is faced with a developmental conflict that must be successfully resolved in order to move on to the next stage. The heart of this conflict is the degree to which parents either frustrate or overindulge the child's expression of pleasurable feelings. Hence, Freud (1940) believed that parental attitudes and the timing of specific child-rearing events, such as weaning or toilet training, leave a lasting influence on personality development.

If frustrated, the child will be left with feelings of unmet needs characteristic of that stage. If overindulged, the child may be reluctant to move on to the next stage. In either case, the result of an unresolved developmental conflict is *fixation* at a particular stage. The person continues to seek pleasure through behaviors that are similar to those associated with that psychosexual stage. For example, the adult who constantly chews gum, smokes, or bites her nails may have unresolved oral psychosexual conflicts.

The Oedipus Complex: A Psychosexual Drama

The most critical conflict that the child must successfully resolve for healthy personality and sexual development occurs during the phallic stage (Freud, 1923, 1940). As the child becomes more aware of pleasure derived from the genital area, Freud believed that the child develops a sexual attraction to the opposite-sex parent and hostility toward the same-sex parent. This is the famous **Oedipus complex,** named after the hero of a Greek myth. Abandoned at birth, Oedipus does not know the identity of his parents. As an adult, Oedipus unknowingly kills his father and marries his mother.

Outward manifestations of the Oedipus complex can include the child's possessiveness of the opposite-sex parent, such as the little boy who defiantly says, "Don't kiss my mommy, Daddy!" or the little girl who competitively proclaims, "When I grow up, I'm going to marry Daddy!" According to Freud, this attraction to the opposite-sex parent plays out as a sexual drama in the child's mind, a drama with different plot twists for boys and girls.

For boys, the Oedipus complex unfolds as a confrontation with the father for the affections of the mother. The little boy feels hostility and jealousy toward his father, but he realizes that his father is more physically powerful. The boy experiences *castration anxiety,* or the fear that his father will punish him by castrating him (Freud, 1933).

To resolve the Oedipus complex and these anxieties, the little boy ultimately joins forces with his former enemy by resorting to the defense mechanism of **identification.** That is, he imitates and internalizes his father's values, attitudes, and mannerisms. There is, however, one strict limitation in identifying with the father: Only the father can enjoy the sexual affections of the mother. This limitation becomes internalized as a taboo against incestuous urges in the boy's developing Superego, a taboo that is enforced by the Superego's use of guilt and societal restrictions (Freud, 1905, 1923).

Competing with Mom for Dad? According to Freud, the child identifies with the same-sex parent as a way of resolving sexual attraction toward the opposite-sex parent—the Oedipus complex. He believed that imitating the same-sex parent also played an important role in the development of gender identity and, ultimately, healthy sexual maturity.

Girls also ultimately resolve the Oedipus complex by identifying with the same-sex parent and developing a strong Superego taboo against incestuous urges. But the underlying sexual drama in girls follows different themes. The little girl discovers that little boys have a penis and that she does not. She feels a sense of deprivation and loss that Freud termed *penis envy*.

According to Freud (1940), the little girl blames her mother for "sending her into the world so insufficiently equipped." Thus, she develops contempt for and resentment toward her mother. However, in her attempt to take her mother's place with her father, she also *identifies* with her mother. Like the little boy, the little girl internalizes the attributes of the same-sex parent.

Freud's views on female sexuality, particularly the concept of penis envy, are among his most severely criticized ideas. Perhaps recognizing that his explanation of female psychosexual development rested on shaky ground, Freud (1924) admitted, "Our insight into these developmental processes in girls is unsatisfactory, incomplete, and vague."

The Latency and Genital Stages

It often happens that a young man falls in love seriously for the first time with a mature woman, or a girl with an elderly man in a position of authority; this is a clear echo of the [earlier] phase of development that we have been discussing, since these figures are able to re-animate pictures of their mother or father.

Sigmund Freud, 1905

Freud felt that because of the intense anxiety associated with the Oedipus complex, the sexual urges of male and female children become repressed during the *latency stage* in late childhood. Outwardly, children in the latency stage express a strong desire to associate with same-sex peers, a preference that strengthens the child's sexual identity.

The final resolution of the Oedipus complex occurs in adolescence, during the *genital stage*. As incestuous urges start to resurface, they are prohibited by the moral ideals of the Superego as well as by societal restrictions. Instead, the person directs sexual urges toward socially acceptable substitutes, who often resemble the person's opposite-sex parent (Freud, 1905).

In Freud's theory, a healthy personality and sense of sexuality result when conflicts are successfully resolved at each stage of psychosexual development. Successfully negotiating the conflicts at each psychosexual stage results in the person's capacity to love, and in expressions of productive living through one's life work, child rearing, and other accomplishments.

CONCEPT REVIEW 11.1

Freud's Psychoanalytic Theory

1. The Id is guided by the _____, while the Ego is guided by the _____.
   a. manifest content; latent content
   b. reality principle; pleasure principle
   c. latent content; manifest content
   d. pleasure principle; reality principle

2. Freud developed the method of _____ to help his patients uncover forgotten memories.
   a. hypnosis   c. free association
   b. catharsis   d. Thanatos

3. The structure of personality that evaluates the morality of behavior is called the
   _____.
   a. Ego   c. libido
   b. Superego   d. repression

4. Eight-year-old Johnny wants to be a truck driver when he grows up, just like his dad. Johnny's acceptance of his father's attitudes and values indicate the process of
   _____.
   a. fixation   c. denial
   b. identification   d. projection

5. Every time four-year-old Felix touches his genitals, his parents call him a "dirty little boy" and slap his hands. According to Freud, Felix's frustration may result in an unresolved developmental conflict called _____.
   a. fixation   c. sublimation
   b. identification   d. denial

6. Seven-year-old Carolyn prefers to play with her girlfriends and does not like playing with boys very much. Carolyn is probably in the _____ stage of sexual development.
   a. anal   c. latency
   b. phallic   d. genital

The Neo-Freudians:
Freud's Descendants and Dissenters

The neo-Freudians followed Freud in stressing the importance of the unconscious and early childhood, but they developed their own personality theories. How did the neo-Freudians generally differ from Freud? What were the key ideas of Jung, Horney, and Adler?

Freud's ideas were always controversial. But by the early 1900s he had attracted a number of followers, many of whom went to Vienna to study with him. Although these early followers developed their own personality theories, they still recognized the importance of many of Freud's basic notions, such as the influence of unconscious processes and early childhood experiences. In effect, they kept the foundations that Freud had established but offered new explanations for personality processes. Hence, these theorists are often called *neo-Freudians* (the prefix *neo* means "new"). The neo-Freudians and their theories are considered part of the psychoanalytic perspective on personality.

In general, the neo-Freudians disagreed with Freud on three key points. First, they took issue with Freud's belief that the primary motivation behind behavior was sexual urges. Second, they disagreed with Freud's contention that personality is fundamentally determined by early childhood experiences. Instead, the neo-Freudians believed that personality can also be influenced by experiences throughout the lifespan. Third, the neo-Freudian theorists departed from Freud's generally pessimistic view of human nature and society.

In Chapter 9, on lifespan development, we described the psychosocial theory of one famous neo-Freudian, Erik Erikson. In this chapter, we'll look at the basic ideas of three other important neo-Freudians: Carl Jung, Karen Horney, and Alfred Adler.

What we properly call instincts are physiological urges, and are perceived by the senses. But at the same time, they also manifest themselves in fantasies and often reveal their presence only by symbolic images. These manifestations are what I call the archetypes. They are without known origin; and they reproduce themselves in any time or in any part of the world.

Carl Jung, 1964

collective unconscious
In Jung's theory, the hypothesized part of the unconscious mind that is inherited from previous generations and that contains universally shared ancestral experiences and ideas.

archetypes
In Jung's theory, the inherited mental images of universal human instincts, themes, and preoccupations that are the main components of the collective unconscious.

Carl Jung: Archetypes and the Collective Unconscious

Born in a small town in Switzerland, **Carl Jung** (1875–1961) was fascinated by the myths, folk tales, and religions of his own and other cultures. After studying medicine, Jung was drawn to the relatively new field of psychiatry because he believed it could provide deeper insights into the human mind (Jung, 1963).

Fascinated by Freud's ideas, Jung began a correspondence with him. At their first meeting, the two men were so compatible that they talked for 13 hours nonstop. Freud felt that his young disciple was so promising that he called him his "adopted son" and his "crown prince." It would be Jung, Freud decided, who would succeed him and lead the international psychoanalytic movement. However, Jung was too independent to relish his role as Freud's unquestioning disciple. As Jung continued to put forth his own ideas, his close friendship with Freud ultimately ended in bitterness.

Jung rejected Freud's belief that human behavior was fueled by the instinctual drives of sex and aggression. Instead, Jung believed that people are motivated by a more general psychological energy that pushes them to achieve psychological growth, self-realization, and psychic wholeness and harmony. Jung (1963) also believed that personality continued to develop in significant ways throughout the lifespan.

In studying different cultures, Jung was struck by the universality of many images and themes, which also surfaced in his patients' dreams and preoccupations. These observations led to some of Jung's most intriguing ideas, the notions of the collective unconscious and the archetypes.

Archetypes in Popular Culture According to Jung, archetypal images are often found in popular myths, novels, and even films. Consider the classic film, *The Wizard of Oz*. The motherless child, Dorothy, is on a quest for self-knowledge and selfhood, symbolized by the circular Emerald City. She is accompanied by her symbolic helpers, the Cowardly Lion (seeking courage), the Tin Woodman (seeking love), and the Scarecrow (seeking wisdom).

Jung (1936) believed that the deepest part of the individual psyche was the **collective unconscious,** which is shared by all people and reflects humanity's collective evolutionary history. He described the collective unconscious as containing "the whole spiritual heritage of mankind's evolution, born anew in the brain structure of every individual" (Jung, 1931).

Contained in the collective unconscious are the **archetypes,** the mental images of universal human instincts, themes, and preoccupations (Jung, 1964). Common archetype themes that are expressed in virtually every culture are the hero, the powerful father, the nurturing mother, the witch, the wise old man, the innocent child, and death and rebirth.

Two important archetypes that Jung (1951) described are the *anima* and the *animus*—the representations of feminine and masculine qualities. Jung believed that every man has a "feminine" side, represented by his anima, and every woman has a "masculine" side, represented by her animus. To achieve psychological harmony, Jung believed, it is important for men to recognize and accept their feminine aspects, and for women to recognize and accept the masculine side of their nature.

Not surprisingly, Jung's concepts of the collective unconscious and shared archetypes have been criticized as being unscientific or mystical. As far as we know, individual experiences cannot be genetically passed down from one generation to the next. Regardless, Jung's ideas make more sense if you think of the collective unconscious as reflecting shared human experiences. The archetypes, then, can be thought of as symbols that represent the common, universal themes of the human life cycle (McAdams, 1994; Stevens, 1983). These universal themes include birth, achieving a sense of self, parenthood, the spiritual search, and death.

The Mandala To Jung, the mandala was the archetypal symbol of the self and psychic wholeness. Mandala images are found in cultures throughout the world. Shown here are a ceremonial Buffalo Robe of the Plains Indians (right); the Bhavacakra or Buddhist Wheel of Life, from Tibet (top left); and a rose window from Chartres Cathedral in France (top right).

Although Jung's theory never became as influential as Freud's theory, some of his ideas have gained wide acceptance. For example, Jung (1923) was the first to describe two basic personality types: *introverts,* who focus their attention inward, and *extraverts,* who turn their attention and energy toward the outside world. We will encounter these two basic personality dimensions again when we look at trait theories later in this chapter. Finally, Jung's emphasis on the drive toward psychological growth and self-realization anticipated some of the basic ideas of the humanistic perspective on personality, which we'll look at shortly.

Karen Horney: Basic Anxiety and "Womb Envy"

Man, [Freud] postulated, is doomed to suffer or destroy. . . . My own belief is that man has the capacity as well as the desire to develop his potentialities and become a decent human being, and that these deteriorate if his relationship to others and hence to himself is, and continues to be, disturbed. I believe that man can change and go on changing as long as he lives.

Karen Horney, 1945

Trained as a Freudian psychoanalyst, **Karen Horney** (pronounced HORN-eye) (1885–1952) emigrated from Germany to the United States during the Great Depression in the 1930s. Horney noticed distinct differences between her American and German patients. Whereas Freud traced psychological problems to sexual conflicts, Horney found that her American patients were much more worried about their jobs and economic problems than their sex lives. Thus, Horney came to stress the importance of cultural and social factors in personality development—matters which Freud had largely ignored (Horney, 1945).

Horney also stressed the importance of social relationships, especially the parent–child relationship, in the development of personality. She believed that disturbances in human relationships, not sexual conflicts, were the cause of psychological problems. Such problems arise from the attempt to deal with *basic anxiety,* which Horney (1945) described as "the feeling a child has of being isolated and helpless in a potentially hostile world."

Horney (1945) described three patterns of behavior that the individual uses to defend against basic anxiety: moving toward, against, or away from other people. Those who move *toward* other people have an excessive need for approval and affection. Those who move *against* others have an excessive need for power, especially power over other people. They are often competitive, critical, and domineering, and need to feel superior to others. Finally, those who move *away from* other people have an excessive need for independence and self-sufficiency, which often makes them aloof and detached from others.

Horney contended that people with a healthy personality are *flexible* in balancing these different needs, for there are times when each behavior pattern is appropriate. As Horney (1945) wrote, "One should be capable of giving in to others, of fighting, and of keeping to oneself. The three can complement each other and make for a harmonious whole." But when one pattern becomes the predominant way of dealing with other people and the world, psychological conflict and problems can result.

Horney also sharply disagreed with Freud's interpretation of female development, especially his notion that women suffer from penis envy. What women envy in men, Horney (1926) claimed, is not their penis but their superior status in society. In fact, Horney contended that men often suffer *womb envy,* envying women's capacity to bear children. Neatly standing Freud's view of feminine psychology on its head, Horney argued that *men* compensated for their relatively minor role in reproduction by creating things through their work and other external accomplishments.

Horney shared Jung's belief that people were not doomed to psychological conflict and problems. Also like Jung, Horney contended that the drive to grow psychologically and achieve one's potential are basic human motives.

Alfred Adler: Feelings of Inferiority and Striving for Superiority

Born in Vienna, **Alfred Adler** (1870–1937) was an extremely sickly child. Yet through determination and hard work, he overcame his physical weaknesses. After studying medicine, he became associated with Freud. But from the beginning of Adler's interest in psychoanalysis, he disagreed with Freud on several issues. In particular, Adler placed much more emphasis on the importance of conscious thought processes and social urges. Eventually, Adler broke away from Freud to establish his own theory of personality.

> *To be a human being means to have inferiority feelings. One recognizes one's own powerlessness in the face of nature. One sees death as the irrefutable consequence of existence. But in the mentally healthy person this inferiority feeling acts as a motive for productivity, as a motive for attempting to overcome obstacles, to maintain oneself in life.*
>
> **Alfred Adler,** 1933

Adler (1933b) believed that the most fundamental human motive was *striving for superiority*—the desire to improve oneself, master challenges, and move toward self-perfection and self-realization. Striving toward superiority arises from universal *feelings of inferiority* that are experienced during infancy and childhood, when the child is helpless and dependent on others. These feelings motivate people to *compensate* for their real or imagined weaknesses by emphasizing their talents and abilities, and by working hard to improve themselves. Hence, Adler (1933a) saw the universal human feelings of inferiority as ultimately being constructive and valuable.

However, when people are unable to compensate for specific weaknesses or when their feelings of inferiority are excessive, they can develop an *inferiority complex*—a general sense of inadequacy, weakness, and helplessness. People with an inferiority complex are often unable to strive for mastery and self-improvement.

At the other extreme, people can *overcompensate* for their feelings of inferiority and develop a *superiority complex*. Behaviors due to a superiority complex might include exaggerating one's accomplishments and importance in an effort to cover up weaknesses, and denying the reality of one's limitations (Adler, 1954).

Although we've only been able to touch on the highlights of the work of Jung, Horney, and Adler, their theories provide a wealth of insights and ideas about human behavior and personality. Like Freud, the neo-Freudians have their own followings among therapists and personality theorists.

CONCEPT REVIEW 11.2

Comparing Psychoanalytic Theorists

Which psychoanalytic theorist made each of the following statements?

1. _____ "Man is a wolf to man."

2. _____ "My own belief is that man has the capacity as well as the desire to develop his potentialities and become a decent human being, and that these deteriorate if his relationship to others and hence to himself is, and continues to be, disturbed."

3. _____ "To be human means to have inferiority feelings."

4. _____ "The whole spiritual heritage of mankind's evolution [is] born anew in the brain structure of every individual."

5. _____ "Sexual life does not begin only at puberty, but starts with clear manifestations after birth."

6. _____ "One should be capable of giving in to others, of fighting, and of keeping to oneself. The three can complement each other and make for a harmonious whole."

Evaluating Freud and the Psychoanalytic Perspective on Personality

> *The psychoanalytic perspective has had a profound influence on Western culture and on psychology, yet it has also been criticized. What are three criticisms of Freud's theory and, more generally, the psychoanalytic perspective?*

Like it or not, Sigmund Freud's ideas have had a profound and lasting impact on our culture and on our understanding of human nature. Today, opinions on Freud span the entire spectrum. Some see him as a genius who discovered brilliant, lasting insights into human nature. Others contend that Freud was a deeply neurotic, driven man who successfully foisted his twisted personal view of human nature onto an unsuspecting public (Crews, 1996, 1986).

The truth, as you might suspect, lies somewhere in between. Although Freud has had an enormous impact on psychology and on society, there are several valid criticisms of Freud's theory and, more generally, the psychoanalytic perspective. We'll discuss three of the most important problems next.

> *Freud's legacy, it is clear, consists chiefly of pseudoscience and cannot be defended on any grounds.*
>
> **Frederick Crews,** 1986

> *Sigmund Freud—along with Karl Marx, Charles Darwin, and Albert Einstein—is among that small handful of supreme makers of the twentieth-century mind whose works should be our prized possession.*
>
> **Peter Gay,** 1989

Inadequacy of Evidence

Freud's theory relies wholly on data derived from his relatively small number of patients and from self-analysis. Most of Freud's patients were relatively well-to-do, well-educated members of the middle and upper classes in turn-of-the-century Vienna. Freud (1916, 1919, 1939) also analyzed the lives of famous historical figures, such as Leonardo da Vinci, and looked to myth, religion, literature, and evolutionary prehistory for confirmation of his ideas. Any way you look at it, this is a rather small and skewed sample from which to draw sweeping generalizations about human nature.

Furthermore, it is impossible to objectively assess Freud's "data." Freud did not take notes during his private therapy sessions. When he does report a case in detail, it is Freud's interpretation of the case that we encounter. For Freud, proof of the validity of his ideas depended on his encountering similar patterns in different patients. So the critical question is this: Was Freud imposing his own ideas onto his patients, seeing only what he expected to see? Some critics think so (e.g., Crew, 1996, 1986; P. Robinson, 1993; Masson, 1984a, 1984b).

Lack of Testability

Many psychoanalytic concepts are so vague and ambiguous that they are impossible to objectively measure or confirm (Crew, 1996). For example, how might you go about proving the existence of the Id or the Superego? Or how could you operationally define and measure the effects of the pleasure principle, the life instinct, or the Oedipus complex?

Psychoanalytic "proof" often has a "Heads I win, tails you lose" style to it. In other words, psychoanalytic concepts are often impossible to *dis*prove, because even seemingly contradictory information can be used to support Freud's theory. For example, if your memory of childhood doesn't jibe with Freud's description of the psychosexual stages or the Oedipus complex, well, that's because you've repressed it. Freud himself was not immune to this form of reasoning (P. Robinson, 1993). When one of Freud's patients reported dreams that didn't seem to reveal a hidden wish, Freud interpreted the dreams as betraying the patient's hidden wish to disprove Freud's dream theory!

As Freud acknowledged, psychoanalysis is better at explaining *past* behavior than at predicting future behavior (Gay, 1989). Indeed, psychoanalytic interpretations are so flexible that a given behavior can be explained by any number of completely different motives. For example, a man who is extremely affectionate toward his wife might be exhibiting displacement of a repressed incestuous urge (he is displacing his repressed affection for his mother onto his wife), reaction formation (he actually hates his wife intensely, so he compensates by being overly affectionate), or fixation at the oral stage (he is overly dependent on his wife).

Nonetheless, several key psychoanalytic ideas *have* been substantiated by empirical research (Westen, 1990). Among these are the ideas that (1) much of mental life is unconscious; (2) early childhood experiences have a critical influence on interpersonal relationships and psychological adjustment in adulthood; and (3) people differ significantly in the degree to which they are able to regulate their impulses, emotions, and thoughts toward adaptive and socially acceptable ends.

Sexism

Many people feel that Freud's theories reflect a sexist view of women. According to Freud (1925), a woman "shares the contempt felt by men for a sex which is the lesser in so important a respect"—namely, the lack of a penis. Because of penis envy and an innate sense of inferiority, Freud claimed, women are more vain, masochistic, and jealous than men. He also believed that women are more influenced by their emotions and have a lesser ethical and moral sense.

As Horney and other female psychoanalysts pointed out, Freud's theory uses male psychology as a prototype. Women are essentially viewed as a deviation from the norm of masculinity (Horney, 1926; Thompson, 1950). Perhaps, Horney suggested, psychoanalysis would have evolved an entirely different view of women if it were not dominated by the male point of view.

To Freud's credit, women were quite active in the early psychoanalytic movement. Several female analysts became close colleagues of Freud (Freeman & Strean, 1987; Roazen, 1976). It was Freud's daughter Anna, rather than any of his sons, who followed in his footsteps as an eminent psychoanalyst. Ultimately, Anna Freud became her father's successor as leader of the international psychoanalytic movement.

The weaknesses in Freud's theory and in the psychoanalytic approach to personality are not minor problems. All the same, Freud made some extremely significant contributions to modern psychological thinking. Most important, he drew attention to the existence and importance of mental processes that occur outside of conscious awareness, an idea that continues to be actively investigated by today's psychological researchers (see Underwood, 1996; Kihlstrom & others, 1992; Erdelyi, 1992).

The great question that has never been answered, and which I have not yet been able to answer, despite my thirty years of research into the feminine soul, is "What do women want?"

Sigmund Freud (E. Jones, 1955)

Anna Freud (1895–1982) Freud's youngest daughter, Anna, became his chief disciple and the founder of a psychoanalytic school in her own right. Expanding on her father's theory, she applied psychoanalysis to therapy with children. She is shown here addressing a debate on psychoanalysis at the Sorbonne University in Paris in 1950.

Freud has fundamentally altered the way we think. He has changed our intellectual manners, often without being aware of it. For most of us Freud has become a habit of mind. . . . He is the major source of our modern inclination to look for meanings beneath the surface of behavior—to be always on the alert for the "real" (and presumably hidden) significance of our actions.

Paul Robinson, 1993

humanistic psychology
The theoretical viewpoint on personality that generally emphasizes the inherent goodness of people, human potential, self-actualization, the self-concept, and healthy personality development.

The Humanistic Perspective on Personality

The humanistic perspective emphasizes free will, self-awareness, and psychological growth. What role do the self-concept, the actualizing tendency, and unconditional positive regard play in Rogers' personality theory? What are key strengths and weaknesses of the humanistic perspective?

By the 1950s, the field of personality was dominated by two completely different perspectives: Freudian psychoanalysis and B. F. Skinner's brand of behaviorism (see Chapter 5). Whereas Freud's theory of personality proposed elaborate and complex internal states, Skinner's ideas on personality went to the opposite extreme.

Skinner (1953, 1954) saw the very concept of personality as unnecessary in a scientific understanding of behavior. Rather than focus on a person's inner mental states, which cannot be directly observed or measured, Skinner believed that the focus should be on observable behaviors and on the environmental factors that shape and maintain those behaviors (see Rogers & Skinner, 1956). As Skinner (1971) wrote, "A person does not act upon the world, the world acts upon him."

The Emergence of the "Third Force"

Another group of psychologists had a fundamentally different view of human nature. In opposition to both psychoanalysis and behaviorism, they championed a "third force" in psychology, which they called humanistic psychology. **Humanistic psychology** is a view of personality that emphasizes human potential and such uniquely human characteristics as self-awareness and free will.

In contrast to Freud's pessimistic view of people as being motivated by unconscious sexual and destructive instincts, the humanistic psychologists saw people as being innately good. Humanistic psychologists also differed from psychoanalytic theorists by their focus on the *healthy* personality. They questioned how personality theories that were based largely on the characteristics of psychologically troubled people, like psychoanalytic theories, could accurately portray normal personality functioning.

In contrast to the behaviorist view that human and animal behavior is due largely to environmental reinforcement and punishment, the humanistic psychologists believed that people are motivated by the need to grow psychologically. They also doubted that laboratory research with rats and pigeons accurately reflected the essence of human nature, as the behaviorists claimed. Instead, humanistic psychologists contended that the most important factor in personality is the individual's *conscious, subjective perception of his or her self.*

The two most important contributors to the humanistic perspective were Carl Rogers and Abraham Maslow. In Chapter 8, on motivation, we discussed **Abraham Maslow's** (1908–1970) famous *hierarchy of needs.* Maslow's (1970) research identified several qualities of *self-actualized* people, summarized in Figure 11.2. As you'll see in this section, Rogers also placed considerable importance on the tendency of human beings to strive to fulfill their potential and capabilities.

FIGURE 11.2 Maslow's Characteristics of Self-Actualized People
Maslow (1970) proposed that human motives are arranged in a hierarchy of needs. Gratification of each need in the hierarchy is required before the next level of motives is activated. At the very top of the hierarchy is the need for self-actualization—the drive toward self-expression, growth, creativity, and the fulfillment of one's potential. From his investigations of psychologically healthy people, Maslow identified attributes that characterize self-actualizers, which are summarized here. Maslow also found that very few people seem to achieve self-actualization as he defined it. (Maslow, 1970.)

Self-actualization
Esteem needs
Belongingness and love needs
Safety needs
Physiological needs

Self-actualized people:
- Realistically perceive themselves, others, and external reality.
- Are spontaneous, natural, and open in their behavior and thoughts.
- Easily accept themselves and others as they are.
- Focus on problems outside the self.
- Have a strong need for privacy and independence.
- Continue to enjoy and appreciate positive aspects of everyday life.
- Tend to be creative.

Carl Rogers:

On Becoming a Person

At bottom, each person is asking, "Who am I, really? How can I get in touch with this real self, underlying all my surface behavior? How can I become myself?"

Carl Rogers, 1961

Carl Rogers (1902–1987) grew up in a large, close-knit family in Oak Park, Illinois, a suburb of Chicago. His parents were highly religious and instilled a moral, ethical atmosphere in the home, which no doubt influenced Rogers' early decision to become a minister. After studying theology, Rogers decided that the ministry was not for him. Instead, he turned to the study of psychology, ultimately enjoying a long, productive, and distinguished career as a psychotherapist, writer, and university professor.

Like Freud, Rogers' personality theory developed out of his clinical experiences with his patients, whom he referred to as "clients" to emphasize their active and voluntary participation in therapy. In marked contrast to Freud, Rogers was continually impressed by his clients' drive to grow and develop their potential.

These observations convinced Rogers that the most basic human motive was the **actualizing tendency**—the innate drive to maintain and enhance the human organism. According to Rogers, all other human motives, whether biological or social, were secondary. He compared the actualizing tendency to a child's drive to learn to walk, despite early frustration and falls—and even to a lowly potato's struggling efforts to send out roots and thrive in a less than ideal environment. To get a taste of the vastly different views of Rogers and Freud, read Critical Thinking Box 11.1, "Freud Versus Rogers on Human Nature."

The Self-Concept

Rogers (1959) was struck by how frequently his clients in therapy said "I'm not really sure who I am" or "I just don't feel like myself." This observation helped form the cornerstone of Rogers' personality theory: the idea of the self-concept. The **self-concept** is the set of perceptions and beliefs that you have about yourself, including your nature, your personal qualities, and your typical behavior.

According to Rogers (1980), people are motivated to act in accordance with their self-concept. So strong is the need to maintain a consistent self-concept that people will deny or distort experiences that contradict their self-concept. For example, if a person who thinks that he is not intelligent were to receive a high grade on a test, he would explain it away as an easy test or luck, rather than admit that he is an intelligent person.

The self-concept begins evolving early in life. Because they are motivated by the actualizing tendency, infants and young children naturally gravitate toward self-enhancing experiences. But as the child develops a greater sense of self-awareness, there is an increasing need for positive regard. *Positive regard* is the sense of being loved and valued by other people, especially one's parents.

Rogers (1959) maintained that most parents provide their children with **conditional positive regard**—the sense that the child is valued and loved only when she behaves in a way that is acceptable to others. The problem with conditional positive regard is that the child learns to deny or distort her genuine feelings. For example, if little Amy's parents scold and reject her when she expresses angry feelings, her strong need for positive regard will cause her to deny her anger, even when it's justified or appropriate. Eventually, Amy's self-concept will become so distorted that genuine feelings of anger are denied, because they are inconsistent with her self-concept as "a good girl who never gets angry." Because of the fear of losing positive regard, she cuts herself off from her true feelings.

actualizing tendency
In Rogers's theory, the innate drive to maintain and enhance the human organism.

self-concept
The set of perceptions and beliefs that you hold about yourself.

conditional positive regard
In Rogers's theory, the sense that you will be valued and loved only if you behave in a way that is acceptable to others; conditional love or acceptance.

CRITICAL THINKING 11.1

Freud Versus Rogers on Human Nature

Freud's view of human nature was deeply pessimistic. He believed that the human aggressive instinct was innate, persistent, and pervasive. Were it not for internal Superego restraints and external societal restraints, civilization as we know it would collapse: the destructive instincts of humans would be unleashed. As Freud (1930/1961) wrote in *Civilization and Its Discontents*:

> *Men are not gentle creatures who want to be loved, and who at the most can defend themselves if they are attacked; they are, on the contrary, creatures among whose instinctual endowments is to be reckoned a powerful share of aggressiveness. As a result, their neighbor is for them not only a potential helper or sexual object, but also someone who tempts them to satisfy their aggressiveness on him, to exploit his capacity for work without compensation, to use him sexually without his consent, to seize his possessions, to humiliate him, to cause him pain, to torture and to kill him.* Man is a wolf to man. *Who, in the face of all his experience of life and of history, will have the courage to dispute this assertion?*

In Freud's view, then, the essence of human nature is destructive. Control of these destructive instincts is necessary; yet societal, cultural, religious, and moral restraints also make people frustrated, neurotic, and unhappy. Why? Because the strivings of the Id toward instinctual satisfaction *must* be frustrated if civilization and the human

race are to survive. Hence, as the title of Freud's book emphasizes, civilization is inevitably accompanied by human "discontent."

A pretty gloomy picture, isn't it? Yet if you watch the evening news or read the newspaper, you may find it hard to disagree with Freud's negative image of human nature. People *are* often exceedingly cruel and selfish, committing horrifying acts of brutality toward strangers and even loved ones.

However, you might argue that people can also be extraordinarily kind, self-sacrificing, and loving toward others. Freud would agree with this observation; yet according to his theory, "good" or "moral" behavior does not disprove the essentially destructive nature of people. Instead, he explains "good" or "moral" behavior in terms of Superego control, sublimation of the instincts, displacement, and so forth.

But is this truly the essence of human nature? Carl Rogers disagreed strongly. "I do not discover man to be well characterized in his basic nature by such terms as *fundamentally hostile, antisocial, destructive, evil,*" Rogers (1957a/1989) wrote. Instead, Rogers believed, people were more accurately described as *"positive, forward-moving, constructive, realistic, trustworthy."*

If this is so, how can Rogers account for the evil and cruelty in the world? Rogers didn't deny that people can behave destructively and cruelly. Yet, throughout his life, Rogers insisted that people were innately good. Rogers (1981/1989) explains the existence of evil in this way:

> *My experience leads me to believe that it is* cultural *factors which are the major factor in our evil behaviors. The rough manner of childbirth, the infant's mixed experience with the parents, the constricting, destructive influence of our educational system, the injustice of our distribution of wealth, our cultivated prejudices against individuals who are different—all these elements and many others warp the human organism in directions which are antisocial.*

In sharp contrast to Freud, Rogers (1964/1989) said we should *trust* the human organism, because the human who is truly free to choose will naturally gravitate toward behavior that serves to perpetuate the human race and improve society as a whole:

> *I dare to believe that when the human being is inwardly free to choose whatever he deeply values, he tends to value those objects, experiences, and goals that will make for his own survival, growth, and development, and for the survival and development of others. . . . The psychologically mature person as I have described him has, I believe, the qualities which would cause him to value those experiences which would make for the survival and enhancement of the human race.*

Two great thinkers, two diametrically opposing views of human nature. What do *you* think? Do you agree with Freud that people are inherently driven by aggressive instincts? Must the destructive urges of the Id be restrained by parents, culture, religion, and society if civilization is to continue? Would an environment in which individuals were unrestrained inevitably lead to an unleashing of destructive instincts?

Or is the opposite the case, as Carl Rogers claimed? Are people naturally good? If people existed in a truly free and nurturing environment, would they invariably make constructive choices that would benefit both themselves and society as a whole?

Like Freud, Rogers believed that feelings and experiences could be driven from consciousness by being either denied or distorted. But Rogers believed that feelings become denied or distorted not because they are threatening but because they contradict the self-concept. In this case, people are in a state of *incongruence:* their self-concept conflicts with their actual experience (Rogers, 1959). Such a person is continually defending against genuine feelings and experiences that are inconsistent with his self-concept. As this process continues over time, a person progressively becomes more "out of touch" with his true feelings and his essential self, often experiencing psychological problems as a result.

How is incongruence to be avoided? The ideal situation is one in which a child experiences a great deal of unconditional positive regard. **Unconditional positive regard** refers to the child's sense of being unconditionally loved and valued, even if she doesn't conform to the standards and expectations of others. In this way, the child's actualizing tendency is allowed its fullest expression. Rogers believed that parents should provide unconditional acceptance and love of their children, whatever their child's behavior.

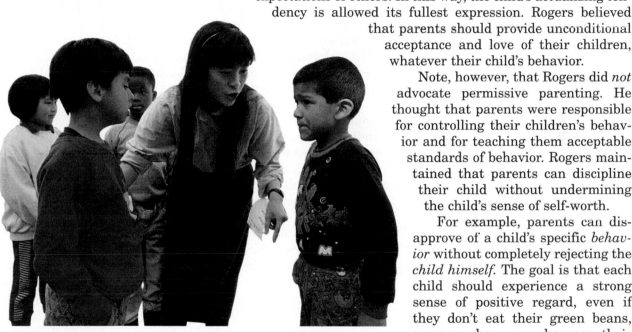

Note, however, that Rogers did *not* advocate permissive parenting. He thought that parents were responsible for controlling their children's behavior and for teaching them acceptable standards of behavior. Rogers maintained that parents can discipline their child without undermining the child's sense of self-worth.

For example, parents can disapprove of a child's specific *behavior* without completely rejecting the *child himself.* The goal is that each child should experience a strong sense of positive regard, even if they don't eat their green beans, scream when you shampoo their hair, or throw a tantrum when you invite your boss over for dinner. In effect, the parent's message should be, "I do not value your behavior right now, but I still love and value *you.*" In this way, the child's essential sense of self-worth can remain intact.

Unconditional Positive Regard Rogers contended that healthy personality development is the result of being unconditionally valued and loved as a person. He advocated that parents and teachers should control a child's inappropriate behavior without rejecting the child himself. Such a style of discipline teaches acceptable behaviors without diminishing the child's sense of self-worth.

The Fully Functioning Person

Rogers (1957b/1989) believed that it is through consistent experiences of unconditional positive regard that one becomes a psychologically healthy, fully functioning person. The *fully functioning person* has a flexible, constantly evolving self-concept. She is realistic, open to new experiences, and capable of changing in response to new experiences.

Rather than defending against or distorting her own thoughts or feelings, the person experiences *congruence:* her sense of self is consistent with her emotions and experiences. The actualizing tendency is fully operational in her, and she makes conscious choices that move her in the direction of greater growth and fulfillment of potential. Rogers (1957b, 1964) believed that the fully functioning person is likely to be creative and spontaneous, and to enjoy harmonious relationships with others.

unconditional positive regard
In Rogers's theory, the sense that you will be valued and loved even if you don't conform to the standards and expectations of others; unconditional love or acceptance.

Evaluating the Humanistic Perspective on Personality

Humanistic psychology has been extremely influential in psychotherapy, which we'll discuss more fully in Chapter 15. Beyond psychotherapy, humanistic theories have also had a significant impact in such diverse areas as education, parenting, and even business management practices (see Rogers, 1980, 1977). But the humanistic perspective has been criticized on two particular points.

First, humanistic theories are hard to validate or test scientifically. Humanistic theories tend to be based on philosophical assumptions or clinical observations, rather than on empirical research. For example, concepts like the self-concept, unconditional positive regard, and the actualizing tendency are very difficult to define or measure objectively.

Second, many psychologists believe that humanistic psychology's view of human nature is *too* optimistic. For example, if self-actualization is a universal human motive, why are self-actualized people so hard to find? And, critics claim, humanistic psychologists have minimized the darker, more destructive side of human nature. Can we really account for all the evil in the world by ascribing it to upbringing, society, or culture?

Rogers disagreed with the accusation that his view of human nature was hopelessly naive. "I am quite aware that out of defensiveness and inner fear individuals can and do behave in ways which are incredibly cruel, horribly destructive, immature, regressive, antisocial, and hurtful," Rogers (1961) wrote. "Yet one of the most refreshing and invigorating parts of my experience is to work with such individuals and to discover the strongly positive directional tendencies which exist in them, as in all of us, at the deepest levels."

The influence of humanistic psychology has waned since the 1960s and early 1970s. Nevertheless, it has made lasting contributions, especially in the realms of psychotherapy, counseling, education, and parenting (Zimring & Raskin, 1992; Lietaer & others, 1990). The humanistic perspective also promoted the scientific study of such topics as the healthy personality and creativity (e.g., Harrington & others, 1987). Finally, the importance of subjective experience and the self-concept has become widely accepted by psychologists (Markus & Cross, 1990; Markus & Kitayama, 1994).

The Social Cognitive Perspective on Personality

The social cognitive perspective stresses conscious thought processes, self-regulation, and the importance of situational influences. What is the principle of reciprocal determinism? What is the role of self-efficacy beliefs in personality? What are key strengths and weaknesses of the social cognitive perspective?

Have you ever noticed how different your behavior and sense of self can be in different situations? Consider this example: You feel pretty confident as you enter your English composition class. After all, you're pulling an A, and your prof nods approvingly every time you participate in the class discussion, which you do frequently. In contrast, your college algebra class is a disaster. You're worried about passing the course, and you feel so shaky about your

self-efficacy
The beliefs that people have about their ability to meet the demands of a specific situation; feelings of self-confidence or self-doubt.

social cognitive theory
Bandura's theory of personality, which emphasizes the importance of observational learning, conscious cognitive processes, social experiences, self-efficacy beliefs, and reciprocal determinism.

skills that you're afraid to even ask a question, much less participate in class. Even a casual observer would notice how differently you behave in the two different situations—speaking freely and confidently in one class, and staring at your desk in hopes that your instructor won't notice you in the other.

The idea that a person's conscious thought processes in different situations strongly influence his or her actions is one important characteristic of the *social cognitive perspective* on personality (Bandura, 1986). According to the social cognitive perspective, people are seen as actively processing information from their social experiences. This information influences their goals, expectations, beliefs, and behavior, as well as the specific environments that they choose.

The social cognitive perspective differs from psychoanalytic and humanistic perspectives in several ways (Meichenbaum, 1995; Pervin, 1997). First, rather than basing their approach on self-analysis or insights derived from psychotherapy, social cognitive personality theorists rely heavily on experimental findings. Second, the social cognitive perspective emphasizes conscious, self-regulated behavior rather than unconscious mental influences and instinctual drives. And third, as in our English-versus-algebra-class example, social cognitive theory emphasizes that our sense of self can vary, depending on our thoughts, feelings, and behaviors in a given situation. Thus, the self-concept is not a global, consistent entity, as implied by the humanistic perspective.

When the social cognitive perspective began to evolve in the late 1950s, it represented an attempt to bridge the clinical insights of psychoanalytic theory and the experimental rigor of learning theories (Grusec, 1992). But this early attempt to bridge psychoanalysis and behaviorism was to be short-lived.

By the early 1960s, the leading proponent of social cognitive theory, **Albert Bandura** (b. 1925), had abandoned both Skinner's radical behaviorism and psychoanalytic notions. Since then, Bandura (1986) has argued that "People are neither driven by inner forces nor automatically shaped and controlled by external stimuli." Instead, his research has repeatedly underscored the *interaction* of behavior, conscious cognitive processes, and our social experiences.

Self-Efficacy We acquire a strong sense of self-efficacy by meeting challenges and mastering new skills specific to a particular situation. With her mother showing her how to ride her new bike, this three-year-old is well on her way to developing a strong sense of self-efficacy in this domain. Self-efficacy beliefs begin to develop in early childhood, but continue to evolve throughout the lifespan as we encounter new and different challenges.

If reading Bandura's name gives you a sense of déjà vu, it's not surprising. In Chapter 5, on learning, we looked at Bandura's now-classic research on *observational learning*—how we learn by observing the actions of others. In Chapter 8, on motivation, we encountered Bandura's (1992a) more recent research on self-efficacy beliefs. **Self-efficacy** refers to the degree to which you are subjectively convinced of your own capabilities and effectiveness in meeting the demands of a particular situation. Bandura's recent research on self-efficacy reflects his growing emphasis on cognitive factors, which is represented in his **social cognitive theory** of personality. As you'll see in this section, both observational learning and self-efficacy play key roles in Bandura's approach to personality.

Multiple Causes of Behavior:
Reciprocal Determinism

It's commonly accepted today that most new behaviors are acquired primarily through observational learning. But as Bandura's research has shown, it's not just the actions of others that we observe and sometimes imitate. We also attend to the *consequences* that follow actions, to the rules and *standards* that apply to behavior in specific situations, and to the ways in which people *regulate their own behavior* (Bandura, 1986, 1992b). Incorporating all this information involves active cognitive processes. And, as we accumulate knowledge, it serves as a guide for our future behavior.

On the one hand, observational learning clearly underscores the social origins of many of our thoughts and actions. On the other hand, people don't simply observe and imitate others. Social cognitive theory also stresses the ongoing human capacity for *self*-regulation, self-reflection, and anticipation of the future. Through planning and self-direction, we identify goals and incentives for our behavior. Furthermore, our ability to reflect on our thoughts and actions allows us to engage in self-evaluation and to modify our future behaviors.

Thus, Bandura contends that our behavior is not determined by instinctual drives, unconscious forces, or a general self-concept. Rather, Bandura (1991b, 1989a) contends, it is our conscious, self-generated goals and standards that exert considerable control over our thoughts, feelings, and actions.

For example, consider your own goal of getting a college education. No doubt your social experiences, such as the influence of family, friends, and teachers, helped you arrive at your conscious formulation of this goal. By consciously choosing this goal, you've greatly influenced your own thoughts, actions, and environmental experiences. You attend college classes and think about new ideas. In fact, you're reading these words trying to make sense out of the social cognitive approach to personality. You plan ahead, schedule study time, prepare for exams, and write papers, all of which in turn influences the consequences you experience in the college environment. And you're evaluating your own performance, not just in comparison to other students but also in terms of the standards you've learned to set for yourself through observing the examples of others.

Bandura explains human functioning as being caused by the interaction of behavioral, cognitive, and environmental factors, a process he calls **reciprocal determinism** (see Figure 11.3). As Bandura (1986) explains, these three factors "all operate interactively as determinants of each other." That is, the environment influences our thoughts and actions, our thoughts influence our actions and the environments we choose, our actions influence our thoughts and the environments we choose, and so on in a circular fashion.

> *If actions were determined solely by external rewards and punishments, people would behave like weather vanes, constantly shifting direction to conform to whatever momentary influence happened to impinge on them.*
>
> **Albert Bandura,** 1986

reciprocal determinism
A model proposed by psychologist Albert Bandura that explains human functioning and personality as caused by the interaction of behavioral, cognitive, and environmental factors.

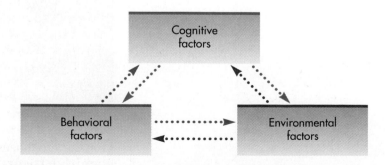

FIGURE 11.3 Reciprocal Determinism (Albert Bandura, 1988)

The Self-Regulation of Behavior

The self-regulation of behavior plays a central role in social cognitive theory (see Bandura, 1989a, 1992a, 1996). We develop the ability to regulate our own behavior through cognitive skills and internalized standards of performance that we've acquired through direct and observational learning.

In infancy and early childhood, our parents and caregivers are the external regulators of much of our behavior. But parents and other models also communicate standards of behavior that the child eventually incorporates as *internal* standards for *self*-control of behavior (Bandura, 1992b). In contrast to Freud's psychoanalytic theory, no special mental entity or unconscious process is required to explain self-control. Self-regulation is simply the result of the child's acquisition of standards, from parents and other models, through the processes of direct and observational learning.

As cognitive skills improve, the child learns how to monitor and evaluate his own actions, to compare his behavior to that of others, and becomes able to set goals and plan ahead. He also develops beliefs about the adequacy of his own capabilities. This process of cognitively integrating information from different situations continues throughout life (Bandura, 1992b).

> *People possess self-directive capabilities that enable them to exercise some control over their thoughts, feelings, and actions by the consequences they produce for themselves. Psychological function is, therefore, regulated by an interplay of self-generated and external sources of influence.*
>
> **Albert Bandura,** 1986

Beliefs of Self-Efficacy:
Anybody Here Know How to Fix a Light Switch?

Collectively, these emerging cognitive skills, abilities, and attitudes represent the person's *self-system* (Bandura, 1978). According to Bandura, it is our self-system that guides how we perceive, evaluate, and control our behavior in different situations. Bandura (in press) has found that the most critical elements influencing the self-system are our beliefs of self-efficacy.

For example, your authors, Don and Sandy, are at opposite ends of the spectrum in their beliefs of self-efficacy when it comes to repairs around the house. Don thinks he can fix anything, whether he really can or not. Sandy likes to describe herself as "mechanically challenged." When a light switch recently broke in our house, it was obvious that Sandy had very little faith in her ability to fix or replace it: she instantly hollered for help. As Don was investigating the matter, he casually asked Sandy whether *she* could replace the light switch.

"Me? You must be kidding," Sandy immediately responded. "It would never occur to me to even *try* to replace a light switch."

Bandura would be quick to point out how Sandy's weak belief of self-efficacy about electrical repairs has guided her behavior: it would prevent her from even attempting to fix a light switch on her own. When Don reassured Sandy that the directions were right on the light-switch package and that it was a very simple task, Sandy still expressed strong self-doubt about her abilities. "I'd probably blow up the house or burn it down or black out the whole neighborhood," she said.

Albert Bandura would, no doubt, smile at how readily Sandy's remark was an everyday confirmation of his research finding that our beliefs of self-efficacy help shape our imagination of future consequences (Bandura, in press, 1992a; Ozer & Bandura, 1990). In Sandy's case, her weak belief of self-efficacy has contributed to her imagination of dire future consequences should she attempt this task.

Bandura's concept of self-efficacy makes it easier to understand why people often fail to perform optimally at certain tasks even though they possess the necessary skills. Sandy has made presentations in front of hundreds of people, knows how to slab a geode with a diamond saw, can easily navigate Chicago's rush-hour traffic, and once single-handedly landed an eight-pound northern pike. In all these situations, she has strong feelings of self-efficacy. But hand her a package containing a light switch and she's intimidated.

Hence, our self-system is very flexible. How we regard ourselves and our abilities varies depending on the situations or tasks we're facing. In turn, our beliefs influence the tasks we are willing to try and how persistent we'll be in the face of obstacles (Bandura, 1996).

With the light switch, Don insisted on proving to Sandy that she was capable of changing it. "Well, maybe if I watched you install a couple of them, I might be willing to try it," Sandy finally offered. Sandy's suggestion illustrates how we acquire new behaviours and strengthen our beliefs of self-efficacy in particular situations: through observational learning and mastery experiences (Bandura, in press, 1990). When we perform a task successfully, our sense of self-efficacy becomes stronger. When we fail to deal effectively with a particular task or situation, our sense of self-efficacy is undermined.

From very early in life, children develop feelings of self-efficacy from their experiences in dealing with different tasks and situations, such as athletic, social, and academic activities (Bandura, 1989b). As Bandura (1992a) points out, developing self-efficacy merely begins in childhood and continues as a lifelong process. Each stage of the lifespan presents new challenges. And just for the record, Sandy *did* successfully replace the broken light switch. Now, about that dripping faucet . . .

The Social Cognitive View of Human Nature

How do social cognitive theorists view human nature? They fall between the extremes of the pessimistic image of destructive urges painted by Freud and the optimistic image of innate goodness painted by the humanistic theorists. Rather than seeing people as controlled solely by external environmental events or unconscious forces, the social cognitive perspective emphasizes the vast potential of human behavior, a potential that is largely self-regulated (see Critical Thinking Box 11.2, "Freud Versus Bandura on Human Aggression").

By emphasizing the reciprocal interaction of mental, behavioral, and situational factors, the social cognitive perspective recognizes the complex combination of factors that influences our everyday behavior. By emphasizing the important role of learning, especially observational learning, the social cognitive perspective offers a developmental explanation of human functioning that persists throughout our lifetime. Finally, by emphasizing the self-regulation of behavior, the social cognitive perspective places most of the responsibility for our behavior, and for the consequences that we experience, squarely on our own shoulders.

Evaluating the Social Cognitive Perspective on Personality

A key strength of the social cognitive perspective on personality is its grounding in empirical, laboratory research. The social cognitive perspective is built on research in learning, cognitive psychology, and social psychology, rather than clinical impressions. And, unlike vague psychoanalytic and humanistic concepts, the concepts of social cognitive theory are scientifically testable—that is, they can be operationally defined and measured. For example, psy-

CRITICAL THINKING 11.2

Freud Versus Bandura on Human Aggression

Freud viewed aggression as a universal, unconscious human instinct which must be controlled by the internal restraints of the Superego and the external restraints of culture, society, and morality. In Freud's eyes, aggressive instincts are part of the irrational, impulsive, and unconscious Id.

Social cognitive theorists, however, discount the importance of unconscious instincts or motives. Instead, they emphasize that behavior is driven by conscious goals and motives. Not surprisingly, Albert Bandura has taken issue with Freud's explanation of war and cruelty as being caused by the failure of the rational Ego, the Superego's restraints, and society's laws to control the Id's destructive impulses (see Box 11.1). Bandura (1986) points out that some of the most horrifying examples of human cruelty have involved conscious, *rational* behavior:

> People frequently engage in *destructive activities,* not *because of reduced self-control, but because their cognitive skills and self-control are too well enlisted*

through moral justification and self-exonerative devices in the service of destructive causes. The infamous extermination procedures of Nazi concentration camps were perfected in laboratories using human victims. In the Nazi value system, where the enslavement and execution of Jewish people were viewed as meritorious acts of patriotism, camp commandants proudly compared execution rates as if they were industrial production figures. This monstrous death

industry required a methodical program of research and efficient and dedicated management. The massive threats to human welfare are generally brought about by deliberate acts of principle, rather than unrestrained acts of impulse. *[Emphasis added.]*

What do *you* think? Is violent, aggressive, and cruel behavior due to unconscious forces that are out of control? Or is it the result of conscious, deliberate motives?

chologists can study self-efficacy beliefs by comparing subjects who are low in self-efficacy in a given situation with subjects who are high in self-efficacy (e.g., Ozer & Bandura, 1990). Not surprisingly, then, the social cognitive perspective has had a major impact on the study of personality (Pervin, 1997).

Some psychologists feel that the social cognitive approach to personality applies *best* to laboratory research. In the typical laboratory study, the relationships among a limited number of very specific variables are studied. In everyday life, situations are far more complex, with multiple factors converging to affect behavior and personality. Thus, an argument can be made that clinical data, rather than laboratory data, may be more reflective of "the whole person."

The social cognitive perspective also ignores unconscious influences, emotions, or conflicts. Some psychologists argue that the social cognitive theory focuses on very limited areas of personality—learning, the effects of situations, and the effects of beliefs about the self (see Engler, 1995). Thus, it seems to lack the richness of psychoanalytic and humanistic theories, which strive to explain the *whole* person, including the unconscious, irrational, and emotional aspects of personality (Westen, 1990).

Humanistic and Social-Cognitive Perspectives

Determine whether each of the following statements is true or false. If a statement is false, rewrite it to correct it.

_____ **1.** According to Carl Rogers, children's impulses are innately good, and they should never be disciplined.

_____ **2.** Carl Rogers strongly advocated the use of conditional positive regard to enhance the psychological well-being of others.

_____ **3.** The humanistic perspective on personality has been criticized for being too optimistic about human nature.

_____ **4.** According to social cognitive theory, people's behavior is determined solely by environmental influences.

_____ **5.** The development of self-efficacy beliefs is complete by late childhood.

_____ **6.** Self-efficacy beliefs can vary from one situation to another.

The Trait Perspective on Personality

Trait theories focus on describing individual differences. A trait is a relatively stable, enduring predisposition to behave in a certain way. How do surface and source traits differ? What are three influential trait theories? How is the expression of personality traits affected by situational demands?

Suppose we asked you to describe the personality of a close friend. How would you begin? Would you describe her personality in terms of her unconscious conflicts, the congruence of her self-concept, or her level of self-efficacy? Probably not. Instead, you'd probably generate a list of her personal characteristics, such as *outgoing, cheerful,* and *generous.* This rather common-sense approach to personality is one that is shared by the trait theories (Funder, 1995; Funder & others, 1995).

The trait approach to personality is very different from the theories that we have encountered thus far. The psychoanalytic, humanistic, and social cognitive theories emphasize the *similarities* among people. They focus on discovering the universal processes of motivation and development that explain human personality (Revelle, 1995). While these theories do deal with individual differences, they do so only indirectly. In contrast, the trait approach to personality *focuses primarily on describing individual differences.*

Trait theorists view the person as being a unique combination of personality characteristics or attributes called *traits.* A **trait** is formally defined as a relatively stable, enduring predisposition to behave in a certain way (Pervin, 1994). A **trait theory** of personality, then, is one that focuses on identifying, describing, and measuring individual differences. Think back to our description of the twins Kenneth and Julian in the chapter prologue. You can probably readily identify their differing personality traits.

People possess traits to different degrees. For example, a person might be extremely shy, somewhat shy, or not shy at all. Hence, a trait is typically described in terms of a range from one extreme to its opposite. Most people fall in the middle of the range (average shyness), while fewer people fall at opposite poles (extremely shy or extremely outgoing).

trait
A relatively stable, enduring predisposition to consistently behave in a certain way.

trait theory
A theory of personality that focuses on identifying, describing, and measuring individual differences.

surface traits
Personality characteristics or attributes that can easily be inferred from observable behavior.

source traits
The most fundamental dimensions of personality; the broad, basic traits that are hypothesized to be universal and relatively few in number.

Surface Traits and Source Traits

Most of the terms that we used to describe Kenneth and Julian are **surface traits**—traits that lie on "the surface" and can be easily inferred from observable behaviors. Other surface traits include attributes like *cheerful, exuberant, spacey, gloomy, forgetful,* and *anxious.* If you try listing the surface traits of three or four people whom you know well, you'll quickly discover that the list of potential surface traits is extremely long!

Gordon Allport, an early personality researcher, actually tried to count the number of surface traits in the English language. Methodically combing through an English-language dictionary, Allport found more than 18,000 words that could be used to describe differences among people! Out of this pool, he identified over 4,000 words that described specific personality traits (Allport & Odbert, 1936; John, 1990).

While you have to admire Allport for his trait of perseverance, his list of 4,000-plus specific personality traits created a problem. For a trait theory to be useful, it needs to identify and organize individual differences in a systematic and workable framework (Goldberg, 1993; John, 1990). Clearly, Allport's pool of 4,000-plus traits was far too large to be of much use to personality researchers.

So how might we narrow down the number of traits to investigate? One approach is to group related traits together. For example, Kenneth was dependable, hard-working, and honest. These surface traits could be grouped together into a broader category, such as "conscientiousness." Trait theorists take a similar, although more systematic, approach: they group related surface traits in order to identify source traits.

Source traits are thought to be more basic than surface traits. As the most basic dimension of personality, a source trait can potentially give rise to a vast number of surface traits (McCrae & John, 1992). Trait theorists believe that there are relatively few source traits, and that these represent a universal way of describing individual personality differences (Goldberg, 1993). Thus, one goal of trait theorists has been to identify the most basic set of universal source traits that can be used to describe all individual differences (Pervin, 1994).

Two Representative Trait Theories:
Raymond Cattell and Hans Eysenck

Raymond Cattell (b. 1905) Cattell was a strong advocate of the trait approach to personality. His research led to the development of the Sixteen Personality Factor Questionnaire, one of the most widely used psychological tests to assess personality.

How many source traits are there? Not surprisingly, trait theorists differ in their answers. For example, pioneer trait theorist **Raymond Cattell** (b. 1905) reduced Allport's list of 4,000 terms to about 171 characteristics by eliminating terms that seemed to be redundant or uncommon (see John, 1990). Cattell collected data on a large sample of people who were rated on each of the 171 terms. He then used a statistical technique called *factor analysis* to identify the traits that were most closely related to one another. After further research, Cattell eventually reduced his list to sixteen key personality factors, which are described in Table 11.2.

TABLE 11.2 Cattell's Sixteen Personality Factors

1. Reserved, unsociable	⟷	Outgoing, sociable
2. Less intelligent, concrete	⟷	More intelligent, abstract
3. Affected by feelings	⟷	Emotionally stable
4. Submissive, humble	⟷	Dominant, assertive
5. Serious	⟷	Happy-go-lucky
6. Expedient	⟷	Conscientious
7. Timid	⟷	Venturesome
8. Tough-minded	⟷	Sensitive
9. Trusting	⟷	Suspicious
10. Practical	⟷	Imaginative
11. Forthright	⟷	Shrewd, calculating
12. Self-assured	⟷	Apprehensive
13. Conservative	⟷	Experimenting
14. Group-dependent	⟷	Self-sufficient
15. Undisciplined	⟷	Controlled
16. Relaxed	⟷	Tense

SOURCE: Adapted from Cattell, 1973.

Raymond Cattell believed that personality could be described in terms of 16 source traits, or basic personality factors. Each factor represents a dimension which ranges between two extremes.

Cattell (1994) believes that these sixteen personality factors represent the essential source traits of human personality. To measure these traits, Cattell developed what has become one of the most widely used personality tests, the *Sixteen Personality Factor Questionnaire* (abbreviated *16PF®*). We'll discuss the 16PF in more detail later in the chapter.

An even simpler model of universal source traits was proposed by **Hans Eysenck** (b. 1916), a British psychologist. Eysenck's methods were similar to Cattell's, but his conception of personality includes just three dimensions. The first dimension is introversion–extraversion, which is the degree to which a person directs his energies outward toward the environment and other people versus inward toward his inner and self-focused experiences. A person who is high on the dimension of *introversion* might be quiet, solitary, and reserved, avoiding new experiences. A person high on the *extraversion* scale would be outgoing and sociable, enjoying new experiences and stimulating environments.

Eysenck's second major dimension is neuroticism–emotional stability. *Neuroticism* refers to a person's predisposition to become emotionally upset, while *stability* reflects a person's predisposition to be emotionally even. Surface traits associated with neuroticism are anxiety, tension, depression, and guilt. At the opposite end, emotional stability is associated with surface traits of being calm, relaxed, and even-tempered.

Eysenck believed that by combining these two dimensions people could be classified into four basic types: introverted-neurotic; introverted-stable; extraverted-neurotic; and extraverted-stable. Each basic type is associated with a different combination of surface traits, as shown in Figure 11.4.

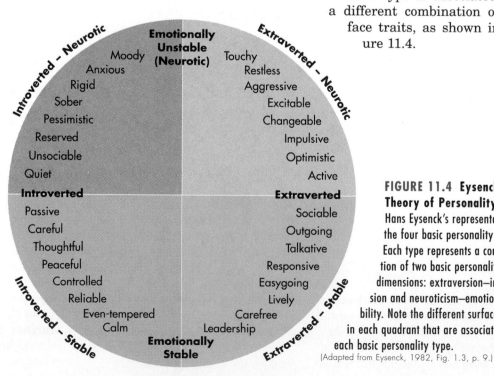

FIGURE 11.4 Eysenck's Theory of Personality Types Hans Eysenck's representation of the four basic personality types. Each type represents a combination of two basic personality dimensions: extraversion–introversion and neuroticism–emotional stability. Note the different surface traits in each quadrant that are associated with each basic personality type. (Adapted from Eysenck, 1982, Fig. 1.3, p. 9.)

In later research, Eysenck identified a third personality dimension, called *psychoticism* (Eysenck & Eysenck, 1975; Eysenck, 1990). A person high on this trait is antisocial, cold, hostile, and unconcerned about others. A person who is low on psychoticism is warm and caring toward others. In the chapter prologue, Julian might be described as above average on psychoticism, while Kenneth was extremely low on this trait.

Eysenck (1990) believes that individual differences in personality are due to biological differences among people. For example, Eysenck has proposed that an introvert's nervous system is more easily aroused than an extravert's nervous system. Assuming that people tend to seek out an optimal level of arousal (see Chapter 8), extraverts would seek stimulation from their environment more than introverts would. And, because introverts would be more uncomfortable than extraverts in a highly stimulating environment, introverts would be much less likely to seek out stimulation.

Eysenck's contention that introverts and extraverts differ physiologically has some tentative research support (see Eysenck, 1990; Stelmack & others, 1993; Stelmack & Geen, 1992). In general, introverts do seem to react more intensely to sensory stimulation than extraverts (Stelmack, 1990). For example, saliva production is a physiological response controlled by the central nervous system. When drops of lemon juice are placed on their tongues, introverts are more physiologically reactive, producing more saliva than extraverts (Eysenck & Eysenck, 1967; Deary & others, 1988).

Do introverts and extraverts actually prefer different environments? Researchers John Campbell and Charles Hawley (1982) found that extraverted students tended to study in a relatively noisy, open area of a college library, where there were ample opportunities for socializing with other students. Introverted students preferred to study in a quiet section of the library, where individual carrels and small tables were separated by tall bookshelves. As Eysenck's theory predicts, the introverts preferred study areas that minimized stimulation, while the extraverts preferred studying in an area that provided stimulation.

Sixteen Are Too Many, Three Are Too Few:
The Five-Factor Model

Many trait theorists felt that Cattell's trait model was too complex and that his sixteen personality factors could be reduced to a smaller, more basic set of traits. Yet Eysenck's three-dimensional trait theory seemed too limited, failing to capture other important dimensions of human personality (see Block, 1995).

Today, the consensus among many trait researchers is that the essential building blocks of personality can be described in terms of five basic personality dimensions, which are sometimes called "the Big Five" (Goldberg, 1993; Briggs, 1992). According to the **five-factor model of personality,** these five dimensions represent the structural organization of personality traits (McCrae & Costa, 1996).

What are the Big Five? Different trait researchers describe the five basic traits somewhat differently (Johnson & Ostendorf, 1993; Zuckerman & others, 1993). However, the most commonly accepted five factors are: extraversion, neuroticism, agreeableness, conscientiousness, and openness to experience. Table 11.3 describes the Big Five traits, as defined by personality theorists Robert McCrae and Paul Costa, Jr. Note that Factor 1, neuroticism, and Factor 2, extraversion, are essentially the same as Eysenck's first two personality dimensions.

five-factor model of personality
A trait theory of personality that identifies five basic source traits (extraversion, neuroticism, agreeableness, conscientiousness, and openness to experience) as the fundamental building blocks of personality.

TABLE 11.3 The Five-Factor Model of Personality

This table shows the five major factors, or source traits, of personality, according to "Big Five" theorists Robert McCrae and Paul Costa, Jr. Note that each factor represents a *dimension*, or range between two extremes. Listed below each major personality dimension are surface traits that are associated with that dimension.

Low ⟷ High	
Factor 1: Neuroticism	
Calm	Worrying
Even-tempered, unemotional	Temperamental, emotional
Hardy	Vulnerable
Factor 2: Extraversion	
Reserved	Affectionate
Loner	Joiner
Quiet	Talkative
Factor 3: Openness to Experience	
Down-to-earth	Imaginative
Conventional, uncreative	Original, creative
Prefer routine	Prefer variety
Factor 4: Agreeableness	
Antagonistic	Acquiescent
Ruthless	Soft-hearted
Suspicious	Trusting
Factor 5: Conscientiousness	
Lazy	Hard-working
Aimless	Ambitious
Quitting	Persevering

SOURCE: Adapted from McCrae & Costa, 1990, Table 1, p. 3.

The Five Dimensions of Personality Contemporary research supports the notion that personality can be described in terms of five source traits: neuroticism, extraversion, agreeableness, conscientiousness, and openness to experience. Judging from this photograph, would you expect the women at the piano to be high or low on the dimension of extraversion?

The five-factor structure of personality has been found in a variety of cultures using a variety of measures. In Canada, Finland, Poland, Germany, and other European cultures, people have been found to describe personality in much the same way, using terms that are generally consistent with the Big Five model (Paunonen & others, 1992). The same finding is seen among Filipinos, an example of the Big Five being found in a non-Western culture (Church & Katigbak, 1989).

How can we account for the seeming universality of the Big Five trait structure? Psychologist David Buss (1991) has one intriguing explanation. Buss thinks we should look at the utility of these factors from an evolutionary perspective. He believes that the Big Five traits reflect the personality dimensions that are the most important in the "social landscape" to which humans have had to adapt. Being able to identify who has social power (extraversion), who is likely to share resources (agreeableness), and who is trustworthy (conscientiousness) enhances our likelihood of survival.

The Great Debate:

Is Behavior Influenced More by Traits or by Situations?

Traits are assumed to be relatively stable, enduring aspects of an individual's personality. According to trait theorists, then, individual traits should be relatively consistent over time and in different situations.

Research has shown that traits are indeed remarkably stable over *time* (Costa & McCrae, 1994; McCrae, 1993). A young adult who is very extraverted, emotionally stable, and relatively open to new experiences is likely to grow into an older adult who could be described in much the same way (McCrae & Costa, 1990). Kenneth's conscientiousness and his willingness to help others were consistent themes throughout his long life. Likewise, Julian's lack of self-control and impulsiveness seemed to be traits that were consistent from childhood to adulthood.

The Continuity of Traits over the Lifespan Kenneth's conscientiousness was a trait that was evident throughout his life. Because he was too old to join the military when the United States entered World War II, Kenneth volunteered his legal expertise to the American Red Cross, providing them with legal services for the western half of the United States.

Traits, then, are relatively consistent over time. But are traits consistent across different *situations*? In other words, if you know that Joan is quite extraverted, can you reliably *predict* how she will behave in different situations, such as during a classroom discussion, at a soccer game, on a date, at a family gathering, or during a job interview?

The great debate over whether people's behavior is influenced more by their traits or by the situation in which they find themselves began in the late 1960s. Social cognitive theorist Walter Mischel fired the opening shot. In a very influential book, *Personality and Assessment* (1968), he reviewed dozens of personality studies. He concluded that, at best, there was only a weak relationship between a person's traits as measured by personality tests and the person's behavior in a specific situation. Mischel claimed that behavior was much more strongly influenced by the specific external situation than by internal traits.

The trait theorists were not about to take this challenge lying down, and a heated debate ensued. Seymour Epstein helped lead the counterattack, pointing out that one shouldn't expect to find a high correlation between a personality trait and behavior on a *single* occasion (Epstein, 1979, 1983a, 1983b; Epstein & O'Brien, 1985). It would be like trying to use a student's math aptitude test score to predict the student's answer on question 5 on an algebra test next Tuesday afternoon.

Similarly, knowing that an individual scored high on neuroticism doesn't necessarily mean that she will feel tense, anxious, and depressed on a particular Friday night. Instead, Epstein argued, we must look at larger numbers of occasions. Using the same two examples, the student with a high aptitude for mathematics will, *on the average,* perform well on arithmetic tests; the person with a high neuroticism score will, *on the average,* experience more frequent bad moods than the person with a low score.

Moreover, trait theorists didn't deny that situations will influence behavior. Situations in which your behavior is limited by social "rules" or expectations are likely to limit the expression of your personality characteristics. For the majority of people, behavior is most likely to reflect personality traits when they're in familiar, informal, or private situations that don't involve a lot of social rules or expectations (Buss, 1989).

Is Behavior More Influenced by Situations or by Personality Traits? These basketball fans are jubilantly celebrating a Chicago Bulls victory. It's doubtful that they would behave the same way in church or during a psychology class. Clearly, situations can and do influence our behavior. For the most part, however, our expression of personality traits tends to be consistent across a wide range of situations.

So what's the bottom line here? Is behavior more strongly influenced by a person's traits or by the situation they happen to be in? Today, most psychologists, including Mischel, generally agree that personality traits are basically consistent in different situations. Human behavior, however, is the result of a complex *interaction* between traits and situations. People *do* respond, sometimes dramatically, to the demands of a particular situation. But the situations that people choose, and the characteristic way that they respond to similar situations, are likely to be consistent with their individual personality dispositions (Mischel & Shoda, 1995; Mischel, 1990).

Personality Traits and Genetics:
Just a Chip off the Old Block?

> *Some theorists believe that personality traits are largely genetic in origin. What is a heritability estimate, and how is it determined? To what degree are personality traits inherited? What is the role of environmental influences on personality? What are key strengths and weaknesses of the trait perspective?*

Do personality traits run in families? Are personality traits determined by genetics? Many trait theorists, like Raymond Cattell and Hans Eysenck, believe that traits are at least partially genetic in origin. This probably doesn't comes as a great surprise to you. Even the casual observer often notices the ways that a child's personality resembles that of his or her parents. For example, our daughter Laura has always been outgoing and sociable, traits that she shares with both her parents. But is she outgoing because she inherited that trait from us? Or is she outgoing because we modeled and reinforced outgoing behavior? Is it even possible to sort out the relative influence of genetics versus environmental experiences on personality traits?

Behavioral Genetics

The field of **behavioral genetics** studies the effects of genes and heredity on behavior. Most behavioral genetics studies on humans involve measuring similarities and differences among members of a large group of people who are genetically related to different degrees. The basic research strategy is to compare the degree of difference among subjects to their degree of genetic relatedness. If a trait is genetically influenced, then the more closely two people are genetically related, the more you would expect them to be similar on that trait.

One way this strategy is applied is by studying identical twins who were separated at birth or in early infancy and raised in different families (Bouchard, 1994). Identical twins reared apart share the same genes but different environments. Any similarities between them are assumed to be due to genetics, while differences are assumed to be due to environmental influences.

Another method is to compare adopted individuals to their adoptive siblings, their adoptive parents, or their biological parents (Plomin & others, 1994). Since the adoptive child is not genetically related to his adoptive siblings, similarities between them must be due to growing up in the same home. And when adoptive children more strongly resemble their biological parents than the adoptive parents on a given trait, behavioral geneticists assume that that trait is subject to genetic influence.

If a trait is genetically influenced, you would expect identical twins to be *most* similar on that trait. Fraternal twins and siblings, who share approximately 50 percent of their genes, would be somewhat similar, but less so than identical twins. And genetically unrelated individuals reared in the same home, such as adopted children, should be even less similar. Finally, you would expect genetically unrelated individuals who grew up in different homes to be the least similar of all.

Using adoption studies and twins-reared-apart investigations, behavioral geneticists can calculate a number called a heritability estimate. A **heritability estimate** is a rough measurement of the degree to which dif-

behavioral genetics
An interdisciplinary field that studies the effects of genes and heredity on behavior.

heritability estimate
A numerical estimate of the degree to which differences within a specific group of people are due to genetics.

IN FOCUS 11.3

Explaining Those Amazing Identical-Twin Similarities

As part of the ongoing "Minnesota Study of Twins Reared Apart" at the University of Minnesota, researchers David Lykken, Thomas Bouchard, and their colleagues (1992) have been studying a very unusual group of people: over 100 pairs of identical and fraternal twins who were separated at birth or in early childhood and raised in different homes. Shortly after the study began in 1980, the researchers were struck by some of the amazing similarities between identical twins—similarities in occupations, hobbies, personality traits, habits, and sometimes even their life histories, despite the fact that the twins had been separated for many years.

One of the most famous cases is that of the "Jim twins," who had been separated for close to forty years. Like many of the other reunited twins, the two Jims had similar heights, postures, and voice and speech patterns. More strikingly, both Jims had married and divorced women named Linda, and then married women named Betty. One Jim named his son James Allan, while the other Jim named his son James Alan. Both Jims bit their nails, chain-smoked Salems, and enjoyed working in their basement workshops. And both Jims had vacationed at the same Florida beach, driving there in the same model Chevrolet (Lykken & others, 1992).

Granted, such similarities could simply be due to coincidence (see Wyatt & others, 1984). Linda, Betty, James, and Alan are not exactly rare names in the United States. And literally thousands of people buy the same model car every year, just as thousands of people vacation in Florida. Besides, if you look closely at any two people of the same

age, sex, and culture, there are bound to be similarities. It's probably a safe bet, for example, that *you* enjoy eating pizza and often wear jeans and T-shirts.

But it's difficult to dismiss as mere coincidences all the striking similarities between identical twins in the Minnesota study. Lykken and his colleagues (1992) point out numerous quirky similarities that occurred in the identical twins they studied but did not occur in the fraternal-twin pairs. For example, in the entire sample of twins, there were only two subjects who had been married five times; two subjects who habitually wore seven rings; and two who left love notes around the house for their wives. In each case, the two were identical twins. And only two subjects independently (and correctly) diagnosed a problem with researcher Bouchard's car—a faulty wheel bearing. Again, the two were members of an identical-twin pair. While Lykken and his colleagues acknowledge that some identical-twin similarities are probably due to coincidence, such as the Jim twins marrying women with the same first names, others are probably genetically influenced.

So does this mean that there's a gene for getting married five times or wearing seven rings? Not exactly. While some physical characteristics and diseases are influenced by a single gene, complex psychological characteristics, such as your personality, are influenced by a large number of genes acting in combination (Plomin, 1990). Unlike fraternal twins and regular siblings, identical twins share the same specific *configuration* of interacting genes. Lykken and his colleagues suggest that many complex psychological traits, including the strikingly similar idiosyn-

crasies of identical twins, may result from a unique configuration of interacting genes.

Lykken and his colleagues call certain traits *emergenic traits* because they appear (or *emerge*) only out of a unique configuration of many interacting genes. Although they are genetically influenced, emergenic traits do not run in families. To illustrate the idea of emergenic traits, consider the couple of average intelligence who give birth to an extraordinarily gifted child. By all predictions, this couple's offspring should have normal, average intelligence. But because of the unique configuration of the child's genes acting in combination, extraordinary giftedness emerges (Lykken & others, 1992).

David Lykken compares emergenic traits to a winning poker hand. All the members of the family are drawing from the same "deck," or pool of genes. But one member may come up with the special configuration of cards that produces a royal flush—the unique combination of genes that produces a genius or an Olympic athlete. And, in fact, history is filled with cases of people with exceptional talents and abilities in varied fields who grew up in average families.

Finally, it's important to point out that there were many differences, as well as similarities, between the identical twins in the Minnesota study. For example, one twin was prone to depression while the other was not; one twin was an alcoholic while the other did not drink. So, even with identical twins, it's important to remember that personality is only *partly* determined by genetics.

ferences within a given population are influenced by genetics. If a particular trait was *completely* due to genetics, it would have a heritability estimate of 100 percent. If genetics played *no* role in the trait at all, it would have a heritability estimate of 0 percent.

It's important to stress that a heritability estimate describes only the degree to which *differences within a specific group of people* are due to genetics. A heritability estimate cannot be used to account for the characteristics of a *particular* individual. Consider your height, which is largely determined by the genes that you inherited. Height has a heritability estimate of 90 percent (Plomin, 1990). This means that within a given group of people, about 90 percent of the *difference* in their heights could be attributed to genetic differences. The remaining 10 percent of the *difference* would be due to environmental differences, such as nutrition and physical health.

Given these research strategies and the heritability estimates they produce, the evidence shows that certain personality traits *are* substantially influenced by genetics. The evidence for genetic influence is particularly strong for extraversion and neuroticism, two of the Big Five personality traits (Plomin, 1990). Twin studies in four different countries involving over 30,000 pairs of twins have yielded heritability estimates of about 50 percent for these two factors (Tellegen & others, 1988; Bouchard & others, 1990a).

Another twin study found that openness to experience and conscientiousness, two other Big Five traits, are also substantially influenced by genetics, although to a lesser degree than extraversion and neuroticism (Bergeman & others, 1993). Interestingly, these researchers found *no* evidence for a genetic effect on agreeableness, which was more strongly affected by shared environmental influences. In other words, both identical and fraternal twins raised together were *more* similar on the trait of agreeableness than twins raised apart. Thus, heredity seems to play a significant role in four of the Big Five personality traits: extraversion, neuroticism, openness to experience, and conscientiousness (Bouchard, 1994).

> *"What runs in families is DNA, not experiences shared in the home. Environmental influences do not operate on a family-by-family basis but rather on an individual-by-individual basis. They are specific to each child rather than general for an entire family.*
>
> **Robert Plomin,** 1989

So is personality completely determined by genetics? Not at all. As behavioral geneticists Robert Plomin and Richard Rende (1991) explain, "The same data that point to significant genetic influence provide the best available evidence for the importance of nongenetic factors. Rarely do behavioral genetic data yield heritability estimates that exceed 50%, which means that behavioral variability is due at least as much to environment as to heredity."

In other words, the influence of environmental factors is at least equal to the influence of genetic factors. Some additional evidence that underscores this point is that identical twins are most alike in early life. As the twins grow up, leave home, and encounter different experiences and environments, their personalities become more different (McCartney & others, 1990).

Why Are Siblings So Different?
(Or, "Mom Always Liked *You* Best!")

Let's start with a simple fact: Overall, sibling personality *differences* are far greater than their *similarities* (Plomin & others, 1990). If you think about it, this seems to contradict what we've been saying in the last couple of paragraphs. Most siblings grow up in the same home, and, as we just noted, environmental influences on personality are as great as genetic effects. And on average, siblings share about 50 percent of their genes. So given that siblings grow up in the same home *and* share about half their genes, why aren't siblings more alike? Or, looking at it the other way, what makes siblings so different?

Plomin and his colleagues suggest that *nonshared experiences* account for much of the personality differences among siblings (Daniels & Plomin, 1987;

Judy Dunn Developmental psychologist Judy Dunn's research has focused on how sibling relationships influence personality. She has described how siblings, despite being brought up in the same home, experience very different psychological and social environments.

Plomin & Rende, 1991; Dunn & Plomin, 1990). Siblings growing up in the same family do not experience identical environmental influences. Most obviously, age and gender differences affect how different children are treated by their parents. Even as toddlers, children are often keenly aware of differences in parental treatment in such areas as affection and discipline (Dunn & Plomin, 1990).

Some differences in parental treatment may well be driven by the child's genetically influenced traits (Plomin, 1989). A rebellious and stubborn child may evoke stricter, harsher parental discipline than a sibling who is more easygoing and cooperative. An impulsive child may experience a great deal of parental control, while a more cautious sibling may be actively encouraged by parents to be more adventurous.

Beyond the parent–child relationship, interaction between siblings can also have a significant effect on children's personalities (Daniels & Plomin, 1985; Dunn & Plomin, 1990). Whether competitive and acrimonious or affectionate and mutually protective, sibling relationships can be important in personality development. For example, Kenneth and Julian were inseparable when they were children. But recall Kenneth's writing to his mother, "I reminded Julian about the boats and I will watch him good." Clearly, even at an early age, Kenneth felt the need to protect and watch over the more impulsive Julian, although they were the same age. No doubt the twins were treated very differently by their parents as well.

Children are also influenced by varied experiences outside the home, such as their relationships with peers and teachers. Illness and accidents are other nonshared environmental influences, like the head injury Julian suffered when he was struck by a car. Even an event that affects the entire family, such as divorce, job loss, or a family move, may be experienced quite differently by each child in the family (Dunn & Plomin, 1990). Thus, even though siblings may grow up in the same family, each child's experiences within that family can be fundamentally different.

Evaluating the Trait Perspective on Personality

While psychologists continue to disagree on how many basic traits exist, they do generally agree that people can be described and compared in terms of basic personality traits. But like the other personality theories, the trait approach has its weaknesses (Block, 1995).

One criticism is that trait theories don't really explain human personality (Pervin, 1994). Instead, they simply label general predispositions to behave in a certain way.

A second criticism is that trait theorists don't attempt to explain how or why individual differences develop. When you think about it, saying that trait differences are partly due to genetics and partly due to environmental influences isn't really saying very much.

A third criticism is that trait approaches generally fail to address other important personality issues, such as the basic motives that drive human

TABLE 11.4 The Major Personality Perspectives

Perspective	Key Theorists	Key Themes and Ideas
Psychoanalytic	Sigmund Freud	Influence of unconscious psychological processes; importance of sexual and aggressive instincts; lasting effects of early childhood experiences
	Carl Jung	The collective unconscious, archetypes, and psychological harmony
	Karen Horney	Importance of parent–child relationship; defending against basic anxiety; womb envy
	Alfred Adler	Striving for superiority, compensating for feelings of inferiority
Humanistic	Carl Rogers	Emphasis on subjective experiences, psychological growth, free will, striving toward capabilities, and inherent goodness
	Abraham Maslow	Behavior as motivated by hierarchy of needs and striving for self-actualization; focus on psychologically healthy people
Social cognitive	Albert Bandura	Reciprocal interaction of behavioral, cognitive, and environmental factors; emphasis on conscious thoughts, self-efficacy beliefs, self-regulation, and goal setting
Trait	Raymond Cattell	Emphasis on measuring and describing individual differences; sixteen source traits of personality
	Hans Eysenck	Three basic dimensions of personality: introversion–extraversion, neuroticism–emotional stability, and psychoticism
	Robert McCrae and Paul Costa	Five-factor model: five basic dimensions of personality: neuroticism, extraversion, openness to experience, agreeableness, conscientiousness

personality, the role of unconscious mental processes, how beliefs about the self influence personality, or how psychological change and growth occur (McAdams, 1992). Conspicuously absent are the grand conclusions about the essence of human nature that characterize the psychoanalytic and humanistic theories. So, while trait theories are useful in describing individual differences and predicting behavior, there are limitations to their usefulness.

As you've seen, each of the major perspectives on personality has contributed to our understanding of human personality. The four perspectives are summarized in Table 11.4.

Our discussion of personality would not be complete without a description of how personality is formally evaluated and measured. In the next section, we'll briefly survey the two main approaches that are used in personality assessment: projective tests and personality tests.

Assessing Personality:
Psychological Tests

Personality can be measured by projective tests and self-report inventories. How are projective tests and self-report inventories administered and scored? What are the strengths and weaknesses of projective tests and self-report inventories?

When we discussed intelligence tests in Chapter 7, we described what makes a good psychological test. Beyond intelligence tests, there are literally hundreds of **psychological tests** that can be used to assess abilities, aptitudes, interests, and personality (see Conoley & Impara, 1995; Aiken, 1994). Any psychological test is useful insofar as it achieves two basic goals: (1) it accurately and consistently reflects a person's characteristics on some dimension, and (2) it predicts a person's future psychological functioning or behavior (Kaplan & Saccuzzo, 1993).

In this section, we'll look at the very different approaches used in the two basic types of personality tests—projective tests and self-report inventories. After looking at some of the most commonly used tests in each category, we'll evaluate the strengths and weaknesses of each approach.

psychological test
A test that assesses a person's abilities, aptitudes, interests, or personality, based on a systematically obtained sample of behavior.

SCIENCE VERSUS PSEUDOSCIENCE 11.4

Is Your Personality Written in the Stars?

Pseudoscientific explanations for personality, such as astrology, have existed long before any of the personality theories described in this chapter. In fact, the history of astrology can be traced back over 4,000 years (Dean & others, 1996). Astrology's basic premise is that the positions of the planets and stars at the time and place of your birth determine your personality and destiny. Originally, astrology was based on the theory that the earth was the center of the solar system, with the stars, the planets, and the sun revolving around the earth (Crowe, 1990). This theory was, of course, scientifically refuted in the early 1600s by Galileo, the Italian astonomer who invented the telescope.

Today, belief in astrological interpretations and predictions remains widespread. Surveys of college students have found that over 30 percent believe in astrology (Duncan & others, 1992; Clarke, 1991). Every year, about 40 million Americans seek astrological guidance from one of the approximately 200,000 practicing astrologers (Glick & others, 1989). About 1,200 North American newspapers carry astrology columns—yet another testament to astrology's widespread popularity (Kurtz & Fraknoi, 1986).

Just how valid is astrology in assessing personality? Can the claims of astrologers be scientifically tested? As it turns out, there is no shortage of scientific investigations of the abilities of astrologers to assess personality characteristics. Let's consider Shawn Carlson's (1985) carefully designed study.

Carlson's (1985) study involved 30 American and European astrologers who were considered to be among the best by their peers in the astrological community. A panel of astrological advisers were also involved in helping Carlson design his study. All the participating astrologers agreed beforehand that Carlson's study was a "fair test" of astrological claims.

In the first part of Carlson's study, the astrologers developed astrological profiles for 177 subjects based on each person's time, date, and place of birth. Each subject was later shown three astrological profiles—one that was based on their time and place of birth, and two randomly chosen astrological profiles of other subjects in the study. The question was simple: Could the subject pick out his own personality profile from the three astrological profiles? If the subjects did no better than merely guessing, you would expect them to be correct about one-third of the time.

In the second part of Carlson's study, 116 of the subjects completed the California Personality Inventory (CPI). As noted in the chapter, the CPI is one of the most widely used personality inventories, and has been shown to be scientifically valid in hundreds of studies (Kramer & Conoley, 1992). All the astrologers in the study were familiar with reading CPI profiles. The astrologers were given a subject's astrological profile and three CPI profiles. All the astrologer had to do was match the person's astrological profile with the same person's CPI profile.

Carlson also presented the subjects with three CPI profiles. One was their own and two were randomly chosen. All the subjects had to do was identify which CPI profile they thought was theirs. If the astrologers or the subjects did no better than merely guessing, you would expect them to be correct only one-third of the time.

The results of Carlson's study? When presented with three astrological profiles, the subjects were correct only 33 percent of the time, meaning that they did *no better than chance* at identifying their own astrological profiles. Interestingly, the subjects were *also* un-able to select their own CPI profile at a rate better than chance! In other words, Carlson's findings cast doubt on the ability of people to subjectively evaluate the accuracy of *any* kind of personality description.

How did the astrologers do when they tried to match a subject's astrological profile with his or her CPI profile? The astrologers were correct only 34 percent of the time—they performed no better than someone merely guessing. Carlson (1985) summarized the results of his study in this way:

> *Great pains were taken to insure that the experiment was unbiased and to make sure that astrology was given every reasonable chance to succeed. It* failed. *Despite the fact that we worked with some of the best astrologers in the country, recommended by the advising astrologers for their expertise in astrology and in their ability to use the CPI, despite the fact that every reasonable suggestion made by the advising astrologers was worked into the experiment, despite the fact that the astrologers approved the design and predicted 50 percent as the "minimum" effect they would expect to see, astrology failed* to perform at a level better than chance.

Carlson's findings are not isolated, by any means (see Dean & others, 1996; French & others, 1991). In a thoughtful review of scientific research on astrology, University of Hawaii researcher Richard Crowe (1990) concluded: "Popular and serious astrology have absolutely no reliable basis in scientific fact. Statistically, astrology does not stand up to any valid test that can be applied."

Projective Tests:

Like Seeing Things in the Clouds

Projective tests developed out of psychoanalytic approaches to personality. In the most commonly used projective tests, a person is presented with a vague image, such as an inkblot or an ambiguous scene, then asked to describe what he "sees" in the image. The person's response is thought to be a projection of his unconscious conflicts, motives, psychological defenses, and personality traits. Notice that this is very similar to the defense mechanism of *projection,* which was described in Table 11.1.

The first projective test was the famous **Rorschach Inkblot Test,** published by Swiss psychiatrist Hermann Rorschach in 1921 (Hertz, 1992). The Rorschach test consists of ten cards, five that show black-and-white inkblots and five that depict colored inkblots. One card at a time, the person describes whatever she sees in the inkblot. The examiner records the person's responses verbatim and also observes her behavior, gestures, and reactions.

Numerous scoring systems exist for the Rorschach. Interpretation is based on such criteria as whether the person reports seeing animate or inanimate objects, human or animal figures, and movement, and whether the person deals with the whole blot or just fragments of it (Exner, 1993).

The Rorschach Inkblot Test Because he died the year after his inkblot test was published, Hermann Rorschach (1884–1922) never knew how popular his projective test would become. The Rorschach Inkblot Test is sometimes used to "break the ice" in clinical interviews.

A more structured projective test is the **Thematic Apperception Test,** abbreviated **TAT,** which was first discussed in Chapter 8. In the TAT, the person looks at a series of cards, each depicting an ambiguous scene. The person is asked to create a story about the scene, including what the characters are feeling and how the story turns out. The stories are scored for the motives, needs, anxieties, and conflicts of the main character, and how conflicts are resolved (Bellak, 1993). As with the Rorschach, interpreting the TAT involves the subjective judgment of the examiner.

The Thematic Apperception Test Developed by psychologist Henry Murray, the TAT involves creating a story about an ambiguous scene, like the one shown on the card this young man is holding. The person is thought to project his own motives, conflicts, and other personality characteristics into the story he creates. According to Murray (1943), "Before he knows it, he has said things about an invented character that apply to himself, things which he would have been reluctant to confess in response to a direct question."

Strengths and Weaknesses of Projective Tests

Although sometimes used in research, projective tests are mainly used to help assess emotionally disturbed individuals (see Kaplan & Saccuzzo, 1993). The primary strength of projective tests is that they provide a wealth of qualitative information about an individual's psychological functioning, information that can be explored further in psychotherapy.

However, there are several drawbacks to projective tests (see Aiken, 1994; Cronbach, 1990). First, the testing situation or the examiner's behavior can influence a person's responses. Second, the scoring of projective tests is highly subjective, requiring the examiner to make numerous judgments about the person's responses. Consequently, two examiners may test the same individual and arrive at different conclusions. Third, projective tests often fail to produce consistent results. If the same person takes a projective test on two separate occasions, very different results may be found. Finally, projective tests are poor at predicting future behavior.

The bottom line? Despite their widespread use, hundreds of studies of projective tests seriously question their *validity* (that the tests measure what they purport to measure) and their *reliability* (the consistency of test results) (see Rorer, 1990). Nonetheless, they remain very popular, especially among clinical psychologists (Butcher & Rouse, 1996).

projective test
A type of personality test that involves a person interpreting an ambiguous image; used to assess unconscious motives, conflicts, psychological defenses, and personality traits.

Rorschach Inkblot Test
A projective test using inkblots, developed by Swiss psychiatrist Hermann Rorschach in 1921.

Thematic Apperception Test (TAT)
A projective personality test that involves creating stories about each of a series of ambiguous scenes.

Self-Report Inventories:

Has Anybody Got an Eraser?

Self-report inventories typically use a paper-and-pencil format and take a direct, structured approach to assessing personality. The person answers specific questions or rates herself on various dimensions of behavior or psychological functioning. Often called *objective personality tests,* self-report inventories contain items that have been shown by previous research to differentiate between people on a particular personality characteristic. Unlike projective tests, self-report inventories are objectively scored by comparing a person's answers to standardized norms collected on large groups of people.

The most widely used self-report inventory is the **Minnesota Multiphasic Personality Inventory (MMPI)** (Butcher & Rouse, 1996). First published in the 1940s and revised in the 1980s, the current version is referred to as the *MMPI-2.* The MMPI consists of over 500 statements. The person responds to each statement with "True," "False," or "Cannot say." Topics include social, political, religious, and sexual attitudes, physical and psychological health, interpersonal relationships, and abnormal thoughts and behaviors (Graham, 1993). Sample MMPI items are shown in Table 11.5.

TABLE 11.5 Simulated MMPI-2 Items

Most people will use somewhat unfair means to gain profit or an advantage rather than lose it.

I am often very tense on the job.

The things that run through my head sometimes are horrible.

Sometimes there is a feeling like something is pressing in on my head.

Sometimes I think so fast I can't keep up.

I am worried about sex.

I believe I am being plotted against.

I wish I could do over some of the things I have done.

SOURCE: MMPI-2®.

The MMPI is widely used by clinical psychologists and psychiatrists to assess patients. It is also used to evaluate the mental health of candidates for such occupations as police officers, doctors, nurses, and professional pilots. What keeps people from simply answering items in a way that makes them look psychologically healthy? Like many other self-report inventories, the MMPI has special scales to detect whether a person is answering honestly and consistently (Butcher & Williams, 1992). For example, if someone responds "True" to items like "I *never* put off until tomorrow what I should do today" and "I *always* pick up after myself," it's probably a safe bet that the person is inadvertently or intentionally distorting his responses.

In contrast to the MMPI, the California Personality Inventory and the Sixteen Personality Factor Questionnaire are personality inventories that are designed to assess normal populations. Of the 462 true–false items on the **California Personality Inventory (CPI),** nearly half are drawn from the MMPI. The CPI provides measures on such characteristics as interpersonal effectiveness, self-control, independence, and empathy. Profiles generated by the CPI are used to predict such things as high school and college grades, delinquency, and job performance (Gough, 1989).

The **Sixteen Personality Factor Questionnaire (16PF®)** was originally developed by Raymond Cattell and is based on his trait theory. The 16PF uses a forced-choice format in which the person must respond to each item by choosing one of three alternatives. Just as the test's name implies, the results generate a profile on Cattell's sixteen personality factors. Each personality factor is represented as a range, with a person's score falling somewhere along the continuum between the two extremes (see Figure 11.5). The 16PF is widely used for career counseling, marital counseling, and evaluating employees and executives (Karson & O'Dell, 1989).

self-report inventory
A type of psychological test in which a person's responses to standardized questions are compared to established norms.

Minnesota Multiphasic Personality Inventory (MMPI)
A self-report inventory that assesses personality characteristics and psychological disorders; used to assess both normal and disturbed populations.

California Personality Inventory (CPI)
A self-report inventory that assesses personality characteristics in normal populations.

Sixteen Personality Factor Questionnaire (16PF)
A self-report inventory developed by Raymond Cattell that generates a personality profile with ratings on sixteen trait dimensions.

FIGURE 11.5 The 16PF: Example Questions and Profiles
The 16PF, developed by Raymond Cattell, is a self-report inventory that contains 185 items. When scored, the 16PF generates a personality profile. In the example shown, personality profiles of airline pilots and writers are compared. Cattell (1973) found that pilots are more controlled, more relaxed, more self-assured, and less sensitive than writers.
(Cattell & others, 1993.)

Strengths and Weakness of Self-Report Inventories

The two most important strengths of self-report inventories are *standardization* and the *use of established norms* (see Chapter 7). Each person receives the same instructions and responds to the same items. The results of self-report inventories are objectively scored and compared to norms established by previous research. In fact, the MMPI, the CPI, and the 16PF can all be scored by computer.

As a general rule, the reliability and validity of self-report inventories are far greater than those of projective tests. Literally thousands of studies have demonstrated that the MMPI, the CPI, and the 16 PF provide accurate, consistent results that can be used to generally predict behavior (Anastasi, 1988).

However, self-report inventories also have their weaknesses. First, despite the inclusion of items that are designed to detect deliberate deception, there is considerable evidence that people can still successfully fake responses and answer in socially desirable ways (Anastasi, 1988). Second, some people are prone to responding in a set way, such as consistently answering "True" whether the item accurately reflects them or not. And some tests, like the MMPI and CPI, include hundreds of items. Taking these tests can become quite tedious, and people may lose interest in carefully choosing the most appropriate response.

Third, people are not always accurate judges of their own behavior, attitudes, or attributes. And some people defensively deny their true feelings, needs, and attitudes, even to themselves (Shedler & others, 1993). For example, a person might indicate that she enjoys parties, even though she actually avoids social gatherings whenever possible.

To sum up, personality tests are generally useful strategies that can provide insights about the psychological makeup of people. But no personality test, by itself, is likely to provide a definitive description of a given individual. In practice, psychologists and other professionals usually combine personality test results with behavioral observations and background information, including interviews with family members, co-workers, or other significant people.

Finally, people can and often do change over time, especially when their life circumstances undergo a significant change. Hence, projective tests and self-report inventories provide a barometer of personality and psychological functioning only at the time of the test.

CONCEPT REVIEW 11.4

Trait Theories and Personality Assessment

1. Trait theories focus on:
   a. individual differences
   b. individual similarities
   c. stages of personality development
   d. universal processes of motivation

2. Surface traits are to source traits as:
   a. aggression is to violent behavior
   b. friendly is to extraversion
   c. conscientiousness is to personality
   d. relaxed is to tense

3. Personality differences among siblings are primarily due to:
   a. shared experiences c. birth order
   b. genetic differences d. nonshared experiences

4. Dana took the same personality test twice within three months. She obtained very different results each time. Which test did she most likely take?
   a. MMPI   c. 16PF
   b. TAT   d. CPI

5. A key strength of the MMPI and the 16PF is:
   a. They provide a wealth of qualitative information about the individual.
   b. They are unstructured.
   c. They are standardized.
   d. Scoring relies on the examiner's expertise and clinical judgment.

Summing Up: Personality

Over the course of this chapter, you've encountered firsthand some of the most influential contributors to modern psychological thought. Their ideas continue to engage today's researchers (see Freiberg, 1996; Mischel & Shoda, 1995; Wiggins, 1996; Bandura, in press). As you'll see in Chapter 15, the major personality perspectives provide the basis for many forms of psychotherapy.

Clearly, the psychoanalytic, humanistic, social cognitive, and trait perspectives each provide a fundamentally different way of conceptualizing personality. That each perspective has strengths and weaknesses underscores the point that no single perspective can explain all aspects of human personality. Indeed, no one personality theory could explain why Kenneth and Julian were so different. And, given the complex factors involved in human personality, it's doubtful that any single theory ever will capture the essence of human personality. Even so, each perspective has made important and lasting contributions to the understanding of human personality.

APPLICATION

Possible Selves: Imagine the Possibilities

Possible selves are the mental images of the selves you might become. How do possible selves influence your behavior, motivation, and decisions?

A key feature of Carl Rogers' (1959) humanistic theory of personality is the importance of a person's self-concept. Contemporary personality psychologists focus on how the self-concept is involved in important cognitive functions, such as information processing, emotions, and goals (see Hermans, 1996; Banaji & Prentice, 1994; Markus & Kitayama, 1994; Markus & Cross, 1990). Researchers have found that one aspect of your self-concept is especially important: how you see yourself in the future. In this Application, we'll look at how the possible selves that you envision yourself becoming in the future can greatly affect your behavior today.

Your Self-Concept: A Multifaceted System

Some psychologists believe that a person's self-concept is not a singular mental self-image, but a *multifaceted system* of related images and ideas (Hermans, 1996; Markus & Kunda, 1986). This collection of related images about yourself reflects your goals, values, emotions, and relationships (Markus & Cross, 1990; Markus & Wurf, 1987).

According to psychologist Hazel Markus and her colleagues, an important aspect of your self-concept has to do with the images of the selves that you *might* become—your **possible selves.** Possible selves are highly personalized, vivid, futuristic images of the self that reflect hopes, fears, and fantasies. As Markus and co-researcher Paula Nurius (1986) write, "The possible selves that are hoped for might include the successful self, the creative self, the rich self, the thin self, or the loved and admired self, whereas the dreaded possible selves could be the alone self, the depressed self, the incompetent self, the alcoholic self, the unemployed self, or the bag lady self."

The Influence of Hoped-for and Dreaded Possible Selves

Possible selves are more than just idle daydreams or wishful fantasies. In fact, possible selves influence our behavior in important ways (Markus & Nurius, 1986; Oyserman & others, 1995). We're often not aware of the possible selves that we have incorporated into our self-concepts. Nevertheless, they can serve as powerful forces that either activate or stall our efforts to reach important goals. Your incentive, drive, and motivation in the here and now can be greatly influenced by your possible selves, as can your decisions and choices about future behavior.

Imagine that you harbored a hoped-for possible self of becoming a professional musician. You would probably practice with greater regularity and intensity than someone who does not hold a vivid mental picture of performing solo at Carnegie Hall or being named Performer of the Year at the American Country Music Awards.

Dreaded possible selves can also influence behavior. Consider Don's father, Kenneth. Although never wealthy, Kenneth was financially secure throughout his long life. Yet Kenneth was a man who had lived through the Great Depression and witnessed first-hand the financial devastation that occurred in the lives of countless people. Though he never expressed it as such, Kenneth harbored a dreaded possible self of becoming penniless. When Kenneth died several years ago, what did

the family find tucked safely under his mattress? A $100 bill.

Notice that the influence of possible selves often has very little to do with how realistic they are. Someone who holds a vivid, negative possible self of "flunking out of college and disgracing my family" may be strongly affected by that image despite acing one course after another.

Conversely, a positive possible self, even if it is not very realistic, can protect an individual's self-esteem in the face of failure (Markus & Nurius, 1986). A high school girl who thinks she is unpopular with her classmates may console herself with visions of a possible self as a successful attorney who snubs her intellectually inferior classmates at her ten-year class reunion. As Hazel Markus and Paula Nurius (1986) explain:

> Positive possible selves can be exceedingly liberating because they foster hope that the present self is not immutable. At the same time, negative possible selves can be powerfully imprisoning because their [emotional impact] and expectations may stifle attempts to change or develop.

Possible Selves, Self-Efficacy Beliefs, and Motivation

In our earlier discussion on self-efficacy, we described how your beliefs about your own capabilities can have a strong impact on your motivation and performance of a particular task. Indeed, self-efficacy beliefs are closely connected to the idea of possible selves. Performing virtually any task involves the construction of a possible self that is capable and competent of performing the action required (see Oyserman & others, 1995; Ruvolo & Markus, 1992).

People who vividly imagine possible selves as "successful because of hard work" persist longer and expend more effort on tasks than do people who imagine themselves as "unsuccessful despite hard work" (Ruvolo & Markus, 1992). The motivation to achieve academically increases when your possible selves include a future self who is successful because of academic achievement (Oyserman & others, 1995).

Applying the Research: Assessing Your Possible Selves

So how can you apply these research findings to *your* life? First, it's important to stress again that we're often unaware of how the possible selves we've mentally constructed influence our beliefs, actions, and self-evaluations. Thus, the first step is to consciously assess the role that your possible selves play in your life.

Take a few moments and jot down the "possible selves" that are active in your working self-concept. To help you in this task, write three responses to each of the following questions (Oyserman & others, 1995):

1. Next year I expect to be . . .
2. Next year I am afraid that I will be . . .
3. Next year I want to avoid becoming . . .

After focusing on the short-term future, take these same questions and extend them further to five years from now or even ten years from now. Most likely, certain themes and goals will consistently emerge. Now the critical questions:

- How are your possible selves affecting your *current* motivation, goals, feelings, and decisions?
- Are your possible selves even remotely plausible?
- Are they pessimistic and limiting?
- Are they unrealistically optimistic?

Finally, ask yourself honestly: What realistic strategies are you using to try to become like the self that you want to become? To avoid becoming the selves that you dread?

These questions should help you gain some insight into whether your possible selves are influencing your behavior in productive, constructive ways. If they are not, now is an excellent time to think about replacing or modifying the possible selves that operate most powerfully in your own self-concept. Why is this so important? Because to a large extent, who any of us becomes is guided by who we *imagine* we'll become. Just imagine the possibilities of who *you* could become!

Summary

Personality

What Is Personality?

- *Personality* is defined as an individual's unique and relatively consistent patterns of thinking, feeling, and behaving. Personality theories attempt to explain how people are similar, why they are different, and why every individual is unique.

- The four major theoretical perspectives on personality are the psychoanalytic, humanistic, social cognitive, and trait perspectives.

The Psychoanalytic Perspective on Personality

- Psychoanalysis was founded by Sigmund Freud. It stresses the unconscious, the importance of sex and aggression, and the influence of early childhood experience. Freud's theory was extremely controversial throughout his lifetime and remains so today.

- Freud believed that behavior is strongly influenced by the unconscious. The contents of the unconscious can surface in disguised form in free associations, dreams, slips of the tongue, and seeming accidents.

- Personality consists of three psychological processes: Id, Ego, and Superego. The Id is fueled by instinctual energy and ruled by the pleasure principle. The Ego is partly conscious and is ruled by the reality principle. The Superego is partly conscious and represents internalized moral values and rules.

- Anxiety results when the demands of the Id or the Superego threaten to overwhelm the Ego. Ego defense mechanisms are used to reduce anxiety by distorting either thoughts or reality. Repression is involved in all ego defense mechanisms.

- The psychosexual stages are age-related developmental periods in which sexual impulses are expressed through different body zones and activities associated with these body areas. The foundations of adult personality are laid down during the first five years of life by the child's progression through the oral, anal, and phallic stages. One result of the Oedipus complex is that children come to identify with the same-sex parent. Fixation at a particular stage may result if the developmental conflicts are not successfully resolved. The latency and genital stages occur during late childhood and adolescence.

- The neo-Freudians believed in the importance of the unconscious and early childhood experience, but disagreed with other aspects of Freud's theory. Carl Jung emphasized psychological growth and proposed the existence of the collective unconscious and the archetypes. Karen Horney emphasized the role of social relationships in protecting against basic anxiety and objected to Freud's views on female development, particularly his idea of penis envy.

Alfred Adler believed that the fundamental human motive was to strive for superiority.

- Freud's theory has been criticized for resting on insufficient evidence, being difficult to test, and being sexist.

The Humanistic Perspective on Personality

- The humanistic perspective was championed as the "third force" in psychology. It emphasized human potential, psychological growth, self-awareness, and free will. Important humanistic theorists were Carl Rogers and Abraham Maslow.

- Rogers believed that the most basic human motive was the actualizing tendency. He viewed the self-concept as the most important aspect of personality. Conditional positive regard by parents or other caregivers causes a person to deny or distort aspects of experience, leading to a state of incongruence with regard to the self-concept. In contrast, unconditional positive regard leads to a state of congruence. The fully functioning person experiences congruence, the actualizing tendency, and psychological growth.

- The humanistic perspective on personality has been criticized for being difficult to scientifically validate or test and for being too optimistic.

The Social Cognitive Perspective on Personality

- The social cognitive perspective stresses the role of conscious thought processes, goals, and self-regulation. Reciprocal determinism emphasizes the interaction of behavioral, cognitive, and environmental factors in behavior and personality.

- Self-efficacy beliefs influence behavior, performance, motivation, and persistence.

- Social cognitive theories emphasize the interaction of multiple factors in determining personality and behavior. While a key strength of this perspective is its grounding in empirical research, it has been criticized for its limited view of human personality, which ignores unconscious conflicts and emotions.

The Trait Perspective on Personality

- The trait perspective focuses on measuring and describing individual differences. Surface traits can be easily inferred from observable behaviors. Source traits are thought to represent the basic, fundamental dimensions of personality.

- Raymond Cattell believed that there were sixteen basic personality factors, while Hans Eysenck proposed that there were three basic personality dimensions. Eysenck believes that the extraversion–introversion dimension may reflect physiological differences.

■ According to the five-factor model, there are five basic personality dimensions: extraversion, neuroticism, agreeableness, conscientiousness, and openness to experience.

■ Traits are generally stable over time and across situations, although situations do influence how and whether traits are expressed.

Personality Traits and Genetics: Just a Chip off the Old Block?

■ Behavioral genetics research uses twin and adoption studies to measure the relative influence of genetics and environment. A heritability estimate is a rough measurement of the degree to which differences within a given population are influenced by genetics. Extraversion, neuroticism, openness to experience, and conscientiousness seem to have a significant genetic component.

■ Nonshared environmental experiences account for much of the difference between siblings.

■ The trait perspective is useful in describing individual differences and predicting behavior. Trait theories have been criticized for their failure to explain human personality and the development of individual differences.

Assessing Personality: Psychological Tests

■ The two basic types of personality tests are projective tests and self-report inventories. Projective tests developed out of the psychoanalytic approach, and include the Rorschach Inkblot Test and the Thematic Apperception Test.

■ Projective tests provide qualitative information about an individual. They have some weaknesses: Responses may be affected by the examiner or the situation; scoring is very subjective; results may be inconsistent; and they do not predict behavior well.

■ Self-report inventories are objectively scored and differentiate among people on particular personality characteristics. Self-report inventories include the MMPI, CPI, and 16PF. The reliability, validity, and predictive value of self-report inventories are high. However, people do not always respond honestly or accurately to items in self-report inventories. Psychological tests provide one measure of personality at a particular point in time.

Key Terms

personality (p. 471)

personality theory (p. 471)

psychoanalysis (p.472)

free association (p. 473)

unconscious (p. 475)

Id (p. 476)

Eros (p. 476)

libido (p. 476)

Thanatos (p. 476)

pleasure principle (p. 476)

Ego (p. 476)

reality principle (p. 476)

Superego (p. 477)

Ego defense mechanisms (p. 478)

repression (p. 478)

displacement (p. 478)

sublimation (p. 478)

psychosexual stages (p. 480)

Oedipus complex (p. 480)

identification (p. 480)

collective unconscious (p. 483)

archetypes (p. 483)

humanistic psychology (p. 488)

actualizing tendency (p. 489)

self-concept (p. 489)

conditional positive regard (p. 489)

unconditional positive regard (p. 491)

self-efficacy (p. 493)

social cognitive theory (p. 493)

reciprocal determinism (p. 494)

trait (p. 498)

trait theory (p. 498)

surface trait (p. 499)

source traits (p. 499)

five-factor model of personality (p. 501)

behavioral genetics (p. 504)

heritability estimate (p. 504)

psychological test (p. 508)

projective test (p. 510)

Rorschach Inkblot Test (p. 510)

Thematic Apperception Test (TAT) (p. 510)

self-report inventory (p. 511)

Minnesota Multiphasic Personality Inventory (MMPI) (p. 511)

California Personality Inventory (CPI) (p. 511)

Sixteen Personality Factor Questionnaire (16PF) (p. 511)

possible selves (p. 514)

Key People

Alfred Adler (1870–1937) Austrian physician who broke with Sigmund Freud and developed his own psychoanalytic theory of personality, which emphasized social factors and the motivation toward self-improvement and self-realization; key ideas included the inferiority complex and the superiority complex.

Albert Bandura (b. 1925) Contemporary American psychologist who is best known for his research on observational learning and his social cognitive theory of personality; key ideas include self-efficacy beliefs and reciprocal determinism.

Raymond Cattell (b. 1905) British-born American psychologist who developed a trait theory that identifies sixteen essential source traits or personality factors; also developed the widely used self-report personality test, the Sixteen Personality Factor Questionnaire (16PF).

Hans Eysenck (b. 1916) German-born British psychologist who developed a trait theory of personality that identifies the three basic dimensions of personality as neuroticism, extraversion, and psychoticism.

Sigmund Freud (1856–1939) Austrian neurologist who founded psychoanalysis, which is both a comprehensive theory of personality and a form of psychotherapy; emphasized the role of unconscious determinants of behavior and early childhood experiences in the development of personality and psychological problems; key ideas include Id, Ego, and Superego, the psychosexual stages of development, and the Ego defense mechanisms.

Karen Horney (1885–1952) German-born American psychoanalyst who emphasized the role of social relationships and culture in personality; sharply disagreed with Freud's characterization of female psychological development, especially his notion that women suffer from penis envy; key ideas included basic anxiety.

Carl G. Jung (1875–1961) Swiss psychiatrist who broke with Sigmund Freud to develop his own psychoanalytic theory of personality which stressed striving toward psychological harmony; key ideas included the collective unconscious and archetypes.

Abraham Maslow (1908–1970) American psychologist who was one of the founders of humanistic psychology and emphasized the study of healthy personality development; developed a hierarchical theory of motivation based on the idea that people will strive for self-actualization, the highest motive, only after more basic needs have been met; key ideas included the hierarchy of needs and self-actualization.

Carl Rogers (1902–1987) American psychologist who was one of the founders of humanistic psychology; developed a theory of personality and form of psychotherapy that emphasized the inherent worth of people, the innate tendency to strive toward one's potential, and the importance of the self-concept in personality development; key ideas included the actualizing tendency and unconditional positive regard.

CONCEPT REVIEW 11.1 Page 481

1. d
2. c
3. b
4. b
5. a
6. c

CONCEPT REVIEW 11.2 Page 485

1. Freud
2. Horney
3. Adler
4. Jung
5. Freud
6. Horney

CONCEPT REVIEW 11.3 Page 498

1. False. Rogers believed it is the parents' responsibility to guide and control their children's behavior.
2. False. Rogers advocated the use of unconditional positive regard.
3. True
4. False. Social cognitive theory holds that human behavior is determined by the interaction of environmental, cognitive, and behavioral factors.
5. False. The development of self-efficacy beliefs continues throughout life.
6. True.

CONCEPT REVIEW 11.4 Page 513

1. a
2. b
3. d
4. b
5. c

Chapter

12

Social Psychology

Prologue: The "Homeless" Man

Remember Erv and Fern, Sandy's parents, from Chapter 5? A few years ago, Fern and Erv got two free plane tickets when they were "bumped" from an overbooked flight. They decided to use their free plane tickets to visit a city they had always wanted to see—San Francisco. Even though Fern was excited about the trip, she was also anxious about visiting the earthquake zone. Erv wasn't especially worried about earthquakes, but he was worried about whether his old army buddy could still beat him at poker. Mostly, they both wanted to see the famous sights, eat seafood, wander through shops, and explore used bookstores, which is Erv's favorite hobby.

As it turned out, Fern and Erv were both quite taken by the beauty and charm of San Francisco. But they were also disturbed by the number of homeless people they saw on the city streets, sleeping in the doorways of expensive shops and restaurants. Especially Fern, who has a heart of gold and is known among her family and friends for her willingness to help others, even complete strangers.

On the third morning of their San Francisco visit, Erv and Fern were walking along one of the hilly San Francisco streets near the downtown area. That's when Fern saw a scruffy-looking man in faded jeans sitting on some steps, holding a cup. Surely this was one of San Francisco's less fortunate, Fern thought to herself. Without a moment's hesitation, Fern rummaged through her purse, walked over to the man, and dropped a handful of quarters in his cup.

"Hey, lady! What the hell d'ya think you're doing!?!" the man exclaimed, jumping up.

"Oh, my! Aren't you homeless!?" Fern asked, mortified and turning bright red with embarrassment.

"Lady, this *is* my home," the man snapped, motioning with his thumb to the house behind him. "I live here! And that's my cup of coffee you just ruined!"

Fortunately, the "homeless" man also had a sense of humor. After fishing Fern's quarters out of his coffee, he chatted with the out-of-towners, enlightening them on the extraordinary cost of real estate near downtown San Francisco. As they parted, the not-so-homeless man ended up recommending a couple of his favorite seafood restaurants to Erv and Fern.

Like Fern, we all try to make sense out of our social environment. We constantly make judgments about the traits, motives, and goals of other people. And, like Fern, sometimes we make mistakes! In this chapter, we will look at how we interpret our social environment, including how we form impressions of other people. We'll explore how our behavior, including our willingness to help others, is influenced by the social environment and other people. In the process, we'll come back to Erv and Fern's incident with the "homeless" man to illustrate several important concepts.

Introduction

What Is Social Psychology?

Social psychology is the scientific study of how people think, feel, and behave in social situations. What kinds of questions do social psychologists try to answer? What is meant by social cognition and social influence?

Why did Fern think the man on the steps was homeless? How did the "homeless" man initially interpret Fern's efforts to help him? And in contrast to Fern, not everyone who feels compassion toward the homeless acts in accordance with that attitude. Why did Fern do so?

These are the kinds of questions that social psychologists try to answer. **Social psychology** is the scientific study of the way individuals think, feel, and behave in social situations (Brehm & Kassin, 1996). It's an area of psychology that explores some of the most basic yet intriguing "people" questions:

- How do we form impressions of other people?
- How do we explain other people's behavior? And how does that explanation differ from the way we explain our own behavior?
- How do people influence one another?
- Why is it that sometimes a person will heroically help a stranger, while in other situations, a crowd of people will ignore someone who desperately needs help?

social psychology
The branch of psychology that studies how people think, feel, and behave in social situations.

social cognition
The study of the mental processes people use to make sense out of their social environment.

social influence
The study of the effect that situational factors and other people have on an individual's behavior.

Social psychologists study an extremely broad range of topics. In this chapter, we're going to focus on two basic areas of social psychology: social cognition and social influence. We'll begin by exploring different dimensions of social cognition. **Social cognition** refers to how we form impressions of other people, how we interpret the meaning of other people's behavior, and how our behavior is affected by our attitudes (Fiske, 1993; Fiske & Taylor, 1991). Later in the chapter, we'll look at **social influence,** which focuses on how our behavior is affected by situational factors and other people. The study of social influence includes such questions as why we conform to group norms, what compels us to obey an authority figure, and the conditions under which people will help a stranger.

Person Perception:
Forming Impressions of Other People

Person perception refers to the mental processes we use to form judgments about other people. What four principles does this process follow? How do social categories, implicit personality theories, and physical attractiveness affect person perception?

Consider the following scenario: You're attending a college in the middle of a big city and commute from your apartment to the campus via the subway. Today you stayed a bit later than usual on campus, so the rush hour is pretty much over. As a seasoned subway rider, you know you're safer when the subway is full of commuters. So as you step off the platform into the subway car, you're feeling just a bit anxious. The car is more than half full. If you want to sit down, you'll have to share a seat with some other passenger. You quickly survey your fellow passengers. In a matter of seconds, you must decide which stranger you'll share your ride home with, elbow to elbow, thigh to thigh. How will you decide?

Even if you've never ridden on a subway, it doesn't matter. We could just as easily use picking a seat on a bus or in a crowded movie theater. What these situations share in common is a task that each of us is confronted with almost every day: On the basis of very limited information, we must quickly draw conclusions about the nature of people who are complete strangers to us. We also have to make some rough predictions as to how these strangers are likely to behave. How do we arrive at these conclusions?

The Interpersonal Context of Person Perception

Person perception refers to the mental processes we use to form judgments and draw conclusions about the characteristics of others. Person perception is an active and subjective process that always occurs in some *interpersonal context* (E. Jones, 1990). Every interpersonal context has three key components:

- the characteristics of the individual you are attempting to size up
- your own characteristics as the perceiver
- the specific situation in which the process occurs

Each component influences the conclusions you reach about other people. As a psychological process, person perception follows some basic principles (see Jones, 1990; Fiske, 1993; Fiske & Neuberg, 1990). We'll illustrate these basic principles using the subway scenario.

Principle 1. *Your reactions to others are determined by your perceptions of them, not by who or what they "really" are.* Put simply, you treat others as you perceive them to be. So, as you step inside the subway car, you quickly choose not to sit next to the big, burly-looking man with a scowl on his face. Why? Because *you* perceive Mr. Burly-Surly as potentially threatening. This guy's picture is probably on the FBI bulletin board at the post office for being an axe murderer, you think. Of course, he could just as easily be a burly florist who's surly because he's getting home late. It

person perception
The mental processes we use to form judgments and draw conclusions about the characteristics and motives of others.

doesn't matter. Your behavior toward him is determined by your subjective perception of him.

Principle 2. Your goals in a particular situation determine the amount and kind of information you collect about others. Your goal in this situation is simple: you want to share a subway seat with someone who will basically leave you alone. Hence, you focus your attention on the characteristics of other people that seem to be relevant to your goal, ignoring details that are unrelated to it (Hilton & Darley, 1991; Swann, 1984). After all, you're not looking for a date for Saturday night, a plumber, or a lab partner for your biology class. If you were, you'd focus on very different aspects of the other people in the situation.

Principle 3. In every situation, you evaluate people partly in terms of how you expect them to act in that situation. Whether you're in a classroom, restaurant, or public restroom, your behavior is governed by **social norms**—the "rules," or expectations, for appropriate behavior in that social situation. Riding a subway is no exception to this principle (Milgram, 1992). For example, you don't sit next to someone else when empty seats are available, you don't try to borrow your seatmate's newspaper, and you avoid eye contact with others.

These "subway rules" aren't posted anywhere, of course. Nevertheless, violating these social norms will draw attention from others and probably make them quite uneasy. So as you size up your fellow subway passengers, you're partly evaluating their behavior in terms of how people-riding-the-subway-at-night-in-a-big-city should behave.

Principle 4. Your self-perception also influences how you perceive others and how you act on your perceptions. Your decision about whom to sit next to is also influenced by how you perceive your *self*. For example, if you think of yourself as looking a bit threatening (even though you're really a mild-mannered biology major), you may choose to sit next to the twenty-something guy with a briefcase rather than the anxious-looking middle-aged woman who's clutching her purse with both hands. In contrast, if you're a young adult female, you probably won't choose to share a seat with a male in your age range because you're concerned that *he* might think that *you* are coming on to him when that's not your intention.

In combination, these four basic principles underscore that person perception is not a one-way process in which we objectively survey other people and then logically evaluate their characteristics. Instead, the context, our self-perceptions, and the perceptions we have of others all interact. Each component plays a role in the judgments we form of others (E. Jones, 1990).

BIZARRO

I'D LIKE TO TALK TO YOU ABOUT THE WAY YOU'VE BEEN DRESSING AT WORK, JIM. IT DOESN'T REALLY BEFIT AN EXECUTIVE OF AN HERBAL TEA COMPANY.

Social Categorization:

Using Mental Shortcuts in Person Perception

As you walk down the aisle of the subway car, you don't carefully weigh the characteristics of your fellow passengers. Instead, you form quick, global impressions of a diverse group of strangers, make a decision in a flash, and sit down as casually as possible. Even with a task as simple as deciding where to sit on the subway, you're integrating a tremendous amount of complex information at split-second speed—faster than any computer. How do you form these impressions of other people so quickly and efficiently?

Social categorization is the mental process of classifying people into groups on the basis of common characteristics. Much of this mental work is automatic and spontaneous, and it often occurs outside of your conscious awareness (Macrae & others, 1994; Bargh & others, 1996).

When you have limited time to form your impressions and limited information about a person, like the other passengers in the subway car, you tend to rely on very broad social categories, such as the other person's gender, race, age, and occupation (Fiske, 1993; Fiske & Neuberg, 1990). So you glance at a person and quickly categorize him as "Asian male, twenty-something, probably a college student."

Using Social Categories We often use superficial cues like clothing and context to assign people to social categories and draw conclusions about their behavior. For example, you might characterize some people in this crowd as belonging to the category of "businessmen" because they are wearing suits and ties—and conclude that they were on their way to or from work. What other sorts of social categories are evident here?

Any given person may be categorized in multiple ways. When we know more about a particular person, more precise subcategories are likely to be used, such as this description of one of our favorite students: "African-American female, twenty-something, psychology major, very smart, sings professionally and in her church choir, good sense of humor."

Using social categories has both disadvantages and advantages. On the one hand, relegating someone to a social category on the basis of superficial information ignores that person's unique qualities. In effect, you're jumping to conclusions about a person that are based on very limited information. Sometimes, these conclusions are incorrect—as Fern was when she categorized the man with a cup in his hand as "homeless."

On the other hand, relying on social categories is a natural, adaptive cognitive process. After all, social categories provide us with considerable basic information about other people. Using social categories allows us to mentally organize and remember information about others more efficiently and effectively (Macrae & others, 1994; Fiske, 1993).

We don't always depend on quick, automatic social judgments. Sometimes we want a more accurate, comprehensive impression of a person. When it's important to your goals to perceive another person as accurately as possible, you're less likely to rely on automatic categorization (Fiske & Neuberg, 1990; Fiske & Taylor, 1991). Instead, you go into mental high gear, consciously and deliberately exerting mental effort to understand the other person better and to form a more accurate impression (Fiske, 1993). You might also check the impressions that you form by seeking additional information, such as calling a job applicant's previous employers.

social norms
The "rules," or expectations, for appropriate behavior in a particular social situation.

social categorization
The mental process of classifying people into groups (or *categories*) on the basis of their shared characteristics.

Implicit Personality Theories:
He's *Not* That Kind of Person!

Closely related to social categories are implicit personality theories. An **implicit personality theory** is a network of assumptions or beliefs about the relationships among various types of people, traits, and behaviors. Through previous social experiences, we form cognitive schemas about the traits and behaviors associated with different "types" of people. When we perceive someone to be a particular "type," we often assume that the person will display these traits and behaviors (Sedikides & Anderson, 1994).

For example, your choice of a seatmate on the subway might well reflect some of your own implicit personality theories. You might feel comfortable sitting next to the silver-haired guy who's reading the *Wall Street Journal*, wearing an expensive suit, and carrying a leather briefcase. Why? Because these superficial characteristics lead you to assume that he's a particular "type" of person—a conservative businessman. And on the basis of your implicit personality theory for "a conservative businessman," you conclude that he's a "law-abiding citizen" who is not likely to try to pick your pocket or whip out a gun and start shooting.

Like social categories, implicit personality theories can be useful as mental shortcuts in perceiving other people. But just like social categories, implicit personality theories are not always accurate. In some instances, they can even be dangerously misleading.

Consider a man named John whom Sandy met when she was a research associate at a University of Chicago research institute. John was a divorced, slightly overweight, middle-aged businessman who had built up a successful contracting and remodeling business. He lived in a quiet suburban neighborhood, where he was well-liked. Every year John threw a block party for his neighbors, and he often helped them with minor home repairs. He was involved in local politics and civic organizations. And John regularly volunteered at a nearby hospital, where he would dress up as "Pogo the Clown," perform magic tricks, and pass out candy to sick and injured children.

Sounds like the kind of person you wouldn't mind knowing, doesn't he? Sandy met John under somewhat different circumstances. When John came to see the psychiatrist for whom Sandy was a research associate, John was shackled in leg irons and handcuffs and flanked by three police officers. The psychiatrist had been appointed by the courts to evaluate John's mental condition. Outside the clinic, a squadron of police had sealed off every possible escape route from the area. Stationed on the roofs of the nearby buildings were police sharpshooters.

Why were so many police guarding a guy who dressed up as a clown and entertained sick children? Because this man was John Wayne Gacy, "the undisputed champion of American serial killers," as *Newsweek* described him (S. Holmes, 1994). Gacy was subsequently convicted of murdering 33 boys and young men, most of whom he had buried in a crawlspace under his suburban home. After years of legal appeals, Gacy was executed in 1994.

One reason Gacy had escaped detection for so many years was that he contradicted the implicit personality theory that most people have for a serial killer. Indeed, most of us find it difficult to believe that a ruthless murderer would also be well-liked by his neighbors and successful in business—or that he would be someone who compassionately visits sick children in the hospital.

Although they can lead us to inaccurate conclusions, implicit personality theories represent another important social cognition strategy in our efforts to make sense out of other people (Fiske & Neuberg, 1990). Like social categories, implicit personality theories simplify information processing about other people and provide a mental framework that helps us organize observations, memories, and beliefs about people (Macrae & others, 1994).

"Pogo the Clown" Dressed as "Pogo the Clown," John would visit sick children in the hospital to cheer them up. He was also a successful building contractor and a local precinct captain. Given that information, what sorts of personal qualities would you expect him to display?

implicit personality theory
A network of assumptions or beliefs about the relationships among various types of people, traits, and behaviors.

Physical Attractiveness:

Can You Judge a Book by Its Cover?

As the subway scenario illustrates, physical appearance cues play a pivotal role in person perception (E. Jones, 1990). Physical attractiveness is particularly influential. We pay lip service to the idea that physical attractiveness is less important than a person's behavior, personality traits, and abilities. That's the point of common sayings like "Beauty is only skin deep" and "You can't judge a book by its cover."

But from childhood on, we are bombarded with images that suggest an entirely different cultural message. In fairy tales, cartoons, movies, and even computer games, the heroes are handsome and the heroines beautiful. The bad guys, wicked witches, and evil stepmothers are ugly. The implicit cultural message in these social schemas is, "What is beautiful is good" (Eagly & others, 1991).

As a result of such cultural conditioning, most people do associate physical attractiveness with a wide range of other desirable characteristics (Feingold, 1992; Eagly & others, 1991). For example, good-looking people are perceived as being more intelligent, happier, and better adjusted than other people. They're also seen as being more socially competent and—surprise!—sexier than less attractive people. However, very good-looking people are also perceived as being more vain and less modest than unattractive people.

Are attractive people *really* better adjusted, smarter, or more assertive than unattractive people? After analyzing dozens of studies, psychologist Alan Feingold (1992) found that there were actually very *few* personality differences between beautiful people and their plainer counterparts. Overall, attractive people tend to be less lonely, more popular, and less anxious in social situations—all characteristics that are related to the advantage that their physical attractiveness seems to confer on them in social situations.

Physical attractiveness is *not* correlated with intelligence, mental health, or even self-esteem (Feingold, 1992). Good-looking people are also well aware of the effect their looks have on other people's judgments of them. Thus, they're more likely than unattractive people to attribute other people's approval of their accomplishments to their looks rather than to their effort or talent (Major & others, 1984).

What Is Beautiful Is Good We are culturally conditioned to associate beauty with goodness and evil with ugliness—an implicit personality theory that has been dubbed the "what is beautiful is good" myth. One example of this cultural conditioning is the classic Disney film *Snow White.* In the scene shown, the wicked stepmother, complete with a wart on her nose, offers the poisoned apple to the innocent and virtuous heroine, Snow White. (The Walt Disney Co.)

Attribution: Explaining the Causes of Behavior

> *Attribution refers to the process of explaining people's behavior. What are the fundamental attribution error, the actor–observer discrepancy, and the self-serving bias? How do these biases shape the attributions we make?*

attribution
The mental process of inferring the causes of people's behavior, including one's own. Also used to refer to the explanation made for a particular behavior.

The process of inferring the cause of, or the "why" behind, someone's behavior, including your own, is called **attribution.** Psychologists also use the word *attribution* to refer to the explanation you make for a particular behavior. The attributions we make have a strong influence on our thoughts and feelings about other people. But as you'll see in this section, our attributions are not always correct.

The Fundamental Attribution Error:
Just a Couple of Bozos?

As you're studying in the college library, the activities of two workers catch your attention. The two men are trying to lift and move a large file cabinet. "Okay, let's lift it and tip it this way," one guy says with considerable authority. In unison, they heave and tip the file cabinet. When they do, all four file drawers come flying out, bonking the first guy on the head. As the file cabinet goes crashing to the floor, you bite your lip to keep from laughing and think to yourself, "Yeah, they're obviously a pair of 40-watt bulbs."

Why did you arrive at that conclusion? After all, it's completely possible that the workers were not dimwits. Maybe the lock on the file drawers broke. Or maybe there was some other explanation for their mishap.

Psychologists have discovered that we tend to follow a consistent pattern when we explain the behavior of other people (Gilbert & Malone, 1995; Leyens & others, 1996). *We tend to spontaneously attribute the behavior of others to internal, personal characteristics, while downplaying or underestimating the effects of external, situational factors.* This bias is so common in individualistic cultures that it's called the **fundamental attribution error** (L. Ross, 1977). Even though it's entirely possible that situational forces are behind another person's behavior, we tend to automatically assume that the cause is an internal, personal characteristic.

However, when the consequences of an attribution are important to us, we respond differently. For example, when a friend fails to call you back as promised, you may be annoyed at first and succumb to the fundamental attribution error: "Sue is such an inconsiderate person." But if you accept this automatic attribution, your relationship with Sue is likely to change for the worse. So, because the consequences of your attribution are important, you give the matter a second thought. Thus, you shift from your initial spontaneous *internal* attribution, and consider possible external, situational factors that might explain her behavior. You wonder if something like a family emergency or other unexpected event came up that kept her from calling you back.

This commonplace example illustrates what social cognition researcher Daniel Gilbert (1989) believes is the natural, two-step process of attribution. Gilbert suggests that people first automatically make an internal attribution ("Sue is an inconsiderate person"). But when the cause of an ambiguous behavior is important to us, we advance to the second step: We exert mental effort and consciously consider possible situational influences in the attempt to "correct" our automatic internal attribution ("Maybe there was a family emergency").

The Actor–Observer Discrepancy:
You're a Klutz, but *I* Slipped on Some Ice!

There is an interesting exception to the fundamental attribution error. When it comes to explaining *our own* behavior, we tend to be biased in the opposite direction: We're more likely to use an *external, situational* attribution than an *internal, personal* attribution. This common attributional bias is called the **actor–observer discrepancy** because there is a discrepancy between the attributions you make when you are the *actor* in a given situation and those you make when you are the *observer* of other people's behavior (Jones & Nisbett, 1971).

fundamental attribution error
The tendency to attribute the behavior of others to internal, personal characteristics, while ignoring or underestimating the effects of external, situational factors; an attributional bias that is common in individualistic cultures.

actor–observer discrepancy
The tendency to attribute one's own behavior to external, situational causes, while attributing the behavior of others to internal, personal causes; especially likely to occur with regard to behaviors that lead to negative outcomes.

For example, if *you* were the one who dropped the file cabinet, you'd probably explain the event very differently. It's not very likely that you would say, "Boy, I am really dumb!" It's much more likely that you would explain your behavior by resorting to a situational explanation: "The librarian told me that the file drawers were locked shut." "I didn't have room to tip the file cabinet the other way."

Once you become aware of the actor–observer discrepancy, it's almost embarrassing to admit how often you succumb to it. Joe got fired because he was incompetent and lazy; you got fired because the boss had it in for you. Jane got her purse snatched because she was careless; you got your pocket picked because the subway was crowded. Some jerk pulled out in front of your car because he's a reckless, inconsiderate moron; you pulled out in front of his car because your view was blocked by a school bus. And so on. In Focus Box 12.1, "Blaming the Victim: Do We Live in a Just World?" discusses a related attributional bias.

IN FOCUS 12.1

Blaming the Victim: Do We Live in a Just World?

Our friend Grace owns a gift shop in a large Chicago shopping mall. About a year ago, Grace was robbed at knifepoint while she was walking to her car after closing up shop for the night. Most of Grace's friends rallied to her support after the incident. But some people also made comments like these: "You of all people should know that shopping mall parking lots aren't safe at night! You should have gotten the security guard to escort you to your car." "It doesn't surprise me at all. You're just way too trusting, Grace. You should leave when everybody else does."

Although well-intentioned, such remarks illustrate an attributional pattern called **blaming the victim.** The

Blaming the Victim This couple's home was destroyed by a wild fire in Alaska. Why do people often "blame the victim" after natural disasters, accidents, and crimes?

innocent victim of a tragedy, crime, disaster, or serious illness is blamed for having somehow caused the misfortune or for not having taken steps to prevent or avoid it. For example, after homes are destroyed by natural disasters like floods or earthquakes, you'll often hear people say things like "They should have known better than to build a house there."

Likewise, many people blame the poor for their dire straits, the sick for bringing on their illness, AIDS patients for being promiscuous or careless, and battered women and rape victims for somehow "provoking" their attackers (see Brehm & Kassin, 1996). Hindsight makes it seem as if the victim should have been able to predict what was going to happen (Carli & Leonard, 1989; Janoff-Bulman & others, 1985).

In part, blaming the victim is another example of the fundamental attribution error—the strong tendency to attribute behavior and events to internal, personal causes, and to downplay external, situational causes. When confronted by an unusual event, people naturally try to identify its cause. The fundamental attribution error makes it more likely that they'll attribute the cause to some sort of personal quality or act of the victim, rather than to the situation or circumstances.

According to social psychologist Melvin Lerner (1980), people also tend to blame the victim because they have

a strong need to believe that the world is fair—that "we get what we deserve and deserve what we get." Lerner calls this the **just-world hypothesis.** Blaming the victim reflects the belief that, since the world is just, the victim must have done *something* to deserve his or her fate.

Why do we have a psychological need to believe in a just world? Well, if you believe that the world is *not* just, then perfectly innocent people—like you, for instance—could also be hit with a tragic misfortune out of the clear blue. If the world is unfair, then no one—including you—is safe from tragic twists of fate and chance, no matter how virtuous, careful, or conscientious you may be. According to the just-world hypothesis, perceiving victims in a negative light reduces your fear of vulnerability. It's a way of psychologically defending yourself against the threatening thought, "It could just as easily have been me" (Thornton, 1992).

In a similar way, people often defend themselves from feelings of vulnerability by *distancing* themselves from victims of tragedies or serious illnesses. Distancing allows you to convince yourself that you are very different from the victim. Participants in one study, for example, believed that they had very little in common with a fictitious profile of a cancer patient, whether they objectively did or not (Pyszczynski & others, 1993).

But if you realistically acknowledge that you may also be threatened by the same misfortunes that others have experienced, your need to defensively distance yourself from their fate may be reduced. For example, the tendency of the participants to distance themselves from a cancer patient was significantly reduced when they were encouraged to express their own fears of being struck by cancer (Pyszczynski & others, 1993).

Blaming the victim is also less likely to occur when we're able to help the victim in some way (Lerner, 1980). In part, helping the victim restores our sense of fairness and justice. By offering assistance, we can put the world back in balance and, to some extent, undo the wrong that has been done (Batson, 1991; Miller & others, 1990). Another way to reduce victim blaming is to imagine how the innocent victim feels. If you feel empathy for the victim, you're less likely to blame him or her (Batson, 1991).

How can we explain the strong tendency to commit the actor–observer discrepancy? One possible explanation is that we simply have more information about the potential causes of our own behavior than we do about the causes of other people's behavior. When you observe another driver turn directly into the path of your car, that's typically all the information you have on which to judge his behavior. But when *you* pull in front of another car, you perceive your own behavior in the context of the many situational factors that influenced your action. You're aware of factors like visibility and road conditions. You also know what motivated your behavior and how differently you have behaved in similar situations in the past. Thus, you are much more aware of the extent to which *your* behavior has been influenced by situational factors (Fiske & Taylor, 1991; E. Jones, 1990; Jones & Nisbett, 1971).

Not surprisingly, then, we're less susceptible to the actor–observer discrepancy with people whom we know well. Because we possess more information about the behavior of our friends and relatives in different situations, we're more aware of the possible situational influences on their behavior (Aron & others, 1992; Sande & others, 1988). We're also better at seeing situations from their point of view.

TABLE 12.1 Some Common Attributional Biases

Bias	Description
Fundamental attribution error	We tend to explain the behavior of other people by attributing their behavior to internal, personal characteristics, while underestimating or ignoring the effects of external, situational factors.
Actor–observer discrepancy	When we are the *actor*, we tend to attribute our own behavior to external causes. When we are the *observer* of someone else's behavior, we tend to attribute their behavior to internal causes.
Blaming the victim	When we're unable to help the victims of misfortune, we tend to blame them for causing their own misfortune, or for not taking steps to prevent or avoid it. Partly due to the *just-world hypothesis*.
Self-serving bias	The tendency to take credit for our *successes* by attributing them to internal, personal causes, along with the tendency to distance ourselves from our *failures* by attributing them to external, situational causes. Most common in individualistic cultures.
Self-effacing (or modesty) bias	The tendency to blame ourselves for our *failures*, attributing them to internal, personal causes, along with the tendency to downplay our *successes* by attributing them to external, situational causes. Most common in collectivistic cultures.

The Self-Serving Bias:
Using Explanations That Meet Our Needs

If you've ever listened to other students react to their grades on an important exam, you've seen the **self-serving bias** in action (Whitley & Frieze, 1985). When students do well on a test, they tend to congratulate themselves and to attribute their success to how hard they studied, their intelligence, and so forth—all *internal* attributions. But when a student blows a test big time, the *external* attributions fly left and right: "They were all trick questions!" "I couldn't concentrate because the guy behind me kept coughing."

In a wide range of situations, people tend to credit themselves for their success and to blame their failures on external circumstances (Schlenker & Weigold, 1992; Schlenker & others, 1990). Psychol-

CULTURE AND HUMAN BEHAVIOR 12.2

Attributional Biases in Collectivistic Versus Individualistic Cultures

Although the self-serving bias is common in individualistic cultures like Australia and the United States, it is far from being universal. In collectivistic cultures, like Asian cultures, an opposite attributional bias is often demonstrated (Bond, 1994; Moghaddam & others, 1993). Called the *self-effacing bias* or *modesty bias,* it involves blaming failure on internal, personal factors, while attributing success to external, situational factors (Markus & Kitayama, 1994, 1991).

This cross-cultural difference in attributional patterns has some practical ramifications. Compared to American students, Japanese and Chinese students are more likely to attribute academic failure to personal factors, such as lack of effort, instead of situational factors (Dornbusch & others, 1996; Matsumoto, 1994). Thus, a Japanese student who does poorly on an exam is likely to say, "I didn't study hard enough." And when a Japanese or Chinese student performs poorly in school, he or she is expected to study harder and longer (Stevenson & Stigler, 1992). In contrast, Japanese or Chinese students tend to attribute academic success to situational factors, such as saying "The exam was very easy" or "There was very little competition this year" (M. Bond & Smith, 1996; Stevenson & others, 1986).

Psychologists Hazel Markus and Shinobu Kitayama (1991) believe that the self-effacing bias reflects the emphasis that interdependent cultures

place on fitting in with other members of the group. As the Japanese proverb goes, "The nail that sticks up gets pounded down." In collectivistic cultures, self-esteem does not rest on doing better than others in the group. Rather, standing out from the group is likely to produce psychological discomfort and tension. As Markus and Kitayama (1994) explain, "For those with interdependent selves, feeling good requires a connection with others, and a connection to others produces good feelings."

Cross-cultural differences are also evident with the fundamental attribution error. In general, members of collectivistic cultures are less likely to commit the fundamental attribution error than members of individualistic cultures (M. Bond & Smith, 1996; Triandis, 1994). That is, collectivists are more likely to attribute the causes of another person's behavior to external, situational factors rather than internal, personal factors—the exact *opposite* attributional bias that is demonstrated in individualistic cultures.

To test this idea in a naturally occurring context, psychologists Michael Morris and Kaiping Peng (1994) compared articles reporting the same mass murders in Chinese-language and English-language newspapers. In one case, the murderer was a Chinese graduate student attending an American university. In the other case, the murderer was an American postal worker. Regardless of whether the murderer was Chinese or American, the news ac-

> *Haughtiness invites ruin; humility receives benefits.*
>
> **Chinese proverb**

counts were fundamentally different depending on whether the *reporter* was American or Chinese.

The American reporters were more likely to explain the killings by making personal, internal attributions. For example, American reporters emphasized the murderers' personality traits, like the graduate student's "bad temper," the postal worker's "history of being mentally unstable," and both murderers' psychological problems.

In contrast, Chinese reporters were more likely to make situational, external attributions to explain the killings. Whether the murderer was American or Chinese, the Chinese reporters emphasized situational factors, such as the fact that the postal worker had recently been fired from his job and the fact that the graduate student had failed to receive an academic award. The Chinese reporters also cited social pressures and problems in American society to account for the actions of the killers.

Clearly, then, the way we account for our successes and failures, as well as the way we account for the actions of others, is yet another example of how human behavior is influenced by cultural conditioning.

ogists explain the self-serving bias as being partly due to an attempt to "save face" and protect self-esteem in the face of failure (Dunning & others, 1995; Banaji & Prentice, 1994).

Although common in many societies, the self-serving bias is far from universal, as cross-cultural psychologists have discovered. We discuss this finding in Culture and Human Behavior Box 12.2, "Attributional Biases in Collectivistic Versus Individualistic Cultures."

self-serving bias
The tendency to attribute successful outcomes of one's own behavior to internal causes and unsuccessful outcomes to external, situational causes.

Person Perception and Attribution

Match each of the following concepts with one of the examples below:

a. fundamental attribution error
b. actor–observer discrepancy
c. self-serving bias
d. self-effacing bias
e. implicit personality theory
f. social categorization

_____ **1.** Dr. Nobuaki, a brilliant young professor who has just joined the faculty, was asked to give a talk about her research to her new colleagues. She began her presentation by saying, "I am very poorly prepared, and my research is not very important. Thank you for being patient with me."

_____ **2.** When Fern saw the man sitting on the San Francisco steps holding a cup, she thought he was a homeless person.

_____ **3.** Your next-door neighbor is a shy, boring, and mild-mannered Latin teacher. When you sign up for a sky-diving class, you are astonished to discover that he is one of the instructors.

_____ **4.** At the very beginning of the marathon, the top three female runners collided and were all forced to drop out because of their extensive injuries. Christine, the surprise winner of the marathon, told a local sports reporter that her win was due to her hard work, running technique, and self-discipline.

_____ **5.** You're sitting in a nice restaurant looking over the menu. From behind you, you hear a loud crash as a tray full of dishes hits the floor. As you watch the waiter scrambling to clean up the mess, you think, "What a klutz!"

_____ **6.** Lynette bought the wrong textbook at the college bookstore. When she brought the book back to the store for a refund, she said, "Your store is so disorganized, it's impossible to tell which books go with which course." You're waiting in line and watching Lynette haggle with the cashier. You think to yourself, "How could anyone be so dumb as to buy the wrong textbook?" What accounts for these different attributions of the mixup?

The Social Psychology of Attitudes

> *An attitude is a learned tendency to evaluate some object, person, or issue in a particular way. What are the three components of an attitude? Under what conditions are attitudes most likely to determine behavior? What is cognitive dissonance, and how does it affect attitudes?*

Are the Republicans or the Democrats better at leading the United States? What's your favorite kind of music? How do you feel about gun control? abortion rights? smoking in public places? gays in the military?

On these and many other subjects, you've probably formed an attitude. Psychologists formally define an **attitude** as a learned tendency to evaluate some object, person, or issue in a particular way (Olson & Zanna, 1993; Zimbardo & Leippe, 1991). Attitudes are typically positive or negative, but they can also be *ambivalent,* as when you have mixed feelings about an issue or person.

As shown in Figure 12.1, attitudes can include three components (Zimbardo & Leippe, 1991; Fazio, 1990). First, an attitude may have a *cognitive component:* your thoughts and conclusions about a given topic or object. An example might be the person who says, "In my opinion, the easy access to guns is contributing to violence in the schools." Second, an attitude may have

attitude
A learned tendency to evaluate some object, person, or issue in a particular way; such evaluations may be positive, negative, or ambivalent.

FIGURE 12.1 The Components of Attitudes
An attitude is a positive or negative evaluation of an object, person, or idea. An attitude may have cognitive, emotional, and behavioral components.

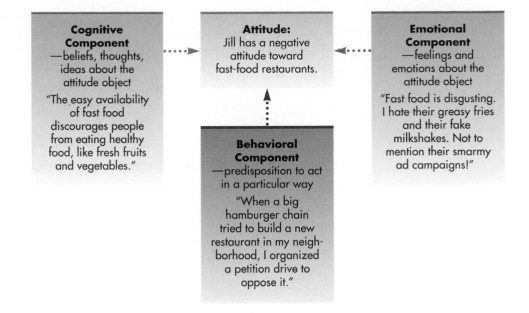

Cognitive Component
—beliefs, thoughts, ideas about the attitude object

"The easy availability of fast food discourages people from eating healthy food, like fresh fruits and vegetables."

Attitude:
Jill has a negative attitude toward fast-food restaurants.

Emotional Component
—feelings and emotions about the attitude object

"Fast food is disgusting. I hate their greasy fries and their fake milkshakes. Not to mention their smarmy ad campaigns!"

Behavioral Component
—predisposition to act in a particular way

"When a big hamburger chain tried to build a new restaurant in my neighborhood, I organized a petition drive to oppose it."

an emotional, or *affective, component:* "I'm really scared and upset by the number of handguns that are floating around." Finally, an attitude can have a *behavioral component,* in which your attitude is reflected in your actions: "I've started a petition drive for stricter gun control laws in my state."

The Effect of Attitudes on Behavior

You may take it for granted that your attitudes tend to guide your behavior. But social psychologists have consistently found that people don't always act in accordance with their attitudes (see Eagly & Chaiken, 1993; Eagly, 1992). For example, you might disapprove of cheating, yet find yourself sneaking a peek at a classmate's exam paper when the opportunity presents itself. Or you might favor a certain political candidate, yet not vote on election day.

Under what conditions are your attitudes most likely to influence or determine your behavior? Social psychologists have found that you're most likely to behave in accordance with your attitudes when:

- *Attitudes are extreme or are frequently expressed* (Eagly & Chaiken, 1993; Bassili, 1993).

- *Attitudes have been formed through direct experience* (Fazio, 1990; Fazio & Zanna, 1981). For example, suppose you once escaped serious injury in an auto accident because you were wearing your seatbelt. You'd probably strongly favor seatbelt use, might actively support a mandatory seatbelt law in your state, and always "buckle up" whenever you get in a car.

- *You are very knowledgeable about the subject* (Wood & others, 1995; Wood, 1982).

- *You have a vested interest in the subject* (Crano, 1995; Sivacek & Crano, 1982). If you personally stand to gain or lose something on a specific issue, you're more likely to act in accordance with your attitudes.

- *You anticipate a favorable outcome or response from others* (Ajzen, 1991; Ajzen & Fishbein, 1980).

cognitive dissonance
An unpleasant state of psychological tension or arousal (*dissonance*) that occurs when two thoughts or perceptions (*cognitions*) are inconsistent; typically results from the awareness that attitudes and behavior are in conflict.

What we've discussed thus far meshes nicely with common sense: people tend to act in accordance with their attitudes when they feel strongly about an issue, have a personal stake in the issue, and anticipate a positive outcome in a particular situation. In short, your attitudes do influence your behavior in many instances. Now, let's consider the opposite question: Can your behavior influence your attitudes?

The Effect of Behavior on Attitudes:
Fried Grasshoppers for Lunch?!

Suppose you have volunteered to participate in a psychology experiment. When you arrive at the lab, you're asked to indicate your degree of preference for a variety of foods, including fried grasshoppers, which you rank pretty low on the list. During the experiment, the experimenter instructs you to eat some fried grasshoppers. You manage to swallow three of the crispy critters. At the end of the experiment, your attitudes toward grasshoppers as a food source are surveyed again.

After the experiment, you talk to a friend who also participated in the experiment. You mention how friendly and polite you thought the experimenter was. As it turns out, your friend had a very different experience. He thought the experimenter was an arrogant, rude jerk.

Here's the critical question: Whose attitude toward eating fried grasshoppers is more likely to change in a positive direction—yours or your friends'? Circle your answer below.

A. You, who encountered a friendly experimenter

B. Your friend, who encountered a rude experimenter

The correct answer is obvious, right? If you're like our students, you probably predicted *A* as the correct answer. Well, before you pat yourself on the back for your keen psychological insight, the correct answer is *B*!

At first glance, the correct answer seems to go against the grain of common sense. So how can we explain this outcome? To begin with, our fried grasshoppers scenario represents the basic design of a classic experiment by psychologist Philip Zimbardo and his colleagues (1965). Zimbardo's experiment and other similar ones underscore the power of cognitive dissonance (see Festinger, 1962). **Cognitive dissonance** is an unpleasant state of psychological tension (dissonance) that occurs when there's an inconsistency between two thoughts or perceptions (cognitions). This state of dissonance is so unpleasant that we are strongly motivated to reduce it (Festinger, 1957).

Cognitive dissonance commonly occurs in situations in which you become uncomfortably aware that your behavior and your attitudes are in conflict. In these situations, you are simultaneously holding two conflicting cognitions: your original attitude versus the realization that you have behaved in a way that contradicts that attitude. If you can easily rationalize your behavior to make it consistent with your attitude, then any dissonance you might experience can be quickly and easily resolved. But when your behavior *cannot* be easily justified, how can you resolve the contradiction and resolve the unpleasant state of dissonance? Since you can't go back and change the behavior, *you change your attitude to make it consistent with your behavior.*

DILBERT

Let's take another look at the results of the grasshopper study, this time from the perspective of cognitive dissonance theory. Your attitude toward eating grasshoppers did *not* change, because you could easily rationalize the conflict between your attitude ("Eating grasshoppers is disgusting") and your behavior (eating three grasshoppers). You probably justified your behavior by saying something like, "I ate the grasshoppers because the experimenter was such a nice guy and I wanted to help him out."

However, your friend who encountered the rude experimenter can't easily explain the contradiction between disliking grasshoppers and voluntarily eating them. Thus, he experiences an uncomfortable state of cognitive dissonance. Since he can't go back and change his behavior, he is left with only one part of the equation that can be changed—his attitude (see Figure 12.2). "You know, eating those grasshoppers wasn't *that* bad," your friend comments. "In fact, they were kind of crunchy." Notice how his change in attitude reduces the dissonance between his previous attitude and his behavior.

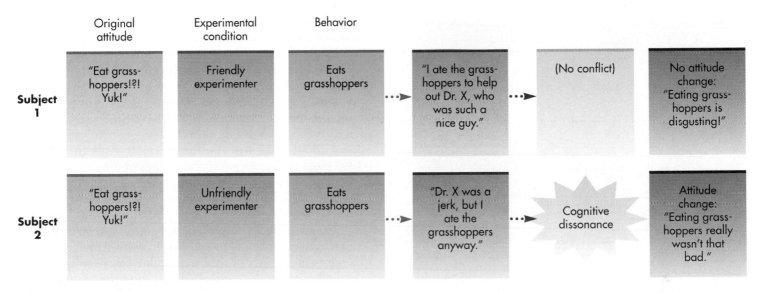

FIGURE 12.2 Cognitive Dissonance: How It Leads to Attitude Change
When your behavior conflicts with your attitudes, an uncomfortable state of tension is produced. However, if you can rationalize or explain your behavior, the conflict (and the tension) is eliminated or avoided. If you *can't* explain your behavior, you may change your attitude so that it is in harmony with your behavior.

Attitude change due to cognitive dissonance is quite common in everyday life. For example, consider the person who painfully quits smoking (because she believes that cigarettes are harmful), only to start smoking again six months later (Franzoi, 1996). "Cigarettes aren't really *that* bad for you," she rationalizes. "Besides, they help me cope with stress."

Cognitive dissonance can also change the strength of an attitude so that it is consistent with some behavior we've already performed. For example, people tend to be much more favorably inclined toward a given political candidate after they have voted for him or her than just before (Regan & Kilduff, 1988; Frenkel & Doob, 1976).

A similar example of cognitive dissonance in action involves choosing between two basically equal alternatives, especially if the decision is important and difficult to undo (Festinger, 1962). Suppose you had to choose between two colleges or two jobs. Each choice has desirable and undesirable features, creating dissonance. But once you actually make the choice, you immediately bring your attitudes more closely into line with that commitment, reducing cognitive dissonance. In other words, after you make the choice, you emphasize the negative features of the choice you've rejected, which is commonly called a "sour grapes" rationalization. You also emphasize the positive features of the choice to which you have committed yourself—a "sweet lemons" rationalization.

Understanding Prejudice

Prejudice refers to a negative attitude toward people who belong to a specific social group. Stereotypes are clusters of characteristics that are attributed to people who belong to specific social categories. What is the function of stereotypes? What problems are associated with the use of stereotypes?

In this section, you'll see how person perception, attribution, and attitudes come together in explaining **prejudice**—a negative attitude toward people who belong to a specific social group. Prejudice is not limited to negative attitudes toward specific racial, ethnic, or religious groups. Other kinds of social groups can also be the target of prejudice, such as homosexuals, disabled people, women, or the elderly. Historically, some groups have suffered more than others from the effects of prejudice, especially people of color and *indigenous populations* (people who are native to a particular area that has come to be dominated by people of another ethnic group or race).

Much of the psychological research on prejudice has focused on relations between whites and African-Americans. Increasingly, however, prejudice has become an "intergroup" affair, as mutual distrust and dislike have taken hold among many different majority *and* minority groups (National Conference of Christians and Jews, 1994; Mackie & Hamilton, 1993). For example, the 1992 riots in Los Angeles were triggered by tensions between African-Americans and white Americans following the initial verdict of not guilty in the trial of the white police officers accused of beating Rodney King. However, *Korean* shopkeepers were the target of much of the violence, reflecting tension between African-Americans and Korean-Americans in that particular community.

Prejudice is ultimately based on the exaggerated notion that members of "other" social groups are very different from members of our own social group. So as you read this discussion, it's important for you to keep two well-established points in mind. First, *racial and ethnic groups are far more alike than they are different* (J. Jones, 1991). And second, any differences that may exist *between* members of racial and ethnic groups are far smaller than differences *among* various members of the same group (Betancourt & López, 1993; Zuckerman, 1990).

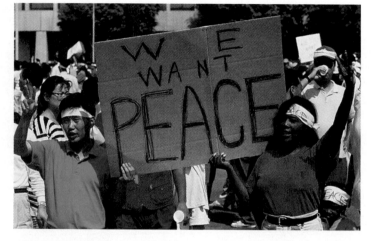

Tension Between Groups Tension and mutual distrust exist among many different racial and ethnic groups in America. During the 1992 Los Angeles riots, for example, some African-Americans vented their frustrations by attacking small businesses that were run by Korean-Americans. But as the photo shows, people can take steps to reduce the distrust that exists between different ethnic groups.

Stereotypes

As we noted earlier, using social categories to organize information about other people seems to be a natural cognitive tendency. Many social categories can be defined by relatively objective characteristics, like age, language, religion, and skin color. A specific kind of social category is a **stereotype**—a cluster of characteristics that are attributed to members of a specific social group or category (Hilton & von Hippel, 1996; Stangor & Lange, 1994). In other words, stereotypes are based on the assumption that people have certain characteristics *because* of their membership in a particular group (Matsumoto, 1994).

Stereotypes typically include qualities that are unrelated to the objective criteria that define a given category (Taylor & Porter, 1994). For example, we can objectively sort people into different categories by age. But our stereo-

prejudice
A negative attitude toward people who belong to a specific social group.

stereotype
A cluster of characteristics that are associated with all members of a specific social group, often including qualities that are unrelated to the objective criteria that define the group.

types for different age groups may include many qualities that have little to do with "number of years since birth." Associating "reckless and irresponsible" with teenagers, "forgetful and incompetent" with the elderly, and "boring and stodgy" with middle-aged adults are examples of associating unrelated qualities with age groups—that is, stereotyping.

Like other social categories, stereotypes simplify social information so that we can sort out, process, and remember information about other people more easily (Macrae & others, 1994). And like our use of other social categories, our tendency to stereotype social groups seems to be a natural cognitive process. Some social psychologists believe that the use of stereotypes is an inescapable fact of social cognition (Lee & others, 1995; Taylor & Porter, 1994). However, relying on stereotypes can have some very negative consequences, as you'll see in the next few sections.

The Problem of Stereotyped Thinking

While forming and using stereotypes may be a "natural" way of categorizing others, stereotypes can easily be misused. And relying on stereotypes can cause numerous problems (Stangor, 1995). Stereotypes often determine what people do *not* see as well as what people do see. Attributing a stereotypic cause for an outcome or event can blind us to the true causes of events (Sanbonmatsu & others, 1994). For example, a teacher might assume that a girl's poor math grades are due to her gender rather than to a lack of preparation or encouragement. (We discussed the myth that "boys are better at math than girls" in Chapter 10, on gender.)

Another drawback is that once they are formed, stereotypes are hard to shake. One reason for this is that stereotypes are not always completely false (Ottati & Lee, 1995). Sometimes they have a kernel of truth, making them easy to confirm, especially when you only see what you expect to see (Swim, 1994; Judd & Park, 1993). However, there's a vast difference between a kernel and the cornfield. When stereotypic beliefs become expectations that are applied to *all* members of a given group, stereotypes can be very misleading and even damaging (Stangor & Lange, 1994).

Consider the stereotype that men are more assertive than women, and that women are more nurturant than men. As noted in Chapter 10, this stereotype does have some truth to it, but only in terms of the *average* difference between men and women (see Eagly, 1995a; Swim, 1994). Thus, it would be inappropriate to automatically apply this stereotype to *every* individual male or female. Doing so would be an example of prejudice.

Equally important, when confronted by evidence that contradicts a stereotype, people tend to discount that information in a variety of ways (Seta & Seta, 1993; Weisz & Jones, 1993). For example, suppose you are firmly convinced that all "Zeegs" are dishonest, sly, and untrustworthy. One day you absent-mindedly leave your wallet on a store's checkout counter. As you walk into the parking lot, you hear a voice calling, "Hey, you forgot your wallet!" It's a Zeeg running after you and waving your wallet in the air. "I was behind you in line and thought you might need this," the Zeeg smiles, handing you your wallet.

Will this experience change your stereotype of Zeegs as dishonest, sly, and untrustworthy? Probably not. It's more likely that you'll conclude that this individual Zeeg is an *exception* to the stereotype. If you run into more than one honest Zeeg, you may create a mental subgroup for individuals who belong to the larger group but depart from the stereotype in some way (Stangor & Lange, 1994). By creating a subcategory of "honest, hard-working Zeegs," you can still maintain your more general stereotype of Zeegs as dishonest, sly, and untrustworthy.

Creating "special cases," or exceptions, allows people to maintain stereotypes in the face of contradictory evidence. Typical of this exception-that-proves-the-rule approach is the person who says, "Hey, I'm not prejudiced! Why, some of my best friends are Zeegs."

From Stereotypes to Prejudice:
In-Groups and Out-Groups

> *An in-group is a group to which we belong, while an out-group is a group to which we do not belong. What effects does in-group/ out-group thinking have on our social judgments, including prejudice and stereotypes? What is ethnocentrism?*

Stereotypes are closely related to another tendency in person perception. That is, people have a strong tendency to perceive others in terms of two very basic social categories: "us" and "them." More precisely, the **in-group** ("us") refers to the group or groups to which we belong, while **out-groups** ("them") refer to groups of which we are not a member. As you'll see, we're more likely to resort to negatively biased stereotypes to describe members of out-groups than fellow members of our in-group (Hilton & von Hippel, 1996; Stangor, 1995).

In-groups and out-groups aren't necessarily limited to racial, ethnic, or religious boundaries. Sometimes, it seems, virtually any characteristic can be used to make in-group and out-group distinctions: Cubs versus White Sox fans, Northsiders versus Southsiders, math majors versus English majors, and so forth.

The Out-Group Homogeneity Effect: They All Look Alike to Me

Two important patterns characterize our views of in-groups versus out-groups. First, when we describe the members of our *in-group,* we typically see them as being quite varied, despite having enough features in common to belong to the same group. In other words, we notice the diversity within our own group.

Second, we tend to see members of the *out-group* as much more similar to one another, even in areas that have little to do with the criteria for group membership (Hilton & von Hippel, 1996; Stangor & Lange, 1994). This tendency is called the **out-group homogeneity effect.** (The word *homogeneity* means similarity or uniformity.)

For example, what qualities do you associate with the category of engineering major? If you're *not* an engineering major, you're likely to see engineering majors as a rather similar crew: male, logical, analytical, conservative, and so forth. However, if you *are* an engineering major, you're much more likely to see your in-group as quite *heterogeneous,* or varied (Park & others, 1992). You might even come up with several subgroups, such as studious engineering majors, party-animal engineering majors, and electrical engineering majors versus chemical engineering majors.

In-Group Bias: *We're* Tactful—*They're* Sneaky

In-group bias is our tendency to make favorable, positive attributions for behaviors by members of our in-group, and unfavorable, negative attributions for behaviors by members of out-groups (see Dovidio & Gaertner, 1993; Hewstone, 1990). We succeeded because we worked hard; they succeeded because they lucked out. We failed because of circumstances beyond our control; they failed because they're stupid and incompetent. We're thrifty; they're stingy. And so on.

in-group
A social group to which one belongs.

out-group
A social group to which one does not belong.

out-group homogeneity effect
The tendency to see members of out-groups as very similar to one another.

in-group bias
The tendency to judge the behavior of in-group members favorably and out-group members unfavorably.

HAGAR

One form of in-group bias is called **ethnocentrism**—the belief that one's culture or ethnic group is superior to others. You're engaging in ethnocentrism when you use your culture or ethnic group as the yardstick by which you judge other cultures or ethnic groups. Not surprisingly, ethnocentric thinking contributes to the formation of negative stereotypes about other cultures whose customs differ from our own (Triandis, 1994; E. Smith, 1993).

The Emotional Basis of Prejudice:
The Perception of Threat

Stereotypes and in-group/out-group bias form the *cognitive* basis for prejudicial attitudes (Hilton & von Hippel, 1996). But as with many attitudes, prejudice also has a strong *emotional* component. In this case, the emotions are intensely negative—hatred, contempt, fear, loathing. *Behaviorally,* prejudice can be displayed in the form of *discrimination*—behaviors ranging from privately sneering at another group to physically attacking members of the out-group.

Intense prejudice is part of what allowed Nazi soldiers to systematically slaughter over 6 million Jews during World War II. Unfortunately, there is no shortage of ethnic hatred in today's world, either. In the name of the in-group, prejudice justifies "ethnic cleansing," or *genocide.* Former neighbors turn on one another and try to obliterate all members of the out-group. Whether it's the Middle East, Asia, Africa, Europe, or the Americas, discrimination and violence occur against men, women, and children *just because they are members of a particular out-group.*

How can we account for the extreme emotions that often characterize prejudice against out-group members? One theory holds that prejudice and intergroup hostility increase when different groups are competing for scarce resources, whether jobs, acreage, oil, water, or political power (Bobo, 1988a, 1988b). Prejudice and intergroup hostility are also likely to increase during times of social change (Staub, 1996; Brewer, 1994).

However, prejudice often exists in the absence of direct competition for resources, changing social conditions, or even contact with members of a particular out-group. What accounts for prejudice in such situations? Increasingly, social psychologists are examining the *emotional* basis of prejudice (see Mackie & Hamilton, 1993; E. Smith, 1993). Research by psychologist Victoria Esses and her colleagues (1993) demonstrates that people are often prejudiced against those groups that are perceived as threatening important in-group norms and values.

For example, a person might be extremely prejudiced against gays and lesbians even though he is not competing with them for jobs or other resources. Instead, his prejudice is fueled by his perception that homosexual behavior threatens his in-group's cherished norms and values, such as a strong commitment to traditional sex roles and family structure (Haddock & others, 1993).

ethnocentrism
The belief that one's own culture or ethnic group is superior to all others, and the related tendency to use one's own culture as a standard by which to judge other cultures.

Overcoming Prejudice at the Group Level

Psychologist Muzafer Sherif demonstrated that prejudice can be overcome when rival groups cooperate to achieve a common goal. How has this finding been applied in the educational setting? What other conditions are essential to reducing tensions between groups? How can we overcome prejudice at the individual level?

At one point, it was believed that simply bringing members of different groups into contact with one another would inevitably reduce prejudice among groups. This is referred to as the *contact theory*. As members of different groups got to know one another as individuals, the theory went, negative stereotypes would be disproved. In time, positive attitudes would naturally replace negative attitudes.

Unfortunately, experience demonstrated that mere contact would not reduce prejudice. Under some circumstances, in fact, contact between different groups can *increase* prejudice by confirming negative stereotypes or failing to meet positive expectations (Amir, 1994; Desforges & others, 1991). And when people mingle with members of out-groups whose behavior and attitudes are unfamiliar or difficult to explain, they can become puzzled, upset, or disturbed (Fiske & Ruscher, 1993).

How can prejudice be combated at the group level? A classic series of studies headed by psychologist **Muzafer Sherif** (b. 1906) helped clarify the conditions that produce intergroup conflict *and* harmony. Sherif and his colleagues (1961/1988) studied a group of eleven-year-old boys in an unlikely setting for a scientific experiment: a summer camp located at Robbers Cave State Park in Oklahoma. Pretending to be camp counselors and staff, the researchers observed the boys' behavior under carefully orchestrated conditions.

The Rattlers Versus the Eagles

The boys were randomly assigned to two groups. The groups arrived at camp in separate buses and were headquartered in different areas of the camp. One group of boys dubbed themselves the Eagles, the other the Rattlers. After a week of separation, the researchers arranged for the groups to meet in a series of competitive games. A fierce rivalry quickly developed, demonstrating the ease with which mutually hostile groups could be created.

The rivalry became increasingly bitter. The Eagles burned the Rattlers' flag. In response, the Rattlers trashed the Eagles' cabin. Somewhat alarmed, the researchers tried to diminish the hostility by bringing the two groups together under peaceful circumstances and on an equal basis—having them go to the movies together, eat in the same dining hall, and so forth. But contact alone did not mitigate the hostility. If anything, these situations only served as opportunities for the rival groups to berate and attack each other. For example, when the Rattlers and Eagles ate together in the same dining hall, a massive food fight erupted!

How could harmony between the groups be established? Sherif and his fellow researchers created a series of situations in which the two groups would need to *cooperate to achieve a common goal*. For example, the researchers secretly sabotaged the water supply. Working together, the Eagles and the Rattlers managed to fix it.

Creating Conflict Between Groups Psychologist Muzafer Sherif and his colleagues demonstrated how easily hostility and distrust could be created between two groups. Competitive situations, like this tug-of-war, increased tension between the Rattlers and the Eagles.

Overcoming Group Conflict To decrease hostility, the researchers created situations that required the joint efforts of both groups to achieve a common goal, such as fixing the water supply. These cooperative tasks helped the boys recognize their common interests and become friends.

On another occasion, the researchers sabotaged a truck that was to bring food to the campers. The hungry campers overcame their differences to join forces and restart the truck. After a series of such joint efforts, the rivalry diminished and the groups became good friends (Sherif, 1956; Sherif & others, 1961/1988).

Sherif successfully demonstrated how hostility between groups could be created and, more important, how that hostility could be overcome. However, other researchers questioned whether these results would apply to other intergroup situations. After all, these boys were very homogeneous: white, middle class, Protestant, and carefully selected for being healthy and well-adjusted (Fiske & Ruscher, 1993; Sherif, 1966). In other words, there were no *intrinsic* differences between the Rattlers and the Eagles; there was only the artificial distinction created by the researchers.

The Jigsaw Classroom: Promoting Cooperation

Social psychologist Elliot Aronson (1992, 1990) tried adapting the results of the Robbers Cave experiments to a very different group situation—a newly integrated elementary school. Realizing that mere contact between black and white children was not dissipating tension and prejudice, Aronson reasoned that perhaps the competitive schoolroom atmosphere was partly at fault. Perhaps tension between racial groups might decrease if cooperation replaced competition.

Aronson and his colleagues tried a teaching technique that stressed cooperative, rather than competitive, learning situations (see Aronson, 1990; Aronson & Bridgeman, 1979). Dubbed the *jigsaw classroom technique,* this approach brought together students in small, ethnically diverse groups to work on a mutual project. Like the pieces of a jigsaw puzzle, each student had a unique contribution to make toward the success of the group. Each student became an expert on one aspect of the overall project and had to teach it to the other members of the group. Thus, interdependence and cooperation replaced competition.

The results? Children in the jigsaw classrooms benefited. They had higher self-esteem and a greater liking for children in other ethnic groups than children in traditional classrooms. They also demonstrated a lessening of negative stereotypes and prejudice, and a reduction in intergroup hostility (see Aronson, 1995, 1987; Aronson & Bridgeman, 1979).

In combination, the Robbers Cave study and the jigsaw classroom experiment illustrate how cooperative efforts between members of different groups can help promote intergroup harmony.

Combating Prejudice at the Individual Level:
No Simple Answers

Many people today agree that prejudice and racism are wrong (see National Conference of Christians and Jews, 1994). However, some psychologists believe that blatant racism has been replaced by a more subtle form of racism (Devine & Zuwerink, 1994; J. Jones, 1991).

Sometimes people who are not *consciously* prejudiced against particular groups nevertheless react in prejudiced ways (Devine & Monteith, 1993; Devine & others, 1991). For example, a white person who is low in racial prejudice might still momentarily hesitate to invite an African-American colleague to her home (Monteith, 1993). Or someone who consciously strives to be nonsexist might be reluctant to consult a female surgeon or feel uncomfortable when he boards a flight and discovers that the pilot is a woman.

Psychologist Patricia Devine and her colleagues argue that prejudice reduction at the individual level is a three-step process (Devine & Zuwerink, 1994; Monteith & others, 1993). First, individuals must decide that prejudiced responses are wrong, and consciously reject prejudice and stereotyped thinking (Hilton & von Hippel, 1996). Second, they must internalize their nonprejudiced beliefs so that they become an integral part of their personal self-concept. Third, individuals must learn to inhibit automatic prejudicial reactions, and deliberately replace them with nonprejudiced responses that are based on their personal standards.

As you can see, prejudice is not a simple phenomenon. Nor is eliminating prejudice likely to be achieved through any single measure. As Devine's research supports, the first step in overcoming prejudice is to become aware of the biases that allow it to flourish, such as in-group bias and the out-group homogeneity effect.

So the next time you find yourself saying, "Oh, those zebras, they're all alike—not like us giraffes," stop and think. Stereotyping may be a "natural" cognitive process, but we don't necessarily have to fall victim to the biases that stereotypes foster. Nor should we act on those biases. Rather, it's important that we make a concerted effort to see each person as he or she really is—a unique individual.

CONCEPT REVIEW 12.2

The Psychology of Attitudes and Prejudice

Which of the following concepts is being illustrated in each of the examples below: cognitive dissonance, stereotyping, in-group bias, ethnocentrism, or out-group homogeneity?

1. Henry's classmate in college was from Sardinia, and he loved to eat sardines for lunch. Henry now believes that the diet of all Sardinians is centered on sardines, and he has little doubt about why the island is called Sardinia. _____

2. A group of employees in the marketing department went out to lunch. They started to complain about the people who worked in accounting. One of them said, "Oh, well, you know those number crunchers are all alike. They just aren't very creative." _____

3. A group of students from Northern State College was watching the antics of a group of students from Western State College at a football game. "Look at how rowdy those guys are. That's disgusting!" one Northern State student observed. A half-hour later, the same student said, "I love going to our football games because everybody's so friendly and laid back. We really know how to let loose and have a good time." _____

4. Georgia thinks that track is a great all-around sport and desperately wants to make the track team. For the first few weeks, she trains hard every day. Gradually, however, she starts missing practice sessions, and on the day of the tryouts she oversleeps, performs poorly, and gets cut in the first round. Georgia says, "Track is so-o-o boring. I'd much rather be on the softball team." _____

5. In an introductory anthropology class, students begin to groan and laugh as they watch a film showing members of a remote tribe eating head lice, grubs, and iguanas. "How repulsive," remarked one gum-chewing student. "Those poor savages are really ignorant and uncivilized," another student agreed, as he put a pinch of chewing tobacco in his mouth. _____

conformity
The tendency to adjust one's behavior, attitudes, or beliefs to group norms in response to real or imagined group pressure.

Conformity: Following the Crowd

Social influence involves the study of how behavior is influenced by the social environment and other people. What factors influence the degree to which people will conform? Why do people conform? How does culture affect conformity?

As we noted earlier in this chapter, *social influence* is the psychological study of how our behavior is influenced by the social environment and other people. If you typically contribute to class discussions, you've probably felt the power of social influence in classes where nobody else said a word. No doubt you found yourself feeling at least slightly uncomfortable every time you ventured a comment or question.

If you changed your behavior to mesh with that of your classmates, you demonstrated conformity. **Conformity** occurs when we change our behavior, attitudes, or beliefs in response to real or imagined group pressure (Kiesler & Kiesler, 1969). However, the fact that we act or present ourselves in the same way as other people doesn't necessarily mean that we're conforming to group standards. As social psychologist David Myers (1996) explains, "Conformity is not just acting as other people act, it is being affected by how they act. It is acting differently from the way you would act alone."

So if everyone in the concert hall rises to give the performer a standing ovation and you do the same because you thought he was fantastic, your behavior does not reflect conformity, even though you're behaving just like everyone else in the concert hall. But if you thought his performance was just so-so, and you stand up and applaud anyway, you're displaying conformity. Notice, you may still *privately* think it was just an average performance, but your *public* behavior conforms to that of the larger group.

At other times we may alter *both* our private beliefs and our outward behavior. As the prevailing group norms change over time, group pressure can influence our perceptions and opinions as well as our behaviors. Clothing fashions and hairstyles are large-scale examples of conformity to norms that shift over time. Males who wear an earring in one ear and females who are adorned with multiple earrings would have drawn stares from other people just a few decades ago.

Group Pressure to Conform:

The Work of Solomon Asch

There's no question that all of us conform to group norms to some degree. The more critical issue is *how far* we'll go to adjust our perceptions and opinions so that they're in sync with the majority opinion—an issue that intrigued psychologist **Solomon Asch** (b. 1907). Asch (1951) posed a straightforward question: Would people still conform to the group if the group opinion was clearly wrong?

To study this question experimentally, Asch (1955) chose a simple, objective task with an obvious answer (see Figure 12.3). A group of people sat at a table and looked at a series of cards. On one side of each card was a standard line. On the other side were three comparison lines. All each person had to do was publicly indicate which comparison line was the same length as the standard line.

Asch's experiment had a hidden catch: All the people sitting around the table were actually in cahoots with the experimenter, except for one—the real subject. Had you been the real subject in Asch's (1956) experiment, here's what you would have experienced:

FIGURE 12.3 Sample Line Judgment Task Used in the Asch Conformity Studies
In Asch's classic studies on conformity, subjects were asked to pick the comparison line that matched the standard line.
(Asch, 1987.)

Standard line   Comparison lines
A   B   C

The first card is shown, and the five people ahead of you respond, one at a time, with the obvious answer: "Line B." Now it's your turn, and you respond the same. The second card is put up. Again, the answer is obvious and the group is unanimous. So far, so good.

Then the third card is shown, and the correct answer is just as obvious: line C. But the first person confidently says, "Line A." And so does everyone else, one by one. Now it's your turn. To you it's clear that the correct answer is line C. But the five people ahead of you have already publicly chosen line A. How do you respond? You hesitate. Do you go with the flow or with what you know?

The real subject was faced with the uncomfortable situation of disagreeing with a unanimous majority on twelve of eighteen trials in Asch's experiment. Notice, there was *no* direct pressure to conform—just the implicit, unspoken pressure of answering differently from the rest of the group.

Over a hundred subjects experienced Asch's experimental dilemma. Not surprisingly, participants differed in their degree of conformity. Nonetheless, the vast majority of Asch's subjects (76 percent) conformed with the group judgment on at least one of the critical trials. When the data for all subjects were combined, the subjects followed the majority and gave the wrong answer on *37 percent* of the critical trials (Asch, 1955, 1957). In comparison, a control group of subjects who responded alone instead of in a group accurately chose the matching line 99 percent of the time.

Although the majority opinion clearly exerted a strong influence, it's also important to stress the flip side of Asch's results. On almost two-thirds of the trials in which the majority named the wrong line, the subjects stuck to their guns and gave the correct answer, despite being in the minority (see Friend & others, 1990).

Factors Influencing Conformity

The basic model of Asch's classic experiment has been used in hundreds of studies exploring the dynamics of conformity (R. Bond & Smith, 1996; Tanford & Penrod, 1984). Why do we sometimes find ourselves conforming to the larger group? There are two basic reasons (see Franzoi, 1996).

First is our desire to be liked and accepted by the group, which is referred to as **normative social influence.** If you've ever been ridiculed and rejected for going against the grain of a unanimous group, you've had firsthand experience with the pressure of normative social influence. Second is our desire to be right. When we're uncertain or doubt our own judgment, we may look to the group as a source of accurate information, which is called **informational social influence.**

Asch performed many variations on his original study. He and other researchers identified several conditions that promote conformity, which are summarized in Table 12.2.

Asch also discovered that conformity *decreased* under certain circumstances. For example, having an ally seemed to counteract the social influence of the majority: Subjects were more likely to go against the majority view if just one other participant did so. Other researchers have found that any dissent increases resistance to the majority opinion, even if the other person's dissenting opinion is wrong (Allen & Levine, 1969). Conformity also lessens even if the other dissenter's competence is questionable, as in the case of a dissenter who wore thick glasses and complained that he could not see the lines very well (Allen & Levine, 1971).

Adolescents and Conformity The adolescent uniform: T-shirts, jeans, and athletic shoes. Think back to your own adolescent years. Do you remember how important it was to you to fit in with other adolescents, especially those in your peer group? Researchers have found that conformity to group norms peaks during early adolescence (Gavin & Furman 1989; B. Brown & others, 1986).

TABLE 12.2 Factors That Promote Conformity

You're more likely to conform to group norms when:

- you are facing a unanimous majority of four or five people.
- you must give your response in front of the group.
- you have not already expressed commitment to a different idea or opinion.
- you find the task is ambiguous or difficult.
- you doubt your abilities or knowledge in the situation.
- you are strongly attracted to a group and want to be a member of it.

SOURCES: Asch, 1955; Campbell & Fairey, 1989; Deutsch & Gerard, 1955; Gerard & others, 1968; Tanford & Penrod, 1984.

Culture and Conformity

Asch's original studies were conducted in the 1950s using U.S. college students as the experimental participants. Would participants today be less likely to conform to the majority's opinion? In general, levels of conformity *have* steadily declined since Asch's original studies in the 1950s (R. Bond & Smith, 1996).

One possible explanation for this finding is that the cultural climate of American society was fundamentally different in the 1950s. The 1950s were an era in which conformity was socially expected. Deviation from the group, especially deviation that appeared the least bit anti-American, was treated with suspicion. So perhaps it's not that surprising that college students during the 1950s were more "conformist" than students during more recent decades.

Do patterns of conformity differ in other cultures? British psychologists Rod Bond and Peter Smith (1996) found in a wide-ranging meta-analysis that conformity is generally higher in collectivistic cultures than in individualistic cultures. Because individualistic cultures tend to emphasize independence, self-expression, and standing out from the crowd, the whole notion of conformity tends to carry a negative connotation.

In collectivistic cultures, however, publicly conforming while privately disagreeing tends to be regarded as socially appropriate tact or sensitivity. Publicly challenging the judgments of others, particularly the judgment of members of one's in-group, would be considered rude, tactless, and insensitive to the feelings of others. Thus, conformity in collectivistic cultures does not seem to carry the same negative connotation that it does in individualistic cultures.

Obedience: Just Following Orders

> *Obedience refers to behaving in direct response to the orders of an authority. What was the basic design of Milgram's obedience experiments? What were the results?*

Stanley Milgram (1933–1984) was one of the most creative and innovative researchers that social psychology has known (Blass, 1992; Zimbardo, 1992; Miller, 1986). Sadly, Milgram died of a heart attack at the age of fifty-one. Though Milgram made many contributions to social psychology, he is best known for his experimental investigations of obedience. **Obedience** is the performance of an action in response to the direct orders of an authority or person of higher status, like a teacher or a supervisor.

Milgram's experimental studies of obedience grew out of his interest in the conformity research and, even more directly, the influence of Solomon Asch himself (Blass, 1992). Milgram was Asch's teaching assistant when Asch spent a year at Harvard as a visiting professor. For his doctoral dissertation, Milgram (1960, 1961) used Asch's experimental design to conduct the first cross-cultural investigations of conformity, comparing French and Norwegian subjects.

Milgram was intrigued by Asch's discovery of how easily people could be swayed by group pressure. But Milgram wanted to investigate behavior that had greater personal significance than simply judging the lengths of lines on a card (Milgram, 1980, 1963). Thus, Milgram posed what he saw as the most critical question: Could a person be pressured by others into committing an immoral act, some action that violated his or her own conscience, such as

normative social influence
Behavior that is motivated by the desire to gain social acceptance and approval.

informational social influence
Behavior that is motivated by the desire to be correct.

obedience
The performance of an action in response to the direct orders of an authority or person of higher status.

hurting a stranger? In his efforts to answer that question, Milgram embarked on one of the most systematic and controversial investigations in the history of psychology: how and why people obey the destructive dictates of an authority figure.

Milgram's Original Obedience Experiment

Milgram was only 28 years old when he conducted his first obedience experiments. At the time, he was a new faculty member at Yale University in New Haven, Connecticut. He recruited participants through direct-mail solicitations and ads in the local paper. Collectively, Milgram's subjects represented a wide range of occupational and educational backgrounds. Postal workers, high school teachers, white-collar workers, engineers, and laborers participated in the study.

Outwardly, it appeared that two subjects showed up at Yale University to participate in each session of the psychology experiment, but the second subject was actually an accomplice working with Milgram. The role of the experimenter, complete with white lab coat, was played by a high school biology teacher. When both subjects arrived, the experimenter greeted them and gave them a plausible explanation of the study's purpose: to examine the effects of punishment on learning.

Setting the Stage: The "Teacher" and the "Learner"

Both subjects drew slips of paper to determine who would be "the teacher" and who "the learner." However, the drawing was rigged so that the real subject was always the teacher and the accomplice was always the learner. The learner was actually a mild-mannered, forty-seven-year-old accountant who had been carefully rehearsed for his part in the drama. Assigned to the role of the teacher, the real subject would be responsible for "punishing" the learner's mistakes by administering electric shocks.

The "Electric Chair" With the help of the real subject who has been assigned the role of "teacher," the experimenter straps the "learner" into the electric chair.

Immediately after the drawing, the teacher and learner were taken to another room, where the learner was strapped into an "electric chair." The purpose of the straps, it was explained, was to prevent excessive movement when the learner got shocked. Although the fact wasn't mentioned, it was obvious that the straps would also keep the learner from escaping the electric chair. The experimenter told both subjects, "Although the shocks can be extremely painful, they cause no permanent tissue damage."

The "Lesson" and a Sample Shock

The teacher was then taken to a different room, from which he could hear but not see the learner. Speaking into a microphone, the teacher tested the learner on a simple word-pair memory task. In the other room, the learner pressed one of four switches to indicate with which alternative the word had previously been paired. The learner's response was registered in an answer box positioned on top of the "shock generator" in front of the teacher. Each time the learner answered incorrectly, the teacher was to deliver an electric shock.

Milgram's (1963) meticulous attention to details greatly enhanced the realism of the situation. The front panel of the bogus shock generator had

Milgram's "Shock Generator" Machine
A young Stanley Milgram sits next to his "shock generator." Milgram went to great lengths to make the shock generator as authentic as possible. Do you think you would have been fooled into believing that this was a real shock generator?

been engraved by professional industrial engravers. Each of the 30 switches, which progressed from 15 to 450 volts, was clearly labeled with its electrical voltage, and each group of switches was also labeled. At the lowest levels, the labels read "Slight Shock" and "Mild Shock." At higher voltages, the label was "Severe Shock." At the highest voltage level, an ominous label simply read "XXX." Whenever the teacher pressed a shock switch, the red light above the switch went on, a buzzing and clicking sound was heard, and the needle on the voltage meter swung to the right. Very convincing details.

Just in case there was any lingering doubt in the teacher's mind about the legitimacy of the shock generator, the *teacher* was given a sample jolt using the switch marked 45 volts. In fact, this sample shock was the only real shock given during the course of the staged experiment.

The Instructions: "You Have No Other Choice, You *Must* Continue"

Each time the learner made an error, the teacher was told to progress to the next level on the shock generator. The teacher was also told to announce the voltage level to the learner before delivering the shock.

At predetermined voltage levels, the learner vocalized first his discomfort, then his pain, and, finally, agonized screams. Some of the learner's vocalizations at the different voltage levels are shown in Table 12.3. After 330 volts, the learner's script called for him to fall silent. If the teacher protested that he wished to stop, or that he was worried about the learner's safety, the experimenter would say, "The experiment requires that you continue" or "You have no other choice, you *must* continue."

According to the script, the experiment would be halted when the teacher-subject refused to obey the experimenter's orders to continue. Alternatively, if the teacher-subject obeyed the experimenter, the experiment would be halted once the teacher had progressed all the way to the maximum shock level of 450 volts.

Either way, after the experiment the teacher was interviewed and it was explained that the learner had not actually received dangerous electric shocks. To underscore this point, a "friendly reconciliation" was arranged between the teacher and the learner, and the true purpose of the study was explained to the subject.

TABLE 12.3 The Learner's Schedule of Protests in Milgram's Obedience Experiment

120 volts	→	Ugh! Hey, *this* really hurts.
150 volts	→	Ugh!!! Experimenter! That's all. Get me out of here. I told you I had heart trouble. My heart's starting to bother me now. Get me out of here, please. My heart's starting to bother me. I refuse to go on. Let me out.
210 volts	→	Ugh!! Experimenter! *Get* me out of here. I've had enough. I *won't* be in the experiment any more.
270 volts	→	(*Agonized scream.*) Let me out of here. Let me out of here. Let me out of here. Let me out. Do you hear? Let me out of here.
300 volts	→	(*Agonized scream.*) I absolutely refuse to answer any more. Get me out of here. You can't hold me here. Get me out. Get me out of here.
315 volts	→	(*Intensely agonized scream.*) I told you I *refuse to answer.* I'm no longer part of this experiment.
330 volts	→	(*Intense and prolonged agonized scream.*) Let me out of here. Let me out of here. My heart's bothering me. Let me out, I tell you. (*Hysterically*) Let me out of here. Let me out of here. You have no right to hold me here. Let me out! Let me out! Let me out! Let me out of here! Let me out! Let me out!

SOURCE: Milgram, 1974a, pp. 56–57.

In Milgram's obedience studies, the learner's script was standardized so that he called out specific protests at certain voltage levels. Some of those protests and the corresponding voltage level at which they occurred are shown here. After the protest at the 330-volt level, the learner made no further protests or sounds.

Shock Level	Switch Labels and Voltage Levels	Number of Subjects Who Refused to Administer a Higher Voltage Level
"Slight Shock"		
1	15	
2	30	
3	45	
4	60	
"Moderate Shock"		
5	75	
6	90	
7	105	
8	120	
"Strong Shock"		
9	135	
10	150	
11	165	
12	180	
"Very Strong Shock"		
13	195	
14	210	
15	225	
16	240	
"Intense Shock"		
17	255	
18	270	
19	285	
20	300	5
"Extreme Intensity Shock"		
21	315	4
22	330	2
23	345	1
24	360	1
"Danger: Severe Shock"		
25	375	1
26	390	
27	405	
28	420	
"XXX"		
29	435	
30	450	26

FIGURE 12.4 The Results of Milgram's Original Study

Contrary to what psychiatrists, college students, and middle-class adults predicted, the majority of Milgram's subjects did not refuse to obey by the 150-volt level of shocks. As this chart shows, five of Milgram's forty subjects (13 percent) refused to continue after administering 300 volts to the learner. Twenty-six of the forty subjects (65 percent) remained obedient to the end, administering the full 450 volts to the learner.

(Milgram, 1974a, p. 35.)

The Results of Milgram's Original Experiment

Can you predict how Milgram's subjects behaved? Of the forty subjects, how many obeyed the experimenter and went to the full 450-volt level? On a more personal level, how do you think *you* would have behaved had you had been one of Milgram's subjects? Do you think *you* would have disobeyed the experimenter and refused to continue? If so, at what voltage level?

Milgram himself asked psychiatrists, college students, and middle-class adults to predict how subjects would behave (see Milgram, 1974a). All three groups predicted that *all* of Milgram's subjects would refuse to obey at some point. They predicted that most subjects would refuse at the 150-volt level, the point at which the learner first protested. They also believed that only a few rare individuals would go as far as the 300-volt level. Finally, *none* of those surveyed thought that *any* of Milgram's subjects would go to the full 450 volts.

As it turned out, they were all wrong. *Two-thirds of Milgram's subjects—twenty-six of the forty—went to the full 450-volt level.* And of those who defied the experimenter, *not one stopped before the 300-volt level.* The actual results of Milgram's original obedience study are shown in Figure 12.4.

Surprised? Milgram himself was stunned by the results, never expecting that the majority of subjects would administer the maximum voltage. Were his results a fluke? Did Milgram inadvertently assemble a sadistic group of New Haven residents who were all too willing to inflict extremely painful, even life-threatening, shocks on a complete stranger?

The answer to both of those questions is no. Milgram's obedience study has been repeated many times in the United States and other countries (see Blass, 1992; Miller, 1986). And, in fact, Milgram (1974a) replicated his own study on numerous occasions, using variations of his basic experimental procedure. In one replication, for instance, Milgram's subjects were forty women. Were female subjects any less likely to inflict pain on a stranger? Not at all. The results were identical.

Were Milgram's subjects heartless, cold, and callous people? Or perhaps they saw through his elaborate experimental hoax, as some critics have suggested (Orne & Holland, 1968). Was it possible that the subjects did not believe that they were really harming the learner?

Again, the answer seems to be no. Milgram's subjects seemed totally convinced that the situation was authentic. And they did not behave in a cold-blooded, unfeeling way. Far from it. As the experiment progressed, many subjects showed signs of extreme tension and conflict. In describing the reaction of one subject, Milgram (1963) wrote, "I observed a mature and initially poised businessman enter the laboratory smiling and confident. Within 20 minutes he was reduced to a twitching, stuttering wreck, who was rapidly approaching a point of nervous collapse."

Making Sense out of Milgram's Findings:
Multiple Influences

> *Milgram and other researchers identified several factors that contributed to the subjects' obedience. What aspects of the experimental situation increased the likelihood of obedience? What factors were later discovered to decrease the level of obedience?*

On the one hand, Milgram's subjects appeared genuinely upset about hurting another person. On the other hand, the majority of them continued to administer stronger and stronger shocks, obediently following the experimenter's commands. How can we explain their willingness to obey?

Milgram, along with other researchers, identified several aspects of the experimental situation that had a strong impact on the subjects (see Milgram, 1965/1992b; Blass, 1992, 1991; Miller, 1986). Here are some of the key forces that influenced subjects to continue obeying the experimenter's orders:

A previously well-established mental framework to obey. Having volunteered to participate in a psychology experiment, Milgram's subjects arrived at the lab with the mental expectation that they would obediently follow the directions of the person in charge—the experimenter. They also accepted compensation upon their arrival, which may have increased their sense of having made a commitment to cooperate with the experimenter.

The situation, or context, in which the obedience occurred. The subjects were familiar with the basic nature of scientific investigation, believed that scientific research was worthwhile, and were told that the goal of the experiment was to "advance the scientific understanding of learning and memory" (Milgram, 1974a). All these factors predisposed the subjects to trust and respect the experimenter's authority (Darley, 1992). Even when subjects protested, they were polite and respectful. Milgram suggested (1974a) that subjects were afraid that defying the experimenter's orders would make them appear arrogant, rude, disrespectful, or uncooperative.

The gradual, repetitive escalation of the task. At the beginning of the experiment, the subject administered a very low level of shock—15 volts. Subjects could easily justify using such low levels of electric shock in the service of science. The shocks, like the learner's protests, escalated only gradually. Each additional shock was only 15 volts stronger than the one before.

The experimenter's behavior and reassurances. Many subjects asked the experimenter who was responsible for what might happen to the learner. In every case, the teacher was reassured that the *experimenter* was responsible for the learner's well-being. Thus, the subjects could believe that they were not responsible for the consequences of their actions; they could tell themselves that their behavior must be appropriate if the experimenter approved of it.

The physical and psychological separation from the learner. Several "buffers" distanced the subject from the pain that he was inflicting on the learner. First, the learner was not visible; he was in a separate room. Only his voice could be heard. Second, punishment was depersonalized: The subject simply pushed a switch on the shock generator. Finally, the learner never appealed directly to the teacher to stop shocking him. The learner's pleas were always directed toward the *experimenter*, as in "Experimenter! Get me out of here!" Undoubtedly, this contributed to the subject's sense that the experimenter, rather than the subject, was ultimately in control of the situation, including the teacher's behavior.

The individual who is commanded by a legitimate authority ordinarily obeys. Obedience comes easily and often. It is a ubiquitous and indispensable feature of social life.

Stanley Milgram, 1963

Conditions That Undermine Obedience:

Variations on a Theme

In a lengthy series of experiments, Milgram systematically varied the basic obedience paradigm. To give you some sense of the enormity of Milgram's undertaking, approximately *1,000* subjects, each tested individually, experienced some variation of Milgram's obedience experiment. Thus, Milgram's obedience research represents one of the largest and most integrated research programs in social psychology (Blass, 1991).

By varying his experiments, Milgram identified several conditions that decrease the likelihood of destructive obedience, which are summarized in Figure 12.5. For example, willingness to obey diminishes sharply when the buffers that separate the teacher from the learner are lessened or removed, as when both of them are put in the same room.

The proximity of the experimenter was another critical element. If the experimenter left the room and spoke to the subject over the telephone instead of face to face, complete obedience dropped to 23 percent. Interestingly, several subjects in this condition found an easy way to reconcile the demands of their conscience with the demands of authority: they simply lied to the experimenter! Over the phone, they assured the experimenter that they were increasing the shock level as ordered—all the while continuing to administer the *lowest* possible shock.

If Milgram's findings seem to cast an unfavorable light on human nature, there are two reasons to take heart. First, when teachers were allowed to act as their own authority and freely choose the shock level, 95 percent of them did not venture beyond 150 volts—the first point at which the learner protested. Clearly, Milgram's subjects were not responding to their own aggressive or sadistic impulses, but rather to orders from an authority figure.

Second, Milgram found that people are more likely to muster up the courage to defy an authority when they see others do so. When Milgram's subjects observed what they thought were two other subjects disobey the experimenter, the real subjects followed their lead 90 percent of the time and refused to continue. Like the subjects in Asch's experiment, we're more likely to stand by our convictions when we're not alone in expressing them.

Despite these encouraging notes, the overall results of Milgram's obedience research painted a bleak picture of human nature. Not surprisingly, the obedience studies were highly publicized—and extremely controversial. Many people were upset by his findings, but his methods drew fire as well. Critical Thinking Box 12.3, "The Ethics of Milgram's Obedience Experiments," describes this controversy.

Experimental variations

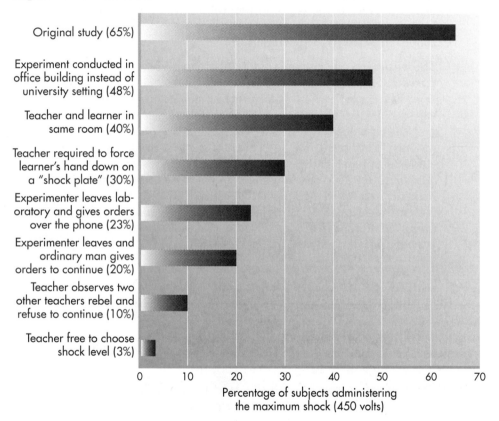

FIGURE 12.5 Factors That Decrease Destructive Obedience
By systematically varying his basic experimental design, Milgram identified several factors that diminish the likelihood of destructive obedience. In this graph, you can see the percentage of subjects who administered the maximum shock in different experimental variations.
(Adapted from data reported in Milgram, 1974a.)

CRITICAL THINKING 12.3

The Ethics of Milgram's Obedience Experiments

Stanley Milgram's obedience experiments are some of the most controversial studies that have been conducted since the discipline of psychology was established (see Blass, 1991; Miller, 1986). His results drew attention from psychologists as well as historians, political scientists, and philosophers. His dramatic experiments also caught the general public's attention. Milgram was interviewed on the CBS News (1979) program *Sixty Minutes* and discussed the obedience experiments in magazines like *Harper's, Psychology Today,* and even *TV Guide* (Milgram, 1973, 1974b, 1976). His 1974 book, *Obedience to Authority,* has been translated into eleven languages and is still in print.

Much of the interest revolved around the sensational results of Milgram's original obedience experiment: two-thirds of his subjects completely obeyed the experimenter's destructive demands and progressed to the full 450-volt level in presumably shocking a complete stranger. But the controversy over Milgram's experiments went beyond his disturbing results. Less than a year after the initial publication of his obedience studies, psychologist Diana Baumrind (1964) fired the first round in the battle over the ethics of Milgram's experimental method.

In an impassioned article in *American Psychologist,* Baumrind (1964) attacked the obedience experiments for the emotional stress, tension, and loss of dignity experienced by Milgram's subjects. To Baumrind, Milgram's experiment was a violation of the trust that a naive subject is likely to place in a researcher. She also believed that Milgram's subjects were likely to experience long-term effects, including a loss of self-esteem and a distrust of authority figures. As Baumrind (1964) wrote:

The subject's personal responsibility for his actions is not erased because the experimenter reveals to him the means which he used to stimulate these actions. The subject realizes that he would have hurt the victim if the current were on. The realization that he has also made a fool of himself by ac-

cepting the experimental set results in additional loss of self-esteem.

In his response to Baumrind, Milgram (1964) noted that he did not set out to create stress in his subjects, and that he and other experts had assumed that few people would proceed beyond a very low level of shock. What was disturbing to people, Milgram suggested, were not so much his methods but his results:

Is not Baumrind's criticism based as much on the unanticipated findings as on the method? The findings were that some subjects performed in what appeared to be a shockingly immoral way. If, instead, every one of the subjects had broken off at "slight shock," or the first sign of the learner's discomfort, the results would have been pleasant, and reassuring, and who would protest?

In fact, many studies conducted before Milgram's obedience research had used deception or mild electric shocks or had involved subjects who believed they faced the possibility of electric shock. These experiments did not result in cries of experimental recklessness or blatant disregard for the psychological well-being of subjects (Miller, 1986). But Milgram's research seemed to touch a nerve that made people very uncomfortable. Few people could read about Milgram's research without wondering, "How would *I* have responded?"

Although Baumrind believed that the subjects were likely to experience serious aftereffects from the experiment, Milgram (1964, 1974b) pointed out that this was not the case. The debriefing procedure that Milgram used was fairly elaborate. The experiment was explained, and subjects were reassured that their behavior was quite normal. A "friendly reconciliation" with the learner was arranged so that the teacher-subject could see that the learner had not been hurt. In a follow-up questionnaire, 84 percent of the participants in Milgram's experiment stated that they were glad to have taken part in the experiment. Only 1.3 percent said they were "sorry to have

The Ethics of Deception In the experimental variation shown, the teacher was ordered to hold the learner's hand down on the shock plate. Some thirty percent of subjects were completely obedient. Was the extreme deception used in Milgram's experiments justified?

been in the experiment." An additional follow-up examination by a psychiatrist a year after the experiment found no signs of harm or traumatic reaction.

Still, the debate over Milgram's studies sensitized psychologists and other social scientists to the ethical issues involved in research with human subjects (Fisher & Fyrberg, 1994). The controversy helped lead to the establishment of ethical safeguards by the American Psychological Association and the federal government regarding experiments involving human subjects (Blass, 1992).

Because of these safeguards, the last Milgram-type obedience studies conducted in the United States occurred in 1976 (Holmes, 1976; Costanzo, 1976). However, obedience research has continued in other countries that have less stringent research guidelines, such as Holland, Spain, and Jordan (Blass, 1992; Meeus & Raaijmakers, 1986).

What do you think? Was the extreme deception used in Milgram's studies unethical? Did Milgram's dramatic and unexpected results justify the emotional stress experienced by his subjects? Could Milgram have reached the same conclusions using less deceptive research methods? Under what conditions is such experimental deception justified?

Asch, Milgram, and the Real World:
Implications of the Classic Social Influence Studies

Conformity and obedience were more than just academic issues to Asch and Milgram. Like countless others, Asch and Milgram struggled to make sense of all-too-real human atrocities. In particular, both were haunted by the systematic slaughter of 6 million European Jews by the Nazis during World War II. The Holocaust also involved killing tens of thousands of others that the Nazis deemed unfit to live: Gypsies, homosexuals, political dissidents, the disabled, and the mentally ill. Unfortunately, it is all too easy to identify other examples of destructive conformity and obedience that have resulted in the brutal sacrifice of innocent people.

There are, of course, enormous differences between a carefully controlled laboratory demonstration of conformity and obedience, on the one hand, and the multitude of complex factors operating in concentration camps, wartime massacres, and religious cults, on the other. Nevertheless, the scientific study of conformity and obedience has produced some important insights.

The first one is the degree to which our behavior is influenced by situational factors. Being at odds with the majority or with authority is very uncomfortable for most people—enough so that our judgment and perceptions can be distorted and we may act in ways that violate our conscience.

More important, perhaps, is the insight that each of us *does* have the capacity to resist group or authority pressure. Because the central findings of these studies are so dramatic, it's easy to overlook the fact that some subjects refused to conform or obey despite considerable social and situational pressure. Consider the response of a subject in one of Milgram's later studies. A thirty-two-year-old industrial engineer named Jan Rensaleer protested when he was commanded to continue at the 255-volt level:

> **Experimenter:** It is absolutely essential that you continue.
>
> **Mr. Rensaleer:** Well, I won't—not with the man screaming to get out.
>
> **Experimenter:** You have no other choice.
>
> **Mr. Rensaleer:** I *do* have a choice. (*Incredulous and indignant:*) Why don't I have a choice? I came here on my own free will. I thought I could help in a research project. But if I have to hurt somebody to do that, or if I was in his place, too, I wouldn't stay there. I can't continue. I'm very sorry. I think I've gone too far already, probably.

Destructive Obedience and Prejudice
Blind obedience to authority combined with ethnic prejudice in Germany during World War II led to the slaughter of millions of Jews in concentration camps (top). When questioned after the war, Nazi officials and soldiers claimed that they were "just following orders." During the 1990s, the Serbian crusade for "ethnic cleansing" of Muslims in Bosnia-Herzegovina resulted in thousands of fellow citizens and former neighbors being driven from their homes and villages (left). During the 1970s and 1980s, the followers of Pol Pot in Cambodia killed three million of their fellow Cambodians (right).

Like some other subjects in the obedience and conformity studies, Mr. Rensaleer effectively resisted the situational and social pressures pushing him in a different direction. In real life situations, people like Raoul Wallenberg, a Swedish diplomat, have done the same. During World War II, Wallenberg supplied Swedish passports to over 20,000 Hungarian Jews, saving them from being deported to the Nazi death camps. When the Soviet army entered Budapest, Wallenberg was arrested and ultimately died in a Soviet prison.

How are such people different from those who conformed or obeyed? Unfortunately, there's no satisfying answer to that question. No specific personality trait consistently predicts conformity or obedience in experimental situations like the ones that Asch and Milgram created (see Blass, 1991; Burger, 1992, 1987). In other words, the social influences that Asch and Milgram created in their experimental situations can be compelling even to people who are normally quite independent.

Finally, we need to reemphasize that conformity and obedience are not completely bad in and of themselves. Quite the contrary: Conformity and obedience are necessary for an orderly society, which is why such behaviors were instilled in all of us as children. The critical issue is not so much whether people conform or obey, because we all do so every day of our lives. Rather, the critical issue is whether the norms we conform to, or the orders we obey, reflect values that respect the rights, well-being, and human dignity of others.

In the next section, we'll look at another dimension of social influence: the factors that influence whether we will help another person.

CONCEPT REVIEW 12.3

Conformity and Obedience

Circle the letter of the correct answer.

1. Five of the six people on the committee have already stated their vote in favor of the proposal. Martin is the last person to vote. Martin is most likely to vote *against* the proposal if:
   a. he is not certain that he understands the proposal.
   b. he privately thinks that the proposal is a bad one.
   c. he wants to continue to be a member of the committee.
   d. he has already openly stated his objections to the proposal.

2. Although Gary prefers to dress casually, he wears a suit and tie to work because he wants to fit in with the other sales representatives. Gary's behavior is best explained as a matter of:
   a. informational social influence
   b. obedience
   c. normative social influence
   d. collectivistic culture

3. If you were a typical subject in Milgram's original obedience experiment, it is very probable that when asked to administer high levels of shock to the learner, you would

   a. obediently do so with no hesitation.
   b. immediately leave the experimental situation.
   c. demand to be paid more money.
   d. do so, but with considerable reluctance.

4. When people first hear about Milgram's obedience research, they are usually surprised by the results because
   a. the subjects were much more obedient than almost everyone would have predicted.
   b. the learners performed significantly better when they were given electric shocks.
   c. the learners so willingly accepted high levels of shock for their mistakes.
   d. the subjects were willing to take part in the experiment for so little money.

5. Conformity and obedience research suggests that
   a. people are innately predisposd to be cruel and aggressive.
   b. people are much less likely to conform or obey if they observe someone else who is defiant in the situation.
   c. only on rare occasions does someone resist group or authority pressure.
   d. extraverted people are most likely to resist group or authority pressure.

Helping Behavior: Coming to the Aid of Strangers

Prosocial behavior describes any behavior that helps another person. What are the components of the model of helping behavior developed by Latané and Darley? What factors increase or decrease the likelihood that people will help others?

Kitty Genovese

The Murder Scene At the end of the sidewalk you can see the railroad station where Genovese parked her car. Along the sidewalk are entrances to shops as well as stairways leading to apartments above the shops. After Genovese staggered to the entrance of her apartment, her attacker returned and stabbed her to death.

If you had been reading the the *New York Times* on March 14, 1964, you might not have even noticed the small story that appeared under the headline, "Queens Woman Is Stabbed to Death in Front of Home." The murder of Catherine Genovese was described in exactly five sentences back on page 28. Two weeks later, however, the story of the murder of twenty-eight-year-old "Kitty" Genovese had moved to the front page. The *Times* headline said it all: "37 Who Saw Murder Didn't Call the Police" (Gansberg, 1964).

The story of Kitty Genovese's murder is chilling. It was about 3:20 a.m. on Friday, March 13, when Kitty returned home from her job managing a bar. Like other residents in her middle-class neighborhood, she parked her car at an adjacent railroad station. Her apartment entrance was only 100 feet away.

As she got out of her car, she noticed a man at the end of the parking lot. When the man moved in her direction, she began walking toward a nearby police callbox, which was under a street light in front of a bookstore. On the opposite side of the street was a ten-story apartment building. As she neared the street light, the man grabbed her and she screamed. Across the street, lights went on in the apartment building. "Oh, my God! He stabbed me! Please help me! Please help me!" she screamed.

"Let that girl alone!" a man yelled from one of the upper apartment windows. The attacker looked up, then walked off, leaving Kitty on the ground, bleeding. The street became quiet. Minutes passed. One by one, lights went off. Struggling to her feet, Kitty made her way toward her apartment. As she rounded the corner of the building moments later, her assailant returned, stabbing her again. "I'm dying! I'm dying!" she screamed.

Again, lights went on. Windows opened and people looked out. This time, the assailant got in his car and drove off. It was now 3:35 a.m. Fifteen minutes had passed since Kitty's first screams for help. A New York City bus passed by. Staggering, then crawling, Kitty moved toward the entrance of her apartment. She never made it. Her attacker returned, searching the apartment entrance doors. At the second apartment entrance, he found her, slumped at the foot of the steps. This time he stabbed her to death.

It was 3:50 a.m. when someone first called the police. The police took just two minutes to arrive at the scene. About half an hour later, an ambulance carried Kitty Genovese's body away. It was only then that people came out of their apartments to talk to the police.

Over the next two weeks, police investigators learned that a total of 38 people had witnessed Kitty's murder—a murder that involved three separate attacks over a period of 35 minutes. Why didn't anyone try to help her? Or even call the police when they first heard her screams for help?

When the *New York Times* interviewed various experts, they seemed baffled, although one expert said it was a "typical" reaction (Mohr, 1964). If there was a common theme in their explanations, it seemed to be "apathy." The occurrence was simply representative of the alienation and depersonalization of life in a big city, people said (see Rosenthal, 1964a, 1964b).

Not everyone bought this pat explanation. In the first place, it wasn't true. As psychologists Bibb Latané and John Darley (1970) later pointed out in their landmark book *The Unresponsive Bystander: Why Doesn't He Help?*:

altruism

Helping another person with no expectation of personal reward or benefit.

prosocial behavior

Any behavior that helps another, whether the underlying motive is self-serving or selfless.

People often help others, even at great personal risk to themselves. For every "apathy" story, one of outright heroism could be cited. . . . It is a mistake to get trapped by the wave of publicity and discussion surrounding incidents in which help was not forthcoming into believing that help never comes. People sometimes help and sometimes don't. What determines when help will be given?

That's the critical question, of course: What factors influence our decision to help another person? Kitty Genovese's death triggered hundreds of investigations into the conditions under which people will help others (see Dovidio, 1984). In this section, we'll summarize the key findings of that research. As we do so, you'll see how these research findings help explain the behavior of the 38 people who could have prevented Kitty Genovese's death.

Altruism and Prosocial Behavior

When we help another person with no expectation of a personal reward or benefit, we're displaying **altruism** (Piliavin & others, 1981). The altruistic act is fundamentally selfless: an individual is motivated purely by the desire to help someone in need.

Everyday life is filled with little acts of altruistic kindness, such as Fern giving the "homeless" man some money or the stranger who thoughtfully holds a door open for you as you juggle an armful of packages.

More dramatic are the altruistic acts of people who risk their lives to save others, often strangers. Such acts may be more common than you might think. Within the same week, we came across two examples reported in our local newspaper. In Boca Raton, Florida, Luis Vega pulled a woman from her stalled car just seconds before an Amtrak train slammed into it at 80 miles per hour (Associated Press, 1994a). Near Providence, Rhode Island, security guard John Santos heard the explosion of a gasoline tanker truck that had overturned and burst into flames, catching the driver on fire. Santos dashed across the highway to help. He used his own hands to put out the flames on the driver and sustained second-degree burns himself (Associated Press, 1994b). Clearly, heroic acts of altruism do occur.

Altruistic actions fall under the broader heading of **prosocial behavior,** which describes any behavior that helps another person, whatever the underlying motive. Note that prosocial behaviors are not necessarily altruistic. Sometimes we help others out of guilt (see Baumeister & others, 1994; McGuire, 1994). And sometimes we help others in order to gain something, such as recognition, rewards, increased self-esteem, or having the favor returned (see Staub, 1978). Table 12.4 summarizes the twelve most common prosocial behaviors reported by college students in a survey by psychologist Anne McGuire (1994).

Prosocial Behavior in Action Everyday life is filled with countless acts of prosocial behavior as people volunteer their time and energy to help others, like these teenagers who volunteered to cook for a church fund-raiser.

TABLE 12.4 Common Helping Behaviors Among College Students

Behavior	Number of Mentions
Helping with homework or schoolwork	121
Listening to someone talk through a problem	90
Giving advice about a situation someone is in	65
Lending a book, notes, household item	60
Giving a ride within the city	57
Bringing or sending flowers, a card, or a small gift	54
Giving directions	52
Opening or holding a door	41
Giving someone a snack	41
Giving a ride a long distance (greater than 20 miles)	33
Answering a short question; giving information	29
While at the store, picking up an item for someone	29

SOURCE: McGuire, 1994, Table 1, p. 49.

As part of a larger study, psychologist Anne McGuire (1994) asked college students to report instances of helping others in a variety of relationships. The twelve examples of helping behavior that the students mentioned most often are listed here.

Latané and Darley's Model of Helping Behavior

Like others, social psychologists **Bibb Latané** (b. 1937) and **John Darley** (b. 1938) were shocked by the inaction of the witnesses to Kitty Genovese's murder (see Evans, 1980). Beginning in the 1960s, Latané and Darley pioneered the study of bystander intervention by conducting ingenious experiments in which people appeared to need help. Often, these studies were conducted using locations in and around New York City as a kind of open-air laboratory.

On the basis of their research findings, Latané and Darley (1970) developed a model of the process people follow when they decide whether or not to help another person. According to this model, people are most likely to help if they answer "yes" to all of the following questions:

1. Do they *notice* the event or incident?

2. Do they believe it is a situation in which *help is needed*?

3. Do they feel some *sense of responsibility* to help?

4. Do they know *how to deal* with the situation?

Factors That *Increase* the Likelihood of Bystanders Helping

Beyond this general model, Latané, Darley, and other researchers identified specific factors that influence the decision to help (see Eisenberg, 1991; Piliavin & Charng, 1990; Dovidio, 1984). First we'll look at factors that increase the likelihood that bystanders will help; then we'll consider the factors that decrease the likelihood of helping behavior.

The "feel good, do good" effect. People who feel good, successful, happy, or fortunate are more likely to help others (see Salovey & others, 1991; Schaller & Cialdini, 1990). Those good feelings can be due to virtually any positive event, such as receiving a gift, succeeding at a task, listening to pleasant music, finding a small amount of money, or even just enjoying a warm, sunny day.

Feeling guilty. We tend to be more helpful when we're feeling guilty. For example, after telling a lie or inadvertently causing an accident, people were more likely to help others (see Baumeister & others, 1994; Cialdini & others, 1973; Regan & others, 1972).

Seeing others who are willing to help. In several chapters, we've noted that people's behavior is often influenced by what they see others do. The same holds true for helping behavior. Whether it's donating blood, helping a stranded motorist change a flat tire, or dropping money in the Salvation Army kettle during the holiday season, we're more likely to help if we observe others do the same (Sarason & others, 1991; Bryan & Test, 1967).

Perceiving the other person as deserving help. We're more likely to help people who are in need of help through no fault of their own. For example, people are twice as likely to

Bystander Intervention In the situation shown here, a bystander is coming to the aid of a stranger. What factors in this situation probably influenced the bystander's decision to help the fallen bicyclist?

give some change to a stranger if they believe the stranger's wallet has been stolen than if they believe the stranger has simply spent all his money (Latané & Darley, 1970).

Knowing how to help. Researcher Ted Huston and his colleagues (1981) interviewed people who had intervened in actual muggings, armed robberies, and bank holdups. This group was then compared to a matched group of people who had not intervened in emergency situations. No clear-cut personality differences emerged between the two groups. However, the groups did differ in one important way: those who intervened had significantly more medical, police, and first aid training. Other research has confirmed that simply knowing what to do contributes greatly to the decision to help someone else (e.g., Clark & Word, 1974).

A personalized relationship. When people have any sort of personal relationship with another person, they're more likely to help that person. Even minimal social interaction with each other, such as making eye contact or engaging in small talk, increases the likelihood that one person will help the other (Solomon & others, 1981; Howard & Crano, 1974).

Factors That *Decrease* the Likelihood of Bystanders Helping

It's equally important to consider influences that decrease the likelihood of helping behavior. As we look at some of the key findings, we'll also note how these factors seemed to play a role in the murder of Kitty Genovese.

The presence of other people. People are much more likely to help when they are alone (Latané & Nida, 1981). If other people are present, helping behavior declines—a phenomenon called the **bystander effect.**

How can we account for this surprising finding? There seem to be two major reasons for the bystander effect (see Dovidio, 1984; Latané & Darley, 1970). First, the presence of other people creates a **diffusion of responsibility.** When you're the only witness to an emergency, the responsibility for intervening falls squarely on your shoulders. However, if other people are present, any of the other bystanders could potentially offer assistance. Thus, the responsibility to intervene is *shared* (or *diffused*) among all the onlookers. Because no one person feels all the pressure to respond, each bystander becomes less likely to help.

Ironically, the sheer number of bystanders seemed to be the most significant factor working against Kitty Genovese. Remember that when she first screamed, a man yelled down, "Let that girl alone!" With that, each observer instantly knew that he or she was not the only one watching the events on the street below. Hence, no single individual felt the full responsibility to help. Instead, there was a diffusion of responsibility among all the bystanders so that each individual's share of responsibility was small indeed (Latané & Darley, 1970).

bystander effect
The phenomenon in which the greater the number of people present, the less likely each individual is to help someone in distress.

diffusion of responsibility
The phenomenon in which the presence of other people makes it less likely that any individual will help someone in distress because the obligation to intervene is shared among all the onlookers.

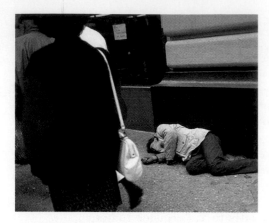

The Bystander Effect In contrast to the situation shown on p. 554, the people in this situation are walking past the man lying on the sidewalk without giving him a second glance. What factors are operating in this situation that make it much less likely that bystanders will help a stranger?

Second, the bystander effect seems to occur because each of us is motivated to some extent by the desire to behave in a socially acceptable way (*normative social influence*) and to appear correct (*informational social influence*). Hence, we often rely on the reactions of others to help us define the situation and guide our response. So if everybody waiting in a room with you acts unconcerned when smoke starts billowing through the air-conditioning vent, you're likely to behave in the same way (Latané & Darley, 1970). In the case of Kitty Genovese, the lack of intervention by any of the witnesses may have signaled the others that intervention was not appropriate, wanted, or needed.

Being in a big city or a very small town. Kitty Genovese was attacked late at night in one of the biggest cities in the world, New York. Are people less likely to help strangers in big cities? Researcher Nancy Steblay (1987) has confirmed that this common belief is true—but with a twist. People are less likely to help a stranger in very big cities (300,000 people or more) *or* in very small towns (5,000 people or less). Either extreme—very big or very small—seems to work against helping a stranger.

Vague or ambiguous situations. When situations are ambiguous and people are not certain that help is needed, they're less likely to offer help (Solomon & others, 1978). For example, in one study *all* the subjects quickly responded when they heard the crash of a man falling off a ladder, followed by a cry of pain: "Oh, my back, I can't move!" But when subjects heard the same crash *minus* the sound of the man crying out in pain, they helped only about 30 percent of the time (Clark & Word, 1972).

The ambiguity of the situation may also have worked against Kitty Genovese. The people in the apartment building saw a man and a woman struggling on the street below, but had no way of knowing whether the two were acquainted. "We thought it was a lovers' quarrel," some of the witnesses later said (Gansberg, 1964). Researchers have found that people are especially reluctant to intervene when the situation appears to be a domestic dispute or a "lovers' quarrel," because they are not certain that assistance is wanted (see Shotland & Straw, 1976).

When the personal costs for helping outweigh the benefits. As a general rule, we tend to weigh the costs as well as the benefits of helping in deciding whether to act. If the potential costs outweigh the benefits, it's less likely that help will be forthcoming from you (see Dovidio & others, 1991). If you find a lost letter near a mailbox, you'll probably be a good guy and drop it in the mailbox. But if no mailbox is in sight, you're less likely to help because you would have to expend much more time and energy to do so (Hedge & Yousif, 1992).

The witnesses in the Genovese case may also have felt that the benefits of helping Genovese were outweighed by the potential hassles and danger of becoming involved in the situation. Many of the witnesses said that they did not want to get involved. Some people simply didn't care. "I was tired. I went back to bed," one witness said blandly (Gansberg, 1964).

Looking Backward:

The Murder of Kitty Genovese

On a small yet universal scale, the murder of Kitty Genovese dramatically underscores the power of situational and social influences on our behavior. Although social psychological research has provided insights about the factors that influenced the behavior of those who witnessed the Genovese murder, it should not be construed as a justification for the inaction of the bystanders. After all, Kitty Genovese's death probably could have been prevented by a single phone call. Like the topics of conformity and obedience, the research on helping behavior has important implications as we go about negotiating daily life.

Consider the stalled car that Sandy recently encountered while driving. One by one, other drivers slowly wove around the stalled car. As Sandy also drove around it, she glanced over and noticed a woman slumped over the steering wheel. Unsure as to whether the woman needed help or not, Sandy kept driving. Besides, she thought, there were many cars on the street, and someone else would probably stop and check on the woman.

Almost instantly, Sandy caught herself: diffusion of responsibility was giving her an excuse to ignore the woman, who probably *did* need help. With this realization, Sandy pulled into the nearest gas station and called 911, asking the dispatcher to send help. Had someone else already reported the matter? No. Despite the large number of cars that had passed the stalled vehicle, Sandy was the first person to call for help.

Granted, that's a minor incident in comparison to the tragic death of Kitty Genovese. Nonetheless, the underlying principles are fundamentally the same. So perhaps if we understand the factors that decrease helping behavior, we can recognize and overcome those obstacles when we encounter someone who needs assistance. After all, if *you* had been the person in the stalled car, or if *you* had been Kitty Genovese, how would *you* have hoped other people would react?

Factors That Influence Helping Behavior

In each of the following examples, first decide if help is "Likely" or "Not likely" to be forthcoming. Second, support your answer by identifying the factor or factors operating in the situation.

1. Mr. Dooley came home elated after having received a large and unexpected bonus at work earlier in the day. During dinner he receives a call from another member of his church asking if he would be willing to help on Saturday with some minor repairs around the church. Likely/Not likely _____

2. Robert is vacationing in another state. His car has broken down right beside a sign that reads "Welcome to Cedar Bluffs, Population 2,821." Likely/Not likely _____

3. While sitting in the middle of a large lecture class, you hear a commotion outside in the hallway, then hear a young woman angrily shout, "Just leave me alone!" Likely/Not likely _____

CONCEPT REVIEW 12.4

4. Just moments after hundreds of people get off a crowded subway train on their way to work, an oddly dressed man in the crowd stumbles and falls as he is walking up the exit steps. Likely/Not likely _____

5. While a family is on a picnic in the woods, a large, mangy dog wanders up. One of the kids notices that the dog has a collar with a name tag. The owner's address on the name tag is in a city and state on the other side of the country. Likely/Not likely _____

6. Three days before Christmas, the local news shows a report of a young, single, working mother whose rental house has burned down because of faulty electrical wiring. In the news report, she tearfully explains that all her possessions, including meager Christmas presents for her two children, were destroyed in the fire. Likely/Not likely _____

social loafing
The tendency to expend less effort on a task when it is a group effort.

The Influence of Groups on Individual Behavior

The presence of other people can strongly influence individual behavior. What are social loafing and social striving, and how does culture affect performance in a group? What are social facilitation and deindividuation, and under what conditions do these phenomena occur?

In our discussions of conformity, obedience, and altruism, we have touched on a variety of ways in which the presence of other people influences an individual's thoughts and behavior. In this section, we'll focus directly on how the behavior of individuals can be affected by being part of a group. As you'll see, the diffusion of responsibility that can occur when a group of people observe someone who needs help also contributes to other aspects of group behavior.

Social Loafing:

When Individual Effort Is "Lost in the Crowd"

The performance and motivation of individuals who are part of a group can be influenced by many different factors (see Guzzo & Dickson, 1996). Whether it's cheering, clapping, or rope pulling, people tend to expend less effort on collective tasks than when performing the same task alone, a phenomenon called **social loafing.** Social loafing is especially pronounced when it's difficult or impossible to assess each individual's contribution to the collective effort. As a general rule, the greater the number of people involved in a collective effort, the lower each individual's output (see Karau & Williams, 1993; Williams & others, 1989; Latané & others, 1979).

Is social loafing inevitable in any group task? Not at all. Psychologists Steven Karau and Kipling Williams (1993) conducted a meta-analysis of over seventy social loafing studies. Collectively, the studies indicate that social loafing is reduced or eliminated when (1) the group is composed of people we know, (2) we are members of a highly valued group, or (3) the task is meaningful or unique. Interestingly, some gender differences also surfaced. Women are generally less likely to engage in social loafing than men. And when the group size increases, the degree of social loafing increases for men, but not for women.

Why does social loafing occur? Much like the diffusion of responsibility that occurs when a group witnesses someone who needs help, there seems to be a similar diffusion of responsibility among group members working on a collective task. The responsibility or effort for attaining the group goal is spread across all the group members, resulting in reduced effort by each individual group member (Latané, 1981). Social loafing can also occur because people expect other group members to slack off. To keep the situation evenhanded or equitable, people reduce their efforts to match the level of effort they expect other group members to display (Jackson & Harkins, 1985).

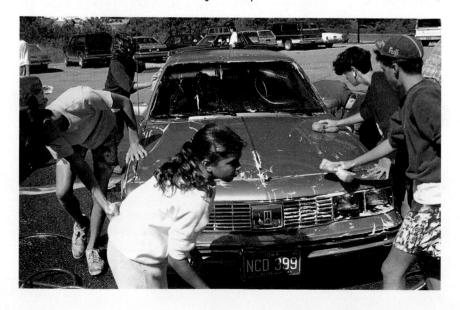

Social Loafing These hard-working teens are demonstrating that social loafing does not always take place. When people know the other members of their group, social loafing is less likely to occur. What other factors make social loafing less likely?

social facilitation
The tendency for the presence of other people to enhance individual performance.

Cultural Variations: Social Striving

Social loafing is a common phenomenon in individualistic cultures. However, cross-cultural psychologists have found that social loafing is not only absent but *reversed* in many collectivistic cultures, including China, Israel, and Japan (M. Bond & Smith, 1996). That is, individuals worked *harder* when they were in groups than when they were alone—a pattern referred to as *social striving* (Matsumoto, 1994; Moghaddam & others, 1993). In the China and Israel studies, those participants who most highly endorsed collectivist values were most likely to demonstrate increased performance and productivity in groups (M. Bond & Smith, 1996).

Why is social loafing less pronounced or even absent in collectivistic cultures? In collectivistic cultures, group success tends to be more highly valued than individual success. The contributions made by individuals to group success are also more highly valued than they are in individualistic cultures (Matsumoto, 1994). Finally, the social norms in collectivistic cultures encourage a sense of social responsibility and hard work within groups (Karau & Williams, 1993).

Social Facilitation:
Individual Performance in the Presence of Others

When your individual efforts go undetected and are "lost in the crowd," individual performance may drop. But what if your individual efforts are *not* lost in the crowd, but instead are the focus of the crowd's attention? Would your performance then be the same in the presence of others as it would be if you were working alone?

Partly, it depends on the complexity of the task that you're trying to perform. When a task is relatively simple or well rehearsed, the presence of other people tends to enhance individual performance, a pattern called **social facilitation.** So when others are watching you perform simple multiplication tables, your individual performance tends to improve. However, if the task is complex or poorly learned, such as a complex memory task, the opposite effect can occur: the presence of other people is likely to *hinder* performance (F. Allport, 1920, 1924; Travis, 1925).

How can this be explained? Several factors are involved (see Geen, 1995, 1991). The presence of others tends to increase our level of arousal and motivation, possibly because of concerns over being favorably or unfavorably evaluated by others. When a task is simple or well learned, increased motivation, spurred on by the anticipation of being positively evaluated, seems to work to our benefit. Under these conditions, social facilitation often occurs: individual performance is *better* in the presence of others. Hence, a well-trained athlete is likely to perform better when others are present than when alone (Guerin, 1986).

However, when the task is complex or poorly learned, arousal coupled with apprehension about being negatively evaluated tends to work against us. Under these conditions, the presence of others can diminish an individual's performance. For example, the apprehensive actor who is not as well rehearsed as he should be may end up missing cues and flubbing lines in front of the opening-night audience.

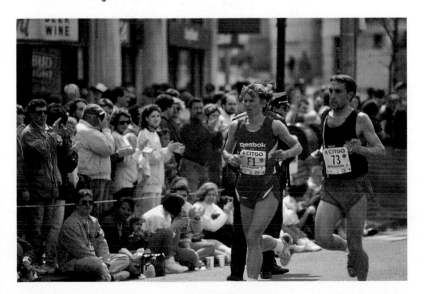

Social Facilitation As the crowd watches and applauds their performance, these professional runners are likely to turn in some of their best running times. When does the presence of other people facilitate the performance of a task? When does it work against us?

Deindividuation:
When Group Members Feel Anonymous

What can happen when you combine the increased arousal due to the presence of others with the diffusion of responsibility that characterizes social loafing and the bystander effect? In combination, increased arousal and a diminished sense of responsibility can lead to deindividuation. **Deindividuation** refers to the reduction of self-awareness and inhibitions that can occur when a person is part of a group whose members feel anonymous.

Because of deindividuation, people may do things that they wouldn't do if they were alone or identifiable. In this way, deindividuation can lead to irresponsible or antisocial behaviors. For example, deindividuation can help explain adolescent acts of vandalism on Halloween. Succumbing to the feeling of anonymity provided by darkness and Halloween masks, groups of otherwise law-abiding teenagers sometimes commit minor acts of vandalism, such as smashing pumpkins, stealing Halloween decorations, and damaging mailboxes.

Much more serious consequences can result from the deindividuation that occurs in a mob or during a riot. The large crowd of people and general social chaos heighten both arousal and the sense of anonymity. This volatile combination can lead to mobs of rioting people who smash windows, steal, and injure innocent bystanders.

Similarly, onlookers are more likely to taunt someone who is threatening a suicidal jump when the incident occurs at night. The darkness of the night adds to the sense of anonymity felt by members of the crowd, who sometimes collectively start chanting, "Jump! Jump! Jump!" Not surprisingly, people are much less likely to urge on the would-be jumper when they are in small groups or during the day, when there is less of a sense of anonymity (Mann, 1981).

How can deindividuation be counteracted? An important element of deindividuation is the reduced sense of self-awareness (Diener, 1980). Thus, one way to counteract deindividuation is to heighten self-awareness. For example, when a mirror was placed above a bowl of Halloween candy, unattended trick-or-treaters were less likely to take more candy than they were told they could take (Beaman & others, 1979). Simply seeing their own faces in the mirror increased personal self-awareness and reduced impulsive, dishonest actions.

Deindividuation: Anonymity and Reduced Self-Awareness The hood and mask of the Ku Klux Klan uniform heightens the sense of anonymity felt by Klansmen. So does the darkness of night at this cross burning. Such factors add to the likelihood that people will commit antisocial acts that they would not commit if alone or if their identity were known.

CONCEPT REVIEW 12.5

Influence of Groups on Individual Behavior

Match each example with the correct concept.
a. social loafing
b. social striving
c. social facilitation
d. deindividuation

_____ **1.** Nina's best running time during practice was 5 minutes and 12 seconds for one mile. During the actual race, however, her time improved to 4 minutes and 42 seconds for one mile.

_____ **2.** As part of a social psychology experiment, female college students wore identical white coats and hoods that concealed their identities. In this anonymous condition, they demonstrated significantly more aggressive behavior than female students who wore name tags and whose faces were not covered.

_____ **3.** A team of workers in a car factory in Thailand is much more productive than are the individual team members when they work alone.

_____ **4.** In a social psychology experiment, university students picked up less litter per person when they were members of a large group than when they worked alone.

_____ **5.** When the Slammers won the playoffs on Friday night, the excitement and chaos following the game turned into a riot, and several stores were looted.

deindividuation
The reduction of self-awareness and inhibitions that can occur when a person is part of a group whose members feel anonymous.

Summing Up: Social Psychology

We began this chapter with a prologue about Fern trying to help a stranger in a strange city. As it turned out, Fern's social perceptions of the man were inaccurate: He was not a "homeless" person living on the streets of San Francisco. As simple as this incident was, it underscored a theme that was repeatedly echoed throughout our subsequent discussions of person perception, attribution, and attitudes. Our subjective impressions, whether they are accurate or not, play a pivotal role in how we perceive and think about other people.

A different theme emerged in our later discussions of conformity, obedience, helping behavior, and the influence of groups. Social and situational factors, especially the behavior of others in the same situation, can have powerful effects on how we act at a given moment. But like Fern, each of us has the freedom to choose how we respond in a given situation. When we're aware of the social forces that influence us, it can be easier for us to choose wisely.

In the final analysis, we are social animals who often influence one another's thoughts, perceptions, and actions, sometimes in profound ways. In the chapter Application, we'll look at some of the ways that social psychological insights have been applied by professional persuaders—and how you can counteract attempts to persuade you.

APPLICATION

The Persuasion Game

Persuasion refers to the deliberate attempt to influence the attitudes or behavior of another person. What are the rules of reciprocity and commitment, and how are these social norms used to persuade others? How can persuasion techniques be resisted?

Our daughter, Laura, then three and a half years old, was happily munching her Cheerios and doodling in the butter on her bread. Don sat across from her at the kitchen table, reading a draft of this chapter. "Don't play with your food, Laura," Don said without looking up.

"Okay, Daddy," Short Stuff chirped. "Daddy, are you in a happy mood?"

Don paused, glancing up. "Yes, I'm in a happy mood, Laura," he said thoughtfully. "Are you in a happy mood?"

"Yes, Daddy," Laura replied as she made the banana peel dance around her placemat. "Daddy, will you get me a Mermaid Barbie doll for my birthday?"

Ah, so young and so clever! From very early in life, we learn the basics of

persuasion—the deliberate attempt to influence the attitudes or behavior of another person in a situation where that person has some freedom of choice. Clearly, Laura had figured out one basic rule: She's more likely to persuade Mom or Dad when they're in "a happy mood."

In this Application, we will look at the tactics used by professional persuaders, such as salespeople, fundraisers, and advertisers. As you'll see, professional persuaders often manipulate people's attitudes and behavior using techniques based on two fundamental social norms: the rule of reciprocity and the rule of commitment. Equally important, we'll give you some practical suggestions to avoid being taken in by persuasion techniques.

The Rule of Reciprocity

The *rule of reciprocity* is a simple but powerful social norm: If someone gives you something or does you a favor, you feel obligated to return the favor. That's why encyclopedia salespeople offer you

a "free" dictionary for listening to their spiel and department stores that sell expensive cosmetics offer "free" makeovers. Technically, you are under "no obligation" to buy anything. Nonetheless, the tactic often creates an uncomfortable sense of obligation, so you *do*

Playing the Persuasion Game This car salesman will use a variety of persuasive techniques to try to persuade this young couple to buy a car from him. Becoming aware of common persuasion techniques can help you make decisions more objectively.

feel pressured to reciprocate by buying their product (Cialdini, 1993).

One strategy that uses the rule of reciprocity is called the *door-in-the-face technique* (see Perloff, 1993; Dillard, 1991). First, the persuader makes a large request that you're certain to refuse. For example, Joe asks to borrow $500. You figuratively "slam the door in his face" by quickly turning him down. But then Joe, apologetic, appears to back off and makes a much smaller request—to borrow $20. From your perspective, it appears that Joe has made a concession to you and is trying to be reasonable. This puts you in the position of reciprocating with a concession of your own. "Well, I can't lend you $500," you grumble, "but I guess I could lend you twenty bucks." Of course, the persuader's real goal was to persuade you to comply with the second, smaller request.

The rule of reciprocity is also operating in the *that's-not-all technique* (see Zimbardo & Leippe, 1991; Burger, 1986). First, the persuader makes an offer. But before you can accept or reject it, the persuader appears to throw in something extra or lower the price to make the deal even more attractive to you. So as you're standing there mulling over the price of the more expensive CD player, the salesperson says, "Listen, I'm offering you a great price but that's not all I'll do—I'll throw in some headphones at no extra charge." From your perspective, it appears as though the salesperson has just done you a favor by making a concession you did not ask for. This creates a sense of obligation for you to reciprocate by buying the "better" package.

The Rule of Commitment

Another powerful social norm is the *rule of commitment*: Once you make a public commitment, there is psychological and interpersonal pressure on you to behave consistently with your earlier commitment. The *foot-in-the-door technique* is one strategy that capitalizes on the rule of commitment (see Perloff, 1993; Cialdini, 1993). Here's how it works.

First, the persuader makes a small request that you're likely to agree with. For example, she might ask you to wear a lapel pin publicizing a fundraising drive for a charity (see Pratkanis & Aronson, 1991). By agreeing to wear the lapel pin, you've made a *commitment* to the fundraising effort. At that point, she has gotten her "foot in the door." Later, the persuader asks you to comply with a second, larger request, such as donating money to the charity. Because of your earlier commitment, you feel psychologically pressured to behave consistently by now agreeing to the larger commitment (Gorassini & Olson, 1995).

The rule of commitment is also operating in the *low-ball technique*. Here, the persuader gets you to make a commitment by deliberately understating the cost of the product you want (Cialdini, 1993). He's thrown you a "low ball," so to speak, one that is simply too good to turn down. In reality, the persuader has no intention of honoring the artificially low price.

Here's an example of the low-ball technique in action: You've negotiated an excellent price (the "low ball") on a used car and filled out the sales contract. The car salesman shakes your hand and beams, then takes your paperwork into his manager's office for approval. Ten minutes pass—enough time for you to convince yourself that you've made the right decision and solidify your commitment to it.

At that point, the salesman comes back from his manager's office looking dejected. "I'm terribly sorry," the car salesman says. "My manager won't let me sell the car at that price because we'd lose too much money on the deal. I told him I would even take a lower commission, but he won't budge."

Notice what has happened. The attractive "low-ball" price that originally prompted you to make the commitment has been pulled out from under your feet. But while you've been waiting, you've had the time to come up with additional justifications to rationalize your commitment to the decision.

What typically happens? Despite the loss of the original inducement to make the purchase—the low-ball price —people often feel compelled to "keep their commitment" to make the purchase even though it is at a higher price (Cialdini, 1993).

Defending Against Professional Persuasion Techniques

How can you reduce the likelihood that you'll be manipulated into making a decision that is not in your best interest? Here are three practical suggestions.

Suggestion 1: Sleep on it. Persuasive transactions typically occur quickly. Part of this is our own doing. We've finally decided to go look at a new CD player, automobile, or whatever, so we're psychologically primed to buy the product. The persuader uses this psychological momentum to help coax you into signing on the dotted line right then and there. It's only later, of course, that you sometimes have second thoughts. So when you think you've got the deal you want, tell the persuader that you always sleep on important decisions before making a final commitment.

Adopting the sleep-on-it rule for important decisions serves several important functions. First, it lets you exercise some control in rapidly occurring transactions. Second, it gets you out of the persuasive situation so you can analyze what actually occurred during the transaction. When you do, you might spot some of the persuasive ploys we've described above. Third, the sleep-on-it rule often provides an opportunity to discover whether the persuader is deliberately trying to pressure or manipulate you. If the persuader responds to your sleep-on-it suggestion by saying something like, "This offer is good for today only," then it's likely that he or she is afraid that your commitment to the deal will crumble if you think about it too carefully or look elsewhere. Finally, adopting the sleep-on-it rule also gives you time to use suggestion 2.

Suggestion 2: Play devil's advocate. Make a list of all the reasons why you should *not* buy the product or make a particular commitment (Pratkanis & Aronson, 1991). Arguing *against* the decision will help activate your critical thinking skills. It's also helpful to discuss important decisions with a friend, who might be able to point out disadvantages that you have overlooked.

Suggestion 3. Pay attention to your gut feelings. Learn to trust your gut feelings when something doesn't feel quite right. If you feel like you're being psychologically pressured or cornered, you probably are. As a general rule, if you feel any sense of hesitation, lean toward the conservative side and do nothing. If you take the time to think things over, you'll probably be able to identify the source of your reluctance.

Some Final Thoughts: Playing the Persuasion Game

Shortly after our daughter was born, we moved from an apartment to the house where we now live. We had exactly three hours on a Saturday afternoon to buy a refrigerator. Did the salesman use any of the techniques described in this Application? Absolutely. In fact, we were *hoping* he would. Yes, he was likable and friendly. Yes, he acted like he had only our best interests at heart. Yes, he brought us some "free"

coffee to get the rule of reciprocity rolling. And, of course, he didn't give us his best offer right off the bat.

But after his third "best" offer, our time was running out. Right on cue, Sandy feigned reluctance and suggested going to a competing store. "You're probably right, Sandy," Don frowned. "I was hoping we could do better."

As we started to collect all the baby-related paraphernalia that new parents drag with them, our salesman

stopped us. Predictably, those familiar words of the "that's not all" technique rolled smoothly off his lips. "Listen," he said. "Just because you're such a nice young couple, that's not all I'm going to do." And that's how we got a "free" icemaker!

The moral here is simple: If you know what to expect when playing the persuasion game, sometimes you can make it work to *your* advantage.

Summary

Social Psychology

What Is Social Psychology?

- Social psychology is the scientific study of the way individuals think, feel, and behave in social situations. Social cognition and social influence are two important areas of research in social psychology.

Person Perception: Forming Impressions of Other People

- Person perception is an active and subjective process and occurs in an interpersonal context. The interpersonal context includes the characteristics of the individual you are judging, your own characteristics, and the situation.

- Person perception is influenced by subjective perceptions, personal goals, social norms, and self-perception.

- People often rely on social categories when they evaluate others. Social categorization may be automatic or deliberate. Using social categories is cognitively efficient, but can lead to inaccurate conclusions.

- Because we expect certain traits and behaviors to go together, we often form and rely on implicit personality theories in person perception. Implicit personality theories provide a mental framework that organizes observations, memories, and beliefs about other people.

- One common implicit personality theory is "what is beautiful is good." Although people tend to associate physical attractiveness with many desirable characteristics, there are few personality differences between attractive and less attractive people.

Attribution: Explaining the Causes of Behavior

- The attribution process refers to how we infer the cause of our own or another person's behavior. Attributions can strongly influence our opinions of other people, but the attribution process is susceptible to many biases.

- Three important attributional biases are the fundamental attribution error, the actor–observer discrepancy, and the self-serving bias. In some collectivistic cultures, people display the modesty or self-effacing bias, and are less prone to making the fundamental attribution error than are people in individualistic cultures.

The Social Psychology of Attitudes

- An attitude is a learned tendency to evaluate an object, person, or issue in a particular way. This evaluation is usually positive or negative, but may be ambivalent. Attitudes can have cognitive, affective, and behavioral components.

- Attitudes are likely to determine behaviors when they are extreme or expressed frequently; when they have been formed through direct experience; when people are very knowledgeable about the attitude object; when people have a vested interest in the subject of the attitude; and when people expect a favorable outcome from acting in accordance with their attitude.

- When behavior conflicts with attitudes, cognitive dissonance may occur, and people may change their attitudes to conform to their behavior.

Understanding Prejudice

- Prejudice refers to a negative attitude toward people who belong to a specific social group.

- Stereotypes are social categories about members of particular social groups. Relying on stereotypes can have many negative consequences. Stereotyped thinking can distort perception and cause us to inaccurately prejudge individuals. Once formed, stereotypes resist change.

- Judgments of others are also influenced by whether they are members of the in-group or an out-group. We're more likely to use negative stereotypes to evaluate members of out-groups. The out-group homogeneity effect, in-group bias, and ethnocentrism are three forms of bias that can result from in-group/out-group thinking.

- Stereotypes form the cognitive basis for prejudicial attitudes. Prejudice also has an emotional component, which often occurs in response to the belief that an out-group somehow threatens the in-group's values or norms.

- Mere contact between members of different groups is not enough to dissolve prejudicial attitudes. Muzafer Sherif demonstrated that intergroup conflict can be decreased when groups engage in a cooperative effort. Cooperative learning is one way of reducing prejudice in classrooms.

- People are sometimes not aware of their prejudiced attitudes. On an individual level, prejudice can be reduced by consciously rejecting prejudiced attitudes, internalizing nonprejudiced beliefs, and deliberately inhibiting prejudicial reactions while replacing them with nonprejudiced responses.

Conformity: Following the Crowd

- Conformity occurs when people change their behavior, attitudes, or beliefs in response to real or imagined group pressure. Sometimes people conform publicly but not privately; at other times, both private beliefs and outward behavior are changed to conform to group norms or pressure.

- Research by Solomon Asch demonstrated the degree to which people will conform to a majority view and the conditions under which conformity is most likely. Normative and informational social influence both contribute to conformity.

- Conformity is generally higher in collectivistic cultures than in individualistic cultures. Conformity to group norms is viewed less negatively in many collectivistic cultures than it is in individualistic cultures.

Obedience: Just Following Orders

- Obedience was studied most extensively by Stanley Milgram. In Milgram's original obedience experiment, each subject ("the teacher") thought he was delivering ever-increasing levels of electric shock to another subject ("the learner"). In contrast to predictions, most of the subjects obeyed the experimenter and progressed to the maximum shock level.

- Milgram identified several powerful aspects of the original experimental situation that influenced subjects to obey the experimenter and continue delivering electric shocks. In later experiments, Milgram also identified several situational factors that made people less likely to obey.

- Asch's research on conformity and Milgram's research on obedience demonstrate the degree to which behavior is influenced by situational factors.

Helping Behavior: Coming to the Aid of Strangers

- The scientific study of helping behavior, altruism, and prosocial behavior was spurred by the murder of Kitty Genovese in front of 38 witnesses. Although no one intervened to save Genovese, sometimes people do help others.

- Bibb Latané and John Darley developed a model to explain the circumstances under which people will help a stranger. Several factors have been identified that increase the likelihood of bystander intervention. Diffusion of responsibility is the most important factor that explains why bystanders do not help another person.

The Influence of Groups on Individual Behavior

- Individual behavior can be strongly influenced by the presence of others. In social loafing, people expend less effort when working as a group on a collective task than when working alone on the same task. Social loafing is less likely when we know the other people in a group, when we are members of a highly valued group, or when a task is meaningful or unique.

- Social loafing is reduced or reversed in some collectivistic cultures. Instead, individuals expend more effort when they are working in a group on a collective task, a phenomenon known as social striving.

- Under some conditions, the presence of others enhances individual performance, a phenomenon called social facilitation. Social facilitation is most likely when a task is simple or well rehearsed. Performance decreases when a task is complex or poorly learned.

- Deindividuation can occur when increased arousal due to the presence of others is combined with diffusion of responsibility and anonymity. Deindividuation can lead to antisocial behaviors, but can be reduced if self-awareness is heightened.

Key Terms

social psychology (p. 520)

social cognition (p. 520)

social influence (p. 520)

person perception (p. 521)

social norms (p. 522)

social categorization (p. 523)

implicit personality theory (p. 524)

attribution (p. 525)

fundamental attribution error (p. 526)

actor–observer discrepancy (p. 526)

blaming the victim bias (p. 527)

just-world hypothesis (p. 527)

self-serving bias (p. 528)

attitude (p. 530)

cognitive dissonance (p. 532)

prejudice (p.534)

stereotype (p. 534)

in-group (p. 536)

out-group (p. 536)

out-group homogeneity effect (p. 536)

in-group bias (p. 536)

ethnocentrism (p. 537)

conformity (p. 541)

normative social influence (p. 542)

informational social influence (p. 542)

obedience (p. 543)

altruism (p. 553)

prosocial behavior (p. 553)

bystander effect (p. 555)

diffusion of responsibility (p. 555)

social loafing (p. 558)

social facilitation (p. 559)

deindividuation (p. 560)

persuasion (p. 561)

Key People

Solomon Asch (b. 1907) American social psychologist who is best known for his pioneering studies of conformity.

John M. Darley (b. 1938) Contemporary American social psychologist who, along with co-researcher Bibb Latané, is best known for his pioneering studies of bystander intervention in emergency situations.

Bibb Latané (b. 1937) Contemporary American social psychologist who, along with co-researcher John Darley, is best known for his pioneering studies of bystander intervention in emergency situations.

Stanley Milgram (1933–1984) American social psychologist who is best known for his controversial series of studies investigating destructive obedience to an authority.

Muzafer Sherif (b. 1906) American social psychologist who is best known for his "Robber's Cave" experiments to study prejudice, conflict resolution, and group processes.

CONCEPT REVIEW 12.1   Page 530

1. d
2. f
3. e
4. c
5. a
6. b

CONCEPT REVIEW 12.2   Page 540

1. stereotyping
2. out-group homogeneity
3. in-group bias
4. cognitive dissonance
5. ethnocentrism

CONCEPT REVIEW 12.3   Page 551

1. d
2. c
3. d
4. a
5. b

CONCEPT REVIEW 12.4   Page 557

1. Likely. The "feel good, do good" effect.
2. Not likely. Robert is a stranger in a very small town.
3. Not likely, for two reasons: (1) diffusion of responsibility; (2) ambiguous situation, possibly a lovers' quarrel.
4. Not likely, for five reasons: (1) diffusion of responsibility; (2) a large city; (3) no personalized relationship with the fallen man; (4) vague situation; (5) personal costs of being late to work outweigh the benefits of stopping to help a stranger.
5. Not likely. Personal costs of getting the dog back to its owner will probably be perceived as outweighing the benefits.
6. Likely, for three reasons: (1) person is perceived as deserving of help through no fault of her own; (2) because the woman speaks to the viewing audience, the situation is more personalized; (3) guilt is likely to motivate helping behavior, especially in people who have much more than the person who needs help.

CONCEPT REVIEW 12.5   Page 560

1. c
2. d
3. b
4. a
5. d

13

Stress, Health, and Coping

Prologue: Thank God It's Friday?

How do you spell *STRESS*? Our friends David and Marie joke that they spell it L-I-F-E. David and Marie are both in their mid-forties, but they have two young children. Like most parents today, they also have full-time jobs. Marie works as an accountant, and David is the computer administrator for a small firm.

Adding to their hectic lives, both Marie and David are taking evening classes at the local community college. Since Marie doesn't have an accounting degree, she's enrolled in an intensive program to prepare her to take the CPA exam. She's at school three nights a week and all day Saturday. Every spare moment when she's not at school or work, Marie immerses herself in accounting books.

David is taking classes to upgrade his computer skills. He had originally been trained as a mainframe programmer, but jobs in that field are hard to come by now. When he was laid off from his last job, it took him over a year to find a new one. On the one hand, he's glad to be employed again. On the other hand, his pay is much lower than at his old job, and he finds his new boss hard to get along with.

Like David, Marie is not completely happy with her job. The Japanese-owned company she works for recently announced that it was moving its North American headquarters from Tulsa to Mexico City. Although the managers announced that no one would be laid off, prospective tenants have twice toured the building to look over the offices. Consequently, Marie has been actively looking for a new job.

Not wanting to jeopardize her current job, Marie has been forced to devise various excuses for leaving work to go to job interviews. She doesn't have a private office, so a simple phone call to a prospective employer presents problems. "It's hard to sound cool, calm, and confident," she laughs, "when you're calling from a Kmart and the PA system is announcing a Blue Light Special in the background."

Going to an interview is even more challenging. After finding a way to duck out of her office, she has to stop somewhere to quickly change into her good suit. "I'm beginning to feel like Superwoman," Marie told us. "So far, I've changed my clothes in a bathroom at the college, two McDonalds, and a Burger King. But I draw the line at phone booths!"

Out of more than a hundred applicants, Marie and two others made the final cut for an extremely promising job. Though the company was supposed to call her within a week to tell her if she had gotten the job, they called instead to tell her that the manager who would make the decision was out of town but would *definitely* call her on Friday. Well, Friday came . . . but the call didn't. As Marie drove home from work that Friday, she felt more and more upset. "They could have at least called me and told me they hired someone else," she thought.

Meanwhile, David was having his own problems that Friday afternoon. The computer network kept crashing, and David had to work later than usual to get it operating again. In turn, this meant that he had to rush to pick up their children—Mandy at her day-care center and Brian at his school. Like David, the children were both tired and cranky after a long week.

Halfway home, David remembered that he had promised Marie that he would stop at the grocery store. Coaxing two tired, hungry, and grumpy kids out of the car and into the crowded grocery store was a challenge in itself. On the way into the store, Mandy stepped in a puddle that was much deeper than she anticipated. Muddy shoes and wet leggings were now added to her misery. As David navigated the cart through the congested store aisles, Mandy squished along behind him while Brian chided her for getting her clothes wet.

In the produce section, Mandy spotted the carefully stacked oranges. Trying to be helpful, she grabbed an orange from the bottom of the stack. The inevitable happened: An avalanche of oranges went bouncing and rolling in every direction. Surrounded by a sea of oranges, Mandy broke into tears. While David tried to calm Mandy down, Brian began rounding up the oranges.

At home, Marie wondered what was keeping David and the kids. As she fixed a quick dinner for the four of them, David burst through the back door, his arms loaded with groceries. Brian walked in and promptly announced that Mandy had knocked over the display of oranges. With that, Mandy began crying again. As the situation degenerated into yet another chaotic scene, David suddenly yelled, "Everyone! Be QUIET!"

Silence filled the kitchen as Marie, Brian, and Mandy looked at David. "What did I ever do to get you two kids, anyway?" David grumbled in frustration.

"Why, don't you know, Daddy?" Brian asked. "You and Mommy had sex!"

David and Marie looked at each other, then started to laugh. "I give up," David said in exasperation as he sat down at the kitchen table.

"Here, Mama, I'll help you with the groceries," Mandy offered. She started to lift a grocery sack off the floor. As she did so, the bag ripped, sending apples, lettuce, *and* oranges across the kitchen floor. Before Mandy could burst into tears for a third time, Marie happily announced, "You remembered the oranges! Thank you, Mandy!"

Although we chose David and Marie, we could just as easily have used a day in the life of any of our friends to illustrate the main topic of this chapter—stress. No doubt you've also had days like the one David and Marie experienced. If you're like most of our students, you probably have ample firsthand experience with the stress of juggling the demands of college, work, and family responsibilities. The simple fact is that all of us face a wide variety of obstacles, frustrations, and challenges as we negotiate daily life. Any way you look at it, stress is an unavoidable part of life.

Introduction

What Is Stress?

What exactly is stress? It's one of those words that is frequently used but is hard to define precisely. When we ask our students what *stress* means to them, we get a number of different answers. Some students focus on the stimuli or events that cause stress: "It's when my mother-in-law comes to visit." "Stress is when I have three final exams on the same day." To psychologists, however, such stress-producing events or situations are more accurately called **stressors.**

Other students respond by focusing on the stress response. "Stress is when I get butterflies in my stomach and I get a tension headache." Early stress researchers, who mostly studied animals, also focused on the physiological response to stressors in their definitions of stress (e.g., Selye, 1956). Although response definitions of stress can be useful, a problem arises when you try to generalize from animal studies to human behavior: Two people can respond very differently to the same objective stressor, such as an impending exam. In other words, response definitions don't adequately account for the psychological and social factors which, researchers have found, play a key role in the stress experience.

How Do You Define Stress?

From a ripped grocery bag to the threat of unemployment, stressors come in all sizes. Any event can produce stress—if you think that you don't have the resources to cope with it.

A Working Definition and Model of Stress

Since the 1960s, psychologists have been actively studying the experience of stress in people, including how people cope with stress and how stress can affect health. As research findings have accumulated, it has become increasingly clear that the human experience of stress is a dynamic process. Biological, psychological, and social factors are all involved in the experience of stress and the effects it produces.

Today, **stress** is widely defined as a negative emotional state occurring in response to events that are perceived as taxing or exceeding a person's resources or ability to cope (Cohen & Herbert, 1996; Lazarus, 1993). This definition emphasizes the important role that a person's perception or appraisal of events plays in the experience of stress. Whether or not we experience stress largely depends on our *cognitive appraisal* of an event and the resources that we have to deal with the event (Tomaka & others, 1993; Lazarus & Folkman, 1984).

If we think that we have adequate resources to deal with a situation, it will probably create little or no stress in our lives. But if we perceive our resources as being inadequate to deal with a situation that we see as threatening, challenging, or even harmful, we'll experience the effects of stress. If our coping efforts are effective, stress will decrease; if ineffective, stress will increase. Figure 13.1 illustrates this dynamic model of stress.

stressors
Events or situations that are perceived as harmful, threatening, or challenging.

stress
A negative emotional state occurring in response to events that are perceived as taxing or exceeding a person's resources or ability to cope.

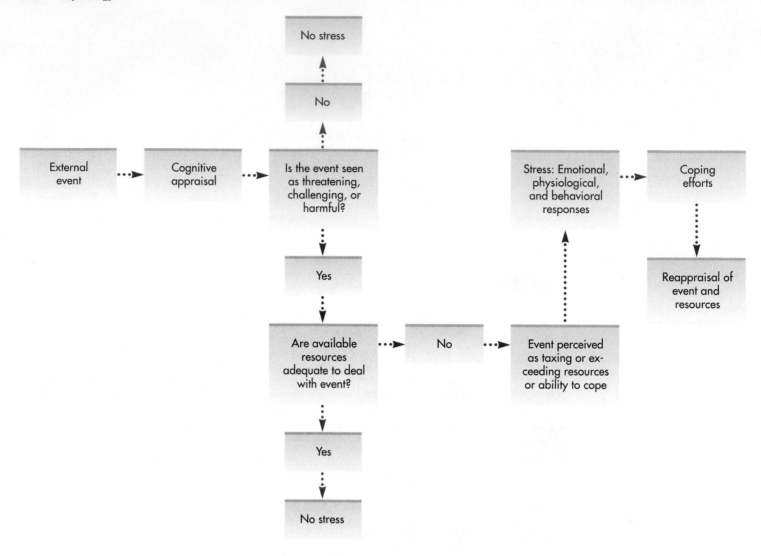

FIGURE 13.1 A Model of Stress
Whether or not we perceive any particular event as a stressor depends on our subjective cognitive appraisal of the event and of our available resources. As we exert coping efforts to deal with a stressful event, we reappraise the event and our resources.

The study of stress is a key topic in one of the most rapidly growing specialty areas in psychology: **health psychology.** Along with stress, health psychologists study how psychological factors influence health, illness, and treatment. They investigate issues such as how to promote health-enhancing behaviors and how people respond in the relationship between patient and health practitioner (Taylor, 1995). In looking at such issues, health psychologists are guided by the *biopsychosocial model.* According to this model, health and illness are determined by the complex interaction of biological, psychological, and social factors (Bernard, 1994).

Throughout this chapter, you'll see the nature of this interaction as we explore the topic of stress in detail. We'll begin by looking at the kinds of events that typically produce stress in our lives and the ways in which stress can affect our health. Later in the chapter, we'll examine how psychological and social factors, such as our personality characteristics and relationships, can influence how we perceive and respond to potential stressors. Toward the end of the chapter, we'll consider the coping strategies that people typically use to deal with stressful events. In the chapter Application, we'll present an effective strategy that can help reduce the amount of stress in your life.

health psychology
The branch of psychology that studies how psychological factors influence health, illness, medical treatment, and health-related behaviors.

TABLE 13.1 Life Events and Stress: The Social Readjustment Rating Scale

Life Events	Life Change Units
Death of spouse	100
Divorce	73
Marital separation	65
Jail term	63
Death of close family member	63
Personal injury or illness	53
Marriage	50
Fired at work	47
Marital reconciliation	45
Retirement	45
Change in health of family member	44
Pregnancy	40
Sex difficulties	39
Gain of new family member	39
Business readjustment	39
Change in financial state	38
Death of close friend	37
Change to different line of work	36
Change in number of arguments with spouse	35
Mortgage or loan for major purchase (home, etc.)	31
Foreclosure on mortgage or loan	30
Change in responsibilities at work	29
Son or daughter leaving home	29
Trouble with in-laws	29
Outstanding personal achievement	28
Spouse begins or stops work	26
Begin or end school	26
Change in living conditions	25
Revision of personal habits	24
Trouble with boss	23
Change in work hours or conditions	20
Change in residence	20
Change in schools	20
Change in recreation	19
Change in church activities	19
Change in social activities	18
Mortgage or loan for lesser purchase (car, TV, etc.)	17
Change in sleeping habits	16
Change in number of family get-togethers	15
Change in eating habits	15
Vacation	13
Christmas	12
Minor violations of the law	11

SOURCE: Holmes & Rahe, 1967.

Sources of Stress

Stressors come in all sizes. Some important sources of stress include life events, daily hassles, conflict, and social and cultural factors. What problems are associated with the life events approach? How do daily hassles and conflict contribute to stress?

From the trivial to the tragic, life is filled with potential stressors. In fact, virtually any event or situation can be a source of stress if you question your ability or resources to deal effectively with it (Lazarus & Folkman, 1984). In this section, we'll survey some of the most important and common sources of stress.

Life Events and Change

Early stress researchers Thomas Holmes and Richard Rahe (1967) believed that any change that required you to adjust your behavior and lifestyle would cause stress. In an attempt to measure the amount of stress people experienced, they developed the *Social Readjustment Rating Scale,* which is shown in Table 13.1. The scale includes 43 life events that are likely to require some level of adaptation. Each life event is assigned a numerical rating that estimates its relative impact in terms of *life change units.*

Life events ratings range from 100 life change units for the most stress-producing (the death of a spouse) to 11 life change units for the least stress-producing (a minor violation of the law, such as a parking ticket). To measure your level of stress, you simply check off the life events you've experienced in the past year and add up the total.

Notice that many of the life events are generally considered to be positive events, such as holidays, an outstanding personal achievement, and even a vacation. According to the life events approach, *any* change, whether positive or negative, is inherently stress-producing.

Holmes and Rahe found that high scores on their life events scale were linked to a greater likelihood of developing serious physical or psychological problems. Accumulating as few as 150 life change units within a year put a person at increased risk for illness. Accumulating over 300 life change units in a year supposedly increased a person's risk of illness to 80 percent (Rahe, 1972; Holmes & Masuda, 1974).

Despite its initial popularity, several problems with the life events approach have been pointed out. First, the link between scores on the Social Readjustment Rating Scale and the development of physical and psychological problems is relatively weak. In general, scores on the Social Readjustment Rating Scale are *not* very good predictors of poor physical or mental health. Instead, researchers have found that most people weather major life events without developing serious physical or psychological problems (Coyne & Downey, 1991; Kessler & others, 1985).

The Social Readjustment Rating Scale, developed by Thomas Holmes and Richard Rahe (1967), was an early attempt to quantify the amount of stress experienced by people in a wide range of situations. Holmes and Rahe reasoned that any life event that required some sort of adaptation or change would create stress, whether the life event was pleasant or unpleasant.

Major Life Events and Stress Would a welcome pregnancy or losing your home in a fire both produce damaging levels of stress? According to the life events approach, any event that required you to change or adjust your lifestyle would produce significant stress—whether the event was positive or negative, planned or unexpected. How was the life events approach modified by later research?

Second, the Social Readjustment Rating Scale does not take into account a person's subjective appraisal of an event, response to that event, or ability to cope with the event (T. W. Miller, 1993; Lazarus & Folkman, 1984; Perkins, 1982). Instead, the number of life change units on the scale is pre-assigned, reflecting the assumption that a given life event will have the same impact on virtually everyone. But clearly, the stress-producing potential of an event might vary widely from one person to another. For instance, if you are in a marriage that is filled with conflict, tension, and unhappiness, getting divorced (73 life change units) might be significantly less stressful than remaining married.

Third, the life events approach assumes that change in itself, whether good or bad, produces stress. However, researchers have found that negative life events have the greatest adverse effects on health, especially when they're unexpected and uncontrollable (Dohrenwend & others, 1993; Perkins, 1982). In contrast, positive or desirable events are much *less* likely to affect your health adversely (see Taylor, 1995).

When positive events do produce stress, it's often due to the hassles or unpleasant activities associated with the positive event. A wedding ceremony, for example, is usually a very joyful occasion. But planning the wedding might involve one headache after another, from finding a reception hall to making sure that feuding relatives aren't inadvertently seated next to each other.

Today, most researchers agree that undesirable events are significant sources of stress, but change in itself is not necessarily stressful. Once again, it's how we evaluate or appraise life events—and whether we have the resources to handle the negative life events—that determines whether stress is experienced (Lazarus, 1993).

Daily Hassles:
"Wait a Second, This Isn't What I Ordered"

Richard Lazarus Psychologist Richard Lazarus has made several influential contributions to the study of stress and coping. His definition of stress emphasizes the importance of cognitive appraisal in the stress response. He also demonstrated the importance of everyday hassles in producing stress.

What made you feel "stressed out" in the last week? Chances are it was not a major life event. Instead, it was probably some unexpected but minor annoyance like getting a splotch of ketchup on your new white T-shirt, misplacing your lecture notes, getting stuck in a long line when you're in a hurry, or even having a bad hair day.

Stress researcher **Richard Lazarus** (b. 1922) and his colleagues suspected that such ordinary irritations in daily life might be an important

TABLE 13.2 Top Ten Daily Hassles in a Survey of College Students and Middle-Aged Adults

College Students	Middle-Aged Adults
1. Troubling thoughts about future	1. Concerns about weight
2. Not getting enough sleep	2. Health of a family member
3. Wasting time	3. Rising prices of common goods
4. Inconsiderate smokers	4. Home maintenance
5. Physical appearance	5. Too many things to do
6. Too many things to do	6. Misplacing or losing things
7. Misplacing or losing things	7. Yard work or outside home maintenance
8. Not enough time to do the things you need to do	8. Property, investment, or taxes
9. Concerns about meeting high standards	9. Crime
10. Being lonely	10. Physical appearance

SOURCE: Kanner & others, 1981.

Do you experience any of these common daily hassles? If you're lucky enough to be both middle-aged and a college student, you probably experience some of the hassles on both lists.

Daily Hassles Life's little hassles and irritants can be a significant source of stress—especially when they pile up. Traffic jams, long lines when you're in a hurry, and misplacing your keys are just a few examples of daily hassles. What daily hassles have you experienced in the last few days?

source of stress. To explore this idea, they developed a scale measuring **daily hassles**—everyday occurrences that annoy and upset people (Kanner & others, 1981; DeLongis & others, 1982). Unlike the Social Readjustment Rating Scale, which measures major life events, the Daily Hassles Scale measures the occurrence of everyday annoyances like losing something, getting stuck in traffic, and even being inconvenienced by lousy weather. You can compare your daily hassles with the top ten hassles reported in a survey of college students and middle-aged adults in Table 13.2.

How important are daily hassles in producing stress? The frequency of daily hassles is linked to both psychological distress and physical symptoms, like headaches and backaches (DeLongis & others, 1988; Weinberger & others, 1987). In fact, the number of daily hassles people experience is a better predictor of physical illness and symptoms than the number of major life events experienced (DeLongis & others, 1982; Burks & Martin, 1985).

Compared to the major impact of being fired or the death of someone near and dear to you, matters like muddy shoes, an avalanche of oranges, and ripped grocery sacks seem pretty insignificant. So why do hassles like missing your bus or locking yourself out of your apartment take such a toll? One explanation is that such minor stressors are *cumulative* (Repetti, 1993; DeLongis & others, 1988). Each hassle may be relatively unimportant in itself, but after a day filled with minor hassles, the effects add up. People feel drained, grumpy, and stressed out—like David in our prologue.

Daily hassles also contribute to the stress produced by major life events (Lazarus & Folkman, 1984). Any major life change, whether positive or negative, can create a ripple effect, generating a host of new daily hassles (Pillow & others, 1996). Getting divorced, for example, often involves finding a new place to live, bickering over who gets what, closing old accounts, opening new accounts, changing insurance plans, and so on. Or beginning a new job can generate new daily hassles like finding transportation to work, juggling child-care responsibilities, and rearranging time schedules.

daily hassles
Everyday, minor events that annoy and upset people.

conflict

A situation in which a person feels pulled between two or more opposing desires, motives, or goals.

Conflict:

Torn Between Two Choices

Another common source of stress is **conflict**—feeling pulled between two opposing desires, motives, or goals (Emmons & King, 1988; Epstein, 1982). There are three basic types of conflict, each with a different potential to be stress-producing. These conflicts are described in terms of *approach* and *avoidance*. An individual is motivated to *approach* desirable or pleasant outcomes and to *avoid* undesirable or unpleasant outcomes.

An *approach-approach conflict* represents a win-win situation—you're faced with a choice between two equally appealing outcomes. Should I go to a movie with Greg or a basketball game with Steve? Should I buy the blue or the red T-shirt? As a rule, approach-approach conflicts are usually easy to resolve and don't produce much stress.

More stressful are *avoidance-avoidance conflicts*—choosing between two unappealing or undesirable outcomes. For example, your history instructor requires either one long term paper or six short essays. Both options are unappealing to you. What do you do? When people feel caught "between a rock and a hard place," a natural response is to delay making a decision (Tversky & Shafir, 1992). By doing so, you're trying to avoid both outcomes. Or you may choose to avoid the decision by bailing out of the situation altogether. In the case of your history course, you may decide to drop it and take it again next semester, hoping that you'll get an instructor who favors multiple-choice exams.

Most stressful are *approach-avoidance conflicts*. Here, a single goal has both desirable and undesirable aspects. For example, suppose you're offered a new job. On the plus side, the higher salary and increased benefits are attractive. On the minus side, you will have to work longer hours. You need the extra money, but keeping up with your college assignments is already a struggle. The result? An approach-avoidance conflict—you're torn between accepting the job and turning it down.

When faced with an approach-avoidance conflict, people often *vacillate,* or repeatedly go back and forth in their minds, unable to decide whether to approach or avoid the goal. From a distance, the desirable aspects of the goal can exert a strong pull. But as you move toward or approach the goal, the negative aspects loom more vividly in your mind, and you pull back (Epstein, 1982). Not surprisingly, people facing approach-avoidance conflicts often find themselves "stuck"—unable to resolve the conflict, but unable to stop thinking about it, either (Emmons & King, 1988). The result is a significant increase in feelings of stress and anxiety.

How can you get "unstuck"? There are several things you can do to resolve an approach-avoidance conflict. First, accept the reality that very few of life's major decisions are likely to be simple, with one alternative standing head and shoulders above the others. Second, see if you can adopt a *partial approach strategy,* in which you test the waters but leave yourself an "out" before making a final decision or commitment.

Third, get as much information as you can about each option. Try to analyze objectively the pros and cons of every option. (We described this strategy of decision making in Chapter 7.) Finally, discuss the issue with a friend or someone outside the conflict. Doing so may help you see other possible rewards or pitfalls that your own analysis might have missed.

CATHY

Once you've gathered and weighed all the information as objectively as you can, make your decision. Sometimes the stress of indecision is far more distressing than coping with the consequences of a decision.

Social and Cultural Sources of Stress

So far we've talked about sources of stress that are unique to the individual. On a broader scale, social conditions can also be an important source of stress. Crowding, crime, unemployment, poverty, racism, inadequate health care, and substandard housing are all associated with increased stress (Graig, 1993; Pearlin, 1993). When people live in an environment that is inherently stressful, they often experience ongoing, or *chronic,* stress (Taylor, 1995).

People in the lowest socioeconomic levels of society tend to have the highest levels of psychological distress, illness, and death (Cohen & Williamson, 1988; Lindheim & Syme, 1983; Kessler, 1979). In a poverty-stricken neighborhood, people are likely to be exposed to more negative life events and to have fewer resources available to cope with those events. Daily hassles are also more common.

Stress can also result when cultures clash (Berry, 1994). For example, Marie sometimes experiences a degree of cultural stress at her job. The company is Japanese-owned, with its headquarters in Tokyo. All the firm's managers and many of its employees are Japanese. Her co-workers often speak Japanese in the office, and Marie has no idea what they're talking about. Marie also feels frustrated and puzzled when a manager appears to publicly agree with a suggestion she makes and then takes a completely different course of action. Such a strategy reflects the Japanese cultural style of avoiding direct social confrontation (Markus & Kitayama, 1991).

As a third-generation American, Marie is accustomed to feeling culturally "at home" in her surroundings. The feelings of being a cultural "outsider" at work are mildly stressful for her. But for refugees, immigrants, and their children, adapting to a new culture can be extremely stress-producing (Shuval, 1993). In Culture and Human Behavior Box 13.1, we describe the stress that can result from adapting to a different culture.

CONCEPT REVIEW 13.1

Defining Stress and Sources of Stress

Determine whether each of the following items is true or false. Rewrite each false statement to correct it.

_____ **1.** According to the biopsychosocial model, physical well-being is wholly determined by stress and social adjustment.

_____ **2.** In the past year, Jan has gotten divorced, changed jobs, moved three times, and lost her closest friend in an auto accident. Because of the number of stress-producing life events Jan has experienced, she is certain to develop a major illness in the next six months.

_____ **3.** The level of stress due to daily hassles is measured by the Social Readjustment Rating Scale.

_____ **4.** The amount of stress you experience depends largely on how you appraise a stressor and your ability to cope with it.

_____ **5.** Lyle can't make up his mind whether to major in cell biology or business. Business is more practical, but he finds the courses boring. He loves the field of cell biology, but he is afraid that he will not be able to find a job in the field. Because he is experiencing an approach-approach conflict, he is likely to experience a low level of stress.

_____ **6.** According to the life events approach, positive life events, such as taking a vacation or getting married, offset the stress caused by negative life events.

CULTURE AND HUMAN BEHAVIOR 13.1

The Stress of Adapting to a New Culture

Refugees and immigrants are often un-prepared for the dramatically different values, language, food, customs, climate, and religions that await them in their new land. Not surprisingly, coping with a new culture can be extremely stress-producing (Johnson & others, 1995). The process of changing one's values and customs as a result of contact with an-other culture is referred to as *accultura-tion.* Thus, the term **acculturative stress** describes the stress that results from the pressure of adapting to a new culture (Williams & Berry, 1991).

Many factors can influence the degree of acculturative stress that a person experiences. For example, when the new society is one that accepts eth-nic and cultural diversity, acculturative stress is reduced (Shuval, 1993). The ease of transition is also enhanced when the person has some familiarity with the new language and customs, advanced education, and social support from friends, family members, and cul-tural associations (Berry, 1994).

Cross-cultural psychologist John Berry has found that the person's atti-tudes about the old and the new culture are important in determining how much acculturative stress is experi-enced. When a person encounters a new cultural environment, they are faced with two fundamental questions:

1. *Should I seek positive relations with the dominant society?* This ques-tion involves the issue of embracing new cultural values and developing positive relationships with members of the dominant culture.

2. *Is my original cultural identity of value to me, and should I try to main-tain it?* This question involves the issue of retaining or rejecting one's original cultural customs and values.

How the person answers these two questions results in one of four possible patterns of acculturation: *integration, assimilation, separation,* or *marginaliza-tion.* The accompanying diagram shows the combination of answers that pro-duces each pattern. In effect, each pat-tern represents a different way of coping with the stress of adapting to a new cul-ture (Berry, 1994; Williams & Berry, 1991). Let's briefly describe each pattern.

Question 2: Is my original cultural identity of value to me, and should I try to maintain it?		Question 1: Should I seek positive relations with the dominant society?	
		Yes	**No**
	Yes	Integration	Separation
	No	Assimilation	Marginalization

Patterns of Adapting to a New Culture

According to cross-cultural psychologist John Berry (1994), there are four basic patterns of adapting to a new culture. Which pattern is followed depends on how the person responds to the two key questions shown.

Integration: Embracing the Old and New Cultures

When an individual answers yes to both questions, he continues to value his original cultural customs and seeks to become part of the dominant society (Berry, 1994). Ideally, the integrated individual feels comfortable in *both* his culture of origin and the culture of the dominant society, moving easily from one to the other (LaFromboise & oth-ers, 1993a). The successfully integrated individual's level of acculturative stress will be low.

Assimilation: Rejecting the Old Culture, Adopting the New Culture

The assimilated individual answers yes to the first question and no to the sec-ond. Hence, the assimilated individual gives up her old cultural identity and tries to become part of the new society. She may adopt the new clothing, reli-gion, and social values of her new envi-ronment and abandon her old customs and language.

Assimilation usually involves a moderate level of stress, partly because it involves a psychological loss—one's previous cultural identity (Berry, 1994). People who follow this pattern also face the possibility of being rejected either by members of the majority culture or by members of the culture of origin (LaFromboise & others, 1993a). The process of learning new behaviors and suppressing old behaviors can also be moderately stressful.

Separation: Rejecting the New Culture, Clinging to the Old Culture

The individual who follows the pattern of separation answers no to the first question and yes to the second. He maintains his cultural identity and avoids contact with the new culture. He may refuse to learn the new language or change his style of dress or eating habits. He may live in a neighborhood that is primarily populated by others of the same ethnic background and limit his socializing to members of his own ethnic group.

In some instances, such with-drawal from the larger society is self-imposed. However, separation can also be the result of discrimination by the dominant society, as when people of a particular ethnic group are discouraged from fully participating in the domi-nant society. Not surprisingly, the level of acculturative stress associated with separation is likely to be very high.

When adult immigrants choose separation, it is often their children who take on the role of negotiating with the new culture. For example, a Viet-namese student in one of our classes described his role as a cultural go-between for his parents. Although his parents have lived in the United States for several years, they have not learned English and interact almost exclusively with other members of the Vietnamese immigrant community. Our student acts as their interpreter when his parents need to see a doctor, deal with govern-ment officials, or speak to the landlord.

Marginalization: Rejecting the Old and New Cultural Identities

Finally, the person who answers no to both questions is out of cultural and psychological contact with *both* her traditional cultural group and the culture of the new society. By taking the path of marginalization, she has lost the important features of her traditional culture, but has not replaced them with a new cultural identity.

The marginalized individual is likely to experience the greatest degree of acculturative stress, feeling as if she doesn't really belong anywhere. Essentially, she is stuck in an unresolved conflict between her traditional culture and her new social environment. She is also likely to experience feelings of alienation and a loss of identity (Berry & Kim, 1988).

Acculturative Stress As this Sikh family crossing a busy street in Chicago has discovered, adapting to a new culture can be a stressful process. What factors can make the transition less stressful? How can the acculturation process be eased?

Physical Effects of Stress:
The Mind–Body Connection

Stress can contribute to health problems both indirectly and directly. How did the work of Cannon and Selye contribute to the early understanding of stress? What endocrine pathways are involved in the fight-or-flight response and the general adaptation syndrome?

From headaches to heart attacks, stress contributes to a wide range of disorders, especially when stress is long-term or chronic (see Pelletier, 1993; Kamarck & Jennings, 1991). Basically, stress appears to undermine physical well-being in two ways: indirectly and directly.

First, stress can *indirectly* affect a person's health by prompting behaviors that jeopardize physical well-being. Many studies have shown that people under chronic stress are more likely to use alcohol, coffee, and cigarettes than people under less stress (e.g., Cohen & Williamson, 1988; Baer & others, 1987). High levels of stress can also interfere with cognitive abilities, like attention, concentration, and memory (Mandler, 1993; Reason, 1988). In turn, such cognitive disruptions can increase the likelihood of accidents and injuries (see Holt, 1993; Quick & Quick, 1984).

Second, stress can *directly* affect physical health by altering body functions, leading to symptoms, illness, or disease. Here's a very common example: When people are under a great deal of stress, their neck and head muscles can contract and tighten, resulting in stress-induced tension headaches (Gannon & others, 1987). But exactly how do stressful events influence bodily processes, such as muscle contractions?

Stress and the Endocrine System

In trying to explain the mind–body connection between stress and health, researchers have focused on how the nervous system, including the brain, interacts with two other important body systems: the endocrine and immune systems. In this section, we'll consider the role that the endocrine system plays in our response to stressful events. In the following section, we'll look at some of the connections between stress and the immune system.

Walter Cannon: Stress and the Fight-or-Flight Response

Imagine hiking alone on an isolated trail in the middle of Yellowstone National Park, lost in your thoughts. A slight movement in the brush on the side of the trail catches your attention. You glance over. Standing only a few yards away from you is a 1,000-pound male moose with a full rack of antlers. That's what happened to your author Don when he was a college student and working in Yellowstone for the summer. Actually, there wasn't one moose. There were five—a massive male and four somewhat smaller female moose.

As Don froze in his tracks, his adrenaline surged. Heartbeat, blood pressure, and pulse skyrocketed. His pupils dilated, and his muscles tensed to the point of trembling. Knowing that the moose could easily charge and kill him, Don inched backward along the trail. The movement caused one of the female moose to bolt. In the pandemonium that ensued, Don ran frantically back down the trail. Thankfully, the five moose thundered off through the pines in the opposite direction.

Whether it's a moose or a mugger, any kind of immediate threat to your well-being is a stress-producing experience that triggers a cascade of changes in your body. As we've noted in previous chapters, this rapidly occurring chain of internal physical reactions is called the **fight-or-flight response.** Collectively, these changes prepare us either to fight or to take flight from an immediate threat. (Notice that Don chose the "flight" option.)

The fight-or-flight response was first described by American physiologist **Walter Cannon** (1871–1945), one of the earliest contributors to stress research. Cannon (1932) found that the fight-or-flight response involved both the sympathetic nervous system and the endocrine system (see Chapter 2).

With the perception of a threat, the hypothalamus and lower brain structures activate the sympathetic nervous system (see left side of Figure 13.2). The sympathetic nervous system stimulates the adrenal medulla to secrete hormones called **catecholamines,** including *adrenaline* and *noradrenaline*. Circulating through the blood, catecholamines trigger the rapid and intense bodily changes associated with the fight-or-flight response. Once the threat is removed, the high level of bodily arousal subsides gradually, usually within about 20 to 60 minutes.

As a short-term reaction, the fight-or-flight response helps ensure survival by swiftly mobilizing internal physical resources to defensively attack or flee an immediate threat. Without question, the fight-or-flight response is very useful if you're suddenly faced with a life-threatening situation, such as a guy pointing a gun at you in a deserted parking lot. However, when exposure to an unavoidable threat is prolonged, the intense arousal of the fight-or-flight response can also become prolonged. Under these conditions, Cannon believed, the fight-or-flight response could prove harmful to physical health.

Hans Selye: Stress and the General Adaptation Syndrome

Does the man shown in the photograph at the right look like someone who had met and conquered stress? **Hans Selye** (1907–1982) was the Canadian endocrinologist whose pioneering scientific investigations confirmed Cannon's

---

fight-or-flight response
A rapidly occurring chain of internal physical reactions that prepare people either to fight or take flight from an immediate threat.

catecholamines
Hormones secreted by the adrenal medulla that cause rapid physiological arousal; include adrenaline and noradrenaline.

general adaptation syndrome
Selye's term for the three-stage progression of physical changes that occur when an organism is exposed to intense and prolonged stress. The three stages are alarm, resistance, and exhaustion.

Pathway 1: Acute stress

Hypothalamus

↓

Sympathetic nervous system

↓

Adrenal medulla

↓

Secretion of catecholamines:
• Increases respiration
• Increases heart rate
• Increases blood pressure
• Increases blood flow to the muscles
• Digestion is inhibited
• Pupils dilate

Pathway 2: Prolonged stress

Hypothalamus

↓

Pituitary

↓

ACTH release

↓

Adrenal cortex

↓

Secretion of corticosteroids:
• Increases release of stored energy
• Reduces inflammation
• Reduces immune system response

FIGURE 13.2 Endocrine System Pathways in Stress Two different endocrine system pathways are involved in the response to stress. Walter Cannon identified the endocrine pathway shown on the left side of this diagram; this is the pathway involved in the fight-or-flight response to immediate threats. Hans Selye identified the endocrine pathway shown on the right side. This second endocrine pathway plays an important role in dealing with prolonged or chronic stressors.

suggestion that prolonged stress could be physically harmful. In 1956 Selye summarized his findings in a book called *The Stress of Life.* The book became a best seller, and *stress* became a household word.

Most of Selye's pioneering research was done with rats that were exposed to prolonged stressors, like electric shock, extreme heat or cold, or forced exercise. Regardless of the condition that Selye used to produce prolonged stress, he found the same pattern of physical changes in the rats. First, the adrenal glands became enlarged. Second, stomach ulcers and loss of weight occurred. And third, there was shrinkage of the thymus gland and lymph glands, two key components of the immune system. Selye believed that these distinct physical changes represented the essential effects of stress—the body's response to any demand placed on it.

Selye discovered that if the bodily "wear and tear" of the stress-producing event continued, the effects became evident in three progressive stages. He called these stages the **general adaptation syndrome.** During the initial *alarm stage,* intense arousal occurs as the body mobilizes internal physical resources to meet the demands of the stress-producing event. Selye (1976) found that the rapidly occurring changes during the alarm stage are the result of the release of catecholamines by the adrenal medulla, as Cannon had previously described.

In the *resistance stage,* the body actively tries to resist or adjust to the continuing stressful situation. The intense arousal of the alarm stage diminishes, but physiological arousal remains above normal and resistance to new stressors is impaired.

If the stress-producing event persists, the *exhaustion stage* may occur. In this third stage, the symptoms of the alarm stage reappear, only this time irreversibly. As the body's energy reserves become depleted, adaptation begins to break down, leading to exhaustion, physical disorders, and, potentially, death.

A Pioneer in Stress Research Does this man look stressed out? With his tie off and his feet up, Canadian endocrinologist Hans Selye looks the very picture of relaxation. Selye's research at the University of Montreal documented the physical effects of exposure to prolonged stress. His popular book, *The Stress of Life,* helped make stress a household word.

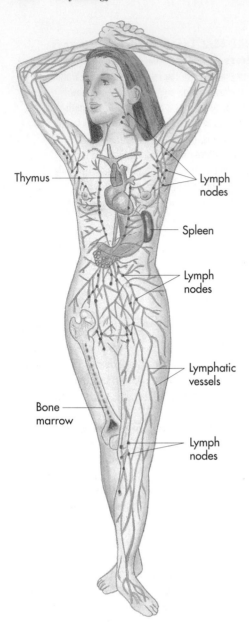

Thymus

Lymph
nodes

Spleen

Lymph
nodes

Lymphatic
vessels

Bone
marrow

Lymph
nodes

FIGURE 13.3 The Immune System
Your immune system battles bacteria, viruses, and
other foreign invaders that try to set up house-
keeping in your body. The specialized white blood
cells that fight infection are manufactured in the
bone marrow and are stored in the thymus,
spleen, and lymph nodes until needed.

Lymphocytes in Action In this color-enhanced
photo, you can see white blood cells, or lymphocytes, attacking and ingesting the beadlike chain
of streptococcus bacteria, which can cause diseases
like pneumonia and scarlet fever.

Selye (1956, 1976) found that prolonged stress activates a different endocrine pathway than the one that Cannon had identified in the fight-or-
flight response. Look again at Figure 13.2. As shown on the right side of the
drawing, this second endocrine pathway involves the hypothalamus, the
pituitary gland, and the adrenal cortex, which is the outer portion of the
adrenal gland. In response to a stressor, the hypothalamus signals the pituitary gland to secrete a hormone called *adrenocorticotropic hormone*, abbreviated *ACTH*. In turn, ACTH stimulates the adrenal cortex to release
stress-related hormones called **corticosteroids,** the most important being
cortisol (see Krishnan & others, 1991; Ritchie & Nemeroff, 1991).

In the short run, the corticosteroids provide several benefits, helping protect the body against the harm caused by stressors (see Baum & others, 1987;
Gray, 1987). For example, corticosteroids reduce inflammation of body tissues and enhance muscle tone in the heart and blood vessels. However, unlike the effects of catecholamines, which tend to diminish rather quickly,
corticosteroids have long-lasting effects. If a stressor is prolonged for days,
weeks, or months, the level of corticosteroids may remain elevated. What was
beneficial in the short run can become harmful in the long run. Continued
high levels of corticosteroids, especially cortisol, can weaken important body
systems, lowering immunity and increasing susceptibility to physical symptoms and illness (see Ader & others, 1991; Solomon & others, 1985).

Selye's pioneering studies are widely regarded as the cornerstone of modern stress research (Taylor, 1995). His description of the general adaptation
syndrome firmly established some of the critical biological links between
stress-producing events and their potential impact on physical health. But as
you'll see in the next section, the endocrine system is only part of the equation in the mind–body connection between stress and health.

Stress and the Immune System

*Stress can undermine health by impairing the immune system.
How did the work of Ader and Cohen challenge the existing view
of the immune system? What is psychoneuroimmunology? How
does the immune system interact with the nervous system? What
kinds of stressors affect immune system functioning?*

Stress can diminish the effectiveness of the immune system. The **immune
system** is your body's surveillance system. It detects and battles foreign invaders, such as bacteria, viruses, and tumor cells. Your immune system comprises several organs, including bone marrow, the spleen, the thymus, and
lymph nodes (see Figure 13.3). The most important elements of the immune
system are **lymphocytes**—the specialized white blood cells that fight bacteria, viruses, and other foreign invaders. Lymphocytes are initially manufactured in the bone marrow. From the bone marrow, they migrate to other
immune system organs, such as the thymus and spleen, where they develop
more fully and are stored until needed (see Tizard, 1992; O'Leary, 1990).

Until the 1970s, the immune system
was thought to be completely independent of other body systems. Many scientists believed that the nervous system,
the endocrine system, and psychological
processes had no impact on immune system functioning. As you'll see in this section, the scientific view of the immune
system has changed dramatically in the
last few decades.

Ader and Cohen: Conditioning the Immune System

The notion that the immune system operated independently was challenged in the mid-1970s, when psychologist **Robert Ader** (b. 1932) teamed up with immunologist Nicholas Cohen. As Ader (1993b) recalled, "You have to understand that as a psychologist, I was not aware of the general position of immunology that there were no connections between the brain and the immune system." In their landmark study, Ader and Cohen (1975) demonstrated that immune system functions could be influenced by the brain. They did so by showing that the immune system response in rats could be classically conditioned.

Conditioning the Immune System
Psychologist Robert Ader (left) teamed with immunologist Nicholas Cohen (right) and demonstrated that immune system responses could be classically conditioned. Ader and Cohen's groundbreaking research helped lead to the new field of psychoneuroimmunology — the study of the interconnections between psychological processes, the nervous system, and the immune system.

Using the same basic procedure that Pavlov used to condition dogs to salivate in response to the sound of a bell (see Chapter 5), Ader and Cohen (1975) paired saccharin-flavored water with a drug that suppressed immune system functioning. After being paired with the immune-suppressing drug, the saccharin-flavored water *alone* suppressed the rat's immune system. As Ader (1993b) explained, "In effect, we had demonstrated that learning processes could influence immune responses. The experiment was a direct and rather dramatic demonstration of a relationship between nervous system function and immune function."

Ader and Cohen's landmark study was important for two reasons. First, it challenged the prevailing scientific view that the immune system operated independently of the brain and psychological processes. Since the publication of Ader and Cohen's research, hundreds of other studies have demonstrated that immune system responses can be conditioned to various stimuli (see Ader & Cohen, 1993, 1991).

Second, Ader and Cohen's study triggered interest in other possible influences on the immune system, including the effects of stress and emotional states. By stimulating diverse lines of research, Ader and Cohen's study helped establish a new interdisciplinary field called psychoneuroimmunology (Maier & others, 1994). **Psychoneuroimmunology** is the scientific study of the interconnections among psychological processes (*psycho-*), the nervous and endocrine systems (*-neuro-*), and the immune system (*-immunology*).

In the last decade, psychoneuroimmunology researchers have made many important discoveries (see Vitkovic, 1995). First, they discovered that the central nervous system and the immune system are *directly* linked. Sympathetic nervous system fibers go into virtually every organ of the immune system, where they directly influence the production and functioning of lymphocytes.

Second, the surfaces of lymphocytes contain receptor sites for neurotransmitters and hormones, including catecholamines and cortisol. Thus, rather than operating independently, the activities of lymphocytes and the immune system are directly influenced by neurotransmitters, hormones, and other chemical messengers from the nervous and endocrine systems (Ader & others, 1991, 1990).

Third, psychoneuroimmunologists have discovered that lymphocytes themselves *produce* neurotransmitters and hormones. These neurotransmitters and hormones, in turn, influence the nervous and endocrine systems. In other words, there is ongoing interaction and communication among the nervous system, the endocrine system, and the immune system. Each system influences *and* is influenced by the other systems (Ader & others, 1995, 1991).

corticosteroids
Hormones released by the adrenal cortex that play a key role in the body's response to long-term stressors.

immune system
Body system that produces specialized white blood cells that protect the body from viruses, bacteria, and tumor cells.

lymphocytes
Specialized white blood cells that are responsible for immune defenses.

psychoneuroimmunology
An interdisciplinary field that studies the interconnections among psychological processes, nervous and endocrine system functions, and the immune system.

Stressors That Can Influence the Immune System

When researchers began studying how stress affects the immune system, they initially focused on extremely stressful events (see Kiecolt-Glaser & Glaser, 1993). For example, researchers looked at how the immune system was affected by such intense stressors as the reentry and splashdown of returning *Skylab* astronauts, being forced to stay awake for days, and going without food for over a week (Kimzey, 1975; Leach & Rambaut, 1974; Palmblad & others, 1979). Each of these highly stressful events, it turned out, was associated with reduced immune system functioning.

Ron Glaser & Janice Kiecolt-Glaser Two of the leading researchers in psycho-neuroimmunology are psychologist Janice Kiecolt-Glaser and her husband, immunologist Ron Glaser. Their research has shown that the effectiveness of the immune system can be lowered by many common stressors—from marital arguments to caring for sick relatives.

Could immune system functioning also be affected by more common negative life events, such as the death of a spouse, divorce, or marital separation? In a word, yes. Researchers consistently found that the stress caused by the end or disruption of important interpersonal relationships impairs immune function, putting the individuals involved at greater risk for health problems (e.g., Kiecolt-Glaser & others, 1987a; Irwin & others, 1987). And perhaps not surprisingly, chronic stressors that continue for years, such as caring for a family member with Alzheimer's disease, also diminish immune system functioning (Kiecolt-Glaser & others, 1991, 1987b).

What about the ordinary stressors of life, such as the pressure of exams? Do they affect immune system functioning? Since 1982, psychologist **Janice Kiecolt-Glaser** (b. 1951) and her husband, immunologist Ronald Glaser, have collected immunological and psychological data from medical students. Several times each academic year, the medical students face three-day examination periods. Kiecolt-Glaser and Glaser (1993, 1991) have consistently found that even the rather commonplace stress of exams adversely affects the immune system.

**Red
Yellow
Green
Blue
Red
Blue
Yellow
Green
Blue
Red**

FIGURE 13.4 The Stroop Color-Word Interference Test Quickly name the ink colors of the words shown in the margin. Researcher Elizabeth Bachen and her colleagues (1992) used a computerized version of the test as a brief stressor. (Adapted from Stroop, 1935/1992, and Bachen & others, 1992.)

Interestingly, recent studies indicate that even brief exposure to a psychological stressor, such as performing a frustrating task for 30 minutes or less, can temporarily alter immune response (Delahanty & others, 1996; Cohen & Herbert, 1996). For example, researcher Elizabeth Bachen and her colleagues (1992) had participants spend about 20 minutes responding to the Stroop Color-Word Interference Test, a frustrating task that you can try for yourself in Figure 13.4. In comparison to control subjects who simply sat quietly for the same length of time, the experimental subjects who took the Stroop Test showed impairment immediately afterward in several aspects of immune system functioning. Even stressors that only last for a matter of minutes, it seems, can alter immune functioning.

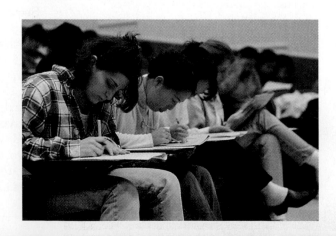

Can Exams Be Hazardous to Your Health? From studies of medical students, Kiecolt-Glaser and Glaser have shown that the common student stressor of taking exams can lower the effectiveness of the immune system.

Taken together, the evidence strongly suggests that a wide variety of stressors are associated with diminished immune system functioning, putting us at greater risk for health problems. In Focus Box 13.2 describes a compelling study that demonstrates the relationship between stress and a health risk to which we are all frequently exposed: the common cold virus.

IN FOCUS 13.2

Stress and the Common Cold

Does stress increase your susceptibility to the common cold? That's certainly what many people believe. But if you think critically about the matter, other explanations are possible. For example, it may be that high-stressed people interact with more people than low-stressed people. In turn, this would mean that high-stressed people have more opportunities for exposure to cold viruses. Or it could be that stressed-out people engage in more health-compromising behaviors, such as smoking, not exercising, eating poorly, and not getting enough sleep.

Psychologist Sheldon Cohen and his colleagues (1993, 1991) tackled such issues in a carefully controlled experiment. Over 400 healthy volunteers underwent a thorough medical examination and completed questionnaires assessing their stress levels and health behaviors. The participants were then given nasal drops containing either a cold virus or salt water. For two days before and seven days after receiving the drops, the participants were quarantined together in apartments. Each day during the study, the participants were medically examined for any signs or symptoms of a cold. Blood samples were also monitored for evidence of infection.

The results? Of the people exposed to cold virus, one factor stood out in determining the rate of infection: the level of stress. The researchers found an almost perfect relationship between the level of stress and the rate of respiratory infection and colds. Put simply, the higher the psychological stress score, the higher the rate of respiratory infection and colds.

Could it be that other factors, such as health-compromising behaviors, were underlying the stress–illness connection? Not at all. The stress–illness effect held even when the researchers took into account the number of participants housed together, whether roommates were also infectious, and the participants' age, sex, smoking, alcohol consumption, exercise, diet, or quality of sleep. In other words, *none* of these factors could account for the relationship between stress and increased susceptibility to infection (Cohen & others, 1993, 1991).

So how does stress increase our susceptibility to colds and infections? Basically, stress reduces the effectiveness of the immune system and its ability to fight off viruses, bacteria, and other foreign invaders (see Kiecolt-Glaser & Glaser, 1993, 1991).

Relationship Between Stress and Susceptibility to a Cold Virus
In a carefully controlled study, psychologist Sheldon Cohen and his colleagues (1991) assessed over 400 healthy volunteers for their level of stress and health behaviors. After exposing the participants to a cold virus, the researchers noted how many of the participants developed colds. As you can see in the graph, the researchers found that level of stress was closely related to the development of colds.

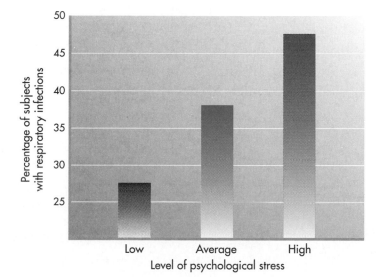

While stress-related immune system decreases may heighten our susceptibility to health problems, exposure to stressors does not automatically translate into poorer health. Your physical health is affected by the interaction of many factors, such as your unique genetic makeup, nutrition, exercise, personal habits, and access to medical care. Also required, of course, is exposure to bacteria, viruses, and other disease-causing agents. As psychologists Sheldon Cohen and Gail Williamson (1988) point out, "Even the most severe stress cannot result in infection without the presence of an infectious agent."

It's also important to keep in mind that the stress-induced decreases in immune functioning that have been demonstrated experimentally are often small. As psychoneuroimmunology researchers are careful to point out, these small decreases in immune function may not translate into an added health risk for most people. As Kiecolt-Glaser and Glaser (1993) explain:

> Our best understanding at this point is that the people most likely to become ill in response to stress are probably those whose immune systems are already compromised to some extent, either by a disease like AIDS or by a natural process like aging. These people start out with poorer immunological defenses, so that small changes associated with stress could have more important consequences. But even young, generally healthy people may find themselves getting sick more often if they are subject to severe or ongoing, long-term stress.

Finally, the simple fact is that some people are more vulnerable to the negative effects of stress than others (Adler & Matthews, 1994). Why? As you'll see in the next section, researchers have found that a wide variety of psychological factors can influence people's reactions to stressors.

CONCEPT REVIEW 13.2

The Physical Effects of Stress

1. Walking home late at night, Yvette is startled and frightened when a prankster sets off a firecracker right behind her. Walter Cannon described Yvette's physiological response as the
   a. startle-stop-stare response
   b. fight-or-flight response
   c. general adaptation response
   d. learned helplessness response

2. Shelley has just been unexpectedly called into her manager's office and told that she is going to be laid off from her job next week. Which phase of the general adaptation syndrome is Shelley most likely experiencing?
   a. alarm stage
   b. resistance stage
   c. exhaustion stage
   d. fight-or-flight stage

3. Although it was very difficult at first, Daniel seems to have adjusted to the daily routine of caring for his father, who has Alzheimer's disease. Nonetheless, Daniel seems tense, and his ability to cope with new stressors is diminished. Daniel is most likely in the _____ stage of the general adaptation syndrome.

   a. alarm
   b. resistance
   c. exhaustion
   d. fight-or-flight

4. Loraine has worked very hard, and under much pressure, for many months to complete her dissertation and prepare for her Ph.D. defense. According to Selye's model, it is very likely that Loraine's adrenal cortex has released higher than usual levels of _____ during this prolonged period of stress in her life.
   a. catecholamines
   b. lymphocytes
   c. teratogens
   d. corticosteroids

5. Dr. Yen believes that psychological processes, the nervous and endocrine systems, and the immune system all interact—that is, each system influences and is influenced by the other systems. Dr. Yen is probably a
   a. quack
   b. cognitive psychologist
   c. psychoneuroimmunologist
   d. systems psychologist

Psychological Factors That Influence Our Response to Stress

Researchers have identified several psychological factors that can affect our response to stress. How do feelings of control, explanatory style, and chronic negative emotions influence stress and health? What is Type A behavior, and what role does hostility play in its relationship to health?

People can vary a great deal in the way they respond to the same stressor, whether it's a rush-hour fender bender or an ominous letter from the Internal Revenue Service demanding more information about a tax return. In part, individual differences in reacting to stressors are due to how people appraise a stressful event and the resources that they have available to cope with the stressful event. But as psychologists and other researchers have learned, several other factors can influence a particular person's response to stress. As you'll see in this section, psychological factors play a key role in how people react to stressors and, ultimately, in the impact that stress can have on health.

Personal Control

Suppose that you've volunteered for a psychology experiment. Sitting in the lab, you're told that you will experience some painful, but harmless, shocks. However, if the shocks become too painful, you can stop them by pushing a button on the panel in front of you. In another room, one of your classmates has volunteered for the same experiment. Unlike you, he does not have a "stop" button. You have some control over the situation, while your classmate does not. Which of you is likely to experience more stress?

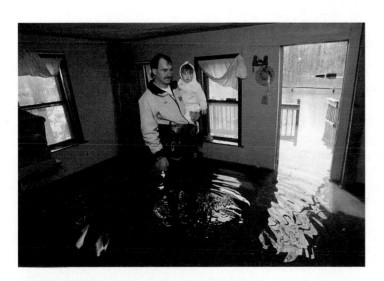

Uncontrollable Stressors There was nothing this family could do to protect their home from catastrophic floodwaters. Psychological research has found that stressors that are beyond our control are especially damaging to physical and mental health.

Psychological research has consistently shown that having a sense of control over a stressful situation reduces the impact of stressors and decreases feelings of anxiety and depression (e.g., Thompson & Spacapan, 1991; Taylor & others, 1991; Neufeld & Paterson, 1989). In fact, those who can control a stress-producing event often show no more psychological distress or physical arousal than people who are not exposed to the stressor (Taylor, 1989; Laudenslager & others, 1983).

In a series of studies with elderly nursing home residents, psychologists Judith Rodin and Ellen Langer (1977) demonstrated the importance of a sense of control. One group of residents—the "high control" group—were given the opportunity to make choices about their daily activities and to exercise control over their environment. For example, they were allowed to select a plant for their room, and were told that they would be responsible for caring for it. They were also given responsibility for making decisions about other matters, such as when they would watch a movie, where they would receive visitors, and so forth.

In contrast, the "low control" group had little control over their daily activities. Decisions were made by others. A staff member selected a plant for each resident's room, and other staff members took care of it. The staff also decided what night the residents saw the weekly movie, what they were served for breakfast, and so on.

Rodin and Langer found that having the freedom to make choices about daily activities and to exercise control over even minor aspects of their environment had powerful effects on the nursing home residents. Eighteen months later, the high-control residents were more active, alert, sociable, and healthier than the low-control residents. The high-control group was also more likely to be alive: twice as many of the low-control residents had died (Rodin & Langer, 1977; Langer & Rodin, 1976).

Now the obvious question: How does a sense of control affect health? If you feel that you can control a stressor by taking steps to minimize or avoid it, you will experience less stress, both subjectively and physiologically (Thompson & Spacapan, 1991). Having a sense of personal control also works to our benefit by enhancing positive emotions, such as self-confidence, feelings of self-efficacy, autonomy, and self-reliance (Burger, 1992). In contrast, feeling a lack of control over events produces all the hallmarks of the stress response. Levels of catecholamines and corticosteroids increase, and the effectiveness of immune system functioning decreases (see Rodin, 1986).

The perceptions of personal control in a stressful situation must be *realistic* to be adaptive (Helgeson, 1992; Taylor & others, 1991). Studies of people with chronic diseases, like heart disease and arthritis, have shown that unrealistic perceptions of personal control contribute to stress and poor adjustment (Affleck & others, 1987a, 1987b). But, even in low-control situations, there is often some aspect of the overall situation that people can realistically influence.

For example, Suzanne Thompson and her colleagues (1993) found that the best-adjusted cancer patients accepted the fact that they could not realistically control the course of their disease. Rather, they focused on what they could realistically do to control the *consequences* of the disease. They exercised control by managing their emotions, seeking medical information, improving their personal relationships, and changing their diet. By doing so, they lowered their subjective level of stress and increased their sense of personal well-being.

How Do You Explain Your Setbacks and Failures? Everyone experiences setbacks, rejection, and failure occasionally. The way you explain your failures has a significant impact on motivation and mental and physical health. If this jewelry store owner explained the failure of his business by blaming a temporary downturn in the economy, he might be more likely to try again in the future.

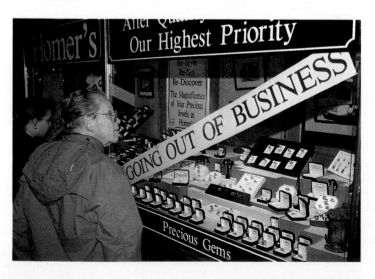

Explanatory Style:
Optimism Versus Pessimism

Everyone experiences defeat, rejection, or failure at some point in their lives. Yet despite repeated failures, rejections, or defeats, some people persist in their efforts. When our friend David was unemployed, for example, he sent out hundreds of résumés and worked at one temporary job after another, from loading boxes in a warehouse to working in a gas station. In contrast, some people give up in the face of failure and setbacks. What distinguishes between those who persist and those who give up?

Psychologist **Martin Seligman** (1991, 1992) believes that how people characteristically explain their failures and defeats makes the difference. People who have an **optimistic explanatory style** tend to use *external, unstable,* and *specific* explanations for negative events. In contrast, people who have a **pessimistic explanatory style** use *internal, stable,* and *global* explanations for negative events. Pessimists are also inclined to believe that no amount of personal effort will improve their situation. Not surprisingly, pessimists tend to experience more stress than optimists.

Let's look at these two explanatory styles in action. Optimistic Olive sees an attractive guy at a party and starts across the room to introduce herself and strike up a conversation. As she approaches him, the guy glances at her, then abruptly turns away. Hurt by the obvious snub, Optimistic Olive retreats to the buffet table. Munching on some fried zucchini, she mulls the matter over in her mind. At the same party, Pessimistic Pete sees an attractive female across the room and approaches her. He, too, gets a cold shoulder and retreats to the chips and clam dip. Standing at opposite ends of the buffet table, here is what each of them is thinking:

> **Optimistic Olive:** What's *his* problem? (*External* explanation: the optimist blames other people or external circumstances)

> **Pessimistic Pete:** I must have said the wrong thing. She probably saw me stick my elbow in the clam dip before I walked over. (*Internal* explanation: the pessimist blames self)

> **Optimistic Olive:** I'm really not looking my best tonight. I've just got to get more sleep. (*Unstable, temporary* explanation)

> **Pessimistic Pete:** Let's face it, I'm a pretty boring guy and really not very good-looking. (*Stable, permanent* explanation)

> **Optimistic Olive:** He looks pretty preoccupied. Maybe he's waiting for his girlfriend to arrive. Or his boyfriend! Ha! (*Specific* explanations)

> **Pessimistic Pete:** Women never give me a second look, probably because I dress like a nerd and I never know what to say to them. (*Global, pervasive* explanation)

> **Optimistic Olive:** Whoa! Who's that hunk over there?! Okay, Olive, turn on the charm! Here goes! (*Perseverance* after a rejection)

> **Pessimistic Pete:** Maybe I'll just hold down this corner of the buffet table . . . or go home and soak up some TV. (*Passivity* and *withdrawal* after a rejection)

Most people, of course, are neither as completely optimistic as Olive nor as totally pessimistic as Pete in all areas of their lives. Instead, they fall somewhere along the spectrum of optimism and pessimism, and their explanatory style may vary somewhat in different situations (Peterson & Bossio, 1993). Even so, a person's characteristic explanatory style, particularly for negative events, is relatively stable across the lifespan (Burns & Seligman, 1989).

Like personal control, explanatory style is related to health consequences. One study showed that explanatory style in early adulthood predicted physical health status decades later. On the basis of interviews conducted at age twenty-five, explanatory style was evaluated for a large group of Harvard graduates. At the time of the interviews, all the young men were in excellent physical and mental health. Thirty-five years later, however, those whom the interviews showed had an optimistic explanatory style were in significantly better health and were more likely to be alive (Peterson & others, 1988). Other studies have shown that a pessimistic explanatory style is associated with poorer physical health, including increased occurrences of infectious disease (Peterson & Seligman, 1987).

Chronic Negative Emotions:
The Hazards of Being Grouchy

Everyone experiences an occasional bad mood. However, some people almost always seem to be unhappy campers—they frequently experience bad moods and negative emotions (Marshall & others, 1992; Watson & Pennebaker, 1989). Are people who are prone to chronic negative emotions more likely to suffer health problems?

optimistic explanatory style
Accounting for negative events or situations with external, unstable, and specific explanations.

pessimistic explanatory style
Accounting for negative events or situations with internal, stable, and global explanations.

Howard S. Friedman and Stephanie Booth-Kewley (1987) systematically compared over 100 studies investigating the potential links between personality factors and five chronic diseases: asthma, arthritis, ulcers, headaches, and coronary heart disease. Their analysis revealed that habitual feelings of anxiety, depression, anger, and hostility are related to the development of chronic diseases. They proposed that a generic "disease-prone personality" may exist that predisposes a person to develop any one of a wide variety of diseases.

How might chronic negative emotions predispose people to develop disease? Not surprisingly, tense, angry, and unhappy people experience more stress than happier people. They also report more frequent and more intense daily hassles than people who are generally in a positive mood (Bolger & Zuckerman, 1995; Bolger & Schilling, 1991).

CALVIN AND HOBBS

Do these unhappy campers actually *experience* more daily problems? Not necessarily. Psychologists Christine A. Marco and Jerry Suls (1993) found that chronically tense, angry, and unhappy people do not necessarily experience a greater number of daily hassles and problems than happy people. However, they do react much more intensely, and with far greater distress, to the stressful events that they do encounter.

Habitually grouchy people also recover much more slowly from the distress evoked by hassles and problems, and their bad moods last longer. In fact, grouches are more likely to be in a bad mood even in the absence of stressful events (Marco & Suls, 1993). All of this adds up to greater amounts of stress for chronically angry, tense, and unhappy people. In turn, chronically unhappy people are at greater risk of stress-related illnesses and symptoms (Friedman, 1991).

What about people who occasionally experience bad moods? Are transient negative moods also associated with health risks? One series of studies investigated the relationship between daily mood and immune system functioning. Participants were given oral doses of a foreign protein to which they produced antibodies for three months (Stone & others, 1994, 1987). During the study, they recorded their mood every day. On the days that they experienced negative events and moods, the effectiveness of their immune system dipped, as measured by a lower level of antibodies produced. But their immune system improved on the days when they experienced positive events and good moods.

Type A Behavior and Hostility

The concept of Type A behavior originated about thirty years ago, when two cardiologists, Meyer Friedman and Ray Rosenman, noticed that many of their heart disease patients shared certain traits. They were typically ambitious, competitive, hard-working, impatient, tense, and hostile. They always seemed to be in a hurry, often doing two or three things at once.

The original formulation of the **Type A behavior pattern** included a cluster of three characteristics: (1) an exaggerated sense of time urgency, often trying to do more and more in less and less time; (2) a general sense of hostility, frequently displaying anger and irritation; and (3) intense ambition

Type A behavior pattern
A behavioral and emotional style characterized by a sense of time urgency, hostility, and competitiveness.

and competitiveness. In contrast, people who were more relaxed and laid back were classified as displaying the *Type B behavior pattern* (Rosenman & Chesney, 1982; Janisse & Dyck, 1988).

Friedman and Rosenman (1974) interviewed and classified more than 3,000 middle-aged, healthy men as either Type A or Type B. For over eight years, they tracked the health of these men. Their findings? Type A men were twice as likely to develop heart disease as the Type B men. This held true even when the Type A men did not display other known risk factors for heart disease, such as smoking, high blood pressure, and elevated levels of cholesterol in their blood. The conclusion seemed clear: Type A behavior pattern was a significant risk factor for heart disease.

Rosenman and Friedman's findings received a great deal of attention in the popular press, and the phrase "Type A behavior" came into wide usage. Type A scales appeared in popular magazines. Are you an ambitious, competitive workaholic? Then you're probably showing Type A behavior. The pat advice: Slow down and don't work so hard, or you'll have a heart attack. In short, anyone with a lot of energy and ambition was accused of being a "Type A" and told to take it easy.

Although early results linking the Type A behavior pattern to heart disease were impressive, studies soon began to appear in which Type A behavior did *not* reliably predict the development of heart disease (see Williams, 1989). These findings led researchers to question whether the different components of the Type A behavior pattern were equally hazardous to health. After all, many people thrive on hard work, especially when they enjoy their jobs (Friedman, 1991). And high achievers don't necessarily suffer from health problems (Robbins & others, 1991).

When researchers focused on the association between heart disease and the separate components of the Type A behavior pattern—time urgency, achievement striving, and hostility—an important distinction began to emerge. Feeling a sense of time urgency and being competitive or achievement-oriented did *not* seem to be associated with the development of heart disease. Instead, the critical component that emerged as the strongest predictor of cardiac disease was hostility. *Hostility* refers to the tendency to feel anger, annoyance, resentment, and contempt, and to hold negative beliefs about human nature in general. Hostile people are also prone to believing that the disagreeable behavior of others is intentionally directed against them. Thus, hostile people tend to be suspicious, mistrustful, cynical, and pessimistic (Barefoot, 1992).

Little wonder, then, that hostile men and women are much more likely than other people to develop heart disease. In one study that covered a twenty-five-year span, hostile men were five times as likely to develop heart disease and nearly seven times as likely to die as nonhostile men (Barefoot & others, 1983). The results of this prospective study are shown in Figure 13.5 on the next page.

The Type A Behavior Pattern The original formulation of the Type A behavior pattern included hostility, ambition, and a sense of time urgency. Type A's always seem to be in a hurry, hate wasting time, and often try to do two or more things at once. Both the man on the far left and the man on the far right would probably qualify as Type A people.

Other studies have tracked individuals over time and found that hostility predicts the development of coronary heart disease independently of the other Type A characteristics (see T. Q. Miller & others, 1996).

Researchers have also found that the level of hostility predicts the severity of heart disease: the higher the hostility, the greater the severity of coronary disease (Barefoot, 1992). In fact, high hostility levels increase the likelihood of dying from *all* natural causes, including cancer (T. Q. Miller & others, 1996; Koskenvuo & others, 1988).

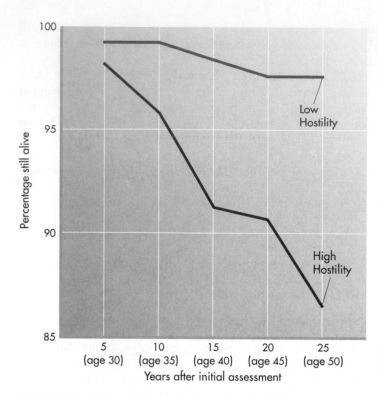

FIGURE 13.5 Hostility and Mortality
Beginning when they were in medical school, over 250 doctors were monitored for their health status for twenty-five years. In this prospective study, those who had scored high in hostility in medical school were seven times more likely to die by age fifty than were those who had scored low in hostility.
(Based on Barefoot & others, 1983, p. 61.)

How does hostility predispose people to heart disease and other health problems? First, hostile Type As tend to react more intensely to a stressor than other people do (Lyness, 1993). They experience larger increases in blood pressure, heart rate, and the production of stress-related hormones.

Second, since hostile men and women are prone to get angry more often than others, they also experience stress more frequently (Lundberg & others, 1989). Finally, because of their cynical attitudes and aggressive behavior, hostile people experience more frequent and more severe negative life events and daily hassles.

In combination, then, the emotional style, attitudes, behaviors, and physiological reactivity of hostile people create more stress in their lives and, ultimately, more stress-related health consequences for them (T. Smith, 1992).

In general, the research evidence demonstrating the role of personality factors in the development of stress-related diseases is impressive. However, it's important to keep in mind that personality characteristics are just some of the risk factors involved in the overall picture of health and disease (Cohen & Herbert, 1996; Adler & Matthews, 1994). We look at this issue in more detail in Critical Thinking Box 13.3, "Do Personality Factors *Cause* Disease?"

CONCEPT REVIEW 13.3

Psychological Factors and Stress

What psychological characteristic is best illustrated by each of the examples below? Choose from the following:

A. High level of personal control
B. Optimistic explanatory style
C. Type A behavior pattern
D. Type B behavior pattern
E. Pessimistic explanatory style
F. Chronic negative emotions

_____ **1.** No matter what happens to her, Lucy is dissatisfied and grumpy. She constantly complains about her health, her job, and how lousy her life is. She dislikes most of the people she meets.

_____ **2.** Stanley is a laid-back, easygoing, and friendly delivery person. He loves his job because its slow pace gives him time to talk to people on his route.

_____ **3.** Cheryl was despondent when she received a low grade on her algebra test. She said,

"I never do well on exams because I'm not very smart. I might as well drop out of school now before I flunk out."

_____ **4.** In order to deal with the high levels of stress associated with returning to college full-time, Pat selected her courses carefully, arranged her work and study schedules to make the best use of her time, and scheduled time for daily exercise and social activities.

_____ **5.** Richard is a very competitive, ambitious stockbroker, who is easily irritated by small inconveniences. If he thinks that someone or something is wasting his time, he blows up and becomes completely enraged.

_____ **6.** Max flubbed an easy free throw in the big basketball game, but told his coach, "My game was off today because I'm still getting over the flu and I pulled a muscle in practice yesterday. I'll do better in next week's game."

CRITICAL THINKING 13.3

Do Personality Factors *Cause* Disease?

■ You overhear a co-worker saying, "Of course he had a heart attack—the guy is a workaholic!"

■ An acquaintance casually remarks, "She's been so depressed since her divorce; no wonder she got cancer."

■ A tabloid headline hails, "New Scientific Findings: Use Your Mind to Cure Cancer!"

Statements like these make health psychologists, physicians, and psychoneuroimmunologists extremely uneasy (see Goleman & Gurin, 1993; Felten, 1993; Friedman, 1992). Why? Throughout this chapter, we've presented scientific evidence that emotional states can affect the functioning of the endocrine system and the immune system. Both systems play a significant role in the development of various physical disorders. We've also shown that personality factors, like hostility and pessimism, are associated with an increased likelihood of developing poor health. But saying that "emotions affect the immune system" is a far cry from making claims like "a positive attitude can cure cancer."

There are several reasons that psychologists and other scientists are cautious in the statements they make about the connections between personality and health. First, many studies investigating the role of psychological factors in disease are *correlational.* That is, researchers have statistical evidence that two factors happen together so often that the presence of one factor reliably predicts the occurrence of the other. For example, high hostility reliably predicts the development of heart disease (T. Q. Miller & others, 1996).

However, correlation does not necessarily indicate causality—only that two factors occur together. It's completely possible that some third, unidentified factor may have caused the other two factors to occur. For example, a person's heart disease and his hostile temperament could both have been caused by a third factor, such as a genetic predisposition to react intensely to stressful situations.

Second, personality factors might indirectly lead to disease via poor health habits. Low control, pessimism, chronic negative emotions, and hostility are each associated with poor health habits (Herbert & Cohen, 1993; T. Smith, 1992; Peterson, 1988). And, in turn, poor health habits are associated with higher rates of illness (Taylor, 1995). That's why psychologists who study the role of personality factors in disease are typically careful to measure and consider the possible influence of the participants' health practices.

Third, it may be that the disease influences a person's emotions, rather than the other way around. After being diagnosed with advanced cancer or heart disease, most people would probably find it difficult to feel cheerful, optimistic, or in control of their lives.

One way researchers try to disentangle the relationship between personality and health is by conducting carefully controlled prospective studies. A *prospective study* starts by assessing an initially healthy group of participants on variables thought to be risk factors, such as certain personality traits. Then the researchers track the health, personal habits, health habits, and other important dimensions of the partici-

pants' lives over a period of months, years, or decades. In analyzing the results, researchers can determine the extent to which each risk factor contributed to the health or illness of the participants. Thus, prospective studies provide more compelling evidence than do correlational studies that are based on people who are already in poor health.

Finally, as we've reminded you throughout this chapter, a person's health at any given time is influenced by the complex interaction of biological, psychological, and social factors (Bernard, 1994). For example, it's well documented that smoking increases the likelihood of developing lung cancer. But why does a nonsmoker get lung cancer in his forties while a three-pack-a-day smoker lives into his nineties? Is it diet? number of friends? health-compromising behaviors? genetics? personality factors? the environment? The bottom line is that it is often impossible to identify precisely why a person develops a particular disease.

One thing is certain: People who are diagnosed with a serious disease do *not* benefit from having a sense of personal guilt added to the psychological load they are already carrying. As Marcia Angell, editor of the *New England Journal of Medicine,* commented, "The dark side of assuming there is a connection between emotions and health is that people who fall ill may blame themselves and feel even guiltier if they get worse" (Angell, 1985/1991). So remember that although stress, emotions, and other psychological factors play a role in physical health, they are just some of the key factors in the complex equation of health and illness.

Social Factors That Influence Our Response to Stress

Social support refers to the resources provided by other people. How does social support benefit health? How can social support sometimes increase stress? What gender differences have been found in social support?

Let's get personal. How many friends do you have? Are you an active member of a club, church, or other organization? How many people are available to you in times of need? Are you involved in a stable, committed relationship? Do you have a best friend to confide in when you're feeling troubled? Are you satisfied with your relationships and friendships, or do you feel socially isolated from other people?

Close Relationships and Physical Health

Psychologists have become increasingly aware of the importance that close relationships play in our ability to deal with stressors and, ultimately, in our physical health. Consider the following research evidence:

The Benefits of Companionship Married people and couples live longer than people who are single, divorced, or widowed. How do close relationships benefit health?

- In a study involving 700 men, those who were more socially isolated were more likely to develop heart disease (Orth-Gomér & others, 1993). In fact, the two leading risk factors for the development of heart disease in these men were smoking and a lack of social relationships.

- Patients with advanced breast cancer who attended weekly support group sessions survived twice as long as a matched group of patients with equally advanced cancer who did not attend support groups. Both groups of women received comparable medical treatment. The added survival time for those who attended support group sessions was longer than that which could have been provided by any known medical treatment (Spiegel, 1993b; Spiegel & others, 1989).

- After monitoring the health of 2,800 people for seven years, researchers found that people who had no one to talk to about their problems were three times as likely to die after being hospitalized for a heart attack than were those who had at least one person to provide such support (Berkman & others, 1992).

- The health of nearly 7,000 adults was tracked for nine years. Those individuals who had few social connections were twice as likely to die from all causes than were those who had numerous social contacts, even when risk factors such as cigarette smoking, obesity, and elevated cholesterol levels were taken into account (Berkman & Syme, 1979; Berkman, 1985).

- Compared to single people, married people are less likely to die from all causes (see Burman & Margolin, 1992). Among people diagnosed with cancer, married individuals are likely to survive longer than people who are single or divorced (Goodwin & others, 1987).

These are just a few of the hundreds of studies conducted in the last few years exploring how our interpersonal relationships influence our health and

The Social Support of Friends Hundreds of studies have documented the beneficial effects of social support, whether it is emotional support (top) or tangible support (above). By listening to us when we're upset, helping us move, or simply being there when we need them, friends help us handle problems and cope with stress.

ability to tolerate stress. Repeatedly, researchers have found that socially isolated people have poorer health and higher death rates than people who have many social contacts or relationships (see Schwarzer & Leppin, 1992; Berkman, 1985). In fact, social isolation seems to be just as potent a health risk as smoking, high blood cholesterol, obesity, and physical inactivity (House & others, 1988).

To investigate the role played by personal relationships in stress and health, psychologists measure the level of **social support**—the resources provided by other people in times of need (Hobfoll & Stephens, 1990). Researchers generally agree that there are three broad categories of social support: emotional, tangible, and informational. Each provides different beneficial functions (Taylor & Aspinwall, 1993; Peirce & others, 1996).

Emotional support includes expressions of concern, empathy, and positive regard. *Tangible support* involves direct assistance, such as providing transportation, lending money, or helping with meals, child care, or household tasks. When people offer helpful suggestions, advice, or possible resources, they are providing *informational support*.

It's possible that all three kinds of social support might be provided by the same person, such as a relative, spouse, or very close friend. More commonly, we turn to different people for different kinds of support. In this chapter's prologue, we described some of the ongoing events in the life of Marie and David. Like many couples, David and Marie primarily rely on each other for emotional support. Marie's mother often provides tangible support by taking care of Mandy or Brian when either of them is sick so that neither David nor Marie needs to miss work. In terms of informational support, Marie often seeks the advice of a co-worker who successfully completed the same accounting program in which Marie is enrolled.

How Social Support Benefits Health:
"I Get By with a Little Help from My Friends"

Social support may benefit our health and improve our ability to cope with stressors in several ways (see Cohen, 1988). First, the social support of friends and relatives can modify our appraisal of a stressor's significance, including the degree to which we perceive it as threatening or harmful (Cohen & McKay, 1984). Simply knowing that support and assistance are readily available may make the situation seem less threatening.

Second, the presence of supportive others seems to decrease the intensity of physical reactions to a stressor (Edens & others, 1992; Kamarck & others, 1990). When people are given stressful tasks to complete in laboratory studies, their physical stress reaction is less intense when a friend is present than if they are alone. Thus, when faced with a painful medical procedure, a legal hearing, or some other stressful situation, many people find the presence of a supportive friend to be calming.

Third, social support can influence our health by making us less likely to experience negative emotions (Cohen & Herbert, 1996; Cohen, 1988). Given the well-established link between chronic negative emotions and poor health, a strong social support network can promote positive moods and emotions, enhance self-esteem, and increase feelings of personal control (Rodin & Salovey, 1989). In contrast, loneliness and depression are unpleasant emotional states that increase levels of stress hormones and adversely affect immune system functioning (Herbert & Cohen, 1993; Weisse, 1992; Kennedy & others, 1990).

social support
The resources provided by other people in times of need, including emotional support, tangible support, and informational support.

Potential Drawbacks of Social Support

Pets and Social Support Pets can be an important source of social support, especially for the elderly and people who live alone. Does the social support of pets translate into a health advantage? In one study of elderly individuals, pet owners reported feeling less stress and were also less likely to go to the doctor than people without pets (Siegel, 1990).

The flip side of the coin is that relationships with others can also be a significant *source* of stress. In fact, negative interactions with other people are often more effective at creating psychological distress than positive interactions are at improving well-being (Lepore, 1993; Rook, 1992).

Clearly, the quality of interpersonal relationships is an important determinant of whether those relationships help or hinder our ability to cope with stressful events (Feeney & Kirkpatrick, 1996). When other people are perceived as being judgmental, their presence may increase the individual's physical reaction to a stressor. In a clever study, psychologist Karen Allen and her colleagues (1991) demonstrated that the presence of a favorite dog was more effective than the presence of a friend in lowering reactivity to a stressor. Why? Perhaps because the dog was perceived as being nonjudgmental, nonevaluative, and unconditionally supportive. Unfortunately, the same is not always true of friends, family members, and spouses.

Stress may also increase when well-meaning friends or family members offer unwanted or inappropriate social support, as when an overly helpful

IN FOCUS 13.4

Providing Effective Social Support

A close friend turns to you for help in a time of crisis or personal tragedy. What should you do or say? As we've noted in this chapter, appropriate social support can help people weather crises and significantly reduce the amount of distress that they feel. Inappropriate support, in contrast, may only make matters worse.

Research by psychologist Stevan Hobfoll and his colleagues (1992) has identified several support behaviors that are typically perceived as helpful by people under stress. In a nutshell, you're most likely to be perceived as helpful if you:

- Are a good listener and show concern and interest.
- Ask questions that encourage the person under stress to express his or her feelings and emotions.
- Express understanding about why the person is upset.
- Express affection for the person, whether by a warm hug or simply a pat on the arm.

- Are willing to invest time and attention in helping.
- Can help the person with practical tasks, like housework, transportation, or responsibilities at work or school.

Just as important is knowing what *not* to do or say. Here are several behaviors that, however well-intentioned, are often perceived as unhelpful:

- Giving advice that the person under stress has not asked for.
- Telling the person, "I know exactly how you feel." It's a mistake to think that you have experienced the identical distress that the other person is going through.
- Talking about yourself or your problems.
- Minimizing the importance of the person's problem by saying things like, "Hey, don't make such a big deal out of it; it could be a lot worse," or "Don't worry, everything will turn out okay."

- Pretending to be cheerful.
- Offering your philosophical or religious interpretation of the stressful event by saying things like, "It's just fate," "It's God's will," or "It's your karma."

Finally, remember that while social support is helpful, it is *not* a substitute for counseling or psychotherapy. If a friend seems overwhelmed by problems or emotions, or is having serious difficulty handling the demands of everyday life, you should encourage him or her to seek professional help from a counselor, social worker, or psychologist. Most college campuses have a counseling center or a health clinic that can provide referrals to qualified mental health workers. Sliding fee schedules, based on ability to pay, are usually available. Thus, you can assure the person that cost need not be an obstacle to getting help—or an additional source of stress!

relative all but moves in with you while you're recovering from an injury or illness. For some suggestions on how to provide helpful social support and avoid inappropriate support behaviors, see In Focus Box 13.4, "Providing Effective Social Support."

Ironically, social support can sometimes backfire, prolonging the recovery from illness. For example, one study found that the wives of middle-aged heart disease patients were *too* helpful. Although the wives were genuinely trying to take care of their husbands, their overprotectiveness actually undermined their husbands' self-confidence and slowed their physical recovery (Coyne & others, 1990).

There are also drawbacks to having a large network of social relationships. Put simply, relationships tend to be reciprocal. If you feel that you have many people that you can call on in time of need, chances are those same people feel that they can call on *you* when things get rough. Providing social support to others can be psychologically and physically taxing, especially when it's long-term. For example, women who were providing long-term care to a relative with Alzheimer's disease experienced high levels of stress and diminished immune system functioning (Kiecolt-Glaser & others, 1991, 1987b).

Gender Differences in the Effects of Social Support

Women may be particularly vulnerable to some of the problematic aspects of social support, for a couple of reasons. First, women are more likely than men to serve as providers of support, which can be a very stressful role (Hobfoll & Vaux, 1993; Shumaker & Hill, 1991). Consider the differences found in one study: When middle-aged male patients were discharged from the hospital after a heart attack, they went home and their wives took care of them. But when middle-aged female heart attack victims were discharged from the hospital, they went home and fell back into the routine of caring for their husbands (Coyne & others, 1990).

Second, women may be more likely to suffer from the *stress contagion effect,* becoming upset about negative life events that happen to other people that they care about (Belle, 1991). Since women tend to have larger and more intimate social networks than men, they have more opportunities to become distressed by what happens to people who are close to them. And women are more likely than men to be upset about negative events that happen to their relatives and friends. In contrast, men are more likely to be distressed only by negative events that happen to their immediate family—their wives and children (Wethington & others, 1987).

In general, men tend to rely heavily on a close relationship with their spouse, placing less importance on relationships with other people. Women, in contrast, are more likely to list close friends along with their spouse as confidants (Shumaker & Hill, 1991). Because men tend to have a much smaller network of intimate others, they may be especially vulnerable to social isolation, especially if their wife dies. Thus, it's not surprising that the health benefits of being married are more pronounced for men than for women (Belle, 1991).

In summary, it should be clear that having a strong network of social support is generally advantageous to your ability to cope with stressors and maintain health. This is especially true when you are fundamentally satisfied with both the quality and the quantity of your relationships. By providing emotional, tangible, and informational support, the people who are close to you can reduce the impact of stressors, bolster your morale, and identify helpful resources in times of need (Coyne & others, 1990).

Coping: How People Deal with Stress

Coping refers to the ways we try to change circumstances, or interpretations of circumstances, to make them less threatening. What are the two basic forms of coping, and when is each form typically used? What are some of the most common coping strategies? How does culture affect coping style?

At this point, you have a good understanding of the kinds of major and minor life events that can function as stressors in our lives. You also know how the physiological effects of stress, especially when long-term, have the potential to undermine physical health. And you've developed insights into how psychological and social factors can intensify or reduce the impact of stressors.

Given that, let's start this final section of the chapter by asking you to think about some of the stressful periods that have occurred in your life. What kinds of strategies did you use to deal with those distressing events? Which strategies seemed to work best? Did any of the strategies end up working against your ability to reduce the stressor? If you had to deal with the same events again today, would you do anything differently?

Two Ways of Coping:

Problem-Focused and Emotion-Focused Coping

The strategies that you used to deal with distressing events are examples of coping. **Coping** refers to the ways we try to change circumstances, or our interpretation of circumstances, to make them more favorable and less threatening (Lazarus, 1993; Folkman & Lazarus, 1991).

As a rule, coping is not a single response. Rather, coping tends to be a dynamic, ongoing process. We may switch our coping strategies as we appraise the changing demands of a stressful situation and our available resources at any given moment. We also evaluate whether our efforts have made a stressful situation better or worse, and adjust our coping strategies accordingly.

When coping is effective, we adapt to the situation and stress is reduced. Unfortunately, coping efforts do not always help us adapt (see Lukoff & others, 1989; Paykel & Dowlatshahi, 1988). Maladaptive coping can involve thoughts and behaviors that intensify or prolong distress or that produce self-defeating outcomes (Bolger & Zuckerman, 1995). The rejected lover who continually dwells on her former companion, passing up opportunities to form new relationships and letting her studies slide, would be demonstrating maladaptive coping.

What characterizes "good," or adaptive, coping? David and Marie, described in the chapter prologue, are examples of people who are coping well with multiple stressors. As they demonstrate, adaptive coping responses serve many functions. Most important, adaptive coping involves realistically evaluating the situation and determining what can be done to minimize the impact of the stressor. Second, adaptive coping involves dealing with the emotional aspects of the situation. In other words, adaptive coping often includes developing emotional tolerance for negative life events, maintaining self-esteem, and keeping emotions in balance. And third, adaptive coping efforts are directed toward preserving important relationships during stressful experiences (Lazarus, 1993; Lazarus & Folkman, 1984).

Researchers have developed numerous ways to study the types of coping responses that people use (see Moos & Schaefer, 1993; F. Cohen, 1991). Two of the leading researchers in this area are psychologists **Richard Lazarus** and **Susan Folkman.** Folkman and Lazarus (1988) developed the *Ways of*

Susan Folkman Psychologist Susan Folkman is well known for her research in stress and health psychology. With co-author Richard Lazarus, Folkman devised a scale called the *Ways of Coping Questionnaire* that is used to identify coping strategies in a wide variety of situations.

coping
Behavioral and cognitive responses used to contend with stressors; involves efforts to change circumstances, or one's interpretation of circumstances, to make them more favorable and less threatening.

TABLE 13.3 Sample Items from the Ways of Coping Questionnaire

	Rarely	Some-times	Often	Very Often	Does Not Apply/ Never
• Tried to maintain a positive attitude about the problem	1	2	3	4	0
• Tried to keep my feelings about the problem to myself	1	2	3	4	0
• Made a plan of action and tried to follow it	1	2	3	4	0
• Daydreamed or imagined a better time or place than the one I was in	1	2	3	4	0
• Asked a relative or friend I respected for advice	1	2	3	4	0

SOURCE: Adapted from Folkman & Lazarus, 1988.

Questionnaires are one way that researchers assess the types of coping strategies that people use. Shown here are sample items from the Ways of Coping Questionnaire, developed by Susan Folkman and Richard Lazarus (1988). Research participants first indicate how stressful they felt a specific situation, like taking final exams, was for them. Then they check off how frequently they used a particular coping strategy to deal with that situation.

Coping Questionnaire, which is a checklist of thoughts and behaviors that people might use to deal with the demands of a stressful situation. Sample items from the Ways of Coping Questionnaire are shown in Table 13.3.

On the basis of their research, Lazarus and Folkman (1984) have described two basic types of coping, each of which serves different purposes. **Problem-focused coping** is aimed at managing or changing a threatening or harmful stressor. In general, we're likely to use problem-focused coping if we think that something can be done to change the situation. But what if we think there's nothing that can be done to alter a situation? In those situations, we tend to rely on **emotion-focused coping:** we direct our efforts toward relieving or regulating the emotional impact of the stressful situation. Although emotion-focused coping doesn't change the problem, it can help you feel better about the situation. Marie and David's ability to see the humor in a trying situation is one example of emotion-focused coping.

People are flexible in the coping styles they adopt, often relying on different coping strategies for different stressors. In this section, we'll look at some common forms of problem-focused and emotion-focused coping.

Problem-Focused Coping Strategies: Changing the Stressor

Problem-focused coping strategies represent actions that have the goal of changing or eliminating the stressor. When a person relies on aggressive or risky efforts to change the situation, he is engaging in *confrontive coping.* For example, in trying to resolve a conflict with a co-worker, a person may confront the co-worker and demand certain changes: "I told Melinda that I thought she treated me very disrespectfully in that meeting and I won't tolerate that kind of unacceptable behavior in the future."

Ideally, confrontive coping is direct and assertive without being hostile. However, confrontive coping is sometimes characterized by hostile or aggressive undertones (Bolger & Zuckerman, 1995). In the above example, adding the phrase "I won't tolerate that kind of unacceptable behavior in the future" communicates an aggressive tone. When it is hostile or aggressive, confrontive coping may well generate negative emotions in the people being confronted, damaging future relations with them (Folkman & Lazarus, 1991).

In contrast, *planful problem solving* involves efforts to rationally analyze the situation, identify potential solutions, then implement them. In effect, you take the attitude that the stressor represents a problem to be solved. Once you assume that mental stance, you follow the basic steps of problem solving (see Chapter 7).

problem-focused coping
Coping efforts primarily aimed at directly changing or managing a threatening or harmful stressor.

emotion-focused coping
Coping efforts primarily aimed at relieving or regulating the emotional impact of a stressful situation.

For example, in the prologue we described Marie's efforts to deal with the possibility of being laid off from her current job. Along with looking for a new job, she went to her manager and asked for additional responsibilities, reasoning that she would be less likely to be let go if she made herself as valuable as possible. Marie's efforts to make herself indispensable to her current employer while at the same time looking for a new job represents planful problem solving in action.

Unlike those who engage in confrontive coping, people who rely on planful problem solving are less likely to convey a sense of hostility toward others. Instead, their manner tends to be calmer and friendlier. Not surprisingly, then, the person who uses planful problem solving is more likely to elicit emotional, tangible, and informational support from others than is the person who engages in confrontive coping (Folkman & Lazarus, 1991).

Problem-Focused Coping People rely on different coping strategies at different times in dealing with the same stressor. After dealing with the emotional impact of losing their home to a wildfire, this California family is engaged in problem-focused coping as they help clear the site before rebuilding.

Emotion-Focused Coping Strategies: Changing Your Reaction to the Stressor

When the stressor is one over which we can exert little or no control, we often focus on dimensions of the situation that we *can* control—the emotional impact of the stressor on us (Thompson & others, 1994). All the different forms of emotion-focused coping share the goal of reducing or regulating the emotional impact of a stressor.

When you shift your attention away from the stressor and toward other activities, you're engaging in the emotion-focused coping strategy called *escape-avoidance.* Just as the name implies, the basic goal is to escape or avoid the stressor and neutralize distressing emotions. Simple examples of using escape-avoidance to deal with a stressful situation might include taking a walk, exercising, immersing yourself in your work or studies, or focusing on other projects. Maladaptive forms of escape-avoidance include drug use or excessive sleeping.

Escape-avoidance can also take the form of *wishful thinking*—imagining that the stressor is magically removed through an act of fate or a miracle. For example, a person who is reluctantly going through a painful divorce might fantasize a miraculous reconciliation. Or someone who is struggling with financial problems might daydream about winning the lottery.

By focusing your attention on something other than the stressor, escape-avoidance tactics tend to provide emotional relief in the short run. Thus, avoidance strategies can be helpful when facing a stressor that is relatively brief and has limited consequences. But avoidance strategies like wishful thinking tend to be counterproductive when the stressor is severe and chronic, as when a person is coping with a serious disease like cancer (Stanton & Snider, 1993). Escape-avoidance strategies are also associated with increased psychological distress in facing other types of stressors, such as adjusting to college (Aspinwall & Taylor, 1992).

In the long run, escape-avoidance tactics are associated with poor adjustment and symptoms of depression and anxiety (Stanton & Snider, 1993; Folkman & others, 1986). That's not surprising if you think about it. After all, the problem *is* still there. And if the problem is one that needs to be dealt with promptly, such as a pressing medical concern, the delays caused by escape-avoidance strategies can make the stressful situation worse.

Seeking social support is the coping strategy that involves turning to friends, relatives, or other people for emotional, tangible, or informational support. As we discussed earlier in the chapter, having a strong network of social support can help buffer the impact of stressors. Confiding in a trusted

CALVIN AND HOBBES

friend gives us an opportunity to vent our emotions and better understand the stressful situation (Lepore & others, 1996).

But as we also noted, seeking social support has potential drawbacks. For example, you may become more upset if the anticipated sympathy and support are not forthcoming from the other person (Major & others, 1990). And many of us have had the painful experience of realizing that we've confided in the wrong person, or said more than we should have, leaving ourselves psychologically or emotionally vulnerable (Folkman & Lazarus, 1991).

When you acknowledge the stressor but attempt to minimize or eliminate its emotional impact, you're engaging in the coping strategy called *distancing*. A relatively common example of distancing is the person who tries to change the meaning of the stressor by claiming that it's "no big deal" or "not that important." Making jokes about the stressful situation is another form of distancing (see Nezu & others, 1988; Robinson, 1983). And sometimes people emotionally distance themselves from a stressor by discussing it in a detached, depersonalized, or intellectual way.

In certain high-stress occupations, distancing can help workers cope with painful human problems. Clinical psychologists, social workers, rescue workers, police officers, and medical personnel often use distancing to some degree to help them deal with distressing situations without falling apart emotionally themselves.

In contrast to distancing, *denial* is a refusal to acknowledge that the problem even exists (Goldberger, 1983). Examples of someone using denial as a coping strategy would be the spouse who ignores obvious signs of marital infidelity, the parent who won't admit that his son has serious problems even after he's been arrested, or the person who refuses to acknowledge a medical diagnosis or condition.

Like escape-avoidance strategies, denial can compound problems in situations that require immediate attention. However, denial can be constructive when it is applied selectively to the stressful situation (Lazarus & Folkman, 1991). For example, one can deny the *implications* of a situation (e.g., "I'm going to die of cancer") without denying the *fact* of the situation (e.g., "I have cancer"). By denying the implications of the stressor, a person may be able to sustain feelings of hopefulness and perseverance in the face of an inevitable outcome.

Perhaps the most constructive emotion-focused coping strategy is *positive reappraisal*. The person who uses positive reappraisal not only tries to minimize the negative emotional aspects of the situation, but also tries to create positive meaning by focusing on personal growth (Folkman & others, 1986). Positive reappraisal seems to be most beneficial when a person is anticipating a stressor or evaluating the outcome of a stressful experience.

A person may use positive reappraisal to redefine a stressor as a personal challenge or to focus on the possibilities for mastery or growth. Or she may engage in *downward comparison*—comparing her circumstances to someone even less fortunate, or imagining a scenario that is even worse (Aspinwall & Taylor, 1993). Making downward comparisons often helps put matters in perspective and generates positive sentiments that the situation is not as bad as it could be.

People sometimes use positive reappraisal to help them make sense out of a stressful experience. This is especially true when people have experienced

Transcending Personal Tragedy Some people cope with tragedy by channeling their energies into helping others with similar problems. Elizabeth Glaser (no relation to researchers Janice Kiecolt-Glaser or Ron Glaser) became infected with the AIDS virus through a blood transfusion during childbirth. After her children tested positive for HIV, Glaser discovered that almost nothing was known about HIV in children. She co-founded the Pediatric Aids Foundation and became a national spokesperson for AIDS awareness and research. She is shown here at a press conference in 1992.

a tragedy, disaster, or catastrophic loss. People who can find some sense of personal meaning in the stressful event—sometimes through their religious faith—tend to cope better with loss than those who see it as senseless (Meichenbaum & Fitzpatrick, 1993; Wortman & others, 1992).

Most people use multiple coping strategies in stressful situations, often combining problem-focused and emotion-focused forms of coping (Lazarus, 1993; Dunkel-Schetter & others, 1992). Different coping strategies may be used at different stages of dealing with a stressful encounter. In the initial stages of a stressful experience, we often rely on emotion-focused strategies to help us step back emotionally from a problem. Once we've regained our emotional equilibrium, we may rely more on problem-focused coping strategies to identify potential solutions to the situation.

CONCEPT REVIEW 13.4

Coping Strategies

Which of the following coping strategies is being illustrated in each of the scenarios below?

A. Confrontive coping
B. Planful problem solving
C. Escape-avoidance
D. Seeking social support
E. Distancing
F. Denial
G. Positive reappraisal

_____ **1.** In trying to contend with her stormy marriage, Bailey often seeks the advice of her best friend, Paula.

_____ **2.** Although Lionel was very disappointed that he did not get the job, he concluded that the preparations he made in putting a professional résumé together, and the knowledge he gained from the interview, were very beneficial experiences.

_____ **3.** Whenever Dr. Mathau has a particularly hectic and stressful shift in the emergency room, she finds herself making jokes and facetious remarks to the other staff members about the patients she has treated.

_____ **4.** Phil's job as a public defender is filled with long days and little thanks. To reduce his frustration and take his mind off his job, Phil routinely jogs in a city park.

_____ **5.** Faced with low productivity and mounting financial losses, the factory manager called a meeting. In the meeting, he bluntly told all his workers, "You people had better start getting more work done in less time, or all of you will find yourselves looking for jobs elsewhere."

_____ **6.** Because of unavoidable personal problems, Martin did very poorly on his last two tests and was very concerned about his GPA. After thinking about ways to compensate for his low scores, he decided to talk with his professor about the possibility of writing an extra paper or taking a makeup exam.

_____ **7.** Despite having failed five out of six quizzes, Sheila still insists that she is going to get at least a B in her linguistics course.

Gender, Culture, and Coping Strategies

Many people assume that men and women cope in fundamentally different ways. In fact, men and women show very similar patterns of coping when they encounter the same type of stressful situation, such as work-related or family-related stress (Lazarus, 1993).

Unlike gender, culture does seem to play a role in our choice of coping strategies. Americans and other members of individualistic cultures tend to emphasize personal autonomy and personal responsibility in dealing with problems. Thus, they are *less* likely to seek social support in stressful situations than are members of collectivistic cultures, like Asian countries (Marsella & Dash-Scheuer, 1988). Members of collectivistic cultures tend to be more oriented toward their social group, family, or community and to seeking help with their problems.

IN FOCUS 13.5

Minimizing the Physical Effects of Stress

Sometimes stressful situations persist despite our best efforts to resolve them. Knowing that chronic stress can jeopardize your health, what can you do to minimize the adverse impact of stress on your physical well-being? Here are three simple suggestions that you should find helpful.

Suggestion 1: Exercise Regularly

Regular exercise, particularly aerobic exercise like walking, swimming, or

Managing Stress Everyone experiences stressful periods in their lives. How does exercise help people cope with stress?

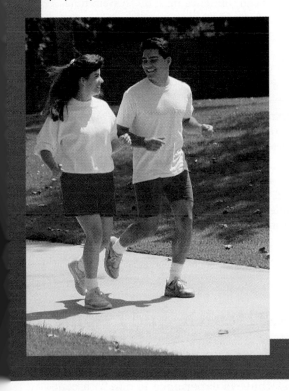

running, is one of the best ways to reduce the impact of stress. Simply walking briskly for 20 minutes four or five times a week will improve your physical health and help you cope with stress. Compared to sofa slugs, physically fit people are less physiologically reactive to stressors and produce less stress hormones (Rejeski & others, 1991, 1992). Psychologically, regular exercise reduces anxiety and depressed feelings, and increases self-confidence and self-esteem (Sacks, 1993).

Regular exercise also buffers the adverse health effects of stress. For example, one study compared the effects of negative life events on physically fit college students and on students who rarely exercised (J. D. Brown, 1991). Of the students who rarely exercised, increased stress was associated with increased physical illness and visits to a health center. But for the physically fit students, increased stress had virtually no impact on their physical health or frequency of health center visits.

Suggestion 2: Avoid or Minimize Stimulants

In dealing with a stressful situation, people often turn to stimulants like coffee or tea to keep them going. Most smokers react to stress by increasing their smoking (Epstein & Jennings, 1985). However, common stimulant drugs like caffeine and nicotine actually increase the physiological effects of stress by raising heart rate and blood pressure (Lovallo & others, 1996; MacDougall & others, 1988). In effect, users of stimulant drugs are already primed

to respond with greater reactivity, exaggerating the physiological consequences of stress (Dembroski, 1985).

The best advice? Avoid stimulant drugs altogether. The next best advice? Make a conscious effort to monitor your use of stimulants, especially when you're under stress. You'll find it easier to deal with stressors when your nervous system is not already in high gear because of caffeine, nicotine, or other stimulants.

Suggestion 3: Regularly Practice a Relaxation Technique

You can significantly reduce stress-related symptoms by regularly using any one of a variety of relaxation techniques (Benson, 1993). One effective relaxation technique is *meditation,* which involves focusing your attention on an object, word, or phrase. We provided you with instructions for a simple meditation technique in Chapter 4.

Another effective technique is *progressive muscle relaxation.* This involves systematically tensing and then relaxing the major muscle groups of your body while lying down or sitting in a comfortable chair. You begin by tensing your facial and jaw muscles, paying careful attention to the feeling of muscle tightness. Then, take a deep breath, hold it for a few seconds, and exhale slowly as you relax your facial and jaw muscles as completely as possible. Notice the difference between the sensations of tension and the warm feelings of relaxation. Progressively work your way down your body, tensing and then relaxing muscle groups.

Individualists also tend to emphasize the importance and value of exerting control over their circumstances, especially circumstances that are threatening or stressful. Thus, they favor problem-focused strategies, like confrontive coping and planful problem solving, which involve directly changing the situation to achieve a better fit with their wishes or goals (Markus & Kitayama, 1991).

In collectivistic cultures, however, a greater emphasis is placed on controlling your personal reactions to a stressful situation rather than trying to control the situation itself. This emotion-focused coping style emphasizes gaining control over inner feelings by accepting and accommodating yourself to existing realities (Thompson & others, 1994; Weisz & others, 1984).

For example, the Japanese emphasize accepting difficult situations with maturity, serenity, and flexibility (Weisz & others, 1984). Common sayings in Japan are "The true tolerance is to tolerate the intolerable" and "Flexibility can control rigidity" (Azuma, 1984). Along with controlling inner feelings, many Asian cultures also stress the goal of controlling the outward expression of emotions, however distressing the situation (Johnson & others, 1995).

These cultural differences in coping underscore the point that there is no formula for effective coping in all situations. That we use multiple coping strategies throughout almost every stressful situation reflects our efforts to identify what will work best at a given moment in time. To the extent that any coping strategy helps us identify realistic alternatives, manage our emotions, and maintain important relationships, it is adaptive and effective.

CONCEPT REVIEW 13.5

Key People in Stress Research

Hans Selye	Robert Ader
Walter Cannon	Janice Kiecolt-Glaser
Richard Lazarus	Martin Seligman

From the above choices, identify the person associated with each of the following descriptions:

1. American psychologist who has conducted extensive research on the role of explanatory style in coping with stress; also developed the learned helplessness model. _____

2. American physiologist who contributed to the study of emotions and described the fight-or-flight response to threat. _____

3. American psychologist who conducted a landmark study demonstrating that learning processes can influence immune system functioning. _____

4. American psychologist who emphasized the importance of cognitive appraisal in emotions and developed a questionnaire to study the role of daily hassles in the experience of stress. _____

5. Canadian endocrinologist who was a pioneer in stress research and described the three-stage response to prolonged stress called the general adaptation syndrome. _____

6. American psychologist who has extensively studied how a wide variety of stressors, including college exams, influence the functioning of the immune system. _____

Summing Up: Stress, Health, and Coping

Stress influences both our physical and our psychological well-being. As we've seen throughout this chapter, people respond to stress in many different ways. Ultimately, the level of stress that we experience is due to a complex interaction of psychological, biological, and social factors. The same is true of the impact of stress on our physical and psychological health. We hope that reading this chapter has given you a better understanding of how stress affects your life, and how you can reduce its impact on your physical and psychological well-being.

While stress is an unavoidable aspect of life, how we choose to cope with stress can minimize its destructive effects. As David and Marie demonstrated in the prologue, people can be remarkably flexible and effective in coping with multiple stressors. In the chapter Application, we'll look at ways to decrease negative reactions to potential stressors so that the problems and hassles of everyday life can be resolved with less stress.

Reducing Stress Through Constructive Thinking

We sometimes create stress in our lives by how we react to events. What is constructive thinking? How can you become a more constructive thinker?

Imagine each of these situations as vividly as you can. As you do so, note the thoughts and emotions that are triggered. Also try to imagine how you would behave in each situation. Remember your responses, because we'll come back to these scenarios shortly.

Situation 1. *You're sitting in a restaurant, waiting for a friend to show up for a lunch date. Your friend is now over 30 minutes late.*

Situation 2. *Your grades come in the mail. Instead of the B you were expecting in Biology, you only got a C.*

Situation 3. *You're getting ready to walk out the door and you can't find your keys.*

Automatic Thoughts and Stress

While everyone experiences stress occasionally, psychologist Seymour Epstein (1992b, 1993) is convinced that many people actually create a good deal of the stress that they experience. How?

According to Epstein's research, self-produced stress is often the result of a chain of events that begins with the automatic and habitual negative thoughts that people generate in response to everyday situations. These automatic thoughts can distort our appraisal of events and magnify the importance or threat of potential stressors. In turn, this distorted appraisal triggers negative emotions that prompt counterproductive or self-defeating behaviors, such as lashing out at others or withdrawing from a challenging situation.

Consider your response to each of the three situations above. Were your automatic thoughts basically positive, negative, or neutral? How did you imagine yourself reacting in each of those situations? Would your reaction have increased or decreased the amount of stress you experienced in the situation?

TABLE 13.4 The Constructive Thinking Inventory

Instructions: Read each item, then decide how well the item describes your behavior using the following 1 to 5 scale.* To determine your score, add up the numbers.

1 = Completely false	2 = Mostly false	3 = Undecided	4 = Mostly true	5 = Completely true

_____ 1. I am the kind of person who takes action rather than just thinks or complains about a situation.

_____ 2. I tend to dwell more on pleasant than unpleasant incidents from the past.

_____ 3. When I am faced with a difficult task, I think encouraging thoughts that help me do my best.

_____ 4. I don't take things personally.

_____ 5. I look at challenges not as something to fear, but as an opportunity to test myself and learn.

_____ 6. I don't worry about things I can do nothing about.

_____ 7. When faced with upcoming unpleasant events, I usually carefully think through how I will deal with them.

_____ 8. If I have an unpleasant chore to do, I try to make the best of it by thinking in positive terms.

_____ 9. I don't feel that I have to perform exceptionally well in order to consider myself a worthwhile person.

_____ 10. I don't let little things bother me.

*Scoring scale appears on page 605.

SOURCE: This brief version of the 106-item Constructive Thinking Inventory is adapted from Epstein, 1993.

If you engaged in what Epstein (1993) calls **constructive thinking,** you responded to each situation with automatic thoughts that would have minimized how much stress you experienced. Do you tend to be a constructive thinker? You can find out by completing the abbreviated version of Epstein's *Constructive Thinking Inventory,* shown in Table 13.4

Because your score is based on an abbreviated version of Epstein's scale, it provides only a rough approximation of your tendency to engage in constructive thinking. If your score fell in the average range or below, take heart. We'll present Epstein's suggestions for enhancing your ability to think constructively.

Constructive Versus Destructive Thinkers

What characterizes constructive thinking? Epstein (1993) describes constructive thinking as problem-solving thinking that has become habitual and automatic. In tackling everyday problems, constructive thinkers spontaneously appraise and construe events using rational, logical, and realistic thought processes. In trying to resolve problems, they naturally tend to be action-oriented, optimistic, and flexible.

Constructive thinkers are very effective at dealing with their own negative emotions (Epstein, 1992a). They don't waste psychological energy holding grudges or ruminating about past injustices. Instead, they are adept at getting along with others. Rather than accelerating potential conflicts, constructive thinkers react in ways that defuse the situation and promote harmony. In short, constructive thinkers display a high degree of "practical" intelligence—they effectively solve everyday problems with minimal personal cost in stress (Epstein & Meier, 1989).

In contrast, destructive thinkers tend to react to events with negative automatic thoughts (see Table 13.5). These thought patterns result in appraisals that intensify physiological arousal, cloud judgment, and magnify the stressfulness of the situation. In other words, destructive thinkers respond to potential stressors in ways that make the situation worse.

Epstein has found that most of the stress that destructive thinkers experience is self-produced (Epstein & Katz, 1992). Compared to constructive thinkers, destructive thinkers experience more negative emotions of all kinds, including anger, depression, and anxiety (Epstein, 1992b). As Epstein (1993) summarizes his research, "The more constructively you think, the happier you feel, and the better your emotional adjustment."

Improving Your Constructive Thinking

Is it possible to change your automatic thoughts and reactions to upsetting events? Can constructive thinking be learned? The answer is yes—with practice (Epstein, 1993). If you'd like to become a more constructive thinker, here's what you can do:

Step 1. Monitor your automatic thoughts. The first step to becoming a more constructive thinker is to increase your awareness of your own automatic reactions. Pay careful attention to the mental imagery and internal self-talk you generate in response to events, especially events that upset you. As you'll quickly discover, your automatic thoughts set the stage for your emotional reaction in the situation.

Consider the automatic thoughts generated in response to each of the three imaginary scenarios at the beginning of this Application. Did you find yourself mentally engaging in any of the destructive thought patterns summarized in Table 13.5?

For example, if you automatically thought that you had been stood up at lunch by your friend, you were *jumping to conclusions*. If you immediately thought your biology professor shafted you on your grade, you were *assuming intentionality*. In the lost keys example, if you instantly thought that someone had taken or moved your keys, you responded by *targeting*. It should be easy to see how these counterproductive

TABLE 13.5 Destructive Automatic Thoughts

Counterproductive Thought Pattern	Description	Example
1. Overestimating significance	Exaggerating or magnifying the importance of an event or situation. Making a mountain out of a molehill.	"This is awful—now *everything* is screwed up."
2. Assuming intentionality	Assuming that other people do things just to irritate or annoy you.	"He parked too close to my car just to make it hard for me to pull out."
3. Jumping to conclusions	Making hasty judgments based on insufficient or imagined evidence.	"I *know* she's cheating on me because she wasn't home when I called her."
4. Targeting	Blaming another person for things that go wrong.	"It's all *your* fault I had a flat tire because *you* didn't notice the tire needed air."
5. "Should" thinking	Dissatisfaction because something is not the way you think it should be.	"I'm miserable because I'm not as successful as I *should* be."
6. Labeling	Labeling people or events and then judging them on the basis of that label.	"Meetings are nothing but wasted time."
7. Overgeneralization	Assuming that what happened in a specific situation will happen again in similar future situations.	"I'll *never* trust a man again because my ex-husband cheated on me."
8. Berating yourself	Blaming yourself or putting yourself down.	"That was a really dumb thing to do! How could I be so stupid?"

SOURCE: Adapted from Epstein, 1993.

thought patterns would make the situation more stressful.

With a little practice, you'll find that it gets easier to psychologically step back, monitor your thoughts, and identify counterproductive thought patterns. It's especially important to do this in situations where you find yourself getting emotionally bent out of shape. Over time, you'll probably discover that because of the way you construe certain situations, those situations are more likely than others to trigger counterproductive thoughts.

Step 2. Use constructive thinking to redefine upsetting events. Once you've become adept at identifying instances of destructive thinking, the next step is to imagine a more constructive automatic thought to substitute in that situation. Remember, constructive thinking essentially comes down to problem-solving thinking that is rational, realistic, optimistic, and action-oriented (Katz & Epstein, 1991).

Using that mental framework, reconsider the three scenarios: late friend, wrong grade, and lost keys. Each of these situations can be con-

strued in a problem-solving way that would minimize how much stress you experience. Before reading further, try to come up with (1) constructive automatic thoughts and (2) constructive responses you could make in each of those situations.

If you use constructive thinking in how you construe the late-friend example, you will recognize that you do not have enough information to determine why your friend is late. Thus, getting annoyed, angry, or anxious is pointless and will only create unnecessary stress. Instead, the constructive thinker recognizes that a rather simple problem needs to be resolved: Should I keep waiting, go ahead and order lunch, or leave?

In the wrong-grade example, either you or your instructor made a mistake in calculating your final grade. Hence, the problem comes down to verifying whether you got the right grade. Rather than getting bent out of shape, resolve the problem in a constructive way: call the instructor and request an appointment to go over your test scores and discuss how the final course grade was determined.

In the lost-keys situation, the constructive thinker would keep the matter in perspective, staying calm and not complicating the situation by becoming angry or accusatory. Rather, the constructive thinker would focus on potential ways to resolve the problem, such as borrowing a set of keys from the landlord or notifying other people that the search for the keys may make him or her late.

Step 3. Use constructive thinking before you act. Armed with your new awareness, the third step is to implement constructive thinking in unfolding situations. As you find yourself starting to get emotionally worked up, look at how your interpretation of the situation is contributing to those emotions. Ask yourself if there is a more constructive way to look at the situation. As Epstein (1993) explains:

At first, you will think of appropriate constructive alternatives only after you have made destructive responses. With practice, you will become increasingly aware of the circumstances in which you tend to make certain destructive responses. You will then be able to make substitutions more quickly, until finally you will make the constructive response without having first made the destructive one. This is the goal you are aiming for.

Of course, you're probably not going to change well-entrenched mental patterns overnight. Epstein notes that people who are prone to self-defeating thinking have often been developing those thought patterns since childhood. Even so, when you consciously focus on developing constructive alternatives to

destructive thoughts and actions, you'll experience an almost immediate payoff: your negative reactions to distressing events won't last as long as they used to. That, in itself, makes Epstein's suggestions a valuable way to reduce the amount of self-produced stress in your life.

Constructive Thinking Score	
Very high:	43 and above
High:	37 to 42
Average:	27 to 36
Low:	21 to 26
Very low:	20 and below

Summary

Stress, Health, and Coping

What Is Stress?

- Stress can be defined as a negative emotional state that occurs in response to events that are appraised as taxing or exceeding a person's resources.

- Health psychologists study stress and other psychological factors that influence health, illness, and treatment. Health psychologists are guided by the biopsychosocial model.

Sources of Stress

- According to the life events approach, any event that requires adaptation produces stress. The Social Readjustment Rating Scale is one way to measure the impact of life events. The life events approach does not take into account a person's subjective appraisal of an event. It also assumes that change, whether good or bad, produces stress.

- Daily hassles are an important source of stress, and also contribute to the stress produced by major life events.

- Stress can also be caused by approach-approach, avoidance-avoidance, or approach-avoidance conflicts. Approach-avoidance conflicts tend to create the most stress.

- Social factors, such as unemployment, crime, and racism, can be significant sources of stress, often producing chronic stress. Stress can also result when people encounter different cultural values. Acculturative stress results from the stress of adapting to a new culture.

Physical Effects of Stress: The Mind–Body Connection

- Stress can affect health indirectly by influencing health-related behaviors, and directly by influencing body functioning.

- Walter Cannon identified the endocrine pathway involved in the fight-or-flight response. This endocrine pathway includes the sympathetic nervous system, the adrenal medulla, and the release of catecholamines.

- In studying the physical effects of prolonged stressors, Hans Selye identified the three-stage general adaptation syndrome, which includes the alarm, resistance, and exhaustion stages. Selye found that prolonged stress involves a second endocrine pathway, which includes the hypothalamus, the pituitary gland, the adrenal cortex, and the release of corticosteroids.

■ Stress affects immune system functioning. Ader and Cohen's discovery that the immune system could be classically conditioned helped launch the new field of psychoneuroimmunology. Subsequent research has discovered that the nervous, endocrine, and immune systems are directly linked and continually influence one another.

■ Stressors that affect immune system functioning include both unusual and common life events, along with everyday pressures. Although stress may increase susceptibility to infection and illness, many other factors are involved in physical health.

Psychological Factors That Influence Our Response to Stress

■ The impact of stressors is reduced when people feel a sense of control over the stressful situation. Feelings of control have both physical and psychological benefits. However, feelings of control must be realistic to be adaptive.

■ The way people explain negative events often determines whether they will persist or give up after failure. People with an optimistic explanatory style use external, unstable, and specific explanations for negative events. People with a pessimistic explanatory style use internal, stable, and global explanations for negative events. A pessimistic explanatory style contributes to stress and undermines health.

■ Chronic negative emotions are related to the development of some chronic diseases. People who frequently experience negative emotions experience more stress than other people. Transient negative moods have also been shown to decrease immune system functioning.

■ Type A behavior can predict the development of heart disease. The most critical health-compromising component of Type A behavior is hostility. Hostile people react more intensely to stressors and experience stress more frequently than nonhostile people.

Social Factors That Influence Our Response to Stress

■ Social isolation contributes to poor health. Social support may be emotional, tangible, or informational. Social support improves the ability to deal with stressors by modifying the appraisal of a stressor, decreasing the physical reaction to a stressor, and making people less likely to experience negative emotions.

■ When the quality of relationships is poor, or when social support is inappropriate or unwanted, relationships may increase stress. Providing social support to others can also be stressful.

■ Women are more likely to be the providers of social support than men, and tend to be more vulnerable to the stress contagion effect. Men are less likely to be upset by negative events that happen to people outside their immediate family.

Coping: How People Deal with Stress

■ Coping refers to the way that people try to change either their circumstances or their interpretations of circumstances in order to make them more favorable and less threatening. Coping may be maladaptive or adaptive.

■ When people think that something can be done to change a situation, they tend to use problem-focused coping strategies, which involve changing a harmful stressor. When people think that a situation cannot be changed, they tend to rely on emotion-focused coping strategies, which involve changing their emotional reactions to the stressor.

■ Problem-focused coping strategies include confrontive coping and planful problem solving.

■ Emotion-focused coping strategies include escape-avoidance, seeking social support, distancing, denial, and positive reappraisal. People usually rely on multiple coping strategies in stressful situations.

■ Men and women tend to use similar coping styles. Culture affects the choice of coping strategies. People in individualistic cultures tend to favor problem-focused strategies. People in collectivistic cultures are more likely to seek social support, and they emphasize emotion-focused coping strategies more than do people in individualistic cultures.

Key Terms

stressors (p. 569)

stress (p. 569)

health psychology (p. 570)

daily hassles (p. 573)

conflict (p. 574)

acculturative stress (p. 576)

fight-or-flight response (p. 578)

catecholamines (p. 578)

general adaptation syndrome (p. 579)

corticosteroids (p. 580)

immune system (p. 580)

lymphocytes (p. 580)

psychoneuroimmunology (p. 581)

optimistic explanatory style (p. 586)

pessimistic explanatory style (p. 586)

Type A behavior pattern (p. 588)

social support (p. 593)

coping (p. 596)

problem-focused coping (p. 597)

emotion-focused coping (p. 597)

constructive thinking (p. 603)

Key People

Robert Ader (b. 1932) American psychologist who, with immunologist Nicholas Cohen, first demonstrated that immune system responses could be classically conditioned; helped establish the new interdisciplinary field of psychoneuroimmunology.

Walter B. Cannon (1871–1945) American physiologist who made several important contributions to psychology, especially in the study of emotions. Described the fight-or-flight response, which involves the sympathetic nervous system and the endocrine system. (Also see Chapter 8.)

Susan Folkman (b. 1938) American psychologist who, with co-researcher Richard Lazarus, developed the cognitive appraisal model of stress and coping.

Janice Kiecolt-Glaser (b. 1951) American psychologist who, with immunologist Ronald Glaser, has conducted extensive research on the effects of stress on the immune system.

Richard Lazarus (b. 1922) American psychologist who helped promote the cognitive perspective in the study of emotion and stress; developed the cognitive appraisal model of stress and coping with co-researcher Susan Folkman. (Also see Chapter 8.)

Martin Seligman (b. 1942) American psychologist who conducted research on explanatory style and the role it plays in stress, health, and illness. Also developed the learned helplessness model (see Chapter 5).

Hans Selye (1907–1982) Canadian endocrinologist who was a pioneer in stress research; defined stress as "the nonspecific response of the body to any demand placed on it," and described a three-stage response to prolonged stress that he termed the *general adaptation syndrome*.

CONCEPT REVIEW 13.1 Page 575

1. False. The biopsychosocial model holds that health and illness are determined by the interaction of biological, psychological, and social factors.
2. False. Exposure to life events is only one of many factors that influence health and illness.
3. False. The Social Readjustment Ratings Scale measures stress due to life events.

4. True
5. False. Lyle is experiencing an approach-avoidance conflict, which is likely to produce a high level of stress.
6. False. According to the life events approach, both positive and negative life events generate stress.

CONCEPT REVIEW 13.2 Page 584

1. b
2. a
3. b
4. d
5. c

CONCEPT REVIEW 13.3 Page 590

1. F
2. D
3. E
4. A
5. C
6. B

CONCEPT REVIEW 13.4 Page 600

1. D
2. G
3. E
4. C
5. A
6. B
7. F

CONCEPT REVIEW 13.5 Page 602

1. Martin Seligman
2. Walter Cannon
3. Robert Ader
4. Richard Lazarus
5. Hans Selye
6. Janice Kiecolt-Glaser

14

Psychological Disorders

Prologue: "Help Me! Fire! Fire! Fire!"

I had just turned thirteen when my dad was hospitalized. At the time, I didn't realize just how sick he was. He nearly died before a diseased kidney was removed, saving his life. As my junior high was only three blocks from the hospital, I visited him every day after school before going to my paper route. It was one of those visits that defined the course of my life.

Lost in my thoughts as I walked through the maze of dim hospital hallways, I took a wrong turn. When I got near the end of the hallway, I realized it was a dead end and started to turn around. That's when her voice pierced the silence, screaming in agony.

"*Help me*! Fire! Fire! Fire! *Please* help me!"

At first I was confused about the direction from which the voice was coming. Then I saw a panic-stricken face against the small window of a steel door. I ran to the door and tried to open it but it was locked.

"Help me, *somebody!* Fire! Fire! Fire!" she screamed again.

"I'll get help!" I yelled back to her but she didn't seem to see or hear me. My heart racing, I ran back down the dim hallway to a nurses' station.

"There's a woman who needs help! There's a fire!" I quickly explained to a nurse.

But instead of summoning help, the nurse looked at me with what can only be described as disdain. "Which hallway?" she said flatly, and I pointed the direction from which I had come. "That's the psychiatric ward down there," she explained. "Those people are crazy."

I stared at her for a moment, feeling confused. *Crazy?* "But she needs help," I finally blurted out.

"That's why she's on the psychiatric ward," the nurse replied calmly. "Which room are you trying to find?"

I didn't answer her. Instead, I walked back down the hallway. I took a deep breath and tried to slow my heart down. As I approached the steel door, the woman was still there, screaming. Standing at the door, I watched her through the wire reinforced glass. She was completely oblivious to my presence.

"There's fire! I *see* fire! Fire! Fire! *Fire!*"

She was probably about twenty-five years old. Her face looked gaunt, dirty, her hair stringy and unkempt. I remember the dark circles under her deep-set eyes, her pupils dilated with sheer, raw panic.

"Listen to me, there's *no* fire," I said loudly, tapping on the glass, trying to get her attention.

"Help me, *please*," she sobbed, laying her cheek against the glass.

"My name is Don," I said, tapping on the glass again. "Listen to me, there's *no* fire."

That's when the attendants came, dressed in white hospital garb. The young woman slapped at their hands as they tried to pull her away from the door. I quickly got next to the glass, trying to see what was happening. *Don't hurt her!* For just an instant I saw her face again and she looked directly into my eyes.

"It's okay, there's *no* fire!" I yelled, then she was gone.

I stood by the steel door, my mind racing. *What was wrong with her? Where did they take her? Why did she think there was a fire? Did she really see flames?*

When I finally got to my dad's hospital room, we talked the entire time about the woman. "If you'd like," my dad finally said, "I can arrange for you to talk to a psychiatrist that I know. He can probably answer your questions better than I can."

A few weeks later, I spent about 30 minutes with the psychiatrist. In very general terms, he talked to me about mental disorders and their treatment. He also explained how psychiatrists usually take a medical approach and clinical psychologists use psychotherapy in trying to help people with psychological disorders. It was at that moment that I knew I wanted to be a clinical psychologist and help people like the woman I had seen.

I never saw that young woman again, nor did I ever find out what happened to her. But I will never forget her face or the sound of her terrified voice. Since that fateful day, I've spent many years of my life working on psychiatric wards, often trying to help people who were just as confused as that young woman.

In this chapter, we'll look at the symptoms that characterize some of the most common psychological disorders, including the one that was being experienced by the young woman I saw that day. As we do, you'll come to better understand how the symptoms of a psychological disorder can seriously impair a person's ability to function. We'll also talk about what researchers have learned about some of the underlying causes of psychological disorders. As you'll see, biological, psychological, and social factors have been implicated as contributing to many psychological disorders.

Introduction

Understanding Psychological Disorders

> *Psychopathology refers to the scientific study of the origins, symptoms, and development of psychological disorders. What characterizes "abnormal" behavior? What is the formal definition of a psychological disorder? What is DSM-IV, and how was it developed? How prevalent are psychological disorders?*

Does the *Far Side* cartoon make you smile? The cartoon is humorous, but it's actually intended to make some serious points. It reflects several common misconceptions about psychological disorders that we hope will be dispelled by this chapter.

First, there's the belief that "crazy" behavior is very different from "normal" behavior. Granted, sometimes it is, like the behavior of the young woman who was screaming "Fire!" when there was no fire. But as you'll see throughout this chapter, the line that divides "normal" and "crazy" behavior is often not as sharply defined as most people think. In many instances, the difference between normal and abnormal behavior is a matter of degree (Frances & others, 1991). For example, as you leave your apartment or house, it's normal to check or even double-check that the door is securely locked. However, if you feel compelled to go back and check the lock seventy-five times, that would be an example of abnormal behavior.

The dividing line between normal and abnormal behavior is also often determined by the social or cultural context in which a particular behavior occurs (Foulks, 1991). For example, among traditional Hindus in India, certain dietary restrictions are followed as part of the mourning process. It would be a serious breach of social norms if an Indian widow ate fish, meat, onions, garlic, or any other "hot" foods within six months of her husband's death (see Triandis, 1994; Shweder & others, 1990b). An American Catholic widow would consider such restrictions absurd. In a similar way, hearing "voices" or talking to disembodied "spirits" is accepted in some cultures, but evidence of serious disturbance in the United States (Mulhern, 1991).

Second, when we encounter people whose behavior strikes us as weird, unpredictable, or baffling, it's easy to simply dismiss them as "just plain nuts," as in the *Far Side* cartoon, or as "crazy," like the nurse's insensitive response in the prologue. Although convenient, such a response is too simplistic. It could also be wrong. Often, unconventional people are labeled as crazy when they're actually just creatively challenging the conventional wisdom with new ideas (Buck, 1992).

Even if a person's responses are seriously disturbed, labeling that person as "crazy" or "just plain nuts" tells us nothing meaningful. What are the person's specific symptoms? What might be the cause of the symptoms? How did they develop? How long can they be expected to last? And how might the person be helped? The area of psychology and medicine that focuses on these questions is called **psychopathology**—the scientific study of the origins, symptoms, and development of psychological disorders. In this chapter and the next, we'll take a closer look at psychological disorders and their treatment.

The *Far Side* cartoon reflects a third troubling issue. There is still a strong social stigma attached to suffering from a mental disorder (Penn & others, 1994). Imagine sitting next to a guy on a plane who grimaces and

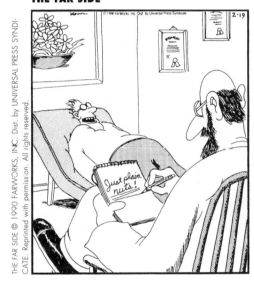

THE FAR SIDE

psychopathology
The scientific study of the origins, symptoms, and development of psychological disorders.

twitches his head and neck every 10 minutes or so. "Are you okay?" you finally ask. The guy jerks his head around to look at you and explains, "I'm taking medication for a pinched nerve that's causing muscle spasms in my neck, but I don't think the medication is working very well." How would you respond to your seatmate? Now imagine the same scene, only the guy jerks his head around and says, "I'm taking medication for schizophrenia and sometimes it makes me grimace and jerk uncontrollably." *Now* what do you think, and how do you react to your fellow passenger?

The important point here is that most of us regard mental and physical disorders very differently. When we are troubled with physical symptoms, we typically seek medical help. And if we're under medical care for a physical problem, we're usually not reluctant to discuss the fact with friends or acquaintances. But at least partly because of the social stigma that can be associated with psychological disorders, people are often reluctant to seek the help of mental health professionals (see Kessler & others, 1994). Many people who are under the care of a mental health professional for serious psychological problems hide the fact, telling only their closest friends—and understandably so. Being labeled as "crazy" carries all kinds of implications, most of which reflect negative stereotypes about people with mental problems (see Penn & others, 1994; Räty, 1990).

The entertainment industry and the news media are major sources of misinformation about mental illness (National Stigma Clearinghouse, 1993). Portrayals of people with psychological disorders in television shows, movies, novels, and even the Sunday comics foster negative stereotypes and myths about psychological problems (Gerbner, 1993). We discuss this issue in more detail in Critical Thinking Box 14.1, "Media Images of Mental Illness."

CRITICAL THINKING 14.1

Media Images of Mental Illness

In the 1980s, it was *Fatal Attraction,* in which Glenn Close portrayed a deranged woman who stalked a man who had had a one-night stand with her. And in the 1990s, it was *Silence of the Lambs.* Jodie Foster played an FBI rookie who enlisted the help of an imprisoned psychopathic killer, played by Anthony Hopkins, to trap *another* psychopathic killer.

Characters with a mental disorder or a history of mental illness have become standard fare in the recycled plot lines of blood and gore that are billed as entertainment. There's no shortage of made-for-TV movies and B-grade movies in which the basic plot involves a "deranged psycho" on the loose and body parts are flying everywhere. To illustrate, here are plot summaries

Just Another Media Psychopath? Anthony Hopkins won an Oscar for his chilling portrayal of "Hannibal the Cannibal," a psychopathic murderer, in *The Silence of the Lambs.* Movie thrillers and TV dramas often use the "homicidal maniac" as a plot device, but how accurate are such portrayals of people with mental illness? Are people with psychological disorders really more dangerous than other people?

of a few recent movie and television listings:

- *The Night Visitor:* Basic plot—Mental patient out for revenge.
- *Portrait of a Killer:* Basic plot—Deranged killer on the loose.
- *Love Butcher:* Basic plot—Young women murdered by homocidal maniac.
- *Madhouse:* Basic plot—The blood fest of a deranged twin sister.

In analyzing U.S. television programming, researcher George Gerbner (1993) found that the typical prime-time television viewer sees an average of three characters per week who are labeled as "mentally ill." How are these characters portrayed?

Gerbner found that people with mental disorders are portrayed in two highly negative, stereotypical ways. One stereotype is that of the mentally disturbed person who is helplessly vic-

The Mentally Ill as Villains on Prime-Time Television
People with psychological disorders are the most stigmatized group on television. This graph shows eight categories of people portrayed as major characters in prime-time television shows. For each category, researchers kept track of the number of villains for every 100 heroes. As you can see, only the mentally ill were portrayed as villains more often than they were portrayed as heroes.
(Gerbner, 1993.)

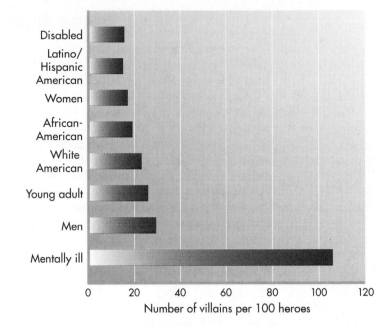

Number of villains per 100 heroes

timized, like the woman with multiple personalities who was murdered as part of the plot in a recent made-for-TV movie.

The other stereotype is that of the mentally disordered person as an evil villain who is unpredictable, dangerous, and violent. Gerbner found that while 5 percent of "normal" television characters are murderers, 20 percent of "mentally ill" characters are killers. And while about 40 percent of normal characters are violent, 70 percent of characters labeled as mentally ill are violent. As Gerbner (1993) summarizes his ongoing analysis of television programs, "The majority of mentally ill characters on television, our most popular media, are not only dangerous but are also touched with a sense of evil."

In fact, people with mental disorders are the *most* stigmatized group on television (National Stigma Clearinghouse, 1993). Characters labeled as mentally ill are portrayed far more negatively than any other group, including African-Americans, Latinos and Hispanic Americans, the disabled, and women (see the accompanying chart).

Television and the movies are not the only perpetrators of negative stereotypes about people with mental disorders. Novels and comic books also routinely use the plot device of the "insane homicidal maniac" or "psychotic killer." And a study of newspaper crime reporting found that "nothing sells newspapers like an insane, unpredictable, gory killer on the loose" (see Gerbner, 1993). Of course, the newspaper accounts are not fictional, underscoring the point that people with mental disorders sometimes do commit violent crimes (Hurley, 1994).

Given the fictionalized accounts and the sensational news stories, it's not surprising that a large percentage of people perceive those with mental disorders as being violent and potentially dangerous (Link & others, 1992). As is true with other stereotypes, people who don't know anyone with a mental disorder are most likely to believe the stereotype (Penn & others, 1994).

Are people with mental disorders significantly more violent and more dangerous than other groups of people? Research has shown that people with a current, severe mental disorder in which they are hallucinating or delusional do have a *slightly* higher level of violent and illegal behavior than do "normal" people (Link & others, 1992). However, we need to put that finding in proper perspective.

First, the statistical risk of violent behavior associated with mental illness is far *lower* than the risks associated with being young, a male, or being poorly educated. Each of these factors contributes much more strongly to the likelihood that a person will behave violently than does having a mental disorder (Link & others, 1992).

Second, the slightly elevated rate of violent behavior by the mentally ill applies *only* to those who are actively suffering severe psychological symptoms, such as bizarre delusional ideas and hallucinated voices. The person with a mental disorder who is *not* suffering from such symptoms is no more likely than the average person to be involved in violent or illegal behavior (Link & others, 1992). So what's the bottom line? The incidence of violent behavior among current or former mental patients is grossly exaggerated in media portrayals.

One of our goals throughout this chapter is to provide you with a more realistic and humane picture of people who experience mental disorders. As you'll see in this chapter, psychological disorders are much more common than most people realize. Perpetuating inaccurate stereotypes of mentally ill people as "homicidal maniacs" and "psychopathic killers" only adds to the burden of people who are already struggling to put their lives back in balance. So the next time you read a movie or television ad with the basic plot line of "a homicidal psycho on the loose," accept it for what it is—a cheap plot device that resembles reality about as closely as, well, *any* television show does.

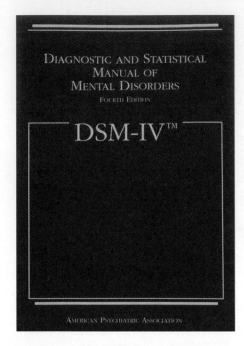

What Is a Psychological Disorder?

Up to this point we've used the terms *psychological disorder* and *mental disorder* interchangeably. And, indeed, the terms mean much the same thing. Psychologists generally prefer the term *psychological disorder,* while psychiatrists tend to prefer the term *mental disorder.* Both terms are widely used in the research literature. But what exactly are we talking about when we say that someone has a *psychological* or *mental disorder*?

A **psychological disorder** or **mental disorder** can be defined as a pattern of behavioral or psychological symptoms that causes significant personal distress, impairs the ability to function in one or more important areas of life, or both (DSM-IV, 1994). An important qualification is that the pattern of behavioral or psychological symptoms must represent a serious departure from the prevailing social and cultural norms. Hence, the behavior of a traditional Hindu woman who refuses to eat onions, garlic, or other "hot" foods following the death of her husband is perfectly normal because that norm is part of the Hindu culture (see Triandis, 1994).

What determines whether a given pattern of symptoms or behaviors qualifies as a psychological disorder? Throughout this chapter, you'll notice numerous references to DSM-IV. **DSM-IV** stands for the *Diagnostic and Statistical Manual of Mental Disorders,* fourth edition, which was published by the American Psychiatric Association in 1994. DSM-IV is a book that describes approximately 250 specific psychological disorders. It includes the symptoms, the exact criteria that must be met to make a diagnosis, and the typical course for each mental disorder. An example of the diagnostic criteria for one mental disorder is shown in Figure 14.1. DSM-IV provides mental health professionals with (1) a common language to label mental disorders and (2) comprehensive guidelines to diagnose mental disorders.

It's important to understand that DSM-IV was not written by a single person or even a single organization. Rather, DSM-IV represents the *consensus* of a wide range of mental health professionals and organizations. In developing DSM-IV, teams of mental health professionals conducted extensive reviews of the research findings for each category of mental disorder. All together, more than 1,000 mental health experts, mostly psychologists and psychiatrists, participated in the development of DSM-IV. More than sixty professional organizations, including the American Psychological Association and the American Psychological Society, reviewed early drafts of DSM-IV. Despite these efforts, the *Diagnostic and Statistical Manual of Mental Disorders* has its critics (see Wilson, 1993; Kirk & Kutchins, 1992). Nevertheless, DSM-IV is the most comprehensive and authoritative set of guidelines available for diagnosing psychological disorders. Thus, we'll refer to it often in this chapter.

■ Diagnostic criteria for 300.14 Dissociative Identity Disorder

A. The presence of two or more distinct identities or personality states (each with its own relatively enduring pattern of perceiving, relating to, and thinking about the environment and self).

B. At least two of these identities or personality states recurrently take control of the person's behavior.

C. Inability to recall important personal information that is too extensive to be explained by ordinary forgetfulness.

D. The disturbance is not due to the direct physiological effects of a substance (e.g., blackouts or chaotic behavior during Alcohol Intoxication) or a general medical condition (e.g., complex partial seizures). **Note:** In children, the symptoms are not attributable to imaginary playmates or other fantasy play.

FIGURE 14.1 Sample DSM-IV Diagnostic Criteria
Each of the more than 250 psychological disorders described in DSM-IV has specific criteria that must be met in order for a person to be diagnosed with that disorder. Shown here are the DSM-IV criteria for dissociative identity disorder, which was formerly called multiple personality disorder. The number 300.14 identifies the specific disorder according to an international code developed by the World Health Organization. The code helps researchers make statistical comparisons of the prevalence of mental disorders in different countries and cultures.
(DSM-IV, 1994, p. 487.)

psychological disorder (mental disorder)
A pattern of behavioral and psychological symptoms that causes significant personal distress, impairs the ability to function in one or more important areas of daily life, or both.

How Prevalent Are Psychological Disorders? Psychological disorders are far more common than most people think. A recent survey found that 1 in 3 American adults had experienced the symptoms of a psychological disorder within the previous year. However, many people who experience such symptoms do not seek help.

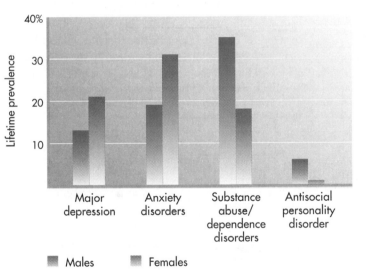

FIGURE 14.2 Gender Differences in the Lifetime Prevalence of Selected Psychological Disorders in the National Comorbidity Survey

(Adapted from Kessler & others, 1994, p. 12.)

DSM-IV
Abbreviation for the *Diagnostic and Statistical Manual of Mental Disorders,* fourth edition; the book published by the American Psychiatric Association that describes the specific symptoms and diagnostic guidelines for different psychological disorders.

The Prevalence of Psychological Disorders:
A Fifty-Fifty Chance?

Just how common are psychological disorders? In 1994 the most comprehensive survey to date on the mental health of U.S. adults was published (Kessler & others, 1994). Called the *National Comorbidity Survey (NCS)*, it surveyed a representative sample of Americans aged fifteen to fifty-four. NCS participants were asked about the symptoms of psychological disorders that they had experienced at (1) any point in their lives and (2) within the previous 12 months.

The NCS results were surprising. First, the researchers found that the prevalence of psychological disorders was much higher than previously thought. Almost one out of two adults—48 percent—had experienced the symptoms of a psychological disorder at some point in their lifetime. The proportion of people who had experienced the symptoms of a psychological disorder in the previous 12 months was 30 percent, or roughly one in three.

Another striking finding was that 80 percent of those who had suffered from the symptoms of a mental disorder in the previous year had *not* sought any type of treatment or help for their symptoms. Although that finding may surprise you, it's consistent with previous research (Narrow & others, 1993; Regier & others, 1993; Manderscheid & others, 1993).

There are two ways we can look at this finding. On the one hand, it's clear that many people who could benefit from mental health treatment do not seek it. This may reflect a lack of awareness about psychological disorders or the fact that a stigma still exists when it comes to seeking treatment for psychological symptoms. It could also be that people lack access to mental health services or lack the financial resources to pay for treatment.

On the other hand, even though the incidence of mental disorders is much higher than previously believed, *most* people seem to weather the symptoms without becoming completely debilitated and without professional intervention. As NCS director Ronald Kessler (1994) explains, "Really serious conditions that demanded immediate treatment affected 3% to 5% of our sample. These people typically had developed several mental disorders over time, not just one disorder that suddenly appeared."

The NCS also found that the prevalence of certain mental disorders differed for men and women. As you can see in Figure 14.2, women had a higher prevalence of anxiety and depression, while men had a higher prevalence of substance abuse disorders (Kessler & others, 1994). The reasons for these gender differences are unknown. Among the areas being actively investigated are genetics, social roles, and degree of willingness to seek professional help and report psychological symptoms (Seeman, 1995).

For the remainder of this chapter, we'll focus on the mental disorders in four DSM-IV categories: anxiety disorders, mood disorders, dissociative disorders, and schizophrenia. The psychological disorders in these four categories are some of the most common disorders encountered by mental health professionals. They're also the ones that our students ask us about most often.

TABLE 14.1 Some Key Diagnostic Categories in DSM-IV

Diagnostic Category	Core Features	Examples of Specific Disorders
Substance-related disorders (see Chapter 4)	Occurrence of adverse social, behavioral, psychological, and physical effects by seeking or using substances such as alcohol, amphetamines, cocaine, marijuana, hallucinogens, and other drugs.	**Substance abuse:** A recurring pattern of impaired ability to function at work, school, or home due to repeated substance use. **Substance dependence:** A maladaptive pattern of substance use usually resulting in drug tolerance, withdrawal symptoms when the drug is discontinued, and compulsive drug-taking behavior that seriously impairs occupational and social functioning.
Somatoform disorders	Persistent, recurring complaints of bodily (or *somatic*) symptoms that have no physical or medical basis.	**Body dysmorphic disorder:** Exaggerated concern and preoccupation about minor or imagined defects in appearance. **Hypochondriasis:** Preoccupation with imagined diseases based on the person's misinterpretation of bodily symptoms or functions.
Sexual and gender identity disorders (see Chapter 10)	Difficulty in the expression of normal sexuality, including confusion about gender identity, decreased sexual desire or arousal, difficulty having or in timing of orgasm, pain or discomfort during sex, or the use of inappropriate objects to produce sexual arousal.	**Fetishism:** Recurrent, intense sexually arousing fantasies, urges, or behaviors usually involving nonliving objects, such as female undergarments, shoes, boots, or other articles of clothing. **Gender identity disorder:** The strong and persistent desire to be the other sex.
Eating disorders (see Chapter 8)	Disturbances in eating behavior that involve obsessive concerns about becoming overweight, a distorted body image, and the inability to maintain a healthy body weight.	**Anorexia nervosa:** Severe restriction of eating and the failure to maintain a normal body weight due to the intense fear of gaining weight. **Bulimia nervosa:** Repeated episodes of binge eating followed by self-induced vomiting, misuse of laxatives, fasting, or excessive exercise.
Impulse-control disorders	Inability to resist an impulse, drive, or temptation to perform an act that is harmful to the self or others.	**Kleptomania:** The impulse to steal objects not needed for personal use or monetary value. **Pyromania:** The urge to set fires for pleasure, gratification, or relief of tension.
Personality disorders	An enduring, rigid pattern of thoughts, behaviors, and personality traits that produce distress and interfere with interpersonal relationships.	**Antisocial personality disorder:** A pervasive pattern of disregard for and violation of the rights of others, deceitfulness, irresponsibility, impulsiveness, and lack of remorse. **Borderline personality disorder:** A pervasive pattern of instability in interpersonal relationships, self-image, emotional control, and self-control.

SOURCE: DSM-IV, 1994.

Table 14.1 describes other categories of mental disorders contained in DSM-IV. Some of these disorders have been discussed in previous chapters. In the chapter Application, we'll look at what you can do to help prevent one of the most disturbing consequences of psychological problems—suicide.

Understanding Psychological Disorders

Identify each of the following statements as either true or false. If an item is false, rewrite it to correct it.

_____ **1.** DSM-IV is the abbreviation for four types of disorders of somatic and mental conditions.

_____ **2.** Women are more likely than men to suffer from anxiety and depression, while men are more likely to suffer from substance abuse.

_____ **3.** Definitions of "normal" behavior are highly consistent across cultures.

_____ **4.** Many people experience the symptoms of a psychological disorder but do not seek treatment.

_____ **5.** According to the National Comorbidity Survey, psychological disorders occur in about 2 percent of the general population in any given year.

_____ **6.** *Psychopathology* refers to the scientific study of psychopaths, or people who are prone to antisocial and violent behavior.

Anxiety Disorders

The main symptom of the anxiety disorders is intense anxiety that disrupts normal functioning. How does pathological anxiety differ from normal anxiety? What characterizes generalized anxiety disorder and panic disorder? What are the phobias, and how have they been explained?

Anxiety is a familiar emotion to all of us—that feeling of tension, apprehension, and worry that often hits during personal crises and everyday conflicts. While unpleasant, anxiety is sometimes helpful. Think of anxiety as your personal, internal alarm system that tells you that something is not quite right. When it alerts you to a realistic threat, anxiety is adaptive and normal. For example, anxiety about your grades may motivate you to study harder.

Anxiety has both physical and mental effects. As your internal alarm system, anxiety puts you on *physical alert,* preparing you to defensively "fight" or "flee" potential dangers. Anxiety also puts you on *mental alert,* making you focus your attention squarely on the threatening situation. You become extremely vigilant, scanning the environment for potential threats (Barlow, 1991). When the threat has passed, your alarm system shuts off and you calm down. But even if the problem persists, you can put your anxious thoughts aside temporarily and attend to other matters.

In the **anxiety disorders,** however, the anxiety is *maladaptive,* disrupting everyday activities, moods, and thought processes. It's as if you're dealing with a faulty car alarm that goes off at the slightest touch and has a broken "off" switch.

Three features distinguish normal anxiety from pathological anxiety. First, pathological anxiety is *irrational.* The anxiety is provoked by perceived threats that are exaggerated or nonexistent, and the anxiety response is out of proportion to the actual importance of the situation. Second, pathological anxiety is *uncontrollable.* The person can't shut off the alarm reaction, even when he or she knows it's unrealistic. And third, pathological anxiety is *disruptive.* It interferes with relationships, job or academic performance, or everyday activities. In short, pathological anxiety is unreasonably intense, frequent, persistent, and disruptive.

anxiety
An unpleasant emotional state characterized by physical arousal and feelings of tension, apprehension, and worry.

anxiety disorders
A category of psychological disorders in which extreme anxiety is the main diagnostic feature and causes significant disruptions in the person's cognitive, behavioral, or interpersonal functioning.

As a symptom, anxiety occurs in many different mental disorders. In the anxiety disorders, however, anxiety is the *main* symptom. Anxiety is manifested differently in each of the anxiety disorders. To help orient you, here's a brief overview of the role played by anxiety in each of the disorders that we'll discuss in this section:

- In *generalized anxiety disorder* and *panic disorder,* the main symptom is intense anxiety that often does not seem to be triggered by anything specific.

- In the *phobias,* severe anxiety occurs in response to a specific object or situation.

- In *posttraumatic stress disorder,* anxiety is triggered by memories of a traumatic experience.

- In *obsessive-compulsive disorder,* pathological anxiety occurs in response to uncontrollable thoughts or urges to perform certain actions.

Generalized Anxiety Disorder:
Worrying About Anything and Everything

Global, persistent, chronic, and excessive apprehension is the main feature of **generalized anxiety disorder.** People with this disorder are constantly tense and anxious, and their anxiety is pervasive. They feel anxious about a wide range of life circumstances, sometimes with little or no apparent justification. The more issues about which a person worries excessively, the more likely it is that he or she suffers from generalized anxiety disorder (DSM-IV, 1994).

Normally, our anxiety quickly dissipates when a threatening situation is resolved. In generalized anxiety disorder, however, when one source of worry is removed, another quickly moves in to take its place. The anxiety can be attached to virtually any object, or none at all. Because of this, generalized anxiety disorder is sometimes referred to as *free-floating anxiety.*

Panic Attacks and Panic Disorder:
Sudden Episodes of Extreme Anxiety

Generalized anxiety disorder is like the dull ache of a sore tooth—a constant, ongoing sense of uneasiness, distress, and apprehension. In contrast, a **panic attack** is a sudden episode of extreme anxiety that rapidly escalates in intensity. The most common symptoms of a panic attack are a pounding heart, rapid breathing, breathlessness, and a choking sensation. The person may also sweat, tremble, and experience light-headedness, chills, or hot flashes. Accompanying the intense, escalating surge of physical arousal are feelings of terror and the belief that one is about to die, go crazy, or completely lose control. A panic attack typically peaks within 10 minutes of onset and then gradually subsides. Nevertheless, the physical symptoms of a panic attack are so severe and frightening that it's not unusual for people to rush to an emergency room, convinced that they are having a heart attack, stroke, or seizure (Shulman & others, 1994).

When panic attacks occur *frequently* and *unexpectedly,* the person is said to be suffering from **panic disorder.** In this disorder, the frequency of panic

---

generalized anxiety disorder
An anxiety disorder characterized by excessive, global, and persistent symptoms of anxiety; also called *free-floating anxiety.*

panic attack
A sudden episode of extreme anxiety that rapidly escalates in intensity.

panic disorder
An anxiety disorder in which the person experiences frequent and unexpected panic attacks.

"Normal" Panic Versus Panic Disorder
These medical workers were helping victims immediately after the bombing in Oklahoma City. When it was announced that a second bomb had been discovered, they ran from the building. Once the threat had passed, they were able to resume their rescue work. The physical arousal of a panic state helps us respond quickly when our lives are threatened. In panic disorder, however, feelings of panic seem to come from out of nowhere and in the absence of realistic threat.

attacks is highly variable and quite unpredictable. One person may have panic attacks several times a month. Another person may go for months without an attack, and then experience panic attacks for several days in a row. Understandably, people with panic disorder are quite apprehensive about when and where the next panic attack will hit (McNally, 1994; Barlow, 1991).

Sometimes the first panic attack occurs after a stressful experience, such as an injury or illness, or during a stressful period of life, such as while changing jobs or during a period of marital conflict (Craske & others, 1990). In other cases, however, the first panic attack seems to come from nowhere. In a recent survey of panic disorder patients, 40 percent could not identify any stressful event or negative life experience that might have precipitated the initial panic attack (Shulman & others, 1994).

Explaining Panic Disorder

Both biological and psychological causes seem to be implicated in panic disorder. On the biological side, family and twin studies have found that panic disorder tends to run in families (Goldstein & others, 1994; Torgersen, 1990). This suggests that some individuals may inherit a greater vulnerability to develop panic disorder. However, many panic disorder patients do not have relatives with the disorder (DSM-IV, 1994). So genetics alone does not provide a complete explanation.

Psychologically, people with panic disorder are unusually sensitive to the signs of physical arousal (Ehlers & Breuer, 1992; Antony & others, 1992). The fluttering heartbeat or momentary dizziness that the average person barely notices signals disaster to the panic-prone. For example, when normal subjects and panic disorder patients are given a substance, like caffeine, that triggers physiological arousal, only the panic disorder patients react with a full-blown panic attack (Margraf & Ehlers, 1989). Why?

According to the *cognitive-behavioral theory of panic disorder,* people with panic disorder tend to misinterpret the physical signs of arousal as catastrophic and dangerous (Rapee & others, 1992; Zinbarg & others, 1992). When their heart starts to pound and their breathing escalates, they interpret their physical symptoms as frightening or dangerous. This interpretation adds to their physiological arousal and intensifies the symptoms.

After a frightening initial attack, the person becomes extremely apprehensive about suffering another panic attack. In turn, he becomes even more keenly attuned to physical changes that might signal the onset of another frightening attack. Ironically, this sensitivity simply increases the likelihood that another panic attack will occur.

The result? After a series of panic attacks, the person becomes behaviorally conditioned to respond with fear to the physical symptoms of arousal (Antony & others, 1992). Once established, such a conditioned response, combined with catastrophic thoughts, can act as a springboard for repeated panic attacks, leading to panic disorder.

The Influence of Culture on Panic Attacks

Syndromes resembling panic disorder have been reported in many cultures (Amering & Katschnig, 1990). The most common symptoms are the sudden onset of heart palpitations, dizziness or faintness, and intense terror. However, other symptoms of panic and the circumstances that trigger panic attacks are influenced by culture (DSM-IV, 1994).

For example, the Spanish phrase *ataque de nervios* literally means "attack of nerves." It's a disorder reported in many Latin American cultures, in Puerto Rico, and among Latinos in the United States. *Ataque de nervios* has many symptoms in common with panic disorder—heart palpitations, dizziness, and the fear of dying, going crazy, or losing control. However, the person experiencing an *ataque de nervios* also becomes hysterical, may scream, swear, strike out at others, and break things. *Ataque de nervios* typically follows a severe stressor, especially one involving a family member. Funerals, accidents, or family conflicts often trigger such attacks (Guarnaccia, 1993). Because *ataque de nervios* tends to elicit immediate social support from others, it seems to be a culturally shaped, acceptable way to respond to severe stress (Liebowitz & others, 1994).

The Phobias:
Fear and Loathing

A **phobia** is an intense, irrational fear that is triggered by a specific object or situation. Encountering the feared situation or object can provoke a full-fledged panic attack in some people (Craske, 1993). People with **specific phobia** are terrified of a particular object or situation and go to great lengths to avoid that object or situation, even though they know that the fear is irrational.

In the general population, *mild* phobias are extremely common. Many people are fearful of certain animals, like dogs or snakes, or mildly uncomfortable in particular situations, like flying in a plane or riding in an elevator. In comparison, the person with a phobia experiences incapacitating terror and anxiety. To be diagnosed as having a psychological disorder, a person's fear and avoidance must significantly interfere with daily life.

About 10 percent of the general population will experience a specific phobia at some point in their lives (Kessler & others, 1994). More than twice as many women as men suffer from specific phobia. Occasionally, people suffer from unusual phobias, such as the elderly woman that Don knew who was terrified of household cleaning supplies (see Table 14.2). But generally, the objects or situations that produce specific phobias tend to fall into four categories:

- *Fear of particular situations,* such as flying, driving, tunnels, bridges, elevators, crowds, or enclosed places

- *Fear of features of the natural environment,* such as heights, water, thunderstorms, or lightning

- *Fear of injury or blood,* including the fear of injections, needles, and medical or dental procedures

- *Fear of animals and insects,* such as snakes, spiders, dogs, cats, slugs, or bats

Agoraphobia: Fear of Panic Attacks in Public Places

One type of phobia deserves special mention—agoraphobia. Compared to the specific phobias, agoraphobia is both more disabling and more complex. Literally, *agoraphobia* means "fear of the marketplace." But rather than fearing public places per se, a person with **agoraphobia** fears having a panic attack in a public place from which it might be difficult to escape or get help (McNally & Louro, 1992). Consequently, people with agoraphobia avoid

TABLE 14.2 Some Unusual Phobias

Ailurophobia	Fear of cats
Algophobia	Fear of pain
Anthropophobia	Fear of men
Cynophobia	Fear of dogs
Monophobia	Fear of being alone
Nyctophobia	Fear of the dark
Ochlophobia	Fear of crowds
Pyrophobia	Fear of fire
Thanatophobia	Fear of death
Xenophobia	Fear of strangers

phobia
An irrational fear triggered by a specific object or situation.

specific phobia
An anxiety disorder characterized by an extreme and irrational fear of a specific object or situation that interferes with the ability to function in daily life.

agoraphobia
An anxiety disorder involving the extreme and irrational fear of experiencing a panic attack in a public situation and being unable to escape or get help.

(1) situations that they think might provoke a panic attack and (2) situations in which they would be unable to escape or get help if they *did* suffer a panic attack.

What kinds of situations are we talking about? Crowds, standing in line, stores or elevators, public transportation, and traveling in a car may all be avoided because of the fear of suffering a panic attack and being unable to escape the situation. Consequently, many agoraphobics become prisoners in their own homes, unable to go beyond their front door. Not surprisingly, then, agoraphobia is the phobia for which people most often seek professional help (D. Sue & others, 1994).

Here's an example to help you understand the distinction between the fear and avoidance in specific phobia as compared to that of agoraphobia. A group of people were seeking treatment to overcome their fear of flying (McNally & Louro, 1992). Half had a diagnosis of specific phobia, and half had been diagnosed with agoraphobia. Those with specific phobia avoided flying because they were afraid that the plane would crash. In contrast, the agoraphobics were *not* worried about dying in a plane crash. Instead, they were afraid that they might have a panic attack during a flight and be trapped on the plane.

Social Phobia Social phobia is far more debilitating than everyday shyness. This pleasant scene shows a happy bride dancing with her mother in the Russian town of Lubavich as the wedding guests look on. For those who suffer from social phobia, dancing in public would be impossible, and even attending the wedding as a guest might cause overwhelming anxiety.

social phobia
An anxiety disorder involving the extreme and irrational fear of being embarrassed, judged, or scrutinized by others in social situations.

Social Phobia: Fear of Social Situations

A second type of phobia also deserves additional comment—social phobia. Social phobia goes well beyond the shyness that everyone sometimes feels at social gatherings. Rather, the person with **social phobia** is paralyzed by fear of social situations, especially if the situation involves performing even routine behaviors in front of others. Eating a meal in public, making small talk at a party, or even using a public restroom can be agonizing for the person with social phobia.

The core of social phobia seems to be an irrational fear of being embarrassed, judged, or critically evaluated by others (Woody, 1996). People with social phobia recognize that their fear is excessive and unreasonable, but they still approach social situations with tremendous anxiety (J. Ross, 1993). In severe cases, they may even suffer a panic attack in social situations. When the fear of being embarrassed or failing in public significantly interferes with daily life, it qualifies as social phobia (DSM-IV, 1994).

Because of their avoidance of social situations, people with social phobia often have very low self-esteem, poor social skills, and few friends. Their fear of evaluation or criticism by others may lead to occupational or academic underachievement. In classroom situations, they may suffer from intense test anxiety or be afraid to ask questions or make comments (Davidson, 1993; J. Ross, 1993).

As with panic attacks, cultural influences can add some novel twists to social phobia. Consider the Japanese disorder called *taijin kyofusho*. *Taijin kyofusho* usually affects young Japanese males. It has several features in common with social phobia, including extreme social anxiety and avoidance of social situations. However, the person with *taijin kyofusho* is not worried about being embarrassed in public. Rather, reflecting the cultural emphasis of concern for others, the person with *taijin kyofusho* fears that his body's appearance or smell, facial expression, or body language will offend, insult, or embarrass other people (Russell, 1989).

Explaining Phobias: Learning Theories

The development of some phobias can be explained in terms of basic learning principles. *Classical conditioning* may well be involved in the development of a specific phobia that can be traced back to some sort of traumatic event. In Chapter 5, on learning, we saw how psychologist John Watson classically conditioned "Little Albert" to fear a tame lab rat that had been paired with loud noise. Following the conditioning, the infant's fear generalized to other furry objects. In much the same way, our neighbor Michelle has been extremely phobic of dogs ever since she was bitten by a German shepherd when she was four years old. In effect, Michelle developed a *conditioned response* (fear) to a *conditioned stimulus* (the German shepherd) that has *generalized* to similar stimuli—any dog.

Operant conditioning can also be involved in the avoidance behavior that characterizes phobias. In Michelle's case, she quickly learned that she could reduce her anxiety and fear by avoiding dogs altogether. To use operant conditioning terms, her *operant response* of avoiding dogs is *negatively reinforced* by the relief from anxiety and fear that she experiences.

Observational learning can also be involved in the development of phobias. Some people learn to be phobic of certain objects or situations by observing the fearful reactions of someone else who acts as a *model* in the situation. The child who observes a parent react with sheer panic to the sight of a spider or mouse may imitate the same behavioral response. People can also develop phobias from observing vivid media accounts of disasters, such as people who become afraid to fly after watching graphic TV coverage of a plane crash.

Although learning principles can explain the genesis of some phobias, they cannot account for all cases of phobia. First, many individuals can't remember any traumatic or upsetting event associated with the feared object or situation. Second, even though many people directly experience traumatic events—an emergency landing in an airplane or a near-drowning—most of those people do not develop phobias associated with the frightening situation or object.

Third, if all phobias were simply due to conditioning, people would be far more likely to be phobic of electrical outlets, stairs, or bicycles than spiders, snakes, and storms. But the simple fact is that people are much more likely to develop phobias of spiders, snakes, and storms than they are of electrical outlets, stairs, or bicycles. Why?

Evolution and Phobias: "Yikes!" and "Yuck!" Responses

In Chapter 5, we noted that humans seem *biologically prepared* to acquire fears of certain animals and situations that were important survival threats in human evolutionary history (Seligman, 1971; McNally, 1987). For example, when pictures of snakes and spiders are paired with mild electric shock, people acquire a more persistent conditioned fear response to the snake and spider pictures than to similarly paired pictures of mushrooms or flowers (Ohman, 1993, 1994). Phobic subjects will even react with heightened anxiety to pictures of snakes and spiders that are flashed so quickly that the subjects are not consciously aware of the image (Ohman & Soares, 1994).

Our evolutionary heritage may set the stage for certain phobias in another way. People also seem predisposed to develop phobias toward creatures that arouse *disgust*, like slugs, maggots, rats, or cockroaches (Webb & Davey, 1993). Such creatures are, of course, relatively

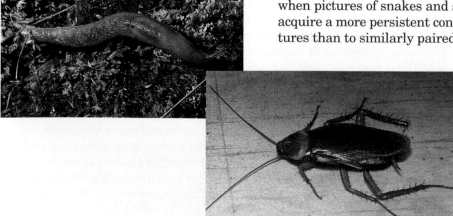

Yuck! It's hard to suppress a shudder of disgust at the sight of a slug sliming its way across the sidewalk . . . or a cockroach scuttling across the kitchen floor. Are such responses instinctive? Why are people more likely to develop phobias for slugs, maggots, and cockroaches than for mosquitoes or grasshoppers?

harmless. (Ever been cornered by a slug?) Instinctively, it seems, many people find them repulsive, possibly because they are associated with disease, infection, or filth. The predisposition to develop phobias for disgusting creatures may reflect a fear of contamination or infection that is also based on human evolutionary history (Ware & others, 1994; Davey, 1993).

In combination, learning principles and biological predispositions provide several useful insights into the development of some phobias. Still, they have shortcomings. For example, they don't adequately explain why some people, but not others, develop a phobia after a traumatic experience. Nor do they adequately explain phobic quirks, such as why your author Don is petrified of balconies more than five stories up, yet will enthusiastically parachute out of a plane that's 5,000 feet above the ground.

Posttraumatic Stress Disorder:

Re-experiencing the Trauma

> *Posttraumatic stress disorder (PTSD) and obsessive-compulsive disorder both involve extreme anxiety and intrusive thoughts. What is PTSD, and what causes it? What is obsessive-compulsive disorder, and what are the most common types of obsessions and compulsions?*

Posttraumatic stress disorder, abbreviated **PTSD,** is a long-lasting anxiety disorder that develops in response to an extreme physical or psychological trauma. Extreme traumas are events that produce intense feelings of horror and helplessness, such as a serious physical injury or threat of injury to yourself or to loved ones (DSM-IV, 1994).

Originally, posttraumatic stress disorder was primarily associated with direct experiences of military combat. However, it's now known that PTSD can also develop in survivors of other sorts of extreme traumas, such as disasters, physical or sexual assault, and random shooting sprees (Sharan & others, 1996; Allodi, 1994; North & others, 1994). Children as well as adults can experience the symptoms of PTSD (Vernberg & others, 1996).

Just *witnessing* the injury or death of others can be sufficiently traumatic for PTSD to occur (Davis & Breslau, 1994). For example, American military personnel assigned to processing the remains of soldiers killed in the Persian Gulf war, although not threatened with death or injury themselves, had a high rate of PTSD (Sutker & others, 1994).

Three core symptoms characterize posttraumatic stress disorder (DSM IV, 1994). First, the person *frequently recalls the event,* replaying it in her mind. Such recollections are often *intrusive,* meaning that they are unwanted and interfere with normal thoughts. Second, the person *avoids stimuli or situations* that tend to trigger memories of the experience and undergoes a general *numbing of emotional responsiveness.* Third, the person experiences the *increased physical arousal* associated with anxiety. He may be easily startled, experience sleep disturbances, have problems concentrating and remembering, and be prone to irritability or angry outbursts (Keane & others, 1992).

Not surprisingly, PTSD seriously interferes with the ability to function in daily life. Along with their PTSD symptoms, people often experience depression and feelings of guilt over surviving the trauma when close friends or relatives did not. Substance abuse is also relatively common, often because people are trying to ease their emotional distress by medicating themselves (Stewart, 1996). Many individuals with PTSD also display other psychological disorders, such as depression, panic disorder, or generalized anxiety disorder (Tomb, 1994; North & others, 1994).

A Half-Century of Psychological Pain
The symptoms of posttraumatic stress disorder can apparently last a lifetime. More than fifty years after the close of World War II, thousands of veterans, now in their 70s and 80s, still suffer from nightmares, anxiety, and other PTSD symptoms (Lee & others, 1995). Some experts estimate that as many as 200,000 World War II veterans may continue to suffer from the symptoms of posttraumatic stress disorder.

posttraumatic stress disorder (PTSD)
An anxiety disorder in which chronic and persistent symptoms of anxiety develop in response to an extreme physical or psychological trauma.

obsessive-compulsive disorder
An anxiety disorder in which the symptoms of anxiety are triggered by intrusive, repetitive thoughts and urges to perform certain actions.

obsessions
Repeated, intrusive, and uncontrollable irrational thoughts or mental images that cause extreme anxiety and distress.

compulsions
Repetitive behaviors or mental acts that are performed to prevent or reduce anxiety.

Posttraumatic stress disorder is somewhat unusual in that the source of the disorder is the traumatic event itself, rather than a cause that lies within the individual. Even well-adjusted and psychologically healthy people may develop PTSD when exposed to an extremely traumatic event (Sutker & others, 1994). However, it's also important to point out that no stressor, no matter how extreme, produces posttraumatic stress disorder in everyone.

So why is it that some people develop PTSD while others don't? Several factors influence the likelihood of developing posttraumatic stress disorder (Tomb, 1994). First, people with a personal or family history of psychological disorders are more likely to develop PTSD when exposed to an extreme trauma. Second, the magnitude of the trauma plays an important role. More extreme stressors are more likely to produce PTSD.

Finally, when people undergo *multiple* traumas, the incidence of PTSD can be quite high. For example, almost 90 percent of a group of Cambodian refugees who had resettled in the United States met the criteria for posttraumatic stress disorder (Carlson & Rosser-Hogan, 1991). These refugees from the Khmer Rouge dictatorship of the 1970s had experienced multiple, extreme stressors—torture, threat of death, the killing of family members, physical hardship, and resettlement in a foreign culture.

Obsessive-Compulsive Disorder:
Checking It Again . . . and Again

When you leave your home, you probably check to make sure all the doors are locked. Sometimes, you may even double- or triple-check just to be on the safe side. But once you're confident that the door is locked, you don't think about it again.

Reprinted from *Health Magazine*

Now imagine you've checked the door *twenty* times. Yet you're still not quite sure that the door is really locked. You know the feeling is irrational, but you feel compelled to check again and again. Imagine you've *also* had to repeatedly check that the coffeepot was unplugged, that the stove was turned off, and so forth. Finally, imagine that you only got two blocks away from home before you felt compelled to turn back and check *again*—because you still were not certain.

Sound agonizing? This is the psychological world of the person who suffers from one form of obsessive-compulsive disorder. **Obsessive-compulsive disorder** is an anxiety disorder in which a person's life is dominated by repetitive thoughts (*obsessions*) and behaviors (*compulsions*).

Obsessions are repeated, intrusive, uncontrollable thoughts or mental images that cause the person great anxiety and distress. Obsessions are not the same as everyday worries. Normal worries typically have some sort of factual basis, even if they're somewhat exaggerated (Freeston & others, 1994). In contrast, obsessions have little or no basis in reality, and are often extremely farfetched.

A **compulsion** is a repetitive behavior that a person feels driven to perform. Typically, compulsions are ritual behaviors that must be carried out in a certain pattern or sequence. Compulsions may be *overt physical behaviors,* such as repeatedly washing your hands. Or they may be *covert mental behaviors,* such as counting or reciting certain phrases to yourself. When the person tries to resist performing the ritual, unbearable

TABLE 14.3 The Most Common Obsessions and Compulsions

Obsession	Description	Examples
Contamination	Irrational fear of contamination by dirt, germs, or other toxic substances. Typically accompanied by cleaning or washing compulsion.	Exaggerated fear that shoes, clothing, or visitors will contaminate your home with germs. Exaggerated worry that you will be contaminated by contact with an unclean object.
Pathological doubt	Feeling of uncertainty about having accomplished a simple task. Recurring fear that you have inadvertently harmed someone or violated a law. Typically accompanied by checking compulsion.	Recurring worry that you did not lock doors or shut off appliances, despite having checked them multiple times. While driving, fear that you might have inadvertently hit and killed someone.
Violent or sexual thoughts	Fear that you have harmed or will harm another person or will engage in some sort of unacceptable sexual behavior. Or the fear that you have done or will do something socially unacceptable. May take the form of intrusive mental images or impulses.	Recurring mental images of attacking a family member, although you feel no hostility toward her. Recurring worry that you will start screaming obscenities in the middle of class.

Compulsion	Description	Examples
Washing	Urge to repeatedly wash yourself or clean your surroundings. Cleaning or washing may involve elaborate, lengthy ritual. Often linked with contamination obsession, but may also be a compulsive ritual that is intended to prevent some sort of unrelated catastrophe.	Strict two-hour showering ritual that requires you to perform each step in a precise order or you must restart. Disinfecting everything in your home that has been touched by a visitor, including doorknobs, floor, furniture, and faucets.
Checking	Checking over and over again to make sure that a simple task has been accomplished. Typically occurs in association with pathological doubt. Checking rituals may take hours.	Checking doors, windows, appliances multiple times yet still feeling uncertain. Checking and rechecking work to make sure you have not made an error. Retracing your route to make sure that you did not inadvertently hit someone while driving.
Counting	Need to engage in certain behaviors a specific number of times, or to count to a certain number before performing some action or task.	Having to count to ten every time a bite of food is taken. Must circle every tree in the front yard sixteen times before leaving home.
Symmetry and precision	Need to have things or actions be perfectly symmetrical. Need to have objects in an exact order or position. Need to do or undo certain actions in an exact fashion.	Entering and reentering a doorway until you walk through exactly in the middle. Precise placement of every item on desk coupled with extreme distress when things are "out of order." Rigid step-by-step ritual for getting dressed, brushing teeth, leaving house, or starting car.

SOURCE: Based on Rasmussen & Eisen, 1992, Table 1, p. 745

As this table shows, obsessions and compulsions tend to fall into a limited number of categories. About three-fourths of obsessive-compulsive patients suffer from multiple obsessions, while slightly more than half report more than one type of compulsion (Rasmussen & Eisen, 1992).

tension, anxiety, and distress result. The most common obsessions and compulsions are described in Table 14.3.

Note that the clinical meanings of *obsessive* and *compulsive* are very different from the meanings intended when people use these words in casual conversation. For example, we may say that someone is "obsessed" with her job, when we mean that she is excessively preoccupied with it. And we may call someone a "compulsive tennis player" when we mean that he really seems to enjoy that activity.

In contrast, the true obsessive-compulsive does *not* find any satisfaction in his obsessions or compulsions. Instead, the obsessions and compulsions he experiences are very distressing and anxiety-provoking (De Silva & Rachman, 1992). The obsessive-compulsive does not repeatedly wash his hands because he enjoys being clean. Rather, he washes his hands because to *not* do so would cause extreme, unbearable anxiety.

People may experience either obsessions or compulsions. More commonly, obsessions and compulsions are *both* present. Often, the obsessions and compulsions are linked in some way. For example, a man who was obsessed with the idea that he might have lost an important document felt compelled to pick up every scrap of paper he saw on the street and other public places.

Other compulsions bear little logical relationship to the feared consequences, like the woman who believed that if she didn't get dressed according to a strict pattern, her husband would die in an automobile accident. In all cases, obsessive-compulsives feel that something terrible will happen if the compulsive action is left undone.

Interestingly, obsessions and compulsions take a similar shape in different cultures around the world. Whether it's Sweden, China, England, the Sudan, India, or Nigeria, obsessions and compulsions occur in surprisingly similar forms. Most common are fears of contamination, compulsive washing or cleaning, checking, and repeating actions (Rapoport, 1989; Rasmussen & Eisen, 1992).

However, the *content* of the obsessions and compulsions tends to mirror the particular culture's concerns and beliefs. In the United States, compulsive washers are typically preoccupied with obsessional fears of germs and infection. But in rural Nigeria and rural India, compulsive washers are more likely to have obsessional concerns about religious purity (Rapoport, 1989).

TABLE 14.4 The Anxiety Disorders

General Anxiety Disorder

- Persistent, chronic, unreasonable worry and anxiety
- General symptoms of anxiety, including persistent physical arousal

Panic Disorder

- Frequent and unexpected panic attacks, with no specific or identifiable trigger

Phobias

- Intense anxiety or panic attack triggered by a specific object or situation
- Persistent avoidance of feared object or situation

Posttraumatic Stress Disorder

- Anxiety triggered by memories of a traumatic experience

Obsessive-Compulsive Disorder

- Anxiety caused by uncontrollable, persistent, recurring thoughts (obsessions) and/or
- Anxiety caused by uncontrollable, persistent urges to perform certain actions (compulsions)

Explaining Obsessive-Compulsive Disorder

Although researchers are far from fully understanding the causes of obsessive-compulsive disorder, biological factors seem to be involved. For example, a deficiency in the neurotransmitter serotonin has been implicated in obsessive-compulsive disorder. When treated with drugs that increase the availability of serotonin in the brain, many obsessive-compulsive patients experience a marked decrease in symptoms (Insel & Winslow, 1992; Jenike, 1992).

In addition, obsessive-compulsive disorder has been linked with dysfunction in specific brain areas, such as the frontal lobes, which play a key role in our ability to think and plan ahead. Another brain area that has been implicated is the caudate nucleus, which is involved in regulating movements (Schwartz & others, 1996). Dysfunctions in these brain areas might help account for the overwhelming sense of doubt and lack of control over thoughts and actions that are experienced in obsessive-compulsive disorder (Rapoport, 1991).

Brain Activity in Obsessive-Compulsive Disorder These PET scans show the change in activity in a brain area called the *caudate nucleus* before (left) and after (right) therapy for obsessive-compulsive disorder. The caudate nucleus is involved in initiating and controlling movement. In obsessive-compulsive disorder, the caudate nucleus is overactive, as indicated by the bright yellow in the left PET scan. After psychotherapy, the obsessions and compulsions cease, and the caudate nucleus becomes less active (right).

PRE   POST
rCd   rCd

Anxiety Disorders

Match each example below with one of the following anxiety disorders: generalized anxiety disorder, panic disorder, specific phobia, posttraumatic stress disorder, obsessive-compulsive disorder, social phobia.

1. Thuan, a Vietnamese refugee, cannot stop thinking about the horrors he experienced while fleeing his country by boat. He sleeps poorly and is often awakened by terrifying nightmares. _____

2. Alayna worries about everything and can never relax. She is very jumpy, has trouble sleeping at night, and has a poor appetite. For the last few months, her anxiety has become so extreme that she is unable to concentrate at work and is in danger of losing her job.

   _____

3. Ever since going through a very painful divorce, Kayla has experienced a number of terrifying "spells" that seem to come out of nowhere. Her heart suddenly starts to pound,

she begins to sweat and tremble, and she has trouble breathing. _____

4. Carl cannot bear to be in small enclosed places, such as elevators, and goes to great lengths to avoid them. Recently he turned down a high-paying job with an air-conditioning repair company because it involved working in crawlspaces. _____

5. Harry disinfects his shoes, clothing, floor, and doorknobs with bleach several times a day. Nevertheless, he is tormented by worries that his apartment may be contaminated by germs from outside. He doesn't allow anyone to come into his apartment for fear they will contaminate his furniture and belongings.

   _____

6. Kathy is so painfully shy that she dropped out of college rather than take a public speaking class. Although she is very bright and hard-working, she is unemployed because she cannot bring herself to go to a job interview.

   _____

Mood Disorders: Emotions Gone Awry

In the mood disorders, disturbed emotions cause psychological distress and impair daily functioning. What are the symptoms of major depression, and what is dysthymic disorder? How prevalent is depression? What is its course?

Let's face it, we all have our ups and downs. When things are going well, we feel cheerful and optimistic. When events take a more negative turn, our mood can sour: we feel miserable and pessimistic. Either way, the intensity and duration of our moods are usually in proportion to the events going on in our lives (Mondimore, 1993). That's completely normal.

In the mood disorders, however, emotions violate the criteria of normal moods. In quality, intensity, and duration, a person's emotional state does not seem to reflect what's going on in his or her life. A person may feel a pervasive sadness despite the best of circumstances. Or a person may be extremely energetic and overconfident with no apparent justification. These mood changes persist much longer than the normal fluctuations in moods that we all experience.

DSM-IV formally defines a **mood disorder** as a serious, persistent disturbance in a person's emotions that causes psychological discomfort, impairs the ability to function, or both. In this section, we'll look at the two most important mood disorders: major depression and bipolar disorder.

mood disorders
A category of mental disorders in which significant and chronic disruption in mood is the predominant symptom, causing impaired cognitive, behavioral, and physical functioning.

Major Depression:

"Like Some Poisonous Fogbank"

The intense psychological pain of **major depression** is hard to convey to those who have never experienced it. In his book *Darkness Visible*, best-selling author William Styron (1990) described his struggle with major depression in this way:

Author William Styron The recipient of the Pulitzer Prize and other awards, Styron's best-selling novels include *Sophie's Choice, The Confessions of Nat Turner,* and *Lie Down in Darkness.* Yet despite his enormous success as a writer, Styron was gripped by the "smothering confinement" of major depression, which he vividly describes in *Darkness Visible.*

All sense of hope had vanished, along with the idea of a futurity; my brain, in thrall to its outlaw hormones, had become less an organ of thought than an instrument registering, minute by minute, varying degrees of its own suffering. The mornings themselves were becoming bad now as I wandered about lethargic, following my synthetic sleep, but afternoons were still the worse, beginning at three o'clock, when I'd feel the horror, like some poisonous fogbank, roll in upon my mind, forcing me into bed. There I would lie for as long as six hours, stuporous and virtually paralyzed, gazing at the ceiling . . .

The Symptoms of Major Depression

The Styron passage gives you a feeling for how the symptoms of depression affect the whole individual—emotionally, behaviorally, cognitively, and physically (see Figure 14.3). *Emotionally,* the person feels an overwhelming sadness. Often, the sadness is accompanied by feelings of guilt, worthlessness, inadequacy, emptiness, and hopelessness. Even if surrounded by close friends and loving family members, the person feels alone and disconnected from others (A. Schwartz & R. M. Schwartz, 1993).

Behaviorally, the depressed person's feelings are reflected in dejected and spiritless facial expressions. Crying spells may occur for no apparent reason. Speech, movements, and gestures seem awkward and slower than usual (Gotlib, 1992). Compared with nondepressed people, the depressed person speaks more slowly and takes longer to respond to the comments of others. Depressed people make less eye contact with others and smile less often than people who are not depressed. Often, depressed people withdraw from activities that they once enjoyed.

Cognitively, memory is often impaired (Burt & others, 1995). Thought processes feel dull and sluggish, and the person may have problems concentrating. It becomes increasingly difficult or impossible to complete what were once routine tasks, such as studying, balancing a checkbook, or making dinner. Because the depressed person is often gripped by a paralyzing indecisiveness, making even simple decisions may seem impossible.

Self-esteem plummets as the person's thoughts become globally pessimistic and negative about themselves, the world, and the future (Beck & others, 1993; Mondimore, 1993). Often, this pervasive negativity and pessimism are manifested in suicidal thoughts or a preoccupation with death. Suicide is always a potential risk in major depression. Approximately 10 percent of those suffering major depression attempt suicide (Zweig & Hinrichsen, 1993).

Physically, major depression is characterized by a general loss of mental and physical energy, along with vague physical aches and pains. Some depressed people experience a sense of physical restlessness and anxiety, demonstrated by fidgeting or aimless pacing. And, in fact, the physical symptoms of anxiety often accompany depression (Wittchen & others, 1994; Liebowitz, 1993).

Many of the artifacts of my house had become potential devices for my own destruction: the attic rafters (and an outside maple or two) a means to hang myself, the garage a place to inhale carbon monoxide, the bathtub a vessel to receive the flow from my opened arteries. The kitchen knives in their drawers had but one purpose for me.

William Styron, 1990

major depression
A mood disorder characterized by extreme and persistent feelings of despondency, worthlessness, and hopelessness, causing impaired emotional, cognitive, behavioral, and physical functioning.

Emotional symptoms

- Feelings of sadness, hopelessness, helplessness, guilt, emptiness, or worthlessness
- Feeling emotionally disconnected from others
- Turning away from other people

Cognitive symptoms

- Difficulty thinking, concentrating and remembering
- Global negativity and pessimism
- Suicidal thoughts or preoccupation with death

Behavioral symptoms

- Dejected facial expression
- Makes less eye contact; eyes downcast
- Smiles less often
- Slowed movements, speech, and gestures
- Tearfulness or spontaneous episodes of crying
- Loss of interest or pleasure in usual activities, including sex
- Withdrawal from social activities

Physical symptoms

- Changes in appetite resulting in significant weight loss or gain
- Insomnia, early morning awakening or oversleeping
- Vague but chronic aches and pains
- Diminished sexual interest
- Loss of physical and mental energy
- Global feelings of anxiety
- Restlessness, fidgety activity

FIGURE 14.3 The Symptoms of Depression

The experience of major depression can permeate every aspect of life. This figure shows some of the most common emotional, behavioral, cognitive, and physical symptoms of that disorder.

Along with a general loss of energy, motivation and drive diminish (Papolos & Papolos, 1992). Appetite and eating patterns are disturbed. People with depression often lose weight because they lose all interest in food. Less commonly, people may eat excessively and gain weight. Sexual interest also diminishes (Nofzinger & others, 1993).

Abnormal sleep patterns are another hallmark of major depression. The amount of time spent in nondreaming, deeply relaxed sleep is greatly reduced or absent (see Chapter 4). Rather than the usual 90-minute cycles of dreaming, the person experiences sporadic REM periods of varying lengths. Spontaneous awakenings occur repeatedly during the night. Very commonly, the depressed person awakens at 3:00 or 4:00 a.m., then cannot get back to sleep, despite feeling exhausted (Benca & others, 1992; Wehr, 1988). Less commonly, some depressed people sleep excessively, sometimes as much as 18 hours a day.

To be diagnosed with major depression, a person must display most of the symptoms described above for two weeks or longer (DSM-IV, 1994). In many cases, there doesn't seem to be any external reason for the persistent feeling of depression. In other cases, a person's downward emotional spiral has been triggered by some negative event or stressful situation (see Frank & others, 1994; Kendler & others, 1993a).

One significant negative event deserves special mention: the death of a loved one. If a family member or close friend dies, it is completely normal to feel despondent and sad for several months as part of the mourning or bereavement process (Zisook & Shuchter, 1993). Even so, most people resume attending to the routine duties of life within a few weeks. Privately, they may still feel a strong sense of loss, but they function adequately if not optimally. As a general rule, if a person's ability to function after the death of a loved one is still seriously impaired after two months, major depression is suspected (DSM-IV, 1994).

Dysthymic Disorder

In contrast to major depression, which significantly impairs a person's ability to function, some people experience a less severe form of depression called dysthymic disorder. Briefly, **dysthymic disorder** is chronic, low-grade depression. It's characterized by many of the symptoms of depression, but the symptoms are less intense. Usually, dysthymic disorder develops in response to some stressful event or trauma. Rather than improving over time, however, the negative mood persists indefinitely. Although the person functions adequately, she has a chronic case of "the blues" that can continue for years (Hirschfeld, 1991).

Some people with dysthymic disorder experience *double depression*. That is, they experience one or more episodes of major depression on top of their ongoing dysthymic disorder. As the person recovers from the episode of major depression, he returns to the less intense depressed symptoms of dysthymic disorder (Bower, 1994a; Lewinsohn & others, 1991b).

The Prevalence and Course of Major Depression

Major depression is often called "the common cold" of psychological disorders, and for a good reason: depression is the most common of all the psychological disorders (Kessler & others, 1994; Gotlib, 1992). In any given year, about 12 million Americans are affected by major depression. When you combine the costs of treating depression, worker absenteeism, reduced work productivity, and the loss of lifetime earnings from depression-related suicides, the cost of major depression is staggering—approximately $44 *billion* a year in the United States alone (Greenberg & others, 1993a, 1993b).

Women are about twice as likely as men to be diagnosed with major depression, though researchers aren't completely certain why depression is more prevalent among women (Nolen-Hoeksema, 1990; Kendler & others, 1993a). If you're female, the lifetime odds are approximately 1 out of 4 that you'll experience major depression. If you're male, the lifetime odds are about 1 out of 8 (Kessler & others, 1994).

Age also seems to play a significant role. Those in the fifteen-to-twenty-four and thirty-five-to-forty-four age brackets are most at risk to develop major depression. Statistical profiles indicate that you're also at greater risk to develop major depression if you have little education or income, are a homemaker, or are divorced, widowed, or separated (Blazer & others, 1994; K. C. Burke & others, 1991). However, people outside these categories are not immune to depression. Styron (1990) was sixty years old, happily married, and immensely successful when he first experienced the "smothering confinement" of major depression.

Most people who experience major depression try to cope with the symptoms without seeking professional help (Kessler & others, 1994). Left untreated, the symptoms of major depression can easily last six months or longer. In about 10 percent of people experiencing major depression, the symptoms become chronic, meaning they last for two years or longer (Coryell & others, 1994a; Hornig-Rohan & Amsterdam, 1994).

When depression is not treated, it may become a recurring mental disorder that progressively becomes more severe. Better than half of all people who have been through one episode of major depression can expect a relapse, usually within two years. With each recurrence, the symptoms tend to increase in severity and the time between major depression episodes decreases (Coryell & others, 1994b; Wells & others, 1992).

Finally, for millions of people with **seasonal affective disorder (SAD)**, repeated episodes of depression are as predictable as the changing seasons, especially the onset of autumn and winter (Faedda & others, 1993). In the most common form of seasonal affective disorder, episodes of depression

dysthymic disorder
A mood disorder involving chronic, low-grade feelings of depression that produce subjective discomfort but do not seriously impair the ability to function.

seasonal affective disorder (SAD)
A mood disorder in which episodes of depression typically recur during the fall and winter and remit during the spring and summer.

recur in the fall and winter months, when there is the least amount of sunlight. Seasonal affective disorder is more common among women and among people who live in the northern latitudes (Rosenthal, 1993).

Bipolar Disorder:

An Emotional Roller Coaster

Bipolar disorder typically involves abnormally intense positive and negative moods. What characterizes a manic episode? What is cyclothymic disorder? How prevalent is bipolar disorder? What factors contribute to mood disorders?

It was about 6:30 a.m. when your author Don arrived for work at 2 Specialty—the hospital psychiatric ward. A few patients sat sipping their morning coffee or looking at the newspaper. As Don walked toward the nurses' station, a tall, overweight young man with black curly hair *zoomed* across the ward and intercepted him.

"Hi! My name's Kelly! What's yours?" he enthusiastically boomed, vigorously shaking hands. Before Don could respond, Kelly moved on to new topics. Within the next 90 seconds, Don heard about: (1) Kelly's plans to make millions of dollars organizing garage sales for other people; (2) several songs that Kelly had written that were all going to skyrocket to the top of the music charts; (3) Kelly's many inventions; and (4) a variety of movie stars, rock stars, and professional athletes, all of whom were Kelly's close friends.

Kelly spoke so rapidly that his words often got tangled up with each other. His arms and legs looked as if they were about to get tangled up, too—Kelly was in constant motion. His grinning, rapid-fire speech was punctuated with grand, sweeping gestures and exaggerated facial expressions. Before Don could get a word in edgewise, Kelly vigorously shook his hand again, and *zoomed* to the other side of the psychiatric ward to intercept another unfamiliar face.

The Symptoms of Bipolar Disorder

Kelly displayed classic symptoms of the mental disorder that used to be called *manic depression* and is today called **bipolar disorder.** In contrast to major depression, bipolar disorder almost always involves abnormal moods at *both* ends of the emotional spectrum. In most cases of bipolar disorder, the person experiences extreme mood swings. Episodes of incapacitating depression alternate with shorter periods of extreme euphoria called **manic episodes.** For most people with bipolar disorder, a manic episode immediately precedes or follows a bout with major depression. However, a small percentage of people with bipolar disorder experience only manic episodes (DSM-IV, 1994).

Manic episodes typically begin suddenly and symptoms escalate rapidly. During a manic episode, people are uncharacteristically euphoric, expansive, and excited for several days or longer. Although they sleep very little, they have boundless energy. To the unfamiliar observer, people experiencing a manic episode may simply seem overly enthusiastic. But to those who know them, the unbridled enthusiasm and unlimited energy are clearly excessive and out of character.

Typically, the person in the midst of a manic episode does not recognize what is happening to him. As a result, he often resists the efforts of others to help. This was certainly true in the case of Kelly: it took four police officers and three of Kelly's fraternity buddies to corral Kelly and bring him to the psychiatric ward at two o'clock in the morning.

Patty Duke and Bipolar Disorder Actress Patty Duke was the youngest person to win an Academy Award for her performance as Helen Keller in *The Miracle Worker.* But as an adult, Duke careened from bouts of suicidal depression to episodes of manic behavior. At one point, she married a man she had known for only five hours. At another time, just moments after accepting an Emmy, she angrily rejected the award and announced she was going to become a doctor. In 1982, Patty Duke was diagnosed with bipolar disorder. Since that time, medication has stabilized her behavior.

bipolar disorder
Often called *manic depression;* a mood disorder involving periods of incapacitating depression alternating with periods of extreme euphoria and excitement.

manic episode
A sudden, rapidly escalating emotional state characterized by extreme euphoria, excitement, physical energy, and rapid thoughts and speech.

During a manic episode, the person's sense of self-esteem is wildly inflated. He exudes supreme self-confidence. Often, he has grandiose plans for obtaining wealth, power, and fame (Mondimore, 1993). Sometimes the grandiose ideas represent *delusional,* or false, beliefs. Kelly's belief that various celebrities were his close personal friends was delusional.

Frenzied goal-directed behavior abounds during a manic episode. Multiple activities, business ventures, shopping sprees, social interactions, or other tasks are initiated, often simultaneously. To an outside observer, the behavior seems disorganized and bizarre. But the manic person believes that he or she is simply seizing golden opportunities. For example, Kelly believed he had invented a new kind of fishing pole that would "revolutionize" game fishing. The hospital staff finally suspended Kelly's telephone privileges after a fishing rod manufacturer called to confirm his order of 10,000 fishing rods.

Kelly's fast-forward speech was loud and virtually impossible to interrupt. During a manic episode, words are spoken so rapidly, they're often slurred as the person tries to keep up with his own thought processes. The manic person feels as if his thoughts are racing along at Warp Factor 10. Attention is easily distracted by virtually anything, triggering a *flight of ideas,* in which thoughts rapidly and loosely shift from topic to topic.

Not surprisingly, the ability to function during a manic episode is severely impaired. Hospitalization is usually required, partly to protect people from the potential consequences of their own poor judgment and inappropriate behaviors. Bolstered by their supreme self-confidence, they do inappropriate things like tell their boss to shove it or show up in the university president's office demanding immediate policy changes, both of which Kelly did. During manic episodes, people can also run up a mountain of bills, disappear for weeks at time, become sexually promiscuous, or commit illegal acts. Very commonly, the person becomes agitated or verbally abusive when others question his grandiose claims (Hendrix, 1993).

Some people experience a milder but chronic form of bipolar disorder called **cyclothymic disorder.** In cyclothymic disorder, people experience moderate but frequent mood swings for two years or longer. These mood swings are not severe enough to qualify as either bipolar disorder or major depression. Often, people with cyclothymic disorder are perceived as being extremely moody, unpredictable, and inconsistent.

The Prevalence and Course of Bipolar Disorder

As in Kelly's case, the onset of bipolar disorder typically occurs in the person's early twenties. The extreme mood swings of bipolar disorder tend to start and stop much more abruptly than the mood changes of major depression. And whereas an episode of major depression can easily last for six months or longer, the manic and depressive episodes of bipolar disorder tend to be much shorter—lasting anywhere from a few days to a couple of months (Winokur & others, 1993).

Annually, about 2 million Americans suffer from bipolar disorder (Hendrix, 1993). Unlike major depression, there are no sex differences in the rate at which bipolar disorder occurs. For both men and women, the lifetime risk of developing bipolar disorder is about 1 percent (Leibenluft, 1996; Kessler & others, 1994).

In the vast majority of cases, bipolar disorder is a recurring mental disorder (Gitlin & others, 1995). A small percentage of people with bipolar disorder display *rapid cycling,* experiencing four or more manic or depressive episodes every year (Maj & others, 1994). More commonly, bipolar disorder tends to recur every couple of years (Coryell & others, 1992). Often, bipolar disorder recurs when the individual stops taking *lithium,* a medication that helps control the disorder (Keck & McElroy, 1993).

cyclothymic disorder
A mood disorder characterized by moderate but frequent mood swings that are not severe enough to qualify as bipolar disorder.

Explaining Mood Disorders

Multiple factors appear to be involved in the development of the mood disorders. In this section, we'll briefly consider three key factors that have been implicated: genetics, brain chemistry, and stressful events.

Genetics and Mood Disorders

Thus far, researchers have not been able to directly identify a specific gene or combination of genes that causes mood disorders (Marshall, 1994; A. Schwartz & R. M. Schwartz, 1993). However, there is ample indirect evidence from family, twin, and adoption studies that some people inherit a *genetic predisposition,* or a greater vulnerability, to develop a mood disorder (Tsuang & Faraone, 1990).

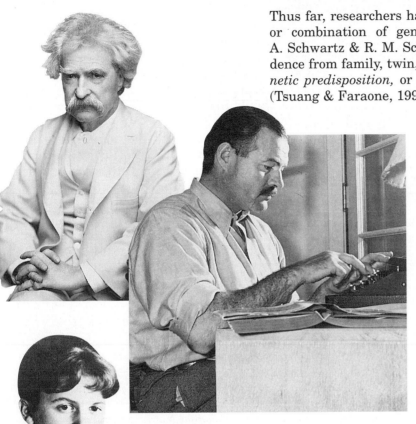

Creativity and Mood Disorders
Mood disorders occur more frequently among creative writers and artists than among the general population, leading some researchers to propose a biochemical or genetic link between mood disorders and the artistic temperament (Jamison, 1993). Writer Mark Twain, novelist Ernest Hemingway, and poet Sylvia Plath all suffered from severe bouts of depression throughout their lives. Plath and Hemingway both committed suicide, as did Hemingway's father, brother, and sister. Hemingway's two sons also suffered from major depression. In 1996, Hemingway's granddaughter, actress Margaux Hemingway, committed suicide one day before the 35th anniversary of her famous grandfather's death.

For example, researchers have consistently found that both major depression and bipolar disorder tend to run in families (Warner & others, 1992; Hammen & others, 1990). If a person has a mood disorder, that person's immediate relatives—children, siblings, or parents—are up to three times more likely than the general population to have a mood disorder (A. Schwartz & R. M. Schwartz, 1993).

Twin studies have shown that if one identical twin suffers from major depression or bipolar disorder, the other twin has about a 70 percent chance of also developing the disorder (Torrey & others, 1994; Kendler & others, 1993b; 1993c). The same 70 percent shared risk rate has been found in studies of identical twins who were adopted and raised apart (Klein & Wender, 1993). These findings strongly suggest that shared genetics rather than shared environmental experiences account for the high rate of similarity of mood disorders in identical twins.

Neurotransmitters and Mood Disorders

There is a great deal of indirect evidence that implicates at least two important neurotransmitters, serotonin and norepinephrine, in major depression. Since the 1960s, several medications, called *antidepressants,* have been developed to treat major depression. In one way or another, the antidepressants seem to lift the symptoms of depression by increasing the availability of norepinephrine and serotonin in the brain.

In general, the antidepressants are highly effective. The symptoms of major depression are alleviated in about 80 percent of the people for whom antidepressants are prescribed (Sargent, 1993). Evidence is also accumulating that continued use of antidepressants can prevent recurrences of major depression (Fava & Kaji, 1994; Kupfer & others, 1992).

In the case of bipolar disorder, the drug lithium has been widely used since the 1960s to treat bipolar disorder and to prevent its recurrence (Sachs & others, 1994; Keck & McElroy, 1993). How lithium works, however, is unknown.

In the next chapter, we'll look more closely at antidepressants, lithium, and other treatments for psychological disorders. For now, simply understand that the effectiveness of these medications provides some of the most compelling evidence that mood disorders involve a disruption in the delicate balance of brain chemistry.

TABLE 14.5 The Mood Disorders

Major Depression

- Loss of interest or pleasure in almost all activities
- Despondent mood, feelings of emptiness, worthlessness, or excessive guilt
- Preoccupation with death or suicidal thoughts
- Difficulty sleeping or excessive sleeping
- Diminished ability to think, concentrate, or make decisions
- Diminished appetite and significant weight loss

Dysthymic Disorder

- Chronic, low-grade depressed feelings that are not severe enough to qualify as major depression

Bipolar Disorder

- One or more manic episodes characterized by euphoria, high energy, grandiose ideas, flight of ideas, inappropriate self-confidence, and decreased need for sleep
- Usually, one or more episodes of major depression
- May alternate rapidly between symptoms of mania and major depression

Cyclothymic Disorder

- Moderate, recurring mood swings that are not severe enough to qualify as major depression or bipolar disorder

Stress and Mood Disorders

Major depression is often triggered by traumatic and stressful events (G. Brown & others, 1994). Exposure to recent stressful events is one of the best predictors of major depression episodes. This seems to be especially true for people who have experienced previous episodes of depression and who have a family history of mood disorders (Kendler & others, 1993a).

But even in people with no family or personal history of mood disorders, chronic stress alone can produce major depression. For example, one study looked at older adults who were caring for spouses whose mental abilities were progressively deteriorating. Almost none of these older adult caregivers had a family history of mood disorders or prior episodes of depression. Nevertheless, 30 percent of them experienced a depressive disorder while caring for their spouse over the course of several years. During the same time period, depression occurred in only 1 percent of those in a matched control group (Dura & others, 1990).

There is some evidence that stressful life events also play a role in the course of bipolar disorder (Johnson & Roberts, 1995). In summary, considerable evidence points to the role of genetic factors, biochemical factors, and stressful life events in the development of mood disorders. However, exactly how these factors interact to cause mood disorders is still being investigated.

CONCEPT REVIEW 14.3

Mood Disorders

1. Since moving to Fairbanks, Alaska, five years ago, Joan has experienced episodes of depression during the fall and winter months. It is likely that Joan suffers from:
   a. bipolar disorder
   b. cyclothymic disorder
   c. selective Alaskan depression (SAD)
   d. seasonal affective disorder (SAD)

2. For as long as she can remember, Mary has felt negative about life. Although good things occasionally happen in Mary's life, they have little impact on her gloomy mood. Mary functions adequately, but she has few friends because she is so pessimistic. Mary probably suffers from:
   a. situational aetiology disorder (SAD)
   b. dysthymic disorder
   c. bipolar disorder
   d. cyclothymic disorder

3. After weeks of feeling dejected, despondent, and dissatisfied with his life, Fred has suddenly become euphoric and energetic. He talks constantly about his far-fetched plans for making huge amounts of money. Fred is most likely suffering from:
   a. bipolar disorder
   b. dysthymic disorder
   c. seasonal affective disorder (SAD)
   d. major depression

4. Bianca, a nineteen-year-old college student, has missed almost all her classes during the last month. She sleeps fourteen hours a day, has withdrawn from friends and family, feels worthless, and cries for no apparent reason. Bianca is most likely suffering from:
   a. major depression
   b. dysthymic disorder
   c. bipolar disorder
   d. cyclothymic disorder

5. Mark is very unpredictable. One week he is a recluse, the next week he is energetic and initiating activities with others. Even though his mood swings occur regularly, they are not severe enough to qualify as bipolar disorder. Mark's consistent moodiness may well be a symptom of:
   a. personality oscillating disorder (POD)
   b. dysthymic disorder
   c. cyclothymic disorder
   d. shifting affective dementia (SAD)

dissociative experience
A break or disruption in consciousness during which awareness, memory, and personal identity become separated or divided.

The Dissociative Disorders:
Fragmentation of the Self

> *A dissociative experience reflects a disruption in awareness, memory, or identity. What are dissociative amnesia and dissociative fugue? What is dissociative identity disorder (DID), and what is thought to cause it? Why are some psychologists skeptical about DID?*

Despite the many changes you've experienced throughout your lifetime, you have a pretty consistent sense of identity. You're aware of your surroundings and can easily recall memories from the recent and distant past. In other words, a normal personality is one in which *awareness, memory,* and *personal identity* are associated and well-integrated.

In contrast, a **dissociative experience** is one in which a person's awareness, memory, and personal identity become separated or divided. While that may sound weird, dissociative experiences are not inherently pathological. In fact, mild dissociative experiences are quite common and completely normal (Kihlstrom & others, 1994; Putnam, 1993). Here are several common examples of minor dissociative experiences, some of which have probably happened to you:

- You become so absorbed in a book or movie that you lose all track of time.

- You feel "spacey" when you're extremely tired or under stress.

- You daydream your way through class, snapping to only when your instructor calls your name for the third time.

- You are so preoccupied with your thoughts while driving that when you get to your destination, you remember next to nothing about the trip.

- You wake up in a strange room on vacation and are momentarily unable to remember where you are or how you got there.

In each of these examples, you've experienced a temporary "break" or "separation" in your memory or awareness—a mild form of dissociation.

In some cultures, dramatic disruptions in an individual's sense of personal identity are perceived as normal and even highly valued (Mulhern, 1991). For example, *spirit possession* is common in many cultures, typically within a religious context (Spanos, 1994; Krippner, 1994). The usual occupant of a human body is supposedly displaced by a "spirit" that takes control of the body. The individual often has no memory for events experienced while the spirit is in control. Another phenomenon that occurs in some cultures is

CALVIN AND HOBBS

Dissociation and Possession A Candomble priestess in Brazil holds a woman who is "possessed" by a Christian saint during a religious ceremony. Such dissociative trance and possession states are common in religions around the world. When dissociative experiences take place within a religious ritual context, they are not considered abnormal. In fact, such experiences may be highly valued (Mulhern, 1991).

a *trance state,* in which the person loses his sense of personal identity or is unaware of his surroundings (Cardeña, 1992).

If spirit possession and trance states sound like bizarre behaviors that only occur in cultures radically different from our own, think again. *Glossolalia,* or "speaking in tongues," is common in some North American Christian churches (Spanos, 1994). Speaking in tongues is another example of a dissociative possession state: the person is temporarily "possessed" by the Holy Spirit, who speaks through the individual in an unknown language. Like trance states and spirit possession, glossolalia is a highly valued experience within a specific cultural and religious context.

As DSM-IV points out, dissociative possession or trance states are *not* considered pathological if: (1) they occur within the context of accepted cultural or religious practices; (2) they occur voluntarily; and (3) they don't cause distress or impair functioning. In fact, people who frequently experience possession or trance states may achieve special status within their culture as spiritual leaders or healers (Mulhern, 1991).

Dissociation and Trauma

More extreme dissociative experiences often occur in victims of accidents, disasters, and other types of trauma, including physical assault and rape (Spiegel & Cardeña, 1991). During traumatic situations, people may feel detached from their surroundings. They may experience *depersonalization*, a sense of being detached from their body or self, feeling as if they are watching themselves act from a distance. Events can seem "unreal" or dreamlike. Perceptual distortions, such as a feeling that time has slowed down or stopped, can also occur.

Such dissociative symptoms seem to be a relatively common way of coping with traumatic experiences (Carlson & Rosser-Hogan, 1991). For example, one study looked at dissociative symptoms in journalists who had witnessed the execution of a condemned prisoner in California. When surveyed a month after the execution, many of the journalists reported a wide range of dissociative symptoms, including emotional numbness and detachment from other people (Freinkel & others, 1994). According to psychiatrist David Spiegel (1993a), dissociative experiences during and after traumatic experiences "are often extremely helpful in allowing the person to defend against overwhelming fear, pain, and helplessness."

Clearly, then, dissociative experiences are not necessarily abnormal. But in the **dissociative disorders,** the dissociative experiences are more extreme and frequent and severely disrupt everyday functioning. Awareness, or recognition of familiar surroundings, may be completely obstructed. Memories of pertinent personal information may be unavailable to consciousness. Identity may be lost, confused, or fragmented (Spiegel & Cardeña, 1991; Kihlstrom & others, 1994).

Until recently, the dissociative disorders were thought to be extremely rare. However, there is increasing evidence that dissociative symptoms and the dissociative disorders are far more common than researchers had believed (Saxe & others, 1993; C. Ross, 1991).

The category of dissociative disorders consists of three basic disorders: *dissociative amnesia, dissociative fugue,* and *dissociative identity disorder,* which was previously called multiple personality disorder.

Dissociative Amnesia and Fugue:

Forgetting and Wandering

Dissociative amnesia refers to the partial or total inability to recall important information which is not due to a medical condition, like an illness, injury, or drug. Usually the person develops amnesia for personal events and information, rather than for general knowledge or skills. That is, the person may not be able to remember his wife's name, but does remember how to read and who Martin Luther King, Jr., was. In most cases, dissociative amnesia is a response to stress, trauma, or an extremely distressing situation, such as combat, marital problems, or physical abuse (Loewenstein, 1993; Spiegel & Cardeña, 1991).

A closely related disorder is dissociative fugue. In **dissociative fugue,** the person outwardly appears completely normal. However, the person has extensive amnesia and is confused about his identity. While in the fugue state, he suddenly and inexplicably travels away from his home, wandering to other cities or even countries. In some cases, people in a fugue state adopt a completely new identity.

Like dissociative amnesia, dissociative fugues are associated with traumatic events or stressful periods (Loewenstein, 1993). Interestingly, when the person "awakens" from the fugue state, he may remember his past life but have amnesia for what occurred *during* the fugue state (DSM-IV, 1994).

Dissociative Identity Disorder

Among the dissociative disorders, none is more fascinating—or more controversial—than dissociative identity disorder, formerly known as *multiple personality disorder.* **Dissociative identity disorder,** abbreviated **DID,** involves extensive memory disruptions for personal information along with the presence of two or more distinct identities or "personalities" within a single person (DSM-IV, 1994). Typically, each personality has its own name, and each will be experienced as if it has its own personal history and self-image. These alternate personalities, often called *alters,* may be of widely varying ages and different genders. The number of alternate personalities can range from two to over a hundred, but having ten to fifteen alters is most common (Goff & Simms, 1993; C. Ross & others, 1989).

Alters are not really separate people. Rather, they constitute a "system of mind" (Kluft, 1993; Putnam, 1991a). That is, the alters seem to embody different aspects of the individual's personality that, for some reason, cannot be

dissociative disorders
A category of psychological disorders in which extreme and frequent disruptions of awareness, memory, and personal identity impair the ability to function.

dissociative amnesia
A dissociative disorder involving the partial or total inability to recall important personal information.

dissociative fugue
A dissociative disorder involving sudden and unexpected travel away from home, extensive amnesia, and identity confusion.

dissociative identity disorder (DID)
Formerly called *multiple personality disorder;* a dissociative disorder involving extensive memory disruptions along with the presence of two or more distinct identities or "personalities."

integrated into the primary personality. The alternate personalities hold memories, emotions, and motives that are not admissible to the individual's conscious mind.

At different times, different alters take control of the person's experience, thoughts, and behavior (Kihlstrom, 1992). Typically, the primary personality is unaware of the existence of the alternate personalities. However, the alters may have knowledge of each other's existence and share memories (Kihlstrom & others, 1994). Sometimes the experiences of one alter are accessible to another alter but not vice versa.

Some researchers claim that there are physiological differences among the different personalities within a single individual. Differences in visual functioning, allergies, brain function, and handedness have been reported (Miller & others, 1991; Henninger, 1992). Although these accounts are intriguing, such physiological differences have yet to be convincingly demonstrated under controlled conditions (Miller & Traggiano, 1992).

Symptoms of amnesia and memory problems are present in virtually all cases of DID. There are frequent gaps in memory for both recent and childhood experiences. Commonly, the person with dissociative identity disorder "loses time" and is unable to recall her behavior or whereabouts during specific time periods. For example, people with DID may discover items in their closet that they don't remember buying, or find themselves in an unfamiliar location with no idea of how they got there (Loewenstein, 1991). They may discover letters in a strange handwriting that they don't remember writing, drawings and paintings that they can't remember creating, or canceled checks that they don't remember writing.

Besides memory problems, people with DID typically have numerous psychiatric and physical symptoms, along with a chaotic personal history (Putnam, 1991a, 1991b; Saxe & others, 1994). Headaches and other physical symptoms are common, as are physical symptoms for which no medical cause can be found. Symptoms of major depression, anxiety, posttraumatic stress disorder, substance abuse, sleep disorders, and self-destructive behavior are also very common. Often, the DID patient has been diagnosed with a variety of other psychological disorders before the DID diagnosis is made (Carlson & others, 1993; Coons & Dua, 1993).

The DID Controversy

Many psychologists and other mental health professionals are very skeptical about dissociative identity disorder (Hayes & Mitchell, 1994). Much of this skepticism is related to the fact that the number of reported cases of DID has risen dramatically in the last two decades (Merskey, 1992). Other psychologists point out that DID is not unique in this regard. Psychological disorders such as obsessive-compulsive disorder and PTSD have also increased in prevalance, partly because psychologists have become more aware of the symptoms (Gleaves, 1996; Davis & Breslau, 1994).

Nevertheless, some psychologists flatly claim that there is no such thing as multiple personality disorder or dissociative identify disorder. Rather, they suggest, DID patients are consciously or unconsciously "faking" the symptoms, responding to a therapist's suggestions, or mimicking the symptoms of sensational DID cases portrayed in the media. As outspoken skeptic Nicholas Spanos (1994) put it:

> Patients learn to construe themselves as possessing multiple selves, learn to present themselves in terms of this construal, and learn to reorganize and elaborate on their personal biography so as to make it congruent with their understanding of what it means to be a multiple.

Although it is certainly possible that some patients may be faking DID symptoms, it seems unlikely that this is the case in all instances of dissociative identity disorder. Psychologists on the other side of this controversy point out that many of these patients experience clear-cut DID symptoms before entering treatment or learning about the disorder (Gleaves, 1996). Instead, they suggest that the increase in DID cases is due to (1) greater clinical awareness of the disorder, (2) improved diagnostic descriptions of DID symptoms, and (3) increased screening for dissociative symptoms.

For example, dissociative identity disorder was once thought to be extremely rare or nonexistent in Puerto Rico, the Netherlands, Belgium, and other countries. However, when formal screening programs for dissociative symptoms were established in these countries, cases of DID and other dissociative disorders were uncovered (Boon & Draijer, 1993; Vanderlinden & others, 1991; Martinez-Taboas, 1991). These DID patients were found to have the same core symptoms as DID patients in the United States, including a history of childhood abuse or trauma.

Is DID a bona fide psychological disorder? Many psychologists think so (Gleaves, 1996). Since DID became an official DSM diagnostic category in 1980, its clinical picture has become progressively better defined. As research on DID and other dissociative disorders continues, questions about the prevalence and nature of this diagnostic category may well be answered. For now, it remains the most controversial diagnostic category in DSM-IV.

Explaining Dissociative Identity Disorder

According to one explanation, dissociative identity disorder represents an extreme form of dissociative coping (Gleaves, 1996). A very high percentage of DID patients report having suffered extreme physical or sexual abuse in childhood—over 90 percent in most surveys (Coons, 1994). In order to cope with the trauma, the child "dissociates" himself or herself from it, creating alternate personalities to experience the trauma (Irwin, 1994).

Over time, alternate personalities are created to deal with the memories and emotions associated with intolerably painful experiences. Feelings of anger, rage, fear, and guilt that are too powerful for the child to consciously integrate can be dissociated into these alternate personalities (Kluft, 1991; Putnam, 1989). In effect, dissociation becomes a pathological defense mechanism that the person uses to cope with overwhelming experiences (Spiegel, 1993a).

Although widely accepted among therapists who work with dissociative identity disorder patients, the dissociative coping theory is difficult to test empirically. The main problem is that memories of childhood are notoriously unreliable (Loftus, 1993b). Since DID is usually diagnosed in adulthood, it is very difficult, and often impossible, to determine whether the reports of childhood abuse are real or imaginary (Frankel, 1993).

Despite the difficulties of objective verification, a few researchers have confirmed memories of childhood abuse with independent evidence, such as medical records and court testimony by family members and social workers (Coons, 1994). Other research has shown a strong correlation between childhood trauma and the frequency of dissociative experiences in adulthood (Spiegel & Cardeña, 1991). For example, in an Australian study of normal adults, psychologist Harvey Irwin (1994) found that a childhood history of sexual abuse or loss of a family member was correlated with proneness to dissociative experiences in adulthood. Even in people who do not have a mental disorder, childhood trauma seems to lead to greater dissociative tendencies in adulthood.

In the next section, we look at a mental disorder that some people mistakenly believe is the same as multiple personality disorder. As you'll see, the symptoms of *schizophrenia* are fundamentally different from those that characterize dissociative identity disorder.

TABLE 14.6 Dissociative Disorders

Dissociative Amnesia

- Inability to remember important personal information, too extensive to be explained by ordinary forgetfulness

Dissociative Fugue

- Sudden, unexpected travel away from home
- Amnesia
- Confusion about personal identity or assumption of new identity

Dissociative Identity Disorder

- Presence of two or more distinct identities, each with consistent patterns of personality traits and behavior
- Behavior is controlled by two or more distinct, recurring identities
- Amnesia; frequent memory gaps

Dissociative Disorders

Match each example below with one of the following terms: dissociative experience, dissociative amnesia, dissociative fugue, dissociative identity disorder.

1. On the day of the Oklahoma City bombing, William had left the federal building just minutes before the bomb blast. When he heard the explosion, he raced back to the scene to help the victims. He remembers feeling as if time had slowed down, as if his surroundings were completely unreal, and as if he were watching himself from a distance. _____

2. Norma has frequent memory gaps and cannot account for her whereabouts during certain periods of time. After she expressed suicidal thoughts, her husband brought her to a community mental health center. While being interviewed by a clinical psychologist, she began speaking in a childlike voice. She claimed that

her name was Donna and that she was only six years old. Moments later, she seemed to revert to her adult voice and had no recollection of speaking in a childlike voice or claiming that her name was Donna. _____

3. Jay, a high school physics teacher in New York City, disappeared three days after his wife unexpectedly left him for another man. Six months later, he was discovered tending bar in Miami Beach. Calling himself Martin, he claimed to have no recollection of his past life and insisted that he had never been married. _____

4. Marian and her brother were recently involved in an automobile accident. Marian was not seriously injured, but her brother was killed. Marian is unable to recall any details from the time of the accident until four days later. _____

Schizophrenia: A Different Reality

Schizophrenia involves severely distorted beliefs, perceptions, and thought processes. How do positive and negative symptoms differ, and what are the core symptoms of schizophrenia? What are the main subtypes of schizophrenia? What are the prevalence and typical course of schizophrenia?

Normally, you've got a pretty good grip on reality. You can easily distinguish between external reality and the different kinds of mental states that you routinely experience, such as dreams or daydreams. But as we negotiate life's many twists and turns, the ability to stay firmly anchored in reality is not a given. Rather, we're engaged in an ongoing process of verifying the accuracy of our thoughts, beliefs, and perceptions.

If any mental disorder demonstrates the potential for losing touch with reality, it's schizophrenia. **Schizophrenia** is a psychological disorder that involves severely distorted beliefs, perceptions, and thought processes. During a schizophrenic episode, people lose their grip on reality, like the woman screaming "Fire!" in the chapter prologue. They experience an entirely different inner world, one that is often characterized by mental chaos, disorientation, and frustration.

Symptoms of Schizophrenia

The characteristic symptoms of schizophrenia can be described in terms of two broad categories: positive and negative symptoms. **Positive symptoms** reflect an excess or distortion of normal functioning. Positive symptoms include: (1) *delusions,* or false beliefs; (2) *hallucinations,* or false perceptions;

schizophrenia
A mental disorder in which the ability to function is impaired by severely distorted beliefs, perceptions, and thought processes.

positive symptoms
In schizophrenia, symptoms that reflect excesses or distortions of normal functioning, and include delusions, hallucinations, and disorganized thoughts and behavior.

and (3) severely disorganized thought processes, speech, and behavior. In contrast, **negative symptoms** reflect a restriction or reduction of normal functions, such as greatly reduced motivation, emotional expressiveness, or speech.

According to DSM-IV, schizophrenia is diagnosed when two or more of these characteristic symptoms are actively present for a month or longer. Usually, schizophrenia also involves a longer personal history, typically six months or more, of odd behaviors, beliefs, perceptual experiences, and other less severe signs of mental disturbance.

In the following sections, we'll describe the positive and negative symptoms that characterize schizophrenia. While these are the core symptoms of schizophrenia, keep in mind that there is enormous individual variation in the onset, intensity, and duration of schizophrenic symptoms (Beratis & others, 1994; Keith & Matthews, 1991).

Delusions: False Beliefs

We've all had the experience of firmly believing something that later turned out to be dead wrong. But when faced with evidence that contradicts our belief, we usually change our views, at least eventually. In contrast, a **delusion** is a falsely held belief that persists in spite of contradictory evidence or appeals to reason (Fauman, 1994; Garety, 1991).

Unlike beliefs that are simply inaccurate or unconventional, schizophrenic delusions are usually bizarre and far-fetched. The person believes that secret agents are poisoning his food, or that the next-door neighbors are actually aliens from outer space who are trying to transform him into a remote-controlled robot. Ignoring any evidence to the contrary, the delusional person clings to his erroneous belief. Even if the delusion is a frightening one, he often becomes so preoccupied with the idea that he can't stop thinking or talking about it (Spitzer, 1992; Butler & Braff, 1991). Not surprisingly, delusional beliefs typically cause great psychological distress and interfere with social or occupational functioning.

Although the content of delusions can be pretty wide-ranging, delusions are almost always centered on the person who is experiencing them. Certain themes also tend to surface consistently. For example, in *delusions of reference,* the delusional person believes that other people are constantly talking about her or that everything that happens is somehow related to her. Thus, the person experiencing delusions of reference grossly misinterprets or distorts the meaning of ordinary events. Traffic lights become symbolic communications from God, radio or television announcers are talking directly to her, and billboards are proclaiming her guilt or innocence to the world.

The basic theme of *delusions of grandeur* is that the person is extremely important, powerful, or wealthy. People may believe that they are the reincarnation of some famous or powerful person, such as Jesus Christ, the Virgin Mary, Marilyn Monroe, or Elvis Presley (Manschreck, 1992). Or they may believe that God has given them the power to control the forces of nature, dictate the plot lines of television programs, or resurrect dead geraniums.

In *delusions of persecution,* the basic theme is that others are plotting against or trying to harm the person or someone to whom the person is close. For example, psychiatrist Robert Howard (1992) reported a case in which an elderly woman became convinced that her upstairs neighbor was transmitting "violet rays" through the ceiling to harm her and her dog. This case has an interesting twist: the woman's dog adapted to her delusional beliefs and behavior. Here's part of Howard's (1992) case description of Ms. A:

> *For protection, she had placed a mattress under the kitchen table and slept there at night. She constructed what she called an "air raid shelter" for her dog from a small table and a pile of suitcases and insisted that the dog sleep*

Glimpses of Schizophrenia This drawing was made by a young man hospitalized for schizophrenia. At the time the picture was drawn, he was hallucinating and extremely paranoid. The drawing provides glimpses of the distorted perceptions and thoughts that are characteristic of a schizophrenic episode. Notice the smaller face that is superimposed on the larger face, which might represent the hallucinated voices that are often heard in schizophrenic episodes.

negative symptoms
In schizophrenia, symptoms that reflect defects or deficits in normal functioning, and include flat affect, alogia, and avolition.

delusion
A falsely held belief that persists in spite of contradictory evidence.

hallucination
A false or distorted perception that seems vividly real to the person experiencing it.

The Hallucinating Brain Researcher David Silbersweig and his colleagues (1995) used PET scans to take a "snapshot" of brain activity during schizophrenic hallucinations. The scan shown above was recorded at the exact instant a schizophrenic patient hallucinated disembodied heads yelling orders at him. The bright orange areas reveal activity in the left auditory and visual areas of his brain but not the frontal lobe, which normally is involved in organized thought processes.

FIGURE 14.4 Incidence of Different Types of Hallucinations in Schizophrenia
Schizophrenia-related hallucinations can occur in any sensory modality. Auditory hallucinations, usually in the form of voices, are the most common type of hallucination that occurs in schizophrenia, followed by visual hallucinations.
(Adapted from data in Mueser & others, 1990; Bracha & others, 1989.)

in it. When I visited Ms. A at her home, it was apparent that the dog's behavior had become so conditioned by that of its owner that upon hearing any sound from the flat upstairs, such as a door closing, it would immediately go to the kitchen and enter the shelter.

That Ms. A slept under the kitchen table and constructed an "air raid shelter" for her dog illustrates just how resistant to reality delusions can be. Because people with schizophrenia find their delusions so convincing, the delusions can sometimes provoke inappropriate or bizarre behavior (Buchanan & others, 1993). In some instances, delusional thinking can lead to dangerous behaviors, such as the person who responds to his delusional ideas by hurting himself or attacking others (Martell & Dietz, 1992).

Hallucinations: False Perceptions

Among the most disturbing experiences in schizophrenia are hallucinations. **Hallucinations** are false or distorted perceptions that seem vividly real (Bentall, 1990). Contrary to what you may think, hallucinations are a relatively common, normal experience. As you may recall from Chapter 4, many people occasionally experience vivid *hypnagogic hallucinations* as they're falling asleep, such as feeling the sensation that they're falling out of bed or hearing the sound of someone shouting their name (Mavromatis, 1987). People also occasionally experience hallucinations as they're waking up, including mildly disturbing hallucinations of being paralyzed (Takeuchi & others, 1992). Such sleep-related hallucinatory experiences are perfectly normal and are not considered symptoms of schizophrenia or any other mental disorder.

Sleep-related hallucinations and schizophrenia-related hallucinations are similar in one respect: both forms of hallucinatory experiences can involve any of the senses (Carter, 1992; Mueser & others, 1990). But they also differ in some important ways. First, schizophrenia-related hallucinations *do* occur in the waking state. Second, sleep-related hallucinations are typically fleeting, lasting a few moments at most. In contrast, the hallucinations of schizophrenia are often ongoing and persistent, such as hallucinated voices that continually tell the person what to do (Andreasen & Flaum, 1991).

As shown in Figure 14.4, the most common hallucinations experienced in schizophrenia are auditory, followed by visual hallucinations (Mueser & others, 1990; Bracha & others, 1989). The most frequent form of auditory hallucination is hearing a voice or voices. The voices may be familiar or unfamiliar, friendly or hostile. Sometimes the voices even talk to each other (Krausz & Müller-Thomsen, 1993).

The content of hallucinations is often tied to the person's delusional beliefs (DSM-IV, 1994). If the person harbors delusions of grandeur, hallucinated voices may reinforce her grandiose ideas by communicating instructions from God or the angels. If the person harbors delusions of persecution, hallucinated voices or images may be extremely frightening, threatening, or accusing. The content of hallucinations and delusions can also be influenced by culture, as we describe in Culture and Human Behavior Box 14.2, "From Cannibals to Computer Games."

When a schizophrenic episode is severe, hallucinations can be virtually impossible to distinguish from objective reality. For example, the young woman in the prologue probably did see very vivid images of fire. But when schizophrenia symptoms are less severe, the person may recognize that the hallucination is a product of his own mind (Amador & others, 1991). As one young man confided to Don, "I know the voices aren't real, but I can't make them stop talking to me." As this young man got better, the hallucinated voices did eventually stop. In some cases of schizophrenia, the auditory hallucinations can last for months or even years (Krausz & Müller-Thomsen, 1993).

CULTURE AND HUMAN BEHAVIOR 14.2

From Cannibals to Computer Games

Around the world, schizophrenia is characterized by delusions and hallucinations (Brislin, 1993). However, the *content* of those delusions and hallucinations can vary tremendously from one culture to another.

As an example of how culture can shape delusional ideas, consider the disorder that has been labeled the *Jerusalem syndrome*. First noticed in 1980, the Jerusalem syndrome has afflicted hundreds of tourists visiting that city. The symptoms? Gradually, the tourist becomes more and more withdrawn. Then suddenly he dons sheets or other makeshift robes and takes to the streets, where he begins preaching. Jerusalem psychiatrist Yair Bar-El, who has treated many of these tourists, notes that Christians tend to believe that they are Jesus Christ, the Virgin Mary, or John the Baptist. Jews, on the other hand, prefer a Hebrew hero like Moses, Samson, or King David. And Muslims tend to simply say that they're the Messiah (Bar-El, 1994).

Another variation of culturally influenced delusional thinking is sometimes seen among the Algonquin Indians in Canada. For the Algonquin, the *Witiko,* a man-eating monster, is an important mythological figure. When the *Witiko syndrome* occurs, an Algonquin believes that he is becoming possessed by the Witiko spirit. As the syndrome progresses, he becomes convinced that he is turning into a Witiko himself. He becomes increasingly obsessed with the craving for human flesh, and may become suicidal to escape the cannibalistic urges (see Matsumoto, 1994; Marano, 1985).

Like delusions, hallucinations tend to incorporate culturally relevant stimuli. As cross-cultural psychologist Richard Brislin (1993) observes:

> *In North America and Europe, these forces keep up to date with technology. In the 1920s, it was voices from the radio; in the 1950s, it was voices from the television; in the 1960s it could be voices from satellites in outer space; and in the 1970s and 1980s it could be spirits transmitted through people's microwave ovens.*

In Third World countries, where modern technology is less common, hallucinated voices are still largely being transmitted the old-fashioned way—from demons, evil spirits, deceased relatives, and other unseen forces. But as technology and societal structures change, the manifestations of delusions and hallucinations also tend to change. In South America, for example, when rural Indians with schizophrenia move to the cities, delusions of radio waves and secret police replace the more traditional delusions about witchcraft, saints, and jungle spirits (Murphy, 1982).

Finally, consider the case of a woman from Zimbabwe who developed peculiar auditory hallucinations after she moved to London (Spence, 1993). Her symptoms? Persistent hallucinations of the music soundtrack from the Mario Brothers Nintendo game! Today, no doubt, some people are hearing hallucinated voices coming from cellular telephones and over the Internet via desktop computers.

Disturbances in Sensation, Thinking, and Speech

It's not unusual to experience occasional disturbances in sensation, thinking, and speech. At a loud, crowded party, you may suddenly feel overwhelmed by the noise, lights, and commotion. Losing your train of thought, inadvertently saying the wrong word, and running words together are mild cognitive and speech glitches that almost everyone sporadically experiences. Such glitches are perfectly normal as long as they don't happen on a regular basis. They also provide a glimpse of the kinds of perceptual, thought, and speech disturbances that can dominate the experience of the person with schizophrenia.

People often report that during a schizophrenic episode, sights, sounds, and other sensations feel distorted. One woman described the sensory distortions in this way:

> *Looking around the room, I found that things had lost their emotional meaning. They were larger than life, tense, and suspenseful. They were flat, and colored as if in artificial light. I felt my body to be first giant, then minuscule. My arms seemed to be several inches longer than before and did not feel as though they belonged to me. (Anonymous, 1990)*

Along with sensory distortions, the person may experience severely disorganized thinking (Braff, 1993). It can be enormously difficult to concentrate, remember, and integrate important information while ignoring irrelevant information (Chen & others, 1994). The person's mind drifts from topic to topic in an unpredictable, illogical manner.

Such disorganized thinking is also often reflected in the person's speech (Barch & Berenbaum, 1996). Ideas, words, and images are sometimes strung together in ways that seem completely nonsensical to the listener. For example, when asked, "How are you today?" a schizophrenic patient responded:

> *Yes, sir, it's a good day. Full of rainbows, you know. They go along on their merry way without concern for asphyxiation or impurities. Yes, sir, like unconcerned flappers of the cosmoblue. (Reported in D. Sue & others, 1994)*

This response is certainly very odd, but notice that it is not completely unintelligible. If you think carefully about this patient's words, you can see how they reflect ideas that are very loosely related to the question that triggered them. Also notice how he made up a new word—*cosmoblue*—by combining the words *cosmos* and *blue*. Creating new words in this way is relatively common in schizophrenia.

Negative Symptoms: Deficits in Behavior, Emotion, and Motivation

Delusions, hallucinations, and disrupted sensations reflect positive symptoms—excesses or distortions in normal functioning. In contrast, negative symptoms reflect marked deficits or decreases in behavioral or emotional functioning.

One commonly seen negative symptom is referred to as *flat affect,* or *affective flattening.* Regardless of the situation, the person responds in an emotionally "flat" way. She consistently shows a dramatic reduction in emotional responsiveness and a lack of normal facial expressions (Raskin & others, 1993; Shtasel & others, 1992). Few expressive gestures are made, and the person's speech is slow and monotonous, lacking normal vocal inflections.

A closely related negative symptom is *alogia*—greatly reduced production of speech. In alogia, verbal responses are limited to brief, empty comments. Alogia is also referred to as *poverty of speech.*

Finally, *avolition* refers to the inability to initiate or persist in even simple forms of goal-directed behaviors, such as dressing, bathing, or engaging in social activities. Instead, the person seems to be completely apathetic, sometimes sitting for hours at a time.

CONCEPT REVIEW 14.5

Symptoms of Schizophrenia

Identify each of the symptoms below as one of the following: (a) delusions of reference; (b) delusions of grandeur; (c) alogia; (d) avolition; (e) hallucinations; (f) flat affect; (g) delusions of persecution.

_____ **1.** Slow, monotonous speech, reduced emotional responsiveness, and few expressive gestures.

_____ **2.** The experience of hearing voices without any actual auditory input.

_____ **3.** Reduced speech production that is limited to brief, empty comments.

_____ **4.** The mistaken belief that others are actively plotting against oneself.

_____ **5.** Apathy and inability to persist in even simple goal-directed behaviors, such as dressing, bathing, or social activities.

_____ **6.** The mistaken belief that other people are constantly talking about oneself.

_____ **7.** The erroneous belief that one possesses extraordinary powers.

Types of Schizophrenia

Figure 14.5 shows the frequency of positive and negative symptoms at the time of hospitalization for schizophrenia. These symptoms are used in diagnosing the particular subtype of schizophrenia. DSM-IV includes three basic subtypes of schizophrenia: *paranoid, catatonic,* and *disorganized.*

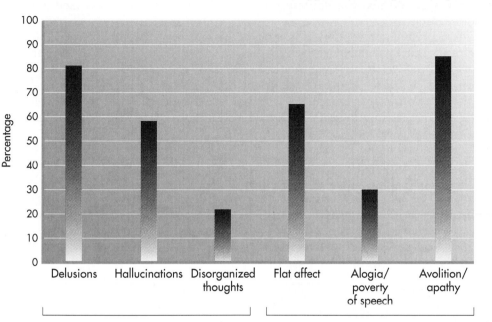

FIGURE 14.5 Presence of Symptoms in Schizophrenia
This graph shows how often specific positive and negative symptoms were present in a study of over 100 individuals at the time they were hospitalized for schizophrenia. Delusions were the most common positive symptom, while avolition, or apathy, was the most common negative symptom.
(Based on data reported in Andreasen & Flaum, 1991.)

The *paranoid type* of schizophrenia is characterized by the presence of delusions, hallucinations, or both. However, the person shows virtually no cognitive impairment, disorganized behavior, or negative symptoms. Instead, well-organized delusions of persecution or grandeur are operating. Auditory hallucinations in the form of voices talking about the delusional ideas are also often evident. Convinced that others are plotting against him, the person reacts with extreme distrust of others. Or the person may assume an air of superiority, confident in the delusional belief of his "special powers." The paranoid type is the most common type of schizophrenia.

The *catatonic type* of schizophrenia is marked by highly disturbed movements or actions. These may include bizarre postures or grimaces, extremely agitated behavior, complete immobility, echoing words just spoken by another person, or imitating the movements of others. The person will resist direction from others and may also assume rigid postures to resist being moved. Catatonic schizophrenia is often characterized by another unusual symptom, called *waxy flexibility*. Like a wax figure, the person can be "molded" into any position, and she will hold that position indefinitely. The catatonic type of schizophrenia is very rare.

The prominent features of the *disorganized type* of schizophrenia are extremely disorganized behavior, disorganized speech, and flat affect. Delusions and hallucinations are sometimes present but they are not well-organized and integrated, like those that characterize paranoid schizophrenia. Instead, a person with the disorganized type experiences delusions and hallucinations that contain fragmented, shifting themes. Silliness, laughing, and giggling may occur for no apparent reason. In short, the person's behavior is very peculiar. This type of schizophrenia was formerly called *hebephrenic schizophrenia,* and that term is still sometimes used.

Finally, the label of *undifferentiated type* is used when an individual displays some combination of positive and negative symptoms that does not clearly fit the criteria for the paranoid, catatonic, or disorganized types.

The Prevalence and Course of Schizophrenia

Every year, there are about 200,000 new cases of schizophrenia in this country. Annually, approximately 1 million Americans are treated for schizophrenia (Rosenstein & others, 1989). All told, about 1 percent of the U.S. population will experience at least one episode of schizophrenia at some point in life (Regier & others, 1993). Worldwide, no society or culture is immune to

TABLE 14.7 Types of Schizophrenia

Paranoid Type

- Well-organized delusional beliefs reflecting persecutory or grandiose ideas
- Frequent auditory hallucinations, usually voices
- Little or no disorganized behavior, speech, or flat affect

Catatonic Type

- Highly disturbed movements or actions, such as extreme excitement, bizarre postures or grimaces, or being completely immobile
- Echoes words spoken by others, or imitates movements of others

Disorganized Type

- Flat or inappropriate emotional expressions
- Severely disorganized speech and behavior
- Fragmented delusional ideas and hallucinations

Undifferentiated Type

- Displays characteristic symptoms of schizophrenia but not in a way that fits the pattern for paranoid, catatonic, or disorganized type

this mental disorder. Most cultures correspond very closely to the 1 percent rate of schizophrenia seen in the United States (Gottesman, 1991).

Young adulthood is prime time for the onset of schizophrenia (Beratis & others, 1994). The onset is typically gradual. Odd behaviors or thoughts are among the first signs. The person may feel tense and nervous, eat less, and have trouble concentrating or sleeping (Keith & Matthews, 1991). Eventually, his behavior and thoughts become more blatantly confused and inappropriate.

The course of schizophrenia is marked by enormous individual variability. Even so, a few global generalizations are possible (Krausz & Müller-Thomsen, 1993; Shepard & others, 1989). The good news is that about one-quarter of those who experience an episode of schizophrenia recover completely and never experience another episode. Another one-quarter experience recurrent episodes of schizophrenia, but often with only minimal impairment in the ability to function.

Now the bad news: For the rest of those who have suffered an episode of schizophrenia—one-half of the total—schizophrenia becomes a chronic mental illness, and the ability to function normally in society may be severely impaired. The people in this last category face the prospect of repeated hospitalizations and extended treatment. Thus, chronic schizophrenia places a heavy emotional, financial, and psychological burden on people with the disorder, their families, and society (Rupp & Keith, 1993; Gerace & others, 1993).

Explaining Schizophrenia

> *Genetics, brain abnormalities, and environmental factors have all been implicated as factors that contribute to the development of schizophrenia. What evidence points to the involvement of genetic factors and brain abnormalities? What environmental factors may contribute to the development of schizophrenia?*

Schizophrenia is an extremely complex psychological disorder. There is enormous individual variability in the onset, symptoms, duration, and recovery from schizophrenia. So it shouldn't come as a surprise that the causes of schizophrenia seem to be equally complex. In this section, we'll survey some of the factors that have been most strongly implicated in the development of schizophrenia: genetics, brain abnormalities, and environmental factors.

Genetic Factors: Evidence from Family, Twin, and Adoption Studies

Studies of families, twins, and adopted individuals have firmly established that genetic factors play a significant role in many cases of schizophrenia. First, family studies have consistently shown that schizophrenia tends to cluster in certain families (Prescott & Gottesman, 1993; Kendler & Diehl, 1993).

Second, family and twin studies have consistently shown that the more closely related a person is to someone who has schizophrenia, the greater the risk that she will be diagnosed with schizophrenia at some point in her lifetime. As you can see in Figure 14.6, the greatest risk occurs in cases of genetically identical (monozygotic) twins. If one identical twin develops schizophrenia, there's about a 48 percent lifetime risk—roughly, odds of 1 in 2—that the other identical twin will also develop schizophrenia (Gottesman, 1991).

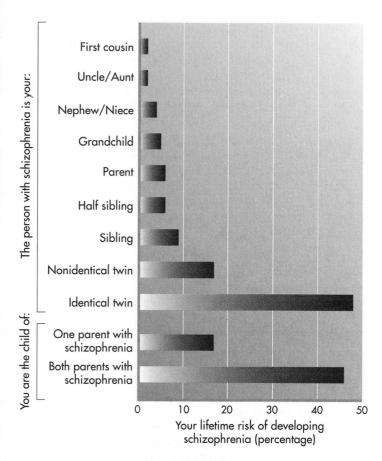

FIGURE 14.6 The Risk of Developing Schizophrenia Among Blood Relatives
The risk percentages shown here reflect the collective results of about forty studies investigating the likelihood of developing schizophrenia among blood relatives. As you can see, the greatest risk occurs if you have an identical twin who has schizophrenia (48 percent lifetime risk), or if both of your biological parents have schizophrenia (46 percent lifetime risk). However, genetics is just one of a number of factors involved in the development of schizophrenia.

(Gottesman, 1991, p. 96.)

Third, adoption studies have consistently shown that if either *biological* parent of an adopted individual had schizophrenia, the adopted individual is at greater risk to develop schizophrenia (Tienari & others, 1994). And conversely, in cases where an adopted individual has already developed schizophrenia, the adopted individual's *biological* relatives are much more likely to suffer from schizophrenia than his adoptive relatives (Kendler & others, 1994; Kety & others, 1994).

However, the evidence of genetic influence provided by family, twin, and adoption studies remains *indirect.* Researchers can only conclude that there are genes that influence the development of schizophrenia somewhere in the human genetic map (Kendler & Diehl, 1993). But they still don't know which genes are involved, how commonly those genes occur, or how genes might trigger schizophrenia.

Ironically, the strongest evidence that points to genetic involvement in schizophrenia—the 50 percent risk rate for a person whose identical twin has schizophrenia—is the same evidence that underscores the importance of environmental factors (Torrey, 1992; Pato & others, 1989). After all, identical twins *are* genetically identical. If schizophrenia were purely a matter of inherited maladaptive genes, then you would expect a risk rate much closer to 100 percent for monozygotic twins. Obviously, nongenetic factors must play a role in explaining why almost half of identical twins with a schizophrenic twin do *not* develop schizophrenia.

Abnormal Brain Chemistry: The Dopamine Hypothesis

The idea that schizophrenia is the result of abnormal brain chemistry is also supported largely by indirect evidence (Csernansky & Newcomer, 1994; Lieberman & Koreen, 1993). One important theory involves the brain neurotransmitter *dopamine.* According to the **dopamine hypothesis,** schizophrenia is related to excess dopamine activity in the brain (Davis & others, 1991).

Two pieces of indirect evidence support this notion. First, antipsychotic drugs, such as Haldol, Thorazine, and Stelazine, *reduce or block dopamine activity in the brain* (Dykstra, 1992). These drugs reduce schizophrenic symptoms in many people. Second, drugs like amphetamines or cocaine *enhance dopamine activity in the brain.* Using amphetamines or cocaine can produce schizophrenia-like symptoms in normal adults and can increase symptoms in people who already suffer from schizophrenia (Syvälahti, 1994).

Although the dopamine hypothesis is compelling, there are inconsistencies. Not all individuals who have schizophrenia experience a reduction of symptoms in response to the antipsychotic drugs that reduce dopamine activity in the brain. And for many patients, these drugs reduce some but not all schizophrenic symptoms (Heinrichs, 1993). So, while it seems likely that dopamine is somehow involved in schizophrenia, its exact role is far from clear.

Abnormalities in Brain Structures and Functioning

Researchers have found that about half of the people with schizophrenia show some type of brain structure abnormality (Cannon & Marco, 1994). For example, MRI studies have found evidence of abnormalities in the frontal lobes, temporal lobes, and basal ganglia (e.g., Breier & others, 1992).

dopamine hypothesis
The view that schizophrenia is related to, and may be caused by, excess activity of the neurotransmitter dopamine in the brain.

Identical Twins but Not Identical Brains
David and Steven Elmore are identical twins but they differ in one important respect—Steven (right) has schizophrenia. Behind each is a CAT scan, which reveals that Steven's brain is slightly smaller with less area devoted to the cortex at the top of the brain. Steven also has larger fluid-filled ventricles, shown in the middle of the brain scan. As researcher Daniel Weinberger comments, "The part of the cortex that Steven is missing serves as perhaps the most evolved part of the human brain. It performs complicated tasks such as thinking organized thoughts. This might help explain why paranoid delusions and hallucinations are characteristic of schizophrenia" (Suddath & others, 1990).

The most consistent finding has been the enlargement of the fluid-filled cavities called *ventricles* located deep within the brain (Raz, 1994). However, researchers aren't certain how enlarged ventricles might be related to schizophrenia. Finally, PET scans have revealed differences in brain activity between schizophrenic and normal individuals.

Although these differences are intriguing, they do not prove that schizophrenia is definitely caused by brain abnormalities. First, about half of the people suffering from schizophrenia do *not* show brain structure abnormalities. Second, the evidence is correlational. Researchers are still investigating whether differences in brain structures and activity are the cause or the consequence of schizophrenia.

Third, the kinds of brain abnormalities seen in schizophrenia are also seen in other mental disorders. Rather than specifically causing schizophrenia, it's quite possible that brain abnormalities might contribute to mental disorders in general. The bottom line is that researchers know that brain abnormalities are present in some cases of schizophrenia, but the exact role played by those abnormalities is unclear (Cannon & Marco, 1994).

Environmental Factors: The Viral Infection Theory

One provocative theory is that schizophrenia might be caused by exposure to an influenza virus or other viral infection during prenatal development or shortly after birth (see Huttunen & others, 1994). A virus might seem an unlikely cause of a serious mental disorder, but viruses *can* spread to the brain and spinal cord by traveling along nerves. According to this theory, exposure to a viral infection during prenatal development or early infancy affects the developing brain, producing changes that make the individual more vulnerable to schizophrenia later in life (Torrey, 1991; Weinberger, 1987).

There is some evidence to support the viral infection theory. First, children whose mothers were exposed to a flu virus during the second trimester of pregnancy do show an increased rate of schizophrenia (Venables, 1996; Huttunen & others, 1994; Barr & others, 1990). Second, schizophrenia occurs more often in people who were born in the winter and spring months, when upper respiratory infections are most common (Torrey & others, 1993). Once again, though, the evidence is correlational. And some researchers have not found such correlations (Takei & others, 1994).

Psychological Factors: Unhealthy Families

Do psychological factors cause schizophrenia? Researchers have investigated such factors as dysfunctional parenting, disturbed family communication styles, and critical or guilt-inducing parental styles as possible contributors to schizophrenia (Miklowitz, 1994; Hahlweg & Goldstein, 1987). However, no single psychological factor seems to emerge consistently as causing schizophrenia. Rather, it seems that those who are genetically predisposed to develop schizophrenia may be more vulnerable to the effects of disturbed family environments (Fowles, 1992).

Strong support for this view comes from a landmark study being conducted by Finnish psychiatrist Pekka Tienari and his colleagues (1994, 1987). In the Finnish Adoptive Family Study of Schizophrenia, researchers are following about 150 adopted individuals whose biological mothers had schizophrenia. As part of their study, the researchers assessed the adoptive family's degree of psychological adjustment, including the mental health of the adoptive parents. The study also includes a control group of about 180 adopted individuals whose biological mothers were *not* schizophrenic.

Tienari and his colleagues (1994) have found that adopted children with a schizophrenic biological mother have a much higher rate of schizophrenia and schizophrenia-related disorders than the children in the control group. This finding provides further confirmation that genetics plays an important role in the development of schizophrenia. However, this was true *only* when the children were raised in a psychologically disturbed adoptive home. When children with a genetic background of schizophrenia were raised in a psychologically healthy adoptive family, they were *no more likely* to develop schizophrenia than the control-group children.

Although adopted children with no genetic history of schizophrenia were less vulnerable to the psychological stresses of a disturbed family environment, they were by no means completely immune to such influences. As Figure 14.7 shows, one-third of the control-group adoptees developed symptoms of a serious psychological disorder if they were raised in a disturbed family environment.

Tienari's study provides strong evidence for the beneficial effects of a healthy family environment. Figure 14.7 shows that children who were genetically at risk to develop schizophrenia clearly benefited from being raised in a healthy psychological environment. Put simply, a healthy psychological environment may counteract a person's inherited genetic vulnerability for schizophrenia. This finding is consistent with other research showing that psychologically healthy family environments can exert protective effects against various mental disorders in vulnerable people (see Jacob, 1987).

So what can we conclude about the causes of schizophrenia? Three broad conclusions are possible. First, genetics plays a significant role. Having a genetic predisposition for schizophrenia puts an individual at greater risk to develop that disorder. Second, disruptions in brain chemistry or abnormalities in brain structure are involved in a significant number of schizophrenia cases. And third, the psychological environment, especially the psychological adjustment of the family, can act as either a catalyst or a buffer for the onset of schizophrenia.

After more than a century of intensive research, schizophrenia remains a baffling disorder. Thus far, no single biological, psychological, or social factor has emerged as the causal agent in schizophrenia (Keefe & Harvey, 1994). Nevertheless, researchers are expressing greater confidence that the pieces of the schizophrenia puzzle are beginning to form a more coherent picture.

Even if the exact causes of schizophrenia remain elusive, there is still reason for optimism. In the last few years, new antipsychotic drugs have been developed that are much more effective in treating both the positive and negative symptoms of schizophrenia (Meltzer, 1993). In the next chapter, we'll take a detailed look at the different treatments and therapies for schizophrenia and other psychological disorders.

FIGURE 14.7 The Finnish Adoptive Family Study of Schizophrenia
In the Finnish Adoptive Family Study, researchers are following two groups of adopted individuals: one group with biological mothers who had schizophrenia and a control group whose biological mothers did not have schizophrenia. This graph shows the strong influence of the adoptive family environment on the development of serious mental disorders.
(Tienari & others, 1994; Tienari, 1991.)

Summing Up: Psychological Disorders

In this chapter, we've looked at the symptoms and causes of several psychological disorders. We've seen that some of the symptoms of psychological disorders represent a sharp break from normal experience. The behavior of the young woman in the prologue was an example of the severely disrupted functioning characteristic of schizophrenia. In contrast, the symptoms of other psychological disorders, like the mood disorders, differ from normal experience primarily in their degree, intensity, and duration.

Psychologists are only beginning to understand the causes of many psychological disorders. The broad picture that emerges reflects a familiar theme: biological, psychological, and social factors all contribute to the development of psychological disorders. In the next chapter, we'll look at how psychological disorders are currently treated.

In the chapter Application, we'll explore one of the most serious consequences of psychological problems—suicide. Since people who are contemplating suicide often turn to their friends before they seek help from a mental health professional, we'll also suggest several ways you can help a friend who expresses suicidal intentions.

APPLICATION

Understanding and Helping Prevent Suicide

Every year, about 300,000 people attempt suicide in the United States. How can you help a friend in a suicidal crisis?

It was a warm October afternoon when Ann made her second attempt. This time she was more determined. She shut the garage door and then methodically sealed the base of the garage door with towels. She moved a reclining lawn chair to the spot where her husband Doug's car was normally parked. Calling Doug at work, she nonchalantly explained that she was going shopping but would be back in a few hours. From the bookcase in the living room, Ann took down her album of wedding photographs and the Bible that her grandmother had given her when she was a little girl. Rummaging through the medicine cabinet, she found the four remaining sleeping pills that her doctor had prescribed and swallowed them.

Ann went back into the garage, sealing the door behind her with more towels. Then she started her car, put it in neutral, and sat down in the lawn chair. She looked at her wedding pictures and began to cry. Setting her wedding album aside, she started reading aloud from her Bible. A short while later, Ann slipped into unconsciousness as the sleeping pills took effect and the garage filled with car exhaust fumes.

Who Commits Suicide?

Ann's story is dramatic, but unfortunately, suicide is all too common. About 30,000 suicides occur each year in this country (U.S. Bureau of the Census, 1995). That number is probably too low, because many suicides are misreported as accidental deaths (Phillips & Ruth, 1993).

In a given year, it's conservatively estimated that about 300,000 people will try to kill themselves (Garland & Zigler, 1993). Women outnumber men by 3 to 1 in the number of suicide *attempts*. However, men outnumber women by 4 to 1 in suicide *deaths*, primarily because men tend to use more lethal methods, such as guns and hanging.

We usually think of suicide as an adult phenomenon, but children as young as five years of age have been known to commit suicide (Lester, 1991). Completed suicides are relatively rare among children aged five to fourteen, but they do occur. Every year, about 12,000 children in that age group are admitted to psychiatric hospitals because of suicidal behaviors (Stillion & others, 1989).

One disturbing trend has been the increase in adolescent suicides. Over the last three decades, the suicide rate for adolescents has increased by about 200 percent, as compared to a 17 percent increase for the general population (Garland & Zigler, 1993). Although this trend has received considerable media attention, the suicide rate of adolescents is still below that of young and middle-aged adults. The highest rate of suicide consistently occurs in the oldest segments of our population, among those aged sixty-five and above (U.S. Bureau of the Census, 1995).

Why Do People Attempt or Commit Suicide?

Fleeting thoughts of suicide are not uncommon (Meehan & others, 1992). But there is a vast difference between having such occasional thoughts and being genuinely intent on self-destruction. Why do people attempt or commit suicide? In general terms, the suicidal person's view of life has become progressively more pessimistic and negative. At the same time, his view of self-inflicted death as an alternative to life has become progressively more positive and permissible (Hughes & Neimeyer, 1990).

Some people choose suicide in order to escape the pain of a chronic illness or the slow, agonizing death of a terminal disease. Others commit suicide because of feelings of depression, guilt, rejection, failure, humiliation, or shame (see Van Egmond & others, 1993). The common denominator is that they see suicide as the only escape from their own unbearably painful emotions (Baumeister, 1990). Ann, for example, was deeply despondent over the fact that she had failed to live up to her own expectations of becoming a highly acclaimed, successful painter.

When faced with a dilemma, the average person tends to see a range of possible solutions to the problem, accepting the fact that none of the solutions may be ideal. In contrast, the suicidal person's thinking and perceptions have become *rigid and constricted*. She can see only two ways to solve her problems: a magical resolution *or* suicide. Because she cannot imagine a realistic way of solving her problems, death seems like the only logical option (Shneidman, 1985).

Helping Prevent Suicide

If someone is truly intent on taking his own life, it may be impossible to prevent him from doing so. But that does not mean that you can't try to help a friend who is expressing suicidal intentions. People often turn to their friends rather than to a mental health professional (Stillion & others, 1989). If a friend confides that he is feeling hopeless and suicidal, these guidelines may help you help your friend.

Guideline 1. If you do not feel comfortable talking to a potentially suicidal person, say so in a way that encourages the person to seek help elsewhere. Your response can be as simple as saying, "I'm not sure what to say or how I can help you. But I really think you need to talk to someone who *can* help you." There are any number of resources you can suggest, including suicide hot lines, local mental health associations, the person's family doctor or religious advisor, the college counseling service, or even 911 or whatever your local emergency number is.

Guideline 2. Don't minimize the person's suicidal intentions. Brushing aside suicidal statements with platitudes like "Don't be silly, you've got everything to live for," or clichés like "Every cloud has a silver lining," is not a helpful response. This is not the time to be glib, patronizing, or superficial (Grollman, 1988).

Instead, ask your friend if she wants to talk about her feelings. Try to be matter-of-fact and confirm that she is indeed seriously suicidal, rather than simply exaggerating her frustration or disappointment. How can you confirm that the person is suicidal? Simply ask her, "Are you *really* thinking about killing yourself?" One sign that she may be serious about her intention to kill herself is talking about specific suicide plans (how, when, and where). Giving away valued possessions, taking care of legal matters, and putting her

affairs in order for no apparent reason are other indications (Grosz, 1990).

Guideline 3. Let the person talk and vent her feelings about whatever is causing her psychological pain. If a person is feeling suicidal, there's a reason. *Ask.* Let the person talk, and try to appreciate your friend's feelings (Lester, 1989). The suicidal person often feels isolated or lonely, with few sources of social support (Heikkinen & others, 1993). An understanding friend who is willing to take the time to listen patiently without passing judgment may provide just the support that the person needs to overcome the suicidal feelings.

Guideline 4. Identify other potential solutions to whatever problems are causing the suicidal person's sense of hopelessness. Remember, the suicidal person has usually lost his ability to imagine a range of potential solutions to his dilemma (Dixon & others, 1994). The suicidal person perceives only two ways out of the dilemma—either a magical solution or suicide, with nothing in between. At this particular moment, the suicidal person is operating with psychological blinders that prevent him from seeing alternative courses of action or alternative ways of looking at his problem.

How can you widen those blinders? Simply saying, "Here are some options you may not have thought about," is a good starting point. You might list alternative solutions to the person's problems, helping him to understand that other potential solutions do exist, even though none may be perfect (Shneidman, 1987).

Guideline 5. Ask the person to delay his decision. Most suicidal people are ambivalent about wanting to die (Richman & Eyman, 1990). If they did *not* have mixed feelings about committing suicide, they probably wouldn't be talking to you. If the person is still intent on suicide after talking about other alternatives, ask him to delay his decision. Delaying even for a few days may give the person enough time to psychologically regroup, consider alternatives, or seek help from other sources.

Guideline 6. Encourage the person to seek professional help. Remember, it's important that the seriously suicidal person receive professional help from a counselor or psychol-

ogist. These guidelines are meant only to help you provide "psychological first aid" in a crisis situation. They do *not* qualify you as a suicide prevention expert. Your goal is to help your friend weather the immediate crisis so that he or she can be directed to a mental health professional (Stillion & others, 1989). The mental health professional will not only help your friend deal with suicidal feelings, but will also help her work through her problems in a constructive way.

Some Final Thoughts

Even if you follow all of these guidelines, there's no guarantee that the person won't attempt or commit suicide. Ann's case clearly illustrates this point. After her first suicide attempt, Ann went into therapy three times a week with a clinical psychologist. Her husband, Doug, participated in many of those counseling sessions, and it appeared that Ann had weathered the crisis that led to her first suicide attempt.

Nevertheless, Ann made the second, much more serious suicide attempt that we described at the beginning of this Application. By all accounts, Ann should have died in the garage on that October afternoon. But she didn't die. Instead, after about 90 minutes, Ann regained consciousness, the garage air thick with the exhaust from her running car. She awoke with extreme nausea and dizziness, her head pounding with excruciating pain. To this day, Ann maintains that angels woke her up and pulled her out of the garage.

After her second suicide attempt, Ann was hospitalized at a psychiatric facility, where she stayed for a month. That was about six years ago. The world looks much different to Ann today. She eventually finished a business degree and now works full time as a hospital administrator.

Ann continues to see her psychologist at least once a month, sometimes more often. "I've got to work at keeping myself mentally healthy," she will tell you without apology or embarrassment. And, most important, Ann has resumed painting her glorious watercolors of flowers and nature scenes. "I may never be famous," she says, smiling, with only a hint of disappointment in her expression, "but at least I'm still here to enjoy painting."

Summary
Psychological Disorders

Understanding Psychological Disorders

■ Distinguishing "normal" from "abnormal" behavior involves consideration of many different factors, including cultural norms. Psychopathology refers to the scientific study of the origins, symptoms, and development of psychological disorders.

■ A psychological disorder is a pattern of behavioral or psychological symptoms that causes significant personal distress and/or impairs the ability to function. The diagnostic criteria for psychological disorders are described in DSM-IV.

■ The prevalence of psychological disorders is much higher than had previously been thought. According to one comprehensive survey, approximately one in two Americans will experience a psychological disorder at some point in their lifetime, while approximately one in three Americans have experienced the symptoms of a psychological disorder in the previous year.

Anxiety Disorders

■ In contrast to normal anxiety, pathological anxiety is irrational and uncontrollable, and is unreasonably intense, frequent, persistent, and disruptive.

■ Generalized anxiety disorder and panic disorder are characterized by intense anxiety that is not triggered by a specific stimulus. Generalized anxiety disorder involves a constant, persistent state of anxiety, while panic disorder involves sudden episodes of extreme, intense anxiety.

■ The phobias involve intense, irrational fear and avoidance of the feared object or situation. Important forms of phobia include specific phobia, social phobia, and agoraphobia, which is fear of having a panic attack in a public or inescapable situation. Learning theories and evolved biological predispositions have been offered as explanations of the development of phobias.

■ Posttraumatic stress disorder develops in response to an extreme psychological or physical trauma. Symptoms include frequent intrusive memories of the trauma, avoidance and emotional numbness, and increased physical arousal.

■ Obsessive-compulsive disorder is an anxiety disorder in which a person's life is dominated by repetitive thoughts (obsessions) and actions (compulsions). Biological factors that have been implicated in obsessive-compulsive disorder include serotonin deficiency and brain dysfunction.

Mood Disorders: Emotions Gone Awry

■ Mood disorders involve serious, persistent disturbances in emotions that cause psychological discomfort and/or impair the ability to function.

■ The symptoms of major depression include negative emotions, extreme pessimism, thoughts of suicide, cognitive impairment, lack of motivation, and sleep disruption for a period of two weeks or longer. Dysthymic disorder is a milder but chronic form of depression.

■ Major depression is the most common psychological disorder. Left untreated, depression may recur and become progressively more severe.

■ Bipolar disorder usually involves periods of depression alternating with manic episodes. A milder form of bipolar disorder is cyclothymic disorder. Bipolar disorder is less common than major depression.

■ Genetics, brain chemistry, and stress have all been implicated in mood disorders. Two neurotransmitters, serotonin and norepinephrine, have also been implicated in depression.

The Dissociative Disorders:
Fragmentation of the Self

■ Dissociative experiences involve a disruption in awareness, memory, and personal identity. Dissociation can be a normal coping response in situations of extreme trauma. In the dissociative disorders, however, dissociative experiences are extreme, frequent, and disruptive.

■ Dissociative amnesia refers to the inability to recall important information which is not due to a medical condition and cannot be explained by ordinary forgetfulness. Dissociative fugue involves amnesia and sudden, unexplained travel away from home.

■ Dissociative identity disorder involves memory gaps and the presence of two or more distinct identities. Some psychologists are skeptical of dissociative identity disorder. According to one theory, DID is caused by trauma in childhood, and represents an extreme form of coping through dissociation.

Schizophrenia: A Different Reality

■ Schizophrenia is a psychological disorder that involves severely distorted beliefs, perceptions, and thought processes. The positive symptoms of schizophrenia represent excesses in normal functioning, and include delusions, hallucinations, and severely disorganized thought processes, speech, and behavior.

■ Negative symptoms reflect deficits or decreases in normal functioning. The negative symptoms of schizophrenia include flat affect, alogia, and avolition.

■ Three subtypes of schizophrenia are paranoid type, catatonic type, and disorganized type, each of which is distinguished by a particular combination of symptoms. When symptoms do not match any of these three subtypes, the diagnosis of undifferentiated type is made.

■ The course of schizophrenia is highly variable. Schizophrenia becomes chronic in about one-half of people who experience a schizophrenic episode. About one-quarter recover completely, and about one-quarter experience recurrent episodes but are able to function with minimal impairment.

■ Family, twin, and adoption studies have shown that genetics contributes to the development of schizophrenia. However, studies of identical twins demonstrate that nongenetic factors play at least an equal role in the development of schizophrenia.

■ Excess dopamine and abnormalities in brain structure and function have been identified as factors that are associated with schizophrenia.

■ Environmental factors that may be involved in schizophrenia include exposure to a virus during prenatal development and a psychologically unhealthy family environment. Adopted children who were genetically at risk to develop schizophrenia were found to be less likely to develop the disorder when raised in a psychologically healthy family.

■ Given the complexity of schizophrenia, it is not surprising that no single factor has emerged as causing this psychological disorder.

Key Terms

psychopathology (p. 611)

psychological disorder (mental disorder) (p. 614)

DSM-IV (p. 614)

anxiety (p. 617)

anxiety disorders (p. 617)

generalized anxiety disorder (p. 618)

panic attack (p. 618)

panic disorder (p. 618)

phobia (p. 620)

specific phobia (p. 620)

agoraphobia (p. 620)

social phobia (p. 621)

posttraumatic stress disorder (PTSD) (p. 623)

obsessive-compulsive disorder (p. 624)

obsessions (p. 624)

compulsions (p. 624)

mood disorders (p. 627)

major depression (p. 628)

dysthymic disorder (p. 630)

seasonal affective disorder (SAD) (p. 630)

bipolar disorder (p. 631)

manic episode (p. 631)

cyclothymic disorder (p. 632)

dissociative experience (p. 635)

dissociative disorders (p. 637)

dissociative amnesia (p. 637)

dissociative fugue (p. 637)

dissociative identity disorder (DID) (p. 637)

schizophrenia (p. 640)

positive symptoms (p. 640)

negative symptoms (p. 641)

delusion (p. 641)

hallucination (p. 642)

dopamine hypothesis (p. 647)

CONCEPT REVIEW 14.1 Page 617

1. False. DSM-IV is the abbreviation for *Diagnostic and Statistical Manual of Mental Disorders,* fourth edition, published by the American Psychiatric Association.
2. True.
3. False. What is considered "normal" behavior varies from one culture to another.
4. True.
5. False. About 30 percent of people surveyed experienced symptoms of a psychological disorder during the previous twelve months, and almost 50 percent experienced symptoms at some point during their lives.
6. False. *Psychopathology* refers to the scientific study of the origins, symptoms, and development of psychological disorders.

CONCEPT REVIEW 14.2 Page 627

1. posttraumatic stress disorder
2. generalized anxiety disorder
3. panic disorder
4. specific phobia
5. obsessive-compulsive disorder
6. social phobia

CONCEPT REVIEW 14.3 Page 634

1. d
2. b
3. a
4. a
5. c

CONCEPT REVIEW 14.4 Page 640

1. dissociative experience
2. dissociative identity disorder
3. dissociative fugue
4. dissociative amnesia

CONCEPT REVIEW 14.5 Page 644

1. f, flat affect
2. e, hallucinations
3. c, alogia
4. g, delusions of persecution
5. d, avolition
6. a, delusions of reference
7. b, delusions of grandeur

Chapter

15 Therapies

Prologue: "A Clear Sense of Being Heard . . ."

How would we describe Marcia? She's an extraordinarily kind, intelligent woman. Her thoughtfulness and sensitivity is tempered by a ready laugh and a good sense of humor. She's happily married, has a good job as a feature writer for a large suburban newspaper, and has two young children, who only occasionally drive her crazy. If Marcia has a flaw, it's that she tends to judge herself and her own performance much too harshly. She's too quick to blame herself when anything goes wrong.

Juggling a full-time career, marriage, and parenting is a challenge for anyone, but Marcia always makes it look easy. The last time we had dinner at Bill and Marcia's home, the meal featured home-grown vegetables, made-from-scratch bread, and fresh seasonings from the herb pots in the kitchen. Outwardly, Marcia appears to have it all. But a few years ago, she began to experience a pervasive sense of dread and unease—feelings that gradually escalated into a full-scale depression. Marcia describes the onset of her feelings in this way:

> *Physically I began to feel as if I were fraying around the edges. I had a constant sense of anxiety, and a recurring sense of being a failure. My daughter Maggie was going through a rather difficult stage. Andy was still a baby. I felt worn out. I started worrying constantly about my children. Are they safe? Are they sick? What's going to happen? Are my kids going to get hurt? I knew that I really didn't have any reason to worry that much, but I did. It finally struck me that my worrying and my anxiety and my feelings of being a failure were not going to go away on their own.*

Marcia decided to seek help. She made an appointment with her therapist—a psychiatrist whom she had last seen ten years before, when she had helped Marcia cope with a very difficult time in her life. In some ways, Marcia's experience with her therapist today is very different from her sessions of ten years ago; but some aspects of their relationship remain the same. As Marcia explains:

> Since I have seen the same therapist at different times in my life, I can say that her approach has changed a great deal since I first worked with her. She was originally very classically psychoanalytic, saying little, listening impassively. She used such standard psychodynamic concepts as transference and looking at historic family relationships as the origin of problems in the present.
>
> In the past two years, we have tried quite different techniques: short-term, solution-oriented therapy and a twelve-step approach. At her suggestion, I joined a twelve-step support group called Emotions Anonymous, and I now attend a group meeting once a week. My therapist has also "prescribed" books for me that use the twelve-step framework. Until we moved to the twelve-step framework, I never had a very clear sense of a progression in therapy. I always felt better after a session, but it would not last very long. I now feel more engaged in a process that has a course to run and that will, I hope, give me coping skills and some needed sense of perspective or ability to detach from a given issue or problem.
>
> How has therapy helped me? My feelings before a therapy session may vary greatly, depending on the issue under discussion. However, I always find the sessions cathartic and I invariably feel great relief. I feel a sense of being understood by someone who knows me but who is detached from me. I have a clear sense of being heard, as though my therapist has given me a gift of listening and of allowing me to see myself as the worthwhile and capable person I am. It is as though therapy allows me to see more clearly into a mirror that my problems have obscured.

Over the course of several months, Marcia made progressive gains as a result of her weekly psychotherapy sessions and attending her support group. Today, Marcia is calmer, more confident, and feels much more in control of her emotions and her life. As Marcia's mental health improved, so did her relationships with her children and her husband.

> Psychotherapy has also helped me communicate more clearly. It has enabled me to become more resilient after some emotional conflict. It has had a preventive effect in helping me to ignore or manage situations that might under certain circumstances trigger depression, anxiety, or obsessive worry. And it makes me a better parent and marriage partner.
>
> Therapy's negative effects? I'm poorer; it costs money. And therapy poses the risk of becoming an end in itself. Psychotherapy has the attraction of being a safe harbor from the petty assaults of everyday life. There's always the danger of losing sight of the goal of becoming a healthier and more productive person, and becoming stuck in the therapy process.

Marcia's experience with psychotherapy reflects many of the themes that we will touch on in this chapter. We'll look at the different forms of therapy that psychologists and other mental health professionals use to help people cope with psychological problems. We'll also consider the growing popularity of self-help groups and how they differ from more structured forms of therapy. Toward the end of the chapter, we'll discuss biomedical approaches to the treatment of psychological disorders. Over the course of the chapter, we'll come back to Marcia's story.

Introduction

Psychotherapy and Biomedical Therapy

Psychotherapy is the use of psychological techniques to treat emotional, behavioral, and interpersonal problems. What is the basic assumption common to all forms of psychotherapy? What is biomedical therapy, and how does it differ from psychotherapy?

psychotherapy
The treatment of emotional, behavioral, and interpersonal problems through the use of psychological techniques designed to encourage understanding of problems and modify troubling feelings, behaviors, or relationships.

People seek help from mental health professionals for a variety of reasons. In Marcia's case, feelings of anxiety and depression were beginning to dominate her life. Although she could still function at work and home, Marcia found it increasingly difficult to deal with the ordinary tasks of daily life. The intensity of her anxious and depressed feelings finally got to the point where Marcia knew she needed professional help—help that well-meaning friends and family could not provide.

Like Marcia, many people seek help because they are suffering from some form of a *psychological disorder*—troubling thoughts, feelings, or behaviors that cause psychological discomfort or interfere with a person's ability to function. As we saw in Chapter 14, psychological disorders are much more prevalent than most people realize. In any given year, approximately one out of three adults experience the symptoms of a psychological disorder (Kessler & others, 1994).

Not everyone who seeks professional help is suffering from a psychological disorder. Many people seek help in dealing with troubled relationships, such as an unhappy marriage or parent–child conflicts. And sometimes people need help with life's transitions, such as coping with the death of a loved one, dissolving a marriage, or adjusting to retirement.

In this chapter, we'll look at the two broad forms of therapy that mental health professionals use to help people: *psychotherapy* and *biomedical therapy.* **Psychotherapy** refers to the use of psychological techniques to treat emotional, behavioral, and interpersonal problems. There are hundreds of types of psychotherapy (Garfield & Bergin, 1994). Although there are many forms of psychotherapy, they all share the assumption that psychological factors play a significant role in a person's troubling feelings, behaviors, or relationships.

Table 15.1 summarizes the diverse range of mental health professionals who use psychotherapy techniques to help people. Although psychotherapy is usually conducted as a one-to-one relationship between the therapist and the person seeking help, it can also be conducted with groups of people, families, or couples.

TABLE 15.1 Who's Who Among Mental Health Professionals

Clinical psychologist	Holds an academic doctorate (Ph.D., Psy.D., or Ed.D.) and is required to be licensed to practice. Has expertise in psychological testing, diagnosis, psychotherapy, research, and prevention of mental and emotional disorders. May work in private practice, hospitals, or community mental health centers.
Psychiatrist	Holds a medical degree (M.D. or D.O.) and is required to be licensed to practice. Has expertise in the diagnosis, treatment, and prevention of mental and emotional disorders. Often has training in psychotherapy. May prescribe medications, electroconvulsive therapy, or other medical procedures.
Psychoanalyst	Usually a psychiatrist or clinical psychologist who has received additional training in the specific techniques of psychoanalysis, the form of psychotherapy originated by Sigmund Freud.
Psychiatric social worker	Holds a master's degree in social work (M.S.W.). Training includes an internship in a social service agency or mental health center. Most states require certification or licensing. May or may not have training in psychotherapy.
Marriage and family therapists	Usually holds a master's degree with extensive supervised experience in couple or family therapy. May also have training in individual therapy. Many states require licensing.
Psychiatric nurse	Holds an R.N. degree and has selected psychiatry or mental health nursing as a specialty area. Typically works on a hospital psychiatric unit or in a community mental health center. May or may not have training in psychotherapy.

In contrast to psychotherapy, the **biomedical therapies** involve the use of medication or other medical treatments to treat the symptoms associated with psychological disorders. The biomedical therapies are based on the assumption that the symptoms of many psychological disorders involve biological factors, such as abnormal brain chemistry. As we saw in Chapter 14, the involvement of biological factors in many psychological disorders is well documented. Not surprisingly, there has been a steadily growing trend to combine biomedical therapy and psychotherapy in treating psychological disorders (Klerman & others, 1994).

Traditionally, only licensed physicians, such as psychiatrists, have been allowed to prescribe the different forms of biomedical therapy. However, that tradition may be changing. In recent years, field trials have been conducted in which clinical psychologists were allowed to prescribe medications to treat psychological disorders (see Fowler, 1995; Youngstrom, 1992). In order to acquire prescription privileges, clinical psychologists would be required to undergo additional training (Chafetz & Buelow, 1994). Eventually, clinical psychologists may be able to prescribe the same medications that psychiatrists use to treat psychological disorders.

We'll begin this chapter by surveying some of the most influential approaches in psychotherapy: psychoanalytic, humanistic, behavioral, and cognitive. As you'll see, each approach makes different assumptions about the underlying causes of psychological problems. And each approach uses different strategies to produce beneficial changes in the way a person thinks, feels, and behaves—the ultimate goal of all forms of psychotherapy. After discussing the effectiveness of psychotherapy, we'll look at the most commonly used biomedical treatments for psychological disorders.

Psychoanalytic Therapy

> *Psychoanalysis is a form of therapy developed by Sigmund Freud and based on his theory of personality. What techniques are used in psychoanalysis, and what is their purpose? What role does insight play in psychoanalytic therapy? What are short-term dynamic therapies?*

When cartoonists portray psychotherapy, they often draw a person lying on a couch and talking while a bearded gentleman sits behind the patient, passively listening. This stereotype reflects some of the key ingredients of traditional **psychoanalysis,** a form of psychotherapy originally developed by **Sigmund Freud** (1856–1939) in the early 1900s. Although psychoanalysis was developed almost a century ago, its assumptions and techniques continue to be influential today.

Sigmund Freud and Psychoanalysis

As a therapy, traditional psychoanalysis is closely interwoven with Freud's theory of personality. As you may recall from Chapter 11, on personality, Freud stressed that early childhood experiences provided the foundation for later personality development. When early experiences result in unresolved conflicts and frustrated urges, these emotionally charged memories are *repressed,* or pushed out of conscious awareness. Although unconscious, these repressed conflicts continue to influence a person's thoughts and behavior, including the dynamics of his relationships with others.

biomedical therapies
The use of medications, electroconvulsive therapy, or other medical treatments to treat the symptoms associated with psychological disorders.

psychoanalysis
A type of psychotherapy originated by Sigmund Freud in which free association, dream interpretation, and analysis of resistance and transference are used to explore repressed or unconscious impulses, anxieties, and internal conflicts.

According to Freud, these conflicts festering in the unconscious are at the core of maladjusted behavior and psychological disorders. To achieve psychological health, Freud believed it is essential to move these conflicts from the unconscious to conscious awareness. Thus, psychoanalysis is designed to help unearth past conflicts so the patient attains *insight* as to the real source of her problems. Central to this process is the intense relationship that gradually forms between the psychoanalyst and the patient. In this relationship, long-standing psychological conflicts are not only recognized but also re-experienced and ultimately resolved.

How can unconscious conflicts be uncovered in psychoanalysis? Freud (1904) believed that unconscious material occasionally surfaces in disguised form. Glimpses of unconscious conflicts can be revealed in dreams, memory lapses, inadvertent slips of the tongue, and even in apparent "accidents," such as clumsily spilling coffee all over a colleague whom you secretly envy.

Freud also developed several techniques to coax a patient's unconscious conflicts to awareness. In the famous technique called **free association,** the patient lies on a couch and spontaneously reports all thoughts, mental images, and feelings as they come to mind. Usually the psychoanalyst sits out of view, occasionally asking questions and encouraging the patient to elaborate on his or her feelings.

Free association can reveal several clues about possible unconscious conflicts or repressed memories (Liff, 1992). Along with the general themes that keep resurfacing in the patient's free associations, the psychoanalyst notes the occasional inadvertent comment that seems puzzling or disconnected from other thoughts. Rather than being dismissed, such remarks are explored for their potential meaning.

Even more significant are blocks in free association, an abrupt change in topic, or sudden silences. Such instances may be signs of **resistance**—the patient's unconscious attempts to block the process of revealing repressed memories and conflicts. To the psychoanalyst, resistance is a signal that the patient is uncomfortably close to uncovering psychologically threatening material.

Another technique that Freud made famous is **dream interpretation** (see Chapters 4 and 11). Because psychological defenses are reduced during sleep, he believed that frustrated desires, impulses, and motives were expressed symbolically in dreams. According to Freud (1933), we consciously remember the *manifest content,* or actual dream images. But beneath these surface images is what Freud called the *latent content*—the true, hidden, and unconscious meaning of the dream that is disguised in dream symbols. We'll let Freud (1911) himself describe what he saw as the symbolic meaning of some common dream images:

> There are some symbols which bear a single meaning almost universally: thus the Emperor and Empress (or the King and Queen) stand for the parents, rooms represent women, and their entrances and exits the openings of the body. . . . Sharp weapons, long and stiff objects, such as tree-trunks and sticks, stand for the male genital; while cupboards, boxes, carriages, or ovens may represent the uterus. Symbols such as a staircase or going upstairs represent sexual intercourse. . . .

In helping the patient process dreams and free associations, the psychoanalyst gently guides him toward areas of psychological conflict. The analyst asks questions, encourages the patient to elaborate on thoughts, and occasionally confronts him with patterns of resistance that have emerged. For example, the analyst might say, "Every time you talk about your father, you seem to hesitate and measure your words carefully. What do you think that might mean?"

More directly, the analyst sometimes makes carefully timed **interpretations,** explaining the possible meaning of dreams, free associations,

---

We ask the dreamer as well to free himself from the impression of the manifest dream, to switch his attention from the dream as a whole to individual parts of its content, and tell us one after another the things that occur to him in connection with these parts, what associations come into his mind when he turns his mental eye on to each of them separately.

Sigmund Freud New Introductory Lectures on Psychoanalysis, 1933

The resistance accompanies the treatment step by step. Every single association, every act of the person under treatment must reckon with the resistance and represents a compromise between the forces that are striving towards recovery and opposing ones.

Sigmund Freud The Dynamics of Resistance, 1912

free association
A technique used in psychoanalysis in which the patient spontaneously reports all thoughts, feelings, and mental images as they come to mind, as a way of revealing unconscious thoughts and emotions.

resistance
In psychoanalysis, the patient's unconscious attempts to block the revelation of repressed memories and conflicts.

dream interpretation
A technique used in psychoanalysis in which the content of dreams is analyzed for disguised or symbolic wishes, meanings, and motivations.

interpretation
A technique used in psychoanalysis in which the psychoanalyst offers a carefully timed explanation of the patient's dreams, free associations, or behavior to facilitate the recognition of unconscious conflicts or motivations.

Freud's Famous Couch This photograph shows Freud's consulting room. During therapy sessions, his patients would lie on the couch. Freud usually sat by the head of the couch, out of the patient's view. He believed that this arrangement encouraged the patient's free flow of thoughts, feelings, and images. Although some traditional psychoanalysts still have the patient lie on a couch, many favor comfortable chairs in which analyst and patient are facing one another.

instances of resistance, or the patient's reactions to the psychoanalyst. The timing of such interpretations is important. If an interpretation is offered before the patient is psychologically ready to confront an issue, she may reject the interpretation or respond defensively, increasing resistance (Henry & others, 1994).

One of the most important processes that occurs in the relationship between the patient and the psychoanalyst is called transference. As Freud (1940) explains, **transference** occurs when the patient unconsciously responds to the therapist as though the therapist were a significant person in the patient's life, often a parent:

> The patient sees in his analyst the return—the reincarnation—of some important figure out of his childhood or past, and consequently transfers on to him the feelings and reactions that undoubtedly applied to this model. . . . This transference comprises positive and affectionate as well as negative and hostile attitudes toward the analyst who, as a rule, is put in the place of one or other of the patient's parents, his father or mother.

The psychoanalyst encourages transference by purposely remaining as neutral as possible. In other words, the psychoanalyst does not reveal personal feelings, take sides, make judgments, or actively advise the patient. This therapeutic neutrality is designed to produce "optimal frustration" so that the patient transfers and projects unresolved conflicts onto the psychoanalyst (Eagle & Wolitzky, 1992).

As these transference feelings become more intense, the patient relives unconscious emotional conflicts that have been repressed since childhood. Only now, these conflicts are being relived and played out in the context of the relationship between the psychoanalyst and the patient. For example, the patient might transfer toward the analyst feelings of anger that he repressed in response to a harsh or rejecting parent. At the appropriate time, the analyst offers interpretations to help the patient perceive and understand the transference that is occurring.

All these psychoanalytic techniques are designed to help the patient see how past conflicts influence her current behavior and relationships, including her relationship with the psychoanalyst. Once these kinds of insights are achieved, the psychoanalyst helps the patient work through and resolve longstanding conflicts. As resolutions occur, maladaptive behavior patterns that were previously driven by unconscious conflicts can be replaced with more adaptive emotional and behavioral patterns.

The intensive relationship between the patient and the psychoanalyst takes time to develop. On average, the traditional psychoanalyst sees the patient four or five times a week over the course of four years or longer (Garfield & Bergin, 1994). Freud's patients were on the couch six days a week (Liff, 1992). Obviously, traditional psychoanalysis is a slow, expensive process that few people can afford. For those who have the time and the money, traditional psychoanalysis is still available.

Short-Term Dynamic Therapies

Today, few psychotherapists practice traditional psychoanalysis lasting for years. The simple fact is that most people entering psychotherapy are not seeking the kind of major personality overhaul that traditional psychoanaly-

transference
In psychoanalysis, the process by which emotions and desires originally associated with a significant person in the patient's life, such as a parent, are unconsciously transferred to the psychoanalyst.

BIZARRO

sis is designed to produce. Instead, people come to therapy expecting help with specific problems. People also expect therapy to provide beneficial changes in a matter of weeks or months, not years.

Research has shown that such expectations are both reasonable and realistic. Regardless of which type of therapy is used, the average duration of therapeutic contact is only about eight sessions. As we'll discuss in more detail later, most people experience significant benefits from therapy in just a few months of weekly therapy sessions.

Today, there are many different forms of *short-term dynamic therapies* based on traditional psychoanalytic notions (Binder & others, 1994). These short-term dynamic therapies have several features in common (Koss & Shiang, 1994). Therapeutic contact lasts for no more than a few months. The patient's problems are quickly assessed at the beginning of therapy. The therapist and patient agree on specific, concrete, and attainable goals. In the actual sessions, most psychodynamic therapists are more directive than traditional psychoanalysts, actively engaging the patient in a dialogue.

As in traditional psychoanalysis, the therapist uses interpretations to help the patient recognize hidden feelings and transferences that may be occurring in important relationships in her life (Liff, 1992). Therapy also focuses on helping the patient identify psychological resources that she can use to cope with the current difficulty as well as future problems (Koss & Shiang, 1994).

Were Sigmund Freud alive today, would he be upset by these departures from traditional psychoanalysis? Not at all. In fact, Freud himself treated some of his patients using short-term psychodynamic therapy that sometimes lasted for only one lengthy session. Several of Freud's patients completed psychoanalysis in as little as two months (Magnavita, 1993).

Despite the fact that traditional, lengthy psychoanalysis is seldom practiced today, it should be clear that Freud's basic assumptions and techniques continue to be influential. Although contemporary research has challenged some of Freud's original ideas, modern researchers are also studying the specific factors that seem to influence the effectiveness of basic Freudian techniques, such as interpretation and transference (Henry & others, 1994). Without question, psychoanalysis has many critics (e.g., Eysenck, 1994, 1985; Szasz, 1988). But it's equally true that the legacy of Freud's contributions to personality theory and psychotherapy have been enormous.

CONCEPT REVIEW 15.1

Psychoanalytic Therapy

Read each of the descriptions below and decide what aspect of psychoanalytic therapy is being illustrated. Choose from: free association, resistance, dream interpretation, interpretation, transference.

_____ **1.** When Jeremy was asked to elaborate on his negative feelings about his wife, he made a few wisecracks about women and then abruptly changed the subject by talking about the Stanley Cup hockey playoffs.

_____ **2.** After Karl told his therapist about a very bizarre dream, the therapist suggested that perhaps the dream was really about Karl's anger and resentment toward his own father.

_____ **3.** Even though his therapist has remained neutral and nonjudgmental during their therapy sessions, Mr. Steinberg has recently begun to express feelings of hostility and anger toward his therapist.

_____ **4.** Dr. Freedman sometimes makes comments about certain aspects of what his patients tell him, but only when he thinks that his patients are psychologically ready to confront the issues he raises.

_____ **5.** Jackie told her therapist that she had been lonely as a child. Her therapist told her to close her eyes and talk about whatever thoughts and feelings came to mind, no matter how trivial or childish they seemed.

Humanistic Therapy

Client-centered therapy is a form of therapy that grew out of the humanistic perspective and was developed by Carl Rogers. What therapeutic conditions and techniques are important in client-centered therapy? How do client-centered therapy and psychoanalysis differ as insight therapies?

The *humanistic perspective* in psychology emphasizes human potential, self-awareness, and freedom of choice. Humanistic psychologists contend that the most important factor in personality is the individual's conscious, subjective perception of his or her self. They see people as being innately good and motivated by the need to grow psychologically. If people are raised in a genuinely accepting atmosphere and given freedom to make choices, they will develop healthy self-concepts and strive to fulfill their unique potential as human beings (Rice & Greenberg, 1992).

Carl Rogers and Client-Centered Therapy

The humanistic perspective exerted a strong influence on psychotherapy. Probably the most influential of the humanistic psychotherapies is **client-centered therapy,** also called *person-centered therapy,* developed by **Carl Rogers** (1902–1987) (Zimring & Raskin, 1992). In naming his therapy, Rogers deliberately used the word *client* rather than *patient.* He believed that the medical term *patient* implied that people in therapy were "sick" and were seeking treatment from an all-knowing authority figure who could "heal" or "cure" them. Instead of stressing the therapist's expertise or perceptions of the patient, client-centered therapy emphasizes the *client's* subjective perception of himself and his environment.

Like Freud, Rogers saw the therapeutic relationship as the catalyst that leads to insight and lasting personality change. But Rogers viewed the nature of this relationship very differently from Freud. According to Rogers (1977), the therapist should not exert power by offering carefully timed "interpretations" of the patient's unconscious conflicts. Advocating just the opposite, Rogers believed that the therapist should be *nondirective.* That is, the therapist must not direct the client, make decisions for the client, offer solutions, or pass judgment on the client's thoughts or feelings. Instead, Rogers believed, change in therapy must be chosen and directed by the client. The therapist's role is to create the conditions that allow the client, not the therapist, to direct the focus of therapy.

What are the therapeutic conditions that promote self-awareness, psychological growth, and self-directed change? Rogers (1980) believed that three qualities of the therapist are critical: genuineness, unconditional positive regard, and empathic understanding. *Genuineness* means that the therapist honestly and openly shares her thoughts and feelings with the client. In effect, the therapist is acting as a model of a genuinely open person who thoughtfully expresses her feelings without the need for defensiveness or pretense. By modeling genuineness, the therapist indirectly encourages the client to exercise more fully this capability in himself.

Second, the therapist must value, accept, and care for the client, whatever her problems or behavior. Rogers called this quality *unconditional posi-*

Carl Rogers Shown on the far right, Rogers contended that human potential would flourish in an atmosphere of genuineness, unconditional positive regard, and empathic understanding. Rogers filmed many of his therapy sessions as part of a research program to identify the most helpful aspects of client-centered therapy.

client-centered therapy
A type of psychotherapy developed by humanistic psychologist Carl Rogers in which the therapist is nondirective and reflective, and the client directs the focus of each therapy session; also called *person-centered therapy.*

tive regard. Rogers believed that a person develops psychological problems largely because she has consistently experienced only *conditional acceptance.* That is, parents, teachers, and others have communicated this message to the client: "I will accept you only *if* you conform to my expectations." Because acceptance by significant others has been conditional, the person has cut off or denied unacceptable aspects of herself and her experience. As a result, the person's self-concept and world view become distorted. In turn, these distorted perceptions affect her thoughts and behaviors in unhealthy, unproductive ways.

The therapist who successfully creates a climate of unconditional positive regard fosters the person's natural tendency to move toward self-fulfilling decisions without fear of evaluation or rejection. Rogers (1977) described this important aspect of therapy in this way:

> *Unconditional positive regard means that when the therapist is experiencing a positive, acceptant attitude toward whatever the client is at that moment, therapeutic movement or change is more likely. It involves the therapist's willingness for the client to be whatever feeling is going on at that moment—confusion, resentment, fear, anger, courage, love, or pride. . . . The therapist prizes the client in a total rather than a conditional way.*

Client-Centered Therapy Rather than "interpreting" the client's thoughts and behavior, the client-centered therapist strives to create a warm, accepting climate that allows the client the freedom to explore troubling issues. The therapist engages in active listening, reflecting both the content and the personal meaning of what the client is saying. In doing so, the therapist helps the client develop a clearer perception and understanding of her own feelings and motives.

Third, the therapist must communicate *empathic understanding* by reflecting the content and personal meaning of feelings being experienced by the client. In effect, the therapist creates a psychological mirror, reflecting the client's thoughts and feelings as they exist in the client's private inner world. The goal is to help the client explore and clarify his feelings, thoughts, and perceptions. In the process, the client begins to see himself, and his problems, more clearly (Egan, 1994).

Empathic understanding requires the therapist to listen *actively* for the personal meaning beneath the surface of what the client is saying (Egan, 1994). To illustrate, consider the following brief excerpt from a client-centered therapy session with an eighteen-year-old female college student:

Client: My parents really bug me. First it was Arthur they didn't like, now it's Peter. I'm just fed up with all their meddling.

Therapist: You really are angry at your folks.

Client: Well, how do you expect me to feel? Here I am with a 3.5 GPA, and providing all sorts of other goodies, and they claim the right to pass judgment on how appropriate my boyfriend is. *(Begins to sob.)*

Therapist: It strikes me that you're not just angry with them. *(Pause)* Maybe you're worried about disappointing them.

Client: *(Crying even more)* I've tried all my life to please them. Sure, their approval is important to me. They're really pleased when I get A's, but why do they have to pass judgment on my social life as well? (Excerpt cited in Davison & Neale, 1994.)

An empathic way of being with another person has several facets. It means entering the private perceptual world of the other and becoming thoroughly at home in it. It involves being sensitive, moment by moment, to the changing felt meanings which flow in this other person, to the fear or rage or tenderness or confusion or whatever that he or she is experiencing.

Carl Rogers A Way of Being, 1980

Notice how the therapist's first response reflects the *content* of what the client has said—her annoyance with her parents. But the therapist's second statement reflects the *personal meaning* of what the client has said—that she's worried about disappointing her parents. By communicating empathic understanding, the therapist helps the client explore and clarify the meaning of her own feelings.

Rogers believed that when the therapeutic atmosphere contains genuineness, unconditional positive regard, and empathic understanding, change is more likely to occur. Such conditions foster feelings of being psychologically safe, accepted, and valued. In this therapeutic atmosphere, change occurs as the person's self-concept and world view gradually become healthier and less distorted. According to Rogers (1977), "As the client becomes more self-aware, more self-acceptant, less defensive and more open, she finds at last some of the freedom to grow and change in directions natural to the human organism." In effect, the client is moving in the direction of *self-actualization*—the realization of his or her unique potentials and talents.

A large number of studies have generally supported Rogers' contention that it is important for the therapist to demonstrate genuineness, unconditional positive regard, and empathic understanding (Greenberg & others, 1994). Such factors promote trust and self-exploration in therapy. However, these conditions, by themselves, may not be sufficient to help clients change (Beutler & others, 1994).

The client-centered approach continues to be developed by therapists, teachers, social workers, and counselors (Lietaer & others, 1990). Along with being influential in individual psychotherapy, the client-centered approach has been applied to marital counseling, parenting, education, business, and even community and international relations (Zimring & Raskin, 1992).

TABLE 15.2 Comparing Insight-Oriented Therapies

Type of Therapy	Founder	Source of Problems	Treatment Techniques	Goals of Therapy
Psychoanalysis	Sigmund Freud	Repressed, unconscious conflicts stemming from early childhood experiences	Free association, analysis of dream content, interpretation, and transference	To recognize, work through, and resolve longstanding conflicts
Client-centered therapy	Carl Rogers	Conditional acceptance and dependence that causes person to develop a distorted self-concept and world view	Nondirective therapist who displays unconditional positive regard, genuineness, and empathic understanding	To develop self-awareness, self-acceptance, and self-determination

Behavior Therapy

Behavior therapy uses the principles of learning theories to directly change problem behaviors. How are classical conditioning principles used to treat specific problem behaviors? How are operant conditioning principles applied to modify problem behaviors?

Psychoanalysis, client-centered therapy, and other insight-oriented therapies maintain that the road to psychologically healthier behavior is increased self-understanding of motives and conflicts. As insights are acquired through therapy, problem behaviors and feelings presumably will give way to more adaptive behaviors and emotional reactions.

However, gaining insight into the source of problems does not necessarily result in desirable changes in behavior and emotions. Even though you fully understand *why* you are behaving in counterproductive ways, your maladaptive or self-defeating behaviors may continue. For instance, an adult

behavior therapy
A type of psychotherapy that focuses on directly changing maladaptive behavior patterns by using basic learning principles and techniques; also called *behavior modification*.

counterconditioning
A behavior therapy technique based on classical conditioning that involves modifying behavior by conditioning a new response that is incompatible with a previously learned response.

who is extremely anxious about public speaking may understand that he feels that way because he was raised by a critical and demanding parent. But having this insight into the underlying cause of his anxiety may do little, if anything, to reduce his anxiety or change his avoidance of such situations.

In sharp contrast to the insight-oriented therapies we discussed in the preceding section, the goal of **behavior therapy** is to modify specific problem behaviors, not to change the entire personality. And, rather than focusing on the past, behavior therapists focus on current behaviors.

Behavior therapists assume that maladaptive behaviors are *learned,* just as adaptive behaviors are. Thus, the basic strategy in behavior therapy involves unlearning maladaptive behaviors and learning more adaptive behaviors in their place. Behavior therapists employ techniques that are based on the learning principles of classical conditioning, operant conditioning, and observational learning to modify the problem behavior.

Techniques Based on Classical Conditioning

Just as Pavlov's dogs learned to salivate to a ringing bell that had become associated with food, learned associations can be at the core of some maladaptive behaviors, including strong negative emotional reactions. In the 1920s, psychologist John Watson demonstrated this in his famous "Little Albert" study. You may recall from Chapter 5 that Watson classically conditioned an infant called "Little Albert" to fear a tame lab rat by repeatedly pairing the rat with a loud clanging sound. Over time, Albert's conditioned fear generalized to other furry objects, including a fur coat, cotton, and a Santa Claus mask (Watson & Rayner, 1920).

Mary Cover Jones: The First Behavior Therapist

Watson himself never tried to eliminate Little Albert's fears. But Watson's research inspired one of his students, **Mary Cover Jones** (1896–1987), to explore ways of reversing conditioned fears. With Watson acting as a consultant, Jones (1924a) treated a three-year-old named Peter who "seemed almost to be Albert grown a bit older." Like Little Albert, Peter was fearful of various furry objects, including a tame rat, a fur coat, cotton, and wool. Because Peter was especially afraid of a tame rabbit, Jones focused on eliminating the rabbit fear. She used a procedure that has come to be known as **counterconditioning**—the learning of a new conditioned response that is incompatible with a previously learned response.

Jones's procedure was very simple (Jones, 1924b; Watson, 1924). The caged rabbit was brought into Peter's view but kept far enough away to avoid eliciting fear (the original conditioned response). With the rabbit visible at a tolerable distance, Peter sat in a highchair and happily munched his favorite snack, milk and crackers. Peter's favorite food was used because, presumably, the enjoyment of eating would naturally elicit a positive response (the desired conditioned response). Such a positive response would be incompatible with the negative response of fear.

Every day for almost two months, the rabbit was inched closer and closer to Peter as he ate his milk and crackers. As Peter's tolerance for the rabbit's presence gradually increased, he was eventually able to hold the rabbit in his lap, petting it with one hand while happily eating with his other hand (Jones, 1924a, 1924b). Not only was Peter's fear of the rabbit eliminated, but he also stopped being afraid of other furry objects, including the rat, cotton, and fur coat (Watson, 1924).

Mary Cover Jones This photograph, taken around 1919, shows Mary Cover Jones as a college student in her early twenties. Although Jones pioneered the use of behavioral techniques in therapy, she did not consider herself a "behaviorist," and ultimately disagreed with many of Watson's views.

IN FOCUS 15.1

Mary Cover Jones: The First Behavior Therapist

Often called "the mother of behavior therapy" for her pioneering studies on the removal of fears, Mary Cover Jones never identified herself as a "behaviorist" (Gieser, 1993). She became associated with the famous founder of behaviorism, John Watson, through her friendship with Rosalie Rayner, a college classmate (Jones, 1974). Rayner, you will recall, was Watson's co-researcher in the famous "Little Albert" study. Rayner married Watson shortly after that study.

Impressed by Watson and Rayner's "Little Albert" study, Jones was intrigued by the possibility of using learning principles to modify behavior. She asked herself, "If fears could be built in by conditioning, as Watson had demonstrated, could they not also be removed by similar procedures?"

In her treatment of three-year-old Peter, described in the text, Jones demonstrated that conditioning could be used to remove fears.

Some fifty years after her landmark study with Peter, Jones (1974) described her motives for the research in this way:

And so we come to Peter. It has always been of the greatest satisfaction to me that I could be associated with the removal *of a fear when I came in contact with this three-year-old in whom a fear of animals was already well-established. I could not have played the role of creating a fear in a child, no matter how important the theoretical implications. When my own children came across the case of Peter in their college textbooks, they too were relieved to find out that I had functioned in this benign capacity in the psychological experiments with children and children's fears.*

After receiving her Ph.D. from Columbia University in 1925, Jones became involved in the Oakland Growth Study, a longitudinal study that followed the lives of some 200 people for over half a century. When Jones began studying them in 1931, the subjects were 10 years of age. She continued the study for 55 years, until 1986. In describing that research, Jones's (1975)

sentiments provide a clear contrast to the assumptions and methods of Watson's early behaviorism:

I have watched the psychobiological development of our study members as they grew from children to adults now in their 50s. I think of what we have learned as we studied these lives in progress. Participants have provided information on somatic [bodily], environmental, family, attitudinal and behavioral growth and change.

It is my one regret that I did not have so extensive an association with little Peter of the fear study. . . . Now I would be less satisfied to treat the fears of a three-year-old, or of anyone else without a later follow-up and in isolation from an appreciation of him as a tantalizingly complex person with unique potentials for stability and change. . . .

Behaviorism has come a long way since the days of John B. Watson.

Laurel, Mary, Arthur, Peter playing together in laboratory. Experimenter put rabbit down on floor. . . . Laurel and Mary stroked the rabbit and chattered away excitedly. Peter walked over, touched the rabbit on the back, exulting, "I touched him on the end."

Mary Cover Jones A Laboratory Study of Fear: The Case of Peter, 1924

systematic desensitization
A type of behavior therapy in which phobic responses are reduced by pairing relaxation with a series of mental images or real-life situations that the person finds progressively more fear-provoking; based on the principle of counterconditioning.

Along with counterconditioning, Jones (1924a) used social imitation or *observational learning* techniques to help eliminate Peter's rabbit fear. As part of the treatment, Peter observed other children petting or holding the tame rabbit. As you can see in Jones's treatment note, Peter imitated the actions of the nonfearful children. For her pioneering efforts in the treatment of children's fears, Jones is widely regarded as the first behavior therapist (Gieser, 1993; Reiss, 1990). For more on the contributions she made to psychology, see In Focus Box 15.1 "Mary Cover Jones: The First Behavior Therapist."

Systematic Desensitization

Mary Cover Jones's pioneering studies in treating children's fears helped set the stage for the later development of a more standardized procedure to treat phobias and other anxiety disorders. Developed by South African psychiatrist Joseph Wolpe in the 1950s, the procedure is called *systematic desensitization* (Wolpe, 1958, 1982). Based on the same premise as counterconditioning, **systematic desensitization** involves learning a new conditioned response (relaxation) that is incompatible with or inhibits the old conditioned response (fear and anxiety).

FIGURE 15.1 A Sample Anxiety Hierarchy Used in Systematic Desensitization
As part of systematic desensitization, the therapist helps the client develop an anxiety hierarchy. The sample anxiety hierarchy shown here illustrates the kinds of scenes that a person who is fearful of dental treatment might list. Relaxation is paired with each scene, starting with the least threatening scene, until the client can successfully imagine the scene while maintaining complete relaxation.

Degree of Fear	Imagined Scene
100	Holding mouth open, eyes closed, listening to the sound of the dental drill as a cavity is repaired
95	Holding mouth open in preparation for an oral injection
90	Lying back in dental chair, eyes closed, as dentist examines teeth
85	Lying back in dental chair, mouth open, listening to the sounds of dental equipment, as dental technician cleans teeth
80	Lying in dental chair, watching dental technician unwrap sterilized dental tools
75	Being greeted by the dental technician and walking back to dental examination chair
70	Sitting in dentist's waiting room
60	Driving to dentist's office for appointment
50	Looking at the bright yellow reminder postcard on the refrigerator and thinking about dental appointment
40	Listening to my sister talk about her last dental visit
30	Looking at television or magazine advertisements depicting people in a dentist's chair
25	Calling dentist's office to make an appointment
20	Thinking about calling dentist's office to set up an appointment
15	Driving past dentist's office on a workday
10	Driving past dentist's office on a Sunday afternoon

Let's illustrate the three basic steps of systematic desensitization by describing the behavioral treatment of a common phobia, fear of dentists. Mild to moderate dental anxiety is very common: 80 percent of American adults experience at least mild anxiety about trips to the dentist. But about 5 percent of adults experience such intense fear of going to the dentist that they avoid dental treatment even when it is medically necessary (Getka & Glass, 1992).

Classical conditioning often plays a role in the acquisition of dental fear (Milgrom & others, 1995). In much the same way that Little Albert was classically conditioned to fear a tame lab rat, many people have acquired a conditioned fear of the dentist's office because it has become paired with a painful or traumatic experience (De Jongh & others, 1995; Davey, 1989).

Three basic steps are involved in systematic desensitization (Morris, 1991). Let's say you're one of the phobic 5 percent of dental patients. First, the behavior therapist teaches you *progressive relaxation,* which involves successively relaxing one muscle group after another until a deep state of relaxation is achieved. Second, the therapist helps you construct a list of specific anxiety-provoking images associated with dental visits. These scenes are arranged in a hierarchy from least anxiety-provoking to most anxiety-provoking (see Figure 15.1). The therapist would also have you create a very relaxing, unrelated *control scene,* such as imagining yourself walking on the beach on a warm, sunny day.

The third step is the actual process of desensitization. After becoming deeply relaxed, you close your eyes and vividly imagine the least threatening scene at the bottom of the hierarchy. After you can maintain complete relaxation while imagining this scene three or four times, you move up to the next scene in your hierarchy. If you start to feel twinges of anxiety or tension, you signal the therapist by raising a finger. The therapist will guide you back to imagining a previous scene or the relaxing control scene. If necessary, the therapist will help you relax again by using the progressive relaxation technique.

Over several sessions, you gradually work your way up the anxiety hierarchy, imagining each scene while maintaining complete relaxation. Very systematically, desensitization to the feared situations occurs as each imagined scene becomes paired with a conditioned response of relaxation rather than anxiety. Once mastered with mental images, desensitization is often continued, step by step, in the actual feared setting. In an interesting twist, new computer technology is providing another avenue for desensitization, which is discussed in In Focus Box 15.2, "Using Virtual Reality to Conquer Phobias."

IN FOCUS 15.2

Using Virtual Reality to Conquer Phobias

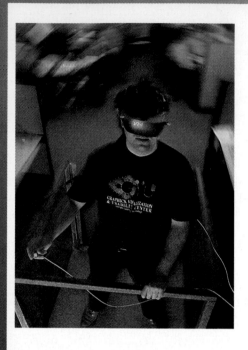

Virtual reality (VR) consists of computer-generated scenes that you view using a special motion-sensitive helmet, as shown in the photograph. Move your head in any direction and an electromagnetic sensor in the helmet detects the movement and the computer-generated scene you see changes accordingly (Kalawsky, 1993). Turning a handgrip lets you move for-ward or backward to explore your artificial world. You can also use a virtual hand to reach out and touch objects, such as an elevator button.

VR technology is now being used experimentally as a treatment for some specific phobias, including fear of flying and fear of heights (Rothbaum & others, 1996, 1995a, 1995b). For example, psychologist Ralph Lamson has used virtual reality as a form of computer-assisted systematic desensitization to help more than sixty patients conquer their fear of heights. Rather than mental images, the person experiences computer-generated images that seem almost real. Once the helmet is donned, patients begin a 40-minute journey that starts in a café and progresses to a narrow wooden plank that leads to a bridge.

Although computer-generated and cartoonlike, the scenes of being high above the ground on the plank or bridge are real enough to trigger the physiological indicators of anxiety. As Lamson (1994) explains, "When people look down, their heart rate and blood pressure go up. They may say, 'Oh my God, I can't do this.'" Lamson encourages the person to stay in the same spot until the anxiety diminishes. Once relaxed, the person continues the VR journey. By the time the person makes the return journey back over the plank, heart rate and blood pressure are close to normal.

How effective is VR in helping desensitize people to their fear of heights? After virtual reality therapy, over 90 percent of Lamson's patients successfully rode a glass elevator up to the fifteenth floor. They also completed self-assigned activities, such as driving across the Golden Gate Bridge and standing on a ladder to clean leaves out of roof gutters.

Researcher Barbara Olasov Rothbaum and her colleagues (1996, 1995a, 1995b) reported similar successes in using VR therapy to treat fear of heights and fear of flying. Rothbaum believes that VR therapy has great potential as a treatment for phobias, especially for patients who have difficulty imagining frightening scenes on their own. VR therapy also has the advantage of providing controlled exposure to fear-provoking situations, such as flying, without the need to leave the therapist's office.

Despite such optimism, VR therapy is not without potential side effects. After wearing the VR helmet for extended periods, some people become dizzy or develop headaches.

In practice, systematic desensitization is often combined with other techniques. For example, in a behavioral treatment program for dental anxiety conducted by Eric Getka and Carol Glass (1992), participants received relaxation training and systematic desensitization. They then visited an actual dental clinic and practiced their relaxation skills there. *Observational learning* was also incorporated into the program: participants watched videotapes of patients calmly receiving routine dental care.

The acid test for such a behavioral treatment package is not just reduction of fear and anxiety, but whether treated subjects actually go to a dentist following treatment. Given these criteria, the behavioral treatment was highly effective. As compared to people with dental anxiety in an untreated control group, treated subjects were much more likely to have actually gone to a dentist on their own in the year following treatment (Getka & Glass, 1992).

The Bell and Pad Treatment

Another problem that has been effectively treated by techniques based on classical conditioning is bedwetting by children over the age of six. (Occasional bedwetting by children under the age of six is not considered a clinical problem.) About 3 percent of girls and 7 percent of boys age seven and older have problems with bedwetting. For some individuals, bedwetting may persist into early adolescence (Kaplan & Busner, 1993).

Children who are chronic bedwetters tend to be very deep sleepers. They spend more time in the very relaxed, deep states of nondreaming sleep than other children (Anch & others, 1988). Behavior therapy is based on the assumption that bedwetting occurs because the child has not learned to wake up when his bladder is full. The goal of the **bell and pad treatment** is to use classical conditioning to pair arousal with the sensation of a full bladder.

First developed in the 1930s, the bell and pad treatment is a very simple and effective procedure (O'Leary & Wilson, 1987). A special insulated pad is placed under the bottom bedsheet. When the child starts to wet the bed, a loud bell goes off, waking the child. After shutting off the alarm, the child uses the bathroom, then changes the sheet. Before going back to bed, he resets the alarm.

Over the course of a few weeks, the child becomes conditioned so that the sensation of a full bladder (the conditioned stimulus) triggers waking arousal (the desired conditioned response). In the process, the child's sleeping cycles are also modified so that the child is not such a heavy sleeper. The bell and pad procedure is effective in about 75 percent of school-aged children who have difficulties with bedwetting (Kaplan & Busner, 1993).

Notice that behavior therapists are not inclined to dwell on the "psychological meaning" of bedwetting. Instead, the behavior therapist attempts to directly modify the problem behavior. In contrast, Freud (1905) explained bedwetting as a form of sexual gratification and regressive behavior caused by extreme anxiety. Not surprisingly, psychoanalytically oriented therapists warn that direct conditioning methods like the bell and pad treatment for bedwetting will lead to symptom substitution, such as sexual problems, later in life. Does it?

Contrary to the predictions of psychoanalytic theory, there is ample evidence that the direct treatment of bedwetting does *not* produce symptom substitution (Kaplan & Busner, 1993; O'Leary & Wilson, 1987). In fact, the bell and pad treatment is significantly more effective in dealing with bedwetting than are the insight-oriented therapies. School-age children who achieve success by using the bell and pad treatment experience a greater sense of self-control, self-esteem, and happiness at being able to remain dry. Sleeping over at another child's house, going to summer camp, and other overnight experiences are no longer dreaded because of the fear of a humiliating "accident."

The Bell and Pad Treatment for Bedwetting On the bedside table is an electronic device that monitors a moisture-sensitive pad that is placed below the bottom sheet of the bed. If the child wets the bed, a loud buzzer and a bright light are activated, waking the child. Over the course of several weeks, the bell and pad device conditions arousal from sleep in response to the body signals of a full bladder.

bell and pad treatment
A behavior therapy technique used to treat nighttime bedwetting by conditioning arousal from sleep in response to body signals of a full bladder.

aversive conditioning
A relatively ineffective type of behavior therapy that involves repeatedly pairing an aversive stimulus with the occurrence of undesirable behaviors or thoughts.

Aversive Conditioning

It was psychologist John Garcia who first demonstrated how taste aversions could be classically conditioned (see Chapter 5). After rats drank a sweet-flavored water, Garcia injected them with a drug that made them ill. The rats developed a strong taste aversion for the sweet-flavored water, avoiding it altogether (Garcia & others, 1966). In much the same way, **aversive conditioning** attempts to create an unpleasant conditioned response to a harmful stimulus like cigarette smoking or alcohol. We'll illustrate how this approach works by describing how your author Don used aversive conditioning as part of a hospital program he conducted to help people quit smoking.

Participants in the stop-smoking program attended daily sessions for a week. Much of the program involved information about the health hazards of smoking, including slides of people with throat, mouth, and lung cancer. At the end of every night's meeting, the participants engaged in a rapid-puffing procedure. They had three minutes to rapidly puff but not inhale five cigarettes. Unbeknownst to the participants, the filters of the cigarettes had been coated with a harmless but very foul-tasting substance.

Imagine the scene: Forty people in close quarters rapidly puffing five cigarettes that tasted absolutely horrible. As the stench of cigarette smoke filled the unventilated room, gruesome slides of cancer victims flashed on the screen. Not surprisingly, this combination of factors left many participants gagging and nauseous.

The goal of this aversive conditioning procedure is to replace the former positive conditioned response to the taste of cigarettes with one that produces distaste, even nausea. Similar aversive conditioning techniques have been used to treat alcohol addiction, sexual deviance, compulsive gambling, and overeating (see Emmelkamp, 1994; Sandler & Steele, 1991). For example, a medication called *Antabuse* is used in aversion therapy for alcohol addiction. If a person taking Antabuse consumes any amount of alcohol, extreme nausea is induced. For some conditions, such as sexual deviance, mild electric shocks are used rather than nausea-producing drugs.

In general, aversive conditioning is not very effective, and its use has been on the decline in recent years (Emmelkamp, 1994). The problem seems to be that aversive conditioning procedures do not generalize well to situations beyond the specific therapy setting. For example, in the case of the stop-smoking class that Don taught, participants could easily counteract the aversive conditioning procedure simply by smoking outside the class. And indeed, at least some of the participants did just that.

Techniques Based on Operant Conditioning

B. F. Skinner's *operant conditioning* model of learning is based on the simple principle that behavior is shaped and maintained by its consequences (see Chapter 5). When a behavior increases as the result of a desirable consequence, *reinforcement* has occurred. When a behavior decreases because it no longer leads to a reinforcer, *extinction* has occurred. And when behavior decreases in response to an unpleasant consequence, *punishment* has occurred.

Behavior therapists have devised a variety of techniques based on the principles of operant conditioning. Often, these operant techniques focus on controlling the consequences of undesired and desired behaviors. Two relatively simple operant techniques are *positive reinforcement* for desired behaviors and *extinction,* or nonreinforcement, for undesired behaviors.

Let's illustrate how operant techniques are used in therapy by describing a behavioral program to treat a four-year-old girl's sleeping problems (Ronen, 1991). When it came to bedtime this child was not a happy camper. She would resist going to bed. After finally falling asleep, she would wake up five to seven times a night, screaming and shouting for hours. She would not stop crying unless her parents let her sleep in their bed. If her parents carried her back to her own bed, she would continue to wake up every hour, returning to their bed and crying.

The first step in the treatment program was to identify specific problem behaviors and determine their *baseline rate,* or how often each problem occurred before treatment began. After measuring the baseline rate, the therapist could target each problem behavior individually and objectively measure the child's progress. The parents next identified several very spe-

token economy
A form of behavior therapy in which the therapeutic environment is structured to reward desired behaviors with tokens or points that may eventually be exchanged for tangible rewards.

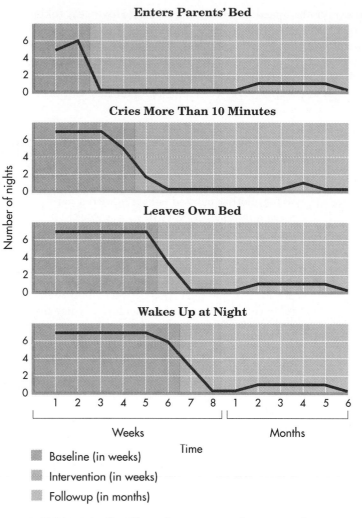

Enters Parents' Bed

Cries More Than 10 Minutes

Leaves Own Bed

Wakes Up at Night

Number of nights

1 2 3 4 5 6 7 8   1 2 3 4 5 6

Weeks   Months

Time

■ Baseline (in weeks)

■ Intervention (in weeks)

■ Followup (in months)

FIGURE 15.2 The Effect of Operant Conditioning Techniques on a Four-Year-Old Girl with Sleeping Problems
These graphs depict the changes in four specific sleep-related problem behaviors of a four-year-old girl over the course of behavioral therapy (Ronen, 1991). The intervention for each problem behavior was introduced separately over the course of several weeks. As you can see, behavior therapy produced a rapid reduction in the rate of each problem behavior. The green area shows the maintenance of desired behavior changes over the course of a six-month followup.

(Adapted from Ronen, 1991.)

cific behavioral goals for their daughter. These goals included not crying when she was put to bed, not crying if she woke up in the night, not getting into her parents' bed, and staying in her own bed throughout the night.

The parents were taught operant techniques to decrease the undesirable behaviors and increase desirable ones. For example, the parents were taught to *extinguish* the girl's screaming and crying: they were to ignore the behavior rather than continue to reinforce it with parental attention. In contrast, desirable behaviors were to be *positively reinforced* with abundant praise, encouragement, social attention, and other rewards.

At first, positive reinforcers were delivered for small gains in desirable behaviors, as when the little girl stayed in her bed for a short period of time. As the treatment progressed, rewards were given only for greater behavioral gains, such as sleeping all night. In Figure 15.2, you can see the little girl's progress for specific problem behaviors during the intervention and follow-up phases.

Operant conditioning techniques have been applied to many different kinds of psychological problems, from habit and weight control to helping autistic children learn to speak and behave more adaptively (Mazur, 1994). Techniques based on operant conditioning have also been successfully used to modify the behavior of people who are severely disabled by retardation or mental disorders (O'Leary & Wilson, 1987).

The **token economy** is an example of the use of operant conditioning techniques to modify the behavior of groups of people (Bloxham & others, 1993). A token economy is a very structured environment, a system for strengthening desired behaviors through positive reinforcement. Basically, tokens or points are awarded as positive reinforcers for desirable behaviors, and withheld or taken away for undesirable behaviors. When a token economy is used with schizophrenic patients in a psychiatric hospital, for example, the patients might receive tokens for getting dressed, interacting appropriately, maintaining personal hygiene, and so forth. The tokens can be exchanged for other reinforcers, such as special privileges or desirable items or activities like additional TV time, a weekend pass, recreational activities, or candy.

Token economies have been used in prisons, classrooms, juvenile correction institutes, and psychiatric hospitals (Mazur, 1994). Token economies have been shown to be effective even with severely disturbed patients who have

TABLE 15.3 Behavior Therapy

Type of Therapy	Founder	Source of Problems	Treatment Techniques	Goals of Therapy
Behavior therapy	Derived from the fundamental principles of learning	Learned maladaptive behavior patterns	Systematic desensitization, bell and pad treatment, aversive conditioning, reinforcement and extinction, token economy, observational learning	To unlearn maladaptive behaviors, and learn adaptive behaviors in their place

been hospitalized for many years (Paul & Menditto, 1992). However, token economies are difficult to implement and require a great deal of staff training and cooperation to be effective. The withholding of privileges from hospital inpatients has also been challenged legally. Consequently, token economies are not in wide use today (Glynn, 1990).

Behavior Therapy

Match each of the behavior therapy examples below with one of the following terms: systematic desensitization, the bell and pad treatment, virtual reality, aversive conditioning, a token economy.

1. In a group home for mentally retarded adults, the residents earn points for performing assigned chores, maintaining personal hygiene, and engaging in appropriate social interaction. Once a week, the points can be exchanged for special privileges. This is an example of _____.

2. Whenever eight-year-old Oswald started to wet his bed, an alarm went off and woke him up. After going to the bathroom, he changed the sheet, reset the alarm, and went back to sleep. After four weeks of this conditioning, Oswald now wakes up automatically whenever he has a full bladder, and he no longer wets the bed. Oswald's treatment illustrates _____.

3. Ten-year-old Mandy bit her nails constantly, so her mother painted her nails with a foul-tasting nail polish every day for a week. Mandy no longer bites her nails, but she does chew on the end of her pencil. Mandy's mother used a form of _____.

4. Mr. Lexington is phobic of small, enclosed places. His therapist first teaches him how to relax completely, then he asks him to come up with a list of anxiety-provoking images associated with his fear. Finally, the therapist asks Mr. Lexington to close his eyes and imagine very clearly the least fearful scene on the list. The therapist is using _____.

5. To help conquer her fear of flying, Carrie's therapist has her put on a special helmet so that Carrie sees computer-generated images that are very similar to what passengers actually see as they board and sit on an airplane. Carrie's therapist is using _____.

Cognitive Therapies

> *The cognitive therapies are based on the assumption that psychological problems are due to maladaptive thinking patterns. What is rational-emotive therapy (RET)? What is Beck's cognitive therapy (CT), and how does it differ from rational-emotive therapy?*

cognitive therapies
A group of psychotherapies that are based on the assumption that psychological problems are due to maladaptive patterns of thinking; treatment techniques focus on recognizing and altering these unhealthy thinking patterns.

rational-emotive therapy (RET)
A type of cognitive therapy, developed by psychologist Albert Ellis, that focuses on changing the client's irrational beliefs.

Whereas behavior therapy assumes that faulty learning is at the core of problem behaviors and emotions, the **cognitive therapies** assume that the culprit is *faulty thinking.* The key assumption of the cognitive therapies could be put like this: Most people blame their unhappiness and problems on external events and situations, but the real cause of unhappiness is the way the person *thinks* about the events, not the events themselves. Thus, cognitive therapists zero in on the faulty patterns of thinking that they believe are causing the psychological problems. Once faulty patterns of thinking have been identified, the second step is to *change* them to more adaptive, healthy patterns of thinking. In this section, we'll look at how this change is accomplished in two influential forms of cognitive therapy: Ellis's *rational-emotive therapy* (RET) and Beck's *cognitive therapy* (CT).

Albert Ellis and Rational-Emotive Therapy

There is nothing either good or bad, but thinking makes it so.

William Shakespeare Hamlet

Albert Ellis A colorful and sometimes controversial figure, Albert Ellis developed rational-emotive therapy (RET). Rational-emotive therapy promotes psychologically healthier thought processes by disputing irrational beliefs and replacing them with more rational interpretations of events.

Shakespeare said it more eloquently, but psychologist **Albert Ellis** (b. 1913) has expressed the same sentiment: "You largely feel the way you think." Ellis was trained as both a clinical psychologist and psychoanalyst. As a practicing psychoanalyst, Ellis became increasingly disappointed with the psychoanalytic approach to solving human problems. Psychoanalysis simply didn't seem to work: his patients would have insight after insight, yet never get any better.

In the 1950s, Ellis began to take a more active, directive role in his therapy sessions. He developed **rational-emotive therapy,** abbreviated **RET.** RET is based on the assumption that "people are not disturbed by things but rather by their view of things" (Ellis, 1991). The key premise of RET is that people's difficulties are caused by their faulty expectations and irrational beliefs. Rational-emotive therapy focuses on changing the patterns of irrational thinking that are believed to be the primary cause of the client's emotional distress and psychological problems.

Ellis points out that most people mistakenly believe that they become upset and unhappy because of external events. Here's an example: Our friend Carrie was upset one day because an attractive co-worker, who had previously seemed to like her, was giving her the cold shoulder. The more she thought about it, the more upset and depressed Carrie felt. When another friend asked Carrie why she was upset, she explained, "Because David is avoiding me, and I want him to like me."

Ellis (1993) would argue that Carrie's common-sense assessment is completely wrong. It's not David's behavior that's really making Carrie miserable—it's Carrie's *interpretation* of the meaning of David's behavior. In rational-emotive therapy, psychological problems are explained by the "ABC" model, as shown in Figure 15.3. According to this model, when an *Activating event* (**A**) occurs, it is the person's *Beliefs* (**B**) about the event that cause emotional *Consequences* (**C**). Notice how this differs from the common-sense view that it is the event (A) that causes the emotional and behavioral consequences (C).

Identifying the core irrational beliefs that underlie personal distress is the first step in rational-emotive therapy. In Carrie's case, the underlying cause of her distress is the common irrational belief that "everyone must love and accept me, or else I am a worthless person."

Common-Sense View

Rational-Emotive Therapy's ABC Model

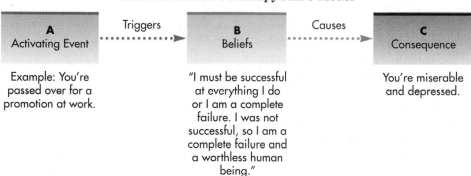

FIGURE 15.3 The "ABC" Model in Rational-Emotive Therapy
Common sense tells us that unhappiness and other unpleasant emotions are caused by unpleasant or disturbing events. This view is shown in the top part of the figure. But Albert Ellis (1993) points out that it is really our *beliefs* about the events, and not the events themselves, that make us miserable, as diagrammed in the bottom part of the figure.

TABLE 15.4 Irrational Beliefs

1. It is a dire necessity for you to be loved or approved by virtually everyone in your community.

2. You must be thoroughly competent, adequate, and achieving in all possible respects if you are to consider yourself worthwhile.

3. Certain people are bad, wicked, or villainous, and they should be severely blamed and punished for their villainy. You should become extremely upset over other people's wrongdoings.

4. It is awful and catastrophic when things are not the way you would very much like them to be.

5. Human unhappiness is externally caused, and you have little or no ability to control your bad feelings and emotions.

6. It is easier to avoid than to face difficulties and responsibilities. Avoiding difficulties whenever possible is more likely to lead to happiness than facing difficulties.

7. You need to rely on someone stronger than yourself.

8. Your past history is an all-important determinant of your present behavior. Because something once strongly affected your life, it should indefinitely have a similar effect.

9. You should become extremely upset over other people's problems.

10. There is a single perfect solution to all human problems, and it is catastrophic if this perfect solution is not found.

SOURCE: Based on Ellis, 1991.

According to rational-emotive therapy, unhappiness and psychological problems can often be traced to people's irrational beliefs. Becoming aware of these irrational beliefs is the first step toward replacing them with more rational alternatives. Some of the most common irrational beliefs are listed here.

The second step in rational-emotive therapy is for the therapist to vigorously *dispute and challenge the irrational beliefs*. The therapist might pose very direct questions to Carrie, like these: "Is there any reason David *should* think highly of you? So what if David does dislike you? Isn't that his perfect right? Is it the end of the world if he does dislike you? And even if David absolutely despises you, how does that make you a worthless person?"

Notice how irrational beliefs reflect "musts" and "shoulds" that are absolutes, such as the notion that "I should be competent at everything I do." Other common irrational beliefs are listed in Table 15.4. When these absolute demands are not satisfied, the person who subscribes to such beliefs responds by saying in effect, "This is terrible, horrible, and I cannot and will not stand it."

The consequences of such thinking are unhealthy negative emotions, like extreme anger, despair, resentment, and feelings of worthlessness. Not only does the person feel miserable, but she also feels that she is unable to control or cope with an upsetting situation. These kinds of irrational cognitive and emotional responses interfere with constructive attempts to change disturbing situations (Ellis & Harper, 1975). According to RET, the result is self-defeating behaviors, anxiety disorders, depression, and other psychological problems.

In challenging a person's irrational beliefs, rational-emotive therapists tend to be very direct and even confrontational (Haaga & Davison, 1991). Rather than trying to establish a warm, supportive atmosphere, rational-emotive therapists rely on logical persuasion and reason to push the client toward recognizing and surrendering his irrational beliefs (Hollon & Beck, 1994). According to Ellis (1991), blunt, harsh language is sometimes needed to push people into helping themselves.

From the client's perspective, rational-emotive therapy requires considerable effort. First, the person must admit her irrational beliefs and accept the fact that those beliefs are irrational and unhealthy, which is not as easy as it sounds. Old mental habits don't always yield easily. Equally challenging, the client must radically change her way of interpreting and responding to stressful events (Haaga & Davison, 1991).

Carrie would learn in therapy how to replace her irrational beliefs with more rational interpretations of adverse events. For example, she could learn to say to herself, "I would *prefer* that David really like me, and it's *disappointing* that he does not, but it's certainly not the end of the world." The long-term therapeutic goal would be to teach Carrie to recognize and dispute her own irrational beliefs in a wide range of situations.

It's important to note that responding "rationally" to unpleasant situations does not mean denying your feelings (Ellis & Bernard, 1985). Ellis believes that it is perfectly appropriate and rational to feel sad when you are rejected, or regretful when you make a mistake. Other appropriate emotional responses include disappointment, annoyance, frustration, and displeasure.

Appropriate emotions are the consequences of rational beliefs such as "I would prefer that everyone like me, but that's not likely to happen," or "It would be nice if I never failed at anything, but it's unlikely that I will always succeed in everything I do." Such healthy mental and emotional responses encourage people to work toward constructively changing or coping with difficult situations (Ellis & Harper, 1975). In effect, the person accepts the fact that his absolute demands are unlikely to be met.

Albert Ellis is a colorful figure whose ideas have been extremely influential in psychotherapy (Haaga & Davison, 1993). Rational-emotive therapy is a popular approach in clinical practice, partly because it is straightforward and simple (Arnkoff & Glass, 1992). It has been shown to be generally effective in the treatment of depression, social phobia, and certain anxiety disorders. Rational-emotive therapy is also useful in helping people overcome self-defeating behaviors, such as excessive need for approval, extreme shyness, and chronic procrastination.

Aaron Beck and Cognitive Therapy

Like Albert Ellis, psychiatrist **Aaron T. Beck** (b. 1921) was initially trained as a psychoanalyst. Beck's development of **cognitive therapy,** abbreviated **CT,** grew out of his research on depression (Beck & others, 1979). Seeking to scientifically validate the psychoanalytic assumption that depressed patients "have a need to suffer," Beck began collecting data on the free associations and dreams of his depressed patients. What he found, however, was that his depressed patients did *not* have a need to suffer. In fact, his depressed patients often went to great lengths to avoid being rejected by others.

Aaron Beck In Aaron Beck's cognitive therapy, called CT, clients learn to identify and change their automatic negative thoughts. Originally developed to treat depression, CT has also been applied to other psychological problems, such as anxiety disorders, phobias, and eating disorders.

Instead, Beck discovered, depressed people have an extremely negative view of the past, present, and future (Beck & others, 1979). Rather than realistically evaluating their situation, depressed patients have developed a *negative cognitive bias,* consistently distorting their experiences in a negative way. Their negative perceptions of events and situations are shaped by deep-seated, self-deprecating beliefs, such as "I can't do anything right," "I'm worthless," or "I'm unlovable" (Beck, 1991). Beck's cognitive therapy essentially focuses on correcting the cognitive biases that underlie depression and other psychological disorders.

Beck's CT has much in common with Ellis's rational-emotive therapy. Like Ellis, Beck believes that what people think creates their moods and emotions. And like RET, CT involves helping clients to identify faulty thinking and to replace unhealthy patterns of thinking with healthier ones.

But in contrast with Ellis's emphasis on "irrational" thinking, Beck believes that depression and other psychological problems are caused by *distorted thinking* and *unrealistic beliefs* (Hollon & Beck, 1994; Arnkoff & Glass, 1992). Rather than logically debating the "irrationality" of a client's beliefs, the CT therapist encourages the client to *empirically test the accuracy of his or her assumptions and beliefs.* Let's look at how this occurs in Beck's CT.

The first step in CT is to help the client learn to recognize and monitor the automatic thoughts that occur without conscious effort or control (Beck, 1991). Because their perceptions are shaped by their negative cognitive biases, depressed people usually have automatic thoughts that reflect very negative interpretations of experiences. Table 15.5 summarizes some of the negative cognitive biases that often operate in depression.

Whether negative or positive, automatic thoughts can control your mood and shape your emotional and behavioral reactions to events (Robins & Hayes, 1993). For example, suppose a classmate seems to snub you in the hall. A psychologically healthy person might automatically think, "Connor must be preoccupied about something. I wonder what's wrong?" Such automatic thoughts are unlikely to provoke a negative emotional reaction.

In contrast, a depressed person is more likely to respond with different automatic thoughts, like these: "Connor is mad at me because of what I said yesterday. Nobody likes me. I always say the wrong thing to people. I'm such a jerk." Not surprisingly, the result of such negative automatic thoughts is a deepened sense of depression, hopelessness, and helplessness.

Once the client has learned how to recognize and monitor his negative automatic thoughts, the therapist moves to the second step of CT. The therapist helps the client learn how to *empirically test* the reality of the

cognitive therapy (CT)
A type of cognitive therapy, developed by psychiatrist Aaron T. Beck, that focuses on changing the client's unrealistic beliefs.

TABLE 15.5 Cognitive Biases in Depression

Cognitive Bias (Error)	Description	Example
Arbitrary inference	Drawing a negative conclusion when there is little or no evidence to support it.	When Joan calls Jim to cancel their lunch date because she has an important meeting at work, Jim concludes that she is probably going out to lunch with another man.
Selective abstraction	Focusing on a single negative detail taken out of context, ignoring the more important aspects of the situation.	During Jacqueline's annual review, her manager praises every aspect of her job performance. In passing, he remarks that she could be a little more confident when she deals with customers over the phone. Jacqueline leaves her manager's office thinking that he is on the verge of firing her because of her poor telephone skills.
Overgeneralization	Drawing a sweeping, global conclusion based on an isolated incident and applying that conclusion to other unrelated areas of life.	Tony spills coffee on his final exam. He apologizes to his instructor, but can't stop thinking about the incident. He concludes that he is a klutz who will never be able to succeed in a professional career.
Magnification and minimization	Grossly overestimating the impact of negative events and grossly underestimating the impact of positive events so that small, bad events are magnified, but good, large events are minimized.	A few days after Emily finds out that she has made the dean's list, she worries about flunking out because she gets a B on an in-class quiz.
Personalization	Taking responsibility, blaming oneself, or applying external events to oneself when there is no basis or evidence for making the connection.	Richard becomes extremely upset when his instructor warns the class about plagiarism. He thinks the instructor's warning was aimed at him, and he concludes that the instructor suspects him of plagiarizing parts of his term paper.

SOURCE: Based on Beck & others (1979), p. 14.

According to Aaron Beck, depressed people perceive and interpret experience in very negative terms. They are prone to systematic errors in logic, or cognitive biases, which shape their negative interpretation of events. The table shows the most common cognitive biases in depression.

automatic thoughts that are so upsetting. For example, if a client reported negative automatic thoughts like those described above, a CT therapist might respond in this way: "Is it *really* true that 'nobody likes you'? What's your evidence for that statement? Surely *somebody* must like you. Didn't Jill invite you to her party last week?" The CT therapist may also assign behavioral tasks to "test" the accuracy of the negative automatic thoughts. To test the belief that "I always say the wrong thing," the therapist might assign the person to initiate a conversation with three acquaintances and note how often he actually said the wrong thing.

Initially, the CT therapist acts as a model, showing the client how to evaluate the accuracy of automatic thoughts. By modeling techniques for evaluating the accuracy of automatic thoughts, the therapist hopes to eventually teach the client to do the same on her own. The CT therapist also strives to create a therapeutic climate of *collaboration* that encourages the client to contribute to the evaluation of the logic and accuracy of automatic thoughts (Robins & Hayes, 1993; Beck & others, 1979). This approach contrasts with the confrontational approach used by the RET therapist, who directly challenges the client's thoughts and beliefs.

Beck's cognitive therapy has been shown to be very effective in treating depression and other psychological disorders, including anxiety disorders, eating disorders, posttraumatic stress disorder, and relationship problems (Beck, 1993; Chambless & Gillis, 1993; Klinger, 1993; Wilson & Fairburn, 1993). Beck's cognitive therapy techniques have even been adapted to help treat psychotic symptoms, such as the delusions and disorganized thought processes that often characterize schizophrenia (Alford & Correia, 1994; Chadwick & others, 1994).

TABLE 15.6 Comparing Cognitive Therapies

Type of Therapy	Founder	Source of Problems	Treatment Techniques	Goals of Therapy
Rational-emotive therapy (RET)	Albert Ellis	Irrational beliefs	Very directive: Identify, logically dispute, and challenge irrational beliefs	Surrender of irrational beliefs and absolutist demands
Cognitive therapy (CT)	Aaron T. Beck	Unrealistic, distorted perceptions and interpretations of events due to cognitive biases	Directive collaboration: Teach client to monitor automatic thoughts; test accuracy of conclusions; correct distorted thinking and perception	Accurate and realistic perception of self, others, and external events

Group and Family Therapy

Group therapy involves one or more therapists working with several people simultaneously. What are some key advantages of group therapy? What is family therapy, and how does it differ from individual therapy?

Individual psychotherapy offers a personal relationship between a client and a therapist, one that is focused on a single client's problems, thoughts, and emotions. But individual psychotherapy has certain limitations (Feldman & Powell, 1992). The therapist sees the client in isolation, rather than within the context of his interactions with others. Hence, the therapist must rely on the client's interpretation of reality and his description of his relationships with others.

Group Therapy

In contrast, **group therapy** involves one or more therapists working with several people simultaneously. Group therapy may be provided by a therapist in private practice or at a community mental health clinic. Often, group therapy is an important part of the treatment program for hospital inpatients (Kibel, 1993). Groups may be as small as three or four people or as large as ten or more people.

Virtually any approach, whether psychodynamic, client-centered, behavioral, or cognitive, can be used in group therapy (Alonso & Swiller, 1993a). And just about any problem that can be handled individually can be dealt with in group therapy.

Some therapy groups are made up of clients who share the same problem, but others are far more diverse. Regardless, the goals of group therapy are the same as those for individual psychotherapy—resolving psychological problems and promoting more adaptive behaviors. The therapeutic success of group therapy often hinges on the group's collective sense of *cohesion,* or togetherness (Bednar & Kaul, 1994).

Group therapy has a number of advantages over individual psychotherapy (Dies, 1993). First, group therapy is very cost-effective: a single therapist can work simultaneously with several people. Thus, it is less expensive for the client and less time-consuming for the therapist. Second, rather than relying on a client's self-perceptions about how she relates to other people, the therapist can observe her actual interactions with others. Observing the way clients interact with others in a group may provide unique insights into their personalities and behavior patterns (Alonso & Swiller, 1993b; Porter, 1993).

group therapy
A form of psychotherapy that involves one or more therapists working simultaneously with a small group of clients.

IN FOCUS 15.3

Self-Help Groups: Helping Yourself by Helping Others

Every month our local newspaper publishes a list of more than 300 self-help and support groups that meet in our area. These groups range from the familiar (Alcoholics Anonymous, Toughlove) to the obscure (Abused by Religion, Cult Awareness Group, Crossdressers of Green County), and from the general (Parents of Adolescents, Effective Black Parenting) to the specific (Multiple Sclerosis—Newly Diagnosed). There are groups for people with particular psychological problems, medical conditions, or problems with substance abuse. There are also groups for people dealing with life's transitions and crises, such as becoming a parent, divorce, retirement, or bereavement.

What this bewildering array of groups have in common is that all of them are organized and led by nonprofessionals. Typically, such groups are made up of members who have a common problem and meet for the purpose of exchanging psychological support (Jacobs & Goodman, 1989). Some groups are focused on psychological growth and change. Other groups have a more practical emphasis, providing information and advice (Carroll, 1993). The groups are either free or charge nominal fees to cover the cost of materials.

In the United States, the number of self-help groups is rapidly approaching 1 million. How many people belong to these groups? Estimates range from 7 million to 15 million people and growing (Christensen & Jacobson, 1994). In comparison, about 16 million people per year use professional mental health services, such as psychotherapy (Rutter, 1994). Clearly, self-help groups play an important and useful role in many people's lives.

The format of self-help groups varies enormously. Some groups are quite free-wheeling, but others are highly structured (McFadden & others, 1992). Meetings may follow a prescribed format, and there may be rules regulating contacts among group members outside the meetings. For example, our friend Marcia attends weekly meetings of a self-help group called Emotions Anonymous. In Marcia's group, each person takes a turn speaking for five minutes. Interruptions are not allowed, and other members simply listen without responding to the speaker's comments.

Many self-help groups follow a twelve-step approach, patterned after the famous twelve-step program of Alcoholics Anonymous. The twelve steps involve themes of admitting that you

have a problem, seeking help from a "higher power," confessing your shortcomings, repairing your relationships with others, and helping other people who have the same problem. These twelve steps have been adapted by many different groups to fit their particular problem. Some psychologists criticize the twelve-step approach for its emphasis on the idea that people are "powerless" to cope with their problems on their own and must depend on a higher power and on other group members (Kasl, 1992).

Just how helpful are self-help groups? Research has shown that self-help groups are often just as effective as therapy provided by a mental health professional, at least for some psychological problems (Christensen & Jacobson, 1994). Given that many people cannot afford professional counseling, self-help groups may be a cost-effective alternative to psychotherapy for some people.

What is not known is *why* self-help groups are effective in helping people solve problems, change behaviors, and grow psychologically. Support and encouragement from others are undoubtedly important. So may be the "helper therapy" principle on which all self-help groups are based: people who help other people are themselves helped. But more research is needed to clarify the elements that contribute the most to a successful outcome. Research is also needed to identify the kinds of people and problems that are most likely to benefit from a self-help approach (Christensen & Jacobson, 1994).

An Alcoholics Anonymous Meeting Founded in 1935, *Alcoholics Anonymous* has more than two million members worldwide. People from all walks of life attend AA, and many credit AA for turning their lives around. Because AA group members are guaranteed anonymity, their faces cannot be shown in the photograph. Many other kinds of self-help groups are modeled on the AA program.

Third, the support and encouragement provided by the other group members may help a person feel less alone and understand that his problems are not unique (Alonso & Swiller, 1993a). Fourth, group members may provide each other with helpful, practical advice for solving common problems and can act as models for successfully overcoming difficulties. Finally, working within a group gives people an opportunity to try out new behaviors in a safe, supportive environment (Porter, 1993). For instance, someone who is very shy and submissive can practice more assertive behaviors and receive honest feedback from other group members.

Group therapy is typically conducted by a mental health professional. In contrast, *self-help groups* and *support groups* are typically conducted by non-professionals. Support groups and self-help groups have become increasingly popular in the United States. And, like Marcia's therapist in the chapter prologue, some therapists recommend self-help groups as an adjunct to traditional psychotherapy. As discussed in In Focus Box 15.3, the potential of these groups to promote mental health should not be underestimated.

Family and Couple Therapy

Most forms of psychotherapy, including most group therapies, tend to see a person's problems—and the solutions to those problems—as primarily originating within the individual himself. **Family therapy** operates on a different premise, focusing on the whole family rather than on an individual. The major goal of family therapy is to alter and improve the ongoing interactions among family members (Lebow & Gurman, 1995). Typically, family therapy involves every member of the family, even young children, and may also include important members of the extended family, such as grandparents or in-laws.

Family therapy is based on the assumption that the family is a *system,* an interdependent unit, not just a collection of separate individuals. The family is seen as a dynamic structure in which each member plays a unique role. According to this view, every family has certain unspoken "rules" of interaction and communication. Some of these tacit rules revolve around issues such as which family members exercise power and how, who makes decisions, who keeps the peace, and what kinds of alliances members have formed among themselves. As such issues are explored, unhealthy patterns of family interaction can be identified and replaced with new "rules" that promote the psychological health of the family as a unit.

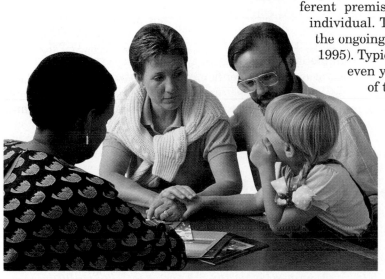

A Family Therapy Session Family therapists typically work with all the members of a family at the same time, including young children. Doing so allows the family therapist to directly observe how family members interact, resolve differences, and exert control over one another. As unhealthy patterns of family interactions are identified, they can often be replaced with new patterns that promote the psychological well-being of the family as a whole.

family therapy
A form of psychotherapy that is based on the assumption that the family is a system and that treats the family as a unit.

Family therapy is often used to enhance the effectiveness of individual psychotherapy (Feldman & Powell, 1992). Very commonly, the therapist realizes that the individual client's problems reflect conflict and disturbance in the entire family system (Lebow & Gurman, 1995). In order for the client to make significant improvements, the family as a whole must become psychologically healthier. Family therapy is also indicated when there is conflict among family members, such as among parents and adolescent children, or when younger children are being treated for behavior problems, such as truancy or aggressive behavior (Kazdin, 1994b).

Many family therapists also provide *marital* or *couple therapy*. The term *couple therapy* is preferred today because such therapy is conducted with any couple in a committed relationship, whether they are married or unmarried, heterosexual or homosexual (Lebow & Gurman, 1995). As is the case with family therapy, there are many different approaches to couple therapy

Couple Therapy Couple therapy focuses on helping people who are in a committed relationship. Couple therapy usually emphasizes improving communication, increasing intimacy, and strengthening the relationship bond.

(Alexander & others, 1994). However, most couple therapies have the goal of improving communication and problem-solving skills and increasing intimacy between the pair.

A current trend in couple therapy is for the therapist to be closely attuned to the cultural and social context within which the couple functions. Therapists are taking greater care not to impose their own expectations on client couples of what constitutes a healthy relationship. This is especially important when the couple is from a different cultural background with different values and expectations about gender roles and about the marital relationship. As you'll see in the next section, psychotherapists are becoming more aware of the importance of culture in the therapist–client relationship.

Culture and Psychotherapy:
Bridging the Culture Gap

> *When psychotherapists and clients hold different cultural values, the effectiveness of psychotherapy can decrease. What cultural values are inherent in Western psychotherapy? How do these values clash with the values of other cultures?*

Like any other aspect of society, psychotherapy reflects the culture in which it has developed. Psychodynamic, humanistic, behavioral, and cognitive therapies are all products of middle-class European and North American culture. The cultural values implicit in these Western forms of psychotherapy are usually taken for granted by most members of "mainstream" American or European culture.

However, these unspoken cultural values can be quite foreign to people whose cultural background is different. They can present cultural barriers to the effective treatment of members of certain ethnic or cultural groups. In this section, we'll discuss the cultural values inherent in most Western psychotherapies that are most likely to conflict with the values of clients from other cultural backgrounds.

Focus on the Individual

Individualistic cultures emphasize the independent, autonomous self, behaving in accordance with internal attributes and motives. Not surprisingly, then, most Western psychotherapies focus on the individual. Problems are presumed to have internal causes and are expected to be solved by the individual himself.

Commonly, the client is encouraged to become more assertive, more self-sufficient, and less dependent on others in making decisions and conducting his or her life. Therapy emphasizes meeting the client's individual needs, even if those needs conflict with the demands of significant others. In the process of developing his individual potential, the client may even be encouraged to disregard the demands of family members.

In many collectivistic cultures, however, the basic psychosocial unit is not the individual, but the family, the group, or the community (Markus & Kitayama, 1991). The needs of the individual are much more strongly identified with the needs of the group to which he or she belongs (Triandis, 1994). Problems and successes reflect on the group as well as the individual. Thus, an individual would never make an important decision without consulting other group members.

For example, traditional Native Americans are less likely than European-Americans to believe that personal problems are due to an internal cause within the individual (Sue, Zane, & Young, 1994). Instead, one person's problems may be seen as a matter for the entire community to resolve.

In traditional forms of Native American healing, treatment is collective rather than individual. Family members, friends, and other members of the community may be asked to participate in the treatment or healing rituals. One type of therapy, called *network therapy,* is conducted in the person's home and can involve as many as 40 to 70 members of the individual's community or tribe. Network therapy has been shown to help prevent and resolve psychological problems in Native American communities (LaFromboise & others, 1993b).

Latino cultures also stress interdependence over independence, with a strong emphasis on the family. But in Latino cultures, the boundaries of the "family" reach beyond the immediate family to include members of the extended family as well. Because the sense of family is so central to Latino culture, psychologist Lilian Comas-Diaz (1993) recommends that members of the client's extended family be actively involved in psychological treatment.

Similarly, members of many Asian cultures define their identities in terms of the groups and the family to which they belong. This difference is reflected in a Japanese psychotherapy called *Naikan therapy* (Reynolds, 1990, 1989). According to Naikan therapy, being self-absorbed is the surest path to psychological suffering. In Naikan therapy, the client meditates on three key themes:

- What he has received from other significant people in his life
- What he has done in return
- The problems that he has caused for these significant people

The goal of Naikan therapy is to replace the focus on the self with a sense of gratitude and obligation toward significant others. Contrast this with psychodynamic and humanistic therapies, in which the client often focuses on how parents and others have failed to meet the client's needs. In Naikan therapy, the client focuses on how much parents and others have done for him—and how he has failed to meet *their* needs!

Cultural Values Even after immigrating to the United States, many people maintain strong ties with their cultural heritage. Here, Arab-American children attend an Islamic school. Notice that the young female students as well as the teacher are wearing the traditional *chador* or veil. The traditional beliefs of some cultures, such as the Islamic belief that women should be modest and obedient to their husbands, may conflict with the values inherent in western psychotherapies.

Seeking Professional Help

In many cultures, people are far more likely to turn to family members or friends than they are to mental health professionals. In many Native American cultures, for example, personal problems are considered to be spiritual rather than "psychological" in nature (LaFromboise & others, 1993b). Thus, traditional Native Americans may turn to spiritual leaders for help rather than psychologists or psychiatrists.

Another barrier is felt by refugees and immigrants who have experienced government oppression in their native lands. They may be understandably reluctant to seek help from psychologists or counselors who are affiliated with government agencies (Nishio & Bilmes, 1993).

Importance of Insight

Psychodynamic, humanistic, and cognitive therapies all stress the importance of a client's insight into thoughts and feelings. Hence, Western psychotherapies encourage the client to explore painful thoughts and feelings.

Many other cultures, however, do *not* emphasize the importance of soul-searching in resolving psychological problems. Asian cultures stress that mental health is enhanced by the avoidance of negative thinking (Sue, Zane, & Young, 1994). In China and many other Asian countries, a depressed or anxious person may be encouraged to *avoid* focusing on upsetting thoughts.

Intimate Disclosure Between Therapist and Client

Many Western psychotherapies are based on the assumption that the client will disclose her deepest feelings and most private thoughts to her therapist. But in many other cultures, intimate details of one's personal life would never be discussed with a stranger. Asians, for example, are brought up to disclose intimate details only to very close friends (Sue, Sue, & Sue, 1994).

The demand for emotional openness may also clash with other cultural values. In Asian cultures, people tend to avoid the public expression of emotions, often expressing thoughts and feelings indirectly or nonverbally (Sue,

TABLE 15.7 APA Ethical Guidelines for Counseling Culturally Diverse Populations

Psychologists should:

- Be aware of research and practice issues related to the specific population being served

- Acknowledge that ethnicity and culture impact on behavior and take those factors into account when working with various ethnic or racial groups

- Be aware of how their own cultural background, experiences, values, and biases influence psychological processes, and make efforts to correct any prejudices and biases

- Incorporate an understanding of the client's ethnic and cultural background into their practice

- Help clients increase their awareness of their own cultural values

- Respect the roles of family members and community structures, hierarchies, values, and beliefs within the client's culture

- Respect clients' religious and spiritual beliefs and values

SOURCE: Excerpted from American Psychological Association, 1993.

Zane, & Young, 1994). In a similar way, Native American cultures tend to value the restraint of emotions rather than the open expression of emotions (LaFromboise & others, 1993b).

Increasing Sensitivity to Cultural Differences

Given such fundamental differences in cultural values, it's not surprising that ethnic minorities are less likely than European-Americans to consult mental health professionals. They're also more likely to drop out after a single session when they do (Sue, Zane, & Young, 1994).

Recognizing the need for psychotherapists to become more culturally sensitive, the American Psychological Association has recommended formal training in multicultural awareness for all psychologists (Edwards, 1995a). The American Psychological Association (1993) has also published a new set of ethical guidelines for psychologists who provide psychological help to culturally diverse populations. Key points of these new guidelines are summarized in Table 15.7.

CONCEPT REVIEW 15.3

Types of Psychotherapy

Match each statement below with one of the following types of psychotherapy: psychoanalytic therapy, behavior therapy, humanistic therapy, cognitive therapy.

1. Our problems are not the result of what happens to us, but instead are a function of our cognitive interpretations and irrational thinking about what happens to us.

_____

2. Maladaptive behavior is learned in the same way as any other behavior. Improvement occurs when the environmental conditions are changed so that adaptive behavior is reinforced and maintained. _____

3. The therapist's role is to be nondirective and to provide the client with unconditional positive regard and empathic understanding.

_____

4. People can regain mental health only by developing insight into their hidden, unconscious conflicts through the techniques of free association, dream interpretation, and transference.

_____

Evaluating the Effectiveness of Psychotherapy

> *Meta-analysis has been used to evaluate the effectiveness of psychotherapy. Is one form of psychotherapy superior to the others? What common factors contribute to effective psychotherapy? What is eclecticism?*

During the last thirty years, hundreds of studies have investigated the effectiveness of the major forms of psychotherapy (see Seligman, 1995; Lambert & Bergin, 1994; Orlinsky & others, 1994). As you might imagine, these studies vary enormously. Some studies focus on a specific psychotherapy, while others compare the effectiveness of two or more types of psychotherapy. The type and severity of psychological problems treated in these studies also vary.

Equally diverse are the measures of improvement used in these studies. Improvement is sometimes measured in terms of social adjustment, job performance, or satisfaction with intimate relationships. Psychological tests, self-reported feelings of improvement, and ratings by other family members have also been used to gauge the effectiveness of psychotherapy.

To help deal with the diversity among psychotherapy studies and arrive at general conclusions, researchers often combine the results of similar studies using a statistical technique called *meta-analysis* (Lipsey & Wilson, 1993). Meta-analysis involves pooling the results of several studies into a single analysis, and essentially creates one large study that can reveal overall trends in the data.

For example, meta-analysis has been used to combine the results of studies assessing the effectiveness of different psychotherapies in treating depression (e.g., Robinson & others, 1990; Dobson, 1989). As you'll see in this section, meta-analysis has helped researchers answer some fundamental questions about the effectiveness of psychotherapy.

Is Psychotherapy More Effective Than No Treatment at All?

Let's start with a simple fact: Most people with psychological symptoms do *not* seek help from mental health professionals (Kessler & others, 1994). This suggests that most people eventually weather their psychological problems without professional intervention.

How do these people cope on their own with psychological difficulties? Probably with the help and support of friends and family, along with self-help strategies, such as common stress-reducing techniques (see Chapter 13). And some people eventually improve simply with the passage of time, a phenomenon called *spontaneous remission* (see Eysenck, 1994, 1952). Given that, here's the critical question: Does psychotherapy offer significant benefits over simply waiting for the possible "spontaneous remission" of symptoms?

The basic strategy to investigate this issue is to compare people who enter psychotherapy with a matched control group of people who do not receive psychotherapy (Kazdin, 1994a). The people in the control group have similar characteristics and roughly the same degree of psychological problems as the people in psychotherapy. At different times over the course of psychotherapy, the treated and untreated groups are compared for signs of improvement. If the treated group improves significantly more than the un-

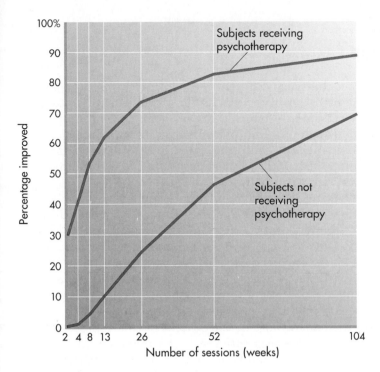

FIGURE 15.4 Psychotherapy Versus No Treatment
This graph depicts the rates of improvement for more than 2,000 people in weekly psychotherapy and for 500 people who did not receive psychotherapy. As you can see, after only eight weekly sessions, better than 50 percent of subjects receiving psychotherapy were significantly improved. After the same length of time, only 4 percent of subjects not receiving psychotherapy showed "spontaneous remission" of symptoms. Clearly, psychotherapy accelerates both the rate and degree of improvement for those experiencing psychological problems.
(Adapted from McNeilly & Howard, 1991.)

treated group, then it's probable that the psychotherapy is the reason for the improvement.

When meta-analysis is used to summarize studies that compare people who receive psychotherapy treatment to no-treatment controls, researchers consistently arrive at the same conclusion: *Psychotherapy is significantly more effective than no treatment.* On the average, the person who completes psychotherapy treatment is better off than about 80 percent of those in the untreated control group (Lambert & Bergin, 1994; Lipsey & Wilson, 1993).

Even more impressively, the benefits of psychotherapy are usually apparent in a relatively short period of time. As shown in Figure 15.4, approximately 50 percent of people show significant improvement by the eighth weekly session of psychotherapy. By the end of six months of weekly psychotherapy sessions, about 75 percent are significantly improved (McNeilly & Howard, 1991; Howard & others, 1986). The gains that people make as a result of psychotherapy also tend to endure long after the therapy has ended, sometimes for years (Lambert & Bergin, 1994). Even brief forms of psychotherapy tend to produce beneficial and longlasting changes (Koss & Shiang, 1994).

Another line of evidence comes from a recent study that used PET scans to measure brain activity before and after ten weeks of psychotherapy for obsessive-compulsive disorder (Schwartz & others, 1996). The psychotherapy patients who improved showed the same changes in brain function that are associated with effective drug therapy for this disorder. In other words, psychotherapy alone produced distinct physiological effects in the brain—effects that were associated with a reduction in symptoms.

So, is psychotherapy effective? In a word, *yes.* Nevertheless, it's important to note that psychotherapy is not a miracle cure. While most people experience significant benefits from psychotherapy, not everyone benefits to the same degree. Some people who enter psychotherapy improve only slightly or not at all.

Is One Form of Psychotherapy Superior?

Given the very different assumptions and techniques used in the major types of psychotherapy, does one type of psychotherapy stand out as more effective than the others? Hundreds of studies have compared the treatment outcomes for different types of psychotherapy. If you look at any individual study, it might show that one type of psychotherapy is more effective than another in treating certain types of problems.

For example, cognitive and behavioral therapies tend to be more successful than insight-oriented therapies in helping people who are experiencing panic disorder, obsessive-compulsive disorder, and phobias (Hollon & Beck, 1994; Kazdin, 1994). Insight-oriented therapies are also less effective than other therapies in the treatment of disorders characterized by severe psychotic symptoms, such as schizophrenia (Mueser & Glynn, 1993).

However, when meta-analysis techniques are used to assess the collective results of treatment outcome studies, a surprising but consistent finding emerges: *In general, there is little or no difference in the effectiveness of different psychotherapies.* Despite sometimes dramatic differences in psychotherapy techniques, all of the standard psychotherapies have very similar success rates (Lambert & Bergin, 1994; Lipsey & Wilson, 1993).

What Factors Contribute to Effective Psychotherapy?

How can we explain the fact that very different forms of psychotherapy are basically equivalent in producing positive results? One possible explanation is that the factors that are crucial to producing improvement are present in *all* effective therapies. Following this line of reasoning, researchers have identified a number of common factors that are related to a positive therapy outcome (Lambert & Bergin, 1994, 1992). Put simply, when these common factors are present in the therapy situation, the outcome is more likely to be successful. Some studies even suggest that common factors may be more important in producing improvement than the specific techniques espoused by different psychotherapies (Elkin & others, 1989; Glass & Arnkoff, 1988).

What are these common factors? First and most important are factors associated with the *therapeutic relationship.* In effective psychotherapies, the therapist–client relationship is characterized by mutual respect, trust, and hope. Both the therapist and the client believe that significant change is possible and can be achieved. Working in a cooperative alliance, both people are actively trying to achieve the same goals. In the context of this therapeutic relationship, the client often experiences *catharsis*—the reduction of emotional and physical tension that occurs simply as a result of talking about his or her psychological problems (Lambert & Bergin, 1994, 1992).

Second, certain *therapist characteristics* are associated with successful therapy. Not surprisingly, people frequently attribute their success in psychotherapy to the personal qualities of the therapist rather than to the specific techniques used. Effective therapists actively help people understand and face their problems. Regardless of orientation, effective therapists tend to be warm, sensitive, and responsive people, and they are perceived as sincere and genuine (Beutler & others, 1994).

Effective therapists are also sensitive to the *cultural differences* that may exist between themselves and their clients (Atkinson & others, 1993; Sue, Zane, & Young, 1994). As you read in the previous section, cultural differences can be a barrier to effective psychotherapy. Increasingly, training in cultural sensitivity and multicultural issues is being incorporated into psychological training programs in the United States (Edwards, 1995a; DeAngelis, 1994b; Hills & Strozier, 1992).

Third, *client characteristics* are important. If the client is motivated, committed to therapy, and actively involved in the process, a successful outcome is much more likely. People who are open to looking at their problems in a different way and who are willing to attempt new behaviors and ways of thinking are more likely to benefit from therapy. The ability to express thoughts and feelings, as well as the client's level of emotional and social maturity, also influence the likelihood of therapeutic success (Garfield, 1994; Koss & Shiang, 1994).

Finally, *external circumstances* often play a role in therapy outcome. Having the support, understanding, and encouragement of family members or a spouse can enhance the effectiveness of psychotherapy. It also helps if the client's living situation is a stable one in which the other people are psychologically well adjusted (Engler & Goleman, 1992).

Therapeutic Sensitivity to Cultural Differences Therapist sensitivity to a client's cultural values can affect the ability to form a good working relationship and, ultimately, the success of psychotherapy. Thus, some clients prefer to see therapists who are from the same cultural background, as is the case of the Korean-American therapist and client shown. In general, therapists have become more attuned to the important role played by culture in effective psychotherapy.

eclecticism
The pragmatic and integrated use of techniques from different psychotherapies.

If you stop to consider the common factors that contribute to effective psychotherapy, you'll notice that none of these factors is specific to any particular brand of psychotherapy. However, this does not mean that differences between psychotherapy techniques are completely irrelevant. Rather, it's important that there be a good "match" between the person seeking help and the specific psychotherapy techniques used. One person may be very comfortable with psychodynamic techniques, such as exploring childhood memories and free association. Another person might be more open to behavioral techniques, like systematic desensitization. For therapy to be optimally effective, the individual should feel comfortable with both the therapist and the therapist's approach to therapy.

Increasingly, such a personalized approach to therapy is being facilitated by the movement of mental health professionals toward **eclecticism**—the pragmatic and integrated use of diverse psychotherapy techniques (Garfield, 1992). Today, therapists identify themselves as eclectic more often than any other orientation (Garfield & Bergin, 1994). *Eclectic psychotherapists* carefully tailor the therapy approach to the problems and characteristics of the person seeking help. For example, an eclectic therapist might integrate insight-oriented techniques with specific behavioral techniques to help someone suffering from extreme shyness.

In summary, it's clear that psychotherapy is generally effective for the moderate kinds of problems that trouble most people. Although diverse, the different psychotherapies are basically equivalent in the positive results they produce. To a large degree, these positive results seem to hinge on common factors that are present in all forms of effective psychotherapy (Lambert & Bergin, 1994).

Still, the optimal situation remains one in which the person is comfortable with the therapist and the specific psychotherapy techniques used. Today's psychotherapists tend to utilize diverse techniques that are tailored to the needs and characteristics of the person seeking help. In summing up the meta-analyses of hundreds of psychotherapy outcome studies, psychologists Michael Lambert and Allen Bergin (1994) put it this way:

> *Psychotherapy facilitates the remission of symptoms. It not only speeds up the natural healing process but also often provides additional coping strategies and methods for dealing with future problems. Psychologists, psychiatrists, social workers, and marriage and family therapists as well as patients can be assured that a broad range of therapies, when offered by skillful, wise, and stable therapists, are likely to result in appreciable gains for the client.*

CONCEPT REVIEW 15.4

Elements of Effective Psychotherapy

Identify each statement below as true or false. If a statement is false, rewrite it to correct it.

_____ **1.** Meta-analysis is the most effective psychoanalytic technique.

_____ **2.** In general, psychotherapy is no more effective than talking with a friend.

_____ **3.** Behavior therapy is the single most effective therapy available for all psychological disorders.

_____ **4.** Because the principles of effective therapy are universal, cultural differences between clients and therapists have no impact on the effectiveness of psychotherapy.

_____ **5.** Regardless of which form of therapy they practice, the most effective psychotherapists are perceived as warm, genuine, and sincere.

_____ **6.** A client's attitude toward therapy has minimal impact on therapy's effectiveness.

Biomedical Therapies

The biomedical therapies are medical treatments for the symptoms of psychological disorders. What are the most important antipsychotic, antianxiety, and antidepressant medications, and how do they achieve their effects? What are their disadvantages? What are lithium and ECT, and how are they used?

Medical treatments for psychological disorders actually predate modern psychotherapy by hundreds of years. In past centuries, patients were whirled, soothed, drenched, restrained, and isolated—all in an attempt to alleviate symptoms of psychological disorders. Today, such "treatments" seem cruel, inhumane, and useless. Keep in mind, however, that these early treatments were based on the limited medical knowledge of the time. As you'll see in this section, some of the early efforts to treat psychological disorders did eventually evolve into treatments that are widely used today.

Historical Treatments for Mental Illness
Left: An early treatment apparatus called the "circulating swing" involved spinning patients. Center: A "tranquilizing chair" was developed in the early 1800s to restrain and sedate unmanageable patients. Right: Found in Peru, this pre-Columbian skull shows the results of primitive surgery on the brain, called *trephining,* presumably as a treatment to allow evil spirits to leave the body.

For the most part, it was not until the twentieth century that effective biomedical therapies were developed to treat the symptoms of mental disorders. Today, the most common biomedical therapy is the use of *psychoactive medications*—prescription drugs that alter mental functions and alleviate psychological symptoms. In fact, of all medical prescriptions written today, 20 percent are for medications used to affect mental processes (Baldessarini, 1990). Although often used alone, psychoactive medications are increasingly being combined with psychotherapy.

Most of the psychoactive medications used today were discovered by accident or in the course of medical research in some other area. Typically, it was only after a medication had been observed to relieve psychological symptoms that scientists began to unravel how the drugs worked (Klerman & others, 1994). In doing so, researchers have gained important insights about the biological underpinnings of many psychological disorders.

Because they are medical treatments, the biomedical therapies must be administered by a psychiatrist or other licensed physician. In fact, family physicians write many of the prescriptions for medications that affect psychological symptoms (Sleek, 1994). But as we noted at the beginning of this chapter, the momentum toward allowing clinical psychologists to prescribe psychoactive medications is growing (Fowler, 1995; Chafetz & Buelow, 1994; Smyer & others, 1993). Some psychologists in the U.S. military are already prescribing medications for the treatment of mental disorders (DeLeon & others, 1995; Youngstrom, 1992). Clinical psychologists in private practice may someday be able to directly prescribe psychoactive medications to help treat psychological disorders.

We'll begin this section by looking at the major categories of psychoactive medications used to treat psychological symptoms. Following that, we'll consider the most controversial biomedical therapy in use today: electroconvulsive shock therapy.

Antipsychotic Medications

For more than 2,000 years, traditional practitioners of medicine in India used a herb derived from the snakeroot plant, a shrub that grows in central Asia. The herbal extract was used to treat diverse medical conditions, including insomnia, epilepsy, and snakebite. But its primary use in traditional Indian medicine was to diminish the psychotic symptoms commonly associated with schizophrenia: hallucinations, delusions, and disordered thought processes (Frankenburg, 1994). The same plant was used in traditional Japanese medicine to treat anxiety and restlessness (Jilek, 1993). In the 1930s, Indian physicians discovered that the herb was also helpful in the treatment of high blood pressure. They also developed a synthetic version of the herb's active ingredient, called *reserpine*.

Reserpine first came to the attention of American researchers as a potential treatment for high blood pressure. But it wasn't until the early 1950s that American researchers became aware of research in India demonstrating the effectiveness of reserpine in treating schizophrenia (Frankenburg, 1994). Almost 2,000 years after reserpine's effectiveness had first been discovered, American clinical trials on reserpine as a treatment for schizophrenia finally began in the 1950s.

It was also during the 1950s that French scientists began investigating the psychoactive properties of another drug, called *chlorpromazine*. Like reserpine, chlorpromazine diminished the psychotic symptoms commonly seen in schizophrenia. Hence, reserpine and chlorpromazine were dubbed **antipsychotic medications.** Because chlorpromazine had fewer side effects than reserpine, it nudged out reserpine as the preferred medication for treating schizophrenia-related symptoms. Today, chlorpromazine is better known by its trade name, *Thorazine,* and is still widely used to treat psychotic symptoms.

How do these drugs diminish psychotic symptoms? Reserpine and chlorpromazine act differently on the brain, but both drugs reduce levels of the neurotransmitter called *dopamine*. Since the development of these early drugs, more than thirty other antipsychotic medications have been developed (see Table 15.8). These antipsychotic medications also act on dopamine receptors in the brain (Klerman & others, 1994).

The first antipsychotics effectively reduced the so-called *positive symptoms* of schizophrenia—hallucinations, delusions, and disordered thinking (see Chapter 14). This therapeutic effect had a revolutionary impact on the number of people hospitalized for schizophrenia. Until the 1950s, patients suffering from schizophrenia were thought to be incurable. These chronic patients formed the bulk of the population on the "back wards" of psychiatric hospitals (Davison & Neale, 1994). With the introduction of the antipsychotic medications, however, the number of patients in mental hospitals decreased dramatically (see Figure 15.5).

TABLE 15.8 Commonly Prescribed Antipsychotic Drugs

	Generic Name	Trade Name
Typical Antipsychotics		
	Chlorpromazine	Thorazine
	Fluphenazine	Prolixin
	Trifluoperazine	Stelazine
	Thioridazine	Mellaril
	Thiothixene	Navane
	Haloperidol	Haldol
Atypical Antipsychotics		
	Clozapine	Clozaril
	Risperidone	Risperdal

SOURCE: Adapted from Julien, 1995, Table 11.1, p. 281.

antipsychotic medications
Prescription drugs that are used to reduce psychotic symptoms; frequently used in the treatment of schizophrenia.

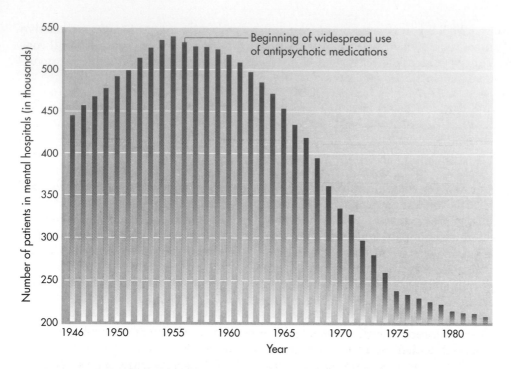

FIGURE 15.5 Change in the Number of Patients Hospitalized for Mental Disorders, 1946–1983

When the first antipsychotic drugs came into wide use in the late 1950s, the number of people hospitalized for mental disorders began to drop sharply.

(Adapted from Julien, 1995, Fig. 11.3, p. 276.)

Drawbacks of Antipsychotic Medications

Even though the early antipsychotic drugs allowed thousands of patients to be discharged from hospitals, these drugs had a number of drawbacks. First, they didn't actually *cure* schizophrenia. Psychotic symptoms often returned if a person stopped taking the medication.

Second, the early antipsychotic medications were less effective in eliminating the so-called *negative symptoms* of schizophrenia—social withdrawal, apathy, and lack of emotional expressiveness (Marder & others, 1993). In some cases, the drugs even made negative symptoms worse. Third, the antipsychotics often produced unwanted side effects, such as dry mouth, weight gain, constipation, sleepiness, and poor concentration (Gerlach & Peacock, 1994).

Fourth, the fact that the early antipsychotics *globally* altered brain levels of dopamine turned out to be a double-edged sword. Dopamine pathways in the brain are involved not only in psychotic symptoms but also in normal motor movements. Consequently, the early antipsychotic medications could produce motor-related side effects—muscle tremors, rigid movements, a shuffling gait, and a masklike facial expression (Barondes, 1993). This collection of side effects occurred so commonly that mental hospital staff members sometimes informally referred to it as the "Thorazine shuffle."

Even more disturbing, the long-term use of antipsychotic medications causes a small percentage of people to develop a potentially irreversible motor disorder called *tardive dyskinesia*. Tardive dyskinesia is characterized by severe, uncontrollable facial tics and grimaces, chewing movements, and other involuntary movements of the lips, jaw, and tongue (Marder & others, 1993).

Closely tied to the various side effects of the first antipsychotic drugs is a fifth problem: the "revolving door" pattern of hospitalization, discharge, and rehospitalization (Davison & Neale, 1994). Schizophrenic patients, once stabilized by antipsychotic medication, were released from hospitals into the community. But because of the medication's unpleasant side effects, inadequate medical follow-up, or both, many patients eventually stopped taking the medication. When psychotic symptoms returned, the patients were rehospitalized. Today, the majority of schizophrenic patients admitted to psychiatric facilities have been hospitalized before. Some patients have "revolved" between hospitals and the community more than forty times (Paul & Menditto, 1992).

The Atypical Antipsychotics

Recently, a new generation of antipsychotic drugs have given rise to increased optimism about the treatment of schizophrenia. Called *atypical antipsychotics,* these drugs act differently on the brain than the older antipsychotic drugs. The first atypical antipsychotics, *clozapine* and *risperidone,* affect levels of the neurotransmitter *serotonin* as well as dopamine in the brain.

antianxiety medications
Prescription drugs that are used to alleviate the symptoms of anxiety.

The atypical antipsychotics have three important advantages over the traditional antipsychotic drugs (Meltzer, 1995, 1994). First, clozapine and risperidone are much less likely to cause the movement-related side effects associated with the older antipsychotic drugs. That's because they block dopamine brain receptors far more *selectively* than the older antipsychotics. Rather than blocking dopamine receptors globally throughout the brain, they act on dopamine receptors primarily in the brain areas associated with psychotic symptoms.

Second, clozapine and risperidone are much more effective than the older antipsychotics in treating the negative symptoms of schizophrenia—apathy, social withdrawal, and flat emotions. And third, a significant proportion of patients who have not responded to any of the traditional antipsychotic drugs improve after taking clozapine or risperidone, sometimes dramatically (Kane, 1994; Marder & Meibach, 1994).

However, new drugs bring the potential of new side effects. In a small percentage of patients, clozapine can cause a life-threatening drop in white blood cells. Thus, patients taking clozapine must be monitored with weekly blood tests. In contrast, risperidone does not produce this dangerous side effect.

Clozapine and risperidone produce greater benefits and far fewer side effects for people suffering from the most severe forms of mental disorder. But it remains to be seen if these new medications can reduce the "revolving door" pattern of repeated hospitalizations. Nevertheless, clozapine and risperidone signal a new generation of antipsychotic medications. Among researchers in this area, there is an increased sense of optimism that even more effective antipsychotic medications will be developed (Meltzer, 1994; Kane, 1994).

Antianxiety Medications

The symptoms of anxiety are well known to almost everyone—feeling tense, jittery, and apprehensive. It's perfectly normal to feel mildly anxious when you're facing a difficult challenge or trying to cope with some crisis. But when anxiety is intense and persistent, it can be disabling, interfering with a person's ability to eat, sleep, and function. At such times, **antianxiety medications** may be prescribed (see Table 15.9).

The best-known antianxiety drugs are the *benzodiazepines,* which include the trade-name drugs *Valium* and *Xanax.* These antianxiety medications calm jittery feelings, relax the muscles, and promote sleep. They take effect rapidly, usually within an hour or so. In general, the benzodiazepines produce their effects by increasing the level of *GABA,* a neurotransmitter that inhibits the transmission of nerve impulses in the brain and slows brain activity (Carlson, 1994).

Taken for a week or two, and in therapeutic doses, the benzodiazepines can effectively reduce anxiety levels. However, the benzodiazepines have several potentially dangerous side effects. First, they can reduce coordination, alertness, and reaction time. Second, their effects can be intensified when they are combined with alcohol and many other drugs, including over-the-counter antihistamines. Such a combination can produce severe drug intoxication, even death.

Third, the benzodiazepines are physically addictive if taken in large quantities or over a long period of time (Maxmen & Ward, 1995). If physical dependence occurs, the person must withdraw from the drug gradually, as

TABLE 15.9 Antianxiety Drugs

	Generic Name	Trade Name
Benzodiazepines		
	Diazepam	Valium
	Chlordiazepoxide	Librium
	Lorazepam	Ativan
	Triazolam	Halcion
	Alprazolam	Xanax
Non-benzodiazepine		
	Buspirone	Buspar

SOURCE: Based on Julien, 1995, Table 4.1, p. 80.

abrupt withdrawal can produce life-threatening symptoms. Because of their addictive potential, the benzodiazepines are less widely prescribed today than they were twenty years ago.

A newer antianxiety drug with the trade name *Buspar* has fewer side effects. Buspar is not a benzodiazepine, and it does not affect the neurotransmitter GABA. In fact, exactly how Buspar works is uncertain. Regardless, Buspar relieves anxiety while maintaining normal alertness. It does not cause the drowsiness, sedation, and cognitive impairment that is associated with the benzodiazepines. And Buspar seems to have a very low risk of dependency and physical addiction (Julien, 1995).

However, Buspar has one major drawback: it must be taken for two to three *weeks* before anxiety is reduced. While this reduces Buspar's potential for abuse, it also reduces its effectiveness for treating acute anxiety. For immediate, short-term relief from anxiety, the benzodiazepines are still regarded as the most effective medications currently available (Lickey & Gordon, 1991). But for the long-term treatment of chronic anxiety, such as in panic disorder or generalized anxiety disorder, Buspar may be the most appropriate antianxiety medication.

Lithium

In Chapter 14, on psychological disorders, we described *bipolar disorder,* more commonly known as *manic depression.* The medication used to treat bipolar disorder is **lithium,** a naturally occurring substance. Lithium counteracts both manic and depressive symptoms in bipolar patients (Barondes, 1993). Its effectiveness in treating bipolar disorder has been well established since the 1960s (Shou, 1993).

The beneficial effects of lithium have been known about for better than a century. Soaking in the famous hot springs in Arkansas or Banff, Canada, has long been suggested to people to help diminish depressed symptoms. The water in those hot springs has a naturally high concentration of lithium. An early version of the soft drink 7-Up included small amounts of lithium (Maxmen & Ward, 1995). Marketed as "lithium soda," the ad campaign claimed that it was the drink that "took the ouch out of the grouch!"

As a treatment for bipolar disorder, lithium stops acute manic episodes over the course of a week or two. Once an acute manic episode is under control, the long-term use of lithium can help prevent relapses into either mania or depression. The majority of bipolar disorder patients respond well to lithium therapy (Shou, 1993; Keck & McElroy, 1993). However, lithium doesn't help everyone. Some people on lithium therapy experience relapses (Sachs & others, 1994).

Like all other medications, lithium has potential side effects. Lithium has a very narrow range between the therapeutic dosage level and the toxic dosage level (Julien, 1995). If the lithium level is too low, manic symptoms persist. If it is too high, symptoms of lithium poisoning may occur, such as vomiting, muscle weakness, and reduced muscle coordination. Consequently, the patient's lithium blood level must be carefully monitored (Shou, 1993).

How lithium works is a complete mystery. Lithium's action is especially puzzling because lithium prevents mood disturbances at both ends of the emotional spectrum—mania *and* depression. Some researchers have suggested that lithium somehow regulates neurotransmission, evening out extremes in both directions (Barondes, 1993).

Recently, bipolar disorder has been treated with an anticonvulsant medicine called *Depakote.* Originally used to prevent seizures in epileptics, Depakote seems to be especially helpful in treating those who rapidly cycle through bouts of bipolar disorder several times a year. It's also useful for

Lithium Water Lithium salt, a naturally occurring substance, was used in many over-the-counter medicines before it was discovered to be helpful in the treatment of mania. As this late-nineteenth-century ad shows, small amounts of lithium salt were also added to bottled water.

lithium
A naturally occurring substance that is used in the treatment of bipolar disorder.

treating bipolar patients who do not respond to lithium (Jefferson, 1995). Depakote is the first new biomedical treatment for bipolar disorder since lithium was approved in 1970.

Antidepressant Medications

The **antidepressant medications** counteract the classic symptoms of depression—hopelessness, guilt, dejection, suicidal thoughts, difficulty concentrating, and disruptions in sleep, energy, appetite, and sexuality. The first effective antidepressant was accidentally discovered when a new drug for tuberculosis was being tested in the 1950s. Unexpectedly, patients experienced relief from depressive symptoms (Carlson, 1994; Kramer, 1993). Since that discovery, three groups of antidepressant drugs have been developed (see Table 15.10).

The first generation of antidepressants consists of two classes of drugs called *tricyclics* and *MAO inhibitors*. Tricyclics and MAO inhibitors affect multiple neurotransmitter pathways in the brain (Golden & Gilmore, 1990). Evidence suggests that these drugs alleviate depression by increasing the availability of two key brain neurotransmitters, *norepinephrine* and *serotonin*.

Once again, though, exactly how tricyclics and MAO inhibitors work is unknown. For example, even though brain levels of norepinephrine and serotonin begin to rise within *hours* of taking a tricyclic or MAO inhibitor, it can take up to six *weeks* before depressive symptoms begin to lift (Richelson, 1993).

Tricyclics and MAO inhibitors have been widely used for many years. In about 75 percent of depressed patients, they effectively eliminate depressive symptoms (Fawcett, 1994; Hornig-Rohan & Amsterdam, 1994). But these drugs can also produce numerous side effects. Tricyclic antidepressants can cause weight gain, dizziness, dry mouth and eyes, and sedation, and, because tricyclics affect the cardiovascular system, an overdose can be fatal. As for the MAO inhibitors, they can interact with a chemical found in many foods, including cheese, smoked meats, and red wine. Eating these foods while taking an MAO inhibitor can result in dangerously high blood pressure, leading to stroke or even death.

The search for antidepressants with fewer side effects led to the development of the second generation of antidepressants. Second-generation antidepressants include *trazodone* and *bupropion*. Although chemically different from the tricyclics, the second generation of antidepressants were generally no more effective than the first generation, and they turned out to have many of the same side effects (Kramer, 1993).

In 1987 the picture changed dramatically with the introduction of a third group of antidepressants, the *selective serotonin reuptake inhibitors,* abbreviated *SSRIs.* Rather than acting on multiple neurotransmitter pathways, the SSRIs primarily affect the availability of a single neurotransmitter—serotonin. Compared to the earlier antidepressants, the new antidepressants act much more selectively in targeting specific serotonin pathways in the brain. The first SSRI to be released was *fluoxetine,* which is better known by its trade name, *Prozac.* Prozac was quickly followed by its chemical cousins, *Zoloft* and *Paxil.*

TABLE 15.10 Commonly Prescribed Antidepressant Drugs

	Generic Name	Trade Name
First-Generation Antidepressants		
Tricyclic antidepressants	Imipramine	Tofranil
	Desipramine	Norpramin
	Nortriptyline	Pamelor, Aventil
	Amitriptyline	Elavil
MAO inhibitors	Phenelzine	Nardil
	Tranylcypromine	Parnate
Second-Generation Antidepressants		
	Trazodone	Desyrel
	Bupropion	Wellbutrin
Selective Serotonin Reuptake Inhibitors (SSRIs)		
	Fluoxetine	Prozac
	Sertraline	Zoloft
	Paroxetine	Paxil
	Venlafaxine	Effexor

SOURCE: Based on Julien, 1995, Table 8.4, p. 198.

antidepressant medications
Prescription drugs that are used to reduce the symptoms associated with depression.

CRITICAL THINKING 15.4

Prozac: Better Living Through Chemistry?

Comic strips, comedy routines, talk shows—the buzz about the new "wonder drug" Prozac seems to be everywhere. Don't like your job? "Hey, take a Prozac," says a co-worker. The kids driving you crazy? Prozac will help. Can't seem to concentrate on your studies? Maybe Prozac is the answer. Need a confidence booster to help you get ahead in that new job? No problem—Prozac ought to do the trick.

Those are just some examples of the hype surrounding Prozac and its chemical cousins, Zoloft and Paxil. The popularity of these new antidepressants is unprecedented and undeniable. Since Prozac was introduced, over 6 million people have taken it in the United States alone—and over 20 million worldwide.

In some ways, that's good news. If anything, depression is underdiagnosed and undertreated. So if a new antidepressant comes along that effectively alleviates depressive symptoms in millions of people and has minimal side effects, that's no small accomplishment. Still, a word of caution is in order. Tinkering with the delicate balance of brain neurotransmitters is not to be taken lightly. Even though Prozac appears to be relatively safe, it hasn't been around long enough for anyone to know what its long-term effects might be (Sleek, 1994; Breggin & Breggin, 1994).

The very popularity of Prozac has drawn media attention to the antidepressant medications and has fueled misconceptions about their effects. It's simply inaccurate to label Prozac, or any other antidepressant, as a "don't-worry-be-happy pill." Prozac does *not* transform a seriously depressed person into someone who is perpetually lighthearted, confident, and on top of the world.

Instead, Prozac and other antidepressants help depressed people recover their *normal* level of psychological and physical energy, including the *normal* experience of the emotional ups and downs of everyday life. Rather than creating a supercharged, ultra-happy, carefree person, Prozac helps the seriously depressed person regain a normal level of functioning. Thus, prescribing antidepressants for depression is analogous to prescribing glasses for the nearsighted or insulin for the diabetic.

Prozac alone, of course, won't solve the problems that often contribute to major depression (Sleek, 1995). However, once a person's depressive symptoms have been alleviated, he or she may be able to cope with and resolve life problems in a healthier way.

Prozac's popularity makes many psychologists and other mental health professionals uncomfortable for another reason (Sleek, 1994). Some psychologists fear that Prozac is being overprescribed—and prescribed for the wrong reasons. According to media headlines, science now provides the opportunity to "change your personality with a pill." Prozac has raised "the prospect of nothing less than made-to-order, off-the-shelf personalities" (see Begley, 1994; Cowley, 1994). And in his best-selling book, *Listening to Prozac,* psychiatrist Peter Kramer (1993) describes how Prozac can be used to "transform your sense of self."

Prescribing Prozac to someone who is suffering from debilitating depression or some other serious psychological disorder is one matter. It's another matter altogether to prescribe Prozac or another drug to "transform" normal people and to make them more outgoing, productive, competitive, or self-confident. Or is it?

Thus far, the media claims that Prozac can enhance normal personality remain just that—anecdotal reports that have gotten a lot of play in the media. No controlled, scientific research has established that Prozac, or any other psychoactive drug, can "transform" normal personality or permanently alter basic personality traits (see Rosenhan & Seligman, 1995; Bower, 1994b).

But for the sake of argument, let's assume that Prozac could transform a normal personality into "better than well" by making a person more mellow, cheerful, self-assured, productive, optimistic, focused, thoughtful, and alive—all qualities that have been attributed to the effects of Prozac (see Begley, 1994; Kramer, 1993). Given this assumption, should Prozac be prescribed to people who are *not* clinically depressed but want to enhance their mental performance, emotional stability, and sense of psychological well-being?

Before you answer, consider the ready availability of nose jobs, facelifts, hair transplants, and tummy tucks. Our society generally approves of cosmetic surgery, especially if the surgery results in improved well-being and self-confidence. Well, if cosmetic surgery to enhance your appearance is okay, why not "cosmetic pharmacology" to chemically enhance your personality?

Here's another thought. Most cultures, including ours, have a long tradition of using psychoactive drugs to improve performance. And most of us already use all sorts of "artificial" substances to change our moods and enhance our performance (Schwartz, 1991). Caffeine, nicotine, chocolate, and Doritos immediately come to mind. Even behaviors such as exercising and listening to music can be used to alter how we feel or think.

According to neuroscientist Richard Restak (1994), the development of psychoactive drugs like Prozac signals the prospect of drugs "aimed not so much at 'patients' as at people who are already functioning on a high level." Restak makes a bold claim: "For the first time in human history, we will be in a position to design our own brain." Assuming that such claims have some foundation, here's the critical issue: *Should* we be in that position? *Should* Prozac or any other psychoactive drug be used to enhance normal personality and psychological functioning? Have a cup of coffee and think it over.

MOTHER GOOSE

© 1995 Grimmy, Inc. Dist. by Tribune Media Services, Inc. Reprinted with permission.

Prozac was specifically designed to alleviate depressive symptoms with fewer side effects than earlier antidepressants. It achieved that goal with considerable success. Although no more effective than tricyclics or MAO inhibitors, Prozac and the other SSRI antidepressants tend to produce fewer, and milder, side effects. But remember, no medication is risk-free. Among Prozac's potential side effects are headaches, nervousness, difficulty sleeping, loss of appetite, and sexual dysfunction (Julien, 1995; Sleek, 1994).

Early reports that Prozac increased suicidal impulses in depressed patients or led to violent behavior have not held up under scrutiny (Mann & Kapur, 1991; Kramer, 1993). If anything, Prozac seems to be more effective than other antidepressants in reducing suicidal urges. Keep in mind, however, that the effects of any medication vary from one individual to the next.

Because of its overall effectiveness and relatively mild side-effect profile, Prozac quickly became very popular. By the early 1990s, an estimated *one million prescriptions per month* were being written for Prozac.

No longer just a widely prescribed drug, Prozac has become a household word. But its very popularity raises some important issues: Is Prozac being overprescribed? Is it being prescribed for the wrong reasons? We tackle those issues in Critical Thinking Box 15.4, "Prozac: Better Living Through Chemistry?"

Electroconvulsive Therapy

As we have just seen, millions of prescriptions are written for antidepressant medications in the United States every year. In contrast, about 40,000 patients a year receive **electroconvulsive therapy** or **ECT** as a medical treatment for severe depression (Abrams, 1992). Electroconvulsive therapy involves using a brief burst of electric current to induce a seizure in the brain, much like an epileptic seizure. While ECT is most commonly used to treat depression, it is occasionally used to treat mania, catatonia, and other severe mental disorders (Rummans, 1993; Fink, 1993).

Zapping the brain with electric current as a treatment for mental illness may seem a bit farfetched, but there actually was a scientific rationale for the development of ECT (Abrams, 1994, 1992). Chemically induced seizures were first used as a treatment for mental disorders in the mid-1700s. Although some patients' psychotic symptoms improved, the effects of chemically produced seizures were both dangerous and unpredictable.

Given the controversy that still swirls around ECT, it's ironic that ECT was originally developed by two Italian doctors in the 1930s as a safer and more controlled alternative to chemically induced brain seizures. By the 1940s and 1950s, ECT was being widely used in the United States and Europe (Abrams, 1994).

Today, ECT is a relatively simple and quick medical procedure, usually performed in a hospital (Khan & others, 1993). The patient lies on a table. Electrodes are placed on one or both of the patient's temples, and she is given a short-term, light anesthesia and muscle-relaxing drugs. To ensure adequate airflow, a breathing tube is placed in the patient's mouth.

While the patient is unconscious, a split-second burst of electricity induces a seizure. The seizure lasts for about a minute. Outwardly, the seizure

electroconvulsive therapy (ECT)
A biomedical therapy used primarily in the treatment of depression that involves electrically inducing a brief brain seizure; also called *shock therapy* and *electric shock therapy*.

typically produces mild muscle tremors. After the anesthesia wears off and the patient wakes up, confusion and disorientation may be present for a few hours. Not uncommonly, the patient experiences a temporary or permanent memory loss for the events leading up to the treatment (Devanand & others, 1994). To treat major depression, a series of six to ten ECT treatments are usually spaced over a few weeks.

ECT is a very effective treatment for severe depression, with a slightly higher overall effectiveness rate than the antidepressant drugs: about 80 percent of depressed patients improve (Maxmen & Ward, 1995). ECT relieves the symptoms of depression very quickly, typically within days. Because of its rapid therapeutic effects, ECT can be a lifesaving procedure for extremely suicidal or severely depressed patients. Such patients may not survive for the several weeks it takes for antidepressant drugs to improve symptoms (Barondes, 1993). In fact, it is not difficult to find former ECT patients who will flatly say that ECT saved their lives.

ECT may also be considered when patients are not helped by antidepressant medications or psychotherapy, or when they cannot tolerate the side effects of medications. For some people, such as elderly individuals, ECT may be less dangerous than antidepressant drugs (Maxmen & Ward, 1995). In general, the complication rate from ECT is very low.

Nevertheless, inducing a brain seizure is not a matter to be taken lightly. ECT has potential dangers. Serious cognitive impairments can occur, such as extensive amnesia (memory loss) and disturbances in language and verbal abilities. However, fears that ECT might produce brain damage have not been confirmed by research (Devanand & others, 1994).

ECT's biggest drawback is that its antidepressive effects can be short-lived. Relapses within four months are relatively common. Researchers are currently investigating the effectiveness of following ECT with various antidepressants in an effort to prolong the benefits of ECT (Khan & others, 1993).

At this point, you may be wondering why ECT is not in wider use. The reason is that ECT is probably the single most controversial medical treatment for psychological disorders (Fink, 1991). Not everyone agrees that ECT is either safe or effective (Breggin, 1991, 1979). For example, ECT has been banned in some countries, like Japan, because of concerns about its safety. Several years ago, voters in Berkeley, California, banned ECT in a public referendum (a judge overturned the referendum results).

Electroconvulsive Therapy ECT is still used in the treatment of depression, especially in people who do not respond to antidepressant medication. In modern ECT, the person is given a short-acting anesthetic and muscle relaxants. A mild seizure, which lasts about a minute, is induced by a brief pulse of electricity.

Much of the controversy over ECT stems from its use in the 1940s and 1950s. At that time, electroconvulsive therapy was a frightening and over-used treatment. Patients were strapped to a table, wide awake, and the shock was administered while they were fully conscious. The electrically induced seizures produced such violent convulsions that patients sometimes suffered fractured spines and broken bones (Maxmen & Ward, 1995).

ECT was also used indiscriminately and inappropriately, often as a routine treatment for schizophrenia. Patients and others claimed that "shock therapy" was used to punish unruly patients and maintain order in institutions (Breggin, 1979).

In most countries today, ECT is conducted very differently (Fink, 1991). Because patients are anesthetized during the seizure, the procedure is painless and psychological trauma is minimized. Muscle-relaxing drugs have reduced the once violent, bone-breaking convulsions to mild muscle twitches. In one survey of patients who had received ECT, two-thirds said that going to the dentist was more upsetting than their ECT treatments (see Maxmen & Ward, 1995).

How does ECT work? Despite more than fifty years of research, psychiatrists still have *no* idea why electrically inducing a convulsion relieves the symptoms of depression (O'Connor, 1993; Kapur & Mann, 1993).

CONCEPT REVIEW 15.5

Biomedical Therapies

Match each statement below with one of the following terms: atypical antipsychotic medications, antipsychotic medications, antidepressant medications, ECT, antianxiety medications, lithium.

1. The most controversial biomedical therapy. _____

2. Used in the treatment of bipolar disorder. _____

3. Drugs that globally reduce dopamine levels in the brain. _____

4. Drugs that produce their effects by increasing brain levels of GABA. _____

5. Drugs that are effective in reducing positive and negative symptoms of schizophrenia. _____

6. A category of psychoactive drugs that includes SSRIs. _____

Summing Up: Therapies

As we've seen throughout this chapter, a wide range of therapies are available to help people who are troubled by psychological symptoms and disorders. Marcia, discussed in our prologue, found a combination of individual psychotherapy and a self-help group to be particularly effective. Some people are helped by one of the biomedical therapies. Often, psychotherapy includes elements from insight, behavioral, and cognitive forms of therapy. Increasingly, people are being helped by a combination of psychotherapy and biomedical therapy, usually one of the psychoactive medications.

As our discussion of the effectiveness of psychotherapy has shown, characteristics of both the therapist and the client are important to the success of psychotherapy. In our chapter Application, "What to Expect in Psychotherapy," we discuss some general ground rules of psychotherapy, dispel some common misunderstandings, and describe the attitudes that should be brought to the therapeutic relationship. The Application will help you understand the nature of the therapeutic relationship and provides information useful to anyone who may be considering entering psychotherapy.

APPLICATION

What to Expect in Psychotherapy

Effective psychotherapy results from a collaborative effort by both therapist and client. What should a client expect from the therapeutic relationship, and what are the client's responsibilities?

The cornerstone of psychotherapy is the relationship between the therapist and the person seeking help. But the therapy relationship is different from all other close relationships. On the one hand, the therapist–client relationship is characterized by intimacy and the disclosure of very private, personal experiences. On the other hand, there are distinct boundaries to the therapist–client relationship. To a therapy client, especially one who is undertaking psychotherapy for the first time, the therapy relationship may sometimes seem confusing and contradictory.

The goal of this Application is to help you develop realistic expectations about the therapist–client relationship and the psychotherapy process. These guidelines are very general, but they should help you better understand the special nature of the therapy relationship. In turn, your awareness of these "ground rules" may increase the likelihood that therapy will produce beneficial results for you. Or, if someone you know is in psychotherapy, this Application may help you understand and support the therapeutic process.

1. Therapy Is a Collaborative Effort

Don't expect your therapist to do all the work for you. If you are going to benefit from psychotherapy, you must actively participate in the therapeutic process. Often, therapy requires effort not only during the therapy sessions, but also *outside* them. Many therapists assign "homework" to be completed between sessions. You may be asked to keep a diary of your thoughts and behaviors, read assigned material, rehearse skills that you've learned in therapy, and so forth. Such exercises are important components of the overall therapy process.

2. Don't Expect Your Therapist to Make Decisions for You

One of the most common misunderstandings about psychotherapy is that your therapist is going to tell you how to run your life. Not so. Virtually all forms of therapy are designed to increase a person's sense of responsibility, confidence, and mastery in dealing with life's problems. Your therapist won't make your decisions for you, but he or she *will* help you explore your feelings about important decisions—including ambivalence or fear. Some people find this frustrating because they want the therapist to tell them what to do. But if your therapist made decisions for you, it would only foster dependency and undermine your ability to be responsible for your own life.

3. Your Therapist Is Not a Substitute Friend

Unlike friendship, which is characterized by a mutual give and take, psychotherapy is focused solely on *you*. Rather than thinking of your therapist as a friend, think of him or her as an expert consultant—someone you've hired to help you deal better with your problems. The fact that your therapist is not socially or personally involved with you allows your therapist to respond objectively and honestly. Part of what allows you to trust your therapist and "open up" emotionally is the knowledge that your therapist is ethically and legally bound to safeguard the confidentiality of what you say.

4. Therapeutic Intimacy Does Not Include Sexual Intimacy

It's very common for clients to have strong feelings of affection, love, and even sexual attraction toward their therapist (Pope & Tabachnick, 1993). After all, the most effective therapists tend to be warm, empathic people who are genuinely caring and supportive (Beutler & others, 1994). However, *it is never ethical or appropriate for a therapist to have any form of sexual contact with a client*. There are *no* exceptions to that statement. Sexual contact between a therapist and a client violates the ethical standards of all mental health professionals.

Lest we make the matter seem completely one-sided, surveys have revealed that many therapists occasionally feel sexually attracted to their clients (Pope & Tabachnick, 1993; Stake & Oliver, 1991). How often does actual sexual contact occur? About 7 percent of male and 2 percent of female therapists admit that they have had sexual contact with clients (Davis & others, 1995; Williams, 1992).

Sexual involvement between client and therapist can be enormously damaging (Pope, 1990). Not only does it destroy the therapist's professional objectivity in the therapist–client relationship, but it also destroys the trust the client has invested in the therapist. When a therapist becomes sexually involved with a client, regardless of who initiated the sexual contact, the client is being exploited.

Just how psychologically devastating can such sexual exploitation be? One survey found that of patients who had had sex with their therapists, 11 percent were hospitalized, 14 percent attempted suicide, and 1 percent killed themselves because of the experience (see M. Beck & others, 1992; Pope & Bouhoutsos, 1986).

Rather than exploiting a client's feelings of sexual attraction, an ethical therapist will help the client understand and work through such feelings. Therapy should ultimately help you develop closer, more loving relationships with other people—but *not* with your therapist.

5. Expect Therapy to Challenge How You Think and Act

As you confront issues that you've never discussed before or even admitted to yourself, you may find therapy to be very anxiety-provoking. Moments of psychological discomfort are a normal, even expected, part of the therapy process.

Think of therapy as a psychological magnifying glass. Therapy tends to magnify both your strengths and weaknesses. Such intense self-scrutiny is not always flattering. Examining how you habitually deal with failure and success, conflict and resolution, disappointment and joy can be disturbing. You may become aware of the psychological games you play, or of how you use ego defense mechanisms to distort reality. You may have to acknowledge your own immature, maladaptive, or destructive behavior patterns. Although it can be painful, becoming aware that changes are needed is a necessary step toward developing healthier forms of thinking and behavior.

6. Don't Confuse Insight with Change

Despite what you've seen in the movies, developing insight into the sources or nature of your psychological problems does not magically resolve them. Nor does insight automatically translate into healthier thoughts and behaviors. Instead, insight allows you to look at and understand your problems in a new light. The opportunity for change occurs when your therapist helps you use these insights to redefine past experiences, resolve psychological conflicts, and explore more adaptive forms of behavior. Even with the benefit of insight, it takes effort to change how you think, behave, and react to other people.

7. Don't Confuse Catharsis with Change

Catharsis refers to the emotional release that people experience from the simple act of talking about their problems. Although it usually produces short-term emotional relief, catharsis in itself does not resolve the problem. Even so, catharsis is an important element of psychotherapy. Discussing emotionally charged issues with a therapist can lessen your sense of psychological tension and urgency, and help you explore the problem more rationally and objectively.

8. Don't Expect Change to Happen Overnight

Change occurs in psychotherapy at different rates for different people. How quickly change occurs depends on many factors, such as the seriousness of your problems, the degree to which you are psychologically ready to make needed changes, and the therapist's skill in helping you implement those changes. As a general rule, most people make significant progress in a few months of weekly therapy sessions (McNeilly & Howard, 1991). You can help create the climate for change by choosing a therapist whom you feel comfortable working with and by genuinely investing yourself in the therapy process.

Summary
Therapies

Psychotherapy and Biomedical Therapy

▪ Psychological disorders can be treated with psychotherapy or biomedical therapy. Psychotherapy is based on the assumption that psychological factors play an important role in psychological disorders and symptoms. The biomedical therapies are based on the assumption that biological factors play an important role in psychological disorders and symptoms.

Psychoanalytic Therapy

▪ Psychoanalysis is a form of therapy developed by Sigmund Freud and based on his theory of personality. The goal of psychoanalysis is to unearth repressed conflicts and resolve them in therapy.

▪ Psychoanalytic techniques and processes include free association, dream interpretation, resistance, interpretation, and transference. Traditional psychoanalysis involves an intensive, long-term relationship between the patient and the psychoanalyst.

▪ Short-term dynamic therapies are based on psychoanalytic ideas, but are more problem-focused and shorter than traditional psychoanalysis. Therapists play a more direc-tive role than traditional psychoanalysts, but still they use psychoanalytic techniques to help the patient resolve unconscious conflicts.

Humanistic Therapy

▪ Client-centered therapy was developed by Carl Rogers. Important aspects of client-centered therapy include a client who directs the focus of therapy sessions and a therapist who is genuine, demonstrates unconditional positive regard, and communicates empathic understanding.

▪ According to Rogers, clients change and grow when their self-concept becomes healthier as a result of these therapeutic conditions.

Behavior Therapy

▪ Behavior therapy assumes that maladaptive behaviors are learned, and uses learning principles to directly change problem behaviors.

▪ Mary Cover Jones was the first behavior therapist, using the procedure of counterconditioning to extinguish phobic behavior in a child.

■ Classical conditioning principles are involved in the use of systematic desensitization to treat phobias, the bell and pad treatment to treat bedwetting, and aversive conditioning to treat harmful behaviors like smoking and alcohol addiction.

■ Operant conditioning techniques include using positive reinforcement for desired behaviors and extinction for undesired behaviors. The token economy represents the application of operant conditioning to modify the behavior of people in groups.

Cognitive Therapies

■ The cognitive therapies are based on the assumption that psychological problems are caused by maladaptive patterns of thinking. Treatment focuses on changing unhealthy thinking patterns to healthier ones.

■ Rational-emotive therapy (RET) was developed by Albert Ellis. RET focuses on changing the irrational thinking that is assumed to be the cause of emotional distress and psychological problems.

■ Rational-emotive therapy involves identifying core irrational beliefs; disputing and challenging irrational beliefs; and teaching clients to recognize and dispute their own irrational beliefs.

■ Cognitive therapy (CT) was developed by Aaron T. Beck. CT is based on the assumption that psychological problems are caused by unrealistic and distorted thinking.

■ Beck's cognitive therapy involves teaching the client to recognize negative automatic thoughts and biases and to empirically test the reality of the upsetting automatic thoughts.

Group and Family Therapy

■ Group therapy involves one or more therapists working with several people simultaneously. Group therapy has these advantages: it is cost-effective; therapists can observe clients interacting with other group members; clients benefit from the support, encouragement, and practical suggestions provided by other group members; and people can try out new behaviors in a safe, supportive environment.

■ Family therapy focuses on the family rather than the individual, and is based on the assumption that the family is an interdependent system. Marital or couple therapy focuses on improving communication, problem-solving skills, and intimacy between members of a couple.

Culture and Psychotherapy:
Bridging the Culture Gap

■ Psychotherapy methods reflect the culture in which they developed. Western psychotherapies reflect individualistic cultural values.

■ Cultural values inherent in many Western psychotherapies include a focus on the individual; an emphasis on the importance of insight; the assumption that clients are willing to seek professional help to solve their problems; and an emphasis on emotional openness and disclosure. These values may not be shared by clients with a different cultural background.

■ The American Psychological Association has established guidelines for psychotherapists who work with culturally diverse populations.

Evaluating the Effectiveness of Psychotherapy

■ Meta-analysis has been used to combine the findings of many different studies on the effectiveness of psychotherapy. In general, psychotherapy has been shown to be significantly more effective than no treatment.

■ Among the standard psychotherapies, no particular form of therapy is superior to the others. However, particular forms of therapy are more effective than others for treating some specific problems.

■ Factors identified as crucial to therapy's effectiveness include: the quality of the therapeutic relationship; therapist characteristics; therapists' sensitivity to cultural differences; client characteristics; and supportive, stable external circumstances.

■ Most psychotherapists today identify their orientation as eclectic, meaning that they integrate the techniques of more than one form of psychotherapy, tailoring their approach to the individual client's needs.

Biomedical Therapies

■ The most common biomedical therapy is psychoactive medication, which must be prescribed by a physician.

■ Antipsychotic medications include reserpine and chlorpromazine, which alter dopamine levels in the brain. While chlorpromazine and reserpine reduce positive symptoms of schizophrenia, they have little or no effect on negative symptoms. They also have potential side effects, including the development of tardive dyskinesia after long-term use.

■ The new atypical antipsychotics include clozapine and risperidone, which affect both serotonin and dopamine levels in the brain. The atypical antipsychotics have fewer side effects and are more effective in treating both the positive and negative symptoms of schizophrenia.

■ Antianxiety medications include the benzodiazepines. The benzodiazepines are effective in the treatment of anxiety, but are potentially addictive and have many side effects. Buspar is a newer antianxiety medication which is apparently nonaddictive.

■ Lithium is effective in the treatment of bipolar disorder, although its mechanism of action is unknown. A new drug called Depakote has recently been introduced as a drug treatment for bipolar disorder.

■ Antidepressant medications include the tricyclics, the MAO inhibitors, and the second-generation antidepressants. New antidepressants, including Prozac, selectively inhibit the reuptake of serotonin. While their effectiveness is similar to that of older antidepressants, the SSRIs have far fewer side effects.

Electroconvulsive therapy (ECT), which involves delivering a brief electric shock to the brain, is used in treating severe depression. There is a great deal of controversy over ECT. Today, ECT procedures are safer than when it was first used. The therapeutic effects of ECT tend to be short-lived, lasting no more than a few months. Partly because it is controversial, ECT is used far less frequently than antidepressant medication in the treatment of depression.

Key Terms

psychotherapy (p. 657)

biomedical therapies (p. 658)

psychoanalysis (p. 658)

free association (p. 659)

resistance (p. 659)

dream interpretation (p. 659)

interpretation (p. 659)

transference (p. 660)

client-centered therapy (p. 662)

behavior therapy (p. 665)

counterconditioning (p. 665)

systematic desensitization (p. 666)

bell and pad treatment (p. 669)

aversive conditioning (p. 669)

token economy (p. 671)

cognitive therapies (p. 672)

rational-emotive therapy (RET) (p. 673)

cognitive therapy (CT) (p. 675)

group therapy (p. 677)

family therapy (p. 679)

eclecticism (p. 687)

antipsychotic medications (p. 689)

antianxiety medications (p. 691)

lithium (p. 692)

antidepressant medications (p. 693)

electroconvulsive therapy (ECT) (p. 695)

Key People

Aaron T. Beck (b. 1921) American psychiatrist who founded cognitive therapy (CT), a psychotherapy based on the assumption that depression and other psychological problems are caused by biased perceptions, distorted thinking, and inaccurate beliefs.

Albert Ellis (b. 1913) American psychologist who founded the cognitive psychotherapy called rational-emotive therapy (RET), which emphasizes recognizing and changing irrational beliefs.

Sigmund Freud (1856–1939) Austrian physician and founder of psychoanalysis who theorized that psychological symptoms are the result of unconscious and unresolved conflicts stemming from early childhood. (Also see Chapter 11.)

Mary Cover Jones (1896–1987) American psychologist who conducted the first clinical demonstrations of behavior therapy.

Carl Rogers (1902–1987) American psychologist who helped found humanistic psychology and developed client-centered therapy. (Also see Chapter 11.)

CONCEPT REVIEW 15.1   Page 661

1. resistance
2. dream interpretation
3. transference
4. interpretation
5. free association

CONCEPT REVIEW 15.2   Page 672

1. a token economy
2. the bell and pad treatment
3. aversive conditioning
4. systematic desensitization
5. virtual reality

CONCEPT REVIEW 15.3   Page 683

1. cognitive therapy
2. behavior therapy
3. humanistic therapy
4. psychoanalytic therapy

CONCEPT REVIEW 15.4   Page 687

1. False. Meta-analysis is a statistical technique used to combine and analyze the results of multiple studies on the same topic or issue.
2. False. Psychotherapy is significantly more effective than no treatment.
3. False. In general, there is little or no difference in the effectiveness of the different forms of psychotherapy.
4. False. For psychotherapy to be effective, psychotherapists must be sensitive to cultural differences.
5. True.
6. False. The client's willingness to change and her attitude toward therapy are essential to psychotherapy's success.

CONCEPT REVIEW 15.5   Page 697

1. ECT
2. lithium
3. antipsychotic medications
4. antianxiety medications
5. atypical antipsychotic medications
6. antidepressant medications

Appendix A

Marie D. Thomas
California State University, San Marcos

Statistics: Understanding Data

Prologue: The Tables Are Turned: A Psychologist Becomes a Research Subject

From December 1994 to December 1995 I participated in a research project designed to compare the effects of "traditional" and "alternative" diet, exercise, and stress-reduction programs.* Volunteers assigned randomly to the *traditional* program were taught to eat a high-fiber, low-fat diet, do regular aerobic exercise, and practice a progressive muscle relaxation technique (described in Chapter 13). Participants in the *alternative* program received instruction in yoga and in a meditation technique, and a diet based on body type and tastes. A *no-treatment* control group was monitored throughout the year for weight and general health but received no diet, exercise, or stress-reduction intervention. (I was in the control group.)

Fifteen thousand invitations to participate in this study were sent in late 1994 to members of a large medical group. Out of that initial pool, 124 volunteers were recruited, and about 40 were randomly selected for each group (*traditional, alternative,* and *no treatment,* or control). The participants included women and men between the ages of 20 and 56. A total of 88 subjects lasted the full year. The researchers were pleased that so many of us stayed with the project; it isn't easy to get people to commit to a year-long study!

*Riegel, B., Simon, D., Weaver, J., Carlson, B., Clapton, P., & Gocka, I. (1996). Ayurvedic Medicine Demonstration Project, 1 R21 RR09726-01. Report submitted to National Institutes of Health, Institute for Alternative Medicine.

Data collection began even before participants found out the group to which they had been randomly assigned. We were mailed a thick packet of questionnaires covering a wide range of topics. The questions asked about our current health status, use of prescription and over-the-counter medications, use of vitamins, and visits to both physicians and alternative health-care practitioners. Another questionnaire focused on self-perceptions of health and well-being. Here we rated our mood, energy level, physical symptoms, and health in general. A lifestyle survey requested information about diet (how often did we eat red meat? how many servings of fruits and vegetables did we consume a day?), exercise (how many times per week did we do aerobic exercise?), and behavior (such as cigarette smoking and consumption of alcoholic beverages). The lifestyle survey also assessed psychological variables such as levels of stress and happiness, and how well we felt we were coping.

At our first meeting with the researchers, we handed in the questionnaires and were told which of the three groups we had been assigned to. We returned early the next morning to have our blood pressure and weight measured and to have blood drawn for tests of our levels of cholesterol, triglycerides, and glucose. The two intervention groups also received a weekend of training in their respective programs. In addition to daily practice of the techniques they had been taught, people in the *traditional* and *alternative* groups were expected to maintain a "compliance diary"—a daily record of their exercise, diet, and relaxation/meditation activities. The purpose of this diary was to determine whether health outcomes were better for people who practiced the techniques regularly. At first I was disappointed when I was randomly chosen for the control group, because I was especially interested in learning the "alternative" techniques. However, I was relieved later, when I found out how much detailed record keeping the intervention groups had to do!

The researchers accumulated even more data over the year-long period. Every three months, our blood pressure and weight were measured. At 6 months and 12 months, the researchers performed blood tests and asked us to fill out questionnaires identical to those at the beginning of the project.

The study included many variables. The most important independent variable (the variable that the researcher *manipulates*) was group assignment: *traditional* program, *alternative* program, and *no-treatment* control. The dependent variables (variables that are not directly manipulated by the researcher but that may change in response to manipulations of the independent variable) included weight, blood pressure, cholesterol level, self-perceptions regarding health, and mood. Since the dependent variables were measured several times, researchers could study changes in them over the course of the year.

This study can help to answer important questions about the kinds of programs that tend to promote health. But the purpose of describing it here is not just to tell you whether the two intervention programs were effective and whether one worked better than the other. Instead, I use this study as a tool for explaining how researchers use statistics to help them summarize findings and draw legitimate conclusions from them. The job of assessing the legitimacy of conclusions drawn from research findings is the domain of *inferential statistics*, which I'll discuss at the end of this appendix. I begin by exploring the task of summarizing findings in ways that are brief yet meaningful and easy to understand. For this, researchers use *descriptive statistics*.

Descriptive Statistics

The study on programs to promote health generated a large amount of data. How did the researchers make sense of such a mass of information? How did they summarize it in meaningful ways? The answer lies in descriptive statistics. **Descriptive statistics** do just what their name suggests—they

descriptive statistics
Statistics used to organize and summarize data in a meaningful way.

frequency distribution
A summary of how often various scores occur in a sample of scores. Score values are arranged in order of magnitude and the number of times each score occurs is recorded.

histogram
A way of graphically representing a frequency distribution; a type of bar chart using vertical bars that touch.

describe data. There are many ways to describe information. In this appendix we examine four of the most commonly used ways: frequency distributions, measures of central tendency, measures of variability, and measures of relationships. Since I don't have access to all the data that the health-promotion researchers gathered, I'll use hypothetical numbers to illustrate these statistical concepts.

Frequency Distributions

Suppose that at the start of the health-promotion study 30 people in the *traditional* group reported getting the following number of hours of aerobic exercise each week:

2, 5, 0, 1, 2, 2, 7, 0, 6, 2, 3, 1, 4, 5, 2, 1, 1, 3, 2, 1, 0, 4, 2, 3, 0, 1, 2, 3, 4, 1

Even with only 30 cases, it is difficult to make much sense of these data. Researchers need a way to organize such *raw scores* so that the information makes sense at a glance. One way to organize the data is to determine how many participants reported exercising 0 hours per week, how many reported exercising 1 hour, and so on, until all the reported amounts are accounted for. If put into a table, the data would look like Table A.1.

This table is one way of presenting a **frequency distribution**—a summary of how often various scores occur. Categories are set up (in this case, the number of hours of aerobic exercise per week), and occurrences of each category are tallied to give the frequency of each one.

What information can be gathered from this frequency distribution table? We know immediately that most of the participants did aerobic exercise less than 3 hours per week. The number of hours per week peaked at 2 hours, and declined steadily thereafter. According to the table, the most diligent exerciser worked out about an hour per day.

Some frequency distribution tables include an extra column that shows the percentage of cases in each category. For example, what percentage of participants reported 2 hours of aerobic exercise per week? The percentage is calculated by dividing the category frequency (8) by the total number of people (30), which yields about 27 percent.

While a table is good for summarizing data, it is often useful to present a frequency distribution visually through graphs. One type of graph is the **histogram** (see Figure A.1). A histogram is like a bar chart with two special features: the bars are always vertical, and they always touch. Categories (in our example, the number of hours of aerobic exercise per week) are placed on the X (horizontal) axis, while the Y (vertical) axis shows the frequency of each category. The resulting graph looks something like a city skyline, with buildings of different heights.

TABLE A.1 A Frequency Distribution Table

Hours of Aerobic Exercise per Week	Frequency
0	4
1	7
2	8
3	4
4	3
5	2
6	1
7	1
	30

A table like this is one way of presenting a frequency distribution. It shows at a glance that most of the people in our hypothetical group of 30 were not zealous exercisers before they began their traditional health-promotion program. Nearly two-thirds of them (19 people) engaged in vigorous exercise for 2 hours or less each week.

FIGURE A.1 A Histogram
This histogram is another way of presenting the data given in Table A.1. Like the table, the histogram shows that most people do, at best, only a moderate amount of aerobic exercise (2 hours or less each week). This is immediately clear from the fact that the highest bars on the chart are on the left, where the hours of exercise are lowest.

Another way of graphing the same data is with a **frequency polygon,** shown in Figure A.2. A mark is made above each category at the point representing its frequency. These marks are then connected by straight lines. In our example, the polygon begins before the "0" category and ends at a category of "8," even though both these categories have no cases in them. This is traditionally done so that the polygon is a closed figure.

Frequency polygons are good for showing the shape of a distribution. The polygon in Figure A.2 looks like a mountain, rising sharply over the first two categories, peaking at 2, and slowly diminishing from there. A distribution like this is asymmetrical, or a **skewed distribution.** This means that, if we drew a line through the middle of the X axis (halfway between 3 and 4 hours), more scores would be piled up on one side of the distribution than on the other. The polygon in Figure A.2 represents a *positively skewed* distribution, indicating that most people had low scores. A *negatively skewed* distribution would have mostly high scores, with fewer scores at the low end of the distribution. For example, if the traditional diet and exercise intervention worked, the 30 participants should, as a group, be exercising more at the end of the study than they had been at the begin-

FIGURE A.2 A Frequency Polygon (Positive Skew)
Like Table A.1 and Figure A.1, this frequency polygon shows at a glance that the number of hours of aerobic exercise weekly is not great for most people. The high points come at 1 and 2 hours, which doesn't amount to much more than 10 or 15 minutes of exercise daily. An asymmetrical distribution like this one, which includes mostly low scores, is said to be positively skewed.

ning. Perhaps the distribution of hours of aerobic exercise per week at the end of the study would look something like Figure A.3—a distribution with a slight negative skew.

In contrast to skewed distributions, a **symmetrical distribution** is one in which scores fall equally on both halves of the graph. A special case of a symmetrical distribution, the normal curve, is discussed in a later section.

A useful feature of frequency polygons is that more than one distribution can be graphed on the same set of axes. For example, the end-of-study hours of aerobic exercise per week for the *traditional* and *alternative* groups could be compared on a single graph. This would allow us to see at a glance whether one group was exercising more than the other after a year of their respective programs.

By the way, Figure A.3 is actually a figment of my imagination. According to the diaries kept by the traditional and alternative program participants, compliance with the exercise portion of the program decreased over time. This does not necessarily mean that these subjects were exercising *less* at the end of the study than at the beginning, but they certainly did not keep up the program as it was taught to them. Compliance with the prescribed diets was steadier than compliance with exercise; compliance by the alternative group dropped between 3 months and 6 months, and then rose steadily over time. There was, however, one major difference between the two intervention groups in terms of compliance. Participants in the alternative group were more likely to be meditating at the end of the study than their traditional-group counterparts were to be practicing progressive relaxation.

FIGURE A.3 A Frequency Polygon (Negative Skew)
When more scores fall at the high end of a distribution than at the low end, the distribution is said to be negatively skewed. We would expect a negatively skewed distribution if a health-promotion program worked and encouraged more hours of aerobic exercise. The more effective the program, the greater the skew.

Hours of aerobic exercise per week at end of study

Measures of Central Tendency

Frequency distributions can be used to organize a set of data and tell us how scores are generally distributed. But researchers often want to put this information into a more compact form. They want to be able to summarize a distribution with a single score that is "typical." To do this they use a **measure of central tendency.**

The Mode

The **mode** is the easiest measure of central tendency to calculate; it is simply the score or category that occurs most frequently in a set of raw scores or in a frequency distribution. The mode in the frequency distribution shown in Table A.1 is 2; more participants reported exercising 2 hours per week than any other category. In this example, the mode is an accurate representation of central tendency, but this is not always the case. In the distribution 1, 1, 1, 10, 20, 30, the mode is 1, yet half the scores are 10 and above. This type of distortion is the reason measures of central tendency other than the mode are needed.

The Median

Another way of describing central tendency is to determine the **median,** or the score that falls in the middle of a distribution. If the exercise scores are laid out from lowest to highest,

0, 0, 0, 0, 1, 1, 1, 1, 1, 1, 1, 2, 2, 2, 2, 2, 2, 2, 2, 3, 3, 3, 3, 4, 4, 4, 5, 5, 6, 7

↑

what would the middle score be? Since there are 30 scores, look for the point that divides the distribution in half, with 15 scores on each side of this point. The median can be found between the 15th and 16th scores (indicated by the arrow). In this distribution, the answer is easy: a score of 2 is the median as well as the mode.

The Mean

A problem with the mode and the median is that both measures reflect only one score in the distribution. For the mode, the score of importance is the most frequent one; for the median it is the middle score. A better measure of central tendency is usually one that reflects *all* scores. This is why the most commonly used measure of central tendency is the **mean,** or arithmetic average. You have calculated the mean many times. It is computed by summing a set of scores, and then dividing by the number of scores that went into the sum. In our example, adding together the exercise distribution scores gives a total of 70; the number of scores is 30, so 70 divided by 30 gives a mean of 2.33.

Formulas are used to express how a statistic is calculated. The formula for the mean is:

$$\bar{X} = \frac{\sum X}{N}$$

In this formula, each letter and symbol has a specific meaning:

$\bar{X}$ is the symbol for the mean.

Σ is sigma, the Greek letter for capital S, and it stands for "sum." (Taking a course in statistics is one way to learn the Greek alphabet!)

---

frequency polygon
A way of graphically representing a frequency distribution; frequency is marked above each score category on the graph's horizontal axis, and the marks are connected by straight lines.

skewed distribution
An asymmetrical distribution; more scores pile up on one side of the distribution than on the other. In a *positively* skewed distribution, most people have low scores; in a *negatively* skewed distribution, most people have high scores.

symmetrical distribution
A distribution in which scores fall equally on both sides of the graph. The normal curve is an example of a symmetrical distribution.

measure of central tendency
A single number that presents some information about the "center" of a frequency distribution.

mode
The most frequently occurring score in a distribution.

median
The score that divides a frequency distribution exactly in half, so that the same number of scores lies on each side of it.

mean
The sum of a set of scores in a distribution divided by the number of scores. The mean is usually the most representative measure of central tendency.

X represents the scores in the distribution, so the numerator of the equation says: "Sum up all the scores."

N is the total number of scores in the distribution.

Therefore, the formula says: "The mean equals the sum of all the scores divided by the total number of scores."

Although the mean is usually the most representative measure of central tendency because each score in a distribution enters into its computation, it is particularly susceptible to the effect of extreme scores. Any unusually high or low score will pull the mean in its direction. Suppose, for example, that in our frequency distribution for aerobic exercise one exercise zealot worked out 70 hours per week. The mean number of aerobic exercise hours would jump from 2.33 to 4.43. This new mean is deceptively high, given that most of the scores in the distribution are 2 and below. Because of just that one extreme score, the mean has become less representative of the distribution. Frequency tables and graphs are important tools for helping us identify extreme scores *before* we start computing statistics.

Measures of Variability

In addition to identifying the central tendency in a distribution, researchers may want to know how much the scores in that distribution differ from one another. Are they grouped closely together or widely spread out? To answer this question, we need some **measure of variability.** Figure A.4 shows two distributions with the same mean but different variability.

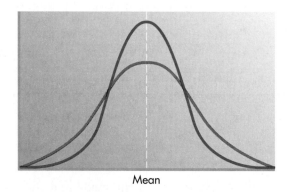

Mean

FIGURE A.4 Distributions with Different Variability
Two distributions with the same mean can have very different variability, or spread. This is shown in these two curves. Notice how one is more spread out than the other; its scores are distributed more widely.

A simple way to measure variability is with the **range,** which is computed by subtracting the lowest score in the distribution from the highest score. Let's say that there are 15 women in the traditional diet and exercise group and that their weights at the beginning of the study varied from a low of 95 pounds to a high of 155 pounds. The range of weights in this group would be 155 − 95 = 60 pounds.

As a measure of variability, the range provides a limited amount of information, because it depends on only the two most extreme scores in a distribution (the highest and lowest scores). A more useful measure of variability would give some idea of the average amount of variation in a distribution. But variation from what? The most common way to measure variability is to determine how far scores in a distribution vary from the distribution's mean. We saw earlier that the mean is usually the best way to represent the "center" of the distribution, so the mean seems like an appropriate reference point.

What if we subtracted the mean from each score in a distribution to get a general idea of how far each score is from the center? When the mean is subtracted from a score, the result is a *deviation* from the mean. Scores that are above the mean would have positive deviations, and scores that are below the mean would have negative deviations. To get an average deviation, we would need to sum the deviations and divide by the number of deviations that went into the sum. There is a problem with this procedure, however. If

measure of variability
A single number that presents information about the spread of scores in a distribution.

range
A measure of variability; the highest score in a distribution minus the lowest score.

TABLE A.2 Calculating the Standard Deviation

Weight X	Mean $\bar{X}$	Weight − Mean $X - \bar{X}$	(Weight − Mean) Squared $(X - \bar{X})^2$
155	124	31	961
149	124	25	625
142	124	18	324
138	124	14	196
134	124	10	100
131	124	7	49
127	124	3	9
125	124	1	1
120	124	−4	16
115	124	−9	81
112	124	−12	144
110	124	−14	196
105	124	−19	361
102	124	−22	484
95	124	−29	841

Sum (Σ) = 1,860 $\Sigma = 0$ $\Sigma = 4,388$

Mean ($\bar{X}$) = 124

$$SD = \sqrt{\frac{\Sigma(X - \bar{X})^2}{N}} = \sqrt{\frac{4,388}{15}} = 17.10$$

To calculate the standard deviation, you simply add all the scores in a distribution (the left-hand column in this example) and divide by the total number of scores to get the mean. Then you subtract the mean from each score to get a list of deviations from the mean (third column). Next you square each deviation (fourth column), add the squared deviations together, divide by the total number of cases, and take the square root.

deviations from the mean are added together, the sum will be 0, because the negative and positive deviations will cancel each other out. In fact, the real definition of the mean is "the only point in a distribution where all the scores' deviations from it add up to 0."

We need to somehow "get rid of" the negative deviations. In mathematics, such a problem is solved by squaring. If a negative number is squared, it becomes positive. So instead of simply adding up the deviations and dividing by the number of scores, we first square each of the deviations, then add together the *squared* deviations and divide by N. Finally, we need to compensate for the squaring operation. To do this, we take the square root of the number just calculated. This leaves us with the **standard deviation.** The larger the standard deviation, the more spread out are the scores in a distribution.

Let's look at an example to make this clearer. Table A.2 lists the hypothetical weights of the 15 women in the traditional group at the beginning of the study. The mean, which is the sum of the weights divided by 15, is calculated to be 124 pounds, as shown at the bottom of the left-hand column. The first step in computing the standard deviation is to subtract the mean from each score, which gives that score's deviation from the mean. These deviations are listed in the third column of the table. The next step is to square each of the deviations (done in the fourth column), then add the squared deviations ($\Sigma = 4,388$) and divide that total by the number of women ($N - 15$). Finally, we take the square root to obtain the standard deviation ($SD = 17.10$). The formula for the standard deviation (SD) incorporates these instructions:

$$SD = \sqrt{\frac{\Sigma(X - \bar{X})^2}{N}}$$

Notice that when scores have large deviations from the mean, the *standard deviation* is also large.

z Scores and the Normal Curve

standard deviation
A measure of variability; expressed as the square root of the sum of the squared deviations around the mean divided by the number of scores in the distribution.

z score
A number, expressed in standard deviation units, that shows a score's deviation from the mean.

The mean and the standard deviation provide useful descriptive information about an entire set of scores. But researchers can also describe the relative position of any individual score in a distribution. This is done by locating how far away from the mean the score is in terms of standard deviation units. A statistic called a **z score** gives us this information:

$$z = \frac{X - \bar{X}}{SD}$$

This equation says that to compute a z score, we subtract the mean from the score we are interested in (that is, we calculate its deviation from the mean) and divide this quantity by the standard deviation. A positive z score indicates that the score is above the mean, while a negative z score shows that the score is below the mean. The larger the z score, the farther away from the mean the score is.

Let's take an example from the distribution found in Table A.2. What is the z score of a weight of 149 pounds? To find out, you simply subtract the mean from 149 and divide by the standard deviation.

$$z = \frac{149 - 124}{17.10} = 1.46$$

A z score of +1.46 tells us that a person weighing 149 pounds falls about 1½ standard deviations above the mean. In contrast, a person weighing 115 pounds has a weight below the mean and would have a negative z score. If you calculate this z score you will find it is −.53. This means that a weight of 115 is a little more than one-half a standard deviation below the mean.

Some variables, such as height, weight, or IQ, if graphed for large numbers of people, fall into a characteristic pattern. Figure A.5 shows this pattern, which is called the **standard normal curve** or the **standard normal distribution.** The normal curve is symmetrical (that is, if a line is drawn down its center, one side of the curve is a mirror image of the other side), and the mean, median, and mode fall exactly in the middle. The X axis of Figure A.5 is marked off in standard deviation units, which, conveniently, are also z scores. Notice that most of the cases fall between −1 and +1 SDs, with the number of cases sharply tapering off at either end. This pattern is the reason the normal curve is often described as "bell-shaped."

The great thing about the normal curve is that we know exactly what percentage of the distribution falls between any two points on the curve. Figure A.5 shows the percentages of cases between major standard deviation units. For example, 34.13 percent of the distribution falls between 0 and +1. That means that 84.13 percent of the distribution falls *below* one standard deviation (the 34.13 percent that is between 0 and +1, plus the 50 percent that falls below 0). A person who obtains a z score of +1 on some normally distributed variable has scored better than 84 percent of the other people in the distribution. If a variable is normally distributed (that is, if it has the standard bell-shaped pattern), a person's z score can tell us exactly where that person stands relative to everyone else in the distribution.

Correlation

So far, the statistical techniques we've looked at focus on one variable at a time, such as hours of aerobic exercise weekly or weight measured in pounds. Life would be simple if it were influenced by only one variable at a time! The world, however, is a far more complicated place. Accordingly, statistical techniques have been devised that allow us to look at the relationship—the

FIGURE A.5 The Standard Normal Curve
The standard normal curve has several characteristics. Most apparent is its symmetrical bell shape. On such a curve, the mean, the median, and the mode all fall at the same point. But not every curve that is shaped roughly like a bell is a standard normal curve. With a normal curve, specific percentages of the distribution fall within each standard deviation unit from the mean. These percentages are shown on the graph.

standard normal curve (standard normal distribution)
A symmetrical distribution forming a bell-shaped curve in which the mean, median, and mode are all equal and fall in the exact middle.

correlation—between two variables. This relationship is assessed by a statistic called the **correlation coefficient.**

In order to compute a correlation coefficient, we need two sets of measurements from the same individuals, or from pairs of people who are similar in some way. To take a simple example, let's determine the correlation between height (we'll call this the X variable) and weight (the Y variable). We start by obtaining height and weight measurements for each individual in a group. The idea is to combine all these measurements into one number that expresses something about the relationship between the two variables, height and weight. However, we are immediately confronted with a problem: the two variables are measured in different ways. Height is measured in inches and weight is measured in pounds. We need some way to place both variables on a single scale.

Think back to our discussion of the normal curve and z scores. What do z scores do? They take data of any form and put them into a standard scale. Remember, too, that a high score in a distribution always has a positive z score, and a low score in a distribution always has a negative z score. To compute a correlation coefficient, the data from both variables of interest can be converted to z scores. Therefore, each individual will have two z scores: one for height (the X variable) and one for weight (the Y variable).

In order to compute the correlation coefficient, each person's two z scores are multiplied together. All these "cross-products" are added up, and this sum is divided by the number of individuals. In other words, a correlation coefficient is the average (or mean) of the z-score cross-products of the two variables being studied:

$$\text{correlation coefficient} = \frac{\sum z_x z_y}{N}$$

A correlation coefficient can range anywhere from -1 to $+1$. The exact number provides two pieces of information: it tells us about the *magnitude* of the relationship being measured, and it tells us about its *direction*. The magnitude, or degree of relationship, is indicated by the size of the number. A number close to 1 (whether positive or negative) indicates a strong relationship, while a number close to zero indicates a weak relationship. The sign ($+$ or $-$) of the correlation coefficient tells us about the relationship's direction. A *positive* correlation means that as one variable increases in size, the second variable also increases. For example, height and weight are positively correlated: as height increases, weight tends to increase also. In terms of z scores, a positive correlation means that high z scores on one variable tend to be multiplied by high z scores on the other variable and that low z scores on one variable tend to be multiplied by low z scores on the other. Remember that just as two positive numbers multiplied together result in a positive number, so two negative numbers multiplied together also result in a positive number. When the cross-products are added together, the sum in both cases is positive. A *negative* correlation, in contrast, means that two variables are *inversely* related. As one variable increases in size, the other variable decreases. For example, professors like to believe that the more hours students study, the fewer errors they will make on exams. In z-score language, high z scores (which are positive) on one variable (more hours of study) tend to be multiplied by low z scores (which are negative) on the other variable (fewer errors on exams), and vice versa, making negative cross-products. When the cross-products are summed and divided by the number of cases, the result is a negative correlation coefficient.

An easy way to show different correlations is with graphs. Plotting two variables together creates a **scatter diagram** or **scatter plot,** like the ones in Figures A.6, A.7, and A.8. These figures show the relationship between

correlation
The relationship between two variables.

correlation coefficient
A measure of the magnitude and direction of the relationship (the correlation) between two variables. The closer the correlation coefficient is to +1 or −1, the stronger the relationship is. A *positive* correlation coefficient indicates that as one variable increases, the other tends to increase. A *negative* correlation coefficient indicates that as one variable increases, the other tends to decrease.

scatter diagram (scatter plot)
A graph that represents the relationship between two variables.

complying with some component of the alternative health-promotion program and some other variable related to health. Although the figures describe relationships actually found in the study, I have made up the specific correlations to illustrate key points.

Figure A.6 shows a moderately strong positive relationship between compliance with the yoga part of the alternative program and a person's energy

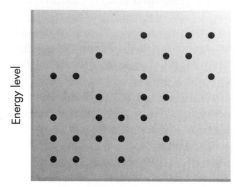

level. You can see this just by looking at the pattern of the data points. They generally form a line running from lower left to upper right. When calculated, this particular correlation coefficient is +.59, which indicates a correlation roughly in the middle between 0 and +1. In other words, people who did more yoga tended to have higher energy levels. The "tended to" part is important. Some people who did not comply well with the yoga routine still had high energy levels, while the reverse was also true. A +1 correlation, or a *perfect*

FIGURE A.6 Scatter Plot of a Positive Correlation

A correlation (or the lack of one) can be clearly shown on a scatter diagram. This one shows a moderately strong positive correlation between subjects' compliance with the yoga component of the alternative health-promotion program and their energy level. The positive direction of the correlation is indicated by the upward-sloping pattern of the dots: from bottom left to top right. This means that if one variable is high, the other tends to be high too, and vice versa. That the strength of the relationship is only moderate is indicated by the fact that the data points (each indicating an individual subject's score) are not all positioned along a straight diagonal line.

positive correlation, would indicate that frequent yoga sessions were *always* accompanied by high levels of energy, and vice versa. What would a scatter diagram of a perfect +1 correlation look like? It would be a straight diagonal line starting in the lower left-hand corner of the graph and progressing to the upper right-hand corner.

Several other positive correlations were found in this study. Compliance with the alternative diet was positively associated with increases in energy and positive health perceptions. In addition, following the high-fiber, low-fat traditional diet was associated with a higher level of coping and high vitamin intake.

The study also found some negative correlations. Figure A.7 illustrates a *negative* correlation between compliance with the meditation part of the

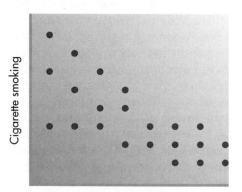

alternative program and cigarette smoking. This correlation coefficient is −.77. Note that the data points fall in the opposite direction from those in Figure A.6, indicating that as the frequency of meditation increased, cigarette smoking decreased. The pattern of points in Figure A.7 is closer to a straight line than the pattern of points in Figure A.6. A correlation of −.77 shows a relationship of greater magnitude than does a correlation of +.59. But though −.77 is a relatively high correlation, it is not a perfect relationship. A *perfect* negative relationship

FIGURE A.7 Scatter Plot of a Negative Correlation

In general, people who engage in meditation more often tend to smoke less. This negative correlation is indicated by the downward-sloping pattern of dots, from upper left to lower right. Because these dots are clustered somewhat closer together than those in Figure A.6, we can tell at a glance that the relationship here is somewhat stronger.

would be illustrated by a straight diagonal line starting in the upper left-hand corner of the graph and ending at the lower right-hand corner.

Finally, Figure A.8 shows two variables that are not related to each other. The hypothetical correlation coefficient between compliance with the aerobic exercise part of the traditional program and a person's level of coping is +.03, barely above zero. In the scatter diagram, data points fall randomly, with no general direction to them. From a *z*-score point of view, when two variables

FIGURE A.8 Scatter Plot of No Correlation
You may be surprised to learn that in this study, compliance with the aerobic exercise portion of the traditional program was not related to level of coping. This scatter diagram shows that lack of relationship. The points fall randomly, revealing no general direction or trend and thus indicating the absence of a correlation.

Level of coping

Compliance with
aerobic exercise program

are not related, the cross-products are mixed—that is, both positive and negative. Sometimes high z scores on one variable go with high z scores on the other, and low z scores on one variable go with low z scores on the other. In both cases, positive cross-products result. In other pairs of scores, high z scores on one variable go with low z scores on the other variable (and vice versa), producing negative cross-products. When the cross-products for the two variables are summed, the positive and negative numbers cancel each other out, resulting in a 0 (or close to 0) correlation.

In addition to describing the relationship between two variables, correlation coefficients are useful for another purpose: prediction. If we know a person's score on one of two related variables, we can predict how he or she will perform on the other variable. For example, in a recent issue of a magazine I found a quiz to rate my risk of heart disease. I assigned myself points depending on my age, HDL ("good") and total cholesterol levels, systolic blood pressure, and other risk factors, such as cigarette smoking and diabetes. My total points (−2) indicated that I had less than a 1 percent risk of developing heart disease in the next 5 years. How could such a quiz be developed? Each of the factors I rated is correlated to some degree with heart disease. The older you are, and the higher your cholesterol and blood pressure, the greater your chance of developing heart disease. Statistical techniques are used to determine the relative importance of each of these factors and to calculate the points that should be assigned to each level of a factor. Combining these factors provides a better prediction than any single factor, because none of the individual risk factors correlates perfectly with the development of heart disease.

One thing a correlation does *not* tell us is *causality*. In other words, the fact that two variables are highly correlated does not mean that one variable directly causes the other. Take the meditation and cigarette smoking correlation. This negative correlation tells us that people in the study who diligently practiced meditation tended to smoke less than those who seldom meditated. Regular meditation may have had a direct effect on the desire to smoke cigarettes, but it is also possible that one or more other variables affected both meditation and smoking. For example, perhaps participation in the study convinced some people that they needed to change their lifestyles completely. Both compliance with the meditation routine and a decreased level of cigarette smoking may have been "caused" by this change in lifestyle. The only way to determine cause and effect is to conduct an experiment, as you saw in Chapter 1. Can you think of a way to test the hypothesis that regularly practicing meditation causes a reduction in the desire to smoke cigarettes?

Inferential Statistics

Let's say that the mean number of physical symptoms (like pain) experienced by the participants in each of the three groups had been about the same at the beginning of the health-promotion study. A year later, the number of symptoms had decreased in the two intervention groups, but had remained stable in the control group. This may or may not be a meaningful result. We would expect the average number of symptoms to be somewhat different for each of the three groups, because each group consisted of different people. And we would expect some fluctuation in level over time, due simply to chance. But are the differences in number of symptoms between the intervention groups and the control group large enough *not* to be due to chance alone? If other researchers conducted the same study with different participants, would they be likely to get the same general pattern of results? To answer such questions, we turn to inferential statistics. **Inferential statistics** tell us the inferences, or conclusions, that we can legitimately draw from a set of research findings.

There are many inferential statistical techniques that can be called into service to answer questions such as the ones raised above. Each of them helps determine whether or not a set of findings can plausibly be explained merely by chance and random variation. If the results of a study are more extreme than would be expected by chance alone, we reject the idea that no *real* effect occurred, and conclude that the manipulation of the independent variable is the reason for the obtained results. In other words, we say that our results are *statistically significant.*

To see how this works, let's go back to the normal curve for a moment. Remember that we know exactly what percentage of a normal curve falls between any two z scores. If we choose one person at random out of a normal distribution, what is the chance that this person's z score is above $+2$? If you look again at Figure A.5, you will see that 2.28 percent of the curve lies above a z score (or standard deviation unit) of $+2$. Therefore, the chance, or *probability,* that the person we choose will have a z score above $+2$ is .0228 (or 2.28 chances out of 100). That's a pretty small chance. If you study the normal curve, you will see that the majority of cases fall between -2 and $+2$ SDs (95.44 percent of the cases, to be exact), so in choosing a person at random, that person is not likely to fall above a z score of $+2$.

When researchers test for statistical significance, they usually employ statistics other than z scores, and they may use distributions that differ in shape from the normal curve. The logic, however, is the same. They compute some kind of inferential statistic that they compare to the appropriate distribution. This comparison tells them the likelihood of obtaining their results if chance alone is operating.

The problem is that no test exists that will tell us for sure whether our intervention or manipulation "worked"; we always have to deal with probabilities, not certainties. Researchers have developed some conventions to guide them in their decisions about whether or not their study results are statistically significant. Generally, if the probability of obtaining a particular result if random factors alone are operating is less than .05 (5 chances out of 100), the results are considered statistically significant. Researchers who want to be even more sure set their probability value at .01 (1 chance out of 100).

Because researchers deal with probabilities, there is a small but real possibility of *erroneously* concluding that study results are significant. The results of one study, therefore, should never be completed trusted. In order to have greater confidence in a particular effect or result, the study should be repeated, or *replicated.* If the same results are obtained in different studies, then we can draw conclusions about a particular intervention or effect with greater certainty.

One final point about inferential statistics. Are the researchers interested only in the changes that might have occurred in the small groups of people participating in the health-promotion study, or do they really want to know whether the interventions would be effective for people in general?

inferential statistics
Statistical techniques that allow researchers to determine whether the outcomes in a study are likely to be more than just chance events and whether they can be legitimately generalized to a larger population.

This question focuses on the difference between a population and a sample. A **population** is a complete set of something—people, nonhuman animals, objects, or events. The researchers who designed this study wanted to know whether the interventions they developed would benefit *all* people (or, more precisely, all people between the ages of 20 and 56). Obviously, they could not conduct a study on this entire population. The best they could do is choose some portion of that population to serve as subjects; in other words, they selected a **sample.** The study was conducted on this sample. The researchers analyzed the sample results using inferential statistics to make guesses about what they would find had they studied the entire population. Inferential statistics allow researchers to take the findings they obtain from a sample and apply them to a population.

So what did the health-promotion study find? Did the interventions work? The answer is yes, sort of. The traditional and alternative groups, when combined, improved more than the no-treatment control group. At the end of the study, participants in the two intervention programs had better self-perceptions regarding health, better mood, more energy, and fewer physical symptoms. Compared with the traditional and the no-treatment groups, the alternative group showed greater improvement in health perceptions and a significant decrease in depression and the use of prescription drugs. Interestingly, participation in the treatment groups did not generally result in changes in health risk, such as lowered blood pressure or decreased weight. The researchers believe that little change occurred because the people who volunteered for the study were basically healthy individuals. The study needs to be replicated with a less-healthy sample. In sum, the intervention programs had a greater effect on health perceptions and psychological variables than on physical variables. The researchers concluded that a health-promotion regimen (either traditional or alternative) is helpful. I hope other studies will be conducted to explore these issues further!

Endnote

Although I briefly saw other study participants at each 3-month data collection point, I never spoke to anyone. The last measurement session, however, was also a celebration for our year-long participation in the project. Approximately 30 people attended my session, and participants from each of the three groups were present. After our blood was drawn and our blood pressure and weight readings were taken, we were treated to breakfast. Then one of the principal researchers *debriefed* us: She gave us some background on the study and told us what she hoped to learn. At this point, participants were given the opportunity to talk about how the study had affected their lives. It was fascinating to hear members of the intervention groups describe the changes they had made over the past year. One woman said that a year ago she could never imagine getting up early to meditate, yet now she looks forward to awakening each morning at 4:00 a.m. for her first meditation session. Other people described the modifications they had made in their diet and exercise patterns, and how much better they felt. While I did not experience either of the interventions, I know that simply being a subject in the study made me more conscious of what I ate and how much I exercised. This could have been a confounding factor—that is, it could have inadvertently changed my behavior even though I was in the control group. In fact, my weight decreased and my level of "good" cholesterol increased over the course of the year.

population
A complete set of something—people, nonhuman animals, objects, or events.

sample
A subset of a population.

We were not paid for our participation in this study, but we received small gifts as tokens of the researchers' appreciation. In addition, we were all given the option of taking any or all of the intervention training at no cost (and some courses in alternative techniques could be quite expensive). The most important thing for me was the satisfaction of participation—the fact that I had stayed with the study for an entire year and, in a small way, had made a contribution to science.

Summary
Statistics: Understanding Data

Descriptive Statistics

■ Descriptive statistics allow us to organize and summarize data in ways that are brief yet meaningful and easy to understand. One descriptive statistic is a frequency distribution, which can be presented in the form of a table, a histogram, or a frequency polygon. Some frequency distributions are positively skewed; that is, most of the scores in the distribution pile up at the low end. Distributions that are negatively skewed have mostly high scores. Symmetrical distributions have equal numbers of scores on both sides of the distribution's midpoint.

■ The mode, the median, and the mean are measures of central tendency of a distribution. The mode is the most frequent score. The median is the middle score in the distribution. The mean is the arithmetic average. To calculate the mean, scores are summed and divided by the total number of scores. The mean is usually the best overall representation of central tendency, but it is strongly influenced by extremely high or extremely low scores.

■ The range and standard deviation are measures of variability or spread of a distribution. The range is the highest score in the distribution minus the lowest score. The standard deviation is the square root of the average of the squared deviations from the mean.

■ A z score expresses a single score's deviation from the mean of a distribution in standard deviation units.

■ The standard normal curve is a symmetrical distribution forming a bell-shaped curve in which the mean, median, and mode are all equal and fall in the exact middle. The percentage of cases that fall between any two points on the normal curve is known. Over 95 percent of the cases fall between two standard deviations above the mean and two standard deviations below the mean.

■ Correlation refers to the relationship between two variables. A correlation coefficient is a number that indicates the magnitude and direction of such a relationship. A correlation coefficient may range from +1 to −1. The closer the value is to +1 or −1, the stronger the relationship is. Correlations close to 0 indicate no relationship. A positive correlation coefficient tell us that as one variable increases in size, the second variable also increases. A negative correlation coefficient indicates that as one variable in-

creases in size, the second variable decreases. A correlation relationship may be presented visually though a scatter diagram.

■ Correlations enable us to predict the value of one variable from knowledge of another variable's value. However, a correlational relationship is not necessarily a causal relationship.

Inferential Statistics

■ Inferential statistics are used to determine whether the outcomes of a study can be legitimately generalized to a larger population. A population is a complete set of something. A sample is a subset of a population.

■ Inferential statistics provide information about the probability of a particular result if only chance or random factors are operating. If this probability is small, the findings are said to be statistically significant—that is, they are probably due to the researcher's interventions.

Key Terms

descriptive statistics (p. A-2)

frequency distribution (p. A-3)

histogram (p. A-3)

frequency polygon (p. A-4)

skewed distribution (p. A-4)

symmetrical distribution (p. A-4)

measure of central tendency (p. A-5)

mode (p. A-5)

median (p. A-5)

mean (p. A-5)

measure of variability (p. A-6)

range (p. A-6)

standard deviation (p. A-7)

z score (p. A-7)

standard normal curve (standard normal distribution) (p. A-8)

correlation (p. A-9)

correlation coefficient (p. A-9)

scatter diagram (scatter plot) (p. A-9)

inferential statistics (p. A-12)

population (p. A-13)

sample (p. A-13)

Appendix B

Industrial/ Organizational Psychology

Marie Waung
University of Michigan, Dearborn

industrial/organizational (I/O) psychology
The branch of psychology that focuses on the study of human behavior at work.

personnel psychology
A sub-area of I/O psychology that focuses on matching people's characteristics to job requirements, accurately measuring job performance, and assessing employee training needs.

What Is Industrial/Organizational Psychology?

I was at a party recently when the inevitable question was asked of me: "What do you do?" When I answered that I am an industrial/organizational psychologist, the people around me looked puzzled. Finally, one man said with a smile, "Oh, is that like *big* psychology—you know, industrial size?" Another person remarked, "Well, you certainly must be well organized!" While the conversation made for a good ice breaker, it was clear that few people at the party were familiar with I/O psychology, even though I/O psychologists have been conducting research for some 100 years. The general unfamiliarity with the field is unfortunate, since its research and applications touch the lives of almost everyone who works.

Industrial/organizational psychology is the branch of psychology that focuses on the study of human behavior at work. The field consists of five major sub-areas (Muchinsky, 1993):

1. **Personnel psychology** This sub-area of I/O psychology focuses on the measurement of human characteristics, such as knowledge, skills, abilities, and personality dimensions. A major goal is to match people's characteristics with the characteristics required in particular jobs. If a good match is made, employees are likely to be more productive. Those working in the area of personnel psychology also apply research findings to the goal of measuring job performance as accurately and fairly as possible. Assessing employee training needs, and developing and evaluating training programs, also fall within the realm of personnel psychology. Personnel psychology is one of the two subfields of I/O psychology that we will discuss in more detail later in this appendix.

Designing for People One sub-area of industrial/organizational psychology is concerned with the human factors involved in the use of workplace procedures and equipment. For example, this factory's procedure for stitching jacket seams requires the sewing-machine operator to hold her arms away from her body—an unnatural, painful position. The employer, attentive to ergonomics, installed a pulley system with slings that allow the operator to work with her arms relaxed.

organizational behavior
A sub-area of I/O psychology that focuses on how the organization and the social environment in which people work affect their attitudes and behaviors.

human factors
A sub-area of I/O psychology that focuses on the design of equipment and the development of work procedures in light of human capabilities and limitations.

ergonomics
The science of applying knowledge about human physical characteristics to the design of equipment that minimizes fatigue and discomfort and maximizes productivity.

vocational and career counseling
A subfield of I/O psychology that combines with counseling psychology to help people choose occupations that match their preferences and needs.

organizational development (OD)
A sub-area of I/O psychology that focuses on bringing about positive change in an organization, such as increased profitability or improved products.

2. Organizational behavior This sub-area of I/O psychology focuses on how the organization and the social environment in which people work affect their attitudes and behaviors. Attitudes that I/O psychologists commonly study are job satisfaction and organizational commitment. Behaviors studied involve the extent to which employees are motivated to perform their jobs well, to attend work, and to remain with the organization. Aspects of the organizational environment looked at include the type of leadership or management, organizational communication patterns, and group processes within the organization. Organizational behavior is the other subfield of I/O psychology that we will look at in more detail later.

3. Human factors The focus of this sub-area is the design of equipment and the development of work procedures in light of human capabilities and limitations. Some of these human factors involve strength, size (human height, girth, arm and leg length), and other physical characteristics. The science of applying knowledge of such physical characteristics to the design of equipment that minimizes fatigue and discomfort and maximizes productivity is called **ergonomics.** Unfortunately, some everyday devices are designed with poor attention to human factors. For example, the first time that my mother used an automatic teller machine, she spent 10 frustrating minutes searching for the screen. She is barely five-foot-two, so the screen was positioned at the top of her head and the sun was shining directly on the screen. An adjustable screen with a sun shield could have prevented this problem. At the other end of the height spectrum, when my six-foot-three husband was shopping for a car, he found that many cars were uncomfortable for him to sit in because his head touched the roof. With the increased dependence on simple technological devices, such as beepers, voice mail systems, and fax machines, and more complicated devices like computers and automated production equipment, the sub-area of human factors is becoming even more important. The proper design of such devices will enable technology to help people become more productive, rather than frustrate them.

4. Vocation and career counseling This sub-area is a combination of I/O psychology and counseling psychology. It focuses on helping people to choose occupations that best match their preferences, needs, and values. In addition, psychologists in this specialty area often help people, as they gain job knowledge and experience, to plan for promotions or for career moves. Two common instruments used to help people select occupations are Holland's Vocational Preference Inventory (1965) and the Strong-Campbell Interest Inventory (Campbell, 1977). These inventories ask people about their preferences in a variety of areas; then, on the basis of the responses, certain types of work are recommended.

5. Organizational development The goal of the final sub-area of I/O psychology—organizational development (OD)—is to bring about positive change in an organization, such as greater profitability or improvement in the quality of products. Techniques for bringing about change include ex-

IN FOCUS B.1

Diversity in the Workplace

Digital Equipment Corporation is one company that has benefited from diversity training. Digitial is a globally based computer firm, with about 120,000 employees worldwide. A group of leaders at Digitial wanted to develop an organizational culture that would value the many differences among Digital's employees. This "valuing differences" philosophy would teach employees to pay attention to the differences among them in positive ways. Each employee would be recognized as a unique individual, as well as being a member of various groups. At Digital, workers would be encouraged to become comfortable with their differences and to realize that these differences were a major asset to the company. Human differences in the workplace add a richness of perspectives, ideas, and methods regarding what should be accomplished and how it should be done.

The valuing-differences culture at Digital was developed, in part, by a con-sulting firm that specializes in race relations (Walker & Hanson, 1992). The consultants began the diversity training by showing employees that sexism and racism are so much a part of American culture that all Americans are to some degree sexist and racist. This approach helped to lower employees' defensiveness about these topics. It helped them to realize that prejudiced ways of thinking did not necessarily make them bad people. Once employee defensiveness was reduced, sessions were held in which people were able to speak openly about gender and race issues. This open dialogue was important to the development of the valuing-differences culture at Digital.

The valuing-differences culture was enhanced through a number of other techniques (Walker & Hanson, 1992). One was the creation of an *awareness and skills training program.* It consisted of sessions designed to raise employees' level of awareness concerning human differences and to teach them about cultures other than their own. Another technique was *celebrating differences events,* sponsored by various employee groups. Events such as Black History Month, Hispanic Heritage Month, and Gay and Lesbian Pride Week helped to make employees feel that the differences among them were to be emphasized, not downplayed. A third technique was the creation of *leadership groups and support groups* designed to provide emotional and career support for employees with similar backgrounds (white females, for example, or Hispanic males). Also established were *core groups,* or small groups of workers who meet on a regular basis to discuss key issues. In this case, the core groups focused on their stereotypes and biased assumptions, and tried to build relationships with those they regarded as different from themselves. Together, these various techniques helped Digital to foster in its work force a real understanding and appreciation of human differences.

amining group processes to determine how interpersonal interactions or problem solving could be improved; probing employee perceptions of weaknesses in management; examining the work group and work procedures; and creating quality circles, in which small groups of employees meet on a regular basis to discuss production problems and how these problems might be reduced. *Diversity training* is a fairly new and increasingly popular OD intervention. Diversity training involves changing the cultural beliefs and attitudes of an organization so that its members better appreciate the differences among human beings. In Focus Box B.1 describes a diversity-training intervention at one large corporation.

Although you now know what I/O psychologists do, you may still have questions about the types of settings in which they work, the training they must have, and their employment outlook. We turn to these topics next.

Work Settings, Type of Training, and Employment Outlook

Many I/O psychologists belong to a division of the American Psychological Association (APA) called the Society for Industrial and Organizational Psychologists (SIOP). Of SIOP members, 89.8 percent hold doctorates, 9.7 percent have master's degrees, and .4 percent have bachelor's degrees (Howard, 1990). The division conducts periodic surveys of its members and, as a result, can supply information on topics such as typical work settings, job duties, and salary levels of I/O psychologists. To work in the field of I/O psychology, a doctorate or a master's degree is generally required. However, some areas that are closely related to I/O are open to those with bachelor's degrees. These will be discussed later in this section.

The principal employment settings of I/O psychologists are presented in Figure B.1. Over 39 percent of I/O psychologists who belong to SIOP and who responded to the latest survey reported working in a university or college; 32.7 percent worked as consultants to organizations; 15.1 percent worked in private organizations (such as utility companies, insurance companies, and companies that make consumer products); and 7.1 percent worked for public organizations (federal, state, and local governments, for example, or the military).

The employment outlook for those with Ph.D.'s and master's degrees appears to be favorable. Of the 1,826 SIOP members who responded to the survey, only 11 were unemployed and seeking employment. However, those who are unemployed may also be those who do not belong to SIOP or who did not complete the survey.

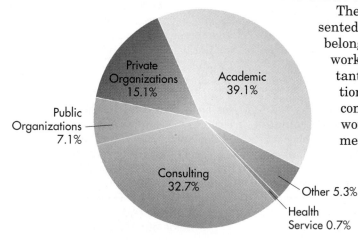

FIGURE B.1 Work Settings of I/O Psychologists

Institutions of higher education are where most I/O psychologists work. Thirty-nine percent of the members of the Society for Industrial and Organizational Psychologists work in colleges and universities. Next come I/O psychologists (32.7 percent) who work as consultants to organizations. Another substantial percentage (15.1 percent) are employed by large private corporations, such as insurance companies and consumer product manufacturers. Public organizations, such as government agencies, employ less than half as many I/O psychologists as private organizations do (7.1 percent vs. 15.1 percent).
(Howard, 1990.)

Although it is very difficult for people with bachelor's degrees to find employment in the field of I/O psychology, some related areas are open to them. For example, jobs for *personnel, training, and labor relations specialists and managers* are open to those with bachelor's degrees. The purpose of these jobs is to help management make effective use of employees' knowledge, skills, and abilities, and to help employees find job satisfaction.

The educational requirements for personnel, training, and labor relations specialists and managers vary widely. Some employers prefer applicants with majors in human resources, public administration, or industrial relations. Others seek those with backgrounds in technical or business areas, while still others want people with well-rounded liberal arts educations. Given the wide variety of skills required for these jobs, an interdisciplinary background that combines social and behavioral sciences and business is useful. In fact, a recent study found that managers who majored in the humanities or social sciences in college tended to be better managers than those who majored in business, engineering, or math/science (Howard, 1986). In addition, managers who majored in humanities or social sciences showed more potential for advancement to higher levels of management than those with other college majors.

Job growth for personnel, training, and labor relations specialists and managers is expected to be higher than the average job growth through the year 2005. However, the job market is likely to remain competitive due to the high number of qualified college graduates and experienced workers (Bureau of Labor Statistics, 1994).

Another I/O-related career in which those with bachelor's degrees may sometimes find employment is that of *management analysts and consultants.* Management analysts and consultants deal with a variety of organizational

job analysis
An assessment of the major responsibilities of a particular job and the human characteristics needed to fill it.

problems, from helping organizations relocate to helping them restructure. Generally, they collect, review, and analyze information, make recommendations, and help to implement those recommendations. Educational requirements vary for these jobs. Those with bachelor's degrees may work in government agencies in entry-level positions as research associates or junior consultants. Most companies prefer that their full-fledged management consultants have master's degrees.

Growth in the demand for management consultants and analysts is expected to be higher than the average job growth through the year 2005. The reason for this expected growth is the greater reliance of private companies and government agencies on outside expertise to improve productivity (Bureau of Labor Statistics, 1994).

Employment interviewer is a third I/O-related field open to those with bachelor's degrees. Employment interviewers typically work for personnel supply firms, matching employers with job applicants and job applicants with employers. An employment interviewer needs sales ability, because he or she is expected to attract clients and job applicants to the personnel supply firm. Self-confidence, as well as strong oral communication and interpersonal skills, are needed too.

Demand for employment interviewers is expected to grow at an average rate. Some of the demand is being curtailed by the increased use of computerized job matches and information systems (Bureau of Labor Statistics, 1994).

JOB ANALYST alternate titles: personnel analyst

Collects, analyzes, and prepares occupational information to facilitate personnel, administration, and management functions of organization: Consults with management to determine type, scope, and purpose of study. Studies current organizational occupational data and compiles distribution reports, organization and flow charts, and other background information required for study. Observes jobs and interviews workers and supervisory personnel to determine job and worker requirements. Analyzes occupational data, such as physical, mental, and training requirements of jobs and workers and develops written summaries, such as job descriptions, job specifications, and lines of career movement. Utilizes developed occupational data to evaluate or improve methods and techniques for recruiting, selecting, promoting, evaluating, and training workers, and administration of related personnel programs. May specialize in classifying positions according to regulated guidelines to meet job classification requirements of civil service system and be known as Position Classifier.

FIGURE B.2 A Sample Job Analysis

The job analysis is a crucial tool in personnel psychology. A thorough job analysis is the first step not only in selecting among job applicants but also in training employees for specific positions and in evaluating their performance. This job analysis is for the job of job analyst itself.

(*Dictionary of occupational titles*, 1991.)

Personnel Psychology

Personnel psychology, as you have learned, is a major subfield of I/O psychology. I have chosen to discuss it in detail in this appendix because it is one of the areas that best represents the work that most I/O psychologists do. For the same reason, following this section on personnel psychology, we will also discuss the subfield of organizational behavior in more detail.

Three major goals of personnel psychologists are: (1) selecting the best applicants for jobs; (2) training employees so that they perform their jobs effectively; and (3) accurately evaluating employee performance. The first step in attaining each of these goals is to perform a job analysis.

The First Step:
Job Analysis

Job analysis is a technique in which the major responsibilities of a job, along with the human characteristics needed to fill it, are determined. Information about the job is usually collected from employees who currently hold the job or from their supervisors. These people may be observed at their work, interviewed, or asked to complete surveys. Figure B.2 presents a job analysis for the position of job analyst itself.

Once a job's requirements are determined and written down in a job analysis, it is easier to achieve the goal of selecting appropriate people for a position.

selection device validity
The extent to which a personnel selection device is successful in distinguishing between those who will become high performers at a certain job and those who will not.

Selection devices, such as tests and interviews, are used to determine which applicants have the knowledge, skills, and abilities specified in a job analysis. For example, a job analysis might reveal that as a salesperson, a dominant, extroverted personality is important. Applicants' personality traits might therefore be measured to screen for those who have these characteristics.

After appropriate applicants have been selected, the job of training them begins. Here, too, the key is to have a clear view of the job procedures, knowledge, and skills needed for effective job performance—that is, to have a good job analysis. Training program developers might begin by comparing the current work procedures, knowledge, and skills of employees with the information obtained from a job analysis. They would then design training programs to eliminate gaps between what currently exists and what is optimal.

Job analysis is also the first step in the design of performance appraisal systems. Before performance can be measured, expected performance must first be defined. Job analysis defines and clarifies what effective performance is so that performance appraisal instruments may be developed.

A Closer Look at Personnel Selection

Have you ever applied for a job and not been hired? If so, you probably wonder what happened. Did you lose the job because of something that you said or did in the interview or, perhaps, because of your responses on an application test? In this section you'll learn about the applicant selection process. While you won't necessarily discover why you weren't picked for a particular job, you will get a better understanding of the selection processes that many companies use. This knowledge may help you to feel better prepared and more relaxed the next time you apply for a job.

The goal in personnel selection is to hire only those applicants who will perform the job effectively. A variety of selection devices are used to choose among applicants. The effectiveness of each device depends, in part, on its appropriateness for a particular job. For example, a test of visual acuity may be a good selection device for the job of airline pilot, but a poor selection device for the job of seamstress (some sewing machine operators are able to sew with their eyes closed!). Personnel psychologists are concerned with the degree to which selection devices are valid. **Selection device validity** refers to the extent to which a selection device is successful in distinguishing between those applicants who will become high performers and those who will not. If a personality measure is used to select salespeople, it is considered valid if those whom it singles out as potential high performers do, indeed, become high performers.

Psychological Tests

Psychological tests are one kind of selection device that employers often use. Such tests are usually classified on the basis of what they measure. Common types of psychological tests are cognitive ability tests, mechanical aptitude tests, motor and sensory ability tests, and personality tests.

Cognitive ability tests measure general intelligence or specific cognitive skills, such as mathematical or verbal ability. Some items from two cognitive ability tests are presented in Figure B.3. *Mechanical ability tests* measure

FIGURE B.3 Sample Items from Two Cognitive Ability Tests
Cognitive ability tests can measure either general intelligence or specific cognitive skills, such as mathematical ability. **(a)** These two items are from the Wonderlic Personnel Test, which is designed to assess general cognitive ability. Employers assume that people who cannot answer most such questions correctly would not be good candidates for jobs that require general knowledge and reasoning skills. **(b)** The chart is from theNon-Verbal Reasoning Test. It assesses reasoning skills apart from the potentially confounding factor of skill with the English language.
(Wonderlic, 1996; Corsini, 1957.)

(a) 1. RESENT/RESERVE — Do these words
    1 have similar meanings
    2 have contradictory meanings
    3 mean neither the same nor opposite
  2. Paper sells for 21 cents per pad. What will 4 pads cost?

(b)

For each item find the picture that goes best with the picture in the first box. Draw a dark line from the upper right corner to the lower left corner in the proper box to show the right answer.

Which room has more of an echo?

Which would be the better shears for cutting metal?

Which man carries more weight?
(If equal, mark C)

Which letter shows the seat where a passenger will get the smoothest ride?

mechanical reasoning and may be used to predict job performance for engineering, carpentry, and assembly work. Figure B.4 presents sample items from the Bennett Test of Mechanical Comprehension. *Motor ability tests* include measures of fine dexterity in fingers and hands (for jobs that require the assembly of products with tiny parts), accuracy and speed of arm and hand movement, and eye–hand coordination. *Sensory ability tests* include measures of visual acuity, color vision, and hearing.

Personality tests may be designed to measure either abnormal or normal personality characteristics. An assessment of abnormal personality characteristics might be appropriate for selecting people for sensitive jobs, such as nuclear power plant operator, police officer, and airline pilot. Recently, tests designed to measure normal personality traits, such as conscientiousness, extroversion, and agreeableness, have become more popular for the selection of employees (e.g., Barrick & Mount, 1991, 1993; Tett & others, 1991). Because of legal restrictions on the use of polygraph tests in the workplace, honesty tests have also become more widely used in recent years. Honesty tests attempt to assess an applicant's level of honesty by asking about past behaviors involving theft or dishonesty, attitudes about theft and the punishment of it, and perceptions about the prevalence of theft. One issue regarding the use of honesty tests is the extent to which people can fake their responses. Although distorting one's responses to an honesty test is possible, it is controlled for, to some extent, by the use of scales designed to detect faking (Ryan & Sackett, 1987). Another issue is the likelihood of "false positives"—test results indicating dishonesty when the applicant in fact is honest. Because of the issues of faking and false positives, the Committee on Psychological Tests and Assessments of the American Psychological Association has expressed concern about the use of honesty tests in personnel selection (Bales, 1988). More research is needed to draw any firm conclusions about the validity of honesty tests.

FIGURE B.4 Sample Items from a Mechanical Ability Test Questions such as these from the Bennett Test of Mechanical Comprehension are designed to assess a person's ability to figure out the physical properties of things. Such a test might be used to predict job performance for carpenters or assembly-line workers.
(Bennett, 1940.)

Work Samples and Situational Exercises

Two other kinds of personnel selection devices are work samples and situational exercises. Work samples are typically used for jobs involving the manipulation of objects, while situational exercises are usually used for jobs involving managerial or professional skills. In both, applicants are given a mini-version of the job to perform. It is assumed that if they do well on this mini-version, they are likely to do well on the actual job. One work sample test for the job of mechanic, for instance, required the applicant to perform tasks such as taking apart and repairing a gear box and installing pulleys and belts. Successful performance on the work sample test did in fact predict successful performance on the job (Campion, 1972). A common situational exercise is the in-basket test, which requires the applicant to sort through a series of memos, directives, reports, letters, and phone messages in a limited amount of time (Frederickson, 1968). The employer evaluates the way in which the applicant organizes and deals with the items.

Matching Job and Applicant A job analysis helps to pinpoint the qualities a person must have in order to succeed at a particular job. Thus, not everyone has the special combination of compassion and toughness needed to be an effective physical therapist.

Selection Interviews

Although the general interview is one of the most commonly used selection devices, it typically possesses low validity. That is, assessments of applicants in general interviews are not strongly related to their subsequent job performance (Hunter & Hunter, 1984). The reason for the low validity of interviews is that they are often unstructured. The questions asked may be vague and unrelated to job performance, such as "Tell me about yourself" and "Why do you want this job?" In addition, different questions are sometimes asked of different applicants; as a result, it is difficult to compare their responses, and employers are forced to evalute them on the basis of different information. Consider how unfair it would be if some students in your class were graded on their exam performance, others on their class attendance, and still others on their physical attractiveness (Berry & Houston, 1993).

In contrast to unstructured interviews, structured ones, if developed and conducted properly, are adequate predictors of job performance. A structured interview should: (1) be based on a job analysis; (2) involve questions that elicit job-related information about the applicant; (3) involve questions that are asked of all applicants in the same order; and (4) be evaluated by a panel of interviewers who record and rate the applicant's responses. When these criteria are met, the interview is likely to be an effective selection tool (Campion & others, 1988).

Organizational Behavior

Organizational behavior (OB) is another subfield we will discuss in detail because of its representativeness of the work that I/O psychologists do. It focuses on how the organization and social environment in which people work affect their attitudes and behaviors. Job satisfaction is the most thoroughly researched attitude among I/O psychologists. The impact of leadership on attitudes and behaviors is another well-researched OB topic. We will examine both these topics here.

Job Satisfaction

Lucy and Jane are both engineers who work in the same department of the same company. Lucy is almost always eager to get to work in the morning. She feels that her work is interesting and that she has plenty of opportunities to learn new skills. In contrast, Jane is unhappy because she feels that she doesn't get the recognition she deserves at work. She also complains that the company doesn't give enough vacation time to employees and that it provides inadequate benefits. Jane can't think of many good things about her job; she's even beginning to feel that her job is negatively affecting her personal life.

Fortunately, Lucy is more typical of American workers than Jane. In a recent telephone poll conducted by the Gallup Organization, 87 percent of those polled reported that they were satisfied with their jobs (Hugick & Leonard, 1991). However, respondents differed as to which aspects of work they were satisfied with. For example, 67 percent of those polled were satisfied with their health insurance and benefits; 88 percent with the interest level of their work; and 79 percent with the amount of job security they had.

Several approaches have been used to explain differences in job satisfaction. One approach is based on a **discrepancy hypothesis,** which consists of three ideas: (1) that people differ in what they want from a job; (2) that people differ in how they evaluate what they experience at work; and (3) that level of satisfaction is based on the difference between what is desired and what is experienced (Lawler, 1973; Locke, 1976). Lucy and Jane, for instance, may not only want different things from their jobs but they may also make different assessments of the same events at work. Although their supervisor may treat them in the same encouraging manner, Lucy may see the boss's encouragment as supportive, while Jane may view it as condescending. As a result, one perceives a discrepancy between desires and experiences, whereas the other does not.

A significant amount of research supports the discrepancy hypothesis. For example, negative discrepancies (getting less than desired) have been related to dissatisfaction. Interestingly, positive discrepancies (getting more than desired) have also been related to dissatisfaction in some cases (Rice & others, 1989). As an example, you might be dissatisfied with a job because it involves more contact with customers than you want or expect.

Another hypothesis to explain job satisfaction is the **social influence hypothesis,** which is based on the idea that people interpret their situations, in part, according to the reactions of others (Salancik & Pfeffer, 1977). For instance, when listening to a comedian, some people will make sure others are laughing before they laugh themselves. Similarly, when evaluating their own job satisfaction, people may be influenced by the attitudes of their co-workers regarding the degree to which the job is satisfying. After hearing Jane complain about the job, Lucy might report a lower level of satisfaction than she would have without Jane's influence. In a laboratory study, people who heard others evaluate a task positively were also likely to evaluate the task positively when they performed it later. Similarly, people who heard others evaluate a task negatively were later likely to evaluate the task negatively (Weiss & Shaw, 1979).

Recently, **dispositional factors** have also been used to explain differences in job satisfaction. Some researchers believe that "job attitudes may reflect a biologically based trait that predisposes individuals to see positive or negative content in their lives" (Staw & Ross, 1985, p. 471). In other words, some people may be prone to negative perceptions and feelings (such as suspicion, fear, worry, and dissatisfaction), whereas others may be prone to positive ones (such as trust, enthusiasm, and satisfaction). In a recent study, researchers who examined identical twins raised apart found support for the idea that a tendency toward positive or negative outlooks may be biologically based. They found that sets of twins had similar levels of job satisfaction and concluded that job satisfaction may be explained, in part, by genetic factors (Arvey & others, 1989).

Discrepancy between desires and experiences, social influence, and inherited dispositions have each been successful in explaining some of the differences in job satisfaction among people. But as is true with most psychological research into human behavior; none of these approaches by itself can completely explain differences in job satisfaction.

Whatever its causes, job satisfaction or lack of it can affect a person's general level of contentment. Job satisfaction has been found to be related to overall life satisfaction (see, for example, Judge & Watanabe, 1993; Lance & others, 1989; Weaver, 1978). In general, satisfaction (or dissatisfaction) in one area of life has been found to spill over into others. Feelings of happiness or unhappiness tend to pervade all aspects of our lives (Weaver, 1978). This

discrepancy hypothesis
An approach to explaining job satisfaction that focuses on the discrepancy, if any, between what a person wants from a job and how that person evaluates what is experienced at work.

social influence hypothesis
The view that a person's level of job satisfaction is influenced by the job satisfaction levels of other people.

dispositional factors hypothesis
The view that a person's level of job satisfaction may be due in part to a genetically based disposition toward a positive or negative outlook.

trait approach to leader effectiveness
An approach to determining what makes an effective leader that focuses on the personal characteristics displayed by successful leaders.

behavioral theories of leader effectiveness
Theories of leader effectiveness that focus on differences in the behaviors of effective and ineffective leaders.

situational (or contingency) theories of leader effectiveness
Theories that focus on how a particular situation influences a leader's effectiveness.

is one reason that high job satisfaction among employees should be a goal of all organizations. In addition to reducing absenteeism and turnover, it contributes to employees' overall levels of happiness. Companies might also provide resources to help employees cope with personal problems, because of the spillover effect just mentioned: happiness in one's personal life is likely to spill over into one's work life.

Leadership

Leadership is one of the most widely researched topics in I/O psychology; thousands of studies have investigated it. Those who have the ability to direct groups toward the attainment of goals are leaders. According to this definition of leadership, one of the functions of a manager is to lead. Keep in mind, though, that managers act not only as leaders but also as negotiators, disturbance handlers, resource allocators, and decision makers (Mintzberg, 1973). Being a good leader is only one aspect of being a good manager.

Leader Effectiveness

I/O psychologists have spent a great deal of time trying to determine what makes someone an effective leader. The **trait approach to leader effectiveness,** one of the earliest approaches to the study of leadership, is based on the idea that leaders are born, not made. According to this view, some people possess certain qualities or characteristics that make them natural leaders. Examples are John F. Kennedy, Martin Luther King, Jr., Norman Schwartzkopf, and Colin Powell. These people presumably share certain characteristics that made them good leaders, and these characteristics would make them good leaders in practically any situation. A large number of traits such as height, physical attractiveness, dominance, flexibility, and intelligence have been examined to see if they determine how effective a leader will be. However, after a substantial amount of research, little connection has been found between personal traits and leader effectiveness (Stogdill, 1948; Hollander & Julian, 1970).

After the failure of the trait approach to identify effective leaders, researchers began to examine the *behaviors* of leaders, in the hope of verifying **behavioral theories of leader effectiveness.** They reasoned that the behaviors of effective and ineffective leaders must differ. One of the most influential studies of leader behavior was conducted at Ohio State University. The researchers identified two major types of leadership behavior: consideration and initiating structure (Fleishman & Harris, 1962). *Consideration* describes leaders who are deeply concerned about their followers and who spend time building trust, respect, and warmth between themselves and their followers. *Initiating structure* describes leaders who are task-oriented, who structure tasks for their followers and who push for things to get done. Initiating structure has been related to high productivity, but also to low job satisfaction and high personnel turnover. In contrast, consideration has been related to high job satisfaction, but also to low productivity in some situations (Bass, 1981; Locke & Schweiger, 1979).

Additional research on initiating structure and consideration behaviors has led researchers to conclude that the *situation* might have an impact on the effectiveness of a leader's behavior. In some situations, initiating structure might be best; in other situations, consideration might be more effective. The theories that developed from this view are called **situational (or con-**

What Makes a Leader? Nelson Mandela is an extraordinarily charismatic leader. Not only did he keep his political organization, the African National Congress, functioning during his twenty-seven years of imprisonment, but he also guided South Africa out of its racist apartheid system with a minimum of violence and turmoil.

tingency) theories of leadership. These theories tend to be complicated but seem to do a better job of explaining leader effectiveness than either trait or behavioral theories.

In the last 15 years or so, researchers have once again become interested in leadership traits. In particular, the trait of charisma has received a lot of attention. Charismatic leaders have extraordinary effects on their followers, thanks to their compelling personalities and highly developed interpersonal skills (House, 1977). Typically, charismatic leaders have a high need for power, are extremely self-confident, and believe strongly in a particular cause. Charismatic leaders are able to change the attitudes and beliefs of their followers, and may even be able to evoke strong compliance from them. The followers are motivated by love, enthusiasm, and devotion to their leader. In some cases, compliance to the wishes of a charismatic leader may be so strong that followers are willing to engage in unethical or illegal behavior. A recent study of U.S. presidents from George Washington to Ronald Reagan revealed that the more charismatic the president, the greater his success with domestic issues (House & others, 1991).

Leader Emergence

Research on the emergence of leaders examines who in a group is likely to become the group leader. This topic differs from that of leader effectiveness, because not everyone who emerges as a leader is a good leader. For example, in a discussion with your classmates, you might find that a particular person dominates the conversation and directs the group's efforts. This person is clearly the group's leader, but the effect of his or her behavior on group productivity and satisfaction may be either positive or negative. Using a technique called *leaderless group discussion,* in which a group is given a problem to solve or a topic to discuss, researchers study the group to see who emerges as the leader. Intelligence, aggressiveness, decisiveness, and dominance are personal qualities that have been related to leader emergence (Lord & others, 1986).

Gender, Ethnicity, and Leadership

Women have entered lower-level management jobs in great numbers in recent years; about 40 percent of all managerial jobs in the United States are held by women (Morrison & Von Glinow, 1990). At higher levels, however, few women are found. Only 2 to 4 percent of upper-level management positions are filled by women (Morrison & Von Glinow, 1990; Snyder & others, 1992). The difficulty that women are having in advancing to high levels in most organizations may be due to subtle, unofficial discrimination that creates an invisible but strong barrier to women's promotion to the top. This barrier is called the **glass ceiling.** It is reinforced by differences in the socialization, educational and training opportunities, and family and child-care responsibilities of males and females.

Yet another powerful reinforcer of the glass ceiling is unfair performance evaluation. Performance appraisal information affects promotion decisions, and to the extent that performance evaluation is biased against women, their opportunities for advancement are limited. And, indeed, Heilman and Stopeck (1985) found that males and females were often evaluated differently for managerial jobs. In particular, attractive female managers tended to receive lower performance evaluations than did less attractive female managers, even when the evaluators were given exactly the same performance information about them. The researchers explained that these results were based on stereotypes. Attractive females were perceived as more feminine than less attractive females, and because femininity is inconsistent with widely held stereotypes regarding the characteristics of successful managers, attractive

glass ceiling
An invisible but strong barrier of subtle, unofficial discrimination that prevents women or minorities from being promoted to the highest levels of leadership in an organization.

females were perceived as less competent—so they received lower ratings. Interestingly, raters were not influenced by the attractiveness of males; attractive and unattractive males received similar performance ratings when evaluators were given the same information about them.

Researchers have found no differences in the leadership effectiveness of men and women working in organizations, and practically no differences in male and female leadership behavior (Bass, 1981; Eagly & Johnson, 1990; Rice & others, 1984). However, some research has found that men tend to be more autocratic, while women tend to be more democratic, with the effectiveness of each style depending on the situation (Eagly & Johnson, 1990).

Little research on leadership and members of racial and ethnic minorities has been conducted, partly because so few minority members have been promoted to leadership positions. One finding is that leaders of different races hold similar values (Watson & Barone, 1976).

The similarities found between male and female leaders and minority and nonminority ones may reflect the fact that people are basically the same regardless of gender or ethnic background. But another explanation may be that women and minorities who are the most similar to those in positions of power (usually Caucasian males) are more likely to be selected for promotions within organizations. For example, a group of males might view a stereotypically "masculine" female as more appropriate for a managerial position than a stereotypically "feminine" female.

Cultivating a diverse work force is likely to be advantageous to organizations because heterogenous groups, compared with homogeneous ones, are more likely to be flexible and creative—two characteristics that are becoming increasingly important in a rapidly changing world. One team of researchers hypothesized that *biculturalism*—a familiarity with, understanding of, and sympathy toward the norms of two different cultures—enables people to be more flexible when leading heterogeneous groups, because it provides them with a greater diversity of skills. Some support was found for this idea. Mexican-Americans high in biculturalism exhibited more leadership behavior than those low in biculturalism (Garza & others, 1982).

Although progress is being made toward diversifying the work force, there is still a great deal of room for improvement, especially at managerial levels. The work of I/O psychologists in areas such as personnel selection, performance appraisal, and leadership will undoubtedly encourage additional progress.

Trends for the Future

Demographers predict that the work force will become increasingly diverse as we move into the twenty-first century, with more women and minorities than ever before. The workplace is also expected to become ever more technical, with employees required to operate and maintain complicated machinery and equipment. Furthermore, organizations are likely to find themselves competing not only nationally, but globally. All these trends have implications for the work of I/O psychologists. Let's take a closer look at each of them.

Increased diversity. Increased diversity in the work force will result in a greater demand for research on the ways in which heterogeneous groups communicate, interact, and make decisions. An understanding of the effects of heterogeneity on group creativity and productivity will be important to the economic competitiveness of the United States. The best ways

Shaping the Jobs of the Future The work of industrial/organizational psychologists is becoming crucial in helping American businesses accommodate an increasingly diverse workforce.

of leading heterogeneous groups also must be determined. As women participate in the work force in record numbers and as our population ages, the need for child care and elder care will continue to grow—yet most companies have made little or no effort to provide on-site care for the children or aging parents of employees. Research on the effects of such day-care programs on employee tardiness, absenteeism, turnover, productivity, and job satisfaction is needed.

Technological advances. Advances in communication—computers, modems, faxes, e-mail, and voice mail—have made it possible for greater numbers of employees to work from their homes. The job satisfaction and productivity of the home workers will need to be compared with those who work on company premises. The advantages of working from home, such as the time and money saved on the daily commute, may be offset by the lack of social contact and abundance of distractions.

Human factors will become more important as technological advances continue. The design of equipment with human capabilities and limitations in mind will be vital to the productivity, and perhaps to the satisfaction, of employees as companies come to depend on more sophisticated techniques and equipment.

Global economy. With more and companies competing for a share of the world market, it will be increasingly important to have systems for selecting manager who are able to function effectively in various cultures. In addition, managers must be trained in the customs and languages of different cultures. Programs to help managers and their families adjust to living in foreign countries will also be needed. Research on the effects of various incentives on employees' willingness to transfer to foreign countries and on their satisfaction with living abroad will also be important.

In the future, I/O psychologists will continue to have a significant impact on the workplace. To keep pace with the trends we've looked at—increased diversity of the work force, technological advances, and a global economy—I/O psychologists will continue to adjust the focus of their research and its applications to meet the changing needs of people at work.

Summary

Industrial/Organizational Psychology

What Is Industrial/Organizational Psychology?

- Industrial/organizational (I/O) psychology is a broad field that studies human behavior at work. It consists of five major sub-areas: personnel psychology, which focuses on evaluating and selecting job applicants, measuring job performance, and assessing employee training needs; organizational behavior, which focuses on how the organization and social environment in which people work affect their attitudes and behaviors; human factors, which is concerned with the design of equipment and work procedures with human capabilities and limitations in mind; vocational and career counseling, which helps people choose appropriate occupations; and organizational development, which focuses on bringing about positive changes in an organization.

Work Settings, Type of Training, and Employment Outlook

- The vast majority of I/O psychologists (about 90 percent) have Ph.D.s, and most of the rest have master's degrees. The employment outlook for these highly trained professionals appears to be quite favorable.

- I/O psychologists may work in colleges or universities, or as consultants to organizations. They may also work for large private corporations or for public institutions, such as government agencies.

- In certain fields related to I/O psychology, jobs are sometimes available for people with bachelor's degrees. These fields include personnel, training, and labor relations specialists and manaers, management analysts and consultants, and employment interviewers.

Personnel Psychology

- A first step in the work of personnel psychologists is to perform a job analysis—a determination of the major responsibilities of a certain job and the human characteristics needed to fill it. A good job analysis is key to successful personnel seletion, effective job training programs, and accurate evaluation of job performance.

- Personnel psychologists use many devices to help them with their goal of selecting the best applicants for jobs. These include psychological tests, work samples and situational exercises, and selection interviews. Personnel psychologists are very concerned about the validity of a selection device—the extent to which it succeeds in distinguishing between those applicants who will become high performers and those who will not.

Organizational Behavior

- One topic extensively studied in the field of organizational behavior is job satisfaction. Researchers have tried to explain different levels of job satisfaction in three ways: the discrepancy hypothesis, which focuses on gaps between what a person wants from a job and what he or she actually experiences; the social influence hypothesis, which looks at how people interpret their situations in relation to others' reactions; and the dispositional factors hypothesis, which links job satisfaction to inherited dispositions.

- Leadership is also a widely studied topic in the field of organizational behavior. Researchers have tried to explain leadership effectiveness by looking at the personal traits of effective leaders, at their distinguishing behaviors, and at situational factors that might influence their success. Of these three approaches, situational theories seem to do the best job. Other aspects of leadership studies are how leaders emerge in a group and how the "glass ceiling" of cultural biases prevents women and members of racial and ethnic minorities from attaining positions of leadership in organizations.

Trends for the Future

- Three important trends will affect the workplace of the twenty-first century. One is an increased diversity in the makeup of the work force, with more women and members of minorities than ever before. The second is greater technical sophistication in the workplace, with an increasing number of complex machines to operate. The third is the growing globalization of our economy and of the companies that do business in it.

Key Terms

industrial/organizational (I/O) psychology (p. B-1)

personnel psychology (p. B-1)

organizational behavior (p. B-2)

human factors (p. B-2)

ergonomics (p. B-2)

vocational and career counseling (p. B-2)

organizational development (OD) (p. B-2)

job analysis (p. B-5)

selection device validity (p. B-6)

discrepancy hypothesis (p. B-9)

social influence hypothesis (p. B-9)

dispositional factors hypothesis (p. B-9)

trait approach to leader effectiveness (p. B-10)

behavioral theories of leader effectivness (p. B-10)

situational (or contingency) theories of leader effectiveness (p. B-10)

glass ceiling (p. B-11)

Glossary

absolute threshold The smallest possible strength of a stimulus that can be detected half the time. (p. 96)

accommodation The process by which the lens of the eye changes shape to focus incoming light so that it falls on the retina. (p. 101)

acculturative stress The stress that results from the pressure of adapting to a new culture. (p. 576)

acetylcholine (uh-seet-ull-KO-leen) Neurotransmitter that produces muscle contractions and is involved in memory functions. (p. 54)

achievement motivation Motivated behavior directed toward excelling, succeeding, or outperforming others at some task. (p. 354)

achievement test A test designed to measure a person's level of knowledge, skill, or accomplishment in a particular area. (p. 314)

action potential A brief electrical impulse by which information is transmitted along the axon of a neuron. (p. 47)

activation-synthesis model of dreaming The theory that brain activity during sleep produces dream images (*activation*), which are combined by the brain into a dream story (*synthesis*). (p. 170)

activity theory of aging The psychosocial theory that life satisfaction in late adulthood is highest when people maintain the level of activity they displayed earlier in life. (p. 420)

actor–observer discrepancy The tendency to attribute one's own behavior to external, situational causes, while attributing the behavior of others to internal, personal causes; especially likely to occur with regard to behaviors that lead to negative outcomes. (p. 526)

actualizing tendency In Carl Rogers's theory of personality, the innate drive to maintain and enhance the human organism. (p. 489)

adolescence The transitional stage between late childhood and the beginning of adulthood, during which sexual maturity is reached. (p. 405)

adolescent growth spurt The period of accelerated growth during puberty, involving rapid increases in height and weight. (p. 452)

adrenal cortex The outer portion of the adrenal gland that secretes corticosteroids. (p. 63)

adrenal glands Pair of endocrine glands that are involved in the human stress response. (p. 63)

adrenal medulla The inner portion of the adrenal gland; secretes epinephrine and norepinephrine. (p. 63)

afterimage A visual experience that occurs after the original source of stimulation is no longer present. (p. 106)

agoraphobia An anxiety disorder involving the extreme and irrational fear of experiencing a panic attack in a public situation and being unable to escape or get help. (p. 620)

AIDS (acquired immune deficiency syndrome) A disease caused by the exchange of body fluids (semen, blood, or blood products) containing the human immunodeficiency virus (HIV), which attacks and weakens the immune system. (p. 462)

algorithm A problem-solving strategy that involves following a specific rule, procedure, or method, which inevitably produces the correct solution. (p. 294)

all-or-none law The principle that either a neuron is sufficiently stimulated and an action potential occurs or a neuron is not sufficiently stimulated and an action potential does not occur. (p. 48)

alpha brain waves Brain wave pattern associated with relaxed wakefulness and drowsiness. (p. 154)

altruism Helping another person with no expectation of personal reward or benefit. (p. 553)

amnesia (am-NEE-zha) Severe memory loss. (p. 276)

amphetamines (am-FET-uh-mins) A class of stimulant drugs that arouse the central nervous system and suppress appetite. (p. 187)

amplitude The intensity or amount of energy of a wave, reflected in the height of the wave; the amplitude of a sound wave determines a sound's loudness. (p. 108)

amygdala (uh MIC dull-uh) An almond-shaped forebrain structure that is part of the limbic system and involved in emotion and memory. (p. 78)

anorexia nervosa An eating disorder in which the individual refuses to maintain a minimally normal body weight, is extremely afraid of gaining weight or becoming fat, and has a distorted perception about the size of his or her body. (p. 348)

anterograde amnesia Loss of memory caused by the inability to store new memories. (p. 277)

antianxiety medications Prescription drugs that are used to alleviate the symptoms of anxiety. (p. 691)

antidepressant medications Prescription drugs that are used to reduce the symptoms associated with depression. (p. 693)

antipsychotic medications Prescription drugs that are used to reduce psychotic symptoms; frequently used in the treatment of schizophrenia. (p. 689)

anxiety An unpleasant emotional state characterized by physical arousal and feelings of tension, apprehension, and worry. (p. 617)

anxiety disorders A category of psychological disorders in which extreme anxiety is the main diagnostic feature and causes significant disruptions in the person's cognitive, behavioral, or interpersonal functioning. (p. 617)

aphasia (uh-FAZE-yuh) The partial or complete inability to articulate ideas or understand spoken or written language due to brain injury or damage. (p. 81)

aptitude test A test designed to assess a person's capacity to benefit from education or training. (p. 314)

archetypes In Jung's theory of personality, the inherited mental images of universal human instincts, themes, and preoccupations that are the main components of the collective unconscious. (p. 483)

arousal theory The view that people are motivated to maintain an optimal level of arousal, which is neither too high nor too low. (p. 350)

association areas Areas of the cerebral cortex where information from different brain centers is combined and integrated. (p. 75)

attachment The emotional bond that forms between an infant and her caretaker(s), especially her parents. (p. 392)

attitude A learned tendency to evaluate some object, person, or issue in a particular way; such evaluations may be positive, negative, or ambivalent. (p. 530)

attribution The mental process of inferring the causes of people's behavior, including one's own. Also used to refer to the explanation made for a particular behavior. (p. 525)

audition The technical term for the sense of hearing. (p. 108)

authoritarian parenting style Parenting style in which parents are demanding and unresponsive toward their children's needs or wishes. (p. 423)

authoritative parents Parenting style in which parents set clear standards for their children's behavior, but are also responsive to the children's needs and wishes. (p. 423)

autonomic nervous system (aw-toe-NOM-ick) Subdivision of the peripheral nervous system that regulates involuntary functions. (p. 59)

availability heuristic A strategy in which the likelihood of an event is estimated on the basis of how easily other instances of the event are available in memory. (p. 301)

aversive conditioning A relatively ineffective type of behavior therapy that involves repeatedly pairing an aversive stimulus with the occurrence of undesirable behaviors or thoughts. (p. 669)

axon The long, fluid-filled tube that carries a neuron's messages to other body areas. (p. 47)

axon terminals Branches at the end of the neuron's axon that contain tiny pouches or sacs called synaptic vesicles. (p. 50)

B

barbiturates (barb-ITCH-yer-ets) A category of depressant drugs that reduce anxiety and produce sleepiness. (p. 184)

basal metabolic rate (BMR) The rate at which the body, when at rest, uses energy for vital body functions. (p. 343)

basilar membrane (BASE-uh-ler) The membrane within the cochlea of the ear that contains the hair cells. (p. 111)

behavior modification The application of learning principles to help people develop more effective or adaptive behaviors. (p. 219)

behavior therapy A type of psychotherapy that focuses on directly changing maladaptive behavior patterns by using basic learning principles and techniques; also called *behavior modification.* (p. 665)

behavioral genetics An interdisciplinary field that studies the effects of genes and heredity on behavior. (p. 504)

behavioral perspective In learning theory, a general explanation of learning that emphasizes the relationship between outwardly observable behaviors and environmental events, rather than mental processes. (p. 197)

behavioral theories of leader effectiveness Theories of leader effectiveness that focus on differences in the behaviors of effective and ineffective leaders. (p. B-10)

behaviorism School of psychology and theoretical viewpoint that emphasizes the study of observable behaviors, especially as they pertain to the process of learning. (p. 7)

bell and pad treatment A behavior therapy technique used to treat nighttime bedwetting by conditioning arousal from sleep in response to body signals of a full bladder. (p. 669)

beta brain waves Brain wave pattern associated with alert wakefulness. (p. 154)

binocular cues (by-NOCK-you-ler) Distance or depth cues that require the use of both eyes. (p. 124)

biological preparedness In learning theory, the idea that an organism is innately predisposed to form associations between certain stimuli and responses. (p. 230)

biological psychology Specialized branch of psychology that studies the relationship between behavior and body processes and systems. (p. 43)

biomedical therapies The use of medications, electroconvulsive therapy, or other medical treatments to treat the symptoms associated with psychological disorders. (p. 658)

bipolar disorder Often called *manic depression;* a mood disorder involving periods of incapacitating depression alternating with periods of extreme euphoria and excitement. (p. 631)

blaming the victim bias The tendency to blame an innocent victim of misfortune for having somehow caused the problem or for not having taken steps to avoid or prevent it. (p. 527)

blind spot The point where the optic nerve leaves the eye, producing a small gap in the field of vision. (p. 103)

brain The main organ of the nervous system, made up of billions of neurons organized into a complex, integrated hierarchy of structures. (p. 64)

brainstem A region of the brain made up of the hindbrain and the midbrain. (p. 70)

brightness The perceived intensity of a color that corresponds to the amplitude of the light wave. (p. 104)

brightness constancy The perception that the brightness of an object remains the same even though the lighting conditions change. (p. 132)

bulimia nervosa An eating disorder in which a person engages in binge eating and then purges the excessive food consumption by self-induced vomiting or, less often, by taking laxatives or enemas. (p. 348)

bystander effect The phenomenon in which the greater the number of people present, the less likely each individual is to help someone in distress. (p. 555)

C

caffeine (kaff-EEN) A stimulant drug found in coffee, tea, cola drinks, chocolate, and many over-the-counter medications. (p. 186)

California Personality Inventory (CPI) A self-report inventory that assesses personality characteristics in normal populations. (p. 511)

Cannon-Bard theory of emotion The theory that emotions arise from the simultaneous activation of the nervous system, which causes physical arousal, and the cortex, which causes the subjective experience of emotion. (p. 368)

case study A highly detailed description of a single individual or event. (p. 28)

CAT scan (computerized axial tomography) An instrument that produces two-dimensional pictures of brain structures using multiple X-rays that are reassembled by a computer. (p. 67)

catecholamines Hormones secreted by the adrenal medulla that cause rapid physiological arousal; include adrenaline and noradrenaline. (p. 578)

cell body The part of a neuron that contains the nucleus. (p. 46)

central nervous system Division of the nervous system that consists of the brain and spinal cord. (p. 57)

centration In Piaget's theory, the tendency to focus, or *center,* on only one aspect of a situation and ignore other important aspects of the situation. (p. 400)

cerebellum (sare-uh-BELL-um) A large, two-sided hindbrain structure at the back of the brain responsible for muscle coordination, fine motor movements, and maintaining posture and equilibrium. (p. 72)

cerebral cortex (suh-REE-brull or SARE-uh-brull) The wrinkled outer portion of the forebrain, which contains the most sophisticated brain centers. (p. 73)

cerebral hemisphere The nearly symmetrical left and right halves of the cerebral cortex. (p. 73)

cholecystokinin (CCK) (*kole*-eh-*sist*-oh-KINE-in) A hormone that seems to play a role in signaling satiation, or fullness. (p. 340)

chromosome A long, threadlike structure composed of twisted parallel strands of DNA; found in the nucleus of the cell. (p. 383)

chunking Increasing the amount of information that can be held in short-term memory by grouping related items together into a single unit, or "chunk." (p. 247)

circadian rhythm (ser-KADE-ee-en) A cycle or rhythm that is roughly 24 hours long; refers to daily fluctuations in many biological and psychological processes. (p. 148)

classical conditioning The basic learning process that involves repeatedly pairing a neutral stimulus with a response-producing stimulus until the neutral stimulus elicits the same response. (p. 199)

client-centered therapy A type of psychotherapy developed by humanistic psychologist Carl Rogers in which the therapist is nondirective and reflective, and the client directs the focus of each therapy session; also called *person-centered therapy.* (p. 662)

clustering Organizing items into related groups during recall from long-term memory. (p. 251)

cocaine A stimulant drug derived from the coca tree. (p. 187)

cochlea (COKE-lee-uh) The coiled, fluid-filled inner-ear structure that contains the sensory receptors for sound. (p. 110)

cognition The mental activities involved in acquiring, retaining, and using knowledge. (p. 287)

cognitive dissonance An unpleasant state of psychological tension or arousal (*dissonance*) that occurs when two thoughts or perceptions (*cognitions*) are inconsistent; typically results from the awareness that attitudes and behavior are in conflict. (p. 532)

cognitive map Tolman's term to describe the mental representation of the layout of a familiar environment. (p. 223)

cognitive-mediational theory of emotion Lazarus's theory that emotions result from the cognitive appraisal of a situation's effect on personal well-being. (p. 371)

cognitive perspective In learning theory, a general approach to the study of learning that stresses the role of expectations, mental representation, and other mental processes in learning. (p. 220)

cognitive therapies A group of psychotherapies that are based on the assumption that psychological problems are due to maladaptive patterns of thinking; treatment techniques focus on recognizing and altering these unhealthy thinking patterns. (p. 672)

cognitive therapy (CT) A type of cognitive therapy, developed by psychiatrist Aaron T. Beck, that focuses on changing the client's unrealistic beliefs. (p. 675)

collective unconscious In Jung's theory of personality, the hypothesized part of the unconscious mind that is inherited from previous generations and that contains universally shared ancestral experiences and ideas. (p. 483)

collectivistic cultures Cultures that emphasize the needs and goals of the group over the needs and goals of the individual. (p. 12)

color The perceptual experience of different wavelengths of light, involving hue, saturation (purity), and brightness (intensity). (p. 104)

color blindness One of several inherited forms of color deficiency or weakness in which an individual cannot distinguish between certain colors. (p. 105)

competence motivation Motivated behavior directed toward demonstrating competence and exercising control in a situation. (p. 353)

comprehension vocabulary The words that are understood by an infant or child. (p. 397)

compulsions Repetitive behaviors or mental acts that are performed to prevent or reduce anxiety. (p. 624)

concepts The mental categories of objects or ideas based on properties that they share. (p. 289)

concrete operational stage In Piaget's theory, the third stage of cognitive development, which lasts from about age seven to adolescence; characterized by the ability to think logically about concrete objects and situations. (p. 401)

conditional positive regard In Carl Rogers's theory of personality, the sense that you will be valued and loved only if you behave in a way that is acceptable to others; conditional love or acceptance. (p. 489)

conditioned reinforcer A stimulus or event that has acquired reinforcing value by being associated with a primary reinforcer; also called a secondary reinforcer. (p. 209)

conditioned response (CR) The learned, reflexive response to a conditioned stimulus. (p. 200)

conditioned stimulus (CS) A formerly neutral stimulus that acquires the capacity to elicit a reflexive response. (p. 200)

cones The short, thick, pointed sensory receptors of the eye that detect color and are responsible for color vision and visual acuity. (p. 101)

conflict A situation in which a person feels pulled between two or more opposing desires, motives, or goals. (p. 574)

conformity The tendency to adjust one's behavior, attitudes, or beliefs to group norms in response to real or imagined group pressure. (p. 541)

consciousness Personal awareness of mental activities, internal sensations, and the external environment. (p. 146)

conservation In Piaget's theory, the understanding that two equal quantities remain equal even though the form or appearance is rearranged, as long as nothing is added or subtracted. (p. 401)

constructive thinking Responding to situations with automatic thoughts that minimize the stress experienced. (p. 603)

context effect The tendency to recover information more easily when the retrieval occurs in the same setting as the original learning of the information. (p. 256)

continuous reinforcement A schedule of reinforcement in which every occurrence of a particular response is reinforced. (p. 215)

control group The group of subjects who are exposed to all experimental conditions, except the independent variable. (p. 23)

coping Behavioral and cognitive responses used to contend with stressors; involves efforts to change circumstances, or one's interpretation of circumstances, to make them more favorable and less threatening. (p. 596)

cornea (CORE-nee-uh) A clear membrane covering the visible part of the eye that helps gather and direct incoming light. (p. 99)

corpus callosum A thick band of nerve fibers that connects the two cerebral hemispheres and acts as a communication link between them. (p. 73)

correlation The relationship between two variables. (p. A-8)

correlation coefficient A measure of the magnitude and direction of the relationship (the correlation) between two variables. The closer the correlation coefficient is to +1 or −1, the stronger the relationship is. A *positive* correlation coefficient indicates that as one variable increases, the other tends to increase. A *negative* correlation coefficient indicates that as one variable increases, the other tends to decrease. (p. A-9)

correlational study A research strategy that allows the precise calculation of how strongly related two factors are to one another. (p. 31)

corticosteroids Hormones released by the adrenal cortex that play a key role in the body's response to long-term stressors. (p. 580)

counterconditioning A behavior therapy technique based on classical conditioning that involves modifying behavior by conditioning a new response that is incompatible with a previously learned response. (p. 665)

creativity A group of cognitive processes used to generate useful, original, and novel ideas or solutions. (p. 328)

critical thinking The active process of trying to minimize the influence of preconceptions and biases while rationally evaluating evidence, determining what conclusions can be drawn from the evidence, and considering alternative explanations. (p. 17)

cryptomnesia (krip-tome-NEE-zha) A memory-distortion phenomenon in which a "hidden," or unremembered, memory becomes the basis for a seemingly "new" memory. (p. 262)

cued recall A test of long-term memory that involves remembering an item of information in response to a retrieval cue. (p. 254)

culture The attitudes, values, beliefs, and behaviors shared by a group of people and communicated from one generation to another. (p. 11)

cyclothymic disorder A mood disorder characterized by moderate but frequent mood swings that are not severe enough to qualify as bipolar disorder. (p. 632)

D

daily hassles Everyday, minor events that annoy and upset people. (p. 573)

deafness The complete or partial loss of hearing. (p. 111)

decay theory The view that forgetting is due to normal metabolic processes that occur in the brain over time. (p. 271)

decibel (DESS-uh-bell) The unit of measurement for loudness. (p. 108)

deindividuation The reduction of self-awareness and inhibitions that can occur when a person is part of a group whose members feel anonymous. (p. 560)

delusion A falsely held belief that persists in spite of contradictory evidence. (p. 641)

dendrites Multiple short fibers that extend from the neuron's cell body and receive information from other neurons or sensory receptor cells. (p. 46)

deoxyribonucleic acid (DNA) The chemical basis of heredity; carries the genetic instructions in the cell. (p. 383)

dependent variable The factor that is observed and measured for change in an experiment; thought to be influenced by the independent variable. (p. 22)

depressants A category of psychoactive drugs that depress or inhibit brain activity. (p. 182)

depth perception The use of visual cues to perceive the distance or three-dimensional characteristics of objects. (p. 124)

descriptive methods Scientific procedures that involve systematically observing behavior in order to describe the relationships among behaviors and events. (p. 27)

descriptive statistics Statistics used to organize and summarize data in a meaningful way. (p. A-2)

developmental psychology The branch of psychology that studies how people change over the lifespan. (p. 381)

difference threshold The smallest possible difference between two stimuli that can be detected half the time. Also called *just noticeable difference*. (p. 97)

diffusion of responsibility The phenomenon in which the presence of other people makes it less likely that any individual will help someone in distress because the obligation to intervene is shared among all the onlookers. (p. 555)

discrepancy hypothesis An approach to explaining job satisfaction that focuses on the discrepancy, if any, between what a person wants from a job and how that person evaluates what is experienced at work. (p. B-9)

discriminative stimulus In operant conditioning, a specific stimulus in the presence of which a particular response is more likely to be reinforced, and in the absence of which a particular response is not reinforced. (p. 212)

displacement In psychoanalytic theory, the Ego defense mechanism that involves unconsciously shifting the target of an emotional urge to a substitute target that is less threatening or dangerous. (p. 478)

display rules Social and cultural rules that regulate the expression of emotions, particularly facial expressions. (p. 364)

dispositional factors hypothesis The view that a person's level of job satisfaction may be due in part to a genetically based disposition toward a positive or negative outlook. (p. B-9)

dissociation The splitting of consciousness into two or more simultaneous streams of mental activity. (p. 175)

dissociative amnesia A dissociative disorder involving the partial or total inability to recall important personal information. (p. 637)

dissociative disorders A category of psychological disorders in which extreme and frequent disruptions of awareness, memory, and personal identity impair the ability to function. (p. 637)

dissociative experience A break or disruption in consciousness during which awareness, memory, and personal identity become separated or divided. (p. 635)

dissociative fugue A dissociative disorder involving sudden and unexpected travel away from home, extensive amnesia, and identity confusion. (p. 637)

dissociative identity disorder (DID) Formerly called *multiple personality disorder;* a dissociative disorder involving extensive memory disruptions along with the presence of two or more distinct identities or "personalities." (p. 637)

dominant gene In a pair of genes, the gene containing genetic instructions that will be expressed whether paired with another dominant gene or with a recessive gene. (p. 384)

dopamine (DOPE-uh-meen) Neurotransmitter that is involved in the regulation of bodily movements and thought processes. (p. 55)

dopamine hypothesis The view that schizophrenia is related to, and may be caused by, excess activity of the neurotransmitter dopamine in the brain. (p. 647)

dream A story-like episode of unfolding mental imagery during sleep. (p. 166)

dream interpretation A technique used in psychoanalysis in which the content of dreams is analyzed for disguised or symbolic wishes, meanings, and motivations. (p. 659)

drive An impulse that activates behavior to reduce a need and restore homeostasis. (p. 336)

drive theories The view that behavior is motivated by the desire to reduce internal tension caused by unmet biological needs. (p. 336)

drug abuse Recurrent drug use that results in disruptions in academic, social, or occupational functioning, or in legal or psychological problems. (p. 181)

drug rebound effect Withdrawal symptoms that are the opposite of a physically addictive drug's action. (p. 180)

DSM-IV Abbreviation for the *Diagnostic and Statistical Manual of Mental Disorders,* fourth edition; the book published by the American Psychiatric Association that describes the specific symptoms and diagnostic guidelines for different psychological disorders. (p. 614)

dyspareunia A sexual dysfunction characterized by genital pain before, during, or after intercourse. (p. 459)

dysthymic disorder A mood disorder involving chronic, low-grade feelings of depression that produce subjective discomfort but do not seriously impair the ability to function. (p. 630)

E

eardrum A tightly stretched membrane at the end of the ear canal that vibrates when sound waves hit it. (p. 109)

eclecticism The pragmatic and integrated use of techniques from different psychotherapies. (p. 687)

ecological perspective In learning theory, a general approach that emphasizes that the study of learning must consider the unique behavior patterns of different species that have evolved in relation to the species' natural environment. (p. 229)

EEG The graphic record of brain activity produced by an electroencephalograph. (p. 154)

Ego Latin for "I"; in Freud's theory of personality, the partly conscious rational component of personality that regulates thoughts and behavior and is most in touch with the demands of the external world. (p. 476)

Ego defense mechanisms In psychoanalytic theory, largely unconscious distortions of thought or perception that act to reduce anxiety. (p. 478)

egocentrism In Piaget's theory, the inability to take another person's perspective or point of view. (p. 400)

elaborative rehearsal Rehearsal that involves focusing on the meaning of information to help encode and transfer it to long-term memory. (p. 248)

electroconvulsive therapy (ECT) A biomedical therapy used primarily in the treatment of depression that involves electrically inducing a brief brain seizure; also called *shock therapy* and *electric shock therapy.* (p. 695)

electroencephalograph (electro-en-SEFF-uh-low-graph) An instrument that uses electrodes placed on the scalp to measure and record the brain's electrical activity. (pp. 67, 154)

embryonic period The second period of prenatal development, extending from the third week through the eighth week. (p. 387)

emotion A distinct psychological state that involves subjective experience, physical arousal, and a behavioral expression or response. (p. 357)

emotion-focused coping Coping efforts primarily aimed at relieving or regulating the emotional impact of a stressful situation. (p. 597)

encoding The process of transforming information into a form that can be entered into and retained by the memory system. (p. 241)

encoding failure The inability to recall specific information because of insufficient encoding for storage in long-term memory. (p. 267)

encoding specificity principle The principle that when the conditions of information retrieval are similar to the conditions of information encoding, retrieval is more likely to be successful. (p. 255)

endocrine system (EN-doe-krin) A system of glands located throughout the body that secrete hormones into the bloodstream. (p. 62)

endorphins (en-DORF-ins) Neurotransmitters that regulate pain perception. (p. 56)

episodic information Long-term memory of personally experienced events; also called *autobiographical memory.* (p. 250)

ergonomics The science of applying knowledge about human physical characteristics to the design of equipment that minimizes fatigue and discomfort and maximizes productivity. (p. B-2)

Eros In Freud's theory of personality, the self-preservation or life instinct, reflected in the expression of basic biological urges that perpetuate the existence of the individual and the species. (p. 476)

ESP or extrasensory perception Perception of sensory information by some means other than through the normal processes of sensation. (p. 123)

ethnocentrism The belief that one's own culture or ethnic group is superior to all others, and the related tendency to use one's own culture as a standard by which to judge other cultures. (pp. 12, 537)

evolutionary theory of sleep The view that the unique sleep patterns of different animals evolved over time to help promote survival and environmental adaptation. (p. 161)

expectancy effect Change in a subject's behavior produced by the subject's belief that change should happen. (p. 25)

experimental group The group of subjects who are exposed to all experimental conditions, including the independent variable. (p. 24)

experimental method A method of investigation used to demonstrate cause-and-effect relationships by purposely manipulating a factor thought to produce change in a second factor. (p. 22)

extinction In learning theory, the gradual weakening and disappearance of conditioned behavior. In classical conditioning, extinction occurs when the conditioned stimulus is repeatedly presented without the unconditioned stimulus. In operant conditioning, extinction occurs when an emitted behavior is no longer followed by a reinforcer. (pp. 202, 215)

F

facial feedback hypothesis The view that expressing a specific emotion, especially facially, causes the subjective experience of that emotion. (p. 368)

family therapy A form of psychotherapy that is based on the assumption that the family is a system and that treats the family as a unit. (p. 679)

female orgasmic disorder In females, sexual dysfunction characterized by consistent delays in achieving orgasm or the inability to achieve orgasm. (p. 459)

fetal period The third and longest period of prenatal development, extending from the eighth week until birth. (p. 388)

fight-or-flight response A rapidly occurring chain of internal physical reactions that prepare people either to fight or take flight from an immediate threat. (pp. 60, 578)

figure–ground relationship A Gestalt principle of perceptual organization that states that we automatically separate the elements of a perception into the feature that clearly stands out (the figure) and its less distinct background (the ground). (p. 129)

five-factor model of personality A trait theory of personality that identifies five basic source traits (extraversion, neuroticism, agreeableness, conscientiousness, and openness to experience) as the fundamental building blocks of personality. (p. 501)

fixed-interval (FI) schedule In operant conditioning, a reinforcement schedule in which a reinforcer is delivered for the first response that occurs after a fixed time interval has elapsed. (p. 217)

fixed-ratio (FR) schedule In operant conditioning, a reinforcement schedule in which a reinforcer is delivered after a fixed number of responses has occurred. (p. 216)

flashbulb memory The recall of very specific images or details surrounding a vivid, rare, or significant personal event. (p. 258)

forebrain The largest and most complex brain region, which contains centers for complex behaviors and mental processes. (p. 73)

forgetting The inability to recall information that was previously available. (p. 265)

formal concept A mental category that is formed by learning the rules or features that define it. (p. 290)

formal operational stage In Piaget's theory, the forth stage of cognitive development, which lasts from adolescence through adulthood; characterized by the ability to think logically about abstract principles and hypothetical situations. (p. 401)

fovea (FOH-vee-uh) A small area in the center of the retina that is composed entirely of cones, where visual information is most sharply focused. (p. 102)

free association A psychoanalytic technique in which the patient spontaneously reports all thoughts, feelings, and mental images as they come to mind. (p. 473)

frequency In hearing, the rate of vibration, or the number of sound waves per second. (p. 108)

frequency distribution A summary of how often various scores occur in a sample of scores. Score values are arranged in order of magnitude and the number of times each score occurs is recorded. (p. A-3)

frequency polygon A way of graphically representing a frequency distribution; frequency is marked above each score category on the graph's horizontal axis, and the marks are connected by straight lines. (p. A-4)

frequency theory In hearing, the view that the basilar membrane vibrates at the same frequency as the sound wave. (p. 111)

frontal lobe The largest lobe of the cerebral cortex; processes voluntary muscle movements and is involved in thinking, planning, and emotional expression and control. (p. 74)

functional fixedness The tendency to view objects as functioning only in their usual or customary way. (p. 297)

functionalism Early school of psychology which emphasized studying the purpose, or function, of behavior and mental experiences. (p. 5)

fundamental attribution error The tendency to attribute the behavior of others to internal, personal characteristics, while ignoring or underestimating the effects of external, situational factors; an attributional bias that is common in individualistic cultures. (p. 526)

G

***g* factor (general intelligence)** The notion of a general intelligence factor that is responsible for a person's overall performance on tests of mental ability. (p. 316)

gate-control theory The theory that pain is a product of both physiological and psychological factors that cause spinal "gates" to open and relay patterns of intense stimulation to the brain, which perceives them as pain. (p. 118)

gender The cultural, social, and psychological meanings that are associated with masculinity or femininity. (p. 431)

gender identity A person's psychological sense of being either male or female. (p. 431)

gender identity disorder A persistent discomfort about one's assigned gender along with the desire to be a member of the opposite sex. (p. 461)

gender roles The behaviors, attitudes, and personality traits that are designated as either masculine or feminine in a given culture. (p. 431)

gender schema theory The theory that gender-role development is influenced by the formation of schemas, or mental representations, of masculinity and femininity. (p. 440)

gender-role stereotypes The beliefs and expectations that people hold about the typical characteristics, preferences, and behavior of men and women. (p. 432)

gene The basic unit of heredity that directs the development of a particular characteristic; the individual unit of DNA instructions on a chromosome. (p. 383)

general adaptation syndrome Selye's term for the three-stage progression of physical changes that occur when an organism is exposed to intense and prolonged stress. The three stages are alarm, resistance, and exhaustion. (p. 579)

generalized anxiety disorder An anxiety disorder characterized by excessive, global, and persistent symptoms of anxiety; also called *free-floating anxiety*. (p. 618)

genotype (JEEN-oh-type) The underlying genetic makeup of a particular organism, including the genetic instructions for traits that are not actually displayed. (p. 384)

germinal period The first two weeks of prenatal development. (p. 387)

Gestalt psychology (geh-SHTALT) A school of psychology founded in Germany in the early 1900s that maintained that our sensations are actively processed according to consistent perceptual rules that result in meaningful whole perceptions, or gestalts. (pp. 8, 122)

glass ceiling An invisible but strong barrier of subtle, unofficial discrimination that prevents women or minorities from being promoted to the highest levels of leadership in an organization. (p. B-11)

glial cells (GLEE-ull) Support cells that assist neurons by providing structural support, nutrition, and removal of cell wastes; also manufacture myelin. (p. 45)

gonads The endocrine glands that secrete hormones that regulate sexual characteristics and reproductive processes; ovaries in females and testes in males. (p. 64)

group therapy A form of psychotherapy that involves one or more therapists working simultaneously with a small group of clients. (p. 677)

H

hair cells The hairlike sensory receptors for sound, found in the basilar membrane of the cochlea. (p. 111)

hallucination A false or distorted perception that seems vividly real to the person experiencing it. (p. 642)

health psychology The branch of psychology that studies how psychological factors influence health, illness, medical treatment, and health-related behaviors. (p. 570)

heritabililty The percentage of variation within a given population that is due to heredity. (p. 321)

heritability estimate A numerical estimate of the degree to which differences within a specific group of people are due to heredity. (p. 504)

heuristic A problem-solving strategy that involves following a general rule of thumb to reduce the number of possible solutions. (p. 294)

hidden observer Hilgard's term for the hidden, or dissociated, stream of mental activity during hypnosis. (p. 175)

hierarchy of needs Maslow's hierarchical division of motivation into levels that progress from basic physical needs to psychological needs to self-fulfillment needs. (pp. 337, 488)

hindbrain A region at the base of the brain that contains several structures that regulate basic life functions. (p. 70)

hippocampus A curved forebrain structure that is part of the limbic system and is involved in learning and forming new memories. (p. 78)

histogram A way of graphically representing a frequency distribution; a type of bar chart using vertical bars that touch.(p. A-3)

homeostasis (home-ee-oh-STAY-sis) The notion that the body monitors and maintains internal states, such as body temperature and energy supplies, at relatively constant levels. (p. 336)

hormones Chemical messengers secreted into the bloodstream by endocrine glands. (p. 62)

hue The property of wavelengths of light known as color, with different wavelengths corresponding to our perceptual experience of different colors. (p. 104)

human factors A sub-area of I/O psychology that focuses on the design of equipment and the development of work procedures in light of human capabilities and limitations. (p. B-2)

humanistic psychology School of psychology and theoretical viewpoint on personality that generally emphasizes the inherent goodness of people, human potential, self-actualization, the self-concept, and healthy personality development. (pp. 9, 488)

hypermnesia (high-perm-NEES-zha) A phenomenon in which a person's memory for past events is presumably enhanced through the use of hypnotic suggestion. (p. 174)

hypnagogic hallucinations (hip-nah-GO-jick) Vivid sensory phenomena that can occur during the onset of sleep. (p. 154)

hypnosis (hip-NO-sis) A cooperative social interaction in which a person responds to suggestions with changes in perception, memory, and behavior. (p. 172)

hypoactive sexual desire disorder A sexual dysfunction characterized by little or no sexual desire. (p. 459)

hypothalamus (hi-poe-THAL-uh-muss) A peanut-sized forebrain structure that is part of the limbic system and regulates behaviors related to survival, such as eating, drinking, and sexual activity. (p. 77)

hypothesis (high-POTH-eh-sis) A tentative statement about the relationship between two or more variables. (p. 18)

I

Id Latin for "the it"; in Freud's theory of personality, the completely unconscious, irrational component of personality that seeks immediate satisfaction of instinctual urges and drives; ruled by the pleasure principle. (p. 476)

identification In psychoanalytic theory, an Ego defense mechanism that involves reducing anxiety by modeling the behavior and characteristics of another person. (p. 480)

identity A person's definition or description of himself or herself, including the values, beliefs, and ideals that guide the individual's behavior. (p. 407)

immune system Body system that produces specialized white blood cells that protect the body from viruses, bacteria, and tumor cells. (p. 580)

implicit personality theory A network of assumptions or beliefs about the relationships among various types of people, traits, and behaviors. (p. 524)

in-group A social group to which one belongs. (p. 536)

in-group bias The tendency to judge the behavior of in-group members favorably and out-group members unfavorably. (p. 536)

incentive theories The view that behavior is motivated by the "pull" of external goals, such as rewards. (p. 337)

independent variable The purposely manipulated factor thought to produce change in an experiment. (p. 22)

individualistic cultures Cultures that emphasize the needs and goals of the individual over the needs and goals of the group. (p. 12)

induction A discipline technique that combines parental control with explaining why a behavior is prohibited. (p. 424)

industrial/organizational (I/O) psychology The branch of psychology that focuses on the study of human behavior at work. (p. B-1)

infancy The first two years of life. (p. 389)

inferential statistics Statistical techniques that allow researchers to determine whether the outcomes in a study are likely to be more than just chance events and whether they can be legitimately generalized to a larger population. (p. A-12)

information-processing model of cognitive development The model that views cognitive development as a continuous process over the lifespan and that studies the development of basic mental processes like attention, memory, and problem solving. (p. 404)

informational social influence Behavior that is motivated by the desire to be correct. (p. 542)

inhalants Chemical substances that are inhaled to produce an alteration in consciousness. (p. 184)

inner ear The part of the ear where sound is transduced into neural impulses; consists of the cochlea and semicircular canals. (p. 110)

insight The sudden realization of how a problem can be solved. (p. 295)

insomnia A condition in which a person regularly experiences the inability to fall asleep, stay asleep, or feel adequately rested by sleep. (p. 163)

instinct theories The view that some motives are innate and due to genetic programming. (p. 335)

instinctive drift The tendency of an animal to revert to instinctive behaviors which can interfere with the performance of an operantly conditioned response. (p. 232)

intelligence The global capacity to think rationally, act purposefully, and deal effectively with the environment. (p. 310)

intelligence quotient (IQ) A global measure of intelligence derived by comparing an individual's score to that of others in the same age group. (p. 311)

interference theory The theory that forgetting is caused by one memory competing with or replacing another. (p. 267)

interneuron Type of neuron that communicates information from one neuron to the next. (p. 45)

interpretation A technique used in psychoanalysis in which the psychoanalyst offers a carefully timed explanation of the patient's dreams, free associations, or behavior to facilitate the recognition of unconscious conflicts or motivations. (p. 659)

intuition Coming to a conclusion or making a judgment without conscious awareness of the thought processes involved. (p. 296)

iridology (EYE-ruh-*doll*-uh-jee) A popular pseudoscience based on the unproven notion that the physical and psychological functioning of an individual is represented in the color and markings of the iris of the eye. (p. 100)

iris (EYE-riss) The colored part of the eye, which is the muscle that controls the size of the pupil. (p. 99)

irreversibility In Piaget's theory, the inability to mentally reverse a sequence of events or logical operations. (p. 400)

J

James-Lange theory of emotion The theory that emotions arise from the perception and interpretation of bodily changes. (p. 366)

job analysis An assessment of the major responsibilities of a particular job and the human characteristics needed to fill it. (p. B-5)

just noticeable difference (jnd) The smallest possible difference between two stimuli that can be detected half the time. Also called *difference threshold*. (p. 97)

just-world hypothesis The assumption that the world is fair, and therefore that people get what they deserve and deserve what they get. (p. 527)

K

kinesthetic sense (kin-ess-THET-ick) The technical name for the sense of location and position of body parts in relation to one another. (p. 120)

L

language A system for combining arbitrary symbols to produce an infinite number of meaningful statements. (p. 302)

latent learning Tolman's term to describe learning that occurs in the absence of reinforcement but is not behaviorally demonstrated until a reinforcer becomes available. (p. 223)

Law of Effect Learning principle espoused by Thorndike that responses followed by a satisfying effect become strengthened and are more likely to recur in a particular situation, while responses followed by a dissatisfying effect are weakened and less likely to recur in a particular situation. (p. 206)

learned helplessness A phenomenon in which exposure to inescapable and uncontrollable aversive events produces passive behavior. (p. 224)

learning A relatively permanent change in behavior as a result of past experience. (p. 196)

lens A transparent structure located behind the pupil that actively focuses, or bends, light as it enters the eye. (p. 101)

levels of processing framework The view that information that is processed at a "deeper" (more meaningful) level is more likely to be remembered than information that is processed at a "shallow" level. (p. 249)

libido In Freud's theory of personality, the psychological and emotional energy associated with expressions of sexuality; the sex drive. (p. 476)

limbic system A group of forebrain structures, including the hypothalamus, thalamus, amygdala, and hippocampus, that form a border around the brainstem; collectively these structures are involved in emotion, motivation, learning, and memory. (p. 78)

linguistic relativity hypothesis The notion that differences among languages cause differences in the thoughts of their speakers. (p. 305)

lithium A naturally occurring substance that is used in the treatment of bipolar disorder. (p. 692)

long-term memory The stage of memory that represents the long-term storage of information. (p. 243)

loudness The intensity (or amplitude) of a sound wave, measured in decibels. (p. 108)

LSD A synthetic psychedelic drug. (p. 188)

lucid dream A dream in which the sleeper is aware that he or she is dreaming. (p. 169)

lymphocytes Specialized white blood cells that are responsible for immune defenses. (p. 580)

M

magnetic resonance imaging scanner (MRI) An instrument that provides three-dimensional, highly detailed views of the brain using electrical signals generated by the brain in response to magnetic fields. (p. 67)

maintenance rehearsal The mental or verbal repetition of information in order to maintain it beyond the usual 30-second duration of short-term memory. (p. 246)

major depression A mood disorder characterized by extreme and persistent feelings of despondency, worthlessness, and hopelessness, causing impaired emotional, cognitive, behavioral, and physical functioning. (p. 628)

male erectile disorder In males, sexual dysfunction characterized by a recurring inability to achieve or maintain an erect penis. (p. 459)

male orgasmic disorder In males, sexual dysfunction characterized by de-layed orgasm during intercourse or the inability to achieve orgasm during intercourse. (p. 459)

manic episode A sudden, rapidly escalating emotional state characterized by extreme euphoria, excitement, physical energy, and rapid thoughts and speech. (p. 631)

marijuana A psychoactive drug derived from the hemp plant. (p. 188)

mean The sum of a set of scores in a distribution divided by the number of scores. The mean is usually the most representative measure of central tendency. (p. A-5)

measure of central tendency A single number that presents some information about the "center" of a frequency distribution. (p. A-5)

measure of variability A single number that presents information about the spread of scores in a frequency distribution. (p. A-6)

median The score that divides a frequency distribution exactly in half, so that the same number of scores lies on each side of it. (p. A-5)

meditation Any one of a number of sustained concentration techniques that focus attention and heighten awareness. (p. 177)

medulla (meh-DULL-uh) A hindbrain structure that controls vital life functions such as breathing, circulation, and muscle tone. (p. 71)

melatonin (mel-uh-TONE-in) A hormone manufactured by the pineal gland that produces sleepiness. (p. 149)

memory The mental processes that enable us to retain and use information over time. (p. 241)

memory consolidation The gradual, physical process of converting new long-term memories to stable, enduring long-term memory codes. (p. 277)

memory trace The brain changes associated with a particular stored memory. (p. 272)

menarche A female's first menstrual period, which occurs during puberty. (p. 452)

menopause The natural cessation of menstruation and the end of reproductive capacity in women. (p. 412)

mental age A measurement of intelligence in which an individual's mental level is expressed in terms of the average abilities of a given age group. (p. 311)

mental image The mental representation of objects or events that are not physically present. (p. 287)

mental set The tendency to persist in solving problems with solutions that have worked in the past. (p. 297)

mescaline A psychedelic drug derived from the peyote cactus. (p. 188)

meta-analysis A statistical technique that involves combining and analyzing the results of many research studies on a specific topic in order to identify overall trends. (p. 19)

midbrain The smallest brain region, which helps coordinate auditory and visual sensations. (p. 72)

middle ear The part of the ear that amplifies sound waves and consists of three small bones, the hammer, the anvil, and the stirrup. (p. 110)

Minnesota Multiphasic Personality Inventory (MMPI) A self-report inventory that assesses personality characteristics and psychological disorders; used to assess both normal and disturbed populations. (p. 511)

misinformation effect A memory-distortion phenomenon in which people's existing memories can be altered by exposing them to misleading information. (p. 263)

mode The most frequently occurring score in a distribution. (p. A-5)

monocular cues (moe-NOCK-you-ler) Distance or depth cues that can be processed by either eye alone. (p. 124)

mood congruence An encoding specificity phenomenon in which a given mood tends to evoke memories that are consistent with that mood. (p. 257)

mood-dependent retrieval An encoding specificity phenomenon in which information encoded in a certain emotional state is most retrievable when the person is in the same emotional state. (p. 257)

mood disorders A category of mental disorders in which significant and chronic disruption in mood is the predominant symptom, causing impaired cognitive, behavioral, and physical functioning. (p. 627)

moon illusion A visual illusion involving the misperception that the moon is larger when it is on the horizon that when it is directly overhead. (p. 134)

moral reasoning The aspect of cognitive development that has to do with the way an individual reasons about moral decisions. (p. 409)

motivated forgetting The theory that forgetting occurs because an undesired memory is held back from awareness. (p. 268)

motivation The forces that act on or within an organism to initiate and direct behavior. (p. 334)

motor neuron Type of neuron that signals muscles to relax or contract. (p. 45)

Müller-Lyer illusion A famous visual illusion involving the misperception of the identical length of two lines, one with arrows pointed inward, one with arrows pointed outward. (p. 133)

myelin sheath (MY-eh-linn) A white, fatty covering wrapped around the axons of some neurons that increases their communication speed. (p. 47)

N

narcolepsy A sleep disorder characterized by excessive daytime sleepiness and brief lapses into sleep throughout the day. (p. 165)

natural concept A mental category that is formed as a result of everyday experience. (p. 290)

naturalistic observation The systematic observation and recording of behaviors as they occur in their natural setting. (p. 27)

negative correlation A finding that two factors vary systematically in opposite directions, one increasing as the other decreases. (p. 31)

negative reinforcement In operant conditioning, a situation in which a response results in the removal, avoidance, or escape of a punishing stimulus, increasing the likelihood of the response being repeated in similar situations. (p. 208)

negative symptoms In schizophrenia, symptoms that reflect defects or deficits in normal functioning, and include greatly reduced emotional expressiveness, motivation, and/or speech. (pp. 641, 644)

nerve Bundle of neuron axons that carries information in the peripheral nervous system. (p. 57)

nervous system The primary internal communication network of the body; divided into the central nervous system and the peripheral nervous system. (p. 56)

neuron Highly specialized cell that communicates information in electrical and chemical form; a nerve cell. (p. 44)

neurotransmitter Chemical messenger manufactured by a neuron. (p. 50)

nicotine A stimulant drug found in tobacco products. (p. 186)

night terrors A sleep disturbance characterized by an episode of increased physiological arousal, intense fear and panic, frightening hallucinations, and no recall of the episode the next morning; typically occurs during stage 3 or stage 4 NREM sleep; also called *sleep terror*. (p. 164)

nightmare A frightening or unpleasant anxiety dream that occurs during REM sleep. (p. 168)

norepinephrine (nor-ep-in-EF-rin) Neurotransmitter involved in learning and memory; also a hormone manufactured by the adrenal glands. (p. 55)

normal curve (**normal distribution**) A bell-shaped distribution of individual differences in a normal population in which most scores cluster around the average score. (p. 315)

normative social influence Behavior that is motivated by the desire to gain social acceptance and approval. (p. 542)

NREM sleep Nondreaming quiet sleep, which is divided into four stages. (p. 154)

O

obedience The performance of an action in response to the direct orders of an authority or person of higher status. (p. 543)

obese Weighing 20 percent or more above one's "ideal" body weight. (p. 346)

object permanence In Piaget's theory, the understanding that an object continues to exist even when it can no longer be seen. (p. 399)

observational learning Learning that occurs through observing the actions of others. (p. 225)

obsessions Repeated, intrusive, and uncontrollable irrational thoughts or mental images that cause extreme anxiety and distress. (p. 624)

obsessive-compulsive disorder An anxiety disorder in which the symptoms of anxiety are triggered by intrusive, repetitive thoughts and urges to perform certain actions. (p. 624)

occipital lobe (ock-SIP-it-ull) An area at the back of each cerebral hemisphere that is the primary receiving area for visual information. (p. 74)

Oedipus complex In Freud's theory of personality, a child's unconscious sexual desire for the opposite-sex parent, usually accompanied by hostile feelings toward the same-sex parent. (p. 480)

olfactory bulb (ole-FACK-toe-ree) The enlarged ending of the olfactory cortex at the front of the brain where the sensation of smell is registered. (p. 113)

operant In operant conditioning, Skinner's term for an actively emitted (or voluntary) behavior that operates on the environment to produce consequences. (p. 206)

operant conditioning The basic learning process that involves changing the probability of a response being repeated by manipulating the consequences of that response. (p. 207)

operational definition A precise description of how the variables in a study will be manipulated or measured. (p.18)

opiates (OH-pee-ets) A category of psychoactive drugs that are chemically similar to morphine and have strong pain-relieving properties. (p. 185)

opponent-process theory of color vision The theory that color vision is the product of opposing pairs of color receptors, red/green, blue/yellow, and black/white; when one member of a color pair is stimulated, the other member is inhibited. (p. 106)

optic nerve The thick nerve that exits from the back of the eye and carries visual information to the occipital lobe and primary visual cortex in the brain. (p. 103)

optimistic explanatory style Accounting for negative events or situations with external, unstable, and specific explanations. (p. 586)

organizational behavior A sub-area of I/O psychology that focuses on how the organization and the social environment in which people work affect their attitudes and behaviors. (p. B-2)

organizational development (OD) A sub-area of I/O psychology that focuses on bringing about positive change in an organization, such as increased profitability or improved products. (p. B-2)

out-group A social group to which one does not belong. (p. 536)

out-group homogeneity effect The tendency to see members of an out-group as very similar to one another. (p. 536)

outer ear The part of the ear that collects sound waves and consists of the pinna, the ear canal, and the eardrum. (p. 109)

P

pain The unpleasant sensation of physical discomfort or suffering that can occur in varying degrees of intensity. (p. 118)

panic attack A sudden episode of extreme anxiety that rapidly escalates in intensity. (p. 618)

panic disorder An anxiety disorder in which the person experiences frequent and unexpected panic attacks. (p. 618)

paraphilia (pair-uh-FILL-ee-uh) Any of several forms of nontraditional sexual behavior in which a person's sexual gratification depends on an unusual sexual experience, object, or fantasy. (p. 460)

parapsychology The study of claims about various forms of extrasensory perception. (p. 123)

parasympathetic nervous system Branch of the autonomic nervous system that maintains normal body functions and conserves the body's physical resources. (p. 61)

parietal lobe (puh-RYE-et-ull) An area on each hemisphere of the cerebral cortex located above the temporal lobe that processes somatic sensations. (p. 74)

partial reinforcement In operant conditioning, a situation in which the occurrence of a particular response is only sometimes followed by a reinforcer. (p. 216)

partial reinforcement effect In operant conditioning, the phenomenon by which behaviors that are conditioned using partial reinforcement are more resistant to extinction than behaviors that are conditioned using continuous reinforcement. (p. 216)

perception The process of integrating, organizing, and interpreting sensations. (p. 95)

perceptual constancy The tendency to perceive objects, especially familiar objects, as constant and unchanging despite changes in sensory input. (p. 131)

perceptual illusion The misperception of the true characteristics of an object or an image. (p. 133)

perceptual set The influence of prior assumptions and expectations on perceptual interpretations. (p. 138)

peripheral nervous system (per-IF-er-ull) Division of the nervous system that includes all the nerves lying outside the central nervous system. (p. 59)

permissive parenting style Parenting style in which parents are extremely tolerant and not demanding; permissive-indulgent parents are responsive to their children, while permissive-indifferent parents are not. (p. 423)

person perception The mental processes used to form judgments and draw conclusions about the characteristics and motives of others. (p. 521)

personality An individual's unique and relatively consistent patterns of thinking, feeling, and behaving. (p. 471)

personality theory A theory that attempts to describe and explain individual similarities and differences. (p. 471)

personnel psychology A sub-area of I/O psychology that focuses on matching people's characteristics to job requirements, accurately measuring job performance, and assessing employee training needs. (p. B-1)

persuasion The deliberate attempt to influence the attitudes or behavior of another person in a situation in which that person has some freedom of choice. (p. 561)

pessimistic explanatory style Accounting for negative events or situations with internal, stable, and global explanations. (p. 586)

PET scan (positron emission tomography) An instrument that provides color-coded images of brain activity by measuring the amount of glucose or oxygen used in different brain regions. (p. 67)

phenotype (FEEN-oh-type) The observable traits or characteristics of an organism as determined by the interaction of genetics and environmental factors. (p. 384)

pheromones (FARE-uh-mones) Chemical signals used by animals to communicate territorial boundaries and sexual receptiveness. (p. 115)

phobia An irrational fear triggered by a specific object or situation. (p. 620)

physical dependence A condition in which a person has physically adapted to a drug so that he or she must take the drug

regularly in order to avoid withdrawal symptoms. (p. 180)

pitch The relative highness or lowness of a sound, determined by the frequency of a sound wave. (p. 108)

pituitary gland (pi-TOO-ih-tare-ee) Endocrine gland attached to the base of the brain that secretes hormones that affect the function of other glands as well as hormones that act directly on physical processes. (p. 63)

place theory In hearing, the view that different frequencies cause larger vibrations at different locations along the basilar membrane. (p. 111)

placebo control group (pluh-SEE-bo) An experimental control group in which subjects are exposed to a fake independent variable. (p. 25)

pleasure principle In Freud's theory of personality, the motive to obtain pleasure and avoid tension or discomfort; the most fundamental human motive and the guiding principle of the Id. (p. 476)

pons A hindbrain structure that connects the medulla to the two sides of the cerebellum; helps coordinate and integrate movements on each side of the body. (p. 72)

population In statistics, a complete set of something—people, nonhuman animals, objects, or events. (p. A-13)

positive correlation A finding that two factors vary systematically in the same direction, increasing or decreasing together. (p. 31)

positive reinforcement In operant conditioning, a situation in which a response is followed by the addition of a reinforcing stimulus, increasing the likelihood of the response being repeated in similar situations. (p. 207)

positive symptoms In schizophrenia, symptoms that reflect excesses or distortions of normal functioning, and include delusions, hallucinations, and disorganized thoughts and behavior. (p. 640)

possible selves The aspect of the self-concept that includes images of the selves that you hope, fear, or expect to become in the future. (p. 514)

posthypnotic amnesia A hypnotic suggestion that suppresses the ability to recall specific information. (p. 174)

posthypnotic suggestion A suggestion made during hypnosis that the person carry out a specific instruction following the hypnotic session. (p. 174)

posttraumatic stress disorder (PTSD) An anxiety disorder in which chronic and persistent symptoms of anxiety develop in

response to an extreme physical or psychological trauma. (p. 623)

prejudice A negative attitude toward people who belong to a specific social group. (p. 534)

premature ejaculation In males, sexual dysfunction characterized by orgasm occurring before it is desired, often immediately or shortly after sexual stimulation or penetration. (p. 459)

prenatal stage The state of development before birth; divided into the germinal, embryonic, and fetal periods. (p. 387)

preoperational stage In Piaget's theory, the second stage of cognitive development, which lasts from about age two to age seven; characterized by increasing use of symbols and prelogical thought processes. (p. 400)

primary reinforcer In learning theory, a stimulus or event that is naturally or inherently reinforcing for a given species, such as food, water, or other biological necessities. (p. 208)

primary sex characteristics Sexual organs that are directly involved in reproduction, such as the uterus, ovaries, penis, and testicles. (p. 452)

proactive interference Forgetting in which an old memory interferes with remembering a new memory. (p. 267)

problem-focused coping Coping efforts primarily aimed at directly changing or managing a threatening or harmful stressor. (p. 597)

problem solving Thinking and behavior directed toward attaining a goal that is not readily available. (p. 292)

procedural information Long-term memory of how to perform different skills, operations, and actions. (p. 250)

production vocabulary The words that an infant or child understands and can speak. (p. 397)

projective test A type of personality test that involves a person interpreting an ambiguous image; used to assess unconscious motives, conflicts, psychological defenses, and personality traits. (p. 510)

prosocial behavior Any behavior that helps another, whether the underlying motive is self-serving or selfless. (p. 553)

prototype The most typical instance of a particular concept. (p. 290)

pseudoscience A fake or false science that makes claims based on little or no scientific evidence. (p. 36)

psychedelic drugs A category of psychoactive drugs that create sensory and perceptual distortions, alter mood, and affect judgment. (p. 188)

psychoactive drug A drug that alters normal consciousness, perception, mood, and behavior. (p. 180)

psychoanalysis Sigmund Freud's theory of personality and form of psychotherapy; emphasizes unconscious determinants of behavior, sexual and aggressive instinctual drives, and the enduring effects of early childhood experiences on later personality development. (pp. 8, 472, 658)

psychological disorder (mental disorder) A pattern of behavioral and psychological symptoms that causes significant personal distress, impairs the ability to function in one or more important areas of daily life, or both. (p. 614)

psychological test A test that assesses a person's abilities, aptitudes, interests, or personality, based on a systematically obtained sample of behavior. (p. 508)

psychology The scientific study of behavior and mental processes. (p. 3)

psychoneuroimmunology An interdisciplinary field that studies the interconnections among psychological processes, nervous and endocrine system functions, and the immune system. (p. 581)

psychopathology The scientific study of the origins, symptoms, and development of psychological disorders. (p. 611)

psychosexual stages In Freud's theory of personality, age-related developmental periods in which the child's sexual urges are expressed through different body areas and the activities associated with those body areas. (p. 480)

psychotherapy The treatment of emotional, behavioral, and interpersonal problems through the use of psychological techniques designed to encourage understanding of problems and modify troubling feelings, behaviors, or relationships. (p. 657)

puberty The stage of adolescence in which an individual reaches sexual maturity and becomes physiologically capable of sexual reproduction. (p. 451)

punishment The presentation of a stimulus or event following a behavior that acts to decrease the likelihood of the behavior being repeated. (p. 209)

pupil In vision, the opening in the middle of the iris of the eye that changes size to let in different amounts of light. (p. 99)

R

random assignment Assigning subjects to experimental conditions in such a way that all subjects have an equal chance of being assigned to any of the conditions or groups in the study. (p. 23)

range A measure of variability; the highest score in a distribution minus the lowest score. (p. A-6)

rational-emotive therapy (RET) A type of cognitive therapy, developed by psychologist Albert Ellis, that focuses on changing the client's irrational beliefs. (p. 673)

reality principle In Freud's theory of personality, the awareness of environmental demands and the capacity to accommodate them by postponing gratification until the appropriate time or circumstances exist. (p. 476)

recall A test of long-term memory that involves retrieving information without the aid of retrieval cues. (p. 254)

recessive gene In a pair of genes, the gene containing genetic instructions that will not be expressed unless paired with another recessive gene. (p. 384)

reciprocal determinism A model proposed by psychologist Albert Bandura that explains human functioning and personality as caused by the interaction of behavioral, cognitive, and environmental factors. (p. 494)

recognition A test of long-term memory that involves identifying correct information out of several possible choices. (p. 254)

reinforcement In operant conditioning, the occurrence of a stimulus or event following a response that increases the likelihood of the response being repeated. (p. 207)

reliability The ability of a test to produce consistent results when administered on repeated occasions under similar conditions. (p. 315)

REM rebound A phenomenon in which a person who is deprived of REM sleep greatly increases the amount of time spent in REM sleep during the first opportunity to sleep uninterrupted. (p. 161)

REM sleep Type of sleep during which rapid eye movements and dreaming occur. (p. 154)

REM sleep behavior disorder A sleep disorder in which the sleeper acts out his dreams. (p. 164)

replicate To repeat or duplicate a scientific study in order to increase confidence in the validity of the original findings. (p. 20)

representative sample A selected segment that very closely parallels the larger population being studied on relevant characteristics. (p. 29)

representativeness heuristic A strategy in which the likelihood of an event is estimated by comparing how similar it is to the typical prototype of the event. (p. 301)

repression Motivated forgetting that occurs unconsciously; in psychoanalytic theory, the unconscious exclusion of anxiety-provoking thoughts, feelings, and memories from conscious awareness. (pp. 268, 478)

resistance In psychoanalysis, the patient's unconscious attempts to block the revelation of repressed memories and conflicts. (p. 659)

resting potential State in which a neuron is prepared to activate and communicate its message if it receives sufficient stimulation. (p. 48)

restorative theory of sleep The view that sleep and dreaming are essential to normal physical and mental functioning. (p. 161)

reticular formation (reh-TICK-you-ler) A network of nerve fibers located in the center of the medulla that helps regulate attention, arousal, and sleep. (p. 72)

retina (RET-in-uh) A thin, light-sensitive membrane located at the back of the eye that contains the sensory receptors for vision. (p. 101)

retrieval The process of recovering information stored in memory so that we are consciously aware of it. (pp. 241, 253)

retrieval cue A clue, prompt, or hint that helps trigger recall of a given piece of information stored in long-term memory. (p. 253)

retrieval cue failure The inability to recall long-term memories because of inadequate or missing retrieval cues. (p. 253)

retroactive interference Forgetting in which a new memory interferes with remembering an old memory. (p. 267)

retrograde amnesia Loss of memory, especially for episodic information. (p. 276)

reuptake The process by which neurotransmitter molecules detach from a postsynaptic neuron and are reabsorbed by a presynaptic neuron so they can be recycled and used again. (p. 50)

rods The long, thin, blunt sensory receptors of the eye that are highly sensitive to light but not color and are primarily responsible for peripheral vision and night vision. (p. 101)

Rorschach Inkblot Test A projective test using inkblots, developed by Swiss psychiatrist Hermann Rorschach in 1921. (p. 510)

S

sample A selected segment of the population used to represent the group that is being studied. (p. 29)

sample A subset of a population. (p. A-13)

saturation The property of color that corresponds to the purity of the light wave. (p. 104)

scatter diagram (scatter plot) A graph that represents the relationship between two variables. (p. A-9)

schedule of reinforcement In operant conditioning, the delivery of a reinforcer according to a preset pattern based on the number of responses or the elapse of a time interval. (p. 216)

schema (SKEE-muh) An organized cluster of information about a particular topic, a mental representation of an action, an object, or an event. (p. 259)

schizophrenia A mental disorder in which the ability to function is impaired by severely distorted beliefs, perceptions, and thought processes. (p. 640)

scientific method A set of assumptions, attitudes, and procedures that guide researchers in creating questions to investigate, generating evidence, and drawing conclusions. (p. 16)

seasonal affective disorder (SAD) A mood disorder in which episodes of depression typically recur during the fall and winter and remit during the spring and summer. (p. 630)

secondary sex characteristics Sexual characteristics that develop during puberty and are not directly involved in reproduction but differentiate between the sexes, such as male facial hair and female breast development. (p. 452)

selection device validity The extent to which a personnel selection device is successful in distinguishing between those who will become high performers at a certain job and those who will not. (p. B-6)

self-actualization Defined by Maslow as "the full use and exploitation of talents, capacities, and potentialities." (p. 338)

self-concept The set of perceptions and beliefs that you hold about yourself. (p. 489)

self-efficacy The degree to which a person is subjectively convinced of his or her ability to effectively meet the demands of a situation; feelings of self-confidence or self-doubt. (p. 355, 493)

self-report inventory A type of psychological test in which a person's responses to standardized questions are compared to established norms. (p. 511)

self-serving bias The tendency to attribute successful outcomes of one's own behavior to internal causes and unsuccessful outcomes to external, situational causes. (p. 528)

semantic information General knowledge of facts, names, and concepts stored in long-term memory. (p. 250)

semantic network model A model that describes units of information in long-term memory as being organized in a complex network of associations. (p. 251)

sensation The process of detecting a physical stimulus, such as light, sound, heat, or pressure. (p. 95)

sensation seeking A personality characteristic reflecting the degree to which an individual is motivated to experience high levels of arousal associated with varied and novel activities. (p. 352)

sensorimotor stage In Piaget's theory, the first stage of cognitive development, from birth to about age two; the period during which the infant explores the environment and acquires knowledge through sensing and manipulating objects. (p. 399)

sensory adaptation The decline in sensitivity to a constant stimulus. (p. 97)

sensory memory The stage of memory that registers information from the environment and holds it for a very brief period of time. (p. 242)

sensory neuron Type of neuron that conveys information to the brain from specialized receptor cells in sense organs and internal organs. (p. 45)

sensory receptors Specialized cells unique to each sense organ that respond to a particular form of sensory stimulation. (p. 95)

sensory threshold The level at which a stimulus is strong enough to be detected by activating sensory receptors. (p. 96)

serial position effect The tendency to remember items at the beginning and end of a list better than items in the middle. (p. 255)

serotonin (ser-ah-TONE-in) Neurotransmitter that is involved in sleep and emotions. (p. 55)

set-point weight The particular weight that is set and maintained by increases or decreases in basal metabolic rate. (p. 344)

sex (1) The biological category of male or female as defined by physical differences in genetic composition and in reproductive anatomy and function. (2) The behavioral manifestation of the sexual urge; sexual intercourse. (p. 431)

sex chromosomes Chromosomes designated as X or Y which determine biological sex; the 23rd pair of chromosomes in humans. (p. 385)

sex-linked recessive characteristics Traits determined by recessive genes located on the X chromosome; in males, these characteristics require only one recessive gene to be expressed. (p. 385)

sexual aversion disorder A sexual dysfunction characterized by active avoidance of genital sexual contact because of extreme anxiety, fear, or disgust. (p. 459)

sexual dysfunction A consistent disturbance in sexual desire, arousal, or orgasm that causes psychological distress and interpersonal difficulties. (p. 459)

sexual orientation The direction of a person's emotional and erotic attraction toward members of the opposite sex, the same sex, or both sexes. (p. 431)

sexually transmitted diseases (STDs) Any of several infectious diseases that are primarily transmitted through sexual intercourse or other intimate sexual contact. (p. 461)

shape constancy The perception of a familiar object as maintaining the same shape regardless of the image produced on the retina. (p. 132)

shaping The operant conditioning procedure of selectively reinforcing successively closer approximations of a goal behavior until the goal behavior is displayed. (p. 214)

short-term memory (working memory) The active stage of memory in which information is stored for about 30 seconds. (p. 242)

situational (or contingency) theories of leader effectiveness Theories that focus on how a particular situation influences a leader's effectiveness. (p. B-10)

Sixteen Personality Factor Questionnaire (16PF) A self-report inventory developed by Raymond Cattell that generates a personality profile with ratings on sixteen trait dimensions. (p. 511)

size constancy The perception of an object as maintaining the same size despite changing images on the retina. (p. 131)

skewed distribution An asymmetrical distribution; more scores pile up on one side of the distribution than on the other. In a *positively* skewed distribution, most people have low scores; in a *negatively* skewed distribution, most people have high scores. (p. A-4)

Skinner box The popular name for an *operant chamber,* the experimental apparatus invented by B. F. Skinner to study the relationship between environmental events and active behaviors. (p. 214)

sleep apnea (APP-nee-uh) A sleep disorder in which the person repeatedly stops breathing during sleep. (p. 164)

sleep disorders Serious disturbances in the normal sleep pattern that interfere with daytime functioning and cause subjective distress. (p. 163)

sleep inertia Feelings of grogginess upon awakening from sleep that interfere with the ability to perform mental or physical tasks. (p. 190)

sleep spindles Short bursts of brain activity that characterize stage 2 NREM sleep. (p. 155)

sleep thinking Repetitive, bland, and uncreative ruminations about real-life events during sleep. (p. 166)

sleepwalking A sleep disturbance characterized by an episode of walking or performing other actions during stage 3 or stage 4 NREM sleep; also called *somnambulism.* (p. 164)

social categorization The mental process of classifying people into groups (or *categories*) on the basis of their shared characteristics. (p. 523)

social cognition The study of the mental processes people use to make sense out of their social environment. (p. 520)

social cognitive theory Bandura's theory of personality, which emphasizes the importance of observational learning, conscious cognitive processes, social experiences, self-efficacy beliefs, and reciprocal determinism. (p. 493)

social facilitation The tendency for the presence of other people to enhance individual performance. (p. 559)

social influence The study of the effect that situational factors and other people have on an individual's behavior. (p. 520)

social influence hypothesis The view that a person's level of job satisfaction is influenced by the job satisfaction levels of other people. (p. B-9)

social learning theory of gender-role development The theory that gender roles are acquired through the basic processes of learning, including reinforcement, punishment, and modeling. (p. 439)

social loafing The tendency to expend less effort on a task when it is a group effort. (p. 558)

social norms The "rules," or expectations, for appropriate behavior in a particular social situation. (p. 522)

social phobia An anxiety disorder involving the extreme and irrational fear of being

embarrassed, judged, or scrutinized by others in social situations. (p. 621)

social psychology The branch of psychology that studies how people think, feel, and behave in social situations. (p. 520)

social support The resources provided by other people in times of need, including emotional support, tangible support, and informational support. (p. 593)

somatic nervous system Subdivision of the peripheral nervous system that communicates sensory information to the central nervous system and carries messages from the central nervous system to the muscles. (p. 59)

source confusion A memory distortion that occurs when the true source of the memory is forgotten. (p. 260)

source traits The most fundamental dimensions of personality; the broad, basic traits that are hypothesized to be universal and relatively few in number. (p. 499)

specific phobia An anxiety disorder characterized by an extreme and irrational fear of a specific object or situation that interferes with the ability to function in daily life. (p. 620)

spinal reflexes Simple, automatic behaviors that are processed in the spinal cord. (p. 58)

split-brain operation A surgical procedure that involves cutting the corpus callosum. (p. 83)

spontaneous recovery In classical conditioning, the reappearance of a previously extinguished conditioned response after a period of time without exposure to the conditioned stimulus. (p. 202)

stage model of memory A model describing memory as consisting of three distinct stages: sensory memory, short-term memory, and long-term memory. (p. 242)

standard deviation A measure of variability; expressed as the square root of the sum of the squared deviations around the mean divided by the number of scores in the distribution. (p. A-7)

standard normal curve (standard normal distribution) A symmetrical distribution forming a bell-shaped curve in which the mean, median, and mode are all equal and fall in the exact middle. (p. A-8)

standardization The administration of a test to a large, representative sample of people under uniform conditions for the purpose of establishing norms. (p. 315)

state-dependent retrieval An encoding specificity phenomenon in which information that is learned in a particular drug state is more likely to be recalled while

the person is in the same drug state. (p. 256)

statistical significance A mathematical indication that research results are not very likely to have occurred by chance. (p. 19)

statistics Mathematical methods used to summarize data and draw conclusions based on the data. (p. 19)

stereotype A cluster of characteristics that are associated with all members of a specific social group, often including qualities that are unrelated to the objective criteria that define the group. (p. 534)

stimulant-induced psychosis Schizophrenia-like symptoms that can occur as the result of prolonged amphetamine or cocaine use. (p. 187)

stimulants A category of psychoactive drugs that increase brain activity, arouse behavior, and increase mental alertness. (p. 186)

stimulus discrimination In learning theory, the occurrence of a learned response to a specific stimulus but not to other similar stimuli. (p. 201)

stimulus generalization In learning theory, the occurrence of a learned response not only to the original stimulus but to other similar stimuli as well. (p. 201)

stimulus threshold The minimum level of stimulation required to activate a particular neuron. (p. 48)

storage The process of retaining information in memory so that it can be used at a later time. (p. 241)

stress A negative emotional state occurring in response to events that are perceived as taxing or exceeding a person's resources or ability to cope. (p. 569)

stressors Events or situations that are perceived as harmful, threatening, or challenging. (p. 569)

structural plasticity A phenomenon in which brain structures physically change in response to environmental influences. (p. 87)

structuralism Early school of psychology which emphasized studying the most basic components, or structures, of conscious experiences. (p. 5)

sublimation In psychoanalytic theory, an Ego defense mechanism that involves redirecting sexual urges toward productive, socially acceptable, nonsexual activities; a form of displacement. (p. 478)

substance P A neurotransmitter that is involved in the transmission of pain messages to the brain. (p. 119)

substantia nigra (sub-STANCE-ee-uh NEE-gruh) An area of the midbrain that is involved in motor control and contains a large concentration of dopamine-producing neurons. (p. 72)

Superego In Freud's theory of personality, the partly conscious self-evaluative, moralistic component of personality that is formed through the internalization of parental and societal rules. (p. 477)

suppression Motivated forgetting that occurs consciously. (p. 268)

suprachiasmatic nucleus (SCN) (soup-rah-*kye*-az-MAT-ick) A cluster of neurons in the hypothalamus in the brain that governs the timing of circadian rhythms. (p. 149)

surface trait Personality characteristics or attributes that can easily be inferred from observable behavior. (p. 499)

survey A questionnaire or interview designed to investigate the opinions, behaviors, or characteristics of a particular group. (p. 28)

symbolic thought In developmental psychology, the child's ability to use words, images, and symbols to represent the world. (p. 400)

symmetrical distribution A distribution in which scores fall equally on both sides of the graph. The normal curve is an example of a symmetrical distribution. (p. A-4)

sympathetic nervous system Branch of the autonomic nervous system that produces rapid physical arousal in response to perceived emergencies or threats. (p. 60)

synapse (SIN-aps) The point of communication between two neurons. (p. 50)

synaptic gap (sin-AP-tick) The tiny space between the axon terminal of one neuron and the dendrite of an adjoining neuron. (p. 50)

synaptic transmission (sin-AP-tick) The process in which neurotransmitters are released by one neuron, cross the synaptic gap, and affect adjacent neurons. (p. 50)

synaptic vesicles (sin-AP-tick VESS-ick-ulls) Tiny pouches or sacs in the axon terminals that contain neurotransmitters. (p. 50)

systematic desensitization A type of behavior therapy in which phobic responses are reduced by pairing relaxation with a series of mental images or real-life situations that the person finds progressively more fear-provoking; based on the principle of counterconditioning. (p. 666)

T

taste buds The specialized sensory receptors for taste that are located on the tongue and inside the mouth and throat. (p. 116)

temperament Inborn predispositions to consistently behave and react in a certain way. (p. 391)

temporal lobe An area on each hemisphere of the cerebral cortex near the temples which is the primary receiving area for auditory information. (p. 74)

teratogens Harmful agents or substances that can cause malformations or defects in an embryo or fetus. (p. 387)

thalamus (THAL-uh-muss) A forebrain structure that processes sensory information for all senses, except smell, and relays it to the cerebral cortex. (p. 77)

Thanatos In Freud's theory of personality, the death instinct, reflected in aggressive, destructive, and self-destructive actions. (p. 476)

Thematic Apperception Test (TAT) A projective personality test that involves creating stories about each of a series of ambiguous scenes; also used to measure achievement motivation. (p. 510)

theory A tentative explanation that tries to integrate and account for the relationship among various findings and observations. (p. 21)

thinking The manipulation of mental representations of information in order to draw inferences and conclusions. (p. 287)

timbre (TAM-ber) The distinctive quality of a sound, determined by the complexity of the sound wave. (p. 108)

tip-of-the-tongue (TOT) experience A memory phenomenon that involves the sensation of knowing that specific information is stored in long-term memory but being temporarily unable to retrieve it. (p. 254)

token economy A form of behavior therapy in which the therapeutic environment is structured to reward desired behaviors with tokens or points that may eventually be exchanged for tangible rewards. (p. 671)

tolerance In drug use, a condition in which increasing amounts of a physically addictive drug are needed to produce the original, desired effect. (p. 180)

trait A relatively stable, enduring predisposition to consistently behave in a certain way. (p. 498)

trait approach to leader effectiveness An approach to determining what makes an effective leader that focuses on the personal characteristis displayed by successful leaders. (p. B-10)

trait theory A theory of personality that focuses on identifying, describing, and measuring individual differences in traits. (p. 498)

tranquilizers Depressant drugs that relieve anxiety. (p. 184)

transduction The process by which a form of physical energy is converted into a coded neural signal that can be processed by the nervous system. (p. 96)

transference In psychoanalysis, the process by which emotions and desires originally associated with a significant person in the patient's life, such as a parent, are unconsciously transferred to the psychoanalyst. (p. 660)

trial and error A problem-solving strategy that involves attempting different solutions and eliminating those that do not work. (p. 293)

triarchic theory of intelligence Sternberg's theory that there are three forms of intelligence: componential, contextual, and experiential. (p. 318)

trichromatic theory of color vision The theory that the sensation of color is due to cones in the retina that are especially sensitive to red light (long wavelengths), green light (medium wavelengths), or blue light (short wavelengths). (p. 105)

two-factor theory of emotion Schachter and Singer's theory that emotion is a result of the interaction of physiological arousal and the cognitive label that we apply to explain the arousal. (p. 370)

Type A behavior pattern A behavioral and emotional style characterized by a sense of time urgency, hostility, and competitiveness. (p. 588)

U

unconditional positive regard In Carl Rogers's theory of personality and client-centered psychotherapy, the sense that you will be valued and loved even if you don't conform to the standards and expectations of others; unconditional love or acceptance. (p. 491)

unconditioned response (UCR) In classical conditioning, the unlearned, reflexive response that is elicited by an unconditioned stimulus. (p. 199)

unconditioned stimulus (UCS) In classical conditioning, the natural stimulus that reflexively elicits a response without the necessity of prior learning. (p. 199)

unconscious In Freud's theory of personality, a term used to describe thoughts, feelings, wishes, and drives that are operating below the level of conscious awareness. (p. 475)

V

vaginismus Sexual dysfunction characterized by persistent, involuntary contractions or spasms of the vaginal muscles, which result in uncomfortable or painful intercourse. (p. 459)

validity The ability of a test to measure what it is intended to measure. (p. 315)

variable A factor that can vary, or change, in ways that can be observed, measured, and verified. (p. 18)

variable-interval (VI) schedule In operant conditioning, a reinforcement schedule in which a reinforcer is delivered for the first response that occurs after an average time interval that varies unpredictably from trial to trial. (p. 218)

variable-ratio (VR) schedule In operant conditioning, a reinforcement schedule in which a reinforcer is delivered after an average number of responses that varies unpredictably from trial to trial. (p. 217)

vestibular sense (vess-TIB-you-ler) The technical name for the sense of balance, or equilibrium. (p. 120)

vocational and career counseling A subfield of I/O psychology that combines with counseling psychology to help people choose occupations that match their preferences and needs. (p. B-2)

W

wavelength The distance from one wave peak to another. (p. 98)

Weber's Law A principle of sensation that holds that the size of the just noticeable difference will vary depending on its relation to the strength of the original stimulus. (p. 97)

withdrawal symptoms Unpleasant physical reactions, combined with intense drug cravings, that occur when a person abstains from a drug on which he or she is physically dependent. (p. 180)

Z

z score A number, expressed in standard deviation units, that shows a score's deviation from the mean. (p. A-7)

References

Abramov, Israel, & Gordon, James. (1994). Color appearance: On seeing red—or yellow, or green, or blue. *Annual Review of Psychology, 45,* 451–485.

Abrams, Richard. (1992). *Electroconvulsive therapy* (2nd ed.). New York: Oxford University Press.

Abrams, Richard. (1994). The treatment that will not die: Electroconvulsive therapy. *Psychiatric Clinics of North America, 17,* 525–530.

Adams, James, L. (1979). *Conceptual blockbusting: A guide to better ideas* (2nd ed.). New York: Norton.

Ader, Robert. (1993a). Conditioned responses in pharmacotherapy research. *Psychological Medicine, 23,* 297–311.

Ader, Robert. (1993b). Conditioned responses. In Bill Moyers & Betty Sue Flowers (Eds.), *Healing and the mind.* New York: Doubleday.

Ader, Robert, & Cohen, Nicholas. (1975). Behaviorally conditioned immunosuppression. *Psychosomatic Medicine, 37,* 333–340.

Ader, Robert, & Cohen, Nicholas. (1991). The influence of conditioning on immune responses. In Robert Ader, David L. Felten, & Nicholas Cohen (Eds.), *Psychoneuroimmunology* (2nd ed.). San Diego: Academic Press.

Ader, Robert, & Cohen, Nicholas. (1993). Psychoneuroimmunology: Conditioning and stress. *Annual Review of Psychology, 44,* 53–85.

Ader, Robert; Cohen, Nicholas; & Felten, David. (1995, January 14). Psychoneuroimmunoloy: Interactions between the nervous system and the immune system. *Lancet, 345,* 99–112.

Ader, Robert; Felten, David; & Cohen, Nicholas. (1990). Interactions between the brain and immune system. *Annual Review of Pharmacology and Toxicology, 30,* 561–602.

Ader, Robert; Felten, David; & Cohen, Nicholas. (1991). *Psychoneuroimmunology* (2nd ed.). San Diego: Academic Press.

Adler, Alfred. (1933a/1979). Advantages and disadvantages of the inferiority feeling. In Heinz L. Anspacher & Rowena R. Ansbacher (Eds.), *Superiority and social interest: A collection of later writings.* New York: Norton.

Adler, Alfred. (1933b/1979). On the origin of the striving for superiority and of social interest. In Heinz L. Anspacher & Rowena R. Ansbacher (Eds.), *Superiority and social interest: A collection of later writings.* New York: Norton.

Adler, Alfred. (1954). *Understanding human nature.* New York: Fawcett.

Adler, Nancy, & Matthews, Karen. (1994). Health psychology: Why do some people get sick and some stay well? *Annual Review of Psychology, 45,* 229–259.

Adler, Tina. (1993, November). Debate over: Qualitative, quantitative both valuable. *APA Monitor, 24* (11), 16.

Affleck, Glenn; Tennen, Howard; & Croog, Sydney. (1987a). Causal attribution, perceived control, and recovery from a heart attack. *Journal of Social and Clinical Psychology, 5,* 339–355.

Affleck, Glenn; Tennen, Howard; Pfeiffer, Carol; & Fifield, Judith. (1987b). Appraisals of control and predictability in reacting to a chronic disease. *Journal of Personality and Social Psychology, 53,* 273–279.

Aggleton, John P. (Ed.). (1992). *The amygdala: Neurobiological aspects of emotion, memory, and mental dysfunction.* New York: Wiley–Liss.

Aghajanian, George K. (1994). Serotonin and the action of LSD in the brain. *Psychiatric Annals, 24* (3), 137–141.

Agosta, William C. (1992). *Chemical communication: The language of pheromones.* New York: Scientific American Library.

Aiken, Lewis R. (1994). *Psychological testing and assessment* (8th ed.). Boston: Allyn & Bacon.

Ainslie, George. (1975). Specious reward: A behavioral theory of impulsiveness and impulse control. *Psychological Bulletin, 82,* 463–496.

Ainsworth, Mary D. Salter. (1979). Attachment as related to mother–infant interaction. In J. G. Rosenblatt, R. A. Hinde, C. Beer, & M. Busnel (Eds.), *Advances in the study of behavior* (Vol. 9). New York: Academic Press.

Ainsworth, Mary D. Salter. (1982). Attachment: Retrospect and prospect. In C. M. Parkes & J. Stevenson-Hinde (Eds.), *The place of attachment in human behavior.* New York: Basic Books.

Ainsworth, Mary D. Salter; Blehar, Mary C.; Waters, Everett; & Wall, Sally. (1978). *Patterns of attachment: A psychological study of the Strange Situation.* Hillsdale, N.J.: Erlbaum.

Ajzen, Icek. (1991). The theory of planned behavior. *Organizational Behavior and Human Decision Processes, 50,* 179–211.

Ajzen, Icek, & Fishbein, M. (1980). *Understanding attitudes and predicting social behavior.* Englewood Cliffs, N.J.: Prentice Hall.

Albert, Marilyn. (1994, September 21). Quoted in Ronald Kotulak, Mental workouts can keep the brain sharp as we age, *Chicago Tribune,* p. 14.

Alcock, James E. (1978–1979). Psychology and near-death experiences. *Skeptical Inquirer, 3,* 25–41.

Alcock, James E. (1981). *Parapsychology: Science or magic?* New York: Pergamon.

Alcock, James E. (1987). Parapsychology: Science of the anomalous or search for the soul? *Behavioral and Brain Sciences, 10,* 553–565.

Alexander, Charles N.; Chandler, Howard M.; Langer, Ellen J.; Newman, Ronnie I.; & Davies, John L. (1989). Transcendental meditation, mindfulness, and longevity: An experimental study with the elderly. *Journal of Personality and Social Psychology, 57,* 950–964.

Alexander, James F.; Holtzworth-Munroe, Amy; & Jameson, Penny. (1994). The process and outcome of marital and family therapy: Research review and evaluation. In Allen E. Bergin & Sol L. Garfield (Eds.), *Handbook of psychotherapy and behavior change* (4th ed.). New York: Wiley.

Alford, Brad A., & Correia, Christopher J. (1994). Cognitive therapy of schizophrenia: Theory and empirical status. *Behavior Therapy 25,* 17–33.

Alkon, Daniel L. (1989, July). Memory storage and neural systems. *Scientific American, 258,* 42–50.

Allen, Karen M.; Blascovich, Jim; Tomaka, Joe; & Kelsey, Robert M. (1991). Presence of human friends and pet dogs as moderators of autonomic responses to stress in women. *Journal of Personality and Social Psychology, 61,* 582–589.

Allen, Keith D.; Loiben, Ted; Allen, Sarah J.; & Stanley, Robert T. (1992). Dentist-implemented contingent escape for management of disruptive child behavior. *Journal of Applied Behavior Analysis, 25,* 629–636.

Allen, Vernon L., & Levine, John M. (1969). Consensus and conformity. *Journal of Experimental Social Psychology, 5,* 389–399.

Allen, Vernon L., & Levine, John M. (1971). Social support and conformity: The role of independent assessment of reality. *Journal of Experimental Social Psychology, 7,* 48–58.

Allodi, Frederico A. (1994). Post-traumatic stress disorder in hostages and victims of torture. *Psychiatric Clinics of North America, 17,* 279–288.

Allport, Floyd H. (1920). The influence of the group upon association and thought. *Journal of Experimental Psychology, 3,* 159–182.

Allport, Floyd H. (1924). *Social psychology.* Boston: Houghton Mifflin.

Allport, Gordon W., & Odbert, H. S. (1936). Trait-names: A psycho-lexical study. *Psychological Monographs, 47* (211).

Alonso, Anne, & Swiller, Hillel I. (Eds.) (1993a). Group therapy in clinical practice. Washington, D.C.: American Psychiatric Press.

Alonso, Anne, & Swiller, Hillel I. (1993b). Introduction: The case for group therapy. In Anne Alonso & Hillel I. Swiller (Eds.), *Group therapy in clinical practice.* Washington, D.C.: American Psychiatric Press.

Amabile, Teresa M. (1983). *The social psychology of creativity.* New York: Springer-Verlag.

Amabile, Teresa M. (1989). *Growing up creative: Nurturing a lifetime of creativity.* New York: Crown.

Amabile, Teresa M., & Tighe, Elizabeth. (1993). Questions of creativity. In John Brockman (Ed.), *Creativity.* New York: Simon & Schuster.

Amador, Xavier F.; Strauss, David H.; Yale, Scott A.; & Gorman, Jack M. (1991). Awareness of illness in schizophrenia. *Schizophrenia Bulletin, 17,* 113–132.

American Association for the Advancement of Science. (1989). Science for all Americans. Washington, D.C.: American Association for the Advancement of Science.

American Psychiatric Association. (1994). *Diagnostic and statistical manual of mental disorders* (4th ed.). Washington, D.C.: American Psychiatric Association.

American Psychological Association. (1986). *Animal Research Survey, 1985–1986.* Washington, D.C.: American Psychological Association.

American Psychological Association. (1992a). *Ethical principles of psychologists and code of conduct.* Washington, D.C.: American Psychological Association.

American Psychological Association. (1992b). *Guidelines for ethical conduct in the care and use of animals.* Washington, D.C.: American Psychological Assocation.

American Psychological Association. (1993). Guidelines for practitioners of psychological services to ethnic, linguistic, and culturally diverse populations. *American Psychologist, 48,* 45–48.

American Psychological Association. (1995a, September). APA's year in review: 1995. *APA Monitor,* pp. 16–27.

American Psychological Association. (1995b). *Behavior research with animals.* Washington, D.C.: American Psychological Association.

Amering, M., & Katschnig, H. (1990). Panic attacks and panic disorder in cross-cultural perspective. *Psychiatric Annals, 20,* 511–516.

Amir, Yehuda. (1994). The contact hypothesis in intergroup relations. In Walter J. Lonner & Roy Malpass (Eds.), *Psychology and culture.* Boston: Allyn & Bacon.

Anand, B. K., & Brobeck, J. R. (1951). Hypothalamic control of food intake in rats and cats. *Yale Journal of Biological Medicine, 24,* 123–140.

Anastasi, Anne. (1988). *Psychological testing* (6th ed.). New York: Macmillan.

Anch, A. Michael; Browman, Carl P.; Mitler, Merrill M.; & Walsh, James K. (1988). *Sleep: A scientific perspective.* Englewood Cliffs, N.J.: Prentice Hall.

Anderson, John R. (1995). *Cognitive psychology and its implications* (4th ed.). New York: Freeman.

Anderson, S. A.; Russell, C. S.; & Schumm, W. R. (1983). Perceived marital quality and family life-cycle categories: A further analysis. *Journal of Marriage and the Family, 45,* 127–139.

Andersson, Bengt-Erik. (1989). Effects of day care: A longitudinal study. *Child Development, 60,* 857–866.

Andersson, Bengt-Erik. (1992). Effects of day care on cognitive and socioemotional competence of thirteen-year-old Swedish schoolchildren. *Child Development, 63,* 20–36.

Andreasen, Nancy C., & Flaum, Michael. (1991). Schizophrenia: The characteristic symptoms. *Schizophrenia Bulletin, 17,* 27–49.

Angell, Marcia. (1985/1991). Quoted in Daniel Goleman, Debate intensifies on attitude and health. In Daniel Goleman, *Psychology updates: Articles on psychology from* The New York Times. New York: HarperCollins.

Angier, Natalie. (1995, February 14). Powerhouse of senses, smell, at last gets its due. *New York Times,* pp. C1, C6.

Anonymous. (1990). First person account: Birds of a psychic feather. *Schizophrenia Bulletin, 16,* 165–168.

Antony, Martin M.; Brown, Timothy A.; & Barlow, David H. (1992). Current perspectives on panic and panic disorder. *Current Directions in Psychological Science, 1,* 79–82.

APA Research Office. (1995). *Profile of all APA members: 1995.* Washington, D.C.: American Psychological Association.

Argyle, Michael, & Martin, Maryanne. (1991). The psychological causes of happiness. In Fritz Strack, Michael Argyle, & Norbert Schwarz (Eds.), *Subjective well-being: An interdisciplinary perspective.* New York: Pergamon Press.

Arkes, H. R., & Boykin, A. W. (1971). Analysis of complexity preference in Head Start and nursery school children. *Perceptual and Motor Skills, 33,* 1131–1137.

Arkin, Arthur M. (1981). *Sleep talking: Psychology and psychophysiology.* Hillsdale, N.J.: Erlbaum.

Arkin, Arthur M. (1991). Sleeptalking. In Steven J. Ellman & John S. Antrobus (Eds.), *The mind in sleep: Psychology and psychophysiology* (2nd ed.). New York: Wiley.

Arkin, Arthur M., & Antrobus, John S. (1991). The effects of external stimuli applied prior to and during sleep on sleep experience. In Steven J. Ellman & John S. Antrobus (Eds.), *The mind in sleep: Psychology and psychophysiology* (2nd ed.). New York: Wiley.

Arling, Greg. (1987). Strain, social support, and distress in old age. *Journal of Gerontology, 42,* 107–113.

Armstrong, Blake G., & Greenberg, Bradley S. (1990). Background television as an inhibitor of cognitive processing. *Human Communication Research, 16* (3), 355–386.

Arnkoff, Diane B., & Glass, Carol R. (1992). Cognitive therapy and psychotherapy integration. In Donald K. Freedheim (Ed.), *History of psychotherapy: A century of change.* Washington, D.C.: American Psychological Association.

Aron, Arthur; Aron, Elaine N.; & Smollan, Danny. (1992). Inclusion of Other in the Self Scale and the structure of interpersonal closeness. *Journal of Personality and Social Psychology, 63,* 596–612.

Aronson, Elliot. (1987). Teaching students what they think they already know about prejudice and desegregation. In Vivian Parker Makosky (Ed.), *G. Stanley Hall Lecture Series* (Vol. 7). Washington, D.C.: American Psychological Association.

Aronson, Elliot. (1990). Applying social psychology to desegregation and energy conservation. *Personality and Social Psychology Bulletin, 16,* 118–132.

Aronson, Elliot. (1992). The return of the repressed: Dissonance theory makes a comeback. *Psychological Inquiry, 3,* 303–311.

Aronson, Elliot. (1995). *The social animal* (7th ed). New York: Freeman.

Aronson, Elliot, & Bridgeman, Diane. (1979). Jigsaw groups and the desegregated classroom: In pursuit of common goals. *Personality and Social Psychology Bulletin, 5,* 438–466.

Arvey, R. D.; Bouchard, T. J.; Segal, N. L.; & Abraham, L. M. (1989). Job satisfaction: Environmental and genetic components. *Journal of Applied Psychology, 74,* 187–192.

Arvidson, K. & Friberg, U. (1980). Human taste response and taste bud number in fungiform papillae. *Science, 209,* 807–808.

Asch, Solomon E. (1951). Effects of group pressure upon the modification and distortion of judgments. In Harold S. Guetzkow (Ed.), *Groups, leadership, and men: Research in human relations. Reports on research sponsored by the Human Relations and Morale Branch of the Office of Naval Research, 1945–1950.* Pittsburgh: Carnegie Press.

Asch, Solomon E. (1955, November). Opinions and social pressure. *Scientific American, 193,* 31–35.

Asch, Solomon E. (1956). Studies of independence and conformity: A minority of one against a unanimous majority. *Psychological Monographs, 70* (9), Whole No. 416.

Asch, Solomon E. (1957). An experimental investigation of group influence. In *Symposium on preventive and social psychiatry.* Walter Reed Army Institute of Research. Washington, D.C.: U.S. Government Printing Office.

Aschoff, Jurgen. (1993). On the passage of subjective time in temporal isolation. *Psychologica Belgica, 33,* 147–157.

Aschoff, Jurgen. (1994). The timing of defecation within the sleep-wake cycle of humans during temporal isolation. *Journal of Biological Rhythms, 9,* 43–50.

Ashcraft, Mark H. (1994). *Human memory and cognition* (2nd ed.). New York: HarperCollins.

Ashton, Heather, & Stepney, Rob (1983). *Smoking: Psychology and pharmacology.* New York: Tavistock.

Aspinwall, Lisa G., & Taylor, Shelley E. (1992). Modeling cognitive adaptation: A longitudinal investigation of the impact of individual differences and coping on college adjustment and performance. *Journal of Personality and Social Psychology, 63,* 989–1003.

Aspinwall, Lisa G., & Taylor, Shelley E. (1993). Effects of social comparison direction, threat, and self-esteem on affect, self-evaluation, and expected success. *Journal of Personality and Social Psychology, 64,* 708–722.

Associated Press. (1994a, March 24). Woman rescued at rail crossing seconds before train hits car. *Tulsa World,* p. 2.

Associated Press. (1994b, March 28) Gasoline tanker explodes: Man burns as some watch. *Tulsa World,* p. 16.

Atkinson, Donald R.; Morten, George; & Sue, Derald Wing. (1993). Counseling racial/ethnic minorities: An overview. In Donald R. Atkinson, George Morten, & Derald Wing Sue (Eds.), *Counseling American minorities: A cross-cultural perspective* (4th ed.). Madison, Wis.: Brown & Benchmark.

Atkinson, Richard C., & Shiffrin, Richard M. (1968). Human memory: A proposed system and its control processes. In Kenneth W. Spence & Janet T. Spence (Eds.), *The psychology of learning and motivation: Advances in research and theory* (Vol. 2). New York: Academic Press.

Averill, James R. (1982). *Anger and aggression: An essay on emotion.* New York: Springer-Verlag.

Averill, James R. (1994). I feel, therefore I am—I think. In Paul Ekman & Richard J. Davidson (Eds.), *The nature of emotion: Fundamental questions.* New York: Oxford University Press.

Axel, Richard. (1995, October). The molecular logic of smell. *Scientific Amerian, 273,* 154–159.

Axelrod, Saul, & Apsche, Jack. (1983). *The effects of punishment on human behavior.* New York: Academic Press.

Azar, Beth. (1994a, August). Brain imaging raises, answers questions. *APA Monitor,* p. 14.

Azar, Beth. (1994b, December). Research improves lives of animals. *APA Monitor, 25* (12), 19.

Azar, Beth. (1996). Influences from the mind's inner layers. *APA Monitor, 27* (2), 1, 25.

Azrin, N. H., & Holz, W. C. (1966). Punishment. In W. K. Honig (Ed.), *Operant behavior: Areas of research and application.* Englewood Cliffs, N.J.: Prentice Hall.

Azuma, Hiroshi. (1984). Secondary control as a heterogeneous category. *American Psychologist, 39,* 970–971.

Babbitt, Roberta L., & Parrish, John M. (1991). Phone phobia, phact or phantasy? An operant approach to a child's disruptive behavior induced by telephone usage. *Journal of Behavior Therapy and Experimental Psychiatry, 22,* 123–129.

Bachen, Elizabeth A.; Manuck, Stephen B.; Marsland, Anna L.; Cohen, Sheldon; Malkoff, Susan B.; Muldoon, Matthew F.; & Rabin, Bruce S. (1992). Lymphocyte subset and cellular immune responses to a brief experimental stressor. *Psychosomatic Medicine, 54,* 673–679.

Baddeley, Alan D. (1989). The psychology of remembering and forgetting. In Thomas Butler (Ed.), *Memory: History, culture, and the mind.* Oxford, England: Basil Blackwell.

Baddeley, Alan D. (1990). *Human memory: Theory and practice.* Boston: Allyn & Bacon.

Baddeley, Alan D. (1992). Working memory: Humans. In Larry R. Squire (Ed.), *Encyclopedia of learning and memory.* New York: Macmillan.

Baddeley, Alan D. (1995). Working memory. In Michael S. Gazzaniga (Ed.), *The cognitive neurosciences.* Cambridge, Mass.: MIT Press.

Baer, John. (1993). *Creativity and divergent thinking: A task-specific approach.* Hillsdale, N.J.: Erlbaum.

Baer, P. E.; Garmezy, L. B.; McLaughlin, R. L.; Pokorny, A. D.; & Wernick, M. J. (1987). Stress, coping, family conflict, and adolescent alcohol use. *Journal of Behavioral Medicine, 10,* 449–466.

Bahrick, Harry P., & Hall, Lynda K. (1991). Lifetime maintenance of high school mathematics content. *Journal of Experimental Psychology: General, 120,* 20–33.

Bahrick, Harry P., & Phelps, Elizabeth. (1987). Retention of Spanish vocabulary over eight years. *Journal of Experimental Psychology: Learning, Memory, and Cognition, 13,* 344–349.

Bailey, Craig H. (1992). Morphological basis of learning and memory: Invertebrates. In Larry R. Squire (Ed.), *Encyclopedia of learning and memory.* New York: Macmillan.

Bailey, J. Michael, & Pillard, Richard C. (1991). A genetic study of male sexual orientation. *Archives of General Psychiatry, 48,* 1089–1096.

Bailey, J. Michael; Bobrow, David; Wolfe, Marilyn; & Mikach, Sarah. (1995). Sexual orientation of adult sons of gay fathers. *Developmental Psychology, 31,* 124–129.

Bailey, J. Michael; Pillard, Richard C.; Neale, Michael C.; & Agyei, Yvonne. (1993). Heritable factors influence sexual orientation in women. *Archives of General Psychiatry, 50,* 217–223.

Bailey, J. Michael, & Zucker, Kenneth J. (1995). Childhood sex-typed behavior and sexual orientation: A conceptual analysis and quantitative review. *Developmental Psychology, 31,* 43–55.

Bailey, Marian Berland, & Bailey, Robert E. (1993). "Misbehavior": A case history. *American Psychologist, 48,* 1157–1158.

Baillargeon, Renée. (1987). Young infants' reasoning about the physical and spatial characteristics of a hidden object. *Cognitive Development, 2,* 179–200.

Baillargeon, Renée. (1994). How do infants learn about the physical world? *Current Directions in Psychological Science, 3,* 133–140.

Baillargeon, Renée, & De Vos, Julie. (1991). Object permanence in young infants: Further evidence. *Child Development, 62,* 1227–1246.

Baker, Robert A. (1990). *They call it hypnosis.* Buffalo, N.Y.: Prometheus.

Baker, Robert A. (1992). *Hidden memories: Voices and visions from within.* Buffalo, N.Y.: Prometheus.

Baker, Robert A. (1996). Hypnosis. In Gordon Stein (Ed.), *The encyclopedia of the paranormal.* Amherst, N.Y.: Prometheus Books.

Baldessarini, R. J. (1990). Drugs and the treatment of psychiatric disorders. In A. Goodman Gilman, T. W. Rall, A. S. Nies, & P. Taylor (Eds.), *The pharmacological basis of therapeutics* (8th ed.). Elmsford, N.Y.: Pergamon Press.

Bales, J. (1988). Integrity tests: Honest results? *APA Monitor, 19,* 1–4.

Balk, David E. (1995). *Adolescent development: Early through late adolescence.* Pacific Grove, Calif.: Brooks/Cole.

Banaji, Mahzarin R., & Prentice, Deborah A. (1994). The self in social contexts. *Annual Review of Psychology, 45,* 297–332.

Bandura, Albert. (1965). Influence of models' reinforcement contingencies on the acquisition of imitative behaviors. *Journal of Personality and Social Psychology, 1,* 589–595.

Bandura, Albert. (1974). Behavior theory and the models of man. *American Psychologist, 29,* 859–869.

Bandura, Albert (1977). *Social learning theory.* Englewood Cliffs, N.J.: Prentice-Hall.

Bandura, Albert. (1978). The self system in reciprocal determinism. *American Psychologist, 33,* 344–358.

Bandura, Albert. (1986). *Social foundations of thought and action: A social cognitive theory.* Englewood Cliffs, N.J.: Prentice Hall.

Bandura, Albert. (1988). Self-regulation of motivation and action through goal systems. In V. Hamilton, G. H. Bower, & N. H. Frijda (Eds.), *Cognitive perspectives on emotion and motivation.* Dordrecht, Netherlands: Kluwer Academic Publishers.

Bandura, Albert. (1989a). Human agency in social cognitive theory. *American Psychologist, 44,* 1175–1184.

Bandura, Albert. (1989b). Regulation of cognitive processes through perceived self-efficacy. *Developmental Psychology, 25,* 729–735.

Bandura, Albert. (1990). Conclusion: Reflections on nonability determinants of competence. In Robert J. Sternberg & John Kolligian, Jr. (Eds.), *Competence considered.* New Haven, Conn.: Yale University Press.

Bandura, Albert. (1991a). Self-regulation of motivation through anticipatory and self-reactive mechanisms. In Richard Dienstbier (Ed.), *Nebraska Symposium on Motivation 1990* (Vol. 38). Lincoln: University of Nebraska Press.

Bandura, Albert. (1991b). Social cognitive theory of self-regulation. *Organizational Behavior and Human Decision Processes, 50,* 248–287.

Bandura, Albert. (1992a). Exercise of personal agency through the self-efficacy mechanism. In Ralf Schwarzer (Ed.), *Self-efficacy: Thought control of action.* Washington, D.C.: Hemisphere.

Bandura, Albert. (1992b). Social cognitive theory. In Ross Vasta (Ed.), *Six theories of child development: Revised formulations and current issues.* Philadelphia: Jessica Kingsley Publishers.

Bandura, Albert. (1996). Failures in self-regulation: Energy depletion or selective disengagement? *Psychological Inquiry, 7,* 20–24.

Bandura, Albert. (in press). *Self-efficacy: The exercise of control*. New York: Freeman.

Bandura, Albert; Ross, Dorothea; & Ross, Sheila A. (1963). Imitation of film-mediated aggressive models. *Journal of Abnormal and Social Psychology, 66,* 3–11.

Bandura, Albert, & Wood, Robert. (1989). Impact of conceptions of ability on self-regulatory mechanisms and complex decision making. *Journal of Personality and Social Psychology, 56,* 407–415.

Barch, Deanna M., & Berenbaum, Howard. (1995). Language production and thought disorder in schizophrenia. *Journal of Abnormal Psychology, 105,* 81–88.

Barclay, Craig R. (1986). Schematization of autobiographical memory. In David Rubin (Ed.), *Autobiographical memory*. New York: Cambridge University Press.

Barclay, Deborah R., & Houts, Arthur C. (1995a). Childhood enuresis. In Charles E. Schaefer (Ed.), *Clinical handbook of sleep disorders in children*. Northvale, N.J.: Aronson.

Barclay, Deborah R., & Houts, Arthur C. (1995b). Parenting skills: A review and developmental analysis of training content. In William O'Donohue & Leonard Krasner (Eds.), *Handbook of psychological skills training: Clinical techniques and applications*. Boston: Allyn & Bacon.

Barefoot, John C. (1992). Developments in the measurement of hostility. In Howard S. Friedman (Ed.), *Hostility, health, and coping*. Washington, D.C.: American Psychological Association.

Barefoot, John C.; Dahlstrom, W. Grant; & Williams, Redford B. (1983). Hostility, CHD incidence, and total mortality: A 25-year follow-up study of 255 physicians. *Psychosomatic Medicine, 45,* 59–63.

Bar-El, Yair. (1994, October 2). Quoted in Associated Press, Syndrome strikes spiritual senseless. *Tulsa World,* p. 10.

Bargh, John A.; Chen, Mark; & Burrows, Lara. (1996) Automaticity of social behavior: Direct effects of trait construct and stereotype activation on action. *Journal of Personality and Social Psychology, 71,* 230–244.

Barinaga, Marcia. (1995, April 14). Dendrites shed their dull image. *Science, 268,* 200–201.

Barlow, David Harrison. (1991). Disorders of emotion. *Psychological Inquiry, 2,* 58–71.

Barnett, Rosalind C.; Marshall, Nancy L.; & Singer, Judith D. (1992). Job experiences over time, multiple roles, and women's mental health: A longitudinal study. *Journal of Personality and Social Psychology, 62,* 634–644.

Barondes, Samuel H. (1993). *Molecules and mental illness*. New York: Scientific American Library.

Barr, Christopher E.; Mednick, Sarnoff A.; & Munk-Jorgensen, Poul. (1990). Exposure to influenza epidemics during gestation and adult schizophrenia: A 40-year study. *Archives of General Psychiatry, 47,* 869–874.

Barrett, Stephen. (1996). "Alternative" health practices and quackery. In Gordon Stein (Ed.), *The encyclopedia of the paranormal*. Amherst, N.Y.: Prometheus Books.

Barrick, M. R., & Mount, M. K. (1991). The Big Five personality dimensions and job performance: A meta-analysis. *Personnel Psychology, 44,* 1–26.

Barrick, M. R., & Mount, M. K. (1993). Autonomy as a moderator of the relationship between the Big Five personality dimensions and job performance. *Journal of Applied Psychology, 78,* 111–118.

Bartecchi, Carl E.; MacKenzie, Thomas D.; & Schrier, Robert W. (1995, May). The global tobacco epidemic. *Scientific American, 272,* 44–51.

Bartoshuk, Linda M., & Beauchamp, Gary K. (1994). Chemical senses. *Annual Review of Psychology, 45,* 419–449.

Bashore, Theodore R., & Rapp, Paul E. (1993). Are there alternatives to traditional polygraph procedures? *Psychological Bulletin, 113,* 3–22.

Basil, Robert. (1991). Graphology and personality: "Let the buyer beware." In Kendrick Frazier (Ed.), *The hundredth monkey and other paradigms of the paranormal*. Buffalo, N.Y.: Prometheus Books.

Bass, B. M. (1981). *Stogdill's handbook of leadership*. New York: Free Press.

Bass, Ellen, & Davis, Linda. (1994). *The courage to heal* (3rd ed.). New York: HarperPerennial.

Bassili, John N. (1993). Response latency versus certainty as indexes of the strength of voting intentions in a CATI survey. *Public Opinion Quarterly, 57,* 54–61.

Bates, John E. (1989). Concepts and measures of temperament. In G. A. Kohnstamm, John E. Bates, & Mary K. Rothbart (Eds.), *Temperament in childhood*. New York: Wiley.

Bates, John E. (1994). Introduction. In John E. Bates & Theodore D. Wachs (Eds.), *Temperament: Individual differences at the interface of biology and behavior*. Washington, D.C.: American Psychological Association.

Batson, C. Daniel. (1991). *The altruism question: Toward a social-psychological answer*. Hillsdale, N.J.: Erlbaum.

Baudry, Michel, & Davis, Joel L. (1992). Neurotransmitter systems and memory. In Larry R. Squire (Ed.), *Encyclopedia of learning and memory*. New York: Macmillan.

Baum, Andrew; Davidson, Laura M.; Singer, Jerome E.; & Street, Stacey W. (1987). Stress as a psychophysiological process. In Andrew Baum & Jerome E. Singer (Eds.), *Handbook of psychology and health: (Vol. 5). Stress*. Hillsdale, N.J.: Erlbaum.

Baum, William, & Heath, Jennifer L. (1992). Behavioral explanations and intentional explanations in psychology. *American Psychologist, 47,* 1312–1317.

Baumeister, Roy F. (1990). Suicide as escape from self. *Psychological Review, 97,* 90–113.

Baumeister, Roy F.; Stillwell, Arlene M.; & Heatherton, Todd F. (1994). Guilt: An interpersonal approach. *Psychological Bulletin, 115,* 243–267.

Baumrind, Diana. (1964). Some thoughts on ethics of research: After reading Milgram's "Behavioral Study of Obedience." *American Psychologist, 19,* 421–423.

Baumrind, Diana. (1967). Child care practices anteceding three patterns of preschool behavior. *Genetic Psychology Monographs, 75,* 43–88.

Baumrind, Diana. (1971). Current patterns of parental authority. *Developmental Psychology Monographs, 4,* 1–103.

Baumrind, Diana. (1995). Commentary on sexual orientation: Research and social policy implications. *Developmental Psychology, 31,* 130–136.

Beal, Carole R. (1994). *Boys and girls: The development of gender roles*. New York: McGraw-Hill.

Beaman, A. L.; Klentz, B.; Diener, E.; & Svanum, S. (1979). Self-awareness and transgression in children: Two field studies. *Journal of Personality and Social Psychology, 37,* 1835–1846.

Bearpark, Helen M. (1994). Insomnia: Causes, effects, and treatment. In Rosemary Cooper (Ed.), *Sleep*. New York: Chapman & Hall.

Beck, Aaron T. (1991). Cognitive therapy: A 30-year retrospective. *American Psychologist, 46,* 368–375.

Beck, Aaron T. (1993). Cognitive therapy: Past, present, and future. *Journal of Consulting and Clinical Psychology, 61,* 194–198.

Beck, Aaron T.; Rush, A. John; Shaw, Brian F.; & Emery, Gary. (1979). *Cognitive therapy of depression*. New York: Guilford Press.

Beck, Aaron T.; Steer, Robert A.; Beck, Judith S.; & Newman, Cory F. (1993). Hopelessness, depression, suicidal ideation, and clinical diagnosis of depression. *Suicide and Life Threatening Behavior, 23,* 139–145.

Beck, Melinda, & Borger, Gloria. (1979, August 20). The polite bandit: A priest on trial. *Newsweek,* p. 26.

Beck, Melinda; Springen, Karen; & Foote, Donna. (1992, April 13). Sex and psychotherapy. *Newsweek,* pp. 52–57.

Beck, Robert C. (1990). *Motivation: Theories and principles* (3rd ed.). Englewood Cliffs, N.J.: Prentice Hall.

Bednar, Richard L., & Kaul, Theodore J. (1994). Experiential group research: Can the canon fire? In Allen E. Bergin & Sol L. Garfield (Eds.), *Handbook of psychotherapy and behavior change* (4th ed.). New York: Wiley.

Beecher, Michael D. (1988). Some comments on the adaptationist approach to learning. In Robert C. Bolles & Michael D. Beecher, *Evolution and learning.* Hillsdale, N.J.: Erlbaum.

Begley, Sharon. (1994, February 7). One pill makes you larger, one pill makes you small. *Newsweek,* pp. 37–40.

Beilin, Harry. (1994). Jean Piaget's enduring contribution to developmental psychology. In Ross D. Parke, Peter A. Ornstein, John J. Rieser, & Carolyn Zahn-Waxler (Eds.), *A century of developmental psychology.* Washington, D.C.: American Psychological Association.

Bell, Alan; Weinberg, Martin; & Hammersmith, Sue. (1981). *Sexual preference: Its development in men and women.* Bloomington: Indiana University Press.

Bellak, Leopold. (1993). *The Thematic Apperception Test, the Children's Apperception Test, and the Senior Apperception Technique in clinical use* (5th ed.). Boston: Allyn & Bacon.

Belle, Deborah. (1991). Gender differences in the social moderators of stress. In Alan Monat & Richard S. Lazarus (Eds.), *Stress and coping: An anthology* (3rd ed.). New York: Columbia University Press.

Belsky, Jay. (1986). Infant day care: A cause for concern. *Zero to Three, 6,* 1–7.

Belsky, Jay. (1992). Consequences of child care for children's development: A deconstructionist view. In Alan Booth (Ed.), *Child care in the 1990s: Trends and consequences.* Hillsdale, N.J.: Erlbaum.

Belsky, Jay, & Rovine, Michael J. (1988). Nonmaternal care in the first year of life and security of infant–parent attachment. *Child Development, 59,* 157–167.

Bem, Daryl J. (1994). Response to Hyman. *Psychological Bulletin, 115,* 25–27.

Bem, Daryl J., & Honorton, Charles. (1994). Does psi exist? Replicable evidence for an anomalous process of information transfer. *Psychological Bulletin, 115,* 4–18.

Bem, Sandra L. (1981). Gender schema theory: A cognitive account of sex typing. *Psychological Review, 88,* 354–364.

Bem, Sandra L. (1987). Gender schema theory and the romantic tradition. In P. Shaver & C. Hendrick (Eds.), *Sex and gender.* Beverly Hills, Calif.: Sage.

Bem, Sandra L. (1989). Genital knowledge and gender constancy in preschool children. *Child Development, 60,* 649–662.

Benca, Ruth M.; Obermeyer, William H.; Thisted, Ronald A.; & Gillin, Christian. (1992). Sleep and psychiatric disorders: A meta-analysis. *Archives of General Psychiatry, 49,* 651–668.

Benderly, Beryl Lieff. (1989, September). Everyday intuition. *Psychology Today,* pp. 35–40.

Bennett, G. K. (1940). *Bennett Test of Mechanical Comprehension.* New York: Psychological Corporation.

Benson, Herbert. (1993). The relaxation response. In Daniel Goleman & Joel Gurin (Eds.), *Mind / body medicine: How to use your mind for better health.* Yonkers, N.Y.: Consumer Reports Books.

Bentall, R. P. (1990). The illusion of reality: A review and integration of psychological research on hallucinations. *Psychological Bulletin, 107,* 82–95.

Beratis, Stavroula; Gabriel, Joanna; & Holdas, Stavros. (1994). Age of onset in subtypes of schizophrenic disorders. *Schizophrenia Bulletin, 20,* 287–296.

Bergeman, C. S.; Chipuer, Heather M.; Plomin, Robert; Pedersen, Nancy L.; McClearn, G. E.; Nesselroade, John R.; Costa, Paul T., Jr.; & McCrae, Robert R. (1993). Genetic and environmental effects on openness to experience, agreeableness, and conscientiousness: An adoption/twin study. *Journal of Personality, 61,* 159–179.

Berger, Kathleen Stassen. (1995). *The developing person through childhood and adolescence* (4th ed.). New York: Worth Publishers.

Berkman, Lisa F. (1985). The relationship of social networks and social support to morbidity and mortality. In Sheldon Cohen & S. Leonard Syme (Eds.), *Social support and health.* New York: Academic Press.

Berkman, Lisa F.; Leo-Summers, Linda; & Horowitz, Ralph I. (1992). Emotional support and survival after myocardial infarction. *Annals of Internal Medicine, 117,* 1003–1009.

Berkman, Lisa, & Syme, S. Leonard. (1979). Social networks, host resistance, and mortality: A nine-year follow-up study of Alameda County residents. *American Journal of Epidemiology, 109,* 186–204.

Berlyne, Daniel E. (1960). *Conflict, arousal, and curiosity.* New York: McGraw-Hill.

Berlyne, Daniel E. (1971). *Aesthetics and psychobiology.* New York: Appleton-Century-Crofts.

Bermond, B.; Fasotti, L.; Nieuwenhuyse, B.; & Schuerman, J. (1991). Spinal cord lesions, peripheral feedback and intensities of emotional feelings. *Cognition and Emotion, 5,* 201–220.

Bernard, Larry C. (1994). *Health psychology: Biopsychosocial factors in health and illness.* Fort Worth, Tex.: Harcourt Brace.

Berndt, Thomas J. (1992). Friendship and friends' influence in adolescence. *Current Directions in Psychological Science, 1,* 156–159.

Berridge, Kent C., & Robinson, Terry E. (1995). The mind of an addicted brain: Neural sensitization of wanting versus liking. *Current Directions in Psychological Science, 4,* 71–76.

Berry, John W. (1994). Acculturative stress. In Walter J. Lonner & Roy Malpass (Eds.), *Psychology and culture.* Boston: Allyn & Bacon.

Berry, John W., & Kim, Uichol. (1988). Acculturation and mental health. In Pierre R. Dasen, John W. Berry, & Norman Sartorius (Eds.), *Health and cross-cultural psychology: Toward applications.* [Vol. 10, Cross-cultural Research And Methodology Series.] Newbury Park, Calif.: Sage.

Berry, L. M., & Houston, J. P. (1993). *Psychology at work.* Madison, Wis.: Brown & Benchmark.

Betancourt, Hector, & López, Steven Regeser. (1993). The study of culture, ethnicity, and race in American psychology. *American Psychologist, 48,* 629–637.

Beutler, Larry E.; Machado, Paulo P. P.; & Neufeldt, Susan Allstetter. (1994). Therapist variables. In Allen E. Bergin & Sol L. Garfield (Eds.), *Handbook of psychotherapy and behavior change* (4th ed.). New York: Wiley.

Beyerstein, Barry. (1996). Graphology. In Gordon Stein (Ed.), *The encyclopedia of the paranormal.* Amherst, N.Y.: Prometheus Books.

Binder, Jeffrey L.; Strupp, Hans H.; & Henry, William P. (1994). Psychodynamic therapies in practice: Time-limited dynamic psychotherapy. In Bruce Bongar & Larry E. Beutler (Eds.), *Comprehensive textbook of psychotherapy: Theory and practice.* New York: Oxford University Press.

Binet, Alfred, & Simon, Théodore. (1905). New methods for the diagnosis of the intellectual level of subnormals. *L'Année Psychologique, 11,* 191–244.

Birnbaum, D. A.; Nosanchuck, T. A.; & Croll, W. L. (1980). Children's stereotypes about sex differences in emotion. *Sex Roles, 6,* 435–443.

Bjorklund, Barbara R. (1995). Language development and cognition. In David F. Bjorklund (Ed.), *Children's thinking: Developmental function and individual differences* (2nd ed.). Pacific Grove, Calif.: Brooks/Cole.

Blackmore, Susan. (1985). Belief in the paranormal: Probability judgements, illusory control, and the chance baseline shift. *British Journal of Psychology, 76,* 459–468.

Blackmore, Susan. (1987). The elusive open mind: Ten years of negative research in parapsychology. *Skeptical Inquirer, 11,* 244–255.

Blair, Sampson Lee, & Lichter, Daniel T. (1991). Measuring the division of household labor: Gender segregation of housework among American couples. *Journal of Family Issues, 12,* 91–113.

Blaney, P. H. (1986). Affect and memory: A review. *Psychological Bulletin, 99,* 229–246.

Blank, Arthur S., Jr. (1994). Clinical detection, diagnosis, and differential diagnosis of post-traumatic stress disorder. *Psychiatric Clinics of North America, 17,* 351–383.

Blass, Elliott M., & Hoffmeyer, M. A. (1991). Sucrose as an analgesic for newborn infants. *Pediatrics, 87,* 215–218.

Blass, Thomas. (1991). Understanding behavior in the Milgram obedience experiment. *Journal of Personality and Social Psychology, 60,* 398–413.

Blass, Thomas. (1992). The social psychology of Stanley Milgram. In Mark P. Zanna (Ed.), *Advances in experimental social psychology* (Vol. 25). San Diego: Academic Press.

Blazer, Dan G.; Kessler, Ronald C.; McGonagle, Katherine A.; & Swartz, Marvin S. (1994). The prevalence and distribution of major depression in a national community sample: The National Comorbidity Survey. *American Journal of Psychiatry, 151,* 979–986.

Block, J. H. (1983). Differential premises arising from differential socialization of the sexes: Some conjectures. *Child Development, 53,* 1335–1354.

Block, Jack. (1995). A contrarian view of the five-factor approach to personality description. *Psychological Bulletin, 117,* 187–215.

Bloxham, G.; Long, C. G.; Alderman, N.; & Hollin, C. R. (1993). The behavioral treatment of self-starvation and severe self-injury in a patient with borderline personality disorder. *Journal of Behavioral Therapy and Experimental Psychiatry, 24,* 261–267.

Blumberg, Mark S., & Wasserman, Edward A. (1995). Animal mind and the argument from design. *American Psychologist, 50,* 133–144.

Bobo, Lawrence. (1988a). Attitudes toward the black political movement: Trends, meaning, and effects on racial policy preferences. *Social Psychology Quarterly, 51,* 287–302.

Bobo, Lawrence. (1988b). Group conflict, prejudice, and the paradox of contemporary racial attitudes. In Phyllis A. Katz & Dalmas A. Taylor (Eds.), *Eliminating racism: Profiles in controversy.* New York: Plenum Press.

Boivin, Diane B.; Duffy, Jeanne F.; & Czeisler, Charles A. (1994). Sensitivity of the human circadian pacemaker to moderately bright light. *Journal of Biological Rhythms, 9* (3/4), 315–322.

Boldizar, Janet P.; Wilson, Kenneth L.; & Deemer, Debra Kay. (1989). Gender, life experiences, and moral judgment development: A process-oriented approach. *Journal of Personality and Social Psychology, 57,* 229–238.

Bolger, Niall, & Schilling, Elizabeth A. (1991). Personality and problems of everyday life: The role of neuroticism in exposure and reactivity to stress. *Journal of Personality, 59,* 355–386.

Bolger, Niall, & Zuckerman, Adam. (1995). A framework for studying personality in the stress process. *Journal of Personality and Social Psychology, 69,* 890–902.

Bolles, Robert C. (1972). Reinforcement, expectancy, and learning. *Psychological Review, 79,* 394–409.

Bolles, Robert C. (1985). The slaying of Goliath: What happened to reinforcement theory? In Timothy D. Johnston & Alexandra T. Pietrewicz (Eds.), *Issues in the ecological study of learning.* Hillsdale, N.J.: Erlbaum.

Bond, Michael Harris. (1986). *The psychology of the Chinese people.* New York: Oxford University Press.

Bond, Michael Harris. (1994). Continuing encounters with Hong Kong. In Walter J. Lonner & Roy Malpass (Eds.), *Psychology and culture.* Boston: Allyn & Bacon.

Bond, Michael Harris, & Smith, Peter B. (1996). Cross-cultural social and organizational psychology. *Annual Review of Psychology, 47,* 205–235.

Bond, Rod, & Smith, Peter B. (1996). Culture and conformity: A meta-analysis of studies using Asch's (1952b, 1956) line judgment task. *Psychological Bulletin, 119,* 111–137.

Bond, Susan B., & Mosher, Donald L. (1986). Guided imagery of rape: Fantasy, reality, and the willing victim myth. *Journal of Sex Research, 22,* 162–183.

Boon, Suzette, & Draijer, Nel. (1993). Multiple personality disorder in the Netherlands: A clinical investigation of 71 patients. *American Journal of Psychiatry, 150,* 489–494.

Bornstein, Marc H., & Lamb, Michael E. (1992). *Development in infancy: An introduction* (3rd ed.). York: McGraw-Hill.

Bornstein, Marc H., & Marks, Lawrence E. (1982, January). Color revisionism. *Psychology Today, 16,* 64–73.

Bouchard, C.; Tremblay, A.; Despres, J. P.; Nadeau, A.; Lupien, P. J.; Theriault, G.; Dussault, J.; Moorjani, S.; Pinault, S.; & Fournier, G. (1990b). The response to long-term overfeeding in identical twins. *New England Journal of Medicine, 322,* 1477–1482.

Bouchard, Thomas J., Jr. (1994, June 17). Genes, environment, and personality. *Science, 264,* 1700–1701.

Bouchard, Thomas J., Jr.; Lykken, David T.; McGue, Matthew; Segal, Nancy L.; & Tellegen, Auke. (1990a). Sources of human psychological differences: The Minnesota Study of Twins Reared Apart. *Science, 250,* 223–250.

Bouchard, Thomas J., Jr., & McGue, Matthew. (1981). Familial studies of intelligence: A review. *Science, 212,* 1055–1059.

Bouman, Jerry L; Grawe, Jeffrey J.; & Hariman, Robert J. (1994). Cocaine-related sudden cardiac death: A hypothesis correlating basic science and clinical observations. *Journal of Clinical Pharmacology, 34,* 902–909.

Bovbjerg, Dana H.; Redd, William H.; Maier, Lisa A.; Holland, Jimmie C.; Lesko, Lynna M.; Niedzwiecki, Donna; Rubin, Stephen C.; & Hakes, Thomas B. (1990). Anticipatory immune suppression and nausea in women receiving cyclic chemotherapy for ovarian cancer. *Journal of Consulting and Clinical Psychology, 58,* 153–157.

Bower, Bruce. (1994a, August 20). Chronic depression: Drugs show promise. *Science News, 146,* 117–118.

Bower, Bruce. (1994b, June 4). Antidepressants may alter personality. *Science News, 145,* 359.

Bower, Gordon H. (1993). The fragmentation of psychology? *American Psychologist, 48,* 905–907.

Bower, T. G. R. (1989). *The rational infant: Learning in infancy.* New York: Freeman.

Bowers, Kenneth S. (1976). *Hypnosis for the seriously curious*. Monterey, Calif.: Brooks/Cole.

Bowers, Kenneth S.; Regehr, Glenn; Balthazard, Claude; & Parker, Kevin. (1990). Intuition in the context of discovery. *Cognitive Psychology, 22,* 72–110.

Boynton, Robort M. (1088). Color vision. *Annual Review of Psychology, 39,* 69–100.

Bracha, H. Stefan; Wolkowitz, Owen M.; Lohr, James B.; Karson, Craig N.; & Bigelow, Llewellyn B. (1989). High prevalence of visual hallucinations in research subjects with chronic schizophrenia. *American Journal of Psychiatry, 146,* 526–528.

Bradbard, Marilyn R.; Martin, Carol L.; Endsley, Richard C.; & Halverson, Charles F. (1986). Influence of sex stereotypes on children's exploration and memory: A competence versus performance distinction. *Developmental Psychology, 22,* 481–486.

Braff, David L. (1993). Information processing and attention dysfunctions in schizophrenia. *Schizophrenia Bulletin, 19,* 233–259.

Braiker, Harriet B. (1989, December). The power of self-talk. *Psychology Today,* pp. 23–27.

Brainerd, C. J. (1996). Piaget: A centennial celebration. *Psychological Science, 7,* 191–195.

Brandon, Thomas H. (1994, April). Negative affect as motivation to smoke. *Current Directions in Psychological Science, 3,* 33–37.

Bransford, John D., & Stein, Barry S. (1984). *The ideal problem solver*. New York: Freeman.

Bray, George A. (1991). Weight homeostasis. *Annual Review of Medicine, 42,* 205–216.

Brecher, Edward M. (1984). *Love, sex, and aging*. Mount Vernon, N.Y.: Consumers Union.

Breedlove, S. Marc. (1994). Sexual differentiation of the human nervous system. *Annual Review of Psychology, 45,* 389–418.

Breggin, Peter R. (1979). *Electroshock: Its brain disabling effects*. New York: Springer.

Breggin, Peter R. (1991). *Toxic psychiatry*. New York: St. Martin's Press.

Breggin, Peter, & Breggin, Ginger Rose. (1994). *Talking back to Prozac*. New York: St. Martin's Press.

Bregman, Elsie O. (1934). An attempt to modify the emotional attitude of infants by the conditioned response technique. *Journal of Genetic Psychology, 45,* 169–198.

Brehm, Sharon S. (1992). *Intimate relationships* (2nd ed.). New York: McGraw-Hill.

Brehm, Sharon S., & Kassin, Saul M. (1996). *Social psychology* (3rd ed.). Boston: Houghton Mifflin.

Breier, Alan; Buchanan, Robert W.; Elkashef, Ahmed; Munson, Robert C.; Kirkpatrick, Brian; & Gellad, Fouad. (1992). Brain morphology and schizophrenia: A magnetic resonance imaging study of limbic, prefrontal cortex, and caudate structures. *Archives of General Psychiatry, 49,* 921–926.

Breland, Keller, & Breland, Marian. (1961). The misbehavior of organisms. *American Psychologist, 16,* 681–684.

Brennan, James F. (1991). *History and systems of psychology* (3rd ed.). Englewood Cliffs, N.J.: Prentice Hall.

Bretschneider, Judy G., & McCoy, Norma L. (1988). Sexual interest and behavior in healthy 80- to 102-year-olds. *Archives of Sexual Behavior, 17,* 109–129.

Breuer, Josef, & Freud, Sigmund. (1895/1957). *Studies on hysteria*. Translated and edited by James Strachey, in collaboration with Anna Freud. New York: Basic Books.

Brewer, Marilyn B. (1994). The social psychology of prejudice: Getting it all together. In Mark P. Zanna & James M. Olson (Eds.), *The psychology of prejudice: The Ontario Symposium* (Vol. 7). Hillsdale, N.J.: Erlbaum.

Brewer, William F., & Treyens, James C. (1981). Role of schemata in memory for places. *Cognitive Psychology, 13,* 207–230.

Brewin, Chris R.; Andrews, Bernice; & Gotlib, Ian H. (1993). Psychopathology and early experience: A reappraisal of retrospective reports. *Psychological Bulletin, 113,* 82–98.

Brickman, Philip; Coates, Dan; & Janoff-Bulman, Ronnie. (1978). Lottery winners and accident victims: Is happiness relative? *Journal of Personality and Social Psychology, 36,* 917–927.

Briere, John, & Conte, Jon. (1993). Self-reported amnesia for abuse in adults molested as children. *Journal of Traumatic Stress, 6* (1), 21–31.

Briggs, Stephen R. (1992). Assessing the five-factor model of personality description. *Journal of Personality, 60,* 253–293.

Brislin, Richard. (1993). *Understanding culture's influence on behavior*. Fort Worth, Tex.: Harcourt Brace College Publishers.

Brock, Dwight B.; Lemke, Jon H.; & Berkman, Lisa F. (1994). Mortality and physical functioning in epidemiologic studies of three older populations. *Journal of Aging & Social Policy, 6* (3), 21–32.

Bronfenbrenner, Urie. (1979). *The ecology of human development*. Cambridge, Mass.: Harvard University Press.

Bronfenbrenner, Urie. (1995). Developmental ecology through space and time: A future perspective. In Phyllis Moen, Glen H. Elder, Jr., & Kurt Lüscher (Eds.), *Examining lives in context: Perspectives on the ecology of human development*. Washington, D.C.: American Psychological Association.

Bronfenbrenner, Urie, & Ceci, Stephen J. (1994). Nature-nurture reconceptualized in developmental perspective: A bioecological model. *Psychological Review, 101,* 568–586.

Brooks-Gunn, Jeanne. (1988). Antecedents and consequences of variations of girls' maturational timing. In Melvin D. Levine & Elizabeth R. McAnarney (Eds.), *Early adolescent transitions*. Lexington, Mass.: Lexington Books.

Brooks-Gunn, Jeanne, & Furstenberg, Frank F., Jr. (1989). Adolescent sexual behavior. *American Psychologist, 44,* 249–257.

Brooks-Gunn, Jeanne, & Reiter, Edward O. (1990). The role of pubertal processes. In S. Shirley Feldman & Glen R. Elliott (Eds.), *At the threshold: The developing adolescent*. Cambridge, Mass.: Harvard University Press.

Broughton, Roger J. (1989). Chronobiological aspects and models of sleep and napping. In David F. Dinges & Roger J. Broughton (Eds.), *Sleep and alertness: Chronobiological, behavioral, and medical aspects of napping*. New York: Raven Press.

Broughton, Roger J. (1990). Narcolepsy. In Michael J. Thorpy (Ed.), *Handbook of sleep disorders*. New York: Dekker.

Brown, Alan S. (1991). A review of the tip-of-the-tongue experience. *Psychological Bulletin, 109* (2), 204–223.

Brown, B. Bradford; Clasen, Donna Rae; & Eicher, Sue Ann. (1986). Perceptions of peer pressure, peer conformity dispositions, and self-reported behavior among adolescents. *Developmental Psychology, 22,* 521–530.

Brown, George William; Harris, Tirril Olivia; & Hepworth, Cathy. (1994). Life events and endogenous depression: A puzzle reexamined. *Archives of General Psychiatry, 51,* 525–534.

Brown, Gregory M. (1994). Light, melatonin, and the sleep-wake cycle. *Journal of Psychiatry and Neuroscience, 19* (5), 345–353.

Brown, Jonathan D. (1991). Staying fit and staying well: Physical fitness as a moderator of life stress. *Journal of Personality and Social Psychology, 60,* 555–561.

Brown, Robert T. (1989). Creativity: What are we to measure? In John A. Glover, Royce R. Ronning, & Cecil R. Reynolds (Eds.), *Handbook of creativity*. New York: Plenum.

Brown, Roger, & Kulik, James. (1982). Flashbulb memories. In Ulric Neisser (Ed.), *Memory observed: Remembering in natural contexts*. San Francisco: Freeman.

Brownell, Kelly D. (1982). The addictive disorders. In C. M. Franks, B. T. Wilson, P. C. Kendall, & Kelly D. Brownell (Eds.), *Annual review of behavior therapy: Theory and practice* (Vol. 8). New York: Guilford Press.

Brownell, Kelly D., & Rodin, Judith. (1994). The dieting maelstrom: Is it possible and advisable to lose weight? *American Psychologist, 49,* 781–791.

Bruhn, Arnold R. (1990). *Earliest childhood memories: Vol. 1. Theory and application to clinical practice.* New York: Praeger.

Bruner, Jerome, (1992). Another look at New Look 1. *American Psychologist, 47,* 780–783.

Bryan, James H., & Test, Mary Ann. (1967). Models and helping: Naturalistic studies in aiding behavior. *Journal of Personality and Social Psychology, 6,* 400–407.

Buchanan, Alec; Reed, Alison; Wessely, Simon; & Garety, Philippa. (1993). Acting on delusions: The phenomenological correlates of acting on delusions. *British Journal of Psychiatry, 163,* 77–81.

Buchanan, Christy Miller; Eccles, Jacquelynne S.; & Becker, Jill B. (1992). Are adolescents the victims of raging hormones? Evidence for activational effects of hormones on moods and behavior at adolescence. *Psychological Bulletin, 111,* 62–107.

Buck, Linda. (1993, June). Quoted in David H. Freedman, In the realm of the chemical. *Discover, 14,* 68–76.

Buck, Linda B. (1995, February 14). Quoted in Natalie Angier, Powerhouse of senses, smell, at last gets its due. *New York Times,* pp. C1, C6.

Buck, Linda B. (1996). Information coding in the vertebrate olfactory system. *Annual Review of Neuroscience, 19,* 517–544.

Buck, Linda, & Axel, Richard. (1991). A novel multigene family may encode odorant receptors: A molecular basis for odor recognition. *Cell, 65,* 175–187.

Buck, Lucien A. (1992). The myth of normality: Consequences for the diagnosis of abnormality and health. *Social Behavior and Personality, 20,* 251–262.

Buck, Ross. (1988). *Human motivation and emotion* (2nd ed.) New York: Wiley.

Buckley, Kerry W. (1982). The selling of a psychologist: John Broadus Watson and the application of behavioral techniques to advertising. *Journal of the History of the Behavioral Sciences, 18,* 207–221.

Buckley, Kerry W. (1989). *Mechanical man: John Broadus Watson and the beginnings of behaviorism.* New York: Guilford Press.

Buhrmester, D., & Furman, W. (1987). The development of companionship and intimacy. *Child Development, 50,* 1101–1115.

Bulcroft, Richard A., & Bulcroft, Kris A. (1991). The nature and functions of dating in later life. *Research on Aging, 13,* 244–260.

Bullock, Theodore H. (1993). Integrative systems research on the brain: Resurgence and new opportunities. *Annual Review of Physiology, 16,* 1–15.

Bureau of Labor Statistics. (1994). *Occupational outlook handbook.* Washington, D.C.: U.S. Department of Labor.

Burger, Jerry M. (1986). Increasing compliance by improving the deal: The that's-not-all technique. *Journal of Personality and Social Psychology, 51,* 277–283.

Burger, Jerry M. (1987). Desire for control and conformity to a perceived norm. *Journal of Personality and Social Psychology, 53,* 355–360.

Burger, Jerry M. (1992). *Desire for control: Personality, social, and clinical perspectives.* New York: Plenum.

Burgio, Louis, D., & Sinnott, Jan. (1990). Behavioral treatments and pharmacotherapy: Acceptability ratings by elderly individuals in residential settings. *Gerontologist, 30,* 811–816.

Buri, J. R.; Louiselle, P. A.; Misukanis, T. M.; & Mueller, R. A. (1988). Effects of parental authoritarianism and authoritativeness on self-esteem. *Personality and Social Psychology Bulletin, 14,* 271–282.

Burke, Deborah M.; MacKay, Donald G.; Worthley, Joanna S.; & Wade, Elizabeth. (1991). On the tip of the tongue: What causes word finding failures in young and older adults? *Journal of Memory and Language, 30,* 542–579.

Burke, Kimberly Christie; Burke, Jack D.; Rae, Donald S.; & Regier, Darrel A. (1991). Comparing age at onset of major depression and other psychiatric disorders by birth cohorts in five U. S. community populations. *Archives of General Psychiatry, 48,* 789–795.

Burks, Nancy, & Martin, Barclay. (1985). Everyday problems and life change events: Ongoing versus acute sources of stress. *Journal of Human Stress, 11,* 27–35.

Burman, Bonnie, & Margolin, Gayla. (1992). Analysis of the association between marital relationships and health problems: An interactional perspective. *Psychological Bulletin, 112,* 39–63.

Burns, Melanie, & Seligman, Martin E. P. (1989). Explanatory style across the life-span: Evidence for stability over 52 years. *Journal of Personality and Social Psychology, 56,* 471–477.

Burt, Diana Byrd; Zembar, Mary Jo; & Niederehe, George. (1995). Depression and memory impairment: A meta-analysis of the association, its pattern, and specificity. *Psychological Bulletin, 117,* 285–305.

Bushman, Brad J. (1993). Human aggression while under the influence of alcohol and other drugs: An integrative research review. *Current Directions in Psychological Science, 2,* 148–152.

Buss, Arnold H. (1989). Personality as traits. *American Psychologist, 44,* 1378–1388.

Buss, David M. (1991). Evolutionary personality psychology. *Annual Review of Psychology, 42,* 459–491.

Buss, David M. (1995). Psychological sex differences: Origins through sexual selection. *American Psychologist, 50,* 164–168.

Butcher, James N., & Rouse, Steven V. (1996). Personality: Individual differences and clinical assessment. *Annual Review of Psychology, 47,* 87–111.

Butcher, James N., & Williams, Carolyn L. (1992). *Essentials of MMPI-2 and MMPI-A interpretation.* Minneapolis: University of Minnesota Press.

Butler, Richard A., & Harlow, Harry. (1954). Persistence of visual exploration in monkeys. *Journal of Comparative and Physiological Psychology, 47,* 258–263.

Butler, Robert W., & Braff, David L. (1991). Delusions: A review and integration. *Schizophrenia Bulletin, 17,* 633–647.

Butters, Nelson, & Delis, Dean C. (1995). Clinical assessment of memory disorders in amnesia and dementia. *Annual Review of Psychology, 46,* 493–523.

Buysse, Daniel J., & Reynolds, Charles F., III. (1990). Insomnia. In Michael J. Thorpy (Ed.), *Handbook of sleep disorders.* New York: Dekker.

Byne, William. (1994, May). The biological evidence challenged. *Scientific American, 270,* 50–55.

Byne, William, & Parsons, Bruce. (1993). Human sexual orientation: The biologic theories reappraised. *Archives of General Psychiatry, 50,* 228–239.

Byrd, Kevin R. (1994). The narrative reconstruction of incest survivors. *American Psychologist, 49,* 439–440.

Cacioppo, John T.; Uchino, Bert N.; Crites, Stephen L.; Snydersmith, Mary A.; Smith, Gregory; Berntson, Gary G.; & Lang, Peter J. (1992). Relationship between facial expressiveness and sympathetic activation in emotion: A critical review, with emphasis on modeling underlying mechanisms and individual differences. *Journal of Personality and Social Psychology, 62,* 110–128.

Cailliet, René. (1993). *Pain: Mechanisms and management.* Philadelphia: F. A. Davis.

Cain, William S. (1982). Odor identification by males and females: Predictions versus performance. *Chemical Senses, 7,* 129–142.

Calkins, Mary W. (1893). Statistics of dreams. *American Journal of Psychology, 5,* 311–343.

Calkins, Susan D., & Fox, Nathan A. (1994). Individual differences in the biological aspects of temperament. In John E. Bates & Theodore D. Wachs (Eds.), *Temperament: Individual differences at the interface of biology and behavior.* Washington, D.C.: American Psychological Association.

Campbell, D. P. (1977). *Manual for the Strong-Campbell Interest Inventory T325 (merged form).* Stanford, Calif.: Stanford University Press.

Campbell, Jennifer D., & Fairey, Patricia J. (1989). Informational and normative routes to conformity: The effect of faction size as a function of norm extremity and attention to the stimulus. *Journal of Personality and Social Psychology, 57* 457–458.

Campbell, John B., & Hawley, Charles W. (1982). Study habits and Eysenck's theory of extraversion–introversion. *Journal of Research in Personality, 16,* 139–146.

Campion, J. E. (1972). Work sampling for personnel selection. *Journal of Applied Psychology, 56,* 40–44.

Campion, M. A.; Pursell, E. D.; & Brown, B. K. (1988). Structured interviewing: Raising the psychometric properties of the employment interview. *Personnel Psychology, 41,* 25–42.

Candland, Douglas Keith. (1995). *Feral children and clever animals.* New York: Oxford University Press.

Cannon, Tyrone D., & Marco, Elysa. (1994). Structural brain abnormalities as indicators of vulnerability to schizophrenia. *Schizophrenia Bulletin, 20,* 89–102.

Cannon, Walter B. (1927). The James-Lange theory of emotion: A critical examination and an alternative theory. *American Journal of Psychology, 39,* 106–124.

Cannon, Walter B. (1932). *The wisdom of the body.* New York: Norton.

Cannon, Walter B.; Lewis, J. T.; & Britton, S. W. (1927). The dispensability of the sympathetic division of the autonomic nervous system. *Boston Medical and Surgical Journal, 197,* 514.

Card, J. Patrick, & Moore, Robert Y. (1991). The organization of visual circuits influencing the circadian activity of the suprachiasmatic nucleus. In David C. Klein, Robert Y. Moore, & Steven M. Reppert (Eds.), *Suprachiasmatic nucleus: The mind's clock.* New York: Oxford University Press.

Cardeña, Etzel. (1992). Trance and possession as dissociative disorders. *Transcultural Psychiatric Research Review, 29,* 287–300.

Carli, Linda L., & Leonard, Jean B. (1989). The effect of hindsight on victim derogation. *Journal of Social and Clinical Psychology, 8,* 331–343.

Carlson, Earl R. (1995). Evaluating the credibility of sources: A missing link in the teaching of critical thinking. *Teaching of Psychology, 22* (1), 39–41.

Carlson, Eve Bernstein; Putnam, Frank W.; Ross, Colin A.; Torem, Moshe; Coons, Philip; Dill, Diana L.; Loewenstein, Richard J.; & Braun, Bennett G. (1993). Validity of the Dissociative Experiences Scale in screening for multiple personality disorder: A multicenter study. *American Journal of Psychiatry, 150,* 1030–1036.

Carlson, Eve Bernstein, & Rosser-Hogan, Rhonda. (1991). Trauma experiences, posttraumatic stress, dissociation, and depression in Cambodian refugees. *American Journal of Psychiatry, 148,* 1548–1551.

Carlson, John G., & Hatfield, Elaine. (1992). *Psychology of emotion.* Fort Worth, Tex.: Harcourt Brace Jovanovich.

Carlson, Neil R. (1994). *Physiology of behavior* (5th ed.). Boston: Allyn & Bacon.

Carlson, Shawn. (1985, December 5). A double-blind test of astrology. *Nature, 318,* 419–425.

Carmichael, L.; Hogan, H. P.; & Walter, A. A. (1932). An experimental study of the effect of language on the reproduction of visually perceived forms. *Journal of Experimental Psychology, 15,* 73–86.

Carroll, Kathleen Whiteman. (1993). Family support groups for medically ill patients and their families. In Anne Alonso & Hillel I. Swiller (Eds.), *Group therapy in clinical practice.* Washington, D.C.: American Psychiatric Press.

Carskadon, Mary A. (1989). Ontogeny of human sleepiness as measured by sleep latency. In David F. Dinges & Roger J. Broughton (Eds.), *Sleep and alertness: Chronobiological, behavioral, and medical aspects of napping.* New York: Raven Press.

Carter, Jerry L. (1992). Visual, somatosensory, olfactory, and gustatory hallucinations. *Psychiatric Clinics of North America, 15,* 347–358.

Cartwright, Rosalind Dymond, & Kaszniak, Alfred. (1991). The social psychology of dream reporting. In Steven J. Ellman & John S. Antrobus (Eds.), *The mind in sleep: Psychology and psychophysiology* (2nd ed.). New York: Wiley.

Case, Robbie. (1985). *Intellectual development: Birth to adulthood.* Orlando, Fla.: Academic Press.

Casey, M. Beth; Nuttall, Ronald; Pezaris, Elizabeth; & Benbow, Camilla Persson. (1995). The influence of spatial ability on gender differences in mathematics college entrance test scores across diverse samples. *Developmental Psychology, 31,* 697–705.

Cattell, Raymond B. (1973, July). Personality pinned down. *Psychology Today,* pp. 40–46.

Cattell, Raymond B. (1994). A cross-validation of primary personality structure in the 16 P.F. by two parcelled factor analysis. *Multivariate Experimental Clinical Research, 10* (3), 181–191.

Cattell, Raymond B.; Cattell, A. Karen S.; & Cattell, Heather E.P. (1993). *16 PF questionnaire* (5th ed.). Champaign, Ill.: Institute for Personality and Ability Testing.

CBS News. (1979, March 31). Transcript of *Sixty Minutes* segment, "I was only following orders," pp. 2–8.

Ceci, Stephen J., & Bruck, Maggie. (1993). Suggestibility of the child witness: A historical review and synthesis. *Psychological Bulletin, 113* (3), 403–439.

Ceci, Stephen J., & Loftus, Elizabeth F. (1994). "Memory work": A royal road to false memories? Special issue: Recovery of memories of childhood sexual abuse. *Applied Cognitive Psychology, 8,* 351–364.

Centers for Disease Control and Prevention. (1993a). Update: Acquired immunodeficiency syndrome: United States, 1991 and 1992. *Morbidity and Mortality Weekly Report, 42* (28), 547–557.

Centers for Disease Control and Prevention. (1993b). Update: Mortality attributable to HIV infection among persons aged 25–44 years: United States, 1991 and 1992. *Morbidity and Mortality Weekly Report, 42* (45), 869–872.

Centers for Disease Control and Prevention. (1994). Update: Heterosexually acquired AIDS: United States, 1993. *Morbidity and Mortality Weekly Report, 43* (9), 155–160.

Chadwick, P. D. J.; Lowe, C. F.; Horne, P. J.; & Higson, P. J. (1994). Modifying delusions: The role of empirical testing. *Behavior Therapy, 25,* 35–49.

Chafetz, Michael D., & Buelow, George. (1994). A training model for psychologists with prescription privileges. *Professional Psychology: Research and Practice, 25,* 149–153.

Chambers, Deborah; & Reisberg, Daniel. (1985). Can mental images be ambiguous? *Journal of Experimental Psychology: Human Perception and Performance, 11,* 317–328.

Chambers, Mark J. (1995). Childhood insomnia. In Charles E. Schaefer (Ed.), *Clinical handbook of sleep disorders in children.* Northvale, N.J.: Aronson.

Chambless, Dianne L., & Gillis, Martha M. (1993). Cognitive therapy of anxiety disorders. *Journal of Consulting and Clinical Psychology, 61,* 248–260.

Chase, Michael H., & Morales, Francisco R. (1990). The atonia and myoclonia of active (REM) sleep. *Annual Review of Psychology, 41,* 557–584.

Chen, E. Y. H.; Wilkins, A. J.; & McKenna, P. J. (1994). Semantic memory is both impaired and anomalous in schizophrenia. *Psychological Medicine, 24,* 193–202.

Cheney, Dorothy L., & Seyfarth, Robert M. (1990). *How monkeys see the world.* Chicago: University of Chicago Press.

Chomsky, Noam. (1965). *Aspects of a theory of syntax.* Cambridge, Mass.: MIT Press.

Christensen, Andrew, & Heavey, Christopher L. (1993). Gender differences in marital conflict: The demand/withdraw interaction pattern. In Stuart Oskamp & Mark Costanzo (Eds.), *Gender issues in contemporary society.* Newbury Park, Calif.: Sage Publications.

Christensen, Andrew, & Jacobson, Neil S. (1994). Who (or what) can do psychotherapy: The status and challenge of nonprofessional therapies. *Psychological Science, 5,* 8–14.

Church, A. T., & Katigbak, M. S. (1989). Internal, external, and self-report structure of personality in a non-Western culture: An investigation of cross-language and cross-cultural generalizability. *Journal of Personality and Social Psychology, 54,* 296–308.

Chwalisz, Kathleen; Diener, Ed; & Gallagher, Dennis. (1988). Autonomic arousal feedback and emotional experience: Evidence from the spinal cord injured. *Journal of Personality and Social Psychology, 54,* 820–828.

Cialdini, Robert B. (1993). *Influence: Science and practice* (3rd ed.). New York: HarperCollins.

Cialdini, Robert B.; Darby, Betty Lee; & Vincent, Joyce E. (1973). Transgression and altruism: A case for hedonism. *Journal of Experimental Social Psychology, 9,* 502–516.

Cioffi, Delia, & Holloway, James. (1993). Delayed costs of suppressed pain. *Journal of Personality and Social Psycyhology, 64,* 274–282.

Clark, Russell D., III, & Word, Larry E. (1972). Why don't bystanders help? Because of the ambiguity? *Journal of Personality and Social Psychology, 24,* 392–400.

Clarke, Dave. (1991). Belief in the paranormal: A New Zealand survey. *Journal of the Society for Psychical Research, 57,* 412–425.

Clarke-Stewart, K. Alison. (1989). Infant day care: Maligned or malignant? *American Psychologist, 44,* 266–273.

Clarke-Stewart, K. Alison. (1992). Consequences of child care for children's development. In Alan Booth (Ed.), *Child care in the 1990s: Trends and consequences.* Hillsdale, N.J.: Erlbaum.

Clay, Rebecca A. (1995, November). Working mothers: Happy or haggard? *APA Monitor, 26* (1) 37.

Cohen, Bruce M.; Renshaw, Perry F.; & Yurgelun-Todd, Deborah. (1995). Editorial: Imaging the mind: Magnetic resonance technology and functional brain imaging. *American Journal of Psychiatry, 152,* 655–658.

Cohen, Frances. (1991). Measurement of coping. In Alan Monat & Richard S. Lazarus (Eds.), *Stress and coping: An anthology* (3rd ed.). New York: Columbia University Press.

Cohen, Neil J. (1984). Preserved learning capacity in amnesia: Evidence for multiple memory systems. In Larry R. Squire & Nelson Butters (Eds.), *Neuropsychology of memory.* New York: Guilford Press.

Cohen, Sheldon. (1988). Psychosocial models of the role of social support in the etiology of physical disease. *Health Psychology, 7,* 269–297.

Cohen, Sheldon, & Herbert, Tracy B. (1996). Health psychology: Psychological factors and physical disease from the perspective of human psychoneuroimmunology. *Annual Review of Psychology, 47,* 113–142.

Cohen, Sheldon, & McKay, Garth. (1984). Social support, stress, and the buffering hypothesis: A theoretical analysis. In Andrew Baum, Shelley E. Taylor, & Jerome E. Singer (Eds.), *Handbook of psychology and health: Vol. IV. Social psychological aspects of health.* Hillsdale, N.J.: Erlbaum.

Cohen, Sheldon; Tyrrell, David A. J.; & Smith, Andrew P. (1991). Psychological stress and susceptibility to the common cold. *New England Journal of Medicine, 325,* 606–612.

Cohen, Sheldon; Tyrrell, David A. J.; & Smith, Andrew P. (1993). Negative life events, perceived stress, negative affect, and susceptibility to the common cold. *Journal of Personality and Social Psychology, 64,* 131–140.

Cohen, Sheldon, & Williamson, Gail M. (1988). Perceived stress in a probability sample of the United States. In Shirlynn Spacapan & Stuart Oskamp (Eds.), *The social psychology of health: The Claremont Symposium on Applied Social Psychology* (4th ed). Newbury Park, Calif.: Sage.

Coile, D. Caroline, & Miller, Neal E. (1984, June). How radical animal activists try to mislead humane people. *American Psychologist, 39,* 700–701.

Colby, Anne, & Kohlberg, Lawrence. (1984). Invariant sequence and internal consistency in moral judgment stages. In William M. Kurtines & Jacob L. Gewirtz (Eds.), *Morality, moral behavior, and moral development.* New York: Wiley.

Colby, Anne; Kohlberg, Lawrence; Gibbs, John; & Lieberman, Marcus. (1983). A longitudinal study of moral judgment. *Monographs of the Society for Research in Child Development, 48,* Nos. 1–2, 1–123.

Cole, K. C. (1995). Innumeracy. In Russell Jacoby & Naomi Glauberman (Eds.), *The Bell Curve debate: History, documents, opinions.* New York: Times Books.

Cole, Michael, & Cole, Sheila R. (1993). *The development of children* (2nd ed.). New York: Freeman.

Coles, Robert, & Stokes, Geoffrey. (1985). *Sex and the American teenager.* New York: Harper & Row.

Collaer, Marcia J., & Hines, Melissa. (1995). Human behavioral sex differences: A role for gonadal hormones during early development? *Psychological Bulletin, 118,* 55–107.

Collins, A. M., & Loftus, Elizabeth F. (1975). A spreading activation theory of semantic processing. *Psychological Review, 82,* 407–428.

Collins, Robert L. (1970). The sound of one paw clapping: An inquiry into the origins of left-handedness. In G. Lindzey & D. B. Thiessen (Eds.), *Contributions to Behavior-Genetic Analysis—The Mouse as Prototype.* New York: Meredith.

Collins, Robert L. (1975). When left-handed mice live in right-handed worlds. *Science, 187,* 181–184.

Collins, W. Andrew, & Gunnar, Megan. (1990). Social and personality development. *Annual Review of Psychology, 41,* 387–416.

Colton, James, & Colton, Sheelagh. (1988). *Iridology: A patient's guide.* Wellingborough, Northamptonshire, U.K.: Thorsons.

Comas-Diaz, Lillian. (1993). Hispanic/Latino communities: Psychological implications. In Donald R. Atkinson, George Morten, & Derald Wing Sue (Eds.), *Counseling American minorities: A cross-cultural perspective* (4th ed.). Madison, Wis.: Brown & Benchmark.

Compas, Bruce E.; Hinden, Beth R.; & Gerhardt, Cynthia A. (1995). Adolescent development: Pathways and processes of risk and resilience. *Annual Review of Psychology, 46,* 265–293.

Connor-Greene, Patricia A. (1993). From the laboratory to the headlines: Teaching critical evaluation of the press reports of research. *Teaching of Psychology, 20* (3), 167–169.

Conoley, Jane Close, & Impara, James C. (1995). *The 12th mental measurements yearbook.* Lincoln: University of Nebraska Press.

Conway, Martin A.; Cohen, Gillian; & Stanhope, Nicola. (1991). On the very long-term retention of knowledge acquired through formal education: Twelve years of cognitive psychology. *Journal of Experimental Psychology: General, 120,* 395–409.

Cook, Michael, & Mineka, Susan. (1990). Selective associations in the observational conditioning of fear in rhesus monkeys. *Journal of Experimental Psychology: Animal Behavior Processes, 16,* 372–389.

Coons, Philip M. (1994). Confirmation of childhood abuse in child and adolescent cases of multiple personality disorder and dissociative disorder not otherwise specified. *Journal of Nervous and Mental Disease, 182,* 461–464.

Coons, Philip M.; Bowman, Elizabeth S.; Kluft, Richard P.; & Milstein, Victor. (1991). The cross-cultural occurrence of MPD: Additional cases from a recent survey. *Dissociation, 4,* 124–128.

Coons, Philip M., & Dua, Vikram. (1993). Psychiatric health care costs of multiple personality disorder. *American Journal of Psychotherapy, 47,* 103–112.

Cooper, Leslie M. (1979). Hypnotic amnesia. In Erika Fromm & Ronald E. Shor (Eds.), *Hypnosis: Developments in research and new perspectives* (2nd ed.). New York: Aldine.

Cooper, Rosemary. (1994). Normal sleep. In Rosemary Cooper (Ed.), *Sleep.* New York: Chapman & Hall.

Cooper, Rosemary, & Bradbury, Sue. (1994). Techniques in sleep recording. In Rosemary Cooper (Ed.), *Sleep.* New York: Chapman & Hall.

Corbett, S. W., & Keesey, R. E. (1982). Energy balance of rats with lateral hypothalamic lesions. *American Journal of Physiology, 242,* 273–279.

Coren, Stanley. (1992). *The left-hander syndrome: The causes and consequences of left-handedness.* New York: Free Press.

Coren, Stanley, & Halpern, Diane F. (1991). Left-handedness: A marker for decreased survival fitness. *Psychological Bulletin, 109,* 90–106.

Coren, Stanley; Ward, Lawrence M.; & Enns, James T. (1994). *Sensation and perception* (4th ed.). Fort Worth, Tex.: Harcourt Brace College Publishers.

Corsini, R. J. (1957). *Non-Verbal Reasoning Test.* Park Ridge, Ill.: London House Press.

Coryell, William; Akiskal, Hapog S.; Leon, Andrew C.; Winokur, George; Maser, John D.; Mueller, Timothy I.; & Keller, Martin B. (1994a). The time course of nonchronic major depressive disorder: Uniformity across episodes and samples. *Archives of General Psychiatry, 51,* 405–410.

Coryell, William; Endicott, Jean; & Keller, Martin. (1992). Rapid cycling affective disorder: Demographics, diagnosis, family history, and course. *Archives of General Psychiatry, 49,* 126–131.

Coryell, William; Winokur, George; Shea, Tracie; Maser, Jack D.; Endicott, Jean; & Akiskal, Hapog S. (1994b). The long-term stability of depressive subtypes. *American Journal of Psychiatry, 151,* 199–204.

Costa, Paul T., Jr., & McCrae, Robert R. (1989). Personality continuity and the changes of adult life. In Martha Storandt & Gary R. VandenBos (Eds.), *The adult years: Continuity and change.* Washington, D.C.: American Psychological Association.

Costa, Paul T., Jr., & McCrae, Robert R. (1994). "Set like plaster?" Evidence for the stability of adult personality. In Todd F. Hetherton & Joel L. Weinberger (Eds.), *Can personality change?* Washington, D.C.: American Psychological Association.

Costanzo, Elaine M. (1976). The effect of probable retaliation and sex-related variables on obedience. *Dissertation Abstracts International, 37,* 4214B. (University Microfilms No. 77–3253).

Cotton, Paul. (1995, January 11). Prognosis, diagnosis, or who knows? Time to learn what gene tests mean. *Journal of the American Medical Association, 273,* 93–95.

Cowan, Nelson. (1994). Mechanisms of verbal short-term memory. *Current Directions in Psychological Science, 6,* 185–189.

Cowan, Nelson; Wood, Noelle L.; & Borne, Dawn N. (1994). Reconfirmation of the short-term storage concept. *Psychological Science, 5,* 103–108.

Cowan, Philip A., & Cowan, Carolyn Pape. (1988). Changes in marriage during the transition to parenthood: Must we blame the baby? In Gerald Y. Michaels & Wendy A. Goldberg (Eds.), *The transition to parenthood: Current theory and research.* Cambridge, England: Cambridge University Press.

Cowan, Philip A., & Cowan, Carolyn Pape. (1992). *When partners become parents.* New York: Basic Books.

Cowley, Geoffrey. (1994, February 7). The culture of Prozac. *Newsweek,* pp. 41–42.

Cowley, Geoffrey. (1995, August 7). Melatonin. *Newsweek,* pp. 46–49.

Coyne, James C., & Downey, Geraldine. (1991). Social factors and psychopathology: Stress, social support, and coping processes. *Annual Review of Psychology, 42,* 401–425.

Coyne, James C.; Ellard, John H.; & Smith, David A. F. (1990). Social support, interdependence, and the dilemmas of helping. In Barbara R. Sarason, Irwin G. Sarason, & Gregory R. Pierce (Eds.), *Social support: An interactional view.* New York: Wiley.

Crabbe, John C.; Belknap, John K.; & Buck, Kari J. (1994, June 17). Genetic animal models of alcohol and drug abuse. *Science, 264,* 1715–1723.

Craik, Fergus I. M. (1994). Memory changes in normal aging. *Current Directions in Psychological Science, 3,* 155–158.

Craik, Fergus I. M.; Byrd, M.; & Swanson, J. M. (1987). Patterns of memory loss in three elderly samples. *Psychology and Aging, 2,* 79–86.

Craik, Fergus I. M., & Lockhart, Robert S. (1972). Levels of processing: A framework for memory research. *Journal of Verbal Learning and Verbal Behavior, 11,* 671–684.

Craik, Fergus I. M., & Tulving, Endel. (1975). Depth of processing and the retention of words in episodic memory. *Journal of Experimental Psychology: General, 104,* 268–294.

Crano, William D. (1995). Attitude strength and vested interest. In Richard E. Petty & Jon A. Krosnick (Eds.), *Attitude strength: Antecedents and consequences.* Hillsdale, N.J.: Erlbaum.

Craske, Michelle G. (1993). Specific fears and panic attacks: A survey of clinical and nonclinical samples. *Journal of Anxiety Disorders, 7,* 1–19.

Craske, Michelle G.; Miller, Patricia P.; Rotunda, Robert; & Barlow, David H. (1990). A descriptive report of initial unexpected panic attacks in minimal and extensive avoiders. *Behaviour Research and Therapy, 28,* 395–400.

Crews, Frederick. (1984/1986). The Freudian way of knowledge. In *Skeptical engagements.* New York: Oxford University Press.

Crews, Frederick. (1996). The verdict on Freud. *Psychological Science, 7,* 63–68.

Crick, Francis, & Koch, Christof. (1992, September). The problem of consciousness. *Scientific American, 267,* 110–117.

Cronbach, Lee J. (1990). *Essentials of psychological testing* (5th ed.). New York: Harper & Row.

Cropley, Arthur J. (1991). Improving intelligence by fostering creativity in everyday settings. In Helga A. H. Rowe (Ed.), *Intelligence: Reconceptualization and measurement.* Hillsdale, N.J.: Erlbaum.

Cropley, Arthur J. (1992). *More ways than one: Fostering creativity.* Norwood, N.J.: Ablex.

Crowder, Robert G. (1992). Sensory memory. In Larry R. Squire (Ed.), *Encyclopedia of learning and memory.* New York: Macmillan.

Crowe, Richard A. (1990). Astrology and the scientific method. *Psychological Reports, 67,* 163–191.

Csernansky, John G., & Newcomer, John W. (1994). Are there neurochemical indicators of risk for schizophrenia? *Schizophrenia Bulletin, 20,* 75–88.

Cumming, Elaine, & Henry, William. (1961). *Growing old: The process of disengagement.* New York: Basic Books.

Cupach, William R., & Canary, Daniel J. (1995). Managing conflict and anger: Investigating the sex stereotype hypothesis. In Pamela J. Kalbfleisch & Michael J. Cody (Eds.), *Gender, power, and communication in human relationships.* Hillsdale, N.J.: Erlbaum.

Cutler, W. B.; Preti, George; Krieger, A.; Huggins, G. R.; Garcia, C. R.; & Lawley, H. J. (1986). Human axillary secretions influence women's menstrual cycles: The role of donor extract from men. *Hormones and Behavior, 20,* 463–473.

Czeisler, Charles A.; Johnson, Michael P.; Duffy, Jeanne F.; Brown, E. N.; Ronda, J. M.; & Kronauer, Richard E. (1990). Exposure to bright light and darkness to treat physiologic maladaptions to night work. *New England Journal of Medicine, 322* (18), 1253–1259.

Czeisler, Charles A.; Kronauer, Richard E.; Allen, J. S.; Duffy, J. F.; Jewett, M. E.; Brown, E. N.; & Ronda, J. M. (1989, June

16). Bright light induction of strong (Type O) resetting of the human circadian pacemaker. *Science, 244,* 1328–1333.

Czeisler, Charles A.; Moore–Ede, Martin C.; & Coleman, Robert M. (1982). Rotating shift work schedules that disrupt sleep are improved by applying circadian principles. *Science, 217,* 460–463.

Czeisler, Charles A.; Shanahan, Theresa L.; Klerman, Elizabeth B.; Martens, Heinz; Brotman, Daniel J.; Emens, Jonathan S.; Klein, Torsten; & Rizzo, Joseph F., III. (1995). Suppression of melatonin secretion in some blind patients by exposure to bright light. *New England Journal of Medicine, 332* (1), 6–11.

Damasio, Antonio R. (1994). *Descartes' error: Emotion, reason, and the human brain.* New York: Putnam.

Damasio, Antonio R., & Damasio, Hanna. (1992, September). Brain and language. *Scientific American, 267,* 62–71.

Damasio, Hanna; Grabowski, Thomas; Frank, Randle; Galaburda, Albert M.; & Damasio, Antonio R. (1994, May 20). The return of Phineas Gage: Clues about the brain from the skull of a famous patient. *Science, 264,* 1102–1105.

Daniels, Denise, & Plomin, Robert. (1985). Differential experience of siblings in the same family. *Developmental Psychology, 21,* 747–760.

Daniels, Denise, & Plomin, Robert. (1987). Why are children in the same family so different from one another? *Behavioral and Brain Sciences, 10,* 1–60.

Darley, John M. (1992). Social organization for the production of evil. Book Review Essay. *Psychological Inquiry, 3,* 199–218.

Darley, John M., & Shultz, Thomas R. (1990). Moral rules: Their content and acquisition. *Annual Review of Psychology, 41,* 525–556.

Dasen, Pierre R. (1994). Culture and cognitive development from a Piagetian perspective. In Walter J. Lonner & Roy Malpass (Eds.), *Psychology and culture.* Boston: Allyn & Bacon.

Davey, Graham C. L. (1989). Dental phobias and anxieties: Evidence for conditioning processes in the acquisition and modulation of a learned fear. *Behaviour Research and Therapy, 27,* 51–58.

Davey, Graham C. L. (1993). Factors influencing self-rated fear to a novel animal. *Cognition and Emotion, 7,* 461–471.

Davidson, Jonathan R. T. (1993). Introduction: Social phobia in review: 1993. *Journal of Clinical Psychiatry, 54* (12, Supplement), 3–4.

Davidson, Julian M., & Myers, L. S. (1988). Endocrine factors in sexual psychophysiology. In Raymond C. Rosen & J. Gayle Beck (Eds.), *Patterns of sexual arousal: Psychophysiological processes and clinical applications.* New York: Guilford.

Davidson, Richard J. (1992). Emotion and affective style: Hemispheric substrates. *Psychological Science, 3,* 39–43.

Davidson, Richard J. (1993). Parsing affective space: Perspectives from neuropsychology and psychophysiology. *Neuropsychology, 7,* 464–475.

Davidson, Richard J. (1994a). Complexities in the search for emotion-specific physiology. In Paul Ekman & Richard J. Davidson (Eds.), *The nature of emotion: Fundamental questions.* New York: Oxford University Press.

Davidson, Richard J. (1994b). Honoring biology in the study of affective style. In Paul Ekman & Richard J. Davidson (Eds.), *The nature of emotion: Fundamental questions.* New York: Oxford University Press.

Davidson, Richard J.; Ekman, Paul; Saron, Clifford D.; Senulis, Joseph A.; & Friesen, Wallace V. (1990). Approach-withdrawal and cerebral asymmetry: Emotional expression and brain physiology I. *Journal of Personality and Social Psychology, 58,* 330–341.

Davis, D. L., & Whitten, R. G. (1987). The cross-cultural study of human sexuality. *Annual Review of Anthropology, 16,* 69–98.

Davis, Glenn Craig, & Breslau, Naomi. (1994). Post-traumatic stress disorder in victims of civilian and criminal violence. *Psychiatric Clinics of North America, 17,* 289–299.

Davis, Kenneth L.; Kahn, René S.; Ko, Grant; & Davidson, Michael. (1991). Dopamine in schizophrenia: A review and reconceptualization. *American Journal of Psychiatry, 148,* 1474–1486.

Davis, Mary Helen; Drogin, Eric Y.; & Wright, Jesse H. (1995). Therapist–patient sexual intimacy: A guide for the subsequent therapist. *Journal of Psychotherapy Practice and Research, 4,* 140–149.

Davis, Michael. (1992). The role of the amygdala in fear and anxiety. *Annual Review of Neuroscience, 15,* 353–375.

Davison, Gerald C., & Neale, John M. (1994). *Abnormal psychology* (6th ed.). New York: Wiley.

Dawson, Drew. (1995). Improving adaptation to simulated night shift: Timed exposure to bright light versus daytime melatonin administration. *Sleep, 18,* 11–18.

Dawson, Drew, & Campbell, Scott S. (1991). Time exposure to bright light improves sleep and alertness during simulated night shifts. *Sleep, 14,* 511–516.

Dawson, Drew, & Encel, Nicola. (1993). Melatonin and sleep in humans. *Journal of Pineal Research, 15,* 1–20.

Dean, Geoffrey. (1991a). Does astrology need to be true? Part 1: A look at the real thing. In Kendrick Frazier (Ed.), *The hundredth monkey and other paradigms of the paranormal.* Buffalo, N.Y.: Prometheus Books.

Dean, Geoffrey. (1991b). Does astrology need to be true? Part 2: The answer is no. In Kendrick Frazier (Ed.), *The hundredth monkey and other paradigms of the paranormal.* Buffalo, N.Y.: Prometheus Books.

Dean, Geoffrey; Mather, Arthur; & Kelly, Ivan W. (1996). Astrology. In Gordon Stein (Ed.), *The encyclopedia of the paranormal.* Buffalo, N.Y.: Prometheus.

DeAngelis, Tori. (1994a, February). People's drug of choice offers potent side effects. *APA Monitor, 25,* p. 16.

DeAngelis, Tori. (1994b, March). Massachusetts now requires multicultural training. *APA Monitor,* p. 41.

Deary, I. J.; Ramsay, H.; Wilson, J. A.; & Riad, M. (1988). Stimulated salivation: Correlations with personality and time of day effects. *Personality and Individual Differences, 9,* 903–909.

de Bono, Edward. (1992). *Seriously creative: Using the power of lateral thinking to create new ideas.* New York: HarperCollins.

DeCasper, A., & Fifer, W. (1980). Of human bonding: Newborns prefer their mothers' voices. *Science, 208,* 1174–1176.

de Charms, Richard. (1968). *Personal causation: The internal affective determinants of behavior.* New York: Academic Press.

De Jongh, A.; Muris, P.; Ter Horst, G.; & Duyx, M. P. M. A. (1995). Acquisition and maintenance of dental anxiety: The role of conditioning experiences and cognitive factors. *Behaviour Research and Therapy, 33,* 205–210.

Delahanty, Douglas L.; Dougall, Angela Liegey; Hawken, Leanne; Trakowski, John H.; Schmitz, John B.; Jenkins, Frank J.; & Baum, Andrew. (1996). Time course of natural killer cell activity and lymphocyte proliferation in response to two acute stressors in healthy men. *Health Psychology, 15,* 48–55.

DeLeon, Patrick H.; Sammons, Morgan T.; & Sexton, John L. (1995). Focusing on society's real needs: Responsibility and prescription privileges? *American Psychologist, 50,* 1022–1032.

Delgado, Jose M. (1969). *Physical control of the mind.* New York: Harper & Row.

DeLisi, Richard, & Staudt, Joanne. (1980). Individual differences in college students' performance on formal operations tasks. *Journal of Applied Developmental Psychology, 1,* 163–174.

DeLoache, Judy S. (1995). Early symbol understanding and use. In Douglas L. Medin (Ed.), *The psychology of learning and motivation: Advances in research and theory* (Vol. 33). New York: Academic Press.

DeLongis, Anita; Coyne, James C.; Dakof, C.; Folkman, Susan; & Lazarus, Richard S. (1982). Relationship of daily hassles, uplifts, and major life events to health status. *Health Psychology, 1,* 119–136.

DeLongis, Anita; Folkman, Susan; & Lazarus, Richard S. (1988). The impact of stress on health and mood: Psychological and social resources as mediators. *Journal of Personality and Social Psychology, 54,* 486–495.

Delprato, Dennis J., & Midgley, Bryan D. (1992). Some fundamentals of B. F. Skinner's behaviorism. *American Psychologist, 47,* 1507–1520.

Dember, W. N., & Earl, R. W. (1957). Analysis of exploratory, manipulatory, and curiosity behaviors. *Psychological Review, 64,* 91–96.

Dembroski, Theodore M. (1985). Overview of classic and stress-related risk factors: Relationship to substance effects on reactivity. In Karen A. Matthews, Stephen M. Weiss, Thomas Detre, Theodore M. Dembroski, Bonita Falkner, Stephen B. Manuck, & Redford B. Williams, Jr. (Eds.), *Handbook of stress, reactivity, and cardiovascular disease.* New York: Wiley.

Dement, William C. (1978). *Some must watch while some must sleep.* New York: Norton.

Dement, William C. (1992a). The proper use of sleeping pills in the primary care setting. *Journal of Clinical Psychiatry, 53,* 50–58.

Dement, William C. (1992b). *The sleepwatchers.* Stanford, Calif.: Stanford Alumni Association in series *The Portable Stanford.*

DePaulo, Bella. (1992). Nonverbal behavior and self-presentation. *Psychological Bulletin, 111,* 203–243.

Desforges, Donna M.; Lord, Charles G.; Ramsey, Shawna L.; Mason, Julie A.; Van Leeuwen, Marilyn D.; West, Sylvia C.; & Lepper, Mark R. (1991). Effects of structured cooperative contact on changing negative attitudes toward stigmatized social groups. *Journal of Personality and Social Psychology, 60,* 531–544.

De Silva, Padmal, & Rachman, Stanley. (1992). *Obsessive-compulsive disorder: The facts.* Oxford, England: Oxford University Press.

Deutsch, Morton, & Gerard, Harold B. (1955). A study of normative and informational social influence upon individual judgment. *Journal of Abnormal and Social Psychology, 51,* 629–636.

DeValois, Russell L., & DeValois, Karen K. (1975). Neural coding of color. In E. C. Carterette & M. P. Friedman (Eds.), *Handbook of perception* (Vol. 5). New York: Academic Press.

Devanand, D. P.; Dwork, Andrew J.; Hutchinson, Edward R.; Bolwig, Tom G.; & Sackeim, Harold A. (1994). Does ECT alter brain structure? *American Journal of Psychiatry, 151,* 957–970.

Devine, Patricia G., & Monteith, Margo J. (1993). The role of discrepancy-associated affect in prejudice reduction. In Diane M. Mackie & David L. Hamilton (Eds.), *Affect, cognition, and stereotyping: Interactive processes in group perception.* San Diego: Academic Press.

Devine, Patricia G.; Monteith, Margo J.; Zuwerink, Julia R.; & Elliot, Andrew J. (1991). Prejudice with and without compunction. *Journal of Personality and Social Psychology, 60,* 817–830.

Devine, Patricia G., & Zuwerink, Julia R. (1994). Prejudice and guilt: The internal struggle to overcome prejudice. In Walter J. Lonner & Roy Malpass (Eds.), *Psychology and culture.* Boston: Allyn & Bacon.

De Vos, George, & Wagatsuma, Hiroshi. (1967). *Japan's invisible race: Caste in culture and personality.* Berkeley and Los Angeles: University of California Press.

deWaal, Frans B. M. (1995, March). Bonobo sex and society. *Scientific American, 271,* 82–88.

Diamond, Marian Cleeves. (1993). An optimistic view of the aging brain: Understanding behavior by understanding its source. *Generations: The Journal of the Western Gerontologist, 17,* 31–37.

Dickinson, Anthony. (1989). Expectancy theory in animal conditioning. In Stephen B. Klein & Robert R. Mowrer (Eds.), *Contemporary learning theories: Pavlovian conditioning and the status of traditional learning theory.* Hillsdale, N.J.: Erlbaum.

Dictionary of occupational titles. (1991). Washington, D.C.: U.S. Government Printing Office.

Diener, Ed. (1980). Deindividuation: The absence of self-awareness and self-regulation in group members. In Paul B. Paulus (Ed.), *Psychology of group influence.* Hillsdale, N.J.: Erlbaum.

Diener, Ed. (1984). Subjective well-being. *Psychological Bulletin, 95,* 542–575.

Diener, Ed, & Diener, Marissa. (1995). Cross-cultural correlates of life satisfaction and self-esteem. *Journal of Personality and Social Psychology, 68,* 653–663.

Diener, Ed, & Emmons, Robert A. (1984). The independence of positive and negative affect. *Journal of Personality and Social Psychology, 47,* 1105–1117.

Diener, Ed; Larsen, Randy J.; Levine, Steven; & Emmons, Robert A. (1985). Intensity and frequency: Dimensions underlying positive and negative affect. *Journal of Personality and Social Psychology, 48,* 1253–1265.

Diener, Ed; Sandvik, Ed; & Pavot, William. (1991). Happiness is the frequency, not the intensity, of positive versus negative affect. In Fritz Strack, Michael Argyle, & Norbert Schwarz (Eds.), *Subjective well-being: An interdisciplinary perspective.* New York: Pergamon Press.

Diener, Ed; Wolsic, Brian; & Fujita, Frank. (1995). Physical attractiveness and subjective well-being. *Journal of Personality and Social Psychology, 69,* 120–129.

Dies, Robert R. (1993). Research on group psychotherapy: Overview and clinical applications. In Anne Alonso & Hillel I. Swiller (Eds.), *Group therapy in clinical practice.* Washington, D.C.: American Psychiatric Press.

Dillard, James Price. (1991). The current status of research on sequential-request compliance techniques. *Personality and Social Psychology Bulletin, 17,* 283–288.

Dillbeck, M. C., & Orme-Johnson, D. W. (1987). Physiological differences between transcendental meditation and rest. *American Psychologist, 42,* 879–881.

Dillingham, S. (1987, September 14). Inaudible messages making a noise. *Insight,* pp. 44–45.

Dinges, David F. (1989). Napping patterns and effects in human adults. In David F. Dinges & Roger J. Broughton (Eds.), *Sleep and alertness: Chronobiological, behavioral, and medical aspects of napping.* New York: Raven Press.

Dinges, David F. (1990). Are you awake? Cognitive performance and reverie during the hypnopompic state. In Richard R. Bootzin, John F. Kihlstrom, & Daniel L. Schacter (Eds.), *Sleep and cognition.* Washington, D.C.: American Psychological Association.

Dinges, David F., & Broughton, Roger J. (1989). The significance of napping: A synthesis. In David F. Dinges & Roger J. Broughton (Eds.), *Sleep and alertness: Chronobiological, behavioral, and medical aspects of napping.* New York: Raven Press.

Dinsmoor, James A. (1992). Setting the record straight: The social views of B. F. Skinner. *American Psychologist, 47,* 1454–1463.

Dixon, Wayne A.; Heppner, P. Paul; & Rudd, M. David. (1994). Problem-solving appraisal, hopelessness, and suicide ideation: Evidence for a mediational model. *Journal of Counseling Psychology, 41,* 91–98.

Dobson, K. S. (1989). A meta-analysis of the efficacy of cognitive therapy for depression. *Journal of Consulting and Clinical Psychology, 57,* 414–419.

Dohrenwend, Bruce P.; Raphael, Karen G.; Schwartz, Sharon; Stueve, Ann; & Skodol, Andrew. (1993). The structured event probe and narrative rating method for measuring stressful life events. In Leo Goldberger & Shlomo Breznitz (Eds.), *Handbook of stress: Theoretical and clinical aspects* (2nd ed.). New York: Free Press.

Domjan, Michael, & Purdy, Jesse E. (1995). Animal research in psychology: More than meets the eye of the general psychology student. *American Psychologist, 50,* 496–503.

Dornbusch, Sanford M.; Glasgow, Kristan L.; & Lin, I-Chun. (1996). The social structure of schooling. *Annual Review of Psychology, 47,* 401–429.

Dornbusch, Sanford M.; Ritter, Philip L.; Leiderman, P. Herbert; Roberts, Donald F.; & Fraleigh, Michael J. (1987). The relation of parenting style to adolescent school performance. *Child Development, 58,* 1244–1257.

Dovidio, John F. (1984). Helping behavior and altruism: An empirical and conceptual overview. *Advances in Experimental Social Psychology, 17,* 361–427.

Dovidio, John F., & Gaertner, Samuel L. (1993). Stereotypes and evaluative intergroup bias. In Diane M. Mackie & David L. Hamilton (Eds.), *Affect, cognition, and stereotyping: Interactive processes in group perception.* San Diego: Academic Press.

Dovidio, John F.; Piliavin, Jane A.; Gaertner, Samuel L.; Schroeder, David A.; & Clark, Russell D., III. (1991). The arousal: cost-reward model and the process of intervention: A review of the evidence. In Margaret S. Clark (Ed.), *Prosocial behavior: Vol. 12. Review of personality and social psychology.* Newbury Park, Calif.: Sage.

Doyle, James A., & Paludi, Michele A. (1995). *Sex and gender* (3rd ed.). Madison, Wis.: Brown & Benchmark.

DSM-IV. (1994). *Diagnostic and statistical manual of mental disorders* (4th ed.). Washington, D.C.: American Psychiatric Association.

Duclos, Sandra E.; Laird, James D.; Schneider, Eric; Sexter, Melissa; Stern, Lisa; & Van Lighten, Oliver. (1989). Emotion-specific effects of facial expressions and postures on emotional experience. *Journal of Personality and Social Psychology, 57,* 100–108.

Duffin, Darian. (1985). Acupuncture and acupressure. In Theresa Hoskins Michel (Ed.), *Pain: International perspectives in physical therapy* (Vol. 1). New York: Churchill Livingston.

Duncan, David F.; Donnelly, William J.; & Nicholson, Thomas. (1992). Belief in the paranormal and religious belief among American college students. *Psychological Reports, 70,* 15–18.

Duncker, Karl. (1945). On problem solving. *Psychological Monographs, 58* (Whole No. 270).

Dunkel-Schetter, Christine; Feinstein, Lawrence G.; Taylor, Shelley E.; & Falke, Roberta L. (1992). Patterns of coping with cancer. *Health Psychology, 11,* 79–87.

Dunn, Judy, & Plomin, Robert. (1990). *Separate lives: Why siblings are so different.* New York: Basic Books.

Dunning, David; Leuenberger, Ann; & Sherman, David A. (1995). A new look at motivated inference: Are self-serving theories of success a product of motivational forces? *Journal of Personality and Social Psychology, 69,* 58–68.

Dura, Jason R.; Stukenberg, Karl W.; & Kiecolt-Glaser, Janice K. (1990). Chronic stress and depressive disorders in older adults. *Journal of Abnormal Psychology, 99,* 284–290.

Durham, Ross M. (1989). *Human physiology: Functions of the human body.* Dubuque, Iowa: Brown.

Dusek, Jerome B. (1996). *Adolescent development and behavior* (3rd ed.). Upper Saddle River, N.J.: Prentice Hall.

Dykstra, Linda. (1992). Drug action. In John Grabowski & Gary R. VanderBos (Eds.), *Master lectures in psychology: Psychopharmacology: Basic mechanisms and applied interventions.* Washington, D.C.: American Psychological Association.

Eagle, Morris N., & Wolitzky, David L. (1992). Psychoanalytic theories of psychotherapy. In Donald K. Freedheim (Ed.), *History of psychotherapy: A century of change.* Washington, D.C.: American Psychological Association.

Eagly, Alice H. (1992). Uneven progress: Social psychology and the study of attitudes. *Journal of Personality and Social Psychology, 63,* 693–710.

Eagly, Alice H. (1995a). The science and politics of comparing women and men. *American Psychologist, 50,* 145–158.

Eagly, Alice H. (1995b). Reflections on the commenters' views. *American Psychologist, 50,* 169–171.

Eagly, Alice H.; Ashmore, Richard. D.; Makhijani, Mona G.; & Longo, Laura C. (1991). What is beautiful is good, but . . . : A meta-analytic review of research on the physical attractiveness stereotype. *Psychological Bulletin, 110,* 109–128.

Eagly, Alice H., & Chaiken, Shelly. (1993). *The psychology of attitudes.* Fort Worth, Tex.: Harcourt Brace.

Eagly, Alice H., & Johnson, Blair T. (1990). Gender and leadership style: A meta-analysis. *Psychological Bulletin, 108,* 233–256.

Ebbinghaus, Hermann. (1885/1987). *Memory: A contribution to experimental psychology.* Translated by Henry A. Ruger & Clara E. Bussenius. New York: Dover Publications.

Ebbinghaus, Hermann. (1908/1973). *Psychology: An elementary textbook.* [German: *Abriss der psychologie.*] Translated and edited by Max Meyer. New York: Arno Press.

Eckensberger, Lutz H. (1994). Moral development and its measurement across cultures. In Walter J. Lonner & Roy Malpass (Eds.), *Psychology and culture.* Boston: Allyn & Bacon.

Edens, Jennifer L.; Larkin, Kenneth I.; & Abel, Jennifer L. (1992). The effects of social support and physical touch on cardiovascular reactions to mental stress. *Journal of Psychosomatic Research, 36,* 371–381.

Edwards, Anthony G. P., & Armitage, Peter. (1992). An experiment to test the discriminating ability of graphologists. *Personality and Individual Differences, 13,* 69–74.

Edwards, Randall. (1995a, February). Future demands culturally diverse education. *APA Monitor,* p. 43.

Edwards, Randall. (1995b, September). Psychologists foster the new definition of family. *APA Monitor, 26,* 38.

Egan, Gerard. (1994). *The skilled helper: A problem-management approach to helping* (5th ed.). Pacific Grove, Calif.: Brooks/Cole.

Ehlers, Anke, & Breuer, Peter. (1992). Increased cardiac awareness in panic disorder. *Journal of Abnormal Psychology, 101,* 371–382.

Eibl-Eibesfeldt, Irenäus. (1973). The expressive behavior of the deaf-and-blind-born. In M. von Cranach & I. Vine (Eds.), *Social communication and movement.* New York: Academic Press.

Eich, Eric. (1980). The cue-dependent nature of state-dependent retrieval. *Memory and Cognition, 8,* 157–173.

Eich, Eric. (1989). Theoretical issues in state-dependent memory. In Henry L. Roediger III & Fergus I. M. Craik (Eds.), *Varieties of memory and consciousness: Essays in honour of Edel Tulving.* Hillsdale, N.J.: Erlbaum.

Eich, Eric. (1995). Searching for mood dependent memory. *Psychological Science, 6,* 67–75.

Eich, Eric; Macaulay, D.; & Ryan, L. (1994). Mood dependent memory for events of the personal past. *Journal of Experimental Psychology: General, 123,* 201–215.

Eisenberg, Nancy. (1991). Meta-analytic contributions to the literature on prosocial behavior. *Personality and Social Psychology Bulletin, 17,* 273–284.

Ekman, Paul. (1980). *The face of man.* New York: Garland Publishing.

Ekman, Paul. (1982). *Emotion in the human face* (2nd ed.). New York: Cambridge University Press.

Ekman, Paul. (1992). Are there basic emotions? *Psychological Review, 99,* 550–553.

Ekman, Paul, & Davidson, Richard J. (1993). Voluntary smiling changes regional brain activity. *Psychological Science, 4,* 342–345.

Ekman, Paul, & Davidson, Richard J. (1994). Epilogue: Affective science: A research agenda. In Paul Ekman & Richard J. Davidson (Eds.), *The nature of emotion: Fundamental questions.* New York: Oxford University Press.

Ekman, Paul, & Friesen, Wallace V. (1978). *Facial Action Coding System: A technique for the measurement of facial movement.* Palo Alto, Calif.: Consulting Psychologists Press.

Ekman, Paul; Friesen, Wallace V.; O'Sullivan, Maureen; Chan, Anthony; Diacoyanni-Tarlatzis, Irene; Heider, Karl; Krause, Rainer; LeCompte, William Ayhan; Pitcairn, Tom; Ricci-Bitti, Pio E.; Scherer, Klaus; Masatoshi, Tomita; & Tzavaras, Athanase. (1987). Universals and cultural differences in the judgments of facial expressions of emotion. *Journal of Personality & Social Psychology, 53,* 712–717.

Elkin, Irene; Shea, T.; Watkins, J. T.; Imber, S. D.; Sotsky, S. M.; Collins, J. H. F.; Glass, D. R.; Pilkonis, P. A.; Leber, W. R.; Docherty, J. P.; Fiester, S. J.; & Parloff, M. B. (1989). National Institute of Mental Health Treatment of Depression Collaborative Research Program: General effectiveness of treatments. *Archives of General Psychiatry, 46,* 971–983.

Elkind, David. (1996). Inhelder and Piaget on adolescence and adulthood: A postmodern appraisal. *Psychological Science, 7,* 216–220.

Ellis, Albert. (1991). *Reason and emotion in psychotherapy.* New York: Carol Publishing.

Ellis, Albert. (1993). Reflections on rational-emotive therapy. *Journal of Consulting and Clinical Psychology, 61,* 199–201.

Ellis, Albert, & Bernard, Michael E. (1985). What is rational-emotive therapy (RET)? In Albert Ellis & Michael E. Bernard (Eds.), *Clinical applications of rational-emotive therapy.* New York: Plenum Press.

Ellis, Albert, & Harper, Robert A. (1975). *A new guide to rational living.* Hollywood, Calif.: Wilshire Book Company.

Ellis, Henry C., & Hunt, R. Reed. (1993). *Fundamentals of cognitive psychology* (5th ed.). Dubuque, Iowa: Brown & Benchmark.

Ellman, Steven J.; Spielman, Arthur J.; Luck, Dana; Steiner, Solomon S.; & Halperin, Ronnie. (1991). REM deprivation: A review. In Steven J. Ellman & John S. Antrobus (Eds.), *The mind in sleep: Psychology and psychophysiology* (2nd ed.). New York: Wiley.

Ellsworth, Phoebe C. (1994). William James and emotion: Is a century of fame worth a century of misunderstanding? *Psychological Review, 101,* 222–229.

Emmelkamp, Paul M. G. (1994). Behavior therapy with adults. In Allen E. Bergin & Sol L. Garfield (Eds.), *Handbook of psychotherapy and behavior change* (4th ed.). New York: Wiley.

Emmons, Robert, & King, Laura. (1988). Conflict among personal strivings: Immediate and long-term implications for psychological and physical well-being. *Journal of Personality and Social Psychology, 54,* 1040–1048.

Emmons, Robert A.; Larsen, Randy J.; Levine, S.; & Diener, Ed. (1983, May). *Factors predicting satisfaction judgments.* Paper presented at the annual meeting of the Midwestern Psychological Association, Chicago.

Empson, Jacob. (1993). *Sleep and dreaming* (2nd ed.). New York: Harvester Wheatsheaf.

Engen, Trygg. (1991). *Odor sensation and memory.* New York: Praeger.

Engler, Barbara. (1995). *Personality theories: An introduction* (4th ed.). Boston: Houghton Mifflin.

Engler, Jack, & Goleman, Daniel. (1992). *The consumer's guide to psychotherapy.* New York: Simon & Schuster.

English, Horace B. (1929). Three cases of the "conditioned fear response." *Journal of Abnormal and Social Psychology, 24,* 221–225.

Epstein, Leonard H., & Jennings, J. Richard. (1985). Smoking, stress, cardiovascular reactivity, and coronary heart disease. In Karen A. Matthews, Stephen M. Weiss, Thomas Detre, Theodore M. Dembroski, Bonita Falkner, Stephen B. Manuck, & Redford B. Williams, Jr. (Eds.), *Handbook of stress, reactivity, and cardiovascular disease*. New York: Wiley.

Epstein, Leonard H.; Valoski, Alice M.; Vara, Linda S.; McCurley, James; Wisniewski, Lucene; Kalarchian, Melissa A.; Klein, Karla R.; & Shrager, Loreen R. (1995). Effects of decreasing sedentary behavior and increasing activity on weight change in obese children. *Health Psychology, 14* (2), 109–115.

Epstein, Mark. (1995). *Thoughts without a thinker: Psychotherapy from a Buddhist perspective.* New York: Basic Books.

Epstein, Seymour. (1979). The stability of behavior: I. On predicting most of the people most of the time. *Journal of Personality and Social Psychology, 37*, 1097–1126.

Epstein, Seymour. (1982). Conflict and stress. In Leo Goldberger & Shlomo Breznitz (Eds.), *Handbook of stress: Theoretical and clinical aspects.* New York: Free Press.

Epstein, Seymour. (1983a). Aggregation and beyond: Some basic issues on the prediction of behavior. *Journal of Personality, 51*, 360–392.

Epstein, Seymour. (1983b). The stability of behavior across time and situations. In R. Zucker, J. Aronoff, & A. I. Rabin (Eds.), *Personality and the prediction of behavior.* San Diego: Academic Press.

Epstein, Seymour. (1992a). Constructive thinking and mental and physical well-being. In Leo Montada, Sigrun-Heide Filipp, & Melvin J. Lerner (Eds.), *Life crises and experiences of loss in adulthood.* Hillsdale, N.J.: Erlbaum.

Epstein, Seymour. (1992b). Coping ability, negative self-evaluation, and overgeneralization: Experiment and theory. *Journal of Personality and Social Psychology, 62*, 826–836.

Epstein, Seymour. (1993). *You're smarter than you think: How to develop your practical intelligence for success in living.* New York: Simon & Schuster.

Epstein, Seymour, & Katz, Lori. (1992). Coping ability, stress, productive load, and symptoms. *Journal of Personality and Social Psychology, 62*, 813–825.

Epstein, Seymour, & Meier, Petra. (1989). Constructive thinking: A broad coping variable with specific components. *Journal of Personality and Social Psychology, 57*, 332–350.

Epstein, Seymour, & O'Brien, E. J. (1985). The person-situational debate in historical and current perspective. *Psychological Bulletin, 98*, 513–537.

Erdelyi, Matthew Hugh. (1992). Psychodynamics and the unconscious. *American Psychologist, 47*, 784–787.

Erdelyi, Matthew Hugh. (1993). Repression: The mechanism and the defense. In Daniel M. Wegner & James W. Pennebaker (Eds.), *Handbook of mental control.* Englewood Cliffs, N.J.: Prentice Hall.

Ericsson, K. Anders, & Kintsch, Walter. (1995). Long-term working memory. *Psychological Review, 102*, 211–245.

Erikson, Erik H. (1964a). *Childhood and society* (rev. ed.). New York: Norton.

Erikson, Erik H. (1964b). *Insight and responsibility.* New York: Norton.

Erikson, Erik H. (1968). *Identity: Youth and crisis.* New York: Norton.

Erikson, Erik H. (1982). *The life cycle completed: A review.* New York: Norton.

Erikson, Erik H.; Erikson, Joan M.; & Kivnick, Helen Q. (1986). *Vital involvement in old age: The experience of old age in our time.* New York: Norton.

Esses, Victoria M.; Haddock, Geoffrey; & Zanna, Mark P. (1993). Values, stereotypes, and emotions as determinants of intergroup attitudes. In Diane M. Mackie & David L. Hamilton (Eds.), *Affect, cognition, and stereotyping: Interactive processes in group perception.* San Diego: Academic Press.

Estes, W. K., & Skinner, B. F. (1941). Some quantitative properties of anxiety. *Journal of Experimental Psychology, 29*, 390–400.

Etscorn, F., & Stephens, R. (1973). Establishment of conditioned taste aversions with a 24-hour CS-US interval. *Physiological Psychology, 1*, 251–253.

Evans, Richard I. (1980). *The making of social psychology: Discussions with creative contributors.* New York: Gardner Press.

Exner, John E., Jr. (1993). *The Rorschach: A comprehensive system: Vol. 1. Basic foundations* (3rd ed.). New York: Wiley.

Eysenck, Hans J. (1952). The effects of psychotherapy: An evaluation. *Journal of Consulting Psychology, 16*, 319–324.

Eysenck, Hans J. (1982). *Personality, genetics, and behavior.* New York: Praeger.

Eysenck, Hans J. (1985). *Decline and fall of the Freudian empire.* New York: Penguin.

Eysenck, Hans J. (1990). Biological dimensions of personality. In Lawrence A. Pervin (Ed.), *Handbook of personality: Theory and research.* New York: Guilford Press.

Eysenck, Hans J. (1994). The outcome problem in psychotherapy: What have we learned? *Behaviour Research and Therapy, 32*, 447–495.

Eysenck, Hans J., & Eysenck, Sybil B. G. (1975). *Psychoticism as a dimension of personality.* London: Hodder & Stoughton.

Eysenck, Sybil B. G., & Eysenck, Hans J. (1967). Physiological reactivity to sensory stimulation as a measure of personality. *Psychological Reports, 20*, 45–46.

Ezzell, Carol. (1992, October 3). Two human chromosomes entirely mapped. *Science News, 142*, 212.

Fackelmann, Kathy A. (1994, July 2). The conscious mind: Karen Ann Quinlan case yields surprising scientific data. *Science News, 146*, 10–11.

Faedda, Gianni L.; Tondo, Leonardo; Teicher, Martin H.; Baldessarini, Ross J.; Gelbard, Harris A.; & Floris, Gianfranco F. (1993). Seasonal mood disorders: Patterns of seasonal recurrence in mania and depression. *Archives of General Psychiatry, 50*, 17–23.

Fagot, Beverly I., & Hagan, Richard. (1991). Observations of parent reactions to sex-stereotyped behaviors: Age and sex effects. *Child Development, 62*, 617–628.

Fagot, Beverly I.; Leinbach, Mary D.; & O'Boyle, Cherie. (1992). Gender labeling, gender stereotyping, and parenting behaviors. *Developmental Psychology, 28*, 225–230.

Fancher, Raymond E. (1973). *Psychoanalytic psychology: The development of Freud's thought.* New York: Norton.

Fancher, Raymond E. (1985). *The intelligence men: Makers of the IQ controversy.* New York: Norton.

Fancher, Raymond E. (1990). *Pioneers of psychology* (2nd ed.). New York: Norton.

Fantz, Robert L. (1961, May). The origin of form perception. *Scientific American, 204*, 66–72.

Fantz, Robert L. (1963). Pattern vision in newborn infants. *Science, 140*, 296–297.

Fantz, Robert L. (1965). Visual perception from birth as shown by pattern selectivity. *Annals of the New York Academy of Sciences, 118*, 793–814.

Farah, Martha J. (1994). Neuropsychological inference with an interactive brain: A critique of the "locality" assumption. *Behavioral and Brain Sciences, 17*, 43–61.

Farah, Martha J. (1995). The neural bases of mental imagery. In Michael S. Gazzaniga (Ed.), *The cognitive neurosciences.* Cambridge, Mass.: MIT Press.

Farber, Ilya B., & Churchland, Patricia S. (1995). Consciousness and the neurosciences: Philosophical and theoretical issues. In Michael S. Gazzaniga (Ed.), *The cognitive neurosciences*. Cambridge, Mass.: MIT Press.

Fauman, Michael A. (1994). *Study guide to DSM-IV*. Washington, D.C.: American Psychiatric Press.

Faust, I. M.; Johnson, P. R.; & Hirsch, J. (1976). Noncompensation of adipose mass in partial lipectomized mice and rats. *American Journal of Physiology, 231,* 538–544.

Faust, I. M.; Johnson, P. R.; & Hirsch, J. (1977a). Adipose tissue regeneration following lipectomy. *Science, 197,* 391–393.

Faust, I. M.; Johnson, P. R.; & Hirsch, J. (1977b). Surgical removal of adipose tissue alters feeding behavior and the development of obesity in rats. *Science, 197,* 393–396.

Fava, Maurizio, & Kaji, Junko. (1994). Continuation and maintenance treatments of major depressive disorder. *Psychiatric Annals, 24,* 281–290.

Fawcett, Jan. (1994). Antidepressants: Partial response in chronic depression. *British Journal of Psychiatry, 165* (Suppl. 26), 37–41.

Fazio, Russell H. (1990). Multiple processes by which attitudes guide behavior: The MODE model as an integrative framework. In Mark P. Zanna (Ed.), *Advances in experimental social psychology* (Vol. 23). San Diego: Academic Press.

Fazio, Russell H., & Zanna, Mark P. (1981). Direct experience and attitude–behavior consistency. In Leonard Berkowitz (Ed.), *Advances in experimental social psychology* (Vol. 14). San Diego: Academic Press.

Feder, H. H. (1984). Hormones and sexual behavior. *Annual Review of Psychology, 35,* 165–200.

Feeney, Brooke C., & Kirkpatrick, Lee A. (1996). Effects of adult attachment and presence of romantic partners on physiological responses to stress. *Journal of Personality and Social Psychology, 70,* 255–270.

Feingold, Alan. (1992). Good-looking people are not what we think. *Psychological Bulletin, 111,* 304–341.

Feingold, Alan. (1994). Gender differences in personality: A meta-analysis. *Psychological Bulletin, 116,* 429–456.

Feinman, S. (1981). Why is cross-sex-role behavior more approved for girls than for boys? A status characteristic approach. *Sex Roles, 7,* 289–300.

Feldman, Larry B., & Powell, Sandra L. (1992). Integrating therapeutic modalities.

In John C. Norcross & Marvin R. Goldfried (Eds.), *Handbook of psychotherapy integration*. New York: Basic Books.

Fellows, Brian J. (1990). Current theories of hypnosis: An overview. *British Journal of Experimental and Clinical Hypnosis, 7,* 81–92.

Felten, David. (1993). The brain and the immune system. In Bill Moyers (Interviewer) & Betty Sue Flowers (Ed.), *Healing and the mind*. New York: Doubleday.

Feltz, D. L., & Landers, D. M. (1983). Effects of mental practice on motor skill learning and performance: A meta-analysis. *Journal of Sport Psychology, 5,* 25–57.

Fenwick, Peter. (1987). Meditation and the EEG. In Michael A. West (Ed.), *The psychology of meditation*. New York: Oxford University Press.

Ferber, Richard. (1994). Sleep disorders in children. In Rosemary Cooper (Ed.), *Sleep*. New York: Chapman & Hall.

Ferguson, N. B. L., & Keesey, R. E. (1975). Effect of a quinine-adulterated diet upon body weight maintenance in male rats with ventromedial hypothalamic lesions. *Journal of Comparative Physiological Psychology, 89,* 478–488.

Fernald, Ann. (1985). Four-month-old infants prefer to listen to motherese. *Infant Behavior and Development, 8,* 181–182.

Fernandez, E. (1986). A classification system of cognitive coping strategies for pain. *Pain, 26,* 141–151.

Festinger, Leon. (1957). *A theory of cognitive dissonance*. Stanford, Calif.: Stanford University Press.

Festinger, Leon. (1962). Cognitive dissonance. *Scientific American, 207,* 93–99. Reprinted in *Contemporary psychology: Readings from Scientific American*. (1971). San Francisco: Freeman.

Field, Tiffany. (1991). Quality infant daycare and grade school behavior and performance. *Child Development, 62,* 863–870.

Field, Tiffany. (1996). Attachment and separation in young children. *Annual Review of Psychology, 47,* 541–561.

Field, Tiffany; Masi, W.; Goldstein, D.; Perry, S.; & Parl, S. (1988). Infant day-care facilitates preschool behavior. *Early Childhood Research Quarterly, 3,* 341–359.

Field, Tiffany; Schanberg, Saul M.; Scafidi, Frank; Bauer, Charles R.; Vega-Lahr, Nitza; Garcia, Robert; Nystrom, Jerome; & Kuhn, Cynthia. (1986, May). Tactile/kinesthetic stimulation effects on preterm neonates. *Pediatrics, 77,* 654–658.

Field, Tiffany M.; Woodson, R.; Greenberg, R.; & Cohen, D. (1982). Discrimination and

imitation of facial expressions by neonates. *Science, 218,* 179–182.

Fieldhouse, Paul. (1986). *Food & nutrition: Customs & culture*. London: Croom Helm.

Fields, H. L., & Levine, J. D. (1984). Placebo analgesia: A role for endorphins. *Trends in Neuroscience, 7,* 271–273.

Fink, Max. (1991). Impact of the antipsychiatry movement on the revival of electroconvulsive therapy in the United States. *Psychiatric Clinics of North America, 14,* 793–801.

Fink, Max. (1993). Who should get ECT? In C. Edward Coffey (Ed.), *The clinical science of electroconvulsive therapy*. Washington, D.C.: American Psychiatric Press.

Finsen, Lawrence, & Finsen, Susan. (1994). *The animal rights movement in America: From compassion to respect*. New York: Twayne Publishers.

Fischbach, Gerald D. (1992, September). Mind and brain. *Scientific American, 267,* 24–33.

Fischer, Kurt W.; Hand, Helen H.; & Russell, Sheryl (1984). The development of abstractions in adolescence and adulthood. In Michael L. Commons, Francis A. Richards, & Cheryl Armon (Eds.), *Beyond formal operations: Late adolescence and adult cognitive development*. New York: Freeman.

Fischer, Kurt W., & Hencke, Rebecca W. (1996). Infants' construction of actions in context: Piaget's contribution to research on early development. *Psychological Science, 7,* 204–210.

Fisher, Celia B., & Fyrberg, Denise. (1994). Participant partners: College students weigh the costs and benefits of deceptive research. *American Psychologist, 49,* 417–427.

Fisher, Kathleen. (1986, March). Animal research: Few alternatives seen for behavioral studies. *APA Monitor*, pp. 16–17.

Fisher, William A., Fisher, Jeffrey D., & Rye, Barbara J. (1995). Understanding and promoting AIDS-preventative behavior: Insights from the theory of reasoned action. *Health Psychology, 14* (3), 255–264.

Fishman, J. A. (1960/1974). A systematization of the Whorfian hypothesis. In John W. Berry & P. R. Dasen (Eds.), *Culture and cognition: Readings in cross-cultural psychology*. London: Methuen.

Fiske, Susan T. (1993). Social cognition and perception. *Annual Review of Psychology, 44,* 155–194.

Fiske, Susan T., & Neuberg, Steven L. (1990). A continuum of impression formation, from category-based to individuating processes: Influences of information and motivation on attention and interpretation. In Mark P. Zanna (Ed.), *Advances in experi-*

mental social psychology (Vol. 23). San Diego: Academic Press/Harcourt.

Fiske, Susan T., & Ruscher, Janet B. (1993). Negative interdependence and prejudice: Whence the affect? In Diane M. Mackie & David L. Hamilton (Eds.), *Affect, cognition, and stereotyping: Interactive processes in group perception.* San Diego: Academic Press.

Fiske, Susan T., & Taylor, Shelley E. (1991). *Social cognition* (2nd ed.). New York: McGraw-Hill.

Flaks, David K.; Ficher, Ilda; Masterpasqua, Frank; & Joseph, Gregory. (1995). Lesbians choosing motherhood: A comparative study of lesbian and heterosexual parents and their children. *Developmental Psychology, 31,* 105–114.

Flavell, John H. (1996). Piaget's legacy. *Psychological Science, 7,* 200–203.

Fleishman, E. A., & Harris, E. F. (1962). Patterns of leadership behavior related to employee grievances and turnover. *Personnel Psychology, 15,* 43–56.

Flynn, James R. (1987). Massive IQ gains in 14 nations: What IQ tests really measure. *Psychological Bulletin, 101,* 171–191.

Folkard, Simon; Arendt, Josephine; & Clark, Mark. (1993). Can melatonin improve shift workers' tolerance of the night shift? Some preliminary findings. *Chronobiology International, 10,* 315–320.

Folkman, Susan; & Lazarus, Richard S. (1988). *Manual for the Ways Of Coping Questionnaire.* Palo Alto, Calif.: Consulting Psychologists Press.

Folkman, Susan, & Lazarus, Richard S. (1991). Coping and emotion. In Alan Monat & Richard S. Lazarus (Eds.), *Stress and coping: An anthology* (3rd ed.). New York: Columbia University Press.

Folkman, Susan; Lazarus, Richard S.; Gruen, Rand J.; & DeLongis, Anita. (1986). Appraisal, coping, health status, and psychological symptoms. *Journal of Personality and Social Psychology, 50,* 571–579.

Ford, M., & Lowery, C. (1986). Gender differences in moral reasoning: A comparison of the use of justice and care orientations. *Journal of Personality and Social Psychology, 50,* 777–783.

Fordyce, Michael W. (1977). Development of a program to increase personal happiness. *Journal of Counseling Psychology, 24,* 511–521.

Fordyce, Michael W. (1981). *The psychology of happiness: A brief version of the Fourteen Fundamentals.* Fort Myers, Fla.: Cypress Lake Media.

Fordyce, Michael W. (1983). A program to increase happiness: Further studies. *Journal of Counseling Psychology, 30,* 483–498.

Foster, Russell G. (1993). Photoreceptors and circadian systems. *Current Directions in Psychological Science, 2,* 34–39.

Foulks, Edward F. (1991). Transcultural psychiatry and normal behavior. In Daniel Offer & Melvin Sabshin (Eds.), *The diversity of normal behavior: Further contributions to normatology.* New York: Basic Books.

Fouts, Roger S., & Rigby, Randall L. (1977). Man–chimpanzee communication. In Thomas A. Seboek (Ed.), *How animals communicate.* Bloomington: University of Indiana Press.

Fowler, Raymond D. (1995, April). Should psychologists prescribe medicine? *APA Monitor, 26,* 3.

Fowles, D. C. (1992). Schizophrenia: Diathesis-stress revisited. *Annual Review of Psychology, 43,* 303–336.

Fox, Nathan A.; Kimmerly, Nancy L.; & Schafer, William D. (1991). Attachment to mother/Attachment to father: A meta-analysis. *Child Development, 62,* 210–225.

Fozard, James L. (1990). Vision and hearing in aging. In James E. Birren & K. Warren Schaie (Eds.), *Handbook of the psychology of aging* (3rd ed.). New York: Academic Press.

Frances, Allen J.; Widiger, Thomas A.; & Sabshin, Melvin. (1991). Psychiatric diagnosis and normality. In Daniel Offer & Melvin Sabshin (Eds.), *The diversity of normal behavior: Further contributions to normatology.* New York: Basic Books.

Frank, Barney. (1996, February 4). Quoted in Claudia Dreifus: And then there was Frank, *The New York Times Magazine,* pp. 22–25.

Frank, Ellen; Anderson, Barbara; Reynolds, Charles F., III; Ritenour, Angela; & Kupfer, David J. (1994). Life events and the research diagnostic criteria endogenous subtype: A confirmation of the distinction using the Bedford College methods. *Archives of General Psychiatry, 51,* 519–524.

Frankel, Fred H. (1993). Adult reconstruction of childhood events in the multiple personality literature. *American Journal of Psychiatry, 150,* 954–958.

Franken, Robert E. (1994). *Human motivation* (3rd ed.). Pacific Grove, Calif.: Brooks/Cole.

Frankenburg, Frances R. (1994). History of the development of antipsychotic medication. *Psychiatric Clinics of North America, 17,* 531–540.

Franz, Carol E.; McClelland, David C.; & Weinberger, Joel. (1991). Childhood antecedents of conventional social accomplishment in midlife adults: A 36-year prospective study. *Journal of Personality and Social Psychology, 60,* 586–595.

Franzoi, Stephen L. (1996). *Social psychology.* Madison, Wis.: Brown & Benchmark.

Fraser, Steven. (Ed.). (1995). *The* Bell Curve *wars: Race, intelligence, and the future of America.* New York: Basic Books.

Frederickson, N. (1968). *Organization climates and administrative performance.* Princeton, N.J.: Educational Testing Service.

Freeman, Lucy, & Strean, Herbert S. (1987). *Freud and women.* New York: Continuum.

Freeston, Mark H.; Ladouceur, Robert; Rhéaume, Josée; Letarte, Hélène; Gagnon, Fabien; & Thibodeau, Nicole. (1994). Self-report of obsessions and worry. *Behavior Research and Therapy, 32,* 29–36.

Freiberg, Peter. (1996, February). Answers are often closer than we think. *APA Monitor, 27,* 24–26.

Freinkel, Andrew; Koopman, Cheryl; & Spiegel, David. (1994). Dissociative symptoms in media eyewitnesses of an execution. *American Journal of Psychiatry, 151,* 1335–1339.

French, Christopher C.; Fowler, Mandy; McCarthy, Katy; & Peers, Debbie. (1991, Winter). Belief in astrology: A test of the Barnum effect. *Skeptical Inquirer, 15,* 166–172.

Frenkel, Oded J., & Doob, Anthony N. (1976). Post-decision dissonance at the polling booth. *Canadian Journal of Behavioural Science, 8,* 347–350.

Freud, Anna. (1946). *The ego and mechanisms of defence.* Translated by Cecil Baines. New York: International Universities Press.

Freud, Sigmund. (1900/1974). *The interpretation of dreams.* In James Strachey (Ed.), *The standard edition of the complete psychological works of Sigmund Freud* (Vols. 4 & 5). London: Hogarth Press.

Freud, Sigmund. (1904/1965). *The psychopathology of everyday life.* Translated by Alan Tyson & edited by James Strachey. New York: Norton.

Freud, Sigmund. (1905/1975). *Three essays on the theory of sexuality.* Translated by James Strachey. New York: Basic Books.

Freud, Sigmund. (1911/1989). *On dreams.* In Peter Gay (Ed.), *The Freud reader.* New York: Norton.

Freud, Sigmund. (1914/1948). On narcissism: An introduction. In *Collected papers: Vol. 4. Papers on metapsychology and applied psychoanalysis.* Translated under the supervision of Joan Riviere. London: Hogarth Press.

Freud, Sigmund. (1915a/1948). Repression. In *Collected papers: Vol. 4. Papers on metapsychology and applied psychoanalysis.* Translated under the supervision of Joan Riviere. London: Hogarth Press.

Freud, Sigmund. (1915b/1959). Analysis, terminable and interminable. In *Collected papers: Vol. 5. Miscellaneous papers* (2nd ed.). Translated under the supervision of Joan Riviere. London: Hogarth Press.

Freud, Sigmund. (1915c/1959). Libido theory. In *Collected papers: Vol. 5. Miscellaneous papers* (2nd ed.). Translated under the supervision of Joan Riviere. London: Hogarth Press.

Freud, Sigmund. (1916/1964). *Leonardo da Vinci and a memory of his childhood.* Translated by James Strachey in collaboration with Anna Freud. New York: Norton.

Freud, Sigmund. (1919/1989). *Totem and taboo: Some points of agreement between the mental lives of savages and neurotics.* Translated and edited by James Strachey, with a biographical introduction by Peter Gay. New York: Norton.

Freud, Sigmund. (1920/1961). *Beyond the pleasure principle.* Translated by James Strachey. New York: Norton.

Freud, Sigmund. (1923/1962). *The ego and the id.* Translated by Joan Riviere and edited by James Strachey. New York: Norton.

Freud, Sigmund. (1924/1948). The dissolution of the Oedipus complex. In *Collected papers: Vol. 2. Clinical papers and papers on technique.* Translated under the supervision of Joan Riviere. London: Hogarth Press.

Freud, Sigmund. (1925/1989). Some psychical consequences of the anatomical distinction between the sexes. In Peter Gay (Ed.), *The Freud reader.* New York: Norton.

Freud, Sigmund. (1926/1947). *The question of lay analysis: An introduction to psychoanalysis.* Translated by Nancy Proctor-Gregg. London: Imago Publishing.

Freud, Sigmund. (1930/1961). *Civilization and its discontents.* Translated & edited by James Strachey. New York: Norton.

Freud, Sigmund. (1933). *New introductory lectures on psychoanalysis.* Translated by W. J. H. Sprott. New York: Norton.

Freud, Sigmund. (1936). *The problem of anxiety.* Translated by Henry Alden Bunker. New York: The Psychoanalytic Quarterly Press and W. W. Norton & Company.

Freud, Sigmund. (1939/1967). *Moses and monotheism.* Translated by Katherine Jones. New York: Vintage Books.

Freud, Sigmund. (1940/1949). *An outline of psychoanalysis.* Translated by James Strachey. New York: Norton.

Friedman, Howard S. (1991). *The self-healing personality: Why some people achieve health and others succumb to illness.* New York: Holt.

Friedman, Howard S. (1992). Understanding hostility, coping, and health. In Howard S. Friedman (Ed.), *Hostility, coping, and health.* Washington, D. C.: American Psychological Association.

Friedman, Howard S., & Booth-Kewley, Stephanie. (1987). The "disease-prone personality": A meta-analytic view of the construct. *American Psychologist, 42,* 539–555.

Friedman, Meyer, & Rosenman, Ray H.. (1974). *Type A behavior and your heart.* New York: Knopf.

Friedman, Michael A., & Brownell, Kelly D. (1995). Psychological correlates of obesity: Moving to the next research generation. *Psychological Bulletin, 117,* 3–20.

Friend, Ronald; Rafferty, Yvonne; & Bramel, Dana. (1990). A puzzling misinterpretation of the Asch "conformity" study. *European Journal of Social Psychology, 20,* 29–44.

Friesen, Wallace V. (1972). *Cultural differences in facial expressions in a social situation: An experimental test of the concept of display rules.* Unpublished doctoral dissertation, University of California, San Francisco.

Frijda, Nico H. (1994). Varieties of affect: Emotions and episodes, moods, and sentiments. In Paul Ekman & Richard J. Davidson (Eds.), *The nature of emotion: Fundamental questions.* New York: Oxford University Press.

Frodi, Ann; Macaulay, Jacqueline; & Thome, Pauline. (1977). Are women always less aggressive than men? A review of the literature. *Psychological Bulletin, 84,* 634–660.

Funder, David C. (1995). On the accuracy of personality judgment: A realistic approach. *Psychological Review, 102,* 652–670.

Funder, David C.; Kolar, David C.; & Blackman, Melinda C. (1995). Agreement among judges of personality: Interpersonal relations, similarity, and acquaintanceship. *Journal of Personality and Social Psychology, 69,* 656–672.

Furnham, Adrian. (1991). Write and wrong: The validity of graphological analysis. In Kendrick Frazier (Ed.), *The hundredth monkey and other paradigms of the paranormal.* Buffalo, N.Y.: Prometheus Books.

Galanter, Eugene. (1962). Contemporary psychophysics. In R. Brown, E. Galanter, E. H. Hess, & G. Mandler (Eds.), *New directions in psychology.* New York: Holt, Rinehart & Winston.

Gallo, Linda C., & Eastman, Charmane I. (1993). Circadian rhythms during gradually delaying and advancing sleep and light schedules. *Physiology and Behavior, 53,* 119–126.

Gallup, George H., Jr., & Newport, Frank. (1991). Belief in paranormal phenomena among adult Americans. *Skeptical Inquirer 15,* 137–146.

Gallup, Gordon G., Jr., & Suarez, Susan D. (1985, October). Alternatives to the use of animals in psychological research. *American Psychologist, 40,* 1104–1111.

Gallup Organization. (1991). *Sleep in America.* Princeton, N.J.: Gallup Organization.

Galluscio, Eugene H. (1990). *Biological psychology.* New York: Macmillan.

Gambrill, Eileen. (1995a). Helping shy, socially anxious, and lonely adults: A skill-based contextual approach. In William O'Donohue & Leonard Krasner (Eds.), *Handbook of psychological skills training: Clinical techniques and applications.* Boston: Allyn & Bacon.

Gambrill, Eileen. (1995b). Assertion skills training. In William O'Donohue & Leonard Krasner (Eds.), *Handbook of psychological skills training: Clinical techniques and applications.* Boston: Allyn & Bacon.

Gannon, L. R.; Haynes, S. N.; Cueves. J.; & Chavez, R. (1987). Psychophysiological correlates of induced headaches. *Journal of Behavioral Medicine, 10,* 411–423.

Gansberg, Martin. (1964, March 27). 37 who saw murder didn't call the police. *New York Times,* pp. 1, 38.

Garcia, John. (1981). Tilting at the paper mills of academe. *American Psychologist, 36,* 149–158.

Garcia, John; Ervin, Frank R., & Koelling, Robert A. (1966). Learning with prolonged delay of reinforcement. *Psychonomic Science, 5,* 121–122.

Garcia, John, & Koelling, Robert A. (1966). Relation of cue to consequence in avoidance learning. *Psychonomic Science, 4,* 123–124.

Gardner, Howard. (1985). *Frames of mind: The theory of multiple intelligences.* New York: Basic Books.

Gardner, Howard. (1993a). *Frames of mind: The theory of multiple intelligences* (2nd ed.). New York: Basic Books.

Gardner, Howard. (1993b). Seven creators of the modern era. In John Brockman (Ed.), *Creativity.* New York: Simon & Schuster.

Gardner, Howard. (1995). Cracking open the IQ box. In Steven Fraser (Ed.), *The Bell Curve wars: Race, intelligence, and the future of America.* New York: Basic Books.

Gardner, Martin. (1981). Fliess, Freud, and biorhythms. In Martin Gardner (Ed.), *Science: Good, bad, and bogus.* Buffalo, N.Y.: Prometheus.

Garety, Philippa. (1991). Reasoning and delusions. *British Journal of Psychiatry, 159,* 14–18.

Garfield, Sol L. (1992). Eclectic psychotherapy: A common factors approach. In John C. Norcross & Marvin R. Goldfried (Eds.), *Handbook of psychotherapy integration.* New York: Basic Books.

Garfield, Sol L. (1994). Research on client variables in psychotherapy. In Allen E. Bergin & Sol L. Garfield (Eds.), *Handbook of psychotherapy and behavior change* (4th ed.). New York: Wiley.

Garfield, Sol L., & Bergin, Allen E. (1994). Introduction and historical overview. In Allen E. Bergin & Sol L. Garfield (Eds.), *Handbook of psychotherapy and behavior change* (4th ed.). New York: Wiley.

Garguilo, J.; Attie, I.; Brooks-Gunn, Jeanne; & Warren, M. P. (1987). Dating in middle school girls: Effects of social context, maturation, and grade. *Developmental Psychology, 23,* 730–737.

Garland, Ann F., & Zigler, Edward. (1993). Adolescent suicide prevention: Current research and social policy implications. *American Psychologist, 48,* 169–182.

Garry, Maryanne, & Loftus, Elizabeth F. (1994). Pseudomemories without hypnosis. *International Journal of Clinical and Experimental Hypnosis, 42* (4), 363–373.

Garza, R. T.; Romero, G. J.; Cox, B. G.; & Ramirez, M. (1982). Biculturalism, locus of control, and leader behavior in ethnically mixed small groups. *Journal of Applied Social Psychology, 12,* 237–253.

Gastil, J. (1990). Generic pronouns and sexist language: The oxymoronic character of masculine generics. *Sex Roles, 23,* 629–642.

Gavin, Leslie A., & Furman, Wyndol. (1989). Age difference in adolescents' perceptions of their peer groups. *Developmental Psychology, 25,* 827–834.

Gay, Peter. (1988). *Freud: A life for our time.* New York: Norton.

Gay, Peter (Ed.). (1989). *The Freud reader.* New York: Norton.

Gazzaniga, Michael S. (1977). *The split brain and conscious experience.* [Motion picture/Concept Films.] New York: Harper & Row.

Gazzaniga, Michael S. (1995). Consciousness and the cerebral hemispheres. In Michael S. Gazzaniga (Ed.), *The cognitive neurosciences.* Cambridge, Mass.: MIT Press.

Geen, Russell G. (1991). Social motivation. *Annual Review of Psychology, 42,* 377–399.

Geen, Russell G. (1995). *Human motivation: A social psychological approach.* Pacific Grove, Calif.: Brooks/Cole.

Geldard, F. A. (1972). *The human senses* (2nd ed.). New York: Wiley.

Geliebter, A.; Westriech, S.; Hashim, S. A.; & Gage, D. (1987). Gastric ballon reduces food intake and body weight in obese rats. *Physiology and Behavior, 39,* 399–402.

Gelman, Rochel, & Baillargeon, Renée. (1983). A review of some Piagetian concepts. In Paul H. Mussen (Ed.), *Handbook of child psychology, Vol. III. Cognitive Development.* New York: Wiley.

George, Mark S.; Ketter, Terence A.; Parekh, Priti I.; Horwitz, Barry; Herscovitch, Peter; & Post, Robert M. (1995). Brain activity during transient sadness and happiness in healthy women. *American Journal of Psychiatry, 152,* 341–351.

Gerace, Laina M.; Camilleri, Dorothy; & Ayres, Lioness. (1993). Sibling perspectives on schizophrenia and the family. *Schizophrenia Bulletin, 19,* 637–647.

Gerard, Harold B.; Wilhelmy, Roland A.; & Conolley, Edward S. (1968). Conformity and group size. *Journal of Personality and Social Psychology, 8,* 79–82.

Gerbner, George. (1993). Images that hurt: Mental illness in the mass media. *The JOURNAL of the California Alliance for the Mentally Ill, 4,* (1), 17–20.

Gerlach, Jes, & Peacock, Linda. (1994). Motor and mental side effects of clozapine. *Journal of Clinical Psychiatry, 55* (9, Supplement B), 107–109.

Geschwind, Norman, & Galaburda, Albert M. (1987). *Cerebral lateralization: Biological mechanisms, associations, and pathology.* Cambridge, Mass.: Harvard University Press.

Gesteland, R. C. (1982). The new physiology of odor. *Environmental Progress, 1,* 94–97.

Getka, Eric J., & Glass, Carol R. (1992). Behavioral and cognitive-behavioral approaches to the reduction of dental anxiety. *Behavior Therapy, 23,* 433–448.

Getzels, Jacob W., & Csikszentmihalyi, Mihaly. (1976). *The creative vision: A longitudinal study of problem finding in art.* New York: Wiley.

Gibbons, B. (1986, September). The intimate sense of smell. *National Geographic, 170,* 324–361.

Gibbons, Vincent P., & Kotagal, Suresh. (1995). Narcolepsy in children. In Charles E. Schaefer (Ed.), *Clinical handbook of sleep disorders in children.* Northvale, N.J.: Aronson.

Gieser, Marlon T. (1993). The first behavior therapist as I knew her. *Journal of Behavior Therapy and Experimental Psychiatry, 24,* 321–324.

Gilbert, Daniel T. (1989). Thinking lightly about others: Automatic components of the social inference process. In James S. Uleman & John A. Bargh (Eds.), *Unintended thought.* New York: Guilford Press.

Gilbert, Daniel T., & Malone, Patrick S. (1995). The correspondence bias. *Psychological Bulletin, 117,* 21–38.

Gilbert, Lucia Albino. (1993). *Two careers/one family: The promise of gender equality.* Beverly Hills, Calif.: Sage.

Gilbert, Lucia Albino. (1994). Current perspectives on dual-career families. *Current Directions in Psychological Science, 3,* 101–105.

Gillespie, George. (1988). Lucid dreams in Tibetan Buddhism. In Jayne I. Gackenbach & Stephen LaBerge (Eds.), *Conscious mind, sleeping brain: Perspectives on lucid dreaming.* New York: Plenum.

Gilligan, Carol. (1982). *In a different voice: Psychological theory and women's development.* Cambridge, Mass.: Harvard University Press.

Gilligan, Carol, & Attanucci, Jane. (1988). Two moral orientations. In Carol Gilligan, Janie Victoria Ward, & Jill McLean Taylor (Eds.), *Mapping the moral domain: A contribution of women's thinking to psychological theory and education.* Cambridge, Mass.: Harvard University Press.

Gilligan, Carol; Ward, Janie Victoria; & Taylor, Jill McLean. (1988). *Mapping the moral domain: A contribution of women's thinking to psychological theory and education.* Cambridge, Mass.: Harvard University Press.

Gitlin, Michael J.; Swendsen, Joel; Heller, Tracy L.; & Hammen, Constance. (1995). Relapse and impairment in bipolar disorder. *American Journal of Psychiatry, 152,* 1635–1640.

Gladue, Brian A. (1994). The biopsychology of sexual orientation. *Current Directions in Psychological Science, 3,* 150–154.

Glass, Carol R., & Arnkoff, Diane B. (1988). Common and specific factors in client descriptions of and explanations for change. *Journal of Integrative and Eclectic Psychotherapy, 7,* 427–440.

Gleaves, David H. (1996). The sociocognitive model of dissociative identity disorder: A reexamination of the evidence. *Psychological Bulletin, 120,* 42–59.

Gleitman, Henry. (1991). Edward Chace Tolman: A life of scientific and social purpose. In Gregory A. Kimble, Michael Wertheimer, & Charlotte White (Eds.), *Portraits of pioneers in psychology.* Washington, D.C., & Hillsdale, N.J.: American Psychological Association & Erlbaum.

Glick, Peter; Gottesman, Deborah; & Jolton, Jeffrey. (1989). The fault is not in the stars: Susceptibility of skeptics and believers in astrology to the Barnum effect. *Personality and Social Psychology Bulletin, 15,* 572–583.

Glynn, Shirley M. (1990). Token economy approaches for psychiatric patients: Progress and pitfalls over 25 years. *Behavior Modification, 14,* 383–407.

Godden, Duncan R., & Baddeley, Alan D. (1975). Context-dependent memory in two natural environments: On land and underwater. *British Journal of Psychology, 66,* 325–331.

Goff, Donald C., & Simms, Claudia A. (1993). Has multiple personality remained consistent over time? A comparison of past and recent cases. *Journal of Nervous and Mental Disease, 181,* 595–600.

Gökcebay, Nilgün; Cooper, Rosemary; Williams, Robert L.; Hirshkowitz, Max; & Moore, Constance A. (1994). Function of sleep. In Rosemary Cooper (Ed.), *Sleep.* New York: Chapman & Hall.

Gold, Steven N.; Hughes, Dawn; & Hohnecker, Laura. (1994). Degrees of repression of sexual abuse memories. *American Psychologist, 49,* 441–442.

Goldberg, Lewis R. (1993). The structure of phenotypic personality traits. *American Psychologist, 48,* 26–34.

Goldberger, Leo. (1983). The concept and mechanisms of denial: A selective overview. In Shlomo Breznitz (Ed.), *The denial of stress.* Madison, Conn.: International Universities Press.

Golden, Robert N., & Gilmore, John H. (1990). Serotonin and mood disorders. *Psychiatric Annals, 20,* 580–586.

Goldman, Ronald, & Goldman, Juliette. (1982). *Children's sexual thinking: A comparative study of children aged 5 to 15 years in Australia, North America, Britain, and Sweden.* Boston: Routledge & Kegan Paul.

Goldman-Rakic, Patricia S. (1992, September). Working memory and the mind. *Scientific American, 267,* 110–117.

Goldsmith, H. Hill; Buss, Arnold H.; Plomin, Robert; Rothbart, Mary Klevjord;

Thomas, Alexander; Chess, Stella; Hinde, Robert A.; & McCall, Robert B. (1987). Roundtable: What is temperament? Four approaches. *Child Development, 58,* 505–529.

Goldsmith, H. Hill, & Harman, Catherine. (1994). Temperament and attachment; individuals and relationships. *Current Directions in Psychological Science, 3,* 53–61.

Goldstein, Avram. (1994). *Addiction: From biology to drug policy.* New York: Freeman.

Goldstein, Risë B.; Weissman, Myrna M.; Adams, Phillip B.; Horwath, Ewald; Lish, Jennifer D.; Charney, Dennis; Woods, Scott W.; Sobin, Christina; & Wickramaratne, Priya J. (1994). Psychiatric disorders in relatives of probands with panic disorder and/or major depression. *Archives of General Psychiatry, 51,* 383–394.

Goleman, Daniel. (1980, February). 1,528 little geniuses and how they grew. *Psychology Today,* pp. 28–53.

Goleman, Daniel. (1991a). Sex roles reign powerful as ever in the emotions. In Daniel Goleman (Ed.), *Psychology updates: Articles on psychology from* The New York Times. New York: HarperCollins.

Goleman, Daniel. (1991b). The experience of touch: Research points to a critical role. In Daniel Goleman (Ed.), *Psychology updates.* New York: HarperCollins.

Goleman, Daniel. (1994, May 31). Miscoding is seen as the root of false memories. *New York Times,* pp. C-1, C-8.

Goleman, Daniel. (1995). *Emotional intelligence.* New York: Bantam.

Goleman, Daniel, & Gurin, Joel (1993). *Mind/body medicine: How to use your mind for better health.* Yonkers, N.Y.: Consumer Reports Books.

Goleman, Daniel; Kaufman, Paul; & Ray, Michael. (1992). *The creative spirit.* New York: Penguin.

Golomb, Claire, & Galasso, Lisa. (1995). Make-believe and reality: Explorations of the imaginary realm. *Developmental Psychology, 31,* 800–810.

Golombok, Susan, & Tasker, Fiona. (1996). Do parents influence the sexual orientation of their children? Findings from a longitudinal study of lesbian families. *Developmental Psychology, 32,* 3–11.

Goodall, G. (1984). Learning due to the response–shock contingency in signalled punishment. *Quarterly Journal of Experimental Psychology, 36B,* 259–279.

Goodenough, Donald R. (1991). Dream recall: History and current status of the field. In Steven J. Ellman & John S. Antrobus (Eds.), *The mind in sleep: Psychology and psychophysiology* (2nd ed.). New York: Wiley.

Goodenough, F. (1932). The expression of emotion in a blind-deaf child. *Journal of Abnormal Social Psychology, 27,* 328–333.

Goodwin, James S.; Hunt, W. C.; Key, C. R.; & Samet, J. M. (1987). The effect of marital status on stage, treatment, and survival of cancer patients. *Journal of the American Medical Association, 258,* 3125–3130.

Gopnik, Alison. (1996). The post-Piaget era. *Psychological Science, 7,* 221–225.

Gorassini, Donald R., & Olson, James M. (1995). Does self-perception change explain the foot-in-the-door effect? *Journal of Personality and Social Psychology, 69,* 91–105.

Gordon, T., & Doyle, J. T. (1987). Drinking and mortality: The Albany Study. *American Journal of Epidemiology, 125,* 263–270.

Gorski, Roger. (1995, February 28). Quoted in Gina Kolata. Man's world, woman's world? Brain studies point to differences. *New York Times,* pp. C1, C7.

Gotlib, Ian H. (1992). Interpersonal and cognitive aspects of depression. *Current Directions in Psychological Science, 1,* 149–154.

Gottesman, Irving I. (1991). *Schizophrenia genesis: The origins of madness.* New York: Freeman.

Gottfried, A. W., & Bathurst, K. (1983). Hand preference across time is related to intelligence in young girls, not boys. *Science, 221,* 1074–1075.

Gottlieb, Gilbert, & Krasnegor, Norman A. (1985). *Measurement of audition and vision in the first year of postnatal life: A methodological overview.* Norwood, N.J.: Ablex Press.

Gottman, John M. (1994). *Why marriages succeed or fail: What you can learn from the breakthrough research to make your marriage last.* New York: Simon & Schuster.

Gottman, John M., & Levenson, Robert W. (1992). Marital processes predictive of later dissolution: Behavior, physiology, and health. *Journal of Personality and Social Psychology, 63,* 221–233.

Gough, Harrison G. (1989). The California Personality Inventory. In Charles S. Newmark (Ed.), *Major psychological assessment instruments* (Vol. 2). Boston: Allyn & Bacon.

Gould, James L., & Gould, Carol Grant. (1994). *The animal mind.* New York: Freeman.

Gould, Stephen Jay. (1993). *The mismeasure of man* (2nd ed.). New York: Norton.

Graham, John R. (1993). *MMPI-2: Assessing personality and psychopathology* (2nd ed.). New York: Oxford University Press.

Graham, Robert B. (1990). *Physiological psychology*. Belmont, Calif.: Wadsworth.

Graig, Eric. (1993). Stress as a consequence of the urban physical environment. In Leo Goldberger & Shlomo Breznitz (Eds.), *Handbook of stress: Theoretical and clinical aspects* (2nd ed.). New York: Free Press.

Gray, D. S., & Gorzalka, B. B. (1980). Adrenal steroid interactions in female sexual behavior: A review. *Psychoneuroendocrinology, 5,* 157–175.

Gray, Jeffrey A. (1987). *The psychology of fear and stress* (2nd ed.). New York: Cambridge University Press.

Gray, John. (1992). *Men are from Mars, women are from Venus: A practical guide for improving communication and getting what you want in your relationships.* New York: HarperCollins.

Greeley, Andrew. (1987, January/February). Mysticism goes mainstream. *American Health,* pp. 47–49.

Green, Celia, & McCreery, Charles. (1994). *Lucid dreaming: The paradox of consciousness during sleep.* New York: Routledge.

Greenberg, Leslie S.; Elliott, Robert K.; & Lietaer, Germain. (1994). Research on experiential psychotherapies. In Allen E. Bergin & Sol L. Garfield (Eds.), *Handbook of psychotherapy and behavior change* (4th ed.). New York: Wiley.

Greenberg, Paul E.; Stiglin, Laura E.; Finkelstein, Stan N.; & Berndt, Ernst R. (1993a). Depression: A neglected major illness. *Journal of Clinical Psychiatry, 54,* 419–424.

Greenberg, Paul E.; Stiglin, Laura E.; Finkelstein, Stan N.; & Berndt, Ernst R. (1993b). The economic burden of depression in 1990. *Journal of Clinical Psychiatry, 54,* 405–418.

Greeno, Catherine G., & Wing, Rena R. (1994). Stress-induced eating. *Psychological Bulletin, 115,* 444–464.

Greenough, William T. (1992). Morphological basis of learning and memory: Vertebrates. In Larry R. Squire (Ed.), *Encyclopedia of learning and memory.* New York: Macmillan.

Greenough, William T. (1993, April 12). Quoted in Ronald Kotulak, Mental workouts pump up brain power. *Chicago Tribune,* p. 12.

Greenough, William T.; Black, James E.; & Wallace, Christopher S. (1987). Experience and brain development. *Child Development, 58,* 539–559.

Gregory, Richard L. (1968, November). Visual illusions. *Scientific American, 212,* 66–76.

Griffiths, Roland. (1994, February). Quoted in Tori DeAngelis, People's drug of choice offers potent side effects. *APA Monitor, 25,* p. 16.

Grimm, Laurence G. (1993). *Statistical applications for the behavioral sciences.* New York: Wiley.

Grollman, Earl A. (1988). *Suicide: Prevention, intervention, postvention* (2nd ed.). Boston: Beacon Press.

Grossman, Michele, & Wood, Wendy. (1993). Sex differences in intensity of emotional experience: A social role interpretation. *Journal of Personality and Social Psychology, 65,* 1010–1022.

Grossmann, K. E., & Grossmann, K. (1990). The wider concept of attachment in cross-cultural research. *Human Development, 33,* 31–47.

Grosz, Richard D. (1990). Suicide: Training the resident assistant as an interventionist. In Leighton C. Whitaker & Richard E. Slimak (Eds.), *College student suicide.* New York: Haworth Press.

Grotevant, Harold D. (1992). Assigned and chosen identity components: A process perspective on their integration. In Gerald R. Adams, Thomas P. Gullotta, & Raymond Montemayor (Eds.), *Adolescent identity formation.* Newbury Park, Calif.: Sage.

Groves, Philip M., & Rebec, George V. (1992). *Introduction to biological psychology* (4th ed.). Dubuque, Iowa: Brown.

Grusec, Joan E. (1992). Social learning theory and developmental psychology: The legacies of Robert Sears and Albert Bandura. *Developmental Psychology, 28,* 776–786.

Guarnaccia, Peter J. (1993). *Ataques de nervios* in Puerto Rico: Culture-bound syndrome or popular illness? *Medical Anthropology, 15,* 157–170.

Guerin, B. (1986). Mere presence effects in humans: A review. *Journal of Experimental Social Psychology, 22,* 38–77.

Gunnar, Megan R. (1994). Psychoendocrine studies of temperament and stress in early childhood: Expanding current models. In John E. Bates & Theodore D. Wachs (Eds.), *Temperament: Individual differences at the interface of biology and behavior.* Washington, D.C.: American Psychological Association.

Gurman, Ernest B. (1994). Debriefing for all concerned: Ethical treatment of human subjects. *Psychological Science, 5* (3), p. 139.

Gustavson, Carl R.; Kelly, Daniel J.; Sweeney, Michael; & Garcia, John. (1976). Prey-lithium aversions I: Coyotes and wolves. *Behavioral Biology, 17,* 61–72.

Guzzo, Richard A., & Dickson, Marcus W. (1996). Teams in organizations: Recent research on performance and effectiveness. *Annual Review of Psychology, 47,* 307–338.

Haaga, David A. F., & Davison, Gerald C. (1991). Cognitive change methods. In Frederick H. Kanfer & Arnold P. Goldstein (Eds.), *Helping people change: A textbook of methods* (4th ed.). New York: Pergamon Press.

Haaga, David F., & Davison, Gerald C. (1993). An appraisal of rational-emotive therapy. *Journal of Consulting and Clinical Psychology, 61,* 215–220.

Hackel, Lisa S., & Ruble, Diane N. (1992). Changes in the marital relationship after the first baby is born: Predicting the impact of expectancy disconfirmation. *Journal of Personality and Social Psychology, 62,* 944–957.

Haddock, Geoffrey; Zanna, Mark P.; & Esses, Victoria M. (1993). Assessing the structure of prejudicial attitudes: The case of attitudes toward homosexuals. *Journal of Personality and Social Psychology, 65,* 1105–1118.

Hahlweg, Kurt, & Goldstein, Michael J. (Eds.). (1987). *Understanding major mental disorder: The contribution of family interaction research.* New York: Family Process Press.

Haidt, Jonathan; Koller, Silvia Helena; & Dias, Maria G. (1993). Affect, culture, and morality, or is it wrong to eat your dog? *Journal of Personality and Social Psychology, 65,* 613–628.

Haight, Barbara Kavanagh. (1992). Long-term effects of a structured life review process. *Journal of Gerontology, 47* (5), 312–315.

Hall, Calvin S., & Van de Castle, R. L. (1966). *Content analysis of dreams.* New York: Appleton-Century-Crofts.

Halliday, Gordon. (1995). Treating nightmares in children. In Charles E. Schaefer (Ed.), *Clinical handbook of sleep disorders in children.* Northvale, N.J.: Aronson.

Halonen, Jane S. (Ed.). (1986). *Teaching critical thinking in psychology.* Milwaukee, Wis.: Alverno Productions.

Halonen, Jane S. (1995a). Demystifying critical thinking. In Diane F. Halpern & Susan G. Nummedal (Eds), *Special Issue: Psychologists teach critical thinking. Teaching of Psychology, 22,* No. 1.

Halonen, Jane S. (1995b). *The critical thinking companion for introductory psychology.* New York: Worth Publishers.

Halpern, Diane F. (1989). *Thought and knowledge: An introduction to critical thinking.* Hillsdale, N.J.: Erlbaum.

Halpern, Diane F., & Coren, Stanley. (1993). Left-handedness and life span: A reply to Harris. *Psychological Bulletin, 114,* 235–241.

Halpern, Diane F., & Nummedal, Susan G. (Eds.). (1995). *Special Issue: Psychologists teach critical thinking. Teaching of Psychology, 22,* No. 1.

Hamburg, David A., & Takanishi, Ruby. (1989). Preparing for life: The critical transition of adolescence. *American Psychologist, 44,* 825–827.

Hamilton, Leonard W., & Timmons, C. Robin. (1990). *Principles of behavioral pharmacology.* Englewood Cliffs, N.J.: Prentice Hall.

Hamilton, Mykol C. (1988). Using masculine generics: Does generic *he* increase male bias in the user's imagery? *Sex Roles, 19,* 785–799.

Hamilton, Mykol C. (1991). Masculine bias in the attribution of personhood. *Psychology of Women Quarterly, 15,* 393–402.

Hammen, Constance; Burge, Dorli; Burney, Elizabeth; & Adrian, Cheri. (1990). Longitudinal study of diagnoses in children of women with unipolar and bipolar affective disorder. *Archives of General Psychiatry, 47,* 1112–1117.

Hansel, C. E. M. (1991). Parapsychology re-viewed. *Contemporary Psychology, 36,* 198–200.

Hardy, John Droubay, & Smith, Timothy W. (1988). Cynical hostility and vulnerability to disease: Social support, life stress, and physiological response to conflict. *Health Psychology, 7,* 447–459.

Hare, B. D., & Milano, R. A. (1985). Chronic pain: Perspectives on physical assessment and treatment. *Annals of Behavioral Medicine, 7* (3), 6–10.

Harlow, Harry F. (1953). Motivation as a factor in new responses. In *Current theory and research in motivation: A symposium.* Lincoln: University of Nebraska Press.

Harlow, John M. (1848, December 13). Passage of an iron rod through the head. *Boston Medical and Surgical Journal, 39* (20), 389–393.

Harlow, John M. (1869). Recovery from the passage of an iron bar through the head. *Publications of the Massachusetts Medical Society, 2,* 327–347.

Harma, Mikko. (1993). Individual differences in tolerance to shiftwork: A review. *Ergonomics, 36* (1–3), 101–109.

Harrington, D. M.; Block, J. H.; & Block, J. (1987). Testing aspects of Carl Rogers' theory of creative environments: Child-rearing antecedents of creative potential in young adolescents. *Journal of Personality and Social Psychology, 52,* 851–856.

Harris, Ben. (1979). What ever happened to Little Albert? *American Psychologist, 34,* 151–160.

Harris, Lauren Julius. (1993a). Do left-handers die sooner than right-handers? Commentary on Coren and Halpern's (1991) "Left-Handedness: A marker for decreased survival fitness." *Psychological Bulletin, 114,* 203–234.

Harris, Lauren Julius. (1993b). Reply to Halpern and Coren. *Psychological Bulletin, 114,* 242–247.

Harter, Susan. (1983) Developmental perspectives on the self-system. In Paul H. Mussen & E. Mavis Hetherington (Eds.), *Handbook of child psychology* (4th ed.): *Vol. IV. Socialization, personality, and social development.* New York: Wiley.

Harter, Susan. (1990). Self and identity development. In S. Shirley Feldman & Glen R. Elliott (Eds.), *At the threshold: The developing adolescent.* Cambridge, Mass.: Harvard University Press.

Havighurst, Robert J.; Neugarten, Bernice L.; & Tobin, Sheldon S. (1968). Disengagement and patterns of aging. In Bernice L. Neugarten (Ed.), *Middle age and aging.* Chicago: University of Chicago Press.

Hawkins, J. David; Catalano, Richard F.; & Miller, Janet Y. (1992). Risk and protective factors for alcohol and other drug problems in adolescence and early adulthood: Implications for substance abuse prevention. *Psychological Bulletin, 112,* 64–105.

Hawkins, John N. (1994). Issues of motivation in Asian education. In Harold F. O'Neil, Jr., & Michael Drillings (Eds.), *Motivation: Theory and research.* Hillsdale, N.J.: Erlbaum.

Hayes, Jeffrey A., & Mitchell, Jeffrey C. (1994). Mental health professionals' skepticism about multiple personality disorder. *Professional Psychology: Research and Practice, 25,* 410–415.

Hayes, John R. (1989). *The complete problem solver* (2nd ed.). Hillsdale, N.J.: Erlbaum.

Hebb, Donald O. (1955). Drives and the C. N. S. (central nervous system). *Psychological Review, 62,* 243–254.

Hedge, Alan, & Yousif, Yousif H. (1992). Effects of urban size, urgency, and cost of helpfulness: A cross-cultural comparison between the United Kingdom and the Sudan. *Journal of Cross-Cultural Psychology, 23,* 107–115.

Hedges, Larry V., & Nowell, Amy. (1995, July 7). Sex differences in mental test scores, variability, and numbers of high-scoring individuals. *Science, 269,* 41–45.

Heider, Eleanor Rosch, & Olivier, Donald C. (1972). The structure of the color space in naming and memory for two languages. *Cognitive Psychology, 3,* 337–354.

Heikkinen, Martti; Aro, Hillevi M.; & Lonnqvist, Jouko K. (1993). Life events and social support in suicide. *Suicide and Life Threatening Behavior, 23,* 343–358.

Heilman, M. E., & Stopeck, M. H. (1985). Being attractive, advantage or disadvantage? Performance-based evaluations and recommended personnel actions as a function of appearance, sex, and job type. *Organizational Behavior and Human Decision Processes, 35,* 202–215.

Heiman, Gary. (1995). *Research methods in psychology.* Boston: Houghton Mifflin.

Heinrichs, R. Walter. (1993). Schizophrenia and the brain: Conditions for a neuropsychology of madness. *American Psychologist, 48,* 221–233.

Helgeson, Vicki S. (1992). Moderators of the relation between perceived control and adjustment to chronic illness. *Journal of Personality and Social Psychology, 63,* 656–666.

Helgeson, Vicki S. (1994). Relation of agency and communion to well-being: Evidence and potential explanations. *Psychological Bulletin, 116,* 412–428.

Hendrix, Mary Lynn. (1993). *Bipolar disorder.* Rockville, Md.: National Institute of Mental Health (NIMH Publication No. 93–3679).

Henley, Nancy M. (1989). Molehill or mountain? What we know and don't know about sex bias in language. In M. Crawford & M. Gentry (Eds.), *Gender and thought: Psychological perspectives.* New York: Springer-Verlag.

Hennessey, Beth A., & Amabile, Teresa M. (1988). The conditions of creativity. In Robert J. Sternberg (Ed.), *The nature of creativity: Contemporary psychological perspectives.* New York: Cambridge University Press.

Henninger, Polly. (1992). Conditional handedness: Handedness changes in multiple personality disordered subject reflects shift in hemispheric dominance. *Consciousness and Cognition, 1,* 265–287.

Henry, William P.; Strupp, Hans H.; Shacht, Thomas E.; & Gaston, Louise. (1994). Psychodynamic approaches. In Allen E. Bergin & Sol L. Garfield (Eds.), *Handbook of psychotherapy and behavior change* (4th ed.). New York: Wiley.

Hepper, Peter G.; Shahidullah, Sara; & White, Raymond. (1990, October 4). Origins of fetal handedness. *Nature, 347,* 431.

Herbert, Tracy Bennett, & Cohen, Sheldon. (1993). Depression and immunity: A meta-analytic review. *Psychological Bulletin, 113,* 472–486.

Herman, C. P., & Polivy, J. (1984). A boundary model for the regulation of eating. In A. J. Stunkard & E. Stellar (Eds.), *Eating and its disorders.* New York: Raven.

Herman, Louis M.; Kuczaj, Stan A., II; & Holder, Mark D. (1993). Responses to anomalous gestural sequences by a language-trained dolphin: Evidence for processing of semantic relations and syntactic information. *Journal of Experimental Psychology: General, 122,* 184–194.

Hermans, Hubert J. M. (1996). Voicing the self: From information processing to dialogical interchange. *Psychological Bulletin, 119,* 31–50.

Herrnstein, Richard J., & Murray, Charles. (1994). *The bell curve: Intelligence and class structure in American life.* New York: Free Press.

Hertel, Paula T., & Rude, Stephanie S. (1991). Depressive deficits in memory: Focusing attention improves subsequent recall. *Journal of Experimental Psychology: General, 120,* 301–309.

Hertz, Marguerite R. (1992). Rorschach-bound: A 50-year memoir. *Professional Psychology: Research and Practice, 23,* 168–171.

Hetherington, A. W., & Ranson, S. W. (1940). Hypothalamic lesions and adiposity in the rat. *Anatomical Record, 78,* 149–172.

Hewstone, Miles. (1990). The "ultimate attribution error"? A review of the literature on intergroup causal attribution. *European Journal of Social Psychology, 20,* 311–335.

Hilgard, Ernest R. (1982). Hypnotic susceptibility and implications for measurement. *International Journal of Clinical and Experimental Hypnosis, 30,* 394–403.

Hilgard, Ernest R. (1986a). *Divided consciousness: Multiple controls in human thought and action.* New York: Wiley.

Hilgard, Ernest R. (1986b, January). A study in hypnosis. *Psychology Today, 20,* 23–27.

Hilgard, Ernest R. (1987). *Psychology in America: A historical survey.* New York: Harcourt Brace Jovanovich.

Hilgard, Ernest R. (1991). A neodissociation interpretation of hypnosis. In Steven J. Lynn & J. Rhue (Eds.), *Theories of hypnosis: Current models and perspectives.* New York: Guilford Press.

Hilgard, Ernest R. (1992). Divided consciousness and dissociation. *Consciousness and Cognition, 1,* 16–32.

Hilgard, Ernest R., & Hilgard, Josephine R. (1983). *Hypnosis in the relief of pain.* Los Altos, Calif.: Kaufmann.

Hilgard, Ernest R., & Marquis, D. G. (1940). *Conditioning and learning.* New York: Appleton-Century-Crofts.

Hills, Hope I., & Strozier, Anne L. (1992). Multicultural training in APA-approved counseling psychology programs: A survey. *Professional Psychology: Research and Practice, 23,* 43–51.

Hillyard, Steven A.; Mangun, George R.; Woldorff, Marty G.; & Luck, Steven J. (1995). Neural systems mediating selective attention. In Michael S. Gazzaniga (Ed.), *The cognitive neurosciences.* Cambridge, Mass.: MIT Press.

Hilton, James L., & Darley, John M. (1991). The effects of interaction goals on person perception. In Mark P. Zanna (Ed.), *Advances in experimental social psychology* (Vol. 24). San Diego: Academic Press/Harcourt.

Hilton, James L., & von Hippel, William. (1996). Stereotypes. *Annual Review of Psychology, 47,* 237–271.

Hines, Terence. (1988). *Pseudoscience and the paranormal: A critical examination of the evidence.* Buffalo, N.Y.: Prometheus Books.

Hines, Terence. (1996). Biorhythms. In Gordon Stein (Ed.), *The encyclopedia of the paranormal.* Amherst, N.Y.: Prometheus Books.

Hirschfeld, Robert M. A. (1991). *When the blues won't go away: New approaches to dysthymic disorder and other forms of chronic low-grade depression.* New York: Macmillan.

Hobfoll, Stevan E.; Lilly, Roy S.; & Jackson, Anita P. (1992). Conservation of social resources and the self. In Hans O. F. Veiel & Urs Baumann (Eds.), *The meaning and measurement of social support.* New York: Hemisphere.

Hobfoll, Stevan E., & Stephens, Mary Ann Parris. (1990). Social support during extreme stress: Consequences and intervention. In Barbara R. Sarason, Irwin G. Sarason, & Gregory R. Pierce (Eds.), *Social support: An interactional view.* New York: Wiley.

Hobfoll, Stevan E., & Vaux, Alex. (1993). Social support: Resources and context. In Leo Goldberger & Shlomo Breznitz (Eds.), *Handbook of stress: Theoretical and clinical aspects* (2nd ed.). New York: Free Press.

Hobson, J. Allan. (1988). *The dreaming brain.* New York: Basic Books.

Hobson, J. Allan. (1989). *Sleep.* New York: Scientific American Library.

Hobson, J. Allan. (1990). Activation, input source, and modulation: A neurocognitive model of the state of the brain-mind. In Richard R. Bootzin, John F. Kihlstrom, & Daniel L. Schacter (Eds.), *Sleep and cognition.* Washington, D.C.: American Psychological Association.

Hobson, J. Allan, & Stickgold, Robert. (1995). The conscious state paradigm: A neurological approach to waking, sleeping, and dreaming. In Michael S. Gazzaniga (Ed.), *The cognitive neurosciences.* Cambridge, Mass.: MIT Press.

Hoffman, Martin L. (1977). Moral internalization: Current theory and research. In Leonard Berkowitz (Ed.), *Advances in experimental social psychology* (Vol. 10). New York: Academic Press.

Hoffman, Martin L. (1988). Moral development. In Marc H. Bornstein & Michael E. Lamb (Eds.), *Developmental psychology: An advanced textbook.* Hillsdale, N.J.: Erlbaum.

Hoffman, Martin L. (1994). Discipline and internalization. *Developmental Psychology, 30,* 26–28.

Hohmann, George W. (1966). Some effects of spinal cord lesions on experienced emotional feelings. *Psychophysiology, 3,* 143–156.

Holahan, Carole K., & Holahan, Charles J. (1987). Self-efficacy, social support, and depression in aging: A longitudinal analysis. *Journal of Gerontology, 42,* 65–68.

Holahan, Carole K., & Sears, Robert R. (1995). *The gifted group in later maturity.* In association with Lee J. Cronbach. Stanford, Calif.: Stanford University Press.

Holden, Constance. (1994, June 17). A cautionary genetic tale: The sobering story of D_2. *Science, 264,* 1696–1697.

Hole, John W., Jr. (1993). *Human anatomy and physiology* (6th ed.). Dubuque, Iowa: Brown.

Holland, A. J.; Sicotte, N.; & Treasure, J. (1988). Anorexia nervosa: Evidence of a genetic basis. *Journal of Psychosomatic Research, 32,* 561–571.

Holland, J. L. (1965). *Manual for the Vocational Preference Inventory.* Palo Alto, Calif.: Consulting Psychologists Press.

Hollander, E. P., & Julian, J. W. (1970). Studies in leader legitimacy, influence, and innovation. In L. Berkowitz (Ed.), *Advances in experimental social psychology,* (Vol. 5). New York: Academic Press.

Hollon, Steven D., & Beck, Aaron T. (1994). Cognitive and cognitive-behavioral therapies. In Allen E. Bergin & Sol L. Garfield (Eds.), *Handbook of psychotherapy and behavior change* (4th ed.). New York: Wiley.

Holmes, David S. (1976). Debriefing after psychological experiments. II. Effectiveness of postexperimental desensitizing. *American Psychologist, 31,* 868–875.

Holmes, David S. (1984). Meditation and somatic arousal reduction: A review of the experimental evidence. *American Psychologist, 39,* 1–10.

Holmes, David S. (1987). The influence of meditation versus rest on physiological arousal: A second examination. In Michael A. West (Ed.), *The psychology of meditation.* New York: Oxford University Press.

Holmes, David. (1990). The evidence for repression: An examination of sixty years of research. In Jerome Singer (Ed.), *Repression and dissociation: Implications for personality theory, psychopathology, and health.* Chicago: University of Chicago Press.

Holmes, Stanley. (1994, April 25). The tortuous tale of a serial killer. *Newsweek,* p. 30.

Holmes, Thomas H., & Masuda, Minoru. (1974). Life change and illness susceptibility. In Barbara Snell Dohrenwend & Bruce P. Dohrenwend (Eds.), *Stressful life events: Their nature and effects.* New York: Wiley.

Holmes, Thomas H., & Rahe, Richard H. (1967). The Social Readjustment Rating Scale. *Journal of Psychosomatic Research, 11,* 213–218.

Holt, Robert R. (1993). Occupational stress. In Leo Goldberger & Shlomo Breznitz (Eds.), *Handbook of stress: Theoretical and clinical aspects* (2nd ed.). New York: Free Press.

Holyoak, Keith J., & Spellman, Barbara A. (1993). Thinking. *Annual Review of Psychology, 44,* 265–315.

Hoppe, Richard B. (1988). In search of a phenomenon: Research in parapsychology. *Contemporary Psychology, 33,* 129–130.

Hopson, Janet L. (1988, July/August). A pleasurable chemistry. *Psychology Today, 22,* 29–33.

Hoptman, Matthew J., & Davidson, Richard J. (1994). How and why do the two cerebral hemispheres interact? *Psychological Bulletin, 116,* 195–219.

Horgan, John. (1994, July). Can science explain consciousness? *Scientific American, 271,* 88–94.

Horney, Karen. (1926/1967). The flight from womanhood. In Harold Kelman (Ed.), *Feminine psychology.* New York: Norton.

Horney, Karen. (1945/1972). *Our inner conflicts: A constructive theory of neurosis.* New York: Norton.

Hornig-Rohan, Mädy, & Amsterdam, Jay D. (1994). Clinical and biological correlates of treatment-resistant depression: An overview. *Psychiatric Annals, 24,* 220–227.

Horton, David L., & Mills, Carol B. (1984). Human learning and memory. *Annual Review of Psychology, 35,* 361–394.

House, James S.; Landis, Karl R.; & Umberson, Debra. (1988). Social relationships and health. *Science, 241,* 540–545.

House, R. J. (1977). A 1976 theory of charismatic leadership. In J. G. Hunt & L. L. Larsen (Eds.), *Leadership: The cutting edge* (pp. 189–207). Carbondale: Southern Illinois University Press.

House, R. J.; Spangler, W. D.; & Woycke, J. (1991). Personality and charisma in the U.S. presidency: A psychological theory of leader effectiveness. *Administrative Science Quarterly, 36,* 364–396.

Howard, A. (1986). College experiences and managerial performance. *Journal of Applied Psychology, 71,* 530–552.

Howard, A. (1990). *The multiple facets of industrial-organizational psychology.* Arlington Heights, Ill.: Society for Industrial and Organizational Psychology.

Howard, George S. (1991). Culture tales: A narrative approach to thinking, cross-cultural psychology, and psychotherapy. *American Psychologist, 46,* 187–197.

Howard, Kenneth I.; Kopta, Stephen M.; Krause, M. S.; & Orlinsky, D. E. (1986). The dose-effect relationship in psychotherapy. *American Psychologist, 41,* 159–164.

Howard, Robert. (1992). *Folie à deux* involving a dog. *American Journal of Psychiatry, 149,* 414.

Howard, William, & Crano, William D. (1974). Effects of sex, conversation, location, and size of observer group on bystander intervention in a high risk situation. *Sociometry, 37,* 491–507.

Howe, Mark L., & Courage, Mary L. (1993). On resolving the enigma of infantile amnesia. *Psychological Bulletin, 113,* 305–326.

Howes, Carollee. (1991). Caregiving environments and their consequences for children: The experience in the United States. In E. C. Melhuish & P. Moss (Eds.), *Daycare for young children.* London: Routledge.

Howes, Carollee, & Hamilton, Claire E. (1992). Children's relationships with caregivers: Mothers and child care teachers. *Child Development, 63,* 859–871.

Hubel, David H. (1995). *Eye, brain, and vision.* New York: Scientific American Library.

Hudspeth, William J., & Pribram, Karl H. (1992). Psychophysiological indices of cerebral maturation. *International Journal of Psychophysiology, 12,* 19–29.

Hugdahl, Kenneth; Satz, P.; Mitrushina, M.; & Miller, E. N. (1993). Left-handedness and old age: Do left-handers die earlier? *Neuropsychologia, 31,* 325–333.

Hughes, Steven L., & Neimeyer, Robert A. (1990). A cognitive model of suicidal behavior. In David Lester (Ed.), *Current concepts of suicide.* Philadelphia: The Charles Press.

Hugick, L., & Leonard, J. (1991). Job dissatisfaction grows; "moonlighting" on the rise. *Gallup Poll News Service, 56,* 1–11.

Hull, Clark L. (1943). *Principles of behavior: An introduction to behavior theory.* New York: Appleton-Century-Crofts.

Hull, Clark L. (1952). *A behavior system: An introduction to behavior theory concerning the individual organism.* New Haven, Conn.: Yale University Press.

Human Capital Initiative. (1993, December). *Human capital initiative: Vitality for life: Psychological research for productive aging: Report 2.* Special issue of the *APS Observer* published by the American Psychological Society.

Hume, K. Michelle, & Crossman, Jane. (1992). Musical reinforcement of practice behaviors among competitive swimmers. *Journal of Applied Behavior Analysis, 25,* 665–670.

Hunt, Earl, & Agnoli, Franca. (1991). The Whorfian hypothesis: A cognitive psychology perspective. *Psychological Review, 98,* 377–389.

Hunter, J. E., & Hunter, R. F. (1984). Validity and utility of alternative predictors of job performance. *Psychological Bulletin, 96,* 72–98.

Hurley, Dan. (1994, July/August). Imminent danger. *Psychology Today, 27,* 54–57, 60–68.

Hurvich, Leo M. (1981). *Color vision.* Sunderland, Mass.: Sinauer.

Huston, Aletha C. (1983). Sex-typing. In Paul H. Mussen (Ed.), *Handbook of child psychology: Vol. IV. Socialization, personality, and social development.* New York: Wiley.

Huston, Ted L.; McHale, Susan M.; & Crouter, Ann C. (1986). When the honeymoon's over: Changes in the marriage relationship over the first year. In Robin Gilmour & Steve Duck (Eds.), *The emerging field of personal relationships.* Hillsdale, N.J.: Erlbaum.

Huston, Ted L.; Ruggiero, Mary; Conner, Ross; & Geis, Gilbert. (1981). Bystander intervention into crime: A study based on naturally-occurring episodes. *Social Psychology Quarterly, 44,* 14–23.

Huttunen, Matti O.; Machon, Ricardo A.; & Mednick, Sarnoff A. (1994). Prenatal factors in the pathogenesis of schizophrenia. *British Journal of Psychiatry, 164* (Supplement No. 23), 15–19.

Hyde, Janet Shibley. (1996). Where are the gender differences? Where are the gender similarities? In David M. Buss & Neil M. Malamuth (Eds.), *Sex, power, conflict: Evolutionary and feminist perspectives.* New York: Oxford University Press.

Hyde, Janet Shibley, & Delamater, John. (1997). *Understanding human sexuality* (6th ed.). New York: McGraw-Hill.

Hyde, Janet Shibley, & Plant, Elizabeth Ashby. (1995). Magnitude of psychological gender differences. *American Psychologist, 50,* 159–161.

Hyman, Ray. (1994). Anomaly or artifact? Comments on Bem and Honorton. *Psychological Bulletin, 115,* 19–24.

Illnerová, Helena. (1991). The suprachiasmatic nucleus and rhythmic pineal melatonin production. In David C. Klein, Robert Y. Moore, & Steven M. Reppert (Eds.), *Suprachiasmatic nucleus: The mind's clock.* New York: Oxford University Press.

Inouye, Sharon L.; Albert, Marilyn S.; & Mohs, Richard. (1993). Cognitive performance in a high-functioning community-dwelling elderly population. *Journal of Gerontology, 48,* 146–157.

Insel, Thomas R., & Winslow, James T. (1992). Neurobiology of obsessive compulsive disorder. *Psychiatric Clinics of North America, 15,* 813–824.

Intons-Peterson, M. J., & Reddel, M. (1984). What do people ask about a neonate? *Developmental Psychology, 20,* 358–359.

Irving, Clive (Ed.). (1995). *In their name: Oklahoma City: The official commemorative volume.* New York: Random House.

Irwin, Harvey J. (1994). Proneness to dissociation and traumatic childhood events. *Journal of Nervous and Mental Disease, 182,* 456–460.

Irwin, M.; Daniels, M.; Smith, T. L.; Bloom, E.; & Weiner, H. (1987). Impaired natural killer cell activity during bereavement. *Brain, Behavior, and Immunity, 1,* 98–104.

Isabella, Russell A.; Belsky, Jay; & von Eye, Alexander. (1989). Origins of infant–mother attachment: An examination of interactional synchrony during the infant's first year. *Developmental Psychology, 25,* 12–21.

Ishihara, Kaneyoshi; Miyake, Susumu; Miyasita, Akio; & Miyata, Yo. (1992). Morningness-eveningness preference and sleep habits in Japanese office workers of different ages. *Chronobiologia, 19,* 9–16.

Iversen, Iver H. (1992). Skinner's early research: From reflexology to operant conditioning. *American Psychologist, 47,* 1318–1328.

Izard, Carroll E. (1989). The structure and function of emotions: Implications for cognition, motivation, and personality. In Ira S. Cohen (Ed.), *The G. Stanley Hall Lecture Series* (Vol. 9) (1988 lectures). Washington, D.C.: American Psychological Association.

Izard, Carroll E. (1990a). The substrates and functions of emotion feelings: William James and current emotion theories. *Personality and Social Psychology Bulletin, 16,* 626–635.

Izard, Carroll E. (1990b). Facial expressions and the regulation of emotions. *Journal of Personality and Social Psychology, 58,* 487–498.

Jackson, Adam J. (1993). *Iridology: A guide to iris analysis and preventive health care.* Boston: Charles E. Tuttle Co.

Jackson, J. M., & Harkins, S. G. (1985). Equity in effort: An explanation of the social loafing effect. *Journal of Personality and Social Psychology, 49,* 1199–1206.

Jacob, Theodore (Ed.). (1987). *Family interaction and psychopathology: Theories, methods, and findings.* New York: Plenum.

Jacobs, Barry L. (1987). How hallucinogenic drugs work. *American Scientist, 75* (4), 388–392.

Jacobs, Bob. (1993, April 12). Quoted in Ronald Kotulak, Mental workouts pump up brain power. *Chicago Tribune,* p. 12.

Jacobs, Bob; Schall, Matthew; & Scheibel, Arnold B. (1993). A quantitative dendritic analysis of Wernicke's area in humans. II. Gender, hemispheric, and environmental factors. *Journal of Comparative Neurology, 327,* 97–106.

Jacobs, M. K., & Goodman, G. (1989). Psychology and self-help groups: Predictions on a partnership. *American Psychologist, 44,* 536–545.

Jacobson, John W.; Mulick, James A.; & Schwartz, Allen A. (1995). A history of facilitated communication: Science, pseudoscience, and antiscience: Science working group on facilitated communication. *American Psychologist, 50,* 750–765.

Jacoby, Russell, & Glauberman, Naomi. (Eds.). (1995). *The* Bell Curve *debate: History, documents, opinions.* New York: Times Books.

Jacox, Ada; Carr, D. B.; & Payne, Richard. (1994, March 3). New clinical-practice guidelines for the management of pain in patients with cancer. *New England Journal of Medicine, 330,* 651–655.

James, William. (1884). What is an emotion? *Mind, 9,* 188–205.

James, William. (1890). *Principles of psychology.* New York: Henry Holt.

James, William. (1892). *Psychology, briefer course.* New York: Holt.

James, William. (1894). The physical basis of emotion. *Psychological Review, 1,* 516–529. (Reprinted in the 1994 Centennial Issue of *Psychological Review, 101,* 205–210.)

James, William. (1899/1958). *Talks to teachers.* New York: Norton.

Jameson, Dorothea, & Hurvich, Leo M. (1989). Essay concerning color constancy. *Annual Review of Psychology, 40,* 1–22.

Jamison, Kay Redfield. (1993). *Touched with fire: Manic-depressive illness and the artistic temperament.* New York: Free Press.

Janisse, Michel Pierre, & Dyck, Dennis G. (1988). The Type A behavior pattern and coronary heart disease: Physiological and psychological dimensions. In Michel Pierre Janisse (Ed.), *Individual differences, stress, and health psychology.* New York: Springer-Verlag.

Janoff-Bulman, Ronnie C.; Timko, Christine; & Carli, Linda L. (1985). Cognitive biases in blaming the victim. *Journal of Experimental Social Psychology, 21,* 161–177.

Janus, Samuel S., & Janus, Cynthia L. (1993). *The Janus report on sexual behavior.* New York: Wiley.

Jedrczak, A. (1986). The TM-Sidhi programme and age-related psychological variables. *Journal of Clinical Psychology, 42,* 162–164.

Jefferson, James W. (1995). Lithium: The present and the future. *Journal of Clinical Psychiatry, 56,* 41–48.

Jenike, Michael A. (1992). Pharmacologic treatment of obsessive compulsive disorders. *Psychiatric Clinics of North America, 15,* 895–920.

Jensen, Arthur R. (1969). How much can we boost I.Q. and scholastic achievement? *Harvard Educational Review, 39,* 1–123.

Jensen, Bernard. (1980). *Iridology simplified.* Escondido, Calif.: Iridologists International.

Jensen, Bernard. (1988). *Beyond basic health.* Garden City Park, N.Y.: Avery.

Jensen, Bernard, & Bodeen, Donald V. (1992). *Visions of health: Understanding iridology.* Garden City Park, N.Y.: Avery.

Jessell, Tom. (1995a). Development of the nervous system. In Eric R. Kandel, James H. Schwartz, & Thomas M. Jessell (Eds.), *Essentials of neural science and behavior.* Norwalk, Conn.: Appleton & Lange.

Jessell, Tom. (1995b). The nervous system. In Eric R. Kandel, James H. Schwartz, & Thomas M. Jessell (Eds.), *Essentials of neural science and behavior.* Norwalk, Conn.: Appleton & Lange.

Jilek, Wolfgang G. (1993). Traditional medicine relevant to psychiatry. In Norman Sartorius, Giovanni de Girolamo, Gavin Andrews, G. Allen German, & Leon Eisenberg (Eds.), *Treatment of mental disorders: A review of effectiveness.* Washington, D.C.: World Health Organization/American Psychiatric Press.

John, Oliver P. (1990). The "Big Five" factor taxonomy: Dimensions of personality in the natural language and in questionnaires. In Lawrence A. Pervin (Ed.), *Handbook of personality: Theory and research.* New York: Guilford Press.

Johnson, C. L.; Stuckey, M. K.; Lewis, L. D.; & Schwartz, D. M. (1982). Bulimia: A descriptive survey of 316 cases. *International Journal of Eating Disorders, 2,* 3–16.

Johnson, Hollyn M. (1994). Processes of successful intentional forgetting. *Psychological Bulletin, 116,* 274–292.

Johnson, John A., & Ostendorf, Fritz. (1993). Clarification of the five-factor model with the abridged Big Five dimensional circumplex. *Journal of Personality and Social Psychology, 65,* 563–576.

Johnson, Katrina W.; Anderson, Norman B.; Bastida, Elena; Kramer, B. Josea; Williams, David; & Wong, Morrison. (1995). Panel II: Macrosocial and environmental influences on minority health. *Health Psychology, 14,* 601–612. (Special issue: Behavioral and Sociocultural Perspectives on Ethnicity and Health.)

Johnson, Marcia K.; Hashtroudi, Shahin; & Lindsay, D. Stephen. (1993). Source monitoring. *Psychological Bulletin, 114,* 3–28.

Johnson, Mark H.; Dziurawiec, Suzanne; Ellis, Hadyn; & Morton, John. (1991). Newborns' preferential tracking of face-like stimuli and its subsequent decline. *Cognition, 40,* 1–19.

Johnson, Mark H., & Magaro, Peter A. (1987). Effects of mood and severity on memory processes in depression and mania. *Psychological Bulletin, 101,* 28–40.

Johnson, Sheri L., & Roberts, John E. (1995). Life events and bipolar disorder: Implications from three biological theories. *Psychological Bulletin, 117,* 434–449.

Johnston, Daniel; Magee, Jeffrey C.; Colbert, Costa M.; & Christie, Brian R. (1996). Active properties of neuronal dendrites. *Annual Review of Neuroscience, 19,* 165–186.

Johnston, Timothy D. (1985). Introduction: Conceptual issues in the ecological study of learning. In Timothy D. Johnston & Alexandra T. Pietrewicz (Eds.), *Issues in the ecological study of learning.* Hillside, N.J.: Erlbaum.

Jones, Edward E. (1990). *Interpersonal perception.* New York: Freeman.

Jones, Edward E., & Nisbett, Richard E. (1971). *The actor and the observer: Divergent perceptions of the causes of behavior.* Morristown, N.J.: General Learning Press.

Jones, Ernest. (1953). *The life and work of Sigmund Freud: Vol. 1. The formative years and the great discoveries: 1856–1900.* New York: Basic Books.

Jones, Ernest. (1955). *The life and work of Sigmund Freud: Years of maturity, 1901–1919.* New York: Basic Books.

Jones, James M. (1991). Psychological models of race: What have they been and what should they be? In Jacqueline D. Goodchilds (Ed.), *Psychological perspectives on human diversity in America.* Washington, D.C.: American Psychological Association.

Jones, Mary Cover. (1924a). A laboratory study of fear: The case of Peter. *The Pedagogical Seminary and Journal of Genetic Psychology, 31,* 308–315.

Jones, Mary Cover. (1924b). The elimination of children's fears. *Journal of Experimental Psychology, 7,* 382–390.

Jones, Mary Cover. (1974). Albert, Peter, and John B. Watson. *American Psychologist, 29,* 581–583.

Jones, Mary Cover. (1975). A 1924 pioneer looks at behavior therapy. *Journal of Behavior Therapy & Experimental Psychiatry, 6,* 181–187.

Jones, Warren H., & Russell, Dan W. (1980). The selective processing of belief-discrepant information. *European Journal of Social Psychology, 10,* 309–312.

Jordon, Henry A. (1969). Voluntary intragastric feeding: Oral and gastric contributions to food intake. *Journal of Comparative and Physiological Psychology, 68,* 498–506.

Josephs, Lawrence. (1987). Dream reports of nightmares and stages of sleep. In Henry Kellerman (Ed.), *The nightmare: Psychological and biological foundations.* New York: Columbia University Press.

Judd, Charles M., & Park, Bernadette. (1993). Definition and assessment of accuracy in social stereotypes. *Psychological Review, 100,* 109–128.

Judge, T. A., & Watanabe, S. (1993). Another look at the job satisfaction–life satisfaction relationship. *Journal of Applied Psychology, 78,* 939–945.

Julien, Robert M. (1995). *A primer of drug action* (7th ed.). New York: Freeman.

Jung, Carl G. (1923/1976). Psychological types. In Joseph Campbell (Ed.), *The portable Jung.* New York: Penguin.

Jung, Carl G. (1931/1976). The structure of the psyche. In Joseph Campbell (Ed.), *The portable Jung.* New York: Penguin.

Jung, Carl G. (1936/1976). The concept of the collective unconscious. In Joseph Campbell (Ed.), *The portable Jung.* New York: Penguin.

Jung, Carl G. (1951/1976). Aion: Phenomenology of the self. In Joseph Campbell (Ed.), *The portable Jung.* New York: Penguin.

Jung, Carl G. (1963). *Memories, dreams, reflections.* Translated by Richard and Clara Winston. New York: Random House.

Jung, Carl G. (1964). *Man and his symbols.* New York: Dell.

Kagan, Jerome, & Fox, Nathan. (1995, November). Interviewed in Beth Azar, Timidity can develop in the first days of life. *APA Monitor, 26* (11), 23.

Kagan, Jerome; Snidman, Nancy; & Arcus, Doreen M. (1992). Initial reactions to unfamiliarity. *Current Directions in Psychological Science, 1,* 171–174.

Kahn, Edwin; Fisher, Charles; & Edwards, Adele. (1991). Night terrors and anxiety dreams. In Steven J. Ellman & John S. Antrobus (Eds.), *The mind in sleep: Psychology and psychophysiology* (2nd ed.). New York: Wiley.

Kahneman, Daniel, & Tversky, Amos. (1982). On the psychology of prediction. In Daniel Kahneman, Paul Slovic, & Amos Tversky (Eds.), *Judgment under uncertainty: Heuristics and biases.* New York: Cambridge University Press.

Kail, Robert. (1991). Developmental change in speed of processing during childhood and adolescence. *Psychological Bulletin, 109,* 490–501.

Kaitz, Marsha; Lapidot, Pnina; Bronner, Ruth; & Eidelman, Arthur I. (1992). Parturient women can recognize their infants by touch. *Developmental Psychology, 28,* 35–39.

Kalat, James W. (1985). Taste-aversion learning in ecological perspective. In Timothy D. Johnston & Alexandra T. Pietrewicz (Eds.), *Issues in the ecological study of learning.* Hillsdale, N.J.: Erlbaum.

Kalat, James W. (1995). *Biological psychology* (5th ed.). Pacific Grove, Calif.: Brooks/Cole.

Kalawsky, R. S. (1993). *The science of virtual reality and virtual environments.* Reading, Mass.: Addison-Wesley.

Kalbfleisch, Pamela J., & Cody, Michael J. (Eds.). (1995). *Gender, power, and communication in human relationships.* Hillsdale, N.J.: Erlbaum.

Kales, J. D.; Kales, A.; Bixler, E. O.; Soldatos, C. R.; Cadieux, R. J.; Kashurba, G. J.; & Vela-Bueno, A. (1984). Biopsychobehavioral correlates of insomnia: V. Clinical characteristics and behavioral correlates. *American Journal of Psychiatry, 141,* 1371–1376.

Kalichman, Seth C. (1995). *Understanding AIDS: A guide for mental health professionals.* Washington, D.C.: American Psychological Association.

Kalin, Ned H. (1993, May). The neurobiology of fear. *Scientific American, 268,* 94–101.

Kamarck, Thomas, & Jennings, J. Richard. (1991). Biobehavioral factors in sudden cardiac death. *Psychological Bulletin, 109,* 42–75.

Kamarck, Thomas W.; Manuck, Stephen B.; & Jennings, J. Richard. (1990). Social support reduces cardiovascular reactivity to psychological challenge: A laboratory model. *Psychosomatic Medicine, 52,* 42–58.

Kamin, Leon J. (1995). The pioneers of IQ testing. In Russell Jacoby & Naomi Glauberman (Eds.), *The Bell Curve debate: History, documents, opinions.* New York: Times Books.

Kamps, Debra M.; Leonard, Betsy R.; Vernon, Sue; Dugan, Erin P.; & Delquadri, Joseph C. (1992). Teaching social skills to students with autism to increase peer interactions in an integrated first-grade classroom. *Journal of Applied Behavior Analysis, 25,* 281–288.

Kandel, Eric R. (1995a). Nerve cells and behavior. In Eric R. Kandel, James H. Schwartz, & Thomas M. Jessell (Eds.), *Essentials of neural science and behavior.* Norwalk, Conn.: Appleton & Lange.

Kandel, Eric R. (1995b). Synaptic integration. In Eric R. Kandel, James H. Schwartz, & Thomas M. Jessell (Eds.), *Essentials of neural science and behavior.* Norwalk, Conn.: Appleton & Lange.

Kandel, Eric R. (1995c). Transmitter release. In Eric R. Kandel, James H. Schwartz, & Thomas M. Jessell (Eds.), *Essentials of neural science and behavior.* Norwalk, Conn.: Appleton & Lange.

Kandel, Eric R. (1995d). Cellular mechanisms of learning and memory. In Eric R.

Kandel, James H. Schwartz, & Thomas M. Jessell (Eds.), *Essentials of neural science and behavior.* Norwalk, Conn.: Appleton & Lange.

Kandel, Eric R., & Hawkins, Robert D. (1993). The biological basis of learning and individuality. In *Mind and brain: Readings from Scientific American.* New York: Freeman.

Kandel, Eric R., & Kupfermann, Irving. (1995). Emotional states. In Eric R. Kandel, James H. Schwartz, & Thomas M. Jessell (Eds.), *Essentials of neural science and behavior.* Norwalk, Conn.: Appleton & Lange.

Kandel, Eric R., & Siegelbaum, Steven. (1995). An introduction to synaptic transmission. In Eric R. Kandel, James H. Schwartz, & Thomas M. Jessell (Eds.)., *Essentials of neural science and behavior.* Norwalk, Conn.: Appleton & Lange.

Kane, John M. (1994). Editorial: Risperidone. *American Journal of Psychiatry, 151,* 802–803.

Kanin, E. J. (1982). Female rape fantasies: A victimization study. *Victimology, 7,* 114–121.

Kanner, Allen D.; Coyne, James C.; Schaefer, Catherine; & Lazarus, Richard S. (1981). Comparison of two modes of stress management: Daily hassles and uplifts versus major life events. *Journal of Behavioral Medicine, 4,* 1–39.

Kaplan, Craig A., & Simon, Herbert A. (1990). In search of insight. *Cognitive Psychology, 22,* 374–419.

Kaplan, Robert M. (1985). The controversy related to the use of psychological tests. In Benjamin B. Wolman (Ed.), *Handbook of intelligence: Theories, measurements, and applications.* New York: Wiley.

Kaplan, Robert M., & Saccuzzo, Dennis P. (1993). *Psychological testing: Principles, applications, and issues* (3rd ed.). Pacific Grove, Calif.: Brooks/Cole.

Kaplan, Steve. (1990). Capturing your creativity. In Michael G. Walraven & Hiram E. Fitzgerald (Eds.), *Annual editions: Psychology: 1990/91.* Guilford, Conn.: Dushkin.

Kaplan, Stuart L., & Busner, Joan. (1993). Treatment of nocturnal enuresis. In Thomas R. Giles (Ed.), *Handbook of effective psychotherapy.* New York: Plenum Press.

Kapur, Shitij, & Mann, J. John. (1993). Antidepressant action and the neurobiologic effects of ECT: Human studies. In C. Edward Coffey (Ed.), *The clinical science of electroconvulsive therapy.* Washington, D.C.: American Psychiatric Press.

Karau, Steven J., & Williams, Kipling D. (1993). Social loafing: A meta-analytic re-

view and theoretical integration. *Journal of Personality and Social Psychology, 65,* 681–706.

Karney, Benjamin R., & Bradbury, Thomas N. (1995). The longitudinal course of marital quality and stability: A review of theory, method, and research. *Psychological Bulletin, 118* (1), 3–34.

Karson, Samuel, & O'Dell, Jerry W. (1989). The 16 PF. In Charles S. Newmark (Ed.), *Major psychological assessment instruments* (Vol. 2). Boston: Allyn & Bacon.

Kasl, Charlotte Davis. (1992). *Many roads, one journey: Moving beyond the twelve steps.* New York: HarperPerennial.

Kastenbaum, Robert. (1986). *Death, society, and the human experience.* Columbus, Ohio: Merrill.

Kastenbaum, Robert. (1992). *The psychology of death.* New York: Springer-Verlag.

Katchadourian, Herant A. (1977). *The biology of adolescence.* San Francisco: Freeman.

Katchadourian, Herant A. (1990). Sexuality. In S. Shirley Feldman & Glen R. Elliott (Eds.), *At the threshold: The developing adolescent.* Cambridge, Mass.: Harvard University Press.

Katz, Lori, & Epstein, Seymour. (1991). Constructive thinking and coping with laboratory-induced stress. *Journal of Personality and Social Psychology, 61,* 789–800.

Katz, Phyllis A., & Ksansnak, Keith R. (1994). Developmental aspects of gender role flexibility and traditionality in middle childhood and adolescence. *Developmental Psychology, 30,* 272–282.

Katzman, Robert. (1993). Education and the prevalence of dementia and Alzheimer's disease. *Neurology, 43,* 13–18.

Kaufman, Alan S. (1990). *Assessing adolescent and adult intelligence.* Boston: Allyn & Bacon.

Kaufman, Lloyd, & Rock, Irvin. (1989). The moon illusion thirty years later. In Maurice Hershenson (Ed.), *The moon illusion.* Hillsdale, N.J.: Erlbaum.

Kawasaki, Guy. (1991). E-mail etiquette. *MacUser, 7* (11), 29–30.

Kazdin, Alan E. (1994a). Methodology, design, and evaluation in psychotherapy research. In Allen E. Bergin & Sol L. Garfield (Eds.), *Handbook of psychotherapy and behavior change* (4th ed.). New York: Wiley.

Kazdin, Alan E. (1994b). Psychotherapy for children and adolescents. In Allen E. Bergin & Sol L. Garfield (Eds.), *Handbook of psychotherapy and behavior change* (4th ed.). New York: Wiley.

Keane, T. M.; Gerardi, R. J.; Quinn, S. J.; & Litz, B. T. (1992). Behavioral treatment of post-traumatic stress disorder. In S. M. Turner, K. S. Calhoun, & H. E. Adams (Eds.), *Handbook of clinical behavior therapy* (2nd ed.). New York: Wiley.

Keating, Daniel P. (1990). Adolescent thinking. In Glen R. Elliott & S. Shirley Feldman (Eds.), *At the threshold: The developing adolescent*. Cambridge, Mass.: Harvard University Press.

Keck, Paul E., & McElroy, Susan L. (1993). Current perspectives on treatment of bipolar disorder with lithium. *Psychiatric Annals, 23,* 64–69.

Keefe, Richard S., & Harvey, Philip D. (1994). *Understanding schizophrenia: A guide to the new research on causes and treatment*. New York: Free Press.

Keesey, Richard E., & Powley, Terry L. (1986). The regulation of body weight. *Annual Review of Psychology, 37,* 109–133.

Kehoe, P., & Blass, Eliott M. (1986). Behaviorally functional opioid systems in infant rats, II. Evidence for pharmacological, physiological, and psychological mediation of pain and stress. *Behavioral Neuroscience, 100,* 624–630.

Keith, Samuel J., & Matthews, Susan M. (1991). The diagnosis of schizophrenia: A review of onset and duration issues. *Schizophrenia Bulletin, 17,* 51–67.

Kelly, I. W.; Rotton, James; & Culver, Roger. (1991). The moon was full and nothing happened: A review of studies on the moon and human behavior. In Kendrick Frazier (Ed.), *The hundredth monkey and other paradigms of the paranormal*. Buffalo, N.Y.: Prometheus Books.

Kendler, Kenneth S., & Diehl, Scott R. (1993). The genetics of schizophrenia: A current genetic-epidemiologic perspective. *Schizophrenia Bulletin, 19,* 261–285.

Kendler, Kenneth S.; Gruenberg, Alan M.; & Kinney, Dennis K. (1994). Independent diagnoses of adoptees and relatives as defined by DSM-III in the provincial and national samples of the Danish Adoption Study of Schizophrenia. *Archives of General Psychiatry, 51,* 456–468.

Kendler, Kenneth S.; Kessler, Ronald C.; Neale, Michael C.; Heath, Andrew C.; & Eaves, Lindon J. (1993a). The prediction of major depression in women: Toward an integrated etiologic model. *American Journal of Psychiatry, 150,* 1139–1148.

Kendler, Kenneth S.; Neale, Michael C.; Kessler, Ronald C.; Heath, Andrew C.; & Eaves, Lindon J. (1993b). A longitudinal twin study of personality and major depression in women. *Archives of General Psychiatry, 50,* 853–862.

Kendler, Kenneth S.; Neale, Michael C.; Kessler, Ronald C.; Heath, Andrew C.; & Eaves, Lindon J. (1993c). The lifetime history of major depression in women: Reliability of diagnosis and heritability. *Archives of General Psychiatry, 50,* 863–870.

Kennedy, Susan; Kiecolt-Glaser, Janice K.; & Glaser, Ronald. (1990). Social support, stress, and the immune system. In Barbara R. Sarason, Irwin G. Sarason, & Gregory R. Pierce (Eds.), *Social support: An interactional view*. New York: Wiley.

Kessen, William. (1996). American psychology just before Piaget. *Psychological Science, 7,* 196–199.

Kessler, Ronald C. (1979). Stress, social status, and psychological distress. *Journal of Health and Social Behavior, 20,* 259–272.

Kessler, Ronald C. (1994, January 22). "Really serious conditions. . . ." Quoted in *Science News, 145,* 55.

Kessler, Ronald C.; McGonagle, Katherine A.; Zhao, Shanyang; Nelson, Christopher B.; Hughes, Michael; Eshleman, Suzann; Wittchen, Hans-Ulrich; & Kendler, Kenneth S. (1994). Lifetime and 12-month prevalence of *DSM-III-R* psychiatric disorders in the United States: Results from the National Comorbidity Survey (NCS). *Archives of General Psychiatry, 51,* 8–19.

Kessler, Ronald C.; Price, Richard H.; & Wortman, Camille B. (1985). Social factors in psychopathology: Stress, social support, and coping processes. *Annual Review of Psychology, 36,* 531–572.

Kety, Seymour S.; Wender, Paul H.; Jacobsen, Bjørn; Ingraham, Loring J.; Jansson, Lennart; Faber, Britta; & Kinney, Dennis K. (1994). Mental illness in the biological and adoptive relatives of schizophrenic adoptees: Replication of the Copenhagen Study in the rest of Denmark. *Archives of General Psychiatry, 51,* 442–455.

Khan, A.; Mirolo, M. H.; Hughes, D.; & Bierut, L. (1993). Electroconvulsive therapy. *Psychiatric Clinics of North America, 16* (2), 497–513.

Kibel, Howard D. (1993). Inpatient group psychotherapy. In Anne Alonso & Hillel I. Swiller (Eds.), *Group therapy in clinical practice*. Washington, D.C.: American Psychiatric Press.

Kiecolt-Glaser, Janice K.; Dura, Jason R.; Speicher, Carl E.; Trask, O. Joseph; & Glaser, Ronald. (1991). Spousal caregivers of dementia victims: Longitudinal changes in immunity and health. *Psychosomatic Medicine, 53,* 345–362.

Kiecolt-Glaser, Janice K.; Fisher, Laura D.; Ogrocki, Paula.; Stout, Julie C.; Speicher, Carl E.; & Glaser, Ronald. (1987a). Marital quality, marital disruption, and immune function. *Psychosomatic Medicine, 49,* 13–34.

Kiecolt-Glaser, Janice K., & Glaser, Ronald. (1991). Stress and immune function in humans. In Robert Ader, David L. Felten, & Nicholas Cohen (Eds.), *Psychoneuroimmunology*. San Diego: Academic Press.

Kiecolt-Glaser, Janice K., & Glaser, Ronald. (1993). Mind and immunity. In Daniel Goleman & Joel Gurin (Eds.), *Mind/body medicine: How to use your mind for better health*. Yonkers, N.Y.: Consumer Reports Books.

Kiecolt-Glaser, Janice K.; Glaser, Ronald; Dyer, Carol S.; Shuttleworth, Edwin C.; Ogrocki, Paula; & Speicher, Carl E. (1987b). Chronic stress and immunity in family caregivers of Alzheimer's disease victims. *Psychosomatic Medicine, 49,* 523–535.

Kiesler, Charles A., & Kiesler, Sara B. (1969). *Conformity*. Reading, Mass.: Addison-Wesley.

Kihlstrom, John F. (1983). Instructed forgetting. *Journal of Experimental Psychology: General, 112,* 73–79.

Kihlstrom, John F. (1984). Conscious, subconscious, unconscious: A cognitive perspective. In Kenneth S. Bowers & Donald Meichenbaum (Eds.), *The unconscious reconsidered*. New York: Wiley.

Kihlstrom, John F. (1985). Hypnosis. *Annual Review of Psychology, 36,* 385–418.

Kihlstrom, John F. (1986). Strong inferences about hypnosis. *The Behavioral and Brain Sciences, 9* (3), 474–475.

Kihlstrom, John F. (1987, September 18). The cognitive unconscious. *Science, 237,* 1445–1452.

Kihlstrom, John F. (1992). Dissociation and dissociations: A comment on consciousness and cognition. *Consciousness and Cognition, 1,* 47–53.

Kihlstrom, John F., & Barnhardt, Terrence M. (1993). The self-regulation of memory: For better and for worse, with and without hypnosis. In Daniel M. Wegner & James W. Pennebaker (Eds.), *Handbook of mental control*. Englewood Cliffs, N.J.: Prentice Hall.

Kihlstrom, John F.; Barnhardt, Terrence M.; & Tataryn, Douglas J. (1992). The psychological unconscious: Found, lost, and regained. *American Psychologist, 47,* 788–791.

Kihlstrom, John F.; Glisky, Martha L.; & Angiulo, Michael J. (1994). Dissociative tendencies and dissociative disorders. *Journal of Abnormal Psychology, 103,* 117–124.

Kilshaw, D., & Annett, M. (1983). Right- and left-hand skill: Effects of age, sex, and hand preference showing superior skill in left-handers. *British Journal of Psychology, 74,* 253–268.

Kimble, Gregory A. (1993). Evolution of the nature-nurture issue in the history of psychology. In Robert Plomin & Gerald E. McClearn (Eds.), *Nature, nurture, and psychology.* Washington, D.C.: American Psychological Association.

Kimura, Doreen. (1992, September). Sex differences in the brain. *Scientific American, 267,* 80–87.

Kimzey, Stephen L. (1975). The effects of extended spaceflight on hematologic and immunologic systems. *Journal of the American Medical Women's Association, 30,* 218–232.

Kinsey, Alfred C., Pomeroy, Wardell B., & Martin, Clyde E. (1948). *Sexual behavior in the human male.* Philadelphia: Saunders.

Kinsey, Alfred C.; Pomeroy, Wardell B.; Martin, Clyde E.; & Gebhard, Paul H. (1953). *Sexual behavior in the human female.* Philadelphia: Saunders.

Kirchner, Wolfgang H., & Towne, William F. (1994, June). The sensory basis of the honeybee's dance. *Scientific American, 270,* 74–80.

Kirk, Stuart A., & Kutchins, Herb. (1992). *The selling of DSM: The rhetoric of science in psychiatry.* New York: Aldine De Gruyter.

Kirsch, Irving; Silva, Christopher E.; Comey, Gail; & Reed, Steven. (1995). A spectral analysis of cognitive and personality variables in hypnosis: Empirical disconfirmation of the two-factor model of hypnotic responding. *Journal of Personality and Social Psychology, 69,* 167–175.

Kitayama, Shinobu, & Matsuda, Takahiko. (1995). Reappraising cognitive appraisal from a cultural perspective. *Psychological Inquiry, 6,* 217–223.

Klahr, David. (1992). Information-processing approaches. In Ross Vasta (Ed.), *Six theories of child development: Revised formulations and current issues.* London: Jessica Kingsley Publishers.

Klein, David C.; Moore, Robert Y.; & Reppert, Steven M. (Eds.). (1991). *Suprachiasmatic nucleus: The mind's clock.* New York: Oxford University Press.

Klein, Donald F., & Wender, Paul H. (1993). *Understanding depression: A complete guide to its diagnosis and treatment.* New York: Oxford University Press.

Klein, Stephen B., & Mowrer, Robert R. (1989). *Contemporary learning theories: Instrumental conditioning theory and the impact of biological constraints on learning.* Hillsdale, N.J.: Erlbaum.

Kleinmuntz, Benjamin, & Szucko, Julian. (1984). A field study of the fallibility of polygraph lie detection. *Nature, 308,* 449–450.

Klerman, Gerald L.; Weissman, Myrna M.; Markowitz, John; Glick, Ira; Wilner, Philip J.; Mason, Barbara; & Shear, M. Katherine. (1994). Medication and psychotherapy. In Sol L. Garfield & Allen E. Bergin (Eds.), *Handbook of psychotherapy and behavior change* (4th ed.). New York: Wiley.

Klinger, Eric. (1993). Clinical approaches to mood control. In Daniel M. Wegner & James W. Pennebaker (Eds.), *Handbook of mental control.* Englewood Cliffs, N.J.: Prentice Hall.

Kluft, Richard P. (1991). Clinical presentations of multiple personality disorder. *Psychiatric Clinics of North America, 14,* 605–629.

Kluft, Richard P. (1993). Multiple personality disorders. In David Spiegel (Ed.), *Dissociative disorders: A clinical review.* Lutherville, Md.: Sidran.

Knittle, Jerome L. (1975). Endocrine and metabolic adaptations to obesity. In George A. Bray (Ed.), *Obesity in perspective.* Bethesda, Md.: National Institutes of Health, Publication No. 75–708.

Koester, John. (1995a). Membrane potential. In Eric R. Kandel, James H. Schwartz, & Thomas M. Jessell (Eds.), *Essentials of neural science and behavior.* Norwalk, Conn.: Appleton & Lange.

Koester, John. (1995b). Propagated signaling: The action potential. In Eric R. Kandel, James H. Schwartz, & Thomas M. Jessell (Eds.), *Essentials of neural science and behavior.* Norwalk, Conn.: Appleton & Lange.

Koester, John, & Siegelbaum, Steven. (1995a). Ion channels. In Eric R. Kandel, James H. Schwartz, & Thomas M. Jessell (Eds.), *Essentials of neural science and behavior.* Norwalk, Conn.: Appleton & Lange.

Koester, John, & Siegelbaum, Steven. (1995b). Local signaling: Passive electrical properties of the neuron. In Eric R. Kandel, James H. Schwartz, & Thomas M. Jessell (Eds.), *Essentials of neural science and behavior.* Norwalk, Conn.: Appleton & Lange.

Koffka, Kurt. (1935). *Principles of Gestalt psychology.* New York: Harcourt, Brace, & Company.

Kohlberg, Lawrence. (1976). Moral stages and moralization: The cognitive-developmental approach. In T. Lickona (Ed.), *Moral development and behavior: Theory, research, and social issues.* New York: Holt, Rinehart & Winston.

Kohlberg, Lawrence. (1981). *The philosophy of moral development: Moral stages and the idea of justice: Vol. 1. Essays on moral development.* New York: Harper & Row.

Kohlberg, Lawrence. (1984). *The psychology of moral development.* New York: Harper & Row.

Kohout, Jessica L., & Gaddy, Catherine D. (1995). *Education and employment in psychology in the next century.* American Psychological Association Research Office. Washington, D.C.: American Psychological Association.

Konishi, Masakazu. (1993, April). Listening with two ears. *Scientific American, 268,* 66–73.

Koriat, Asher. (1993). How do we know that we know? The accessibility model of the feeling of knowing. *Psychological Review, 100,* 609–639.

Koskenvuo, M.; Kapiro, J.; Rose, R. J.; Kesnaiemi, A.; Sarnaa, S.; Heikkila, K.; & Langinvanio, H. (1988). Hostility as a risk factor for mortality and ischemic heart disease in men. *Psychosomatic Medicine, 50,* 330–340.

Koss, Mary P., & Shiang, Julia. (1994). Research on brief psychotherapy. In Allen E. Bergin & Sol L. Garfield (Eds.), *Handbook of psychotherapy and behavior change* (4th ed.). New York: Wiley.

Kosslyn, Stephen M. (1995). Introduction: Thought and imagery. In Michael S. Gazzaniga (Ed.), *The cognitive neurosciences.* Cambridge, Mass.: MIT Press.

Kosslyn, Stephen M.; Ball, Thomas M.; & Reiser, Brian J. (1978). Visual images preserve metric spatial information: Evidence from studies of image scanning. *Journal of Experimental Psychology: Human Perception and Performance, 4,* 47–60.

Kosslyn, Stephen M., & Sussman, Amy L. (1995). Roles of imagery in perception: Or, there is no such thing as immaculate perception. In Michael S. Gazzaniga (Ed.), *The cognitive neurosciences.* Cambridge, Mass.: MIT Press.

Kramer, Jack L., & Conoley, Jane Close (Eds.). (1992). *The eleventh mental measurements yearbook.* Lincoln: Buros Institute of Mental Measurements/University of Nebraska Press.

Kramer, Peter D. (1993). *Listening to Prozac: A psychiatrist explores antidepressant drugs and the remaking of the self.* New York: Viking.

Krausz, Michael, & Müller-Thomsen, Tomas. (1993). Schizophrenia with onset in adolescence: An 11-year followup. *Schizophrenia Bulletin, 19,* 831–841.

Krieger, Jean. (1990). Obstructive sleep apnea: Clinical manifestations and pathophysiology. In Michael J. Thorpy (Ed.), *Handbook of sleep disorders.* New York: Dekker.

Krippner, Stanley. (1994). Cross-cultural treatment perspectives of dissociative disorders. In Steven Jay Lynn & Judith W. Rhue (Eds.), *Dissociation: Clinical and theoretical perspectives*. New York: Guilford Press.

Krishnan, K. Ranga Rama; Doraiswamy, P. Murali; Venkataraman, Sanjeev; Reed, Deborah A.; & Ritchie, James C. (1991). Current concepts in hypothalamo-pituitary-adrenal axis regulation. In James A. McCubbin, Peter G. Kaufmann, & Charles B. Nemeroff (Eds.), *Stress, neuropeptides, and systemic disease*. San Diego: Academic Press.

Kronauer, Richard E. (1994). Circadian rhythms. In Rosemary Cooper (Ed.), *Sleep*. New York: Chapman & Hall.

Kübler-Ross, Elisabeth. (1969). *On death and dying*. New York: Macmillan.

Kuhl, Patricia K; Williams, Karen A.; Lacerda, Francisco; Stevens, Kenneth N.; & Lindblom, Bjorn. (1992, January 31). Linguistic experience alters phonetic perception in infants by 6 months of age. *Science, 255*, 606–608.

Kunoh, Hiroshi, & Takaoki, Eiji. (1994). *3-D planet: The world as seen through stereograms*. San Francisco: Cadence Books.

Kupfer, David J.; Frank, Ellen; Perel, James M.; Cornes, Cleon; Mallinger, Alan G.; Thase, Michael E.; McEachran, Ann B.; & Grochocinski, Victoria J. (1992). Five-year outcome for maintenance therapies in recurrent depression. *Archives of General Psychiatry, 49*, 769–773.

Kupfermann, Irving, & Kandel, Eric R. (1995). Learning and memory. In Eric R. Kandel, James H. Schwartz, & Thomas M. Jessell (Eds.), *Essentials of neural science and behavior*. Norwalk, Conn.: Appleton & Lange.

Kurcinka, Mary Sheedy. (1991). *Raising your spirited child*. New York: HarperCollins.

Kurdek, Lawrence A. (1995). Developmental changes in relationship quality in gay and lesbian cohabiting couples. *Developmental Psychology, 31*, 86–94.

Kurtz, Paul. (1994, Winter). The new skepticism. *Skeptical Inquirer, 18*, 139–147.

Kurtz, Paul, & Fraknoi, Andrew. (1986). Scientific tests of astrology do not support its claims. In Kendrick Frazier (Ed.), *Science confronts the paranormal*. Buffalo, N.Y.: Prometheus Books.

LaBerge, Stephen. (1992). Physiological studies of lucid dreaming. In John S. Antrobus & Mario Bertini (Eds.), *The neuropsychology of sleep and dreaming*. Hillsdale, N.J.: Erlbaum.

LaFromboise, Teresa; Coleman, Hardin L. K.; & Gerton, Jennifer. (1993a). Psychological impact of biculturalism: Evidence and theory. *Psychological Bulletin, 114*, 395–412.

LaFromboise, Teresa D.; Trimble, Joseph E.; & Mohatt, Gerald V. (1993b). Counseling intervention and American Indian tradition: An integrative approach. In Donald R. Atkinson, George Morten, & Derald Wing Sue (Eds.), *Counseling American minorities: A cross-cultural perspective* (4th ed.). Madison, Wis.: Brown & Benchmark.

Lamb, Michael E.; Sternberg, Kathleen J.; & Prodromidis, Margardita. (1992). Non-maternal care and the security of infant–mother attachment: A reanalysis of the data. *Infant Behavior and Development, 15*, 71–83.

Lamb, Michael E.; Thompson, Ross A.; Gardner, William; & Charnov, Eric L. (1985). *Infant–mother attachment: The origins and developmental significance of individual differences in Strange Situation behavior*. Hillsdale, N.J.: Erlbaum.

Lambert, Michael J., & Bergin, Allen E. (1992). Achievements and limitations of psychotherapy research. In Donald K. Freedheim (Ed.), *History of psychotherapy: A century of change*. Washington, D.C.: American Psychological Association.

Lambert, Michael J., & Bergin, Allen E. (1994). The effectiveness of psychotherapy. In Allen E. Bergin & Sol L. Garfield (Eds.), *Handbook of psychotherapy and behavior change* (4th ed.). New York: Wiley.

Lamson, Ralph. (1994, November). Quoted in Virtural therapy, *Psychology Today, 27*, 21.

Lamson, Ralph. (1996, February 12). Quoted in Jill Jordon Sieder, The latest head trip: Virtual reality technology may be a cost-effective therapy. *U.S. News & World Report*, p. 55.

Lancer, C. E.; Lautenschlager, G. J.; Sloan, C. E.; & Varcar, P. E. (1989). A comparison between bottom-up, top-down, and bidirectional models of relationships between global and life satisfaction events. *Journal of Personality, 57*, 601–624.

Landau, Barbara. (1994). Where's what and what's where: The language of objects in space. L. R. Gleitman & Barbara Landau (Eds.), Lexical acquisition, *Lingua* (Special Issue), *92*, 259–296.

Landau, Barbara, & Jackendoff, Ray. (1993). "What" and "where" in spatial language and spatial cognition. *Behavioral and Brain Sciences, 16*, 217–265.

Lane, C. E.; Lautenschlager, G. J.; Sloan, C. E.; & Varca, P. E. (1989). A comparison between bottom-up, top-down, and bidirectional models of relationships between global and life satisfaction facets. *Journal of Personality, 57*, 601–624.

Lane, Harlan. (1992). *The mask of benevolence: Disabling the deaf community*. New York: Knopf.

Lang, Peter J. (1994). The varieties of emotional experience: A meditation on James-Lange theory. *Psychological Review, 101*, 211–221.

Lang, Peter J.; Greenwald, M. K.; Bradley, M. M.; & Hamm, A. O. (1993). Looking at pictures: Affective, facial, visceral, and behavioral reactions. *Psychophysiology, 30*, 261–273.

Lange, Carl G., & James, William. (1922). *The emotions*. Translated by I. A. Haupt. Baltimore: Williams & Wilkins.

Langer, Ellen, & Rodin, Judith. (1976). The effects of choice and enhanced personal responsibility for the aged: A field experiment in an institutional setting. *Journal of Personality and Social Psychology, 34*, 191–198.

Langley, Pat, & Jones, Randolph. (1988). A computational model of scientific insight. In Robert J. Sternberg (Ed.), *The nature of creativity*. New York: Cambridge University Press.

Larsen, Randy J., & Diener, Ed. (1987). Affect intensity as an individual difference characteristic: A review. *Journal of Personality and Social Psychology, 21*, 1–39.

Larsen, Randy J.; Diener, Ed; & Emmons, Robert A. (1986). Affect intensity and reactions to daily life events. *Journal of Personality and Social Psychology, 51*, 803–814.

Larson, Jeffry H.; Crane, D. Russell; & Smith, Craig W. (1991). Morning and night couples: The effect of wake and sleep patterns on marital adjustment. *Journal of Marital and Family Therapy, 17*, 53–65.

Larson, Mark, & Ham, Mark. (1993). Stress and "storm and stress" in early adolescence: The relationship of negative events with dysphoric affect. *Developmental Psychology, 29*, 130–140.

Larwood, Laurie, & Gutek, Barbara A. (1987). Working toward a theory of women's career development. In Barbara A. Gutek & Laurie Larwood (Eds.), *Women's career development*. Newbury Park, Calif.: Sage.

Lashley, Karl S. (1928). *Brain mechanisms and intelligence*. Chicago: University of Chicago Press.

Lashley, Karl. (1929). *Brain mechanisms and intelligence*. Chicago: University of Chicago Press.

Lashley, Karl. (1950). In search of the engram. In *Symposium of the Society for*

Experimental Biology (Vol. 4). New York: Cambridge University Press.

Lask, Bryan. (1995). Night terrors. In Charles E. Schaefer (Ed.), *Clinical handbook of sleep disorders in children*. Northvale, N.J.: Aronson.

Latané, Bibb. (1981). The psychology of social impact. *American Psychologist, 36,* 343–356.

Latané, Bibb, & Darley, John M. (1970). *The unresponsive bystander: Why doesn't he help?* New York: Appleton-Century-Crofts.

Latané, Bibb, & Nida, Steve A. (1981). Ten years of research on group size and helping. *Psychological Bulletin, 89,* 308–324.

Latané, Bibb; Williams, Kipling; & Harkins, S. (1979). Many hands make light the work: The causes and consequences of social loafing. *Journal of Personality and Social Psychology, 37,* 822–832.

Laudenslager, M. C.; Ryan, S. M.; Drugan, R. C.; Hyson, R. L.; & Maier, S. F. (1983). Coping and immunosuppression: Inescapable but not escapable shock suppresses lymphocyte proliferation. *Science, 231,* 568–570.

Laumann, Edward O.; Gagnon, John H.; Michael, Robert T.; & Michaels, Stuart. (1994). *The social organization of sexuality: Sexual practices in the United States.* Chicago: University of Chicago Press.

Laurence, J.-R., & Perry, C. (1983). Hypnotically created memory among highly hypnotizable subjects. *Science, 222,* 523–524.

Laursen, Brett, & Collins, W. Andrew. (1994). Interpersonal conflict during adolescence. *Psychological Bulletin, 115* (2), 197–209.

Lavie, Peretz. (1989). To nap, perchance to sleep—ultradian aspects of napping. In David F. Dinges & Roger J. Broughton (Eds.), *Sleep and alertness: Chronobiological, behavioral, and medical aspects of napping.* New York: Raven Press.

Lawler, E. E., III. (1973). *Motivation in work organizations.* Pacific Grove, Calif.: Brooks/Cole.

Lawrence, D. H. (1928/1960). *Lady Chatterley's lover.* Hammondsworth, U.K.: Penguin.

Lawton, Carolyn; France, Karyn G.; & Blampied, Neville M. (1991). Treatment of infant sleep disturbance by graduated extinction. *Child and Family Behavior Therapy, 13,* 39–56.

Lazarus, Richard S. (1984). On the primacy of cognition. *American Psychologist, 39,* 124–129.

Lazarus, Richard S. (1991a). Cognition and motivation in emotion. *American Psychologist, 46,* 352–367.

Lazarus, Richard S. (1991b). *Emotion and adaptation.* New York: Oxford University Press.

Lazarus, Richard S. (1993). From psychological stress to the emotions: A history of changing outlooks. *Annual Review of Psychology, 44,* 1–21.

Lazarus, Richard S. (1994). Universal antecedents of the emotions. In Paul Ekman & Richard J. Davidson (Eds.), *The nature of emotion: Fundamental questions.* New York: Oxford University Press.

Lazarus, Richard S. (1995). Vexing research problems inherent in cognitive-mediational theories of emotion—and some solutions. *Psychological Inquiry, 6,* 183–197.

Lazarus, Richard S., & Folkman, Susan. (1984). *Stress, appraisal, and coping.* New York: Springer.

Leach, C. S., & Rambaut, P. C. (1974). Biochemical responses of the *Skylab* crewmen. *Proceedings of the Skylab Life Sciences Symposium, 2,* 427–454.

Leahy, Thomas Hardy. (1992). *A history of psychology: Main currents in psychological thought.* Englewood Cliffs, N.J.: Prentice Hall.

Lebow, Jay L., & Gurman, Alan S. (1995). Research assessing couple and family therapy. *Annual Review of Psychology, 46,* 27–57.

LeDoux, Joseph E. (1994a). Memory versus emotional memory in the brain. In Paul Ekman & Richard J. Davidson (Eds.), *The nature of emotion: Fundamental questions.* New York: Oxford University Press.

LeDoux, Joseph E. (1994b, June). Emotion, memory, and the brain. *Scientific American, 270,* 50–57.

LeDoux, Joseph E . (1995). Emotion: Clues from the brain. *Annual Review of Psychology, 46,* 209–235.

Lee, Kimberly L.; Vaillant, George T.; Torrey, William C.; & Elder, Glen H. (1995). A 50-year prospective study of the psychological sequelae of World War II combat. *American Journal of Psychiatry, 152,* 516–522.

Lees, G. J. (1993). The possible contributions of microglia and macrophages to delayed neuronal death after ischemia. *Journal of the Neurological Sciences, 114,* 119–122.

Leibel, Rudolph L., & Hirsch, Jules (1984). Diminished energy requirements in reduced-obese patients. *Metabolism, 33,* 164–170.

Leibenluft, Ellen. (1996). Women with bipolar illness: Clinical and research issues. *American Journal of Psychiatry, 153,* 163–173.

Leichtman, Michelle D., & Ceci, Stephen J. (1995). The effects of stereotypes and suggestions on preschoolers' reports. *Developmental Psychology, 31* (4), 568–578.

Leitenberg, Harold, & Henning, Kris. (1995). Sexual fantasy. *Psychological Bulletin, 117* (3), 469–496.

Lemperers, J. D.; Flavell, E. R.; & Flavell, John H. (1977). The development in very young children of tacit knowledge concerning visual perception. *Genetic Psychology Monographs, 95,* 3–53.

Lent, R. W., & Hackett, G. (1987). Career self-efficacy: Empirical status and future directions. *Journal of Vocational Behavior, 30,* 347–382.

Lepore, Stephen J. (1993). Social conflict, social support, and psychological distress: Evidence of cross-domain buffering effects. *Journal of Personality and Social Psychology, 63,* 857–867.

Lepore, Stephen J.; Silver, Roxane Cohen; Wortman, Camille B.; & Wayment, Heidi A. (1996). Social constraints, intrusive thoughts, and depressive symptoms among bereaved mothers. *Journal of Personality and Social Psychology, 70,* 271–282.

Lerner, M. R.; Gyorgyi, T. K.; Reagan, J.; Roby-Shemkovitz, A.; Rybczynski, R; & Vogt, R. (1990). Peripheral events in moth olfaction. *Chemical Senses, 15,* 191–198.

Lerner, Melvin J. (1980). *The belief in a just world: A fundamental delusion.* New York: Plenum Press.

Lester, David. (1989). *Questions and answers about suicide.* Philadelphia: Charles Press.

Lester, David. (1990, Summer). Biorhythms and the timing of death. *Skeptical Inquirer, 14,* 410–412.

Lester, David. (1991). A cross-cultural look at the suicide rates of children and teenagers. In Antoon A. Lennaars & Susan Wenckstern (Eds.), *Suicide prevention in schools.* New York: Hemisphere Publishing.

LeUnes, Arnold D., & Nation, Jack R. (1989). *Sport psychology.* Chicago: Nelson-Hall.

LeVay, Simon. (1991, August 30). A difference in hypothalamic structure between heterosexual and homosexual men. *Science, 253,* 1034–1037.

LeVay, Simon, & Hamer, Dean H. (1994, May). Evidence for a biological influence in male homosexuality. *Scientific American, 270,* 44–49.

Levenson, Michael R.; Kiehl, Kent A.; & Fitzpatrick, Cory M. (1995). Assessing psychopathic attributes in a noninstitutionalized population. *Journal of Personality and Social Psychology, 68,* 151–158.

Levenson, Robert W. (1992). Autonomic nervous system differences among emotions. *Psychological Science, 3,* 23–27.

Levenson, Robert W.; Carstensen, Laura L.; & Gottman, John M. (1994). The influence of age and gender on affect, physiology, and their interrelations: A study of long-term marriages. *Journal of Personality and Social Psychology, 67,* 56–68.

Levenson, Robert W.; Ekman, Paul; & Friesen, Wallace V. (1990). Voluntary facial action generates emotion-specific autonomic nervous system activity. *Psychophysiology, 27,* 363–384.

Levenson, Robert W.; Ekman, Paul; Heider, Karl; & Friesen, Wallace V. (1992). Emotion and autonomic nervous system activity in the Minangkabau of west Sumatra. *Journal of Personality and Social Psychology, 62,* 972–988.

Levin, Harvey S.; Papanicolaou, Andrew; & Eisenberg, Howard. (1984). Observations on amnesia after nonmissile head injury. In Larry R. Squire & Nelson Butters (Eds.), *Neuropsychology of memory.* New York: Guilford Press.

Levin, William C. (1988). Age stereotyping: College student evaluations. *Research on Aging, 10,* 134–148.

Levy, Alan S., & Heaton, Alan H. (1992). Preliminary results of the 1992 weight loss practices survey. Division of Consumer Studies, Food and Drug Administration, Washington, D.C.

Levy, Becca, & Langer, Ellen. (1994). Aging free from negative stereotypes: Successful memory in China and among the American Deaf. *Journal of Personality and Social Psychology, 66,* 989–997.

Levy-Shiff, Rachel. (1994). Individual and contextual correlates of marital change across the transition to parenthood. *Developmental Psychology, 30,* 591–601.

Lewinsohn, Peter M.; Redner, Julie E.; & Seeley, John R. (1991a). The relationship between life satisfaction and psychosocial variables: New perspectives. In Fritz Strack, Michael Argyle, & Norbert Schwarz (Eds.), *Subjective well-being: An interdisciplinary perspective.* New York: Pergamon Press.

Lewinsohn, Peter M.; Rohde, Paul; Selley, John R.; & Hops, Hyman. (1991b). Comorbidity of unipolar depression: I. Major depression with dysthymia. *Journal of Abnormal Psychology, 100,* 205–213.

Lewis, R. J., & Janda, L. H. (1988). The relationship between adult sexual adjustment and childhood experiences regarding exposure to nudity, sleeping in the parental bed, and parental attitudes toward sexuality. *Archives of Sexual Behavior, 17,* 349–362.

Lewontin, Richard. (1970, March). Race and intelligence. *Bulletin of the Atomic Scientists,* pp. 2–8.

Lewy, Alfred J., & Sack, Robert L. (1987). Phase typing and bright light therapy of chronobiological sleep and mood disorders. In Angelos Halaris (Ed.), *Chronobiology and psychiatric disorders.* New York: Elsevier.

Lewy, Alfred J.; Sack, Robert L.; & Singer, Clifford M. (1990). Bright light, melatonin, and biological rhythms in humans. In Jacques Montplaisir & Roger Godbout (Eds.), *Sleep and biological rhythms: Basic mechanisms and applications to psychiatry.* New York: Oxford University Press.

Leyens, Jacques-Philippe; Yzerbyt, Vincent; & Corneille, Olivier. (1996). The role of applicability in the emergence of the overattribution bias. *Journal of Personality and Social Psychology, 70,* 219–229.

Lickey, Marvin E., & Gordon, Barbara. (1991). *Medicine and mental illness: The use of drugs in psychiatry.* New York: Freeman.

Lieberman, Jeffrey A., & Koreen, Amy R. (1993). Neurochemisty and neuroendocrinology of schizophrenia: A selective review. *Schizophrenia Bulletin, 19,* 371–386.

Liebowitz, Michael R. (1993). Depression with anxiety and atypical depression. *Journal of Clinical Psychiatry, 54,* No. 2 (Supplement), 10–14.

Liebowitz, Michael R.; Salmán, Ester; Jusino, Carlos M.; Garfinkel, Robin; Street, Linda; Cárdenas, Dora L.; Silvestre, Joao; Fyer, Abby J.; Carrasco, José L.; Davies, Sharon; Guarnaccia, Peter; & Klein, Donald F. (1994). *Ataque de nervios* and panic disorder. *American Journal of Psychiatry, 151,* 871–875.

Lietaer, Germain; Rombauts, Jan; & Van Balen, Richard (Eds.). (1990). *Client-centered and experiential psychotherapy in the nineties.* Leuven, Belgium: Leuven University Press.

Liff, Zanvel A. (1992). Psychoanalysis and dynamic techniques. In Donald K. Freedheim (Ed.), *History of psychotherapy: A century of change.* Washington, D.C.: American Psychological Association.

Lilie, Jamie K., & Rosenberg, Russell P. (1990). Behavioral treatment of insomnia. In Michel Hersen, Richard M. Eisler, & Peter M. Miller (Eds.), *Progress in behavior modification* (Vol. 25). Newbury Park, Calif.: Sage.

Lindheim, R., & Syme, S. L. (1983). Environments, people, and health. *Annual Review of Public Health, 4,* 335–359.

Link, Bruce G.; Andrews, Howard; & Cullen, Francis T. (1992). The violent and illegal behavior of mental patients reconsidered. *American Sociological Review, 57,* 275–292.

Lipsey, Mark W., & Wilson, David B. (1993). The efficacy of psychological, educational, and behavioral treatment: Confirmation from meta-analysis. *American Psychologist, 48,* 1181–1209.

Little, J. D. (1993). Physiological principles in the treatment of difficulty in waking from sleep. *Australian and New Zealand Journal of Psychiatry, 27,* 502–505.

Livingstone, Margaret, & Hubel, David. (1988, May 6). Segregation of form, color, movement and depth: Anatomy, physiology, and perception. *Science, 240,* 740–749.

Lockard, R. B. (1971). Reflections on the fall of comparative psychology: Is there a message for us all? *American Psychologist, 26,* 168–179.

Locke, E. A. (1976). The nature and causes of job satisfaction. In M. D. Dunnette (Ed.), *Handbook of industrial and organizational psychology.* Chicago: Rand McNally.

Locke, E. A., & Schweiger, D. M. (1979). Participation in decision-making: One more look. In B. M. Staw (Ed.), *Research in organizational behavior* (Vol. 1). Greenwich, Conn.: JAI Press.

Lockhart, Robert S. (1992). Coding processes: Levels of processing. In Larry R. Squire (Ed.), *Encyclopedia of learning and memory.* New York: Macmillan.

Lockhart, Robert S., & Craik, Fergus I. M. (1990). Levels of processing: A retrospective commentary on a framework for memory research. *Canadian Journal of Psychology, 44* (1), 87–112.

Loeb, G. E. (1985, February). The functional replacement of the ear. *Scientific American, 252,* 104–111.

Loewenstein, George. (1994). The psychology of curiosity: A review and reinterpretation. *Psychological Bulletin, 116,* 75–98.

Loewenstein, Richard J. (1991). An office mental status examination for complex chronic dissociative symptoms and multiple personality disorder. *Psychiatric Clinics of North America, 14,* 567–604.

Loewenstein, Richard J. (1993). Psychogenic amnesia and psychogenic fugue: A comprehensive review. In David Spiegel (Ed.), *Dissociative disorders: A clinical review.* Lutherville, Md.: Sidran.

Loftus, Elizabeth F. (1992). When a lie becomes memory's truth: Memory distortion after exposure to misinformation. *Current*

Directions in Psychological Science, 1, 121–123.

Loftus, Elizabeth F. (1993a). Desperately seeking memories of the first few years of childhood: The reality of early memories. *Journal of Experimental Psychology: General, 122,* 274–277.

Loftus, Elizabeth F. (1993b). The reality of repressed memories. *American Psychologist, 48,* 518–537.

Loftus, Elizabeth F.; Donders, Karen; Hoffman, Hunter G.; & Schooler, Jonathan W. (1989). Creating new memories that are quickly accessed and confidently held. *Memory and Cognition, 17,* 607–616.

Loftus, Elizabeth F.; Garry, Maryanne; Brown, Scott W.; & Rader, Marcella. (1994). Near-natal memories, past-life memories, and other memory myths. *American Journal of Clinical Hypnosis, 36,* 176–179.

Loftus, Elizabeth F., & Ketcham, Katherine. (1991). *Witness for the defense: The accused, the eyewitness, and the expert who puts memory on trial.* New York: St. Martin's Press.

Loftus, Elizabeth F., & Ketcham, Katherine. (1994). *The myth of repressed memory: False memories and allegations of sexual abuse.* New York: St. Martin's Press.

Loftus, Elizabeth F., & Palmer, J. C. (1974). Reconstruction of automobile destruction: An example of the interaction between language and memory. *Journal of Verbal Learning and Verbal Behavior, 13,* 585–589.

Logothetis, Nikos K., & Sheinberg, David L. (1996). Visual object recognition. *Annual Review of Neuroscience, 19,* 577–621.

Lonetto, Richard, & Templer, Donald I. (1986). *Death anxiety.* Washington, D.C.: Hemisphere.

Lord, Charles G.; Ross, Lee; & Lepper, Mark R. (1979). Biased assimilation and attitude polarization: The effects of prior theories on subsequently considered evidence. *Journal of Personality and Social Psychology, 37,* 2098–2109.

Lord, R. G.; DeVader, C. L.; & Alliger, G. M. (1986). A meta-analysis of the relation between personality traits and leadership perceptions: An application of validity generalization procedures. *Journal of Applied Psychology, 71,* 402–410.

Lovallo, William R.; al'Absi, Mustafa; Pincomb, Gwen A.; Everson, Susan A.; Sung, Bong Hee; Passey, Richard B.; & Wilson, Michael F. (1996). Caffeine and behavioral stress effects on blood pressure in borderline hypertensive Caucasian men. *Health Psychology, 15,* 11–17.

Lucas, F.; Bellisle, F.; & Di Maio, A. (1987). Spontaneous insulin fluctuations and the preabsorptive insulin response to food ingestion in humans. *Physiology and Behavior, 40,* 631–636.

Lugaresi, Elio, & Montagna, Pasquale. (1990). Fatal familial insomnia. In Michael J. Thorpy (Ed.), *Handbook of sleep disorders.* New York: Dekker.

Lukoff, David; Snyder, Karen; Ventura, Joseph; & Neuchterlein, Keith H. (1989). Life events, familial stress, and coping in the developmental course of schizophrenia. In Thomas W. Miller (Ed.), *Stressful life events.* Madison, Conn.: International Universities Press.

Lundberg, U.; Hedman, M.; Melin, B.; & Frankenhaeuser, M. (1989). Type A behavior in healthy males and females as related to physiological reactivity and blood lipids. *Psychosomatic Medicine, 51,* 113–122.

Lykken, David. (1983, April). Polygraph prejudice. *APA Monitor,* p. 4.

Lykken, David T.; McGue, Matthew; Tellegen, Auke; & Bouchard, Thomas J., Jr. (1992). Emergenesis: Genetic traits that may not run in families. *American Psychologist, 47,* 1565–1577.

Lyles, J. N.; Burish, T. G.; Krozely, M. G.; & Oldham, R. K. (1982). Efficacy of relaxation training and guided imagery in reducing the aversiveness of cancer chemotherapy. *Journal of Consulting and Clinical Psychology, 50,* 509–524.

Lynch, Gary. (1986). *Synapses, circuits, and the beginnings of memory.* Cambridge, Mass.: MIT Press.

Lyness, Scott A. (1993). Predictors of differences between Type A and B individuals in heart rate and blood pressure reactivity. *Psychological Bulletin, 114,* 266–295.

Lynn, Richard. (1987). The intelligence of the Mongoloids: A psychometric evolutionary and neurological theory. *Personality and Individual Differences, 8,* 813–844.

Lynn, Steven Jay, & Nash, Michael R. (1994). Truth in memory: Ramifications for psychotherapy and hypnotherapy. *American Journal of Clinical Hypnosis, 36,* 194–208.

Lytton, Hugh, & Romney, David M. (1991). Parents' differential socialization of boys and girls: A meta-analysis. *Psychological Bulletin, 109,* 267–296.

Maccoby, Eleanor E., & Martin, John A. (1983). Socialization in the context of the family: Parent–child interaction. In Paul H. Mussen (Ed.), *Handbook of child psychology: Vol. IV. Socialization, personality, and social development.* New York: Wiley.

MacDougall, James M.; Musante, Linda; Castillo, Sara; & Acevedo, Marcela C. (1988). Smoking, caffeine, and stress: Effects on blood pressure and heart rate in male and female college students. *Health Psychology, 7,* 461–478.

Macedonio, Michele. (1984). Regulation of energy balance. In Jean Storlie & Henry A. Jordon (Eds.), *Evaluation and treatment of obesity.* New York: Spectrum.

MacKenzie, Brian. (1984). Explaining race differences in IQ: The logic, the methodology, and the evidence. *American Psychologist, 39,* 1214–1233.

Mackie, Diane M., & Hamilton, David L. (1993). Affect, cognition, and stereotyping: Concluding comments. In Diane M. Mackie & David L. Hamilton (Eds.), *Affect, cognition, and stereotyping: Interactive processes in group perception.* San Diego: Academic Press.

Macklin, E. D. (1987). Nontraditional family forms. In M. B. Sussman & S. K. Steinmetz (Eds.), *Handbook of marriage and the family.* New York: Plenum Press.

Macrae, C. Neil; Milne, Alan B.; & Bodenhausen, Galen V. (1994). Stereotypes as energy-saving devices: A peek inside the cognitive toolbox. *Journal of Personality and Social Psychology, 66,* 37–47.

Magnavita, Jeffrey J. (1993). The evolution of short-term dynamic psychotherapy: Treatment of the future? *Professional Psychology: Research and Practice, 24,* 360–365.

Mahowald, Mark W., & Schenck, Carlos H. (1990). REM-sleep behavior disorder. In Michael J. Thorpy (Ed.), *Handbook of sleep disorders.* New York: Dekker.

Maier, Steven F. (1989). Learned helplessness: Event covariation and cognitive changes. In Stephen B. Klein & Robert R. Mowrer (Eds.), *Contempory learning theories: Instrumental conditioning theory and the impact of biological constraints on learning.* Hillsdale, N.J.: Erlbaum.

Maier, Steven F.; Seligman, Martin E.; & Solomon, Richard L. (1969). Pavlovian fear conditioning and learned helplessness: Effects of escape and avoidance behavior of (a) the CS=UCS contingency, and (b) the independence of the US and voluntary responding. In B. A. Campbell and R. M. Church (Eds.), *Punishment and aversive behavior.* New York: Appleton-Century-Crofts.

Maier, Steven F.; Watkins, Linda R.; & Fleshner, Monika. (1994). Psychoneuroimmunology: The interface between behavior, brain, and immunity. *American Psychologist, 49,* 1004–1017.

Maj, Mario; Magliano, Lorena; Pirozzi, Raffaele; Marasco, Cecilia; & Guarneri, Manuela. (1994). Validity of rapid cycling as a course specifier for bipolar disorder. *American Journal of Psychiatry, 151,* 1015–1019.

Major, Brenda; Carrington, Patricia I.; & Carnevale, Peter J. (1984). Physical attractiveness and self-esteem: Attribution for praise from an other-sex evaluator. *Personality and Social Psychology Bulletin, 10,* 43–50.

Major, Brenda; Cozzarelli, Catherine; Sciacchitano, Anne Marie; Cooper, M. Lynne; Testa, Maria; & Mueller, Pallas M. (1990). Perceived social support, self-efficacy, and adjustment to abortion. *Journal of Personality and Social Psychology, 59,* 452–463.

Makin, Jennifer W. (1989). Attractiveness of lactating females' breast odors to neonates. *Child Development, 60,* 803–810.

Maltz, Wendy. (1991). *The sexual healing journey: A guide for survivors of sexual abuse.* New York: HarperCollins.

Manderscheid, Ronald W.; Rae, Donald S.; Narrow, William E.; Locke, Ben Z.; & Regier, Darrel A. (1993). Congruence of service utilization estimates from the Epidemiologic Catchment Area Project and other sources. *Archives of General Psychiatry, 50,* 108–115.

Mandler, George. (1993). Thought, memory, and learning: Effects of emotional stress. In Leo Goldberger & Shlomo Breznitz (Eds.), *Handbook of stress: Theoretical and clinical aspects* (2nd ed.). New York: Free Press.

Mandler, Jean. (1990). A new perspective on cognitive development in infancy. *American Scientist, 78,* 236–243.

Mann, J. J., & Kapur, S. (1991). The emergence of suicidal ideation and behavior during antidepressant pharmacotherapy. *Archives of General Psychiatry, 48,* 1027–1033.

Mann, Leon. (1981). The baiting crowd in episodes of threatened suicide. *Journal of Personality and Social Psychology, 41,* 703–709.

Mann, Traci. (1994). Informed consent for psychological research: Do subjects comprehend consent forms and understand their legal rights? *Psychological Science, 5* (3), 140–143.

Manschreck, Theo C. (1992). Delusional disorders: Clinical concepts and diagnostic strategies. *Psychiatric Annals, 22,* 241–251.

Marano, Lou. (1985). *Windigo psychosis: The anatomy of an Emic-Etic confusion.* In Richard C. Simons & Charles C. Hughes (Eds.), *The culture-bound syndromes: Folk illnesses of psychiatric and anthropological interest.* Boston: D. Reidel Publishing.

Marañon, Gregorio. (1924). Contribution à l'etude de l'action emotive de l'adrenaline. *Revue Francaise d'Endocrinologie, 2,* 301–325.

Maratsos, Michael. (1983). Some current issues in the study of the acquisition of grammar. In Paul H. Mussen (Ed.), *Handbook of child psychology: Vol. III. Cognitive development.* New York: Wiley.

Marcia, James E. (1980). Identity in adolescence. In Joseph Adelson (Ed.), *Handbook of adolescent psychology.* New York: Wiley.

Marcia, James E. (1991). Identity and self-development. In R. M. Lerner, A. C. Petersen, & Jean Brooks-Gunn (Eds.), *Encyclopedia of adolescence* (Vol. 1). New York: Garland.

Marco, Christine A., & Suls, Jerry. (1993). Daily stress and the trajectory of mood: Spillover, response assimilation, contrast, and chronic negative affectivity. *Journal of Personality and Social Psychology, 64,* 1053–1063.

Marder, Stephen R.; Ames, Donna; Wirshing, William C.; & Van Putten, Theodore. (1993). Schizophrenia. *Psychiatric Clinics of North America, 16,* 567–587.

Marder, Stephen R., & Meibach, Richard C. (1994). Risperidone in the treatment of schizophrenia. *American Journal of Psychiatry, 151,* 825–835.

Margraf, Jürgen, & Ehlers, Anke. (1989). Etiological models of panic: a) Medical and biological aspects; b) Psychophysiological and cognitive aspects. In Roger Baker (Ed.), *Panic disorder: Theory, research and therapy.* Chichester, England: Wiley.

Markus, Hazel, & Cross, Susan. (1990). The interpersonal self. In Lawrence A. Pervin (Ed.), *Handbook of personality: Theory and research.* New York: Guilford Press.

Markus, Hazel Rose, & Kitayama, Shinobu. (1991). Culture and the self: Implications for cognition, emotion, and motivation. *Psychological Review, 98,* 224–253.

Markus, Hazel Rose, & Kitayama, Shinobu. (1994). The cultural construction of self and emotion: Implications for social behavior. In Shinobu Kitayama & Hazel Rose Markus (Eds.), *Emotion and culture: Empirical studies of mutual influence.* Washington, D.C.: American Psychological Association.

Markus, Hazel, & Kunda, Ziva. (1986). Stability and malleability of the self-concept. *Journal of Personality and Social Psychology, 51,* 858–866.

Markus, Hazel, & Nurius, Paula. (1986). Possible selves. *American Psychologist, 41,* 954–969.

Markus, Hazel, & Wurf, Elissa. (1987). The dynamic self-concept: A social psychological perspective. *Annual Review of Psychology, 38,* 299–337.

Marlatt, G. Alan; Baer, John S.; Donovan, Dennis M.; & Kivlahan, Daniel R. (1988). Addictive behaviors: Etiology and treatment. *Annual Review of Psychology, 39,* 223–252.

Marlatt, G. Alan, & Rohsenow, Damaris J. (1980). Cognitive processes in alcohol use: Expectancy and the balanced placebo design. In N. K. Mello (Ed.), *Advances in substance abuse* (Vol. 1). Greenwich, Conn.: JAI Press.

Marler, Peter. (1967). Animal communication symbols. *Science, 35,* 63–78.

Marschark, Marc. (1992). Coding processes: Imagery. In Larry R. Squire (Ed.), *Encyclopedia of learning and memory.* New York: Macmillan.

Marsella, Anthony J., & Dash-Scheuer, Alice. (1988). Coping, culture, and healthy human development: A research and conceptual overview. In Pierre R. Dasen, John W. Berry, & Norman Sartorius (Eds.), *Health and cross-cultural psychology: Toward applications.* [Vol. 10, Cross-cultural Research and Methodology Series.] Newbury Park, Calif.: Sage.

Marshall, Donald S. (1972). Sexual behavior on Mangaia. In Donald S. Marshall & Robert C. Suggs (Eds.), *Human sexual behavior: Variations in the ethnographic spectrum.* Englewood Cliffs, N.J.: Prentice Hall.

Marshall, Eliot. (1994, June 17). Manic depression: Highs and lows on the research roller coaster. *Science, 264,* 1693–1695.

Marshall, Elizabeth L. (1996). *The Human Genome Project: Cracking the code within us.* New York: Franklin Watts.

Marshall, Grant N.; Wortman, Camille B.; Kusulas, Jeffrey W.; Hervig, Linda K.; & Vickers, Ross R., Jr. (1992). Distinguishing optimism from pessimism: Relations to fundamental dimensions of mood and personality. *Journal of Personality and Social Psychology, 62,* 1067–1074.

Marshall, J. F., & Teitelbaum, P. (1974). Further analysis of sensory inattention following lateral hypothalamic damage in rats. *Journal of Comparative and Physiological Psychology, 86,* 375–395.

Martell, Daniel A., & Dietz, Park E. (1992). Mentally disordered offenders who push or attempt to push victims onto subway tracks in New York City. *Archives of General Psychiatry, 49,* 472–475.

Martens, Brian K.; Lochner, David G.; & Kelly, Susan Q. (1992). The effects of variable-interval reinforcement on academic engagement: A demonstration of matching theory. *Journal of Applied Behavior Analysis, 25,* 143–151.

Martin, Carol L., & Halverson, Charles F., Jr. (1981). A schematic processing model of sex typing and stereotyping in children. *Child Development, 52,* 1119–1134.

Martin, Carol L., & Halverson, Charles F., Jr. (1983). The effects of sex-typing schemas on young children's memory. *Child Development, 54,* 563–574.

Martin, Jack, & Jessell, Thomas M. (1995). The sensory systems. In Eric R. Kandel, James H. Schwartz, & Thomas M. Jessell (Eds.)., *Essentials of neural science and behavior.* Norwalk, Conn.: Appleton & Lange.

Martin, Laura. (1986). "Eskimo words for snow": A case study in the genesis and decay of an anthropological example. *American Anthropologist, 88,* 418–423.

Martinez-Taboas, Alfonso. (1991). Multiple personality in Puerto Rico: Analysis of fifteen cases. *Dissociation, 4,* 189–192.

Maslow, Abraham H. (1968). *Toward a psychology of being* (2nd ed.). Princeton, N.J.: Van Nostrand.

Maslow, Abraham H. (1970). *Motivation and personality* (2nd ed.) New York: Harper & Row.

Masson, Jeffrey M. (February, 1984a). Freud and the seduction theory: A challenge to the foundations of psychoanalysis. *The Atlantic, 253,* 33–60.

Masson, Jeffrey M. (1984b). *The assault on truth: Freud's suppression of the seduction theory.* New York: Farrar, Straus & Giroux.

Masters, William H., & Johnson, Virginia E. (1966). *Human sexual response.* Boston: Little, Brown.

Masters, William H.; Johnson, Virginia E.; & Kolodny, Robert C. (1995). *Human sexuality* (5th ed.). New York: HarperCollins.

Matarazzo, Joseph D. (1981). Obituary: David Wechsler (1896–1981). *American Psychologist, 36,* 1542–1543.

Matchett, G., & Davey, Graham C. L. (1991). A test of a disease-avoidance model of animal phobias. *Behaviour Research and Therapy, 29,* 91–94.

Mathews, Judith R.; Hodson, Gary D.; Crist, William B.; & LaRoche, G. Robert. (1992). Teaching young children to use contact lens. *Journal of Applied Behavior Analysis, 25,* 229–235.

Matlin, Margaret W. (1985). Current issues in psycholinguistics. In Theodore M. Shlechter & Michael P. Toglia (Eds.), *New directions in cognitive science.* Norwood, N.J.: Ablex.

Matlin, Margaret W. (1989). *Cognition* (2nd ed). Fort Worth, Tex.: Holt, Rinehart & Winston.

Matlin, Margaret W., & Foley, Hugh J. (1992). *Sensation and perception* (3rd ed.). Boston: Allyn & Bacon.

Matsumoto, David. (1994). *People: Psychology from a cultural perspective.* Pacific Grove, Calif.: Brooks/Cole.

Matsumoto, David. (1995). Lazarus's vexing research problems are even more vexing than he thinks. *Psychological Inquiry, 6,* 228–230.

Matsumoto, David; Kitayama, Shinobu; & Markus, Hazel. (1994). Culture and self: How cultures influence the way we view ourselves. In David Matsumoto (Ed.), *People: Psychology from a cultural perspective.* Pacific Grove, Calif.: Brooks-Cole.

Mauro, Robert; Sato, Kaori; & Tucker, John. (1992). The role of appraisal in human emotions: A cross-cultural study. *Journal of Personality and Social Psychology, 62,* 301–317.

Mavromatis, Andreas. (1987). *Hypnagogia: The unique state of consciousness between wakefulness and sleep.* New York: Routledge & Kegan Paul.

Maxmen, Jerrold S., & Ward, Nicholas G. (1995). *Essential psychopathology and its treatment* (2nd ed.). New York: Norton.

May, R. B. (1963). Stimulus selection of preschool children under conditions of free choice. *Perceptual and Motor Skills, 16,* 203–206.

Mayer, Richard, & Goodchild, Fiona. (1990). *The critical thinker: Thinking and learning strategies for psychology students.* Dubuque, Iowa: Brown.

Mazur, James E. (1994). *Learning and behavior* (3rd ed.). Englewood Cliffs, N.J.: Prentice Hall.

McAdams, Dan P. (1992). The five-factor model *in* personality: A critical appraisal. *Journal of Personality, 60,* 329–362.

McAdams, Dan P. (1994). *The person: An introduction to personality psychology* (2nd ed.). New York: Harcourt Brace Jovanovich.

McCall, Robert B. (1988). Science and the press: Like oil and water. *American Psychologist, 43,* 87–91.

McCarley, Robert W., & Hobson, J. Allan. (1977). The neurobiological origins of psychoanalytic theory. *American Journal of Psychiatry, 134,* 1211–1221.

McCartney, Kathleen; Harris, Monica J.; & Bernieri, Frank. (1990). Growing up and growing apart: A developmental meta-analysis of twin studies. *Psychological Bulletin, 107,* 226–237.

McCaul, K. D., & Malott, J. M. (1984). Distraction and coping with pain. *Psychological Bulletin, 95,* 516–533.

McClelland, David C. (1984). *Motives, personality, and society: Selected papers.* New York: Praeger.

McClelland, David C. (1985). *Human motivation.* Glenview, Ill.: Scott, Foresman, & Co.

McClelland, David C.; Atkinson, John W.; Clark, Russell A.; & Lowell, Edgar L. (1953). *The achievement motive.* New York: Appleton-Century-Crofts.

McClintock, Martha K. (1971). Menstrual synchrony and suppression. *Nature, 229,* 244–245.

McClintock, Martha K. (1992, October). Quoted in John Easton, Sex, rats, and videotapes: From the outside in. *The University of Chicago Magazine, 85* (1), 32–36.

McClure, Harold M., & Novembre, Francis J. (1996). Simian immunodeficiency virus variants: Threat of new lentiviruses. *American Journal of the Medical Sciences, 311,* 30–38.

McConnell, James V. (1989). Reinvention of subliminal perception. *The Skeptical Inquirer, 13,* 427–428.

McCoy, Robert. (1996). Phrenology. In Gordon Stein (Ed.), *The encyclopedia of the paranormal.* Amherst, N.Y.: Prometheus Books.

McCrae, Robert R. (1993). Moderated analyses of longitudinal personality stability. *Journal of Personality and Social Psychology, 65,* 577–585.

McCrae, Robert R., & Costa, Paul T., Jr. (1990). *Personality in adulthood.* New York: Guilford Press.

McCrae, Robert R., & Costa, Paul T., Jr. (1996). Toward a new generation of personality theories: Theoretical contexts for the five-factor model. In Jerry S. Wiggins (Ed.), *The five-factor model of personality: Theoretical perspectives.* New York: Guilford Press.

McCrae, Robert R., & John, Oliver P. (1992). An introduction to the five-factor model and its applications. *Journal of Personality, 60,* 175–215.

McFadden, Lisa; Seidman, Edward; & Rappaport, Julian. (1992). A comparison of espoused theories of self- and mutual help: Implications for mental health professionals. *Professional Psychology: Research and Practice, 23,* 515–520.

McFarlan, Donald. (Ed.). (1991). *The Guinness book of world records.* New York: Bantam.

McGuire, Anne M. (1994). Helping behaviors in the natural environment: Dimensions and correlates of helping. *Personality and Social Psychology Bulletin, 20,* 45–56.

McHugh, P. R., & Moran, T. H. (1985). The stomach: A conception of its dynamic role in satiety. *Progress in Psychobiology and Physiological Psychology, 11,* 197–232.

McKellar, Peter. (1972). Imagery from the standpoint of introspection. In Peter W. Sheehan (Ed.), *The function and nature of imagery*. New York: Academic Press.

McNally, Richard J. (1987). Preparedness and phobias: A review. *Psychological Bulletin, 101,* 283–303.

McNally, Richard J. (1994). Cognitive bias in panic disorder. *Current Directions in Psychological Science, 3,* 129–132.

McNally, Richard J., & Louro, Christine E. (1992). Fear of flying in agoraphobia and simple phobia: Distinguishing features. *Journal of Anxiety Disorders, 6,* 319–324.

McNeilly, Cheryl L., & Howard, Kenneth I. (1991). The effects of psychotherapy: A reevaluation based on dosage. *Psychotherapy Research, 1,* 74–78.

Mebert, C. J. (1991). Variability in the transition to parenthood experience. In Karl Pillemer & Kathleen McCartney (Eds.), *Parent–child relations throughout life*. Hillsdale, N.J.: Erlbaum.

Meehan, Patrick J.; Lamb, Jane A.; Saltzman, Linda E.; & O'Carroll, Patrick W. (1992). Attempted suicide among young adults: Progress toward a meaningful estimate of prevalence. *American Journal of Psychiatry, 149,* 41–44.

Meeus, Wim H., & Raaijmakers, Quinten A. (1986). Administrative obedience: Carrying out orders to use psychological-administrative violence. *European Journal of Social Psychology, 16,* 311–324.

Meichenbaum, Donald H. (1995). Cognitive-behavioral therapy in historical perspective. In Bruce Bongar & Larry E. Beutler (Eds.), *Comprehensive textbook of psychotherapy: Theory and practice*. New York: Oxford University Press.

Meichenbaum, Donald, & Fitzpatrick, Deborah. (1993). A constructivist narrative perspective on stress and coping: Stress inoculation applications. In Leo Goldberger & Shlomo Breznitz (Eds.), *Handbook of stress: Theoretical and clinical aspects* (2nd ed.). New York: Free Press.

Mellinger, G. D.; Balter, M. B.; & Uhlenhuth, E. H. (1985). Insomnia and its treatment: Prevalence and correlates. *Archives of General Psychiatry, 42,* 225–232.

Melton, Gary B. (1989). Public policy and private prejudice: Psychology and law on gay rights. *American Psychologist, 44,* 933–940.

Meltzer, Herbert Y. (1993). New drugs for the treatment of schizophrenia. *Psychiatric Clinics of North America, 16,* 365–386.

Meltzer, Herbert Y. (1994). Clozapine and other atypical neuroleptics: Efficacy, side effects, optimal utilization. *Journal of Clinical Psychiatry Monograph 12* (2), 38–42.

Meltzer, Herbert Y. (1995). The role of serotonin in schizophrenia and the place of serotonin-dopamine antagonist antipsychotics. *Journal of Clinical Psychopharmacology, 15,* Suppl. 1, 2S-3S.

Meltzoff, Andrew N. (1988). Infant imitation and memory: Nine-month-olds in immediate and deferred tests. *Child Development, 59,* 217–225.

Meltzoff, Andrew N., & Moore, M. Keith. (1977). Imitation of facial and manual gestures by human neonates. *Science, 198,* 75–78.

Meltzoff, Andrew N., & Moore, M. Keith. (1983). Newborn infants imitate adult facial gestures. *Child Development, 54,* 702–709.

Melzack, Ronald. (1990, February). The tragedy of needless pain. *Scientific American, 262,* 27–33.

Melzack, Ronald. (1993). Pain: Past, present, and future. *Canadian Journal of Experimental Psychology, 47* (4), 615–624.

Melzack, Ronald, & Wall, Patrick D. (1965). Pain mechanisms: A new theory. *Science, 150,* 971–980.

Melzack, Ronald, & Wall, Patrick D. (1983). *The challenge of pain*. New York: Basic Books.

Mendelson, Carole R., & Boggaram, Vijayakumar. (1991). Hormonal control of the surfactant system in fetal lung. *Annual Review of Physiology, 53,* 415–440.

Mento, A. J.; Steel, R. P.; & Karren, R. J. (1987). A meta-analytic study of the effects of goal setting on task performance: 1966–1984. *Organizational Behavior and Human Decision Processes, 39,* 52–83.

Merckelbach, Harald; Arntz, Arnoud; Arrindell, Willem A.; & De Jong, Peter J. (1992). Pathways to spider phobia. *Behaviour Research and Therapy, 30,* 543–546.

Merikle, P. M. (1988). Subliminal auditory messages: An evaluation. *Psychology and Marketing, 5,* 297–316.

Merskey, H. (1992). The manufacture of personalities: The production of multiple personality disorder. *British Journal of Psychiatry, 160,* 327–340.

Mervis, Carolyn B., and Rosch, Eleanor. (1981). Categorization of natural objects. *Annual Review of Psychology, 32,* 89–115.

Merzenich, Michael. (1994, September 21). Quoted in Ronald Kotulak, Mental workouts can keep the brain sharp as we age. *Chicago Tribune,* p. 14.

Messenger, John. (1972). Sex and repression in an Irish folk community. In Donald S. Marshall & Robert C. Suggs (Eds.), *Human sexual behavior: Variations in the ethnographic spectrum*. Englewood Cliffs, N.J.: Prentice Hall.

Michael, Robert T.; Gagnon, John H.; Laumann, Edward O.; & Kolata, Gina. (1994). *Sex in America: A definitive survey*. New York: Warner Books.

Miklowitz, David J. (1994). Family risk indicators in schizophrenia. *Schizophrenia Bulletin, 20,* 137–149.

Milewski, A. (1976). Infants' discrimination of internal and external pattern elements. *Journal of Experimental Child Psychology, 22,* 229–246.

Milgram, Stanley. (1960). *Conformity in Norway and France: An experimental study of national characteristics*. Doctoral dissertation, Harvard University, Cambridge, Mass.

Milgram, Stanley. (1961, December). Nationality and conformity. *Scientific American, 205,* 45–51.

Milgram, Stanley. (1963). Behavioral study of obedience. *Journal of Abnormal Psychology, 67,* 371–378.

Milgram, Stanley. (1964). Issues in the study of obedience: A reply to Baumrind. *American Psychologist, 19,* 848–852.

Milgram, Stanley. (1965/1992). Some conditions of obedience and disobedience to authority. In Stanley Milgram, *The individual in a social world: Essays and experiments* (2nd ed.). Edited by John Sabini & Maury Silver. New York: McGraw-Hill.

Milgram, Stanley. (1973, December). The perils of obedience. *Harper's Magazine,* 61–67.

Milgram, Stanley. (1974a). *Obedience to authority: An experimental view*. New York: Harper & Row.

Milgram, Stanley. (1974b, June). Interview by Carol Tavris: The frozen world of the familiar stranger: An interview with Stanley Milgram. *Psychology Today,* pp. 71–80.

Milgram, Stanley. (1976, August 21). Obedience to authority: A CBS drama deals with the shocking results of a social psychologist's experiment. *TV Guide,* pp. 24–25.

Milgram, Stanley. (1980). Interview by Richard I. Evans. In Richard I. Evans (Ed.), *The making of social psychology: Discussions with creative contributors*. New York: Gardner Press.

Milgram, Stanley. (1992). On maintaining social norms: A field experiment in the subway. In Stanley Milgram, *The individual in a social world: Essays and experiments* (2nd ed.). Edited by John Sabini & Maury Silver. New York: McGraw-Hill.

Milgrom, Peter; Mancl, Lloyd; King, Barbara; & Weinstein, Philip. (1995). Origins of childhood dental fear. *Behaviour Research and Therapy, 33,* 313–319.

Miller, Arthur G. (1986). The obedience experiments: A case study of controversy in social science. New York: Praeger.

Miller, George A. (1956/1994). The magical number seven, plus or minus two: Some limits on our capacity for processing information. *Psychological Review, 101,* 343–352.

Miller, Neal E. (1985, April). The value of behavioral research on animals. *American Psychologist, 40,* 423–440.

Miller, Neal E. (1995). Clinical-experimental interactions in the development of neuroscience. *American Psychologist, 50,* 901–911.

Miller, Patricia H. (1993). *Theories of developmental psychology* (3rd ed.). New York: Freeman.

Miller, Scott D.; Blackburn, Terrell; Scholes, Gary; White, George L.; & Mamalis, Nick. (1991). Optical differences in multiple personality disorder: A second look. *Journal of Nervous and Mental Disease, 179,* 132–135.

Miller, Scott D., & Triggiano, Patrick J. (1992). The psychophysiological investigation of multiple personality disorder: Review and update. *American Journal of Clinical Hypnosis, 35,* 47–61.

Miller, Thomas W. (1993). The assessment of stressful life events. In Leo Goldberger & Shlomo Breznitz (Eds.), *Handbook of stress: Theoretical and clinical aspects* (2nd ed.). New York: Free Press.

Miller, Todd Q.; Smith, Timothy W.; Turner, Charles W.; Guijarro, Margarita L.; & Hallet, Amanda J. (1996). A meta-analytic review of research on hostility and physical health. *Psychological Bulletin, 119,* 322–348.

Miller-Jones, Dalton. (1989). Culture and testing. *American Psychologist 44,* 360–366.

Milner, Brenda. (1965). Memory disturbance after bilateral hippocampal lesions. In Peter M. Milner & Steven E. Glickman (Eds.), *Cognitive processes and the brain: An enduring problem in psychology: Selected readings.* Princeton, N.J.: Van Nostrand.

Milner, Brenda. (1970). Memory and the medial temporal regions of the brain. In Karl H. Pribram & Donald E. Broadbent (Eds.), *Biology of memory.* New York: Academic Press.

Mindell, J. A. (1993). Sleep disorders in children. *Health Psychology, 12,* 152–163.

Mineka, Susan, & Cook, Michael. (1993). Mechanisms involved in the observational conditioning of fear. *Journal of Experimental Psychology: General, 122,* 23–38.

Mintzberg, H. (1973). *The nature of managerial work.* New York: Harper & Row.

Mischel, Walter. (1966). Theory and research on the antecedents of self-imposed delay of reward. *Progress in Experimental Personality Research, 3,* 85–132.

Mischel, Walter. (1968). *Personality and assessment.* New York: Wiley.

Mischel, Walter. (1977). Self-control and the self. In Theodore Mischel (Ed.), *The self: Psychological and philosophical issues.* Totowa, N.J.: Rowman & Littlefield.

Mischel, Walter. (1981). Objective and subjective rules for delay of gratification. In G. d'Ydewalle & W. Lens (Eds.), *Cognition in human motivation and learning.* Hillsdale, N.J.: Erlbaum.

Mischel, Walter. (1983). Delay of gratification as process and as person variable in development. In David Magnusson & Vernon L. Allen (Eds.), *Human development.* New York: Academic Press.

Mischel, Walter. (1990). Personality dispositions revisited and revised: A view after three decades. In Lawrence Pervin (Ed.), *Handbook of personality: Theory and research.* New York: Guilford Press.

Mischel, Walter, & Shoda, Yuichi. (1995). A cognitive-affective system theory of personality: Reconceptualizing situations, dispositions, dynamics, and invariance in personality structure. *Psychological Review, 102,* 246–268.

Mischel, Walter; Shoda, Yuichi; & Rodriguez, Monica L. (1989, May 26). Delay of gratification in children. *Science, 244,* 933–938.

Mitler, Merrill M. (1994). Sleep and catastrophes. In Rosemary Cooper (Ed.), *Sleep.* New York: Chapman & Hall.

Modgil, Sohan, & Modgil, Celia. (1986). Lawrence Kohlberg: Consensus and controversy. In Sohan Modgil & Celia Modgil (Eds.), *Lawrence Kohlberg: Consensus and controversy.* Philadelphia: Falmer Press.

Moghaddam, Fathali M.; Taylor, Donald M.; & Wright, Stephen C. (1993). *Social psychology in cross-cultural perspective.* New York: Freeman.

Mohr, Charles. (1964, March 28). Apathy is puzzle in Queens killing: Behavioral specialists hard put to explain witnesses' failure to call police. *The New York Times,* pp. 21, 40.

Mondimore, Francis Mark. (1993). *Depression: The mood disease* (rev. ed.). Baltimore: Johns Hopkins University Press.

Monteith, Margo J.; Devine, Patricia G.; & Zuwerink, Julia R. (1993). Self-directed versus other-directed affect as a consequence of prejudice-related discrepancies. *Journal of Personality and Social Psychology, 64,* 198–210.

Mook, Douglas G. (1996). *Motivation: The organization of action* (2nd ed.). New York: Norton.

Moore, Keith L. (1993). *Before we are born: Essentials of embryology and birth defects* (4th ed.). Philadelphia: Saunders.

Moore, T. E. (1988). The case against subliminal manipulation. *Psychology and Marketing, 5,* 355–372.

Moore-Ede, Martin C. (1993). *The twenty-four hour society: Understanding human limits in a world that never stops.* Reading, Mass.: Addison-Wesley.

Moos, Rudolf H., & Schaefer, Jeanne A. (1993). Coping resources and processes: Current concepts and measures. In Leo Goldberger and Shlomo Breznitz (Eds.), *Handbook of stress: Theoretical and clinical aspects* (2nd ed.). New York: FreePress.

Morawetz, D. (1977). Income distribution and self-rated happiness: Some empirical evidence. *The Economic Journal, 87,* 511–522.

Morelli, Gilda A.; Rogoff, Barbara; Oppenheim, David; & Goldsmith, Denise. (1992). Cultural variation in infants' sleeping arrangements: Questions of independence. *Developmental Psychology, 28,* 604–613.

Morgan, Christiana, & Murray, Henry A. (1935). A method of investigating fantasies: The Thematic Apperception Test. *Archives of Neurology and Psychiatry, 4,* 310–329.

Morin, Charles M. (1993). *Insomnia: Psychological assessment and management.* New York: Guilford.

Morokoff, Patricia J. (1994, Summer). Issues in adult treatment of childhood sexual abuse. *The Health Psychologist, 16,* 6–7, 10.

Morris, Michael W., & Peng, Kaiping. (1994). Culture and cause: American and Chinese attributions for social and physical events. *Journal of Personality and Social Psychology, 67,* 949–971.

Morris, Richard J. (1991). Fear reduction methods. In Frederick H. Kanfer & Arnold P. Goldstein (Eds.), *Helping people change: A textbook of methods* (4th ed.). New York: Pergamon Press.

Morrison, A. M., & Von Glinow, M. A. (1990). Women and minorities in management. *American Psychologist, 45,* 539–550.

Mortensen, Preben Bo, & Eaton, W. W. (1994). Predictors for readmission risk in schizophrenia. *Psychological Medicine, 24,* 223–232.

Moruzzi, Gustav, & Magoun, Herbert. (1949). Brainstem reticular formation and activation of the EEG. *Electroencephalography and Clinical Neurophysiology, 1,* 455–473.

Moscovitch, Morris. (1985). Memory from infancy to old age: Implications for theories of normal and pathological memory. *Annals of the New York Academy of Sciences, 444,* 78–96.

Mounts, Nina S., & Steinberg, Laurence. (1995). An ecological analysis of peer influence on adolescent grade point average and drug use. *Developmental Psychology, 31,* 915–922.

Muchinsky, P. M. (1993). *Psychology applied to work.* Pacific Grove, Calif.: Brooks/Cole.

Mueser, Kim T.; Bellack, Alan S.; & Brady, E. U. (1990). Hallucinations in schizophrenia. *Acta Psychiatrica Scandinavica, 82,* 26–29.

Mueser, Kim T., & Glynn, Shirley M. (1993). Efficacy of psychotherapy for schizophrenia. In Thomas R. Giles (Ed.), *Handbook of effective psychotherapy.* New York: Plenum Press.

Mulhern, Sherrill. (1991). Embodied alternative identities: Bearing witness to a world that might have been. *Psychiatric Clinics of North America, 14,* 769–786.

Murphy, H. B. M. (1982). Culture and schizophrenia. In Ihsan Al-Issa (Ed.), *Culture and psychopathology.* Baltimore, Md.: University Park Press.

Murphy, K. R. (1993). *Honesty in the workplace.* Pacific Grove, Calif.: Brooks/Cole.

Murray, Bridget. (1995, November). Gender gap in math scores is closing. *APA Monitor, 26* (11), p. 43.

Murray, Henry A. (1938). *Explorations in personality.* New York: Oxford University Press.

Murray, Henry A. (1943). *Thematic Apperception Test Manual.* Cambridge, Mass.: Harvard University Press.

Musto, David F. (1991, July). Opium, cocaine and marijuana in American history. *Scientific American, 265,* 40–47.

Muth, Denise K.; Glynn, Shawn M.; Britton, Bruce K.; & Graves, Michael F. (1988). Thinking out loud while studying text: Rehearsing key ideas. *Journal of Educational Psychology, 80,* 315–318.

Myers, David G. (1996). *Social psychology* (5th ed.). New York: McGraw-Hill.

Myers, David G., & Diener, Ed. (1995). Who is happy? *Psychological Science, 6* (1), 10–19.

Nadel, Lynn, & Zola–Morgan, Stuart. (1984). Infantile amnesia: A neurobiological perspective. In Morris Moscovitch (Ed.), *Infant memory.* New York: Plenum Press.

Nadon, Robert; Hoyt, Irene P.; Register, Patricia A.; & Kihlstrom, John F. (1991). Absorption and hypnotizability: Context effects reexamined. *Journal of Personality and Social Psychology, 60,* 144–153.

Naeye, Robert. (1994, July). The brain at work. *Discover,* pp. 30–31.

Narrow, William E.; Regier, Darrel A.; Rae, Donald S.; Manderscheid, Ronald W.; & Locke, Ben Z. (1993). Use of services by persons with mental and addictive disorders: Findings from the National Institute of Mental Health Epidemiologic Catchment Area Program. *Archives of General Psychiatry, 50,* 95–107.

Nash, Michael. (1987). What, if anything, is regressed about hypnotic age regression? A review of the empirical literature. *Psychological Bulletin, 102* (1), 42–52.

National Association for the Education of Young Children. (1989). *Quality child care.* Washington, D.C.: National Association for the Education of Young Children.

National Association for the Education of Young Children. (1990). *How to choose a good early childhood program.* Washington, D.C.: National Association for the Education of Young Children.

National Conference of Christians and Jews. (1994). *Taking America's pulse: The National Conference Survey on Intergroup Relations.* New York: National Conference of Christians and Jews.

National Stigma Clearinghouse. (1993, July/August). Press release: Prime-time TV portrayals of mentally ill as villains perpetuate stigma, advocates charge. Albany, N.Y.

Neher, A. (1991). Maslow's theory of motivation: A critique. *Journal of Humanistic Psychology, 31,* 89–112.

Neimark, Edith D. (1975). Longitudinal development of formal operational thought. *Genetic Psychology Monographs, 91,* 171–225.

Neimark, Edith D. (1979). Current status of formal operations research. *Human Development, 22,* 60–67.

Neisser, Ulric. (1992). Amnesia, infantile. In Larry R. Squire (Ed.), *Encyclopedia of learning and memory.* New York: Macmillan.

Neisser, Ulric (Chair); Boodoo, Gwyneth; Bouchard, Thomas J., Jr.; Boykin, A. Wade; Brody, Nathan; Ceci, Stephen J.; Halpern, Diane F.; Loehlin, John C.; Perloff, Robert; Sternberg, Robert J.; & Urbina, Susana. (1996). Intelligence: Knowns and unknowns. *American Psychologist, 51,* 77–101.

Neisser, Ulric, & Harsch, Nicole. (1992). Phantom flashbulbs: False recollections of hearing the news about *Challenger.* In Eugene Winograd & Ulric Neisser (Eds.), *Affect and accuracy in recall: Studies of "flashbulb" memories.* New York: Cambridge University Press.

Nelson, Anna. (1995, November/December). Quoted in Cybershrink. *Psychology Today, 28,* 20–21.

Nelson, Charles A. (1995). The ontogeny of human memory: A cognitive neuroscience perspective. *Developmental Psychology, 31,* 723–738.

Nelson, Katherine. (1993). The psychological and social origins of autobiographical memory. *Psychological Science, 4,* 7–14.

Neter, Efrat, & Ben-Shakhar, Gershon. (1989). The predictive validity of graphological inferences: A meta-analytic approach. *Personality and Individual Differences, 10,* 737–745.

Neufeld, Richard W. J., & Paterson, Randolph J. (1989). Issues concerning control and its implementation. In Richard W. J. Neufeld (Ed.), *Advances in the investigation of psychological stress.* New York: Wiley.

Nevid, Jeffrey S.; Fichner-Rathus, Lois; & Rathus, Spencer A. (1995). *Human sexuality in a world of diversity* (2nd ed.). Boston: Allyn & Bacon.

Nevitt, Amy. (1995). *Fetal alcohol syndrome.* New York: Rosen.

New prairie dog vacuum catching on in Southwest. (1992, January 24). *Tulsa World,* p. C-7.

Newcombe, Nora, & Huttenlocher, Janellen. (1992). Children's early ability to solve perspective-taking problems. *Developmental Psychology, 28,* 635–643.

Nezu, Arthur M.; Nezu, Christine M.; & Blissett, Sonia E. (1988). Sense of humor as a moderator of the relation between stressful events and psychological distress: A prospective analysis. *Journal of Personality and Social Psychology, 54,* 520–525.

Nichelli, Paolo; Grafman, Jordan; Pietrini, Pietro; Alway, David; Carton, John C.; & Miletich, Robert. (1994, May 19). Brain activity in chess playing. *Nature, 369,* 191.

Nickerson, Raymond S., & Adams, Marilyn J. (1982). Long–term memory for a common object. In Ulric Neisser (Ed.), *Memory observed: Remembering in natural contexts.* San Francisco: Freeman.

NIH/CEPH (National Institute of Health/Centre d'Etude du Polymorphisme Humain) Collaborative Mapping Group. (1992, October 2). A comprehensive genetic linkage map of the human genome. *Science, 258,* 67–75.

Nisbett, Richard. (1995a). Dangerous, but important. In Russell Jacoby & Naomi Glauberman (Eds.), *The* Bell Curve *debate: History, documents, opinions*. New York: Times Books.

Nisbett, Richard. (1995b). Race, IQ, and scientism. In Steven Fraser (Ed.), *The* Bell Curve *wars: Race, intelligence, and the future of America*. New York: Basic Books.

Nishio, Kazumi, & Bilmes, Murray. (1993). Psychotherapy with Southeast Asian American clients. In Donald R. Atkinson, George Morten, & Derald Wing Sue (Eds.), *Counseling American minorities: A cross-cultural perspective* (4th ed.). Madison, Wis.: Brown & Benchmark.

Nofzinger, Eric A.; Thase, Michael E.; Reynolds, Charles F., III; Frank, Ellen; Jennings, Richard; Garamoni, Gregory L.; Fasiczka, Amy L.; & Kupfer, David J. (1993). Sexual function in depressed men: Assessment by self-report, behavioral, and nocturnal penile tumescence measures before and after treatment with cognitive behavior therapy. *Archives of General Psychiatry, 50,* 24–30.

Nolen-Hoeksema, Susan. (1990). *Sex differences in depression*. Stanford, Calif.: Stanford University Press.

Norris, Joan E., & Tindale, Joseph A. (1994). *Among generations: The cycle of adult relationships*. New York: Freeman.

North, C.; Gowers, S.; & Byram, V. (1995). Family functioning in adolescent anorexia nervosa. *British Journal of Psychiatry, 167,* 673–678.

North, Carol S.; Smith, Elizabeth M.; & Spitznagel, Edward L. (1994). Posttraumatic stress disorder in survivors of a mass shooting. *American Journal of Psychiatry, 151,* 82–88.

Nuckolls, James G. (1992). Data presented at National Institutes of Health Technology Assessment Conference on Methods of Voluntary Weight Loss and Control, March 30–April 1, Bethesda, Maryland.

O'Connor, M. Kevin. (1993). Hypotheses regarding the mechanism of action of electroconvulsive therapy, past and present. *Psychiatric Annals, 23,* 15–18.

O'Leary, Ann. (1990). Stress, emotions, and human immune function. *Psychological Bulletin, 108,* 363–382.

O'Leary, K. Daniel, & Wilson, G. Terence. (1987). *Behavior therapy: Application and outcome* (2nd ed.). Englewood Cliffs, N.J.: Prentice Hall.

Oakley, B. (1986). Basic taste physiology: Human perspectives. In H. L. Meiselman & R. S. Rivlin (Eds.), *Clinical measurement of taste and smell*. New York: Macmillan.

Ochse, R. (1990). *Before the gates of excellence: The determinants of creative genius*. New York: Cambridge University Press.

Ochsner, Kevin N., & Kosslyn, Stephen M. (1994). Mental imagery. In V. S. Ramachandran (Ed.), *Encyclopedia of human behavior*. San Diego: Academic Press.

Ofshe, Richard, & Watters, Ethan. (1994). *Making monsters: False memories, psychotherapy, and sexual hysteria*. New York: Scribner's.

Ogbu, John U. (1986). The consequences of the American caste system. In Ulric Neisser (Ed.), *The school achievement of minority children: New perspectives*. Hillsdale, N.J.: Erlbaum.

Ogden, Jenni A., & Corkin, Suzanne. (1991). Memories of H.M. In Wickliffe C. Abraham, Michael Corballis, & K. Geoffrey White (Eds.), *Memory mechanisms: A tribute to G. V. Goddard*. Hillsdale, N.J.: Erlbaum.

Ohman, Arne, & Soares, Joaquim J. F. (1994). "Unconscious anxiety": Phobic responses to masked stimuli. *Journal of Abnormal Psychology, 103,* 231–240.

Olds, James. (1958). Self-stimulation of the brain. *Science, 127,* 315–324.

Olds, James. (1962). Hypothalamic substrates of reward. *Physiological Reviews, 42,* 554–604.

Olds, M. E., & Fobes, J. L. (1981). The central basis of motivation: Intracranial self-stimulation studies. *Annual Review of Psychology, 32,* 523–574.

Olds, Sally Wendkos. (1989). *The working parents' survival guide*. Rocklin, Calif.: Prima Publishing.

Olivardia, Roberto; Pope, Harrison G.; Mangweth, Barbara; & Hudson, James I. (1995). Eating disorders in college men. *American Journal of Psychiatry, 152,* 1279–1285.

Oliver, Mary Beth, & Hyde, Janet Shibley. (1993). Gender differences in sexuality: A meta-analysis. *Psychological Bulletin, 114,* 29–51.

Olness, Karen. (1993). Hypnosis: The power of attention. In Daniel Goleman & Joel Gurin (Eds.), *Mind/body medicine: How to use your mind for better health*. Yonkers, N.Y.: Consumer Reports Books.

Olson, James M., & Zanna, Mark P. (1993). Attitudes and attitude change. *Annual Review of Psychology, 44,* 117–154.

Olton, David S. (1992). Tolman's cognitive analysis: Predecessors of current approaches in psychology. *Journal of Experimental Psychology: General, 121,* 427–428.

Orlinsky, David E.; Grawe, Klaus; & Parks, Barbara K. (1994). Process and outcome in psychotherapy—*noch einmal*. In Allen E. Bergin & Sol L. Garfield (Eds.), *Handbook of psychotherapy and behavior change* (4th ed.). New York: Wiley.

Orme-Johnson, D. W. (1987). Transcendental meditation and reduced health care utilization. *Psychosomatic Medicine, 49,* 493–507.

Orne, Martin T., & Holland, Charles H. (1968). On the ecological validity of laboratory deceptions. *International Journal of Psychiatry, 6,* 282–293.

Orth-Gomér, Kristina; Rosengren, Annika; & Wilhelmsen, Lars. (1993). Lack of social support and incidence of coronary heart disease in middle-aged Swedish men. *Psychosomatic Medicine, 55,* 37–43.

Ortony, Andrew; Clore, Gerald L.; & Collins, Allan. (1988). *The cognitive structure of emotions*. New York: Cambridge University Press.

Ortony, Andrew, & Turner, Terence J. (1990). What's basic about basic emotions? *Psychological Review, 97,* 315–331.

Ottati, Victor, & Lee, Yueh-Ting. (1995). Accuracy: A neglected component of stereotype research. In Yueh-Ting Lee, Lee J. Jussim, & Clark R. McCauley (Eds.), *Stereotype accuracy: Toward appreciating group differences*. Washington, D.C.: American Psychological Association.

Owsley, Cynthia; Ball, Karlene; Sloane, Michael E.; Roenker, Daniel L.; & Bruni, John R. (1991). Visual/cognitive correlates of vehicle accidents in older drivers. *Psychology and Aging, 6,* 403–415.

Oyserman, Daphna; Grant, Larry; & Ager, Joel. (1995). A socially contextualized model of African American identity: Possible selves and school persistence. *Journal of Personality and Social Psychology, 69,* 1216–1232.

Ozbayrak, Kaan R., & Berlin, Richard M. (1995). Sleepwalking in children and adolescents. In Charles E. Schaefer (Ed.), *Clinical handbook of sleep disorders in children*. Northvale, N.J.: Aronson.

Ozer, Elizabeth M., & Bandura, Albert. (1990). Mechanisms governing empowerment effects: A self-efficacy analysis. *Journal of Personality and Social Psychology, 58,* 472–486.

Paivio, Allan. (1986). *Mental representations: A dual coding approach*. New York: Oxford University Press.

Palmblad, J.; Petrini, B.; Wasserman, J.; & Akerstedt, T. (1979). Lymphocyte and granulocyte reactions during sleep deprivation. *Psychosomatic Medicine, 41,* 273–278.

Papolos, Demitri F., & Papolos, Janice. (1992). *Overcoming depression* (rev. ed.). New York: HarperCollins.

Papoušek, Mechthild; Papoušek, Hanus; & Bornstein, Marc H. (1985). The naturalistic vocal environment of young infants: On the significance of homogeneity and variability in parental speech. In Tiffany M. Field & N. Fox (Eds.), *Social perception in infants*. Norwood, N.J.: Ablex.

Park, Bernadette; Ryan, Carey S.; & Judd, Charles M. (1992). Role of meaningful subgroups in explaining differences in perceived variability for in-groups and out-groups. *Journal of Personality and Social Psychology, 63* (4), 553–567.

Parrott, W. Gerrod. (1995). But emotions are sometimes irrational. *Psychological Inquiry, 6,* 230–232.

Pato, Carlos N.; Lander, Eric S.; & Schultz, S. Charles. (1989). Prospects for the genetic analysis of schizophrenia. *Schizophrenia Bulletin, 15,* 365–372.

Patterson, Charlotte J. (1992). Children of lesbian and gay parents. *Child Development, 63,* 1025–1042.

Patterson, Charlotte J. (1995a). Sexual orientation and human development: An overview. *Developmental Psychology, 31,* 3–11.

Patterson, Charlotte J. (1995b). Families of the lesbian baby boom: Parents' division of labor and children's adjustment. *Developmental Psychology, 31,* 115–123.

Patterson, Charlotte J. (1995c). Lesbian mothers, gay fathers, and their children. In Anthony R. D'Augelli & Charlotte J. Patterson (Eds.), *Lesbian, gay and bisexual identities across the lifespan: Psychological perspectives*. New York: Oxford University Press.

Paul, Diane B., & Blumenthal, Arthur L. (1989). On the trail of Little Albert. *The Psychological Record, 39,* 547–553.

Paul, Gordon L., & Menditto, Anthony A. (1992). Effectiveness of inpatient treatment programs for mentally ill adults in public psychiatric facilities. *Applied and Preventive Psychology, 1,* 41–63.

Paunonen, Sampo V.; Jackson, Douglas N.; Trzebinski, Jerry; & Fosterling, Friedrich. (1992). Personality structure across cultures: A multimethod evaluation. *Journal of Personality and Social Psychology, 62,* 447–456.

Pavlov, Ivan. (1904/1965). On conditioned reflexes. In Richard J. Herrnstein & Edwin G. Boring (Eds.), *A source book in the history of psychology*. Cambridge, Mass.: Harvard University Press.

Pavlov, Ivan. (1927/1960). *Conditioned reflexes: An investigation of the physiological activity of the cerebral cortex* (Translated by G. V. Anrep). New York: Dover Books.

Pavlov, Ivan. (1928). *Lectures on conditioned reflexes*. New York: International Publishers.

Pavot, William; Diener, Ed; & Fujita, Frank. (1990). Extraversion and happiness. *Personality and Individual Differences, 11,* 1299–1306.

Paykel, Eugene S., & Dowlatshahi, D. (1988). Life events and mental disorder. In Shirley Fisher & James Reason (Eds.), *Handbook of life stress, cognition, and health*. New York: Wiley.

Payne, John W. (1976). Task complexity and contingent processing in decision making: An information search and protocol analysis. *Organizational Behavior and Human Performance, 16,* 366–387.

Payne, John W. (1985). Psychology of risky decisions. In George Wright (Ed.), *Behavioral decision making*. New York: Plenum Press.

Payne, John W.; Bettman, James R.; & Johnson, Eric J. (1993). *The adaptive decision maker*. Cambridge, England: Cambridge University Press.

Payton, Jack R. (1992, May 16). The sad legacy of Japan's outcasts. *Chicago Tribune,* section 1, p. 21.

Pearlin, Leonard I. (1993). The social contexts of stress. In Leo Goldberger & Shlomo Breznitz (Eds.), *Handbook of stress: Theoretical and clinical aspects* (2nd ed.). New York: Free Press.

Peirce, Robert S.; Frone, Michael R.; Russell, Marcia; & Cooper, M. Lynne (1996). Financial stress, social support, and alcohol involvement: A longitudinal test of the buffering hypothesis in a general population study. *Health Psychology, 15,* 38–47.

Pekala, Ronald J. (1987). The phenomenology of meditation. In Michael A. West (Ed.), *The psychology of meditation*. New York: Oxford University Press.

Pelletier, Kenneth R. (1993). Between mind and body: Stress, emotions, and health. In Daniel Goleman & Joel Gurin (Eds.), *Mind/body medicine: How to use your mind for better health*. Yonkers, N.Y.: Consumer Reports Books.

Pendergrast, Mark. (1995). *Victims of memory: Incest accusations and shattered lives*. Hinesburg, Vt.: Upper Access.

Penfield, Wilder, & Perot, Phanor. (1963). The brain's record of auditory and visual experience: A final summary and discussion. *Brain, 86,* 595–696.

Penn, David L.; Guynan, Kim; Daily, Tamara; Spaulding, William D.; Garbin, Calvin P.; & Sullivan, Mary. (1994). Dispelling the stigma of schizophrenia: What sort of information is best? *Schizophrenia Bulletin, 20,* 567–577.

Pennisi, Elizabeth. (1994, November 26). Gut counts calories even when we do not. *Science News, 146,* 359.

Pepler, Debra J., & Craig, Wendy M. (1995). A peek behind the fence: Naturalistic observations of aggressive children with remote audiovisual recording. *Developmental Psychology, 31* (4), 548–553.

Pepperberg, Irene. (1993). Cognition and communication in an African gray parrot (*Psittacus erithacus*): Studies on a nonhuman, nonprimate, nonmammalian subject. In Herbert L. Roitblat, Louis M. Herman, & Paul E. Nachtigall (Eds.), *Language and communication: Comparative perspectives*. Hillsdale, N.J.: Erlbaum.

Perkins, D. V. (1982). The assessment of stress using life events scales. In Leo Goldberger & Shlomo Breznitz (Eds.), *Handbook of stress: Theoretical and clinical aspects*. New York: Free Press.

Perkins, Daniel N. (1981). *The mind's best work*. Cambridge, Mass.: Harvard University Press.

Perloff, Richard M. (1993). *The dynamics of persuasion*. Hillsdale, N.J.: Erlbaum.

Perls, Thomas T. (1995, January). The oldest old. *Scientific American, 272,* 70–75.

Pert, Candace B., & Snyder, Solomon H. (1973). Opiate receptor: Demonstration in the nervous tissue. *Science, 179,* 1011–1014.

Pervin, Lawrence A. (1990). A brief history of modern personality theory. In Lawrence A. Pervin (Ed.), *Handbook of personality: Theory and research*. New York: Guilford Press.

Pervin, Lawrence A. (1994). A critical analysis of current trait theory. *Psychological Inquiry, 5,* 103–113.

Pervin, Lawrence A. (1997). *Personality: Theory and research* (7th ed.). New York: Wiley.

Peters, Roger, & McGee, Rob. (1982). Cigarette smoking and state-dependent memory. *Psychopharmacology, 76* (3), 232–235.

Petersen, Anne C. (1988). Adolescent development. *Annual Review of Psychology, 39,* 583–607.

Peterson, Christopher. (1988). Explanatory style as a risk factor for illness. *Cognitive Therapy and Research, 12,* 117–130.

Peterson, Christopher, & Bossio, Lisa M. (1993). Healthy attitudes: Optimism, hope, and control. In Daniel Goleman & Joel Gurin (Eds.), *Mind/body medicine: How to use your mind for better health*. Yonkers, N.Y.: Consumer Reports Books.

Peterson, Christopher; Maier, Steven F.; & Seligman, Martin E. P. (1993). *Learned helplessness: A theory for the age of personal control.* New York: Oxford University Press.

Peterson, Christopher, & Seligman, Martin E. P. (1987). Explanatory style and illness. *Journal of Personality, 55,* 237–265.

Peterson, Christopher; Seligman, Martin E. P.; & Vaillant, George E. (1988). Pessimistic explanatory style as a risk factor for physical illness: A thirty-five-year longitudinal study. *Journal of Personality and Social Psychology, 55,* 23–27.

Peterson, Dale, & Goodall, Jane. (1993). *Visions of Caliban: On chimpanzees and people.* Boston: Houghton Mifflin.

Peterson, Mary A., & Gibson, Bradley S. (1994). Must figure–ground organization precede object recognition? An assumption in peril. *Psychological Science, 5,* 253–259.

Petitto, Laura Ann, & Marentette, Paula F. (1991, March 31). Babbling in the manual mode: Evidence for the ontogeny of language. *Science, 251,* 1493–1496.

Petraitis, John; Flay, Brian R.; & Miller, Todd Q. (1995). Reviewing theories of adolescent substance abuse: Organizing pieces of the puzzle. *Psychological Bulletin, 117,* 67–86.

Petri, Herbert L. (1996). *Motivation: Theory, research, and applications* (4th ed.). Pacific Grove, Calif.: Brooks/Cole.

Phillips, D. P., & Brugge, J. F. (1985). Progress in neurophysiology of sound localization. *Annual Review of Psychology, 36,* 245–274.

Phillips, David P., & Ruth, Todd E. (1993). Adequacy of official suicide statistics for scientific research and public policy. *Suicide and Life Threatening Behavior, 23,* 307–319.

Phillips, Deborah. (1991). Day care for young children in the United States. In E. C. Melhuish & Peter Moss (Eds.), *Day care for young children.* London: Routledge.

Phillips, Deborah A., & Howes, Carollee. (1987). Indicators of quality in child care: Review of research. In Deborah A. Phillips (Ed.), *Quality in child care: What does research tell us? Research Monograph of the National Association for the Education of Young Children: Vol. 1.* Washington, D.C.: National Association for the Education of Young Children.

Phillips, Susan D. (1982). Career exploration in adulthood. *Journal of Vocational Behavior, 20,* 129–140.

Phillips, Susan D., & Blustein, David L. (1994). Readiness for career choices: Planning, exploring, and deciding. *The Career Development Quarterly, 43,* 63–75.

Piaget, Jean. (1952). *The origins of intelligence in children.* Translated by Margaret Cook. New York: International Universities Press.

Piaget, Jean. (1972). Intellectual evolution from adolescence to adulthood. *Human Development, 15,* 1–12.

Piaget, Jean. (1973). The stages of cognitive development: Interview with Richard I. Evans. In Richard I. Evans (Ed.), *Jean Piaget: The man and his ideas.* New York: Dutton.

Piaget, Jean, & Inhelder, Bärbel. (1958). *The growth of logical thinking from childhood to adolescence: An essay on the construction of formal operational structures.* Translated by Anne Parsons and Stanley Milgram. New York: Basic Books.

Piaget, Jean, & Inhelder, Bärbel. (1974). *The child's construction of quantities: Conservation and atomism.* London: Routledge and Kegan Paul.

Piirto, Jane. (1992). *Understanding those who create.* Dayton, Ohio: Ohio Psychology Press.

Piliavin, Jane Allyn, & Charng, Hong-Wen. (1990). Altruism: A review of recent theory and research. *Annual Review of Sociology, 16,* 27–65.

Piliavin, Jane Allyn; Dovidio, John F.; Gaertner, Samuel L.; & Clark, Russell D., III. (1981). *Emergency intervention.* New York: Academic Press.

Pillow, David R.; Zautra, Alex J.; & Sandler, Irwin. (1996). Major life events and minor stressors: Identifying mediational links in the stress process. *Journal of Personality and Social Psychology, 70,* 381–394.

Pinker, Steven. (1994). *The language instinct: How the mind creates language.* New York: Morrow.

Pinker, Steven. (1995). Introduction: Language. In Michael S. Gazzaniga (Ed.), *The cognitive neurosciences.* Cambridge, Mass.: MIT Press.

Plomin, Robert. (1989). Environment and genes: Determinants of behavior. *American Psychologist, 44,* 105–111.

Plomin, Robert. (1990). The role of inheritance in behavior. *Science, 248,* 183–188.

Plomin, Robert. (1993). Nature and nurture: Perspective and prospective. In Robert Plomin & Gerald E. McClearn (Eds.), *Nature, nurture, and psychology.* Washington, D.C.: American Psychological Association.

Plomin, Robert; Chipuer, Heather M.; & Loehlin, John C. (1990). Behavioral genetics and personality. In Lawrence A. Pervin (Ed.), *Handbook of personality: Theory and research.* New York: Guilford Press.

Plomin, Robert, & Daniels, Denise. (1987). Why are children in the same family so different from each other? *Behavioral and Brain Sciences, 10,* 1–16.

Plomin, Robert, & Neiderhiser, Jenae. (1992). Genetics and experience. *Current Directions in Psychological Science, 1,* 160–163.

Plomin, Robert; Owen, Michael J.; & McGuffin, Peter. (1994, June 17). The genetic basis of complex human behaviors. *Science, 264,* 1733–1739.

Plomin, Robert, & Rende, Richard. (1991). Human behavioral genetics. *Annual Review of Psychology, 42,* 161–190.

Plutchik, Robert. (1984). Emotions: A general psychoevolutionary theory. In Klaus R. Scherer & Paul Ekman (Eds.), *Approaches to emotion.* Hillsdale, N.J.: Erlbaum.

Polk, Thad A., & Newell, Allen. (1995). Deduction as verbal reasoning. *Psychological Review, 102,* 533–566.

Pollitt, Katha. (1993, September/October). Are women morally superior to men? Debunking "difference" feminism. *Utne Reader,* No. 59, pp. 101–109.

Poloma, Margaret M., & Pendleton, Brian F. (1990). Religious domains and general well-being. *Social Indicators Research, 22,* 255–276.

Pope, Kenneth S. (1990). Therapist–patient sexual involvement: A review of the research. *Clinical Psychology Review, 10,* 477–490.

Pope, Kenneth S., & Bouhoutsos, Jacqueline C. (1986). *Sexual intimacy between therapists and patients.* New York: Praeger.

Pope, Kenneth S., & Tabachnick, Barbara G. (1993). Therapists' anger, hate, fear, and sexual feelings: National survey of therapist responses, client characteristics, critical events, formal complaints, and training. *Professional Psychology: Research and Practice, 24,* 142–152.

Porter, Kenneth. (1993). Combined individual and group psychotherapy. In Anne Alonso & Hillel I. Swiller (Eds.), *Group therapy in clinical practice.* Washington, D.C.: American Psychiatric Press.

Porter, R. H., & Moore, J. D. (1981). Human kin recognition by olfactory cues. *Physiology and Behavior, 27,* 493–495.

Poulin-Dubois, Diane; Serbin, Lisa A.; Kenyon, Brenda; & Derbyshire, Alison. (1994) Infants' intermodal knowledge about gender. *Developmental Psychology, 30,* 436–442.

Povinelli, Daniel J. (1993). Reconstructing the evolution of mind. *American Psychologist, 48,* 493–509.

Powlishta, Kimberly K. (1995a). Intergroup processes in childhood: Social categorization and sex role development. *Developmental Psychology, 31,* 781–788.

Powlishta, Kimberly K. (1995b). Gender bias in children's perceptions of personality traits. *Sex Roles, 32,* 223–240.

Pratkanis, Anthony R., & Aronson, Elliot. (1991). *Age of propaganda: The everyday use and abuse of persuasion.* New York: Freeman.

Premack, David, & Premack, Ann Jones. (1983). *The mind of an ape.* New York: Norton.

Prescott, Carol A., & Gottesman, Irving I. (1993). Genetically mediated vulnerability to schizophrenia. *Psychiatric Clinics of North America, 16,* 245–268.

Preti, George; Cutler, W. B.; Garcia, C. R.; Huggins, G. R.; & Lawley, H. J. (1986). Human axillary secretions influence women's menstrual cycles: The role of donor extract of females. *Hormones and Behavior, 20,* 474–482.

Prinzmetal, William. (1995). Visual feature integration in a world of objects. *Current Directions in Psychological Science, 4,* 90–94.

Pullum, Geoffrey K. (1991). *The great Eskimo vocabulary hoax and other irreverent essays on the study of language.* Chicago: University of Chicago Press.

Putnam, Frank W. (1989). *Diagnosis and treatment of multiple personality disorder.* New York: Guilford Press.

Putnam, Frank W. (1991a). Recent research on multiple personality disorder. *Psychiatric Clinics of North America, 14,* 489–502.

Putnam, Frank W. (1991b). Dissociative disorders in children and adolescents: A developmental perspective. *Psychiatric Clinics of North America, 14,* 519–531.

Putnam, Frank W. (1993). Dissociative phenomena. In David Spiegel (Ed.), *Dissociative disorders: A clinical review.* Lutherville, Md.: Sidran.

Pyszczynski, Tom; Greenberg, Jeff; Solomon, Sheldon; Sideris, John; & Stubing, Mari Jo. (1993). Emotional expression and the reduction of motivated cognitive bias: Evidence from cognitive dissonance and distancing from victims' paradigms. *Journal of Personality and Social Psychology, 64,* 177–186.

Quick, James C., & Quick, Jonathan D. (1984). *Organizational stress and preventive management.* New York: McGraw-Hill.

Rabinowitz, D. (1970). Some endocrine and metabolic aspects of obesity. *Annual Review of Medicine, 21,* 241–258.

Rachlin, Howard. (1974). Self-control. *Behaviorism, 2,* 94–107.

Rahe, Richard H. (1972). Subjects' recent life changes and their near-future illness reports. *Annals of Clinical Research, 4,* 250–265.

Rakic, Pasko. (1995). Corticogenesis in human and nonhuman primates. In Michael S. Gazzaniga (Ed.), *The cognitive neurosciences.* Cambridge, Mass.: MIT Press.

Ramachandran, Vilayanur S. (1992a, May). Blind spots. *Scientific American, 266,* 86–91.

Ramachandran, Vilayanur S. (1992b). Filling in gaps in perception: Part 1. *Current Directions in Psychological Science, 1,* 199–205.

Randi, James. (1980). *Flim-flam!* New York: Lippincott & Crowell.

Randi, James. (1982). *The truth about Uri Geller.* Buffalo, N.Y.: Prometheus.

Rapee, Ronald M.; Brown, Timothy A.; Antony, Martin M.; & Barlow, David H. (1992). Response to hyperventilation and inhalation of 5.5% carbon dioxide-enriched air across the *DSM-III-R* anxiety disorders. *Journal of Abnormal Psychology, 101,* 538–552.

Rapoport, Judith L. (1989). *The boy who couldn't stop washing: The experience and treatment of obsessive-compulsive disorder.* New York: Dutton.

Rapoport, Judith L. (1991). Basal ganglia dysfunction as a proposed cause of obsessive-compulsive disorder. In Bernard J. Carroll & James E. Barrett (Eds.), *Psychopathology and the brain.* New York: Raven Press.

Raskin, Allen; Pelchat, Rodney; Sood, Ramn; Alphs, Larry D.; & Levine, Jerome. (1993). Negative symptom assessment of chronic schizophrenia patients. *Schizophrenia Bulletin, 19,* 627–635.

Rasmussen, Steven A., & Eisen, Jane L. (1992). The epidemiology and clinical features of obsessive-compulsive disorder. *Psychiatric Clinics of North America, 15,* 743–758.

Ratcliff, Roger, & McKoon, Gail. (1994). Retrieving information from memory: Spreading-activation theories versus compound-cue theories. *Psychological Review, 101,* 177–184.

Räty, Hannu. (1990). A world without mental illness: Concepts of mental health and mental illness among a student group. *Social Behaviour, 5,* 315–326.

Rawlings, Steve W., & Saluter, Arlene F. (1995). *Household and family characteristics: March 1994.* U.S. Bureau of the Census, Current population reports, Series P20-483. Washington, D.C.: U.S. Government Printing Office.

Rawlins, William K. (1992). *Friendship matters: Communication, dialectics, and the life course.* Hawthorne, N.Y.: Aldine de Gruyter.

Raz, Sarah. (1994). Gross brain morphology in schizophrenia: A regional analysis of traditional diagnostic subtypes. *Journal of Consulting and Clinical Psychology, 62,* 640–644.

Reason, James. (1988). Stress and cognitive failure. In Shirley Fisher & James Reason (Eds.), *Handbook of life stress, cognition, and health.* New York: Wiley.

Reed, Stephen K. (1996). *Cognition: Theory and applications* (4th ed.). Pacific Grove, Calif.: Brooks/Cole.

Reese, Ellen. (1986). Learning about teaching from teaching about learning: Presenting behavioral analysis in an introductory survey course. In Vivian Parker Makosky (Ed.), *The G. Stanley Hall Lecture Series* (Vol. 6). Washington, D.C.: American Psychological Association.

Regan, Dennis T., & Kilduff, Martin. (1988). Optimism about elections: Dissonance reduction at the ballot box. *Political Psychology, 9,* 101–107.

Regan, Dennis T.; Williams, Margo; & Sparling, Sondra. (1972). Voluntary expiation of guilt: A field experiment. *Journal of Personality and Social Psychology, 24,* 42–45.

Regier, Darrel A.; Narrow, William E.; Rae, Donald S.; Manderscheid, Ronald W.; Locke, Ben Z.; & Goodwin, Fredrick K. (1993). The de facto U.S. mental and addictive disorders service system: Epidemiologic catchment area prospective one-year prevalence rates of disorders and services. *Archives of General Psychiatry, 50,* 85–94.

Reisberg, Daniel, & Chambers, Deborah. (1991). Neither pictures nor propositions: What can we learn from a mental image? *Canadian Journal of Psychology, 45,* 336–348.

Reisenzein, Rainer. (1983). The Schachter theory of emotion: Two decades later. *Psychological Bulletin, 94,* 239–264.

Reisenzein, Rainer; Meyer, Wulf-Uwe; & Schützwohl, Achim. (1995). James and the physical basis of emotion: A comment on Ellsworth. *Psychological Review, 102,* 757–761.

Reiss, B. K. (1990). *A biography of Mary Cover Jones.* Berkeley, Calif.: Wright Institute.

Rejeski, W. Jack; Gregg, Edward; Thompson, Amy; & Berry, Michael. (1991). The effects of varying doses of acute aerobic exercise on psychophysiological stress responses in highly trained cyclists. *Journal of Sport and Exercise Psychology, 13,* 188–199.

Rejeski, W. Jack; Thompson, Amy; Brubaker, Peter H.; & Miller, Henry S. (1992). Acute exercise: Buffering psychosocial responses in women. *Health Psychology, 11,* 355–362.

Renner, Michael, & Rosenzweig, Mark. (1987). *Enriched and impoverished environments: Effects on brain and behavior.* New York: Springer Verlag.

Renzulli, Joseph S. (1986). The three-ring conception of giftedness: A developmental model for creative productivity. In Robert J. Sternberg & Janet E. Davidson (Eds.), *Conceptions of giftedness.* New York: Cambridge University Press.

Repetti, Rena L. (1993). Short-term effects of occupational stressors on daily mood and health complaints. *Health Psychology, 12,* 125–131.

Rescorla, Robert A. (1968). Probability of shock in the presence and absence of CS in fear conditioning. *Journal of Comparative and Physiological Psychology, 66,* 1–5.

Rescorla, Robert A. (1988). Pavlovian conditioning: It's not what you think it is. *American Psychologist, 43,* 151–160.

Rest, James R. (1983). Morality. In Paul H. Mussen, John H. Flavell, & Ellen M. Markman (Eds.), *Handbook of child psychology* (4th ed.): *Vol. III. Cognitive development.* New York: Wiley.

Restak, Richard M. (1994). *Receptors.* New York: Bantam.

Revelle, William. (1995). Personality processes. *Annual Review of Psychology, 46,* 295–328.

Reynolds, David K. (1989). *Pools of lodging for the moon: Strategy for a positive life-style.* New York: Morrow.

Reynolds, David K. (1990). *A thousand waves: A sensible life-style for sensitive people.* New York: Morrow.

Riccio, David C.; Rabinowitz, Vita C.; & Axelrod, Shari. (1994). Memory: When less is more. *American Psychologist, 19,* 917–926.

Rice, Laura N., & Greenberg, Leslie S. (1992). Humanistic approaches to psychotherapy. In Donald K. Freedheim (Ed.), *History of psychotherapy: A century of change.* Washington, D.C.: American Psychological Association.

Rice, R. W.; Instone, D.; & Adams, J. (1984). Leader sex, leader success, and leadership process: Two field studies. *Journal of Applied Psychology, 69,* 12–31.

Rice, R. W.; McFarlin, D. B.; & Bennett, D. E. (1989). Standards of comparison and job satisfaction. *Journal of Applied Psychology, 74,* 591–598.

Richardson, John, & Simpson, Carl. (1982). Children, gender, and social structure: An analysis of the contents of letters to Santa Claus. *Child Development, 53,* 429–436.

Richelson, Elliott. (1993). Treatment of acute depression. *Psychiatric Clinics of North America, 16,* 461–478.

Richman, Joseph, & Eyman, James R. (1990). Psychotherapy of suicide: Individual, group, and family approaches. In David Lester (Ed.), *Current concepts of suicide.* Philadelphia: Charles Press.

Rimm, Eric B.; Giovannucci, Edward L.; Willett, Walter C.; Colditz, Graham A.; Ascherio, Alberto; Rosner, Bernard; & Stampfer, Meir J. (1991, August 24). Prospective study of alcohol consumption and risk of coronary disease in men. *Lancet, 338,* 464–468.

Riskin, Joy Dana, & Frankel, Fred H. (1994). A history of medical hypnosis. *Psychiatric Clinics of North America, 17,* 601–609.

Rissman, Emilie F. (1995). An alternative animal model for the study of female sexual behavior. *Current Directions in Psychological Science, 4,* 6–10.

Ritchie, James C., & Nemeroff, Charles B. (1991). Stress, the hypothalamic-pituitary-adrenal axis, and depression. In James A. McCubbin, Peter G. Kaufmann, & Charles B. Nemeroff (Eds.), *Stress, neuropeptides, and systemic disease.* San Diego: Academic Press.

Roazen, Paul. (1976). *Freud and his followers.* New York: Meridian Books.

Robb, Brian J. (1994). *River Phoenix: A short life.* New York: HarperPerennial.

Robbins, Ann S.; Spence, Janet T.; & Clark, Heather. (1991). Psychological determinants of health and performance: The tangled web of desirable and undesirable characteristics. *Journal of Personality and Social Psychology, 61,* 755–765.

Roberts, Elizabeth J. (Ed.). (1980). *Childhood sexual learning: The unwritten curriculum.* Cambridge, Mass.: Ballinger.

Robin, Nina, & Holyoak, Keith J. (1995). Relational complexity and the functions of the prefrontal cortex. In Michael S. Gazzaniga (Ed.), *The cognitive neurosciences.* Cambridge, Mass.: MIT Press.

Robins, Clive J., & Hayes, Adele M. (1993). An appraisal of cognitive therapy. *Journal of Consulting and Clinical Psychology, 61,* 205–214.

Robins, Lee N.; Schoenberg, Sandra P.; Holmes, Sandra J.; Ratcliff, Kathryn S.; Benham, Alexander; & Works, Jane. (1985). Early home environment and retrospective recall: A test for concordance between siblings with and without psychiatric disorders. *American Journal of Orthopsychiatry, 55,* 27–41.

Robinson, Daniel N. (1993). Is there a Jamesian tradition in psychology? *American Psychologist, 48,* 638–643.

Robinson, John A. (1986). Autobiographical memory: A historical prologue. In David C. Rubin (Ed.), *Autobiographical memory.* New York: Cambridge University Press.

Robinson, L. A.; Berman, J. S.; & Neimeyer, R. A. (1990). Psychotherapy for the treatment of depression: A comprehensive review of controlled outcome research. *Psychological Bulletin, 100,* 30–49.

Robinson, Paul. (1993). *Freud and his critics.* Berkeley: University of California Press.

Robinson, Vera M. (1983). Humor and health. In Paul E. McGhee & Jeffrey H. Goldstein (Eds.), *Handbook of humor research: Vol. II. Applied studies.* New York: Springer-Verlag.

Roche, Suzanne M., & McConkey, Kevin M. (1990). Absorption: Nature, assessment, and correlates. *Journal of Personality and Social Psychology, 59,* 91–101.

Rock, Irvin. (1995). *Perception.* New York: Scientific American Library.

Rodin, Judith. (1978). Has the distinction between internal versus external control of feeding outlived its usefulness? In George A. Bray (Ed.), *Recent advances in obesity research* (Vol. 2). London: Newman.

Rodin, Judith. (1981). Current status of the internal-external hypothesis for obesity: What went wrong? *American Psychologist, 36,* 361–372.

Rodin, Judith. (1982). Obesity: Why the losing battle? In Benjamin B. Wolman (Ed.), *Psychological aspects of obesity: A handbook.* New York: Van Nostrand Reinhold.

Rodin, Judith. (1985). Insulin levels, hunger, and food intake: An example of feedback loops in body weight reduction. *Health Psychology, 4* (1), 1–24.

Rodin, Judith. (1986, September 19). Aging and health: Effects of the sense of control. *Science, 233,* 1271–1275.

Rodin, Judith, & Langer, Ellen. (1977). Long-term effects of a control-relevant intervention with the institutionalized aged. *Journal of Personality and Social Psychology, 35,* 897–902.

Rodin, Judith, & Salovey, Peter. (1989). Health psychology. *Annual Review of Psychology, 40,* 533–579.

Rodin, Judith; Silberstein, Lisa; & Striegel-Moore, Ruth. (1985). Women and weight: A normative discontent. In Richard A. Dienstbier & Theo B. Sonderegger (Eds.), *Nebraska Symposium on Motivation, 1984: Psychology and gender.* Lincoln: University of Nebraska Press.

Roediger, Henry L., III. (1992). Retrieval processes in memory. In Larry R. Squire (Ed.), *Encyclopedia of learning and memory.* New York: Macmillan.

Roemer, Lizabeth, & Borkovec, Thomas D. (1993). Worry: Unwanted cognitive activity that controls unwanted somatic experience. In Daniel M. Wegner & James W. Pennebaker (Eds.), *Handbook of mental control.* Englewood Cliffs, N.J.: Prentice Hall.

Rogers, Carl. (1957a/1989). A note on "The Nature of Man." In Howard Kirschenbaum & Valerie Land Henderson (Eds.), *The Carl Rogers reader.* Boston: Houghton Mifflin.

Rogers, Carl. (1957b/1989). A therapist's view of the good life: The fully functioning person. In Howard Kirschenbaum & Valerie Land Henderson (Eds.), *The Carl Rogers reader.* Boston: Houghton Mifflin.

Rogers, Carl. (1959). A theory of therapy, personality, and interpersonal relationships, as developed in the client-centered framework. In S. Koch (Ed.), *Psychology: A study of a science: Vol. 3. Formulations of the person and the social context.* New York: McGraw-Hill.

Rogers, Carl. (1961). *On becoming a person.* Boston: Houghton Mifflin.

Rogers, Carl. (1964/1989). Toward a modern approach to values: The valuing process in the mature person. In Howard Kirschenbaum & Valerie Land Henderson (Eds.), *The Carl Rogers reader.* Boston: Houghton Mifflin.

Rogers, Carl. (1977). *Carl Rogers on personal power: Inner strength and its revolutionary impact.* New York: Delacorte Press.

Rogers, Carl R. (1980). *A way of being.* Boston: Houghton Mifflin.

Rogers, Carl. (1981/1989). Notes on Rollo May. In Howard Kirschenbaum & Valerie Land Henderson (Eds.), *Carl Rogers: Dialogues.* Boston: Houghton Mifflin.

Rogers, Carl, & Skinner, B. F. (1956, November 30). Some issues concerning the control of human behavior: A symposium. *Science, 124,* 1057–1066.

Rogers, Susan M., & Turner, Charles F. (1991). Male–male sexual contact in the U.S.A.: Findings from five sample surveys, 1970–1990. *Journal of Sex Research, 28,* 491–519.

Rogers, T. B.; Kuiper, N. A.; & Kirker, W. S. (1977). Self–reference and the encoding of personal information. *Journal of Personality and Social Psychology, 35,* 677–688.

Rogler, Lloyd H.; Malgady, Robert G.; Costantino, Guiseppe; & Blumenthal, Rena. (1993). What do culturally sensitive mental health services mean? The case of Hispanics. In Donald R. Atkinson, George Morten, & Derald Wing Sue (Eds.), *Counseling American minorities: A cross-cultural perspective* (4th ed.). Madison, Wis.: Brown & Benchmark.

Rogo, D. Scott. (1985). *The search for yesterday: A critical examination of the evidence for reincarnation.* Englewood Cliffs, N.J.: Prentice Hall.

Rogoff, Barbara, & Chavajay, Pablo. (1995). What's become of research on the cultural basis of cognitive development? *American Psychologist, 50,* 859–877.

Rogoff, Barbara, & Morelli, Gilda. (1989). Perspectives on children's development from cultural psychology. *American Psychologist, 44,* 343–348.

Rollin, Bernard E. (1992). *Animal rights and human morality.* Buffalo, N.Y.: Prometheus Books.

Romney, A. Kimball; Brewer, Devon D.; & Batchelder, William H. (1993). Predicting clustering from semantic structure. *Psychological Science, 4,* 28–34.

Ronen, Tammie. (1991). Intervention package for treating sleep disorders in a four-year-old girl. *Journal of Behavior Therapy and Experimental Psychiatry, 22,* 141–148.

Rook, Karen S. (1992). Detrimental aspects of social relationships: Taking stock of an emerging literature. In Hans O. F. Veiel & Urs Baumann (Eds.), *The meaning and measurement of social support.* New York: Hemisphere.

Rorer, Leonard G. (1990). Personality assessment: A conceptual survey. In Lawrence A. Pervin (Ed.), *Handbook of personality: Theory and research.* New York: Guilford Press.

Rosch, Eleanor H. (1973). Natural categories. *Cognitive Psychology, 4,* 328–350.

Rosch, Eleanor H. (1978). Principles of categorization. In Eleanor H. Rosch &

Barbara B. Lloyd (Eds.), *Cognition and categorization.* Hillsdale, N.J.: Erlbaum.

Rosch, Eleanor H. (1987). Linguistic relativity. *Et Cetera, 44,* 254–279.

Rosch, Eleanor H., & Mervis, Carolyn B. (1975). Family resemblances: Studies in the internal structure of categories. *Cognitive Psychology, 7,* 573–605.

Rose, G. A., & Williams, R. T. (1961). Metabolic studies on large and small eaters. *British Journal of Nutrition, 15,* 1–9.

Rose, Kenneth Jon. (1988). *The body in time.* New York: Wiley.

Rose, Richard J. (1995). Genes and human behavior. *Annual Review of Psychology, 46,* 625–654.

Rose, Steven. (1993). *The making of memory: From molecules to mind.* New York: Doubleday.

Rose, Susan A., & Feldman, Judith F. (1995). Prediction of IQ and specific cognitive abilities at 11 years from infancy measures. *Developmental Psychology, 31,* 685–696.

Rosenberg, Harold. (1993). Prediction of controlled drinking by alcoholics and problem drinkers. *Psychological Bulletin, 113,* 129–139.

Rosenfeld, J. P. (1995). Alternative views of Bashore and Rapp's (1993) alternatives to traditional polygraphy: A critique. *Psychological Bulletin, 117,* 159–166.

Rosenhan, David L., & Seligman, Martin E. P. (1995). *Abnormal psychology* (5th ed.). New York: Norton.

Rosenman, Ray H., & Chesney, Margaret A. (1982). *Stress, Type A behavior, and coronary disease.* In Leo Goldberger & Shlomo Breznitz (Eds.), *Handbook of stress: Theoretical and clinical aspects.* New York: Free Press.

Rosenstein, Marilyn J.; Milazzo-Sayre, Laura J.; & Manderscheid, Ronald W. (1989). Care of persons with schizophrenia: A statistical profile. *Schizophrenia Bulletin, 15,* 45–58.

Rosenthal, Abraham M. (1964a, May 3). Study of the sickness called apathy. *The New York Times Magazine,* Section VI, pp. 24, 66, 69–72.

Rosenthal, Abraham M. (1964b). *Thirty-eight witnesses.* New York: McGraw-Hill.

Rosenthal, Norman E. (1993). *Winter blues: Seasonal affective disorder: What it is and how to overcome it* (rev. ed.). New York: Guilford Press.

Rosenthal, Robert. (1994). Science and ethics in conducting, analyzing, and reporting psychological research. *Psychological Science, 5* (3), 127–134.

Rosenzweig, Mark R. (1996). Aspects of the search for neural mechanisms of memory. *Annual Review of Psychology, 47,* 1–32.

Ross, Barbara. (1991). William James: Spoiled child of American psychology. In Gregory A. Kimble, Michael Wertheimer, & Charlotte White (Eds.), *Portraits of pioneers in psychology.* Washington, D.C.: American Psychological Association.

Ross, Bruce M. (1992). *Remembering the personal past: Descriptions of autobiographical memory.* New York: Oxford University Press.

Ross, Colin A. (1991). Epidemiology of multiple personality disorder and dissociation. *Psychiatric Clinics of North America, 14,* 503–517.

Ross, Colin A.; Norton, R.; & Wozney, K. (1989). Multiple personality disorder: An analysis of 236 cases. *Canadian Journal of Psychiatry, 34,* 414–418.

Ross, Jerilyn. (1993). Social phobia: The consumer's perspective. *Journal of Clinical Psychiatry, 54* (12, Supplement), 5–9.

Ross, Lee. (1977). The intuitive psychologist and his shortcomings: Distortions in the attribution process. In Leonard Berkowitz (Ed.), *Advances in experimental social psychology* (Vol. 10). New York: Academic Press.

Ross, Lee, & Anderson, Craig A. (1982). Shortcomings in the attribution process: On the origins and maintenance of erroneous social assessments. In Daniel Kahneman, Paul Slovic, & Amos Tversky (Eds.), *Judgment under uncertainty: Heuristics and biases.* New York: Cambridge University Press.

Rossman, Martin L. (1993). Imagery: Learning to use the mind's eye. In Daniel Goleman & Joel Gurin (Eds.), *Mind/body medicine: How to use your mind for better health.* Yonkers, N.Y.: Consumer Reports Books.

Rothbart, Mary K.; Derryberry, Douglas; & Posner, Michael I. (1994). A psychobiological approach to the development of temperament. In John E. Bates & Theodore D. Wachs (Eds.), *Temperament: Individual differences at the interface of biology and behavior.* Washington, D.C.: American Psychological Association.

Rothbaum, Barbara Olasov; Hodges, Larry F.; Kooper, Rob; Opdyke, Dan; Williford, James S.; & North, Max. (1995a). The efficacy of virtual reality graded exposure in the treatment of acrophobia. *American Journal of Psychiatry, 152,* 626–628.

Rothbaum, Barbara Olasov; Hodges, Larry F.; Kooper, Rob; Opdyke, Dan; Williford,

James S.; & North, Max. (1995b). Virtual reality graded exposure in the treatment of acrophobia: A case report. *Behavior Therapy, 26,* 547–554.

Rothbaum, Barbara Olasov; Hodges, Larry F.; Opdyke, Dan; Williford, James S.; & North, Max. (1996). Virtual reality exposure therapy in the treatment of fear of flying: A case report. *Behaviour Research and Therapy, 34,* 477–486.

Rumbaugh, Duane M. (1977). *Language learning by a chimpanzee: The Lana project.* New York: Academic Press.

Rummans, Teresa A. (1993). Medical indications for electroconvulsive therapy. *Psychiatric Annals, 23,* 27–32.

Rupp, Agnes, & Keith, Samuel J. (1993). The costs of schizophrenia: Assessing the burden. *Psychiatric Clinics of North America, 16,* 413–423.

Russell, James A. (1980). A circumplex model of affect. *Journal of Personality and Social Psychology, 39,* 1161–1178.

Russell, James A.; Lewicka, Maria; & Niit, Toomas. (1989). A cross-cultural study of a circumplex model of affect. *Journal of Personality and Social Psychology, 57,* 848–856.

Russell, John G. (1989). Anxiety disorders in Japan: A review of the Japanese literature on *shinkeishitsu* and *taijinkyofusho. Culture, Medicine, and Psychiatry, 13,* 391–403.

Russell, Tanya G.; Rowe, Wayne; & Smouse, Albert E. (1991). Subliminal self-help tapes and academic achievement: An evaluation. *Journal of Counseling and Development, 69,* 359–362.

Rutter, Virginia. (1994, April). Oops! A very embarrassing story. *Psychology Today,* pp. 12–13, 95.

Ruvolo, Ann Patrice, & Markus, Hazel Rose. (1992). Possible selves and performance: The power of self-relevant imagery. *Social Cognition, 10,* 95–124.

Ryan, A. M., & Sackett, P. R. (1987). Pre-employment honesty testing: Fakability, reactions of test takers, and company image. *Journal of Business and Psychology, 1,* 248–256.

Ryan, E. B. (1992). Beliefs about memory across the life span. *Journal of Gerontology: Psychological Sciences, 47,* 41–47.

Sachs, Gary S.; Lafer, Beny; Truman, Christine J.; Noeth, Mary; & Thibault, Amy B. (1994). Lithium monotherapy: Miracle, myth and misunderstanding. *Psychiatric Annals, 24,* 299–306.

Sack, Robert L.; Blood, Mary L.; & Lewy, Alfred J. (1992a). Melatonin rhythms in night shift workers. *Sleep, 15,* 434–441.

Sack, Robert L., & Lewy, Alfred J. (1993). Human circadian rhythms: Lessons from the blind. *Annals of Medicine, 25,* 303–315.

Sack, Robert L.; Lewy, Alfred J.; Blood, Mary L.; Keith, L. D.; & Nakagawa, Hiroki. (1992b). Circadian rhythm abnormalities in totally blind people: Incidence and clinical significance. *Journal of Clinical Endocrinology and Metabolism, 75,* 127–134.

Sacks, Michael H. (1993). Exercise for stress control. In Daniel Goleman & Joel Gurin (Eds.), *Mind/body medicine: How to use your mind for better health.* Yonkers, N.Y.: Consumer Reports Books.

Sakheim, David K., & Devine, Susan E. (Eds.). (1992). *Out of darkness: Exploring Satanism and ritual abuse.* New York: Lexington Books.

Salancik, G. R., & Pfeffer, J. (1977). An examination of needs satisfaction models of job satisfaction. *Administrative Science Quarterly, 22,* 427–456.

Salens, Lester B. (1984). *Obesity and energy metabolism.* Bethesda, Md.: National Institutes of Health, Publication No. 86–1805.

Salovey, Peter; Mayer, John D.; & Rosenhan, David L. (1991). Mood and helping: Mood as a motivator of helping and helping as a regulator of mood. In Margaret S. Clark (Ed.), *Prosocial behavior: Vol. 12. Review of personality and social psychology.* Newbury Park, Calif.: Sage.

Salthouse, Timothy. (1993). Speed mediation of adult age differences in cognition. *Developmental Psychology, 29,* 722–738.

Saluter, Arlene F. (1994). *Marital status and living arrangements: March 1993.* U.S. Bureau of the Census, Current population reports, Series P20-478. Washington, D.C.: U.S. Government Printing Office.

Sanbonmatsu, David M.; Akimoto, Sharon A.; & Gibson, Bryan D. (1994). Stereotype-based blocking in social explanation. *Personality and Social Psychology Bulletin, 20,* 71–81.

Sande, Gerald N.; Goethals, George R.; & Radloff, Christine E. (1988). Perceiving one's own traits and others': The multifaceted self. *Journal of Personality and Social Psychology, 54,* 13–20.

Sandelowski, M.; Holditch-Davis, D.; & Harris, B. G. (1992). Using qualitative and quantitative methods: The transition to parenthood among infertile couples. In Jane F. Gilgun, Kerry Daly, & Gerald Handel (Eds.), *Qualitative methods in family research.* Newbury Park, Calif.: Sage.

Sandler, Jack, & Steele, Holly Villareal. (1991). Aversion methods. In Frederick H. Kanfer & Arnold P. Goldstein (Eds.), *Helping people change: A textbook of methods* (4th ed.). New York: Pergamon Press.

Sanduleak, Nick. (1986). The moon is acquitted of murder in Cleveland. In Kendrick Frazier (Ed.), *Science confronts the paranormal*. Buffalo, N.Y.: Prometheus.

Sarafino, Edward P. (1994). *Health psychology: Biopsychosocial interactions* (2nd ed.) New York: Wiley.

Sarason, Irwin G.; Sarason, Barbara R.; Pierce, Gregory R.; Shearin, Edward N.; & Sayers, Merlin H. (1991). A social learning approach to increasing blood donations. *Journal of Applied Social Psychology, 21,* 896–918.

Sargent, Marilyn. (1993). *Depressive illnesses: Treatments bring new hope*. Rockville, Md.: National Institute of Mental Health (NIH Publication No. 93-3612).

Saufley, W. H.; Otaka, S. R.; & Bavaresco, J. L. (1985). Context effects: Classroom tests and context independence. *Memory and Cognition, 13,* 522–528.

Savage-Rumbaugh, E. Sue. (1993). Language learnability in man, ape, and dolphin. In Herbert L. Roitblat, Louis M. Herman, & Paul E. Nachtigall (Eds.), *Language and communication: Comparative perspectives*. Hillsdale, N.J.: Erlbaum.

Savage-Rumbaugh, E. Sue, & Lewin, Roger. (1994, September). Ape at the brink. *Discover, 15,* 91–98.

Savin-Williams, Ritch C.; & Berndt, Thomas J. (1990). Friendship and peer relations. In S. Shirley Feldman & Glen R. Elliott (Eds.), *At the threshold: The developing adolescent*. Cambridge, Mass.: Harvard University Press.

Saxe, Glenn N.; Chinman, Gary; Berkowitz, Robert; Hall, Kathryn; Lieberg, Gabriele; Schwartz, Jane; & van der Kolk, Bessel A. (1994). Somatization in patients with dissociative disorders. *American Journal of Psychiatry, 151,* 1329–1334.

Saxe, Glenn N.; van der Kolk, Bessel A.; Berkowitz, Robert; Chinman, Gary; Hall, Kathryn; Lieberg, Gabriele; & Schwartz, Jane. (1993). Dissociative disorders in psychiatric inpatients. *American Journal of Psychiatry, 150,* 1037–1042.

Scanlon, Matthew, & Mauro, James. (1992, November/December). The lowdown on handwriting analysis: Is it for real? *Psychology Today, 25,* 46–53.

Scarr, Sandra. (1984, May). PT conversation: What's a parent to do? *Psychology Today, 18,* 59–63.

Scarr, Sandra. (1992). Developmental theories for the 1990s: Development and individual differences. *Child Development, 63,* 1–19.

Scarr, Sandra, & Eisenberg, Marlene. (1993). Child care research: Issues, perspectives, and results. *Annual Review of Psychology, 44,* 613–644.

Scarr, Sandra, & Weinberg, Richard A. (1976). IQ test performance of black children adopted by white families. *American Psychologist, 31,* 726–739.

Schachter, Stanley. (1971a). *Emotion, obesity, and crime*. New York: Academic.

Schachter, Stanley. (1971b). Some extraordinary facts about obese humans and rats. *American Psychologist, 26,* 129–144.

Schachter, Stanley, & Singer, Jerome E. (1962). Cognitive, social, and physiological determinants of emotional state. *Psychological Review, 69,* 379–399.

Schacter, Daniel L. (1995a). Consciousness: Introduction. In Michael S. Gazzaniga (Ed.), *The cognitive neurosciences*. Cambridge, Mass.: MIT Press.

Schacter, Daniel L. (1995b, April). Memory wars. *Scientific American, 272,* 135–139.

Schacter, Daniel L., & Moscovitch, Morris. (1984). Infants, amnesics, and dissociable memory systems. In Morris Moscovitch (Ed.), *Infant memory*. New York: Plenum Press.

Schaie, K. Warner. (1994). The course of adult intellectual development. *American Psychologist, 49,* 304–313.

Schaie, K. Warner. (1995a). Brain-astics: Mind exercises to keep you sharp. *New Choices in Retirement Living, 35,* 22–28.

Schaie, K. Warner. (1995b). *Intellectual development in adulthood: The Seattle Longitudinal Study*. New York: Cambridge University Press.

Schaie, K. Warner, & Willis, Sherry L. (1986). Can decline in adult intellectual functioning be reversed? *Developmental Psychology, 22,* 223–232.

Schaie, K. Warner, & Willis, Sherry L. (1996). *Adult development and aging* (4th ed.). New York: HarperCollins.

Schaller, Mark, & Cialdini, Robert B. (1990). Happiness, sadness, and helping: A motivational integration. In Richard M. Sorrentino & E. Tory Higgins (Eds.), *Handbook of motivation and cognition: Vol. 2. Foundations of social behavior*. New York: Guilford Press.

Schanberg, Saul M., & Field, Tiffany M. (1987). Sensory deprivation stress and supplemental stimulation in the rat pup and preterm human neonate. *Child Development, 58,* 1431–1447.

Schank, Robert C. (1988). Creativity as a mechanical process. In Robert J. Sternberg (Ed.), *The nature of creativity*. New York: Cambridge University Press.

Schattschneider, Doris. (1990). *Visions of symmetry: Notebooks, periodic drawings, and related work of M. C. Escher*. New York: Freeman. Page 169. Notes on page 301.

Schatzman, Morton, & Fenwick, Peter. (1994). Dreams and dreaming. In Rosemary Cooper (Ed.), *Sleep*. New York: Chapman & Hall.

Scheibel, Arnold B. (1994, July). Quoted in Daniel Golden, Building a better brain. *Life*, p. 66.

Scherer, Klaus R., & Wallbott, Harald G. (1994). Evidence for universality and cultural variation of differential emotion response patterning. *Journal of Personality and Social Psychology, 66,* 310–328.

Schiffman, Susan S. (1983). Taste and smell in disease. *New England Journal of Medicine, 308,* 1275–1279, 1337–1343.

Schindler, R. A., & Merzenich, M. M. (Eds.). (1985). *Cochlear implants*. New York: Raven.

Schlenker, Barry R., & Weigold, Michael F. (1992). Interpersonal processes involving impression regulation and management. *Annual Review of Psychology, 43,* 133–168.

Schlenker, Barry R.; Weigold, Michael F.; & Hallam, J. R. (1990). Self-serving attributions in social context: Effects of self-esteem and social pressure. *Journal of Personality and Social Psychology, 58,* 855–863.

Schmidt, Frank L. (1992). What do data really mean? Research findings, meta-analysis, and cumulative knowledge in psychology. *American Psychologist, 47,* 1173–1181.

Schneider, Allen M., & Tarshis, Barry. (1995). *Elements of physiological psychology*. New York: McGraw-Hill.

Schneider, David J. (1993). Mental control: Lessons from our past. In Daniel M. Wegner & James W. Pennebaker (Eds.), *Handbook of mental control*. Englewood Cliffs, N.J.: Prentice Hall.

Schooler, Jonathan W.; Ohlsson, Stellan; & Brooks, Kevin. (1993). Thoughts beyond words: When language overshadows insight. *Journal of Experimental Psychology: General, 122,* 166–183.

Schulz, R., & Schlarb, J. (1987–1988). Two decades of research on dying: What do we know about the patient? *Omega, 18,* 299–317.

Schuman, Marjorie. (1980). The psychophysiological model of meditation and altered states of consciousness: A critical review. In Julian M. Davidson & Richard J. Davidson (Eds.), *The psychobiology of consciousness*. New York: Plenum.

Schwartz, Arthur, & Schwartz, Ruth M. (1993). *Depression: Theories and treatments: Psychological, biological, and social perspectives*. New York: Columbia University Press.

Schwartz, James H. (1995a). Neurotransmitters. In Eric R. Kandel, James H. Schwartz, & Thomas M. Jessell (Eds.), *Essentials of neural science and behavior*. Norwalk, Conn.: Appleton & Lange.

Schwartz, James H. (1995b). The neuron. In Eric R. Kandel, James H. Schwartz, & Thomas M. Jessell (Eds.), *Essentials of neural science and behavior*. Norwalk, Conn.: Appleton & Lange.

Schwartz, Jeffrey M.; Stoessel, Paula W.; & Phelps, Michael E. (1996). Systematic changes in cerebral glucose metabolic rate after successful behavior modification treatment of obsessive-compulsive disorder. *Archives of General Psychiatry, 53,* 109–117.

Schwartz, Mark S., & Schwartz, Nancy M. (1993). Biofeedback: Using the body's signals. In Daniel Goleman & Joel Gurin (Eds.), *Mind/body medicine: How to use your mind for better health*. Yonkers, N.Y.: Consumer Reports Books.

Schwartz, Richard S. (1991). Mood brighteners, affect tolerance, and the blues. *Psychiatry, 54,* 397–403.

Schwarzer, Rolf, & Leppin, Anja. (1992). Possible impact of social ties and support on morbidity and mortality. In Hans O. F. Veiel & Urs Baumann (Eds.), *The meaning and measurement of social support*. New York: Hemisphere.

Scott, Allene J. (1994). Chronobiological considerations in shiftworker sleep and performance and shiftwork scheduling. *Human Performance, 7* (3), 207-233.

Seachrist, Lisa. (1995, December 9). Testing genes: Physicians wrestle with the information that genetic tests provide. *Science News, 148* (24), 394–395.

Sedikides, Constantine, & Anderson, Craig A. (1994). Causal perceptions of intertrait relations: The glue that holds person types together. *Personality and Social Psychology Bulletin, 20,* 294–302.

Seeman, Mary V. (Ed.). (1995). *Gender and psychopathology*. Washington, D.C.: American Psychiatric Press.

Segall, Marshall H. (1994). A cross-cultural research contribution to unraveling the nativist/empiricist controversy. In Walter J. Lonner & Roy Malpass (Eds.), *Psychology and culture*. Boston: Allyn & Bacon.

Segall, Marshall H.; Campbell, Donald T.; & Herskovits, Melville J. (1963). Cultural differences in the perception of geometric illusions. *Science, 193,* 769–771.

Segall, Marshall H.; Campbell, Donald T.; & Herskovits, Melville J. (1966). *The influence of culture on visual perception*. Indianapolis: Bobbs-Merrill

Seidman, Stuart N., & Rieder, Ronald O. (1994). A review of sexual behavior in the United States. *American Journal of Psychiatry, 151,* 330–341.

Sekuler, Robert, & Blake, Randolph. (1994). *Perception* (3rd ed.). New York: McGraw-Hill.

Seligman, Martin E. P. (1970). On the generality of the laws of learning. *Psychological Review, 77,* 406–418.

Seligman, Martin E. P. (1971). Phobias and preparedness. *Behavior Therapy, 2,* 307–320.

Seligman, Martin E. P. (1990). *Learned optimism*. New York: Knopf.

Seligman, Martin E. P. (1992). *Helplessness: On development, depression, and death*. New York: Freeman.

Seligman, Martin E. P. (1995). The effectiveness of psychotherapy: The *Consumer Reports* study. *American Psychologist, 50,* 965–974.

Seligman, Martin E. P., & Maier, Steven F. (1967). Failure to escape traumatic shock. *Journal of Experimental Psychology, 37B,* 1–21.

Selye, Hans. (1956). *The stress of life*. New York: McGraw-Hill.

Selye, Hans. (1976). *The stress of life* (rev. ed.). New York: McGraw-Hill.

Seta, John J., & Seta, Catherine E. (1993). Stereotypes and the generation of compensatory and noncompensatory expectancies of group members. *Personality and Social Psychology Bulletin, 19,* 722–731.

Shakin, M.; Shakin, D.; & Sternglanz, S. H. (1985). Infant clothing: Sex labeling for strangers. *Sex Roles, 12,* 955–964.

Shanahan, T. L., & Czeisler, Charles A. (1991). Light exposure induces equivalent phase shifts of the endogenous circadian rhythms of circulating plasma melatonin and core body temperature in men. *The Journal of Clinical Endocrinology and Metabolism, 73* (2), 227–234.

Shapiro, Johnna K. (1995). Dr. Kohlberg goes to Washington: Using congressional debates to teach moral development. *Teaching of Psychology, 22* (4), 245–247.

Shapiro, K. L. (1991, July). Use morality as basis for animal treatment. *APA Monitor*, p. 5.

Sharan, Pratap; Chaudhary, Geeta; Kavathekar, Surabhi A.; & Saxena, Shekhar. (1996). Preliminary report of psychiatric disorders in survivors of a severe earthquake. *American Journal of Psychiatry, 153,* 556–558.

Shatz, Carla J. (1992, September). The developing brain. *Scientific American, 267,* 34–41.

Shaywitz, Bennett A.; Shaywitz, Sally E.; & Gore, J. C. (1995, February 16). Sex differences in the functional organization of the brain for language. *Nature, 373,* 607–615.

Shedler, Jonathan; Mayman, Martin; & Manis, Melvin. (1993). The *illusion* of mental health. *American Psychologist, 48,* 1117–1131.

Sheingold, Karen, & Tenney, Yvette J. (1982). Memory for a salient childhood event. In Ulric Neisser (Ed.), *Memory observed: Remembering in natural contexts*. San Francisco: Freeman.

Shepard, Michael; Watt, David; Falloon, Ian; & Smeeton, Nigel. (1989). The natural history of schizophrenia: A five-year follow-up study of outcome and prediction in a representative sample of schizophrenics. *Psychological Medicine, 19* (Monograph Supplement 15), 1–46.

Shepard, Roger N. (1990). *Mind sights: Original visual illusions, ambiguities, and other anomalies, with a commentary on the play of mind in perception and art*. New York: Freeman.

Sherif, Muzafer. (1956, November). Experiments in group conflict. *Scientific American, 195,* 33–47.

Sherif, Muzafer. (1966). *In common predicament: Social psychology of intergroup conflict and cooperation*. Boston: Houghton Mifflin.

Sherif, Muzafer; Harvey, O. J.; White, B. Jack; Hood, William R.; & Sherif, Carolyn W. (1961/1988). *The Robbers Cave experiment: Intergroup conflict and cooperation*. Middletown, Conn.: Wesleyan University Press.

Shields, Stephanie A. (1987). Women, men, and the dilemma of emotion. In Phillip Shaver & Clyde Hendrick (Eds.), *Sex and gender: Review of personality and social psychology*. Newbury Park, Calif.: Sage Publications.

Shiffman, Saul; Paty, Jean A.; Gnys, Maryann; Kassel, John D.; & Elash, Celeste. (1995). Nicotine withdrawal in chippers and regular smokers: Subjective and cognitive effects. *Health Psychology, 14,* 301–309.

Shiffrin, Richard M., & Nosofsky, Robert M. (1994). Seven plus or minus two: A commentary on capacity limitations. *Psychological Review, 101,* 357–361.

Shimamura, Arthur P. (1995). Memory and frontal lobe function. In Michael S. Gazzaniga (Ed.), *The cognitive neurosciences.* Cambridge, Mass.: MIT Press.

Shneidman, Edwin. (1985). *Definition of suicide.* New York: Wiley.

Shneidman, Edwin S. (1987). A psychological approach to suicide. In Gary R. VanderBos & Brenda K. Bryant (Eds.), *Cataclysms, crises, and catastrophes: Psychology in action.* Washington, D.C.: American Psychological Association.

Shotland, R. Lance, & Straw, Margret K. (1976). Bystander response to an assault: When a man attacks a woman. *Journal of Personality and Social Psychology, 34,* 990–999.

Shou, Mogens. (1993). *Lithium treatment of manic-depressive illness: A practical guide.* (5th ed.). Basel, Switzerland: Karger.

Shtasel, Derri L.; Gur, Raquel E.; Gallacher, Fiona; Heimberg, Carolyn; Cannon, Tyrone; & Gur, Ruben C. (1992). Phenomenology and functioning in first-episode schizophrenia. *Schizophrenia Bulletin, 18,* 449–462.

Shulman, Ian D.; Cox, Brian J.; Swinson, Richard P.; Kuch, Klaus; & Reichman, Jaak T. (1994). Precipitating events, locations and reactions associated with initial unexpected panic attacks. *Behaviour Research and Therapy, 32,* 17–20.

Shulman, Michael, & Mekler, Eva. (1985). *Bringing up a moral child: A new approach for teaching your child to be kind, just, and responsible.* Reading, Mass.: Addison-Wesley.

Shumaker, Sally A., & Hill, D. Robin. (1991). Gender differences in social support and physical health. *Health Psychology, 10,* 102–111.

Shuval, Judith T. (1993). Migration and stress. In Leo Goldberger & Shlomo Breznitz (Eds.), *Handbook of stress: Theoretical and clinical aspects* (2nd ed.). New York: Free Press.

Shweder, Richard A., & Haidt, Jonathan. (1993). The future of moral psychology: Truth, intuition, and the pluralist way. *Psychological Science, 4,* 360–365.

Shweder, Richard A.; Mahapatra, Manamohan; & Miller, Joan G. (1990). Culture and moral development. In James W. Stigler, Richard A. Shweder, & Gilbert Herdt (Eds.), *Cultural psychology.* New York: Cambridge University Press.

Siegal, Michael. (1991). *Knowing children: Experiments in conversation and cognition.* Hillsdale, N.J.: Erlbaum.

Siegler, Robert S. (1983). Information processing approaches to cognitive development. In Paul H. Mussen & W. Kessen (Eds.), *Handbook of child psychology: Vol. I: History, theory, and methods* (4th ed.). New York: Wiley.

Siegler, Robert S. (1989). Mechanisms of cognitive development. *Annual Review of Psychology, 40,* 353–379.

Siegler, Robert S. (1991). *Children's thinking* (2nd ed.). Englewood Cliffs, N.J.: Prentice Hall.

Siegler, Robert S. (1992). The other Alfred Binet. *Developmental Psychology, 28,* 179–190.

Siegler, Robert S., & Ellis, Shari. (1996). Piaget on childhood. *Psychological Science, 7,* 211–215.

Silbersweig, David A.; Stern, Emily; & Frackowaik, R. S. J. (1995, November 9). A functional neuroanatomy of hallucinations in schizophrenia. *Nature, 387,* 176–184.

Silva, Christopher E., & Kirsch, Irving. (1992). Interpretive sets, expectancy, fantasy proneness, and dissociation as predictors of hypnotic response. *Journal of Personality and Social Psychology, 63,* 847–856.

Silverman, Irwin, & Eals, Marion. (1996, August). Quoted in: Azar, Beth. "Why men lose keys—and women find them." *APA Monitor, 27,* (8), 32.

Simon, Allie; Worthen, David M.; & Mitas, John A. (1979). An evaluation of iridology. *Journal of the American Medical Association, 242* (13), 1385–1389.

Simon, Bernd; Pantaleo, Giuseppe; & Mummendey, Amelie. (1995). Unique individual or interchangeable group member? The accentuation of intragroup differences versus similarities as an indicator of the individual self versus the collective self. *Journal of Personality and Social Psychology, 69,* 106–119.

Sinclair, Robert C.; Hoffman, Curt; Mark, Melvin M.; Martin, Leonard L.; & Pickering, Tracie L. (1994). Construct accessibility and the misattribution of arousal: Schachter and Singer revisited. *Psychological Science, 5,* 15–19.

Singer, Barry, & Benassi, Victor A. (1981, January/February). Occult beliefs. *American Scientist, 69,* 49–55.

Singer, Peter. (1990). *Animal liberation* (2nd ed.) New York: New York Review of Books.

Sivacek, John, & Crano, William D. (1982). Vested interest as a moderator of attitude–behavior consistency. *Journal of Personality and Social Psychology, 43,* 210–221.

Sivak, M.; Olson, P. L.; & Pastalan, L. A. (1981). Effect of driver's age on nighttime legibility of highway signs. *Human Factors, 23,* 59–64.

Skinner, B. F. (1935). Two types of conditioned reflex and a pseudo type. *Journal of General Psychology, 12,* 66–77.

Skinner, B. F. (1938). *The behavior of organisms: An experimental analysis.* New York: Appleton-Century-Crofts.

Skinner, B. F. (1948). *Walden Two.* New York: Macmillan.

Skinner, B. F. (1948/1992). Superstition in the pigeon. *Journal of Experimental Psychology: General, 121,* 273–274.

Skinner, B. F. (1953). *Science and human behavior.* New York: Macmillan.

Skinner, B. F. (1954). A critique of psychoanalytic concepts and theories. *Scientific Monthly, 79,* 300–305.

Skinner, B. F. (1956). A case history in scientific method. *American Psychologist, 11,* 221–233.

Skinner, B. F. (1961, November). Teaching machines. *Scientific American, 205,* 90–102.

Skinner, B. F. (1967). B. F. Skinner . . . An Autobiography. In E. G. Boring & G. Lindzey (Eds.), *A history of psychology in autobiography* (Vol. 5). New York: Appleton-Century-Crofts.

Skinner, B. F. (1971). *Beyond freedom and dignity.* New York: Bantam.

Skinner, B. F. (1974). *About behaviorism.* New York: Knopf.

Skinner, B. F. (1987). Whatever happened to psychology as the science of behavior? *American Psychologist, 42,* 780–786.

Slamecka, Norman J. (1992). Forgetting. In Larry R. Squire (Ed.), *Encyclopedia of learning and memory.* New York: Macmillan.

Sleek, Scott. (1994, April). Could Prozac replace demand for therapy? *APA Monitor,* p. 28.

Sleek, Scott. (1995, February). Prozac under new scrutiny by researchers, practitioners. *APA Monitor,* p. 31.

Sloane, Martin C. (1981). A comparison of hypnosis vs. waking state and visual vs. nonvisual recall instructions for witnesses/victims memory retrieval in actual major crimes. Florida State University Ph.D. thesis. *Dissertation Abstracts International, 42,* 6, 2551-B. University Microfilms No. 8125873.

Smetana, Judith G., & Asquith, P. (1994). Adolescents' and parents' conceptions of parental authority and personal autonomy. *Child Development, 65,* 1147–1162.

Smith, Barbara A.; Fillion, Thomas J.; & Blass, Elliott M. (1990). Orally mediated sources of calming in 1- to 3-day-old human infants. *Developmental Psychology, 26,* 731–737.

Smith, Carlyle, & Lapp, Lorelei. (1991). Increases in numbers of REMs and REM density in humans following an intensive learning period. *Sleep, 14* (4), 325–330.

Smith, David E., & Seymour, Richard B. (1994). LSD: History and toxicity. *Psychiatric Annals, 24*, 145–147.

Smith, Eliot R. (1993). Social identity and social emotions: Toward new conceptualizations of prejudice. In Diane M. Mackie & David L. Hamilton (Eds.), *Affect, cognition, and stereotyping: Interactive processes in group perception.* San Diego: Academic Press.

Smith, Marilyn C. (1983). Hypnotic memory enhancement of witnesses: Does it work? *Psychological Bulletin, 94* (3), 387–407.

Smith, Randolph A. (1995). *Challenging your preconceptions: Thinking critically about psychology.* Pacific Grove, Calif.: Brooks/Cole.

Smith, S. M.; Glenberg, A. M.; & Bjork, R. A. (1978). Environmental context and human memory. *Memory and Cognition, 6*, 342–355.

Smith, Timothy W. (1992). Hostility and health: Current status of a psychosomatic hypothesis. *Health Psychology, 11*, 139–150.

Smyer, Michael A.; Balster, Robert L.; Egli, Dan; Johnson, Dale L.; Kilbey, M. Marlyne; Leith, Nancy J.; & Puente, Antonio E. (1993). Summary of the report of the ad hoc task force on psychopharmacology of the American Psychological Association. *Professional Psychology: Research and Practice, 24*, 394–403.

Snyder, R. A.; Verderber, K.; Langmeyer, L.; & Myers, M. (1992). A reconsideration of self- and organization-referent attitudes as "causes" of the glass ceiling effect. *Groups and Organization Management, 17*, 260–278.

Snyder, Solomon H. (1984). Drug and neurotransmitter receptors in the brain. *Science, 224*, 22–31.

Snyder, Solomon H. (1986). *Drugs and the brain.* New York: Scientific American Books.

Snyder, Solomon H. (1990, August 9). Planning for serendipity. *Nature, 346*, 508.

Snyderman, Mark, & Rothman, Stanley. (1987). Survey of expert opinion on intelligence and aptitude testing. *American Psychologist, 42*, 137–144.

Snyderman, Mark, & Rothman, Stanley. (1988). *The IQ controversy, the media, and public policy.* New Brunswick, N.J.: Transaction Books.

Soares, Joaquim J. F., & Ohman, Arne. (1993). Preattentive processing, preparedness and phobias: Effects of instruction on conditioned electrodermal responses to masked and non-masked fear-relevant stimuli. *Behaviour Research and Therapy, 31*, 87–95.

Solomon, George F.; Amkraut, Alfred A.; & Rubin, Robert T. (1985). Stress, hormones, neuroregulation, and immunity. In Susan R. Birchfield (Ed.), *Stress: Psychological and physiological interactions.* Washington, D.C.: Hemisphere.

Solomon, Henry; Solomon, Linda Zener; Arnone, Maria M.; Maur, Bonnie J.; Reda, Rosina M.; & Roth, Esther O. (1981). Anonymity and helping. *Journal of Social Psychology, 113*, 37–43.

Solomon, Linda Zener; Solomon, Henry; & Stone, Ronald. (1978). Helping as a function of number of bystanders and ambiguity of emergency. *Personality and Social Psychology Bulletin, 4*, 318–321.

Solso, Robert L. (1991). *Cognitive psychology* (3rd ed.). Boston: Allyn & Bacon.

Spangler, William D. (1992). Validity of questionnaire and TAT measures of need for achievement: Two meta-analyses. *Psychological Bulletin, 112*, 140–154.

Spanos, Nicholas P. (1986). Hypnotic behavior: A social-psychological interpretation of amnesia, analgesia, and "trance logic." *The Behavioral and Brain Sciences, 9*, 449–502.

Spanos, Nicholas P. (1987–1988, Winter). Past–life hypnotic regression: A critical view. *Skeptical Inquirer, 12*, 174–180.

Spanos, Nicholas P. (1989). Hypnosis, demonic possession, and multiple personality: Strategic enactments and disavowals of responsibility for actions. In Colleen A. Ward (Ed.), *Altered states of consciousness and mental health: A cross-cultural perspective.* Newbury Park, Calif.: Sage.

Spanos, Nicholas P. (1994). Multiple identity enactments and multiple personality disorder: A sociocognitive perspective. *Psychological Bulletin, 116*, 143–165.

Spanos, Nicholas P.; Brett, P. J.; Menary, E. P.; & Cross, W. P. (1987). A measure of attitudes toward hypnosis: Relationships with absorption and hypnotic susceptibility. *American Journal of Clinical Hypnosis, 30*, 139–150.

Spanos, Nicholas P.; Burnley, Caroline E.; & Cross, Patricia A. (1993). Response expectancies and interpretations as determinants of hypnotic responding. *Journal of Personality and Social Psychology, 65*, 1237–1242.

Spanos, Nicholas P.; Williams, V.; & Gwynn, M. I. (1990). Effects of hypnotic, placebo, and salicylic acid treatments on wart regression. *Psychosomatic Medicine, 52* (1), 109–114.

Spearman, Charles E. (1904). "General intelligence" objectively determined and measured. *American Journal of Psychology, 15*, 201–293.

Spence, Janet T., & Buckner, Camille. (1995). Masculinity and femininity: Defining the undefinable. In Pamela J. Kalbfleisch & Michael J. Cody (Eds.), *Gender, power, and communication in human relationships.* Hillsdale, N.J.: Erlbaum.

Spence, Sean A. (1993). Nintendo hallucinations: A new phenomenological entity. *Irish Journal of Psychological Medicine, 10*, 98–99.

Sperling, George. (1960). The information available in brief visual presentations. *Psychological Monographs, 74* (Whole No. 48).

Sperry, Roger W. (1982). Some effects of disconnecting the cerebral hemispheres. *Science, 217*, 1223–1226.

Sperry, Roger W. (1995). The future of psychology. *American Psychologist, 50*, 505 506.

Spiegel, David. (1993a). Dissociation and trauma. In David Spiegel (Ed.), *Dissociative disorders: A clinical review.* Lutherville, Md.: Sidran.

Spiegel, David. (1993b). Social support: How friends, family, and groups can help. In Daniel Goleman & Joel Gurin (Eds.), *Mind/body medicine: How to use your mind for better health.* Yonkers, N.Y.: Consumer Reports Books.

Spiegel, David; Bloom, J. R.; Kraemer, H. C.; & Gottheil, E. (1989). Effect of psychosocial treatment on survival of patients with metastatic breast cancer. *Lancet, 2*, 888–891.

Spiegel, David, & Cardeña, Etzel. (1991). Disintegrated experience: The dissociative disorders revisited. *Journal of Abnormal Psychology, 100*, 366–378.

Spielberger, Charles D., & Starr, Laura M. (1994). Curiosity and exploratory behavior. In Harold F. O'Neil, Jr., & Michael Drillings (Eds.), *Motivation: Theory and research.* Hillsdale, N.J.: Erlbaum.

Spielman, Arthur J., & Glovinsky, Paul B. (1991). Psychology and sleep: The interdependence of sleep and waking states. In Michael J. Thorpy & Jan Yager (Eds.), *The encyclopedia of sleep and sleep disorders.* New York: Facts on File.

Spira, James L., & Spiegel, David. (1992). Hypnosis and related techniques in pain management. In Dennis C. Turk & Caryn S. Feldman (Eds.), *Noninvasive approaches to pain management in the terminally ill.* New York: Haworth Press.

Spirduso, Waneen W., & MacRae, Priscilla Gilliam. (1990). Motor performance and aging. In James E. Birren & K. Warren Schaie (Eds.), *Handbook of the psychology of aging* (3rd ed.). New York: Academic Press.

Spiro, Rand J. (1980). Accommodative reconstruction in prose recall. *Journal of Verbal Learning and Verbal Behavior, 19,* 84–95.

Spitzer, L., & Rodin, J. (1981). Human eating behavior: A critical review of studies in normal weight and overweight individuals. *Appetite: Journal for Intake Research, 2,* 293–329.

Spitzer, Manfred. (1992). The phenomenology of delusions. *Psychiatric Annals, 22,* 252–259.

Spock, Benjamin, & Rothenberg, Michael B. (1985). *Dr. Spock's baby and child care* (rev. and updated ed.) New York: Simon & Schuster/Pocket Books.

Springer, Sally P., & Deutsch, Georg. (1993). *Left brain, right brain.* (4th ed.). New York: Freeman.

Squire, Larry R. (1987). *Memory and the brain.* New York: Oxford University Press.

Squire, Larry R., & Butters, Nelson. (1992). *Neuropsychology of memory.* New York: Guilford Press.

Squire, Larry R., & Knowlton, Barbara J. (1995). Memory, hippocampus, and brain systems. In Michael S. Gazzaniga (Ed.), *The cognitive neurosciences.* Cambridge, Mass.: MIT Press.

Squire, Larry R.; Knowlton, Barbara J.; & Musen, G. (1993). The structure and organization of memory. *Annual Review of Psychology, 44,* 453–495.

Squire, Larry R.; Ojemann, J. G.; Miezin, F. M.; Petersen, S. E.; Videen, T. O.; & Raichle, Marcus E. (1992). Activation of the hippocampus in normal humans: A functional anatomical study of memory. *Proceedings of the National Academy of Sciences, 89,* 1837–1841.

Sroufe, Alan. (1995, September). Quoted in Beth Azar, The bond between mother and child. *APA Monitor, 26* (9), 28.

Stacy, Alan W.; Widaman, Keith F.; & Marlatt, G. Alan. (1990). Expectancy models of alcohol use. *Journal of Personality and Social Psychology, 58,* 918–928.

Staddon, J. E. R. (1988). Learning as inference. In Robert C. Bolles & Michael D. Beecher (Eds.), *Evolution and learning.* Hillsdale, N.J.: Erlbaum.

Stafford, Laura, & Dainton, Marianne. (1994). The dark side of "normal" family interaction. In William R. Cupach & Brian H. Spitzberg (Eds.), *The dark side of inter-personal communication.* Hillside, N.J.: Erlbaum.

Stake, Jayne E., & Oliver, Joan. (1991). Sexual contact and touching between therapist and client: A survey of psychologists' attitudes and behavior. *Professional Psychology: Research and Practice, 22,* 297–307.

Stangor, Charles. (1995). Content and application inaccuracy in social stereotyping. In Yueh-Ting Lee, Lee J. Jussim, & Clark R. McCauley (Eds.), *Stereotype accuracy: Toward appreciating group differences.* Washington, D.C.: American Psychological Association.

Stangor, Charles, & Lange, James E. (1994). Mental representations of social groups: Advances in understanding stereotypes and stereotyping. In Mark P. Zanna (Ed.), *Advances in experimental social psychology* (Vol. 26). San Diego: Academic Press.

Stangor, Charles, & Ruble, Diane N. (1987). Development of gender role knowledge and gender constancy. In Lynn S. Liben & Margaret L. Signorella (Eds.), *Children's gender schemata.* New Directions for Child Development Series No. 38. San Francisco: Jossey-Bass.

Stanton, Annette L., & Snider, Pamela R. (1993). Coping with a breast cancer diagnosis: A prospective study. *Health Psychology, 12,* 16–23.

Stanton, H. E. (1989). Using rapid change techniques to improve sporting performance. *Australian Journal of Clinical & Experimental Hypnosis, 17* (2), 153–161.

Staub, Ervin. (1978). *Positive social behavior and morality: Social and personal influences* (Vol. 1). New York: Academic Press.

Staub, Ervin. (1996). Cultural-societal roots of violence: The examples of genocidal violence and of contemporary youth violence in the United States. *American Psychologist, 51,* 117–132.

Staw, B. M., & Ross, J. (1985). Stability in the midst of change: A dispositional approach to job attitudes. *Journal of Applied Psychology, 70,* 469–480.

Steblay, Nancy Mehrkens. (1987). Helping behavior in urban and rural environments: A meta-analysis. *Psychological Bulletin, 102,* 346–356.

Steele, Claude M. (1986, January). What happens when you drink too much? *Psychology Today, 20,* 48–52.

Steele, Claude M. (1995, November 6). Quoted in Connie Leslie, You can't high-jump if the bar is set low. *Newsweek,* pp. 82–84.

Steele, Claude M., & Aronson, Joshua. (1995). Stereotype threat and the intellectual performance of African Americans. *Journal of Personality and Social Psychology, 69,* 797–811.

Steele, Claude M., & Josephs, Robert A. (1990). Alcohol myopia: Its prized and dangerous effects. *American Psychologist, 45,* 921–933.

Stein, Barry E.; Wallace, Mark T.; & Meredith, M. Alex. (1995). Neural mechanisms mediating attention and orientation to multisensory cues. In Michael S. Gazzaniga (Ed.), *The cognitive neurosciences.* Cambridge, Mass.: MIT Press.

Stein, Marvin, & Miller, Andrew H. (1993). Stress, the immune system, and health and illness. In Leo Goldberger & Shlomo Breznitz (Eds.), *Handbook of stress: Theoretical and clinical aspects.* New York: Free Press.

Steinberg, Laurence. (1990). Autonomy, conflict, and harmony in the family relationship. In S. Shirley Feldman & Glen R. Elliott (Eds.), *At the threshold: The developing adolescent.* Cambridge, Mass.: Harvard University Press.

Steinberg, Laurence; Darling, Nancy E.; Fletcher, Anne C; Brown, Bradford B.; & Dornbusch, Sanford M. (1995). Authoritative parenting and adolescent adjustment: An ecological journey. In Phyllis Moen, Glen H. Elder, Jr., & Kurt Luscher (Eds.), *Examining lives in context: Perspectives on the ecology of human development.* Washington, D.C.: American Psychological Association.

Steinhausen, Hans-Christoph. (1994). Anorexia and bulimia nervosa. In Michael Rutter, Eric Taylor, & Lionel Hersov (Eds.), *Child and adolescent psychiatry: Modern approaches.* Boston: Blackwell Scientific Publications.

Steinhausen, Hans-Christoph, & Seidel, R. (1993). Correspondence between the clinical assessment of eating-disordered patients and findings derived from questionnaires at follow-up. *International Journal of Eating Disorders, 14,* 367–379.

Steinhausen, Hans-Christoph, & Vollrath, M. (1993). The self-image of adolescent patients with eating disorders. *International Journal of Eating Disorders, 13,* 221–229.

Stelmack, Robert M. (1990). Biological bases of extraversion—psychophysiological evidence. *Journal of Personality, 58,* 293–311.

Stelmack, Robert M., & Geen, R. G. (1992). The psychophysiology of extraversion. In A. Gale & M. W. Eysenck (Eds.), *Handbook of individual differences: Biological perspectives.* New York: Wiley.

Stelmack, Robert M.; Houlihan, Michael; & McGarry-Roberts, Patricia A. (1993). Personality, reaction time, and event-related potentials. *Journal of Personality and Social Psychology, 65,* 399–409.

Stenberg, C. R., & Campos, J. J. (1990). The development of anger expressions in infancy. In Nancy Stein, Bennett Leventhal, & Tom Trabasso (Eds.), *Psychological and biological approaches to emotion.* Hillsdale, N.J.: Erlbaum.

Stepper, Sabine, & Strack, Fritz. (1993). Proprioceptive determinants of emotional and nonemotional feelings. *Journal of Personality and Social Psychology, 64,* 211–220.

Stern, Marilyn, & Karraker, Katherine Hildebrandt. (1989). Sex stereotyping of infants: A review of gender labelling studies. *Sex Roles, 20,* 501–522.

Stern, Yaakov; Alexander, Gene E.; & Prohovnik, Isak. (1992). Inverse relationship between education and parietotemporal perfusion deficit in Alzheimer's disease. *Annals of Neurology, 32,* 371–377.

Stern, Yaakov; Gurland, B.; & Tatemichi, T.K. (1994, April 6). Influence of education and occupation on the incidence of Alzheimer's disease. *Journal of the American Medical Association, 271* (13), 1004–1007.

Sternberg, Robert J. (1982). Lies we live by: Misapplication of tests in identifying the gifted. *Gifted Child Quarterly, 26,* 157–161.

Sternberg, Robert J. (1985). *Beyond IQ: A triarchic theory of human intelligence.* New York: Cambridge University Press.

Sternberg, Robert J. (1986). *Intelligence applied: Understanding and increasing your intellectual skills.* San Diego: Harcourt Brace Jovanovich.

Sternberg, Robert J. (1988a). *The triarchic mind: A new theory of human intelligence.* New York: Viking.

Sternberg, Robert J. (1988b). A three-facet model of creativity. In Robert J. Sternberg (Ed.), *The nature of creativity.* New York: Cambridge University Press.

Sternberg, Robert J. (1990). *Metaphors of mind: Conceptions of the nature of intelligence.* New York: Cambridge University Press.

Sternberg, Robert J. (1991). Theory-based testing of intellectual abilities: Rationale for the Triarchic Abilities Test. In Helga A. H. Rowe (Ed.), *Intelligence: Reconceptualization and measurement.* Hillsdale, N.J.: Erlbaum.

Sternberg, Robert J. (1995). For whom the bell curve tolls: A review of *The Bell Curve. Psychological Science, 6,* 257–261.

Stevens, A. (1983). *Archetypes.* New York: Quill.

Stevens, Albert, & Coupe, Patty. (1978). Distortions in judged spatial relations. *Cognitive Psychology, 10,* 422–437.

Stevens, Gwendolyn, & Gardner, Sheldon. (1982). *The women of psychology: Volume I. Pioneers and innovators.* Cambridge, Mass.: Schenkman.

Stevenson, Harold W., & Lee, Shin-Ying. (1990). Contexts of achievement: A study of American, Chinese, and Japanese children. *Monographs of the Society for Research in Child Development, 55* (Serial No. 221, Nos. 1–2).

Stevenson, Harold W.; Lee, Shin-Ying; & Stigler, James W. (1986). Mathematics achievements of Chinese, Japanese, and American children. *Science, 236,* 693–698.

Stevenson, Harold L., & Stigler, James. (1992). *The learning gap: Why our schools are failing and what we can learn from Japanese and Chinese education.* New York: Summit Books.

Stewart, Sherry H. (1996). Alcohol abuse in individuals exposed to trauma: A critical review. *Psychological Bulletin, 120,* 83–112.

Stewart, V. M. (1973). Tests of the "carpentered world" hypothesis by race and environment in America and Zambia. *International Journal of Psychology, 8,* 83–94.

Stillings, Neil A.; Feinstein, Mark H.; Garfield, Jay L.; Rissland, Edwina L.; Rosenbaum, David A.; Weisler, Steven E.; and Baker-Ward, Lynne. (1987). *Cognitive science: An introduction.* Cambridge, Mass.: MIT Press.

Stillion, Judith M.; McDowell, Eugene E.; & May, Jacque H. (1989). *Suicide across the life span: Premature exits.* New York: Hemisphere.

Stogdill, R. M. (1948). Personal factors associated with leadership: A survey of the literature. *Journal of Psychology, 25,* 35–71.

Stone, Arthur A.; Cox, Donald S.; Valdimarsdottir, Heiddis; Jandorf, Lina; & Neale, John M. (1987). Evidence that secretory IgA antibody is associated with daily mood. *Journal of Personality and Social Psychology, 52,* 988–993.

Stone, Arthur A.; Neale, John M.; Cox, Donald S.; Napoli, Anthony; Valdimarsdottir, Heiddis; & Kennedy-Moore, Eileen. (1994). Daily events are associated with a secretory immune response to an oral antigen in men. *Health Psychology, 13,* 440–446.

Strack, Fritz; Martin, Leonard L.; & Stepper, Sabine. (1988). Inhibiting and facilitating conditions of the human smile: A non-obtrusive test of the facial-feedback hypothesis. *Journal of Personality and Social Psychology, 54,* 768–777.

Stratton, Kathleen R.; Howe, Cynthia J.; & Battaglia, Frederick C. (Eds.). (1996). *Fetal alcohol syndrome: Diagnosis, epidemiology, prevention, and treatment.* Washington, D.C.: National Academy Press.

Street, Warren R. (1994). *A chronology of noteworthy events in American psychology.* Washington, D.C.: American Psychological Association.

Strickland, Bonnie R. (1995). Research on sexual orientation and human development: A commentary. *Developmental Psychology, 31,* 137–140.

Stromswold, Karin. (1995). The cognitive and neural bases of language acquisition. In Michael S. Gazzaniga (Ed.), *The cognitive neurosciences.* Cambridge, Mass.: MIT Press.

Stroop, J. Ridley. (1935/1992). Studies of interference in serial verbal reactions. *Journal of Experimental Psychology: General, 121,* 15–23.

Stryker, Susan. (1996, July/August). Portrait of a new man. *Utne Reader,* No. 76, 76–79.

Stuart, Richard B., & Davis, Barbara. (1972). *Slim chance in a fat world.* Champaign, Ill.: Research Press.

Stunkard, A. J.; Sorensen, T. I. A.; Hanis, C.; Teasdale, T. W.; Chakraborty, R.; Skull, W. J.; & Schulsinger, F. (1986). An adoption study of human obesity. *New England Journal of Medicine, 314,* 193–198.

Styron, William. (1990). *Darkness visible: A memoir of madness.* New York: Vintage.

Substance Abuse and Mental Health Services Administration. (1994). *National Household Survey on Drug Abuse: Population Estimates 1993.* Rockville, Md: U. S. Department of Health and Human Services. DHHS Publication No. (SMA) 94-3017.

Suchman, Anthony L., & Ader, Robert. (1989). Placebo response in humans can be shaped by prior pharmacologic experience. *Psychosomatic Medicine, 51,* 251.

Suddath, Richard L.; Christison, George W.; Torrey, E. Fuller; Casanova, Manuel F.; & Weinberger, Daniel R. (1990, March 22). Anatomical abnormalities in the brains of monozygotic twins discordant for schizophrenia. *New England Journal of Medicine, 322,* 789–794.

Sue, David; Sue, Derald; & Sue, Stanley. (1994). *Understanding abnormal behavior* (4th ed.). Boston: Houghton Mifflin.

Sue, Stanley; Zane, Nolan; & Young, Kathleen. (1994). Research on psychotherapy with culturally diverse populations. In Allen E. Bergin & Sol L. Garfield (Eds.), *Handbook of psychotherapy and behavior change* (4th ed.). New York: Wiley.

Suess, G. J.; Grossmann, K. E.; & Sroufe, L. Alan. (1992). Effects of infant attachment to mother and father on quality of adaptation in preschool: From dyadic to individual organisation of self. *International Journal of Behavioral Development, 15* (1), 43–65.

Sumerlin, J. R., & Norman, R. L. (1992). Self-actualization and homeless men: A known-groups examination of Maslow's hierarchy of needs. *Journal of Social Behavior and Personality, 7,* 469–481.

Super, Donald E. (1990). Career and life development. In Duane Brown, Linda Brooks, & Associates (Eds.), *Career choice and development: Applying contemporary theories to practice.* San Francisco: Jossey-Bass.

Supercharge your mind for success. (1995, March/April). Advertisement in *Psychology Today, 28* (2), 71.

Sutker, Patricia B.; Uddo, Madeline; Brailey, Kevin; Vasterling, Jennifer J.; & Errara, Paul. (1994). Psychopathology in war-zone deployed and nondeployed Operation Desert Storm troops assigned graves registration duties. *Journal of Abnormal Psychology, 103,* 383–390.

Swann, William B. (1984). Quest for accuracy in person perception: A matter of pragmatics. *Psychological Review, 91,* 457–477.

Swim, Janet K. (1994). Perceived versus meta-analytic effect sizes: An assessment of the accuracy of gender stereotypes. *Journal of Personality and Social Psychology, 66,* 21–36.

Syvälahti, E. K. G. (1994). Biological factors in schizophrenia: Structural and functional aspects. *British Journal of Psychiatry, 164* (Supplement 23), 9–14.

Szasz, Thomas. (1988). *The myth of psychotherapy: Mental healing as religion, rhetoric, and repression.* Syracuse, N.Y.: Syracuse University Press.

Taft, Lois B., & Nehrke, Milton F. (1990). Reminiscence, life review, and ego integrity in nursing home residents. *International Journal of Aging and Human Development, 30,* 189–196.

Takei, Noriyoshi; Sham, Pak; O'Callaghan, Eadbhard; Murray, Graham K.; Glover, Gyles; & Murray, Robin M. (1994). Prenatal exposure to influenza and the development of schizophrenia: Is the effect confined to females? *American Journal of Psychiatry, 151,* 117–119.

Takeuchi, Tomoka; Miyasita, A.; Sasaki, Y.; & Inugami, M. (1992). Isolated sleep paralysis elicited by sleep interruption. *Sleep, 15,* 217–225.

Tanford, Sarah, & Penrod, Steven. (1984). Social influence model: A formal integration of research on majority and minority influence processes. *Psychological Bulletin, 95,* 189–225.

Tannen, Deborah. (1990). *You just don't understand: Women and men in conversation.* New York: Ballantine.

Tart, Charles T. (1979). Measuring the depth of an altered state of consciousness, with particular reference to self-report scales of hypnotic depth. In Erika Fromm & Ronald E. Shor (Eds.), *Hypnosis: Developments in research and new perspectives* (2nd ed.). New York: Aldine.

Tart, Charles T. (Ed.). (1990). *Altered states of consciousness* (3rd ed.). San Francisco: HarperCollins.

Tart, Charles T. (1994). *Living the mindful life: A handbook for living in the present moment.* Boston: Shambhala.

Tavris, Carol. (1989). *Anger: The misunderstood emotion* (2nd ed.). New York: Simon & Schuster.

Tavris, Carol. (1992). *The mismeasure of women.* New York: Simon & Schuster.

Taylor, Donald M., & Porter, Lana E. (1994). A multicultural view of stereotyping. In Walter J. Lonner & Roy Malpass (Eds.), *Psychology and culture.* Boston: Allyn & Bacon.

Taylor, Shelley. (1989). *Positive illusions: Creative self-deceptions and the healthy mind.* New York: Basic Books.

Taylor, Shelley E. (1995). *Health psychology* (3rd ed.). New York: McGraw-Hill.

Taylor, Shelley, & Aspinwall, Lisa G. (1993). Coping with chronic illness. In Leo Goldberger & Shlomo Breznitz (Eds.), *Handbook of stress: Theoretical and clinical aspects* (2nd ed.). New York: Free Press.

Taylor, Shelley E.; Helgeson, Vicki S.; Reed, Geoffrey M.; & Skokan, Laurie A. (1991). Self-generated feelings of control and adjustment to physical illness. *Journal of Social Issues, 47,* 91–109.

Tellegen, Auke; Lykken, David T.; Bouchard, Thomas J.; Wilcox, Kimerly J.; Segal, Nancy L.; & Rich, Stephen. (1988). Personality similarity in twins reared apart and together. *Journal of Personality and Social Psychology, 54,* 1031–1039.

Terman, Lewis M. (1916). *Measurement of intelligence.* Boston: Houghton Mifflin.

Terman, Lewis M. (1926). *Genetic studies of genius: Vol. I. Mental and physical traits of a thousand gifted children* (2nd ed.). Stanford, Calif.: Stanford University Press.

Terman, Lewis M., & Oden, Melita H. (1947). *Genetic studies of genius: Vol. IV.*

The gifted child grows up: Twenty-five years' follow-up of a superior group. Stanford, Calif.: Stanford University Press.

Terman, Lewis M., & Oden, Melita H. (1959). *Genetic studies of genius: Vol. V. The gifted at mid-life: Thirty-five years' follow-up of the superior child.* Stanford, Calif.: Stanford University Press.

Terrace, Herbert S. (1981). A report to an academy, 1980. *Annals of the New York Academy of Sciences, 364,* 115–129.

Terrace, Herbert S. (1985). In the beginning was the "name." *American Psychologist, 40,* 1011–1028.

Tett, R. P.; Jackson, D. N.; & Rothstein, M. (1991). Personality measures as predictors of job performance: A meta-analytic review. *Personnel Psychology, 44,* 703–742.

Thomas, Alexander, & Chess, Stella. (1977). *Temperament and development.* New York: Brunner/Mazel.

Thomas, Alexander, & Chess, Stella. (1980). *The dynamics of psychological development.* New York: Brunner/Mazel.

Thomas, Alexander, & Chess, Stella. (1986). The New York Longitudinal Study: From infancy to early adult life. In Robert Plomin & Judith Dunn (Eds.), *The study of temperament: Changes, continuities, and challenges.* Hillsdale, N.J.: Erlbaum.

Thomason, Sarah G. (1984). Do you remember your previous life's language in your present incarnation? *American Speech, 59* (4), 340–350.

Thomason, Sarah G. (1986–1987, Summer). Past tongues remembered? *Skeptical Inquirer, 11,* 367–375.

Thommen, George S. (1987). *Biorhythms: Is this your day?* New York: Crown.

Thompson, Clara. (1950/1973). Some effects of the derogatory attitude toward female sexuality. In Jean Baker Miller (Ed.), *Psychoanalysis and women.* Baltimore, Md.: Penguin Books.

Thompson, Richard F. (1993). *The brain: A neuroscience primer* (2nd ed.). New York: Freeman.

Thompson, Richard F. (1994). Behaviorism and neuroscience. *Psychological Review, 101,* 259–265.

Thompson, Ross A. (1986). Temperament, emotionality, and infant social cognition. In Jacqueline V. Lerner & Richard M. Lerner (Eds.), *Temperament and social interaction in infants and children.* New Directions for Child Development, No. 31. San Francisco: Jossey-Bass.

Thompson, Suzanne C.; Nanni, Christopher; & Levine, Alexandra. (1994). Primary versus secondary and central versus consequence-related control in HIV-positive men. *Journal of Personality and Social Psychology, 67,* 540–547.

Thompson, Suzanne C.; Sobolew-Shubin, Alexandria; Galbraith, Michael E.; Schwankovsky, Lenore; & Cruzen, Dana. (1993). Maintaining perceptions of control: Finding perceived control in low-control circumstances. *Journal of Personality and Social Psychology, 64,* 293–304.

Thompson, Suzanne C., & Spacapan, Shirlynn. (1991). Perceptions of control in vulnerable populations. *Journal of Social Issues, 47,* 1–21.

Thorndike, Edward L. (1898). Animal intelligence: An experimental study of the associative processes in animals. *Psychological Review Monograph Supplement, 2,* Serial No. 8.

Thorndike, Edward L. (1903) *Educational psychology.* New York: Teachers College.

Thorndike, Edward L. (1911). *Animal intelligence.* New York: Macmillan.

Thorne, Barrie. (1986). Girls and boys together, but mostly apart. In Willard W. Hartup & Zick Rubin (Eds.), *Relationships and development.* Hillsdale, N.J.: Erlbaum.

Thorne, Barrie, & Luria, Zella. (1986). Sexuality and gender in children's daily worlds. *Social Problems, 33,* 176–190.

Thornton, Bill. (1992). Repression and its mediating influence on the defensive attribution of responsibility. *Journal of Research in Personality, 26,* 44–57.

Thorpy, Michael J. (1991). History of sleep and man. In Michael J. Thorpy & Jan Yager (Eds.), *The encyclopedia of sleep and sleep disorders.* New York: Facts on File.

Thorpy, Michael J., & Ledereich, Philip S. (1990). Medical treatment of obstructive sleep apnea syndrome. In Michael J. Thorpy (Ed.), *Handbook of sleep disorders.* New York: Dekker.

Thorpy, Michael J., & Yager, Jan (Eds.). (1991). *The encyclopedia of sleep and sleep disorders.* New York: Facts on File.

Thurgood, Delores H., & Clarke, Julie E. (1995). *Summary report 1993: Doctoral recipients from United States universities.* National Research Council Office of Scientific and Engineering Personnel. Washington, D.C.: National Academy Press.

Thurstone, Louis L. (1937). *Primary mental abilities.* Chicago: University of Chicago Press.

Tienari, Pekka. (1991). Interaction between genetic vulnerability and family environment: The Finnish Adoptive Family Study of Schizophrenia. *Acta Psychiatrica Scandinavica, 84,* 460–465.

Tienari, Pekka; Sorri, Anneli; Lahti, Ilpo; Naarala, Mikko; Wahlberg, Karl-Erik; Moring, Juha; Pohjola, Jukka; & Wynne, Lyman C. (1987). Genetic and psychosocial factors in schizophrenia: The Finnish Adoptive Family Study. *Schizophrenia Bulletin, 13,* 477–484.

Tienari, Pekka; Wynne, Lyman C.; Moring, Juha; Lahti, Ilpo; Naarala, Mikko; Sorri, Anneli; Wahlberg, Karl-Erik; Saarento, Outi; Scitamaa, Markku; Kaleva, Merja; & Läksy, Kristian. (1994). The Finnish Adoptive Family Study of Schizophrenia: Implications for family research. *British Journal of Psychiatry, 164* (Supplement), 20–26.

Tizard, Ian. (1992). *Immunology: An introduction* (3rd ed). Philadelphia: Saunders.

Todd, James T., & Morris, Edward K. (1992). Case histories in the great power of steady misrepresentation. *American Psychologist, 47,* 1441–1453.

Tolman, Edward C. (1932). *Purposive behavior in animals and men.* New York: Appleton-Century-Crofts.

Tolman, Edward C. (1948). Cognitive maps in rats and men. *Psychological Review, 55,* 189–208.

Tolman, Edward C., & Honzik, C. H. (1930a). "Insight" in rats. *University of California Publications in Psychology, 4,* 215–232.

Tolman, Edward C., & Honzik, C. H. (1930b). Introduction and removal of reward, and maze performance in rats. *University of California Publications in Psychology, 4,* 257–275.

Tolman, Edward C.; Ritchie, B. F.; & Kalish, D. (1946/1992). Studies in spatial learning. I. Orientation and the short-cut. *Journal of Experimental Psychology: General, 121,* 429–434.

Tomaka, Joe; Blascovich, Jim; Kelsey, Robert M.; & Leitten, Christopher L. (1993). Subjective, physiological, and behavioral effects of threat and challenge appraisal. *Journal of Personality and Social Psychology, 65,* 248–260.

Tomarken, Andrew J.; Davidson, Richard J.; Wheeler, Robert E.; & Doss, Robert C. (1992). Individual differences in anterior brain asymmetry and fundamental dimensions of emotion. *Journal of Personality and Social Psychology, 62,* 676–687.

Tomb, David A. (1994). The phenomenology of post-traumatic stress disorder. *Psychiatric Clinics of North America, 17,* 237–250.

Torgersen, S. (1990). Genetics of anxiety and its clinical implications. In Graham D. Burrows, Martin Roth, & Russell Noyes, Jr. (Eds.), *Handbook of anxiety: Vol. 3.*

The neurobiology of anxiety. Amsterdam: Elsevier.

Torrey, E. Fuller. (1991). A viral-anatomical explanation of schizophrenia. *Schizophrenia Bulletin, 17,* 15–18.

Torrey, E. Fuller. (1992). Are we overestimating the genetic contribution to schizophrenia? *Schizophrenia Bulletin, 18,* 159–170.

Torrey, E. Fuller; Bowler, Ann E.; Rawlings, Robert; & Terrazas, Alejandro. (1993). Seasonality of schizophrenia and stillbirths. *Schizophrenia Bulletin, 19,* 557–562.

Torrey, E. Fuller; Bowler, Ann E.; Taylor, Edward H.; & Gottesman, Irving I. (1994). *Schizophrenia and manic-depressive disorder: The biological roots of mental illness as revealed by the landmark study of identical twins.* New York: Basic Books.

Travis, L. E. (1925). The effect of a small audience upon eye–hand coordination. *Journal of Abnormal and Social Psychology, 20,* 142–146.

Triandis, Harry C. (1994). *Culture and social behavior.* New York: McGraw-Hill.

Triandis, Harry C. (1996). The psychological measurement of cultural syndromes. *American Psychologist, 51,* 407–415.

Trimble, Joseph E. (1994). Cultural variations in the use of alcohol and drugs. In Walter J. Lonner & Roy Malpass (Eds.), *Psychology and culture.* Boston: Allyn & Bacon.

Tsuang, Ming T., & Faraone, Stephen V. (1990). *The genetics of mood disorders.* Baltimore, Md.: Johns Hopkins University Press.

Tulving, Endel. (1962). Subjective organization in free recall of "unrelated words." *Psychological Review, 69,* 344–354.

Tulving, Endel. (1983). *Elements of episodic memory.* Oxford: Clarendon Press/Oxford University Press.

Tulving, Endel. (1985). How many memory systems are there? *American Psychologist, 40,* 385–398.

Tulving, Endel. (1995). Organization of memory: *Quo vadis?* In Michael S. Gazzaniga (Ed.), *The cognitive neurosciences.* Cambridge, Mass.: MIT Press.

Turk, Dennis C. (1994, April). Perspectives on chronic pain: The role of psychological factors. *Current Directions in Psychological Science, 3* (2), 45–48.

Turk, Dennis C.; Meichenbaum, Donald; & Genest, Myles. (1983). *Pain and behavioral medicine: A cognitive-behavioral perspective.* New York: Guilford Press.

Turk, Dennis C., & Nash, Justin M. (1993). Chronic pain: New ways to cope. In Daniel Goleman & Joel Gurin (Eds.), *Mind/body medicine: How to use your mind for better health.* Yonkers, N.Y.: Consumer Reports Books.

Turk, Dennis C., & Rudy, Thomas E. (1992). Cognitive factors and persistent pain: A glimpse into Pandora's box. *Cognitive Therapy and Research, 16* (2), 99–122.

Turner, Patricia J., & Gervai, Judit. (1995). A multidimensional study of gender typing in preschool children and their parents: Personality, attitudes, preferences, behavior, and cultural differences. *Developmental Psychology, 31,* 759–772.

Turner, Terence J., & Ortony, Andrew. (1992). Basic emotions: Can conflicting criteria converge? *Psychological Review, 99,* 566–571.

Tversky, Amos. (1972). Elimination by aspects: A theory of choice. *Psychological Review, 80,* 281–299.

Tversky, Amos, & Kahneman, Daniel. (1982). Judgment under uncertainty: Heuristics and biases. In Daniel Kahneman, Paul Slovic, & Amos Tversky (Eds.), *Judgment under uncertainty: Heuristics and biases.* New York: Cambridge University Press.

Tversky, Amos, & Shafir, Eldar. (1992). Choice under conflict: The dynamics of deferred decision. *Psychological Science, 3,* 358–361.

U.S. Bureau of the Census. (1992). *Sixty-five plus in America.* Current population reports, Special Studies, Series P-23, No. 178. Washington, D.C.: U. S. Government Printing Office.

U. S. Bureau of the Census. (1995). *Statistical abstract of the United States: 1995* (115th ed.). Washington, D.C.: U. S. Government Printing Office.

U.S. National Center for Health Statistics. (1990). *Vital and health statistics.* Series 10. Washington, D.C.: U.S. Government Printing Office.

Umberson, Debra; & Gove, Walter R. (1989). Parenthood and psychological well-being: Theory, measurement, and stage in the family life course. *Journal of Family Issues, 10,* 440–462.

Underwood, Geoffrey (Ed.). (1996). *Implicit cognition.* New York: Oxford University Press.

Unger, Rhoda K., & Crawford, Mary. (1993). Commentary: Sex and gender: The troubled relationship between terms and concepts. *Psychological Science, 4,* 122–124.

Unger, Rhoda K., & Crawford, Mary. (1996). *Women and gender: A feminist psychology* (2nd ed.). New York: McGraw-Hill.

Usher, JoNell Adair, & Neisser, Ulric. (1993). Childhood amnesia and the beginnings of memory for four early life events. *Journal of Experimental Psychology: General, 122,* 155–165.

Uttal, William R. (1981). *A taxonomy of visual processes.* Hillsdale, N.J.: Erlbaum.

van den Boom, Dymphna C., & Hoeksma, Jan B. (1994). The effect of infant irritability on mother–infant interaction: A growth-curve analysis. *Developmental Psychology, 30,* 581–590.

Van Egmond, Marjan; Garnefski, Nadia; Jonker, Daan; & Kerkhof, Ad. (1993). The relationship between sexual abuse and female suicidal behavior. *Crisis, 14,* 129–139.

Vandell, Deborah Lowe, & Corasaniti, Mary Ann. (1990). Child care and the family: Complex contributors to child development. In Kathleen McCartney (Ed.), *Child care and maternal employment: A social ecology approach.* New Directions for Child Development, No. 49. San Francisco: Jossey-Bass.

Vanderlinden, Johan; Van Dyck, Richard; Vandereycken, Walter; & Vertommen, Hans. (1991). Dissociative experiences in the general population in the Netherlands and Belgium: A study with the Dissociative Questionnaire (DIS-Q). *Dissociation, 4,* 180–184.

Venables, Peter H. (1996). Schizotypy and maternal exposure to influenza and to cold temperature: The Mauritius study. *Journal of Abnormal Psychology, 105,* 53–60.

Vernberg, Eric M.; La Greca, Annette M.; Silverman, Wendy K.; & Prinstein, Mitchell J. (1996). Prediction of posttraumatic stress symptoms in children after Hurricane Andrew. *Journal of Abnormal Psychology, 105,* 237–248.

Vitkovic, Ljubisa. (1995). Neuroimmunology and neurovirology. In Stephen H. Koslow (Ed.), *The neuroscience of mental health II: A report on neuroscience research: Status and potential for mental health and mental illness.* Rockville, Md.: National Institute of Mental Health. NIMH Publication No. 95–4000.

Voyer, Daniel; Voyer, Susan; & Bryden, M. P. (1995). Magnitude of sex differences in spatial abilities: A meta-analysis and consideration of critical variables. *Psychological Bulletin, 117,* 250–270.

Vygotsky, Lev S. (1978). *Mind in society: The development of higher psychological processes.* Edited by Michael Cole, Vera John-Steiner, Sylvia Scribner, & Ellen Souberman. Cambridge, Mass.: Harvard University Press.

Vygotsky, Lev S. (1987). *Thinking and speech.* Translated by Norris Minick. New York: Plenum.

Wachs, Theodore D., & King, Beverly. (1994). Behavioral research in the brave new world of neuroscience and temperament: A guide to the biologically perplexed. In John E. Bates & Theodore D. Wachs (Eds.), *Temperament: Individual differences at the interface of biology and behavior.* Washington, D.C.: American Psychological Association.

Wadsworth, Barry J. (1996). *Piaget's theory of cognitive and affective development: Foundations of constructivism* (5th ed.). White Plains, N.Y.: Longman.

Wagner, Hugh L. (1990). The spontaneous facial expression of differential positive and negative emotions. *Motivation and Emotion, 14,* 27–43.

Waldman, Irwin D.; Weinberg, Richard A.; & Scarr, Sandra. (1994). Racial group differences in IQ in the Minnesota Transracial Adoption Study: A reply to Levin and Lynn. *Intelligence, 18,* 29–44.

Walker, B. A., & Hanson, W. C. (1992). Valuing differences at Digital Equipment Corporation. In S. E. Jackson (Ed.), *Diversity in the workplace: Human resources initiatives.* New York: Guilford Press.

Walker, Lawrence J. (1984). Sex differences in the development of moral reasoning: A critical review. *Child Development, 55,* 677–691.

Walker, Lawrence J. (1989). A longitudinal study of moral reasoning. *Child Development, 60,* 157–166.

Walker, Lawrence J.; De Vries, Brian; & Trevethan, Shelley D. (1987). Moral stages and moral orientations in real-life and hypothetical dilemmas. *Child Development, 58,* 842–858.

Wallace, B., & Persanyi, M. W. (1989). Hypnotic susceptibility and familial handedness. *Journal of General Psychology, 116* (4), 345–350.

Wallace, R. K. (1987). *The Maharishi technology of the unified field: The neurophysiology of enlightenment.* Fairfield, Iowa: MIU Press.

Wallace, R. K., & Bensen, Herbert. (1972, February). The physiology of meditation. *Scientific American, 226,* 84–90.

Wallach, Hans. (1987). Perceiving a stable environment when one moves. *Annual Review of Psychology, 38,* 1–27.

Wangensteen, O., & Carlson, A. (1931). Hunger sensation after total gastrectomy. *Proceedings of the Society for Experimental Biology, 28,* 545–547.

Ware, Jacqueline; Jain, Kumud; Burgess, Ian; & Davey, Graham C. L. (1994). Disease-avoidance model: Factor analysis of common animal fears. *Behaviour Research and Therapy, 32,* 57–63.

Warner, Virginia; Weissman, Myrna M.; Fendrich, Michael; Wickramaratne, Priya; & Moreau, Donna. (1992). The course of major depression in the offspring of depressed patients: Incidence, recurrence, and recovery. *Archives of General Psychiatry, 49,* 795–801.

Wasserman, Edward A. (1993). Comparative cognition: Beginning the second century of the study of animal intelligence. *Psychological Bulletin, 113,* 211–228.

Waterman, Alan S. (1985, December). Identity in the context of adolescent psychology. In Alan S. Waterman (Ed.), *Identity in adolescence: Processes and contents.* New Directions in Child Research Series, No. 30. San Francisco: Jossey-Bass.

Watkins, L. R., & Mayer, D. L. (1982). Organization of the endogenous opiate and nonopiate pain control systems. *Science, 216,* 1185–1193.

Watson, D. L., & Tharp, R. G. (1985). Self-directed behavior: *Self-modification for personal adjustment* (4th ed.). Monterey, Calif.: Brooks/Cole.

Watson, David, & Clark, Lee Anna. (1994). Emotions, moods, traits, and temperaments: Conceptual distinctions and empirical findings. In Paul Ekman & Richard J. Davidson (Eds.), *The nature of emotion: Fundamental questions.* New York: Oxford University Press.

Watson, David, & Pennebaker, James W. (1989). Health complaints, stress, and distress: Exploring the central role of negative affectivity. *Psychological Review, 96,* 234–254.

Watson, J. G., & Barone, S. (1976). The self-concept, personal values, and motivational orientations of black and white managers. *Academy of Management Journal, 19,* 36–48.

Watson, John B. (1913). Psychology as the behaviorist views it. *Psychological Review, 20,* 158–177.

Watson, John B. (1924). *Behaviorism.* New York: Norton.

Watson, John B. (1924/1970). *Behaviorism.* New York: Norton.

Watson, John B. (1930). *Behaviorism* (rev. ed.). Chicago: University of Chicago Press.

Watson, John B., & Rayner, Rosalie. (1920). Conditioned emotional reactions. *Journal of Experimental Psychology, 3,* 1–14.

Watson, Robert I., & Evans, Rand B. (1991). *The great psychologists: A history of psychological thought.* New York: Harper-Collins.

Weaver, C. N. (1978). Job satisfaction as a component of happiness among males and females. *Personnel Psychology, 31,* 831–840.

Weaver, Charles A., III. (1993). Do you need a "flash" to form a flashbulb memory? *Journal of Experimental Psychology: General, 122,* 39–46.

Webb, K., & Davey, Graham C. L. (1993). Disgust sensitivity and fear of animals: Effect of exposure to violent or revulsive material. *Anxiety, Coping and Stress, 5,* 329–335.

Webb, Wilse B. (1975). *Sleep: The gentle tyrant.* Englewood Cliffs, N.J.: Prentice Hall.

Webb, Wilse B. (1989). Development of human napping. In David F. Dinges & Roger J. Broughton (Eds.), *Sleep and alertness: Chronobiological, behavioral, and medical aspects of napping.* New York: Raven Press.

Webb, Wilse B. (1994). Sleep as a biological rhythm: A historical review. *Sleep, 17,* 188–194.

Webb, Wilse B., & Dinges, David F. (1989). Cultural perspectives on napping and the siesta. In David F. Dinges & Roger J. Broughton (Eds.), *Sleep and alertness: Chronobiological, behavioral, and medical aspects of napping.* New York: Raven Press.

Wechsler, David. (1944). *The measurement of adult intelligence* (3rd ed.). Baltimore: Williams & Wilkins.

Wechsler, David. (1974). *Manual for the Wechsler Intelligence Scale for Children* (rev.). New York: Psychological Corporation.

Wegner, Daniel M. (1989). *White bears and other unwanted thoughts: Suppression, obsession, and the psychology of mental control.* New York: Viking.

Wehr, Thomas A. (1988). Sleep and biological rhythms in affective illness. In David J. Kupler, Timothy H. Monk, & Jack D. Barchas (Eds.), *Biological rhythms and mental disorders.* New York: Guilford Press.

Weinberg, Richard A. (1989). Intelligence and IQ: Landmark issues and great debates. *American Psychologist, 44,* 98–104.

Weinberg, Richard A.; Scarr, Sandra; & Waldman, Irwin D. (1992). The Minnesota Transracial Adoption Study: A follow-up of IQ test performance at adolescence. *Intelligence, 16,* 117–135.

Weinberger, Daniel R. (1987). Implications of normal brain development for the pathogenesis of schizophrenia. *Archives of General Psychiatry, 44,* 660–669.

Weinberger, Daniel. (1995, June). Quoted in Joel L. Swerdlow, "Quiet miracles of the brain," *National Geographic, 187,* 2–41.

Weinberger, M.; Hiner, S. L.; & Tierney, W. M. (1987). In support of hassles as a measure of stress in predicting health outcomes. *Journal of Behavioral Medicine, 10,* 19–31.

Weinstein, Lissa N.; Schwartz, David G.; & Arkin, Arthur M. (1991). Qualitative aspects of sleep mentation. In Steven J. Ellman & John S. Antrobus (Eds.), *The mind in sleep: Psychology and psychophysiology* (2nd ed.). New York: Wiley.

Weisberg, Robert W. (1988). Problem solving and creativity. In Robert J. Sternberg (Ed.), *The nature of creativity.* New York: Cambridge University Press.

Weisberg, Robert W. (1993). *Creativity: Beyond the myth of genius.* New York: Freeman.

Weiss, H. M., & Shaw, J. B. (1979). Social influences on judgments about tasks. *Organizational Behavior and Human Performance, 24,* 136–140.

Weisse, Carol Silvia. (1992). Depression and immunocompetence: A review of the literature. *Psychological Bulletin, 111,* 475–489.

Weisz, Carolyn, & Jones, Edward E. (1993). Expectancy disconfirmation and dispositional inference: Latent strength of target-based and category-based expectancies. *Personality and Social Psychology Bulletin, 19,* 563–573.

Weisz, John R.; Rothbaum, Fred M.; & Blackburn, Thomas C. (1984). Standing out and standing in: The psychology of control in Japan and America. *American Psychologist, 39,* 955–969.

Wells, Gary L. (1993). What do we know about eyewitness identification? *American Psychologist, 48,* 553–571.

Wells, Kenneth B.; Burnam, M. Audrey; Rogers, Williams; Hayes, Ron; & Camp, Patti. (1992). The course of depression in adult outpatients: Results from the Medical Outcomes Study. *Archives of General Psychiatry, 49,* 788–794.

Wenar, Charles. (1994). *Developmental psychopathology: From infancy through adolescence* (3rd ed.). New York: McGraw-Hill.

Werker, Janet, & Desjardins, Renee. (1995). Listening to speech in the 1st year of life: Experiential influences on phoneme production. *Current Directions in Psychological Science, 4,* 76–81.

Wertenbaker, Lael. (1984). *The eye: Window to the world.* Tarrytown, N.Y.: Torstar Books.

Wertheimer, Max. (1912/1965). Experimentelle Studien über das Sehen von Bewegung. *Zeitschrift für Psychologie, 61,* 162–163, 221–227. Portions of original publication translated and reprinted in Richard J. Herrnstein & Edwin G. Boring (Eds.), *A source book in the history of psychology.* Translated by Don Cantor. Cambridge, Mass.: Harvard University Press.

Wertsch, James V., & Tulviste, Peeter. (1992). L. S. Vygotsky and contemporary developmental psychology. *Developmental Psychology, 28,* 548–557.

Wertsch, James V., & Tulviste, Peeter. (1994). Lev Semyonovich Vygotsky and contemporary developmental psychology. In Ross D. Parke, Peter A. Ornstein, John J. Rieser, & Carolyn Zahn-Waxler (Eds.), *A century of developmental psychology.* Washington, D.C.: American Psychological Association.

West, Michael A. (1987). Traditional and psychological perspectives on meditation. In Michael A. West (Ed.), *The psychology of meditation.* New York: Oxford University Press.

Westen, Drew. (1990). Psychoanalytic approaches to personality. In Lawrence A. Pervin (Ed.), *Handbook of personality: Theory and research.* New York: Guilford Press.

Wethington, Elaine; McLeod, Jane D.; & Kessler, Ronald C. (1987). The importance of life events for explaining sex differences in psychological distress. In Rosalind C. Barnett, Lois Biener, & Grace K. Baruch (Eds.), *Gender and stress.* New York: Free Press.

Wheeler, Anthony. (1990, Fall). Biological cycles and rhythms vs. biorhythms. *Skeptical Inquirer, 15,* 75–82.

White, G. L.; Fishbein, S.; & Rutstein, J. (1981). Passionate love and the misattribution of arousal. *Journal of Personality and Social Psychology, 41,* 56–62.

White, Lon; Katzman, Robert; & Losonczy, Katalin. (1994). Association of education with incidence of cognitive impairment in three established populations for epidemiologic studies of the elderly. *Journal of Clinical Epidemiology, 47,* 363–371.

White, Robert W. (1959). Motivation reconsidered: The concepts of competence. *Psychological Review, 66,* 297–333.

White, Sheldon H. (1994). G. Stanley Hall: From philosophy to developmental psychology. In Ross D. Parke, Peter A. Ornstein, John J. Rieser, & Carolyn Zahn-Waxler (Eds.), *A century of developmental psychology.* Washington, D.C.: American Psychological Association.

Whitley, Bernard E., & Frieze, Irene H. (1985). Children's causal attributions for success and failure in achievement settings: A meta-analysis. *Journal of Educational Psychology, 77,* 608–616.

Whorf, Benjamin L. (1956). Science and linguistics. In J. B. Carroll (Ed.), *Language, thought, and reality: Selected papers of Benjamin Lee Whorf.* Cambridge, Mass.: MIT Press.

Whyte, Jamie, & Schaefer, Charles E. (1995). Introduction to sleep and its disorders. In Charles E. Schaefer (Ed.), *Clinical handbook of sleep disorders in children.* Northvale, N.J.: Aronson.

Wiedemann, Carl F. (1987). REM and non-REM sleep and its relation to nightmares and night terrors. In Henry Kellerman (Ed.), *The nightmare: Psychological and biological foundations.* New York: Columbia University Press.

Wiggins, Jerry S. (1996). *The five-factor model of personality: Theoretical perspectives.* New York: Guilford.

Wilcoxon, Hardy C.; Dragoin, W. B.; & Kral, P. A. (1971). Illness-induced aversions in rat and quail: Relative salience of visual and gustatory cues. *Science, 171,* 826–828.

Wilkie, C. F., & Ames, E. W. (1986). The relationship of infant crying to parental stress in the transition to parenthood. *Journal of Marriage and the Family, 48,* 545–550.

Wilkinson, T. R. (1992). How fast should the night shift rotate? *Erogonomics, 35,* 1425–1446.

Williams, C. L., & Berry, John W. (1991). Primary prevention of acculturative stress among refugees. *American Psychologist, 46,* 632–641.

Williams, John E., & Best, Deborah L. (1990). *Measuring sex stereotypes: A multination study.* Newbury Park, Calif.: Sage.

Williams, John E., & Best, Deborah L. (1994). Cross-cultural views of women and men. In Walter J. Lonner & Roy Malpass (Eds.), *Psychology and culture.* Boston: Allyn & Bacon.

Williams, Kipling D.; Nida, S. A.; Baca, L. D.; & Latané, B. (1989). Social loafing and swimming: Effects of identifiability on individual and relay performance of intercollegiate swimmers. *Basic and Applied Social Psychology, 10,* 73–81.

Williams, Martin H. (1992). Exploitation and inference: Mapping the damage from therapist–patient sexual involvement. *American Psychologist, 47,* 412–421.

Williams, Redford B. (1989). *The trusting heart: Great news about Type A behavior.* New York: Times Books/Random House.

Williams, Robert L.; Gökcebay, Nilgün; Hirshkowitz, Max; & Moore, Constance A. (1994). Ontogeny of sleep. In Rosemary Cooper (Ed.), *Sleep.* New York: Chapman & Hall.

Wilson, G. Terence, & Fairburn, Christopher G. (1993). Cognitive treatments for eating disorders. *Journal of Consulting and Clinical Psychology, 61,* 261–269.

Wilson, Mitchell. (1993). DSM-III and the transformation of American psychiatry: A history. *American Journal of Psychiatry, 150,* 399–410.

Windholz, George. (1990). Pavlov and the Pavlovians in the laboratory. *Journal of the History of the Behavioral Sciences, 26,* 64–73.

Winokur, George; Coryell, William; Endicott, Jean; & Akiskal, Hapog. (1993). Further distinctions between manic-depressive illness (bipolar disorder) and primary depressive disorder (unipolar depression). *American Journal of Psychiatry, 150,* 1176–1181.

Winstead, Barbara A. (1986). Sex differences in same-sex friendships. In Valerian J. Derlega & Barbara A. Winstead (Eds.), *Friendship and social interaction.* New York: Springer-Verlag.

Winter, Ruth. (1976). *The smell book.* Philadelphia: Lippincott.

Wise, R. A. (1996). Addictive drugs and brain stimulation reward. *Annual Review of Neuroscience, 19,* 319–340.

Wittchen, Hans-Ulrich; Zhao, Shanyang; Kessler, Ronald C.; & Eaton, William W. (1994). DSM-III-R generalized anxiety disorder in the National Comorbidity Survey. *Archives of General Psychiatry, 51,* 355–364.

Wolpe, Joseph. (1958). *Psychotherapy by reciprocal inhibition.* Stanford, Calif.: Stanford University Press.

Wolpe, Joseph. (1982). *The practice of behavior therapy.* New York: Pergamon Press.

Wood, David. (1988). *How children think and learn.* New York: Blackwell.

Wood, James M., & Bootzin, Richard R. (1990). The prevalence of nightmares and their independence from anxiety. *Journal of Abnormal Psychology, 99* (1), 64–68.

Wood, Robert, & Bandura, Albert. (1991). Social cognitive theory of organizational management. In Richard M. Steers & Lyman W. Porter (Eds.), *Motivation and work behavior.* New York: McGraw-Hill.

Wood, Wendy. (1982). The retrieval of attitude-relevant information from memory: Effects on susceptibility to persuasion and on intrinsic motivation. *Journal of Personality and Social Psychology, 42,* 798–810.

Wood, Wendy; Rhodes, Nancy; & Biek, Michael. (1995). Working knowledge and attitude strength: An information-processing analysis. In Richard E. Petty & Jon A. Krosnick (Eds.), *Attitude strength: Antecedents and consequences*. Hillsdale, N.J.: Erlbaum.

Wood, Wendy; Rhodes, Nancy; & Whelan, Melanie. (1989). Sex differences in positive well-being: A consideration of emotional style and marital status. *Psychological Bulletin, 106*, 249–264.

Woodward, Amanda L.; Markman, Ellen M.; & Fitzsimmons, Colleen M. (1994). Rapid word learning in 13- and 18-month-olds. *Developmental Psychology, 30*, 553–566.

Woodworth, Robert S. (1958). *Dynamics of behavior*. New York: Holt.

Woody, Shelia R. (1996). Effects of focus of attention on anxiety levels and social performance of individuals with social phobia. *Journal of Abnormal Psychology, 105*, 61–69.

Worrall, Russell S. (1986). Iridology: Diagnosis or delusion? In Kendrick Frazier (Ed.), *Science confronts the paranormal*. Buffalo, N.Y.: Prometheus.

Wortman, Camille B.; Sheedy, Collette; Gluhoski, Vicki; & Kessler, Ron. (1992). Stress, coping, and health: Conceptual issues and directions for future research. In Howard S. Friedman (Ed.), *Hostility, coping, and health*. Washington, D.C.: American Psychological Association.

Wujec, Tom. (1988). *Pumping ions: Games and exercises to flex your mind*. New York: Doubleday.

Wundt, Wilhelm. (1874). *Grundzüge der physiologischen Psychologie* (Principles of physiological psychology) (5th ed.). Leipzig, Germany: Engelmann. English version published by Macmillan Publishers, New York, 1904.

Wyatt, J. W.; Posey, A.; Welker, W.; & Seamonds, C. (1984). Natural levels of similarities between identical twins and between unrelated people. *The Skeptical Inquirer, 9*, 62–66.

Yapko, Michael D. (1994a). Suggestibility and repressed memories of abuse: A survey of psychotherapists' beliefs. *American Journal of Clinical Hypnosis, 36*, 163–171.

Yapko, Michael D. (1994b). *Suggestions of abuse: True and false memories of childhood sexual trauma*. New York: Simon & Schuster.

Yarnell, Phillip R., & Lynch, Steve. (1970, April 25). Retrograde memory immediately after concussion. *Lancet, 1*, 863–865.

Youngstrom, Nina. (1992, October). Training brings psychologists closer to prescribing drugs. *APA Monitor, 23*, 31.

Yu, Bolin; Zhang, W.; Jing, Qicheng; Peng, R.; Zhang, G.; & Simon, Herbert A. (1985). STM capacity for Chinese and English language materials. *Memory and Cognition, 13*, 202–207.

Zajonc, Robert B. (1984). On the primacy of affect. *American Psychologist, 39*, 117–123.

Zammit, G. K. (1988). Subjective ratings of the characteristics and sequelae of good and poor sleep in normals. *Journal of Clinical Psychology, 44*, 123–130.

Zeigler, H. P.; Jacquin, M. F.; & Miller, M. G. (1985). Trigeminal orosensation and ingestive behavior in the rat. *Progress in Psychobiology and Physiological Psychology, 11*, 163–196.

Zgourides, George. (1996). *Human sexuality: Contemporary perspectives*. New York: HarperCollins.

Zhang, D.-M.; Bula, W.; & Stellar, E. (1986). Brain cholecystokinin as a satiety peptide. *Physiology and Behavior, 36*, 1183–1186.

Zhdanova, Irina V.; Wurtman, Richard J.; & Schomer, Donald L. (1995). Sleep-inducing effects of low doses of melatonin ingested in the evening. *Clinical Pharmacology and Therapeutics, 57*, 552–562.

Zillmann, Dolf. (1983). Transfer of excitation in emotional behavior. In John T. Cacioppo & Richard E. Petty (Eds.), *Social psychophysiology: A sourcebook*. New York: Guilford Press.

Zimbardo, Philip G. (1992). Foreword. In Stanley Milgram, *The individual in a social world: Essays and experiments* (2nd ed.). New York: McGraw-Hill.

Zimbardo, Philip G., & Leippe, Michael R. (1991). *The psychology of attitude change and social influence*. New York: McGraw-Hill.

Zimbardo, Philip G.; Weisenberg, Matisyohu; Firestone, Ira; & Levy, Burton. (1965). Communicator effectiveness in producing public conformity and private attitude change. *Journal of Personality, 33*, 233–256.

Zimmer, Carl. (1993, June). Making senses. *Discover, 14* (6), 78–85.

Zimring, Fred M., & Raskin, Nathaniel J. (1992). Carl Rogers and client/person-centered therapy. In Donald K. Freedheim (Ed.), *History of psychotherapy: A century of change*. Washington, D.C.: American Psychological Association.

Zinbarg, Richard E.; Barlow, David H.; Brown, Timothy; & Hertz, Robert M. (1992). Cognitive-behavioral approaches to the nature and treatment of anxiety disorders. *Annual Review of Psychology, 43*, 235–267.

Zisook, Sidney, & Shuchter, Stephen R. (1993). Uncomplicated bereavement. *Journal of Clinical Psychiatry, 54*, 365–372.

Zola-Morgan, S. (1995). Localization of brain function: The legacy of Franz Joseph Gall (1758–1828). *Annual Review of Neuroscience, 18*, 359–383.

Zola-Morgan, Stuart, & Squire, Larry R. (1993). Neuroanatomy of memory. *Annual Review of Neuroscience, 16*, 547–563.

Zoltoski, Rebecca K., & Gillin, J. Christian. (1994). The neurochemistry of sleep. In Rosemary Cooper (Ed.), *Sleep*. New York: Chapman & Hall.

Zuckerman, Marvin. (1979). *Sensation seeking: Beyond the optimal level of arousal*. Hillsdale, N.J.: Erlbaum.

Zuckerman, Marvin. (1983). *Biological bases of sensation seeking, impulsivity, and anxiety*. Hillsdale, N.J.: Erlbaum.

Zuckerman, Marvin. (1990). Some dubious premises in research and theory on racial differences. *American Psychologist, 45*, 1297–1303.

Zuckerman, Marvin; Kuhlman, D. Michael; Joireman, Jeffrey; Teta, Paul; & Kraft, Michael. (1993) A comparison of three structural models for personality: The Big Three, the Big Five, and the Alternative Five. *Journal of Personality and Social Psychology, 65*, 757–768.

Zusne, Leonard; & Jones, Warren H. (1989). *Anomalistic psychology: A study of magical thinking* (2nd ed.). Hillsdale, N.J.: Erlbaum.

Zweig, Jason, & Clash, James M. (1993, June 21). Show your hand. *Forbes, 151*, 240.

Zweig, Richard A., & Hinrichsen, Gregory A. (1993). Factors associated with suicide attempts by depressed older adults: A prospective study. *American Journal of Psychiatry, 150*, 1687–1692.

Illustration Credits

CHAPTER OPENERS

Phoebe Beasley is the artist who created the art used in the chapter openers.

Chapter 1: *Repeat Again, I Do Believe,* collage on acrylic, 16 × 40" (detail) **Chapter 2:** *Temporary Shelter,* collage on acrylic, 36 × 48" (detail) **Chapter 3:** *105 Countdown #2,* collage on acrylic, 30 × 40" (detail) **Chapter 4:** *Shaded Lives,* collage, 30 × 40" (detail) **Chapter 5:** *We're More Alike,* collage 36 × 36" **Chapter 6:** *His Grandmother's Quilt,* collage, 30 × 40", flopped **Chapter 7:** *Yellow Legal Pad #2,* collage, 36 × 24" (detail) **Chapter 8:** *Practice Session,* collage, 30 × 40", collection of Mr. and Mrs. E.C. Hanes (detail) **Chapter 9:** *Fine China,* original hand-pulled serigraph, 26 × 31" **Chapter 10:** *Love Lesson For All Seasons,* collage, 40 × 30" (detail) **Chapter 11:** *Two Generations,* collage, 30 × 40" **Chapter 12:** *Precipitation,* collage, 30 × 40", collection of Louise Grantham (detail) **Chapter 13:** *In Resignation,* collage 36 × 24", flopped **Chapter 14:** *Absolution,* collage, 24 × 36" (detail), flopped **Chapter 15:** *Training Ground #2,* collage, 48 × 24" (detail)

CHAPTER 1

p. 2 *(top)* Lana Tyree/Gamma-Liaison Network; **p. 2** *(bottom)* Steve Gooch/The Daily Oklahoman/Saba; **p. 4** A. Glauberman/Photo Researchers, Inc.; **p. 5** Corbis-Bettmann; **p. 6** *(top & bottom left)* Corbis-Bettmann; **p. 6** *(bottom right)* Wellesley College Archives; **p. 8** *(top left)* Culver Pictures; **p. 8** *(top center)* Corbis-Bettmann; **p. 8** *(top right)* Archives of the History of American Psychology, University of Akron; **p. 8** *(bottom)* Stock Montage; **p. 9** *(top)* Courtesy Carl Rogers Memorial Library; **p. 9** *(bottom)* Courtesy of Brandeis University; **p. 11** Figaro Magahn/Photo Researchers, Inc.; **p. 15** Ralf-Finn Hestoff/Saba Press Images; **p. 19** Wayne Hoy/The Picture Cube; **Fig. 1.4** Leichtman, Michelle & Ceci, Stephen J. (1995). "The Effects of Stereotypes and Suggestions on Preschoolers' Reports." *Developmental Psychology, 31*(4), 568–578. Copyright © 1995 by the American Psychological Association. Adapted with permission; **p. 27** Baron Hugo Van Lawick/National Geographic Society Image Collection; **Tables 1.2 and 1.3** From *Sex in America* by Michael et al. Copyright © 1994 by CGS Enterprises, Inc., Edward O. Laumann, Robert T. Michael & Gina Kolata. By permission of Little, Brown & Company; **p. 35** Beate Rettberg-Beck.

CHAPTER 2

p. 43 Ted Kawalerski/The Image Bank; **p. 46** CNRI/Science Source/ Photo Researchers, Inc.; **p. 50** Courtesy Tim Murphy and Gil Wier, The University of British Columbia; **p. 57** Biophoto Associates/Science Source/Photo Researchers, Inc.; **p. 65** Stock Montage; **p. 66** The Hulton Getty Picture Collection, Ltd.; **p. 67** *(top left)* Dan McCoy/Rainbow; **p. 67** *(bottom left)* Hank Morgan/Science Source/ Photo Researchers, Inc.; **p. 67** *(right)* Scott Camazine/Science Source/Photo Researchers, Inc.; **p. 68** *(left a & b)* Courtesy Jordan Grafman, National Institute of Neurological Disorders & Stroke; **p. 68** *(right)* Beringer-Dratch/The Picture Cube; **p. 70** Nestle/Petit Format/Science Source/Photo Researchers, Inc.; **p. 74** Martin M. Rotker; **p. 76** Damasio, H., Grabowski, T., Frank, R., Galaburda, A. M., Damasio, A. R., "The Return of Phineas Gage: Clues About The Brain From The Skull Of A Famous Patient," *Science;* 264: 1102–1105, 1994; **p. 77** AP/Wide World Photos; **p. 84** Courtesy California Institute of Technology; **p. 85** Dan McCoy/Rainbow; **p. 87** Bryn Alan; **p. 88** Courtesy T. A. Jones and W. T. Greenough; **p. 89** Barlettani-Sestini/Gamma-Liaison Network.

CHAPTER 3

p. 95 Paul Conklin/Monkmeyer Press Photos; **p. 99** John Downer/ Planet Earth Pictures; **p. 100** From book, *Visions of Health—Understanding Iridology* by Bernard Jensen & Dr. Donald V. Bodeen. Avery Publishing Group; **p. 101** Lennart Nilsson/Bonnier Alba AB, *Behold Man;* Little, Brown & Co.; **p. 104** Jerome Wexler/Photo

University of Wisconsin; **p. 350** *(all photos)* Courtesy of the authors; **p. 351** A. Ramey/PhotoEdit; **p. 354** Doug Pensinger/Allsport; **p. 357** *(top)* Tony Freeman/PhotoEdit; **p. 357** *(bottom)* Ogust/The Image Works; **Fig. 8.4** Russell, James A. (1980). "A Circumplex Model of Affect." *Journal of Personality and Social Psychology, 39,* p. 1168. Copyright © 1980 by the American Psychological Association. Reprinted with permission; **Fig. 8.5** Levenson, Robert W., Ekman, Paul, & Friesen, Wallace V. (1990). "Voluntary facial action generates emotion-specific autonomic nervous system activity." *Psychophysiology, 27,* pp. 363–384. Copyright © 1990, reprinted by permission of Cambridge University Press; **p. 362** Bernard Gottfryd/Woodfin Camp & Associates; **p. 363** *(both photos)* From Ekman, P., Friesen, W. V., O'Sullivan., M. (1988), "Smiles When Lying" *Journal of Personality and Social Psychology; 54,* 414–420. Photos courtesy of Paul Ekman; **p. 364** *(top)* From Eibl-Eibesfeldt, I. (1970). *Ethology: The Biology of Behavior.* New York: Holt. Photo Courtesy I. Eibl-Eibesfeldt; **p. 364** *(all bottom photos)* From Matsumoto, D., & Ekman, P. (1989) Japanese and Caucasian Facial Expressions of Emotion. JACFEE. Photographs courtesy of Paul Ekman; **p. 369** *(top & bottom)* Treë; **p. 371** Nancy Richmond/The Image Works.

CHAPTER 9

p. 382 *(top left)* Nancy Sheehan/PhotoEdit; **p. 382** *(top center)* Merrill Vincent/PhotoEdit; **p. 382** *(top right)* M. Ferguson/PhotoEdit; **p. 382** *(bottom)* D. Young-Wolff/PhotoEdit; **p. 383** CNRI/Science Photo Library/Photo Researchers, Inc.; **p. 385** Biophoto Associates/Photo Researchers, Inc.; **p. 388** *(all photos)* Petit Format/Nestle/Science Source/Photo Researchers, Inc.; **p. 389** *(top)* Elizabeth Crews/The Image Bank; **p. 389** *(bottom)* Petit Format/Science Source/Photo Researchers, Inc.; **p. 390** Courtesy of the authors; **p. 392** John Lei/Stock, Boston; **p. 395** Stephen Agricola/The Image Works; **Fig. 9.5** Marc H. Bornstein & Micael E. Lamb, *Development in Infancy, 3rd ed.* Copyright © 1992 McGraw-Hill. Reproduced with permission of McGraw-Hill, Inc.; **p. 397** Romilly Lockyer/The Image Bank; **p. 399** *(top)* Bill Anderson/Monkmeyer Press Photos; **p. 399** *(bottom)* Elizabeth Crews/The Image Works; **p. 400** Laura Dwight; **p. 401** *(all photos)* Bill Armstrong; **p. 403** Courtesy Renée Baillargeon, University of Illinois at Urbana-Champaign; **Fig. 9.6** Baillargeon, Renée, & DeVos, Julie (1991). "Object Permanence in Young Infants: Further Evidence." *Child Development, 62,* pp. 1227–1246. Reprinted with permission of the Society for Research in Child Development; **p. 405** Sovfoto/Eastfoto; **p. 406** Bob Daemmrich/Stock, Boston; **p. 407** Sarah Putman/The Picture Cube; **Table 9.3** From *Childhood and Society* by Erik H. Erikson. Copyright 1950, © 1963 by W. W. Norton & Company, Inc., renewed © 1978, 1991 by Erik H. Erikson. Reprinted by permission of W. W. Norton & Company, Inc.; **Fig. 9.7** Stephen A. Anderson, Candyce S. Russell, Walter R. Schumm (1983). "Perceived Marital Quality and Family Life-Cycle Categories: Further Analysis." *Journal of Marriage and the Family, 45*(1), 127–139. Copyrighted 1983 by the National Council on Family Relations, 3989 Central Ave. NE, Suite 550, Minneapolis, MN 55421. Reprinted by permission; **p. 416** *(top right)* Michael Newman/PhotoEdit; **p. 416** *(bottom left)* Michelle Bridwell/PhotoEdit; **p. 416** *(bottom right)* Myrleen Ferguson/PhotoEdit; **p. 417** *(top)* Robert Rathe/Stock, Boston; **p. 417** *(bottom)* Jonathan Novrok/PhotoEdit; **p. 418** K. Kurita/Gamma-Liason Network; **p. 420** Joel Gordon; **p. 424** Lew Merrim/Monkmeyer Press Photos.

CHAPTER 10

p. 431 Mike Okoniewski/The Image Works; **p. 432** David Young-Wolff/PhotoEdit; **Table 10.1** From Williams, John E., & Best, Deborah L. (1994) "Cross-cultural views of women and men." In Walter J. Lonner & Roy Malpass (Eds.), *Psychology and Culture.* Copyright © 1994 by Allyn & Bacon. Adapted by permission; **Fig. 10.1** From *Sex in America* by Michael et al. Copyright © 1994 by CGS Enterprises, Inc., Edward O. Laumann, Robert T. Michael, and Gina Kolata;

Fig. 10.2 From "Sex Differences in the Brain" by Doreen Kimura. Copyright © 1992 by Scientific American, Inc. All rights reserved; **p. 435** © 1995, *Newsweek;* Inc. All rights reserved. Reprinted with permission. Photo by Douglas Levere.; **p. 437** *(both photos)* Myrleen Ferguson/PhotoEdit; **Fig. 10.3** Richardson, John and Simpson, Carl (1982). "Children, gender, and social structure: An analysis of the contents of letters to Santa Claus." *Child Development, 53,* 429–436. © The Society for Research in Child Development, Inc.; **p. 439** *(top)* Tony Freeman/PhotoEdit; **p. 439** *(bottom)* Myrleen Ferguson/Photo Edit; **p. 440** *(top)* Tom McCarthy/The Picture Cube; **p. 440** *(bottom)* From *Good Night, Sleep Tight! Shh . . .* by Gyo Fujikawa. Copyright © 1990 by Gyo Fujikawa. Reprinted by permission of Random House, Inc.; **p. 442** Jonathan Novak/PhotoEdit; **p. 443** John Chiasson/Gamma-Liaison Network; **p. 445** Frans Lanting/Minden Pictures; **p. 447** Burke Uzzle; **p. 449** Deborah Davis/PhotoEdit; **p. 451** Jerry Koontz/The Picture Cube; **p. 452** Bob Daemmrich/The Image Works; **Figs. 10.5 and 10.6** From *Sex in America* by Michael et al. Copyright © 1994 by CGS Enterprises, Inc., Edward O. Laumann, Robert T. Michael, and Gina Kolata; **p. 455** Sotographs/Gamma-Liaison Network; **p. 457** *(both photos)* Treë; **p. 458** Pam Francis/Gamma-Liaison Network; **p. 461** © Loren Cameron. Photograph originally published in *Body Alchemy;* Ceis Press, 1996. Reprinted by permission of Cleis Press; **p. 462** Lee Snider/The Image Works.

CHAPTER 11

p. 470 Courtesy Don Hockenbury; **p. 473** Mary Evans/Sigmund Freud Copyrights/Photo Researchers, Inc.; **p. 474** *(top)* Culver Pictures; **p. 474** *(bottom)* Corbis-Bettmann; **p. 476** Tony Freeman/PhotoEdit; **p. 477** Michael Newman/PhotoEdit; **p. 478** Eric Futran/Gamma-Liaison Network; **p. 480** Paul Gish/Monkmeyer Press Photos; **p. 482** Karsh/Woodfin Camp & Associates; **p. 483** *(top)* Photofest; **p. 483** *(center left)* Courtesy Dharma Publishing; **p. 483** *(center right)* Scala/Art Resource, NY; **p. 483** *(bottom)* Transparency #3416 (2). Courtesy Department of Library Services, American Museum of Natural History, Photo P. Hollembeak; **pp. 484 and 485** UPI/Corbis-Bettmann; **p. 487** Corbis-Bettmann; **Fig. 11.2** From *Motivation and Personality, 2nd ed.* by Abraham H. Maslow. Copyright 1954 by Harper & Row Publishers, Inc. Copyright © 1970 by Abraham H. Maslow. Reprinted by permission of Addison-Wesley Educational Publishers Inc.; **Box 11.1** First quotation from *Civilization and Its Discontents* by Sigmund Freud, translated by James Strachey. Translation copyright © 1961 by James Strachey, renewed 1989 by Alix Strachey. Reprinted by permission of W. W. Norton & Company, Inc.; Second quotation from *Carl Rogers: Dialogues,* edited by Kirschenbaum and Henderson. Copyright © 1989 by Howard Kirschenbaum and Valerie Land Henderson. Reprinted by permission of Houghton Mifflin Company. All rights reserved; Third quotation from *The Carl Rogers Reader,* edited by Kirschenbaum and Henderson. Copyright © 1989 by Howard Kirschenbaum. Reprinted by permission of Houghton Mifflin Company. All rights reserved; **p. 490** *(top)* Courtesy Carl Rogers Memorial Library; **p. 490** *(bottom)* Stock Montage; **p. 491** Russell D. Curtis/Photo Researchers, Inc.; **p. 493** Jean Hangarter/The Picture Cube; **Fig. 11.3** *Social Foundations of Thought & Action* by Albert Bandura, © 1986. Adapted by permission of Prentice-Hall, Inc., Upper Saddle River, NJ; **p. 497** *(left)* Stock Montage; **p. 497** *(right)* Courtesy Albert Bandura, Stanford University; **p. 499** Courtesy Mary Cattell; **Table 11.2** Cattell, Raymond B. (1973) "Personality Pinned Down." *Psychology Today.* Reprinted with permission from Psychology Today Magazine, Copyright © 1973 (Sussex Publishers, Inc.); **Fig. 11.4** *Personality, Genetics and Behavior* by H. J. Eysenck. Copyright © 1982. Reproduced with permission of Greenwood Publishing Group, Inc., Westport, CT. Reprinted with permission; **p. 502** Mike McGovern/The Picture Cube; **p. 503** *(top)* Courtesy Don Hockenbury; **p. 503** *(bottom)* Michael Springer/Gamma-Liaison Network; **p. 506** The Maudsley Institute of Psychiatry, London; **p. 507** Courtesy

CHAPTER 12

CHAPTER 13

CHAPTER 14

CHAPTER 15

APPENDIX B

Name Index

Subject Index